ZELLIG S. HARRIS

PAPERS IN STRUCTURAL AND TRANSFORMATIONAL LINGUISTICS

D. REIDEL PUBLISHING COMPANY / DORDRECHT-HOLLAND

Library of Congress Catalog Card Number 74–118128

Printed in The Netherlands by D. Reidel, Dordrecht

PAPERS IN STRUCTURAL AND TRANSFORMATIONAL LINGUISTICS

FORMAL LINGUISTICS SERIES

Editor:

H. HIŻ, *University of Pennsylvania*

Consulting Editors:

ZELLIG S. HARRIS, *University of Pennsylvania*

HENRY M. HOENIGSWALD, *University of Pennsylvania*

VOLUME 1

PREFACE

The papers reprinted in this volume carry out what has been called the distributional method, i.e. the analysis of occurrence-restrictions, beyond phonemics. The establishment of the phoneme marked the beginning of structural linguistics both in content and in method. In respect to content: Before phonemics, the physical nature of speaking suggested that the entities of language are sounds which differ from each other on a continuous scale, and whose wave-forms are decomposable into superposed elements (sine-waves), and change continuously through the duration of speaking. Phonemics showed that none of these properties are relevant to structural entities: phonemes can be realized by physical events other than sounds; they do not superpose, and their differences and transitions are discrete. In respect to method: The pre-phonemic descriptive approach in grammar was to record the physically obtainable data (sounds as heard) and to note how those sounds occurred in speech – what combinations of them constituted words, what sequence of words occurred, and so on. Phonemics showed that new entities, the phonemes, could be defined as classifications of these sounds based on their occurrence-relations. The occurrence-restrictions (i.e., the restrictions on combination) of the originally observed sounds are thereupon replaced, equivalently, by the occurrence-restriction which determines membership of sounds in phonemes, plus the occurrence-restrictions on the phonemes.

This methodological approach, of defining more freely combining new elements on the basis of occurrence-restrictions of old elements, has proved applicable in many further situations in structural linguistics. For example, it has produced more freely combining phonological entities such as the phonemic long components out of which phonemes can be obtained (Paper I). It has led to constructionally-definable morphological entities: e.g., when morphemes are defined on the basis of relations among morpheme alternants (IV), including non-contiguous ones (V); or when certain morphemes are shown to be resultants of several morphemic components (VII). Even syntactic entities are obtained with this approach: locally, when we ask what morpheme sequences are substitutable for (i.e. have the same occurrence-restrictions as) the single morphemes of elementary sentences (VI); constructionally (from local to global), when we ask what sub-sequences in a sentence are such that all sentences are regularly composed of contiguous adjoinings of them (XVII); globally, when we ask how elementary sentences can be defined on the basis of relations among sentence transforms (XXIII).

The hierarchical defining of new elements, one level in terms of another, provides a more compact description of the combinations which occur in language. But not only that: It also changes the character of structural linguistics from a science of classificational lists to one of relational types. This development stems from the following: Every linguistic classification is based on a relation in respect to occurrence in combinations. When the classification of the observed data into phonemes, and of these into other entities, and so on, is carried out wherever possible, we find that while the classes are necessarily different in each case, and while the effect of the classificatory relation is in each case the equivalent of certain occurrence-restrictions, the relations which show up in the various cases are of only a few types. And while classes (relations) of physical events with their occurrence-restrictions are the primitives of the grammar, it is the types of relation that are the primitives of the meta-grammar. There are behavioral relations which replace the original data: phonemic distinction on the basis of the pair-test (XXXVI) replaces the data of sounds; acceptability-ordering (XXVII) replaces the characterization of what is in the language. There are substitutive relations (free and complementary variants): among phoneme variants and components; and among sentence transforms. And there are sequential relations: on phonemes to define morphemes stochastically (II); on morphemes to define those phrases which can be sentence components (VI); on words to define strings (XVII), or to define elementary sentences (XXIII); on strings to define sentences (XVII – permitting then a stochastic definition of sentence from words). Finally, there are operator-relations: on elementary sentences to produce other sentences (XXVII, XXX). Occurrence-restrictions among segments of the sentences of a discourse involve quite different relations: one of these appears in XIX; another is the scope over which reference can stretch.

That occurrence-relations are relevant to structure is clear from the fact that for each set of entities not all combinations occur as utterances of the languages. But occurrence-relations have also an interpretational relevance, because the entities and distinctions which they define have a useful interpretation in the behavioral or meaningful character of language. This is clear in the case of phonemes, where phonemic distinction indicates what is and is not repetition in the language; so also in the case of morphemes, which correspond to the rough subdivisions of meaning in the language; and so in the case of elementary sentences, which express assertion. Going beyond this, when the analysis of occurrence-relations is carried out as far as possible on the observed data, it produces a separation between the information-bearing properties and the paraphrastic properties of language (XXX). It permits a decomposition of each sentence into information-bearing components (of various kinds) and, separately, other components. The information-bearing components are then found to have a separate structure (a grammar), with very little restriction on combination (i.e., on what information can be expressed), while the non-information-bearing components have a different and restrictive grammar. Thus the analysis of occurrence-relations, which led first to phonemics, leads finally to the distinguishing of two structurally and interpretationally different systems which together produce language.

CONTENTS

DISCOURSE ANALYSIS

TRANSFORMATIONS

ABOUT LINGUISTICS

STRUCTURAL LINGUISTICS. 1: METHODS*

* See the later treatment in (*Methods in*) *Structural Linguistics*, University of Chicago Press, Chicago 1951.

SIMULTANEOUS COMPONENTS IN PHONOLOGY

1.0. This paper[1] investigates the results that may be obtained when phonemes, or utterances in general, are broken down into simultaneously occurring components: as when the English phoneme /b/ is said to consist of voicing plus lip position plus stop closure, all occurring simultaneously.[2]

1.1. The analysis presented here rests on the fact that two independent breakdowns of the flow of speech into elements are physically and logically possible. One is the division of the flow of speech into successive segments; this is used throughout phonology and morphology, and gives us the standard elements (allophones or positional variants; phonemes; morphemes; words; phrases) of descriptive linguistics. The other is the division of each segment into simultaneous components, as when the single sound [¹á] (high-pitched loud-stressed low mid vowel) is said to be the resultant of three components: high pitch, loud stress, and low-mid vowel articulation. It is this type of breakdown, only little used in phonemics today, that is investigated here.

1.2. This investigation will show that intonations, prosodemes and 'secondary phonemes', pitch and stress morphemes and phonemes, and suprasegmental features in general, can all be obtained as a result of the single operation of analyzing the utterances of a language into simultaneous components. It will show that the various limitations of phonemic distribution, including defective distribution of phonemes, can be compactly expressed by means of the same operation. When this operation is carried out for a whole language, it breaks all or most of the phonemes into new sub-elements (components). Each of the old phonemes will be a particular simultaneous combination of one or more of these new elements; and the total number of different components will be much smaller than the previous total number of different phonemes. It will be possible to select and symbolize the components in such a way as to show immediately the limitations of distribution, and in many cases the phonetic composition, of the phonemes in which they occur.

1.3. It will be seen that the linguistic status of these components varies with their length. Components which are precisely the length of a phoneme, i.e. which represent merely the simultaneous breakdown of each phoneme by

Language **20**, No. 4 (1944), 181–205.

itself, enable us to eliminate phonemes of defective distribution and to indi-cate the phonetic composition of each phoneme (§ 5.3, 4).[3] We shall also permit some components to have the length of more than one phoneme, i.e. we shall say that such a component stretches over a sequence of phonemes. When phonemes are written with such long components, we shall be able to know the limitations of distribution of any phoneme by looking at the components of which it is composed (§ 5.2). Some of these long components will extend over all the phonemes of an utterance or linguistic form. These components will turn out to constitute the intonational or other contours of the language (§ 5.1).

In the following sections, these three groups of components which differ as to their length will be kept separate.

PRESENT TREATMENT

2.0. We have then a large number of linguistic situations which, it will turn out, can all be described by means of the analysis into simultaneous com-ponents. It will be helpful if we briefly note how these situations are usually treated at present.

2.1. *Pitch and Stress.* There is a particular group of phonetic features which has customarily been separated from the rest of the linguistic material even though simultaneous with it. This is pitch and stress. The extraction of these features out of the flow of speech is due to the fact that they constitute morphemes by themselves, independent of the rest of the speech, with which they are simultaneous. In *You.* : *You?* : *Yes.* : *Yes?* we have four different sound-sequences, and four different meanings. These must therefore have four different phonemic compositions. This requirement would be satisfied if we had phonemic /U/ and /E/ as high-pitched vowels contrasting with low-pitched /u/ and /e/. Then we would write /yuw/, /yUw/, /yes/, /yES/. However, the pitch features which are symbolized by /U, E/ have the specific meaning of interrogation. We therefore wish to consider some part of /yUw/, /yES/ as the morphemes 'you', 'yes' and another part as the morpheme 'interrogation'. This can be done only if we consider /U, E/ to consist of two simultaneous components /u, e/ and /'/. Then the phonemes /u, e/ are part of the mor-phemes for 'you' and 'yes'; and the phoneme /'/, or rather the rising pitch which extends over the whole utterance, is the morpheme for interroga-tion.

In most languages that have been investigated, pitch and stress have been found to constitute the elements of special morphemes (such as phrase and sentence intonation or the English contrastive stress). These elements are pronounced simultaneously with the other morphemes of the language. It would be impossible to isolate the other morphemes without extracting the pitch and stress morphemes that occur simultaneously with them. Perhaps as a result of this, it has been customary to extract pitch and stress features even when they form part of the phonemic make-up of ordinary segmental morphemes (words and parts of words). Thus we do not usually say that a language has ten vowels, five loud and five weak, but rather that it has five vowel phonemes plus two degrees of stress.

2.2. *Relations among Phonemes*, and the limitations of distribution of particular phonemes, are not presented in linguistics as an essential part of the individual phonemes. There exists no method which would enable us to say '/b/ is phonemic everywhere except after /s/' or '/t/ is a phoneme except after initial /k/, etc.' Instead we say that /b/ and /t/ are phonemes, and then tack on statements which correct the phonemic list by pointing out that /b/ does not occur after /s/, i.e. that there is no allophone occurring after /s/ which is assigned to /b/. If a number of phonemes have identical distributions, a single statement is devoted to them all. We say, for example, that English /ŋ/ occurs before no consonant other than /g, k/, or that morpheme-medial clusters in English hardly ever include both a voiceless consonant and a voiced one which has a voiceless homorganic counterpart: we get /ft/, /ks/ in *after* and *axiom*, but not /vt/, etc.[4] If a phoneme occurs in few positions as compared with other phonemes in the language, as is the case with English /ŋ/, we say that it is defective in distribution. But the writing system which we create does not reveal all these limitations. Given the phonemes of a language, a person would not know how to avoid making non-extant sequences unless he kept in mind the distribution statements.

The phonologists of the Prague Circle tried to indicate some of these limitations of distribution by saying that a phoneme which does not occur in a given position is 'neutralized' by one which does, and that an 'archiphoneme' symbol can be written to represent either phoneme in that position. Thus /b/ and /p/ are neutralized after /s/, and can then be represented by the archiphoneme P, which would indicate the 'common element' of both: /sPin/ instead of /spin/. This did not in itself prove to be a productive method of description. In the first place, most cases of 'neutralization' involve not merely two phonemes that directly neutralize each other. Usually several phonemes occur in a given position while several others do not, and 'neutralization' may be said to exist between the two whole classes of phonemes; thus after word-initial /s/ we find /p, t, k, f, l, w, y, m, n/ and the vowels, but not /b, d, g, v, θ, ð, š, ž, s, z, r, ŋ, h/. To select /p/ and /b/ out of the two lists and assign them to a separate archiphoneme P implies some further and hitherto unformulated method of phonemic classification on phonetic grounds. And what shall we do with /θ/ or /š/ or /z/?[5]

Related to these limitations of individual phonemes are other distributional facts. In a particular language, certain positions have the greatest number of phonemic contrasts, and others have the least: in Swahili every phoneme may occur in the position after pause, but only the five vowels ever occur before pause or between consonants. There are also limitations upon clustering: in English, not more than three consonants occur in succession initially, nor more than four or five (depending on the inclusion of foreign names) medially in a morpheme. These clusters may be further limited in the order of the phonemes: /t/ occurs after /p/ and /k/ before word-juncture, but not before them. In our present descriptions, facts of this type are not automatically derivable from any other information given. They must be separately stated, and are not represented in the phonemic writing itself.

A less important point in which our present method of description is inadequate is the phonetic similarity among the allophones of various phonemes. Thus English /p, t, k/ all have identically varying allophones in identically varying positions (strongly aspirated initially, unaspirated after /s/, etc.); /k, g, ŋ/ have identical places of articulation in identical environments (fronted allophones after front vowels, etc.). These similarities are recognized in the grammar when we describe the variation in allophones of all the analogous phonemes in one statement, as was done above. But the similarities among these phonemes are not explicit in the phonemic inventory or directly marked in the transcription.

2.3. *Breaking an Allophone into two Phonemes.* Whereas the two previous types of treatment have been fairly clear-cut, there is a group of linguistic facts in which the usual treatment is ambiguous: in some cases simultaneous elements are separated out and in other cases they are not, with no very clear criteria to decide whether the separation is to be performed or not.

It is customary to divide an allophone x into two successive allophones $x_1 x_2$ if we can then assign x_1 and x_2 to two otherwise recognized phonemes whose sequence is complementary to x. Thus we may break up English [č] into two successive phonemes /tš/, considering the retracted [t] as a positional variant of /t/ and the fronted [š] off-glide as a positional variant of /š/. We do this because phonemes /t/ and /š/ have already been recognized in English, but do not (except here) occur next to each other. We therefore consider the two successive parts of [č] as the allophonic values of the two phonemes /t/ and /š/ when they do occur next to each other. Certain accessory criteria influence us in deciding to consider the allophone as a combination of the allophones of two phonemes. The positions in which [č] occurs should be

such in which sequences of the same type as /tš/ also occur. The new allophones, back [t] before a palatal spirant /š/, and [š] off-glide after a stop /t/,
should have some phonetic similarity to other allophones of the phonemes
to which they will be assigned, and should if possible have the same relation
to them that analogous allophones have in analogous positions. Finally, the
original allophone [č] should have some of the phonetic qualities which
characterize a sequence of two phonemes in English (e.g. it should be longer
than a single phoneme; or should have the tongue moving not directly from
the alveolar stop to the position of the next sound, but going out of its way
via the spirant off-glide).

In practice, however, this last criterion is often disregarded. Among
speakers who distinguish the initials of *tune* and *tool*, many pronounce in
tune a simple consonant – a palatalized post-dental blade stop with no
recognizable [y] off-glide; nevertheless we consider that allophone to represent the phonemic sequence /ty/. Similarly the nasalized alveolar flap in
painting, which contrasts with the alveolar nasal continuant in *paining*, is not
considered a new phoneme occurring only after loud-stressed vowel and before zero-stressed vowel, but is assigned to the sequence /nt/.[6] Analyses of
this type constitute an important departure in method, because we are here
analyzing a sound segment into two simultaneous parts and assigning one
part to one phoneme and the other to another. In the case of /ty/ we may
say that the post-dental occlusion is the allophone of /t/ and the simultaneous
palatalization is the allophone of /y/. In the case of /nt/, we may say that
nasalization combined with obstruction of the breath in the dental-alveolar
area is the allophone of /n/, and the alveolar flap movement is the normal
allophone of /t/ between loud and zero-stressed vowels. In each case we have
avoided the introduction of a new phoneme with defective distribution, by
assigning the sound to a sequence of previously recognized phonemes.

In all these cases we have an allophone broken up into components each
of which we consider an allophone of phonemes which had already been
recognized in other positions. As an extension of this analysis we have the
occasional setting up of a new suprasegmental phoneme to account for a
whole sequence of allophones which always appear together. Thus in Moroccan Arabic a new suprasegmental emphatic phoneme[7] is set up to account
for the emphatic allophones. Phonetically, we have [ṣog] 'drive' (with cerebral
[ṣ]) but [flus] 'money' (with post-dental [s]); [daṛ] 'house' (with cerebral [ḍ]
and [ṛ]), but [dær] 'he built'; [lanba] 'lamp' (with low back [a]), but [læbs]
'dressing'. We could write this phonemically by considering [ṣ, o, ḍ, a, ṛ] to
be different phonemes from [s, u, d, æ, r] respectively. But we notice that to
say this would indicate a greater phonemic distinction than actually exists.
In [lanba] ~ [læbs], the difference between [a] and [æ] is phonemic; for there

is nothing in the neighboring phonemes to indicate that the vowel is [a] in one word and [æ] in the other. But in [ḍaṛ] ~ [dær] the difference between [a] and [æ] need not be considered phonemic; for [æ] never occurs next to [ḍ], and we could say that [a] is the positional variant of the /æ/ phoneme next to /ḍ/ and other emphatics (i.e. cerebrals). This crux is avoided by breaking each emphatic phoneme into two simultaneous parts: a regular consonant or vowel, and an emphatic component: [ṣ] is analyzed as /s/ plus /'/, [o] as /u/ plus /'/, etc. It is then shown that when this emphatic component occurs after consonants it affects a sequence of phonemes, but when it occurs after vowels it affects only the preceding phoneme: /s'ug/ = [ṣog], /d'ær/ = [ḍaṛ], /læ'nba/ = [lanba]. But it must be noted that this new phoneme was not inescapable. We could have written each of the Moroccan emphatic sounds as a new emphatic phoneme, and added a statement that in certain positions emphatic phonemes occur with each other to the exclusion of non-emphatic phonemes. However, such a statement would be at least as complicated as the equivalent statement which gives the domain of the single emphatic phoneme, and would leave us with a large number of extra and defectively distributed phonemes instead of the single emphatic /'/.

INTRODUCTION OF SIMULTANEOUS COMPONENTS

3.0. The various linguistic situations mentioned in §§ 2.1–3 can all be compactly described by the use of simultaneous components. In order to introduce these components, all we need do is to permit the segmental elements of our linguistic description to be resolved into any number of simultaneous component sub-elements.

3.1. This is not a new operation in linguistics: it is used implicitly when pitch and stress features are extracted as separate phonemes, and it is used when we analyze English flapped [n] as /nt/. There is no particular reason to admit such analysis in these cases and to deny it in such cases as the Greek aspiration (which, like stress, occurred in most forms only once within a word) or English voicelessness (which, like the Moroccan Arabic emphatic, occurs over a sequence of phonemes). No new methods or postulates are therefore required to extend the analysis of simultaneous components into all the phonemes of a language.

3.2. It may also be noted that this operation involves us in no theoretical difficulties. It does not prevent us from having a statable physical character for our linguistic elements. The traditional phonemes indicate explicit physical events: time-stretches of sound (sound-waves), or sets of simultaneous motions of the 'vocal organs'. The new component elements also indicate explicit physical events: time-stretches of sound-waves[8], or motions of particular vocal organs.[9] The only difference is that phonemes are elements which can, in general, occur only after one another, while components are elements which can also occur simultaneously with each other (as well as after each other).

3.3. If we are to permit our segmental elements to be resolved into components, we must bear in mind that there are many different ways in which any elements can be broken down into sub-elements. There are a great many ways in which components – various numbers of them and variously grouped – can be arranged so that every combination of components recognized in the arrangement will yield a particular phoneme. Such expressions of phonemes in terms of components are not in themselves of value to linguistics. The advantage they offer in reduction of the number of elements may be more than offset if connecting them with the distributional and phonetic facts requires more complicated statements than are required for regular phonemes. We consider the possibility of such analysis into components only because, as will be shown below, we can select the components in a way that will enable us to give simpler statements of the facts about phonemes.

3.4. We can now say in general terms what we must do when we analyze phonemes into components. We take a list of phonemes, each with its phonetic and distributional description; we select a number of components; we select some method for combining these components simultaneously (e.g. not more than three components at a time), in such a way that each combination permitted by the method will identify a phoneme, and that the grammar becomes simpler and briefer when written in terms of the components.

PROPERTIES OF THE COMPONENTS

4.0. Since the components are to be physical elements (§ 3.2), we must consider the phonetic values that they can have (§ 4.1). Furthermore, it will be seen that in special cases a component (or its phonetic value) may extend over more than one phoneme; and it will be important to note what happens when we get such LONG COMPONENTS (§ 4.2). The work that a component can do in the description of a language depends on its length. Components whose length is that of one phoneme can be used to describe the phonetic composition of phonemes (§ 5.4) or the dissection of a single allophone into two or more phonemes (§ 5.3). Components whose length is that of two or three phonemes (or thereabouts) can be used to indicate the limitations of distribution of any phoneme which contains them (§ 5.2). And components which can extend over long sequences of phonemes are used in the descriptions of intonational and other contours (§ 5.1).

4.1. *Phonetic Values*

Since the components are to identify phonemes, or more generally speech sounds, each component must have a stated phonetic value in each environment in which it occurs. As in the case of phonemes, there is no reason to require that its phonetic value be identical in all the environments. The component can therefore have different phonetic variants (allophones) in various positions, and the environmental factor which determines the particular allophone may be anything outside the component itself: other components with which it is concurrent, neighboring components or pauses, position of the component within the sequence of segments, etc.

Again as in the case of phonemes, it is not required that components have a constant phonetic value throughout their duration. A component may have a phonetic value which changes in a fixed way in respect to its endpoints: e.g. falling tone, increase in nasality, voiceless beginning and voiced ending.

Finally, if we are ready to admit partial overlapping among phonemes[10], we may agree to have different components in different environments represent the same phonetic value. So long as we do not have a component in one environment represent two phonetic values which are not freely interchangeable, or two components or component-combinations in the same environment represent the same phonetic value, we are preserving the bi-unique one-to-one correspondence of phonemic writing. (The term bi-unique implies that the one-to-one correspondence is valid whether we start from the sounds or from the symbols: for each sound one symbol, for each symbol one sound.)

4.2. *Length Values*

Whereas the considerations of phonetic value are comparable for phonemes and for components, we find that in the matter of length there is an important restriction upon phonemes which can be lifted in the case of components. In the operations which lead to the setting up of phonemes, one of the most important steps is segmenting the flow of speech into successive unit lengths, such that every allophone or phoneme consists of exactly one of these lengths.[11] In analyzing out the components, we make use of this segmentation, because what we break down are phonemes or allophones, not just random parts of the speech flow. However, there is no reason for us to restrict every component to the length of one phoneme. If a component is always common to a sequence of phonemes, we can say that its length is the length of the sequence. This will enable us to describe the limitations of phoneme sequences. When particular phonemes occur next each other (e.g.

English /sp/ in /spin/), while others do not (e.g. /sb/), we will say that the phonemes which occur next to each other all have some one component in common. The length of a component will therefore always be an integral number of phoneme-lengths – 1, 2, 3, etc. – but need not be just one.

It follows that just as a component may have different phonetic variants in different positions, so it may have different lengths in different environments. When the Moroccan Arabic emphatic occurs after a vowel, it affects only the preceding vowel; when it occurs after a consonant, it affects a whole neighborhood, including several consonants and vowels.

OBTAINING THE COMPONENTS

5.0. The greatest advantage from the analysis into components comes from the components with a length of two or more phonemes. These components enable us to express situations which could not be symbolized by the fixed-length phonemes. We shall investigate these components first. The first technique we shall use will yield the syntactic contours. The second will yield a way of treating the limitations of distribution of phonemes. The third will yield special cases of segmental phonemes. Finally we shall consider the components whose length is that of only one phoneme.

5.1. *Automatic Sequences expressed by Long Components*

Our first operation is to extract those components which appear only in fixed patterns.

Intonations

We first consider the case where some connection among particular successive components in successive allophones is readily noticeable to us – that is, where we do not have to conduct a search to find a series of components which we can extract. Since we are assuming that no simultaneous elements have as yet been extracted, we have our language material in the form not of phonemes but of allophones, with each future phoneme, or at least each vowel, represented by many allophones[12]: loud and middle-pitched [a], loud and high-pitched [a], very loud and middle-pitched [a], soft and low-pitched [a], etc. As a result of our past experience with languages, we may tend to scrutinize particularly the various stresses or pitches of each successive allophone in an utterance. However, we may also happen to note fixed patterns in the sequence of other features in successive allophones: e.g. a decrease in sharpness of articulatory movements from the beginning to the end of English utterances. Or we may notice a fixed pattern composed of several phonetic features of successive allophones: decrease in sharpness plus level tone during most of the utterance, followed by a falling tone at the end, in certain types of English statement.

In any case, we look for successions of phonetic features which recur in various utterances. We note that the occurrence of these features is limited: only certain sequences appear. For instance, we find the relative pitch sequence 1221130 (where 3 = highest pitch and 0 = lowest) in *I don't know where he's going.* | *We can't tell when they're coming.* | etc. Among utterances with the same stress positions we do not find other pitch sequences ending in 30. For utterances with these stresses then, we tentatively count the above pitch sequence as one of the fixed patterns. We then see if we can in any way reduce the number of fixed patterns. We note that before the final 30, the slightly raised pitch 2 occurs wherever a mildly loud stress occurs; we therefore consider pitch 2 to be an allophone of pitch 1 in stressed position. Other pitch sequences can also be considered special cases of this one: occurrences of relative high pitch 4 at one or more places in such utterances will always be accompanied by a loud contrastive stress (*Wé can't tell when they're coming.* 4221130), and can therefore also be considered an allophone of pitch 1. As a result of such manipulations a large number of pitch sequences ending in 30 become identical. They are all cases of one fixed sequence: as many relatively low tones as vowels (with slightly raised tones under stress and fairly high tones under contrastive stress) followed by a middling high tone on the last stressed vowel with a drop to zero (lowest) pitch on the vowels or consonants after it.

In English, a number of other sequences will not be reducible to this. For instance, there is the sequence in which every loud-stressed vowel, and every vowel or consonant after the last loud stress, has a higher pitch than the preceding one, while every zero-stressed vowel has the same pitch as the preceding loud stressed: *You're not going over to Philadelphia?* 012233333456.

By investigating all these intonations, we obtain a small number of pitch-sequence patterns, occurring over whole utterances or over sections of utterances (phrases, etc.). In phonemics, if we were dealing with a fixed sequence of segmental phonemes as long as these sequences of pitch, we should have to consider it as composed of the observable successive elements; and the fact that only a very few of the possible sequences of these elements occur could only be stated as a limitation upon their distribution. Since, however, components are not restricted as to length, we can say in this case that each of these pitch sequences is a single component whose length is that of a whole utterance or phrase. This is permissible, since the successive parts of the sequence are not independent of each other (e.g. before 30, only 1's occur) and may all be considered parts of one element. And it is advantageous, since we thus avoid having to state limitations of distribution for individual phonemic tones.

The essential operation here is to put two successive sounds or sound features into one unit if they always occur together in a particular environment. This is often done in phonemics, as when we consider the aspiration after initial [p, t, k] to be not a separate phoneme but part of the allophones of /p, t, k/ in that position.[13] Similarly, in these few fixed sequences of pitch or the like, we consider the parts of each sequence to be automatically dependent upon each other, so that the whole sequence is one phonemic element.[14]

Components of Components

If we wish to reduce the number of such dependent-sequence elements, we analyze them in turn into components on the basis of phonetic similarity (since there are no limitations of distribution among them) in the same way that this will be done for segmental phonemes (see § 5.4 below). That is, we break up the sequences into any simultaneous components which seem most convenient, and the combinations of which uniquely identify each sequence: e.g. the direction of pitch change after the last loud stressed vowel, the degree of change there, etc.

Stress

An analogous operation is performed when we have word or morpheme junctures phonemically established and note that some feature always occurs exactly once between each two junctures, or that some phonetic feature has fixed patterns between junctures. Thus we may note that there is never more than one loud stress between word junctures in English, and that the other vowels between these junctures have medium or weak stress, usually in fixed patterns: e.g. 1030 in *distribution, independent*, etc. Certain facts about the stresses are thus automatic: the number of loud stresses, the occurrence of some of the weak stresses. We therefore mark as phonemic only the remaining non-automatic facts: the place of the loud stress, and where necessary the place of any secondary stress. In a similar way, English contrastive stress (1040 in *distribution, not production*) would be discovered, since when it does occur it hardly ever appears more than once between two word junctures. This operation, however, will not discover features which do not appear in a limited number of fixed sequences, e.g. pitch in languages where all sequences occur and where the different sequences cannot be reduced into special cases of one another.

In dealing here with dependent sequences, it has been assumed that the phonetic features comprising the sequences would be readily noticed by the linguist. This is usually the case not only because pitch and stress are so frequently the features concerned, but also because it is relatively easy to notice phonetic features which show recurrent patterns in many sequences of allophones. Nevertheless, the analysis in no way depends upon a lucky finding of these phonetic features. It is possible to discover any fixed sequences methodically by the laborious process of taking each allophone (or each of a class of allophones, e.g. vowels) in many utterances and seeing in what respect the allophone after it is limited: e.g. given a low-pitched, sharply-articulated, weak-stressed vowel at the beginning of various utterances, can we find examples of every grade of pitch, sharpness, and stress in the vowel after it, or do only certain grades occur?

Segmental Allophones

The net result of this operation has been not only to produce a number of phonemic sequences of phonetic features (e.g. pitch-sequence phonemes), but also to extract these same phonetic features (e.g. pitch) from the recorded flow of speech. The recurring fixed patterns helped us to notice these phonetic features and gave us the basis for extracting them as a single independent element. But by doing so we are left with the original sequence of allophones minus these features. If we now go back to the allophones, we shall find that the extraction of these dependent-sequence elements (e.g. pitch) has reduced the allophones, which had originally differed in these features, to the conventional phonemes: the variously stressed and pitched [a]'s are now identical /a/, since they no longer represent classes of actual sounds but only features of sounds – namely, all the features except stress and pitch. What we thus obtain out of our original allophones equals the conventional phonemes merely because it has been customary for linguists to extract pitch and stress features, so that our usual phonemes are even now not classes of sounds but classes of sounds minus their pitch and stress features. The original allophones with which we began here were pure classes of freely varying or complementary sounds, and when we extracted the dependent sequences, which in most cases are composed of the pitch and stress features, we obtained the conventional phonemes.

The fact that most of these fixed sequences of sound components have meanings, or correlate with morphological constructions, is a matter apart. This fact is independently recognized by including them in the list of morphemes of the language. Dependent sequences may turn out to be phonemic without being morphemes, e.g. word-stress, varying rhythms and melodies of speech.

5.2. *Limitations of Distribution expressed by Long Components*

In our second operation we consider the usual type of limitation of distribution, in which a phoneme that occurs in most environments is limited by never appearing in certain positions. Here no solution is possible within the methods of segmental phonemics. The difficulty with the archiphoneme device, and with the statements about distributional relations between phonemes, is that they seek only to find a relation or common factor among the phonemes that can or cannot occur in a given environment. But there also exists a relation between the phonemes which occur in a given environment and that environment itself, namely the fact that they occur next to each other. That relation exists, for instance, between English /ŋ/ and /k/, but not between /ŋ/ and /t/. If we are willing to break phonemes up into simultaneous components, we restate this relation as a factor common to /ŋ/ and /k/ but not to /t/; and we say that /ŋ/ and /k/ each contain a certain component (say, back position) and that this component spreads over the length of two phonemes when the first is nasal. /ŋt/ therefore does not occur, nor /nk/, because the component of mouth position always extends identically over both phoneme places. If we mark N for nasal without regard to mouth position, and s for stop without regard to mouth position, and ⁻ for alveolar and ⁼ for velar position, then we say that the latter two marks always have 2-phoneme length when the first is /N/.[15] Thus /N̄s/ = /nt/ and /N̿s/ = /ŋk/; there is no way to write /nk/, since ⁻ is so defined that it cannot be stopped after the /N/.

By the use of components which are defined so as to extend over a number of phoneme places, we thus circumvent the limitation in distribution of the phonemes. This is not merely a trick, concealing the limitations of the phonemes in the definitions of the components. For the components are generalized phonemes: they appear concurrently with each other as well as next each other, and they may have a length of several phoneme-places as well as of one phoneme-place. And when we write with these components it is natural that various ones will have various lengths; each of them has to have some stated length, and the components symbolized by ⁻ and ⁼ are simply among those that in some situations have 2-phoneme length.

Since we should like our new elements, the components, to have as general a distribution as possible, we try to select them in such a way that the components which occur under (or together with) a two-length component should also occur without it. Thus given English morpheme-medial /sp/ but not /sb/, we say that the component common to /s/ and /p/ is unvoicing, or fortisness, and that its length is that of the cluster in which it is present. /sp/ is then a sequence of sibilant plus stop, with overriding unvoicing. The same sequence occurs with the unvoicing absent: /zb/ in *Asbury*. As in the case above, /sb/ and /zp/ cannot be written in terms of components, because of our definition of the length of the unvoicing.

General Formula

The procedure of obtaining these 2-length (and longer) components can be stated generally. If we have a sequence of two phonemes xy, we can select any number of factors which they have in common (both may be oral, both articulated in a certain position, both voiced or both voiceless, both explosive as against implosive, etc.). If one of these two phonemes does not occur with some third phoneme (say xc does not occur), we can then say that xy have significantly that component in common which c lacks. We call this component γ, and say that it has 2-phoneme length. Then x consists of this component γ plus some residue w, and y consists of the same γ plus some other residue u; thus /s/ = unvoicing plus sibilant articulation, /p/ = unvoicing plus lip and nose closing. We try to identify some other sequence of phonemes with these residues, and in particular to have the phoneme c equal the residue u, since the phoneme c is already known as lacking the component γ; in this case such a sequence would be /zb/, where /z/ = sibilant articulation, /b/ = lip and nose closing.[16]

$$
\begin{array}{ll}
\text{If } xy \text{ occurs} & \text{then } xy = \gamma + (wu) \\
xu \text{ does not occur} & x = \gamma + (w) \\
wu \text{ occurs} & y = \gamma + (u)
\end{array}
$$

Then our new elements are w, u, and the 2-length γ, and all possible sequences of them occur. There is no longer any limitation of distribution: w and u occur alone (intervocalic /z/ and /b/) and together as wu (cluster /zb/), and each of these occurs with γ in the combinations $\gamma + w = $ /s/, $\gamma + u = $ /p/, $\gamma + wu = $ cluster /sp/.[17] If we represent unvoicing by a small circle, we may paraphrase our general formula as follows:

$$
\begin{array}{ll}
\text{Since /sp/ occurs} & \text{/sp/} = \circ + (zb) \\
\text{/sb/ does not occur} & \text{/s/} = \circ + (z) \\
\text{/zb/ occurs} & \text{/p/} = \circ + (b)
\end{array}
$$

Assimilations

In Moroccan Arabic, the clusters /šš/, /žž/, /šž/ all occur, as well as the clusters /ss/ and /zz/; and there are morphemes which contain both /š/ and /ž/, or both /s/ and /z/, not contiguous to each other and in any order. But no morpheme containing /s/ or /z/ ever contains also /š/ or /ž/ anywhere within its bounds, nor does /s/ or /z/ ever occur in a morpheme with /š/ or /ž/. This complete statement of limitations[18] can be eliminated if we extract the feature † as a component and define it as having the length of a morpheme[19] and the phonetic value of retracting the tongue when in sibilant position (and as having zero phonetic value when the tongue is not in sibilant position). In doing this we can simply follow the formula above. /š…ž/ occur in one morpheme and represent our xy; /š…z/ do not occur in one morpheme and represent our xc. The factor common to /š, ž/ and absent in /z/ (our γ component) is †, a component of morpheme length. Then /ž/ (our y) consists of † (our γ) plus a residue (our u), and we identify this residue with /z/ (our c), which fits in with the fact that /š…z/ does not occur. And since /s…z/ does occur, we consider /s/ to be the residue of /š/ when the † component is extracted: /š/ = † + /s/, /ž/ = † + /z/, /šž/ = † + /sz/, etc. We now have three elements /s/, /z/, and †, each with its stated length and phonetic value, and all sequences of them occur.[20] /s/ in /iams/ 'yesterday', /zz/ in /zzit/ 'the olive', /sz/ in /†sz'r/ (=/šž'ŗ/) 'tree', /ss/ and /z/ in /†ssrzm/ (=/ššržm/) 'the window', etc.

/šš/ occurs	/šš/ = † + (ss)
/šs/ does not occur	/š/ = † + (s)
/ss/ occurs	/s/ = (s)

Note that † has a defined phonetic value when it occurs with some phonemes (the sibilants) and zero phonetic value when it occurs with other phonemes within its length.

Frequently the γ + u and the u, i.e. the phonemes which do and which do not occur next to the γ + w, represent whole classes of phonemes. In Swahili, /t, d, k, g, s, z, l, r, n/ occur after /n/, but the other consonants /p, b, f, v, m, h, θ, ð, γ/ do not.

/nt/ occurs	/nt/ = ‾ + (mp)
/np/ does not occur	/n/ = ‾ + (m)
/mp/ occurs	/t/ = ‾ + (p)

We call /n/ a 2-length component having the value of a dental nasal when occurring by itself, and stated other values (mostly, retarding of the tongue) when occurring simultaneously with various other components. Hence the n-component by itself = /n/. When the n-component is simultaneous with a labial, its value is tongue retarding, so that (n+p) = /t/. Since the n-component has the length of two phonemes, it will always stretch over the p whenever n occurs before it, so that /n p/ = /n(n+p)/ = /nt/. In terms of fixed-length phonemes, the distributional statements seem paradoxical: we are saying that p occurs after /n/, but when it does, it isn't /p/ at all but /t/. This apparent paradox brings out the difference, and the profit, in speaking in terms of components. For in terms of components we have two statements: 1. t = (p+n), d = (b+n), etc.; 2. n has 2-phoneme length when over consonants. Initially, or after m or vowels, we may have the components which constitute /p/, or those which constitute /t/ (i.e. the p components plus the n component): /paka/ 'cat', /tatu/ 'three'. After /n/, the components which comprise /p/ may indeed occur, but they then fall under the length of the n component, and their conjunction with that component yields /t/:/amen-tizama/ 'he saw me'. If we take an /n/, we can say that the /p/ components may follow it (in which case the n component extends over them); or we may say that the /t/ components follow it, since the segment following /n/ will actually contain precisely the /t/ components (/p/ components plus the n component). It makes no difference which we say, since either statement describes the same situation. This type of description, which cannot differentiate between /np/ and /nt/ in Swahili, corresponds exactly to the Swahili situation where /np/ does not exist phonemically as against /nt/. When we speak in terms of components, therefore, we do not have to make statements of limitation of distribution such as that the phoneme /p/ does not occur after the phoneme /n/.

A component may have a particular length when it occurs in one environment, and another when it is in other positions. In the case of the Moroccan Arabic emphatic (§ 2.3), we find the following sequences: /tæ/, /ta/ (rare), /ṭa/ (the /ṭ/ being domal unaspirated), but not /ṭæ/ (except across word juncture). We say that /ṭ/ and /a/ each contain a 2-place component ' whose phonetic value in general is to pull consonants and vowels to central position. The lack of /ṭæ/ is explained by the fact that /æ/ does not contain the ' component. We call /æ/ the residue of /a/ after the ' is extracted. Then since /tæ/ does occur, we call /t/ the residue of /ṭ/ after ' is extracted. Now /a/ = '+/æ/, /ṭ/ = '+/t/, /ṭa/ = '+/tæ/, and every combination occurs. We write /mæt/ 'he did' but /gæt'/ for [gaṭ] 'pliers', and /t'ab/ for [ṭab] 'he repented'. However, in this case we also have /ta/ occurring, though rarely, as in [banka] 'bank'. The only way to write it is to restrict our previous statement: ' is a 2-place component only when it appears with a consonant; on the rare occasions when it appears concurrently with a vowel (written after the vowel) it is a one-place component. Now we add /ta/ = /tæ/+'; we write /bæ'nka/ 'bank'.

/ṭa/ occurs	/ṭa/ = (t'æ)
/ṭæ/ does not occur	/ṭ/ = (t')
/tæ/ occurs	/a/ = (æ')
/ta/ occurs rarely	/ta/ = t(æ')

This situation is repeated for all the vowels and nine of the consonants, and the length of ' when placed after a consonant turns out to be several phonemes, not all contiguous. However, all these additional results can be obtained merely by repeating the investigation sketched above.

The technique of using these components to express limited distribution may simplify the description of morphophonemic alternation. For example, German has (to take only one pair) contrasting /t, d/ before vowels, as in *bunte* 'colored ones', *Bunde* '(in) the group', but only /t/ before open junction (- or ⁂, and in certain types of clusters). The lack of the sequence /d-/ involves morphophonemic complications, since morphemes ending in /d/ before a vowel, end in /t/ before open juncture: /bunt/, /bunde/ 'group'. The /t-/ is the *xy* of our formula, and /d-/ is the *xc* which does not occur. We recognize a 2-place component having the phonetic value of unvoicing (but having zero value on certain phonemes such as /e/) which is common to /t/ and open juncture /-/ but lacking in /d/. If we write this component as ‾, we can say that open juncture equals ‾, and /t/ = /d/ + ‾. Since /e/ does not contain the ‾ component, /d/ is free to occur before it. However, since we also have /t/ before /e/, we must define ‾ as having 2-place length only when it occurs by itself (i.e. when it equals open juncture) and as having one-place length otherwise. We now have /bund‾, bunde‾/ = *bunt*, *bunte*, and /bund‾, bunde/ = *Bund*, *Bunde* (where the overhanging ‾ is the phonemic open juncture). The writing is still phonemic; /bund‾/ 'group' and /bund‾/ 'colored' are still identical. But now we need not say that there is a morphophonemic alternation in the word for 'group'. The morpheme is /bund/ in both environments; the unvoicing heard before open juncture is not part of the morpheme /bund/ but is an automatic part of open juncture. This juncture consists of the component ‾, which is a 2-place component in this position. Note that since open juncture is phonemic, we should have to write it one way or another, if in no other way than by a space. We can equally well write this open juncture with one or more of the new components, so long as the sum of their phonetic values in that position equals the phonetic value of open juncture (and pause). In contrast with this, the morpheme 'colored' is /bund̄/, as in the inflected form /bunder/; when it occurs before open juncture the ‾ component of the juncture and the ‾ component of the last place in the morpheme coincide, and we have /bund‾/.

/t-/ occurs	/t-/ = ‾ + (d with or without‾
/d-/ does not occur	/t/ = ‾ + (d)
/d/ + vowel occurs	open juncture = ‾

In view of the possibilities of a component coinciding with a 2-length component extending over the next place, this case does not eliminate the practical lexical problem: given /bund‾/ we do not know whether the morpheme is /bund/ or /bund̄/. But in terms of components we need no longer say that /*Bund*/ has two forms.

Dissimilations

In all the foregoing cases there has been a physical similarity between the phonemes that occur together, which is not shared by the phonemes that do not occur in such combinations. The matter is somewhat more difficult when it is the dissimilar phonemes that occur together while the similar ones do not.

In classical Greek, only one aspirate occurs in a stem with its affixes, except for a very few morphemes, and there is a morphophonemic alternation between aspirates and non-aspirates, as when an aspirate-initial stem is reduplicated with the homorganic non-aspirate: φύω 'I produce', pf. πέφῦκα. We analyze φ into /p/ plus a component ' having the length of a stem plus its affixes, and the phonetic value of aspiration after one of the voiceless stops (which one, to be stated in terms of the phonetic structure of the word) and zero after every other phoneme. It is now possible to write /'pépūka/, with the ' component anywhere in the word, and with no need for morphophonemic statements.[21]

In Moroccan Arabic, double consonants are common (e.g. /tt/ in /fttš/ 'he searched', etc.), but no two different phonemes pronounced in the same mouth position (labial, dental, palatal, laryngal) ever occur next each other (with certain exceptions): there is no /fb, bf, td, gx, ṣh/[22], etc. If we try to pin this limitation upon a component of one of the phonemes, say /f/ among the labials, we must recognize that component in all the other homorganic phonemes – /b/ and /m/ – since the limitation applies equally to them. In order to enable the component to have any effect upon the neighborhood of the labial (so as to preclude another labial there), it must be present also in the neighboring position. We are thus faced with the need for a component which occurs in all the labials and in the place next to each labial, and which permits only a doubling of that labial, or a non-labial, to occur, but no different labial. This can be done by a 3-length component whose phonetic value is defined as follows: in its middle length, labial (so that this component serves to distinguish, say, the labial voiced stop /b/ from the dental voiced stop /d/); in its first and third lengths, labial if the other components are identical with those of the middle length, and laryngal otherwise. If this component is simultaneous in its middle length with the components for voiced stop, it will yield /b/ in that position; and if on either side there are again the voiced-stop components alone, this component will yield with them another /b/; while if the components there are anything else, say voiceless continuant, this component, extending over them, will with them yield a corresponding laryngal voiceless continuant, /ḥ/.[23]

If, as in English, there are no double consonants, we have to say that certain components, one or another of which is present in every consonant, have 3-phoneme lengths and have some stated value in their middle length and some contrary value in their end lengths, if the other components are identical with those of the middle length.

Clusterings

Further extensions of our method are necessary when we treat some of the more complicated limitations upon clusters, especially when limitations of order are present, i.e. when certain phonemes occur in one order but not in another. For example, English has morpheme-medial clusters like /rtr/, /ndy/, as in *partridge, endure*, but never clusters like /trt/, with any one of the consonants /r, l, m, n, ŋ, y, w/ in the middle. We cannot say simply that phonemes in the class of /r/ do not occur after stops, because in clusters of two consonants we have /rt, kr, lr, pt/ (*curtain, secret, walrus, reptile*; but no stop other than /t/ or /d/ after another stop). We require, therefore, a component extending over the length of a cluster and having the following phonetic values: in first position, general consonant value (serving incidentally to distinguish consonants from vowels; this because any consonant may occur here); in second position, continuant or /t, d/ if it follows a stop, otherwise general consonant value; in third position, continuant if it follows a stop (but if the stop is /t, d/, this value only if a continuant precedes it), otherwise, vocalic value. This value of the consonant-component permits any clusters of two except stop plus /p, b, k, g/, and then permits the third place to have continuant value (and to remain a member of the cluster) only if the preceding two are continuant and stop; otherwise the component has non-consonant value and thus changes the third position into a vowel. This statement does not allow for clusters with middle /s/, as in *sexton*, and omits several details which would be taken care of in the other components for the individual phonemes. However, it is included here to show that even fairly complicated clusterings can be described by single components.

Summary

The net result of this technique is the extraction of 2-length and longer components from all sequences that can be matched against non-occurring sequences (a sequence being an environment and the phoneme that occurs in it); e.g. from English /rtr/ matched against /trt/. These components do part of the work of identifying and phonetically describing the phoneme over which they extend (e.g. the ' gives the aspiration component of Greek φ), so that only a residue of the original phoneme is required to accompany them (in this case /p/ to accompany ': /'p/ = φ). This residue in turn can designate another phoneme which occurs without the component (/p/ = π). Meanwhile, the length of the component, covering an environment and the phoneme that occurs in it, takes care of the original limitation in distribution. In the simplest cases this may be just a special limitation between contiguous phonemes, when in a given environment only such phonemes occur as are similar in some respect to that environment: the extracted component then has a single phonetic value throughout its length (so /n̄s̄/ for English /nt/). In other cases, the phonemes which occur in an environment may be no more similar to it than those which do not; in fact, it may be precisely the phonemes similar to the environment that never occur in it: the extracted component will then have different phonetic values in different parts of its length (so the Moroccan labial component). More generally, these components can be set up to express the fact that particular phonemes occur in one order and not in another (English morpheme-medial /pt/ occurs, /tp/ does not), and that only certain types of clusters occur; in such cases the phonetic values of the components may vary according to what phonemes or components adjoin it (just as allophones of phonemes vary in value according to what phonemes adjoin them).

Where two groups of phonemes are completely separated, so that no member of one group occurs with a member of the other, the extracted component always keeps its particular length (e.g. when in Moroccan Arabic neither /š/ nor /ž/ occurs near either /s/ or /z/). Where the separation is not complete (so that Moroccan /ṭ/, for example, occurs with /a/ but not with /æ/, while /t/ occurs with both /a/ and /æ/), the extracted component must have different lengths in different positions: with /ṭ/ it has 2-phoneme length so as to exclude /æ/, but with /a/ it has 1-phoneme length so as not to exclude /t/.[24] Where the limitation of distribution operates only between adjoining phonemes, their common component extends only over the sequence in question (i.e. the environment, and the phoneme which occurs in it to the exclusion of some other phoneme): so in English /ŋk/ or in Swahili consonant clusters. Where the limitation operates across unaffected phonemes, or throughout some stated limits such as a cluster or a morpheme, then the extracted component has zero value over those phonemes which happen to occur in its length but are not party to the limitation which it expresses: e.g. the Moroccan limitation on the occurrence of /š, ž/ and /s, z/ is operative throughout word limits; and the voiced–voiceless separation in English morpheme-medial clusters applies only to phonemes with voiced or voiceless homorganic counterparts and hence does not affect /r, l, m, n, ŋ, y, w/ if they occur in the same cluster (thus /ŋgz/ in *anxiety*, but /ŋkš/ in *anxious*; there is no /ŋkz/).

5.3. *Defective Distribution expressed by Simultaneous Components*

Our third operation is to try to break up into simultaneous components any allophones which cannot be assigned to the existing phonemes and which have a very defective distribution in themselves. This is the case with the nasalized alveolar flap of *painting*, which occurs only after loud-stressed and before weak-stressed vowels. In this position it contrasts with all the consonant phonemes, so that we would be forced to recognize it as a new phoneme occurring only in this one environment.[25] Since we cannot set up this restricted allophone as complementary to some single previously recognized phoneme, we ask if it may not be complementary to some sequence of previously recognized phonemes. We find that /nt/ is one of the very few sequences which occur between vowels under other stress conditions without also occurring after loud and before weak-stressed vowels. The nasalized flap is therefore in complementary distribution with this sequence and is analyzed into two simultaneous components, one an allophone of /n/ in this position (V́-tV) and the other an allophone of /t/.

There is, of course, a morphophonemic consideration: *painting* can be divided into two morphemes, the first of which would have a morphophonemic alternation between /nt/ and the nasalized flap if we recognized the latter as being anything but /nt/. This consideration is not important here, but might be resorted to in other cases. In any event, it is not essential to such analysis. When we break up the palatalized post-dental blade stop into simultaneous allophones of /t/ before /y/ and of /y/ after /t/ (/tyuwn/ for *tune*), we have no morphophonemic advantage, since when a morpheme ending with /t/ comes before a morpheme beginning with /y/, we get not the palatalized stop but /č/ (or /tš/) by morphophonemic alternation.

From the point of view of relations between allophones, this operation means that we extend complementary distribution to apply not only to single allophones but also to sequences of allophones. From the point of view of the physical nature of allophones, it means that we no longer require an allophone to be an observable complete sound; we extend the term to include observable components of a sound. The net result is to eliminate some potential phonemes of exceptionally limited distribution.

5.4. *Phonetic Similarity expressed by Short Components*

In carrying out the distributional analysis, we shall have extracted components from various phonemes in whatever language we investigate. It may be profitable to continue this extraction until all phonemes have been reduced to combinations of components.

When long components have been set up for all the important distributional limitations, we proceed to analyze those phonemes which have not been broken up, or the residues of the phonemes which have been broken up. Each of these phonemes or residues may be analyzed into simultaneous components so chosen as to distinguish the phonemes phonetically one from the other in the simplest manner. 'Simplest' can be determined with the aid of a few obvious criteria: where possible we should utilize components already recognized in the previous analysis, stating that in this position (or in this combination) the component has only 1-phoneme length, since it affects only the phoneme which it identifies phonetically. For example, if in a particular language we have had to recognize front, middle, and back consonants because they follow /m, n, ŋ/ respectively, whereas all vowels occur after each of these three nasals, we may nevertheless use the front, middle, and back components to differentiate vowels, with the proviso that they do not have 2-component length when they occur with vowels, and hence do not preclude the occurrence of a front vowel (say /i/) after a back nasal /ŋ/.[26] This means in effect that the limitations of distribution among certain phonemes are used as a partial guide to show us what phonetic differences among the other phonemes are the relevant ones.

Another criterion is the parallelism of allophones among different phonemes. If the allophones of English /p, t, k/ are all analogous in that they all have comparable differences of aspiration in identical environments (as [pʰ, tʰ, kʰ] after word-juncture but [p, t, k] after /s/, etc.), we can say that a particular component γ is contained in each of them and that this γ (which may be the combination of the unvoicing and the stop components) is strongly aspirated after word-juncture, unaspirated after /s/, etc.

The physical movements of articulation may also offer certain absolute factors common to various phonemes: /p, t, k/ are generally voiceless, fortis, stopped. Since the components will in the last analysis have to identify articulatory (as well as acoustic) events, it is desirable to reflect these as closely as possible. However, as is well known, the correlation with articulatory events will rarely coincide completely with our other criteria, not even with our criterion of complementary distribution for phonemes. To take the simplest example, there are sounds in the /t/ phoneme which are not stops (in *butter*, etc.).

Some components which are commonly extracted by linguists merely because they consist of pitch or stress features have no basis for being thus extracted except the phonetic considerations of this section. Such, for example, are the tones in languages where each vowel in a morpheme has an arbitrary phonemic pitch.[27] As far as distributional simplicity goes we could just as well state that a language has not, say, 5 vowels and 3 tones, but 15 vowel phonemes (high /í/, mid /i/, low /ì/ – all of which might differ in quality as well as pitch; high /é/, etc.). If these vowels have not already been completely broken down into components on distributional grounds, we may now extract the tones as components on grounds of phonetic simplicity.

5.5. *Manipulating the Components*

When all the phonemes of a language are completely analyzed into components, various additional problems are met. A set of components which

conveniently express certain limitations of distribution (e.g. of the voiced –
unvoiced group in English as against /r, l, m, n, ŋ, y, w/) may conflict with
a different analysis which results from a different limitation but which involves some of the already-analyzed phonemes of the first group (e.g. /s/
which in certain respects behaves like /r, l, m, n, ŋ, y, w/). Sometimes the
only way to resolve such difficulties is to reconsider the phonemic system.
This is, of course, permissible since in grouping allophones together into
phonemes there are often alternative ways of grouping within the basic
phonemic criteria.[28] We choose one way for our phonemic statement, but
a slightly different grouping of some of the allophones may be more convenient for the component analysis. Furthermore, we sometimes obtain an
extremely complicated component analysis for the distributional limitations
and clusterings of the phonemes throughout the vocabulary of the language,
where a much simpler system may be possible if we eliminate from consideration certain morphemes (often borrowed ones) which have a different
phonetic structure from the rest.[29] It is often possible to identify phonemically the parts of the vocabulary which we wish to exclude from consideration, and perhaps to give them a separate component analysis. For all these
reasons, any attempt at a component analysis of a whole phonemic system
requires considerable attention to the detailed facts of the language. No
examples of such systems will therefore be presented here. It has been possible, however, to carry out the analysis for a few languages, and to obtain
sets of components which had only mildly complicated phonetic values, and
which required very few statements about distribution (so that practically
every combination or sequence of components occurred).

ARE THE COMPONENTS USABLE?

6.1. *Their Status in Descriptive Linguistics*

Having worked through specific cases of analysis into components, we may
now ask: What is the status in linguistic science of the new techniques and
the new elements which they produce? At present the phonemic elements of
linguistic analysis are obtained by segmenting the flow of speech and calling
each group of mutually substitutable segments ('free variants') an allophone.
Now the components described in this paper are not complete physical
events; therefore, they cannot actually be substituted for each other to see
if any two of them are free variants or 'repetitions' of each other. First,
therefore, we must move as before from unique sounds to allophones, which
in general have the relative length of a phoneme (that is, are not composed
of smaller segments which in turn are allophones of phonemes). Only then
can we proceed to analyze the allophones into simultaneous components,

producing a new set of elements instead of the previous allophones. The operation of complementary distribution can be performed upon the new elements as well as upon the old. Theoretically, therefore, we could break the allophones into components and then do all the complementary grouping on the components. Actually, it is more efficient to group the complementary allophones into tentative phonemes, and to analyze these tentative phonemes into components. We can then try to group the components by complementary distribution in order to get fewer components, each having wider coverage. If certain limitations of occurrence exist for some components, we may even try to express their limitations in turn by a second extraction of components, on much the same grounds that we used in expressing phonemic limitations by components, in order to obtain the most general and least limited set of elements.

We thus obtain for the language a new set of elements, each of which occurs with fewer limitations than the original phonemes. This is so because each setting up of a component of more than one-phoneme length takes care of at least one limitation of phonemic occurrence; this is equally true of the automatic-sequence components (§ 5.1) which replace the highly limited distribution of phonemic pitch and stress.[30] In some cases the components can be so selected that practically every possible combination and sequence of the components actually occurs. Any combinations and sequences that do not occur will, of course, have to be stated.

The new elements are still, like the phonemes, in bi-unique correspondence with speech events: given the writing we know uniquely what sounds to pronounce, and given the sounds we know uniquely how to write them.[31] The components are essentially similar to phonemes in that both are distributional symbols with phonetic values. That is to say, the observed physical events are always sounds, and the criteria for classifying them into linguistic elements – whether phonemes or components – are always distributional.

The components are merely generalizations of the phonemes, extending the very development which gives us phonemes out of sounds. In writing allophones we have one distinguishable sound per symbol (hence closely abiding by the physical event); but there are many symbols and each usually has a highly restricted occurrence. In writing phonemes we often have several distinguishable sounds per symbol, usually but not always having considerable phonetic similarity (hence abiding rather less closely by the physical event); but there are fewer symbols with a wider distribution for each. In writing components we usually have more distinguishable sounds per symbol, sometimes with no common feature (hence abiding much less by the physical event); but there are fewer symbols yet, with much wider distribution for each. It follows that analysis into components completes what phonemics can only do in part: the transfer of the limitations of sounds from distributional restriction to positional variation in phonetic value. This is not an argument for the use of components: phonemics is undoubtedly the more convenient stopping point in this development, because it fits alphabetic writing; but we must recognize the fact that it is possible to go beyond it.

6.2. *Practical and Historical Considerations*

The use of components will clearly be practicable only within narrow limits. Components which enter into supra-segmental morphemes (e.g. sentence intonations) are now extracted and must be extracted in order to permit isolation of morphemes in general. Components which resolve major distributional limitations, e.g. Moroccan' or †, can easily be extracted and written among the segmental phonemes. Such components are especially worth extracting if many morphophonemic statements are thereby eliminated.[32] One-length components produce little saving and would not normally be extracted except for cases like vowel tones (§ 5.4), where the extraction is due chiefly to tradition or is desirable because the tones have morphophonemic alternations under various syntactic pitches.

Analysis into components may be of interest to linguists even where it is not used to simplify the writing system, for components may offer correlations with historical change, and may in a sense quantify the structural importance of various phonemic limitations. The connection with linguistic change derives from the fact that many phonemic limitations are produced by single historical changes[33] or by a related series of them, so that the long components may represent the effect of events in history. The structural quantification derives from the fact that some non-occurrences of phonemes are represented by long components and others merely by the non-occurrence of one component with a particular other component in a position where the first component otherwise occurs. Let us take the non-occurring */sbin/ and */stend/ in English. If the cluster-long unvoicing component is ‾, we may say that *spin* is /z̄bin/; the sequence /z̄b/ (=/sb/) is impossible since ‾ always extends over the whole cluster in which it occurs. On the other hand the general vowel component contained in /e/ occurs after /st/, but only with the particular quality component of /æ/ and not that of /e/: *stand* but not **stend*. There is no long component excluding the /e/ quality component from the position after /t/ or before /n/ or between clusters, since the /e/-quality component occurs in those positions: *tend, spend*. Therefore all we have is the fact that while the general vowel component occurs in between /st/ and /nd/, it does not occur there with the /e/-quality component, although it does occur with that component elsewhere. We may then say that forms like */sbin/ are excluded from the phonetic structure as it is described by our components, while forms like */stend/ are not excluded. True, the same considerations which led us to set up a long component in the first case and not in the second could have led us directly to such a judgment concerning these two forms. But no form of expression creates new information: the only question is the availability and organization which it gives to the information. The difference in terms of components is perhaps more clear-cut than a direct discussion of each form, and in setting up the components we may have used relevant considerations which we should not have thought of in a direct discussion.[34]

SUMMARY

7. This paper has tried to show that many linguistic facts can be discovered and described by the application of a single operation: the analysis of speech into simultaneous components. Automatic sequences of phonetic features yield intonations, word stresses, and the like. Defectively distributed phonemes complementary to sequences of phonemes are broken up into allophones of those sequences. Limitations of phonemic distribution, including neutralization, cluster limits, and certain automatic morphophonemic changes, are resolved by components having a length of more than one phoneme. Phonemes and residues not otherwise broken up are analyzed into components of one-phoneme length on the basis of phonetic considerations. The length of a component can vary in different positions, and can be bounded by phonemic environment or by junctures. The phonetic value of a component can vary in different positions, and can be determined by its concurrent components, or its neighboring components, or the section of the components's length. Whole phonemic systems can be replaced by component systems.

No one technique is essential, but rather the method of attack. Different devices will have to be used in different situations. For each language, it will be necessary to state what system of combination of the components is being used, what the length and phonetic value of each component is, and what limitations of occurrence remain among the components.

It has been shown that this analysis creates a new set of elements out of the original allophones or phonemes, and that these elements have the same status as phonemes and are, indeed, merely generalized phonemes. Analysis into simultaneous parts is the only operation aside from segmentation into allophones that produces usable elements for descriptive linguistics.

NOTES

[1] I am glad to express here my thanks to Dr. Henry Hoenigswald and the members of the linguistic seminar at the University of Pennsylvania for valuable criticism and for linguistic material. I am particularly indebted to Dr. Roman Jakobson for an interesting conversation on the phonetic breakdown and grouping of phonemes. I owe an exceptionally heavy debt to Dr. Bernard Bloch, who has helped me state many of the more difficult points.

[2] This example of phonetic components is given here only for introductory simplicity. The analysis presented below is primarily distributional rather than phonetic.

[3] E.g. it is this technique that enables us, in languages which have a phonemic tone on each vowel (Fanti, Chinese, etc.), to extract the tones as separate phonemic elements.

[4] Voiced-voiceless sequences like /rp/ in *carpet* are not counted here, since /r/ has no voiceless homorganic counterpart.

[5] The Prague Circle more closely approached the technique of dividing elements into simultaneous components, but purely on arbitrary phonetic grounds, when they said that the difference between two phonemes was not *a* vs. *b*, but *a* vs. $a + x$ (where x is a Merkmal denoting the extra features which differentiate *b* from *a*). See N. S. Trubetzkoy, *Grundzüge der Phonologie* (Travaux du Cercle Linguistique de Prague, 7) 1939, 67.

[6] Y. R. Chao gives other "cases of one homogeneous sound represented by two or three piece symbols, each of which represented some aspect or aspects of the sound" in his article 'The Non-Uniqueness of Phonemic Solutions of Phonetic Systems', *Bulletin of the Institute of History and Philology* 4 (Academia Sinica; Shanghai), 1934, 371.

[7] Z. S. Harris, 'The Phonemes of Moroccan Arabic', *JAOS* 62 (1942), 309–18. (Paper X of this volume.)

[8] It is possible, by Fourier analysis, to replace periodic waves by a sum of simpler periodic waves. The original waves (e.g. sound waves) can then be considered the resultants which are obtained by adding together all their component waves.

[9] E.g. vibration of the vocal cords, giving 'voice'. This might be the phonetic value of a particular component in a particular position, whereas the phonetic value of a particular phoneme in a particular position might be, for example, voice plus closing off of the nose plus closing of the lips (English /b/). A phonetic system of this kind without the phonemic limitation is Otto Jespersen's analphabetic system, presented in his *Lehrbuch der Phonetik*, 2nd ed., Leipzig-Berlin, 1912, and elsewhere.

[10] Bernard Bloch, 'Phonemic Overlapping', *American Speech* 16 (1941), 278–84.

[11] The lengths are not absolute (so many hundredths of a second) but relative. This means that an allophone [p], for instance, is not composed of two shorter allophones 'p-closure' and 'p-release'.

[12] We will assume that these allophones satisfy all the criteria for phonemes – that is, that complementary allophones have been grouped together – except that allophones having different stress and pitch have been considered different sounds and hence not grouped together under one symbol. It is impossible to obtain the conventional phonemes until intonational components have been extracted from the allophones.

[13] This operation is used implicitly throughout phonemics to keep us from breaking sounds down into smaller and smaller segments ad infinitum. We do not consider the lip closing and the lip opening of intervocalic /p/ to be separate phonemes, because they always occur together in that position.

[14] A fuller discussion of the character of these contour components is given in note 30 below.

[15] Linguistic forms which are written in components will be set between diagonals, in the same way as forms written phonemically. It is convenient to use identical brackets for these two systems, because many linguistic forms cited in this paper are written partly in phonemes, partly in components: e.g. /†sz'r/ 'tree'. We write in components only those parts of a form which are under discussion. This is permissible because phonemics is merely a special case of component analysis; the extension from phonemics into components can be carried out to any degree desired. In the analysis of Moroccan Arabic

cited in note 7, the phonemes are of the usual kind except for the component /'/ (§ 2.3 above), which is included among the phonemes. – In some cases, where it is clear that a symbol indicates a component, the diagonals are omitted. The use of non-alphabetic marks like the horizontal bar (§ 5.2) is not in general desirable; but only such marks can depict on paper the effect of a long component that extends over more than one phoneme.

[16] More briefly: Given that xy occurs, we select u such that xu does not occur. Then $y = \gamma + u$ (where γ has 2-phoneme length, when two phonemes are present), and $x = \gamma + w$, where w is selected so that wu occurs.

[17] Note that in this example γ does not occur alone.

[18] Aside from an unrelated limitation between /s/ and contiguous /z/.

[19] Or of a word, except for one enclitic. That is, when † occurs, it extends from one word juncture to the next.

[20] See note 18.

[21] The morphophonemic alternation of φ for π + ' (e.g. in ἀφ' ὧν) can also be avoided, if the ' component is written where it is heard. In the few cases of two aspirates within a word, a second ' would have to be written over the extra aspirate, and the statement of the length of ' would have to be adjusted accordingly. In the case of the reduplication there is a real elimination of a morphophonemic statement: the stem initial in /'pépūka/ (or /pép'ūka/) is /p/, which is duly present in the reduplication.

[22] For the phonetic values of these phonemes see op. cit. in note 7.

[23] The laryngal value for the ends of the labial component is not essential, though it seemed most convenient for various reasons. It would also be possible to assign merely a 'non-labial' value to the ends of the labial component, leaving it to the components in the neighboring positions to decide whether they are laryngal, dental, or palatal. They cannot be labial because a 'non-labial' component extends over them.

[24] Or we may say that with /t/, absence of that component has 1-phoneme length so as not to exclude /a/ (which contains the component).

[25] Rather than include it in one of the vowel phonemes, which would confuse all the general statements about the distribution of vowel phonemes and their allophones.

[26] In varying measure, this is the case in English (within a morpheme), Swahili, and Fanti.

[27] E.g. Fanti. See W. E. Welmers and Z. S. Harris, 'The Phonemes of Fanti', JAOS 62 (1942), 319.

[28] Y. R. Chao, op. cit. in note 6.

[29] Leonard Bloomfield, The Structure of Learned Words. A Commemorative Volume Issued by the Institute for Research in English Teaching, Tokyo 1933, 17–23.

[30] We have seen that the 2- and 3-place components of § 5.2 and the fixed-sequence components of § 5.1 differ in effect, in that the former describe limitations of distribution and the latter describe contours. It is of interest to notice wherein these two types of long components differ structurally and wherein they are similar.

They are similar in that they are all expressions for limitations of distribution of different segments. In the case of the pitch contours, we begin with allophonic segments that contain pitch and stress features in them. We notice that there are limitations upon the distribution of these segments. For instance, after a sequence of segments in which each loud-stressed segment is higher-pitched than the preceding, we never get a low-pitched segment: after Is your brother? we never get a low going, but only a going which is pitched even higher than brother. And in Is your brother going? we do not get a low pitched ing. We express this limitation of distribution by saying that all the segments of the utterance contain a particular component in common, and that this component has various phonetic values at various parts of its stretch: low pitch on the first low-stressed vowel, higher pitch on the next, etc. Exactly this is what we do with the 2- and 3-place components: We notice that after /s/ we never have /b/, but only /p/. We express this by saying that both successive segments have a particular component in common, and that this component has fortis value throughout its stretch.

The differences between the two types of long components are four. First, the phonetic values of the contour components are usually all pitch and stress features, which we are accustomed to consider a thing apart, while the phonetic values of the other components may seem to us to be arbitrarily extracted from the rest of the segment, as when we distinguish the closure of /b/ from its lip position.

Second, since the contour components are often constituents of simultaneous morphemes (e.g. the question intonation), we often cannot obtain the phonemes of the segmental morphemes (e.g. *your* or *brother*, without regard to intonation) until after the contour components have been extracted. Therefore we usually extract the contour components while working on sequences of allophonic segments, whereas we extract the other long components by working on sequences of phonemes.

Third, whereas the long components usually extend over a definite small number of phonemes, the contour components usually extend over a variable (and much larger) number – as many as there may be in a linguistic form or utterance of a particular type.

Fourth, we usually have many more positional variants of a contour component than of a 2- or 3-place component. The 1221130 of *I don't know where he's going* (§ 5.1) and the 2230 of *Bud Clark fumbled* are positional variants of the 230 in *He told him*. The phonemic component environment, which determines the number of 1's and the number and place of 2's in all these variants, is the simultaneous sequence of stress contours. The 2- or 3-place components usually have fewer though more complicated positional variants, as when the Swahili n component indicates tongue retarding with labial components, but velar occlusion with h (n + p = t, n + b = d, n + h = k).

[31] If only the first of these were true, we should have morphophonemic writing. We may permit partial overlapping among our components, i.e. the same sound feature may be represented in different environments by different components, but that is no bar to phonemic writing.

[32] This will in general happen only in cases of automatic morphophonemic alternation.

[33] See now Henry Hoenigswald, 'Internal Reconstruction', *Studies in Linguistics*, 1944.

[34] Various other facts about the phonetic structure also transpire from a component analysis. One can tell, by looking at the combinations of components representing the phonemes, which phonemes ever occur next to each other and which never do (i.e. whether they have a long component in common), which phonemes replace each other in complementary environments (i.e. whether all their one-length components are identical), which phonemes have the smallest number of different phonemes next to them (i.e. the ones that contain the largest number of long components).

II

FROM PHONEME TO MORPHEME

0.1. *Introduction*

The following investigation[1] presents a constructional procedure segmenting
an utterance in a way which correlates well with word and morpheme boundaries. The procedure requires a large set of utterances, elicited in a certain
manner from an informant (or found in a very large corpus); and it requires
that all the utterances be written in the same phonemic representation, determined without reference to morphemes. It then investigates a particular
distributional relation among the phonemes in the utterances thus collected;
and on the basis of this relation among the phonemes, it indicates particular
points of segmentation within one utterance at a time. For example, in the
utterance /hiyzkwikər/ *He's quicker* it will indicate segmentation at the points
marked by dots: /hiy.z.kwik.ər/; and it will do so purely by comparing this
phonemic sequence with the phonemic sequences of other utterances.

The interest of this procedure is as follows. At present we have distributional procedures for finding the phonemes of a language, and we have procedures
for testing morphologically whether any arbitrary segment is or is not a
morph, by describing its distributional relations to other segments. We lack,
however, any direct procedure for finding the segments which morphological
analysis would show to be morphs. We have had to depend upon various
indirect methods, or upon distributional or semantic guesses, to tell us what
segments seemed worth testing for morphemic status.[2] The procedure described below may serve to fill this gap. It segments each utterance to which
it is applied. When we test the resulting segments by the usual morphological
methods, we find that most of our procedurally-obtained segmentations
occur at the word and morpheme boundaries for that utterance.[3] This procedure can therefore provide the segments for morphological analysis, even
though it does not tell us directly that any particular segment of an utterance
(e.g. the /ər/ above) is a morph, or a word; and obviously it cannot tell us
anything about its meaning. The decision as to morphemic status is made,
as before, with the usual morphological methods. And when these distributional methods are applied to our procedurally obtained segments, they

Language **31**, No. 2 (1955), 190–222.

not only test the morphemic aptness of the segmentation but also adjust it (whenever it does not fall on morpheme boundaries) to accord with morpho-logical relations. For methodological purposes and for special problems – though certainly not for practical work – this procedure can therefore replace the less orderly search for morphemic segments. In particular, all or almost all word boundaries come out from the procedure.

This completes a chain of procedures covering phonology and morpholo-gy: first, the procedure that starts with the sounds of utterances and yields a phonemic spelling of them, then the present procedure which starts with the phonemic spelling of utterances and yields a segmentation of them into phonemic sequences; and lastly, the morphological procedures which de-scribe the structure of the utterance as a distribution of these segments (and in so doing correct the segmentation to obtain better structural elements). The present procedure requires only activities which are already available at its position in the chain: a phonemic representation of utterances, and the known activities of eliciting (asking an informant for utterances) and count-ing. In particular, it involves no reference to the meaning of morphemes – that is, no knowledge or judgment of meanings or meaning-differences, and no reliance on the speaker's ability to respond in terms of the meaning or meaning-differences of morphemes.

0.2. *Plan of the Paper*

In this paper, the method will be presented empirically. One can raise deeper questions about the method: what relation between phonemes and mor-phemes makes it possible to find morpheme boundaries from a particular distributional relation among phonemes? Why should we have expected the particular relation described here to yield these boundaries? What impli-cations may be drawn from this result, what further investigations suggested? These questions will be touched upon in § 6, but only briefly, because they require an independent discussion, too ramified to serve as an introduction or conclusion to the present procedure (which requires enough space as it is).

The procedure will therefore be described without theoretical introduction. We will simply consider a particular way of counting phoneme distributions; and we will see how the segmentations indicated by this counting procedure coincide with the morpheme boundaries as we know them from morphologi-cal analysis. There is first a basic procedure, which gives the bulk of the desired correlations. To this are added several related procedures which in-crease the correlation between the counting method and morphological boundaries.

The basic procedure (§ 1) is to ask how many different phonemes occur (in various utterances) after the first n phonemes of some test utterance.[4] It will be found that the number of these possible successors to the first n phonemes varies with n: in the test utterance of § 1, 14 different phonemes occur (in one sentence or another) after the first two phonemes of the test utterance, while 29 occur after the first three. We segment the test utterance at the points where the number of successors reaches a peak.[5] To carry out this procedure, it is necessary that each phoneme be pronounceable. This raises certain difficulties, as in the case of junctures, which are discussed in § 2.

By the side of the basic procedure a number of modifications may be considered. The most fruitful of these are: to carry out the procedure backward from the end of the test utterance (§ 3.1); to consider the insertion of phonemic sequences at each point of the test utterance (§ 3.2); and to include an additional count of how many $(n+2)$th successors can be found after each $(n+1)$th successor (§ 3.3). Major additional results are obtained when we consider not only the number of phonemes at each point but also which particular phonemes are the ones that occur there. In all the utterances that begin with /hiyzk/ there are 11 phonemes which ever occupy the sixth place: /l, r, w, y, i, e, æ, a, ə, o, u/. We call this the VARIETY of phonemes after utterance-initial /hiyzk/.[6] In § 4 we correlate the variety of successors at each point, and their number, with the phoneme whose successors they are.[7] With the aid of this we find a periodicity in each sentence. If we segment the utterance on the basis of this periodicity we obtain an even higher agreement with morphemic segments as we know them through morphological analysis. Indeed, this periodicity would suggest to us that sentences can be segmented into morphemic elements, even if we did not know beforehand that such elements exist in language.

How fully all these methods correlate with the boundaries derived from morphological analysis will be briefly considered in § 5. The relation of such methods to linguistic structure is touched upon in § 6. A summary is given in § 7.

1. THE BASIC PROCEDURE: SUCCESSOR COUNTS

We take any utterance U written as a sequence of phonemes. (For the relevance of phonemic contours and junctures, see § 2.) We collect many utterances which begin with the first phoneme of our test utterance U, and count how many different phonemes occupy the second position in these utterances: these are the successors of the first phoneme of U. Then we collect many utterances which begin with the first TWO phonemes of U, and count how many different phonemes occupy the third position in these utterances: these are the successors of the first two phonemes of U. And so on down to the end of U. That is to say, for each utterance-initial sequence of U up to its nth phoneme ($n = 1, 2, \ldots$ up to the last phoneme of the utterance), we count all the different $(n+1)$th phonemes in the various (associated) utterances that begin with this same sequence of n phonemes. As we proceed along the phonemes of U, we find that for each n of U the number of successors, i.e. $(n+1)$th phonemes in the associated utterances, falls, then rises to a peak, then falls again, rises to a peak again, and so on. At the points at which this number reaches a peak, we place our tentative segmentation of U.

For example, consider the short utterance *He's clever* /hiyzklevər/. We collect utterances beginning with /h/: *When did you come? | Humans act like simians. | His ship's in. | He's out. | Hell, what's the use? | Had to, sorry. | Have you got it? | Harping on it won't help. | Hot coffee. | Her timing's off. | Hunting's a dumb thing to do. | Hope for the best. | Who is it? | Hook and ladder company.* The first phoneme in all of these is /h/, as in our test utterance. The second is one of the following: /w, y, i, e, æ, a, ə, o, u/. This is the variety of phonemes in second position, in those utterances whose first-position phoneme is the same as in *He's clever*; the number of successors for /h/[8] is 9.

We next collect utterances beginning with /hi/: *Hip-high in water. | Hit it back! | Hickory nuts are still available. | Hidden meanings were discovered.* And so on. When we continue this collection of utterances beginning with /hi/ we find one or another of the following phonemes in the third position after /hi/: /p, t, k, d, g, ð, s, č, z, l, m, n, h, y/. This is the variety of phonemes in third position, in those utterances whose first two positions have the same phonemes as *He's clever*; the successor count for /hi/ is 14.

In Table I, two test utterances are compared. In various utterances beginning with /h/ there are 9 different phonemes following the /h/; in those that begin with /hi/ there are 14 phonemes after the /hi/; in those that begin with /hiy/ there are 29 phonemes after /hiy/: /p/ in *Heaps of them*, /d/ in *He didn't*, and so on. In utterances beginning with /hiyz/ there are again 29 phonemes after /hiyz/, as in *He's pretending, He's trying to*, etc.; in those that begin with /hiyzk/ there are 11 phonemes after /hiyzk/, as in *He's cranky, He's quiet*, etc.; in those that begin with /hiyzkl/ there are 7 phonemes following, as in *He's clinching it, He's close*; and so on.

The second test utterance is *He's quicker*. Up to the first /k/ the string of phonemes is the same as before, so that the associated utterances and the count of successors at each position are the same. When we get to /hiyzkw/ we find, in new utterances beginning with this sequence, that 6 different phonemes follow the /hiyzkw/; 10 phonemes follow the /hiyzkwi/ in associated utterances that begin with that; and so on.

In *He's clever* we find peak numbers for the successors to /y/, /z/, /r/, dividing the utterance into /hiy/, /z/, and /klevər/. In *He's quicker* we have

TABLE I

T N	J 28 r	L 14 e	J 28 k	L 10 i	K 6 w	K 11 k	J 29 z	J 29 y	L 14 i	K 9 h
p	B	D	B	A			B	A	A	
t	B	A	B	A			B	A	A	
k	B	C	B	A			B	B	D	
b	B	C	B	D			B	A	C	
d	B	A	B				B	B	D	
g	B	C	B				B	B		
f	B	D	B				B	B	D	
θ	B		B				B	B	A	
v	B		B	D			B	B	A	
ð	B		B				B	A	A	
s	B	D	B				B	B	C	
š	B		B				B	B	D	
č	B		B				B	A		
z	B		B	A			B	B	A	
ž	B		B				B	B	A	
j	B		B				B	A	A	
l	B		B			B	B	B	A	
r	B		B			B	B	B	C	
m	B	D	B	A			B	A	D	
n	B		B				B	B		
ŋ						B				B
h	B		B	D			B	B	D	
w	B	C	B				B	B		

T N	J 28 r	L 1 e	N 1 v	L 8 e	K 7 1	K 11 k	J 29 z	J 29 y	L 14 i	K 9 h
p	B			D			B	A	A	
t	B						B	A	A	
k	B	A		D			B	B	D	
b	B						B	A	C	
d	B			D			B	A	D	
g	B						B	B		
f	B						B	B	D	
θ	B						B	B	A	
v	B						B	B	A	
ð	B						B	A	A	
s	B						B	B	C	
š	B						B	B	D	
č	B						B	A		
z	B			D			B	B	A	
ž	B			D			B	B	A	
j	B						B	A	A	
l	B					B	B	B	A	
r	B			D		B	B	B	C	
m	B			D			B	A	D	
n	B			D			B	B		
ŋ						B				B
h	B						B	B		
w	B						B	B		

		A	B	D	B	B	D		A		D	B	A	D	B	B	B	D	B	B
y	D	B	B	B	D	B				B	B		B	B	B	B	D	B	B	B
i	B	B	B	B	B	B				B	B		B	B	B	B	B	B	B	B
e	B	B	B	B	B	B				B	B		B	B	B	B	B	B	B	B
æ	B	B	B	B	B	B				B	B		B	B	B	B	B	B	B	B
a	B	B	B	B	B	B				B	B		B	B	B	B	B	B	B	B
ə	C	C	C	C	B	C		D		C	C		B	C	C	B	C	C	B	B
o	C	D	D	C	C	C				C	D		C	C	C	D	C	C	C	C
u	C	C	C	D	C	C				C	C		C	D	C	C	D	C	C	C

total

	A	B	C	D	average
	8	6	2	1	11.2
	6	21	2	4	2.3
	21	27	1	1	14.2
	7		2	2	14.3
			5	1	10.6
	1		1		5.9
		27			14.8
	8	6	2	4	11.2
	6	21	1	1	2.3
	21	27	1	1	14.2
	7		2	2	14.3
			4	1	10.6
	1	27	6	1	14.3 / 10.6
	8	6	1		2.3 / 11.2
		27	5	5	14.8 / 2.5
	4	27	1	1	14.8

Notes:

If a point in a given column and row is filled (by A, B, C, or D), the phoneme at the head of the row occurs as the $(n+1)$th successors to the sequence (above) ending in the nth phoneme at the top of the column. For example, the sequence /hi/ may be followed by /k/ (as in *hickory*) but not by /f/; here $n=2$ and /k/ is one of the $(n+1)$th phonemes. The sequence /hiyzkle/ may be followed by /t/; here $n=7$ and /p/ is one of the $(n+1)$th phonemes.

N: the number of $(n+1)$th successors to the sequence that ends in the nth phoneme beneath the number.

T: the type of successor variety (§ 4) after the same phoneme sequence.

A, B, C, D: the number of $(n+2)$th successors to the sequence indicated by the column and row in question (§ 3.3); for example, the number of such successors to /hip/ is A, the number of such successors to /hiyk/ is B. The totals below indicate how many $(n+1)$th successors to the sequence ending in the nth phoneme at the top of the column have A $(n+2)$th successors, how many have B $(n+2)$th successors, and so on. The average is of the B, C, D $(n+2)$th successors only (notes 17 and 18), per $(n+1)$th phoneme.

peaks for the successors to /y/, /z/, the second /k/, and /r/, dividing the utterance into /hiy/, /z/, /kwik/, /ər/. Very small rises in number, such as the 8 for the successor to /e/, are not in general a basis for segmentation (§ 5). In this simple example, then, the peaks accord with the boundaries of words and morphemes. We will see below that in some situations the results are not so simple, and auxiliary operations will be introduced to obtain such cuts in the utterance as will correlate with the usual morphemic segmentation.

Sources of Data. The procedure requires a large number of associated utterances sectionally identical with U, some in their first phoneme, others in their first two phonemes, and so on. We could draw these utterances from some written corpus; but the corpus would have to be prohibitively large if we are to be able to find in it, for any U we choose, enough associated utterances for each *n* of U. The only practicable way of finding the required utterances is to elicit them from an informant, i.e. to ask him for any utterances beginning with /h/, then for any utterances beginning with /hi/, and so on. Such eliciting in no way prejudices our result, since it merely selects, from among the utterances which the informant can make, those whose first *n* phonemes are the same as in U. It cannot bring up successors which would not occur normally, for example, eliciting cannot make an informant produce an utterance with /v/ as successor to /hiyzk/. And such eliciting does not involve knowledge of morpheme boundaries on the part of the informant or the investigator.

2. PROBLEMS OF PHONEMIC REPRESENTATION

The procedure above measures the change of successor variety as we proceed through the phonemes of an utterance. In order to obtain a clear picture of how the growing string of its phonemes affects the successor variety, it would be natural to consider at each phonemic position all the phonemic distinctions that are made at that position. Such a representation of the successive phonemic distinctions in an utterance is precisely its phonemic spelling. However, simplifications of phonemic systems have led to various departures from the pure successive representation of simple segmental phonemes. Intonations are sometimes marked by contour indicators like /?/ or by tone-numbers at the change points, although the tones are pronounced not by themselves but simultaneously with the vowels and with some of the consonants. Stress is marked before the syllable or over the vowel symbol, but it is pronounced throughout the syllable. Juncture is written as a phonemic mark among the phonemes; it is pronounced as part of the neighboring consonants and vowels. Long vowels (and consonants) are sometimes written as doubles. And restricted phonemes can be expressed by long components.

For graphic representation it does not matter how these nonsegmental phonemic distinctions are marked, so long as their placing is defined. But in a procedure which measures the effect of successive marks, each phonemic contribution should be marked in the place where it physically occurs. In particular, eliciting from informants (who are not acquainted with the phonemic analysis) requires that each successive phonemic location be pronounced with all the phonemic distinctions it introduces, and that there be no phonemic element which is unpronounceable (such as a zero phoneme), since the effect of such a phoneme upon the successor variety could not be communicated by the informant.

The required phonemic writing is exemplified in Table II. Instead of a segmental juncture phoneme, we write a suprasegmental juncture symbol over the first phoneme which exhibits junctural phenomena: thus /p̟̂/ indi-

TABLE II

```
5 29  8 12  7 29  7 14 14 29 29 10  7  7  2  1 28  7  9 29
ð  ə  n  a  y  t  r  e  y  t  s  p  r  i  t  i  y  l  o  w

         29  7 14  9 28 28
             +           +                               +
   ð  ə  n  á  y  t  r  è  y  t  s  p  r  ì  t  i  y  l  ó  w
      2                                             31  1
          5  5  1  1 29 29
                   +                                     +
   ð  ə  n  á  y  t  r  è  y  t  s  p  r  ì  t  i  y  l  ó  w
      2                                             31  1
```

The night-rate (nitrate) 's pretty low

```
   10 13 29 27 16 11 28 10 29
   b  a  y  t  æ  k  s  i  y

   10 13 29 10 14  5  2  2 29
            +              +
   b  à  y  t  æ  k  s  i  y
      2        3     1
      2        3     3+
```

By taxi

Notes:

Numbers below the letters indicate tones. (The last line applies to the statement intonation 231 of *By taxi/./* and the question intonation 233 + of *By taxi/?/.*) Eliciting sequences from an informant would be difficult if we were to treat junctures as segmental phonemes – for instance, if after obtaining the successors to /ð/, and the successors to /ðə/, we were to ask next for the successors to /ðə +/. Accordingly, instead of segmental junctures, we use junctural allophones of neighboring phonemes. A plus over a letter indicates the prejunctural allophone; the following phoneme then appears in its postjunctural allophone.

cates the prejunctural allophone of /p/. Instead of intonation (and stress) contours, we write a suprasegmental tone (and stress) symbol beneath (and above) the first phoneme with which the contour is audible. The contour and juncture phenomena on any following phonemes are unmarked since they depend automatically on the first mark; for example, the continuation of a tone on successive vowels, or the appearance of a post-junctural /r/ after a pre-junctural /t̟/ in /náytrèyt/. Analogously, long vowels are written as single phonemes.

In Table II we obtain, when junctures and contours are not specified, the following peak-segmentation: /ðə.nayt.reyt.s.pritiy.low./. The phonemic representation here does not specify as between *night-rate* and *nitrate*, and the count yields the fuller division, into *night-rate*. What we get at each point are the successors both for *night-rate* and for *nitrate*; after the first /t/ the successors for *night*, being a peak, include and thus mask the successors for *nit-*. In the second line, where the junctural allophones of *night-rate* are specified, we get the same segmentation, correlating with the morphology of *night-rate*, but with lower successor-counts in *rate* since the successors due to *nit-* (and due to *night-ray*) are absent. And in the third line, where the junctural allophones of *nitrate* are specified, we get /ðə.naytreyt.s. pritiy.low./ which correlates with morphology, with no segmentation after /nayt/.

In the second set we obtain, when junctures and contours are not specified, a segmentation /bay.t.æks.iy./ *By taxi*. The peak after /t/ is due to *bite*; this morphemic division would not satisfy the remainder of the utterance, but that is not known when we are eliciting successors to /bayt/, and in any case that would be a morphological rather than a phoneme-count consideration. The peak after /s/ is due to *by tax*. In the next line we take the counts both for *By taxi* and for *By taxi?*, specifying juncture and contours in each case. The counts for both cases are the same, and correlate with morphology: /bay.tæksiy./.

Operating without Juncture. These results suggest that when we apply the successor count to utterances in a complete phonemic writing, we get a segmentation which agrees well with morphological analysis. Nevertheless, there are reasons for using a simplified phonemic representation which does not specify junctures and intonation or stress contours. One might ask, How do we know that any segmentation obtained without specifying junctures or contours would also be obtained in the real utterance, which specifies junctures and contours? In particular, could it perhaps introduce unjustified correlations with morpheme boundaries, i.e. segmentations which agree with morphological analysis but which would not be obtained if we had specified the junctures and contours? To answer this, we first note from Table II that segmentations which correlate with morpheme boundaries can be obtained both with and without specifying junctures and contours. Indeed, when junctural phenomena are specified, the segmentation accords all the better with morphological analysis (cf. also *Summers, we're out* in Table IV). Hence any correlation with morphology that is obtained without specifying junctures or contours appears to be valid as far as it goes, since it would in general also be obtained when these are included.[9]

One might then ask further, Granted that the segmentation obtained without specifying the junctures is generally similar to (but not quite as good as) that for the complete phonemic writing, why nevertheless should we wish to omit the junctures and contours? The answer is as follows. First, many utterances have alternant forms with and without juncture (e.g. after *a*). Second, informants who are not linguistically trained usually cannot maintain particular junctural and contour allophones as they repeat the sectional strings of phonemes, e.g. they cannot repeat /sêmərẑwìyt̄/ of *Summers, we're out* as distinct from the /sêmərẑwìy̆r/ of *Summers, we rent a cabin*, even though the juncture is different. Third, not all phonemes are equally audible, and their presence in an utterance is not equally definite. In particular, junctures are often less audible; and if we are given a sentence pair which is distinguished by a juncture, we often mishear or are uncertain. Hence a test which counts the effect of juncture equally with that of other phonemes is hard to carry out.[10]

In view of this, it is permissible and preferable to use just the segmental phonemes for most test utterances in making successor counts. As to alternative analyses of the segmental phonemes, it matters little which one is used, so long as the same analysis is used for the test utterance and all associated ones. For the segmentation is decided not on the basis of the actual successor count, but on how the count rises and falls; and this is more or less the same no matter what the phonemic analysis.[11]

3. MODIFICATIONS OF THE PROCEDURES

Various modifications of the basic procedure can be devised. The three modifications presented below yield segmentations that agree more closely with morphological analysis.

3.1. *Predecessor Count (Backward)*

The first modification is to carry out a predecessor count, going backward from the end of the utterance, similar to the successor count forward from the beginning. This means taking the last phoneme of a test utterance, then its last two, then its last three, and so on, and asking in each case for various utterances that could end with this sequence. We count the predecessors in the associated utterances, i.e. what different phonemes occur in $(n+1)$th place counting backward before these utterance-final n phonemes. We segment the test utterance before each peak; the agreement with morphology can be seen in Tables IV and VII.[12]

In English and many other languages, there are three main situations in which a backward test corrects the results of a forward test. The first is where we fail to get a peak before a morpheme because it is in grammatical agreement with some preceding morpheme. For example, in *It disturbs me* we get only 3 successors to /itdistərb/, because -*s* is always present here after *it* unless -*ed* or -*ing(ly)* occurs; in *They disturb me* that is not the case, and we get 29 successors (and a segmentation) after /ðeydistərb/. In such cases, when we test the utterance backward, we find 18 predecessors (indicating a segmentation) before /zmiy/.

The second situation is when we fail to get a peak after a morpheme which is rather limited in its distribution in respect to what follows it. For example, in *Let me qualify this* we get only one successor to /letmiykwal/, namely /i/: *qualify, qualitatively at least ...*, etc. But when we work backward, we find about 13 predecessors before /ifayðis/, suggesting a segmentation here. A special case arises when a morpheme has a morphophonemic form of limited distribution. In *He's a dramatic speaker*, we find only one successor /t/ after /hìyzədræmǽ/, and only one successor /i/ after /hìyzədræmǽt/, since *dramat* as alternate of *drama* occurs only before -*ic* (and -*is personae*). But backward, we find about 15 predecessors (yielding a segmentation) before /ikspiykər/: *She's a terrific speaker, forensic*, etc.

The third and most important situation is that of sectional homonyms (§ 5), where the first part of a morpheme is identical with some whole morpheme: e.g. *They left* has a peak after /ðeyl/ because this is homonymous with *they'll*; but when we go backward we get no peak before /eft/, only before /left/.

The backward operation is then no closer an approximation to morpheme boundaries than is the forward[13]; but it is a check on the forward operation. In many cases the two will yield peaks at the same points. These will usually be points of morpheme boundary for the test utterance; but not necessarily, for we may be dealing with a case where both the beginning and the end of the stretch happen to have homonyms.[14] In some cases, one direction yields a peak at a given location where the other does not. Then either the peak is wrongly due to a sectional homonym, or the lack of a peak is wrongly due to a directionally limited morpheme or alternant. The decision among these possibilities can be made only by morphological tests or with the procedure of § 4.

3.2. *Insertion*

The procedure of § 1 is sometimes inadequate for morphemic correlation chiefly because it measures the dependences of successor count or variety only in respect to what precedes. Carrying this procedure out backward yields, in addition, the dependences on what follows in the utterance. Even the sum of these two operations will not give perfect morphemic correlation, because it has to count the dependence due to each side separately. Morphemes, however, are set up in the grammar on the basis of their relation to a whole sentence. If we wish to find divisions that will correlate more fully with the morphemic boundaries, and to do this by a constructional procedure of counting phonemic variety instead of by the morphological procedure of comparing utterances and substitution, we have to replace the successor and predecessor operations by a single operation of insertion.

We take a test sentence, and insert between the nth and $(n+1)$th phonemes any phonemic sequences (containing whatever morphemes or morpheme parts) such that the total constitutes an utterance of the language. For example, if our test sentence is *This is new* /ðisiznyuw/, we insert between /ð/ and /i/ such phonemic sequences as /əčæl/ making /ðəčælisiznyuw/ *The chalice is new*, or /æth/ to make *That hiss is new*, or /owzpiypəlsedðəčæl/ *Those people said the chalice is new*, and so on. Then we insert other sequences between /i/ and /s/: /yzmarkssowðætðəbak/ making *These marks show that the box is new*. Then we insert fitting sequences between /s/ and /i/: /buk/ making *This book is new*, /ilnəs/ *This illness is new*, /meyk/ *This make is new*, /tuw/ *This too is new*, /əðərwən/ *This other one is new*, etc. And so for every other position in the test utterance. We now count the end-variety of the insertions – how many different first phonemes and how many different last phonemes there were in all the insertions at a given position. Where this count is at a peak we introduce a segmentation. In the example above, we have an end-variety peak for the insertions between /ðis/ and /iznyuw/.

In cases of agreement, limited bound morphemes, and morpheme alternants, the insertion end count shows at a given location how the location has different degrees of morphemic independence in the two directions. In the case of homonyms, the interference is reduced by the fact that each insertion has to fit into the whole utterance. Even when we have homonyms both forward and backward, as in *The silo walls were up*, the undesired peak will often be kept out by the fact that the insertions would have to fit both homonyms at the same time.

The method of insertion is, however, considerably less convenient and direct for informant testing than the forward or even the backward procedures.

3.3. *Counting the (n+2)th*

One important modification gives a closer approximation to the morpheme boundaries. This is to count at location n not only how many different $(n+1)$th phonemes occur, but also how many different $(n+2)$th phonemes occur for each $(n+1)$th.[15]

What can this additional information show about the nth place? To answer this, we consider whether there are any regularities in the sequence of successor counts. If there are any connections between neighboring counts, we might learn something about the nth place not only from its own successor count, but also from the next successor count, at the $(n+1)$th place. In looking over all the tables of data, we see that the successor counts generally decrease as we proceed through the phonemes from one peak to the next, except for slight rises at some of the vowels: *He'll admit my family* has the sequence of counts 9, 14, 29, 29, 18, 12, 4, 2, 29, 8, 12, 28, 10, 13, 2, 3, 1, 1, 28; *...a dramatic* has 22, 13, 7, 2, 1, 1, 1, 1, 28. We can draw some empirical conclusions from the results. For example (in English), if the $(n+1)$th phoneme is a consonant and has around 10 successors, there is likely to be a peak (i.e. a morpheme boundary) after the nth phoneme. If the $(n+1)$th phoneme has only 1 or 2 successors, it is likely that there is no peak (and no morpheme boundary) after the nth place, i.e. the nth and $(n+1)$th phonemes are together inside a morpheme.[16]

The regularity is statistical: it may not appear in the successive counts of a particular test utterance. But we can bring its effect into play by recording for each nth phoneme of our utterance not only how many successors can occupy the $(n+1)$th place (in the associated utterances), but also how many $(n+2)$th successors each of these successors could have there, i.e. how many different phonemes can occupy the $(n+2)$th place for each phoneme in the $(n+1)$th place in the associated utterances. For this purpose it is not necessary to give the exact number of the $(n+2)$th phonemes, as was done in note 15. Because of the numbers which are characteristic for each inter-peak place, as indicated for English in note 16, it suffices to record whether they are, say, around 28 (category A) or around 15 (B), or around 6 (C), or around 2 (D).[17] Then we find that if two phonemes are inside the same morpheme, the second will have fewer of its $(n+2)$th successors in the higher categories and more in the lower.

In Table III, we see a correlation between the distribution of A, B, C, D and morpheme boundaries (as these are known from morphology). When there is a word peak at n, there are usually 29 successors (initial in the next word); and usually of these, 20 have 8 to 18 successors (as second phonemes of the word), 8 have 5 to 7 successors, 1 (namely /u/) has 1 successor. When

TABLE III
Count of $(n+2)$th phonemes for each $(n+1)$th phoneme

It disturbed ...

	i	t	d	i	s	t	ɚ	r	b	d
A	6			2					2	
B	1	20	5	1	4					20
C	1	8	4	4	11	2				8
D	8		1	10	7	3	1	1	1	
Q	16	28	10	17	22	5	1	1	3	28

... family

	f	æ	m	i	l	i	y
A					1		
B	8	1	1				20
C		7					8
D	2	5	1	3		1	
Q	10	13	2	3	1	1	28

... left

	l	é	f	t
A			1	
B	7	3		20
C				8
D		13		1
Q	7	16	1	29

Some ...

	s	ə	m
A		3	
B	8	2	20
C	6		8
D	1	9	1
Q	15	14	29

He's a dramatic ...

	h	ì	y	z	ə	d	r	æ	m	ǽ	t	i	k
A		8										1	
B	5		20	20	15	6	3						20
C	3	2	8	8	7	5	2						8
D	1	4	1	1		2	2	2	1	1	1		
Q	9	14	29	29	22	13	7	2	1	1	1	1	28

Notes:

Q: the total number of $(n+1)$th successors to the nth phoneme above.
A: Of the total in Q, so many had about 28 $(n+2)$th successors in turn.
B: Of the total in Q, so many had about 15 $(n+2)$th successors in turn.
C: Of the total in Q, so many had about 6 $(n+2)$th successors in turn.
D: Of the total in Q, so many had about 2 $(n+2)$th successors in turn.

some of the successors have about 28 successors in turn (A), that means that there can be a word boundary after these successors. Aside from these cases of A, we find that as we proceed inside a morpheme the average number of $(n+2)$th phonemes per $(n+1)$th always decreases. In *some* the total number of $(n+1)$th successors to n decreases only from 15 to 14; but the average of $(n+2)$th successors per $(n+1)$th decreases clearly, from 8 B + 6 C + 1 D to 2 B + 9 D.

Results

We have found that the $(n+2)$th average decreases monotonically in most inter-peak stretches, and that the first, second, and third places after a peak (or utterance beginning) have characteristic $(n+2)$th averages. Now we can use this information in checking on some peculiar counts (chiefly those due to vowel–consonant differences, or to somewhat limited bound morphemes, or to certain morphophonemics).

For example, in *family* there is a slight peak in the $(n+1)$th count from 10 after /f/ to 13 after /fæ/; but the $(n+2)$th average falls from 8 B+2 D to 1 B+7 C+5 D. In *left* there is a bigger peak in the $(n+1)$th count, from 7 after /l/ to 16 after /le/; but the $(n+2)$th average falls clearly from 7 B to 3 B+13 D. In both cases, then, the peak for the $(n+1)$th count does not indicate a morpheme boundary. On the other hand, in *disturbed* we have a peak of 22 after /dis/ which is not relatively larger than these others (though it reaches a higher number); but the $(n+2)$th average shows that there is a segmentation here: it first drops (within *dis-*) from 5 B+4 C+1 D to 1 B+ 4 C+10 D, and then rises to 4 B+11 C+7 D to fall again to 2 C+3 D and on to just 1 D. This means that more successors to /dis/ than to /di/ had a high number of successors in turn, which is due to the fact that many successors to /dis/ were the initial phonemes of new morphemes and therefore had the relatively high successor variety which characterizes the early part of a morpheme.

Finally, in *He's a dramatic*...we see another 22 after /hiyzə/. This 22 is not a peak, but the sequence 22, 13, 7, etc. begins with suspiciously high numbers. When we consider the $(n+2)$th average for these 22, we find that it is little lower if at all than the $(n+2)$th average of the two preceding positions, which were word boundaries. For /hiyz/ we have 20 B+8 C+1 D, while for /hiyzə/ 15 B+7 C[18]; thereafter there is a clear drop to 6 B+5 C+2 D and on to 3 B+2 C+2 D and to 2 D. We judge then that in respect to the $(n+2)$th average /hiyzə/ appears like a word boundary; and morphological investigation shows that in this position /ə/ and a morphophonemic alternant /ən/ fill out between them the position of a morpheme. For contrast, note that in...*we're out* (Table IV) the $(n+1)$th count is rather similar: 29 after /wiyr/ and 20 after /wiyræ/. But when we check the $(n+2)$th average there, we find that it drops sharply from the 20 B+8 C+1 D for the 29 successors of /wiyr/ to (4 A+) 2 B+7 C+7 D for the 20 successors of /wiyræ/. We therefore do not suspect a morpheme boundary after /wiyræ/ as we do after /hiyzə/ above.

4. SEQUENCES OF SUCCESSOR VARIETY

The operation of § 1 counts the successor variety at each n. The location of cuts depends only on the peaks of the successor counts. The modifications of § 3 deal only with the counts. We now consider a related operation, which uses the procedure of § 1, but differs in one respect. Instead of merely counting how many different successors there are at n, we list the specific ones which are there. The importance of this new step is that we find certain recurring sequences of successor varieties.

Recurring sequences of exactly the same successor varieties are rare; but it is possible to group certain similar varieties into classes in such a way that repeating sequences of those classes are common. For example, in *He's clever*, /hiy/ and /hiyz/ both have the same number of successors, 29, and the variety which makes up this number is identical: all the phonemes except /ž, ŋ/ – i.e. all the phonemes that occur at utterance initial. Let us call this variety J. Again, in Table I, /hiyzklevər/, /hiyzkwik/, and /hiyzkwikər/ all have 28 successors, again identical: all the phonemes except /ž, ŋ, u/. We will call this variety J 28; often it will be sufficient, as we will see, simply to call it J. After /h/ we find 9 successors – the 7 vowels and /y, w/. After /hiyzk/ we find 11 successors – the above and /l, r/. In each case these are all the phonemes that would occur after the nth phoneme, /h/ and /k/ respectively, when these consonants are first in an utterance. Let us call this variety K; when a sequence ending in a consonant x has the K variety of successors, that means it has the same successors that x has when x is in utterance initial. K after phoneme x therefore indicates the phonemes that occur in second place in all utterances beginning with x; it almost always includes all the vowels, and usually also a few consonants, depending on the phoneme x. We further notice that /hiyzkl/ has 7 successors, just the vowels, which is what follows /l/ after utterance initial consonant, and /hiyzkw/ has only 6 of the vowels, as does /w/ after an utterance-initial consonant. We can call these varieties K': when a sequence ending in consonants xy has the variety of successors K', it has the same successors that xy have when they are an utterance-initial cluster.[19] We may compare this with /hiyzklev/, which has only one successor, and is thus quite different from initial /v/.

For each language we notice that not all varieties of successors occur, at one point or another; only certain classes or types of varieties (e.g. J or K) occur as successors, at least with any frequency; and some particular classes (e.g. J) occur very frequently. What is even more important, only certain sequences of these successor-variety types (J, K, etc.) occur. We have here, then, a situation which is well known in phonology and morphology; and we can carry out on these successor varieties the same kind of linguistic operations that we carry out on allophones or morphemes. We find that it is possible to group certain similar varieties into classes, like the class K above, in such a way that regularities can be asserted about the occurrence of these classes: a certain one always occurs with a certain other; or one can be treated as a positional alternant of another; or most of the stretches from peak to peak exhibit a few fixed sequences of these classes. And if in some utterance the peaks do not come at the boundaries of these regular sequences of variety classes, we may find that the stretch covered by the regular sequence of varieties correlates better with morphological boundaries than does the stretch from peak to peak.

4.1. For English, we set up empirically the following classes of successor varieties:

J: all phonemes except /ž, ŋ/.

K   (after x): those phonemes which occur after utterance-initial consonant x – the vowels and from 0 to 8 consonants, depending on x.

K′ (after $[z]xy$): those phonemes which occur after the utterance-initial
consonant cluster $(z)xy$ – the vowels and from 0 to 2 consonants.

L: any number of consonants only, as successor variety to vowels or
post-vocalic /w, y, h/, or as successor variety to a consonant which
precedes a consonant whose successor variety is J.

M: a small number (usually 10 or fewer) of consonants and vowels, not
satisfying the conditions for K, K′; usually we say that x has successor variety M only if M contains some phonemes which are not
included in K.

N: vowels only, usually 4 or fewer.

In terms of these, we find that in inter-peak stretches, i.e. after one successor peak (or from the beginning of an utterance) up to and including the
next peak, the sequences can generally be expressed by the following formula:

$$\begin{array}{l}\text{Syllabic character} \\ \quad \text{of the } n\text{th phoneme:} \\ \text{Its successor variety:}\end{array}\quad \begin{pmatrix}\text{consonant}\\ \text{K (K′ K′)}\end{pmatrix} \begin{array}{c}\text{vowel}\\ \text{L}\end{array} \begin{pmatrix}\text{w, y, h}\\ \text{L}\end{pmatrix} \begin{bmatrix}\text{consonant vowel}\\ \text{M N}\quad \text{L}\end{bmatrix}\begin{pmatrix}\text{w, y, h}\\ \text{L}\end{pmatrix}\begin{bmatrix}\quad\end{bmatrix} \begin{pmatrix}\text{consonant}\\ \text{L or M}\end{pmatrix} \text{J}$$

All parenthetic sections can be independently omitted. The square brackets
may yield one or several consonants (of which only the last or none has
successor N) before the vowel, and the whole sequence in square brackets
may be repeated several times. The only case where the first vowel with
successor L is lacking is the case where the first vowel in the inter-peak
stretch has successor variety J, i.e. is the last phoneme of the stretch; this
occurs in *a, the*. The chief additional observation is that the number of
phonemes in each variety falls sharply as we go through the inter-peak
stretch[20]; and the numbers in N, K, K′ (which contain vowels) are smaller
than the numbers in L, M for the same position between peaks.[21]

That this summary satisfies most of the inter-peak stretches can be seen
from the data in Table IV. What is of interest, however, is that when apparent
irregularities are interpreted as special cases of this very sequence, we obtain
a closer correlation with the usual morpheme boundaries than the numerical

TABLE IV

This table shows the results of § 1, § 3.1, and § 4. The number ABOVE a phoneme indicates the number of $(n+1)$th successors to the utterance from the beginning up to and including that phoneme (the nth); the capital letter above it indicates the type of successor variety after that phoneme. The number BELOW a phoneme indicates the number of predecessors to the utterance end, from that phoneme to the close of the utterance; the capital letter below it indicates the type of predecessor variety before that phoneme. J yields a segmentation after the phoneme below it; Z yields a segmentation before the phoneme above it. Dots are placed after each J (in French after I, E, F) and before each Z to show the segmentation from each direction, so as to facilitate comparison with the dots placed between phonemes. The latter dots indicate (not phonemic junctures but) the division of this utterance as it is established by the usual morphological methods: a colon marks a division between words; a single dot marks a division which has a bound morpheme (or morpheme variant) on at least one side. Small differences in phonemics and in successor numbers are due to differences between informants.

Small raised letters refer to the notes after the table.

```
K   L   J · K   L   N   L   J · J · K   L   J
7   2   29  10  3   1   1   28  28  7   9   28
y   u   w : b   a   ð   ə   r · d : m   i   y
```

You bothered me

```
L   J · K   L   J · K   L   L   M[a] J · K   L   J
16  29  10  17  22  5   1   1   3    29  7   9   28
i   t : d   i   s · t   ə   r   b  · d : m   i   y
```

It disturbed me

```
K   L   J[i] · L   J · J · K   L   J · J · L   J[i] · J
15  14  29     17  29  29  7   11  29  29  22  28   29
s   ə̂  m      ə   r · z : w   ì   y · r : æ̂  w    t
```

Summers we're out

Without juncture after the second /r/. With juncture, the last three phonemes have L 20, L 4, J 29, and there is no homonym at /... æw/

```
K   L   J · J · L   M[r] N   L   J · K   L   J · K   L   N   L   N   L   J
9   14  29  29  18  12   4   2   29  8   12  28  10  13  2   3   1   1   28
h   i   y · l : æ̂  d  · m   i   t : m   a   y : f   æ   m   i   l   i   y
```

He'll admit my family

The M 12 suggests a possible boundary after /æd/.

```
K   L   L   J · J · L   L   J · L   J · K   L   J · K   K'
10  3   6   29  29  11  1   28  12  28  9   14  20  8   1
d   o   h   g · z : a   h   r : i   n · d   i   s   p   y
```

```
L   L   J · L   M[m] N   L   J · K   K'  L   J · L   J
1   1   28  1   2    1   1   28  11  6   9   28  2   28
u   w   t · ə   b  · l   i   y : k   w   i   k · ə   r
```

Dogs are indisputably quicker

```
K   L   J · J · J · K   K'  L   N   L   N[m] L   J · K   L   M[g] L   J
9   14  29  29  22  13  7   2   1   1   1    28  15  12  7    4   28
h   ì   y · z : ə : d   r   æ̂  m   æ̂  t  · i   k : s   í   ŋ  · ə   r
```

He's a dramatic singer

```
K  K'  L  J · K  Lm  J · K  L  J · K  L  L  J · L  J
9  5   1  29   10 19  28  8  12 28 5  4  1  29 11 28
h  w   ə  t :  d  i · d:h i  y:θ i  ŋ  k:ə v
22 1   7  18   23 1   3  9  19 4  22 15 3  12 23 6
Z  S   S·Z"h·Z S  T   S  S  T·Z S  T' T·Z T
```

What did he think of ?

The sectional homonym *ink of* has not enough predecessors to make a peak backwards. T 3 is low because few verbs occur before *he think of*. For a cut at S 9 before /hiy/, see § 4.2

```
K  K'  L  J · K  Lm  J · K  L  J · K  L  L
9  5   1  29   10 19  28  8  12 28 5  4  1
h  w   ə  t :  d  i · d:h i  y:θ i  ŋ
20 1   1  8    15 1   3  10 6  4  17 3  4
Z  S   S  T ·  Z  S   T' S  S  T · Z  S  T'
```

```
J · L  Jh · L  J · J · K  L  J · K  L  L  J
29 11 28 1   28 26 6  2  24 7  3  1  28
k : ə  v  ĭ   n · z : w  ə  r : f  o  h  r
11 22 3  8   8  17 23 24 3  23 20 6  3
T · Z  T' S  T · Z' · Z · Zh T · Z  S  T' T
```

What did he think ovens were for ?

S 10 before /hiy/ can be suspected of being a low Z. The grammatical position and the selection permit few words before this *he*

```
L  J · K  L  J · K  L  L  La J · Jh · M  L  L  Jh · L  M  L  J
10 28 11 11 27 7  6  6  3  28 21 9   2  9  28 4   10 2  28
i  t : k  ə  n · t  e  y  n · z : ž  l  u  w  m  ĭ  n  ž  m
22 19 21 1  1  7  7  3  7  16 22 1   1  1  2  1   5  13 9
Z · Z"h · Z  S  T' R  S  T' T · Z' · Z T' S  T'  R  S  R  S  T
```

It contains aluminum

The M 10 after /ĭn/ can be taken as a J which is very low because of selection; it comes from the homonymous *It contains a loom in* ... The S 13 before /žm/ may be taken as a Z low because of selection; many of the 13 predecessors come from words ending in *-um* (which might be morphologically analyzed as a separate morpheme). The R 7 before /teynz/ raises the question of a morpheme boundary here (§ 4.2 end). See § 4.1

```
K  L  J · Jh · L  Lm  J · K  L  J · L  M  L  L  N  L  N  L  J
6  4  29 29 13 1   28 14 15 28 18 10 2  4  1  1  2  1  28
ð  e  y : l  e  f · t : s  ə  m : ž  l  u  w  m  ĭ  n  ž  m
24 12 4  24 2  3   18 23 7  7  22 1  1  1  2  1  5  13 9
Z  S  T · Z  S  T' · Z" · Z  S  T · Z  T' S  T' R  S  R  S  T
```

They left some aluminum

```
K  L  J · K  K'  L  L  J · J · K  L  J
6  4  29 14 7   8  1  29 29 14 13 28
ð  e  y : s  w   a  y  p · t : s  ə  m
23 10 4  23 1   3  3  9  18 23 8  9
Z  S  T · Z  S   S  T' T · Z" · Z  S  T
```

They swiped some

With voiceless allophone of /w/ after /s/, hence no homonymy with *wipe*, going backwards

J	·	K	K′	L	J	·	K	L	L	N	L	J	·	L	J	·	K	L	Nᵐ	L	J
22		10	7	10	28		15	8	8	2	1	28		9	28		10	8	1	1	28
ə	:	b		r	i		k	:	s	a	y	l		o	w	:	i	z	: b	e	t	·	ə	r
22		23	3	9	8		22	4	3	27	17	4		24	18		24	9	14	24	8
Z	·	Z	R	S	T	·	Z	S	T	· Zʰ	S	R	·	Z	·	Z′ʰ	· Z	S	T	· Z	T

A brick silo is better

K	J	·	K	L	Jⁱ	·	K	L	J	·	K	L	L	L	J	·	J	·	K	L	J	·	L	J
5	29		15	12	28		7	5	29		7	1	8		29	29		7	2		29	9		27
ð	ə	:	s	a	y		l	o	w	:	w	o	h	l	·	z	:	w	ə		r	:	ɔ̆	p
24	3		23	10	2		27	15	3		23	16	1	8		18	23		24	5		23	11
Z	S	·	Z	S	T	·	Zⁱ	S	T	·	Z	S	T′	T	·	Z′	· Z	· Zʰ	T	·	Z	T

The silo walls were up

K	J	·	K	L	Jʰ	·	K	L	J	·	K	L	L	L	J	·	K	L	M	J	·	L
5	29		15	12	28		7	5	29		7	5	11	28	10	11	9		14	5
ð	ə	:	s	a	y		l	o	w	:	l	a	y	k	: b	i	l		d	·	i
23	23		22	1	4		9	10	3		22	7	3	13	23	3	4		11	22
Z	·	Zʰ	· Z	S	T′	R	S	T	·	Z	S	T′	T	· Z	S	T′	T	· Z

J	·	L	J	·	J	·	K	L	L	N	L	J	·	K	L	N	L	J
29		9	29		21		7	2	8	1	1	27		8	8	1	1	27
ŋ	:	i	z	:	ə	: w	o	h	t	ə		r	:	t	æ	w	ə		r
4		22	17		24		22	2	1	15	22	7		23	23	23	24	6
T	·	Z	· Z′ʰ	· Z	· Z	S	T′	T	· Zʰ	T	·	Z	· Zʰ	· Zʰ	· Zʰ	T

The silo-like building is a water tower

For the final Z sequences, see § 4.2 end

Notes:

ᵃ A cut is lacking here because the following morpheme is in grammatical agreement (in the direction in which we are going). The cut would be obtained in the reverse direction.

ᵍ A cut is lacking because our morpheme occurs in this grammatical position with only a few successors. The cut would be obtained in the reverse direction.

ʰ An inappropriate cut is obtained here because the first part of the morpheme (proceeding in the direction in which we are going) is homonymous with a whole morpheme. When our morpheme occurs in other grammatical positions this cut may be avoided; and it is avoided in the reverse direction.

ⁱ Same as the preceding, except that the remainder of our morpheme is homonymous with still another morpheme. For this reason the cut is obtained also in the reverse direction.

ᵐ A cut is lacking because our morpheme occurs here in a morphophonemic form that has only one or a few successors. The cut would be obtained in the reverse direction.

ʳ A cut is lacking because the bound morpheme here has too few successor morphemes. The cut would be obtained in the reverse direction.

peaks had afforded. Our cuts will now be made not simply at peaks, but at the points where the above sequence ends, namely after J.

For example, one successor variety X which seems not to belong to any of these classes is the 22 consonants which we obtain after /ə/ in some (not all) of the instances where /ə/ comes at utterance beginning or after a peak (in /əbrík/ *a brick* but not in /sə́məlúwminəm/ *some aluminum*). We notice that this X appears before KK' *(a brick, a dramatic)*; in fact all the sequences of variety classes which occur after X are sequences which occur after J. We notice further that X includes all the consonants except /ž, ŋ/, which are precisely all the consonants of J. Finally the $(n+2)$th variety for each of the 22 members of X is the same as the $(n+2)$th variety for the corresponding 22 consonants in J. Hence we tentatively include the X successor variety of /ə/ as a variant of J, thus assuring a segmentation after the /ə/ which has X successors. This assignment is made independently of any complementary relation to *an*, but it will be supported when we find that there is a sequence *an* whose successors are precisely the vowel members of J. In contrast, the 22-consonant variety after /wiyrǽ/ of *we're out* is not classified in J, because it includes /ž, ŋ/, and because its $(n+2)$th average $(4 A+2 B+7 C+7 D)$ is far smaller than the $(n+2)$th average of J $(27 B+1 C+1 D)$.

In *It contains aluminum* we find the following successors after the successive phonemes of /əluwminəm/: J 21, M 9, L 2, L 9, J 28, L 4, M 10, L 2, J 28. Now the inter-peak sequence MLLJ does not otherwise occur, but the sequence LMLLJ does (see the formula above). If we wish to interpret this case in terms of our formula, we can regard it as the sum of two morphemic possibilities: One of these would take /ə/ as a separate morpheme, with successor J; then the next phoneme /l/ is the first of a word (with roughly the same successors as when it is the first of an utterance) and hence has successor K. The sequence would be JKLLJ. The other possibility would take /ə/ as the first phoneme of a longer word (since it occurs after a peak) with certain successors L (*adrenalin, ascorbic acid, allusions*, etc.); then the next phoneme /l/ is the second of the word and has a smaller number of successors M (*ulterior, albinos, alert...*, etc.). The sequence would be LMLLJ. Both possibilities would fit after *It contains*. But if a string of phonemes can yield both JKLLJ and also LMLLJ (if the first phoneme may constitute a whole morpheme or homonymously the beginning of a longer morpheme), then the sum of both JKLLJ and LMLLJ for that string of phonemes will be JMLLJ. For J includes L, so that we cannot observe the presence of L in the total successors to /ə/; and M includes K, so that we cannot observe the presence of K in the total successors to /əl/. We therefore interpret the aberrant JM...as being merely a resultant of JK... and LM... This means that there are two (homonymous) morphemic analyses here, *a l...* and *al...*;

and this correlates with the morphological analysis. Whether we locate a segmentation here depends on which analysis fits the remainder of the utterance. In this way we can recognize certain homonymous alternatives, which are added together (and therefore hidden) by the successor counts. Some but not all of these cases could also be recognized directly if we specified the junctural allophones.

When a small successor peak occurs, the sequence of variety-classes established here may help in deciding whether a cut should be placed after the peak. For example in *a water tower* we find the following class and number of successors for /əwohtər/: J 21, K 7, L 2, L 8, N 1, L 1, J 27. In considering the small peak at L 8, we ask whether it might not be taken as an unusually low J. If we did, then our next inter-peak stretch would be N 1, L 1, J 27, which would be an otherwise unknown type of inter-peak sequence. And if we try to correct this by saying that the N 1 is just an unusually low case of K, yielding the known sequence KLJ, then we face the unusual situation of having an inter-peak stretch begin with such a low successor count as 1. Hence we make no cut between L and N here.[22] In contrast, an unusually high M, even if it does not reach a peak, will often be found to correlate with the morphologically establishable morpheme boundaries, as in *admit* /ædmit/ with L 18, M 12, N 4, L 2, J 29.

4.2. Similar sequences can be set up for the classes of predecessor varieties, going backward. Most inter-peak stretches turn out to have the same sequence, if we group the predecessor-varieties into the following classes:

> Z: All the consonants and /ə/, except that /ð/ is often lacking, /ž/ extremely rare (depending on dialect), and /h/ almost only after /o/. /ə/ is frequently lacking, especially in what will turn out to be certain grammatical positions.
>
> T (before x): all or most vowels and a few consonants, the consonants being some (not necessarily all) of those which appear before x when x is the utterance-final consonant.
>
> T′: only the vowels, as predecessors to consonants (including /w, y/).[23]
>
> S: consonants, predecessors to vowels.
>
> R: some vowels and some consonants (including some not included in T).

The sequence of these before a peak (or from utterance end) up to and including the preceding peak usually follows this formula:

$$
\begin{array}{l}
\text{Syllabic character} \\
\quad \text{of the } n\text{th phoneme:} \\
\quad \text{Its predecessor variety}
\end{array}
\qquad
Z
\begin{pmatrix} \text{vowel} \\ S \end{pmatrix}
\begin{bmatrix} \text{consonant} & \text{vowel} \\ T' \quad R & S \end{bmatrix}
\begin{pmatrix} \text{consonant} \\ T' \end{pmatrix}
\begin{array}{c} \text{consonant} \\ T \end{array}
$$

Parenthetic sections are independently omissible. In the square brackets there may be none or several R, and one or no T'; and the parenthetic sequences may be repeated.[24] In the few inter-peak stretches which end on /ə/ instead of a consonant, the predecessor of /ə/ is a restricted S instead of T. The numbers in each predecessor class generally go down as we go backward in the inter-peak stretch and in the utterance.

Here again we can analyze irregular phenomena by interpreting them in terms of this sequence. Various rarer predecessor varieties can be assigned to the above classes on the basis of the sequences in which they occur. For example, a variety Z', of all voiced phonemes except the sibilants, occurs often before /z/ when /z/ is before a peak or at utterance end; and a variety Z", of all voiced phonemes except /d/, occurs often before /d/ in similar circumstances. We notice that the sequence before it often starts (going backward) with T, rather than T'; thus, the predecessors for /əvinz/ *ovens* are ZT'STZ', where the sequence ZT'ST is just what we expect before Z. Because of this, as also because the $(n+2)$th precedessor – i.e. the predecessor variety of each member of Z' or Z" – is the same as for the corresponding member of Z – we regard the Z' predecessor variety of /z/ and the Z" predecessor variety of /d/ as two alternants of Z. We can find this situation even in what seem to be the ordinary predecessors of /s, t/ before peaks or at utterance ends; and we can regard those predecessor varieties as alternants of Z' and Z" respectively. For we sometimes find that before /s, t/ also the sequence starts (backward) with T rather than T', as in /swaypt/ *swiped* Z 23, T' 1, S 3, T' 3, T 9, T 18. Our formula admits ZT'ST'T but not ZT'ST'TT; hence we interpret the last T 18 as a low Z". Later we will find that in certain positions the unique predecessor varieties of /z, s, əz/ (before peak or utterance end) complement each other, as do those of /d, t, əd/, and that these can be analyzed as alternants of a complete Z variety.[25]

In *What did he think of* we find for /didhiy/ Z 23, S 1, T 3, S 9, S 19, T 4. The sequence is irregular. The peak of 19 would suggest a cut before /iy/, interpreting S 19 as a low Z. But this would leave ZSTS, which does not otherwise occur. The fact that the numbers decrease in grammatically restricted positions permits us to consider the S 9 as a very low grammatically-reduced Z (the members of this S 9 being all included in Z), yielding two regular sequences ZSTZST which correlate with the morphemic division *did he.*

In *The silo walls were up* we have for /saylow/ Z 23, S 10, T 2, R 27, S 15, T 3, with an unusually high R before /low/. In such cases we may suspect that the peak is due not to a sharp increase of variety in the middle of a regular sequence, but rather to adding two alternative (homonymous) morphemic analyses (*low* and words like *furlough, hollow, silo*), one of which contributes a predecessor Z at this point and the other R or T' (whence the vowel members of this R 27 variety). The resultant is Z+R, and the segmentation is optional, depending on which analysis fits the rest of the utterance. If the sentence had not *silo* but *hollow* /halow/ – where the predecessors would be Z 23, S 2, R 27, S 15, T 3 – it would be clear that only the R contribution and not the Z is relevant for the R 27 in this utterance; because if we took the Z contribution and placed a cut there, the preceding Z 23, S 2 would have to constitute an inter-peak stretch in conflict with the formula above. In this way we are able in some cases (for *hollow* but not for *silo*) to reject a homonymous analysis of one section because it makes a neighboring section irregular.

In general, a small peak can be disregarded if it occurs inside an undividable sequence, e.g. in another /saylow/ where the predecessors are Z 22, S 1, T' 4, R 9, S 10, T 3. But where the sequence is divisible, an R which is not low may be suspected of including a (morpheme-bounding) Z as one of the alternative analyses: e.g. *admit* /ædmit/ Z 23, T' 1, R 7, S 3, T 10; *contains* /kənteynz/ Z 21, S 1, T' 1, R 7, S 7, T' 3, T 7, Z' 16. In this way we recognize the possibility of a segmentation before *mit* and *tain*.

In some cases we find a possible but rare situation, which calls our attention to the need for a morphological decision (§ 0.2) at that point. E.g. in *tower* /tæwər/ Z 23, Z 23, Z 23, Z 24, T 6, the string of Z raises our suspicions; it is due to a number of overlapping homonyms.

4.3. An interesting application of the sequence method arises in the case of French. If we look at the numbers of the successors in Table V, it seems that there are many peaks which do not correlate with the morphological boundaries of the sentences. However, we notice dependences among some of the successor varieties. For example, both /il/ and /ilsə/ have almost all the consonants and vowels as successors. But whereas each successor of /il/ has in turn a fair number of successors, we find after /ilsə/ that each consonant successor has about the same number of successors in turn as after /il/, while each vowel successor has very few successors in turn. Thus /p/ has many successors both after /il/ and after /ilsə/ (*il peut, il pleut, il pense, il prend; il se plaint, ils se parlent, il se propose, il se peint*). But whereas /e/ has many successors after /il/ (*il épouse, il écrit, il éclate, il écarte*), it has only one or two after /ilsə/ (*il se hérisse*). Let us call the variety after /il/ I and that after /ilsə/ E. Then we notice that the varieties neighboring E are restricted: chiefly, either E appears after a /ə/, in which case there will always be the particular successor variety F preceding it, or else E appears after some other vowel, in which case F may follow if a consonant plus vowel follow the /ə/ but not if two consonants or a vowel follow the /ə/. With this and some other regularities in mind we group the successor varieties as follows:

TABLE V

```
Iʰ · I   F   E · Hʳ  E'  F · Gʳ  H   Gˢ  H   Hʳ  G   G   F   E·
33  32  20  27  30  33  19  12  11   8   2   2   1   1  15  27
i   l : s   ə · r · e   t : ɛ̃ · k   õ · v   n   a   b   l   ə :
I · I'· Gʳ  H   G   G   Hʳ  I · E · H   G   I'ʰ  Gʳ  H   H   H   I
35  33  17  15   2   1   1  31  31  22  14  30  22   7   5   1  31
d · i : a   p   ə   r   t   e : œ̃ : p   a   r   a · p   l   y   i
```

Il serait inconvenable d'y apporter un parapluie

The E 27 after /ilsə/ comes largely from *se*, a homonym of the *se-* here. The G 17 after /... dia/ and the high G 22 after /para/ are suspect of being low I″ in view of the high $(n+2)$th average after them

```
G   I · Iʰ · Hᵐ  E   F · Eᵐ · Hᵐ  I   H   Eⁱ · Hʳ  E'ʰ · H   F   G   H   H   G   H   Gᵍ  H   H   I
11  32  34  16  31  19  32  11  33  24  31  23  32  18  16  16  15   9   2   1   1  31
ɛ   l : a   v   e   t : e   t · e : s   ã   s · i   b   l : o   t   r   ə · f   w   a
```

Elle avait été sensible autrefois

The high H 23 after /sãs/ suggests a low I″. Analyzing the 16 after /ible/ as F is supported by the high $(n+2)$th average, and by the free alternant /iblə/) here, which ends with F 16, E 27. A peak after /otrə/ would have been obtained if we had had *l'autre* here

```
I · E · H   H   I · I · E · H   E'  F · E   F · G   H   H   G   G   Hʳ  G   I
36  32  16   2  34  34  32  19  32  13  26  18  21  13   1   1   1   1   1  31
l   ə : ʃ   w   a : d · e : s   i   ɲ   e   t : a   r   b   i   t   r · ɛ   r
```

Le choix des signes est arbitraire

Comparison of many utterances shows additional automaticities of /ə/, among them that certain cases of I (after I or utterance beginning) occur before consonant plus vowel, whereas before a following consonant cluster they always have an additional /ə/ (with E as its successor variety). Such I E sequences then yield a single cut, not two

Notes:

For superscript letters see the notes to Table IV.

ˢ Same as r; but the successor morphemes in turn have few predecessor morphemes, so that a cut would not be obtained in the reverse direction either.

I: All consonants but /ɲ/ and most vowels; with many successors after each of these, in the $(n+2)$th place, except for a few rare vowels and for fewer consonants (e.g. /z/).

I″: Over half (usually) of the I (with fewer vowel successors after vowels), with $(n+2)$th average lower than for I and higher than for G, H.

I′: I plus /ɲ/.

E: I, except that the $(n+1)$th vowels have very few $(n+2)$th successors, and some of the $(n+1)$th vowels may be missing.

E′: E plus /ɲ/.

F: A few consonants and almost all the vowels, the vowels having many successors in $(n+2)$th place and the consonants relatively few.

H: Varies from most vowels and consonants, to most vowels and a few consonants, but always with a middling number of $(n+2)$th successors, clearly lower than in I or the vowel members of F; and down (as we proceed to the next cut) to very few vowels and consonants, with very few $(n+2)$th successors each.

G: Consonants only, varying from most with a good number of $(n+2)$th successors each, down to very few with very few $(n+2)$th successors each; rarely there are one or a few vowels in addition to many consonants, the vowels having very few $(n+2)$th successors.

The sequence of these classes of successor variety are usually:

$$\text{I}$$
$$[\text{G H}] \qquad (\text{F}) \quad \text{E}$$
$$(\text{E}) \quad \text{F}$$

There may be from one to three G, followed by one to three H, or the reverse; this sequence may be repeated several times, or omitted entirely.[26] This is followed by the sequence EF or FE, or by E or F alone, or by I.

We locate our segmentations at the end of this sequence, i.e. after I (or I′), EF, FE, and E (or E′) or F alone. Since I′ and E′ include /ɲ/, which characterizes G as against I and E, we conclude that I′=I+G, E′=E+G− in other words, that I′ and E′ indicate the possibility of alternative analyses, with and without a segmentation at that point. Whether or not we segment after I′ and E′ therefore depends on the surrounding sequences. The numbers for each class decrease as we proceed through a stretch between segmentations, and sometimes through a whole utterance or successive parts of an utterance. I′ will be found to correlate with the end of a bound morpheme.

In the three French sentences, all the word boundaries, and some of the morpheme boundaries within a word, are given by these sequence-end segmentations. The other morpheme boundaries are missed because of morphophonemically or morphologically limited distribution, but only one of these would remain undiscovered after repeating the procedure backward. In addition, there are several segmentations due to homonyms, at points where there are no morpheme boundaries in these utterances; but of these too only one would remain after going backward.

5. CORRELATION OF THE CUTS WITH MORPHEMIC BOUNDARIES

It is of interest to note briefly under what conditions our procedure undercuts (i.e. fails to get a segmentation at a morphemic boundary) or over-cuts (i.e. yields a segmentation at a point where there is no morpheme boundary).

We may fail to get a segmentation in the case of nonsegmental morphemes.[27] For example, if a tone contour and a stress contour extend over the same phonemic stretch, our procedure will fail to distinguish them. We may also fail to find the second parts of discontinuous morphemes. In both cases, indirect evidence of the morphemic situation may nevertheless be found by this procedure. Finally, we may fail to get a segmentation for morpheme alternants which are restricted to a few following environments (e.g. *left* and *dramatic* in Table IV), or for morphemes which have a small morphological selection in the following position (§ 6.3).

On the other hand, we may get a peak where there is no morphemic boundary, due to nonmorphemic restrictions of phoneme distribution. For example, in a language (such as English) with a certain short-range periodicity of consonants and vowels[28], there are positions in which only consonants or only vowels or both may occur. Thus the number of phonemes which can occur as successors in a particular position is affected not only by the relation to morpheme boundary but also by this kind of syllabic periodicity. The variation in number of possible successors becomes greater if there are many more consonants than vowels or, as in Thai, many more tone-bearing vowels than consonants. One way of reducing the disturbing effect of this syllabic periodicity is to use a phonemic analysis with an approximately equal number of consonants and vowels.[29] Another way is to use not the actual successor counts, but the ratio of the count after the *n*th phoneme to the number of successors that ever occur after the *n*th phoneme, or after the same short stretch of phonemes. This is the ratio of the actual successor count to the number of successors permitted by the syllabic structure in that position. This separates in part the phonemic restrictions due to syllabic structure from the phonemic restriction due to the particular utterance, and thus shows how much restriction is due to the occurrence of the nth phoneme in this particular string, i.e. in this particular morphemic complex (cf. Table VII).

We may also get a peak where there is no morpheme boundary in cases of sectional homonyms. If our test utterance begins with /ðəsaylow/ *The silo*, we will get a peak at /ðəsay/ because of all the phonemes (in the associated utterances) that can follow *The sigh*. This will not happen if the sectional homonym (*sigh* in *silo*) is excluded by the intervening environment, e.g. if the test utterance is *The brick silo*. Many sectional homonyms are avoided if we specify junctural allophones: for example, /tæks/ is a sectional homonym of /tæksiy/, but /tæks̓/ is not a sectional homonym of /tæksiy̌/ (Table II). Going backward corrects some of these cases; e.g. we will get no peak before /iy/, since only the first part of *taxi* has a homonym here. But in *silo*, where both parts have homonyms, we may get a peak before /low/ (in *The silo walls were up*, not in *The silo-like building*). The variety-sequence method of § 4 also corrects some of these cases (e.g. *aluminum* § 4.1, *silo* § 4.2), the more so since it requires that the residue (after the sectional homonym, e.g. the /iy/ above) should have the same successor-characteristics as the other segments.

Furthermore, since there are segmentations at virtually all word boundaries and most morpheme boundaries, under-cutting or over-cutting usually occurs between correct cuts. The problems of morphological testing are thus limited to short stretches (note 3).

6. SUCCESSOR COUNTS AND LANGUAGE STRUCTURE

The method presented here involves a special case of a more general characteristic of language structure. Since the physical events which are observed in linguistics are in general occurrences of sounds relative to each other, it is reasonable to suppose that the structural features of a language can be expressed as particular types of relative occurrence of sounds. The question is whether we can find procedures for investigating these occurrences such as will yield, in some orderly way, the structural features (already or not yet known) which are of interest to us. One can look at such a set of procedures as successively investigating how the actual occurrence of sounds departs from a random occurrence, each investigation dealing with a departure from equiprobability that has not been treated by the preceding investigations, i.e. showing the extra contribution to nonrandomness at that level. The method of successor varieties belongs to such a set of investigations. These investigations will be briefly noted here with special reference to the morpheme-boundary correlation.

6.1. *Over Stretches Shorter than a Morpheme*

The frequency of each successor to each sound or phoneme can be studied in terms of the (transitional) probability of each phoneme in respect to its immediate neighbor alone.[30] In general, frequency of occurrence correlates with what may be considered language USE (or communication) as against language STRUCTURE; beyond this point the investigations will ask whether a sound (a subsequently defined element) EVER occurs in a given environment (or never, within a very large corpus) rather than how frequently it occurs there. Count and variety therefore do not include frequency.

Over a stretch only a few sounds in length, the successor and predecessor varieties of each sound determine the grouping of sounds into phonemes. Over slightly longer stretches, the successor and predecessor varieties of each phoneme describe the phoneme distribution (phoneme classes, specially limited phonemes), and such phonologic periodicities as syllabic structure.

6.2. *Existence of Morphemic Segments*

When the successor count is applied not over arbitrary short stretches, but always to the whole stretch from the beginning of the utterance, we find a new periodicity over and above all the preceding ones. It is not only that we find a rise and fall of the counts: when we consider the sequences of $(n+2)$th averages, and also the sequences of successor varieties, we find fairly regular periodicities. We find further that the beginnings and ends of utterances are almost always marked by certain of these sequences. We then segment at the points where sequences that characterize utterance boundaries appear within an utterance; these correlate in general with word boundaries. Other periodicities between word boundaries lead to subsidiary segmentations which correlate with morpheme boundaries.

When we know that a language must contain morphemes, these procedures yield segmentations which we can test to see if they satisfy morphemic relations. But if we had not known that such things as morphemes and words exist at all, then these procedures would reveal to us that every utterance is a succession of periodicities, and that these periodicities are occurrence relations of phonemes which depend on the whole string of phonemes (i.e. on everything that has been said) thus far in the utterance. The existence of something of the nature of words and morphemes could thus be discovered from this procedure.

6.3. *Degrees of Independence*

Morphological analysis in linguistics sets up as the morphemes of a language those phonemic stretches which are independent of (do not co-occur with) every other morpheme in at least one utterance. All morphemes have thus a certain minimum independence. Morphological methods do not – and in their present form cannot – distinguish among various degrees of independence; yet there are different degrees. In the successor count procedure different degrees of independence yield different results. Low degrees do not yield peaks, or yield them only in particular circumstances. High degrees yield peaks regularly. Methods like the successor count could be used for obtaining an indication of morphemic independence.

The major types of reduced independence are as follows. (1) Agreement, in which a morph is required in one position if a particular other morph occurs in another; e.g. -*s* after *It contain*. The successor count yields a peak if the position is not fixed in respect to what precedes; if the position is fixed there is no peak. The count responds therefore to the conditions rather than the fact of dependence. (2) Morpheme alternants, as *dramat* for *drama*. The successor count yields no peak for alternants which occur in very restricted environments. (3) Bound morphemes (e.g. English *-ing*, or the *con-* and *-tain* of *contain*) have in general fewer neighbors than free morphemes. Hence the successor count at their end is in general lower than at the end of words. (4) The selection of a morpheme is the variety of other morphemes with which it occurs; thus, the verb selection of *people* is the list of verbs with which that noun occurs. Morphemes, and even words, end on reduced peaks if their selection in the next position is so small as to reduce the number of next phonemes.

6.4. *Over Stretches Longer than a Word*

In many cases, the successor counts, both peaks and troughs, become some-what lower as we go from the beginning of an utterance to its end, or up to some medial point. This is in part due to the mounting restrictions of the grammatical structure. Some information about the grammatical structure, and the location of such divisions as phrase boundaries (or similar domains within which selection operates) can be found by means of secondary differences in the counts.

7. SUMMARY

This paper presents a method for counting, at each phonemic position n of a test utterance, all the phonemes that occur in the $(n+1)$th place (in any utterances) after the particular string of phonemes from the beginning of the test utterance up to n. When this count is made for each n of the utterance, it is found to rise and fall a number of times. If we segment the test utterance after each peak, we will find that the cuts accord very well with the word boundaries and quite well with the morpheme boundaries of that utterance. While the method works for a complete phonemic writing of the utterances, it is not disrupted but only somewhat reduced in effectiveness if we fail to specify junctures or contours. The disturbing effect of syllabic structure and the like can be reduced, e.g. by taking the ratio of the successor count at n to the successors that ever occur after the nth phoneme even in other (syllabically similar) positions.

The method can also be applied backward through the utterance, or by insertions at each point within the utterance. This yields independent corrections on the forward results. In addition, we can consider the average of $(n+2)$th successors for each $(n+1)$th successor at n. And we can note not only the count but the actual variety (list) of successors at each n, and group these successor varieties into certain frequently occurring types. In these last two additions we obtain a new result: we find recurring sequences, in respect to the class of the *n*th phoneme, of the $(n+2)$th average and of variety types; and we find that the utterance is largely a repetition of these regular sequences. If we segment the utterance at those points where the sequence looks as it does at utterance beginning or end, we get a segmentation which agrees very well with the word and morpheme boundaries for that utterance.

The regularity of these sequences means that this method could have led to the discovery of morpheme-like segments, even if we had not known otherwise that morphemes exist. The method as a whole can be viewed as part of an orderly set of kindred methods capable of yielding a large part of language structure in terms of the relative occurrences of sounds, these occurrences being the physical events of language. In particular, the present method can serve for the gap in procedures between phonology and morphology: using nothing more than phoneme distribution, it provides utterance segments which can be tested with fair success by morphological method, and can thereby be automatically corrected, where necessary, to yield the elements of morphology.

TABLE VI

---

16   21   25 · 19   13   30 · 12   20 · 14   10   30ʰ · 11   34 ·
d   a   s : k   a   n : j   a : ʔ   i   m   e   r :

14   10   30 · 14   9   30 · 21   15   9   2   1   25 · 2   30
n   o   x : m   ā l : š   t   u   d   ī   r · e   n

Das kann ja immer noch mal studieren 'That fellow might yet study'

5   13   24 · 24ʰ · 24 · 24ʰ · 24ʰ · 19   2ᵃ   24 · 15   24 · 5   24 · 18   3   5
h   e   m : l   o : l   a   k   x · u : e   t : h   a · s   f   a
21   8   5 · 21   13 · 21   7   12   18 · 20 · 24   5 · 21   20 · 21   8 · 26ʰ

7 · 1   24 · 5 · 24 · 11   8   4   2   1   1   24 · 10   23 · 24 · 24
r · i   m : h a · x   a   d   a   š · i   m : š   e · l · o
21 · 25   5

HEBREW: *They did not take his new books;* backwards: *They did not take the books*

The 20 predecessors to /a/ have a very low $(n+2)$th average, and so differ from the set of 20 or 21 predecessors which occur at the points where cuts are made.

19   24 · 5   24 · 5   24ʰ · 20 · 3   17   9   3   2ʳ   23ʰ · 23 · 11   23 · 5   24 ·
k   ə · š   e · h i   t · k   a   r   a   v · t   i : e   l : h a ·

19   17   6   2   1   1   23 · 10   1   24 · 19   16   16   23 · 23ʰ · 23 · 24 · 23
s   a   n   d   l   a r · i   ya : k   a   r   a · t   i : l · o

HEBREW: *When I approached the shoemaker's I called him*

TABLE VII

Telugu

Dravidian languages furnish a severe test of the present method, because of their morpho-phonemic complexity and their many one-phoneme morphemes. In the sentences tested (the last obtained by Lisker, the others given to me by Krishnamurti), peaks are found at all word boundaries. Of the morpheme boundaries within words (as we know them from morphological analysis), about half are marked by peaks when the count is made in one direction, more when the count is made in both directions. We never get peaks at points where there are no morphological boundaries; but in some instances where a morpheme boundary may be variously placed (by alternative morphological analyses) or where it occurs in the middle of a long consonant, the peak appears not at the morpheme boundary but at the phoneme next to it.

The results of the count accord more closely with morphological analysis when we apply the correction of § 5 – i.e. when we take not the actual number of phonemes occurring after the nth phoneme in a particular sentence, but the ratio of that number to the number of phonemes that ever occur after this (nth) phoneme. Thus, about 40 phonemes occur after vowels in various contexts. (The sequence VV occurs only across word boundaries; but since we do not use morphological information in making these counts, all we know about each vowel occurrence is that it can be followed by roughly any consonant or any vowel.) Hence if a given vowel in the nth place of a test utterance has 13 successors, we say that occurrence in this nth place has restricted the number of possible successors from 40 to 13 – a restriction of about 68 %. In contrast with vowels, most consonants have a total of only about 15 different successors in various contexts: every consonant is followed by the vowels, and most consonants have particular other consonants as occasional successors; CC is followed only by a vowel. If, therefore, a typical consonant in the nth place of a test utterance has 5 successors, we say that occurrence in this nth place has restricted the number of possible successors from 15 to 5 – about 67 %, or as much as the restriction from 40 to 13 after a vowel.

We get still better accord with morphological boundaries when we find the recurring sequences of successor varieties, as in § 4. Some successor varieties consist of consonants only (after a vowel inside a word), some consist of most vowels plus a few consonants (after a consonant inside a word), and so on.

When I obtained these sentences and made the counts on them I had no knowledge of Telugu. I acquired the relevant morphological information only after obtaining the numbers and working out the peaks (including the C-V restrictions) by direct work with an informant

```
→ 12   13   12[a] · 40 · 10   17[b]   12   38 · 7   7   12[c]   40 · 11   40
    c    e   pp · ē : m   ā    t    a : v   i   n · i : p   ō
   11    1   1 · 17 · 10    1    1    2 · 10   2   6 · 14 · 11[a]   13 ←
```

Having heard what is said, go

```
→ 9   14[b]   2   25 · 7   3   3   1   2[d]   22 · 11   8   1[d]        22 · 2   40
   g    ō    d    a : v    i   r   i   g · i : p   a   ḍ · ḍ a : d   i
```

The wall, having broken, fell down

```
   c    ē   t · u    l    u : k    a    ḍ    u    k · k    o    n · n    ā · n    u
  11    1   2   2[d]   1    1 · 7    1    2    3    4 · 12    1 · 5    1    7 · 4[a]   25 ←
```

Table VII continued

I wash my hands

→ 7 4 17 4 3ᵉ 1 2 2 3ᵃ · 1ᵉ 1ᵉ 1 34 · 8 4 3
  p r a t y · ē k a m · a · y · n a : k r o

→ 1 1 34 · 6 8 1 3 2 1ᵈ 6 · 2 3ᵃ · 11 · 3 2ᵈ 3 34
  t t a : v i s a y ā · l · ē m · i : l ē · v u

There is no special news

Notes:

ᵃ This is a peak when the number is taken in proportion to the total number of possible successors after V, C, CC, etc. – that is, the restriction (mentioned in the headnote to this table) is at a minimum here. Going backwards, all counts of about 10 predecessors before a consonant are minima of restriction.

ᵇ When the adjustment referred to in fn. a is made here, this is not a peak.

ᶜ Since /n/ has many consonant successors, this is not a peak.

ᵈ A peak is missing because of morphophonemic alternation. Double consonants were tested as both single and repeated phonemes, with minor differences as shown.

ᵉ A peak is missing because of selectional limitations of distribution. The last sentence is presented here as given, even though the first word is a rare Sanskrit form, and *krotta* is a spelling-pronunciation of *kotta*.

NOTES

[1] I have had the advantage of discussing the subject of this paper with Noam Chomsky. Bernard Bloch and Charles F. Hockett have devoted a great amount of their time to a careful reading of the paper, which now appears considerably modified as a result of their valuable criticism. For data and comments on particular languages I am indebted to Henry M. Hoenigswald (German), Carol Schatz (French), Fred Lukoff (Korean), and Leigh Lisker and Bh. Krishnamurti of Andhra University (Telugu). The English data were obtained with the aid of the Committee on the Advancement of Research of the University of Pennsylvania.

[2] We are concerned here only with the segmentation at morpheme boundaries. The fact that some of the morphs are alternants of each other (allomorphs), and together comprise a single morpheme, is not relevant here. In /hiy iz leyt/ *He is late*, there are three morphemic segments, even though the middle one is an alternant of a morpheme unit. We are here seeking a method that will locate cuts after the third and fifth and last phonemes (not counting junctures) in this sequence. Such a method will give us the morphemic segments of an utterance, whether or not some of these are alternants of other segments.

[3] In some cases a segment, when morphologically tested, turns out not to constitute a morph. In almost all such cases the lack of correlation between this segmentation and the desired morphemic boundaries affects only a small portion of the utterance, and is automatically corrected by the ancillary procedures discussed in § 3 and § 4, or else by morphological analysis. For example, in /itdistərbdmiy/ *It disturbed me*, the segmentation comes out /it.dis.tərbd.miy./: we lack a cut at the morpheme boundary before /d/. But this affects only the segment /tərbd/, which contains two morphs instead of one. When we test the morphological relations of this stretch, we find that it is not a morphemic segment, but that it can be divided into two morphemic segments. Analogously, in

/ðətæksiy/ *The taxi*, we get /ðə.tæk.s.iy./, with two cuts at points that are not morpheme boundaries. But when we test morphologically, we find that /s/ and /iy/ and even their sum /siy/ cannot be morphemic segments in this position, whereas the somewhat larger sum /tæksiy/ can be. Almost all cases where our segmentations do not coincide with morpheme boundaries fall within short stretches of this type; cf. § 5.

⁴ Note that we are asking not the frequency of the various phonemes, but only which ones EVER occur in that position. In the example of § 1, the test utterance is /hiyzklevər/ *He's clever*. After the first 5 phonemes of that utterance we find 11 different successors: that is, in all the sentences that begin with /hiyzk/ we can find 11 different phonemes after the /k/. Some of these are more frequent than others: the successor /ə/ is frequent, as in /hiyzkəvərd/ *He's covered*, /hiyzkəmiŋ/ *He's coming*; the successor /r/ is less so, as in /hiyzkreyziy/ *He's crazy*; and the successor /y/ is rare, as in /hiyzkyuwrd/ *He's cured*. We ask only how many different successors there are to the first 5 phonemes. We next consider the first 6 phonemes of the test sentence, and find that in all the utterances which begin with /hiyzkl/ there are only 7 different phonemes that ever occur after the /l/, again without regard to how frequent they are.

⁵ This is a special case, though the most common one. More generally: we segment the utterance at those points where the number and variety of successors (see below) is similar to that at utterance end. This formulation is needed, for example, in cases where strong syllabic and other phonemic restrictions are not corrected for (§ 5). It is also needed if, contrary to Table II, we wish to apply this procedure to a phonemic writing in which the juncture /+/ is kept as a separate segmental phoneme, e.g. /²hìyz + ³kwíkər¹ +/ for *He's quicker*.

⁶ The LIST of phonemes which occurs in any utterance after a particular utterance-initial sequence may be called the SUCCESSOR VARIETY for that sequence; while the NUMBER of phonemes in that list is the SUCCESSOR COUNT for that sequence.

⁷ Though we are here correlating the variety with the phoneme which it follows, we must remember that the variety and the count depend upon the whole utterance-initial sequence. In the example above, the 11-phoneme variety occurs after the phoneme /k/, but it is the successor variety of utterance-initial /hiyzk/, not of /k/ in general. After /k/ in general we can find other phonemes in addition, for example /s/ after /k/ in *pixie*. The results of § 4 are obtained by correlating the successors of an utterance-initial sequence with the last phoneme of that sequence.

⁸ Here and in similar cases, it is understood that we refer to utterance-initial sequences.

⁹ The examples above suggest (without assuming morphological knowledge) that junctures and intonation or stress contours have a special relation to morpheme boundaries. Junctures and some contours correlate with morpheme boundaries; other contours correlate with phrase or sentence boundaries without regard to morphemes and words. In contrast, if we dropped some segmental phonemes (e.g. the vowels), we would not obtain a segmentation similar to that obtained with these phonemes included. This applies also to tones and stresses which are not part of long contours, such as the tones in 'tone languages'. Such tones have distributions like those of other phonemes of the language. We can therefore tell whether, in a given language, tones are parts of a contour (and can be omitted in these tests) by seeing what kind of phonemic distribution they have.

¹⁰ More exactly: if we want to segment an utterance which has a junctural pair, like the two sets in Table II, the junctural allophones must be specified. But if we are segmenting some other utterance, we can usually get a successor count for the segmental phonemes alone that is almost the same as (not better than) the count we get if we specify junctural allophones and contours. And this with less work and confusion on the informant's part.

¹¹ In general, different phonemic representations will give somewhat different successor counts; necessarily, since the different analyses mean that the same allophonic facts are represented by different phoneme sequences. In most cases these differences will not suffice to yield different peaks, i.e. different locations for our tentative segmentations. But sometimes this will happen. In particular, phonemes with great restrictions of occurrence usually

yield very low successor counts (e.g. the successor of /o/ is usually only /h, w, y/; and this may raise a neighboring moderate count to a relative peak. A particular phonemic analysis may eliminate certain of these undesired low counts. But some difficulties are unavoidable, for frequently, when we are dealing with very restricted allophones, our phonemic representation will have to have one or another serious restriction, especially since solutions by means of long components cannot be used here (since they involve unpronounceable and nonsuccessive elements).

[12] When we counted the successors of n we approximated the morpheme dependence at position $(n + 1)$ upon the preceding phonemic sequence; but we made no use of any morphemic dependence of position n upon the following phonemic sequence. Sometimes (or always, depending on the structure of the language) the dependence upon the preceding sequence suffices to show whether there is a morpheme boundary before position $(n + 1)$. When it does not suffice, we may be able to find out whether there is a morpheme boundary before position $(n + 1)$ by counting the predecessors of position m from the end (where the utterance is of length $n + m$), thus finding the dependence of position $(m + 1)$ from the end ($=$ position n from the end) upon the phoneme sequence which follows it.

[13] Of course, all the inadequacies of the forward operations can also occur in the backward operation if the positions are reversed: if a morpheme in a particular position is in grammatical agreement with something later in the sentence; if a morpheme or alternant has limited distribution in respect to what precedes it; if the last few phonemes of a morpheme are identical with the total phonemes of some other morpheme. As an example of the limited morpheme: in *It disturbs me* we find, on going backward, only 2 predecessors before /tərbzmiy/: /s/ and /r/ (in *It perturbs me*); but on going forward we find a peak of 15 successors after /itdis/.

[14] E.g. *The silo walls were up* has a successor peak after /ðəsay/ (*The sigh ...*) and also a predecessor peak before /lowwohlzwərɔ́p/ (*... low walls were up*). In this case we would get a segmentation in the middle of *silo*.

[15] For example, in *It disturbed me* we find 16 successors after the first /i/. Of these successors, which are in the $(n + 1)$th place, 6 had 29 successors after them in turn, in the $(n + 2)$th position: *it, if, itch, is, ill, in*; after these 6 successors a new morpheme could begin in the $(n + 2)$th place. Of the other 10 successors, 1 had 18 successors (/y/: *eat, eager, easy, each, either, aeons*, etc.), 1 had 10 successors (/m/: *imp, imbibe, immune, immediate*, etc.), and 8 had from 1 to 4 successors (/ŋ/: *ink, English*; /d/: *idiot*; etc.).

[16] To put it differently, the roughly decreasing numbers as we go from peak to peak (when we interpret peaks as word or morpheme boundaries) mean that there are in English about 29 ways of choosing the initial phoneme of a word; then depending upon the choice of the initial there are about 6 to 18 ways of choosing the second phoneme; and depending on the choice of the second phoneme (and somewhat on the first too) there are about 2 to 15 ways of choosing the third phoneme; about 1 to 10 ways of choosing the fourth; and 1 to 3 ways of choosing each following phoneme up to the end of the morpheme.

[17] These categories depend on the decreasing numbers between peaks. If we say that the $(n + 2)$th phonemes for a given $(n + 1)$th are in category B, we mean that there are about as many $(n + 2)$th phonemes here as we would expect to find if the $(n + 1)$th were the first phoneme of an utterance. On the basis of the successor varieties of § 4, we can go back and modify these categories, so as to obtain categories which closely characterize the first few (and, backward, the last few) places of an utterance. Thus modified, the calculations of the present section yield segmentations that agree even more closely with morphological boundaries. The adjusted categories are: A for the class J and high-count M of § 4; B for the class K and high-count L of § 4; C for middle-count L and N, and low-count M; D for low-count L and N. Part of this adjustment can be obtained simply by doubling the value of every successor vowel, thus correcting for some of the difference between the possible number of vowel and consonant successors. The adjusted categories are used in Table I above; for purposes of the arithmetic averaging there we set $B = 15$, $C = 5$, $D = 1$. Then if after n, 6 of the $(n + 1)$th phonemes have successors in category B (i.e. about 15 successors each) and 2 have successors in category C, and 1 has its successor

in category D, the total in $(n+2)$th place is $6\,B+2\,C+1\,D$, and the $(n+2)$th average per $(n+1)$th phoneme is 11.2.

[18] If the adjusted categories of fn. 17 are used, there is no drop at all between /hiyz/ and /hiyzə/. The 29 successors to /hiy/ then have the following total of $(n+2)$th successors in turn: $6\,A+21\,B+1\,C+1\,D=$ an average of 14.2 per $(n+1)$th phoneme in the numerical values of fn. 17 and Table 1 above. The 29 successors to /hiyz/ have the following total for their successors: $27\,B+1\,C+1\,D=$ an average of 14.3. The 22 successors to /hiyzə/ have for their successors: $22\,B=$ an average of 15. The average is virtually the same, A not being counted since its distribution differs from that of B, C, D. Almost all the $(n+2)$th places (including the C and D) have the distribution we would expect if the $(n+2)$th phoneme were the second of an utterance, that is, if there were a word boundary after the nth phoneme.

[19] This does not mean that there is necessarily a morpheme boundary before xy in this sequence.

[20] Thus the J 28 above is merely J at a later point of the sentence, or at a grammatically more limited point. However, after consonants of rare occurrence, a vowel may have low L successor even near the beginning of an utterance, as in *they* /ðey/, where the successors are K 6, L 4, J 28.

[21] K and L can occur in first position; K' and L in second or third position; M, N, L can occur in the same medial positions.

[22] The rise in L 8 can also be eliminated by correcting for the vowel-consonant distribution, as in § 5.

[23] Before some consonants, T consists only of the vowels (i.e. they are always the first of a postvocalic cluster). In these cases we may write T' before S, and T before Z; but one could also adopt some different convention. Similarly K' after a few consonants contains only vowels, and is hence identical with N.

[24] If a sequence ends in R instead of T, we understand (since R includes T) that it sometimes is a morpheme separate from the following stretch, and sometimes constitutes a single morpheme with the following stretch.

[25] Recognizing this /t/ as a separate morpheme is less obvious than recognizing the /d/ (and so for /s/ as compared with /z/) because /t/ has the same predecessors when it ends a morpheme as when it is a suffix. However, the predecessor variety tells us that in a certain utterance position the sequences preceding /t/ are the same as those which can themselves end an utterance (and have the same $[n+2]$th predecessors), whereas in other positions we find fewer and more restricted sequences preceding the /t/. The phonetic possibilities may be the same in both positions, but the variety that we find is different. This is precisely the difference between the present method and a study of phonetic structure. In those cases where the predecessors to /t/ are the same as those we would find before a peak or utterance end, i.e. where the sequence ends in T rather than T', we place a tentative cut.

[26] I.e. 0 or 1 G followed by 0 or 1 H, repeated up to 10 or 15 times.

[27] Note also that segmental morphemes which consist of one phoneme are not easily separated out, since their boundary may be overshadowed by the neighboring boundary. In any case, a plateau of two high numbers (as in 9, 14, 29, 29 for /hiyz/ *He's*) indicates two segmentations, even though there are not two separate peaks.

[28] This can be established by purely distributional investigations of the successors and predecessors of phonemes, as in J. D. O'Connor and J. L. M. Trim, 'Vowel, Consonant, and Syllable – a Phonological Definition', *Word* 9 (1953), 103–22.

[29] Ibid. Particularly valuable here would be the phonemic system used by Stanley S. Newman, 'On the Stress System of English', *Word* 2 (1946), 171–87.

[30] For the inclusion of such considerations in the bases of phonology, see Charles F. Hockett, *A Manual of Phonology* (Indiana University Publications in Anthropology and Linguistics), 1955.

III

MORPHEME BOUNDARIES WITHIN WORDS:
REPORT ON A COMPUTER TEST

For the science of linguistics we seek objective and formally describable operations with which to analyze language. The phonemes of a language can be determined by means of an explicit behavioral test (the pair test, involving two speakers of the language) and distributional simplifications, i.e. the defining of symbols which express the way in which the outcomes of that test occur in respect to each other in sentences of the language. The syntax, and most of the morphology, of a language is discovered by seeing how the morphemes occur in respect to each other in sentences. As a bridge between these two sets of methods we need a test for determining what are the morphemes of a language, or at least a test that would tentatively segment a phonemic sequence (as a sentence) into morphemes, leaving it for a distributional criterion to decide which of these tentative segments are to be accepted as morphemes.

The locating of morpheme boundaries within a word, by a recurrent process in the manner of the paper 'From Phoneme to Morpheme' (*Language* **31** (1955), 190–222; Paper II of this volume) has now been carried out on a computer.[1] Briefly, the method is as follows: given the first m phonemes of a given n-phoneme sentence, for every m, $1 \leqslant m \leqslant n$, we count how many different phonemes follow these first m phonemes in all sentences which begin with these m phonemes. The same procedure can be used to count the predecessors of the last m phonemes of the sentence, for each m. The points in the given sentence at which the number of successors (or predecessors) forms a peak are, to a first approximation, the boundaries between the morphemic segments of the given sentence.

Since the corpus used in the computer test consisted of words, not sentences, the test could yield not word boundaries within a sentence but only morpheme boundaries within a word. The latter are much harder to determine than word boundaries within a sentence. In the present test, morpheme boundaries were sought from the beginning of each word up to the first hyphen or (if there was no hyphen) up to the end of the word. Since the dictionary was in conventional spelling, the test dealt not with sequences of

Transformations and Discourse Analysis Papers, 73 (1967).

phonemes but with sequences of letters, which give a less fine resolution of morpheme boundaries than do sequences of phonemes.

Testing from a virtually complete dictionary of the language gives results that have certain interest over and above an informant-test. However, an informant-test could also include words constructed by the informant on the basis of productive morpheme-combining rules; these would accentuate the morpheme boundaries.

Any tests using phonemes, informants, and whole sentences, should therefore give even stronger correlation than that obtained here between the next-neighbor count and morphologically justified morpheme boundaries. Furthermore, most of the words used in the present test were selected for being difficult words based on Latin morphemes only a fraction of whose combinations appear in English.

Forty-eight words were tested in the first computer test reported here. All are given below, with the count of predecessors, successors, and (for many words) the average of successors for each successor, as they were given by the computer.[2] For each word, the program carried out the method of the second paragraph above (substituting 'word' for 'sentence'), checking all words in the dictionary for next-neighbor letters to the first (and last) m letters of the test word, for each m.

In many cases, the actual number of next-neighbors rose to a peak at the points of morphological boundary:

	1	1	2	1	1	2	20	5	13	25	←
	d	i	s	t	u	r	b	a	n	c	e
→	15	24	24	8	2	2	4	2	1	1	
	10.4	9.2	6.4	3.9	1.5	2	1.7	1	1	0	

The numbers above the word count the different predecessor letters (in all words of the dictionary) to the sequence of letters up to the end of the given word. The first line below counts the different successors to the initial sequence. And the second line below gives the average of different successors for each successor to the initial sequence. Thus there are 15 different second letters in the set of words beginning with d; and these 15 have an average of 10.4 different letters in third place, following them.

	5	9	24	26	←
	a	p	p	l	e
→	26	14	7	5	
	15	7.7	4.6	4.2	

In other cases, the peak consisted not of the number of next-neighbors, but of the ratio of the number of next-neighbors of the initial or final sequence in the given word to the number of next-neighbors to the preceding (or following) triple of letters whenever that triple might occur. This ratio measures the reduction in next-neighbors due to the whole initial or final sequence in the given word as against the purely phonological requirements of the local environment (vowels, consonant clusters, and word-juncture). Thus, in

	1	4	2	2	9	19	17	25	←
	d	e	f	o	r	m	i	t	y
→	15	26	9	5	4	4	3	1	

fewer letters can follow *orm* in all words containing *orm* than can follow *for* in all words containing *for*; hence the 4 after *m* represents a higher ratio than the 4 after *r*. Similar cases are seen in: *afterward, alligator, antithetical, deflationary, deformity, development, distastefully, perfection,* etc.

In judging the next-neighbor count, it has to be understood that we cannot recognize a peak until the next-neighbor count has begun to drop. Hence, if the first letter of a word is a separate morpheme, we cannot recognize it in the forward count; nor can a last-letter morpheme be recognized in the backward count. More generally, single-letter morphemes cannot be recognized directly. In all these cases we have to use other indications: the count in the reverse direction, an overly high average of next-neighbors per next-neighbor, etc.[3]

Every morpheme boundary appeared as a peak in at least one of the two directions. In these 48 words there were 83 interior points at which a morphemic segmentation would be made on purely morphological grounds. 49 of these points have a next-neighbor peak in both directions. The remaining 34 points appeared as a peak in only one direction. In about half of these cases, the other direction did not show a peak because the morphemes (almost entirely Latin) had very few neighbors in that direction (English having taken over only a few of the words composed of those morphemes in Latin): forward peaks are missed in *alliterate* (after *liter*), *aluminum* (after *alum*), *anomalous* (after *nom*) *antepenultimate* (after *pen*), *devitalize* (after *vit* and *al*), *dormant, periodic* (after *od*, even though this is obtainable as a word boundary), *pestiferous* (after *fer*); backward peaks are missing in *inclined* (before *clin*), *perfection* (before *fect*).

In the other half of the cases, the second direction did not show a peak because the morphemic segment is morphophonemically limited to the environment in this second direction: *antipathetical* (*pathet-*), *applicability* (*ap-, plic-, abil-*), *application* (*ap-, plic-*), *apposition* (*ap-*), *disembody* (*em-*), *permissible* (*miss-*). Of the same nature are the combining forms in *altitude, pestiferous* (attributable to *-itude, -ifer*), and in *autograph,* where the two directions gave different preferences for the point of segmentation. An artificial morphophonemic form appears in *permalloy* (*perm-* from *permanent*).

In addition, there were 17 peaks[4] which did not occur at morpheme boundaries of the given word. These were due to morphemic homonyms of initial or final nonmorphemic segments of the given word. Thus the existence of a final suffix *-us* (frequent in the science dictionaries) produced a maximum of predecessors before *-us* in all words ending in *-ous*, etc. The suffixes *-ally* produced a morphologically wrong peak in *dismally*; *-er* produced it in *answer, another*; and the prefix *dis-* produced it in *discus, dismally, disulfide*; and *de-* produced it in *deign, devilishly*.

In no case was there a peak in the opposite direction.[5] In many cases, the fact that the peak in question did not come at a morpheme boundary for the given word could be recognized by the fact that further next-neighbor counts (in the next one or two positions), and average of next-neighbors per next-neighbor, are low in comparison with phonologically comparable words which have morpheme-boundary peaks in both directions at the corresponding point. Compare, for example,

		4		7		1		1		5		24		12		26		←
	d		i		s		u		l		f		i		d		e	
→		15		24		24		5		2		4		2		1		
		10.4	9.2		6.4		1.4		2.5		1.5		1		0			

with

		1		1		4		3		18		15		11		25		←
	d		i		s		e		m		b		o		d		y	
→		15		24		24		11		5		6		5		2		
		10.4	9.2		6.4		2.5		2		2		1.2		.5			

where the low count of next-neighbor and average of next-neighbors per next-neighbor after *u* in comparison with *e* suggests that *u* is not the first letter of a morpheme, whereas *e* is.

		2		1		3		5		4		20		23		6		21		←
	A		F		T		E		R		W		A		R		D		
→		26		14		5		1		20		5		3		1		1	

		2		1		3		5		8		19		16		25		17		
	A		L		L		I		G		A		T		O		R	
		26		25		14		10		1		1		3		1		2	
		15		7.8		5.1		1.8		1		3		.6		2		1	

1	2	7	3	11	18	21	24	18	26
A	L	L	I	T	E	R	A	T	E
26	25	14	10	1	1	2	3	3	0
15	7.8	5.1	1.8	1	1	2	1.5	1	0

8	1	1	4	2	20	5	13	26
A	L	L	O	W	A	N	C	E
26	25	14	22	4	2	1	2	0
15	7.8	5.1	3.3	2	1	1	0	0

6	2	9	13	5	13	12	26
A	L	T	I	T	U	D	E
26	25	8	8	1	1	2	0
15	7.8	3.8	1.6	1	2	.5	0

3	1	1	4	16	13	27	15
A	L	U	M	I	N	U	M
26	25	10	7	6	6	1	0
15	7.8	2.7	2.3	1.7	3	0	0

0	2	3	5	13	26	23
A	L	U	M	N	U	S
26	25	10	7	4	1	0
15	7.8	2.7	2.3	1.5	0	0

0	13	15	5
A	N	E	W
26	22	15	0
15	7.1	2.6	0

4	1	1	1	9	10	24	26	23
A	N	O	M	A	L	O	U	S
26	22	18	7	2	5	8	1	2
15	7.1	3.9	2	3	2.4	1.1	2	1

0	2	11	12	8	26	17
A	N	O	T	H	E	R
26	22	18	6	1	1	1
15	7.1	3.9	1.2	1	1	1

0	1	1	5	26	17
A	N	S	W	E	R
26	22	8	1	1	4
15	7.1	1.5	1	4	1

2	1	1	1	2	1	1	5	1	5	9	21	24	18	26
A	N	T	E	P	E	N	U	L	T	I	M	A	T	E
26	22	12	21	7	3	2	1	1	1	1	1	1		
15	7.1	7.3	3.4	2.5	1.7	1	1	1	1	1	1	1		

1	1	1	1	4	2	7	3	13	15	22	14	26	21	–	–
A	N	T	I	P	A	T	H	E	T	I	C	A	L	L	Y
26	22	12	23	11	7	2	5	1	1	1	2	1	2	1	
15	7.1	7.3	7.1	4.6	1.9	3	6.7	1	1	1	–	1	–		

2	1	1	2	2	3	23	14	26	26	18
A	N	T	I	Q	U	A	R	I	A	N
26	22	12	23	1	3	2	3	3	1	2
15	7.1	7.3	7.1	3	3	2.5	10	–	2	–

1	1	1	2	7	3	13	13	19	9	22	6	25	25
A	N	T	I	T	H	E	T	I	C	A	L	L	Y
26	22	12	23	9	4	7	1	1	2	1	1	1	–
15	7.1	7.3	7.1	3.5	2.5	1	1	2	13.5	1	1	–	–

0	5	9	24	26
A	P	P	L	E
26	14	7	5	
15	7.7	4.6	4.2	

2	1	4	1	8	6	23	6	13	8	19	17	25
A	P	P	L	I	C	A	B	I	L	I	T	Y
26	14	7	5	4	1	3	2	1	1	1	0	0
15	7.7	4.6	4.2	1.5	3	2.3	1.5	1	1	1	0	0

9	2	9	5	12	11	20	14	21	24	18
A	P	P	L	I	C	A	T	I	O	N
26	14	7	5	4	1	3	4	2	1	0
15	7.7	4.6	4.2	1.5	3	2.3	1.2	1	0	0

2	3	16	1	6	14	14	21	24	18
A	P	P	O	S	I	T	I	O	N
26	14	7	5	3	2	3	2	1	1
15	7.7	4.6	1.4	1.3	1.5	2	1	1	1

5	1	13	20	11	3	5	8	20
A	U	T	O	G	R	A	P	H
26	18	7	22	7	1	4	1	5
15	3.8	5.3	5.5	1.1	4	.8	5	1

0	1	5	10	5	17	25
A	U	T	O	P	S	Y
26	18	7	22	12	2	1
15	3.8	5.3	5.5	2.4	1.5	1

0	12	17	9	26	17
C	L	E	V	E	R
15	6	16	2	2	0

3	1	2	4	15	15	24	26	23
D	A	N	G	E	R	O	U	S
15	23	15	2	1	4	1	1	2
10.4	8.5	3.3	1.5	4	1	1	2	1

1	1	2	3	11	10	8	10	12	23	21	25
D	E	F	L	A	T	I	O	N	A	R	Y
15	26	9	4	2	5	1	1	4	1	1	0
10.4	8.3	4.5	3	2	7	1	2	1	1	0	0

5	7	10	1	3	11	20	14	21	24	18
D	E	F	O	R	M	A	T	I	O	N
15	26	9	5	4	4	4	1	2	1	1
10.4	8.3	4.5	1.4	1.7	3.3	1.2	2	1	1	1

1	1	4	2	2	9	19	17	25
D	E	F	O	R	M	I	T	Y
15	26	9	5	4	4	3	1	0
10.4	8.3	4.5	1.4	1.7	3.3	1	0	0

0	3	7	5	18
D	E	I	G	N
15	26	11	1	0
10.4	8.3	2.4	0	0

10	1	2	1	1	1	6	22	19	11	23
D	E	V	E	L	O	P	M	E	N	T
15	26	6	3	2	1	5	1	1	1	2
10.4	8.3	4.7	1.3	1	5	1.4	1	1	2	1.5

1	1	1	2	11	21	6	6	25	25
D	E	V	I	L	I	S	H	L	Y
15	26	6	7	14	3	2	3	1	0
10.4	8.3	4.7	4	1.6	1.3	1	1	0	0

1	2	3	4	10	19	11	17	5	26
D	E	V	I	T	A	L	I	Z	E
15	26	6	7	2	2	1	1	2	1
10.4	8.3	4.7	4	1.5	1	1	2	1	0

2	1	1	1	1	1	3	10	12	23	21	25
D	I	S	C	I	P	L	I	N	A	R	Y
15	24	24	3	7	2	2	1	3	5	2	0
10.4	9.2	6.5	5.5	1.6	1.5	1.5	2	3	1.4	1	0

0	9	5	11	26	23
D	I	S	C	U	S
15	24	24	8	5	1
10.4	9.2	6.5	5.5	1.4	4

3	1	1	5	2	5	12	21	24	18
D	I	S	C	U	S	S	I	O	N
15	24	24	8	5	1	4	3	1	2
10.4	9.2	6.5	5.5	1.4	4	1.8	1	2	1

1	1	1	3	1	2	2	1	9	18	6	23
D	I	S	E	M	B	A	R	R	A	S	S
15	24	24	11	5	6	2	3	1	1	1	1
10.4	9.2	6.5	2.5	2	2	2	1.3	1	1	1	1

1	1	1	4	3	18	15	11	25
D	I	S	E	M	B	O	D	Y
15	24	24	11	5	6	5	2	0
10.4	9.2	6.5	2.5	2	2	1.2	5	0

0	1	1	7	1	3	21	20	13	26	21
D	I	S	I	N	C	L	I	N	E	D
15	24	24	4	9	5	1	1	3	0	0
10.4	9.2	6.5	4.3	2.4	1	1	2	1	0	0

1	4	4	4	22	6	25	25
D	I	S	M	A	L	L	Y
15	24	24	5	6	3	1	0
10.4	9.2	6.5	2.4	2.2	1.3	0	0

1	1	1	3	3	1	3	17	17	8	6	25	25
D	I	S	T	A	S	T	E	F	U	L	L	Y
15	24	24	8	7	4	1	4	1	1	2	1	0
10.4	9.2	6.5	3.9	1.6	1	2	.5	1	2	1	0	0

5	1	1	2	1	1	2	20	5	13	26
D	I	S	T	U	R	B	A	N	C	E
15	24	24	8	2	2	4	2	1	1	0
10.4	9.2	6.5	3.9	1.5	2	1.7	1	1	0	0

1	4	7	1	1	5	24	12	26
D	I	S	U	L	F	I	D	E
15	24	24	5	2	4	2	1	0
10.4	9.2	6.5	1.4	2.5	1.5	1	0	0

0	2	2	8	29	11	23
D	O	R	M	A	N	T
15	22	18	5	1	2	0
10.4	8.5	2.6	1.4	2	.5	0

6	1	1	5	18	8	14	21	24	18
P	E	R	F	E	C	T	I	O	N
14	24	23	7	2	1	7	5	1	4
–	7.6	6.7	1.9	1	7	1.7	1.6	4	1.3

5	2	2	5	18	12	24	13
P	E	R	I	O	D	I	C
14	24	23	24	13	5	3	2
–	7.6	6.7	5.3	1.8	2.3	1.3	1

2	1	1	1	8	1	7	20	25
P	E	R	M	A	L	L	O	Y
14	24	23	5	4	2	1	1	0
–	7.6	6.7	3.8	1.8	.5	1	0	0

3	1	1	9	2	5	10	14	8	24	26
P	E	R	M	I	S	S	I	B	L	E
14	24	23	5	8	1	2	3	2	2	1
–	7.6	6.7	3.8	1.1	2	2	1.3	1.5	.5	1

7	1	1	3	19	12	26	21
P	E	R	S	O	N	A	L
14	24	23	10	2	7	4	4

1	1	3	14	19	3	15	15	24	26	23
P	E	S	T	I	F	E	R	O	U	S
14	24	7	8	5	3	1	1	1	1	2

0	1	15	5	14	26	17
Q	U	I	C	K	E	R
1	7	18	3	10	2	0

NOTES

[1] The work was programmed by Dr. Philip Rabinowitz, and the program was run by him on the CDC computer at the Weizmann Institute of Science in Rehovot. The English dictionary used was the one arranged on tape by Dr. A. F. Brown (now at Lehigh University) at the University of Pennsylvania, giving a forward and reverse alphabetization of the entries in Webster's Unabridged Dictionary and in a number of major specialized science dictionaries.

[2] Since the dictionary did not list plural, past, and -*ing* suffixes for each word, the computer results were adjusted to what they would have been if the given word with these suffixes were in the dictionary.

[3] Certain other morphemic segmentations can not be directly recognized by this method, e.g. infixed and intercalated morphemes (or that alternant of the past-tense morpheme which appears in *took*). Secondary indications of this situation can be drawn from the number sequences, including the average of next-neighbors per next-neighbor.

[4] Or somewhat more, depending on interpretation of the number sequences.

[5] Although such a situation could occur.

IV

MORPHEME ALTERNANTS IN LINGUISTIC ANALYSIS

The purpose of this paper is to suggest a technique for determining the morphemes of a language, as rigorous as the method used now for finding its phonemes. The proposed technique differs only in details of arrangement from the methods used by linguists today. However, these small differences suffice to simplify the arrangement of grammars.

THE PRESENT TREATMENT OF MORPHEMES

1.0. In essence, the present treatment uses the following criterion: Every sequence of phonemes which has meaning, and which is not composed of smaller sequences having meaning, is a morpheme.[1] Different sequences of phonemes constitute different morphemes; occurrences of the same sequence with sufficiently different meanings constitute homonyms.

In some cases, this criterion dissociates certain morphemes which we wish, because of the grammatical structure, to unite. Various methods are used at present to get around this contradiction. In cases 1–3 below, different sequences of phonemes are considered as different forms of the same morpheme. In cases 4–5, sequences of phonemes are called not morphemes but processes and the like. In case 6, a special relation is seen between different morphemes.

1.1. Tübatulabal[2] *puw* 'to irrigate', *u·buw* 'he irrigated' would have to be analyzed as containing different morphemes, since the phoneme sequence /puw/ does not occur in the second word. Similarly, *pǝlǝ·la* 'to arrive', *ǝ·bǝlǝ·la* 'he arrived'; for every morpheme which begins with a voiced stop after a prefix there is a similar morpheme beginning with the homorganic voiceless stop in word-initial. In spite of the phonemic difference between the members of each of these pairs, we wish to consider each pair a single morpheme, since in other cases we have a single morpheme in the position of both members of these pairs: *wǝ·ʔin* 'to pour', *ǝ·wǝ·ʔin* 'he poured'. We say that there is a regular alternation in the language: a voiced stop is replaced by the homorganic voiceless stop in word-initial.

Similarly, Early Hebrew[3] had *ró·š* 'head', *ro·šó·* 'his head', but *máwt* 'death', *mo·tó·* 'his death'. Since unstressed /aw/ never occurs before a consonant, we say that it is regularly replaced by /o·/.

1.2. We would also have to say that there are different morphemes in *knife* and *knives*. However, the connection between these is too obvious to be disregarded in the grammar, and the difference occurs also in several other pairs: *wives*, but *strifes*. We therefore create a morphophonemic symbol, say /F/, which represents /v/ before /-z/ 'plural' and /f/ elsewhere, and say that there is but one English morpheme /najF/. Or we give a morphophonemic formula: /f/ is replaced by /v/ before /-z/ 'plural' in the following morphemes – *knife, wife,....*

The use of morphophonemic statements or symbols is however of little use in the next case, and of no use in case 4–6.

1.3. By the criterion of § 1.0, Heb. *'i·r* 'city' and *'a·ri·m* 'cities' contain different morphemes.[4] Since the difference between *'i·r* and *'a·r-* is not found between other morphemes with identical meanings, it seems awkward to state it in a morphophonemic formula: /i/ is replaced by /a/ in *'i·r* before *–i·m*. Some linguists have called such pairs morpholexical alternants of one morpheme.[5]

1.4. In Greek μένω 'I remain', μεμένηκα 'I have remained', λύω 'I loose', λέλυκα 'I have loosed', the meaning of the reduplication is the same in all cases, but the phonemic sequences vary so much that they are not commonly considered to constitute a single morpheme. Instead, reduplication is often called a morphological process, a special kind of affix, and the like.

1.5. Much the same is true of vowel changes which correlate with meaning changes. They cannot be expressed by morphophonemic formulas, since these formulas state the alternate forms of a single morpheme, whereas *take* and *took* are not the same morpheme, having different meanings. Such vowel changes are usually described as special kinds of morphological modification, though they may alternate with additive suffixes like *-ed* 'past time'.

1.6. There remain cases of morphemes which complement each other but are entirely dissimilar in their phonemic sequences: *am, are, is, be*, etc. These are considered different morphemes, but with a special mutual relation of suppletion.

PROPOSED TREATMENT OF MORPHEMES

2.0. It is proposed here to arrange the morphemes of a language more clearly by carrying out rigorously three linguistic procedures, the first and third of which are in common use today.

2.1. We divide each expression in the given language into the smallest sequences of phonemes which have what we consider the same meaning when they occur in other expressions, or which are left over when all other parts of the expression have been divided off. This is identical with the criterion of § 1.0. The resultant minimum parts we call not morphemes, but MORPHEME ALTERNANTS.

It is useful to generalize this definition of morpheme alternant by taking sequence to mean not only additive sequence (the addition of phonemes), but also zero (the addition of no phonemes), negative sequence (the dropping of a phoneme), and phonemic component sequence (the addition of a physiological feature of phonemes). In *He cut it* there is a zero morpheme meaning 'past time' after *cut*. In Hidatsa, we have a minus morpheme, consisting of dropping the final vowel mora, with the meaning of command [6]: *cixic* 'he jumped', *cix* 'jump!', *ika·c* 'he looked', *ika* 'look!'. In *took* we have two morphemes: *take*, and /ej/ ~ /u/ 'past time'. The latter occurs also in *shook* as compared with *shake*. It is a combination of negative and additive sequences: dropping /ej/ and adding /u/. Another negative-additive morpheme is /a/ ~ /e/ 'plural', which occurs in *men* as compared with *man*. Lastly, we have a phonemic component morpheme in *to believe*, *to house*, etc., if we wish to divide these words into *belief*, *house*, etc. plus a morpheme consisting of voicing the final consonant and having the grammatical meaning 'verb'.

As in the case of ordinary additive morphemes, zero and the others can be recognized only by comparison with other morphemes. Thus in deciding whether to recognize a minus morpheme in Hidatsa we are faced with the following choice: Consider *cixic*, *ika·c*, also *kikuac* 'he set a trap', *kiku* 'set a trap!'. If we call *cix*, *ika*, *kiku* single morphemes (functioning both as stems and as command), then the morphemes meaning '(he) did' would be *ic*, *·c*, *ac*, etc. We would have no way of indicating which of these forms occurs after each stem except by listing all the stems. Linguistic procedure chooses the simpler arrangement: it considers the stems to be *cixi*, *ika·*, *kikua*, and the suffix always -*c*. Then the command forms must be analyzed as having two morphemes, the stem plus the dropping of the last mora. [7]

Note that at this stage of the analysis every element, here called morpheme alternant, has only one sequence of phonemes: *knife* and *knive-* are two separate morpheme alternants.

2.2. From the list of morpheme alternants which results from the preceding step, we take any two or more alternants which have what we consider the same meaning (but different phonemes) and no one of which ever occurs in the same environment as the others. [8] The two or more alternants which meet these conditions are grouped together into a single MORPHEME UNIT: *am*, which occurs only in phrases with *I*, and *are*, which never occurs with *I*, are put into one morpheme unit. In many cases when we take one alternant and try to find another to group with it, we fail: e.g. in the case of *walk*, *rain*. In such cases we say that the single alternant constitutes a morpheme unit by itself. A morpheme unit is thus a group of one or more alternants which have the same meaning and complementary distribution. To make these units more similar to our present morphemes, and more serviceable for grammatical structure, we now add a further condition: In units consisting of more than one alternant, the total distribution of all the alternants (i.e. the combined range of environments in which each of them occurs) must equal the range of environments in which some unit with but a single alternant occurs. Thus the combined environments of *am, are, be* are included in the environments in which *walk* occurs: *I am, they are, to be*, as compared with *I walk, they walk, to walk*. The case is different with *twenty* and *score*, even though they have the same meaning and never occur in the same environment.[9] For there is no morpheme unit in English which consists of only one alternant and which occurs in the combined distribution of *twenty* and *score*. Therefore, we consider the alternants *am, are, be* as being members of a single morpheme unit; but of the alternants *twenty* and *score*, each constitutes a morpheme unit by itself.

A few examples of alternants which can be grouped together into units: *knife* and *knive-*: *knive-* occurs only before /-z/ 'plural', *knife* never does; the sum of the positions in which both occur equals the range of positions in which the single alternant *fork* occurs.

go and *wen-*: *wen-* only before *-t* 'past', *go* never; *walk* occurs in both positions.

/-əz/ (only after alternants ending in /s, š, č, z, ž, ǰ/ but not after all of these), /-s/ (only after alternants ending in the other voiceless phonemes), /-z/ (only after alternants ending in the other voiced phonemes), /-ən/ (after *ox*), zero (after *sheep*), /a/ ~ /e/ (with *man*), etc., meaning 'plural'; the total range of environments equals that of zero 'singular', the suffix *-ful*, and other single-alternant morpheme units.

/-əz, -s, -z/ (all these in the same environments as above), zero (only after the /-əz, -s, -z/ alternants of 'plural'), and no more, all meaning 'possessed by' or the like.

/-əd, -t, -d/, zero (after *cut*), /ej/ ~ /u/ (with *take*, etc.), and several other alternants, 'past'; no two of these occur after the same alternant, and the combined environments in which they all occur equals the distribution of *-s* '3d sg. pres.'.

One might ask why it is necessary to perform this step formally, instead of merely recognizing that various suffixes (e.g. *-ed*) have occasional variant (suppletive) forms like vowel change (e.g. /ej/ ~ /u/), or that reduplication is an affix having special phonemic similarity to its stem. The drawback in the latter method is that it tells both the special form and the morphological status of the affixes at the same time. This makes it difficult to treat these two features separately, to discuss the special forms together with the special forms of other suffixes and stems (i.e. with the other groupings of alternants), and to discuss the morphological status on the same plane as the morphological status of affixes which do not have special forms. In the proposed method, reduplication is described as a group of morpheme alternants, grouped into a unit, between whose members a particular kind of difference exists; the status of these alternants in the morphology is irrelevant here and would be discussed in the section dealing with the relations between morpheme units.

2.3. We now have a list of morpheme units. We take each unit which consists of more than one alternant, and note the difference between its alternants. If we find another morpheme unit having an identical difference between its alternants, we can describe both units together. Thus the difference between *knife* and *knive-*, which make up one unit, is identical with the difference between *wife* and *wive-*, which make up another, and with the difference between *leaf* and *leave-*, and so on. Instead of listing both members of each unit, we now list only one representative of each unit with a general statement of the difference which applies to all of them: Each of the units *knife*, *wife*,..., has an alternant with /v/ instead of /f/ before /-z/ 'plural'.

In cases like this we can readily see that the units in question have identical relations between their alternants. In other cases it is far more difficult to see that the differences between alternants is identical in various units. For example, in Tübatulabal there are many units whose alternants differ in length of vowel: *ya·yaŋ* 'to be timid', after the reduplication morpheme (which means 'past time') *-yayaŋ*; *ta·wak* 'to see', after reduplication- *dawə·g-*; but *pələ·la* 'to arrive', after reduplication *-bələ·la*; the reduplication vowel, too, is short before some morphemes, long before others. Swadesh and Voegelin[10] showed that a general statement can be made for all these differences in vowel length. They first investigated each morpheme unit to see whether any of its vowels had basic length or basic shortness. A vowel is here said to have basic length if it is long in all the alternants of the unit[11]: e.g. the second /ə/ in *pələ·la*. A vowel has basic shortness if it is short in all the alternants of the unit[12]: e.g. the second /a/ in *ya·yaŋ*. Vowels which do not have basic length or shortness may be called neutral. Then the general statement is: In every morpheme alternant, counting from the beginning of the word, every odd-numbered vowel which is neutral is long, and every even-numbered vowel which is neutral is short.[13] The length of the neutral vowels in each alternant of any particular unit is therefore determined by the number of vowels which precede the alternant within the same word: in *ta·wak* the first neutral vowel of the morpheme is the first vowel of the word, and therefore long; in *a·-dawə·g-* the same first neutral vowel of the morpheme is the second vowel of the word, hence short. As a result of this general statement, it is no longer necessary to list the alternants which differ in vowel length.[14] We merely indicate which vowels of each unit have basic length or shortness.

In the case of some morpheme units, the difference between the alternants is expressed in two or more general statements: e.g. the difference in consonants between *ta·wək* and *-dawə·g-* is expressed in the statement that all morphemes with voiced stops have alternants with voiceless stop when the stop is at word boundary, while the difference in vowel length was expressed above.

THE RESULTANT ANALYSIS

3.0. We can now describe the six cases of § 1.1–6 as being all particular instances of one general operation.

3.1. The Tüb. alternants *puw* and *-buw*, both 'irrigate', are grouped together into one morpheme unit. For the first alternant occurs only at word initial, the second never; and the total range of positions in which both occur equals that of the single-alternant unit *hu·da* 'to be up (sun)'. Similarly, Heb. *máwt* and *mo·t-'*, both 'death', are grouped into one unit (compare *ró·š* and *ro·š-'* 'head').

3.2. *knife* and *knive-* satisfy the condition for composing one unit.

3.3. Heb. *'i·r* and *'a·r-* 'city' are grouped into one unit: *'a·r-* occurs only before *-i·m* 'plural', *'i·r* never; the combined positions of both equal the positions in which *su·s* 'horse' occurs.

3.4. Greek με, λε, and other reduplication prefixes, meaning 'perfect aspect', are alternants of one morpheme unit: με occurs only before morphemes beginning with /m/, λε only before those beginning with /l/, and so on (with other alternants before special types of morphemes); the combined range of environments of all these alternants equals the range of the ε- verb prefix (augment). A similar case is that of the echo words in languages of India. Thus, in Kota[15], *puǰ* is 'tiger', *puǰ-ɟiǰ* is 'any tiger'; *kaḷn* is 'thief', *kaḷn-ɟiḷn* is 'some thief'. *ɟiǰ, ɟiḷn,* and the other echo words have the same meaning; *ɟiǰ* occurs only after morphemes of the form CVǰ, *ɟiḷn* only after morphemes of the form CVḷn, and so on. The combined range of positions of all these echo words beginning with *ɟi* is equal to the range of any single alternant which occurs as second member in compounds and which (unlike the echo words) is not restricted to particular first members. We therefore group all these echo words into one morpheme unit with the meaning 'any, some, and the like', and say that the general form of the unit is *ɟiX*, where *X* is whatever follows the initial CV of the first member of the compound.

3.5. The form *took* is divided into *take* plus /ej/∼/u/; /ej/∼/u/ is an alternant which is grouped with /d/ and other alternants into a morpheme unit meaning 'past time', since they all satisfy the conditions for such grouping.

3.6. The forms *am, are, be, i-* (before /z/ '3d sg. pres.'), *-as, -ere* (both after *w-*, which is an alternant grouped with /d/ 'past time') are all grouped into one morpheme unit.

4.0. It is not enough to show that all such relations between alternants are special cases of one relation, namely that between the alternants of one morpheme unit. For there are differences between these cases, and we must see if it is possible to arrange these differences systematically as subdivisions of the operation of grouping alternants into units. It appears that we can record these differences in a simple manner if each time we group alternants into one unit we answer four questions: (1) What is the difference between the alternants of this unit? (2) In what environments does each alternant occur? (3) What similarity is there, if any, between the alternant and the environment? (4) What morpheme units have this difference between their alternants?

4.1. *The Difference between the Alternants.* In some morpheme units the alternants are the same except for one or two phonemes: e.g. the cases in § 3.1–3. In other units there are many alternants, all (or most) having some phonemic structure in common: e.g. the reduplication alternants in § 3.4 have the form Ce. In both cases we say that the alternants differ in only part of their phonemic sequence. In other units, however, such as in § 3.5–6, the alternants differ entirely.

4.2. *The Environment in which each Alternant occurs.* When a morpheme unit occurs in a given context, the alternant which appears there is determined by the environment of neighboring alternants. Each alternant of that unit occurs only in the neighborhood of particular other alternants; and often, if we investigate each of the morphemes in whose neighborhood the given alternant occurs, we will find that there is a common feature to all of them.

However, we will find that it is not enough to say that there is a common feature to all the environments in which a particular alternant occurs. It is not enough to say that all the environments in which /-əz/ 'plural' occurs have a common feature, namely that they all end in a sibilant or affricate. For while it is true that every time we have /-əz/ we find before it a morpheme ending in /s, š, č, z, ž, ǰ/, e.g. *fox, foxes*, the statement seems to be false when we consider *ox, oxen*. Since *ox* ends in /s/ we might have expected the /-əz/ alternant to occur after it. The catch lies in this: that every time /-əz/ occurs it has a morpheme ending in a sibilant or affricate before it, but not every morpheme ending in a sibilant or affricate has the /-əz/ alternant after it. After we have counted all the morphemes before /-əz/ – and all of them end in /s, š, č, z, ž, ǰ/ – we have left over one or two morphemes which end in sibilants without having /-əz/ after them. We therefore say that /-əz/ occurs only after morphemes ending in /s, š, č, z, ž, ǰ/ but not after all of them. The case is different with the Hebrew alternant *mawt*. This alternant occurs only with main stress; that is, whenever we find *mawt*, we find the stress on it. The other alternant, *mo·t*, occurs only before the stress. Here we can turn the statement around, as we could not in the case of /-əz/. We can say that whenever the stress is on the unit *mawt*, the alternant which appears is *mawt*, and whenever the environment is stressed after the unit, the alternant which appears is *mo·t*. After we have counted all the unstressed occurrences, where the alternant is *mo·t*, we have no unstressed occurrences left over where the alternant is something else. We therefore say that *mo·t* occurs only in un-stressed environments and in all unstressed environments. The difference between these two cases is seen again in the Menomini *e*[16], which is an alternant of the morpheme juncture /-/. In most cases, when a Menomini morpheme follows another within one word, there is no extra sound between them, and we may mark the junction between them with a hyphen. However, every time the first morpheme ends in C and the second begins in C, we find an *e* between the two morphemes, appearing, we might say, in place of the hyphen. This *e* also occurs between certain morphemes ending in V and certain ones beginning in /w/. As in the cases of /-əz/ and *mo·t*, we must distinguish the two environments: the first is any morphemes ending and beginning in C; the second is certain particular morphemes ending in V and beginning in /w/. Hence we say that the alternant *e* for /-/ (morpheme juncture) occurs in all environments of the form ...C-C..., and in certain environments of the form ...V-w....

A special case of environments which consist of a phonemic feature is that of junctures (boundaries of words, etc.). Some alternants occur only at word boundary and at any word boundary: e.g. Tüb. *ta·wək* as compared with *-dawə·g-*.[17]

In some morpheme units, what is common to all the environments in which a particular alternant occurs is the presence of a morpheme from a particular grammatical class. Thus, the contraction which occurs in Meno-mini[18] between certain morphemes ending in Vw and others beginning in /ε/, occurs between all such morphemes if the first is a verb stem and the second an inflectional suffix.

In other units, a given alternant appears only next to particular morpheme units (*knive-* only before /-z/ 'plural', *am* only with *I*), or only next to particular morpheme alternants (zero alternant of 'possessed by' only after the /-s, -z, -ez/ alternants of 'plural').

A special problem of morpheme division may be mentioned here. In some cases, not only does a morpheme unit have a unique alternant which occurs only when it is next to a particular second unit, but the second unit also has a unique alternant when it adjoins the first; e.g. *children*, if it is divided into /čild/, alternant of /čajld/ only before *-ren*, and *-ren*, alternant of /-z/ 'plural' only after *child*. Such situations often result from vowel contraction; e.g. Menomini morpheme units ending in /ɛ̄/[19] have alternants with /y/ (instead of /ɛ̄/) before morpheme units beginning with /o/; and units beginning with /o/ have alternants with /ā/ (instead of /o/) after units ending in /ɛ̄/: instead of having the sequence /...ɛ̄-o .../ we have /... y-ā .../. Each morpheme functions as the environment which determines the alternant of the other. In such cases it is sometimes hard to decide where to put the division between the two alternants. Thus *children* could alternatively be divided into /čildr/ and *-en*; from the point of view of grammatical arrangement each of the two points of division has advantages and disadvantages. In another Menomini contraction[20], the sequence of certain morpheme units ending in /aw/ followed by certain other units beginning in /ɛ/ has not /...aw-ɛ.../ but /...ō.../. We could say that the unit ending in /aw/ had an alternant ending in /ō/, and the one beginning in /ɛ/ had an alternant without the /ɛ/; or we could divide differently. The choice is immaterial here, and can be decided only by seeing which division would be more similar to the division of other morpheme sequences.

4.3. *Similarity between the Alternant and its Environment.* In many morpheme units there is no recognizable similarity between the alternants and the environments in which they occur; e.g. between *am* and *I*, between *i-* (alternant of *am*) and /-z/ '3d sg. pres.', between /ej/ ~ /u/ and *take*. In some cases, however, there is identity in phonemic feature (partial assimilation) or in phonemes (repetition or total assimilation); e.g. /-s/ 'plural' occurs only after alternants ending in voiceless phonemes and is identically voiceless with the phoneme preceding it, while the voiced alternant /-z/ occurs only after voiced phonemes. Identity in whole phonemes is rarer: the consonant of the Greek reduplication, and the *X* of the Kota *ǫiX*.

4.4. *Morpheme Units in which the Difference occurs.* Some differences between the alternants of a morpheme unit occur in all the units of that language which have the particular phoneme involved in the difference; e.g. the difference between alternants with voiced and with voiceless stops occurs in all Tübatulabal units, if they but have a voiced stop at either end. Other differences occur in many units, but not in all; e.g. the difference between alternants ending in /f/ and in /v/ occurs in *wife*, *life*, etc., but not in *fife*.

Still other differences appear only in one unit; e.g. the differences between the alternants in § 3.3, 6.

5.0. To sum up: The difference between alternants of a unit may be partial or complete. It may occur in all units which have a stated feature (e.g. a given phoneme in a certain position), or in some units having a stated feature in common, or in a unique unit (or in several units which have no stated feature in common). The range of environments which determine the appearance of the alternant in question may consist of all morphemes which have a stated feature, or of only some of the morphemes having that feature, or of a unique morpheme (or of several morphemes having no common feature).

It now becomes a simple matter to recognize wherein one grouping of alternants into a unit differs from another (see § 4.0).

5.1. If the difference between alternants of a unit is complete, it necessarily applies only to one unit.[21] If the difference is partial, it may occur in one, some, or all units which have a stated feature.

5.2. If there is a phonemic or morphologic feature which is present only in the units in which the difference under discussion occurs (and in no other units), then we may name the feature in a general statement and there is no need to list the units in which the difference occurs: all Hebrew morphemes with /aw/ had alternants with /o·/. On the other hand, if there is a feature which is common to all the units in which the difference under discussion occurs, but which is also present in other units (in which this difference does not occur), then we may either list all the units, or else make a mark upon their common feature to distinguish these units from the other units in which the difference does not occur: see *knife* in § 5.4.

But if the unit in which the difference occurs is unique, or if there are several units which have no common feature, then we must list all of them.

5.3. The method of describing the environment in which an alternant occurs is similar to the method of describing the units in which the difference occurs.

If whenever a certain feature is present in the environment only a given alternant (and no other one of its own unit) occurs i.e., if the given alternant is the only one of its unit to occur when that feature is present in the environment, then we name the feature in a general statement and there is no need to list all the environments in which the given alternant occurs: Hebrew units with /aw/ always had alternants with /o·/ when the unit was unstressed. Similarly, if a certain feature is always present in the environment when a given alternant appears, but if some other alternants of the same unit also have that feature in their environment, then we may either list all the specific environments in which the given alternant appears, or else mark these environments to distinguish them from other environments which have the same feature: /ej/ ∼ /u/ alternant of -ed 'past time' appears only with morphemes having the structure CejC, but not all morphemes CejC are followed by the /ej/ ∼ /u/ alternant, since *rake* and other morphemes of this structure are followed by the -ed alternant.

If the environment in which the alternant occurs is unique, or if there are several environment morphemes which have no common feature, then we must list all of them.

5.4. A few examples:

Early Hebrew: All units having /aw/ have alternants with /oˑ/ instead, when any stressed morpheme follows within the word. (Both the units and the environments to which this applies include all those which have the features stated here.)

Menomini[22]: Some units ending in /n/ have alternants ending in /s/ instead, before all morphemes beginning with /e/. (The units involved here are only some of those having the stated feature /n/. Therefore they must be listed or marked. Bloomfield writes the units which do not have the /s/ alternant with N, and those which have the /s/ alternant with n, thus distinguishing the two groups.)

Kota: The unit for 'any, some, and the like' has alternants of the form *ạiX* after any morpheme CVX. (The unit is unique; the environment is any unit having the stated feature.)

English: Some units ending in /f/ have alternants ending in /v/ instead, before /-z/ 'plural'. (We may write all these units with F: /najF/, but /fajf/. The environment, being unique, need not be specially marked.)

The unit /čajld/ has the alternant /čild/ before -ren 'plural'.

The unit -ed 'past time' has the alternant /ej/ ∼ /u/ with some units of the form CejC. (Note that here it is the environmental morphemes that have to be listed or marked.)

The unit /-z/ 'plural' has the alternant /-s/ after most morphemes which end in a voiceless phoneme, and in no other environments. (The unit is unique. The environments have to be listed or marked. However, since the cases where an alternant other than /-s/ occurs after the stated feature are relatively rare, it is simpler to list the cases where /-s/ does not occur. They may be listed in connection with the alternants with which they occur; i.e. we list the alternants of 'plural': /-əz/ after /s, š, .../, -en after *ox*, ..., /-s/ after the other morphemes ending in a voiceless phoneme.)

5.5. Statements made for unique alternants are best included in the dictionary rather than the grammar. Units referred to in general statements are written with one base form representing all the alternants and containing any special marks which the general statement may require. By applying to the base form all the general statements which refer to it we obtain the alternants which occur in the environments named in the general statements.

CONCLUSION

Possible advantages of the method described here are:

6.1. It prescribes three explicit procedures which, if rigorously followed, will lead to a unique[23] arrangement of the phenomena described here for a particular language.

6.2. It presents regular phonology, morphophonemics, sandhi, morphological processes like vowel change, morpholexical variation, suppletion, and the like as cases of a single linguistic relation, described in § 2.2. The differences between these cases are systematized in §§ 4 and 5.

6.3. It leaves not merely less, but a simpler morphology. This is necessarily so, because the procedure of § 2.2 (especially the condition concerning the total range of environment) removes from consideration as a separate morpheme unit any alternant which has a more specialized distribution than the rest of its class and which is complementary to other over-specialized alternants. The morphology describes the relations between morpheme units, all those in a given class now having roughly the same distribution.

6.4. It simplifies our general picture of linguistic structure, i.e. of what relations can be discovered between the elements of linguistic expressions. For it shows that we can arrange alternants into units in exactly the same manner as we arrange sound types (positional variants) into phonemes.

7.1. *Summary.* The method of arranging the morphemes of a language consists of three steps: (1) dividing each phonemically written linguistic expression into the smallest parts which recur with the same meaning in different expressions, each such part to be called a morpheme alternant; (2) grouping into a distinct morpheme unit all alternants which satisfy the following conditions: (a) have the same meaning (b) never occur in identical environments, and (c) have combined environments no greater than the environments of some single alternant in the language; (3) making general statements for all units which have identical difference between their alternants.

7.2. Every statement, general or particular, about the alternants must contain three pieces of information: (a) what is the difference between the alternants; (b) in what environments does each alternant occur; (c) in what units does the difference occur. It is seen that various groupings of alternants into units differ on these three counts.

NOTES

[1] L. Bloomfield, *Language*, New York 1933, 161.
[2] M. Swadesh and C. F. Voegelin, 'A Problem in Phonological Alternation', *Lg.* **15** (1939), 4.
[3] Z. S. Harris, 'Linguistic Structure of Hebrew', *JAOS* **61** (1941), 155.
[4] *Ibid.*, 159.
[5] L. Bloomfield, 'Menomini Morphophonemics', *TCLP* **8** (1939), 105.
[6] R. H. Lowie, Z. S. Harris, and C. F. Voegelin, *Hidatsa Texts* (Indiana Historical Society Prehistory Research Series 1), 1939, 192, fn. 38.
[7] Cf. Bloomfield, *Language*, 217, where it is shown that the relation between masculine and feminine adjectives in French can be most simply described by regarding the feminine forms as basic.
[8] This excludes synonyms, i.e. morphemes of approximately similar meaning, which usually occur in the same positions: *a fine youngster, a fine lad.*
[9] As in *a score of voices*, but *twenty voices*. However, we may consider that *twenty* occurs in the same position as *score* in *a twenty* 'a $20 bill'.
[10] *Lg.* **15** (1939), 5ff. The formulation presented here is a restatement, in terms of morpheme alternants, of their morphophonemic analysis.
[11] Or if it is always short while each of its neighboring vowels is either always long or always short.
[12] Unless it is next to a basically long vowel, in which position even a neutral vowel is always short.
[13] But a neutral vowel next to one with basic length is always short.
[14] Certain additional general statements involving /ʔ/, etc., must be applied before the statement about vowel length.
[15] M. B. Emeneau, 'An Echo-Word Motif in Dravidian Folk Tales', *JAOS* **58** (1938), 553–70; 'Echo Words in Toda', *New Indian Antiquary* **1** (1938), 109–17.
[16] Bloomfield, *TCLP* **8**, 105–15, no. 10-2.
[17] What is called external sandhi, therefore, differs from internal sandhi merely in that the former contains statements which have word juncture as a necessary part of their determining environments, while the latter does not. In some languages, alternants next to word juncture may differ so much from those which are not, and differences determined by word juncture may have so many features in common, that it becomes convenient to arrange all statements involving word juncture environments together. In other languages, however, where many statements apply to environments both within words and across word juncture, it is simpler not to distinguish external from internal sandhi.
[18] Bloomfield, *TCLP* **8**, 105–15, no. 18.
[19] *Ibid.*, no. 15.
[20] *Ibid.*, no. 18.
[21] E.g. the complete difference between *go* and *wen-* exists only between these two sequences of phonemes, hence (barring homonyms) only in this particular unit. However, the partial difference between *knife* and *knive-* can occur between any two sequences of phonemes that contain /f/ and /v/.
[22] Bloomfield, *TCLP* **8**, 105–15, no. 13.
[23] Except for sequences of unique alternants (see last paragraph of § 4.2). Such cases should be indicated in a special list of alternative possibilities.

V

DISCONTINUOUS MORPHEMES

This paper attempts to generalize the term MORPHEME so as to apply not only to sequences of successive phonemes but also to broken sequences. In so doing, it offers a method of expressing one of the possible relations between morphemes as previously understood.[1] The relation in question is that which obtains between two or more morphemes that always occur together (in a given environment). The essence of the method is that any two or more continuous morphemes which always occur together shall be considered to constitute together a single new morpheme. Since this relation between continuous morphemes is a type of grammatical agreement, the method here proposed obviates the necessity of separately treating this type of agreement.

1. It is convenient to summarize the forms that may be found among the continuous morphemes, so that we may see to what extent the new forms will differ.

Most morphemes in most languages have been described as sequences of consecutive phonemes: for instance /iŋ/ in *speaking, writing.*

Rarely, it is convenient to recognize a minus morpheme, which consists of the dropping of any phoneme occupying a particular position, e.g. the dropping of the last consonant, which constitutes a morpheme meaning 'masculine' in Bloomfield's analysis of French adjectives.[2]

Morphemes involving replacement of one phoneme by another may then be considered as consisting of the dropping of one phoneme and the adding of the other (i.e. as combinations of the first two types). Thus *men* contains two morphemes: *man*; and $-/æ/+/e/$[3], which means 'plural'.

It is also necessary to recognize that some morphemes do not consist of the traditional phonemes at all, but of phonemic contours which may extend over many phonemes. An example is the rising intonation /?/ which indicates a question in American English.

Lastly, morphemes which are complementary to each other in distribution, and which satisfy certain other criteria, may be conveniently considered as being merely alternants (positional variants) of one morpheme. Thus the /s/ which occurs in *The book- are here*, the /z/ which occurs in *The boy- are here*, and the −/æ/+/e/ which occurs in *The man- are here* may all be included in one morphemic unit {s}[4] which has these three variants in these three environments.[5]

GENERALIZING THE MORPHEME DEFINITION

2.0. In this section it will be seen that the definition of MORPHEME as implicitly used by most linguists today can be extended to include discontinuous morphemes.

Why do we consider *paper* as one morpheme rather than two? Roughly, it is because every time the form occurs, with the meaning of 'paper', it is the whole phonemic sequence /peypər/ that appears; we do not find /pey/ without /pər/, or /pər/ without /pey/, yielding partial meanings whose combination, in the combined form /peypər/, would be 'paper'.[6]

In the continuous morphemes, the fundamental criterion which determines that the whole of a sequence of phonemes constitutes one morpheme rather than two, is the fact that the whole sequence occurs together in a certain class of positions and with certain meanings, and that parts of the sequence do not occur separately with parts of the total meaning of the sequence. Precisely this criterion is found to apply to what will be proposed below as discontinuous morphemes.

2.1. In some cases we have two unique (continuous) morphemes which always occur together, though not next each other. In Yokuts, whenever *na'aṣ* occurs, a verb with the suffix *-al* occurs with it; and whenever the verb-suffix *-al* occurs, *na'aṣ* occurs nearby. Together, they indicate uncertainty of the action; it would presumably be impossible to give the descriptive meaning of each one of them, since they never occur separately: *hina' ma' na'aṣ xat-al* 'Perhaps you might eat', *tunaċ na'aṣ so:g-al* '(He) might pull out the cork', *xatxat-al na'aṣ* '(He) might eat repeatedly'.[7] Instead of saying that we have here two morphemes which always occur with each other, we can say that we have just one morpheme whose phonemes are not consecutive: *na'aṣ...-al* (with the rarer variant *-al...na'aṣ*). We thus obviate the need for a restrictive statement about the two continuous morphemes. Such simple discontinuous morphemes are infrequent.[8]

2.2. On the other hand, repeated (continuous) morphemes appear in many languages. In Gk. σοφῶν ἀδελφῶν 'of wise brothers', we have a continuous morpheme ῶν 'genitive plural' about which the special statement must be made that it occurs twice in this phrase. We might say: if ῶν occurs after ἀδελφ-, and if σοφ- occurs before, then ῶν will also occur after σοφ-; i.e.

noun and adjective agree as to gender, number, and case. However, since the two occurrences of ὧν always appear together and are always identically replaced, as in σοφῷ ἀδελφῷ 'to a wise brother', we might say alternatively: there is a morpheme ...ῶν ...ῶν which occurs in σοφ- ἀδελφ-, and in other adjective-noun sequences; similarly, there is a morpheme ...ῷ ...ῷ, etc. When we say this, no special statement is needed about the concurrence of the two ὧν forms: they occur together because they are parts of one morpheme.

2.3. This type of analysis does not require that the two parts of the morpheme be identical. In σοφῷ ἀνδρί 'to a wise man', we say that there is a morpheme ...ῳ ...ί which occurs in σοφ- ἀνδρ-, and in other sequences of adjective plus third-declension noun.

2.4. Following the practice of grouping complementary morphemes of identical meaning into single morphemic units, we consider such morphemes as ...ῷ ...ῷ and ...ῷ ...ί to be both variants of the dative (masculine) singular morpheme[9], the second variant occurring when the noun is of the third declension.

2.5. The single ὧν which occurs in ἀδελφῶν 'of brothers', the ...ῶν ...ῶν which occurs in σοφῶν ἀδελφῶν, and the ...ῶν ...ῶν ...ῶν which occurs in τῶν σοφῶν ἀδελφῶν 'of the wise brothers', are all complementary to each other, since the first occurs only with single nouns, the second only with a sequence of two morphemes of the article, adjective, or noun class[10], the third only with a sequence of three morphemes of the article, adjective, or noun class. We may therefore say that ὧν, ...ῶν ...ῶν, ...ῶν ...ῶν ...ῶν, etc. are all variants of one morphemic unit {ὧν} 'genitive plural'. Which variant of the unit occurs depends on the environment, i.e. on the number of morphemes of the article, adjective, or noun class appearing together. Similarly, ῷ, ...ῷ ...ῷ, ...ῷ ...ί, ...ῷ ...ῷ ...ῷ, etc. are all variants of one morphemic unit {ῷ} 'dative (masculine) singular'; which of these variants occurs depends on the number and declension of the morphemes in the environment.

2.6. One of the major advantages of this method, i.e. of considering morphemic repetitions as variants of one morpheme, is the fact that the environment of each variant often turns out to be syntactically identical with the environment of every other variant of the same morphemic unit. The morphemic unit can in such cases be referred to the syntactic domain as a whole, while the particular variants of the unit each occur with particular morphemic forms of that domain. Thus the morphemic units {ὧν} and {ῷ} always occur over the whole of a noun phrase in Greek, and may in fact be considered suffixes of the noun phrase as such. If the phrase consists of only one noun, the variant is ὧν (or ῷ). If the phrase consists of two stem morphemes – say adjective and noun or article and noun – the variant is ...ῶν ...ῶν (or ...ῷ ...ῷ); and so on.

The syntactic domain of a repetitive morpheme may be more complicated. In the Semitic languages, the domain of the feminine morpheme and of the plural morpheme is the noun phrase and the following verb (or the preceding verb, if there is no following verb within the clause contour). Thus in Modern Hebrew there are the following types of clauses:

iš diber	A man spoke.
iša dibra.	A woman spoke.
iš cair diber.	A young man spoke.
iša cəira dibra.	A young woman spoke.
iš cair mədaber.	A young man is speaking.
iša cəira mədaberet.	A young woman is speaking.
iša cəira dibra ləiš cair.	A young woman was talking to a young man.

The morphemic unit {*a*} 'feminine' consists of an /a/[11] repeated after each noun (including adjective) in a noun phrase and after the following verb. However, as the last example shows, the domain of the {*a*} does not extend to nouns following the nouns and verb.

3.0. A complicated example of discontinuous repetitive morphemes may be found in the Bantu languages. There every noun stem always occurs with a particular class prefix, and every adjective, pronoun, or preposition which follows it, and the verb whose subject the noun is, all have the same class prefix or one related to it. In Swahili[12] we find utterances like the following[13]:

1. *walikuʒa *wanawake* they-came women two (two women came)
   wawili
2. **watu wa-ulaa* people of-Europe come
   wamewanza
3. **mtu mwenye nguvu* man having strength
4. *huyu *mke wa-ʒamaa* this woman of-countryman mine, she-told-me
   yangu, amenambia
5. **čio ča-'alimu* school of-religion closed
   čimekuiʒa
6. **mikono haina nguvu* arms having-no strength
7. *hiki *kiti kizuri* this chair fine from-Europe, it-got-broken
   ča-ulaa, kimevunʒika

In each utterance, the word marked with an asterisk is a noun which occurs only with the singular or plural class prefix preceding it. The morpheme *tu* 'person' appears here after the singular *m* and plural *wa* ('person class'), as does the morpheme for 'woman'. The morphemes *io* 'school' and *ti* 'chair' appear after the singular *ki* (variant *č*: 'thing class'). The morpheme *kono* 'arm' occurs with the plural *mi* ('tree class'). The nouns which occur with a particular class prefix often have some aspect of meaning in common: e.g. those that occur with *m* and *wa* refer to human beings. The class prefixes may therefore be said to have this class meaning.

The other morphemes in the utterances listed above occur with various class prefixes, depending on the one that precedes the noun. The class prefix of the noun is repeated before the adjective (as *wili* 'two', *zuri* 'fine'), before the verb whose subject the noun is (as *likuža* 'came,' *mevunžika* 'got broken'; the variant of *m* before verbs is *a* as in *amenambia*[14]), and after any one of a class of demonstrative morphemes which includes the pronouns (as *hu* 'this', where *yu* is the variant of the class prefix *m*). The class prefix is also repeated before other morphemes, which make a following noun phrase into an adjective of the preceding noun phrase: *a-* 'of', *wenye* 'having', etc. Thus *ulaa* 'Europe', which can occur as a noun phrase by itself, combines with *a-* into *a-ulaa* 'of Europe', which has the syntactic position of an adjective and is preceded by a repetition of the class prefix of the noun before it: *watu wa-ulaa, kiti ča-ulaa.* The noun after *a-* has its own class prefix[15], unrelated to that of the preceding noun but repeated in any adjectives which follow the post-*a-* noun and refer to it: *žamaa yangu* 'countryman of-me' ('class 3' prefix *y* before *-angu*).[16]

3.1. It is possible to summarize all this by saying that the class prefixes have discontinuous forms. The prefix in utterance 1 above would be *wa... wa... wa...*, a variant of {*wa*} indicating person class plural; in utterance 3 *m... m...*, and in utterance 4 *...yu m... w... a...*, both of these being variants of {*m*} indicating person class singular; and in utterance 7 *...ki ki... ki... č... ki...*, a variant of {*ki*} indicating thing class singular. The domain of the discontinuous parts (whether repetitions or phonemically different parts) of the new morphemes could in all cases be summarized by saying that the parts of the new morpheme occupy as many of the following positions (marked by dashes) as occur in the utterance: demonstrative- -noun -adjective -adjectivizer (+noun) -verb. If any other morphemes occur, they do not affect the parts of the new morpheme. If various sections of this domain do not occur, the parts of the new morpheme which would appear with them of course do not occur either. We can now deal directly with our few discontinuous prefixes, the particular variant of each being always determined by the form of the domain. Given the prefix {*m*} indicating single human beings, if the domain is -noun the variant will be *m...*; if the domain is demonstrative- -noun -verb, the variant will be *...yu m... a...*[17]: thus if the environment is -*tu* we obtain *mtu*; if the environment is *hu- -ke -menambia* we obtain *huyu mke amenambia*.

Instead of having to describe special relations among the prefixes (e.g. between the *m* of *mke* and the *a* of *amenambia*) and the repetition of the class-prefix, we now list merely a few morphemes with somewhat complicated variants, which spread out over a syntactically recognizable domain.[18]

3.2. One feature of special selection remains: particular nouns occur with particular class-prefixes. Even this limitation can be avoided by considering the class prefix, with all its discontinuous parts, as part of each noun.[19] The morpheme for 'chair' is then not *ti* but {*kiti*,} where the *ki* part represents all the variants discussed above: e.g. in the environment *hi- - -zuri -a-ulaa* 'this fine – from Europe', the variant of {*kiti*} is ...*ki kiti ki... č...*. Similarly, the morpheme for 'man' is then not *tu* but {*mtu*}[20]; and 'woman' not *ke* but {*mke*}, which in the environment *hu- - -menambia* 'this – told me' would be ...*yu mke a...*.

If this combining of prefix and noun into one morpheme is carried out, it will be necessary to mention that most nouns in the language begin with one of only five phonemes (the others begin with the zero prefix which would not appear here), and that it is only the first phoneme or the first pair of phonemes which (with many variants) is repeated throughout the domain of the new noun.[21] That is to say, all nouns have discontinuous repeated parts (varying with the environment), but there are only some six sets of discontinuous parts for each environment, and each noun has one or another of these six; which one it is, is indicated by the initial phoneme of the noun, since it is only that initial which (with its variants) is repeated. It will further have to be mentioned that most of the nouns that have a similar initial (the initial that repeats through the domain) also have some broad similarity in meaning: e.g. those whose repeated initial is *m* refer to human beings. This would be on a par with such facts as the meaning-element common to English morphemes which begin with *sl* (*slush, slide, slick*, etc.), though the Bantu correlation is far more thoroughgoing.

CONCLUSIONS

The considerations of §§ 2–3 show the possibility of a general treatment of morphemes which occur together.

4.1. Given some particular environment, if two morphemes X and Y depend on each other so that neither occurs without the other (in that environment), we say that X and Y constitute together one new morpheme Z which simply occurs in the environment.[22] The environment may be stated in terms of particular morphemes, e.g. Swahili *hi- - -zuri* 'this fine –', or in terms of morpheme classes and syntactic constructions, e.g. demonstrative-

(noun) -adjective. The more general the environment is, the greater advantage there is in combining X and Y, which are mutually dependent within it, into one morpheme Z. And the greater the variability of the environment (e.g. if it is a noun phrase which may consist of any number of nouns, adjectives, etc.), the more different types of repetition and variation of dependent morphemes are expressed by the single discontinuous morpheme. Thus the Swahili noun phrase may be *kiti* alone, or *hiki kiti*, or *kiti kizuri*, or *hiki kiti kizuri*, etc., and the discontinuous noun, whether {*kiti*} or any other, has corresponding variants for each form of the noun phrase.[23]

4.2. An apparent loss of descriptive efficiency arises here. If each Swahili noun partakes of one out of only six repeated initials, does that not mean that the six initials are more general, and should be treated separately from the many individual nouns? But, for that matter, all Swahili morphemes partake of only some 21 phonemes; yet we do not on the whole consider the phonemes to be general classifiers of morphemes. It is true that we discuss the phonemes independently of the morphemes, and similarly we should discuss the repeated initials independently of the individual nouns. But we should discuss them merely as a feature of the phonemic composition of a class of Swahili morphemes, namely the fact that these morphemes are discontinuous and that the discontinuity consists in the repeating of the initial (or of a substitute for it) in stated positions throughout a certain domain. All this does not require us to set up the repeated initial as a separate morpheme.

The fact that these repeated initials often have an element of meaning – the meaning common to all the nouns that begin with them – permits us to set them up as separate morphemes only if we are prepared to set up the *sl* of English *slide, slick*, etc. as a separate morpheme on a similar basis.[24] If we wish to recognize such formally dependent but semantically general elements as morphemes, we should reject the extension of § 3.2. However, we should keep the basic method of § 3.1, which places the agreeing morphemes into one repeated morpheme.

4.3. The condition stated in the first sentence of § 4.1 is exactly that which determines whether two consecutive phonemes are parts of the same morpheme. The new discontinuous morpheme is thus distributionally the same as the old continuous morphemes. The only difference between new and old is in the very feature which distinguishes them, i.e. in their continuity. The difference in continuity, therefore, does not correlate with any other difference between them, and in the new definition, which takes no note of continuity, the continuous morphemes are merely a special case, and a simple one, of morphemes as a whole.

NOTES

[1] Where it is necessary to distinguish between morphemes recognized without applying the method here proposed, and the morphemes which result from the application of this method, the former will be called continuous morphemes, and the latter new.

[2] Leonard Bloomfield, *Language*.

[3] Read: minus /æ/ plus /e/. In the pair *man* : *men*, it is of course arbitrary to consider *men* rather than *man* as containing two morphemes. We might have said that *man* consists of *men* plus a morpheme indicating 'singular'. We might also have said that *man* and *men* are two unrelated single morphemes. The choice among these ways of analyzing *man* and *men* depends on the relation of these morphemes to other morphemes in the language, and to the utterances in which they occur.

[4] Braces { } will be used to indicate morphemic units.

[5] See Z. S. Harris, 'Morpheme Alternants in Linguistic Analysis', *Lg.* 18 (1942), 169–80 (Paper IV of this volume), where it is shown that such groupings of morphemes into one morphemic unit can be performed, without arbitrariness or resort to meaning, on the basis of distributional criteria.

[6] More rigorous criteria, with less reliance upon meaning, can be stated, but are not necessary for the present purpose.

[7] Stanley Newman, *Yokuts Language of California*, 1944, 120.

[8] Leonard Bloomfield, *Language*, 180. The late Manuel J. Andrade showed me in 1940 a similar case in his Guatemalan material.

[9] These morphemes can of course be broken down into case, number, and (usually) gender morphemes, but that is not relevant here.

[10] E.g. it occurs also in τ— ἀδελφ—, as in τῶν ἀδελφῶν 'of the brothers'.

[11] Or /et/ after the present tense morpheme.

[12] I am indebted to Nathan Glazer for obtaining these utterances from our informant, and for his valuable collaboration in the Swahili research of the Intensive Language Program of the American Council of Learned Societies.

[13] The phonetic value of a space is to indicate loud stress on the second vowel before it. The letters may be pronounced with their usual values for an approximation to Swahili sounds.

[14] When an object of the verb is stated, its class prefix may also be repeated before the verb, after the subject class prefix.

[15] In the case of *ulaa*, it is *u* ('class 6'). The noun *laa* occurs with the class prefix *u*. The sequence *a-ulaa* occurs with the class prefix of the noun which precedes it.

[16] When a noun is followed by an adjective plus an adjectival noun phrase (i.e. a noun phrase preceded by *a*-), the adjectival noun phrase comes last. Hence there is no confusion as to whether an adjective refers directly to the head noun or to the noun that is preceded by *a*- (even if both are of the same class): if the adjective follows the *a*- noun, it refers to it.

[17] Allowing for variations which depend on the particular demonstrative, etc.

[18] These few discontinuous morphemes may indeed be considered to be the ultimate noun class of the language, since the nouns may be considered to modify these class prefixes in somewhat the same way that the adjectives modify the nouns. The formal relation, however, is not the same, since nouns are limited to particular class prefixes whereas adjectives are not limited to particular nouns.

[19] I am indebted for this suggestion to Freeman Twaddell, and have also profited from a discussion of the question with Bernard Bloch.

[20] The 'person class' plural *wa* would have to be broken into two morphemes, one a plural having the same domain as the class prefixes, the other a variant of the 'person class' prefix which occurs only in the environment of the new plural morpheme.

[21] Since the domain of the class prefix now becomes the domain of the noun, or rather of its first phoneme or two.

[22] X and Y would traditionally be described as being in agreement. The present method replaces this agreement relation by a single morpheme Z. The method can clearly be

extended so as to replace other types of grammatical agreement by single morphemes, but the results would not be as simple as in this limited type.

[23] The fact that we have to state the environment in order to know the form of our discontinuous morpheme in each particular occurrence, means that the environment functions as an independent factor in determining the variant of our new morpheme. Therefore it is possible to generalize the present method, and to take any two morphemes, and treat any factor which determines their coexistence as part of their environment. However, it is descriptively advantageous to do so only if the environment or the variation is of a general character, or correlates with other features of the language.

[24] With a by-product of such forlorn morphemes as -ide, -ick, etc.

VI

FROM MORPHEME TO UTTERANCE

1.0. This paper presents a formalized procedure for describing utterances directly in terms of sequences of morphemes rather than of single morphemes.[1] It thus covers an important part of what is usually included under syntax. When applied in a particular language, the procedure yields a compact statement of what sequences of morphemes occur in the language, i.e. a formula for each utterance (sentence) structure in the language.

1.1. At present, morpheme classes are formed by placing in one class all morphemes which are substitutable for each other in utterances, as *man* replaces *child* in *The child disappeared.* The procedure outlined below consists, essentially, in extending the technique of substitution from single morphemes (e.g. *man*) to sequences of morphemes (e.g. *intense young man*). In so far as it deals with sequences, it parallels the type of analysis frequently used in syntax, so that the chief usefulness of this procedure is probably its explicitness rather than any novelty of method or result.

1.2. The reason for a procedure of the type offered here is not far to seek. One of the chief objectives of syntactic analysis is a compact description of the structure of utterances in the given language. The paucity of explicit methods in this work has made syntactic analysis a tedious and often largely intuitive task, a collection of observations whose relevance is not certain and whose interrelation is not clear. Partly as a result of this, many grammars have carried little or no syntactic description. In many of the descriptions that have been written, the lack of explicit methods has permitted the use of diverse and undefined terms and a reliance on semantic rather than formal differentiation.

If we now seek a clearer method for obtaining generalizations about the structure of utterances in a language, it should preferably deal with the simplest observables. These are the morphemes, which are uniquely identifiable and easy to follow. Constructs such as 'morphological levels' may be useful in particular cases, but there is an advantage in avoiding them if we can achieve the same results by direct manipulation of the observable morphemes. The method described in this paper will require no elements other

Language **22**, No. 3 (1946), 161–83.

than morphemes and sequences of morphemes[2], and no operation other than substitution, repeated time and again.

THE ELEMENTS

2.0. We assume, then, that we have isolated the morphemes of the language. An exact list of the morphemes is of course required for any description of the language, no matter what method is followed. It is possible to obtain somewhat different lists of morphemes, depending on certain choices made at the start.

2.1. We might say that a particular phoneme sequence which has widely divergent meanings represents more than one morpheme: homonyms such as *pair* and *pear*, or *make* in *What make is it?* and *She's on the make*. Alternatively, we may say that the sequence (/peyr/ or /meyk/) constitutes only one morpheme under any circumstances.

2.2. We may say that each morpheme can have only one phonemic form, so that for example the English plural endings /s/, /z/, /əz/ (as in *books, chairs, glasses*) constitute three morphemes, and *am, are* constitute two morphemes. Alternatively, we may include each of these sets in a single morpheme, if we say that different phoneme sequences constitute positional variants of one morpheme when they are complementary to each other.[3]

2.3. We could say, as is usually done, that repeated morphemes express concord, as in Latin feminine *-a* in *mēnsa parva* 'the small table' or the modern Hebrew article *ha* (and feminine *-a*) in *haiša haktana* 'the small woman'. Alternatively, we could say that in each of these cases we have not a repeated word-suffix or word-prefix, but rather a single phrase-infix consisting, in the case of the Hebrew article, of the phonemes /ha/ before every noun-morpheme (including adjectives) in a noun phrase. This would mean that instead of our being given a morpheme *ha* and having to state that it occurs only with certain syntactic selections, we are given a morpheme which we may write *ha... ha...* and which has no further limitations of selection, but either occurs or does not occur in a phrase, just as do the other morphemes. If the phrase contains the morpheme for 'man' and 'small', it is *iš katan* 'small man'; if it also contains the morpheme for 'the', it is *haiš hakatan*; if it also contains the morpheme for 'feminine', it is *iša ktana*; if it contains both, it is *haiša haktana*.[4]

2.4. In the alternatives presented in §§ 2.2–3 above we find that in each paragraph the first method yields phonemically simple morphemes about which statements of selection remain to be made. Thus, we would have to say somewhere that the plural morpheme /s/ occurs only after morphemes ending in a voiceless consonant; that *am* occurs only after *I*; that when *parv-*

is in one phrase with *mēnsa* it always has -*a* following; and that whenever *ha* occurs with one noun it will also occur with all other nouns in the phrase. The second method in each case offers phonemically more complicated morphemes which have fewer special limitations of selection as distinguished from other morphemes.

Each method clearly has its advantages and its uses. The syntactic procedure to be indicated below can be carried out regardless of the method followed in setting up the morphemes. However, as will be seen, the fewer limitations of selection we have to deal with, the simpler will be this syntactic procedure. Therefore, in the examples used in this paper it will be assumed that the morpheme list for the language concerned has been constructed by the second method, i.e. that we have included in the phonemic form and definition of the morpheme as many of its limitations as we could.

THE OPERATION

3.0. The procedure to be indicated below consists essentially of repeated substitution: e.g. *child* for *young boy* in *Where did the – go ?*. To generalize this, we take a form *A* in an environment *C – D* and then substitute another form *B* in the place of *A*. If, after such substitution, we still have an expression which occurs in the language concerned, i.e. if not only *CAD* but also *CBD* occurs, we say that *A* and *B* are members of the same substitution-class, or that both *A* and *B* fill the position *C – D*, or the like.

The operation of substitution is basic in descriptive linguistics. Not only is it essential in phonemics, but it is also necessary for the initial setting up of morphemes, for the recognition of morpheme boundaries.

3.1. *Morpheme Classes.* The first step in our procedure is to form substitution classes of single morphemes. We list, for the language concerned, all single morphemes which replace each other in the substitution test, i.e. which occur in the same environments (have the same selection). If any of them do not occur in the same order, they are placed in a special sub-class. Thus, Moroccan Arabic *n-* 'I will' and -*t* 'I did' are mutually substitutable, although they occur at different points in the order of morphemes: *ana nmši ld'aru* 'I'll go to his house', *ana mšit ld'aru* 'I went to his house'.

3.2. In making these substitution classes of morphemes we may be faced with many problems. In some languages, relatively few morphemes occur in exactly the same environments as others: *poem* occurs in *I'm writing a whole – this time*, but *house* does not. Both morphemes, however, occur in *That's a beautiful –*. Shall we say that *poem* and *house* belong in general to the same substitution class, or that they have some environments in common and some not?

It will be seen that the method proposed in §§ 3.5–9 below can be used no matter how this problem is met.[5] However, in order to keep the examples of §§ 4–6 as simple as possible, it will be assumed here that morphemes having slightly different distributions are grouped together into one class if the distributional differences between their environments correspond to the distributional differences between the morphemes. That is, if *poem* and *house* differ distributionally only in the fact that *poem* occurs with *write* and *house* with *wire*, and in comparable differences, and if *write* and *wire* in turn differ only in that *write* occurs with *poem* and *wire* with *house*, and in comparable differences, we put *poem* in one class with *house*, and simultaneously put *write* in one class with *wire*.

3.3. Other differences of environment are less easily handled. English *cover* occurs after both *un-* and *dis-*, while *dress* occurs only after *un-*, *connect* only after *dis-*, and *take* after neither (but *connected* occurs also after *un-*). On the other hand, *cover, dress, connect,* and *take* all occur before *-ing*, and in environments like *Let's not — it just now*. Here again, shall we group these into the same morpheme class, or into four different classes? That is, should the classes to be used in our method below be set up on the basis of relation to *-ing*, or on the basis of relation to *un-*? We find that the selections which these four have in common (their occurrence before *-ing* and in *Let's not – it just now*) differentiate them from other large substitution classes, such as *India, child,* or *to, from,* which do not occur in these positions. On the other hand, the selections in which they differ do not differentiate or equate morphemes in a way that is useful in analyzing many utterances. Although *un-* occurs before some of the morphemes which occur before *-ing*, we also find *un-* before a few of the morphemes which occur not before *-ing* but in *the – man:* e.g. *just, true.*[6]

As in the case of § 3.2, the method to be described below is applicable regardless of the definition of morpheme class that we select. If we put *cover, dress, connect,* and *take* into four different classes on the basis of relation to *un-*, we will be able to group the classes together later on the basis of their relation to *-ing*. And if we treat them as members of one class on the basis of *-ing*, we will have to note that they differ distributionally (as sub-classes) with respect to *un-*. For brevity, we will here consider them as members of one morpheme class.

3.4. In some cases of morphemes having one environment but not another in common, both the similarity and the difference are relevant for utterance structure. Thus *cover, note, find* all occur in *-ing, We'll – his path,* as well as in *–s* ('plural'), *You can have my –*. But *think* occurs only in the first two types of environment, and *child* only in the last two.[7] In general, practically all morphemes which occur in *–ing* also occur in many environments like

We'll — his path. Similarly, almost all morphemes which occur in *—s* ('plural') occur also in many environments like *You can have my —*. We will therefore recognize these two sets of positions as being diagnostic, and will say that every morpheme which occurs in several environments of one of these two sets is a member of the substitution class which is identified as occurring in that set of positions. There will be two such classes: *cover, note, find, think*; and *cover, note, find, child*. The fact that many morphemes occur in both classes is not relevant at this point, since some do not.[8]

3.5. *Morpheme Sequences.* The chief novelty in the procedure which is offered here is the extension of substitution classes to include sequences of morphemes, not merely single morphemes. We now ask not only if A and B each occur in the environment $C-D$ but also if AE together, or FGH, also occur in that environment. If they do, then A, B, AE, FGH are all substitutable for each other. We may say that they are all members of one substitution class, which is now not merely a class of morphemes but a class of morpheme sequences. The single morphemes in the class are merely the special cases where the sequence consists of one.

Thus we note that in *Please put the book away* we can substitute for *book* not only other single morphemes like *bottle* or *brandy* but also sequences of two and more morphemes like *books, bank-book, brandy bottle, bottle of brandy, silly green get-up*. These sequences differ in various respects: in *brandy bottle* each of the component morphemes could have been substituted singly for *book*; in *books* only the first could; in *silly green get-up* no one of the morphemes could (in most utterances) have alone been substituted for *book*. These differences, however, are not relevant to the essential criterion of our present procedure, which is merely whether or not the sequences are substitutable for each other.

3.6. In the case above, and in most applications of this procedure, we have single morphemes for which the sequences can be substituted. That means that the sequences of morphemes do not yield new classes; we simply group them with various morpheme classes which we have already obtained in the usual manner described in § 3.1. We may say that in any such application of our procedure, we reduce sequences to the status of single morphemes (or of environmental classes of single morphemes).

However, there may be sequences of morphemes which occur in environments where single morphemes do not occur, i.e. where they cannot be replaced by any single morpheme. Such sequences may or may not be useful as elements of the utterance structure. For example, Semitic roots plus verb patterns occur in environments in which no single morpheme occurs. They occur before verb suffixes, after verb prefixes, and in various sentence positions such as (in early Semitic) before an accusative noun (presumably with command intonation): thus, in classical Arabic, root *ftḥ* 'open' and pattern (*i*)--*a*- 'command' in *iftaḥ ilbāba* 'open the door!'. In all these environments we always find the sequence of some root plus some pattern; we never find a single morpheme here. We may consider this sequence to constitute an element in the utterance structure, calling it, say, verb stem.

3.7. Since our procedure now permits us to make any substitutions of any sequences, it may become too general to produce useful results. For example, we might take the utterance *I know John was in* and substitute *certainly* for *know John*, obtaining *I certainly was in*. This substitution conceals the fact that the morphemes of *I know John was in* can be said as two utterances instead of as one, if we make the single change of pronouncing its intonation twice, over the first two words and again over the last three, instead of once over all five. That is, it conceals the fact that *I know John was in* can be described as two sentences strung under one sentence intonation. It further conceals the fact that *certainly* may also occur in a different place in the sentence: *I was certainly in*, whereas *know John* would occur only in the one position. And it conceals the concord of *was* with *John*: for if we substituted *we* for *I*, we would still have *was* in *We know John was here*, but *were* in *We certainly were here*. All this suggests that substitution of sequences be so carried out as to satisfy all manipulations of that environment which forms the frame of the substitution.[9]

3.8. In the following sections (§§ 4, 5), this procedure will be carried out, in a very sketchy manner, for English and for Hidatsa, a Siouan language of North Dakota. There will of course be no attempt to approach even remotely a complete analysis for either language. The purpose of these descriptions is only to show the general lines of the procedure; countless details, as well as some of the types of utterance in each language, will be omitted.

3.9. Equations will be used to indicate substitutability. $BC = A$ will mean that the sequence consisting of a morpheme of class B followed by a morpheme of class C can be substituted for a single morpheme of class A. In cases where unclarity may arise, we shall write $B + C$ for the sequence BC. When we want to say that A substitutes for B only if C follows, we shall write $AC = BC$.

ENGLISH

4.1. *The Morpheme Classes.* For the purposes of the English examples, we shall set up the following classes of morphemes, on the criterion that for each class there are particular sentence positions which can be filled by any member of that class and by these alone.[10]

N: morphemes which occur before plural *-s* or its alternants, or after *the* or adjectives: *hotel, butter, gain, one*[11]*, two.*

V: before *-ed* past or its alternants; before *-ing*; after *N* plus *should, will, might*, etc.: *go, gain, take, think, will* ('desire'), *have, do*. We may distinguish several sub-classes such as those listed below, while *V* without any sub-class mark will be used to indicate all the sub-classes together.

V$_b$: *be, appear, become, get, keep, stay*, etc. (but not *have*). These occur between *N* and adjectives other than *V -ing: The stuff will stay fresh.*[12]

V$_c$: verbs which occur between *N* and *V -ing: stop, try, be* in *Mac will — walking.*

V$_d$: the transitive verbs which occur before *N: make, buy, want* (but not *go, sleep*) in *I'll — butter.*

V$_e$: intransitive verbs which do not occur before *N: go, sleep.*

V$_f$: verbs which occur before two independent *N*'s: *make, consider, want* (but not *buy, go*) in *I'll — this book a best seller.*

V$_g$: verbs (often causative in meaning) which occur before *NV* (a noun phrase followed by a verb phrase): *make, let, see* (but not *consider, buy, go*) in *I'd like to — newcomers try it.*

V$_h$: verbs which occur before *N to V: cause, teach, dare, want* (but not *make, go*) in *The other kids — Junior to do it.*

R: between *N* and *V* (the *V* lacking *-ing, -ed*); *NRV* occurs initially, or after a list of *V* including *think, guess* (*I think the boy can win it*): *will, do, shall, can, may, must, ought* (but not *to*). The *-s* of 3rd-person-singular concord does not occur with these, nor does *-ing*. *Should* can be considered as *shall+-ed*, and so on.

have, be: appearing in *R* positions and in some other positions. These two have the *-s, -ed*, and *-ing* occurring after them. After *have* the *V* is followed by *-en* (if that particular member of the class *V* ever has *-en*, it has it also after *have*), and after *be* by *-en* or *-ing: we are going, we have taken*[13], as compared with *we did go*. When a position is discussed below in which *R, had, be* can all occur equally, the abbreviation *R$_a$* will be used to indicate all three.

A: between *the* and *N*, never before plural *-s: young, pretty, first.*

D: between *the* and *A*, but not between *the* and *N: rather, very, now, not.* Many of these, e.g. *now*, occur in various positions in the utterance (after *V: Don't look now*; before *V: He now wishes it weren't*; at the beginning of an utterance, with a level /,/ intonation: *Now, what's up?*). Some adverbs, e.g. *very*, do not occur in most of these positions. When we wish to indicate only the more widely-occurring ones, to the exclusion of *very* and the like, we write *D$_a$*. In more detailed analysis, many more sub-classes of *D* would be necessary.

T: before *N*, or *A*, or *DA*, but not before *V* (unless *-ing* or *-ed* or *-en* follow it): *a, my, some*. These may all be considered as substituting for *the* and so forming an article-class. Here we must include *all*, which, in addition to occurring in the above positions also occurs before *T* (*all the very good people* as well as *all very good people*); also the cardinal numbers, which occur not only in *T* position but also after *T* (*my two very uncertain suggestions* as well as *the two very new suggestions, two very new suggestions*, parallel to *the very new suggestions*).

I: before or after *V*, after *from, before*, but not after *A* or *T* or before plural *-s*: *it, all, some, now, here*.[14] Some morphemes in this class do not occur after *from, before*, etc., or after utterance-initial *V*: *he, I*. Others do not occur before *V* unless *NV* precedes them: *me*.

P: before *N, T, A, D, I*, and before *V* only if *-ing* follows: *of, from*. Several morphemes in this preposition class also occur after certain *V;* when they are in this position we mark them P_b: *up, off, over* (*walk off, beat up*). Some prepositions (marked P_c) sometimes alternate with zero when an *N* which precedes P_cN is placed after the $(P_c)N$: *to, for* in *They're giving a present to the boss, They're buying a present for the boss*, are replaced by zero in *They're giving the boss a present, They're buying the boss a present*. This does not occur with *from* as in *He's receiving a raise from the boss*.

-Nn: After *N* and before anything which follows *N*: *-let, -eer, -er, -ess*, (*playlet, engineer, Londoner, lioness*).

-Vv: After *V* and before anything which follows *V*: past *-ed*, 3rd person singular *-s* (*rowed, rows*).

-Aa: After *A* and before anything which follows *A*: *-er, -est, -ish* (*older, oldest, oldish*).

-Nv: after *N* and before anything which follows V[14]: *-ize, -(i)fy* (*colonize, beautify*).

-Na: *-ful, -ish, -th, -'s* (*beautiful, boyish, sixth, parent's*).

-Vn: *-ment, -ion, -er, -ing* (*atonement, abolition, writer, writing* in *Writing is just what he hates*).

-Va: *-able, -ing, -ed, -en* (*likable, a shining light, the cooked meal, his shaven head*).

-An: *-ness, -ty* (*darkness, cruelty*).

-Av: *-en, -ize,* (*darken, solemnize*).

-Ad: *-ly* (*really*).

Nv-: before *N*, and after anything which precedes V[15]: *be-, en-* (*bedevil, enshrine*).

Xd'-: before morphemes of several classes, chiefly *N* or *A*. The combination, consisting of these morphemes plus *Xd'-*, may be marked *D'*. It occurs chiefly after *V* (often with intervening *N*, etc., as in *Are you asleep?*): *a-* (*astray, afresh, asleep, ashore*). *D'* is used here to indicate the adverbs which occur in this post-V position, since it is a position in which both D_a and A occur. D' sometimes occurs after N: *A day ashore.*

Av-: en- *(enlarge).*

Na-: pre-, anti-, pro- *(pre-war, anti-war, pro-war).*

Ap-: be- *(below, behind).*

Xx-: before any morpheme class or sequence, and after anything which preceded that same morpheme class. The environment of the morpheme which follows is not affected by the addition of the *Xx-* morpheme, except that it now contains that addition itself: *dis-, re-, pre- (disorder, recall, preview).*

S: stems which occur only next to affixes, i.e. next to the 16 classes *-Nn* to *Xx-* immediately preceding. These stems cannot be assigned to any of the preceding classes *N, V, A, D,* etc., except by seeing if they occur with the same affixes as *N,* etc. Thus, in *society, social,* it would have been possible, instead of considering *soci-* as *S* (as we do here), to consider it as *A* when it occurs before *-ety* and *N* when it occurs before *-al* (compare *superiority, A -An* and *communal N -Na).* However, what is *nat-* in *native?* It could be either *N* or *V* before *-ive,* since *-ive* is both *-Na* and *-Va: massive, adoptive.* We therefore put all such morphemes in the class *S.* Many of the affixes in the classes above occur not only next to *A, N,* or *V,* but also next to *S.*

&: conjunctions between any two sequences: *and, but (I wanted to go, but couldn't make it.)* In some environments (e.g. in the example above) the member of *&* is preceded by /,/ intonation; in other environments the /,/ intonation does not occur (e.g. *war and peace* without /,/).

B: in *-NV* /,/ *NV* or in *NV* /,/ *NV: if, since, as, while (If you go, I won't).* The last subordinative and sometimes also the others lack the preceding /,/ intonation when they are in the middle of the utterance: *We fix it while you wait.* Some members of this class occur after *A* or *N,* etc., before *NV, VN (Little as there is of it,—. Man though he is,—.)* These will be marked B_a.

Finally, there remain various independent morphemes, some of which occur almost anywhere in utterances, often set off by /,/: *then, now, thus.* Others are set off either by /,/ or by quote-intonation, or have /./ by themselves: *yes, no.* Others usually have /!/ intonation by themselves: *hello, oh.*

4.2. We now consider sequences of these thirty-odd morpheme classes, to see what sequences of morphemes can be substituted for single morphemes.

Sequences of morpheme classes which are found to be substitutable in virtually all environments for some single morpheme class, will be equated to that morpheme class: $AN=N$ means that *good boy,* for example, can be substituted for *man* anywhere.[16] If we write $DA=A$ (*quite old* for *old*), then DA can be substituted for A wherever A appears, e.g. in $AN=N$ (*old fellow* for *man*, where we can substitute *quite old* for *old*, and obtain *quite old fellow* $DAN=AN=N$).[17] There is nothing to prevent us from substituting DA for A even in the equation $DA=A$. We would then obtain $DDA=A$: *really quite old* for *old*.

If, however, it proves impossible to substitute the equivalents of a symbol for that symbol in some of its occurrences, we distinguish those occurrences by giving the symbol a distinctive raised number. For instance, N -$s=N$: *paper* + -s = *paper*; and *papers* can be substituted for *paper* in most environments. However, we cannot substitute N -s for the first N in this very equation: we cannot substitute *papers* for the first *paper* and then add -s again (*papers* + -s), as this equation would seem to indicate. We therefore write N^1 -$s=N^2$ and state that wherever N^2 occurs we can substitute for it any N^1 or another N^2, while for N^1 we can only substitute any member of N^1 (never N^2). Then it becomes impossible to construct a sequence *papers* + -s, since *papers* is N^2 and -s is added only to N^1.

The procedure in assigning these raised numbers which indicate uni-directional substitutability is in essence as follows: we assign raised [1] to each class symbol, say X, when it first appears. Next time the X appears in an equation, we assign it the same number [1] if the equivalents of this X can be substituted for X^1 in every equation which has so far been written. If the new X cannot be substituted for all the preceding X^1 we number it X^2. If we later obtain an X which cannot be substituted for all the preceding X^1 or X^2, we will number it X^3, and so on. If some symbols never go above [1] we can dispense with the raised number for them and merely write the symbol without numbers.

On the left-hand side of the equations, each raised number will be understood to include all lower numbers (unless otherwise noted). Thus in $TN^2=N^3$ we have not only *the men* (N^2) equalling N^3, but also *the man* (N^1). Any N^1 can be substituted for the N^2 on the left side. On the right-hand side, however, each number indicates itself alone: N^3 on the right can only substitute for another N^3, and $N^{1,2}$ for an N^1 or an N^2.

4.3. Morpheme sequence equations for English now follow.

4.31. Equations involving N^1, V^1, A^1 are almost all cases of word formation, i.e. of adjoining morphemes within one loud-stress unit.

N^1 -$Nn=N^1$: e.g. for *engineer* we can substitute *engine* in *I saw the*—.
A^1 -$An=N^1$: *darkness* for *smell* in *I don't like the*—*here*.
V^1 -$Vn=N^1$: *abolition* for *bread* in *We demand*—. Note that *abolition* (V^1 -Vn) is N^1 and can be followed by -Nn: *abolitionist*.

N^1 -Nv = V^1: e.g. *colonize* for *conquer* in *The French Government* — *ed North Africa.*

Nv- N^1 = V^1: *enchant* for *scare* in *He* — *s them.*

A^1 -Av = V^1: *sharpen* for *break* in *Don't* — *the knife.*

Av- A^1 = V^1: *enlarge* for *print* in *Do you want to* — *it?*

A^1 -Ad = D: *beautifully* or *really* for *well* in *It's* — *finished.*

Ap- A^1 = P: *below* for *at* in *It fell* — *the dividing line.*

D_a V^1 = V^1: *cordially despise* for *like* in *I* — *him* (this applies if there is no /,/ or /!/ after D_a; P N for D_a is rare in this position).

Xd'-+ any class (chiefly N^1 or A^1) = D', where D' represents a class of words which occur almost always after V, though not always immediately after: *asleep* in *He is* —, *He fell* —, *He is fast* —; *ashore* in *A day ashore.*

Xx-+ any class = that class: e.g. *dislike* for *like* in *He really* — *s it.*

S+ any affix = the class indicated by the second letter in the affix mark: e.g. S -Vn = N^1: *nature* for *life* in *He loves* —.

all + T = T: *all my* for *some* in *We lost* — *books.* When *all* is not followed by T, it may itself be a member of T: *all* for *the* in — *assertions are arbitrary.*

T + *cardinal number* = T: *Which two* for *which* in — *really modern composers?* When cardinal numbers are not preceded by T, they may themselves be members of T: *two* for *the* in the sentence above.

As a result of these equations, we may consider affixes not as distinct elements in the sentence structure, but merely as elements altering the substitution class of the neighboring morphemes. The affix classes will no longer appear in our picture of the sentence structure (except for special cases of selection), since any structure into which they enter can also be composed of N, V, A, D, and P morphemes.

4.32. We next obtain equations in which A^2 is necessary, though N^1 is still adequate.

A^1 -Aa = A^2: e.g. *oldish* for *old* in *Aren't they a bit* — ?.

V^1 -Va = A^2: *likeable* for *oldish* in *My* — *uncle.* Note that the V^1 can be obtained from N^1 -Nv: *A heartening* (N^1 -Nv -Va) *thought.*

D A^2 = A^2: *completely false* for *false* in *That's a* — *statement.* (D here from A -Ad.)

A^2 N^1 = N^1: *peculiar fellow* for *Senator* in *Isn't he a* — ?[18]

A^2 A^2 N^1 = A^2 N^1: Two adjoining A in a particular order, which we will call the 'usual' (e.g. as between *ambitious* and *young*, *ambitious* is first in the usual order), will be stressed $\hat{A}\acute{A}$ (reduced loud, medial)[19]: *ambitious young, pretty dark,* substitutable for *funny* in *She is a* — *girl.* If the adjectives are not in the usual order, or if they are in the usual order but with greater note given to the second A, or if no usual order obtains between them, or if the second A is composed of $D\ A$, the pattern is $\hat{A}$ /,/ $\hat{A}$: *pretty, dark; dark, pretty; young, ambitious; ambitious, very young* in *She is a—girl*.[20]

4.33. Equations involving N^2 and N^3 develop the noun-phrase.

N^1 -$s=N^2$: *papers* for *paper* in *I'll get my—out*.
N^2 -$Na=A^2$: e.g. *parents'* for *big* in —*day at school*.
Na- $N^2=A^2$: *pro-war* for *big* in *a—industrialist*.
$N^2N^2=$N^{1,2}: *family heirloom* substitutable for *boy* in *It's a—*. *Albert Einstein* for *Jim* in —*was here*.

Any sequence including one loud stress and one or more reduced loud (or medial) stresses $=N^{1,2}$, V^1, or $A^{1,2}$, according to which of these may be substituted for the sequence. Most of these $=N^1$: *blackbird* (AN), *by-pass* (PN), *get-up* (VP_b), *our third motor-boat crash* (NNN). Some ending in $A^2=A^{1,2}$: *air-minded* (N^1A^2, the A^2 being a sequence of V^1 -Va). Others $=V^1$: *They by-passed it; They'll railroad* ($N^1N^1=V^1$) *the strike leader* ($N^1N^1=N^1$; N^1 from V^1 -Vn).

$T\ N^2=N^3$: *the orchestra* or *these pointless, completely transparent jokes* for *butter* in *I don't like—*.
$T\ A^2$ (with no N following)$=N^3$: *The longer* or *the uncertain* in —*is what interests us more*. The -s 'plural' does not occur after this N^3 substitute, except in special cases.
$N^3PN^4=N^3$: *This piece of junk* for *the book* in *Who brought—here?*. The occurrence of $N^3\ PN^3$ in the position of N^3 or N^4 in the equations below is restricted by various special selections for particular P. Repetition is not frequent except when P is *of*: *This piece of junk of my mother's$=$* $N^3PN^3PN^3=N^3PN^3=N^3$ (*my mother's* is $T\ N$ -$Na=T\ A^2=N^3$).

4.34. Equations requiring V^2 to V^4 develop the verb phrase.

R_a *not*$=R_a$: *will not* or *have not* or *was not* for *will* or *have* or *was* in *I will go.; Has he gone?; I was going*.
$R_a\ N$ *not*$=\ R_a\ N$: *did he not* for *did he* in *But—attempt it?*.
have V^1 -*en*$=V^2$: *have eaten* for *know* in *I—it.; I will—it*.
$V_c^1\ V^2$ -*ing*$=$*have* V_c^1 -*en* V^2 -*ing*$=V^2$: *be eating* or *stop eating* or *have stopped eating* for *know* in *I—it now*.
$V_b^1A^2=$*have* V_b^1 -*en* $A^2=V_e^2$: *is gone* or *has been gone* or *seems neat* or *is grayish* for *comes* in *He—now*. Note that A^2 on the left-hand side represents both *neat* (A^1) and *grayish* (A^2).
$R\ V^1=R=V^2$: *will go* or *will* for *go* in *We—today*.

$R\ N^4\ V^2\ ? = have\ N^4\ V^1$ -en $? = be\ N^4\ V^1$ -en $? = be\ N^4\ V^1$ -ing $? = R_a\ N^4\ ? = N^4\ V^2\ ?$: *Did you talk* or *Haven't you gone* or *Are you taken* or *Are you going* or *Were you* in — *with him?*.

$V^2\ P_b = V^2$: *walk off* (V^1) or *have walked off* (V^2) for *escape* in *We'll — before them*. The appearance of V^2 on both sides of the equation means that we can also obtain $V^2\ P_b\ P_b = V^2$, etc. This occurs in *walk on over* or *fly on up* for *go* in *Let's —*. However, the selection and number of these sequences of P_b is highly restricted, and detailed equations would have to be given to indicate the selections which actually occur.

$V_d^2\ N^4 = V_e^2$: *take it* for *go* in *I'll — now*. When V^2 includes P_b, there are certain V, P_b, and N for which the order is VNP_b (*I'll knock your opponent down.*), while for others the order is VP_bN (*I'll take over my father's estate*). The N^4 will be identified below.

$V_f^2\ N^4\ N^4 = V_e^2$: *make Harding President* for *vote* in *We're going to —*.

$V_g^1\ N^4\ V^3 = V^3$: *make him vote* for *vote* in *We'll — your way*.

$V_b^2\ N^4\ to\ V^3 = V^3$: *force him to vote* for *vote* in *We'll — your way*.

$V_d^2\ N_1^4\ P_c\ N^4 = V_d^2\ N^4\ N_1^4 = V_e^3$: For P_c and certain N, we find both the first sequence (e.g. *I'll make a party for my husband.*), and the second (e.g. *I'll make my husband a party*). The N_1 with the subscript is used only to identify the N in its two positions. The first sequence is identical with the usual order, as in *I'll get a nickel from my dad.*

$V_d^2\ N^4\ V^4$ (all under one sentence intonation) $= V_d^2\ N^4 = V_e^2$: *know he is* for *know it* in *I — now*. The $N^4\ V^4$ is thus the object of the V_d^2. The V^4 indicates a full verb phrase, e.g. *was* as well as *is* in the example above.

$V^3\ to\ V^3 = V^3$: *try to escape* or *kill the guard to avoid getting caught* in *Let's — here*. Note that *avoid getting caught* is $V_c^1\ V_b^1$ -ing V^1 -en $= V_c^1\ V_b^1$ -ing $A^2 = V_c^1\ V_e^2$ -ing $= V^2$.

V^3 -Vv $= V^4$: *walked* or *walked off* or *had eaten* or *tried to escape* for *walk* or *have eaten* in *I — alone*. The -Vv is added to the first V or R of the whole V^3 phrase.

$V^4\ D_a = V^{3,4}$: *travel smoothly* for *go* in *We'll — in this place*.

$V^4\ P\ N^4 = V^{3,4}$: *travel in this place* for *go* in *Let's — today*. For certain $P\ N$ and D_a the order is $V^3\ D_a\ P\ N$; for others it is $V^3\ P\ N\ D_a$; compare the two examples above.

4.35. The noun phrase is completed with the introduction of N^4. $N^3\ N^4\ V_d^4 = N^3\ N^4\ V_e^4\ P = N^4$: *The clock he fixed* or *The house he slept in* for *The clock* in — *is all right now*. The second N in the sequence usually has reduced stress, while the first N^3 and the end of the V^4 phrase (if it is not sentence-final) usually have a level tone. The sequence $N^3\ N^4\ V^4$ here is therefore distinguished formally, as well as in its environment, from the sequence

$N^3 N^2 V^4 = N^3 V^4$ (with $N^3 N^2 = N^3$; since we have seen that $N^2 N^2 = N^2$ and this can be built up into an N^3 by completing the noun phrase before the first N^2): *The family heir-loom broke.*

Since $V_a^2 N^4$ (*fixed it*) $= V_e^2$, and since V_e^2 occurs in this equation only if P follows, we see that $V_a^2 N^4$ (without P) is excluded from this sequence. We may have $N^3 V_a^2 N^4$ (*He fixed it.*), and we may have $N^3 N^4 V_a^2$ (*the clock he fixed*); but we never have the first N^3 and the last N^4 together in one sequence (there is no *the clock he fixed it*). We may therefore say that the first N^3 replaces the last N^4. This indicates the semantic connection between these two noun phrases, since each of them represents the object of V_a^2.

$I = N^4$: *it* for *the room* in *Was—very hot?* For each morpheme here we can substitute a whole noun phrase, including I, i.e. anything equalling N^3.

$N^4 A^2 P N^4 = T A^2 N^2 V^1 \text{-}Va = V^3 \text{-}ing = N^4$: *strawberries fresh from the field* or *the best drinks obtainable* or *having you* all substitutable for *hope* in *It was only—that kept me going.*

$P N^4 = D_a = D'$: These three classes, represented by *in a moment* or *eventually* or *ashore*, all occur *We'll do these things—*, and less freely in—, *we'll do these things.* However, since style and selection features differ markedly for PN and D_a, detailed statements would be needed to specify in each equation which is more frequent.

$N^3 /,/ = P N^4 /,/$: *Some day*, for *in a moment*, in the utterances above. This applies only to particular N^3; detailed statements of selection or equations involving particular sub-classes of N would be necessary.

Quoted material $= N^4$ (with special quote-intonation); "*Not today, thanks*" or "*wanted*" for *this* in *He said—in a loud voice.*

4.36. Subordinations and Coordinations.

$A^2 B_a = N^4 B_a = B$: *Little as* or *Child though* or *Since* in—*he is, I like him.*

$B N^4 V^4 = P N^3 N^4 V^4 = N^4 V^3 \text{-}ing = V^3 \text{-}ing = P N^4$: *If he goes home* or *In the event that he goes home* or *Everyone having left* or *Being at home* are all substitutable for *At night* in—, *he'll lock up the house.*

any class $+ \& +$ same class $=$ same class: *records and new needles* ($N^2 \& N^2$) for *records* (N^2) in *I have—for you today.*

$V^4 /,/ \& V^4 = V^4$: *found it but lost it again* for *found it* after *We.*

4.37. Equations involving whole utterances.

$P N^4, N^4 V^4 = N^4 V^4, P N^4 = P N^4 N^4 V^4 = N^4 V^4 P N^4$: *At night, it's too hard.; It's too hard, at night.; At night it's too hard.; It's too hard at night.* The morpheme $/,/$ before or after $P N^4$ or any of its substitutes underscores the conditional meaning.

$\&+$ any utterance $=$ that utterance: *But John!* for *John!*; *And I know that too.* for *I know that too.* Only a few conjunctions occur frequently in this position.

$N^4\ V^4\ /,/\ \&\ N^4\ V^4 = N^4\ V^4$: For any $N^4\ V^4$ utterance we may substitute two $N^4\ V^4$ sequences with a conjunction between them, and with reduced loud stress on the second: *I know, but I can't tell.* for *I know.*

4.4. A check of the preceding equations will show that all morpheme classes and all sequences of morphemes, except the independent ones in the last paragraph of § 4.1, occur in positions where they can be replaced by N^4 or V^4. We can therefore state in terms of these classes what sequences of morphemes occur in English utterances. The great majority of English utterances are a succession of the following forms:

$N^4\ V^4$ with $/./$, $/?/$, or other intonations; with $N^4\ (=PN^4=D_a)$, independent morphemes, and successive repetitions introduced by $\&$, set off by $/,/$.

Independent morphemes and almost all others except affixes (classes *-Nn* to *Xx-* in § 4.1), occurring singly or with affixes, with $/./$, $/?/$, $/!/$, and other intonations: *Yes.; Why?; No!; Come!*[21]*; John!; English.; Here.*

HIDATSA

5.1. A particularly brief sketch will be given for Hidatsa, which is of interest here because its structure is very different from that of English. For the most part, Hidatsa consists of morphemes which are not in themselves nouns, verbs, etc., but which combine with affixes of nominal, verbal, or other meaning.

Most morphemes of Hidatsa may be grouped into the following classes on the basis of substitutability:

S: stems, which occur with any affixes or with no affix (or zero), and next to other stems: *ika·* 'look' in *ika·c* 'he looks', *ika·s* 'watcher', *ika·ʔi·s* 'the one who always watches', *ikako·wiha·k* 'finishing to look'; *ko·wi* 'end', *ko·wic* 'it is the end', *ko·wihe·c* 'he finished'.

P: prefixes, which occur before almost any stem and with each other. There are special selections and relative order among them, as also among the suffixes: *ki-* 'suus' in *ki·ka·k* 'looking at their own'; *aru-* 'place or object, future' in *aruʔika* 'something to look at'.

Pr: a group of mutually exclusive personal prefixes: *w-* 'I', *r-* 'you', *i-* (or zero, etc.) 'he', in *wiru·hic* 'I stand up', *riru·hiʔi* 'do you stand up', *iru·hic* 'he stands up'.

Inst: about 70 stems occur in most cases only with instrumental prefixes: *-saki-* 'split' in *pasakic* 'he split with a stick', *rusakic* 'he split with the hand', *kasakic* 'he split by pounding'.

Pinst: about 6 prefixes which occur only with *Inst* stems: see above.

U: utterance-final suffixes which occur at the end of (as well as within) stretches of speech: *-c* 'it is', vowel repetition '?': *wahkuc* 'he is here' *wahku$^{\wp}$u* 'is he here?'.

F: clause-final suffixes which can be substituted for *U* if the utterance continues: *-k* '-ing', *-wa* 'when' in *wu$^{\wp}$usiak* 'we arriving,...', *wu$^{\wp}$usi$^{\wp}$awa* 'when we arrived' (cp. *wu$^{\wp}$usi·$^{\wp}$ac* 'we arrived'). In the equations below, *F* will be taken to include *U*, since no statements are needed for *F* that do not apply also to *U*.

N: non-clause-final suffixes. Some of these are final in the stress-group (word) and others are not, but none of them normally occur at the end of a sequence of words such as have *U* or *F* at their end: *-s* 'naming suffix' in *wa·$^{\wp}$ahtu·$^{\wp}$as* 'the skulls'; *-se* 'by', *-a$^{\wp}$a* 'several' in *a·ta$^{\wp}$ase* 'by their several houses'.

Post: a few postpositive morphemes which occur after word-final affixes (sometimes at the end of an utterance): *isa* 'again' in *wa·hacisa* 'we go again'.

Ind: a very few stems which occur with no affixes, as calls or whole utterances: *ho·* 'yes', *riskare* 'friend'.

5.2. We proceed to state what sequences of morphemes can be substituted for single morphemes of the classes named above.

$S^1\ S^1 = S^2$: *ris·i* 'dance' and *hiri* 'make' in *wa$^{\wp}$o·ris·ihirak* 'making a dance' (*o·* is nominalizing prefix, member of *P*).

Pinst Inst $= S^2$: we can substitute *rusaki* 'split by hand' for *aciwi* 'follow' in *wa$-c$ 'I did $-$'.

Pr $S^2 = S^3$: *wa* 'I' $+aciwi$ 'follow'; *wi* 'I' or *i* 'he' $+ru·hi$ 'stand up'.

$PS^3 = S^3$: *hiru* 'bone', *aruhiru* 'skeleton'. There is considerable limitation of selection for individual members of *P* and for sub-classes.

$S^3\ S^3 = S^3$: *ika·* for *ikako·wi* in $-c$ (see under *S* in § 5.1). Substitution of *Pr* S^2 and PS^3 from the preceding equation for S^3 permits sequences like $P\ S^1\ P\ S^1 = S^3$, or *Pr* $S^1\ P\ Pr\ S^1$ as in *wahku·ciwa·wa·ha·$^{\wp}$ac* 'we want to get': *wah-* '1st person', *ku·ci* 'get', *wa·-* 'something' (a prefix of the second stem), *wa·-* '1st person', *he·* 'want', *-a$^{\wp}$a* 'severally, i.e. plural', *-c* 'verbalizer'.

$S^3\ N = S^4$: *ikahke·* 'he caused to look', substitutable for *ika·* in *wi$^{\wp}$ika·c* 'he looked at me', *wi$^{\wp}$ikahke·c* 'he makes me look'. Substitution from the preceding equations gives us results like this: $S^3\ S^3\ N = S^4, P\ S^3\ P\ S^3\ N = S^4$; see the example in the equation above, where the *-a$^{\wp}$a* plural applies to both stems with their prefixes. Here too there are some individual members and sub-classes of *N* which have restricted distribution.

S^4 S^4 $F=S^4$ F: we can substitute *araxe·xak* 'holding' or *ika·k* 'looking' or *ika·c* 'he looked' for *ixpase araxe·xak* 'holding by the wing' (*ixpa* 'wing', *-se* 'by').[22]

S^4 S^4 $U=S^4$ $F S^4$ $U=S^4$ U: *haruk kara·k re·ware·c* 'thereupon running he went, they say'[23] can be replaced in context by *re·ware·c* 'he went, they say', or by *re·c* 'he went' alone, but not by any single morpheme. Similarly, *tahe·ruk aruʔisiak hap·e·hisahic* 'If he kills him it will be bad. It will be dark.'[24] can be replaced in its context by *aruʔisiac* 'It will be bad'.

5.3. In terms of the classes of morpheme sequences, we can now say that most utterances in Hidatsa, in the style of talking summarized here, consist of S^4 U (representing stretches of speech of any length), or S^3 N ($=S^4$ representing usually a single stress-unit, e.g. a person's name uttered by itself), or *Ind* (again a single word occurring as an utterance with its separate intonation). *Post* occurs in several positions in *S U* utterances, and we may say that its syntactic value within the *S U* formula is zero: *Post S U=S U Post=S U*.

DISCUSSION

6.0. Having sketched how our procedure could be applied in two languages, we may now ask what kind of description it has given us. The following sections attempt an interpretation of the linguistic status of this analysis, and a summary of the kind of results that it yields.

6.1. *Position Analysis.* The procedure begins by noting the environments of each morpheme and by putting in one class all those morphemes that have similar distributions. However, in many cases the complete adherence to morpheme-distribution classes would lead to a relatively large number of different classes: *hotel* would be *N*, *think* would be *V*, and *take* would be in a new class *G* since it has roughly the distribution of both *hotel* and *think*. In order to avoid an unnecessarily large number of classes, we say that *take* is a member of both *N* and *V*. This means that we are no longer studying the morpheme *take* or *think*. We are studying the positions, Bloomfield's 'privileges of occurrence', common to both *take* and *think*, or those common to both *take* and *hotel*.[25]

This means that we change over from correlating each morpheme with all its environments, to correlating selected environments (frames) with all the morphemes that enter them. The variables are now the positions, as is shown by the fact that the criterion for class membership is substitution. The element which occurs in a given class position may be a morpheme which occurs also in various other class positions. We merely select those positions in which many morphemes occur, and in terms of which we get the most convenient total description.[26]

6.2. *Stopping Point.* One might ask how we can tell where to stop the analysis. This is answered by the nature of the work. All we do is to substitute one sequence for another in a given context. When we have the formula for English utterances with assertion intonation, we find that all we can substitute for it is another utterance, with the same or another intonation. When more work has been done on sentence sequences and what is called stylistics, we may find that in certain positions within a sequence of sentences only $N\ V\ /./$, say, ever occurs, to the exclusion of $V\ /!/$. When we have such information, we will be able to extend the substitution procedure to sentences and sequences of utterances (whether monologs or conversations).

6.3. *Resultant Construction Formulae.* The final result, for each language which can be analyzed in this manner, takes the form of one or more sequences of substitution classes ('utterance constructions', 'sentence types'). The formulae tell us that these are the sequences which occur. The final formulae therefore give us the limitations upon the freedom of occurrence of morphemes in the language, for they imply that no sequence of morphemes occurs except those which can be derived from the formula.[27]

The utterance formulae are thus rather like the formulae for the phonetic structure of a language, and even like phonemic writing: all of these are formulae showing what occurs in the language. The signs used in the utterance formulae have value: N has the values $A\ N$, $T\ A\ N$, $T\ A$, etc.; and each of these has specific morphemes as values. Supplying morpheme values for the signs of the formula will give us expressions in the language.

This is not quite the whole story, for there are further limitations of selection among the morphemes, so that not all the sequences provided by the formulae actually occur.[28] Individual limitations of selection cannot be described in these formulae; at best, the more important among them can be stated in special lists or in the dictionary. Limitations applying to various groups of morphemes in each class can, however, be included if we give our formulae the form of charts. The second dimension which the chart provides enables us to state selections among sub-groups in the several columns (each column representing a position, i.e. a class), by placing along one horizontal line the sequences of subgroups that actually occur.

6.4. The procedure outlined here could be paralleled by a series of substitutions beginning with the whole utterance and working down, instead of beginning with single morphemes and working up. In that case we would have to find formal criteria for breaking the utterance down at successive stages. This is essentially the difficult problem of determining the immediate constituents of an utterance.[29] It is not clear that there exists any general method for successively determining the immediate constituents, when we begin with a whole utterance and work down. In any case, it would appear that the formation of substitution classes presents fewer theoretical difficulties if we begin with morphemes and work up.

IMPLICIT IN THE FORMULAE

7.0. We have seen the application and the interpretation of the procedure outlined here. This is perhaps all that is required of a procedure. However, in order to fit it into the rest of the description of a language we should find out how much of the information which we expect from syntactic description is derivable from this procedure.

7.1. *Suprasegmental Features.* The intonational and other suprasegmental features, as well as the pauses, are generally included in the equations. When one sequence is substitutable for another in an utterance, it is understood that the intonations, pauses, etc. of the utterance remain unchanged under the substitution. If the substitution is associated with a change in intonation, as in *Who* for *John* in —*got lost*, we state that fact. Some substitution groups may require not only particular sequences but also particular suprasegmental features; e.g. any English sequence with loud stress followed by reduced loud stress may equal N (§ 4.33). The domains of suprasegmental features often coincide with the sequences which we recognize in our substitution equations; e.g. /,/ and slight pause separating adverbial phrases in certain positions in English.

In general, therefore, the formulae are based not only on the sequences involved but also on the suprasegmental features of the sequences substituted and of the utterances in which they are substituted. The formulae may thus correlate with phonemic junctures which express the limits of suprasegmental features.

7.2. *Morphologic Boundaries.* The formulae also correlate with non-phonemic (structural) junctures, such as may be set up to mark the boundaries of intervals which serve as elements of the utterance structures.

7.3. *Morphologic Relations.* Many of the relations between a morpheme class and other morpheme classes, or the interval or utterance in which it occurs, can be derived from the formulae, although they are not explicitly stated there for their own sake. The formulae show what morpheme classes (or sequences) are syntactically zero, like Xx- prefixes and -Aa suffixes in English (§ 4.31); we can even learn from them that in English most prefixes, but relatively few suffixes, are syntactically zero.

The formulae show which morpheme classes occur by themselves in utterances, and which classes are bound not to other morpheme classes (as are most affixes) but to constructions, i.e. to sequences of classes: e.g. English *&*

is limited to any class or extant class sequence; English T is bound to a following noun phrase as a sort of phrase prefix (§ 4.33); Hidatsa suffixes operate on the whole preceding word, whereas prefixes operate usually only on the immediately following stem (§ 5.2). The fact that English -Vv suffixes (-*ed*) are best added not to V^1 (verb morphemes) but to V^3 (verb phrases including object, etc.), shows that -*ed* may be regarded as a suffix of the whole verb phrase. In general, a class may be considered as bound to the level indicated by the number with which it is associated; i.e. it is bound to whatever is substitutable for the symbol-and-number combination that accompanies it in the equations.

We can also learn from the formulae which morpheme classes are the heads and which are the closures of the sequences in which they appear: the closure is the class which always appears last; and the head is the class which can always substitute for the sequence, e.g. an N morpheme for an N-phrase sequence. The formulae can thus show which sequences are endocentric (e.g. $A\ N = N$) and which are exocentric (e.g. $T\ A = N$).

It goes without saying that adequate information about the morpheme classes can be derived not from sketchy examples of the equational procedure such as we have given, but from detailed analyses of all the mutually substitutable sequences of the language.

7.4. *Order.* The formulae are devised in part on the basis of the order of classes in each sequence, and can therefore be used to show it explicitly or by means of the raised numberings.

7.5. *Always or Sometimes.* They also enable us to indicate if certain classes occur always or only sometimes in a given sequence. If we write $D\ A = A$ and $A\ N = N$, and are free to apply or not to apply the results of one equation in the other, then we can derive from these equations the fact that N, $A\ N$, and $D\ A\ N$ all occur.

7.6. *Selection.* Some of the features of selection, the restrictions on particular morphemes which occur only with particular other morphemes, are indicated in these formulae, or derivable from them. Some selection, such as that between I and *am* as against *he* and *is*, is included in the list of variant forms of the morphemes. Selections of concord are listed as special domains of the morpheme in question (§ 2.3 above).

We can also consider selections and order among sub-classes, e.g. the fact that certain Hidatsa stems are always the last stem in the word, or that *ought* alone among English preverbs usually has *to* after it. This can be expressed by the formulae if they are allowed to become more complicated in form, and especially if they are made into two-dimensional diagrams. Lastly, the formulae in themselves are statements of selection, saying for instance that $N\ V$ sequences occur, but not $N\ T$.

7.7 *Meaning.* The formulae can be used as a source of information on the grammatical meaning of the morpheme classes symbolized in them. To do this, it is necessary to say that morpheme classes or class sequences which replace each other in various equations, i.e. which occur in identical morpheme-class environments, have similar functions or grammatical meanings. Thus the N^3 of N^3 N^4 V_d^4 (§ 4.35) is shown to replace the N^4 which is otherwise found after V_d; both of these represent the object of the V_d.

7.8. *Comparability of Language Structures.* The nature and number of the morpheme classes that have to be set up for a particular language, the forms and number of the equations, and the number of levels which have to be differentiated by raised figures for some of the class symbols, all permit comparisons between the descriptions of one language and another. Such comparisons must not be made too lightly, since considerable choice remains in the setting up of equations for any language. In particular, there may be room for ingenuity in keeping the raised numbers of certain symbols – say N, V, S – at a minimum for each language; so that of two sets of equations for a language, one might reach up to N^8 while the other does not go beyond N^4. Undoubtedly, the procedures of setting up equations and assigning the raised numbers can be made more explicit and, if desired, standardized for greater convenience in structural comparative research. An analysis of this type for Moroccan Arabic comes out rather similar to the English, ending up with N^5 V^3 and N^4 N^4 for the former as against N^4 V^4 for the latter, while the Hidatsa equations are very different, ending with S^4 U. This fits in with the general similarity between Indo-European and Semitic structure as against Siouan.[30]

7.9. *Testing Morphological Cruces.* In § 6.1 it was seen that the values of the symbols in the equations are not morphemes but positions, indicating whatever morphemes occupy these positions (irrespective of what other positions these morphemes may occupy in other equations). Therefore, when we wish to know the analysis of a particular utterance, it is impossible merely to replace each morpheme by its class symbol (e.g. *I know it* $= N^4$ V^1 $N^4 = N^4$ V^1) since many morphemes may be members of several classes. W. F. Twaddell has suggested[31] that such analyses of utterances be carried out by repeated substitution tests on the basis of the equations, in what he termed 'experimental substitution at all levels'. To carry this out, we would ask what substitutions are permitted by the equations for each morpheme or morpheme sequence of our utterance, in the class environment which it has in that utterance. This is repeated until we know unambiguously to what class each occurrence of each morpheme in our utterance belongs.

We take, for example, the utterance *She made him a good husband because she made him a good wife.* We know that there is a difference in meaning between the two occurrences of *made*; and since we know this without any outside information beyond hearing the sentence, it follows that indication of the difference, in meaning and in construction, can be derived from the structure of the utterance. We proceed to analyze the utterance, going backward along the equations as far as may be necessary to reveal this difference. First, we know that the utterance is an instance of $N^4\ V^4$ & $N^4\ V^4 = N^4\ V^4$. At this stage the two halves of the sentence are still identical in structure. Each V^4 has the structure V^2 (*make*) N^4 (*him*) N^4 (*a good husband/wife*)$+$-Vv (-ed). The equations show the two cases of this sequence (§ 4.34): $V_f^2\ N^4\ N^4 = V_e^2$ (*make Harding President*) and $V_d^2\ N^4\ N^4 = V_e^3$ (*make my husband a party*). We cannot tell which of these applies to each of our V^4, or whether both go back to the same one, because *make* is equally a member of V_d and V_f.[32] We find, however (§ 4.34), that $V_d^2\ N^4\ N_1^4 = V_d^2\ N_1^4\ P_c$ N^4 (where the subscript number merely identifies the N which has different positions in the two sequences). We try now to discover whether either V^4 in our utterance has the structure $V_d^2\ N^4\ N^4$, by applying to each V^4 the substitution which is possible for $V_d^2\ N^4\ N^4$. To do this we interchange the two instances of N^4 and insert between them an instance of P_c. In the first V^4 we get a meaningless utterance which would practically never occur: *she made a good husband* (N_1) *for* (P_c) *him* (N) in place of *she made him* (N) *a good husband* (N_1). In the second V^4, however, the substitution gives us an equivalent and not unusual utterance: *she made a good wife* (N_1) *for* (P_c) *him* (N) in place of *she made him* (N) *a good wife* (N_1). Clearly, then, the second V^4 in our utterance is analyzable into $V_d^2\ N^4\ N^4 +$-$Vv = V_e^3 +$-Vv. Since the first V^4 can not be analyzed in this way, it can equal only the one remaining $V\ N\ N$ construction, namely $V_f^2\ N^4\ N^4 +$-$Vv = V_e^2 +$-Vv.[33]

We have thus found that the two halves of the original utterance are formally different in the substitutions which can be performed upon them. The whole analysis could of course have begun with morphemes. We could have assigned class symbols to each morpheme, and upon reaching the two occurrences of *made* would not have known whether to indicate each of them by V_d, V_f, or any one of several other symbols. We would then have had to decide the question by carrying out on the $N\ N$ following them the very substitutions attempted above.

EXCLUDED FROM THE FORMULAE

8.0. Having seen what syntactic facts can be derived from the formulae, we now ask which ones cannot be included in them and must be found by separate investigations and expressed in separate statements.

8.1. The great bulk of selection features, especially those that distinguish between individual morphemes, cannot be expressed except by very unwieldy formulae. Although it may be of theoretical interest to know that two-dimensional diagrams of such detailed selections are conceivable, in practice this information can only be given in lists and statements appended to the formulae.

8.2. This is true also of such relations among morphemes as the families of mutually replacing English suffixes, e.g. *-id, -or* in *squalid: squalor, candid: candor,* etc.[34]

8.3. The formulae also cannot in themselves indicate what meanings may be associated with the various positions or classes.

Thus, in Hidatsa, of two formally equivalent words (with noun suffixes) before the clause-final word (which ends in a verbalizing *F*), the first will normally indicate the subject and the second the object: *ruwac·iri istacu rux·iak* 'one of them his eye opening (when one of them opened his eye)'. Such information about the meaning of positions and constructions have to be given in separate statements accompanying the formulae.[35]

8.4. The formulae will also fail to give information about the complete distribution of any one morpheme, which may occur in various classes (§ 3.4), or about the frequency of morphemes or classes, or about the phonemic structure of various classes (e.g. the fact that Hidatsa *F* or various English affixes are unstressed).

9. We have seen that by extending the term substitution class from single morphemes to sequences of morphemes, we arrive at formulae equating various sequences which are substitutable for each other in all or certain utterances of the language in question. We have seen further that when the setting up of equations is continued until no new results are forthcoming, we obtain succinct statements for the sequences of morphemes which constitute the utterances of the language. The procedure of constructing these equations has here been investigated in order to see what syntactic information it gives or fails to give.

It is clear that the usefulness of this procedure will vary from language to language, the more so in view of the fact that many languages (e.g. to some extent Hidatsa) reveal comparatively little difference between the structure of all utterances and the structure of minimum utterances, and in view of the fact that some languages have great freedom in the distribution of minimum utterances within all utterances.

NOTES

[1] I am indebted to Rulon S. Wells for several valuable discussions of this paper, and to C. F. Voegelin and Bernard Bloch for helpful criticisms. In view of the fact that methods

as mathematical as the one proposed here have not yet become accepted in linguistics, some apology is due for introducing this procedure. However, the advantage which may be gained in explicitness, and in comparability of morphologies, may offset the trouble of manipulating the symbols of this procedure. Furthermore, the proposed method does not involve new operations of analysis. It merely reduces to writing the techniques of substitution which every linguist uses as he works over his material. One works more efficiently when one thinks with pencil and paper.

[2] And, of course, phonemic constituents of suprasegmental 'morphemes' (if we wish to call them that), e.g. stress, intonations, and pauses.

[3] The conditions may be phonemic or morphological.

[4] In effect, such a treatment of concord takes some of the features of selection, e.g. the fact that all nouns in the Hebrew phrase agree as to the article, and puts these facts into the phonemic form of the repeated morpheme. As a result, not only the physical recurrence of a repeated phoneme, but also its special position (e.g. before every noun of the phrase), is now given when we describe that morpheme. Such treatment permits a simpler syntactic statement, because the information about the recurrence of the repeated morpheme would otherwise have to be given somewhere in the course of the syntactic description. The syntactic equations to be offered below will suffice to describe what morphemes occur together and in what order, but will not be able to describe conveniently the agreements among the morphemes in a sequence. To do so would require various devices; e.g. instead of writing NN (N for noun), we would have to write something like $^{ha}N\,^{ha}N$, meaning that we can have either NN or $haN\,haN$ but not $haNN$. Hence it is preferable to get as much of this information out of the way as possible before we attack the sequences. Not only the obvious cases of repeated morphemes but also more complicated types of agreement can be stated as being merely the special forms of particular morphemes. For further discussion of this treatment of repeated morphemes as single morphemes, see *Lg.* 21 (1945), 121–7. (Paper V of this volume.)

[5] If *poem* and *house* are placed in one class N, overlooking the difference in their distribution, then *write* and, say, *wire (I'm wiring a whole house this time)* would be placed together in a class V since the distributional difference between them corresponds to that between *poem* and *house*. We would then obtain a statement connecting N and V. If we kept *poem* and *house* in separate classes, and *write* and *wire* in separate classes, we would obtain two statements, one connecting *write* and *poem*, and another connecting *wire* and *house*. These two statements together would equal the one statement about N and V.

[6] The criterion which decides for *-ing*, and against *un-*, as the relevant environment in determining substitution classes is therefore a criterion of usefulness throughout the grammar, a configurational consideration. It will be seen below that the classes defined on the basis of *-ing* can be replaced by certain sequences of classes, which is not the case for any classes based on the *un-* environment. Special statements will have to be made later about the selection of *un-*, which in part will run across the boundaries of the classes set up on the basis of *-ing*, etc.

[7] With variant *-ren* plus vowel change for plural *-s*.

[8] This would give us a class V including *cover, note, find, think,* and a class N including *cover, note, find, child*. It would permit individual morphemes to be members of more than one class. Alternatively, we could put *cover, note, find* into a class G, *think* into V, *child* into N. Then each morpheme could only belong to one class, and morphemes having wider distributions, or having the distributions of two classes, would find themselves in a new class. Bernard Bloch uses yet another solution in his analysis of Japanese. He would regard the noun *cover*, which occurs in positions of N, and the verb *cover*, which occurs in positions of V, as two independent morphemes whose homonymy is syntactically irrelevant. That is, he uses class membership as a necessary condition for morpheme identity. Any of these methods of classification can be followed rigorously, and may be advantageous for particular purposes. Any one of them can be used in the method discussed below without affecting the final result.

[9] Such substitutions as *certainly* for *know John* can be precluded by analyzing the utterance

into immediate constituents. However, the analysis into immediate constituents requires a technique different from that used in this paper, a technique based on comparing the apparent structures of utterances and parts of utterances. In this paper, on the other hand, we seek to arrive at a description of the structure of an utterance, without having any prior way of inspecting these structures or of saying whether two utterances are equivalent in structure. Therefore, the analysis into immediate constituents is not used here, and we must state other methods of excluding such substitutions as *certainly* for *know John*.

[10] This does not mean that every member of the class occurs in all the positions in which any other member occurs (note 5). A particular morpheme may occur in several classes (note 8). Some morphemes occur in two or more classes in the list below; cf. class-cleavage in Leonard Bloomfield, *Language*, New York 1933, 204. The statement of the environments of each morpheme class given here is far from complete, and is merely sufficient to identify the class.

[11] In such expressions as *the one I saw, a good one*.

[12] If subdivisions are not recognized here they will have to be dealt with as special types of selection (§ 7.6).

[13] We may include *have* and *be* in R in some environments, e.g. in relation to *not: have not taken* parallel to *will not take* as against *don't get going*. Note that when *do, have*, or *be* have *-ing* after them they are in the position of V, not of R.

[14] There are special utterances like *the here and now*, but in general these limitations hold.

[15] For the remaining morpheme classes of this type, the analogous statement of environment will not be made, since the class mark (*-Na, Na-*, etc.) is sufficient indication.

[16] This is true only within the broad limits of what utterances frequently occur in the culture. There are also limitations when *man* is preceded by an adjective A (e.g. *young man*). There would then be two adjectives, the A of *good boy*, and the A of *young man*, which together should yield *young good boy* $(A\ A\ N = A\ N = N)$. The conditions under which the two adjectives would occur next to each other in this way are mentioned in § 4.32.

[17] The standard procedure being as follows: since $D\ A = A$ permits us to substitute $D\ A$ for A wherever A appears, we write $D\ A$ in place of the first A in this very equation: if $D\ A = A$, then $D\ D\ A = A$, i.e. $D\ D\ A = D\ A = A$.

[18] We determine that it is A^2 rather than A^1 in this equation by testing whether *peculiar* (A^1) can be replaced by *older, oldish* (A^2). In constructing all these equations we may use either of two working procedures. One is to obtain a large amount of data, including many sequences which have the same environment as N^1; we may then sort out, from among these, those sequences which consist of A followed by N, and see whether the A is always A^1 or also sometimes A^2: e.g. we see whether among the sequences having the same environment as *senator* we have not only *peculiar fellow* but also *older fellow*. The other procedure is to set up equations as working hypotheses, on the basis of whatever data we have, and then try various substitutions for each symbol in our equations, until we discover which symbols are mutually substitutable. Thus on the basis of *He's a peculiar fellow* we may write tentatively $A\ N^1 = N^1$. Then we would test to see if A is A^1 or A^2 by seeing if we can substitute *older* for *peculiar* and still get an English utterance. The two procedures are, of course, epistemologically equivalent.

[19] See George L. Trager and Bernard Bloch, 'The Syllabic Phonemes of English', *Lg.* 17 (1941), 228.

[20] When we have the stress pattern `´^` the medially-stressed morpheme is in class D: *pretty young* is $D\ A$ in *She's a pretty young girl to be out this time of night*. It parallels *very young* in *He's a very young fellow*. The addition of emphasis stress, and other changes in the environment, complicate these stress statements. Exact statements will be necessary, however, since various morphemes (e.g. *first*) occur in both A and D.

[21] $V\ !$ can substitute for $N\ V$ in many utterances: *Come into the house!* for *He came into the house*. Therefore $V\ !$ can be considered as equalling $N\ V$, with the morphemic intonation *!* substituting syntactically for N. This cannot be done for $N\ !$, since the stretch of speech immediately following $N\ !$ has the complete intonation of an independent minimum

utterance: *John, why don't you come!* Therefore *N!* too must be taken as an independent minimum utterance.

[22] The position of this phrase in the sentence may be seen in II 5, p. 205, of R. H. Lowie, Z. Harris, and C. F. Voegelin, *Hidatsa Texts* (Indian Historical Society, Prehistory Research Series 1.6), May 1939, from which volume most of the Hidatsa examples given here have been taken. The analysis in §§ 5.1–3 is tentative.

[23] *Ibid.*, II 31, p. 207.

[24] *Ibid.*, I 49, p. 195.

[25] This is also done, in essence, by Bloomfield's class cleavage (*Language*, 204), and by his functions of form classes (*ibid.*, 196), which in essence provide for the syntactic equivalence of words and sequences of words (phrases). Needless to say, the whole procedure described here owes much to Bloomfield's method.

[26] It may be necessary to point out that this positional analysis is strictly formal, as compared with form-and-meaning analyses like the one in Otto Jespersen's *Analytic Syntax*, Copenhagen 1937.

[27] Of course, from the formula $N\ V$ we derive many sequences that occur: e.g. $T\ A\ N\ V$ (*The old order changeth*) since $T\ A\ N = N$, and so on.

[28] Some of these limitations can be included by giving the signs more than one alternative value depending on the value of the other signs, somewhat as phonemic letters are given various allophonic values. We could say that after N^4, English V^4 has two values: simple V^4, and $V^4\ N^4$. The utterance sequence $N\ V$ could represent both $N\ V$ and $N\ V\ N$ (see § 4.4). The more limitations of selection we wish to indicate by these equations, the more raised numbers we may need. This may not always be the case; but if we wished for example to indicate which noun stems occur with which -*Nn* suffixes we would require a long list of equations, involving several numerically differentiated resultant N's, before the first N^1 -$Nn = N^1$ equation of § 4.3.

[29] Bloomfield, *Language*, ch. 13. Note also Kenneth L. Pike, 'Taxemes and Immediate Constituents', *Lg.* **19** (1943), 65–82, and the method of analysis used for Japanese by Bloch, 'Studies in Colloquial Japanese II', *Lg.* **22** (1946), 200–48.

[30] Cf. also a comparable brief analysis of Kota in *Lg.* **21** (1945), 283–9, based on the data supplied in M. B. Emeneau, *Kota Texts*, Part I, Berkeley and Los Angeles 1944 (see Paper XIII of this volume.)

[31] In a private communication.

[32] All members of V_f are also members of V_d: V_d are verbs which occur before N, V_f are verbs which occur before $N\ N$ (as well as before N). Cf. § 4.1.

[33] We can check this by noting that if in the first V^4 we substitute a verb which is not a member of V_f, we get a sequence which hardly ever occurs, and whose meaning is not changed by the substitution of $N^4\ P_c\ N^4$: *She bought him a good husband* would not differ in meaning (if it occurred) from *She bought a good husband for him.* But if we try another member of V_f, for instance *think*, we find again that the substitution gives a 'meaningless' (non-occurring) utterance, or in any case one with a greatly altered meaning: *She thought him a good husband* as against *She thought a good husband for him.* Verbs in V_f are therefore verbs which involve obvious change in meaning when the $N_1\ P_c\ N$ substitution is imposed upon them; verbs not in V_f do not involve any reportable change in meaning under that substitution. Therefore the *made* in *made him a good husband* functions as a member of V_f.

[34] Such families of morphemes came to my notice in Stanley Newman's and Morris Swadesh's material on English.

[35] See, for example, Edward Sapir, *Language*, New York 1921, 86ff.

VII

COMPONENTIAL ANALYSIS OF A PARADIGM

The linguistic structure of an utterance is presumed to be fully stated by a list of the morphemes which constitute it, and by their order. The difference between two utterances is expressed by the difference in morphemic constituency between them. Frequently, however, we find that there is a set of morphemes in a language, such that each morpheme in the set is identified by its contrast with all the others in the set. Such morphemes are often arranged in paradigms, and the various crisscrossing relationships among the morphemes of the paradigm are often called categories. Thus there are such Latin morphemes as *-us, -um, -ī, -ōs* which are defined by their membership in a paradigm, and which are considered as expressing, within the paradigm, such categories as case and number.

The presence of these categories is not a happy situation for structural linguistics, which is most useful if it can define everything in terms of some stock of elements (phonemes, morphemes) which are all on a par with each other. It is therefore of interest to note that the categories represented in a paradigm can be set up by means of the very methods which are used to set up the more traditional morphemes. Just as the morphemes *the* and *a* can be isolated by comparing, say, *You've lost the job* with *You've lost a job*, so also the categories of singular and plural can be isolated by comparing certain utterances, even in a language in which these appear not as distinct morphemes but as categories in a paradigm. One important difference between isolating the traditional morphemes and isolating these categories is that the categories are not readily identifiable as consisting of any particular phonemes in the utterances. Another is that it is usually necessary to consider not a simply localized substitution, like *the* for *a* in *You've lost ( ) job*, but a more diffuse substitution, on the order of *-ose are ... -s* for *-is is* :0 in *Th( ) my book ( )*: *Those are my books* as compared with *This is my book*. We will therefore call these morphemically analyzed categories COMPONENTS.[1]

In order to see how this componential representation of paradigmatic categories can be carried out, we consider the morphemes for 'I', 'you', etc. in Modern Hebrew.

If we consider the following 17 utterances, and many sets of utterances of the same type, we would set up a class (C) of 17 morphemes -*ti* 'I did', *a-* 'I will', *y...u* 'they will', etc.[2]

lo limádti	*oto davar.*	I did.....................	not teach him a thing.				
,, *limádta*	,,	,,	you (m.) did	,,	,,	,, ,, ,,
,, *limadt*	,,	,,	you (f.) did	,,	,,	,, ,, ,,
,, *limed*	,,	,,	he did	,,	,,	,, ,, ,,
,, *limda*	,,	,,	she did...................	,,	,,	,, ,, ,,
,, *limádnu*	,,	,,	we did	,,	,,	,, ,, ,,
,, *limadtem*	,,	,,	you (m. pl.) did	,,	,,	,, ,, ,,
,, *limadten*	,,	,,	you (f. pl.) did	,,	,,	,, ,, ,,
,, *limdu*	,,	,,	they did	,,	,,	,, ,, ,,
,, *alamed*	,,	,,	I will	,,	,,	,, ,, ,,
,, *tlamed*	,,	,,	you (m.) *or* she will	,,	,,	,, ,, ,,
,, *tlamdi*	,,	,,	you (f.) will...............	,,	,,	,, ,, ,,
,, *ylamed*	,,	,,	he will	,,	,,	,, ,, ,,
,, *nlamed*	,,	,,	we will	,,	,,	,, ,, ,,
,, *tlamdu*	,,	,,	you (m. pl.) will	,,	,,	,, ,, ,,
,, *tlamédna*	,,	,,	you (f. pl.) *or* they (f. pl.) will	,,	,,	,, ,, ,,
,, *ylamdu*	,,	,,	they (m.) will	,,	,,	,, ,, ,,

Every member of the class *V* (*katav* 'write', *ba* 'come', and other verbs) occurs with every one of these *C* morphemes. At this stage of the analysis, the 17 morphemes isolated by comparing the utterances listed above would constitute a separate class of morphemes, restricted in their use to occur only with members of the class *V*.

However, we find additional environments in which some members of *C* occur while others do not. The first nine occur in *lo limad* ( ) *oto davar etmol* '( ) didn't teach him a thing yesterday', but not in *lo* ( )*lamed* ( ) *oto davar maxar* '( ) won't teach him a thing tomorrow'; the last eight occur in the latter but not in the former.[3] We therefore extract a component T common to the first nine and to their differentiating environments, and another component I common to the last eight and their differentiating environments. The residues of the nine T morphemes may be identified with the residues of the eight I morphemes if we find a convenient way of matching pairs of these residues.

This pairing may be carried out on the basis of the particular members of the *N* class[4] with which each member of *C* occurs:

WITH	THERE OCCUR ONLY	
	+T	+I
ani 'I'	*-ti* 'I did'	*a-* 'I will'
ata 'you (m.)'	*-ta* 'you (m.) did'	*t-* 'you (m.) will'
at 'you (f.)'	*-t* 'you (f.) did'	*t...i* 'you (f.) will'
hu 'he'	*-0* (zero) 'he did'	*y-* 'he will'
hi 'she'	*-a* 'she did'	*t-* 'she will'
anáxnu 'we'	*-nu* 'we did'	*n-* 'we will'
atem 'you (m. pl.)'	*-tem* 'you (m. pl.) did'	*t...u* 'you (m. pl.) will'
hem 'they (m.)'	*-u* 'they (m.) did'	*y...u* 'they (m.) will'
hen 'they (f.)'	*-u* 'they (f.) did'	*t...na* 'they (f.) will'
aten 'you (f. pl.)'	*-ten* 'you (f. pl.) did'	*t...na* 'you (f. pl.) will'

We can therefore identify the residue (X) of *-ti* with the residue (X) of *a-*, and so on: $X+$T$=$*-ti*, $X+$I$=$*a-*; $Y+$T$=$*-ta*, $Y+$I$=$*t-*, etc.

In the environment *ani vəhu* ( ) *oto bəyáxad* 'I and he ( ) him together', the only members of C which occur are in *limádnu* and *nlamed*. In *ata vəhem* ( ) *oto bəyáxad* 'you (m.) and they (m.) ( ) him together', only *limadtem* and *tlamdu* occur, and in *at vəhen* ( ) only *limadten* and *tlamédna*. In *hu vəhi* ( ) *oto bəyáxad* 'He and she ( ) him together', only *limdu* and *ylamdu* occur, and in *hi vəišti* ( ) 'she and my wife ( )' only *limdu* and *tlamédna* occur. If we consider only the presence of *və* 'and' in N *və* N, we find that only the last five of the ten morphemic residues occur in N *və* N ( ). We may therefore extract a P component from these five and from their environment N *və* N, and may seek a basis for identifying the residues of these five with some of the remaining five morphemes.

The basis for pairing the residues of these two new subclasses – of those morphemes which contain P and those which do not – may be found in a more detailed consideration of the occurrence of our ten residues with particular members of the class N. The residue of *-nu/n-* 'we' occurs not only with *anáxnu* 'we' but also with any N *və* N where one of the two N is *ani* 'I' or *anáxnu* 'we' and the other N is any other member of the N class: *ani vəhi limádnu oto* 'I and she taught him', *anáxnu vəhamore haxadaš nlamed otxa* 'We and the new teacher will teach you'. No other one of our ten morphemes occurs in these environments. Analogously, the residue of *-tem/t...u* 'you (m. pl.)' is the only one that occurs with any N *və* N where one N is *ata* or *atem* and the other is any member of N (including these two) except *ani* and *anáxnu*: e.g. *ata vəhu tlamdu oto* 'you (m.) and he will teach him'. Similarly, only *-ten/t...na* 'you (f. pl.)' occurs with N *və* N where one N is *at* or *aten* and the other is *at, aten, hi, hen* or any member of N containing the F component to be defined below: e.g. *at vəaxoti tavóna* 'You and my sister will come'. The residue of *-u/y...u* 'they (m.)' is the only one that occurs with any *N və N* where neither *N* is *ani, anáxnu, ata, at,* or *atem,* and where not more than one *N* includes F: *hu vəhi ydabru ito* 'He and she will talk with him', *habanai vəozro sidru et ze* 'The builder and his helper arranged it'. Similarly, only *-u/t...na* 'they (f.)' occurs with *N və N* where each *N* is either *hi* or *hen* or an *N* including F: *hi vəhabaxura tdabérna* 'She and the girl will talk'.

Of the five morphemes containing P, then, only the first (*-nu/n-*) occurs with *ani* in either *N* position of *N və N*; we therefore pair it with the *-ti/a-* morpheme which also occurs with *ani*. Only the second ever occurs with *ata* or *atem* in each *N* position; we therefore pair it with the *-ta/t-* morpheme which occurs with *ata*. An analogous restriction to *at* leads to the pairing of *-ten/t...na* with *-t/t...i*. The third morphemic residue occurs only with *hu, hi, hem, hen* or the members of *N* not listed here, in either *N* position[5]: we pair it with the morpheme 0/y-, which occurs with *hu*. Analogously, we pair *-u/t...na* with *-a/t-* on the basis of *hi*. We can express these matchings by five morphemic components: *1* contained in *-ti/a-* and *-nu/n-*, *2* contained in *-ta/t-* and *-tem/t...u*, *A* contained in *-t/t...i* and *-ten/t...na*, *3* contained in 0/y- and *-n/y...u*, *B* contained in *-a/t-* and *-u/t...na*.

If we consider the limitations of occurrence of these morphemes or their segments in respect to the *-a* 'feminine' morpheme, we find that *N* occurring with *A* or *B* always has the *-a* morpheme, whereas *N* occurring with *2* or *3* does not.[6] The restriction upon *B* as against *3* is clear: *habaxura sidra et ze* 'The girl arranged it', *habaxura vəhaxavera šela tsadérna et ze* 'The girl and her friend (f.) will arrange it'; as against *habaxur sider et ze* 'The fellow arranged it', *habaxur vəhaxavera šelo ysadru et ze* 'The fellow and his friend (f.) will arrange it'. No *N* with the *-a* 'feminine' morpheme substitutes for *habaxur* in the last two utterances, nor can *baxur* substitute for *baxura* or *xavera* in the first two.[7] We may therefore say that the *-a/t-* and *-u/t...na* residues, *hi* 'she' and *hen* 'they (f.)', and *-a* 'feminine' all contain a component F which is absent in 0/y-, *-u/y...u, hu* 'he', and *hem* 'they (m.)'.

The same component F can be extracted from *A* as against *2*. Just as *hi* contains F, so does *at* 'you (f.)': *hi baxura haguna* 'She's a decent girl', *at baxura haguna* 'You (f.) are a decent girl', *ata baxur hagun* 'You (m.) are a decent fellow'. Since *A* occurs with *at* but not with *ata*, we extract the F component from *A* also.

Further consideration shows a limitation of occurrence of *2* and *3* in respect to *at* and *hi*, as well as to *ata* and *hu*, respectively. Before *3, hi* or *hen* sometimes constitutes one member of *N və N* (see note 5), whereas *at* does not. Similarly, *ata vəat* 'You (m.) and you (f.)' occurs before *2*, but *ata vəani* 'You and I' does not. Hence the component *2* may be extracted from *at, aten,* and the *A* morphemes which occur with these, and *3* may be extracted from *hi, hen,* and the *B* morphemes which occur with them.

Component *A* is thus replaceable by the combination of components *2* and F; and *B* by the combination of components *3* and F.

We now have a set of components in terms of which each member of *C* may be identified and differentiated from each other one, without residue:

MORPHEME	REPRESENTED BY COMPONENTS	MORPHEME	REPRESENTED BY COMPONENTS
-ti 'I did'	*1* T	*a-* 'I will'	*1* I
-ta 'you (m.) did'	*2* T	*t-* 'you (m.) will'	*2* I
-t 'you (f.) did'	*2* F T	*t...i* 'you (f.) will'	*2* F I
-0 'he did'	*3* T	*y-* 'he will'	*3* I
-a 'she did'	*3* F T	*t-* 'she will'	*3* F I
-nu 'we did'	*1* P T	*n-* 'we will'	*1* P I
-tem 'you (m. pl.) did'	*2* P T	*t...u* 'you (m. pl.) will'	*2* P I
-ten 'you (f. pl.) did'	*2* F P T	*t...na* 'you (f. pl.) will'	*2* F P I
-u 'they (m.) did'	*3* P T	*y...u* 'they (m.) will'	*3* P I
-u 'they (f.) did'	*3* F P T	*t...na* 'they (f.) will'	*3* F P I

NOTES

[1] It can be shown that they are identical in analytic status with all other morphemic 'long components', which can be set up for morphology in much the same way that phonemic long components are set up for phonology. Cf. *Lg.* **20** (1944), 181–205. (Paper I of this volume.)

[2] If a vowel adjoins *limed* with no intervening juncture (i.e. within the same word) the preceding vowel is replaced by zero *(limdu).* Aside from that, if any phonemes (except the unstressed *na*) adjoin *limed* with no intervening juncture, the vowel of *limed* which is nearest to them is replaced by *a*. The forms are cited here in phonemic transcription, so that such segments as the *ə* between two initial consonants are not shown.

[3] E.g. *lo limádnu oto davar etmol* 'We didn't teach him a thing yesterday', *lo alamed oto davar maxar* 'I won't teach him a thing tomorrow'.

[4] Where *N* indicates a class of noun morphemes containing *ani* 'I', *hu* 'he', *hamore haxadaš* 'the new teacher', etc.

[5] But only one of the two *N* positions can be occupied by any one of the group *hi, hen,* and *N* plus *-a* 'feminine'. Before *-u/t ... na*, both *N* positions are occupied by morphemes of this group.

[6] And *N* occurring with *1* sometimes has the *-a* and sometimes does not.

[7] *N + -a* may substitute for *N* without *-a*, e.g. *habaxur* in such environments as *N və N* *(habaxur vəaxi sidru et ze* 'The fellow and my brother arranged it', *habaxura vəaxi sidru et ze* 'The girl and my brother arranged it'); or in the *N* of *VN = V (limádti et habaxur* 'I taught the fellow', *limádti et habaxura* 'I taught the girl'); or in the second *N* of *N sě PN* *= N (ze hamakom šel habaxur* 'That's the fellow's place', *ze hamakom šel habaxura* 'That's the girl's place'); etc.

IMMEDIATE-CONSTITUENT
FORMULATION OF ENGLISH SYNTAX

English syntax is presented here in terms of immediate constituents, the classical method of descriptive linguistics first made explicit in Bloomfield's *Language*. The formulation here is such as to facilitate comparison with a string-analysis of English syntax (where the differences are small) and with transformational analysis (where the differences are large).

The following gives a fairly detailed description of English sentence structure, omitting certain complex and rare forms, almost all idioms, and all deeper distinctions of meaning. (The latter would require at least detailed subclassifications of the word-classes, or transformational analysis.)

1. CLASSES OF WORDS

The following marks will be used for classes of words:

T: article: *the, a*; with special restrictions: *some, no, every, any.*

D: adverb: *quite, just*; with restrictions: *not*; also A*ly* (*quietly*, etc.). Many subclasses.

D_t: certain D before T: *scarcely, hardly, barely; all* can replace or follow *these; many* can replace *them: Hardly a man came; barely all the people; many a book.*

D_b: D which are objects of *be: He is here, out, in, nearby.*

Q: quantifiers: *few, many*, the numbers.

A: adjective: *large.*

A_c: color names: *red.*

A_d: a few A which occur after N to modify it: *the people present.*

A_s: A whose subject can be derived from a sentence (i.e. N̄-types 5–9): *To go is fine, That he went is true.*

N: noun: *book.* Subclasses include N of time, of measure.

N_s: nouns whose subject can be N̄-types 5–9: *That he went is a fact, To go now is a good plan.*

V: verb: *go.*

Transformations and Discourse Analysis Papers, 45 (1963).

V_s: verbs whose subject can be $\bar{N}$-types 5-9: *surprised me, satisfies us, suffices for this purpose.*

P: preposition: *in, near, of, after.*

P_c: prepositional conjunction: *after coming home, before he came home, without looking.* They occur in positions of C_s before a sentence or a clause with V*ing.*

C_s: subordinate conjunction: *because, since, while, when, as.*

C: coordinate conjunction: *and, or, but* (often more simply: *but not*), and often comma. With certain restrictions, C includes C_c: comparative conjunction: *than* (always with preceding *-er, more, less*), *as* (always with preceding *as* A, *as* D, *as much,* etc.).

2. THE MAJOR ASSERTION SENTENCE STRUCTURE

Except for special cases to be mentioned below, each English assertion sentence is:

I. $\boxed{\text{APP} \quad \bar{\text{N}} \quad \text{APP} \quad \text{V} \quad \text{OBJ} \quad \text{APP}}$

The capitalized word SENTENCE will hereafter mean the contents of the above box.

APP   means zero or more sentence-appendices (words, phrases, or clauses) listed below; APP can also occur before OBJ, if OBJ does not begin with a short $\bar{N}$. (e.g. *He relies on his charms at such times. He avoids at such times the more dangerous curves of the road. He avoids the more dangerous curves of the road at such times. He avoids the road at such times.* There does not occur: *He avoids at such times it.*)

$\bar{N}$ means noun-phrase of any type listed below.

V   means a single verb word, from the verb subclasses (V_v, V_o, etc.) listed below.

OBJ   means whatever object is appropriate to the preceding V according to the list below.

If the object contains a V within it, then that V must in turn have its object. Every one of these Sentence-sections, and every subsection within it (down to almost every word in each, except *the, a, and*) can be repeated by using C: $\bar{N}$ C $\bar{N}$ V OBJ; etc.

3. THE NOUN-PHRASE

3.1. $\bar{N}$ means any of the following word-sequences or single words:

(1) D_t T Q $\dot{N}_o$'s A A_c N_t 's cpda N_{so} $\dot{N}$–N A_d

$$\begin{cases} [\text{P } \bar{\text{N}}] \\ \bar{\text{A}} \text{ APP} \\ \text{to V APP} \end{cases} \begin{cases} [\text{V}en \text{ OBJ-n APP}] \text{ [wh-APP] } [,\bar{\text{N}},] \\ [\text{V}ing \text{ OBJ APP}] \end{cases}$$

Here every item is optional (i.e. may be absent) except N (the main N of the noun-phrase); if this N is a count-noun (like *chair, plate*, which in the singular must have article preceding it) then T also is required and not optional.

D_t, T, Q include various special words which have special restrictions (e.g. in relation to *not*). When Q is a number it can be many words long (e.g. 2734).

Ṅ indicates N with optional Q Ṅ's A cpda N- before it.

N_o is N which indicates the owner or creator of the main N following it: *the young boy's blue bicycle; the boy's younger sister's blue bicycle*.

A (which includes V*en*, V*ing*) is repeatable; where A occurs there may be several adjectives, in a more or less fixed order according to certain subclasses: *small dark Venetian vase*; not: *dark small*.

every A and D and P (and V) can have before it one or more D which modify it: *almost entirely dark vase; foolishly vociferously angry* (*foolishly* modifying here not *vociferously* but *vociferously angry*).

A_c can have A before it: *pale blue*.

N_t is N which indicates the type of N; it can have compounds before it but not other modifiers: *the boy's little-girl's bicycle* (*the little-girl type of bicycle belonging to the boy*); *the boy's small girl's bicycle* (*small and girl-style bicycle*).

cpda indicates the various types of compound adjective: N-N *life-size*, N-A *stone-grey*, A-N *left-wing*, N-V*en smoke-filled*, N-V*ing fire-eating*.

N_{so} is N indicating source, place, or material of N: *city ordinance, cotton dress*. Like N_t, it can have compounds before it; but if it has other modifiers it becomes cpda: *big-city ordinances*.

Ṅ- is a noun compounded onto the following N. It is repeatable, yielding Ṅ-Ṅ-N, etc.; and any of these N may be V*ing*, though with certain restrictions in respect to the other N of the compound. As in all compounds, the first Ṅ- has main stress (and may have some modifiers of its own or of the other N- before it); the N- (and last N) following it have low stress and can have no modifiers (Q, A, etc.) immediately before them; N- is rarely plural. N-V*ing book-publishing*, V*ing*-N *writing-paper*, N-V*ing*-N *road-building-programs* (but in *road-building laborers* we have N-V*ing*-N, i.e. a cpda: compound noun used as adjective, followed by a noun).

N can also be V*ing*.

items in square brackets [   ] are single modifiers (of which no part appears without the rest); items joined by a bracket { occur in either order (e.g. Ā [P Ñ] or [P Ñ] Ā). Modifiers after N are repeatable (with or without comma; and of course, like everything else, with C), and may have commas around them even if not repeated, and occur usually but not always in the order shown here.

P may be preceded by another P: *out of.*

Ā indicates A with modifiers: A P Ñ, A *to* V OBJ, A *to* V OBJ-n, A C A, rarely D D A, very rarely D A; or combinations of these (here D indicates *not*): *berries fresh from the field, people to build it, houses to build, houses for them to build, people tired but happy, fields not equally fertile, fields equally fertile.* Ā also includes A_s plus Ñ-types 7, 8, or the *wh*-clauses below: *people uncertain whether to go.*

to V: *to* V OBJ; *to* V OBJ-n; *for* Ñ *to* V OBJ-n. If N is N_s, also *for* Ñ *to* V OBJ: (Ñ-type 6): *the plan for him to build it.*

V*en* OBJ-n indicates (*almost*) any V whose object begins with Ñ, plus the suffix *en* (*ed*), plus the object of that V but minus its first Ñ: *the books taken, people ordered to go.*

V*ing* OBJ indicates any V with suffix *ing* plus the object of that V: *the man ordering people to go.*

wh- indicates all clauses with *wh* words except *what*- and *wh-ever*, i.e.: *who, which, whose* N^1, *that* plus a Sentence which lacks its Ñ subject: *the man who came;*
whom, which, whose N^1, *that*, or zero (omitted *that*) plus a Sentence which lacks any one Ñ from the object of the V (or from the object of a V which is within the object of the V): *the man that I saw, the man I saw; the man that I wanted him to meet; the man whom I wanted him to ask to come.*

where, when (*whither, whence*), *why*, very rarely *how*, or zero plus Sentence: *the place where I sat, the place I sat.*

P plus *whom, which, whose* N plus a Sentence which may lack a P Ñ from the object of its V: *the man on whom I rely, the wall near which I planted the tree.*

P plus *where, when*, plus a Sentence: *the place near where I sat.*

If N is N_s, also Ñ-type 7, 8 and *what* plus Sentence lacking Ñ of subject or object: *the idea that he took it, the question what causes it or what it causes.*

Post-N modifiers containing V or A may have APP which modify them, independent of the APP on the larger Sentence in which they are included: *fruit picked too early because labor is short may not ripen.*

,Ñ, represents a noun-phrase in apposition to the preceding Ñ: *the person whom you should see, a man well-known here.* In a few cases (e.g. if the apposition is an occupation-name) the comma is dropped: *my friend the carpenter.*

3.2. Other noun-phrases:

(2) Pronouns: *He* (*him* after V or P); *this*, etc.

(3) Names.

(4) *the* A: *The large is better.*

(5) ($\bar{N}$ APP) V*ing* OBJ APP: (*People*) *fighting sham battles amuses me.* The subject of *amuses* is not *people*. Parentheses indicate omittability.

(6) (*for* $\bar{N}$ APP) *to* V OBJ APP: (*For him*) *to do it when he is called is important.*

(7) *That* Sentence: *That he did it amuses me.*

(8) *Whether* Sentence: *Whether he did it is the question.*[2]

(9) *wh*-clauses as in the list under (1) above, but adding *which* N and *what* to each listing that contains *which*, and omitting *that* or the zero variant (the zero which represents a dropped *that*, etc.), and excluding the $\bar{N}$ P *wh* forms: *What she cooked is indeed a question; What she cooked tastes good.* Also all these *wh*-clauses (preceding in (9)) with *-ever* added to the *wh*-word: *whatever she cooks.*

$\bar{N}$-types (5)–(8) occur as subject only if the following main V (first except for auxiliary V_v) is of a certain subclass which we may call V_s (e.g. *amuse, surprise, interest, worry*), or if it is *be* plus a certain subclass of A or N which we may call A_s, N_s (e.g. *is amusing, is important, is true, is a fact, is a plan*); V_t *en*, V_w *en* (passives of V_t, V_w) are also in A_s: *That he went is known to me, whether he went was questioned.* Types (5)–(8) do not occur for $\bar{N}$ in objects of V.

$\bar{N}$-types (2)–(9) can have after them the same modifiers which occur after N, but only rarely, and in almost all cases with commas before and after each modifier; and hardly ever after types (5)–(8) (or after type 9 before V_s, *is* A_s, *is* N_s). (Before V_s, A_s, N_s, types (5)–(9) represent subjects fashioned out of whole sentences, hence these do not take the modifiers of N or of other $\bar{N}$).

$\breve{N}$ represents $\bar{N}$ without D_t T and excluding types (4), (6)–(9) (or (4)–(9)).

4. THE VERB-PHRASE

V occurs in the following subclasses, according to what object the verb takes. A particular verb may be a member of several subclasses, e.g. *take it* V_n, *take to it* V_{pn}. Each V has past or present tense except after V_v, V_{nv}, *to*, or before *ing*.

V_v auxiliaries, whose "object" is V OBJ: *can, may, will.* Don't occur in object of any V (incl. of V_v) or with *to, -ing.*

V_h have, whose "object" is V*en* OBJ: *have gone. have* is also in V_n, V_{tv}.

V_0 taking no object: *exist, sleep*.

V_n: object is N: *take it, find it*.

V_{pn}: object is P Ñ: *rely on him*. Different V_{pn} occur with different P, and so do different V_{npn}.

V_{npn}: object is Ñ P Ñ: *base Ñ on Ñ, attribute Ñ to Ñ, combine Ñ with* (or: *and*) *Ñ, give Ñ to Ñ, tell Ñ to Ñ*.

V_d: verbs with attached *up, out, in*, etc.: *lash out*.

V_{dn}: V_d with Ñ object: *look it up, cross it out* (not *cross out it*, etc.)

V_a: object is A (usually only a few A): *shine bright, shine red, loom large*.

V_b: *be*, whose objects are: V*ing* OBJ (except: V_h, usually V_b, and of course V_v); Ñ (usually agreeing in number and gender with N of the subject); any A or Ā; P Ñ (all P); D_b; *to* V OBJ; V*en* OBJ-n; *for* N *to* V OBJ-n (*this is for me to do*).

V_{tv}: object is *to* V OBJ: *want, try, begin*. (*ought to* is in V_v, for it does not occur in objects of V.)

V_g: object is V*ing* OBJ: *try, begin*.

V_{pg}: object is P V*ing* OBJ with particular P: *refrain from smoking, get to drinking*.

V_{nsn}: object is Ñ *as* Ñ: *view it as a victory, appoint him as secretary*. (Second Ñ may lack T even if it is count-noun.)

V_{nn}: object is Ñ Ñ; includes many V_{nsn} (*appoint him secretary*), and certain V_{npn} with inverted order of Ñ (*give a book to him*, give him a book; and also *tell, write, take*, etc.), also new V: *name, call*.

V_{na}: object is Ñ A: *consider him foolish* (many of these are also V_{nn}).

V_{nsa}: object is Ñ *as* A: *view him as (being) foolish*.

V_{nv}: object is Ñ V OBJ: *make him go, let him go* (also: *let go of it, let go*).

V_{ntv}: object is Ñ *to* V OBJ: *want him to go, prefer, order*.

V_{ng}: object is Ñ V*ing* OBJ: *catch him going, see him coming*.

V_t: object is *that* Sentence: *believe* that *he came, know, say, report*, that *may be dropped*.[3]

V_{nt}: object is Ñ *that* Sentence: *tell him* that *they came*.

V_{pnt}: object is P Ñ *that* Sentence: *report to him* that *they came*.

V_w: object is all the *wh* clauses of Ñ-types (8), (9) except those with *-ever*: *wonder whether he came, ask whom he will see*.

5. SENTENCE MODIFIERS

APP indicates any of the following; except for type (1), and after type (2), these are (usually) separated by comma from the rest of the Sentence:

1. verb-modifiers: a few D, A*ly*, and P N and certain N of measure which occurs only after V: *out, down, fairly, poorly, stood at attention*,

ran ten yards; or only before V (but after V_v): *just* (*He just left*), *not* (always after V_v, hence after *do, did* if no other V_v is present).

2. A*ly* and P Ñ and certain N of time and measure, which modify the V or the Sentence as a whole: *Quietly she came, She quietly came, She came quietly; Clearly, he was here; With a great rush, he ran up to them; Tuesdays, he comes late; Today he came late.*

Types 1 and 2 contain many subclasses, each with particular restrictions as to the Sentence positions in which it occurs and as to its occurrence next to other members of APP in the same Sentence position.

3. various idioms: *in general, so to speak.*
4. C_s or P_c plus Sentence: *Because in general he is late, we left. We left after he came.*
5. certain C_s or P_c plus APP V*ing* OBJ APP: *While saying this, we left. We left without speaking.*
6. special C_s forms, e.g. A *as* (or: *though*) Ñ(V_v) *be*, Ñ *that* (or: *though*) Ñ(V_v) *be: sick as he was, fool that he is.*
7. a few P_c plus APP Ñ APP V*ing* OBJ APP (Ñ accusative if pronoun): *Without him seeing us, we left.*
8. V*ing* OBJ APP: *Believing it was late, we left.*
9. Ñ APP V*ing* OBJ APP (Ñ nominative): *They being late, we left.*
10. Ñ APP object-of-*be* APP: *The children in bed, we left.* (rare).
11. object-of-*be* APP: *Long aware of this problem, we always sought to avoid it.*

Types 10 and 11 are obtained by dropping *be* (rather: *being*) from the subordinate Sentence.

12. (*as*) Ñ(V_v) V_t (or: V_w): *He's here, (as) I think; Has he, I wonder, returned?*
13. Ñ-types 6–9 occur after It V_s OBJ: *It sufficed for her to do it; It surprised me that he came.*

6. OTHER SENTENCE STRUCTURES

Aside from the main assertion Sentence, there are other Sentences:

II.   APP OBJ Ñ APP V APP: *This I like.* If the object has two parts (Ñ or P Ñ, and Ñ, P Ñ, A, V-OBJ, clause) then one of the parts remains after the V: *Him I told that they came; That they came I told him.* If a V which is inside an object is moved to before the Ñ, its object and APP moves with it: *To buy the books quickly I advised him long ago.*

III. certain D (mostly of place) V_o (or V_b) $\bar{N}$: *Nearby stood a tree; So is he; There's a man here.*

IV. A*ly is how*-clause; P $\bar{N}$ (or N of time, etc., or D) *is where* (or: *when, how, why*)-clause; *Because* Sentence *is why*-clause: *Bitterly is how he spoke; In his room is where he is; Tuesday is when he will do it; Because it was late is why we left.* Clause here indicates Sentence lacking an APP (or: P $\bar{N}$ OBJ).

V. a few rare rearrangements: e.g. *Would that* Sentence (*Would that he came*).

VI. yes-no question: same as I except that V_v precedes $\bar{N}$: *He will go, Will he go?* If the assertion had no V_v, the question uses *do, does, did,* as V_v instead of the tense: *He walked, Did he walk?* If the assertion verb is V_b or V_h (without V_v), the whole V_b or V_h precedes $\bar{N}$: *He is tired, Is he tired?; He has gone, Has he gone?*

VII. *Wh* question: The *wh*-clause of $\bar{N}$-type 9 (but including the $\bar{N}$ P *wh* forms which are excluded there) with the same changes as in VI above: *whom he will see, whom will he see?; what he is, what is he?; wherever he has gone, wherever has he gone?* If there is no subject $\bar{N}$ (after *who,* and possibly after *what, which, which* N, *whose, whose* N), there is no change: *who came, who came?*.

VIII. Imperative: a Sentence with *you* as subject $\bar{N}$ and *should* as V_v, dropping *you should: You should wash yourself, Wash yourself!*

NOTES

[1] Also $\bar{N}$ P plus any of the three preceding forms (except *who*): *the book, the cover of which tore.*

[2] Also *whether, why, how, where,* P *where, when,* P *when* plus *to* V OBJ APP; *whom, what, which, which* $\bar{N}$, *whose, whose* $\bar{N}$ (or P plus any of these) plus *to* V OBJ-n APP: *whether to do it is a question; near where to sit is a problem, whom to see.* These forms replace the subject $\bar{N}$ of the Sentence by *to,* and are natural only before *is* N_s or after N_s or V_w.

[3] Also, rarely, V_t, whose object is *that* Sentence minus the tense: *I insist that he come; I prefer he go now.* This can be considered a dropping of *should: I prefer (that) he (should) go now.*

IX

TRANSFER GRAMMAR

0. INTRODUCTION

The problem treated here is that of the difference between languages.[1] Can this be measured? The method outlined here enables us to measure the difference in grammatical structure, and to establish what is the minimum difference (or the maximum similarity) between any two language systems. Presumably, any method of specifying difference can contribute toward a classification of structural types among languages (as distinct, say, from a genetic classification). The method is also relevant to a proceduralized system of translation, and indeed can be put in the form of routine instructions for machine translations; and this not only because of the inherent connection between transfer and translation, but also because sentence-pairs under translation are used in certain transfer foundations (see § 5). The method may also be relevant for the learning or teaching of foreign languages; it suggests that it may prove possible to acquire a language by learning only the differences between the new language and the old (leaving those features which are identical in both to be carried over untaught); but here educational and psychological considerations enter in addition to any linguistic technique of minimizing the difference between the languages.[2]

One can construct purely structural transfers between the phonologies of two languages, or their morphophonemics, or their morphologies (only the last is discussed here, § 2). And one can construct transfers between paired items in the two languages – paired by some useful criterion. We discuss below sounds paired phonetically (§ 3) rather than purely structurally, and words (§ 4) and sentences (§ 5) paired by translation.

1. DEFINING DIFFERENCE BETWEEN LANGUAGES

We begin by defining difference between languages as the number and content of the grammatical instructions needed to generate the utterances of one language out of the utterances of the other. If A is some large set of utterances in one language, and B is a set in another, then the list of changes that have to be made on A in order to transform A into B will be considered the difference B–A (i.e. it represents what there is in B over and above A; or, given A, how much more has to be done to get from there to B). In certain cases, the list of changes that transform the set B back into the set A may not be simply the reverse of B–A, but may be a different list; this would be A–B (what there is in A over and above B). If among various lists of changes that would transform A into B we find one that is the smallest in number and content (under some way of measuring content), we will call it the least or minimum difference B–A. We will consider whether a least difference exists, how it can be found, and under what circumstances B–A is the reverse of A–B (in which case the amount of difference is independent of the direction).

A grammar may be viewed as a set of instructions which generates the sentences of a language. Since the set of instructions B–A generate sentences (of B) from other sentences (of A), it can be viewed as an appendix to the grammar of A.[3] That is to say, B can be obtained from the grammar of A plus the added instructions of B–A (which would take us from A to B). This would compare with the independent grammar (or grammars) of B, which generate the sentences of B directly, starting from scratch. Thus the difference B–A, or the transfer instruction, can be presented as a grammatical appendix to A, or as part of an indirect grammar of B (going via A). It is for this reason that it may be called a transfer grammar.

One can also consider a set of grammatical instructions Z, which does not in itself generate any known language, but is so selected that if we add to Z certain additional instructions A–Z we will get the sentences of A, while if we add to Z other additional instructions B–Z will get the sentences of B. Then Z is a grammatical base common to A and to B; and both A and B are obtained by an indirect grammar which goes via Z. One can select Z for various purposes, e.g. for translation or teaching convenience, or for minimality (such that the sum of Z and A–Z and B–Z is least). Then the difference between A and B is the sum of A–Z plus the reverse of B–Z.

2. STRUCTURAL TRANSFER

One form of transfer is the difference between two whole grammatical structures. For example, we can consider for each language what are its major morpheme classes (and their subclasses down to some level), and what are the main combinations of these classes into its various successively larger constructions (word, phrase, clause, or the like) until we get up to its whole sentences. We can ask what changes would have to be made in such a structural sketch of one language in order to obtain out of it a structural sketch of the other (at about the same level of detail). Such a list of changes would generate the utterances of one language out of those of the other, since the grammatical sketches of each language yield the utterances of that language (up to some level of detail), so that transferring from one sketch to the other will suffice to transfer from one set of sentences to the other.

2.1. *Corresponding Morpheme Classes*

The very sketchy structures (see Table 1) of Korean, English, and Hebrew will give some impression of what can be done here.

B: affixless particles, occurring as whole sentences.

C: conjunctions, occurring between two like constructions, sometimes before a single construction.

D: generally affixless adverbs, insertable in whole clause or verb constructions.

R: roots, most of them appearing both as a part of some N and as a part of some V (i.e. common to N and to V).

N: nouns, each is head of a noun-phrase M which contains one or several N; there are from zero or one M up to several in each clause; N with affixes may occur in positions of V or A.

M: see N.

n: noun-vowel morphemes, $R + n = N$.

proM: pronouns, substituents for noun phrase.

A: adjectives, occurring with N or in position of N.

a: adjectival noun-vowel morphemes, $R + a = A$ (or rather, $=$ adjective-position N).

V: verbs, each is head of a verb-phrase W containing one or two or so V; there is usually one W in each clause; there may be several W in WCW constructions; V or W with affixes may occur in positions of N or A.

W: see V.

v: verb-vowel morphemes, $R + v = V$.

proW: pro-verbs, substituents for verb phrase.

P: prepositions, occurring primarily before M.

T: article; in Hebrew, and perhaps in English, T can be viewed as a member of mm.

vn: $V + vn = N$, and in general:

xy: $X + xy = Y$, e.g. $M + mm$ affix $= M$; $N + na$ affix $= A$.

Korean clause-finals and sentence-finals (verb affixes occurring only at clause and sentence end respectively) can be viewed as special subclasses of ww (with important distributional characteristics absent from ww in English or Hebrew).

Korean e genitive occurs only in $NeN = N$, hence is like some occurrences

TABLE I

Major morpheme classes

K:	B⁻	D		N⁺		V⁺			mm	ww	vv	nv⁻	vn					? ¿ . . !
E:	B	C	D	N⁺	proM A⁺	V⁺	proW P	T	mm	ww	vv	nv	vn	na	va	aa	ad⁻	. , ? !
H:	C	D⁻		R⁺	n proM a	v	P		mm	ww	nn	vv⁻	vn	na⁻			ad⁻	. , ? !

of certain P, or else like an nn which yields only non-final N (since Ne could be viewed as non-final N).

Korean nv can also be analyzed as V (the verbs i, ha), yielding N + V = last part of a clause; if we take i, ha as verbalizing suffixes, they yield N + nv = V.

Korean vn (participles, gerund) change a V or clause (V with preceding N) to N.

A clause is defined as a substructure of a sentence, ending in /,/, such that a sentence is merely a sequence of clauses, at most with C between them. A sentence is a structure, ending in one of /.?¿!/, such that a discourse is a sequence of sentences.

$^-$ indicates that there are very few members in the class.

$^+$ indicates that there are very many members in the class.

From this table we can read off K–E, E–H, K–H; E–K is the reverse of K–E, and so on. When we say, for example, that C occurs both in E and in H, we mean that both E and H have a class of morphemes with roughly the distribution stated for C. The detailed distributions of Hebrew C and the English C may be quite different. Some of the differences will appear in the very sketchy distributional statements below, but many more are not indicated here. It may be possible to minimize the differences between two languages by classifying the morphemes in both with maximal use of approximately the following criterion: If some morphemes A of language A have (major and regular) similarities of distribution with some morphemes B of B, we form a class z representing the common distributions of A and B. Then the distribution of A is z plus A–z (which are the additional distributions of A over and beyond z), and the distributional difference between A and B is the sum of A–z and reversed B–z. When we do this for all the morphemes of languages A and B, we are constructing a joint system of morpheme classes in much the same way as we construct morpheme classes for a single language (there too we maximize the grouping of morphemes with similar distributions). To some extent this has been done in Table I, for example when Korean clause finals and sentence finals were considered to correspond with (or be in the same joint class as) ww.

2.2. Corresponding Morphological Structures

Table II gives the occurrence of the above classes in each language. The sentences of each language are built out of the classes via the intermediate structures shown in the column for that language. The transfer instructions are those that carry us from one column to another, and in particular from each row (e.g. the W of K) to the corresponding row in the other column (e.g. the W of E). To take a simple example, V of E minus V of K consists in the inclusion of A ar. We can generate each structure of English by adding

TABLE II
Major morphological structures

	K	E	H
Sentence with! =	clause with particular ww name with vocative suffix	M W some A	M W A some D
Sentence with.or?or¿ =	some B some M {M + certain mm,} {clause,} clause	B M D some A clause	
Clause =	{M} W	{C} {D} MW {PM}	{C} {D} MW {PM} M ($proM_3$) (P) M
W =	(D) (V + gerund) V ww	{D} {ww} {V to} $V^{PM}_{(M)}$ {D} proW	(ww) {V le} $V^{(D)}_{(et)}$ M} (D)
V =	V{vv} N nv	V{vv} N nv A av	R v (vv)
M =	{N} N (-N) (mm)	T{{D}A}N(mm) (T){D}A when no N follows M P M M to V M wh S	(mm) Ñ {Ñ} ($proM_3$) ((še) PM) (šeS) (mm) Ñ (M̂) {Ñ} ($proM_3$) ((še) PM) (šeS)

N =	(Ne)N before N or mm also clause + participle V + gerund	{N}N +' on first N, ' on others N{nn} V vn A an	R n (nn) V vn A an
-N =	final bound N stems		
A =		A {aa} N na V va	R a N na
D =		A ad	
X =		X C X some X(,)X	X C X some X(,)X

Notes:

( ) indicates zero or one, { } indicates zero or more, otherwise each item occurs once.

$proM_3$: third-person pronoun.

' main stress, ` secondary stress.

English mm extends over following W.

Hebrew mm extends over all N and following W (but the article is zero over Ṅ, W).

X^y_z indicates that both xy and xz occur.

H: *la* 'to'; *et* accusative preposition, *še* 'that'.

K: *e* genitive.

E: *wh* relative: ww includes preverbs (*can*, etc.) and tenses.

to the corresponding Korean structure whatever is the difference between the two.

The same remarks hold for this table as for the preceding one. Except that there is more room here for modification and for ingenuity in so stating the structures, and in so arranging their substructurings, as to bring out maximum similarity between any two languages. Also, the instructions needed to change a line of K to the corresponding line in E can be stated in various ways, some of which can be simpler or can be more similar to other instructions required elsewhere.

Even these rough tables show the greater similarity between E and H as against K, the former two being members of families which have (and to an even greater extent had) considerable structural similarities.

3. PHONETIC AND PHONEMIC SIMILARITY

Languages differ from each other in their sounds and in the phonemic relations among the sounds. This is a matter of no importance for written translation, where each morpheme can be treated as a primitive entity. However, it is relevant for language-learning, and for linguistic distance and type.

3.1. *Phonetic Correspondences*

The most direct way to measure phonetic difference is to match those sounds (sound types, sets of similar free variants) which are closest in the two languages. For example, we set Korean m corresponding to English m, Korean i corresponding to English i. The phonetic differences in a corresponding pair may be small or large, and will have to be stated. The practical relevance of this matching is obvious, since a learner will usually substitute his own sounds for the nearest ones in the new language, or hear the new ones as the sounds nearest them in his own language. In some cases the differences and similarities between certain sounds of A and the possibly matchable sounds of B are such as to permit a number of alternative pairings: e.g. Korean æ could be matched with English e (different in that it is lower), or with English æ (different in that it is higher).[4] However, there are gross similarities among most languages in respect to kinds of sounds (e.g. often labial, dental, palatal; stops, spirants, vowels; voiced, voiceless), so that the candidates for pairing are usually within a small group: to English p or b (or the p allophone) one could only match Korean pp, ph, or p (or the allophone b), but not, say, m or t or i. Finally, there may be new sounds in A, i.e. ones which are left over after pairings, or are so different from anything in B that they are not paired with any sound of B.

The list of phonetic pairings and new sounds constitutes one set of differences between A and B, covering all the utterances of those languages. The phonetic elements common to each pair constitute the common Z, and the differences are the A–Z and the B–Z.

To this may be added the differences in types of sequences (clustering, etc.) between the sounds of A and the corresponding sounds of B. Learning considerations may favor certain correspondences as against others, in order to center the attention on certain phonetic differences or types of new sequences which are easier to learn (easier in general, or easier for the speakers of the particular language).

3.2. *Corresponding Phonemic Statuses*

The grammar of a language lists its sound types and their phonemic relations (how they are grouped into phonemes). Once we have the sound correspondences, the remaining phonological difference between A and B lies in the phonemic status of the corresponding and new sounds. This would seem to be quite a job, since in each language each of the sounds may be a free or a positional variant of some other sound, or may contrast with any particular sound in one or all positions, or may constitute a whole phoneme by itself, and so on.

It is possible to combine the sound correspondences and their phonemic statuses in some chart such as Table III, upon which the transfer instructions can then draw.

Where the corresponding sounds are written differently for the two languages, the spelling for one of the languages is put in parentheses.

Example of alternative statement: If K. u were matched with E. u, then K. ʉ and ø would be matched with E. ə and ʌ; but E. ə and ʌ are positional variants of each other (ə being unstressed), while K. ʉ and ø are full phonemes without stress restrictions. K. l occurs in the special cluster ll, where E. l does not (except across juncture); on the other hand, English has many clusters lacking in Korean.

K. tt has been matched with E. d, and K. th with E. t (and so for the whole series), which is the way Koreans usually interpret English sounds (Lukoff). Other matchings are possible instead.

The entries in each column list the sounds that have the particular phonemic status stated at the top of that column, for one language. And the entries in each row list the sounds that have the particular phonemic status stated at the head of that row, for the other language. The chart is so arranged that the entries at a given column-row intersection show how the phonemic status of the given sound differs in the two languages.

For each sound in Table III we can change its phonemic status, from that

TABLE III

E (columns) / K (rows)	x is a whole phoneme or phonemic sequence (except for variants noted elsewhere)	ditto, but x occurs in important positions where it is absent (E) / lacking (K) in the other language	x is a positional variant (of y: x/y)	x contrasts with y: x/y	x does not occur as a sound type but y occurs in the position where x occurs in the other language
E	m, n, ŋ; i, e, ae, a, o; u(K. ʉ); a(K. ø); uw(K. u)	ss (E. z), pp(b), tt(d), kk(g); ph(E. p), th(t), kh(k), ch(č); y, w; clusters		p/b etc.; l/r; ši/s; f/h	x/h; x̌/h; mᵇ/m, nᵈ/n.; q̌/l
K		1	pʰ/p, etc.	flap d/d	flap t

K row, additional category — *x does not occur as a sound type nor does y (if x/y)*: v, θ, ð, ž, j, the pre-r vowels of the column in which it is, to that of the row in which it is. Then we get an over-all change from the phonemic status of the sounds of the column language (English in Table III) to the phonemic status of the corresponding sounds in the row language (here, Korean): K–L. And analogously from the row language to the column language. The chart thus serves the purposes of transfer, since the instructions required to generate one language from the other can be read off from it.[5] It is uniquely reversible, and in it K–E is the reverse of E–K.

It is possible to modify the chart for various purposes. For example, whenever a sound appears more than once (or whenever a phonetic similarity between the two languages has not been expressed as a correspondence) there is room for some rearrangement of what sound types shall be taken as corresponding, and what is the resulting phonemic difference. Thus we can say that the Korean l/r phoneme corresponds in certain positions (where its variant is l) to the English l phoneme; and in other positions (where its variant is a flap r) to the English r phoneme; while the Korean ll phoneme corresponds phonetically to English double l across juncture, or is a new sound cluster corresponding to nothing in English.[6] Or we can say that the Korean ll phoneme corresponds to the English l phoneme, while the Korean l/r phoneme (with its l variant) corresponds to the English r phoneme.

If such modifications can be carried out all the way, the resulting chart would have each sound appearing only once, and its column and row would indicate its full difference of phonemic status in the two languages. In doing this, the headings of the columns and rows would be modified (and increased) to suit the particular sounds and their differences in status. Such a modified chart would give the most organized set of instructions for generating the phonemic statuses of one language out of the other, and would thus measure the difference between the two languages in this respect.

For teaching purposes, special considerations are involved. Certain changes in phonemic status (for corresponding sounds) seem especially hard to learn. If two sound types are positional or free variants of each other in one's language, it is quite hard to pronounce their corresponding sounds as contrasting phonemes in another language[7]; or in general if x is a positional variant of y, it is hard to pronounce x in the position where y occurs in one's own language: e.g. for an English speaker to pronounce unaspirated p in word initial. In such cases it may be preferable to assign the correspondences on the basis of some other (perhaps less obvious) phonetic similarity; so that for example if an English speaker has to learn initial unaspirated p, it might be presented as the correspondent of English b (with the phonetic instruction that it should be devoiced), rather than as the correspondent of English p (with the phonetic instruction that it should be deaspirated).

4. MORPHEMES AND MORPHOPHONEMES

Any transfer between two languages will have to substitute the morphemes of one language for those of the other. In most cases this is a matter for a dictionary-like listing. However, some languages have many cognates in common, or many borrowings in one or both directions, or many international words; the latter may comprise a large part of the vocabulary of technical articles even though not of the language as a whole. In such cases, it may be worth-while to set up instructions that would generate the words of one language from the semantically corresponding words in the other which have sufficient phonetic similarity (or whose phonetic difference is sufficiently regular); this would replace listing of translations for these words. For example, in many international words the English sound a corresponds to o in other languages. This is specifically the case for words which are spelled with o in English (and in the other languages), e.g. *comic, historic*; and such facts may be usable in the transfer instructions.

Such vocabulary-transfers mean that for a certain set of words or affixes, we can say that the morphemes in both languages are composed of the same common elements or spelling; except that in this case the elements are not the phonetically corresponding sounds or phonemes, but rather the sounds or phonemes that occupy corresponding positions (i.e. replace each other) in the two-language forms of this common vocabulary. These pairs of vocabulary-corresponding phonemes bear some resemblance to morphophonemes, i.e. to phonemes which replace each other in different positional variants of a morpheme; however the morphemic groups here within which the replacement occurs are not allomorphs but translations.

In contrast, morphophonemics proper, which connects the allomorphs of a single language, is usually very different from language to language. This applies even to the regular and phonetically 'reasonable' morphophonemics of the various languages; though some assimilations, such as devoicing at word end, occur under fairly similar circumstances in different languages. And it applies far more to the irregular morphophonemics and suppletions, which occur in particular morphemes and have no phonetic basis. Here no transfer instructions can be devised, except to drop the morphophonemics of the old language and to add that of the new. In language learning, and in constructing any translation procedure, these two steps have to be included.

When it comes to the actual listing of words or morphemes in one language and their translation in the other, we find that one word may have several translations, due to the different ways in which ranges of meaning are covered by vocabulary in different languages. Where two different words in one's own language are translated into the same foreign word (i.e. vocabulary transfer is many-one), no special instructions are needed; nor is it even necessary to call attention to the fact that the two translations are the same. But the transfer is then not uniquely reversible; for, starting from the other language one would not know which reverse translation to use. When one word in one's own language has two translations in the foreign, we meet the same one-many transfer that the foreigner meets (above) in reversing our many-one situation. (And the difference in translation may not coincide with any difference in meaning perceived by the native.)

Sometimes it is not of great moment which translation is used, though violence may thereby be done to style and subtleties of meaning; in this case we may call the two translations free variants for the transfer. Where the choice of translation is important, and is determinable by something in the environment of the given word, we may speak of the two translations as positional variants of the transfer of the given word. (The positions being the environment of the given word in the starting language.) The determining environment is often a grammatical or other necessarily-occurring feature; in this case we can consider that the starting material is not merely the word in question, but the two environmentally distinguished occurrences of the word plus its environment, and each of these then has only one translation. E.g. *table* in N position may have a different translation from *table* in V position, *check* in *check up* may have a different translation than in *check in*. Or the determining environment may be the presence in the same sentence or discourse of other words drawn from one part of the vocabulary rather than from another (e.g. *masses* in sentences containing *uprising, classes* may translate differently than *masses* in sentences containing *charge, field*). In such cases the instructions may have to call for a sampling of certain neighboring words (often from among the members of particular word classes only); the unique translation would then be not of the original word alone, but of the word in the neighborhood of certain particular word sets.

5. MORPHOLOGICAL TRANSLATABILITY

The transfers of §§ 2, 3 were based on certain similarities and differences of the whole set of utterances A and the whole set B in grammatical structure and in sounds. They do not lead us from any sentence of A to the particular sentence in B which is the translation of A. The transfer of § 4 does something of this, since it takes us from the words of A to their translations in B. But this is far from enough. For one thing many words do not occur alone (e.g. prepositions, verbs in many languages), so that they cannot really be isolated for translation, and are often translated in stilted or non-comparable forms (e.g. 'speak – parler'). More important, certain morphemes and words have a great variety of translations, depending on environmental structure. This holds especially for those with more 'grammatical' meanings, like articles, prepositions, cases, tenses, and affixes in general. Often these can be adequately translated only when their environments are grammatically defined. Finally, translating the morphemes ('word-by-word') is in any case not enough for translation, since the grammatical interrelation of the morphemes in each language is a matter of the subdivision of the sentence into constituents (in successive inclusion), which will often differ in the two languages; and the order of the morphemes within each constituent will often differ. The analysis of a sentence into successively included constituents, and the composition and order of smaller constituents (down to morpheme classes) within each constituent, is therefore necessary for any method of translation that is to be reducible to mechanical procedures. And it is in general an interesting transfer question, to ask how sentences which would translate each other differ grammatically, i.e. what grammatical changes have to be made in a sentence of A to obtain the particular sentence (or sentences) in B which would translate it (given the transfer of dictionary morphemes).

5.1. *Pairing by Translation*

We therefore introduce a transfer relation between each sentence of A and its translation in B, or between each grammatical construction of A and its translation in B (i.e. the part which is common to all the B translations of the various A sentences containing the A construction). A new consideration is thus added, which alters many of the correspondences of § 2. Where in § 2 many constructions and subdividings had no parallel, here we can find – on a translation basis – a parallel in one language to almost everything in the other. (Almost everything in any language can be translated into any other.) Furthermore, different grammatical constructions in A may be translated by only one or a few grammatical constructions in B; and two A constructions which are similar in A may go into two (or more) quite different B constructions.

In the matter of morpheme classes, N and V, for example, were matched in English and Korean by their distribution, and A was unmatchable. If we ask how these appear in translation-paired sentences, we find that English N morphemes translate generally into Korean N morphemes, English V into Korean V, English A into Korean V+vn (participle), English N+na into Korean N. English A thus has a translation correspondent in Korean, even though it doesn't have a morpheme-class correspondent. And even though the structural breakdown of § 2.2 shows English N+na as substitutable for A, these two are translated into different constructions in Korean.

In the structural analysis of § 2.2 we find, for example, no Korean parallel to the M wh S structure of English (*The man who came; The man whom I saw*). But under translation, we find that M wh S is usually translated in Korean by V + vn N, which also translates English V + va N and AN.

5.2. *Translation Correspondences*

We can move in a more or less orderly fashion, from the actual pairs of each sentence and its translation to the summarized transfer instructions, by means of a chart like Table IV.

TABLE IV

H \ E	V + ed	preverb + V	V to V	It's A that N V.	I
V + pers.	√				
pers. + V		√			
V lə V		√	√		
A še pers. + V		√		√	
ani					√
(ani) e —					√
ani) —ti					√

Preverbs are *will, shall, can, could, may*, etc. V + pers. indicates that the personal elements are suffixed; pers. + V that these are prefixed. ani e — or e — is a prefixed 'I'; ani —ti or —ti is a suffixed 'I'.

Across the top we list various sentence types (or independent sub-structures of sentences) in one language (English) – each representing the many sentences which have that structure in English grammar. Down the left side we do the same for the sentence types (or sub-sentence structures) of the other language (Hebrew). Then we check which column is a translation of which row (and which row is a translation of which column).

When we find that a structure in one language is translated into two or more structures in the other, as in the case of English *V to V* or Hebrew *A še pers. + V*, we try to sub-classify it into two or more structures, each of which will have only one translation. If the structure is in terms of classes, we may succeed in this by dividing a class into subclasses. If possible, we find some property that distinguishes these subclasses. E.g. if we wish to subdivide the preverbs so as to match the Hebrew future tense, we note that the preverbs *will* and *shall* differ somewhat from the others, and have some

TABLE V

H \ E	V+ ed	will shall	preverbs not listed else-where +V	V to V	may might should +V	It's A that N $\{^{Ved}_{will\ v}\}$	I am $\{^A_N\}$	I will V	I Ved
V + pers.	✓								
pers. +V		✓							
yaxol muxrax $\}$ lə V etc.			✓						
other V + lə V				✓					
efšar naxon $\}$ še pers. V etc.					✓				
other A + še $\}$ pers. V / V pers.						✓			
ani $\{^{-A}_{-N}\}$							✓		
ani e + pers. + V								✓	
ani V + pers. + ti									✓

characteristics of a tense: *will* and *shall* replace *-ed* when certain replacements occur elsewhere in the sentence (e.g. when *yesterday* is replaced by *tomorrow*), and *will* probably has a frequency more similar to that of −*ed* than to that of other preverbs, such as *can, may*.[8] Since *will* and *shall* are the two preverbs which translate the Hebrew tense *pers.* + V, just as −*ed* translates the Hebrew tense V + *pers.*, we are glad to find grounds within English grammar for separating them off from the other preverbs. When we cannot find a property that would subdivide our structure so as to fit the other language, we simply list the members of the smaller subclass: thus in Hebrew V *lə* V, the first V is divided into two sub-classes, the smaller one consisting of yaxol *can*, muxrax *must*, etc., and translating the English preverbs. We can also separate off from the preverbs those members which are translated into *A še pers.* + V: namely, *may, might, should*.

If the structure is in terms of morphemes, and sometimes also when it is in terms of classes, we can achieve unique translations only by finding some diagnostic element in the environment. Thus I is translated as (ani) e− if *will* V (or, in Hebrew, its correspondent *pers.* + V) follows; as (ani) − ti if V + *ed* (or V + *pers.*) follows; and as ani otherwise. Hence we subdivide I plus its environments into these three sub-classes, each consisting of I plus certain environments, and each having a unique translation in Hebrew.

Finally, some structures or sentences of A will resist any separation into unique translations. This happens when the two or more translations of the A form are distinguished by semantic or stylistic differences which are not readily expressed (or expressible) in A: a semantic example is Hebrew ata *you m. s.g.*, at *you f. sg.*, atem *you pl.* for English *you*; a stylistic example is English *will* and *shall* for Hebrew *pers.* + V. Non-unique translations also occur when there are recognized ambiguities in A: *He tied it* may refer to equalling a mark or to making a knot. Whether or not the two uses are considered homonyms in the original language, they are homonyms for the transfer, in the sense of having separate translations. In this case the ambiguity can often be resolved by adding various environments; but these are usually not classifiable in a simple grammatical way, and the problem reduces to that of vocabulary translation.

In general, the work of breaking down both the top and the side listings so as to reduce cases of double translation can be carried on almost without end, and will soon get us involved in what are called individual idioms. One simply stops the work at some level of detail, with structures which have roughly unique translations in the other language. The amended chart now looks something like Table V.

Within the given limits of detail, such an amended chart gives a one-one transfer between the languages. Starting with the broken-down structures

listed here for English, one can change each listing to its Hebrew counterpart
and thus obtain the Hebrew sentences which translate the English. These
changes therefore constitute H–E, i.e., they show what instructions have
to be added to English to obtain Hebrew. Going the other way, reversing
each change, we start with Hebrew and end up with English: this is E–H
(what is necessary to obtain E over and above H). Since each of the changes
is a replacement of one linguistic structure by another, they can be viewed
as a kind of grammar (of a transformational type): H–E is a grammatical
appendix to E; and the grammar of E plus H–E yields H, and is thus an
indirect grammar of H (via E). In this breakdown, E–H is the reverse of
H–E, and each measures the morphological difference under translation (for
translationally paired sentences) between the two languages.

5.3. *Common Grammatical Base*

One can also try to construct the simplest and most inclusive in-between
grammar, which would have a common part for each structural pair (e.g.
$V+affix$ as a common part for $V+pers.$ and $V+ed$). Then certain changes
would yield E out of this Z, and other changes would yield H out of this Z.
The difference between E and H would be the sum of these E–Z and H–Z
changes. Given certain kinds of similarities between languages such a
formulation in terms of an in-between grammar may be simpler than a
direct E–H.

5.4. *One-Way Translation Correspondences*

After we have the one-one chart, we can consider a further problem. The
categories of the broken-down listings are often not natural ones for each
language taken by itself. They were constructed so as to yield a one-one
relation. But for many purposes, e.g. translation or language learning, a
many-one relation from the native to the new language is no trouble at all.
The only trouble lies in the fact that the reverse would be one-many (i.e.
would have several translations among which we could not choose). If we
are not interested in the reverse, we can simplify our listings to make many-
one (as well as one-one) correspondences. For example, going from English
to Hebrew, we could match both *preverb + V* (except *may, might, should*) and
V to V with Hebrew *V lə V*. We can even try to give this a new one-one form
by considering *preverb + V* as a sub-class of *V to V*, different only in that *to*
has a variant zero after preverbs.[9] Similarly, we can consider *will V* as
different from *preverb + V*, and closer to *V+ed*, something which is made
easy by the fact that the concepts of future and past "tenses" are common,
and are associated with *will* and *ed*.

In this way we obtain a revised grammar of English based as far as possible on the categories of Hebrew, to the extent that such categories can be supported in English. The changes necessary to obtain Hebrew out of this revised version of English structure are fewer than before. We can thus work toward a minimum H–E. The same can be done in the other direction. But in the other direction we would revise Hebrew grammar in an English direction, and the resulting E–H (E over and above revised H) is not in general the inverse of H–E (H over and above revised E).[10]

NOTES

[1] In working on this subject I have had the advantage of many conversations with Fred Lukoff, and the Korean examples used here, as well as various general points, are due to him. For the Korean phonemes and morphology, see Fred Lukoff, *Spoken Korean*.

[2] This investigation of structural difference does not suffice to define distance among language structures. For example, we will not be able to say that the difference between English and German is some specified function of the English–Danish and the Danish–German differences. However, we can now try to go further and define a distance (metric) among language structures with the aid of the measurement of difference discussed here.

[3] Even in the grammar of a single language by itself, it is possible to generate some of the sentences of the language out of other sentences of the same language by particular grammatical transformations. However the conditions for these transformations are quite different from those that carry us from the sentences of one language to those of another.

[4] The relation of one matchable pair to the others often is decisive for determining which phonemes to match. For example, since English has two front vowels higher than its æ, and Korean has two higher than its æ, it is far simpler to match E and K i-i, e-e, æ-æ, rather than E e-K æ.

[5] The chart does not show what are the phonetic differences (and similarities) between corresponding sounds, nor does it show most of the differences in phonemic sequence (clustering, etc.). These were considered in § 3.1.

[6] Double l occurs in English only across juncture. In Korean there is an L sound, with some phonetic similarities to a long l (and analyzed by Lukoff as a cluster of two Korean l) which often occurs across morpheme boundary: kil *road*, killo *by the road* (though there is no Korean open juncture here). However, there are also cases of Korean L not astride morpheme boundary; hence it would not be desirable to write every Korean L as l-l for English readers, but rather to write it as a cluster of l plus l – new for English readers.

[7] E.g. a Korean says kil *road*, kiri *road* (as subj.); but in speaking English he will have to pronounce, by the side of *keel, teary*, also *tear, mealy*.

[8] If *will V* had from the start been listed as a separate English entry, it (with *shall V*) would have had a unique Hebrew translation (except for differences in the range of the tenses). However *will* is most naturally seen in English structure as a member of the preverb group (rather than as a tense), and is not easily distinguishable grammatically from the preverbs *may, might*.

[9] In doing so, we use the fact that preverbs look somewhat like verbs (*I can*, like *I see*), even though from other points of view they are not verbs (*I can* is analyzable as *I* + preverb + zero pro-verb).

[10] It should be clear that only the form of the grammar is revised in each instance. The revised grammar is still a grammar of that language, which correctly generates the sentences of the language.

STRUCTURAL LINGUISTICS.
2: LANGUAGE STRUCTURES

X

THE PHONEMES OF MOROCCAN ARABIC*

0. 1. Moroccan Arabic is divergent from the other modern Arabic dialects in important phonological aspects, chiefly in the change of most occurrences of short vowels to ǝ, and of a·>æ·, in the lessening of phonetic distinction between emphatic and corresponding non-emphatic consonants (e.g. between ṭ and t), and in the loss of distinction between dental spirants and stops (e.g. between θ and t) in some parts of Morocco. Moroccan Arabic is used as a trade language in many Atlantic seaports of Africa south of Morocco, and many of its phonological features are present also in the Arabic of Algeria and Tunisia. Dialects of various Moroccan cities differ from each other both in the phonetic ranges of phonemes and in their phonemic system. The material presented here is based mostly on the speech of Mr. and Mrs. Abdul Kader Larbi of Casablanca; Mrs. Larbi comes from Casablanca, and Mr. Larbi from the town of Bir Rshid, 40 km from that city. Wherever their dialects differed, the forms used here are those spoken by Mrs. Larbi.

1. 0. In these sections are listed the sound types (positional variants) which I was able most clearly to distinguish, with the environments in which each occurs. Each sound type symbol represents a great number of individual sounds which occurred both in repetitions of a particular utterance (e.g. the initial sounds in various repetitions of dæ·r 'he built') and in different utterances (e.g. the initial sound of dyæ·li 'my' and the final sound of bǝrd 'cold'). The individual sounds included in a sound type varied freely over a phonetic range, but these free variations are in most cases not mentioned here. In including various individual sounds in a single sound type, the following condition was always satisfied: in no case does the difference between any two sounds included in a single sound type constitute the only regular phonetic difference between two morphemes. This condition made it necessary, for instance, to exclude the somewhat domal ḍ of ḍǝrṭ 'I circled' from membership in the sound type of the very similar post-dental d of dǝrt 'I built.'

Journal of the American Oriental Society 62, No. 4 (1942), 309–18. Read at the Centennial Meeting of the Society, Boston 1942.

1.1-12. Except as otherwise noted, the vowel sound types listed in these sections occur at the beginning of an utterance (i.e. after the utterance juncture #), at the end of an utterance (i.e. before #), between consonants and next to long vowels (rarely), but not next to short vowels. The long vowels in 1.8-11 do not occur before #.

1.1-9. The vowels in these paragraphs do not occur next to the emphatic consonants[1] ṭ, ḍ, ṣ, ẓ, ṛ, q, or next to any consonant which is next to ṭ, ḍ, or ṣ. They occur next to every other consonant, except as otherwise noted.

1.1. i and u occur also before š; i does not occur in Vy_C[2], nor u in Vw_C; i also occurs in CC_a#. Before # they occur only if C precedes them, i.e. in C_#, and after # they occur only as rare free variants of i̯, u̯ before C (i.e. in #_C). u does not occur before d, n, ḥ, ʿ. Semi-vocalic i̯, u̯ occur only in #_C, V_#, and V·_C/#: kursi 'chair', žibu ' give! (pl.)', siði̯r 'go', flu̯š 'money', mədhia 'busy (f.)', u̯ža and uža 'and he came', i̯ži and iži 'he comes', i̯mšiu̯ 'he goes', žæ·u̯ 'they came', sæ·i̯r 'going'.

1.2. An open ɔ occurs only before ṛ, ḥ, ʿ, ă: dfɔṛ 'finger nail', rɔḥ 'go', irɔ̈aḥ 'he will go'.

1.3. A centered o occurs only before d or n: gǔʿod 'have a seat!'.

1.4. æ occurs in the environments stated above, except before w or #; it is rare next to r or before a cluster of two different consonants: æmmən 'believer'.

1.5. A very open æ, or fronted a, occurs only before #: bra 'needle', bka 'he cried'.

1.6. A back a occurs only before w: daw 'light'.

1.7. A rather low centered ʌ occurs next to r and before clusters of two different consonants and C#; in some of these clusters it varies freely with a: rʌmla 'sand', kbʌr 'taller'.

1.8. i· and u· vary freely with iy and uw respectively; i· does not occur after V or VC, or next to γ, ḥ, and neither occurs before s, x, ʿ, ḥ: msæ·fri·n 'traveling (pl.)', ddiyti 'I took', yu·m and yuwm 'day'.

1.9. Close æ·, approaching e·, varies with open æ·, the latter occurring most frequently next to k, g, x, γ, ḥ, ʿ: dæ·u̯ 'they took', snæ·n 'teeth', bræ·wæ·t 'needles', bkæ·t 'she cried'.

1.10-3. Except as otherwise noted, vowel sound types listed in these paragraphs occur only next to ṭ, ḍ, ṣ, ẓ, ṛ, q, or next to a consonant which is next to ṭ, ḍ, or ṣ.

1.10. Close e· is a rare variant of ey, ɪy, and occurs also next to γ, ḥ: he·rək 'your grace'. bγeyti 'you want', rẓɪyna 'resin'.

1.11. o· (varying with ow) and low back a· occur also in a few (foreign) forms in environments not containing any of the emphatic consonants listed above; o· does not occur directly before ṭ, ḍ, ṣ, q, s, x (though it occurs after these): ḍo·ṛ 'turn!', ṣowf 'wool', bqa·t 'she remained', ṣna·n 'stench', ga·ṭ 'pliers', garsown 'servant', la·nba 'lamp', bla·nša 'fiatiron'.

1.12. o, back a, and close e varying with i; o occurs also before ă: oṣʎl 'he arrived', qobba 'steeple', bṛa 'letter', bqa 'he remained', ṭeḥan 'gall bladder', soăq 'market'.

1.13. ʎ often varies with ə, and occurs only in positions in which ə occurs, next to the emphatics listed above (except ṛ): ṭlʎb 'he begged', wʎqt 'time'. (All vowels marked ˘ are very short.)

1.14. The central shwa ə occurs only in C_CC/#, if the first C after ə is not w, ', ḥ, or h; it does not occur next to ṭ, ḍ, ṣ, q, or next to a consonant adjoining ṭ, ḍ, ṣ; a more exact statement of the positions in which it occurs will be given in 3.2: ktəb 'he wrote', ktəbt 'I wrote', kətbət 'she wrote', xədma 'work', qsəm 'he divided', γadyən 'are about to', žayən 'are coming'.

1.15. ŭ occurs in the position of ə before w, q, k, g, and varies with ə after w; ŏ varies with ŭ before q [3]: sŭwwəl 'he asked', sŭqti 'be quiet (f.)', tŭqlæ·t 'fried food', wŭldət and wəldət 'she bore', nŏqra 'silver'. ŭ also occurs in C_qV, where ə would not occur: sŭqʷor 'sugar'.

1.16. ă occurs in the position of ə next to ' and before ḥ; it occurs in #'_C, and in o/ə_ṭ/ḍ/ṣ/q: 'ămlət 'she worked', ṣbăḥ 'morning', 'ărež 'cripple', 'ăməlt 'I worked', soăq 'market'.

1.17. ə occurs in i/o/u_s/x/r/ḥ: fluəs 'money', riəḥ 'wind', məsloəx 'castrated'.

1.18-34. Except as otherwise noted, all consonant sound types listed in these paragraphs occur before and after #, before and after most consonants including themselves, and before and after any vowel except for the limitations recorded in 1.1-17. E.g. ṭ occurs next to a· but not next to æ·; l occurs next to the vowels in 1.10-3 if ṭ, ḍ, or ṣ is next to the vowel or next to a consonant adjoining the vowel, it occurs before fronted a if # follows the a, and so on for the conditions stated in the other paragraphs above.

1.18-25. Of the consonants in these paragraphs, no member of one of the following pairs occurs next to the other member: td, kg, sz, šž; and no one of t, d, k, g, s, z, š, ž occurs next to any one of ṭ, ḍ, q, ṣ.

1.18. Slightly aspirated k and post-dental t occur only before vowels; k does not occur before u: kæ·s 'glass', tæ·ni 'second'.

1.19. Unaspirated k, t (which are released in certain positions, § 1.35) occur before consonants and #: mʌrtək 'your wife', mæ·t 'he died'.

1.20. A post-dental affricate approaching tˢ, but distinct from the succession of Moroccan t and s, varies freely with t after æ.[4]

1.21. kʷ, gʷ, qʷ, all with labialized release, occur before u, o: sŭqʷor 'sugar'.

1.22. g, q do not occur before u, o; in some morphemes g and q vary freely, while other morphemes have only g or only q[5]: bgʌr and bqʌr 'cow', gləs 'he sat', qraʿ 'ringworm', ɣrʌq 'it sank', ɣrəg 'he parched'.

1.23. s, z, and post-alveolar š, ž: sbæʿ 'lion', nsi·bu 'father in law', zrəb 'hurry', šʌržəm 'window', šəmăʿ 'candle', žəmăʿ 'Friday'.

1.24. Slightly affricate ȝ and ǯ occur as free variants of z, ž, especially after post-dental consonants: sfənǯ 'oil doughnut'.

1.25. Post-dental d, domal unaspirated ṭ, ḍ, ṣ[6]: dæ·r 'he built', ḍa·ṛ 'house', dərt 'I built', ḍəṛt 'I circled', ka·ɣəṭ 'paper', ṣbʌ̆ʿ 'finger', nṣɪybu 'I find him'.

1.26. A domal emphatic ẓ seems to occur in ẓɪyna 'dozen' (cp. zi·na 'beautiful'), in roẓẓa 'turban', and in a few other morphemes.

1.27. b[7], f, m, l, x and ɣ (voiceless and voiced palato-velar spirants), ʿ and ḥ (voiced and voiceless pharyngal spirants), and h occur without any restrictions which can be stated now, except that ʿ does not occur in #_C: bɣa 'he wants', firma 'farm', lu·n 'color', təxzənt 'I hide', ṣbʌ̆ʿ 'finger', ḥe·rək 'your grace', hæ·da 'this'.

1.28. A voiced bilabial spirant β varies freely with the stop b before and especially between vowels: kŭβæ·r 'taller ones', ṣβăḥ 'morning'.

1.29. A back ḷ occurs in ḷḷah 'Allah', cp. la 'no' with fronted a.

1.30. The alveolar tongue-tip trill r does not occur in morphemes containing ṭ, ḍ, ṣ, ẓ (?), or q: bra 'needle' with fronted a.

1.31. A domal tongue-tip trill ṛ occurs in morphemes containing ṭ, ḍ, ṣ, ẓ (?), or q, and in a few other words (often of foreign origin): ḍhəṛ 'back', bṛa 'letter' (with back a), gaṛṛo 'cigarette'.

1.32. n does not occur before k, g, or q: bənt 'daughter', ktəbna 'we wrote'. Vocalic ṇ varies with nə in #_CC: ṇtkəlləm and less frequently nətkəlləm 'I converse'.

1.33. ŋ occurs only before k, g, q: zʌ̆ŋqa 'street.'

1.34. w and y occur only before or after short vowels (including #_əCC and V·_V); w occurs also in Vy_C/#, Vw_C, and y in Vy_C: yæmmən 'he believes', yəbyi 'he wants', wiržaʿu 'and they will return', wəldət 'she bore', nă·ʿṭæyw 'we will give', nă·ʿṭæywh 'we will give it', dæ·wi 'speaking', lwŭžh 'the face', ɣadya 'f. is about to', ɣadyən 'are about to', sŭwwəl 'he asked'.

1.35. Stops are released before #, and before other stops when a consonant precedes them; other consonants are also released, e.g. m before n in certain positions, but the complete statement is not available at this writing (indicating release by ' in this paragraph): ikət'bu 'they write', kət'bət' 'she writes', æ mm'nu 'believers.' The release is phonetically distinct from ə, as in æmmənt 'I believed'.

1.36. Four levels of stress may be distinguished, which will be marked in this paragraph and in 2.22 as follows: zero (no mark), light ˈ, medium ˆ,

heavy ': ʿ*ă*r*ə́*ž 'crippled', m*ʌ*́rtək 'your wife', f*ə́*ttəšt 'I looked', msæ̀·fri^·n 'traveling'.

1.37. The tones which are heard in utterances are most easily described in terms of the length of the whole utterance rather than in terms of each vowel in the utterance. Three tone successions are most frequently heard. In all three types, the zero and light stressed vowels are relatively low in pitch. In the first type, one or several medium or heavy stressed vowels at the end of the utterance are low, the stressed [8] vowel preceding them is high, and all the preceding stressed vowels are midway between high and low. The tone of the stressed vowels thus begins on mid, rises to high on one stressed vowel, and falls to low on those that follow it (in this section stress is not marked, and every medium and heavy stressed vowel is marked with tone: ' for high, ⁻ for mid, ' for low): æ̀·na ží̯yt hæ̀·d ssβ*ǎ*ḥ 'I came this morning'; æ̀·na mā bγéyt ši hæ̀·d lḥæ̀·ža 'I don't need this thing'.

In the second type, the last stressed vowel is high, and all preceding ones are mid. ə̄nta štīh yǽ·ms 'Did you see him yesterday?'; ə̄nta štīh yǣ·ms hə*n*á 'Did you see him here yesterday?'.

In the third type, the first and last stressed vowels in the utterance are high, the others mid: fí·l lmrā dyǽ·lək 'Where is your wife?'; ímta ží̯yt llǽ·hn 'When did you come here?'.

2.0. These sound types may be grouped into phonemes in the usual way by applying the following three conditions: (a) No two sound types included in one phoneme ever occur in the same environment, unless they vary freely (i.e. in repetitions of a single morpheme) in that environment; (b) No single sound type is to be represented by a succession of more than one phonemic symbol (see § 3.0); (c) The resultant phonemic writing must be bi-uniquely correlated with speech, i.e. any utterance can be written phonemically in only one way, and any sequence of phonemes can be pronounced in only one linguistically distinct way.

2.1. If no consonantal sound type listed in **1.10-3** is included in a single phoneme with any one of the consonants excluded from that list, then i and close e have phonemically different (complementary) environments, and may be grouped into one phoneme /i/.[9] We then write kursi, ṭiḥan for the pronuncations recorded in 1.1, 12. See 2.20 for the relation of y to /i/.

2.2. u, ɔ, centered o, o are analogously included in one phoneme /u/. We write kursi, ruḥ, gŭʿud, uṣʌl (1.1, 2, 3, 12). See 2.20 for the relation of w to /u/. (We may also include in /u/ the short ŭ before CV· described in note 3.)

2.3. æ, fronted a, ɑ, ʌ, back ə are included in the phoneme /a/. We write ammən, bra, daw, ramla, bṛa (1.4, 5, 6, 7, 12).

2.4. i·, e·, and the sequences of sound types iy, ey, ɪy may be included in one phoneme /i·/. In doing this, we are counting a succession of two sound types as representing one phoneme. While this does not conflict with condition (b) of 2.0, it may require justification. The successions ey, iy, ɪy do not contrast with either of the single sound types i·, e·, included in this section, or with each other: iy varies freely with i· and is complementary in environment to e·, ey, and so on. This applies to all cases of iy. Furthermore, the phoneme /i·/ is written with two symbols, and it will be seen in 3.1 that the second symbol can be considered a distinct phoneme, representing the second members of these sequences. In view of this, we may also include in /i·/ the sequence yə after V or VC (but not elsewhere), since the other sound types included in /i·/ do not occur in this position. Analogously, we may include the sequence iš. We now write ddi·ti, bγi·ti, žai·n, ri·ḥ (1.1, 8, 10, 14, 17).

2.5. u·, uw, o·, ow are included in /u·/. Here we may include the sequences uš, oš, oă, əă. We write yu·m, ṣu·f, flu·s, məṣlu·x, su·q, iru·ḥ (1.1, 2, 8, 11, 16, 17).

2.6. æ· and close æ· are included in /æ·/: dæ·u (1.9).

2.7. a· must be put by itself into a phoneme /a·/ even though it is mostly complementary to æ·, because there are a few words in which it is not associated with emphatic consonants: cp. la·nba with flæ·n 'so-and-so', læ·bəs 'dressing' (1.11).

2.8. ə (except after Vy, VCy; see 2.4), ǎ, ŭ, ŏ may be included in /ə/. Whereas ă after V was included as part of /u·/ (2.5), ă next to ʿ and before ḥ, in the position of ə, may be included in /ə/. We write ṭləb, ktəb, səwwəl, nəqra, ʿəmlət, sβəḥ (1.13, 14, 15, 16).

2.9. Since #ʿCV never occurs, whereas #ʿăCV does, ă in #ʿ_CV may be considered phonemically zero, or the sequence ʿă in #_CV may be included in /ʿ/ phoneme. We write ʿməlt, ʿrəž (1.16); cp. the writing ʿəmlət in 2.8 where the ă was included in /ə/ before CC. Similarly, ŭ in C_qV, where it is not in the position of ə, is phonemically zero. We write sqʷur (1.15).

2.10. Aspirated and unaspirated t and the tˢ affricate are included in /t/: tæ·ni, mæ·t (1.18, 19, 20).

2.11. Aspirated and unaspirated k and kʷ are included in /k/: kæ·s, martək (1.18, 19, 21).

2.12. g and gʷ are included in /g/, q and qʷ in /q/: qraʿ, squr (1.21, 22). Since some morphemes are regularly distinguished by the difference between g and q, it is a phonemic difference; morphemes in which the two sounds vary freely must be considered to have two phonemic forms, e.g. bgar and bqar. The sequence ŭq in C_V may be included in /q/ (2.9).

2.13. s, š, d, ḍ, ṭ, ṣ, probably ẓ, f, m, l, x, γ, ḥ, h each constitutes a phoneme by itself, written with the same letter: /s/, etc. (1.23, 25, 26, 27).

2.14. z and ʒ are included in /z/, ž and ǯ in /ž/ (1.23, 24). The initial stop in ʒ and ǯ is very short, so that these sound types are distinct from the initial sequences of dzəwwəž 'you marry', džæ·ž 'chicken'.

2.15. b and β are included in /b/. We write ṣbəḥ (1.27, 28).

2.16. ʿ and ʿă are included in /ʿ/ (1.27, 2.9).

2.17. n, ṇ, and ŋ are included in /n/: bənt, zənqa (1.32, 33).

2.18. ḷ should probably be considered a separate phoneme, for even though a perfect pair to ḷḷah may not be found, it would be rather involved to say that "ḷ is the variant of /l/ before ah #" (1.29).

2.19. r and ṛ must be considered phonemically distinct /r/, /ṛ/, though they are largely complementary, since ṛ occurs in some morphemes which contain no other emphatic consonant: bra (with fronted a), bṛa (with back a) (1.30, 31).

2.20. w and y can be included in the /u/ and /i/ phonemes respectively, for they never occur in the same environment as the sound types included in those phonemes (1.1, 34). Some occurrences of w and y have already been included in /u·/, /i·/: iy, ey, ɪy, yə in /i·/, uw, ow in /u·/ (2.4, 5). We now write nə'ṭaiu, nə'ṭaiuh, luəžh, ɣadia, səuuəl (1.34), while the morphemes with other variants of /i, u, i·, u·/ remain as they are written in 2.1, 2, 4, 5. In no case does this lead us to write contrasting sound sequences with an identical sequence of phonemes: e.g. [yuwm] is written /iu·m/, while [sŭwwəl] is written /səuuəl/. On the contrary, this writing gives us a much simpler statement of the distribution of the sound types i, u, y, w, etc. We now can say that the positional variants of these two phonemes are of the following types: consonantal in V_, _V (next to short vowels, on either side) and in #_CC, semi-vocalic in -/#_C[10], V_#, V·_C/#, and vocalic in C_C/# (and /i/ in CC_a#). When there is a sequence of /i/ and /u/ we consider whether each is a consonant or vowel, starting from the last. Thus in /dua/ 'he talked' the /u/ is next to a vowel and hence itself consonantal: [dwa]. In /duua/ 'medicine' one might ask if the first /u/ is in C_C (which would make it [u]) or in C_V (which would make it [w]); but we proceed from the simpler case of the second /u/ which precedes a vowel and is therefore itself consonantal; this puts the first /u/ between two consonants, thus making it a vowel: the sounds are [duwa].

It will be seen that this writing simplifies certain cases of morphemes which appeared to have two phonemic forms. The morpheme u- 'and', as in ušra 'and buying', is [w-] before vowels, as in [wišri] 'and he buys'. The morpheme-root for 'dress' is lbs, for 'go' is syr, and for progressive action is æ· (or a·) after the first C of the root: thus 'dressing' is læ·bəs, but 'going' is sæ·ir. When i and y are both included in one phoneme /i/, the root for 'go' becomes sir, and the formation of sæ·ir becomes, like læ·bs[11], a simple ordered sum of root plus the progressive-action morpheme.

2.21. As far as can be seen at present, the release of particular consonants described in 1.35 is not a phonemic feature, but is free in some positions in the word (minimum utterance) and conditioned (always present or absent) in others.

2.22. It appears that stress is automatically placed within each minimum utterance, and that its position can be described in terms of the arrangement within the utterance of the phonemes which have been set up above. In any free morpheme or sequence of free and following bound morphemes, medium stress occurs on the last V·, and heavy stress on the first short V if there are no V· in the word; all other V· in the utterance have light stress, and all other V zero stress: see the examples in 1.36 (the ă of ʿărəž is not phonemically a V, see 2.9). This does not apply to bound morphemes preceding free morphemes in a minimum utterance; these prefixes have zero stress in most positions, and it will be shown in 3.4 that it is possible to establish a juncture between these prefixes and the following free forms, so that one can always know which is the first V of the free form: i-kətbu 'they write', nə-tkəlləm 'I converse', nə-tkəllmu 'we converse'. In utterances which are composed of several minimum utterances (i.e. of several utterances – words – each of which occasionally occurs by itself), each of the minimum utterances is stressed in accordance with the above statements.[12]

2.23. The first and second tone successions described in 1.37 contrast phonemically, as in hūua žá yæ̀·ms 'He came yesterday' and hūua žā yæ̀·ms 'Did he come yesterday?' The second tone succession may be marked by the contour phoneme /ʔ/ placed immediately after the word containing ': huua ža yæ·ms? The first one, however, is more difficult to determine, because the number of words with ' which follow the ' differs in various utterances. In the morphological analysis of the language it is possible to show that utterances having this first tone succession are divisible into three parts, the second of which contains the ' while the third has low tones throughout, no matter how many words it contains. When that division is exactly stated, it is possible to write a phrase juncture after the word containing the high tone. We can then say that all vowels after this phrase juncture are low, so that there is no longer any ambiguity about how many low vowels there are after the high tone. It is now possible to consider this tone succession as a fixed contour, ' immediately before the phrase juncture and ' after it (with ˉ on all stressed vowels before the '), and to write one phonemic mark /./ after the utterance, instead of indicating the tones on each stressed vowel.

The third tone succession contrasts with neither of the preceding ones, since the utterances in which it occurs always begin with a morpheme of the interrogative group; these morphemes never occur at the beginning of

utterances having the other tone contours. While it is possible to consider
this third tone succession a positional variant of either /./ or /?/, we will
include it in the latter because it is more similar to /?/ than to /./ both in form
and in meaning.

2.24. If we put all the above results together, we find we have 34 linear
phonemes: Vowels: /i, u, a, ə, i·, u·, æ·, a·/; Consonants: /f, b, t, d, ṭ, ḍ,
k, g, q, s, z, š, ž, ṣ, ẓ, x, γ, ḥ, ʿ, h, l, ḷ, r, ṛ, m, n/. In addition we have two
tone contours /./ and /?/, and three junctures which were not explicitly
stated but which are necessary for the elimination of phonemic stress and
for the exact statement of the tone contours: word boundary /#/, juncture
following prefix /-/, juncture following phrase /,/.

Some of these phonemes have more limited distribution than others. /ə/
occurs only before CC or C#; /æ·/ never occurs in the environment
described in **1.10-3** and /a·/ hardly ever except in that environment, and much
the same can be said for /r/ and /ṛ/; /ẓ/ and /ḷ/ are very rare. The inclusion
of w in /u/ may lead one to ask if any other consonants can be phonemically
identified with particular vowels, but this proves to be impossible, for, as a
result of the inclusion of w in /u/, /a/ now occurs next to vowels as well as
consonants; e.g. /a/ and any consonant now contrast, in that each can occur
in C_V: dau 'light', štu 'I saw him'.

3.0. It is possible to simplify the phonemic system by dropping the second
condition of 2.0. The representation of a single sound by a combination of
phonemic symbols is common today in regard to stress and tone features.
For a high-pitched or loud [a] is but one sound, and if we separate off the
tone features for inclusion into tone phonemes, we might also separate off the
feature of front or back articulation of the [a] and include that in a new
phoneme, too. In the present phonemic analysis, there would be no gain if
we separate off some feature which is present in only one or two phonemes,
say the nasal feature of m and n, for that would add a nasalization phoneme
while eliminating only one or two of our present phonemes. When tones are
separated off from each vowel sound one of two advantages is always in
view: Either there are two or three tone features each of which is common to
all vowels, so that instead of writing each vowel sound as one out of, say,
18 vowel phonemes, we write it as a combination of one vowel phoneme (out
of 6) and one tone phoneme (out of 3). Or else it is possible to show that
successions of tone or stress features show a certain regularity which the
vowel qualities do not show, e.g. that no matter what the quality of the
vowels, the last long one in a word is always loudest. Such a situation can
best be described by considering the loudness of each vowel as a separate
feature and saying that there is a word contour consisting of loud stress on

the last vowel. The following sections will indicate a few cases where we may gain either of these two advantages.

3.1. One question open to us is whether to consider the long vowels as single phonemes (writing, say, U for long u), or sequences of short vowel plus length phoneme (writing u·), or sequences of short vowels (writing uu). Writing them as new single phonemes is wasteful, since the length feature is common to several vowels, and can be considered a linear phoneme, occupying a definite time in the flow of speech. Since we have to distinguish long u from long w (which is written /u/), one will have to be written /uu/ and the other /u·/.[13] It is more convenient to use · for the second part of long vowels rather than of long consonants (including consonantal values of /u, i/), because long vowels have a limited distribution; e.g. they never occur before #, so that we can say that · never occurs next to #. Furthermore, the second part of long vowels often differs considerably from the first part, and these phonetic values can now be considered the variants of /·/. We would now replace 2.4–7 by the following statement: The second part of a long i, e, u, o, æ, or a, also y after i, e, or ɪ before C, and w after u or o before C, and ă after o or ɔ, and ŏ after o, u, or i, and ə after Vy or VCy are all included in the phoneme /·/, which occurs only after the phonemes /i, u, a, æ/. Since the short /i/ before /·/ must now include all the first halves of the previous single phoneme /i·/, we must add to 2.1, as a variant of /i/, the sound type y in V_ə, VC_ə (see end of 2.4).

The question of how to write long consonants, e.g. T, t·, or tt for a long t, is analogous. Either t· or tt would be sufficient, without introducing any new phonemes. If we write /·/ for the second half of long consonants it will simplify the statement of the occurrence of ə[14] and of the 'intensive' verb forms[15]; the only repeated phonemes would then be /uu/ and /ii/, which must be distinct from /u·, i·/. If we repeat the letter for long consonants, we would have a simpler distribution of /·/, the consonantal /uu/ and /ii/ would become like all the consonants in their double writing, we would have a morphological parallel between 3-consonant 'intensives' like kllm 'to speak' and 4-consonant roots like fršx 'to break', and we would have a simpler description of the prefix l- 'the'.[16] It seems preferable, therefore, to consider long consonants as repetitions of the consonant: mra 'wife', mrra 'itch'.

3.2. Another type of advantage may be gained from considering /ə/. That /ə/ is phonemically distinct from other vowels or zero, is seen in bərd 'wind, cold' as against brəd 'it grew cold', sæ·fərt 'I traveled' as against sæ·frət 'she traveled', kbər 'it grew' compared with kbar 'tall, large', xədma 'work' compared with firma 'farm'. The phoneme occurs, however, in very limited positions: only in C_C#, C_CC#, or C_CCV (or in C_CC plus ha 'her' or ni 'me'). What is more, if we consider semi-vocalic m and vocalic n, l before

CCV as free variants of mə, nə, lə in that position, we can say the converse: assuming that /ə/ is not written, the sounds it represents will always occur after the first of three C preceding V (or ha or ni) and after the first of either 2 or 3 C preceding #. Before V, therefore, or in 2-consonant words, /ə/ is automatic. Contrasting positions occur only in CCC#: bərd, brəd, sæ·fərt, sæ·frət. It is sufficient to say that /ə/ is phonemic, and need be written, only if it occurs in the position of the dash in C_CC#. In addition to this unique phonemic position, the sounds included in /ə/ will always occur automatically in C_CCV and CC_C# (counting a repeated consonant as one C, and each occurrence of ə as a V[17]). We write /sfənž/ 'oil doughnut', /bərd/ 'wind' but /brd/ 'cold', /nəfs/ 'self', /bənt/ 'daughter', but /žbl/ 'hill' pronounced [žbəl], /lγlm/ 'the sheep' for [ləγləm], /smk/ 'you name' for [smək], /msæ·fr/ 'traveling' for [msæ·fər], /ntkllm/ 'I converse' for [ṇtkəlləm], /xdma/ 'work' for [xədma], and /ktəbt/ 'I wrote' but /ktbt/ 'she wrote' for [kətbət], /ktb/ 'he wrote' for [ktəb], /nktb/ 'I write' for [nəktəb], /nktbu/ 'we write' for [nkətbu].

Objection may be raised against considering a particular sound to be phonemic in one position and non-phonemic elsewhere. But the procedure of putting a particular sound in a particular environment into one phoneme and the same sound (as far as we can tell) in another environment into another phoneme has been used elsewhere in this analysis: e.g. ŏ after i was included in /i·/, but after u or o in /u·/ (2.4, 5); ă after V was included in /u·/, when in #ʿ_C it was included in /ʿ/ or considered automatic, and in other positions it was included in /ə/. The advantage of eliminating /ə/ where possible is that its occurrence in speech is so regular that no note need be taken of it except in the one position mentioned.

Instead of the statement given above, ə could have been considered automatic in C_CC before either V or #, and phonemic only when it occurred in _C#; in that case some of the writings above would have to be changed. The first statement is to be preferred because it leaves ə phonemic in fewer morphemes (perhaps only in certain nouns and before the verbal suffix t 'I did'). When the morphological structure is completely worked out, it may be possible to set up a juncture before all suffixes; this would permit a somewhat simpler statement of the occurrence of ə, and would take care of the suffixes ha and ni mentioned above.

The elimination of most /ə/ puts to the test the inclusion of w in /u/, for now w will occur next to consonants in new positions[18]: [yuwm] 'day' is written /iu·m/ (/u/ next to /·/ is always vocalic, /i/ next to V is consonantal); [sŭwwəl] 'he asked' is written /suul/ (/u/ next to V is consonantal, and in general any repeated phoneme is consonantal); [oṣχl] 'he arrived' is written /uṣl/ (the semi-vocalic value of the o variant is almost vocalic); [wχṣlət] 'she arrived' is written /uṣlt/ (consonantal or semi-vocalic w in #_CC); [l-ṳŭžh] 'the face' is /l-užh/; [l-užu·ha] 'the faces' is /l-užu·ha/.

3.3. The emphatic consonants also present an opportunity for non-unique analyses. Instead of considering t, ṭ, etc., as distinct phonemes, and calling u, o, etc., variants of a single phoneme, we might have considered u and o, for example, distinct phonemes and called ṭ the variant of /t/ next to /o/. This would certainly have been possible in the case of ḷ and ẓ, which occur only next to vowels. Several of the emphatic consonants, however, occur in positions where they are not associated with vowels, so that there is no back vowel which can be said to determine them as emphatic variants of non-emphatic phonemes: e.g. kli·t 'I ate', qli·t 'I fried' (see **1.10-3**), qsəm 'he divided'. We would therefore be left with a few distinct emphatic phonemes as well as two sets of vowel phonemes (one set occurring next to emphatic phonemes or emphatic variants of other phonemes, as well as in a few words like la·nba). A third possible analysis would be to separate off the feature of back position from the consonants (and from the few cases of [a·] not next to emphatics), and consider it a distinct phoneme, thus writing these sound types with a combination of two phonemic marks.

After this paper was written, Mr. Charles Ferguson, who took up the informant work with Mr. and Mrs. Larbi, suggested that the most convenient analysis would be to have a separate phoneme /ʾ/ for back position, and use it both for the so-called emphatic consonants and for the distinction between a· and æ·. This turns out to be distinctly superior, because the feature of back position serves as a prosodic feature, affecting not one phoneme but a sequence of them. The only phonemes for which /ʾ/ indicates a back position are /t, d, s, z, k, l, r, i, u, a/; other phonemes occurring within the sequence (scope) affected by /ʾ/ do not have different variants in this position. The scope of /ʾ/ is: preceding consonants up to a vowel (including automatic ə) or juncture; /r/ anywhere within the word; vowel preceding /ʾ/ or next (except for /k, r/ also next but one C) to any consonant affected by /ʾ/. We now substitute /ʾ/ for the list of emphatics in **1.10-3**, and add /ʾ/ as a phoneme, eliminating /ṭ, ḍ, ṣ, ẓ, q, ḷ, ṛ, æ·/ (æ· becomes a variant of /a·/, the sound [a·] now occurring only in the environment of /ʾ/). And we write: /da·r/ for [dæ·r] 'he built' but /dʾa·r, ddʾa·r/ for [ḍa·ṛ, ḍḍa·ṛ] 'house, the house', /ma·t/ for [mæ·t] 'he died' but /ga·tʾ/ for [ga·ṭ] 'pliers', /sbaʿ/ for [sbæʿ] 'lion' but /sʾbʿ/ for [ṣbx̌ʿ] 'finger', /zi·na/ for [zɪyna] 'dozen', /kubba/ 'bundle' but /kʾubba/ for [qobba] 'steeple', /la/ 'no' (with fronted a) but /llʾah/ for [ḷḷah] 'Allah' (with back a) and /bla··ʾnša/ for [bla·nša] 'flatiron' (note that the /ʾ/ here affects no consonants, by its post-vocalic position), /bra/ 'needle' but /dʾhur/ for [ḍhọṛ] 'back' and /brʾa/ for [bṛa] 'letter' and /garrʾu/ for [gaṛṛo] 'cigarette',

/la·bs/ for [læ·bəs] 'dressing' but /la·'nba/ for [la·nba] 'lamp' and /ba·'nka/ for [ba·nka] 'bank'.

3.4. All junctures should formally be considered here, for they could not be recognized by the terms of the second condition of 2.0. The junctures are not in themselves heard as sounds, and when we write aspirated k before V as /k/ but unaspirated k before V as /k#/ we are using a sequence of two phonemic marks for the single sound type of unaspirated k.

We have to count as phonemic those junctures which are necessarily mentioned as environments of sound types which we consider automatic or include as positional variants of phonemes. Such junctures have occurred in two somewhat different connections. In the first case, there were certain sound types which did not vary freely with other sounds and which we were able to include in existing phonemes only by stating that they occurred next to a juncture and were thereby complementary to other sound types in the phoneme. Thus we were able to include unaspirated t, k in /t, k/ only by pointing out that these sounds occurred at the end of minimum utterances, whereas the other sound types included in /t, k/ do not occur there. This is permissible phonemic writing, for when we hear a released but unaspirated k we know that it is written phonemically /k#/ and when we see /k#/ we know it indicates the unaspirated k sound. Similarly, it is only because we recognize a morpheme juncture after l 'the' that the u in [l-u̯ŭžh] 'the face' does not contrast with the u in [kursi] 'chair'; we write /l-užh, kursi/ and pronounce the first /u/ as a semi-vowel (with following automatic ə) because it follows a juncture, and the second /u/ as a vowel because it is between consonants. Other sound types whose complementary environment always includes # are: the fronted a (1.4), ʿă (1.27, 2.9), vocalic ṇ (1.32).

In the second case, we have certain features of sound which do not occur regularly in relation to a long flow of speech, but which can be shown to occur regularly in small segments of the flow of speech. Thus the succession of the four types of stress described in 1.36 shows no regularity in a long stretch of talking; but if we divide the stretch into minimum utterances, with # between each one, we find that within each segment from # to # (more exactly from - to #) the various stresses occur with a regularity described in 2.22. We therefore consider the occurrence of each stress automatically determined by the position of /#/, V, and /·/, and treat it as a positional variant of the combination of these phonemes. This is permissible, for when we hear a long vowel with medium stress, we know that the juncture /#/ follows the consonant after that vowel (long vowels, i.e. /·/, never occur before # or CC#; therefore, if the medium stressed vowel is the last before #, there is always one C between the vowel and #). And when we see /i·n#/, we know it indicates medium stress on the long vowel.

Similarly, in order to find regularity in the tone successions, we had to fix certain points as ending utterances within the flow of speech. Then we could say that all vowels preceding /./ are low up to the juncture /,/, and the stressed vowel preceding /,/ is high, and all preceding stressed vowels up to the next /./ (or /?/) are mid. Other features of sound whose position is regular within each segment, when once speech is divided into segments, are: the automatic ə; consonant release (2.21); and the feature of back position, which does not occur in all words (and must therefore be marked /'/ when it does occur), but which affects phonemes only within a morpheme, never across word juncture. Thus /'/ indicates back position of /r/ in /d'hur/ 'back' but not in /na·d'#u-rkb/ 'he rose and rode'.

The advantage of these junctures is that in addition to helping to set up successive (linear) and simultaneous (contour) phonemes, they also divide the flow of speech into morphologically distinct segments: morphemes, words, and the like. The junctures recognized here are:

/-/ between prefixes and stems (stems being the smallest utterances that ever occur by themselves); used for stress, /'/, /u, i/.

/#/, usually written as a blank space, between words; used for /u, i, a, ə, t, k, ʻ, n, '/, release, stress. Given a flow of speech, words (as referred to here) are the smallest utterances which sometimes occur by themselves and into which the whole speech can be divided with no bound forms left over; if the utterance includes a prefix followed by a stem, both must be counted into one word, since if the stem were counted as a separate word the prefix, being a bound form which never occurs by itself, would be left over.

/,/ after the verb, in a sentence ending in /./; used for tone contours.

/./ after a sentence (utterance) having the first tone contour (2.23).

/?/ after a sentence having the second or third tone contours (2.23).

The segments of various length (word, etc.) are not defined by the morphological terms used in this section, but by the points in which the junctures are placed, and the place of the junctures is in turn determined by the sound types in whose environment junctures are included.

4.1. The phonemes of this dialect are:

Linear phonemes: /f, t, k, b, d, g, s, š, x, ḥ, h, z, ž, γ, ʻ, l, r, m, n/ occurring next to any phoneme (including non-linear ones and themselves) except before /·/.

/i, u/ occurring next to any phoneme (including themselves and /·/).

/a/ occurring next to any phoneme except itself and /ə/.

/ʾ/ occurring next to any phoneme except itself and except after non-linear phonemes.

/·/ occurring only after /i, u, a/ and before any phoneme except itself, /ə/, and the non-linear phonemes.

/ə/ occurring only in C_CC#.

Non-linear phonemes (junctures and contours): /-/, /#/, /,/, /?/, /./, in increasing order of size of segment, occurring next to any phoneme except /·, ə/ and except before /ʾ/; none of these occurs next to itself or to the others, except that /,/, /?/, /./ always occur at a point where /#/ occurs.

It will be noticed that few of these phonemes have serious limitations of occurrence. It is an aim of phonemic analysis to have as few phonemes as possible, each with greatest freedom of occurrence, all sequences of phonemes constituting different morphemes. Thus, before the emphatic consonants and /æ·/ were replaced by /ʾ/, there were considerable limitations upon their occurrence. No emphatic consonant, for instance, occurred after any non-emphatic consonant which had an emphatic counterpart (1.18-25): e.g. tṭ, sṭ did not occur, but ṣt, bṭ, did. Introduction of /ʾ/ removed the need for this remark; in describing the phonetic value of /ʾ/ it is merely stated that /ʾ/ indicates back position of /t, s/ but not of /b/ and that its scope is the two consonants preceding it: then /ttʾ, stʾ, btʾ/ indicate ṭṭ, ṣṭ, bṭ.[19]

4.2. The phonemic sequences which make up words can be easily constructed from the distributional statements. It will be noted that some words begin or end with double consonants, but never end in long vowels: /tlffətt/ for [tləffətt] 'I turned', /tlfft/ for [tləffət] 'he turned', /tlfftt/ for [tləfftət] 'she turned', /ttlfft/ for [ttləffət] 'you will turn'. Many words contain only consonants and automatic ə. The fact that automatic ə does not enter between two like consonants, and it is often phonetically zero (or vocalization of the consonant) after m, n, l, yields sequences of 3 or more consonants phonetically, as above and in /mtʿa·lma/ 'servant girl'. Otherwise, phonetic clusters of consonants usually consist of two. Relatively few words have short vowels, except before #.

NOTES

* A few months after this paper was read, Mr. Charles Ferguson took over the work in this language, and I am glad to thank him here for new examples and valuable suggestions which he has since given to me.

[1] For lack of a better name, the usual term 'emphatic' will be used here for these consonants. They are pronounced with the blade or back of the tongue further back in the mouth than it is for the corresponding non-emphatic consonants. q is velar and the others domal or pre-palatal. The emphatic stops are all unaspirated.

[2] C represents any consonant, V any vowel, # word boundary; the dash _ indicates the position in which the sound under discussion does or does not occur, according to the preceding statement. Specifically phonemic writing will be placed between slanting bars

/.../; phonetic writing will usually be written with no special marker, but will sometimes be placed in square brackets [...]. A single slanting bar between two symbols means that either symbol can occur in the position of the first one: _VC/# means '_VC or _V#'.

3 Mr. Ferguson notes the possibility of a phonemic /u/ in words such as kŭβæ·r 'taller ones', tŭqæ·l 'heavy ones', ṣŭγa·r 'small ones', compare ṣγi·r 'small', kbʌr 'taller'.

4 This sound was rare with Mrs. Larbi, and never occurred in Mr. Larbi's speech, but is common in other Moroccan dialects.

5 Morphemes which have both forms in Casablanca have g in some Moroccan dialects, q in others. Mrs. Larbi pronounced them with g more often than Mr. Larbi did.

6 Mr. Larbi, who studied in the Koran schools, also has θ and ð as free variants of t and ḍ respectively in words which have these spirants in the school language and in other Moroccan dialects. However, since he pronounces the spirants chiefly when he is trying to speak 'correctly', i.e. in the school pronunciation, it may be judged that these sounds are not distinguished from t, ḍ in his native dialect.

7 Mr. Larbi, who speaks some French, sometimes pronounces p in words which are borrowed from French; more often he says these words with b, as Mrs. Larbi always does.

8 Medium or heavy stressed vowels will be referred to as stressed vowels.

9 This condition applies to all the vowel phonemes, 2.1–8. In general, if sound type a occurs in the environment of c (but not of d) and sound type b occurs in the environment of d (but not of c), the grouping of a and b into one phoneme will hold only if sound types c and d are not grouped together into one phoneme, but enter distinct phonemes.

10 For the juncture /-/, see 3.4.

11 After ə is eliminated, 3.2.

12 In certain cases, which cannot as yet be exactly stated, a word is stressed on its last short vowel when a short unstressed word follows it; this depends on the position of the words in the sentence: tá giltí liya 'you said to me'.

13 This is necessary only after ə is eliminated in 3.2, for until then long w is always distinguished from long u by having ə or some other vowel next to it.

14 See 3.2, especially note 17.

15 These are forms in which the second consonant is lengthened: kləm 'word', kəlləm 'he spoke'. If we wrote kəl·əm, we could say that the morpheme for 'intensity' consists of the phoneme /·/.

16 Before morphemes beginning with certain consonants, this prefix has the form of the first consonant of the morpheme: l–bi·t 'the room', ḍ–ḍa·ṛ 'the house'. If we marked long consonants with /·/, we would have to write ḍ–·a·r, so that these morphemes would begin with /·/ when the prefix 'the' preceded them.

17 Thus in /ntkllmu/ 'we converse' the ə which would precede two consonants before the final vowel would fall between two like consonants, but the two are counted as one (representing phonetically one long consonant): [ṇtkəllmu]. The description of stress in 2.22 applies after the automatic ə is inserted; ə is stressed whenever it is in the position of a stressed short vowel.

18 See note 13.

19 Some partial limitations remain in this analysis. E.g. t occurs next to d in positions where an automatic ə would come between them, but not otherwise (1.18–25).

XI

NAVAHO PHONOLOGY AND HOIJER'S ANALYSIS

0. GENERAL EVALUATION

Linguists who are interested in American Indian languages owe a debt of gratitude to Hoijer for organizing and presenting Sapir's copious Navaho material, with his own additions.[1] The presentation is carefully done, with useful arrangements of the information on allophones, phonemic clusters, and morphophonemics. Considerable attention is paid to the phonetic values of the positional variants, and to individual peculiarities of distribution among the phonemes. On pp. 15–7, for example, Hoijer gives a very neat treatment of the x, h, x^w, h^w phonemes. He lists 10 sets of environments in which various allophones or freely varying pairs of allophones are heard, and then shows by a simple chart that they can all be grouped into the four phonemes mentioned above.[2]

Particularly noteworthy is the great amount of space devoted to morphophonemics (pp. 31–59), a welcome addition to the small list of publications on the subject.

The manner of talking about the evidence is direct and clear. In some places there appears a type of statement which is ultimately deductive in character; and while no brief need be held for one type of treatment rather than another, it is preferable to maintain consistency of form of statement in any one exposition. Thus where Hoijer says: "Since the point of syllabic division for a short-voweled open syllable lies in the following consonant rather than immediately before it, all consonants following such syllables are mechanically lengthened", it might have been more in keeping to write: "Since all consonants following short-voweled open syllables are mechanically lengthened, we shall say that the point of syllabic division for such syllables lies in the following consonant rather than immediately before it." The observable is, of course, the consonant length; 'syllabic division' is just a construct, a name given to this and other observables.

Sapir's Navaho analysis was even more interesting in the morphology than in the phonology. It is therefore to be hoped that Hoijer will soon give

International Journal of American Linguistics, **11**, No. 4 (1945), 239–46.

us a detailed presentation of Navaho morphology as a companion volume to the present excellent publication.

1. THE PHONEMES

Hoijer gives the following table of Navaho phonemes:

b			m	m'	s	z		ʒ	c	c'		a	a·	aⁿ	a·ⁿ
d	t	t'	n	n'	š	ž		j	č	č'		e	e·	eⁿ	e·ⁿ
					ł	l		λ	λ	λ'		i	i·	iⁿ	i·ⁿ
					y	y'						o	o·	oⁿ	a·ⁿ
					x	γ									
g	k	k'			xʷ	γʷ						'	`	^	ˇ tones
	kʷ				h										
	ʔ				hʷ										

His table is constructed on the basis of the chief phonetic characteristics of each phoneme, as given in pp. 8–18 and 26. It is interesting to see how the stock of phonemes, and their interrelations (as indicated by a chart) can be differently stated on the basis of the detailed allophonic information, and the distributional information, which Hoijer gives.

1.1. *Allophonic Patterning*

The Navaho stops g, k, t are often pronounced as affricates, with a continuant glide following the stop (e. g. gγ, kh, kx, th, tx); this is true to a lesser extent of some of the other stops. It is therefore possible to consider the 9 affricates in the table above as being stops, whose allophones, like those of most other stops, contain stop and continuant parts. ʒ would then be the stop counterpart of z, and j that of ž, and λ that of l, in the same way that g is the stop counterpart of γ. Furthermore, c', č', λ' are similar to the glottalized stops in that the glottal release follows the oral release (§§ 7, 9, 11).

The relevant part of the table may now be changed to read:

ʒ	c	c'	s	z
j	č	č'	š	ž
λ	λ	λ'	ł	l
g	k	k'	x	γ

1.2. *Limitations of Phonemic Distribution*

The limitations of distribution which affect large groups of phonemes and very many occurrences (e.g. what phonemes occur at the end of a syllable), do not fit perfectly with the arrangement of the phonemes along the lines of their phonetic characters (such as in the tables above). Hoijer describes such limitations under the heading "clusters". In clusters of two consonants across syllable juncture, any consonant may be the second, while only those that occur at syllable final may be the first: this is, of course, merely another way of saying that there are no limitations in syllable initial position, while only 11 consonants (mostly the continuants, indicated here as C′) occur in syllable final.[3] Hoijer very conveniently gives a complete table of the clusters that occur (pp. 19–20). There are only a few other clusters, of two and three consonants. Instead of discussing these as clusters, they too may be described as peculiarities of distribution of the few phonemes which are involved in them. These are chiefly ʔ and some of the continuants. The only consonants which occur before C- (where - indicates syllable juncture) are n (once) and ʔ; and the C following them is always s, š, ž, ł, or h (these being C″, a subset of C′). The only consonant which occurs between juncture and C (i.e. in -C) is ʔ; the C being only d, n, or j.

Aside from such individual limitations, Navaho utterances are sequences of syllables which may be generalized in terms of consonants and vowels: beginning with one C after word or syllable juncture (rarely ʔC or V after syllable juncture), followed by one or two V, the first of them having a tone, and then nothing more or C before either juncture (rarely ʔš before word juncture, or ns or ʔC″ before syllable juncture).

1.3. *Juncture Phonemes*

At least two junctures must be included in the list of phonemes. The syllable juncture - is a phoneme in at least some cases since allophones having a slight hiatus are put into one phoneme with allophones having no hiatus, on the basis of the former occurring next to the juncture (p. 19).[4] The juncture is therefore the differentiating environment which makes the one allophone complementary to the other, and must hence be phonemic. If every occurrence of Hoijer's syllable boundary is accompanied by special allophones of the neighboring phonemes, then this boundary is always a phonemic juncture.

The juncture preceding the stem syllable must apparently be considered a phonemic juncture, in at least some cases. In § 13b a free variation which occurs in prefinal syllables does not occur after stem syllable juncture. This and similar special stem-syllable allophones of other phonemes make it necessary to consider the juncture preceding the stem syllable as a new phoneme: e.g. the inorganic h of pp. 39–40 is inorganic only if the juncture is phonemic. There are also many morphophonemic alternations peculiar to the stem; this would require that the stem juncture be also recognized morphophonemically.

There are slight differences in the consonant clusters before and after word juncture as against those before and after syllable juncture. More important is the fact that the assimilation of the c series and the č series takes place not simply within but throughout, the word. If the component ˇ is extracted from the č series, its domain will be from the word juncture preceding it to the word juncture following it, and this word juncture must then be phonemic. The stretch between word junctures would have certain morphological properties too, and can perhaps be marked by the occurrence of other phonemes (e.g. the stem juncture) more generally than merely by the occurrence of the ˇ component.

1.4. *Reduction of the Phonemic Stock*

The limitations of distribution of various phonemes can be used to reduce the number of independent phonemes in Navaho without complicating the interrelations among them.[5]

Among the phonemes з, c, c', s, z and j, č, č', š, ž there is a limitation of distribution (pp. 11–4): no word occurs which contains some phoneme of the first set and also some phoneme of the second set. For each word, therefore, which contains any of these phonemes, it suffices to mark just once for the whole word whether all the phonemes of this group are of the first set or of the second. We can use the mark ˇ for the second set; aside from this, then, the two sets will be identical. The phonemic writing would be ˇ sà·z *joint* (for šà·ž) as against zàs *snow*. The five phonemes of the second set are then dropped, and the phonemic component ˇ added.[6]

The phoneme m is in general rare. It never occurs as syllable final, although n does. The nasal vowels a^n, $a·^n$, etc., cannot be analyzed as vowel plus n, because they contrast with Vn (tìn *ice*, -tíⁿ *a living object lies*, -tí *hurt*); but they can be analyzed as vowel plus m, since that sequence does not otherwise occur.[7] It is thus possible to drop the eight nasalized vowel phonemes: a^n is phonemically to be written am. This hardly requires any special statement about the distribution of m or of the vowels; on the contrary, it makes the distribution of m more like that of n and most of the other continuants.[8]

It is further possible to drop the length phoneme, since the distribution of V· does not seem to differ materially from that of VV (when the two vowels are not identical). We need merely say that V· is to be analyzed phonemically as VV, constituting the special case when the two vowels are identical. This is possible because there is no aa as against a·, and because clusters of non-identical vowels such as ao do occur.[9] V· and VV are similar also in respect to the tones: whereas single vowels have either the low tone or the high, V· and VV may also have the rising and falling tones (p. 30). We thus drop the four long vowels and remove the restriction on vowel clusters that the component vowels be non-identical.[10]

A syllabic n also occurs in Navaho, written as n plus tone (ǹ or ń). Its distribution is seen to be exactly that of CV (pp. 11, 28). It would be most convenient, both distributionally and morphophonemically (because ń occurs as optional alternant of ní, etc.), to analyze syllabic n as consisting actually of the consonant n plus the syllabic. The Navaho syllabic should then be considered to be not the vowels but the tonemes. The vowels then become merely quality indications occurring simultaneously with the tonemes; and we would say that after n the quality restricting phonemes sometimes fail to occur with the toneme (i.e. we have the syllabic without specific vowel color).

We may also reduce the number of tonemes from four to two without complicating the statement of their distribution. Since the rising and falling tones occur only on VV (including V· which are now analyzed as a sequence of two like vowels), we may analyze ǎi as àí, ê· as éè, and so on, while ái becomes áí, and à· becomes àà. Whereas previously the second vowels of clusters had no tone, now no vowel occurs but with a toneme.

Since between every two junctures there occur two tonemes if VV occurs and one toneme otherwise, the question arises whether junctures and tonemes cannot be made interdependent. This requires not only that we be able to determine the occurrence of one from the occurrence of the other, but that we be also able to determine the point of occurrence of one from the point of occurrence of the other. In order to determine the exact point of occurrence of one in respect to the other, it would be necessary to check all the consonant clusters to make sure that it is possible to tell from the number and identity of the consonants where the point of juncture occurs. The material presented by Hoijer makes this seem possible. It also seems possible to eliminate one of the two tonemes, since absence of toneme over a vowel could be interpreted phonemically: á could be interpreted as á, and a as à. Such non-writing of one of the two remaining tonemes would cause confusion only in the syllabic n, and there only if the ordinary syllable juncture is also not written. For here we would have three values to indicate, ń, ǹ, and n. If ˋ is being eliminated as a mark, ǹ could be written by n plus some low-toned vowel cluster that does not otherwise occur.

The remaining phonemic question concerns the prosodic patterns (intonation contours, emphases, etc.) of phrase, utterance, or other lengths. Hoijer says (p. 7): "Though the speakers of Navaho, like those of any other speech community, vary the prosodic patterns of their utterances for socially effective gesture-like purposes, there appear to be no phonemically distinctive accentual phonemes belonging to the word, the phrase, or the sentence which stand over and above the accentual patterns formed by the succession of syllables constituting the utterance." Since the prosodic patterns could be socially effective only if they are conventional, it would seem to follow that there are some prosodic morphemes, which presumably can be analyzed as consisting of contour phonemes – unless they are indeed as hard to analyze and to reduce to constituent parts as gestures are. The investigation of the morphemic and if possible phonemic constituents of prosodic patterns, and of the more gesture-like parts of communication in general, is one of the next problems of linguistics. It would be particularly interesting to see how this works out in a tone language like Navaho, and we may hope that Hoijer's further work may enable him to state what regularities occur.

The limitations of distribution thus permit us to reconsider the phonemic allocation of certain allophones (e.g. assigning length to the several vowels, or nasalization to m). Such reallocations are convenient for descriptive linguistics when the new phonemes have less complicated limitations of distribution than did the old. Reducing the number of phonemes at the cost of complicating their distributions would not be desirable in most cases.

1.5. *Morphophonemic Interrelations*

After a distributionally irreducible number of phonemes is obtained, so that each phoneme contrasts which each other in every position[11], it is still possible to reduce the number of elements by considering each phoneme to be composed of more than one simultaneous component: e.g. t' may be analyzed as not one phoneme but two simultaneous phonemes (or phonemic components) t plus ʔ. This break-down may be used to simplify our statements of morphophonemic alternations in the language. Let us suppose that ata contrasts with at'a, but that some morphemes (say, t'a) contain the t' whenever they occur, while in cases of a morpheme ending in t (say, at) coming before a morpheme beginning with ʔ (say, ʔa), the two morphemes together are pronounced with a single t' between them (at'a, instead of at + ʔ a). Then although this t' is a single phoneme contrasting with t in ata (and let us say also with the sequence tʔ in atʔa), it is the morphophonemic resultant of t plus ʔ. It would be convenient if we could describe the t' as being in general composed of these two parts (t and ʔ or ʔ), for then instead of saying that when a morpheme ending in t is followed by one beginning with ʔ these two phonemes are replaced by a third phoneme t', we can say that when a morpheme ending in t is followed by one beginning with ʔ the two phonemes occur simultaneously (t + ʔ above it).

The Navaho material shows that a large part of the many morphophonemic alternations could be thus more simply expressed if the phonemes are broken up into simultaneous components along certain lines. Some of these have already been broken up on distributional grounds. Thus -t'a *to feather an arrow* is replaced by -t'aⁿ in the presence of perfective affixes (p. 34). Since nasalized aⁿ is now not a separate phoneme but merely the sequence of a plus m, we do not have to say that a is replaced by aⁿ, but that perfective affixes include the phoneme m in these cases. Similarly, the breaking up of the rising and falling tones into sequences of ' and `, and writing out the tones of vowel clusters (àì instead of ài), eliminates many morphophonemic statements, e.g. the first two vowels in the base form ná-ìid-ł- are changed if we write nâil- but not if we write náíl- (p. 50). And the suffix -í *he who* (p. 40) seems to suffer a trivial phonemic change to i when it follows nà·-gé *is carried about*, if the writing is nà·-géi, but suffers no change if we write ná·-géí. The writing VV instead of V· also eliminates some morphophonemic statements of a trivial kind: if we write ʔàs-ʒá-nííš instead of ʔàs-ʒá-ní·š for *Is it the woman?* (p. 32) we find that the constituent morphemes ʔàs-ʒán + -í + -íš suffer no phonemic change (except for the placing of the-). In other cases, however, the morphophonemic statements would be simpler if we were writing V· instead of VV, as for example in the positions in which all vowels are lengthened or shortened: dé *horn*, bì-dè·ʔ *his horn* and k'à·ʔ *arrow*, bì-k'àʔ *his arrow* both show change of length, whereas the phonemic analysis bì-dèèʔ and k'ààʔ would require a more complicated statement of the alternation ("repetition of the vowel"). If many occurrences of the syllable juncture can be made automatic, additional morphophonemic statements would be avoided, since many of the alternations described by Hoijer consist of dropping or moving the juncture.

The glottal stop ʔ figures frequently in the morphophonemic statements, alternating with zero (tó *water*, bì-tòʔ *his water*), moving across juncture, and combining with stops (usually the voiced stops) to make glottalized stops: dì·-t'à·š *we two start off* contains the base morphemes di- + ì·d- + ʔà·š (p. 31).[12] ʔ also alternates with h: -bà·ʔ, -bà·h *to go to war*.

The phoneme h is also frequent in morphophonemic alternations. By itself it alternates with ʔ, y, d, or zero. Before voiceless continuants it often drops: dà-sì-tí" *he lies on top* from the base morphemes dàh-sì-tí" (p. 41). With voiced continuants it coalesces to form voiceless continuants: dò-sé·h *you two belch* from the base morphemes dòh-zé·h (pp. 47–8, 51.2). By the side of these cases in which h-ł is replaced by ł, h-z by s, etc., there are morphemes in which voiced and voiceless phonemes alternate without the presence of h: gìz, -gìs *to wash*, etc. (p. 35). There are also many cases of assimilation in respect to voicelessness, e.g. base-form šγ to phonemic šx, złγ to sx (pp. 43–7). It is therefore convenient to consider ł as being simultaneous h + l, s as simultaneous h + z, etc., and to say that where base-form h-z is replaced by s it is merely that the two neighboring phonemes occur simultaneously; where z alternates with s, it is the addition of the simultaneous h component in one variant of the morpheme; and where base-form šγ is replaced by šx, the simultaneous h component of the first phoneme extends over the cluster.[13]

The phoneme d enters into morphophonemic alternations in a rather unexpected manner. Not only does it alternate like ʔ, with h, in the manner in which voiced-voiceless phonemes alternate (-kà·ⁿh,-kà·ⁿd *to sweeten*; -k'à·ⁿh,-k'á·ⁿʔ *to burn*; -gìs, gìz *to wash* pp. 34–5), but it also coalesces with various continuants with voicing or stop-making effect (and in the case of m, n, with glottalizing effect, pp. 43–6). Base-form i·d-ł- is replaced by i·l-, d-m by m', d-n by n', d-z by ʒ, d-l by λ or l (depending at least in part on the kind of juncture), d-γ by g, etc.

The phoneme y also enters into special morphophonemic statements which are difficult to summarize: h-y is replaced by h; d-y by z or d, š-y by s or š, ły by s, etc. Special alternations involve s, z, š, ž, and d, l, ł, and h, γ, y; these are admirably summarized in pp. 43–8.

The morphophonemic alternations also give us a basis for grouping many of the phonemes in phonetic series: when l combines with the simultaneous h component, we get not some arbitrary voiceless continuant, but ł; when it combines with the stop-making d we get λ. Similarly h+z yield s, d+z yield ʒ; h+γ yield x, d+γ yield g.

Among the vowels there are fewer morphophonemic alternations of quality, although e· is frequently replaced by i (rarely by a or o, p. 34) and although some contractions are phonetically distant, such as the replacing of base-form Ci-ni by Có- (p. 55; cf. pp. 48–55).

On the basis of all the morphophonemic alternations noted here, it is possible to say that the morphophonemic statements for Navaho would be simpler if instead of speaking in terms of the phonemes we spoke in terms of certain phonemic components: m, n, z, l, γ, y, d (a stop-making component), h (a devoicing component), ʔ (a glottalizing component), ˇ (a blade-al-veolarizing component extending over a word), a, e, i, o, two or three junctures, and one or two tones. Various simultaneous combinations of these would constitute the phonemes: z by itself would be the phoneme z; d+z would be the phoneme ʒ; h+z would be the phoneme s; h+z+ˇ would be the phoneme š. Only certain simultaneous combinations would occur: e.g. there would be no phoneme composed of d+h+m (there is no p in Navaho), no combination with h+ʔ would occur, and ˇ would occur only with z; and the vowels would never combine simultaneously with any consonant component (since nasalized vowels would be the sequence Vm). Despite the many remaining limitations of occurrence in this reduced phonemic stock, the limitations are fewer than in the larger stock, and many morphopho-nemic statements are eliminated or simplified (as when base-form d plus z becomes componental d+z instead of phonemic ʒ).

The phonemes kʷ, hʷ, xʷ, γʷ have been tentatively omitted from the above list. Their rarity, plus the fact that many combinations of the above-listed components do not occur, makes it seem possible that they could be identified as otherwise non-occurring combinations of recognized components or phonemes. This can only be done, however, if at all, on the basis of an exhaustive survey of the positions in which they occur.

Unlike Hoijer's phonetic chart of phonemes presented above, this list of components cannot very well be represented in chart form, since the relations among them are distributional and complicated and cannot be fairly indicated by the geometric properties of the chart.

2. MORPHOPHONEMIC ALTERNATIONS

There are a considerable number of regular or almost regular alternations, that is alternations for which the conditions are phonemic (or almost completely so: cf. §§ 20, 26, 29, 30, 31, 33).

Certain sequences of vowels, tones, or consonants are occasionally replaced in rapid speech by somewhat different sequences. These must of course be recognized as morphophonemic alternations, unless one chooses to eliminate rapid speech from the description. Thus Ci-Ca (where the juncture is stem juncture) may be replaced by Ca-Ca, etc. (§§ 17, 20, 21).

The phonemically different forms of one morpheme may be each considered a complementary positional variant of the morpheme. Alternatively and equivalently, base forms can be constructed, whose constituents are not phonemes but morphophonemes, and from which, in each environment, the appropriate variant of the morpheme can be derived by substituting for the morphophonemes the appropriate phonemes (following stated rules). Hoijer constructs such base forms and notes something of their character. He points out that although phonemically every vowel occurs with one tone or another, there are some base forms whose vowels have no tone (p. 50): these zero tone morphophonemes are replaced by high tonemes when they occur in one syllable with high tonemes, and by low tonemes otherwise. These base forms would also give the direction of assimilation of the ˇ component: for while it is a phonemic fact that ˇ affects all the z-containing phonemes in a word, it is a morphophonemic fact that whether any word contains ˇ or does not is determined by whether the last z-containing phoneme in the base forms from which the word was derived contained the ˇ component.[14]

Each of these base forms is one morpheme, and consists of one syllable or just one consonant, with juncture on either side. The various morphophonemic alternations affecting the syllable juncture result occasionally in the combination of two or more morphemes into one syllable, or the spreading of the phonemes of one morpheme over two syllables (e.g. by moving the final consonant of the morpheme across the syllable juncture into the next syllable). Even in the phonemic form, syllable juncture and morpheme boundary usually come at the same point in the word.

In addition to all the regular or partially regular alternations, there are so many individual replacements that a set of general rules for deriving phonemic forms from base forms, like those devised for Tübatulabal by Swadesh and Voegelin and for Menomini by Bloomfield, seems impossible here. Hoijer does, however, give very handy tables showing the base-form sources for each phoneme (pp. 55–9).[15]

Quite a few types of replacement of phoneme for morphophoneme are involved in deriving the morphemic variants from the base forms. These are the dropping or replacing of C or CV, the dropping or adding of a component (e.g. voicelessness), the changing of tone, and the dropping or moving of syllable juncture.

NOTES

[1] Harry Hoijer, *Navaho Phonology* (University of New Mexico Publications in Anthropology, 1). The University of New Mexico Press, Albuquerque, 1945. The only misprint which merits correction is cí- and cò- on p. 42 (§ 30.1), which is a misprint for Cí- and Cò-.

[2] Only 9 of these environments are numbered, but the second of them (§ 13b) contains x and h varying freely in prefinal syllables, and only x in stem syllables. It is therefore necessary to distinguish between these two: x and h are free variants of one allophone in a stated environment, while x alone is another allophone in another phonemic environment – after the stem juncture. Both of these allophones are members of the phoneme h. This is, of course, a case of partial overlapping, but it yields the simplest phonemic statement permitted by the data, and one which meets the practical requirements of phonemics (i.e. given the phoneme in an environment, we know what sound it represents; and given the sound in an environment, we know what phoneme it represents).

[3] The phonemic status of syllable juncture will be seen in § 1.3 below.

[4] Cf. also the syllable juncture between long or long and short vowels, p. 28.

[5] In considering here the reduction of the phonemic stock, the purpose is not to have fewer phonemes, come what may, but rather to have a simpler statement of the phonetic facts about the language. Reducing the number of phonemes, or the complexity of allophonic variation within each phoneme, often aids in this direction. Eliminating the limitations of distribution upon each phoneme is yet a greater aid. Often, these three objectives clash with one another. However, when we use the limitations of distribution of phonemes as a basis for reducing their number, we serve two purposes simultaneously. An example of this is seen in the present section.

[6] The direction of assimilation is morphophonemic, since it can be recognized only if we compare other forms of the morphemes involved in the word. See § 2 below.

[7] Morphophonemically, it would be more convenient to analyze nasalized vowel as vowel plus n in some form, since nasalized vowel is sometimes replaced by vowel plus n: Pà-yá-ní *he who eats* from a base form Pà-yá^n + -í. However, this is phonemically impossible.

[8] The new phoneme m will now occur like ʔ before C plus word juncture (p. 27, except that ʔ occurred only in the word-final cluster ʔš, while m would occur in many word-final clusters: sè·ms for sè·^{n}s *wart*, cì·mh for cì·^{n}h *exposed*, etc.). It will also occur like ʔ and n before C-. New types of cluster will be created by writing xá-dâ·mʔš *since when?* and dí·mʔs-kám *four days* (pp. 24–5), since clusters of three consonants in one syllable do not otherwise occur; the new element of distribution is that m would be the only consonant

occurring before CC (in particular, ʔC) before syllable or word juncture. A more serious difficulty is the fact that clusters like aⁿi occur by the side of clusters like ai (p. 28). If the former are written ami, the vowel cluster would be broken up, and contrast with V-mV (with consonant m) may be avoided only by dint of the syllable juncture. This would therefore be an undesirable writing, but may be avoided by writing aim for aⁿi, since clusters like aiⁿ do not seem to occur; this would conform to long nasalized vowels such as a·ⁿ, which would be written aam (for VV instead of V· see below). Another difficulty, of a morphophonemic nature, is the fact that vowel assimilations include nasalization: bòⁿ-zó·ⁿz *stinger* from a base form bì-zó·ⁿz (p. 29). If the new phonemic form is bòmzóómz, we have to say that not only the vowel but also the following m, if any, is assimilated.

⁹ Clusters of long vowels, or of long and short ones, which we would now call clusters of three and four vowels, always contain syllable juncture, so that not more than two vowels (or one long vowel) are in one syllable (p. 28).

¹⁰ This will be found to simplify some of the morphophonemic statements of vowel contraction (pp. 48–55).

¹¹ More exactly, in every position which is sufficiently regular for us to consider.

¹² Note also the rapid-speech variant of t', n', č', for ʔd, ʔn, ʔj (in one syllable, p. 25).

¹³ However, this and the other components do not extend automatically over all clusters.

¹⁴ In the base forms, the ˇ does not extend, but is present or absent with each morphophoneme containing the z component. The extension of the ˇ over the whole word, which expresses the phonetic assimilation, occurs only in the phonemic forms derived from the bases.

¹⁵ In such derivations, as in morphophonemic statements in general, it is necessary to state the environment exactly. A slip in this regard occurs on p. 43, where the table shows ì·d plus d yielding ì·, just as ì·d plus ł yields ì·l. The actual form is bì·h-nì--t'à·h *we two put our heads into it* from the base bì·h-ni-ì-d-d-ʔà·h: hence the alternation is not phonemic ì· from morphophonemic base ì·d-d, but phonemic ì·-t' from morphophonemic base ì·d-d-ʔ.

XII

YOKUTS STRUCTURE AND NEWMAN'S GRAMMAR

1. GENERAL EVALUATION

Newman's long-awaited Yokuts grammar is[1] a major addition to American Indian linguistics. More than that, it is a model contribution to descriptive linguistic method and data. It is written clearly and to the point, in a manner that is aesthetically elegant as well as scientifically satisfactory. It is sufficiently detailed, more so than is usual among American Indian grammars, to enable the reader to become familiar with the language and to construct correctly his own statements about the language.[2] Phonology and morphology are treated fully; syntax is only briefly touched upon, as is customary in grammars of American Indian languages. The meanings of classes of morphemes and the translation of utterances are more careful and sensitive than is usually the case; cf. at random the meaning of the aorist suffix in § 18:2, or of the non-directive gerundial -taw in § 19:9. Although it is perhaps not the custom for linguists to study carefully the grammars of languages not related to their work, this is one of the few grammars which students and workers in linguistics should read with close attention to the method of handling descriptive and comparative data.

2. COMPARATIVE MATERIAL

Newman's work is a simultaneous grammar of six Yokuts dialects, with most of the material coming from Yawelmani. One of the most interesting features of the book is the manner in which Newman has combined the data from the several dialects, and has based his interpretations and generalizations upon their combined weight. For every phoneme and morpheme and for every statement of their distributions, Newman gives the forms for each dialect; complicated dialectal divergences are more fully discussed, as in § 22:19.

No formal attempt is made to reconstruct the common earlier form of these dialects at the time when their divergence from each other began, but

International Journal of American Linguistics **10**, No. 4 (1944), 196–211.

Newman reconstructs particular features of that earlier common language. In addition he is occasionally able to adduce from his data evidence as to the relative date of linguistic developments, and even indications of developments which were in process at the time he obtained the data.

Some of these historical deductions are based upon the usual method of comparing features from the various related dialects. Thus, he reconstructs a bit of the morpheme stock of the earlier common language by finding cognates, including petrified forms, in the present dialects (§ 6:9). More frequently, he bases his reconstructions on the distribution of phonemes (§ 1:13), variant forms of a morpheme (§ 26:1, where relative dating is suggested), and morpheme classes or relations (§§ 18:25, 19:12, 15:25, 15:30, 18:13, 12:25) in the various dialects. Major structural features of the earlier common language are also reconstructed from comparative evidence, in one case showing identity with the structure of the present dialects (§ 21:8), and in another revealing a structural feature (prefixation) which has been lost (except for one petrified morpheme) in all the dialects (§ 25:18).

Analogous comparative evidence – the different variants of a morpheme, each differently distributed, in the various dialects – enable Newman to say that morphological leveling has in one case occurred in the several dialects (§ 15:18) and is in another case under way at the present time (§ 7:6).

Special interest is attached to Newman's utilization of structural features of a single dialect (instead of comparative evidence from several dialects) as a basis for statements about linguistic history. In one case, he reconstructs morphemes of an early Yokuts stage on the basis of the phonemic form, distribution, and semantic function of present morphemes which he suggests have a petrified morpheme in common (-tin and -taw, § 19:10). In other cases, he relates the existence of certain morphemes, which do not have the full distribution of their class, to structural features of the language: the fact that it makes no structural difference whether certain suffixes are preceded by stem or stem plus suffix has contributed to the formation of petrified stems (consisting of an original stem plus suffix, § 12:3); and the fact that bi-consonantal stems plus the suffix -in, when followed by other suffixes, look exactly like tri-consonantal stems followed by those suffixes, has contributed to the formation of analogized new tri-consonantal stems consisting of the two consonants of the original bi-consonantal stem plus n as the third stem consonant (fake bases, § 12:23). Finally, the distribution in one of the dialects of three extra vowels (in addition to the vowel phonemes common to all the dialects), and the fact that individuals sometimes vary between these and other vowels in a given morpheme, with younger informants rarely pronouncing the extra vowels leads Newman to say that these extra vowels may belong to a series which is in process of disappearing from the language (fn. 12).

3. DESCRIPTIVE METHOD

Modern linguistic grammars are notoriously hard to read. Although Newman's study is clearly written, one can hardly grasp the structure of Yokuts from a first reading of the book. In this case, perhaps two readings and some leafing around will suffice to give the reader a picture of the language; in many other published grammars, the reader who wishes to have a picture of the language structure has to reanalyze the whole material for himself, taking merely the elements and their distributions as reported by the author of the grammar and hardly utilizing the author's analysis. This situation arises from the fact that linguists do not yet have a complete common language. At first blush, one might think that they do. The acceptance of phonemes and morphemes as formal elements of a language description gives all linguists a fixed base to which they refer their picture of the language. This differs essentially from the situation in most other social sciences. For example, most of the academic sociological writing is not based on an explicit set of fundamental terms and does not even reveal a general agreement as to what aspects of social events are relevant, i.e. worth observing, in respect to any particular question. In psychology, most research and writing is couched in the terms of some one of the better-known theories; and material presented in one of the systems can often not be translated into another system, because not only the method of treating the data but even the selection of what variables to observe differs in the various systems. Descriptive linguistics is in a class apart, in that it has formally obtainable elements. It is this formal basis of getting phonemes and morphemes that enabled Bloomfield to say that any two linguists must agree on the observation of linguistic data. That is to say that, differently from the case in the other sciences of human action, any two investigators of a particular language would agree on what are the relevant or significant features of the flow of speech – i.e. what features to observe in that language – and how to treat these features in setting up the elements for the description of that language.

Past this point, however, there is often no agreement, even though it might seem that agreement would be almost automatic, since all that has to be done is to state the distribution of the elements which have been obtained. If linguists differ in their arrangement of allophones into phonemes in a particular language, no confusion need result so long as the differences, or the methods used in arranging the allophones, are explicitly stated. However, when it comes to stating the relations among the elements, their distribution in respect to each other – and this is the bulk of the phonology and of the morphology – the reader of a grammar will often not understand what the author is doing, what method of arrangement he is following, and what validity his statements and interpretations have. It does not follow from this that science would profit from having all linguists use one fixed method. But it does follow that we would profit from knowing exactly what methods are being used, and what are the differences among the methods. If in reading a grammar we could state explicitly what the author is doing in every section, we would be able to make much more use of his work, of his analysis, than we usually can today.

The method used by Newman is particularly worth investigating. For it is a consistent method, more so than is usually found in grammars, and the material is meticulously arranged in terms of that method. Furthermore, in addition to the excellence of Newman's work, this grammar takes on special methodological importance as perhaps the fullest example of Sapir's mature linguistic methods. Sapir had a consistent and very productive way of handling linguistic material. The fact that he left his Navaho grammar unfinished means that we have no study which can fully reveal his methods. One of the merits of the Yokuts grammar, written when Sapir was alive and by one of his chief students, is that it follows the general lines of Sapir's work.

4. CONFIGURATIONAL INTERPRETATION

In the paragraphs which follow, no attempt will be made to present a complete analysis of the linguistic methods used by Newman, or to note where they parallel Sapir's own work or differ from it.

The nub of the method is to describe language as a system or pattern of elements – phonemes or morphemes, depending on the level of discussion. To take the simplest case, long consonants are phonemicized as double consonants because "in each case the phonetic entity articulated as a long consonant is the configurational equivalent of two phonemes" (§ 1:15).

The relations between elements in the configuration are always described in terms of the pattern. Therefore Newman says: "In order to preserve that inflexible rule of Yokuts syllabic structure which does not permit the juxtaposition of two vowels, the glottal stop is interposed as a hiatus-filler between two vowels that should morphologically follow each other" (§ 1:13). Similarly, Newman says that a certain vowel change "serves to protect the stem-plus-suffix unit from forming a triconsonantal cluster" (which never occurs, § 2:15). Since the elements are observed only as parts of the system, and occur only in the positions which are mentioned when the system is described, one can picture the configuration as determining the nature of its elements (requiring or employing them): "The strict vocalic and syllabic requirements of the base do not apply to the theme" (§ 12:1); "The regular stem paradigm employs a zero suffix for the subjective case" (§ 24:24).

The difference between two partially similar forms is frequently described here as a process which yields one form out of the other. Thus when bases or themes have several vocalic forms, the various forms are said to be the result of vowel-change processes operating upon the base or theme (§ 6:2, 22:28). The difference between a base and a base-plus-suffix is described as the result of the process of suffixation (§ 6:1, 20:11). This is a traditional manner of speaking, especially in American Indian grammar (e.g. in the Handbook edited by Boas). It has, of course, nothing to do with historical change or process through time: it is merely process through the configuration, moving from one to another or larger part of the pattern. Although, as will be seen below, such terms are less used today, they fit in very well with the method used by Newman, because this method is in general modelled on moving systems. In several places, the model is that of a living organism: "When morphological operations call for a triconsonantal cluster medially, protection may be afforded by the insertion of the protective vowel after the stem, or by the truncation of the initial suffix consonant" (§ 3:4); "In its typical morphological behavior Yokuts adds a suffix to a stem which has undergone dynamic vowel processes" (§ 6:1). Once, it is a solar system model: "Each of the base types at one time moved, more or less, in its own unique orbit" (§ 7:4).

The configuration is treated as though it were a pattern of meanings as well as, basically, of forms. Summaries are offered of the meanings of various formal parts of the pattern. Thus Newman makes the following neat analysis of final as against thematizing (the major type of non-final) suffixes: "Some general functional differences characterize these two formal types of suffix. Final suffixes include a) all tense suffixes, whether their tense reference is pure, as in Wikchamni -si, aorist (past or present tense), or mixed, as in Yawelmani -'at, durative passive aorist; b) all suffixes of mode; c) all gerundial suffixes; d) all the case suffixes of the noun. Thematizing suffixes include a) all suffixes of modal derivation; b) all suffixes referring purely to voice or c) purely to aspect; d) all nominalizing suffixes; e) all verbalizing suffixes" (§ 6:7). In this passage he has correlated a difference in meaning with the difference in position of the two suffix classes. In other cases Newman also points out partial similarities as well as differences in meaning of different forms: "Suffixes whose function is purely that of defining voice are thematizing in type. But suffixes which express a mixed voice and tense or voice and gerundial function are of the final type, as Yawelmani -it, passive aorist, or -tin, passive gerundial" (§ 14:1). "Modal functions, referring to an attitude or affective disposition with regard to an activity, are primarily expressed in Yokuts by means of particles. In addition to this formally loose means of conveying notions of modality, there are only a few suffixes of a modal character. But these are to be distinguished into two groups. On the one hand, a set of modal ideas of a comparatively external and casual nature, such as the desiderative ('desire to act upon, try to act upon'), the hortatory or prioritive ('must act upon, act upon... before doing anything else'), and the exclusive ('do nothing else but act upon'), is conveyed by thematizing suffixes; for convenience of reference, these elements are classed as suffixes of modal derivation. In contrast, the category of mode proper, including such concepts as the imperative, the dubitative, and the precative, is expressed by final suffixes" (§ 16:1). The search for elements of similar meaning, i.e. the attempt to make exact statements of the patterned meanings, leads Newman to find identities between suffixes different in form and position: "A number of factors make the distribution of causative suffixes one of the most ramified formal pictures of a single semantic function in the language. In the formation of the causative, morphological cleavages are characterized, not only by the variable of suffix form (e.g., Yawelmani -a·la/ for bases I, Yawelmani -e / for bases II), but also by the variable of stem form (e.g., Cukchansi -e/ with the long causative stem of base IIA1 but with the strong stem of bases IIA2 and IIB). Not infrequently two causative processes overlap in their affiliations, offering optional methods of forming the causative" (§ 14:41). Note that there is a formal relation among all these causative suffixes: either they are complementary to each other in that they occur with different bases, or else they vary relatively freely with each other if they occur with the same base.

Largely as a result of the attempt to find meaning patterns, this method puts forms into classes which are given meaning names. The morphemes put into such a class will of necessity have some formal features in common; but they may also differ from each other in some relevant formal features. Thus, Newman sets up a class of gerundials: "The term 'gerundial' is applied to verbal derivatives whose predication is subordinate to that of the main verb. Syntactically, gerundials cannot take a grammatical subject; the agent of a gerundial activity is either appropriated from the main verb or expressed in the possessive case. But these semantic and syntactic characteristics belong to verbal nouns as well as to gerundials. The two types of subordinates, however, are sharply distinguished in morphology: verbal nouns, like all nouns of Yokuts, must appear with one of the six case endings (subjective, objective, indirect objective, possessive, ablative, locative); gerundials, on the other hand, are true verbs in that they cannot take any of the case endings" (§ 19:1). Certain of the gerundials, however, differ from the others

in their grammatical position and cut across classes which have been previously set up: "The agent of the gerundial activity (expressed by -taw)
appears in the possessive case. Although this syntactic treatment is characteristic of passives, the suffix-taw is clearly not passive, for it takes its own
grammatical object when used with active stems, and it may, in addition, be
attached to medio-passive stems; genuinely passive suffixes cannot, of course,
be added to stems which are already passive or medio-passive in voice"
(§ 19:9). "The agent of this gerundial activity (expressed by -'as) is indicated
by the possessive case, a syntactic feature which marks the precative gerundial as a non-finite verb. But in spite of its non-finite character, this verb
may stand alone without the support of an independent, finite verb in the
sentence; Yawelmani xat'asnim is acceptable as a complete predication. No
other gerundial has been found to assume the force of a complete, independent predication" (§ 19:11).

The attempt to establish a basic pattern leads to important generalizations
about the total structure of the language. "Each morphological process of
Yokuts is accompanied by stem changes. In contrast to the root consonants,
which are the inflexible, unchanging phonological units of Yokuts, the root
vowels undergo a variety of changes in assuming their stem form. The
extensive system of vocalic change can be conceived as operating on two
planes: on the one hand, dynamic vowel processes effect ablaut changes
which are not to be explained in terms of mechanical phonetic conditions;
on the other hand, a number of phonetic processes introduce additional
vowel changes of a purely mechanical nature. In the formation of stems these
two planes interact; a stem which has suffered dynamic changes may, in turn,
be subjected to secondary phonetic changes" (§ 2:8). "A thematic verb root
(i.e. base plus suffix) may be built upon the stem of another theme as well as
upon the stem of a base; i.e. the root of a given thematic verb may be not
only secondary in its base derivation, but tertiary or even quaternary in the
strict numerical sense. Theoretically, there is no limit to the number of
thematic layers that can lead up to a theme. The practice of avoiding formal
elaboration of any kind in Yokuts, however, sets a vaguely defined but
comparatively narrow limit to thematic luxuriance" (§ 12:1).

The interest in configuration makes it particularly easy to recognize the
status of an element (phoneme or morpheme, or 'process' – i.e. inter-
element relation) in respect to the other elements. Thus, after showing that
morphemes ending in vowels have a glottal stop after the vowel when they
are final, Newman says "If the Yokuts glottal stop was ever an organic
consonant in final position, it has been reinterpreted and leveled to the
status of a protective, inorganic element wherever it occurred finally"
(§ 1:13). Productive features are always noted as such (§ 15:30, 25:1). As a

result of this we often get very useful observations: After noting that continuative suffixes are not productive, Newman adds "The lack of vitality (of this suffix category) is indicated by the limited and sporadic application of the processes involved and by the specializations of meaning that frequently emerge: e.g. Yawelmani 'work' as the continuative of 'grasp', Gashowu 'wait on table' as the continuative of 'pour'. Such semantic specialization, while it represents the normal practice in English, is exceptional and anomalous in Yokuts" (§ 15:30). And since a configurational feature is presumed to operate upon all elements in its sphere, any lack of that feature in a form where it is to be expected, i.e. any exception, leads the linguist to search for an independent interfering pattern: The addition of vowel suffixes is accompanied by the dropping of the preceding vowel, e.g. the i of hɔ·yin *get sent*. This does not happen in forms like panwix *bring*. Newman states it: "A zeroing of the last vowel in the prevocalic normal stem of the IIAb theme would result in a triliteral cluster, which is prohibited in Yokuts. The resistance of this vowel to a zero-grade reduction is undoubtedly due to syllabic interference, for identical morphological processes create verbal themes of type hɔ·yin and panwixa" (§ 12:13).

Finally, the configurational interpretation offers hints of past or current changes in the language, since historical changes are undoubtedly determined in part by the structure of the language at the time: "The form of the future suffix differs considerably among the dialects. Undoubtedly the set of future suffixes in modern Yokuts represents, on the one hand, a deposit of several distinct historical sets and, on the other, a phonetic differentiation between suffixes of an originally uniform set. The process of differentiation is the more apparent, for a suffix containing the consonant n or 'n, generally with a vowel of the i series, is the most widely distributed future suffix in Yokuts. However, the particular details of the historical process have been obliterated by a regimentation of future suffixes into a firmly integrated pattern" (§ 18:11). "The statistical rarity of base IB is due to its anomalous position in the configuration of bases. Because it is the only base ending in a strong vowel, base IB often requires special phonetic treatment in some of the stem formations and special truncated suffixes. Special morphological processes frequently set this base off from the other bases. Among the nouns of theme type IB, corresponding in form to the reduced stem of base IB, the dialects have developed a bewildering variety of sub-classifications and special phonetic processes in their attempt to reinterpret this formal unit to a satisfactory configurational status. By a wide margin, in short, base IB is configurationally the most isolated and behavioristically the most aberrant, formal unit in Yokuts. In view of this, it is hardly surprising that base IB is being leveled out of existence" (fn. 34).

5. CONFIGURATIONAL INTERPRETATION AND STRUCTURAL STATEMENT

The method described above differs in several inessential respects from the type of descriptive analysis which is more widely used today. It may be of interest to note some of these differences.

The great attention to meaning evident in Newman's work is not common in modern grammars. In this Newman's work is undoubtedly superior. Nevertheless, it may be argued that the different grammatical statuses should be kept apart rigorously and clearly: the configuration is always one of linguistic forms, and the meanings are always external statements about forms or groups of forms. The technique of arranging a grammar in two independent ways, in terms of form and of meaning, which Jespersen tried to work out in his *Philosophy of Grammar*, is apparently not attempted today by any linguist. It is impossible to carry out in any explicit or objectively agreed upon way because it is impossible to divide meanings into elements of meaning, to compare one meaning with another, or in general to work out a structure of meanings. Sapir never patterned his linguistic material by meaning, nor does Newman. Newman does, however, note similarities of meaning in some cases even where there are no similarities of form. Thus he notes that certain non-final suffixes (desiderative, hortatory, etc.) are modal as are also certain final suffixes (imperative, precative, etc.). He lists the first group as suffixes of modal derivation (ch. 16) and the other group as modal suffixes (ch. 17). There is of course no harm in pointing out their similarity of meaning and in assigning them similar names. However, it must be recognized that these similarities exist primarily for people in the grammatical tradition of the western world. There is apparently no basis for finding any connection between the two groups in terms of Yokuts language or Yokuts speakers. To the extent that every grammar is a transference from the described language to the language in which the description is written, Newman's technique is of course necessary. If, however, we seek to describe a language in a way that is maximally independent of the language, culture, or experience of the describing linguist, we would recognize no meaning similarities except where there are formal similarities. This formal basis for meaning statements could suffice even to bring out niceties such as are pointed out by Newman.

Somewhat related to the question of meaning is the grouping of elements into classes which are given formal names (e.g. IA2) or meaning names (e.g. gerundial). Sometimes such classes are set up on the basis of one criterion and do not correlate with any other formal criterion (but only with meaning features). For example, Newman gives a list showing the relative order of various classes of suffixes:

I. Thematizing suffixes
   A. Affiliated with the base systems
   B. Affiliated with the theme systems
      1. Verb-forming suffixes
      2. Noun-forming suffixes
II. Auxiliary suffixes
III. Final suffixes

What may not be clear to the reader is that these are not classes of suffixes which are differentiated on various grounds and which also are restricted to the above order. Rather, this relative order is the chief criterion for classifying the suffixes as they are above. Group I in the list above consists merely of those suffixes which do not occur finally. Group IB is defined on the basis of the fact that its members occur both after bases and after other suffixes. There is therefore no new information in saying that group IB occurs after group IA. On the other hand, there are two cases of formal correlation in the list above. About noun forming suffixes, which are defined by the fact that the case endings follow them, this list gives the added information that they occur after but not before verb forming suffixes. And about the auxiliaries, which are defined by features of stress and vowel harmony, this list gives the added fact that they occur after the thematizing suffixes. It is desirable that the correlation between form and form (e.g. the two facts about noun forming suffixes) should be distinguished from statements which contain only one fact and do not correlate it with any other.

In general, the technique of classification and naming can be replaced by the technique of stating relations. Thus, Newman calls a base plus non-final suffix a theme, and obtains classes of themes according to the non-final suffix which went into making them. We could just as well speak in terms of base- and base-plus-suffix, and avoid the term 'theme'. We can similarly side-step the stem-classes of bases and themes. For the base-stems are merely various changes in the vowels of the base (e.g. the zero stem eliminates the second base vowel, yielding the stem hiby- from the base *hibe·y *bring water*); most of them affect only the final vowel of the base, but some also change the first vowel. The theme stems are similar except that they only affect the final vowel of the theme (i.e. of the suffix which had been added to the base).

Whenever a suffix is added to a base or a theme (base plus suffix), vowel changes occur in the base or in the last suffix before the new addition; these vowel changes are called the stem. Each suffix is associated with a particular vowel change or stem, so that when it is added to any base, or to any base having a given phonemic structure, that particular vowel change takes place. When a suffix is added after another suffix (i.e. onto a theme) the vowel changes that take place in the preceding suffix (i.e. in the theme) are generally similar to the vowel changes which occur in a base when that suffix is added to a base. Newman recognizes a long series of stems, and notes for each stem what suffixes go with it. We could just as well avoid the term 'stem' as a morphological factor and as a classifier of suffixes: all we need say is that each suffix consists of certain phonemes preceded by a vowel change; in some cases this vowel change varies slightly according to the phonemic structure of the base preceding the suffix, or according to the phonemic structure of a prior suffix. Instead of talking about bases and themes, stems and classes of suffixes (classed by the stems), we now talk about bases and suffixes only. This is not to say of course, that one of these ways of talking is superior to the other. They are only ways of talking, and each may be useful for particular purposes. If when we use the method of distinguishing various classes and types of elements – themes, stems, etc. – we find that many similarities remain among them, e.g. the similarities between base and theme in respect to their stems (vowel changes), then we may prefer to use the latter method which would not put base and theme under different names, but would distinguish between them only where necessary.

Another term that is disappearing today, no doubt under the influence of Bloomfield's Language, is 'process'. There is involved here a method, not merely a term. Newman uses "process" to indicate a relation between two forms one of which may be viewed as consisting of the other plus some change or addition. Thus, the addition of suffixes to a base is a process, as is the assimilation of a pre-glottal-stop vowel to the quality of the vowel after the glottal stop (§ 2:18), and the changing of vowels in the base when suffixes are added. All such cases can be viewed differently, without bringing in the time or motion analogy implicit in 'process'. Instead of talking about the word ćumo··'uy *that which was devoured* and ćuma··'an (*he*) *is devouring* as the resultants of adding the suffix 'uy and 'an to the base *ćo·mu, we can say that the two words contain each the morpheme ćo·mu and respectively the suffixes 'uy and 'an, each suffix containing a vowel change. We now have not a process from base to word via suffixation, but an inventory of the elements (morphemes) present in two utterances. We can then rearrange this inventory by listing all the utterances in which a given morpheme occurs. The same information that was previously given in terms of a process, from base to word, is now given in terms of a catalog of the components of words. Some of these component parts are bases and others are suffixes, but that does not mean that the bases underlie the word more than do the suffixes, nor that the suffixes are added to the bases rather than bases being added to suffixes; it merely means that some morphemes are initial and non-final (bases), some are non-initial (suffixes).

Similarly, if we speak of the assimilation of o· to a· before 'an we have a process yielding ćuma·-'an. But we speak in morphophonemic terms and say that all vowel morphophonemes before 'a have the phonetic quality a: we then write morphophonemically ćumo·-'an and pronounce ćuma·-'an. Or we can speak in terms of morphemes and say that all initial morphemes ending in the phonemes e· and ɔ· have complementary variants ending in a· which occur only before non-initial morphemes beginning with 'a. Finally, we can speak of all suffixes which begin with 'a as beginning really with ⁻'a, where V̄ = a (i.e. ⁻ is a supra-segmental morphophoneme which changes the quality of the vowel under it to a). All four descriptions above are, of course, equivalent. In the last three we avoid implying the primacy of the base over the vowel umlauting. Instead of a process or change, they give us a number of elements, morphophonemes or morphemes, so defined that when these elements occur next to each other their phonemic forms are what we actually hear.

Lastly, we consider the Dynamic Vowel Processes, in which each vowel of a base is shown to change in various ways as suffixes are added; each stem is obtained by applying a vowel process to each vowel of the base (or theme). Newman gives a complete table of these on pp. 23–4 which greatly simplifies the description of the vowel changes (stems) associated with each suffix. From a general structural point of view we may note that all these processes are composed of a few changes: the adding of a mora or the dropping of the second or all moras (a > a·, a > zero, a· > a, a· > zero); the change of i > e, u > ɔ (morphophonemically written o; these occur chiefly before · but not always), a or ɔ > i, i or u > a; the addition of ' before or after the first mora. Since each of these changes occurs only when particular suffixes occur, we can consider them as part of the suffixes, so that the dubitative suffix is not al but ⁻al, where V̄ = zero (i.e. *giyi *touch* plus a suffix beginning with ⁻ has the phonemic form giẏ). Here again we no longer talk about process and change or the priority of the base; we merely note the adjacent occurrence of initial morphemes (bases) and non-initial morphemes (suffixes). We may say that the suffixes begin with an element whose phonetic value extends over the last preceding vowel (or both vowels of the preceding morpheme). Or we may say that the suffix begins with a non-phonetic morphophonemic symbol, and that the preceding morpheme has complementary phonemic forms each of which occurs before particular morphophonemic symbols.

Both Newman's method and the alternative methods indicated above are essentially similar in that they describe particular events or relations in terms of general systemic relations. This was indeed the great contribution of Sapir's talking about configuration and pattern. The type of model Sapir and Newman used pictured the particular relation as supporting or being controlled by the general relation. Thus Newman can say that in pilaw *in the road* there has been added to the morpheme pil- *road* and -w *in* a protective vowel in order to preserve the general pattern of not more than one consonant finally (§ 22:3). Today, the tendency is to use as model the deductive system of scientific description, so that we might say that no final clusters occur and deduce from that that when the morpheme pil- occurs before the morpheme -w it has a phonemic form ending in a vowel. A protective form protects a general pattern; a deduced form is a special case of a general statement, which statement would not have been true if the actually occurring forms had not fitted in with it.

The deductive style of talking constantly seeks the most general statements which are valid for all the material surveyed. Once a statement has been made, it is not necessary (though it may be helpful) to repeat it for each actually occurring case; this is one of the reasons for the disuse of repetitive paradigms in modern grammars. It is important to ask if this description in terms of a catalog of elements and a minimum of most general statements about their occurrence may not miss much of the heuristic value of Sapir's way of working, with its intuitive insights and utilization of signposts. The answer is that the particular methods characteristic of Sapir and of Newman's work are essentially aids in the process of research. Each worker will use whatever models and habits of thinking come most naturally to him. The productiveness and elegance of Sapir's and Newman's method is apparent from their work, and many, in our culture perhaps most, workers will profit from these techniques. However, once an intuitive guess has been checked, it is no longer intuitive but an observed fact; and the explicit search for most general statements parallels intuitive pattern-thinking in finding interfering factors, inorganic status of particular elements, etc.

6. YOKUTS STRUCTURE

Newman's findings will be summarized here because of the interest both of Newman's analysis and of the grammatical system of Yokuts. As a test case of the differences in method discussed above, the method used in this summary will upon occasion differ from Newman's.

The rather large stock of phonemes is given by Newman on pp. 13 and 19–20. Only two points in the phonemic system seem to be of special interest: the glottal stop, and the interrelation of the vowels.

There are 12 glottalized phonemes and a glottal stop. The glottalized phonemes configurate as single phonemes, although they pair with every other phoneme except the non-aspirate stops and affricates and the voiceless continuants.[3] The ' is automatic in certain positions (§ 1:13) and has special

vowel changes before it (§ 1:12, 2:18, 2:22, 3:3). Certain suffixes begin with
a 'floating glottal stop', i.e. if a voiced continuant precedes them it is glotte-
lized; otherwise the suffix merely begins with a segmental ' (§ 1:8). Finally,
the glottalized voiced continuants do not occur after a consonant. This leads
to morphophonemic alternants: e.g. the tribe name čɔy̓nim̓ni' is čɔy̓en̓mani
in the plural (§ 1:17). We can describe the last two facts by saying that the '
is addable to and removable from glottalized continuants. It would therefore
be desirable to consider the glottalization as separate element. And since a
glottalized consonant configurates as one consonant, we must consider
glottalization as a suprasegmental phoneme which can occur simultaneously
with most of the segmental phonemes. In some positions it occurs between
phonemes, and is then a segmental glottal stop. If we make an exact statement for the occurrence of this supra-segmental phoneme, and for the
limitations of the phonemes in its neighborhood, we would include the fact
that it operates only on the first of any two successive consonants; i.e. it may
occur over a whole cluster but can have phonetic effect only on the first part.
Then we may write čɔy̓nim̓ni' and čɔy̓en̓mani without requiring alternants of
the root, and pronounce as above.

A more involved case is that of the vowel harmony. Of the ten common
Yokuts vowel phonemes, Newman shows that four, a, ɔ, i, u, are basic; only
these and their lengthened forms (a·, ɔ·, e·, o·) occur in bases. Three chief
cases of vowel harmony or assimilation connect a with ɔ, i with u (and their
respective lengthened forms). First: Almost all suffixes contain only the
vowels a and i. When suffixes containing a come after a stem whose last
vowel is ɔ, they have ɔ instead of a; and when suffixes containing i occur after
stems whose last vowel is u, they have u instead of i (§ 2:5–6).[4] Thus the
agentive is hine· in ṭun-hań-hine· *the door which is being closed*, but huno· in
ṭun-huno· *one who is closing the door*. Second: Before certain suffixes the last
vowel of the base changes to i, if it is a or ɔ, but remains unchanged if it is u;
and before other suffixes the last vowel of the base changes to a if it is i or u,
but remains unchanged if it is ɔ (§ 2:11, 8:21–4, 10:19, 11:7–17). Thus before
the future zero suffix, *bo·huṭ *mature* has the form buh'aṭ', and *če·niš
sweep the form čin'aš, but *sɔ·wɔn *swell up* has the form sɔw'ɔn without
change of vowel. Third: Before a consonantal suffix, noun themes have
special forms ending in i or a. However, among nouns adding i, if the last
vowel of the theme is u, the added i is replaced by u; and among the nouns
adding a, the added vowel is replaced by ɔ if the last vowel of the theme is ɔ
(§ 22:4–9, 24:22). Thus we have (added vowel in parentheses):

wɔdɔ·diṣ (a)   *heel*
'oy'uy (a)   *chaparral cock*

šama' (a)	*mouth*
nɔh'ɔ' (ɔ)	*bear*
k̓ɔčɔ'yi' (i)	*rat*
ho'su' (u)	*cayote*
t̓ayt̓'ay (i)	*bluejay*
šɔhgɔy (i)	*elk*

If we now consider what is common to these three cases, we find that a does not follow (or, in the second case, replace) ɔ, nor does i follow u. Articulatorily, we may say that a is the low front vowel, ɔ low back, i high front, u high back. Then if a vowel is followed (or, in the second case, replaced) by one of the same height, the second vowel must also be of the same mouth position: the second will not differ from the first in position alone.[5] This may be expressed more simply if we actually break each vowel up into two suprasegmental components, mouth position and height, and say that the position component of the first vowel extends over the second if the second has the same height component as the first. All the limitations mentioned above then become special cases of this one limitation.

We now consider the general limitations upon the sequences of phonemes that make up an utterance. Newman describes this in terms of two syllabic structures, CV and CVC, which occur in certain sequences. The statements he makes in ch. 3 may be summarized directly in terms of the utterance, without reference to syllables, by some formula such as the following (· is length; ✳ utterance juncture; items in parentheses may or may not occur in that position; items written above each other are mutually exclusive; and the section in square brackets can be omitted or repeated without theoretical limit):

$$✳C[V(Ç)C]V(C)✳$$

Thus we have ki *this* (such short words are rare), ho·gaw *directly*, biwi·nelse·nit *from one who is made to sew*.

Stress (ch. 4) is not phonemically marked, being automatic in respect to word or phrase juncture. Newman shows that many words (especially pronouns, particles, etc.) lose their stress when they are not phrase-final. In rapid speech, several words may be grouped together with only the last one stressed. Yokuts therefore really has a phrase stress rather than a word stress; the effect of a word stress is given merely by the fact that verbs and nouns, the main word types in Yokuts, usually occur in phrase-final and hence usually have the stress.

Before we go on to the morphology of Yokuts, it will be useful to note what morphemes have more than one phonemic form (or: what different phonemic sequence we choose to consider as different forms of one morpheme). It appears that very many Yokuts morphemes have more than one phonemic form within one dialect, each form occurring in different environments and hence being complementary to the others. Some of these variant forms result from automatic morphophonemic alternations, i.e. are determined by the phonemic environment. The greatest group of these is connected with the restriction on what phoneme sequences occur in an utterance. The formula above shows that no Yokuts utterance contains sequences CCC, VV, CC※, V·C※ [6], ※V, etc. It often happens that when one morpheme occurs next to another, the sum of their two phonemic sequences would yield a sequence not described by the formula above, i.e. containing some sequence which cannot be derived from the formula. To take a simple case, we have a morpheme xaya· *place* which occurs with the suffix -ši' in xaya·ši' *he placed it*. When this morpheme occurs before the suffix -t we would seem to obtain the sequence V·C※ which is not included in the formula. In all such cases we find that the morpheme in question has a variant form which occurs in the environment in question such that the variant form plus the environments do not yield a sequence which is excluded from the formula. In our case above, the word is xaya-t *he was placed*, and the original morpheme is not xaya· but xaya·/xaya, the latter form occurring before C※. Every morpheme then has variant forms which occur in such environments that no sequence of morphemes yields a sequence of phonemes not included in the formula. This fact is what makes the formula correct, and is equivalent to Newman's protective features.

In general, the many alternations which fall under the statement above are determined by the phonemic environment: e.g. CVCV· morphemes have variant CVCV before C※ suffixes. In the case of the extra last vowel which noun stems have before consonantal suffixes (§ 22:3), we find that some stems have a (ɔ), others i (u). There is no way of predicting which stem will have which vowel height. The only way we can treat this as an automatic alternation is to say not that the stem adds a vowel (but which vowel?) before consonantal suffixes, but that it drops a vowel (whichever it has) before vocalic suffixes. This means that the high or low vowel will have to be considered as part of the stem.[7]

There are other automatic variations not connected with the statement above. If the facts about vowel harmony and limitations in the neighborhood of ' are not expressed in terms of supra-segmental components, we must state them here, by saying, for example, that all suffixes whose first vowel is i have variant forms with u which occur only after morphemes whose last vowel is u.

Many morpheme variations in Yokuts do not depend on the phonemic environment. I.e. certain morphemes have two or more forms, each of which is used in the neighborhood of certain other morphemes (not phonemes). Thus all the morphemes containing u have forms with ə instead of u in most (but not all) of the cases when · follows the u; this ə· is phonemically identical with the ə· in morphemes which have ə as their short vowel. Morphophonemically, Newman writes o· for the ə· which varies with u (§ 2:2, 11).

Most of the morpheme variations which depend upon a morphemic rather than phonemic environment are to be found in the suffixes. Thus, the Yawelmani dialect has a consequent auxiliary suffix which has the form e·xə· after suffixes (including reduplication), but 'e·xə· with floating ' after initial morphemes (§ 15:18). The future suffix has one form (Yawelmani ') after ·, another (Yaw. en) otherwise (§ 18:12). Particularly complicated are the environments in which the variant forms of the causative (§ 7:4–7, 14:13–4) and objective (§ 23:3) occur, described by Newman under cleavage of the base types. In this category of morpheme variation we must also include the repetitive suffix. Newman shows that reduplication (ch. 11) occurs only in bases having two consonants, and has the meaning of repetition (giẏgiẏ *touch repeatedly*), while the repetitive suffix -da· never occurs after these bases and has the same meaning. It is therefore possible to consider -da· and reduplication, in spite of their difference in form, as variants of one morpheme.

As a last example of morpheme variation we may note the possibility of two interpretations of the plural morpheme. In Yokuts there is a morpheme of generally plural meaning consisting of vowel change (in the base) plus i before a zero subjective case ending, and vowel change plus h before the other (non-zero) case endings. We may consider the i to be part of the plural morpheme, with the subjective case after it marked by zero, because in the singular the subjective case is marked by zero. On the other hand, we may say, as does Newman implicitly, that the subject case has two variants: zero after the singular but i after the plural, and the plural has two variants: vowel change plus h before the oblique case and just vowel change alone before the subjective case. The i can be assigned to either but not both of the adjacent morphemes, plural and subjective.

Knowing in what way morphemes vary in Yokuts, we can now consider what is the stock of Yokuts morphemes. In several cases we find that morphemes which occur in particular positions also have particular types of phonemic form. Some morphemes occur by themselves in a word, without following suffixes; these are adverbial particles, interjections, etc. (ch. 27). Others have a special unproductive system of suffixes, rather different from the others; these are for the most part pronouns, interrogatives, etc. (ch. 26). All morphemes which occur initially in the word and which do not occur finally (i.e. never constitute a word by themselves) have the following form:

2 or 3 consonants for the odd-numbered phonemes, 1 vowel quality which occurs in the first two even-numbered phoneme places, and zero or 1 length which occurs in either of the even numbered places. The combinations deducible from this statement give 6 possible sequences (CVCV, CV·CVC, etc.) listed by Newman in § 7:1, but the statement above suffices to indicate just what phonemic material is needed to identify any initial morpheme uniquely. When we say CV·CVC we have to specify that the two vowels are identical (the V· being the lengthened form of the V) and that not both vowels can be lengthened. Such limitations are summarized in the statement above. Each of these initial morphemes has a specific meaning, neither verbal nor nominal, e.g. *'a·mal 'help' (§ 13:9).

In addition to these, there are other morphemes which are never initial. Some of these are always final, the others never. Of those that are never final, certain ones (called auxiliaries) do not have vowel harmony with the preceding morpheme, and the stress of the preceding morpheme is placed as though the auxiliary were a separate word (§ 6:30, ch. 15). Another, wiyi, occurs with special initial proclitic morphemes (instead of the usual bases) and with particular suffixes after it; it is celerative in meaning and informal in style (ch. 10, § 15:4). All other non-initial morphemes, both final and non-final (except nominalizing suffixes), occur in general with any initial morpheme at all, have the vowel harmony variants, and are part of the stress unit (the stress is on the penult vowel of the word or word-phrase, including these suffixes in the word). Some of these non-final suffixes occur only after initial morphemes; the majority, however, occur after initial morphemes or other suffixes. A few final suffixes, called case-endings, occur only with any one of a group of non-final suffixes, called nominalizing. And the nominalizing suffixes always have a case suffix after them. Most nominalizing suffixes occur only after particular initial morphemes. Among the non-final suffixes in a word, the nominalizing are always last. Auxiliaries may occur after non-final non-nominalizing suffixes.

With each suffix is associated a modification of the vowels of the preceding initial morpheme (addition or dropping of moras, limited changes in quality, addition of '). Each suffix occurs with only one particular vowel change (base plus vowel change is called stem in this grammar), but each vowel change occurs with one or more suffixes. There is no reason to consider these vowel changes as separate morphemes, since no meaning is in general assignable to them; furthermore they are limited in that any given suffix occurs with only one of them. The vowel changes could be considered as classifiers of suffixes, but that does not mean very much; classes of suffixes formed according to like vowel changes would correlate with nothing else, and it is not useful to set up classes that do not tie in with some other feature. It seems best therefore simply to consider the vowel changes as being part of the suffixes. There is no particular reason why morphemes should consist of whole phonemes. All that morphemics requires of phonemics is that it should be possible to identify each morpheme phonemically. A dropping or a change of phoneme is as good as a phoneme in constituting a morpheme. The suffixes therefore merely begin with phonemic vowel change, i.e. with components which change the preceding vowel phonemes, and then continue with ordinary phonemes. We can say that the causative is a·la· and is added only to the W+Z stem of the base: base *giẏi *touch* plus stem change W+Z yields giẏ- plus suffix a·la· yields giẏa·la·-. But we can also say that the causative is ‾a·la·, where V̄=zero: *giẏi+‾a·la·-=giẏa·la·-.

There are some special cases. In the noun there is an absolute form (marked by a vowel-change) which occurs only before the zero subjective case-ending, and an oblique form which occurs before all the other case-endings. Following the method used above, we consider the absolutive vowel change to be part of the subjective case ending; and since the suffixed part of the subjective case is zero we find that the vowel change is itself the subjective case morpheme. The oblique vowel change could be considered to be merely the first part of each oblique case-ending. But since it is common to a group of suffixes which have some relevant meaning in common, it would be more useful to consider it as a morpheme in itself, having general oblique meaning in contrast to the subjective-absolutive morpheme and occurring only before specific oblique cases; the oblique case morphemes, which only occur after this oblique morpheme, would then indicate specific meanings over and above the general oblique meaning.

Similarly, in the noun plural, we may have plural absolutive and oblique general morphemes (vowel changes plus i and h respectively), the latter occurring only before the same specific oblique case morphemes mentioned above.

There remain a few other morphemes with special phonemic forms. One is the reduplication suffix which alternates with the repetitive and which may be said to have the phonemic form of repeating the phonemes of the morpheme preceding it: it may be written as $C^1V^1C^2V^2$, where C^1 means the first consonant of the preceding morpheme, and so on. Another is a discontinuous dubitative morpheme na'aṣ...al. The facts in the case are that the particle na'aṣ always occurs before an initial morpheme which has the dubitative suffix al after it, and wherever al occurs after an initial morpheme, na'aṣ occurs before that initial morpheme. We may therefore consider the two elements as constituting a single morpheme, and thus avoid the necessity of making statements about the mutual limitations of their occurrence. There remain also a few special cases of initial morphemes such as the analogical bases (§ 12:19).

7. THE STRUCTURE OF YOKUTS AND OF SEMITIC

It is a remarkable feature of Yokuts structure that very many of its features are similar to features of Semitic structure. The case is sufficiently unusual to merit some indication of the similarities.

There are some similarities in the phonemic stock. Yokuts has three stops in each position: intermediate, aspirated, glottalized. Semitic apparently also had three stops in each position: voiced, voiceless and emphatic (with no labial emphatic). There is some slight evidence that the Semitic emphatic may have originally been doubly articulated sounds. Among the phonemic differences may be mentioned the absence of laryngals in Yokuts and the fact that Semitic had only three vowels.

The sequence of phonemic classes which make up an utterance is in general almost identical in the two structures. The formula given above for the Yokuts utterance can be used almost unchanged for Semitic.

There are also a number of similarities in the types of morpheme variation. Both structures very rarely have assimilation or metathesis of consonants. Both have a fair amount of vowel assimilation, although Semitic does not have the particular feature of vowel harmony. Semitic also has no truncation of consonants in suffixes, as Yokuts has. Both have some vowel assimilation across glottal stop.

Many similarities may also be seen in the phonemic structure of morphemes. Semitic has roots consisting (like Yokuts bases) for the most part of 2 or 3 consonants (and in some cases, vowels); there is some evidence that at an early period certain roots contained vowels which may have been independent morphemes rather than parts of the root. Semitic also had reduplication which, as in Yokuts, yields new roots to which suffixes are then added. Whereas Yokuts has only a few morphemes composed entirely of vowel change in the preceding morpheme, Semitic has many of these; on the other hand vowel changes in Semitic are only rarely parts of suffixes. Both structures, however, copiously use vowel change as morphemes or parts of morphemes. Semitic differs from Yokuts in two types of morphemes: doublings of root consonants, and prefixes.

One of the chief similarities between the two structures is in the status of the verb system as a formal nucleus of the morphology. In both, verbalizing and nominalizing suffixes are added to roots which are in themselves neither verbal nor nominal. In both, each verbal affix is added to all roots while each nominalizing affix is added only to particular roots. In both, there has been practically no borrowing of verb forms, while nouns are borrowed; and both have greater dialectal variation in the noun system. In Semitic there are more petrified noun stems than in Yokuts, and also a fair number of original noun roots. In both, nominalizing affixes and case endings always occur together, and in both there are a few new roots analogically formed within the language. The semantic function of some Yokuts noun suffixes are very like Semitic ones (§ 20:31). Yokuts has, however, many more suffixes, especially of verb aspects and the like, than does Semitic.

A number of syntactic similarities also appear. The syntactic position of the verbal noun (§ 20:3, 11) is very similar to that in Semitic.

It is impossible at present, of course, to say how many of these similarities are unusual among languages, how many of them are all the result of merely a few basic structural similarities (e.g. the greater borrowing of nouns is related to their unproductivity), and how important these features are relative to the rest of the two structures.

NOTES

[1] *Yokuts Language of California*, by Stanley Newman (Viking Fund Publications in Anthropology, 2), 247 pp., $2.50. 10 Rockefeller Plaza, New York 1944 (see Paper XIV of this volume.)

[2] The only misprint which might confuse the reader is the formula CVCr instead of the correct CWCr on p. 67.

[3] I.e. there is g, k, k̲, z, c, c̲, m, m̲, etc. The phonetic values of the phonemes are so evenly patterned that one could say that there are 4 stops and 2 affricates, to which voicing or glottalization may be added; 3 nasals and 3 voiced continuants, to which glottalization may be added; 3 voiceless continuants, and h and '.

[4] If the suffix vowels are a-i or i-a only the first harmonizes.

[5] But if the second vowel is of a different height it may be of either mouth position.

[6] A few exceptions are given by Newman in note 22.

[7] We cannot consider the vowel as the first part of the suffix, because each suffix occurs after both i and a last vowels, while each stem occurs with only one of them.

XIII

EMENEAU'S KOTA TEXTS

M. B. Emeneau: *Kota Texts: Part One* (University of California Publications in Linguistics, Vol. 2, No. 1), University of California Press, Berkeley – Los Angeles, 1944.

In this first major publication to result from his years in India, Emeneau shows how valuable it is for linguists to obtain the thorough and unhurried acquaintance with a language community which these years in India gave him. Emeneau publishes here eleven myths and tales in phonemic transcription, with translation and brief notes (38–191). This is preceded by a sketch of Kota grammar (15–29) and a short text with detailed linguistic analysis (30–5).

Kota is one of a small group of isolated Dravidian languages spoken in the Nilgiri Hills of South India. Almost no linguistically valid work has been done before on Kota, and little enough on the whole Dravidian family. Emeneau's work in Dravidian is the major achievement in this field. He is a master of linguistic method, and has produced in his brief sketch of Kota a model of compact description. The sketch introduces a number of innovations in analysis and presentation, not least of which is the very neat manner of indicating the many successively included quotations in Kota by successive subscript numerals (§ 4). The large body of texts permits other linguists to test Emeneau's analysis, and to search for morphological details and for syntactic and stylistic features.

Emeneau lists his phonemes in groups of those which have correspondingly differing positional variants in corresponding environments, thus achieving a very compact statement. He says that there are two prosodemes of vowel quality, short (unmarked) and long (marked by /·/), yielding /a/, /a·/, etc. This type of interpretation (for which he refers to Trager's 'Theory of Accentual Systems' in the *Sapir Memorial Volume*) is based on the fact that the /·/ phoneme differs from the others by being not an independent phoneme but some sort of process, a lengthening of the vowel (or consonant) phonemes. Such a view is of course entirely admissible and often convenient.

Language **13**, No. 4 (1945), 283–9.

It is however also possible to take a different view of /·/. It may be considered as merely a phoneme whose positional variants are second moras of
long vowels: after /a/ the positional variant of /·/ is another /a/-quality mora,
and so on. Complete phonemic overlapping is not involved, since the /a/-
mora is a member of /·/ only after /a/, in which position it is not a member of
/a/. Furthermore, in many languages it will be found that the second mora of
each vowel is not even identical with the first mora; they may all contain
some common phonetic feature (in Moroccan Arabic, an approximation of
the tongue toward centered vowel position) thus making it all the easier to
consider them variants of one phoneme in the usual sense. It should also be
noted that /·/ is not phonetically suprasegmental; it represents features of
sound which occur not simultaneously with other segmental phonemes but
among them in the time succession. It is often convenient, therefore, to
consider /·/ a prosodeme or suprasegmental phoneme only if it has peculiar
limitations of distribution, especially if it functions like stress patterns or
intonation contours.[1]

Emeneau recognizes four secondary phonemes, or junctures: utterance
final /./, /?/, /d̵/, and phrase-final /,/ occurring within the utterance. He also
notes: 'Within a phrase, i.e. a section of utterance between two secondary
phonemes, the first or only syllable of the first word has primary stress
accent, the first or only syllable of each succeeding word has secondary stress
accent. All other syllables are unaccented'. This could be integrated with the
juncture listing, by recognizing a word-juncture phoneme whose phonetic
value is a stress contour (loud on the first vowel after the preceding juncture,
zero otherwise), and by saying that all the other junctures, in addition to
marking the intonation or pause by which they are defined, also mark a
particular stress contour which extends over the stretch between any two
occurrences of them and is phonetically equivalent to the contour between
word junctures. The first vowel in a phrase would then have two loud stresses,
one due to its position relative to the word junctures and the other due to its
position relative to the other junctures, and would therefore be extra loud.
Since there is thus a phonetic and distributional feature common to all the
non-word junctures, this situation might perhaps be described by recognizing
a single phrase (non-word) juncture which would always have the phrase-
stress contour value.[2] The three intonations would then be phonemic
components which only occur simultaneously with the phrase juncture (i.e.
they would be quality differentiations of it). Phrase juncture plus assertion
intonation equals the /./ phoneme. Phrase juncture occurring alone equals the
/,/ phoneme. The chief convenience in this analysis lies in our being able to
say that the stress contour occurs automatically between every two word
junctures and again between every two phrase junctures, instead of saying

that it occurs over every previously undefined stretch between any secondary phoneme and any (identical or other) secondary phoneme.

In a very clear section entitled 'Phonological Operations' (§§ 5–14), Emeneau gives the morphophonemic statements. The model he uses is explicitly stated: For every morpheme he assumes a base form, which is composed not of phonemes but of morphophonemes. When the morphemes occur in words (i.e. in speech), the morphophonemes of their base forms are replaced by the corresponding phonemes: morphophoneme k by phoneme /k/, and so on. In some cases the replacement is not by the corresponding phoneme but by some other; e.g. morphophoneme n, when it is due to follow a morphophoneme ḷ, is replaced by phoneme /ṇ/. This occasional non-corresponding replacement is, of course, the only reason for the setting up of base forms and morphophonemes.

In the Kota material, two levels of replacement are distinguished. Morphophonemic operative rules, whether automatic (applying to all cases of the morphophonemes involved) or non-automatic (applying to the morphophonemes only in particular morphemes), yield words from the base forms of the one or more morphemes of which each word is composed. The words themselves, however, have different phonemic forms in different environments; these differences in forms are given by rules of external sandhi, which, as is noted in § 8, often coincide with the morphophonemic operative rules. The need to set up a second base form, the basic word by the side of the basic morpheme, and the inconvenience of having two sets of replacement rules which largely coincide, can be avoided if we accept Emeneau's fundamental model, but in a slightly modified form. We would set up base forms of morphemes, whose elements are morphophonemes, and say that when these morphemes occur in speech (not merely in the word) the morphophonemes are replaced by phonemes. Whether a given morphophoneme is replaced by its analogous phoneme or by some other phoneme, depends on the other morphophonemes, junctures, and morphemes which occur around it in the utterance. Non-automatic replacements will then be those that involve some particular morphemes; automatic replacements will be all others. If a replacement involves certain neighboring morphophonemes to the exclusion of any juncture, it is what Emeneau calls a morphophonemic rule, i.e. it operates only between morphemes within a word: morphophoneme y is replaced by zero when it follows morphophoneme č within a word (piṛčuko 'he clenched', from base forms piṛč-, -yuko; cf. poḷŋgyuko 'he had social intercourse according to caste or intercaste rules'). If the replacement operates whether or not a juncture appears in the immediate environment, it is equivalent both to a morphophonemic rule and to a rule of external sandhi: morphophonemes ty are replaced by zero when they precede morphophoneme t or ⁎t (where ⁎ indicates word juncture; kati·r- 'knife-to cut', ka⁎tač 'knife and stick', from base forms katy 'knife', tayr[3], tač). If a replacement occurs only when a juncture is in the immediate environment, it is what Emeneau calls a rule of external sandhi: we would say morphophoneme X is replaced by phoneme Y when it precedes ⁎Z (not Z alone). In all these cases, the only juncture in question is word boundary; no Kota replacement is affected by features across a phrase juncture.

The coalescing of morphophonemics and external sandhi, by making juncture part of the environment which determines replacements, is merely a very minor modification of the Kota analysis. The model used by Emeneau in this analysis is probably the clearest way of treating morphophonemic phenomena, and most convenient for many languages. It is worth noting, however, that it is possible to present the same facts in quite a different manner. Instead of using the model of base forms composed of morphophonemes, it is possible to speak directly in terms of the observable morphemes and phonemes. We then say that each morpheme is composed of phonemes, but that in some cases we find two or more morphemes which are complementary to each other and function distributionally as one morpheme. We therefore treat these two or more as positional variants of one functional morpheme and state in what environment each variant occurs. If the difference between the variants affects only one or two phonemes, we may accept one variant as being primary, and say that when the given morpheme (in its primary variant) occurs in a particular environment, these phonemes are replaced by others. This parallels the non-automatic morphophonemic or external sandhi rules. If the difference appears in all morphemes which have a particular phoneme or phoneme sequence, we say just that, and so parallel the automatic rules: all morphemes ending in /ty/ have variants without the /ty/ when a morpheme beginning with /t/ follows (after zero or ⁎ juncture). The whole morphophonemics and sandhi thus becomes a series of statements about variants of morphemes.

When we consider Emeneau's syntax (§§ 15–31) and morphology (§§ 32–68) sections, we find a summary description of word classes, utterance types, and constructions of word classes, nouns, verbs, and particles. It may be instructive to see how this analysis can be summarized in a slightly different presentation.

If we ask what morpheme classes Emeneau has found, we obtain the following:

noun-stems (*n*, §§ 32–4)	verb stem derivation (*S*, §§ 48–53)[4]
verb-stems (*v*, §§ 42–7)	verb stem extensions (*e*, § 59)
interjections (*i*, § 16)	non-finite (gerundial) stem extensions (*g*, § 63)

particles (*P*, called particles of the second class, or indicators of sensations, §§ 16, 65)

relation suffixes (*R*, § 31)

particle nominalizers (the suffix -n, § 23)

particle suffixes (*p*, § 67)

secondary noun derivation suffixes (*s*, § 36)

case-suffixes (*c*, §§ 33–4)

deverbal noun derivation (*d*, § 17)

denominal verb derivation (*D*, occurring with only a few noun stems, § 17)

tense and modal suffixes (*m*, §§ 55–8, 61)

the suffix -k of the argumentative and voluntative (§§ 54, 57)

personal suffixes (three sub-classes E^1, E^3, E^4, § 54)

finite suffixes invariant for person (*f*, § 60)

non-finite suffixes invariant for person (*F*, §§ 62–3)

Each morpheme in a morpheme class has essentially the same distribution relative to the other morpheme classes as any other morpheme in the same class. There are, however, various special sub-classes within some of the classes, consisting of morphemes which have distributions partially different from those of the other members of their class. There are many such sub-classes among the verb stems (§§ 43–7); verb stems also differ in the form of the transitive suffix that occurs with them, or in their non-occurrence with the transitive suffix (§§ 48–52). Among the noun stems, the pronouns (personal § 38, demonstrative § 39) and the numerals (§ 40) have special restrictions. So also does the noun stem gīX 'the like' (§ 27)[5] which occurs only as second noun in the copulative construction, i.e. as N^2 in N^1 $N^2 = N$.

While each noun and verb stem has here been considered a single morpheme, many of them have two forms (called by Emeneau absolute and oblique for nouns, S^1 and S^2 for verbs). It is not necessary to regard these dual forms as constituting dual morphemes, or as involving any process other than morphophonemic alternation.

In the case of the nouns, where both forms are identical in most stems, we need merely take the stem before oblique case suffixes as normal. Usually, the noun in the absolute case is identical with this, but with a zero case suffix. When we find a stem which has a different form in the absolute (e.g. marm 'tree', mart-k 'to yonder tree'), we may say that the change itself is the suffix of the absolute case (e.g. change of t to m); or we may say that here, as elsewhere, the absolute case suffix is zero, but that these stems have a special positional variant which occurs only before the zero suffix.[6]

In the case of the verbs, we can say that each stem has a special positional variant when it occurs before certain suffixes. The variant ($= S^2$) is marked in most cases by the addition of y, less frequently t; but some stems have more complicated variations (§§ 43–7). Even the situation described in § 59, where S^2 + the morpheme uḷ $= S^1$, can be described in these terms. We would say that the verb stems occur (a) before person-invariants like -ve·ro· 'must' (§ 60), and (b) before future, voluntative, imperative, and other suffixes, as well as (c) before potential, irrealis, present, past, argumentative, and other suffixes. We would further say that the stems have their special variant form when they occur before the (c) suffixes, or before uḷ + the (b) suffixes.

Similarly, the two third person forms -a and -o (indicated by E^1 and E^2) can be considered variants of one morpheme. We say that the morpheme -o has a variant -a when it follows the potential or irrealis morphemes, and in some other positions. E^1 below will therefore represent Emeneau's E^1 and E^2.

The interrelations among these morpheme classes can be expressed in a manner which will show their relation to the immediate constituents of the utterance types. To do so we need merely indicate by means of equations what sequences of morphemes can be substituted for what single morpheme classes in the utterances in which they occur.[7]

In the first place, if we include the zero of the absolute case as a case suffix, and one or two zero suffixes for the verb stem (e.g. the singular person after the imperative, or a zero member of d), then neither the noun stems nor the verb stems ever occur without suffixes, and the latter need not be mentioned in our final statements about the structure of utterances. In particular:

$n\ s = n$ (I.e. a primary noun stem can be substituted for a secondary one which is composed of some noun stem plus a derivation suffix.)

$v\ d = n$ (I.e. a primary noun stem is distributionally equivalent to a verb stem plus deverbal noun-deriving suffix.)

$n\ c = N$ (I.e. noun stems, whether primary n or composed of $n\ s$ or $v\ d$ to which n is equivalent, always occur with case suffixes; this sequence will be marked N.[8])

$n\ D = v$

$v\ S = v$

$v\ e = v$

$v\ g\ F = v\ F$ (Stems before non-finite endings F may or may not have the intervening suffixes of g: in S^2 -mel 'if one does' and S^2 -ṭ -mel 'if one has done' the stem and stem plus ṭ are distributionally equivalent.)

$m\ E^{1,3,4} = E^{1,3,4}$ (Since the tense and modal suffixes never occur without a personal suffix, it is sufficient to indicate only the personal suffix. If we are willing to accept a few zero members of m, e.g. in the indicative present and the imperative, we can also say that E never occurs without m, so that writing E will always indicate mE.)

$v\ E^1 = V$ (Whether v is primary or composed of nD, vS, etc., when it occurs with E^1 it is in utterance final position, and will be marked V.)

$v\ E^3 = V$ (Emeneau indicates in § 54 and fn. 5 that this can be taken either as V or as utterance-final N. Since other N are not restricted to utterance final, and since other utterance-final N are preceded by /,/ as in § 19, whereas V and the present $v\,E^3$ are not, it seems more convenient to consider this equivalent to V in distribution.)

$v\,E^4$ -k $=V$ (This occurs only with the argumentative and voluntative members of m.[9])

$v\,f=V$ (I.e. $v\,f$, $v\,E^4$ -k, $v\,E^3$, $v\,E^1$ can each be substituted for any of the others.)

$F=V^1$ (V^1 will indicate verbs followed by /,/ rather than by /./, /č/, or /?/. § 61 suggests that there are also sequences of the form vmE^1 which are equivalent to V^1, i.e. restricted to occur before /,/.)

$v\,E^4=N$ (E^4 without the -k; note that this equals N, not n; i.e. it does not take case-endings.)

P -n $=N$ (The sequence P -n occurs in the series of N that precede a V.)

$P\,p=P$

$X\,R=X$ (Where X may be either N, V, or V^1.)

$X\,X=X$ (Where X may be N, V^1, or P, and the double writing indicates repetition of the particular stem, sometimes in a slightly variant form, with a repetitive or intensive meaning, § 29).

$N^1\,N^2=N$ (For only a few pairs of members of N, or for the morpheme gĭX which occurs only in N^2; the meaning is 'N^1 and N^2', but a single N can be substituted for the phrase, § 27.)

$N,\,N=N$ (Meaning 'N and N', § 27; or with relations set by their case-endings, § 23.)

$N\,N=N$; $Nd\,N=N$ (The first is the attribute of the second; d is a suffix of N in first position. vE^4 perhaps does not occur in second position, § 25.)

$N\,N\,s=N$ (This rare construction may be considered exocentric; or else the s may be considered the head, with each member the attribute of its successor, thus making the construction parallel to the one above, § 26.)

quoted material $=N$ (E.g. in § 24.)

NV^1, $NV^1=NV^1$ (Repeated clauses can be replaced by one, § 21.)

NV^1, $NV=NV$ (The V clause can substitute for one preceded by V^1, § 21.)

$V=NV$ (§ 20.)

Since it is possible to replace either side of each equation by the other side, we can now express all the sequences of morphemes discussed here in terms of only a few morpheme classes: P, N, V, and I. Each utterance of Kota, i.e. every stretch of speech between one occurrence of /./, /č/, /?/ (or silence) and another[10], may be described as consisting of one of the following sequences (or their equivalents): N, N or $N\,V$ or I or P or N (§§ 18–20).

NOTES

[1] Here, as in the other cases below, the alternative analyses are given only for their own sake and as examples of possible methods of analysis. They are in no way presumed to correct or amplify Emeneau's interpretation.

[2] Identical in phonetic form, but not in extent, with the phonetic value of the word juncture.

[3] Replacement of ay by i· is due to another rule.

[4] This includes the transitive suffix, whose chief form is č, and the mediacy suffix, whose chief form is kč. Since the two apparently do not occur together, and since the transitive meaning is implicit in the mediacy suffix, the latter could be broken into two: -k- 'mediacy', -č- transitive. This partition, however, would have the drawback of yielding a morpheme which is limited to occur only with the transitive.

[5] X represents whatever follows the $C\check{V}$ of the preceding noun stem: puj 'tiger', puj gij 'tigers and the like'. The 'and' is not part of the meaning of gĭX, since it occurs in all cases of the construction $N^1 N^2 = N$, as in im a·v 'buffaloes and cows'.

[6] Equivalently, we may say that the pre-oblique case form is a variant of the other.

[7] Emeneau has already done this in part in the equations S^2 -uḷ $= S^1$, etc., in § 59.

[8] If we do not wish to regard the absolute case as a zero suffix, but prefer to say that when there is no suffix it is merely the noun stem by itself that occurs (in absolute meaning), we would have to replace this equation by $nc = n$, indicating that a noun stem without case ending occurs in the same environments as a noun stem with case ending.

[9] There are restrictions on the concurrence of $E^{3,4}$ and members of m. Some tense-modal suffixes occur with E^3, others with E^4. The indicative present-future occurs with either one.

[10] Each ends in one of these three. If they were grouped into one class, marked, say, by z, we could say that each utterance is of the form N, Nz or NVz and so on. This is an added reason for distinguishing them from /,/ as was done above.

XIV

STRUCTURAL RESTATEMENTS: I

The series of papers of which this is the first will attempt to restate in summary fashion the grammatical structures of a number of American Indian languages. The languages to be treated are those presented in Harry Hoijer and others, *Linguistic Structures of Native America*, New York 1946.[1] These restatements are not based on new field work, but on the contributions in this volume and on the chief published treatments of the languages in question, as well as on limited manuscript material. While the other publications and manuscript material have been consulted for additional details and for purposes of checking results, the chief basis for each restatement is the corresponding contribution in *LSNA* (to which the reader is referred throughout), since a major purpose in the present series is comparability with these contributions.

The justification for this series is therefore not the presentation of new data, but the testing and exploring of statements of morphological structure. The statements in this series will differ from those in *LSNA* partly in the use of somewhat different techniques and compact formulations, but chiefly in being restricted to the distributional relations among the elements of the language. The present restriction to distributional relations carries no implication of the irrelevance or inutility of other relations of the linguistic elements, in particular their meanings. Information concerning the meanings is not derivable from the distributional statements, and is clearly necessary for any utilization of the language. However, because of the differences between the distributional relations and such other relations as those of meaning and phonemic similarity, and because of the independence of each type of relation in respect to the other types, it becomes desirable to examine each type of relation separately.

SWADESH' ESKIMO[2]

1. *Morpheme Alternants and Morphophonemes*[3]

A great deal of the complexity of Eskimo grammar derives from the fact

International Journal of American Linguistics 13, No. 1 (1947), 47–58.

that many morphemes have variant phonemic forms in various environments.[4] Some of these phonemic differences among the alternants of particular morphemes can be expressed by regular phonological statements. E.g. when a (suffix) morpheme beginning with two consonants follows in close juncture after a morpheme ending in a consonant, the suffix has an alternant lacking the first of the two consonants (Swadesh, 33–4); this fits in with the fact of phonemic distribution that consonants occur in clusters of one or two and no more.[5]

In the case of other morphemes, the alternation among their positional variants can be expressed compactly with the aid of morphophonemic symbols. E.g. certain morphemes containing the phoneme i in many environments have alternants with a instead of i when a vowel follows. Swadesh (33) writes the i in these morphemes as ĭ, while the i in other morphemes (which do not have this and other alternations characteristic of i) is not specially marked.[6] Of the many suffixes, certain ones have correspondingly different alternants in correspondingly different environments; Swadesh (32) marks each such group of suffixes with a particular morphophonemic juncture, and offers compact statements of the phonemic alternations which occur in the environment of each such juncture.

The alternations of one group of stems in various environments do not correspond to the alternations of other groups of stems in those environments (e.g. tikĭq *forefinger* has the variant tikiɣ before -it *plural*, while alĭq *harpoon line* has the variant aɣl before -it). Kleinschmidt, Barnum, and Thalbitzer discuss this under the heading of various 'classes' of stems, and deal with it in those sections of the grammar in which they indicate the suffixes with which these stems occur. Since these stems, however, do not differ in the suffixes with which they occur but only in the phonemic alternations of their variants, the information concerning their differences (i.e. concerning their variants) can be given (as is done by Swadesh) at the point where phonemic variations within morphemes is treated.[7]

Various groups of suffixes also have special variants in particular environments. For example, after the N_d group of morphemes (demonstrative sub-group of nouns) the various C morphemes (case-endings) have variants different from those which they have after other N morphemes: inuɲnut *to people*, isuanut *to its end*, but qaβuɲa *to the south*, aβuɲa *to the north;* qaqqamit *from the mountain*, uβlaamit *from morning*, but qaβaɲɲa *from the south*, aβaɲɲa *from the north*.[8]

Among the alternations of morphemes in different environments we may also consider the varying and repeated forms of the number and case morphemes, and the various forms of the person morphemes, after these morphemes are separated out in section 3 below.

2. Morpheme Classes

P: particles, not occurring with any of the non-initial morphemes listed below (except in one specially noted case), and in most cases having each by itself the phonemic characteristics of a word. These may be subdivided as follows:

P_a: frequently occurring alone as a whole utterance: aak *yes.*

P_b: occurring usually as utterance introducers: imaqa *imagine!....*

P_c: occurring usually before words containing M_s (verbs with subordinate mood suffixes) and before words containing C_r (relative case): nauk *although.* For greater detail, this group could be further subdivided, since various members of P_c occur before particular members of M_s.

P_d: occurring chiefly before words containing M_v: imannat *so many,* qaɲa *when?*

P_e: a sub-group of P_d which also occurs with a suffix following it, the suffix being -nit *from, as against,* a member of C_o (plus plural): itsaq *years ago* (member of P_d), itsaɣ-nit *as compared with years ago.*

tak-: an emphatic morpheme prefixed occasionally to S_{nd} morphemes.

S: stems, occurring initially in the word, with non-initial (suffix) morphemes following within the word. In some cases these suffixes are zero and we may say that the stem constitutes the whole word. Various sub-groups of S may be distinguished according to the particular suffixes which sometimes occur directly after them.

S_{vi}: intransitive verb stems, which sometimes occur directly before Q_a suffixes, but never immediately before Q_b suffixes: au *to rot.*

S_{vt}: transitive verb stems, which sometimes occur immediately before Q_b suffixes, but never immediately before Q_a: tuqut *to kill.* S_v will be used to indicate both S_{vi} and S_{vt}.

S_x: stems which occur both in S_{vi} or S_{vt} positions and in S_n positions.

S_n: nominal stems, which sometimes occur immediately before Q_c or C suffixes: iɣlu *house.*

S_{nd}: demonstratives, occurring directly before C suffixes (which in this position have special variants), but not before Q_c; and occurring occasionally after tak-: ma- *here.*

S_{ni}: interrogatives and some other pronouns, occurring before C and -t *plural,* but not before Q_c: kik- *who?*

S_{nr}: stems which always occur with Q_c; there are various sub-groups, one of which always occurs with C_r: kisi *alone.*

S_{np}: personal pronoun stems which occur only with particular ones of Q_c: uβa- occurs only with -na *I;* iliβ- only with -t (iβlit *thou*).

S_{nn}: numerals, entering into special sequences with each other. Except for atausiq *one,* these never occur without either the dual or the plural suffix following them, and have two plural suffixes: sisamat *four*, sisamait *four groups*.

T: non-initial morphemes, which always follow a member of S or another T; one group follows C. Those T which occur after S_{vi} will be marked with a $_{vi}$ subscript. Those T which occur after no S other than S_n will be marked with subscript $_n$; and so on. Each T morpheme is thus marked with a subscript indicating after what group of S it occurs. Each T will also be provided with a second subscript, to indicate whether it is ever followed immediately by Q_a (in which case it would be similar to S_{vi}), or by Q_b (thus being similar to S_{vt}), or by Q_c or C (which would be similar to S_n). T_{vn} will then indicate a T morpheme which sometimes occurs directly after S_v, and sometimes occurs directly before Q_c or C morphemes [9]; occasionally, of course, this T_{vn} will occur before or after other T morphemes, in which position its specific T_{vn} status could not be determined without additional data about the other environments in which it occurs. The subscript $_x$ will be used to indicate $_{vi}$, $_{vt}$, and $_n$ equally: T_{xn} thus marks a morpheme which occurs occasionally after S_{vi}, S_{vt}, or S_n (as well as after T), and which is sometimes followed by Q_c or C, but never by Q_a or by Q_b. Furthermore, the first subscript of each T also indicates which sub-groups of T it occurs directly after : T_{vn} does not follow T morphemes whose second subscript is $_v$, but only those whose second subscript is $_n$ (or $_x$, if the last subscript before $_x$ is $_n$). The following sub-groups of T may be noted: T_{nn} (never directly after S_v, nor directly before Q_a or Q_b), T_{xn}, T_{vn}, T_{vv} (never directly after S_n nor directly before Q_c or C), T_{xv} (after anything, but never directly before Q_c or C), T_{vn}, T_{xx} (followed by whatever would follow the predecessor of T_{xx}; e.g. $S_n T_{xx}$ could be followed by T_{nv} or Q_c, while $S_v T_{xx}$ could be followed by T_{vv} or Q_a), T_{vtvi} (never after S_{vi} or S_n, nor before Q_b or Q_c), T_{xvi}, T_{xvt}, T_{cv} (only after C and before M_v).

M: The modal morphemes in this group are merely a special case of the T_v morphemes. They are listed separately only because they are the last of any sequence of T, and because every Q_a or Q_b has a member of M_v preceding it, though it may have no other T in the word.

M_{vi}: the last T_{vvi}, always present before Q_a: -βu- *intransitive*.

M_{vt}: the last T_{vvt}, always present before Q_b: -βa- *transitive*.

M_{vs}: those M_v (whether M_{vi} or M_{vt}), after which the members of Q_b containing recurrent ('fourth') person sometimes occur: -γa- *because, when* ....

M_n: a small group of 'participial' T_{vn} which occur only directly before C or Q_c (but directly after S_v or any T whose second subscript is $_v$): -ni- *abstract nominalizer*.

C: case-endings, occurring directly after S_n and after every M_n, and after every sequence of T morphemes (excluding T_{cv}) if the last subscript in the sequence is n.[10] In particular:

C_a: absolutive, which has grammatical concord as to plural with Q_a in the following word (within the utterance). This morpheme has many alternants, among them -q (unnuaq *night*), -k (inuk *man*), zero (iɣlu *house*).

C_r: relative, which has grammatical concord as to plural with Q_c in the following word (within the utterance). This morpheme is -p (iɣlup *of the house*).

C_o: the other (adverbial or local) members of C: -mi *in*, -mit *from*, -mut *to*, -kut *through*, -mik *by means of*, -tut *like*.

D: dual (-k) and plural (-t) morphemes, which occur, within the word, in the position of C_r and C_a: iɣluk *two houses*, iɣlut *houses*.

Q_a: personal ('subject') pronouns which occur after M_{vi}: -q *he did, he does* (lists in Kleinschmidt, 19–20 Table 2 under 'ohne suff.'; Thalbitzer, 1033; Barnum, 117–20).

Q_b: personal ('subject-object') pronouns which occur after M_{vt}: -aa *he … him* (lists in Kleinschmidt, 19–20 Table 2; Thalbitzer, 1034; Barnum, 123).

Q_c: personal ('possessive') pronouns which occur directly after S_n, or after every sequence of T or M the last subscript in which is $_n$: -ɣa *my* (lists in Kleinschmidt, 19–20, Table 1; Thalbitzer, 1021–2; Barnum, 19).

E: enclitics, occurring, within the word, after all the morpheme classes listed above: -lu *and*.

3. *Morphemic Components*

The further analysis of the structure can be facilitated by a breakdown of Q_a, Q_b, and Q_c into morphemic components. Whereas each member of these classes, say -tik *of you two* (Q_c), has been considered as a single whole morpheme, it is possible to consider it now as a combination of morphemic components. In the case of -tik, these components would be C_a, dual, and second person. In order to admit this breakdown in the present analysis, it will have to be based not on meaning but on distribution.[11] This distributional differentiation, however, will be not in respect to the rest of the word (since all members of Q_c are identical in distribution in respect to the rest of the word in which they occur), but in respect to other members of Q_a, Q_b, Q_c and D in other words.

Since the positions of C_a and C_r have been defined, we notice that some members of Q_c are substitutable for C_a (the whole utterance remaining otherwise unchanged), and as many other members are substitutable for C_r. On this basis we say that half the members of Q_c contain C_a (e.g. -ɣa *my* in iɣlu-ɣa *my house*), while the other half contain C_r (e.g. -ma *my, of my* in iɣlu-ma *of my house*).

Two or more words containing C (some of which may begin with S_n, others with S_{nd}) may occur in sequence; the last of these may contain Q_c and the others not: uqautsit makkua tusaɣkaβit *words, these, thy-heard-ones*. In such cases it is noticed that if the first words contain the plural suffix, only certain members of Q_c occur in the last word; if the first words contain the dual suffix, only certain other members of Q_c occur in the last word; and if the first words contain no D suffix, again only particular members of Q_c occur in the last word. On this basis, we divide Q_c into three parallel groups, the members of the first group containing the plural of the preceding S, the members of the second containing the dual, and the members of the third containing neither. The grammatical agreement among the words in the sequence is then expressed by saying that the plural morpheme does not occur in each word independently, but occurs over all the words in the sequence at once. I.e. in this environment the plural and the dual are discontinuous morphemes, suffixed to the sequence as a whole; if the plural occurs here, its phonemic form consists of sections which are appended to each word in the sequence. Similarly, the member of C appended to each word in the sequence is the same (in the example above, the first two words have C_r and the Q_c of the last word contains C_r). The C morphemes are therefore discontinuous in this environment in the same way as the D morphemes.

In other cases, we have a sequence of two words, the first containing C_r and the second any C (not necessarily C_r), which may be included in Q_c: umiap suyua *of the boat, its front*. Here we notice that if the first word lacks the plural suffix, only certain members of Q_c occur in the second word; and if the first has the plural, certain other Q_c occur in the second. This division of Q_c is not the same as in the paragraph above. Hence we can redivide Q_c along a new criterion: those which contain the plural of the preceding C_r and those which contain the singular of the preceding C_r. In accordance with the last paragraph, both -i *his...s* and -it *their...s* (both are Q_c containing C_a) contain the plural of their preceding S and agree with the plural of the other C_a words in the sequence, while -a *his one* and -at *their one* (also Q_c containing C_a) do not contain the plural of their S and agree with the lack of plural in the other C_a words of that sequence.[12] In terms of the present paragraph, both -it *their...s* and -at *their one* contain the plural of their own person agreeing with the plural of the C_r word which comes before in the sequence, while -i *his...s* and -a *his one* do not contain the plural, again in agreement with the C_r word.

In a similar way, we find differences of distribution and an agreement between members of Q_c which occur in sequences with morphemes meaning

I, those occurring with morphemes meaning *thou*, those occurring with S_n words or morphemes meaning *he* (*she*), and those occurring in a special subset of the positions of the last members mentioned.[13] The Q_c thus contain elements agreeing with person.

When a word contains Q_c but no C_o, we can now analyze each Q_c as containing the following components: either C_a or C_r; either singular or dual or plural of the S-part of the word to which the Q_c is suffixed; first, second, or third (or, in some positions, fourth) person (as possessor of the S-part); and singular, dual, or plural of the person. In words which contain C_o after the Q_c (e.g. nuna-βti-nit *from our land*) only half the Q_c members occur. I.e. the Q_c are not differentiated as to C_a and C_r in this case, and we may say that they do not contain C_a or C_r: the C_o which follows the Q_c replaces the C_a or C_r which is contained in the Q_c when there is no C_o following.[14]

The members of Q_a can also be considered as combinations of morphemic components. In a sequence consisting of word with C_a and word with Q_a, only half of Q_a occur if the C_a lacks plural suffix, while the other half occur if the C_a has the plural: inu-k pisuɣ-pu-q *the man went*, inu-it pisuɣ-pu-t *the men, they went*. Similarly, particular Q_a occur according to the person of the C_a word.[15] We therefore analyze each Q_a into a person component and a number component.

We now note the limitations of Q_b in respect to sequences consisting of word with C_r plus word with C_a plus word with Q_b. If D follows the C_r we find only particular Q_a morphemes occurring, the rest occurring if D does not follow C_r. There is a similar subgrouping of the Q_b morphemes in agreement with the presence or absence of D morphemes after C_a. This subgrouping, however, criss-crosses with sub-grouping in agreement with D after C_r. Finally, it is also possible to obtain separate sub-groupings of Q_b in agreement with the person of the C_r-containing word and in agreement with the person of the C_a containing word. On the basis of all this we consider each Q_b as a combination of four components: person ('subject'); its number; another person ('object'); the number of this other person.

The various agreements as to D noted in the last few paragraphs can be expressed by saying that in the sequence environments[16] $-C_r...-CR...$, $-C_a...-M_{vi}R...$, $-C_r...-M_{vt}R...R$, and $-C_a...-M_{vt}RR...$ the D morphemes are discontinuous, being composed of sections one of which occurs in each position within the sequence (if the D morpheme occurs in that sequence).

The many Q_a, Q_b and Q_c morphemes have now been reduced distributionally to various combinations of four R components and the previously recognized D, C_a, and C_r.[17] There is gain rather than loss in considering the person references of Q_a and Q_c, and the double references of Q_b, as being all the same elements R rather than different possessive, subject, object, etc., pronouns. It is characteristic of Eskimo that not only are these pronouns different in meaning from English subject, object, etc., but they also do not differ in meaning from each other except in ways related to the difference in their positions. The R of Q_a, and to a lesser extent of Q_b, are often phonemically identical or similar to the corresponding R of Q_c. The third person singular member of Q_a has in many environments the variant -q, identical with the C_a suffix. From the point of view of English, tikipputit (S_v M_{vi} R) can be translated *thy arrival* (as though it were S_n C_a R) or *thou arrivest*; tikippuq (also S_v M_{vi} R) can be translated *arrival* (as though it were S_n C_a) or *he arrives*.

Various special distributional limitations can be conveniently stated in terms of these components. For example, the two R in a Q_b morpheme are never the same. We do not have a given person as both 'subject' and 'object' in a Q_b; English *he stabs himself* would be translated in the same way as *he is stabbed* or *(someone) stabs him*, i.e. kapiβuq (S_v M_{vi} R). The first three persons of R have much the same distribution. The fourth or recurrent, meaning *he himself* or *his own*, occurs almost only[18] in -C...(-C) -M_v R_3 and -M_{vs}(R_a)... -$M_v$$R_3$($R_a$).

In a similar but much simpler analysis, the negative-modal morphemes (Thalbitzer, 1036–45) can be broken down into combinations of a negative component (member of T_{vv} and occurring last before M) plus the previously recognized M morphemes.

4. *Equivalence of Morpheme Sequences*

A compact description of the structure of utterances in terms of the morpheme classes can be obtained if we equate every morpheme class or sequence of morpheme classes to any other sequence which substitutes for it within the utterance.

We begin with the classes S_v and S_n and their equivalents.

$S_n = N^1$. This and the next equation are merely a change of symbols so as not to confuse the syntactic status of N and V sequences with the specific morpheme classes S_n and S_v. S_n includes all the subgroups of S_n, within the distributional limitations noted in § 2 above.

$S_v = V^1$.

$S_n T_{nn} = N^1$. The sequence of S_n and T_{nn} can be substituted for S_n (i.e. the sequence occurs in the same utterance positions and word positions as does S_n). Since the S_n of this equation can itself be the resultant of $S_n T_{nn} = N^1$ (since $S_n = N^1$), this equation permits a whole series of T_{nn} after an initial S_n.

$S_x T_{xn} = N^1$.

$S_v \ T_{vn} = N^1$.

$S_v \ T_{vv} = V^1$. E.g. tuqut *kill* (S_{vt}), tuqutsi *kill-things* ($S_{vt} \ T_{vtvi} = V_i^1$).

$S_x \ T_{xv} = V^1$.

$S_n \ T_{nv} = V^1$. E.g. iγlu-qaq *have a house*, substitutable for tikip *arrive*.

$N \ T_{xx} = N$. E.g. iγlu-inaq *only a house*.

$V \ T_{xx} = V$.

tak- $S_{nd}^1 = S_{nd}^2$. S_{nd}^2 is included in S_n above.

When N or V are not substitutable for all the preceding N or V, they are given a higher raised numeral than the ones for which they do not substitute.

$V \ M_n = N^2$. To this N^2 we can no longer add, say, T_{nn}, since T_{nn} is added only to N^1.

$N^2 \ C \ T_{cv} = V^2$. A raised numeral on the left hand side of the equation represents itself and all lower numerals.

$V^2 \ M_v = V^3$.

$V^2 \ M_{vs} = V_s^3$.

$N^2 \ R = N^3$.

$N^3 \ (S_{nd}) \ N^3 = N^3$. When C is added here it is added as one discontinuous suffix to each word in this sequence.

$N^3 \ C_r \ N^3 = N^3$.

$N^3 \ C_o \ N^3 = N^3$. This is reported to be rare.

$V_s^3 \ (N_r^3) \ N_a^3 \ N = N$. See below.

$P_c \ V_s = V_s$.

$N^3 \ C_o = P_d$.

$P_e \ C_o = P_d$.

$P_d \ V^3 = V^3$.

$N^3 \ C_o \ V^3 = V^3$.

In what follows it is noteworthy that although V sometimes occurs with one R (Q_a) and sometimes with two R (Q_b), and although the N_a preceding it sometimes agrees with and refers to the 'subject' R of the V (when it is Q_a) and sometimes the 'object' R of the V (the second R or Q_b), we can nevertheless make a simple distributional statement in the matter: V always has an R agreeing as to plural and person with a preceding N_a, and only sometimes does it also have an R agreeing with a preceding N_r.

$N^3 \ C_a \ V^3 \ R = V^3 \ R = N_a^4 \ V^3$. The presence of only one R indicates that the $V^3 = V^2 \ M_{vi}$.

$N^3 \ C_r \ V^3 \ R \ N_a^4 = N_r^4 \ N_a^4 \ V^3$. The presence of two R (one listed after the V^3 and the other included in the N_a^4) indicates that the $V^3 = V^2 \ M_{vt}$.

$N^4 \ D = N^5$. If the N^4 has discontinuous parts, so has the D.

$(N_r^5) \ N_a^5 \ V_s^3 \ (N_r^5) \ N_a^5 \ V^3 = (N_r^5) \ N_a^5 \ V^3$.

P_b utterance = utterance.

Bearing in mind the fact that for each symbol henceforth used we can carry out the substitutions permitted by the equations above, we can now say that every utterance consists either of P_a or else of

$$N_a^5 \text{ with} \begin{cases} V^3 \ (N_r^5) \text{ or} \\ N_a^5 \text{ or} \\ P_d \end{cases}$$

or any single word.

5. *Utterance Structure*

If we consider not the particular distributional interrelations among the morpheme classes, as expressed in § 4, but their relation to word and utterance juncture, we find that the structure of any minimum utterance (word) is either P or else

$$S \text{ (a number of } T) \begin{cases} ((M_n) \, CT_{cv}) M_v \, R \\ (M_n) \qquad\qquad\quad C \end{cases} (D)(R(D))(E)$$

The order is generally as indicated, except that the separation of R, D, and C components is not always subject to a clear ordering, and that C_o morphemes occur after $R(D)$.

All utterances are sequences of these minimum utterances within the limitations noted in § 4.

The final statement can be varied by various alternative formulations. For example, D could become an always-occurring rather than sometimes-occurring suffix of N^4 (i.e. of N and of R) if we added a zero singular to the dual and plural. Conversely, R could be reduced to a sometimes-occurring suffix of V if one of the persons, say R_3, were regarded as automatic to V, so that the mere occurrence of V included the occurrence of R_3 unless another R is specified. This could not be done to the second (R) in the formula above, since all the members of this R are occasionally absent, so that no one of them could be regarded as automatically present. In a similar fashion, M_v and C could be reduced to sometimes-occurring classes; in the case of C either C_a or C_r could be considered automatic with every N. All these variations, however, would not make a considerable change in the structural formulation.

A number of the characteristics of Eskimo as compared with other languages appear in this statement of the distributional structure: e.g. the large number of morphophonemic variations in phonemic environments (especially of morpheme-boundary consonants); the long stringing of non-initial morphemes; the fact that S and either $M_v R$ or C occur in every non-P word (and that the occurrence of one member of each of these classes

excludes the occurrence of any other member in that word). Other characteristics of Eskimo do not appear here: chiefly, the fact that there are very
many T morphemes; and the specific action or situation meanings of many
of the T (e.g. -siaq *obtained*, -kuluk *lonely*, -miu *inhabitant of*, -ɣnit *to smell
of*).

NEWMAN'S YAWELMANI[19]

1. *Phonemic Composition of Morphemes*

A major characteristic of Yokuts is the fact that morphemes of particular
distributional classes have very limited types of phonemic composition. For
example, all morphemes of class V^1 (not including V_a^1) consist of either 2 or 3
consonants in the odd-numbered phonemic positions, one discontinuous
vowel occupying both even-numbered phonemic positions, and the length
phoneme in one or neither of the even-numbered positions: xata *eat*, xaya·
place, 'ilik *sing*, 'a·mal *help*.

Even more noteworthy are the vowel changes which take place in each
morpheme when another morpheme is suffixed to it: huloṣ-'an *he is sitting
down*, hulu'ṣu-' *he will cause to sit down*, hulṣ-atin *desire to sit down*. These
vowel changes are associated with the individual suffix before which they
occur, since the same type of vowel change will occur in all morphemes when
-atin follows them. The vowel changes are not associated with the individual
morpheme in which they occur, since the morpheme (e.g. the hlṣ" *sit down*
above) has various changes, depending on which suffix follows it. We can
therefore say that each of these vowel changes is simply part of the associated
suffix, a part which extends over the preceding morpheme and which consists
not of adding phonemes to that preceding morpheme but of replacing
vowels, length, and ' within it. The number of different types of vowel change
is considerably smaller than the number of different suffixes, so that there are
many cases of different suffixes beginning with the same vowel change. This
can be likened to the fact that different suffixes begin with the same phoneme;
or each type of vowel change can be considered as a morphophonemic
juncture such that each suffix occurs after one of another of these morphophonemic junctures.

A less ramified peculiarity of the phonemic composition of morphemes is
the vowel harmony of suffixes. In the case of Yokuts, this term refers to the
fact that the vowels in all suffixes (except the two morphemes comprising
M_a) are the same as the last vowel of the preceding morpheme as to mouth
position if they are the same as to height: dɔs-hɔtin *desire to report*, 'uṭ'-
hatin *desire to steal*. This can be expressed by saying that morphemes which
contain a vowel determining or determined by vowel harmony contain in
that position not a full vowel but rather two vocalic components, height

and position, the position being a long component extending across morpheme boundary onto the next vowel place which has identical height component.

Aside from these characteristics, Yawelmani has few peculiarities in the phonemic composition of morphemes. There is a reduplicating element, i.e. one composed not of particular phonemes but of a recurrence of whatever phonemes were contained in the preceding morpheme; this is a positional variant of -da· *repeatedly*, and occurs only after two-consonant morphemes and after three-consonant morphemes before -wiyi- *do, say*. There are few discontinuous morphemes, the number of these being reduced by the fact that the verb has no subject or object pronoun affixes and hence no agreement as to number, etc., with neighboring nouns. Lastly, it appears to be unnecessary to recognize any zero morphemes (morphemes whose phonemic composition is zero phonemes), since the three zero morphemes (subjective singular, verbal noun, future) which do occur are associated each with a characteristic (and not common) vowel change in the preceding morpheme. We can say that these morphemes consist of the respective vowel changes and are therefore phonemically identifiable.

2. *Morpheme Alternants and Morphophonemes*

Few morphemes have suppletively different positional alternants. Thus there is -e· (with a particular vowel change in the preceding morpheme) *causative* which occurs only after three-consonant V^1 while -a·la· (with another vowel change) occurs after two-consonant V^1. There is -' *future* which occurs after morphemes ending in · while -en occurs after other morphemes. And -da· *repeatedly* alternates with a variant consisting of reduplication, as noted above.

There are very few cases of morphophonemic alternation involving consonants. In contrast, all the different vowel changes (different as to the vowels which are changed and as to the consonantal environment in which the change occurs) which go to make up a single vowel change type, are ultimately morphophonemic variants of that vowel change type.[20]

3. *Morpheme Classes*

P: particles, not occurring in one word-structure with any other morphemes. They may be subdivided as follows:

P_a: occurring only initially in utterances: 'ama' *and*, 'angi *is it that?*[21]

P_b: occurring anywhere within the utterance: 'e·man *to no avail*.

P_c: between any two words of like class: yɔw *and* (yɔw is also a member of P_a), 'i' *or*.

gi *interrogative*, always after some word.

P_d: each occurring as an utterance by itself: 'ɔhɔm *no* (also in P_b), hiyuk *hello*.

I: initial morphemes within word and, except for P, within utterance. This includes the following distinct classes:

V^1: verb bases, which occur directly before M_i or other M_{vv}, M_{vn}, and which undergo, before these medial suffixes, the major vowel changes organized by Newman in *LSNA*, 235 and *Yokuts*, 23–4 (as compared with the much simpler pre-suffixal vowel changes which occur in the remaining initials or in M).

V_a^1: a few verb initials having the phonemic and morphophonemic characteristics of V^1M, but not morphemically divisible: hɔẏle· *hunt*.

wiyi *do, say*, occurring after Q, but otherwise like a member of V^1.

Q: a group of four-, two-, and three-consonant morphemes (the first two types never occurring except before wiyi, and the first one not reduplicated) which occur before wiyi: t'apwiyi *slap*.

N^1: noun initials or roots, occurring sometimes before M and sometimes directly before F_n (with or without intervening D): k'ać *obsidian*.

N_p: personal and demonstrative nouns, occurring before F_n and before both the dual and the plural members of D: na· *I*.

N_i: interrogatives, occurring before the subjective and two other members of F_n (which two varies with the particular N_i) plus -uk:

N_l: place names, occurring only before the -w *locative* member of F_n: 'alt(a)-w *Altaw*, 'a·lit *salt grass*.

M: medial morphemes, occurring after I and before F. Sub-classes:

M_{vv}: occurring after V^1 and before F_v: atin *desire to*. Some of these occur only directly after V^1 and are marked M_i; the others sometimes occur after other M_{vv}.

M_{vn}: after V^1 or V^2 and before F_n: -n *verbal noun*.

M_{nv}: after N and before F_v: -na· *procure*.

M_{nn}: after N and before F_n:-iyin *one who has*, -hal *plural number*.

M_{npnp}: a morpheme which occurs after ma·- *you*, a member of N_p, and before D, with the meaning *and I*: mak' *you and I*, ma'ak' *you two*.

M_a: two auxiliary suffixes, whose vowels are not affected by vowel harmony[22] and which occur before only 5 members of F_v: -xɔ· *durative*.

D: two plural-dual suffixes, occurring before F_n. In particular:

dual: occurring only after N_p.

plural: occurring after N and N_p.

F_v: word-final suffixes which occur after V^1, M_{vv}, M_{nv}: -en *future*. Five of these, which also occur after M_a, are marked F_a.

F_s: subordinating word-final suffixes which occur after V^1, M_{vv}, M_{vn}, but differ from F_v in that they do not usually occur in an utterance without another word containing F_v (i.e. there are utterances with F_v words, and utterances with F_s words and F_v words, but only rarely utterances with F_s words alone): -e·ni *in order to.*

F_n: six case morphemes occurring after N: -nit *ablative.*[23]

uk: a morpheme occurring after all N_i F_n: wa·tinuk *of whom?*

4. *Equivalence of Morpheme Sequences*

V_{cc}^1 -in $= V^1$. V_{cc}^1 indicates those V^1 which contain only two consonants. -in *become, get to be,* is a member of M_{vv}. This sequence (Newman's fake base) has the V^1M internal structure, but the distribution of a pure V^1. Next to other members of V^1, -in has the effect of any other M_{vv}. Compare he·xin *get fat* ($= V^1$) and lɔgwin *get pulverized* ($= V^1M$).

Q wiyi $= V^1$.

V^1 $M_i = V^2$.

V^2 $M_{vv} = V^2$. This provides for more than one M_{vv}: xat-hatin-xas *do nothing but desire to eat,* xat-hatin *desire to eat.*

V^2 $M_{vn} = N$.

The medials which occur with V occur with any member of V. Among the few exceptions is -le· with a unique vowel change *continue;* it occurs with only a few V^1, all with three consonants and no length in first vowel place: lɔgiw-le· *keep pulverizing.* In contrast, the medials which occur after N, in the next two equations, each occur after a few particular members of N. Although no limit is set by these equations on the number of medials which occur together, after either V or N, there are never more than a few in a single word, and any particular medial is not repeated.

N^1 $M_{nv} = V^2$.

N^1 $M_{nn} = N^1$.

V^2 M_a $F_a = V^3$.

V^2 $F_v = V^3$. E.g. hɔy̆le·-hin *he hunted.*

V^2 $F_s = V_s^3$.

N_p^1 $M_{npnp} = N_p^2$.

$N_i = N^2$. This is necessary because D does not occur after N_i.

N_p^2 $D = N^2$.

N^1 *plural* $= N^2$.

N^2 $F_n = N^3$.

N_l *locative* $= N^3$. The locative is a member of F_n.

We now proceed to sequences of separate words.

N_x^3 $N_{obj}^3 = N_x^3$. $_x$ indicates any member of F_n included in the N^3; $_{obj}$ indicates the objective case member of F_n included in the N^3: yɔlɔwč-in yɔkɔ·či *of the one who is assembling the people* can be replaced in its utterance by the first word (whose F_n is possessive case) alone.

$N_x^3 \; N_{pos}^3 = N_x^3 \cdot {}_{pos}$ indicates the possessive case member of F_n: k'ač-a min *your obsidian* can be replaced in its utterance by the first word (*obsidian*, whose F_n is objective case) alone.

$N_x^3 \; N_x^3 = N_x^3$. Two nouns having the same case are in apposition and may be replaced by a single one having that case: ṭa·nit pilnit *from that road (from that, from road)*. This can be expressed by saying that the F_n is a discontinuous morpheme extending over one or more N. We might have written the equations differently: $N^2 \; N^2 = N^2$, and then $N^2 \; F_n = N^3$ as above, where the N^2 would now represent either one N^2 or more (depending on whether the N^2 in this last equation was a resultant of the preceding $N^2 \; N^2 = N^2$ equation). A special case of this is the nominal sentence: nɔ·čɔ(') be·mamguč *A clever fellow – Humming Bird.* (where both N have the subjective member of F_n).

$V_s^3 \; N_{obl}^3 = V_s^3 \cdot {}_{obl}$ indicates any member of F_n except the subjective.

$V^3 \; N^3 = V^3$.

$V_s^3 \; V^3 = V^3$. The last three equations, each of which is repeatable, permit within a single utterance a number of verb clauses, each containing a number of nouns or noun phrases in addition to its verb (excluding subjective case nouns in V_s clauses), and with all clauses but one containing V_s rather than V. Yawelmani utterances apparently tend to be short, and do not eke out all the possibilities of this structure within one utterance. Note, for example, taxan'an kew mam bine·te·ni *he is coming here to ask you*, containing V^3, N_p+the locative member of F_n, N_p+the objective member of F_n, and V_s^3. The first two words constitute a V^3 clause, and the second two a V_s^3 clause.

We now consider the relation of P to utterances.

$V^1 \; M_{vn} = P$. This occurs with very few morphemes of these classes: 'ut't'al *solely*.

word+gi=that word. ma'gi *was it you* is substitutable for ma' *you* in the identical environment.

word P_c word=either word (or any word of their class). We can substitute kaẏiw for kaẏiw yɔw be·mamguč in 'ama' kaẏiw yɔw be·mamguč pana· hin *And Coyote and Humming Bird arrived*, and still have a Yawelmani utterance.

some words of utterance+P_b+remaining words of utterance=that utterance.

P_a + utterance = that utterance.

We can now say that every utterance consists either of P_d or of N_{sub}^3 (*sub* for subjective member of F_n) or of V^3.

5. *Utterance Structure*

If we consider the morpheme classes in relation to word and utterance juncture, we find that the structure of any minimum utterance is either P or

else N_i F_n -uk or else $I(M_i)$ (a number of M) $\begin{cases} (M_a) \ F_v \text{ or } F_s \\ (D) \quad F_n \end{cases}$

All utterances are sequences of these minimum utterances, in almost any order.

NOTES

[1] Hereinafter abbreviated *LSNA*. This series originated as a review of the book. The importance of the volume, and the opportunity which it offered for exploration into the comparability of structural formulations, led to a change of plan whereby this series is written as an independent restatement of the *LSNA* structures, while a separate review, by W. D. Preston, appears elsewhere.

[2] Morris Swadesh, 'South Greenlandic (Eskimo)', *LSNA*, 30–54. Sources used in addition to Swadesh are: S. Kleinschmidt, *Grammatik der grönländischen Sprache*, Berlin 1851, on which Swadesh' own study was based; William Thalbitzer, 'Eskimo', in Franz Boas (ed.), *Handbook of American Indian Languages*, Part 1 (BAE-B 40, Washington 1911), 967–1069; Francis Barnum, *Grammatical Fundamentals of the Innuit Language*, Boston 1901; Franz Boas, *Eskimo Lexicon*, 1883, listed as Ms 342 in C. F. Voegelin and Z. S. Harris, *Index to the Franz Boas Collection* (Language Monograph, 22), 1945, and now in the Boas Collection of the Library of the American Philosophical Society. Because of the differences in geographic dialect and in phonetic transcription among these sources, Eskimo forms cited will in most cases be taken from Swadesh-Kleinschmidt. When other forms are cited, they will be given in Swadesh' phonemicization.

[3] The phonemes are taken as in Swadesh, 30–2. A few minor modifications seem possible, though they may lead to a less convenient set of phonemes. It may be possible to consider ŋ (the nasal homo-organic with q) as a positional variant of q and a free variant of γ in particular forms, instead of taking it as a phoneme. The rare phoneme y, which occurs only between u and a (in which position it is phonemically distinct from i), may perhaps be phonemicized as a repetition of the preceding vowel plus i: puyak *oxidized blubber* (contrasting with puiaq *bird's crop*) could be written puuiak if the sequence uu/aa + i/y + u/a (where / indicates *or*) does not occur otherwise; to date, I have noticed no case of this sequence. None of these phonemic changes would, however, simplify the morphophonemic statements.

[4] I.e. there are many cases of morphemes, often but little different from each other phonemically, which are complementary to each other in distribution and can hence be regarded as positional variants of one morpheme.

[5] E.g. -γşuaq *evil, large*, after nuna *land* (nunaγşuaq) has the variant şuaq after uyaγak *stone* (uyaγaγşuaq). Summary formulations of such morphophonemic relations are given by Swadesh. While similar data is given in greater detail by Thalbitzer and the others, it is not only diffuse but is also intermingled with sub-phonemic sound alternations which Swadesh treats as positional variants of phonemes.

[6] Compare aki in aki-γa *my coat*, aki-a *his coat*, with morphophonemic nipỉ in nipi-γa *my voice*, nipa-a *his voice*.

[7] In giving the variants of each morpheme or group of morphemes, we state the environments in which each variant occurs. Thus, many morphemes have certain variants before the plural suffix and before the various case suffixes (except the absolutive). Rather than say that these case suffixes are added to the plural stem, which is undesirable since the

forms are plural neither in meaning nor in grammatical concord, we give both plural suffix and case suffixes as the environment in which the prior morphemes have the variants in question.

[8] Thalbitzer, 1050 (where it is treated as a different inflection).

[9] In effect, each T morpheme changes the syntactic status (i.e. the selection of final verb or noun suffixes) of whatever precedes it to that indicated by its second subscript. T_{vn} occurs only after a morpheme having verbal status, and changes it into a noun.

[10] E.g. after T_{vn}, T_{vn} T_{xx}, etc.

[11] Meaning alone is in any case not adequate, since, for example, it would be hard to assign a distinctive meaning to the Ca element.

[12] Note iɣlua *his (one) house*, iɣluat *their (one) house*, iɣlui *his houses*, iɣluit *their houses*.

[13] This last group contains the recurrent or fourth person which occurs in the positions indicated at the end of section 3.

[14] Since we describe Q_c (or Q_c plus C_o) as containing both C and D as well as person, it is convenient to say that even when the person (Q_c) is lacking we have both C and D present. By the side of iɣlu *house* (with Ca) and iɣlup *of the house* (with C_r) we have iɣlut *house* (with D). We can analyze iɣlup as containing not only D but C_a D or C_r D, these last two being identical phonemically. With the other members of C this phonemic identity does not occur: iɣlumut *to the house*, iɣlunut *to the houses*. If we analyze iɣlut in this way, C_a and C_r become similar to C_o in respect to D, and the forms which sometimes have Q_c suffixes always have C (instead of having the C_r and C_a absent if D follows without Q_c, as it does in iɣlut). There is nothing morphophonologically irregular in considering that iɣlut contains a zero C_a or C_r, since C_a is in any case zero after iɣlu, and the -p of iɣlup would drop before a following -t (two consonants do not occur at the end of a word).

[15] Plus the added conditions for the recurrent person.

[16] R indicates the personal reference parts of Q_a, Q_c, Q_b (the last containing two independent R). The ... indicate the position within the environment of the portions of D, after the respective R or other morpheme.

[17] If we could state with phonemic or morphophonemic regularity what portions of each Q were D, C, and R, we would break each Q up into these successive morphemes. This is indeed possible for various members of Q in various Eskimo dialects. However, since a statement of the phonemic variants of each component, in the environment of each Q, would be very complicated and irregular, it seems best to list the Q as morphemes, by and large, and to carry out a componental breakdown only for grammatical analysis.

[18] Parentheses indicate that the enclosed element sometimes occurs in this environment, but not always. R_3 indicates the third person member of R. The a subscript of R is only to indicate that the two R so treated are identical.

[19] Stanley S. Newman, 'The Yawelmani Dialect of Yokuts', *LSNA*, 222–48; Stanley Newman, *Yokuts Language of California*, New York 1944 (see Paper XII of this volume.)

[20] The vowel changes which are included under a single type appear identical only after Newman's configurational analysis. Without benefit of this analysis they would appear to differ as between bases (V^1) having different phonemic composition, and particularly as between bases and 'themes' (initials other than V^1, or sequences of any initial plus medials). For this reason, the setting up of Newman's stem types (types of vowel changes) is a compact morphophonemic organization.

[21] This could be divided into two morphemes, an introductory 'an (in P_a) plus the interrogative gi which is noted below.

[22] This can be expressed by saying that a semi-open morphophonemic juncture occurs before M_a (across which the long vowel components do not extend, as they do not extend across open word juncture), or by saying that the vowel places of M_a are occupied not by the distance vowel components (which extend in vowel harmony) but by whole vowels.

[23] These are the subjective and 5 oblique cases. The subjective consists of -i after the plural morpheme and of a particular vowel change (with zero additive suffix) otherwise. The 5 oblique cases all begin with identical vowel changes, but it does not seem useful to recognize this vowel change as a general oblique morpheme, since there is perhaps only

one (syntactic or morphological) distribution which these 5 have as against the subjective and which we could say is the special distribution of the general oblique morpheme $(V_a{}^3 N_{obl} = V_a{}^3$. There is, of course, a disadvantage in recognizing the general oblique morpheme, since we would then have to specify a special limitation of distribution applying between it and the 5 specific oblique cases.

XV

STRUCTURAL RESTATEMENTS: II

1. FROM PHONEME TO MORPHEME

Since the present Restatements[1], of which this one is concerned with
Voegelin's Delaware[2], are limited to the morphologies of the languages
under consideration, we assume that we have given all the requisite utterances
in phonemic representation. Each utterance is for us a sequence (or combination) of phonemes. Within each utterance we now separate off small
sequences of phonemes one from the other. We may say that between each
such small sequence and its neighbors a morpheme boundary is placed; and
we may call the sequence which lies between two such boundaries a morphemic segment. The placing of the morpheme boundaries is thus an
operation carried out on the phonemes of an utterance.

In general we may consider the placing of morpheme boundaries to be
carried out in the usual way, by comparing various utterances which are
identical in part of their phonemic sequence. If we compare nšé·ʈu·n *my lip*
with wšé·ʈu·n *his lip*, we would place a morpheme boundary after the first
phoneme: n *my*, w *his*, šé·ʈu·n *lip*. When such comparisons are carried out
for a large corpus, we obtain morphemic segments which are repeated in
various environments throughout the corpus (as šé·ʈu·n is repeated here).

1.1. In several cases in Delaware the placing of morphemic boundaries is
not as simple as in the example above. If we compare máxke·w *it is red* with
máxke·k *that which is red* (§ 4.3)[3], we might separate off w *it is* and k *that
which is*. However, since máxke· does not occur by itself, we can consider
máxke·w as a single morphemic segment, and say (in § 3 below) that all
morphemes ending in w have alternants without the w when they occur
before k *that which*.

1.2. The morphemic segment need not be an additive sequence of phonemes. If we compare entawəle·lɔ́ntank *when he is glad* with we·le·lɔ́ntank
one who is glad (§ 4.9), we would separate off enta *when* and $(-V1+e\cdot)$[4] *one
who*. We have here a morpheme which consists not only of an (added) phoneme but also of an associated subtraction of a phoneme.

International Journal of American Linguistics **13**, No. 3 (1947), 175–86.

1.3. The sequence of phonemes which is separated off as a morphemic segment is in some cases not continuous. The sequence əli *indeed* occurs only in the environment (§ 5.9–12)[5]

$$1/2p. + i \cdot lu \cdot + (pl.)|1/2p. —Verb + n + (pl.)$$

all with one stress: ki·lu·waktəlilu·si·né·yo *you fellows indeed are burning.* This environment also occurs less frequently without əli. The two subsequences separated by the vertical bar also occur independently of each other: ki·lú·wa *you fellows,* aləmí·ḳi·n *she began to grow indeed*; in the latter case only n *indeed* occurs (also with third person prefix), without əli. In considering the morphemic segmentation of all these utterances, we seek to satisfy the following conditions: first, əli is not an independent phonemic sequence but occurs only in the neighborhood of n (and the rest of the environment above); second, the n which occurs here in the absence of əli is identical with the n which occurs in the presence of əli.[6] If we are prepared to say that the presence of əli varies freely (from the point of view of descriptive linguistics) with its absence in the above environment, we can set up a single morphemic segment əli...n and identify it (in § 3 below) as a free variant of n. If we wish to distinguish the cases in which əli occurs from those in which it does not, we can satisfy our two conditions by setting up əli...n as a positional variant of n. In order to differentiate the environment in which the əli...n variant occurs from that in which n occurs by itself, we would then have to set up a zero morpheme* which indicates the occurrence of the elaborated form. Then in the environment 1st p. + i·lu· + 1st p. + Verb – the variant of the n morpheme would be n; and in the environment 1st p. + i·lu· + 1st p. + * + Verb – the variant of the n morpheme would be əli...n.[7]

1.4. Structurally more important cases of discontinuous morphemes may be found in what is often called grammatical agreement. In the sequence seen above

person i·lu· (pl.)   person Verb (pl.)

the personal prefix is the same in both positions, and the plural is either present or absent in both of its positions at once. The occurrence of a particular personal prefix in one of the positions is thus dependent upon its occurrence in the other. We can express this by setting up discontinuous morphemes, e.g. k...k *you,* which, when they occur in these environments, occupy both positions at once.

Another environment in which the person and plural morphemes have repeated phonemic forms is (§ 5.8)

person Verb (pl.)   person haḳay (pl.)

as in kənihilá·wəna khaкayéna *we killed ourselves.* We may segment this
utterance into the following morphemes

person Verb (pl.) haкay

with the understanding that person and plural morphemes are discontinuous
in this environment, their repeated parts occurring around haкay.

A more complicated environment of the discontinuous person morpheme
is (§ 6.20)

person maNí·h object   person Verb n

as in nəmaNí·ha təlišenkí·xin *I made him lie down.* Here it is the object of
maNí·h and the subject of the verb that agree. We separate off the following
morphemes:

person maNí·h object   Verb n

and state that in this environment the object morpheme contains two phonemic parts, one appended to maNí·h as object and the other to the following
verb (as formal subject).

1.5. A somewhat different case of a phonemic sequence whose occurrence
depends upon the occurrence of some other sequence is that of i·w *negative.*
It occurs only in the environment: negative particles + person + verb +
− (+ plural). The negative particle position is filled by one of a small class of
morphemes: ku· *not,* kači *don't,* or (if other particles precede) mata *not*
(§ 5.4). Since the i·w is not independent, we may say that it is simply part of
the negative morphemic segments: ku· ... i·w, etc. The environment of these
discontinuous morphemes is now − + person + verb (+ pl.), and the fact that
all morphemes of this class have a discontinuous phonemic part ... i·w is
worth noting under the phonemic constitution of morphemes but does not
otherwise affect the morphological statements. After certain imperative
suffixes the discontinuous portion is not ... i·w but something else; these
other sequences would be listed in § 2 below as positional variants of the
forms with discontinuous ... i·w.

1.6. Various possibilities may be seen in the setting up of the preterite
morpheme. After nouns (§ 3.11; including the plural of the possessor, if
present), and participles (verb -- V1 + e·; including the plural of the subject,
if present; and usually including the suffix əpan *momentaneous* § 5.6), and
after a few verbs there occasionally occur the following suffixes: a *preterite
(singular)* [8] and inka *preterite plural* if the personal prefix (possessor or
subject) is 1st or 2nd person; inka *preterite undifferentiated as to number* if the
prefix is 3rd person. We could divide the first inka into the same a *preterite*

as in the singular, plus ink *plural*. The same sequence inka after 3rd person prefix would then have to be morphemicized differently: we could not segment it into ink *plural* + a *preterite*, but only into ink *undifferentiated number* + a *preterite*, or else into a single inka segment. There is of course no point in merely deciding one way or another. The morphemic segmentation of an utterance becomes unsystematic and subjective if individual choices can be made at various points. This arbitrariness can be avoided if the segmentation of each utterance results only from the carrying out of stated operations of grouping upon the phonemes of the utterance. If these stated operations do not provide a unique segmentation in some particular utterance, as in the case of inka after 3rd person, we may leave the phonemic sequence unsegmented, with a statement of the problem; or we may explicitly add to our original set of stated operations an additional one the application of which (throughout our corpus) will provide a unique segmentation of the phonemic sequence in question.

1.7. There are also other problems of alternative segmentations. If we consider the inanimate transitive suffixes mən, əmən, amən, тamən, ntamən it seems possible to separate off a segment mən. However, it is not clear what could be done with the remaining portions, and what descriptive advantage could result from the segmentation.

Another problem is that of the partial dependence of the person-pluralizing suffix on the personal affixes. The personal affixes occur whether a plural suffix follows or not, but (except for certain nouns which occur without personal affixes) we find the plural suffix occurring only in environments which contain a personal affix. This partial dependence could be stated without being further integrated in the structure. Alternatively, a zero singular could be defined, so that person and number-of-person would each become classes of morphemes some member of which is present with almost every noun or verb; this has some support in the fact that absence of plural morpheme indicates singular (not merely unspecified number).

2. MORPHEMIC COMPONENTS

Although the setting up of morphemes begins as an expression of the regularities of the occurrence of phonemes within utterances (i.e. an expression of the restrictions upon randomness of their occurrence), we are sometimes led to morphemes having zero or very diverse phonemic constitution. This happens when there are certain differing phonemic sequences which have partially similar or intertwined restrictions on occurrence: most simply, if A is subject both to the restrictions upon B and also to the restrictions upon C, we may redefine A as being not a simple morpheme but a combination of two morphemic components B' and C' (alternants of B and C, or members of the same classes as B and C). This is done without regard to the phonemes of A: whether the phonemes can indeed be divided into two parts, and whether the parts are similar to B and C. Such analysis is sometimes convenient in the case of paradigmatic interrelations of morphemes[9], or in the case of incomplete paradigmatic sets of affixes like the imperative or speaker-addressee systems of Delaware which are discussed below.

The speaker-addressee system consists of the following morphemes: a·n *I*, enk *we exclusive*, ankw *we inclusive (I and you)*, an *you sg.*, e·kw *you pl.* (§ 4.4). In other Delaware forms, person and plural are indicated by separate morphemes. If we try to extract a *plural* morphemic component from the above group we might select the kw and k, leaving a·n and en to be alternants of the *I* morpheme, and an and e· alternants of the *you* morpheme.

The imperative affixes, which include person and number of adressee and of object, present a more complex picture. They are: тam *1st person addressee* (i.e. *let's-*), l (i·l after animate transitive verbs) *2nd person sg. addressee*, kw (i·kw after an.tr.) *2nd person pl. addressee* (u· if object is *him*), i·ne·n *us* (1st person plural object, necessarily after an.tr.verbs), zero *me*, −i·l *him*. For example: ne·yó·тom *let's see him*, mí·li·l *give thou me*, né·wi·kw *see ye me*, né·yu· *see ye him*, ne·wí·ne·n *see us*, ne·w *see thou him* (§ 4.2). In the case of inanimate transitives ending in amən, the ən is replaced by a instead of l, by u· before kw, and by u·...u·kw before тam. We now attempt to define each of these morphemes as some combination of underlying component morphemes, the underlying ones being so selected as to have a more regular distribution than the above morphemes have. There are various ways in which these underlying morphemes can be selected. Two considerations which affect the choice are: first, that it would be convenient to have a morpheme *imperative* which would underlie all of the above[10]; second, that in each singular-plural pair the sg. be marked by lack of the pl. morpheme rather than by a special sg. morpheme.[11] One set of underlying morphemes would therefore be: l *imperative* (alternants: i·l after animate intransitive; the l is lacking before all person or number suffixes except zero); тam *1st person addressee* (undifferentiated as to number); zero *2nd person addressee;* kw *plural of addressee* (occurs only after 2nd person, since there is no 3rd person addressee; alternants: u· after *him*, zero after ne·n); zero *me* (1st person object); −i· (dropping of i·, together with an automatic dropping of the following l) *him*; ne·n *plural* (occurs only after *me*). We thus obtain an imperative suffix which occurs (sometimes with zero alternant) in every imperative form, and several person and plural suffixes which are taken as alternants of the other person and plural morphemes.

3. MORPHEME ALTERNANTS

Once the utterances have been morphemically divided, we can take the resulting morphemic segments, and consider any number of them which are complementary to each other as alternants of a single morpheme.[12] A large part of Delaware morphology can be simplified by listing in advance all the sets of morphemic segments which alternate with each other in stated environments. Each set of positional variants can be considered thereafter as a single morpheme. We do not thereby evade the stating of these variations, but we sever the discussion of these private alternations among members of a complementary set from the discussion of the external relations of the whole set with other sets – relations which are not affected by which member of the set is present in any particular case.

3.1. Many of the sets of complementary alternants are given by Voegelin in his section 2 (*Phonology*, pp. 137–42: 'Morpheme Alternants in Prefixation and Suffixation'). Other such sets may be extracted from the morphology. In most cases, the phonemic similarity among the members of these additional sets will be less than in the sets included in Voegelin's phonology. Nevertheless, the members of each set are complementary to each other in environment, so that the relations among the members can be treated separately from the (morphological) relations among the resulting sets.

The major sets of complementary morphemic segments are in the personal affixes, the plural, the stem forms, and the transitive-intransitive suffixes. Before considering these, we may note a number of smaller sets of morphemic alternants.

The əli...n *indeed* of § 1.3 above would have to be listed as a free (or positional) variant of n *indeed*.

The repeated-phoneme forms of personal and plural affixes in § 1.4 above would be listed as alternants of the contiguous-phoneme forms (k...k alternant of k), the alternation taking place in the domains exemplified by the environments in § 1.4 above.

The various negative particles (as also the various final phonemes which replace...i·w) may be considered alternants of a single negative morpheme to the extent that the environments in which one occurs are explicitly different from those in which the others occur (see § 1.5 above).

The morpheme ке *intransitivizer* (§ 6.18) has an alternant zero before the t variant of wə *he*, and the ak variant of nə I.

The following morphemic segments, all indicating *diminutive* can be considered alternants of each other, each occurring in the stated environments (§ 6.37, 39): тət after nouns, тi after modal prefixes and the imperative suffix, тu after verbs without these (alternatively: тu after the prefixed and 'inverse' alternants of the personal affixes).

3.2. The many Delaware plurals can be grouped together into a few morphemes. We consider first the plurals of subject or possessor affixes.

ALTERNANT	ENVIRONMENT
ak	animate intransitive morpheme + w variant of wə *he* (§ 3.5, 12)
mo	animate morphemes + kə *you* (§ 3.8)
e·yo	inanimate transitive morpheme + kə or wə (§ 3.9); n *indeed* + kə or wə
wa·w	other occurrences of the prefixed alternants of kə or wə
e·n	inan. trans. morpheme + nə *I* or kə *you* (§ 3.4); n *indeed* + nə or kə
na·n	other occurrences of the prefixed alternants of nə or kə
hti·	suffixed to variant of wə *he* (§ 4.7, 10)
kw-forms	en *I* and an *you* suffixed variants of nə, kə respectively (§ 4.4)
kw	imperative morpheme + zero *you* (addressee § 4.2)
u	same + (−i) *him* morpheme (§ 4.2).

To this may be added the plurals which follow the inanimate intransitive: ní·ske·w *it is dirty*, ní·ske·yo *they are dirty*. These are complementary to the above (which do not occur with inan. intr.). We can say that these are plurals of the verb proper (there being no person affix); or we can say that there is a zero affix *indefinite (3rd) person* which these suffixes pluralize.

a	inan. intr. ending in w (§ 4.3)
u·l	inan. intr. ending in t.

We now consider the plurals of nouns and of the object (goal) suffixes of transitive verbs.

a	inanimate nouns; inan. tr. verbs (§ 3.10)
ak	animate nouns (§ 3.12: if nə or kə present, or if obviative suffix absent); agentive s suffix (§ 4.10); an. tr. morpheme of verbs (except when subject prefix is wə)
ink	before a *preterite* after nə, kə (§ 3.11)
hti·	after participle prefix (-- V1 + e·) + the ti variant of t *he* (§ 4.10)
i·k	after the participle prefix + the other possessor-subject suffixes (§ 4.10.1)
ne·n	after imperative suffix + zero *1st person* object (§ 4.2).

The morphemic segments in the first list cannot be grouped into fewer than two morphemes, because e·n, na·n are not entirely complementary to ak, mo, e·yo, wa·w. True, the former occur after nə *I* (nə + na·n *we exclusive*) and the latter after wə *he*, but both occur after kə *you*: kə + na·n *you and I* (1st person plural inclusive); kə + wa·w *you fellows*. We can consider e·n, na·n to be alternants of wa·w, etc., in the environment in which they are complementary (i.e. after nə), and a separate morpheme in the environments in which they contrast with wa·w (i.e. after kə). If we do this, we will be adhering closely to the environmentally determined basis of morphemic definition: morphemes contrast only in respect to environments, and identical phonemic sequences (even with identical meanings) may thus come out as morphemically different in different environments. The wa·w after kə and wə and its alternant na·n after nə would constitute the plural morpheme; the na·n after kə would be a separate morpheme *and I*. Alternatively, we could consider na·n to be the same morpheme *and I* (i.e. *plus a member of the first person*) after nə and kə, and wa·w to be another morpheme *plural* (i.e. *plus a member or members of the same person*) after kə and wə. If we first recognize na·n and wa·w as different morphemes after kə, and then ask to which of these morphemes we should assign the na·n that occurs after nə, we have two choices. We could assign it to the na·n morpheme because of phonemic identity; or we could assign it to the wa·w morpheme so as to complete its distribution (otherwise the wa·w plural would occur only after 2nd and 3rd person and not after 1st). Meaning cannot affect this decision. The meaning of na·n in nə + na·n *we exclusive* can be taken as identical with the meaning of na·n in kə + na·n *we inclusive* or with that of wa·w in wə + wa·w *they*: we can translate nə + na·n as *I and others of the first person* (i.e. *two or more people who are first person in respect to this utterance*), or else as *I and others of the same person*.[13] The linguistic reflection of the meaning consideration would be how the morphemes occur in longer linguistic contexts. However, there would probably be no contextual preference for assigning the na·n of nə + na·n to na·n as against to wa·w.

The kw-forms mentioned in the first list would have to be variously assigned: the kw of e·kw *you pl.* as alternant of wa·w, the kw of ankw *you and I* as alternant of na·n, and the k of enk *we exclusive* as alternant of the na·n of nə + na·n (§ 2 above).

The kw and u· after the imperative l (i·l) suffix are alternants of wa·w (§ 2 above).

The object and noun plurals of the third list above have to be recognized as constituting a morpheme distinct from the subject plural of the first list. This is unavoidable because of such sequences as subject-person + verb + object-person + plural.[14] If there are no plurals or two plurals there would be no uncertainty, but when there is one plural it would have to be indicated which person is pluralized. Similarly in person (possessor) + noun + plural, we would have no indication of whether this was the plural of the person or the plural of the noun.

The plural of the second list is complementary to both subject and object plurals, since it occurs with inanimate intransitive verbs, with which no subject occurs. We may consider it an alternant of the subject plural wa·w, occurring when the subject of the verb is zero. Alternatively, we could consider it an alternant of the object plural. This would be on the analog of the noun, for the object plural occurs with nouns whether they have a possessor (subject) personal prefix or not. The latter case, of noun without possessor prefix could be compared to inanimate intransitive verbs which have no subject prefix.

We are thus left with but a few morphemes: *and I* (na·n), subject-plural, object-plural. The ink of wə…inka (§ 1.6 above) might be added as a morpheme of this class indicating unstated number. There are a number of other environments in Delaware in which number is not differentiated, and perhaps these might be considered to include (zero) alternants of the same morpheme (cf. § 3.5, 10, 13; 4.2, 3, 4, 6, 7).

3.3. There are several systems of personal affixes in Delaware. One is prefixed nə *I*, kə *you*, wə *3rd person* (alternant: suffixed w after the an. intr. morpheme), luwa *the other one* (obviative, suffixed as subject only to the an. intr. morpheme). These occur as possessor prefixes of nouns, and as subject (nə, kə also as object) of verbs. Another set is the suffixed a·n *I* (en before k *plural*, ak finally in an. tr. verbs), an *you* (e· before kw *plural*, at finally in an. tr. verbs), t *him* (k after əkw *by him* and after verbs ending in a consonant), li *the other one*. These last occur only when modal particles (enta *when*, etc.) are prefixed to the verb. A third set occurs only after the imperative morpheme (§ 2 above): ʈam *1st person*, zero *thou*, zero *me*, −i· *him*. A fourth set occurs as the second personal affix (in some cases subject, in others object) by the side of the first two sets: i *me*, əlu *by me*, a·w *him*, əkw *by him*, a *the other* (as object, or after 3rd person+noun).

The first three sets can be considered as alternants of each other for the most part, although a distinction has to be made between object and subject occurrences (ʈam and zero both indicate 1st person after imperative, but constitute different morphemes). The problem becomes more complex when we seek to state the relation between the fourth set and the first two. In terms of meaning we could say that the first two sets are in general neither subject nor object but rather indicate the involvement of a particular person; the morpheme of the fourth set is then explicitly object or subject and indicates implicitly whether the morpheme of the other set is subject or object. Thus: ku·lhá·li *you keep me*, ku·lhá·-ləl *you are kept by me, I keep you* (əl variant of əlu). However, in terms of distribution, we find that not all combinations occur. For example, əlu *by me* occurs only after kə *you*, not after wə *he*. It appears that only as many combinations occur as would indicate all subject-object relations among the persons (*I-you, I-him, you-me*, etc., together with *he-the other one*). Therefore if we consider our elements to be the persons and the subject-object relation, we will have unrestricted distribution for our new elements. It then appears that there is a simple connection between these new elements and the limitation upon distribution of the original morphemes (əlu, etc.). When a verb contains morphemes from both the first and fourth sets, they are restricted as follows: the precedence of the two persons involved agrees with the relative precedence of second-first-third-other person. E.g. if a verb includes 2nd and 3rd persons, irrespective of which is subject, the 2nd person will come first in the word (see the example above). The first morpheme is always taken from the first set (prefixes), and the second morpheme from the fourth set (suffixes). As a result, the 2nd person is always the prefix kə, whether it indicates subject or object. The 1st person is i (object) or əlu (subject) when 2nd person is present in the verb; otherwise the 1st person takes precedence and is marked by nə, whether subject or object, leaving the 3rd person to take second place as aw (object) or əkw (subject). Thus we have kə…əlu *I-you*, kə…i *you-me*, kə…əkw *he-you*, kə…aw *you-him*, etc. Essentially the same arrangement obtains when the second set of original morphemes occurs in place of the first (i.e. when modal particles precede the verb). These combine with the fourth set in the same way that their first-set alternants did, although they are suffixed after the fourth set instead of being prefixed: entawəlahalíe·kw *when you fellows kept me*, entawəlahalóle·kw *when I kept you fellows*.

The third (imperative) set, which does not combine with the other three, also contains, although incompletely, person and subject–object distinctions.

Given the morphemes and the rules of combination stated above, we can now establish a bi-unique correspondence between Delaware words and our person and object elements[15], 1, 2, 3, 4[16], G. Thus nu·lhála *I keep him* is 1 + verb + 3G (a variant of a·w), while 3 + 1G for the same verb would be nu·lhálɔkw *he keeps me*.

The same G could be used to distinguish subject-plural (P) from object-plural (GP): nu·lhálku·k *they keep me* is 3 (which is əkw, here ku, when after nə) + P (ak, here ·k, after əkw) + 1G (nə); ku·lhalku·ná·nak *they keep us* is 3 (əkw) + P (ak) + 2G (kə) + *and I* G (na·n).[17]

It should be noted that the new elements 1, 2, 3, 4, G (with P and P' from § 3.2 above) do not merely represent a meaning analysis of the affixes. They can be used as morphemes, each a particular set of alternants selected from among the alternants of the original morphemes. Thus 1 has the following alternants: nə when there is 3G or no person + G and no modal particle, əlu if there is 2G, ꞇam after imperative, en before P after modals, ak finally after an.tr. + modals, a·n otherwise after modals, i before G[18] if the other person is 2 or modal + 3, nə before G if the other person is 3 without modal, zero after imperative. 2 is simpler: zero after imperative, e· before P + modals, at finally after an. tr. + modals, an otherwise after modals, kə otherwise (all this without regard to what other person if any is present, and to whether G follows, i.e. whether the 2 is object or not). The listing of alternants of 1, 2, 3, 4, G, P, P' can be given in a much more organized fashion by presenting them as the result of the operation of the rules stated above (relative order 2134, etc.).

3.4. Characteristically for Algonquian, Delaware verb stems V and instrumentals I (which follow verb stems) occur with various suffixes: inanimate intransitive, animate intransitive, inanimate transitive, and animate transitive (§ 6.11–32). Each V or I occurs with at most one out of each of these four groups of suffixes: nihi *kill* with an. tr. 1 in nníhila *I killed him* (a is variant of a·w), and with inan. tr. tu·n in nní·tu·n (ni· variant of nihi) *I killed it;* but maxk *find* with an. tr. aw in máxkaw *find him*, and with inan. tr. amən in nəmáxkamən *I found it*. Since all the inan. tr. morphemes are thus complementary to each other in the V or I which precede them, we can consider them all as alternants of one morpheme. There are usually several V or I that occur with a particular pair of alternants such as 1 and tu·n above. We may mark each such set of V or I as a particular sub-class of V or I, and say, for example, that the 1 alternant of the an. tr. morpheme and the tu·n alternant of the inan. tr. occur after the V_1 sub-class of V. However some members of these alternant pairs are also members of other alternant pairs. For example pi·l *clean* and other V occur before tu·n *inan. tr.* in mpi·lí·tu·n *I cleaned it*, but before h *an. tr.* in mpi·lí·ha *I cleaned him*. We may call these V_2, and say that the alternant of an. tr. after V_1 is 1 and after V_2 is h, while the alternant of inan. tr. after $V_{1,2}$ is tu·n.

In this manner we obtain an. intr. si (and su), and inan. intr. te·, after certain V. The an. intr. has alternants e· after V_a; i after V_b.[19] The an. tr. has alternants 1 after $V_{c,f}$; h after V_d; šuw after V_e; aw after V_g, I_c; w after V_h, I_b, e; m after $V_{a,b}$, I_g; zero after $I_{a,d,f}$. The inan. tr. morpheme has alternants tu·n after $V_{b,c,d}$; ꞇu·n after V_e; ꞇamən after V_f; ntamən after V_a, I_g; amən after V_g, $I_{b,c,d}$; mən after V_h, $I_{e,f}$; əmən after I_a.

3.5. There are also a number of alternants of the stems themselves. When a stem, or the an. intr. morpheme following a stem, ends in a vowel, it has an alternant with a different final vowel when w *he* (alternant of wə after an. intr.) or luwa *the other* follows (§ 6.1–10).

Some stems have alternants with reduplicated initial syllable when they are followed by ma *habituative* (§ 5.7).

There are some 'non-initial' stems for body-parts which occur only with some other stem immediately preceding (§ 6.41). It may be possible to consider these as alternants of the ordinary 'initial' stems for the same body parts. This may be relatively simple where the phonemes are much the same: xkán *bone*, i·kane in nča·ki·kaného *I tapped him on the bone*. Where this is not the case, such alternation can be based only on the analog of the above: nnáxk *my hand*, but i·lǝnče in nkǝši·lǝnčé·na *I washed his hands with my own hands*.[20] These stems with two alternants would then occur in both initial and non-initial positions. It may even be possible to consider the instrumentals I (short non-initial stems indicating *by body-part or by activity*) as alternants of particular initial stems.

4. MORPHEME CLASSES

The following morpheme classes may be noted in Delaware for the purposes of the structural statements to be given below.[21]

F: Particles which do not occur with other stems (§ 6.43).
F_1: Particles which occur as first of two stems.
F_2: Particles which occur only as second of two stems.
N: Noun stems (§ 6.42).
N_2: Stems which occur only after a preceding noun stem.
V: Verb stems.
V_2: Stems which occur only after a preceding verb stem (§6.41, 44).
I: Instrumentals, a sub-class of V_2, but occurring rarely after V_2 (§ 6.29, 40).
R: Person affixes 1, 2, 3, 4.
G: Object (goal) component.
P: Plural suffixes.
M: Modal prefixes: enta *when*, e·li *while*, etc. (§ 4.4).
Q: Negative prefixes and particles, except kači (§ 5.4).
N_v: The suffixes he· and i which change a noun into an intransitive verb (§ 6.35–6).

In addition to these, the following individual morphemes will appear in the structural statements:

an. tr. suffix
an. intr. suffix
inan. tr. suffix
inan. intr. suffix
l *imperative* (see § 2 above).
ке *intransitivizer* suffix (§ 6.18, and § 3.1 above).
ǝтi *reciprocal* suffix (§ 6.34).

lx 2-*goal transitivizer* suffix (§ 6.19).

—ən *intransitivizer* (consisting of dropping the ən of those alternants of inan. tr. which end in mən, § 3.10; 6.18).

kači *don't* (§ 5.4).

n *indeed* directive predicator suffix (§ 5.9–12, and § 1.3 above).

ma *past habituative* suffix (§ 5.7).

e *if*, suffix occurring last except for á *ought* (§ 5.2).

əpan *past momentaneous* suffix, occurring last except for inka *preterite* (§ 5.5).

—V1+e· *participle* prefix (§ 4.9–11, and § 1.2 above).

s *agentive* suffix, occurring with participles (§ 4.9).

nk *locative* suffix after nouns (usually without preceding person, § 3.6).

Ti *diminutive* suffix (§ 6.37–9, and § 3.1 above).

a *preterite* final suffix (§ 3.11; 5.6; and § 1.6 above. Although it occurs after some verbs as well as after nouns and participles, the incidence after verbs is very small.).

á *ought* final suffix (§ 5.3).

5. MORPHEME SEQUENCES

The following equations indicate substitutability of the equated sequences within longer constructions.

$F_1 + F_2 = F$. (E.g. kwə́Ti *one*, ní·ša *two* are substitutable for the sequences kwəTá·š *six*, ni·ša·š *seven*.)

$V_i + \text{an. tr.}_i = \text{Vat}$. (The subscript $_i$ indicates any one of the sub-classes of § 3.4 above.)

$V_i + \text{inan. tr.}_i = \text{Vit}$.

$V_i + \text{an. intr.}_i = \text{Vai}$.

$V + \text{inan. intr.} = \text{Vii}$.

$V + V_2 + \text{an. intr.} = \text{Vai}$.

$V + \text{ələnč} + h = V + I$. (ələnč *by finger* is V_2, h *with fingers* is I, § 6.29.)

$I_i + \text{an. tr.}_i = \text{Iat}$.

$I_i + \text{inan. tr.}_i = \text{Iit}$.

$V_x + \text{Iat} = \text{Vat}$. ($V_x$ includes the V_2 above and other V, § 6.21.)

$V_x + \text{Iit} = \text{Vit}$.

$N + N_2 = N'$. (N' to indicate that the equation cannot be repeated.)

$N + \text{Nv} = \text{Vai}$.

$V + \text{aw} + \text{ke} = \text{Vai}$. (aw is an alternant of an. tr.)

$V + \text{an. tr.} + \text{əTi} = \text{Vai}$. (Alternatively, əTi could be added to the morpheme class GR as an object pronoun; its position after an. tr. would be unexceptionable.)

V + an. intr. + lx + GR = Vat. (Hence two object pronouns may follow lx, one more than follow Vat.)

V + inan. tr. − ən + aw + GR = Vat. (Substituting the an. tr. alternant aw for the ən of inan. tr. alternants which end in ən makes room for two objects.)

V + inan. tr. − ən + N = Vit + GR. (nná·təm tə́ntay *I'm going after the fire*, nna·təmə́na *I went after it* with a as GR and təmən as inan. tr.)

Beyond this point, it is more convenient to state all the remaining sequences of morphemes within a stress-unit word in the form of a diagram.[22] Beginning from the left-hand edge, if we draw a line which never turns back leftward (but goes to the right, or up, or down) and never crosses a horizontal bar, then the sequence of morphemes (or morpheme classes) through which the line passes is a sequence that occurs in Delaware.

Morphemes placed above and below each other are substitutable for each other. Morphemes which are to the right or left of each other occur together in some sequence, unless they are completely separated by a horizontal bar (in which case they do not occur together in any sequence). The chief shortcoming in this diagram lies in its failure to show much of the relative order of the morphemes.[23] The order of morphemes in the diagram is in general that which occurs in speech, except for the following major departures: the main part of n, and the i·w portion of Q and kači, occur just before GP, as does Ti; l is a final suffix which may be said to occupy the position after it, at, ai; e and əpan occur in the position just before a and á; ma is a final suffix

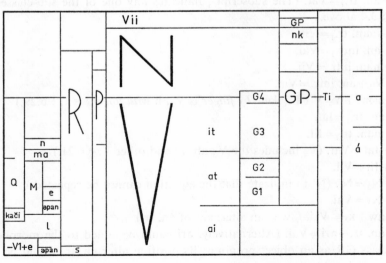

Fig. 1.

(position of a and á); when R and s occur after M, l, or − Vl + e; they occupy the position before GP, as P always does. The departures from the actual order of the morphemes were necessary partly because many of the morphemes had alternants with different positions, but chiefly because morphemes which substituted for each other had to be placed one over the other no matter where they occurred in speech; and morphemes which were most clearly dependent on others in their distribution had to be placed in the column adjoining those others if possible.

NOTES

[1] See 'Structural Restatements: I', *IJAL* **13** (1947), 47–58. (Paper XIV of this volume.)

[2] C. F. Voegelin, 'Delaware, an Eastern Algonquian Language', in Hoijer and others, *Linguistic Structures of Native America*, 130–57.

[3] Section references are to Voegelin's article in *LSNA*, cited in note 2.

[4] Read: minus first vowel plus e·. The phonemic constitution of this morpheme could also be considered as a change of the first vowel into e·.

[5] Elements in parentheses are occasionally present, occasionally not. The dash marks the point at which the əli occurs. The Verb includes intransitive or transitive, and (after animate intransitive) goal suffixes. The first pronoun with i·lu· may also be replaced by the verb maн̇i· *cause* (§ 6.20). 1/2 p. represents 1st or 2nd person.

[6] The only difference between the two occurrences being precisely in the presence of əli in the environment.

[7] The procedure here is similar to that in setting up junctures, which are zero elements defined so as to differentiate two occurrences of what would otherwise be identical environments. This zero yields a simpler system than would keeping the əli as a separate morpheme, only if we can identify the zero as an alternant of some other (zero) morphemes in the language.

[8] The sg. or pl. is of the noun or the participle (= referent) proper. Since the sg. in Delaware is in general indicated merely by lack of the plural suffix, we could consider the a as indicating the preterite alone.

[9] For example in the Eskimo restatement, *IJAL* **13** (1947), 50–3. (Paper XIV of this volume.)

[10] If we do not break these morphemes up into underlying ones, we can distinguish the imperative from the other verb forms by this particular set of addressee-object suffixes. If, however, we break these suffixes up into underlying person and number morphemes which would be considered as alternants of the other person and number morphemes, then we require some environmental distinction for the imperative verbs to differentiate them from the 'independent' verbs which also have the same person and number morphemes (though different alternants of them).

[11] This is generally the case in Delaware. Aside from fitting into the general Delaware pattern, considerations of economy are involved. If there are only two forms, sg. and pl., we can define singular as being merely absence of the pl. form; then any formal features of the sg. can be used instead as some other morphological element (if any is needed in that case).

[12] It should be clear that description in terms of morpheme alternants in no way replaces description in terms of morphophonemes. Although some cases can be equally conveniently treated in either manner, morpheme alternants are used primarily in cases in which morphophonemic representation is not convenient.

[13] In either case, there is nothing formal or cultural which requires us to translate it as *I and he*.

[14] Due to the dependence of plural on person (§ 1.7 above), the object plural could be defined as that which occurs, if at all, only if two person affixes are present in the verb, while the subject plural occurs, if at all, if either one or two person affixes are present. If the plural of inanimate intransitive verbs is taken as an alternant of the subject plurals, then we can say that the subject plural occurs if at all when zero or one or two person affixes are present.

[15] For convenience we will admit, not a general element of subject-object relation, but a specific element G (goal) indicating object.

[16] The number 4 indicates the obviate person *(the other one)*. It is a restricted morpheme, occurring as subject-possessor when a 3rd person subject-possessor is present in the neighborhood (though two 3rd persons, usually indicating the identical person, also occur in each other's neighborhood), and as object of a 3rd person subject, and as suffix to a noun when its possessor-prefix is 3rd person (§ 3.5, 13; 4.6).

[17] When the object is plural, the G of person and plural could be considered as one long object (goal) component extending necessarily over both morphemes: $3P + G/2P'$ (P' for *and I*).

[18] G without other person, i.e. G referring to 1, when the 1st person is the object.

[19] The subscripts are used here to indicate in what way alternants of the various morphemes occur after the same sub-classes of V or I. Thus V_b occurs before alternants i, m, tu·n of the three morphemes, while V_a occurs before alternants e, m, ntamən. We may write m as an. tr.$_{a,b}$ (i.e. that variant of the an. tr. morpheme which occurs after $V_{a,b}$). Then tu·n is inan. tr.$_b$, and so on.

[20] The non-initial stems are of course complementary to all initial stems. The question is what distributional basis there is for combining the pairs which refer to the same body-part.

[21] This would not constitute an adequate list for other purposes.

[22] The diagram is presented here not as a clearer display of forms, but as a compact expression of their complex relative distributions. It does not repeat distributional statements made in English, but replaces them.

[23] Among the other shortcomings are the repetition of əpan and GP. Since the geometric relations correspond to the distributional relations among the morphemes, the correspondence loses from placing a morpheme in two geometric positions. The diagram is also unable to show that $- V1 + e·$ occurs usually with the 3rd person morpheme of R, and that a *preterite* occurs after very few non-participle verbs, and that every $3 + N$ is followed by G4 (obviative).

STRING ANALYSIS AND COMPUTATION*

* See the later *String Analysis of Sentence Structure*, Papers on Formal Linguistics, 1, Mouton, The Hague 1962.

XVI

COMPUTABLE SYNTACTIC ANALYSIS:
THE 1959 COMPUTER SENTENCE-ANALYZER

ABSTRACT

0. Each sentence-structure is a sequence of marks, each mark a class (category) of words. An attempt is made to describe every sentence as composed of a center string (a particular sequence of marks found in every sentence) and various substrings X which are adjoined at stated points Y (Y ≡ 'relative center' of X) within any (center or sub-) string.

1. Of the operators $F_x(Y)$ which adjoin these substrings X (to their relative center Y), the great majority are recursive with respect to the word categories defined. (Without this the denumerable set of sentences would not be obtainable from a finite vocabulary and set of operations.) For many operators $F_x(Y)$ in English, $F = G(Y)$, i.e. the substring X which is adjoined to Y contains within itself an occurrence of Y. Substrings are nested when the relative center of a right (left) substring is a non-rightmost (leftmost) element of another string. Otherwise, substrings are disjoint. (In this case, the associativity of substring-adjoining can lead to certain ambiguities.)

2. Some 30 string-adjoining operators are listed, these being all the main ones for English. A partial ordering is imposed upon them by the fact that the point of application Y of some substrings is in other (previously imported) substrings.

3. The operators $F_x(Y)$, with the sentence-center, can be arranged into a generator which will generate all and only the sentences of the language. Special provision has to be made for operators (especially F_e) whose string-adjoining depends (but not in a completely simple way) upon the operand (the point of application). There are also substrings which replace an element, rather than being adjoined to it.

4. To compute the structure of a sentence is to state a general procedure for scanning the marks of any sentence and deciding what is its center and what are the substrings, to what adjoined. Various related methods of computation are discussed, and it is of interest to see in what respects more is needed than a finite-state device. It is necessary to distinguish first-order strings, and second-order strings which are fixed sequences of the first; this can be expressed as a network of trees having a stateable type of general structure. Nesting of (second-order) strings can be computed by a repeating finite-state recognizer which scans only strings that do not contain strings. The fact that element (string, etc.) A requires the presence of element B can be expressed by counting A as an inverse of B in respect to the larger structure.

5. At various steps of the analysis we may find not one decision but two or more alternative ones, either because a word can be a member of two different classes, or more generally because a sequence can have two different statuses within the string that includes it. The undecidability at a given stage of the analysis is expressed by a decision variable which can take as values the various possible decisions. Further computation then includes this variable, and resolves it on the basis of the neighborhood of other marks in the larger string. The variable may be given preferred values, for one analysis of the string, with the

Excerpts from *Transformations and Discourse Analysis Papers (TDAP)*, 15 (1959). Sections 4 and 5 are a discussion of computational problems related to *String Analysis of Sentence Structure* (Papers on Formal Linguistics, 1), Mouton & Co., The Hague, 1962.

other values being checked later for other analyses. In this way, there is an ordering of analyses; and instead of indecisions along the way, we have a (small) set of alternative analyses for a sentence, each internally decided.

6. The substring analysis of sentence structure, presented here, is compared briefly with the related transformational analysis.

0. INTRODUCTION

This paper presents a preliminary discussion of the theoretical basis for a computable syntactic analysis, and of the major methods which were found useful in carrying it out. The flowcharts and specific methods for the various sections of the computer program (carried out on a Univac in 1959) are given by the authors of *TDAP* 16–20, and a comparison of the present method with functor analysis is made by Henry Hiż in *TDAP* 21. Somewhat different plans, which have not been worked out on the computer, have been presented by the writer in *TDAP* 11, 14.

'Syntactic analysis' means here a procedure for recognizing the structure of each particular sentence, taken as a string of elements (words). To state the structure of a string is:

(1) to assign its words to word-classes,

(2) to divide the word-class sequence (and its substrings) into substrings (on the basis of stated criteria),

(3) to say what combinations of substrings are admitted.

This can be interpreted as giving the grammatical relations among the substrings: e.g. determining whether substring X is the center, or the adjunct, of Y; or whether X is the subject or main verb or object of the sentence.[1]

We will speak of recognizing the structure of a sentence if, given a proposed structure, we can offer an effective test for deciding whether the sentence is or is not a case of the proposed structure. Recognizability for the unbounded number of different sentences is based on recognizability for a small number of structurally different substrings: for every sequence of words, the criteria for division and combination of substrings enable us to say whether that sequence is or is not a part of one (or more) of the listed substrings.[2] (Division into substrings is based on recognizing the word-class composition of each substring; combination of substrings is based on recognizing the permitted points of entry for each substring.)

We will speak of computing the recognition of sentence structure if, given a sentence and a set (which may be recursively defined) of structures, we can offer an effective procedure for deciding of which structure (or structures) of the set the sentence is a case, or if it is a case of no structure (i.e. is not a sentence). Such a procedure is described in the present series of papers.[3]

It will be seen that the computation is not carried out in a simple left-to-right manner with finite memory, but requires separate levels or re-runs of computation, or a back-and-forth search for environmental criteria derived from a theory or model of the structure of the given language (here presented as a well-formedness requirement). For each word of the sentence, the computation decides (on the basis of its decisions for all previously scanned words of that sentence) to what substring or substrings this word may belong in its given environment.

It may be useful to distinguish syntactic recognition from two other syntactic activities: procedures for discovery of syntactic structure in a set of sentences, given only a very general theory of language structure; and procedures for generating the sentences of a language, given a compact formulation of the set of structures.

All of these syntactic activities can utilize either of two closely interrelated types of syntactic formulation:

(1) how a sentence is composed out of parts of it: Here we compute what is the center substring of the sentence, and what are the substrings that are adjoined to the center (or to other substrings): a sentence is well formed if it consists of a well-formed center substring plus well-formed substrings adjoined only at permitted points of other substrings. This is the method of analysis presented in the present series of papers.

(2) how a sentence is derived from other sentences: Here we state what are the kernel substrings and connectives, and in what transformations these kernels appear in the given sentence. This transformational analysis will be given in a later series of papers.

1. RECURSIVE OPERATIONS

Computability of substring identification is based on the fact that the strings have a recursive structure. This is necessarily the case: Natural language is a denumerable set of strings (sentences) of a finite vocabulary, and is produced by a finite set of processes for combining substrings (and by finite speakers). This situation can occur only when some of the string-forming processes (or cycles of them) are repeatable without limit, and when the resultant of the nth repetition is recursively characterizable in terms of the resultant of the $(n-1)$th repetition. The language description can thus begin with a few primitive sentence types which are their own centers, each a sequence of certain word categories; i.e. here $S = \Sigma$.[4] All other sentences are derived from these, by (mostly) repeatable substring-adjoining operations whose resultant string (in the new sentence) is assigned to the same category as their operand word or string (in the old sentence). Each category, then, is a set of strings (including single words), a subset of the set of all strings. The operations are thus recursive with respect to these categories; and it is in this sense that the word 'recursive' will be used here.

For recognition of sentence structure it is necessary not only that all structures be obtained from a finite number of recursive operations, but also that the nth resultant of the recursive operations be uniquely decomposable into the n applications of the operators. This is indeed the case, as follows:

Each string is produced by concatenation, with: substring $a \frown$ substring $b =$ substring ab. Hence given a set of substrings and their points of application, it follows that a string is uniquely decomposable into substrings (aside from associativity, considered below). In particular, we can decompose a string into all substrings which are the result of recursive operations. E.g. let

$$F_a(0, N^i) = N \equiv N^0$$
$$F_a(n, N^i) = A \frown F_a(n - 1, N^i) \equiv N^n$$

where N indicates a (single) word of the word-category N, and N^i indicates a word-sequence (assigned to the string-category N) resulting from the ith application of a recursive operation on N. Every N^i occupies the position of a noun-phrase in some English sentences.

Then given a string which contains …AAN… (e.g. ….*decomposable recursive substring*…), we can recognize the substrings which are due to the repetition of F_a. The recognizability of these substrings may be obliterated if the recursively imported substring is changed, e.g. by automatic changes due to a neighboring element in the whole string, or by a later operation in whose operand this substring is included. However, in actual languages, many recursively imported substrings survive unchanged; and even those which are changed may be recognized if we know what kind of changes to correct for.

A recursive operation is simply iterative when the adjoined substring is different from the original mark or substring (the value of $F(0)$) to which it is first adjoined: e.g. the successive adjoinings of A to N above. But it presents new problems of analysis when the adjoined substring contains a section structurally identical with the original mark or substring to which it is first adjoined. In this case the operator F is itself the resultant of an operator G operating on N^i: $F = G(N^i)$. Examples in English: $PN \equiv G_p(N^0)$, as in *toys of plastic*, where G_p is the left concatenation of P onto N; NWV − (or *which* NWV −) $\equiv G_v(N^0)$, as in *toys which the children liked*, where G_v is the right concatenation of WV − onto N.[5] Since

$$[G(N^j)] (N^i) = F(N^i) = N^{i+1}$$

we can substitute $[G(N^j)] (N^i)$ for N^i or N^j in this expression. If we begin with $j = 0 = i$, we obtain either of the following (or a combination of them):

$[G(N)]$ $\{[G(N)]\ (N)\} = FF(N^0) = F(N^1)$, when $G(N) = F$ is repeated on the N which is the operand of the first $G(N)$: *(toys of plastic) from Germany, toys which the children liked which we brought;*
$[G\{[G(N)]\ (N)\}]\ (N) = F(N^0)$, when $G(N)$ operates on the N which is the operand of G itself: *toys of (plastic from Germany), toys which the children which we brought liked.*

These two expressions are different in the order of application of G; as linguistic expressions they are semantically different.

If the string produced by $G(N)$ is similar to the string N at the point of application of G, then the strings produced by the two expressions are identical; i.e. the order of application is associative, and both expressions produce a concatenation of $G(N)$-strings: NPNPN. If the above condition does not hold, the strings are different; for the first expression, it is a concatenation of $G(N)$-strings as above: NNWV-NWV-; but for the second it is a nesting of $G(N)$-strings: N(N(NWV-) WV-).

In the latter case, then, we have a complicated, but not ambiguous situation:

$$F(0, W^i) = N \equiv N^0$$
$$F(j+1, N^i) = F(j-1, N^i)^\frown F(i, N^i)^\frown WV- \equiv N^{j+1} \quad i, j \geqslant 0;$$
$$i \leqslant j$$

for $j = 0$, we obtain	N	N	WV- *(the book he took...)*
for $j = 1$, $i = 0$ we obtain	N NWV-	N	WV- *(the book I bought he disliked...)*
for $j = 1$, $i = 1$ we obtain	N	NNWV-	WV- *(the book the man I met, bought...)*

However, in the former case above, we obtain ambiguous strings:

$$F(0, N^i) = N \equiv N^0$$
$$F(j+1, N^1) = F(j-i, N^i)^\frown P^\frown F(i, N^i) \equiv N^{j+1} \quad i, j \text{ as above}$$

$j = 0$:	N	P N	*(the house with white railings...)*
$j = 1$, $i = 0$:	NPN	P N	*(the house with white railings on Charles Street...)*
$j = 1$, $i = 1$:	N	P NPN	*(the firm with an office on Charles Street...)*

It is clear that when a right-adjoined substring has the same ending as the original mark or substring to which it is adjoined (or when a left-adjoined substring has the same beginning as the original mark or substring), the successive adjoinings are syntactically associative: (NPN) P (N) is syntactically indistinguishable from (N) P (NPN) (even though the meanings of the two are different).

2. STRING-ADJOINING OPERATORS

We can characterize all the substrings of English sentences by means of a reasonably small number of operations, almost all of them recursive. The major ones of these are listed here. We use the following symbols:

F_x is the operation of adjoining a string consisting of, or characterized by, X.

Y_x^i (a member of the string-category Y) is the resultant of the ith application of F_x to the word-category Y, i.e. the ith adjoining of X to Y. For any Y, X; Y is included in Y_x^0.

For example, N_a^2 is AAN, the result of twice applying F_a to N. N_a^0 is a single N, or any string derived from N to which A has not yet been adjoined, but can be.

We list first the major repeatable operations which adjoin single words as left adjuncts, to N or to left adjuncts of N. Each of these sends N with i adjuncts into N with $i+1$; e.g. $F_n : N_n^i \rightarrow N_n^{i+1}$ (F_n operates on N_n^i to yield N_n^{i+1}). The count of how many adjoinings there are is not in general important in language, and will be omitted here.[6] What is important, as we shall see, is the initial state of the operand. E.g. for F_n, $N_a^0 = N$; that is, the first application of the noun-compounding operates only on a single N word (as given in the dictionary). In contrast, for F_a, $N_a^0 = N_n^i$; that is, the first application of the adjective-adjoining operates on a compound noun of any length (resulting from any number of applications of the compounding operation) including a single N. Equations between the initial operand of one operator and the ith resultant of another impose an ordering on the operators: F_a is applied after F_n.

2.1. *Repeatable Left Adjuncts to* N *and to Adjuncts of* N

F_n : adjoins N— to left of N; operates on N_n to yield N_n, with $N_n^0 = N$; compound noun: *vacuum tube.*

F_a: adjoins A_r (see note 11) to left of N_n^i, yielding N_a, with $N_a^0 = N_n^i$ (for any i): AN *old hat*, AAN *nice old hat*, AN-N *miniature vacuum tube*, etc.[7]

F_d: adjoins D to left of A_r, yielding A_d, with $A_d^0 = A_r$ (and $A_r^0 = A$): DDAAN *quite unusually nice old hats*.[8]

2.2. *Non-Repeating Left Adjuncts to* N

To the left of these a number of additional one-word strings may be adjoined by non-repeating operators:

F_q: adjoins quantifiers to the left of N_a or of $F_d . N_a^i$, $i > 0$[9]: *five very small tubes, a few old tubes*; a few members of this quantifier class Q occur to the left of T, when F_t operates (below): *all the tubes, many a tube, many tubes.*

F_t: adjoins T (*the, a, some*) to the left of the operands of F_q, with or without the F_q: $F_t.F_q.N_a$ *the five small tubes*, $F_t.N_a$ *a tube*. F_t must be applied if the initial (rightmost) N of N_a is in the 'countable' subset of N and without plural suffix.

F_0: adjoins a certain subset E of adverbs (*just, only*, etc.) to the left (very rarely to the right) of the operands of F_t with or without the F_t: $F_e.F_t.F_q.N_a$ *just the five tubes*, $F_e.N_a$ *only Beethoven.*

We may call all resultants of 2.1,2 first-order N-strings. The specification of initial operands for each P shows that all combinations of the operators of 2.1,2 occur, except that F_d operates only if F_a has operated; except for F_t with countable N, any and all operators may not occur for a given occurrence of an N.

2.3. *Right Adjuncts to* N

We now consider another set of repeatable operators which adjoin to the right of N (more exactly to the right of the resultant of 2.1,2) a string headed by the subscript of F:

F_p adjoins PN to N: *tubes of glass*; F_p also operates on A_d when it is not part of N_a.[10]

F_g adjoins V*ing*+to N: *workers downing tools.*

F_a adjoins V*en*+to N: *conclusions based on evidence.*

F_v adjoins NWV- to N: *people you may meet.*

F_w adjoins *wh*... strings (*wh*— words plus NWV—, or WV+, etc.) to N: *people whom you may meet, people who may meet you.*

F_h adjoins *that* plus NWV— or WV+ to N: *people that you may meet, people that may meet you.* F_{h+} adjoins *that* NWV+ to a subset of N: *the reports that the sherpa reached the top first.*

2.4. *Non-Repeating Right Adjuncts to* N

To this we can add a set of apparently non-repeating operations[11]:

F_{t+} adjoins *to*V+ to N: *boats to transport refugees* (with *in order* or *so as* occasionally prefaced).

F_t— adjoins *to*V— to N: *refugees to transport.*

F_{ft} adjoins *for* N *to* V— to N: *refugees for us to transport.*

2.5. *Operators on* N *and* V

There are operators which operate both on N and also, as both right and left operators, on V (rarely W) or WV or WV+ (or the Σ string); F_p, F_g, F_s, F_{t+} are also in this class (often encased in commas). These additional operators (almost always encased in commas) are:

> F_n: adjoins a whole first- or second-order N-string: , *a serious problem in itself,*: apposition.
> F_{na}: adjoins ,NV*en*+,: , *its pages torn,*.
> F_{ng}: adjoins ,NV*ing*+,: , *everyone catching what he could,*.
> F_{pg}: adjoins ,PV*ing*+,: *in seeking help*.
> F_{png}: adjoins ,PNV*ing*+,: *with everyone rushing to his defense*.
> F_{we}: adjoins ,*wh...ever* plus NWV− or WV+,: , *whichever he prefers,*.
> F_l: adjoins words of class C5 (*because*, etc.) plus NWV+: *because they will demand equality*.
> F_k: adjoins words of class C4 (*as, while*, etc.) plus NWV+ or strings which can appear as object of *is*: *as he wrote it, while there*.

The extent to which these operators occur naturally as right operators on N, and the position in which they occur naturally when operating on strings containing V, depends on the particular operator, on the extent to which other operators have acted on the adjoined string, etc. E.g. *A book, its pages flying apart*, is more natural than *A book, the pages flying apart,*; but we can more readily find the latter adjoined to a string containing V: *A book was found in the park, the pages flying apart*.[12]

As right operators on N, these occur with each other in all or almost all combinations; some combinations are rare or varyingly unnatural: e.g. F_p or F_v after any other operator (especially after those of 2.5), F_{t+} and F_{t-} after any operator. Hence we can use a general symbol F_r for any right operator on N (2.3–5), and say that any F_r operating on N_r^i yields N_r^{i+1}, with $N_r^0 = N$ (or, better, = a first-order N-string). This will permit all combinations without limit on repetition; all limitations would have to be stated in addition. N_r^i, $i > 0$, may be called a second-order N-string.

2.6. *Operators on* V

We have seen that some of the operators above are also left and right operators on V-containing strings. Such also are:

> $F_{d'}$ which adjoins adverbs of the set D' (most but not all of D above) to these V-containing strings: *usually is, will always go*.

2.7. *Operators on all Constituents (and)*

Finally, we have to consider the repeatable operator F_c which adjoins to the left of Y the conjunction *and* (or *or*, or *but not*, or in certain positions comma) plus another case of Y: F_c sends Y into Y. Here Y ranges over (a) every operand (of any operator), (b) every adjoined string (due to any operator except F_t), (c) every resultant of an operand plus its adjoined strings. We may call each of these strings in (a), (b), (c) a constituent of the sentence (or of a constituent).[13]

3. GENERATING SENTENCES BY OPERATORS

This series of operators, together with a well-formedness requirement, can be used to generate the sentences of English. Thus, the major sentence type[14], consists of the following:

(1) possibly, strings adjoined by the operators of 2.5,6;

(2) a word of the N class to which strings may be adjoined by any of the operators of 2.1–5, 7;

(3) a word or suffix of the W class[15];

(4) a word of the V class (belonging to one or another subset V_i) to which strings may be adjoined by the operators of 2.5–7;

(5) a succession of words (called the 'object') determined by the V subset: these object-strings consist of one or two (rarely more) classes, usually N, V, rarely A, D, P, with fixed words or affixes in some cases[16];

(6) when the object of a V_i contains some V_i, the sentence continues, to complete the object $+i$ required by the V_i;

(7) the completed object may be followed by strings adjoined by the operators of 2.5–7;

(8) in the object or in any adjoined string, any N which appears may have strings adjoined to it by the operators of 2.1–5,7; and any V may be operated on by 2.5–7.

3.1. N' *Generator*

We write N' for the generator which satisfies the left operators of 2.1, 2 and 2.7 (since this right operator F_0 may enter in among the left operators); it is roughly (omitting some details, e.g. countable N) as sketched in Figure 1.

3.2. V' *Generator*

Similarly, V' is the much simpler generator which satisfies the operators of 2.5–7.

A few examples of $+_i$ for various values of i are[17]:

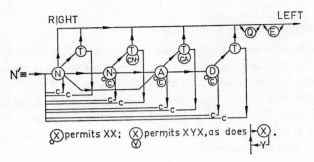

Fig. 1.

for i=	$+_i$ *consists of:*
e	V_j *en* $+_j$
b (with following *en*)	V_k *en* $+k$ (with first $\bar{N}$ omitted from $+k$, k ranging over particular values: namely, those with N in $+_k$)
t	*to* $V_j +_j$
n	$\bar{N}$
nn	$\bar{N}\bar{N}$
ng	$\bar{N}$ V'_j *ing* $+_j$

3.3. N" *Generator*

For N′ followed by the generator which satisfies all the operators of 2.3–5, 7, we write N″ (giving here only a selection of F_r: F_p, F_g, F_v, and two types of F_w[18]; see Figure 2).

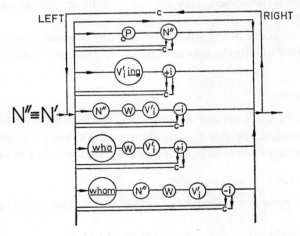

Fig. 2.

3.4. S, Σ *Generators*

The sentence is then generated by the following sequence:

$$S \equiv \quad N'' \quad W \quad V'_i \quad +_i$$
$$\text{(subject) (main verb) (object)}$$

with N'', V' for every N, V in the object or in any substring, and with F_c possibly operating on any constituent, and with possibly substrings adjoined by 2.5 at the beginning or end.

The sentence with no adjoined strings, then, consists of a single word N, a word or affix W, a word V_i, and $+_i$ where each required part of the object is filled by a single word. Such a sentence satisfies the definition of the sentence-center Σ (notes 1 and 4).

3.5. *Generator Power*

The N'' that appears inside N'', in the object or in any substring, has a different output from the N'' that constitutes the subject of the sentence. E.g. if N'' includes F_v, the N'' inside the F_v has an output to the W of that F_v; and if the N'' inside that F_v in turn contains an F_v, the N'' of the second F_v has an output to the W of the second F_v; only after the second F_v is completed can we go on to complete the first F_v. Hence we cannot merely loop each N'' to the original subject of N'' of the sentence. Each time an N'' is generated, we have to know in what part of the overall generator we are. A simple record can be kept of this, but it can allow for nested repetitions of N'' inside N'' only up to a finite number.

We can, however, describe the generator needed for any sentence containing any given number k of words. If all the words in it (except the few words needed for the sentence-center) are used up in the greatest number of repetitions of a single operator on a particular operand in the sentence, and if n is the number of words in the string adjoined by that operator, then the given operator can occur at most k/n times in generating a sentence of k words. A generating device constructed out of these operators in which each n-word-adjoining operator appears as a loop k/n times at each point (in any loop) at which it can be adjoined will generate all sentences (of the type considered here) of up to k words, as well as a great number of longer sentences.

3.6. *Other* S *types;* N-*Replacers*

The remaining types of English sentences can be generated on the basis of the above, or in a comparable way. Thus, for each sentence generated as above, we obtain additional sentences by replacing each N'' by certain N-replacer strings: *the* A_1; *that which* N'' $WV'_i - _i$; *for* N'' *to* $V'_i + _i$; and the strings formed by F_g, F_{t+}, certain F_w and F_h.[19]

4. COMPUTATIONAL TREE NETWORK

In considering the computation of the string structure of a sentence, the most general arrangement, one which is most natural to a general purpose digital computer, is to match the successive word-categories of a sentence or of parts of a sentence, and the successive substrings of a sentence (of various first-order and second-order types), with the successive marks along some branch of a tree or state diagram.

The tree represents all possible sequences of the elements by the successive node points along the branches. It can be modified by loops wherever an element or sequence is repeatable with nothing depending elsewhere on the number of repetitions (zero, one, or more): the looping elements may be considered a repeatable set, a single node of the tree. Each sentence, or section of a sentence, is a particular path through the branches of the tree; structurally different sentences are different paths. The particular conditions of each language make particular specializations of the tree possible.

While it is not possible to create a finite tree that would correspond to all and only the sentences of a language, it is possible to create for this purpose a network of trees of the following kind: Certain sequences of word-categories, whose membership and boundaries can be determined independently of the rest of the sentence (except for ambiguities and special cases), are represented by a local tree. The output of the tree is a replacement for the whole sequence – either a symbol for it or a bracketing around it – and is a node in another tree which reads the same sentence over again, but with a single symbol instead of the local sequence. This hierarchy of trees is continued until we have a tree which represents every sentence, and whose nodes are the outputs of lower-level trees.

For example, a local tree whose nodes are word-categories can represent all left identities operating (directly or indirectly) on N. Each tree has a starting-point (N reading leftward), and all of its branches have an end-point (when a bounding element of the set is met, or when an element not in the ordered – or unordered – set is met). Every endpoint (i.e. every path through the local tree) determines an output. There may be one or more outputs to the particular tree; and every endpoint determines one of these (though some endpoints, due to homonymities, may determine more than one).

Once we have entered upon a local tree, the set of elements that may follow (immediately, or farther along) can in general be grouped into certain sets:

(1) one or more final sets, each of which determines exit from the tree with a particular output (decision);

(2) possibly a non-final set or sequence of elements which have to be gone through (without which the elements of the final set do not have final status);

(3) possibly a set (or sequence of sets) of looping elements, such that if any of these are met before the final sets, the local tree continues as though the looping elements were not there.

Each tree can therefore be summarized as a sequence of the particular a_i and b sets and the various c_j sets that are needed in constructing it. And for each tree whose nodes are the output of a lower-level tree, the distinct nodes are not sets of elements of the sentence, but sets of paths through sections of the sentence.[20]

For example, one of the tests for deciding an undetermined N/V (i.e. N or V) classification (e.g. whether *study* is N or V in *a very clear study*) is briefly as follows: If the predecessor of the N/V word is A, we enter upon the following local tree (going leftward): (1a) The set T1, B, and sentence beginning exits from the tree with replacement of N/V by N; (1b) the set R/B exits from the tree leaving N/V unresolved, but with a note that the local tree will become testable if the R/B is resolved; (1c) the complement set to 1a, 1b, and 3 (i.e. everything not in these sets) exits from the local tree with N/V unresolved; (3) the set A, D, and C if between these, loops to continue the local tree. Thus if to the left of our A N/V we find DCD (*remarkably and unexpectedly clear study*), we proceed leftward in search of an exit symbol. If with or without set 3 we find T1 (*a very clear study*) or B (*their clear study*), we exit and classify *study* as N (it cannot be V in this statement). If we find R/B instead, we exit as noted above (*this clear study* would be like 1a if we can show that *this* is here an adjectival B, not a pronoun R). If we find anything else, e.g. T2 or V, we exit without resolution (*the clear study* might have *study* as V, as in *Those who are in the clear study* ...).

Another example in very rough form: In determining the local tree for left identities on N, we enter the tree leftward from N and have: (1a) the set B, TQ, and T if not preceded by TQ, is included as leftmost element of the local tree and then exits from it; (1b) the complement set to 1a and 3 exits from the local tree without being included in it; (3) a complicated ordered set (with loops) of N, M, L, A, G, S, D, Q, C carries the local tree on.

The set 2 of necessary but non-final elements in a local tree may be found in the second-order local trees that determine verb objects. For example, when we enter the object-finding tree after the verb *base*, we have: (1a) the set *on N* is included as final element in the tree and exits from it; (1b) the complement set to 1a, 2, 3 exits from the tree with failure of finding the object; (2) the set N is necessary non-final element before 1a, since the required object is *N on N*; (3) any right identity before or after 2 continues the tree.

The local tree is thus a set of paths from some starting-point, producing as output a decision or a choice of decisions. The starting-point is the head of the substring, and the decision is (1) where the substring ends, and (2) what its value is in the including string.

5. NON-UNIQUE VALUES

5.1. *Decision Variables*

While in most cases a path in a tree leads to one decision output, in some cases a path leads to an indecision among two or more specific outputs. E.g. in the dictionary, the entry *symbol* leads to one output, N; but the entry *study* leads to the alternative classification N or V. In the local strings, the entry T after reading N leftwards leads to one output: ending the Ñ-string to the left of T; e.g. *[the undefined symbol]* (where square brackets bound the Ñ-string). The entry V after N (leftward) leads to one output: ending the Ñ-string to the right of V; e.g. *include [undefined symbols]*. But the entry *that* after reaching N (leftward) leads to a double output: ending the Ñ-string either to the left or to the right of *that*; e.g. *We consider that [inadequate preparation] was responsible...* and *He disregarded [that inadequate preparation]*.

In all these cases, the situation is not simply indeterminate. Rather, there are always some specific two (rarely more) single outputs, at least one of which must hold for the given case. In most cases, it is possible to determine which output holds; the only problem is that we cannot determine this at the given level of information (dictionary, or local strings), but only after we can survey a larger neighborhood in the sentence. Hence such multiple outputs are marked not as indecisions, but as a set of possible decisions, or a variable taking the particular possible decisions as its values; the resolution of the variable is then left to a later larger-neighborhood survey.

We now consider how a variable output in a local tree determines a point in a higher-order tree. If both outputs are in the same 1_i, 2, or 3_j set of the higher tree (4 above), the two outputs are equivalent as far as further analysis is concerned. Thus if an unresolved A/N appears in the neighborhood TA−N, in which position both A and N are in the 3 (looping) set of the N tree, both values of the variable would lead to the same decision in the N tree. If a section of a sentence is represented by a path in a local tree which ends in two or more outputs that are in different sets of the higher tree, they obviously determine different paths, and in general different outputs, in the higher tree. The other nodes in the higher tree will be the same on both paths (aside from yet other variable points), since both paths continue as a representation of the remaining section of the same sentence. Hence the double output of the lower tree determines in the higher tree a pair of paths which consist otherwise of the same sequence of nodes; we may say that the double output determines a node-pair, or a variable node, in a single path in the simplified higher tree. The higher tree may then itself have a variable output at the end of its paths, either because that path contained a variable node due to a lower tree output, or because the substring it represents (even without any variable) permits more than one analysis.

In the English analysis, variable decisions originate and are resolved as follows:

(1) In the dictionary some words are given the alternative of two or more classifications: N/V, etc.

(2) In the word-complex program some word sequences are sent into a new classification for the sequence as a whole (e.g. *per cent*), while others (e.g. *because of*) are given both the new classification for the sequence and also alternatively the old word-for-word classification. In these cases, the sequence classification will be used in the first analysis of the sentence, the other classification to be used only on the alternative-readings program.[21]

(3) In the alternative-classifications program, certain dictionary variables are resolved, provided that the environment (i.e. the neighboring elements) is one that does not occur for one of the values of the variable.

(4) In computing local substrings, no variables are resolved (except if both values are in one set of the local tree). However, the fact that we are surveying a number of immediately neighboring elements often enables us to recognize that in the given neighborhood one of the values of the variable is far more likely to hold than the other. We then use that value in following the local tree, but record the other values for use in the alternative-readings program. In this later program, when we take the alternative branch of the local tree, the only section of the sentence that will have to be recalculated in local trees is the section covered by this local tree, and at most the immediately neighboring trees.

If one value of the variable is not heavily supported by its neighbors, the variable is left with an indication of all the paths into which its values fit (one for each value). This can be marked by indicating each of these paths with a new kind of path-selector variable whose values are 1 (indicating that this path is being followed in this reading) and 0 (indicating that this path is not). The sentence will then be analyzed for each value separately, first following one path through to the well-formedness check, and then automatically returning (because of the variable path-selector) and taking the alternative path through to the well-formedness check. In this way, we see which value yielded a well formed sentence; if both did, the sentence can be ambiguous.

Computing a local string can add variable decisions of its own, which arise even when the points on its path contain no variable: e.g. when we see two N elements in succession and cannot be sure (on local grounds) whether they constitute two N̄-strings (two noun phrases) or one N̄-string (a compound noun); or when we find *that* at the left of certain N̄-string paths (as above). In the case of such new variable decisions, if one of the outputs is far more likely to hold than the other, that output is followed for the preferred first analysis, with the other value marked for alternative-readings. If there is no strong preference, a path-selector variable is used to indicate the two alternative paths.

(5) When second-level substrings are determined, by means of higher local trees, certain of the path-selector variables can be resolved (both those due to original dictionary variables, and those due to new variable outputs of the local tree). This happens when one of the locally possible paths requires a certain neighborhood of other local strings (something which could not be considered when the local strings were being set up). For example, *to class* can be a PN-string (*He went from class to class.*) or a T-verb string *(To class people by abilities is insidious.)*. As a T-string, however, it requires an object (here: *people*). If that neighboring string which is required by one of the values of our variable string is not present, then that value is discarded, and the variable resolved. If the required neighbor is present, we may assume that the corresponding value of the variable is more likely, and use it for the first analysis; but the other value may nevertheless be the correct one (or both may be), so that the other value also has to be checked in an alternative reading.

Computing the second-level substrings also adds new variable decisions of its own, primarily in deciding where a substring ends. Since almost all second-level substrings contain verbs, and end at the end of the verb object, this becomes a question of where the verb object ends. The lack of unique decision may arise because some of the nodes in the tree are variables due to preceding variable decisions. Or it may arise because the type or position of the substring permits the verb to have either its full object or the short object; if following the verb we find local strings to satisfy each of these requirements, we may assume that the full object is to be taken for first analysis (since the strings required for it were found), but the (rarer) short object would also have to be tried in alternative reading. Finally, variable decisions arise frequently because a verb may belong to several subsets (each subset requiring a particular sequence of local strings as object). If in a particular sentence we find after a verb such strings as would satisfy more than one of its object-requirements, we mark the end of each possible object with a variable object-ending mark. The sentence will then have to be analyzed (for well-formedness) for each of these object-endings.

(6) After the second-order substrings have been computed, it is possible to check the well-formedness of the including substring, or of the sentence as a whole. To do this, we have to give each (second-order) substring a unit value in the including substring, or in the sentence: as N, as W, as object, or as an identity. In some cases, when we come up to a substring from the beginning of the sentence, the information up to that point permits two readings (usually, either Ñ or identity). We then give a variable value to the substring. As before, if the neighborhood makes one value much more likely than the other, we follow that value in the analysis and use the other value for alternative readings. If not, the sentence is analyzed twice, once for each value.

To summarize the types of variables: There are intermediate variables, which indicate the set of decisions made possible when a given length of neighborhood is surveyed, where we expect that a later step, surveying more of the environment, will enable us to reject some of the decisions in the originally permitted set. Such are the alternative classifications in the dictionary (where the textual neighborhood surveyed is zero), or the classification variables M and U (with values N and zero, i.e. N-replacer or identity), E (values C or zero), $X (\equiv N/V)$, $Y (\equiv Q/T)$, $Z (\equiv S/W)$, $F (\equiv A/V)$, for indicating the status of a string or element in the sentence structure, when the neighborhood up to that string cannot give us a more specific decision. In such cases, tests to decide among the alternative values are carried out as soon as a larger neighborhood has been surveyed. In the case of the dictionary classifications, we have the tests of *TDAP* 17. In the case of the U variable, as soon as we reach the first free W, we stop and see if there have been any definite N: if not, we resolve U as N; if yes, U is resolved as zero.

Like the definite symbols, the variables may have different values in different neighborhoods. Thus PN is a variable (zero or necessary part of object) after certain verbs, but is zero in most other positions. & (*so, therefore*, etc.) is a variable (zero or sentence-connective) after verb-object, but is zero elsewhere. H (for the word *that*) is a variable (string head or R/B pronoun as in 5.1(6) above); in some positions it is only one of these.

Those variables which are not resolved, but whose immediate neighborhood suggests that one value is far more likely to be correct than the other, are marked in such a way that the other value is read only if the first value fails to yield well-formedness (or if we wish to see if the less probable value also yields well-formedness, in addition to the more likely value). Such are the dictionary values retained in the word-complex program, the alternatively classified words included in local bracketing, the symbol Y for strings that are more likely zero than N, the symbol # for object-endings (?) which are very likely (but not certainly) the correct object-ending for the given sentence. The method of reading the sentence with these less probable values is given in the alternative-readings program (*TDAP* 20).

Finally, there are variables whose values are used in different readings of the whole sentence, since we cannot tell which values will fit into a well-formed reading of the sentence. These variables are used for the unresolved alternatively classified words or strings whose immediate neighborhood does not favor one of their values: especially the lone N/V, V/A, Q/T, N7, and S/W (the latter for unsolved, usually paired, -*ed* suffixes). Another type is the ? which marks the end of each possible object reading for the given verb of the sentence. In a sentence containing i 2-decision points, j 3-decision points, ... there are $2^i.3^j$ ... readings (paths through the tree), each differing from the others in from 1 to i+j+ ... points. To cover each reading, we have to mark the points which are held fixed while the various values of the remaining point are tested. This can be done by path-selector variables (having the two values of a closed and open switch), or by special devices in special circumstances: e.g. successively changing the last ? to +, where + means the last possible-object-ending (=the object ending accepted in the current reading).

At the end there remain no decision variables, only sets of possible (i.e. well-formed) readings of the sentence.

All the decision variables described above apply to elements or strings whose classification is uniquely decidable in most neighborhoods, but some of which may have two or more possible classifications in particular neighborhoods (i.e. fit into two or more analyses of well-formedness for the whole sentence). One type of non-unique analysis, however, is in general undecidable: the ambiguity due to associativity of identities as in *many (books (and lectures))* vs *(many) books (and lectures)*, or in *the people (in the car (from New York))* vs *the people (in the car) (from New York)*. Only the pairings of specific words can distinguish these constructions.

5.2. *Alternative Reading upon Failure of Well-Formedness*

The use of decision-variables enables us to represent a sentence as a sequence of marks (categories, substrings, etc.) even when some values are not uniquely decided. In order to decide the remaining undecided points (after some variables have been resolved by later information), we have to follow out the computation for a particular assignment of values for each variable (keeping a record of the other possible values), and see whether the result (the output of the final tree along the assigned branch) is well-formed. If it is not, we have to try other values of the variables. However, we do not have to try all combinations of all values of all variables in the sentence. For a failure of well-formedness permits one or more specific diagnoses of what was lacking toward well-formedness: e.g. there may have been one free Ñ too many or too few, or the object may not have matched what the verb subset required. For each diagnosis, only certain alternative paths can offer hope of a well-formed reading. For example, there may have been a U-string which was read as Ñ but has an alternative reading as zero (when the diagnosis says that there is one Ñ too many). If there are several possible diagnoses, or several unused alternative paths, there are possible orderings of the alternative readings, indicating e.g. which solutions may share an alternative path and so should be read in sequence, or which are more likely.

When the sentence is being read for an alternative value at a particular point, it is not in general necessary to recompute the whole sentence, but only the tree in which the alternative point occurred and whatever higher-level trees have nodes affected by this changed tree-output.

5.3. *The Set of all Alternative Readings*

Even if a particular reading, i.e. a particular choice of values for each decision variable in a sentence, is well-formed, we cannot say that there may not be other well-formed readings of the sentence or that the first reading was the one intended. It is therefore necessary to check all possible readings (at least until strong likelihoods are established for what is the intended reading in given types of alternatives). Here again we have diagnoses, and often an ordering among them. Once a well-formed reading has been established, any other well-formed reading can only be due to decision variables (alternative paths) within the sentence, and only to particular combinations of these (often only at particular distances from each other). In general, two interrelated variables are necessary to permit a second well-formed reading: e.g. that in one position there be a word or sequence which could have been read as a second Ñ but was not, and that in a corresponding position there be a word or sequence which have been read as a second WV— but was not. As in 5.2, some readings can best be tested in a particular order; and each reading requires a re-computing only of the sub-trees affected by the variables which are being re-evaluated.

Aside from this, there are certain combinations which are permanent ambiguities, and which depend on different values of a single decision-variable: e.g. Ñ *are* V *ing* N^0 when the V may either have zero object or Ñ object *(They are visiting relatives)*. In such cases, the two readings are marked as such in the original tree.

6. SUBSTRING ANALYSIS AND TRANSFORMATIONAL ANALYSIS

Syntactic analysis by means of substrings describes the structure of a sentence (and its substrings) as a combination of certain well-formed parts (substrings). Syntactic analysis by means of transformations describes the structure of a sentence as a transform of certain well-formed kernel sentences. The two analyses come out to be quite similar, at least in English. The similarities and differences will be discussed in a later paper. Two grounds for the similarity, however, are of such general character as to be mentioned here: (1) the fact that transformational processes, like substring-adjoining, must include recursiveness; (2) the fact that most substring-adjoining operators parallel particular transformations.

6.1. *Recursion of Kernel Structure*

We have seen that substring analysis recursively adjoins substrings to particular word-categories, making them string-categories. As a result, the sentence-center (which is a particular sequence of word-categories: $NWV_i +_i$), can be expanded by the adjoining of substrings. Or: it remains the same sequence, but now of string-categories rather than of word-categories (3.4): Any sentence of this type is $N''\ W'\ V'_i +_i$ (where X' is the resultant of recursive operations on X). Hence the sentence-center of the major type has the following relation to any sentence of the major type: All sentences consist structurally of the same sequence of the same category marks as the sentence-center, except that each category may have been operated on by recursive operations.[22] S itself can be defined as obtained recursively from Σ (note 4).

Similarly, in the case of transformations. The kernel has a given structure, e.g. the same $NWV_i +_i$. The transformations operate on this, mostly permuting the category-marks or adding individual words or affixes. It would seem at first that all we can say is that a given sentence is structurally the result of particular transformation(s) operating on particular kernel(s). However, it is possible to see that the transformations must operate in such a way that many sentences have a structure recursively characterizable (via transformations) in terms of the structure of the kernel. To see this, we note that each transformation φ_i operates on the string structure (i.e. the word-category sequence) of a kernel K, or on the string structure of the transform of a kernel $\varphi_j K$. If the string structure of $\varphi_j K$ differs from that of K, the same transformation φ_i cannot operate on it; i.e. φ_i cannot iterate. If we have transformations which iterate, or products of transformations $\varphi_i...\varphi_j$

which repeat cyclically, it must be that (in some analysis of string structure) there is a 1-1 correspondence between the sections (substrings) of $\varphi_i K$ and the word-categories (sections) of K, or between those of $\varphi_i \ldots \varphi_j \varphi K$ and of φK. That is to say, it must be that for some transformations, in the course of successive applications on one or more kernels, the same substring analysis recurs regularly. Otherwise, it would not be possible to generate a denumerable set of sentences out of a finite vocabulary, a finite set of kernel structures, and a finite set of transformations. Therefore, in the transformational analysis, we will again be dealing (though somewhat differently from the present analysis) with recursive operations carried out on an original string whose structure persists through the resultants of the successive recursive operations.

It follows from this that every sentence must contain precisely one kernel S^1 whose transformations are not of the connecting types. Or, to put it differently: given the types of transformations that exist in English, every sentence on which further transformations can still operate must contain sections (obtained via other transformations) which are recursively related to the sections of some one-kernel sentence S^1. This S^1 corresponds to what is the center Σ under substring analysis, though it is not identical with it. Hence in transformational analysis every sentence is the product of recursive or (less frequently) non-recursive transformations and has a central kernel.

6.2. *Parallelism of Transformations and of Substring-Adjoining Operators*

It is of interest that every repeatable substring-adjoining operator corresponds to a particular transformation (of the type which transforms an unconnected sentence into a connected one). This is clear in the case of the verb-containing right operators, whose word-category composition is that of a sentence-center or close to it. Here the substring head functions as the connective between the including sentence or substring and the included (adjoined) substring: (1) *that* in *Some scientists supported the proposal that the bomb should be made*; (2)-*ing* in *I saw some dogs prowling in the rubble* (the substring begins at *prowl*); etc. In the case of operators whose substring is exactly a sentence-center plus a head, e.g. (1) above, we find corresponding conjunctional transformations. In the case of operators whose substring has one N less than Σ, as in (2) above, we find corresponding word-sharing transformations.

The recursive left operators, which adjoin single words to N or A or V, and the right operators which do not contain V (e.g. F_p, F_n,), are not sentence-like. However, to each one of them there corresponds an English sentence type which contains the special verb *is*, and which is transformable into an adjunct.

TO	WHICH PRODUCES	THERE CORRESPONDS
F_n:	N_1-N_2	The N_2 is of N_1, or N_2 is a N_1, etc.: *steel desk – The desk is of steel; Steinway piano – The piano is a Steinway.*
F_a:	AN	The N is A: *well-formed string – The string is well-formed.*
F_d:	A_1d A_2	The A_2n is A_1: *exceptionally beautiful – The beauty is exceptional.*[23]
F_d:	Ad V, or V Ad	The Ving is A: *dances beautifully – The dancing is beautiful.*
F_p:	N_1 PN$_2$	The N_1 is PN$_2$: *the man in charge – The man is in charge.*[24]
F_{-a}:	N_1 A PN$_2$	The N_1 is A PN$_2$: *the artist responsible for this – The artist is responsible for this.*
F_n,:	N_1, N_2,	The N_1 is N_2: *fascism, still a serious danger, – Fascism is still a serious danger.*[25]

As to the non-recursive N-replacer substrings (3.6), those which contain a verb correspond to sentence structures which are transformable into equivalents of N'.

In contrast, the non-repeating left operators (2.2) and the verb-less N-replacers (3.6) do not correspond to sentences: F_t produces TN (*the man*), but we cannot find a sentence (such as *man is the*) which would transform into *the man*; F_e produces EN$_a$ (e.g. *only quartets*), but we find no sentence which would transform into this.

On the other hand, there are various transformations which do not clearly correspond to any substring-adjoining operators of the types we have considered. These are chiefly the non-connecting transformations, which transform an unconnected sentence into an unconnected sentence, e.g. the active-passive, or *A man walks→There is a man walking*. Such sentences are transforms of kernels, but their structure is so similar to that of a sentence-center that they can be given a center-and-substring analysis which does not correspond to their kernel under transformation.

We have thus seen that the great bulk of the substrings, whose application produces all sentences out of the sentence-center, are related in their composition to sentences; so that the adjoining or inserting of these substrings corresponds to the connecting of separate sentences by means of transformations. In particular, this is the case for the recursive substring operators. Substring analysis turns out therefore not merely to decompose a sentence S_i into parts, but in particular to decompose S_i largely into parts that correspond to other Σ, which have been adjoined to the Σ of S_i. Transformational analysis, by asking a different question, finds additional differentiations in S_i and its parts: e.g. that some substrings correspond to more than one transformation; or that some sentences are derivable from others even though the substrings in them do not make this clear.

NOTES

[1] X is the center of XY (or of Y), and Y is the adjunct of XY (or of X) in sentences S_1, if for every S_1 we can obtain a sentence S_2 by replacing XY by X, but not in general by replacing XY by Y, and if X is the smallest part of XY for which this holds. X, Y range over the set of word-categories defined for each language; for certain purposes they can be taken to range over the individual words or morphemes (word-parts) of the language.

If for every sentence composed of the class or constituent (§ 2.7) sequence ABC there exists a sentence AC, the centers are A and C; but this definition would not specify to which center B is the adjunct. If, in addition, for every sentence ABD there exists a sentence AD, we can add to the definition that Y is adjunct of X only if in all sentences of the form S_2 (here $= AC \lor AD$) every X is replaceable by XY yielding a sentence (an S_1). The analysis is of interest, of course, only if S_2 (and S_1) are convenient types of S for a characterization of language structure, not if they leave inconvenient residues of S types. If X is the center of some sentence section, and X also appears elsewhere in S_1, a unique decision as to which occurrence of X is the center requires the addition either of simplicity conditions (over the structure of the adjunct or the types of S in which X is center) or else of co-occurrence similarities (X_1 and not X_2 is the center if, in the set of word-triples for which $X_1 X_2 Y$ occurs, the dependence of X_1 values on Y values is great in comparison with the dependence of X_2). With a definition thus strengthened, the choice of centers is unique, including the center Σ of a whole sentence, except in unimportant respects (e.g. in X *and* X, either X could be taken as center).

[2] However, the assignment of word sequences to substrings is not unique; so that for some sentences, the fact that a sentence is a case of one structure does not exclude its being recognized as also a case of some other structure.

[3] As before, the structural assignment need not be unique: a given word in a given position may fit into two or more structural assignments. This is not a failure of the computation, but a specific and known homomorphic mapping (homonymous ambiguity) of the set of structures onto the set of sentences.

[4] The major word categories are: A adjective *(recursive, ...)*, N noun *(operation, ...)*, V verb *(recognize, ...)*, T article *(the, ...)*, W tense or auxiliary *(-ed, will, ...)*, P preposition *(of, ...)*, D adverb *(recursively, ...)*, C conjunction *(and, because)*, V + verb with its full object *(took the book, elected the man president)*, V — verb with one $\bar{N}$ or N'' missing from its object *(took, elected president)*. $V_i +_i$ indicates that the object is of type i which is called for by a V of subset i. (The matching subscripts may be omitted, since they are understood); see note 17. S sentence, Σ sentence-center; for the major S type considered here, Σ is $NWV_i +_i$.

[5] G(N) itself does not in turn produce a new N, and hence is not recursive. But in some cases it is formed out of some other recursive operation: If G'(P) is the left concatenation of P onto P, forming e.g. *over near* from *near*, and *out over near* from *over near*, etc., we have: $G'(0, P^i) = P = P^0$ and $G'(n, P^i) = P^{i+1}$. Then G(N) consists in the left concatenation of P^i (i.e. of the resultant of G'(P)) to N.

[6] Although a greater number of repetitions, or a wider variety of words in the adjoined substrings, gives an increasingly bizarre effect (in different degrees for different operations).

[7] There are various additional operations of this type. E.g. F_{a-} operates on N to yield compound nouns (A-N: *wild-flowers*); thus F_n and F_{a-} both produce N_n and can operate

on each other's resultants. F_n can also operate on A (including V*ing* and V*ed*) to yield compound adjectives (N-A: *stone-cold*). F_a can in some cases operate on N_p (i.e. $N_a{}^0 = N_p{}^i$) as in *a veritable bull in a china shop*.

[8] F_d can operate on A even when it is not part of N_a: *This is very nice*. But F_a operates only on N_a; A appearing elsewhere are not repeatable: we don't have *This is nice old*. V (not all) with *-ing, -ed* can also be adjoined by F_a; or additional operators have to be set up for them: *burning interest, broken tubes*. We do not say that F_d operates on N_a, since it does not operate on $N_a{}^0$ (e.g. on N-N or on N). We cannot say that F_a adjoins A_d to N_a, because only the exterior A can be preceded by D; i.e. F_d operates after F_a: there is no DADAN (without commas). F_d also operates on PN: *completely at ease*.

[9] We do not write N_d, since this would indicate a recursive operation on N, and would include the non-existent F_d on $N_a{}^0$. If either the operator F_x or the operand Y are limited, we write $F_x.Y$ for their permitted resultants, not $Y_x{}^1$. A number of detailed restrictions are omitted in this survey. Also omitted are distinctions among some operators (and hence some word-classes) which are grouped together into F_q and into F_e.

[10] $A_r \cdot F_p$ (and A_r with several other F_r, chiefly F_k and F_e, the various F not repeated) is itself a right operator (with difficulty repeatable) on N; we may write it F_{-a}: *children lost in thought*.

[11] F_{t-} also (infrequently) adjoins a hyphenated *to* V— to the right of A; the resultant may be written A_r, with $A_r{}^0 = A$: *a hard-to-distinguish thin line*. (The *to* V— is not hyphenated when A_r is not in N_a: *This is hard to distinguish*.) There are other infrequently-met operators which hyphenate strings to the right of A in N_a, or simply adjoin the strings to A.

[12] There are other, less-frequently occurring, right operators both on N and on V-containing strings. A right substring which is adjoined almost only to Σ is *,which NWV—,*: as in *I found her there, which I had long hoped to do*.

[13] I.e. (a) N, W, WV, etc.; (b) N—, A, D, PN, V*ing* +, V*en* +, *wh*-strings, NV*ing* +, C4 NWV +, etc.; (c) N_a, A_d, N_r, A_r, YCY, etc. In addition, Y can be $F_t.A_d$ and $F_t.F_n$ *(the old and the new plans* and *the dress and the shoe sales)*; and there are some special and infrequent cases, such as the value of Y being two non-contiguous constituents: e.g. the subject and the object, as in *He speaks English and I French*. Among the types of strings excluded from the values of Y are (aside from certain special cases) the adjoinings due to two or more operations (which may be the same); e.g. there is no AACAA: *nice large and new beautiful* (without comma).

[14] Subsidiary sentence types occur chiefly: sentences in which certain N-replacer substrings, not adjoined to N, occupy the position of N in the major type; questions; imperatives; object-subject-verb arrangements.

[15] One member of W is zero. If we do not admit zero members, we would have to say that W may or may not occur here.

[16] For example, the subset V_e (containing the single verb *have*, which is also a member of other subsets) has as object $V_i en + i$ (i.e. a verb of any subject i plus the suffix *en* plus the object of type i); the subset V_g (*is, like*, etc.) has as object $V_i ing + i$; the subset V_n *(sell, find)* has N; the subset V_{nt} *(find, know)* has N *to* $V_i + i$; etc.

[17] In $V_i - i$, the — equals: $+ i$ minus one N''; or $+ i$ P (i.e. $+ i$ PÑ minus the last Ñ). Ñ is a match between (a) the set of strings produced by the N' generator and (b) the sequence of marks to the left of each N in a sentence; the first approximation to Ñ is the longest string (out of b) which ends on the right with this N and which is a member of the set N'. A second approximation is obtained if part of the Ñ can be reassigned to some other element in the well-formedness of the sentence: e.g. *the* ANN = Ñ may be reassigned into TA = Ñ plus NN = Ñ, or into TAN = Ñ plus N = Ñ (both yielding two Ñ in the sentence); ACAN = Ñ may be assigned into A (as an object) plus C plus AN = Ñ and into D (as object or right identity) plus C plus DAN = Ñ (if an appropriate V precedes).

[18] Repetition with C of any circled element X or any succession of these XY, i.e. the adjoining of CX to X and of CXY to XY, is not shown here, but is to be carried out in accordance with 2.7.

[19] In certain positions, e.g. the second N″ of an object, few or none of these strings can besubstituted for N″. Note that while F_r produce adjunct strings adjoined to an N′ (and together with that N′ constitute an N″-string), the N-replacers are strings (mostly similar to some F_r) which occupy the position of an N′ in an including string.

[20] The local-tree network can be completed by considering the dictionary also to be a tree, which in this case follows not the sequence of a text, but the sequence in the matched word and classification in the dictionary. (The entry – the word – reaches immediately to the output; but the analogy to the tree will become useful when we consider the variable output here as in the later trees.) Symbols from the computer program of TDAP 16-20 are: T1 = a, an; B = adjectivized pronouns (e.g. $their$); R = pronouns; T2 = the; Q = quantifiers (e.g. few); M = words not in the dictionary (mostly nouns); L = numbers; G = V + ing; S = V + en; N7 = measure nouns (e.g. $minutes$).

[21] See 5.2, 3.

[22] The two relations of sentence-center to sentence (note 1 and 6.1) are not a surprising correlation, but the result of simplicity considerations in the construction of the analysis. The categories in respect to which the adjoinings were recursive (in 1 above) were determined on this basis: roughly, $\bar{N}^1$ is that set of word sequences that can replace N^0 (i.e. N) in a sentence.

[23] A_d indicates D composed of A plus the adverbializing suffix $-ly$; An indicates N composed of A plus nominalization (in this case, the dropping of $-ful$). Various restrictions on the correspondences of substring and sentence are not mentioned here, but will be discussed in a later paper.

[24] Under given conditions, these substrings correspond to other sentence transforms. For example, if F_p contains Ving of N_2, the corresponding sentence is often N_2 WV + (where + is zero): $barking\ of\ dogs$ – $dogs\ bark$.

[25] The substring adjoined, usually between commas, by F_n, is more exactly not N″ but any string which can be the object of is in a sentence; compare the operator F_k.

XVII

INTRODUCTION TO STRING ANALYSIS

String analysis has developed out of an attempt to carry out syntactic analysis on a computer, just as, some ten years earlier, transformational analysis developed out of the attempt to normalize texts for discourse analysis. The arrangement of syntax for computability, following in part the method presented in 'From Morpheme to Utterance' (*Language* 22 (1946), 161–83; Paper VI of this volume) was based on an effective procedure for finding in each sentence a sequence (in general, broken) of words which was itself a sentence, belonging to a certain set of minimal sentence structures. This minimal sentence was called the center of the given sentence, and its meaning had an important and central relation to the meaning of the given sentence; this relation can be specified independently of the given sentence. The remainder of the sentence consisted of adjunctions to the center or to the adjunctions; an effective procedure was presented for an ordered determining of these adjunctions, and the ordered adjunctions had an interpretation independent of the given sentence. The original version of this analysis, made for the Univac sentence-decomposing program of 1959, is given in *Computable Syntactic Analysis* (TDAP 15), 1959 (Paper XVI of this volume).[1]

1. DECOMPOSITION PRODUCTS

The string (or center-and-adjunct) analysis decomposes without residue each sentence of a language into: one elementary sentence which does not contain any (smaller) elementary sentence as a proper part of it (called the center of the original sentence); plus additional parts, members of a finite set of families of structures called adjuncts, which are not in themselves sentences and which are adjoined to the center or to some part of the center or to an adjunct or to some part of an adjunct. For example, in the sentence above, the center is: *analysis decomposes [each] sentence into sentence plus parts.*[2] The remainder of the sentence, which may consist of many and long adjunct-sections, we try to decompose into a reasonably small list of different adjuncts each adjoined (inserted) according to simple rules. For example, in

Department of Linguistics, University of Pennsylvania, 1961.

the first sentence above, the material after *parts* is not all one adjunct, but a succession of adjuncts some of which contain other adjuncts within them:

(1) *V en* (passive participle of verb) plus its object: *called adjuncts.*

(2) *wh S⁻*, i.e. wh-word (e.g. *which*) plus sentence minus a noun[3]: *which are sentences* (the N which is missing, or rather is replaced by *-ich*, is the subject of *are sentences*).

(3) *not* (an adverb, *D*), and *in themselves* (a *PN*) are two adjuncts of the verb *are* in adjunct (2).

(4) *which are adjoined to the center* repeats (by means of *and*) the structure of adjunct (2).

(5) *to some part* repeats (by means of *or*) the verb-object of the preceding adjunct (4). So do the following *to an adjunct, to some part.*

(6) *of the center* and *of an adjunct* (both *PN*) are adjuncts of the nouns which they follow (and which are themselves parts of the adjuncts listed under (5)).

We have here:

(1) Two adjunct-structures adjoined to verbs: *D* and *PN*. These appear here to the right of the verb, but also may occur to the left.

(2) Three types of adjuncts adjoined to the right of nouns: *V en* plus its object; *wh S⁻*; *PN*.

(3) An adjoining, to the right of a sequence of grammatical classes[4], of an identical (or in some environments a specifiedly different) sequence preceded by a conjunction (*and, or*). This occurs in (4) and (5) above.

2. SOME PROPERTIES OF ADJUNCTS

Note that each adjunct structure is specified as adjoining a particular class or sequence (or type of sequence, as in (3) above), to its right or its left.[5] For a given adjunct structure the situation may be that it may occur with the element to which it is anchored wherever that anchor-element may occur – in any position of any center or adjunct; or it may be that it occurs next to its anchor-element only in a particular position of a particular center or adjunct structure.[6]

A few adjuncts[7] are not repeatable, e.g. the article class. Many are repeatable, e.g. *the books which I read which I didn't like.* Many (almost all?) adjuncts and parts of centers or adjuncts are repeatable with a conjunction *C*: i.e. after (in some cases before) any one of these, *X*, we may have *CX*. The words in the second *X* will in general be different, but the class sequence will be the same as in the first *X* (or will be stated as equivalent to it); see (3) above. If any adjuncting (including via conjunction) is repeatable once, there seems to be no limit to the number of times it can be repeated (except for the human burden involved in constructing and in understanding the sentence).

The setting up of a body of adjuncts which may adjoin particular elements is essential to the present analysis. If we merely sought some subsection of a sentence which was itself a sentence, and called everything else adjunct, we could find various 'centers'; e.g. we could pick out, from the first sentence above, the words ... *each sentence ... does ... contain ... parts ...*; but the residue would not have the form of any combination of otherwise occurring adjunct structures.[8] The center of a sentence, then, is a minimal sentence such that the residue of the original sentence can be decomposed into adjunct-structures. The adjunct-structures are sequences of morpheme or word (or fixed word-sequence) classes, each of which is defined as occurring at a particular point of another structure (center or adjunct), or appended (in English usually, but not necessarily, contiguous) to a particular class (in any structure), with some suitable conditions such as the following:

(1) The addition of each adjunct to any sentence to which it may be appended yields a sentence.

(2) There is a finite number of adjunct-structures, as of center-structures.

(3) Each adjunct-structure is adjoinable to more than one other structure. (This condition is of course satisfied by adjuncts which are adjoined to a particular class in whatever structure the class occurs.[9])

The adjuncts have in general the interpretation of being modifiers of the element or sequence which they adjoin. The center, while not a modifier, does not necessarily bear the central meaning of the sentence.

3. DETERMINING THE STRINGS

The first tentative extraction of centers (and hence adjunct stretches as remainders) can be carried out without previously determined word classes, but simply on the basis of finding the same sequence of words as in the proposed center occurring as an independent sentence. All that is required, therefore, is a segmentation of sentences into words or morphemes; in many languages this can be obtained by an analysis of phoneme succession, without any considerable morphological analysis. However, we then proceed to express each tentative adjunct remainder as a combination of one or more adjunct structures. In order to do this, we have to set up classes with word (or word-sequences) or morphemes as their members. Each adjunct structure is then defined as a particular sequence of classes, adjoined to a particular class or structure. And each word sequence which we wish to consider as being adjunctional in a particular sentence must be shown to be a combination of such adjunct structures. Finding the center and adjunct structures is not hard if we begin with short sentences in a language in which the morphology is known. Given a very short sentence, we check (via an informant) if any proper part of it (not necessarily connected) is also a sentence. If so, we list the residue as a tentative adjunct (possibly a combination of adjuncts), and note what are the elements or sequences to which we may tentatively say the adjunct is adjoined (and on which side). When we extract the tentative adjuncts of another sentence, we test them to see if they contain one or more of the previously recognized adjunct structures, appropriately adjoined. In addition to known and new adjunct structures, we may find previously recognized structures adjoined in a somewhat new way, or structures that are similar but not identical to ones previously recognized.[10] In some cases we may have to redefine our grammatical classes, or at least to establish new subsets of them, as for example if it turns out that a particular adjunct structure occurs not after all members of some grammatical class but only after an identifiable subset of it.

4. PROBLEM SITUATIONS

The extractability of adjuncts is improved if we correct for automatic differences which may appear in the host string (whether center or adjunct) when a particular adjunct is adjoined to it. For example, we may note that *not* in *does not contain*, is not simply an addendum to *does contain*. For in addition to *does not contain* there is *"does not contain* (*"* here for emphatic stress), and of forms without *not* we find *"does contain* (normally with *"*) and without *"* only *contains*. However, we can take *does* before a verb to be a variant of *-s* after a verb, the variant appearing (inter alia) when certain *D* adjuncts or *"* are adjoined to the verb. Then extracting *not* from *does not contain* leaves *contains*, which is eminently acceptable, just as we would extract *not* from *may not contain*, leaving *may contain*.[11]

Various sentence-structures may be found which do not admit directly of a center-and-adjunct analysis. In particular, this is the case with sentences which include another (undeformed) sentence as a required part of their structure. For example in *I said (that) the control is excessive* or *that he's wrong is certain* we can find minimal sentences (centers) *the control is excessive* and *he's wrong*, and each residue has a structure which recurs in all sentences of its type: *N t V' (that)* ... (where *V'* includes *say, claim*, etc. and the parentheses indicate omittability), and *That...is A'* (where *A'* is an adjective subset including *certain, clear, odd*, etc.). The residues are not themselves independent sentences, and would be considered by the present analysis to be adjuncts of the stated center. However, they differ from adjuncts in certain respects; e.g. differently from adjuncts, these residues would themselves become sentences if we replace *that* (if present) plus the center-sentence by a sentential pronoun (a pro-nominalized sentence) such as *this*: *I said this, this is certain.* We can describe these structures, then, either as containing a center plus an adjunct which is close to being a center; or else as consisting of a center that includes a center (considering, e.g. $N \, t \, V'$ *pro-sentence*, as in *I said this*, as itself a center).

Another special problem is that of conjunctions. In English we may find after almost any constituent (structural sub-section) X, of a sentence a conjunction C followed by a sequence X_2 structurally identical (or stated equivalent) to that constituent: $X_1 \, C \, X_2$. We may say that the $C \, X_2$ is an adjunct of X_1. This can also be said when X is a whole sentence structure S. However, it is also possible to say in the case of $S \, C \, S$ or $C \, S, \, S$ that we have conjoined centers rather than considering the conjunctional S to be the adjunct of the other.

The process of determining what is the center and what are adjuncts and to what these adjoin, first for very short sentences and then for longer ones, is not hard to grasp. The difficulty, as in much of linguistics, lies in the complexity of the material, in the fact that there will be many sub-types of each center or of the rules about adjoining of various adjuncts, and so on. Some of the special conditions that may be met have been mentioned here. There can be many more special conditions: for example, some center-structures may be unexpandable (i.e. may take no adjuncts).

5. INVESTIGATING THE PROPERTIES OF STRINGS

Once there is a list of center and adjunct structures that describes the great bulk of sentences of the language, we can investigate the properties of these strings. Among the properties whose investigation is suggested by work so far are:

(1) What kind of morpheme and word classes and subclasses are required for this string analysis of the language; what kind of strings are defined in terms of the same depth of classification, whereas other strings require further sub-classification in order to specify either their composition or what they adjoin;

(2) length, complexity, etc. of the various strings; whether the greater variety of adjuncts, or the more frequently occurring adjuncts, or the longer ones, occur to the right or to the left of the symbol or string they adjoin (in English, right-adjoined adjuncts are of greater variety, and longer; though not so much in the case of sentence-adjuncts);

(3) what types of strings are characterized by the presence of particular class-arrangements or elements (the latter could be called markers of the string, or its head if they are at the beginning of the string); what are the types and positions of the markers, and how this relates to other properties

of the respective strings (e.g. to the left or right position of adjuncts): in English, most right-adjoined adjuncts have their markers on their left, e.g. *that, wh-, to (V), for (N to V)*, conjunctions;

(4) in what cases (as characterized by types of adjuncts or types of adjoined classes) an adjunct is adjoined to a symbol independently of its string position, and in what cases an adjunct is adjoined to a particular symbol in a particular position of a particular string;

(5) what special situations, e.g. degeneracies, result from the operation of the rules of adjoining adjuncts; and what sub-classifications or other specifications can eliminate the degeneracy (in English, $N_1 P N_2 P N_3$ can result from adjoining $P N$ twice to N_1, and also from adjoining one $P N$ to N_1 and another $P N$ to N_2. If we know that the two N in an $N P N$ structure (with particular P) have certain subset relations to each other, then given a particular $N_1 P N_2 P N_3$ we may be able to say that it is unlikely that $P N_3$ is adjoined to N_1, or the like);

(6) what adjunct (and conjunction) types are repeatable (with or without conjunction), and if there is any limit on repeatability;

(7) what departures there are from connectedness within a string (see note 9);

(8) to what extent restrictions on grammatical constructions and word co-occurrences operate only between the various (often primarily the neighboring) parts of one string or between an element and the adjuncts adjoined to it, but not for example between the adjuncts of one element and the adjuncts of another even if neighboring one. In English, there may be some restrictions among the successive adjunct structures of one element, e.g. $N_1 P N P N$ and $N_1 P N$ *wh* S^-, but not N_1 *wh* $S^- P N$ with both adjuncts to the initial N_1. But, for example, in $N_1 P N_2 t V D$ there is dependence of word co-occurrence between N_2 and N_1, or between D and V, but not between the two unrelated adjuncts N_2 and D.[12]

6. STRUCTURAL MODEL

The end-result of a center-and-adjunct analysis is, then, a structure in terms of a set of strings, each string being a sequence of grammatical classes, and the classes being such aggregates of words or morphemes[13] as are necessary and sufficient to distinguish the various strings and their points of insertion (adjunction):

(1) there is a set of center-structures;

(2) and a set of adjunct-structures, each adjoinable at a specified position in respect to specified grammatical classes or strings (center or adjunct) or parts of a string;

(3) each center-string with zero or more adjuncts is a sentence.[14]

NOTES

1 A formal treatment of string analysis is given in *String Analysis of Sentence Structure*, Mouton & Co., The Hague, 1962.

2 Square brackets enclose material which is necessary to the center of the given sentence but which appears as an adjunct in other, related, centers: if the noun here were not a singular count noun, the bracketed word would be an adjunct (e.g. ... *decomposes each theory* ... would have as center ... *decomposes theory* ...). The center includes the object required by its verb. After a certain subset of verbs which includes *decompose, subdivide*, the object is *N into M*, where *N* indicates nouns and *M* indicates mass or aggregate nouns (e.g. *nothingness, list*) or plural nouns (e.g. *sentences*) or count-noun *and* (or *plus* or *with*) *N*. (Count-noun indicates nouns that require *the, a, each*, etc.)

3 If the word is *where, when*, etc. what follows is a full sentence structure.

4 For present purposes it will suffice to say that a grammatical class is a class of words or affixes, selected so that its members will have the same occurrence in respect to other grammatical classes in the formulation of centers and adjuncts. A structure of a sequence of words is a mapping of it onto its grammatical classes. E.g. *of the center* is an adjunct, and *PN* is its structure.

5 Many sentence-adjunct structures may also occur at specified interior points of the structure they adjoin. Conceivably, there may be adjuncts which occur at a distance from their adjoined element. In English this happens almost only when two or more adjuncts occur in succession, e.g. *V PN PN*.

6 E.g. in the case of count-nouns, the article (*the, a, each, one*, etc.) is required (hence not an adjunct) before them in most positions, but it is an adjunct (since it is not required) before them in some cases when they open a verb object.

7 Henceforth, 'adjunct' and 'center' will often be used instead of 'adjunct-structure' and 'center-structure'.

8 The interest in selecting the center, therefore, depends entirely on the possibility of finding a reasonably simple set of adjunct-structures whose permitted combinations, when extracted from the sentences of the language, leave a reasonably simple set of center structures. The considerations here are comparable to those that determine how classes and constructions are set up in the usual structural (descriptive) linguistics.

9 The center-structure may be called the center string (of grammatical classes) and the adjunct structures may be called substrings (each consisting of a sequence of one or more grammatical class symbols). In many languages it will be seen that all strings are connected except for the insertion of (connected) other strings. Thus, if string X consists of initial and final parts X_1 and X_2, we may find $Y_1X_1X_2Y_2$ but not $Y_1X_1Y_2X_2$. If the latter form occurs in a language, it may be that the words of X_1 and X_2 contain markers (affixes, sub-class membership, etc.) indicating that they go together, so that we can collect these related parts by permutation and obtain an artificial form $Y_1X_1X_2Y_2$. On the basis of comments by Henry Hiż, it may be more correct to say that restricted intercalation may occur in various conditions, perhaps always provided that there are some grammatical features or sub-class relations (such as a word in one section being a classifier of a word in another) which would make it possible (for the hearer) to collect the sections that belong to one string.

10 Recognizing and characterizing a family of related and similar substrings is aided by a tentative use of transformational criteria. For instance, adjoined to the right of *N* we find various adjuncts which begin with *wh-* (or *P wh-*): *who met him, whom she met, which surprised him, which he doubted, on whom he relied, whom he relied on, near which he lived, where he lived*, etc. We can describe these as one structure (or family of structures) if we say that after *wh-* there always follows a sentence one of whose nouns has been replaced by the pronominal morpheme after *wh*: *-o* replacing a subject noun, *-om* replacing an object or adjunct noun, *-ich* replacing any noun, *-ere* replacing *in* plus noun, etc. We then have to say that the adjunct structure is *wh-* plus the pronominal morpheme plus a sentence

minus the pronouned noun; and if the pronouned noun had a *P* before it, that *P* may appear before the *wh-*.

[11] More generally, we may note certain unusual structures which occur only in the neighborhood of particular other symbols or structures. For example, *N t* (*t*: tense or auxiliary) occurs after conjunctions or in a sequence of matched or related sentences: *He won't go but I may*. We also find it after certain (matched) sentence structures which have conjunctions before them: *Since he won't go, I may*. We can say that the *N t* is a variant form of *N t V* (plus object of the verb), the *V* being that of the matched sentence: i.e. it is morphophonemically *N t V* with zero variant of the same *V* that occurs in the corresponding positions of the matched sentence: *Since he won't go, I may (go)*.

[12] It should be recognized, as pointed out by Henry Hiż, that the properties of adjuncts presented here reflect to some extent the particular situation in English. In languages in which word-order is more free, and in which inflection is more important, other properties may appear more characteristic.

[13] Note that we do not have to add 'or sequences', for the strings are not defined in terms of sequences, except insofar as a certain sequence of morphemes or morpheme classes may be defined as a member of a word class which is used in defining a string. Beyond this point, we can say about any sequence of grammatical classes either that it is part of the composition of some string, or else that part of it belongs to one string and the next part of it is the beginning or end of another string which is insertable at the given point.

[14] It may be useful to distinguish center-and-adjunct analysis from constituent analysis of sentences, as generally used in structural linguistics. In constituent analysis every sentence is decomposed into parts which are not themselves sentences. Each of these parts is further decomposed into one or more parts which are either the same as itself (with possibly other material in addition), or else which are different and smaller (i.e. are at a deeper level) than itself. Thus: *Sentence = noun-phrase⌒ verb-phrase* (the concatenation mark ⌒ indicates succession); or, if we use (*M*) to indicate the possible presence of sentence-modifiers and conjunctioned clauses: *Sentence = (M)⌒ noun-phrase⌒ (M)⌒verb-phrase⌒(M)*. Of the verb phrase we may say (in English): *verb-phrase = tense ⌒verb⌒object*. Further: *noun-phrase = noun*, or else *article ⌒noun*, or else *the ⌒adjective*. But in addition: *noun-phrase = noun-phrase ⌒ adjective* or *wh-clause*; here we have an entity which is decomposed into a structurally identical entity plus something else. In constituent analysis, this latter is only one of the various types of decomposition, and is specifically not the first decomposition of a sentence; whereas in center-and-adjunct analysis we precisely use this decomposition, in a strong form, to separate out the center.

XVIII

A CYCLING CANCELLATION-AUTOMATON
FOR SENTENCE WELL-FORMEDNESS

INTRODUCTION

This paper attempts to specify what is the simplest device sufficient to recognize sentence structure, i.e. to state for arbitrary sequences of words whether they are well-formed sentences of a natural language. If each word in the sentence is represented by its explicit string-analysis relations, then the sufficient device is one which scans this string-representation of the sentence, cancels every sequence which consists of a symbol followed by its inverse, and repeats the scanning until no more cancellations occur. The device thus requires a memory only one symbol long. In addition, it must retain the uncancelled residue of the sentence after each scan, in order to cycle through it on the next scan; and storage is also needed for the various string-representations which a given sentence can have.

   The representation is obtained directly from string theory of sentence structure. String theory characterizes sentences as the resultants of specific nestings (and rarely encirclings) and disjoint adjoinings (and, rarely, intercalations) of certain strings, each string being a particular sequence of word-categories. If word-category X, when it is part of a particular string, has a string relation to categories $Y Z$ on its right (or left), then X is represented by X followed by the left inverses $Z\backslash\ Y\backslash$ (or preceded by the right inverses $/Z\ /Y$) of the representation of $Y Z$ (except for exocentrics, below). A word-category may have different representations of this type due to its occurrence in different strings. Each sequence of representations of the successive words of a sentence is a representation of that sentence. For each representation of a sentence, the device eliminates all pairs of symbols of the form X /X or $X\backslash\ X$, and then cycles to eliminate such pairs that have been brought together by the preceding cancellation. If the whole sentence-representation is thus cancelled, the sentence was well-formed, i.e. grammatical, for that particular string-representation, and hence meaning, of it. The number of scans is at most $n/2$ for a sentence representation of n symbols; and the maximum storage needed to keep all the representations of a sentence can be determined in advance, as a function of the number and type of word-categories in the sentence.

The detailed problem here is not the study of the particular automaton proposed, but the word-representation methods which made it possible to apply so simple a device. Indeed, since the representation expresses in a principled way the relations of requirement and permission which a given word has to all environing words, it can be studied as a notation for the modalities of requirement and permission.

The cancellation is made possible by the fact that there are explicit and few relations within and between strings, all expressible as inverses, and that all nestings are cancellable so that symbols which are inverses of each other are brought together (after a sufficient number of scannings) no matter how far apart they were in the sentence. Disjoint adjuncts are also readily cancellable.

However, some consequences of language structure require special adjustment of this inverse-representation; for example:

Delays: Sequences of the form $X \backslash X / X X$ will cancel only if scanned from the right. If the scanning is to be from the left, or if the language also yields sequences of the form $Y Y \backslash Y / Y$ which can only be cancelled from the left, then it is necessary to insert a delay $I \backslash I$, to the right of every left inverse (and to the left of every right inverse) which can enter linguistically into such combinations: yielding $X \backslash I \backslash I X / X X$ and $Y Y \backslash Y I \backslash I / Y$, which cancel from either direction.

Conjugates: There are also certain rare linguistic situations (including intercalation; see note 1) which yield a non-cancellable sequence of the form $Z \backslash X \backslash Z X$. An $X \backslash$ which can enter linguistically into such a situation has to be representable by its Z-conjugate $Z X \backslash Z \backslash$, which enables the $X \backslash$ and Z to permute and the sequence to cancel. If a string $A B$, represented by A / A, encircles X, once or repeatedly, then the relation of encirclement requires each A to be represented by $X A X \backslash$: then, e.g., $A A X B B$ yields $X A X \backslash X A X \backslash X / A / A$, cancelling to X.

Exocentrics: Another problem is that of a string $X Y$ which occurs in the position of a category Z, i.e. which occurs where a Z was linguistically expected: here the X would be represented by $Z Y \backslash$, so that $Z Y \backslash Y$ would cancel to Z. (This includes grammatical idioms.)

Markers: If in any linguistic situation requiring a special representation one of the participating words occurs only in that situation or in few others, then that word can be treated as a marker for that situation, and all the special representations required to make the sequence regular can be assigned to the marker. Thus in the English intercalation with *respectively* (see note 1), we have the form $Z \backslash X \backslash Z X$ *respectively*, which will cancel if *respectively* is represented as $/X /Z X Z$. This makes uncouth but not un-bounded representations for the markers (e.g. for the *wh-* words in English below), but it saves us from having alternative representations for more widely occurring word-categories. Similarly, certain classes of verbs (V_h, V_w in the list below) occur as (adverbial) interruptions in sentences: e.g. *Celsius, I think, is Centigrade.* Rather than put the inverse of these verbs as an alternative representation of every noun (so that the noun plus verb inter-ruption should cancel), we put the inverse of the noun onto the representation of these particular verbs.

Among the linguistic phenomena (in addition to the above) which were inconvenient for the inverse-representation were:

Restricted permission: Whereas a segment that may occur anywhere in a sentence would be represented by X /X (which cancels independently of its neighbors), a segment that is permitted to occur only next to certain symbols must have its inverse included in the representation of each word-category that permits it: if A can occur to the left of N, then N must be represented as $/A N$, but also as N (for the case where no A occurs). Furthermore, if the permitted segments are ordered, e.g. T can occur to the left of A or of N, then either N must have a representation $/A /T N$ as well as N, or else the representations of N must be $/T N$, and $/A N$, and of A: $/T A$.

Dependent repetition: A special case of the above is that of conjunction, which permits repetition, i.e. it permits recurrence of the preceding word-category but not of others (hence *N and N, V and V,* but not *N and V*). One or other of the participating words has to carry inverses that restrict the category after *and* to being the same as the one before *and*; and we must allow for sequences which may intervene between the category and *and*. For example, we may give each category X a representation $X X\backslash and\backslash$.

Variable for permuted repetition: If a single symbol or string-head (see p. 292) X is repeatable, provision is made by allowing one of the repre-sentations of X to be $X X\backslash$ or $/X X$. If there is a set ζ of single symbols or string-heads which may repeat in any order, we could include in the re-presentation of each of these the inverses of each member of the set. Thus if N can be followed by *Ving* strings or W string in any order, we could represent N by N, N *Ving*$\backslash$, $N W\backslash$, and *Ving* by *Ving, Ving Ving*$\backslash$, *Ving W*$\backslash$, and W by W *Ving*$\backslash$, $W W\backslash$. However, such representations can each con-tribute to the conditions of requiring a delay (as above), with the result that the number of delays required in a given occurrence of N would be not one (as given above) but a function (<1) of the number of words which follow this N in the sentence. We can avoid having such a dependent number of delays if we define a variable ζ, such that in the above example N would be represented by N, $N \zeta$ *Ving*$\backslash$, $N \zeta W\backslash$, and *Ving* would be represented by

Ving, and *W* by *W*. The variable would be used as follows. If a word *X*, in a sentence in which *m* words follow *X*, has a representation *R* containing a variable ζ, which ranges over certain symbols ζ_1, ζ_2, ... ζ_k, then *R* is to be replaced by a set of representations R_1, R_2, ... R_s, where R_i differs from *R* only in having in place of ζ one of the permutations (different from that in R_j, $j \neq i$) of $m < n$ occurrences of the ζ_i, each ζ_i taken from 0 to *n* times. This situation arises only in the variable *z* (with *x* for reduced range) for the left inverses in the representation of *N* (see notes 15 and 17). Thus it is the number of representations, rather than the number of delays within one representation, which is dependent on the number of words following *X* in the sentence.

Excision: Certain strings lose one of their words *X* in certain environments. Since the *X* is expected in that string, i.e. the string-representation contains *X*\, we have to add the *X* to the excision-marker if there is one, or at some other appropriate point, in order to cancel the *X*\. If the marker is at the wrong end of the string for cancellation, e.g. is to the left of *X*, we have to set up in addition to *X*\ an alternative /*X* which the marker on the left can cancel. Such is the case with the *wh*-markers.

One of the features of language which is least convenient for the inverse-representations is the case of words which occur in a great many strings. Another is zero elements, whose string-relations have to be included in the representation of neighboring word-categories.

A list of the representations for the word-categories of English (in effect, an automaton-style grammar) is appended, together with the analysis of a sample sentence.

1. Before developing the inverse-representation, we consider a cycling automaton with larger memory, which does not require any special representation of words.

If in a sentence of a language we replace each successive word by the word-category to which it belongs, we obtain a sentence-form: from *The night will end* we have *T N t V*. Each sentence-form can be characterized as being a case of some string of the language, where a string is a particular sequence of word-categories into which, at stated interior or boundary points, a string may be inserted whole: *T N t V* has the string *T* inserted before the *N* of the string *N t V*. An elementary string is one into which no string has been inserted: e.g. *N t V*, *T* are elementary strings. The well-formedness of a sentence-form can be checked by seeing whether each elementary string in it is well-formed and is inserted at a stated point of another string. Since, for any two elementary strings $A_1 A_2$, $B_1 B_2$, in a sentence-form, either they are disjoint, yielding $A_1 A_2 B_1 B_2$, or one is wholly inserted (nested) in the other, yielding $A_1\ B_1\ B_2\ A_2$, the section of a sentence-form from the beginning of any one of its component strings A up to the end of A contains no material except A itself and strings which have been inserted into A.[1] We can therefore consider simple programs which will check whether an arbitrary sequence of word-categories is a well-formed sentence-form by checking first each deepest-nested (i.e. elementary) string, and erasing the string if it is well-formed, thus making the string in which it had been nested available, as a now deepest-nested string, for a repetition of the same program.

A simple device of this type would simply contain a list of the elementary strings of the language (perhaps a hundred or so common strings and a few hundred idiomatic complexes[2], not counting the rarest ones). At each successive word-category of the sentence-form we would check whether, for each $n < m$ (m: the largest number of words in any elementary string), the n word-categories beginning with it match any elementary string of n categories. If it does, we would erase these n word-categories from the sentence-form and then repeat the program on the shortened sentence-form. Thus if the sentence form was

T   N   which   N   P   N   tV$_n$ tV$_b$ P   A   N
(The attitudes which people in power express are for public effect)

we first match an elementary string (T) at T, then another $(P\ N)$ at the first P, and another elementary string (A) at A. Erasing these two strings we obtain

N   which   N   tV$_n$ tV$_b$ P   N
(Attitudes which people express are for effect)

Repeating the program on this, we match an elementary string at *which*. Erasing this *which N* tV_n we obtain

N   tV$_b$ P   N
(Attitudes are for effect)

which is an elementary string, and is erased when we repeat the program.

Such a program does not check whether the strings have been inserted only at permitted points of other strings. To check this, we would always (except at the final step) have to match in the sentence-form a section of particular structure, which we may call a string of depth one, namely a string which contains in it only elementary strings (i.e. a string such that any strings which are inserted into it do not themselves contain any strings inserted into them). When this section has been matched we would erase only the elementary (deepest-nested) strings (of depth zero). In the above example, we would on the first scan have matched the string of depth one:

which N P N tV$_n$

and have erased the contained elementary string *P N*, leaving

T N which N tV$_n$ tV$_b$ P A N

which would be matched as consisting of a string containing within it three elementary strings, properly inserted: *T, which N tV$_n$*, and *A*. After these are erased the remaining *N tV$_b$ P N* matches an elementary string without insertions and is erased.

The memory, or ability to look back or see simultaneously, which this device would require would be at most as long as the longest string which contains inserted in it only elementary strings.

Since some elementary strings are identical with the initial portion of other elementary strings, a match beginning at a particular point does not exclude the possibility of some other match beginning at the same point. At each point in the sentence-form we must attempt to match all strings which begin with the word-category at that point. If we can make more than one match we enter, from that point on, upon more than one different string-analysis of the sentence-form in question. If any one of the string-analyses (i.e. the successive matchings at successive points of the sentence-form) leads to an erasing of the whole sentence-form, then the sentence was well-formed for that string-analysis (i.e. had that string structure).

Furthermore, since certain words are members of more than one word-category, the sequence of words in a sentence may be represented by more than one sequence of word-categories. If while word *w* is a member of category *W*, the word *u* is a member both of word-category *U* and of word-category *V*, then from the sentence *w u* we obtain two sentence-forms, *W U* and *W V*. A sentence is well-formed if any one of its sentence-forms is erasable by the above device, for any string-analysis of the sentence-form.[3]

2. The simpler cycling device, which interestingly enough suffices for the same purpose, consists merely of erasing (cancelling) each sequence of two symbols one of which is the inverse of the other. It thus has to match sequences two symbols long.

To make this device possible we have to work not with the usual sentence-forms, but with a new representation of them. In the sentence-form introduced above we have a sequence of word-categories, corresponding to the successive words of the sentence. In the new representation, we replace each word-category by a disjunction of sequences of symbols: each component symbol in a sequence represents one string relation of the given word-category (in one of its string occurrences); and each symbol sequence represents the sum of all the string relations of the given word-category in a particular string occurrence of it. E.g.

word:	*leave*
word-category:	V_{na} (i.e. verb requiring for object $N\ A$, as in *leave him happy*, or $N\ E$, as in *leave him here*)
new representation:	$V\ A\backslash\ N\backslash$ or $V\ E\backslash\ N\backslash$. This is the disjunction of sequences. In each sequence, V indicates that a verb has been added to the string, $N\backslash$ indicates that N is required on the right in the string, an $A\backslash$ (or $E\backslash$) preceding it indicates that an A (or E) is required thereafter on the right in the string.

Specifically (2.1):

For any two word-categories X, Y, if (a) the sequence $X\ Y$ occurs as part of a string (i.e. Y is the next string member to the right of X), or (b) Y is the head of a string s, s being insertable to the right of X, or (c) Y is the head of a string inserted to the right of the string headed by X, then for this occurrence of X, Y in a sentence-form, $X \to Y\backslash$ (read: X is represented by $Y\backslash$, or: the representation of X includes $Y\backslash$) and $Y \to Y$, or alternatively $X \to X$, and $Y \to /X$.[4] Here $Y\backslash$ is the left inverse of Y, $/X$ is the right inverse of X, and the sequences $Y\backslash\ Y$, $X\ /X$ (but not, for example, $X\ X\backslash$) will be cancelled by the device here proposed.

The reason for the two equivalent forms is that the representation indicates merely the possibility of next-occurrence between two categories; and this is a mutual relation.

The occurrence relations listed above are the only ones that hold between two word-categories, in the string theory of sentence structure. Hence if two categories in a sentence-form have any string relation to each other, one is represented by the inverse of the other; and we can choose whether to locate the relation at one or the other category: i.e. whether $X \to Y\backslash$ or $Y \to /X$. A sentence-form is well-formed if the word-categories in it occur in accordance with string properties, i.e. if they have particular ones of the above occurrence-relations to other word-categories in the sentence-form. The relative occurrence of inverses thus constitutes a test of well-formedness; the inverses serve as a notation for the modalities of requirement and permission.[5] If a string analysis recognizes, say, Y as occurring to the right of X, i.e. the occurrence of Y to the right of X is well-formed, then one of these is represented by the inverse of the other, and the sequence $Y\backslash\ Y$ or $X\ /X$ is cancelled. Each cancellation thus indicates that a particular well-formedness requirement has been met: if a whole sentence-form is cancelled to an identity, it was well-formed.

It follows that if a word-category Z occurs as a freely occurring string, i.e. without any further members of its own string and without restriction to particular points of insertion in other strings, then its contribution to the well-formedness of the sentence-form is that of an identity (i.e. a cancellable sequence). The representation would be $Z \to 1$, or $Z \to Z \backslash Z$ (While such categories are rare in languages, an approximation to this in English is the category of *moreover, however, thus*, etc.)

If, in a given occurrence in a string, a word-category has more than one of the string-relations listed above, its representation will be the sum of all the string-relations which it has in that occurrence. Thus if a string consists of the sequence $X\,Y\,Z$ we have an inverse-relation between X and Y, and between Y and Z. The possible representations of the string (all of them equivalent) would be:

$$
\begin{array}{lllll}
\text{category} & : & X & Y & Z \\
\text{representations:} & & X & /X\,Y & /Y \\
\text{or:} & & X & /X\,Z\backslash & Z \\
\text{or:} & & Y\backslash & Y\,Y & /Y \\
\text{or:} & & Y\backslash & Y\,Z\backslash & Z
\end{array}
\left. \vphantom{\begin{array}{l}1\\2\\3\\4\end{array}} \right\} \text{from the pairs X Y, Y Z}
$$

$$(2.2)$$

If X has string-relations to two categories Y, Z both on the same side of X, then the cancellation procedure requires that in the representation of X that part which expresses its relation to the nearer neighbor be nearer to that neighbor than is the rest of the representation of X. E.g. let X have a next-member Z and an adjoined string-head Y, both on its right. Since, in string theory, adjoined strings interrupt between the element to which they are adjoined and its next string members, the resultant sequence of categories would be $X\,Y\,Z$ (and not $X\,Z\,Y$), so that the representation of X would always have the inverse of the representation of Y to the right of (i.e. nearer to Y than) the inverse of the representation of Z:

$$
\begin{array}{lllll}
\text{category} & : & X & Y & Z \\
\text{representation} & : & Z\backslash\,Y\backslash & Y & Z \\
\text{or} & : & Z\backslash\,X & /X & Z \\
\text{or} & : & X\,Y\backslash & Y & /X \\
\text{but not, for example:} & : & Y\backslash\,Z\backslash & Y & Z \\
\text{nor} & : & Y\backslash\,X & Y & /X
\end{array}
$$

$$(2.3)$$

for these last would not cancel.[6]

This accords with the notation $(X\,Y)\backslash = Y\backslash\,X\backslash$ and $/(X\,Y) = /Y\,/X$, and $(X\backslash)\backslash = X = /(/X)$. For, since to have a string-relation to something is to be the inverse of it, the representation of X in 2.3 is the inverse of the representation of the $Y\,Z$ sequence.

Rule 2.1a, restricting inverses to next neighbors in a string, is clearly sufficient to ensure cancellation of well-formed resultants of string theory. However, certain string structures make other cancellable arrangements desirable. For example, many strings have a distinct string-head which it would be convenient to regard as relating to the whole string-remainder at once, and as being the inverse of the whole remainder. E.g. if X is the head of a string $X\,Y\,Z$, we may prefer, not

category	:	X	Y	Z
representation:		$X\,Y\backslash$	$Y\,Z\backslash$	Z

but rather

representation:	$Z\backslash\,Y\backslash$	Y	Z.

Similarly each verb subcategory calls in a particular object-sequence, and could best be considered as the inverse of the whole object: If the verb subcategory V_{na} (e.g. *leave*) has category sequence $N\,A$ as object (*leave him happy*), we set:

category	:	V_{na}	N	A
representation:		$V\,A\backslash\,N\backslash$	N	A.

It is therefore desirable to generalize (2.1) into (2.4):

(a') if X, Y are any two categories in a string, then $X \rightarrow Y\backslash$ and $Y \rightarrow Y$, or else $X \rightarrow X$ and $Y \rightarrow /X$, with the provision as in 2.3 that if the representation of X also includes (by a', or by b or c of 2.1) the inverse of Z, with Y nearer to X than Z is, then the inverses in the representation of X are in the inverse order to the nearness of the categories neighboring X.

This generalization of the basis for representation by inverses adds to table (2.2), for example, the following representations for a string $X\,Y\,Z$:

category	:	X	Y	Z	
representation:		$X\,X$	$/X$	$/X$	
		$X\,Y\backslash$	Y	$/X$	from the pairs X Y, X Z
		$Z\backslash\,X$	$/X$	Z	
		$Z\backslash\,Y\backslash$	Y	Z	
		X	Y	$/Y\,/X$	
		X	$Z\backslash$	$Z\,/X$	from the pairs X Z, Y Z
		$Z\backslash$	Y	$/Y\,Z$	
		$Z\backslash$	$Z\backslash$	$Z\,Z$	

$$(2.5)$$

In all of these, a representation of a category contains the inverses of categories to which the given category is related, but may contain the positive only of that category itself. E.g. we do not set $X \to Y$, $Y \to {}^/YZ$, $Z \to {}^/Z$. Without this restriction, many more cancellable representations would be possible. In addition, each category has precisely as many symbols in its representation as string relations that are stated for it. Both of these restrictions may be removed in some cases to provide a more convenient representation. For example, if X is followed by string heads Y, Z, or $Y Z$ (ordered), then $X \to Y \backslash$ or $Z \backslash$ or $Z \backslash Y \backslash$; or if we want X to remain in order to be cancelled by something else, $X \to X Y \backslash$, $X Z \backslash$, $X Z \backslash Y \backslash$. But if X can also be followed by $Z Y$ as well as $Y Z$, and we want X to remain, then a simpler representation is [7]:

$$X \to X$$
$$Y \to {}^/XX$$
$$Z \to {}^/XX$$

Y has only one relation, to X; and the fact that Y begins with the inverse of X enables Y to sense whether the necessary X is there. But since this sensing leads to a cancellation of X, the X is reinstated in the representation of Y.

In all these representations, each symbol senses whether its inverse symbol is present next to it on the proper side. This is the only situation which is recognizable in the present device, and recognition is carried out by cancellation. If the symbol whose presence has to be sensed, i.e. which is needed to indicate the well-formedness of the senser, is not a next neighbor of the senser, it can be moved over to next neighbor position in the following manner: if there are sentence-forms in which some symbol sequence Z (not equal to identity) intervenes between X and its senser ${}^/X$, we can provide X with an alternative Z-conjugate representation which moves X over the Z: $X \to Z X Z \backslash$. If the sequence of category-representations $X . Z . {}^/X$ is rewritten $Z X Z \backslash . Z . {}^/X$ we can cancel the $Z \backslash Z$ and then the $X {}^/X$, leaving the unrelated Z.[8]

These criteria suffice for many special situations. In some cases, a particular word X (such as the markers discussed in the summary above) requires the presence of particular other words or classes Y at a distance from it, i.e. with intervening Z, after all cancellable material has been cancelled: $Y Z X$ occurs, but not $Z X$ without Y. The representation of X then has to include ${}^/Z {}^/Y Z$ so as to reach and check the presence of Y. Thus the representation for *than* will check for a preceding *-er, more, less*; the representations for *neither, nor* will check for a preceding *not* (or negative adverb like *hardly*) or a following *nor*: *More people came than I had called; He can hardly walk, nor can he talk.* If a string-head heads many strings which occur in the same sentence positions, as in the case of *wh*-words, the inverse of the string-head is attached to the symbol which the string adjoins, while the string-head itself carries all the inverses of all its various strings: *books which fell* is N W$_n^{\backslash}$. W V\ t\. tV, while *book which I like* is N W$_n^{\backslash}$.W N V\ t\ N\.N.tV /N. If the string-head consists of two words (or requires a certain word before it) the extra word can be listed as required by the main head: *books of which I heard* is N W$_n^{\backslash}$.P. /P W V\ t\ N\.N.tV.[9] If the string-head is zero the inverse of the whole string has to be attached to the symbol which the string adjoins: *books I like* is N N V\ t\ N\.N.tV /N.

There are certain conditions which the representations must meet. No two different categories should have the same representation (unless the string relations of one are a subset of the string relations of the other), for then we could cancel sentence-forms that have one category instead of the other. This excludes, for example, the first and last representations in (2.5) above. No proper part of a whole string should cancel out by itself, for then if only that part (or its residue in the string) occurred instead of the whole string, it would cancel as though it were well-formed. If a proper part of a string is itself a string (and so should cancel), then it should be considered a distinct string; otherwise the extra material in the longer string has the properties of a string adjoined to the shorter string. E.g. in *NtV N* (*He reads books*) and *NtV* (*He reads*) we have two distinct strings, with appropriate representations for their parts.

Since the rules given above permit many possible representations for each string, one can consider additional criteria for determining these more narrowly: e.g. should sensing always be in one direction; should the sensing function be arranged so that the less frequent symbols sense the more frequent; should there be the fewest or the shortest representations for each category?

In some situations only one representation is possible. Thus the noun *N* has various left adjunct strings of one category each, e.g. adjective *A*, article *T*. Even if we were willing to represent each of these by *N*, we would not be able to because they are ordered: *N, T N, A N, T A N* all occur, but not *A T N* (*the star, green star, the green star*, but not *green the star*). We have to give these categories, therefore, the following representations (in addition to others):

$$
\begin{array}{ccc}
T & A & N \\
T & A & N \\
{}^{/}T\,A & & {}^{/}T\,N \\
& {}^{/}A\,N. &
\end{array}
$$

Then the above examples would cancel down to *N* for the following representations: *N, T.$^{/}$T N, A.$^{/}$A N, T.$^{/}$T A.$^{/}$A N*; but no representations would cancel *green the star* (*A T N*).

On the whole, it does not matter in which direction the sequence of symbols representing the sentence is scanned. The only serious problem arises when a symbol is flanked by two inverses: $X\backslash.X.^{/}X\,X$ or $X\,X\backslash.X.\,^{/}X$. Here cancellation can be completed only from the direction of the positive symbol. E.g. in $X\backslash.X.^{/}X\,X$ we can cancel if we move from right to left (first cancelling the middle $X^{/}X$ and then the closed-in ends $X\backslash\,X$); but if we move from left to right we first cancel the $X\backslash\,X$ on the left and then have as residue an un-cancellable $^{/}X\,X$. This situation can be avoided by introducing a delay into the representation. Thus, if the category represented here by $X\backslash$ was represented instead by $X\backslash I\backslash I$ (adding a meaningless $I\backslash I$ as delay), then we would have had $X\backslash I\backslash I.X.^{/}X\,X$, in which a left to right scan would first cancel the $I\backslash I$ and the $X^{/}X$, and then cycle to cancel the now closed-in ends $X\backslash\,X$. The delay thus enforces a different choice of cancellations in a sequence of like symbols with inverses in both directions, and would be added (without any knowledge of the individual sentence) to every representation $X\backslash$ which is able to meet on its right $X.^{/}X\,X$ (and, if we wish to ensure cancellation in either direction, also to every representation $^{/}X$ which is able to meet on its left $X\,X\backslash.X$). This occurs in English when a verb which requires a noun as object (and the representation of which is $V\,N\backslash$), or certain string-heads like *that* (in the representation $Wt\backslash\,N\backslash$) meet a compound-noun ($N.^{/}N\,N$). These representations are therefore corrected to $V\,N\backslash I\backslash I,\ W\,t\backslash\,N\backslash I\backslash I$ so that, e.g.,

$$\begin{array}{ccc} \text{take} & \text{book} & \text{shelves} \\ V\,N\backslash I\backslash I\ . & N\ . & ^{/}N\,N \end{array}$$

cancels from the left (as well as from the right) to V.

Almost all word-categories occur in more than one string-relation (in the sense of 2.1) to other categories. For example N may occur with the string A inserted to its left, or with the string T inserted to its left: $A\,N$, $T\,N$. An A which is inserted to the left of N may occur with T, also inserted left of N, on its left, or else without this T: $T\,A\,N$, $A\,N$. A verb V may occur with its whole object on its right, or with the N section of its object indicated only by a *wh*-word (or zero) on its left: *I told the boy to come; the boy whom I told to come* (where the *whom* contains the reference to the *the boy* of the object). All these are recognized, in the string-analysis of the language, as different strings or string-combinings. Each of these requires a different representation.

WORD-CATEGORY	REPRESENTATIONS
N	N, $^{/}T\,N$, $^{/}A\,N$
A	A, $^{/}T\,A$
V_{nt} (i.e. V requiring object N *to* V)	$V_{nt}\,V\backslash$ to$\backslash$ $N\backslash$, V_{nt} $^{/}N\,V\backslash$ to$\backslash$.

Given a sentence-form containing $T\ N$, if we use for N the representation N or $/A\ N$, the result will be $T.\ N$ or $T./A\ N$ and will not cancel; but if we use the representation $/T\ N$, the result is $T./T\ N$ and cancels. But given a sentence-form containing only N, if we use for N the representation $/T\ N$, it will not cancel. Similarly, given *I told the boy to come*, the representation $V\ V\backslash to\backslash N\backslash$ for *told* will enable the object to cancel $(V_{nt}\ V\backslash to\backslash N\backslash.T./T\ N.to.V)$ while $V_{nt}/N\ V\backslash to\backslash$ will not. But in *whom I told to come* only the $V_{nt}\ /N\ V\backslash to\backslash$ representation will cancel $(whom \rightarrow W\ N\ V\backslash t\backslash N\backslash)$; $W\ N\ V\backslash t\backslash N\backslash.N.t.V_{nt}/N\ V\backslash to\backslash.to.V$ cancels to W, which will be cancelled by the preceding noun.

We can now state how the device operates: Given a sentence-form, we replace each successive word-category in it by the disjunction of inverse-representations of that category determined above (selecting for each string relation only one of the alternatives shown in 2.2 and in 2.3 and in 2.5). We then obtain a set of representations of the sentence-form by taking all the different combinations of category-representations for each successive category.[10] We now scan each sentence-form-representation in one direction (left to right or right to left), cancelling every sequence of the form $X\backslash X$ or X/X. Upon reaching the end of the sentence-representation, we repeat this last process (i.e. we scan the reduced sentence-representation and cancel) until there is a scan in which no cancellation takes place. (In this case no cancellation could occur in any further scans. Note that the maximum number of scans for a sentence-representation of n symbols is $n/2$.) If now everything in the sentence-representation has been cancelled, then the given representation (indicating a particular set of string-relations of the categories in the sentence-form) was well-formed; i.e. the sentence was well-formed for the represented string-analysis of it. If, however, there is a non-empty residue in the sentence-representation, then this was not the case.

In considering the amount of storage needed to hold all the representations of a sentence form, we note that some of the most frequent categories have only one representation, with two or so additional ones to allow for conjunction and adverbs (which could be represented otherwise if desired): t (tense; also $t\ t\backslash C\backslash$, $t\ D\backslash$, $/D\ t$), T (article; also $/D\ T$), V_0 (verb having no object; also $V_0\ V\backslash C\backslash$, $V_0\ D\backslash$). Every sentence (except imperatives and certain colloquial forms) has at least one t. Every word-category in the sentence-form replaces one word of the sentence, except that the t_s members of t are only suffixes.

We now list the word-categories of English with their inverse-representations:

, (comma)$\rightarrow C$, or nothing (i.e. $\rightarrow C$, or else omitted in the sentence representation).

& (e.g. *moreover, however*)→& /&; if we accept *and* as operating on these, then also: & &\ C\.[11]

t (tense: *will, can*; includes subset of present, past→t$_s$)→t; t not\; tD\; /D t; t t\ C\.

T (article: *the, a, some*)→T; /D T.

the→T$_t$[12], but *the* is also a member of T.

not→not; but it is also included in D$_a$.

D (adverbs of the sentence)→D; D D\; D D\ C\.

D$_a$ (adverbs primarily of adjectives)→D$_a$; /D$_a$ D$_a$; /T D$_a$; /Q D$_a$; /N's D$_a$; /A D$_a$; D$_a$ D$_a$\ C\.

Q (quantifiers, numbers)→Q; /T Q; /D$_a$ Q; /Q Q; /N's Q; Q Q\ C\.

A (adjectives)→A; /T A; /Q A; /N's A; /D$_a$ A; /A A; A P\; A to\ ; A A\ C\. Also rarely→/T$_t$ N, /D$_a$ /T$_t$ N for *the A* occurring in N position (N-replacer); *The good is oft*...[13]. Also, rarely→A /A, /D A/A A /A D\, A /A to\, for occurrence of A in sentence-adverb positions (*Tired, he arose.*). Also→/N A for compound adjective (*stone-gray*).

N's→N's; /T N's; /Q N's; /N's N's; /A N's; /D$_a$ N's; N's N's\ C\. Proper names are included in N. Also→/T$_t$ N, /A /T$_t$ N; *The new woman's is better.*

possessive pronoun (*his, her*)→N's; N's N's\ C\.

nominalized possessive (*his, hers*)→N; NE\ ; N P\; N N\ C\; *His is better.*

N (noun)→N; /T N; /Q N; /N's N; /A N; /N N. There are also the following representations bearing left inverses X\; to each of these may be appended, on its left, any of the right inverses which have just been listed[14]: N N\ (apposition); N E\; N A$_d^\backslash$ (post-N adjectives; *present* N x P\ A\ (*wars lethal to mankind*)[15]; N x A\ C\ A\ (*flowers fresh and upright*); N x A\ Dà/ (*bombs indescribably destructive*); N P\ (*time for work*); N to\ (*books to read, people to read it*); N for\ (*books for you to read*); N V en\ (*paintings stolen*); N Ving\ (*plans arriving today*); N x W$_n^\backslash$ (*men whom...*) N x W$_n$ P\ N\ (*men the names of whom...*); N x N V\ t\ N\ (N with zero *whom, who, which*, as in *people I know*); N x V\ t\ N\ (N with zero *where, when, how, why, in which*, etc. as in *the way I do it*); N N\ C\, or N N\ C\ followed by any of the left inverses above: N N\ C\ P\, etc. Also rarely →D x N /N, as in *A child, he did not understand*[16]; and→D x Ω$_b^\backslash$ as in *The children in bed, we left* (for Ω, see below).

N$_s$: nouns which, as predicates, take nominalized sentences as subject: *That we'll go is a promise*: inverses as for N.

count-N (N which do not occur in the singular without article or N's; e.g. *chair*)→as for N, except that T or N's is included immediately to the left of this N.

N$_m$ (nouns measuring time, etc.)→D. E.g. *He sat all day*; but N$_m$ are also included in N. Also→/A D; /Q D, /T D.

pronouns (*he, this, such*): representation as for N, but without any of the right inverses on the left of N.

E (post-N adverbs; *here, only*)→E z.[17]

A_d→A_dz.

P (preposition: *of, in*)→P z N\; P /N; /D P z N\; /D P /N; P P\ C\; D N\; D /N; D D\ N\ ; D /N D\.[18] P includes *to, for*.

to→to (in object of V and after *for*, W); to x V\; to x N V\ (*books to read*→N to\.to N V\.V /N); also N V\ for *to V* occurring in the position of N or in apposition to N_s (*To go is important. The plan to go*); and D V\ for adverbial occurrence *To tell the truth, he's gone*).

for→for x N V\ to\ N\ (*books for him to read*); also N V\ to\ N\ when *for* heads a string which occurs in the position of N or in apposition to N_s; and D V\ to\ N\ (for adverbial occurrence).

F→(post-V adverbs; *down, fast*)→F; F D\; F F\ C . With some restrictions, the prepositional complements can be included here: *look it up*.

Since verbs occur in a number of subcategories, each of which is followed by a particular category-sequence as object, we represent each sub-scripted verb-category by V followed by inverses of its object categories Ω_i.[19] Hence each V_i→V_i $\Omega_i^\backslash$, and in addition→V_i $V_i^\backslash$ C\; V_i V\ C\ $\Omega_i^\backslash$ (these provide, respectively, for conjunction between verbs before object, and between verbs with object: *bought and sold books* V_n $V_n^\backslash$ C\.C.V_n N\.N; *bought books and disappeared* V_n V\ C\ N\.N.C.V). Also, each one-word t_s V_i→V_i V\ t\ N\ d C\ $\Omega_i^\backslash$ and each V_i→V_i V\ $t_g^\backslash$ N\ d C\ $\Omega_i^\backslash$ (to provide for a separate conjoined C N t_g V Ω after each N t_g V Ω); the t_g=t or *to* or *ing* added to the V. Also each V_i (except V_0)→V c_i $\Omega_i^\backslash$ (to provide for verb-omitting conjoined clauses like *He plays violin and she piano*); the c_i=zero or c_i Ω_i N\ C\.[20] Rarely, V_i→V_i D\ C\ $\Omega_i^\backslash$; V_i d N\d C\ $\Omega_i^\backslash$; (for *He went, and fast; He came and she too*). In addition, certain V_i→V_i F\ $\Omega_i^\backslash$; V_i $\Omega_i^\backslash$ F\: certain adverbs F follow the object, or precede it (with stylistic preferences). And every V_i→V_i D\ $\Omega_i^\backslash$; V_i $\Omega_i^\backslash$ D\; adverbs of sentence or verb may follow the object or precede it.

V_b (*be*)→V_b Ving\; V_b Ven\; V_b N\; V_b /N; V_b A\; V_b /A; V_b P\; V_b /P; V_b E\; V_b /E; V_b /Ω_b (for use in the question). The set of objects whose inverses are listed here, i.e. Ving, Ven, N, A, P, E, may be called Ω_b.

V_z (*have*)→V_z Ven\; V_z N\; V_z /N; V_z /Ω_z (for use in the question).

V_0 →V_0: *sleep*.

V_g →V_g Ving\: *try*.

V_t →V_t to\: *try*.

V_n →V_n N\; V_n /N: *take*.

V_p →V_p P\; V_p /P *rely*.

V_{np}→V_{np} P\ d N\; V_{np} /N P\ N\; V_{np} /N P\; V_{np} /N /P N [21]: *attribute*.

$V_a \rightarrow V_a$ A\: *loom.*

$V_h \rightarrow V_h$ V\ t\ N\ d that\; V_h V\ t\ N\; V_h /N V\ t\: *think*; also /t /N D.[22]

$V_{h'} \rightarrow V_{h'}$ V\ N\ d that\; $V_{h'}$ V\ N\; $V_{h'}$ /N V\: *insist.*

$V_w \rightarrow V_w$ W\: *wonder*; also /t /N D.

$V_{nh} \rightarrow V_{nh}$ V\ t\ N\ d that\ d N\; V_{nh} V\ t\ N\ d N\; V^{nh} /N V\ t\ N\: *tell.*

$V_{ph} \rightarrow V_{ph}$ V\ t\ N\ d that\ d P ; V_{ph} V\ t\ N\ P\; V_{ph} /N V\ t\ P\: *report.*

$V_{pw} \rightarrow V_{pw}$ d W\ d P\: *ask of.*

$V_{nt} \rightarrow V_{nt}$ V\ to\ d N\; V_{nt} /N V\ to\: *order.*

$V_{ng} \rightarrow V_{ng}$ Ving\ d N\; V_{ng} /N Ving\: *feel.*

$V_{vn} \rightarrow V_{nv}$ V\ N\; V_{nv} /N V\: *make.*

$V_{nn} \rightarrow V_{nn}$ N\ d N\; V_{nn} /N N\: *elect.*

$V_{na} \rightarrow V_{na}$ A\ N\; V_{na} /N A\; V_{na} /A N\; V_{na} E\ N\; V_{na} /N E\; V_{na} /E N\ *leave.*

$V_i \rightarrow V_i \Omega_i^\}$; but also $\rightarrow t_s$ followed by $V_i \Omega_i^\}$ (*shake* is the category $V_n \rightarrow V_n$ N\; as in *can shake*; or the category sequence $t_s V_n \rightarrow t_s V_n$ N\, as in *I shake*).

V_is (present tense)$\rightarrow t_s V_i \Omega_i^\}$ (*shakes* is the category sequence $t_s V_n$, as in *He shakes*).

V_i pure past$\rightarrow t_s V_i \Omega_i^\}$ (*shook*).

$V_i$en (participle)$\rightarrow V_i$ en $\Omega_i^\}$ (*have shaken it*); V_i en z $\Omega_i^\}$ N (i.e. the appropriate $\Omega_i^\}$ but without its rightmost N: *shaken* is then V instead of V N\, as in the passive *is shaken*).

$V_i$ed$\rightarrow t_s V_i \Omega_i^\}$; V_i en $\Omega_i^\}$; V_i en z $\Omega_i^\}$ N (for verbs with -ed, which can be past or participle: *announced*).

V_n en, V_n ed$\rightarrow$also A (*the announced intention*).

V_i ing$\rightarrow V_i$ ing z $\Omega_i^\}$ this representation will cancel after all representations of Ving and $V_i$ing, and after the N Ving\ representation of N:
like reading books, the man reading books;
D $\Omega_i^\}$ (as subordinate clauses: *Reading books, he learned much*);
$N_i \Omega_i^\}$ (as N-replacer: *Reading books is helpful; his plan of reading books*);
N (for the many Ving which occur as N: *road-building, building plans*);
A (for certain Ving which occur in A position: *a biting comment*).

The words containing the *wh*-morpheme are represented by various partially similar sequences of inverses, depending on what can follow them. In this list, $W_n^\}$ cancels W and W_n, while $W_v^\}$ cancels W and W_v.

	after N $W_n^\}$:	after V $W_v^\}$, also:	after N $W_n^\} P$; V $W_v P$:
that[23]	W t\		
	W V\ t\		
	W t\ N\ d		
	W N V\ t\ N\ d		

	after NW_n\:	*after VW_v\, also:*	*after NW_n\ P; VW_v P:*
who	W t\ W V\ t\		
which	W t\ W V\ t\ W t\ N\ d W N V\ t\ N\ d	W_v N V\ to\	/P W V\ to\ N\ d /P W V\ t\ N\ N\ d /P W P V\ t\ N\ N\ d /P W P V\ to\ N\ N\ d /P W V\ t\ N\ d /P W V\ to\ d /P W P V\ t\ N\ d /P W P V\ to\ d
what		W_v t\ W_v V\ t\ W_v t\ N\ W_v N V\ t\ N\ W_v N V\ to\	/P W_v V\ to\ N\ /P W_v V\ t\ N\ N\ /P W_v P V\ t\ N\ N\ /P W_v P V\ to\ N\ /P W_v V\ t\ N\ /P W_v V\ to\ /P W_v P V\ t\ N\ /P W_v P V\ to\
whom	W t\ N\ d W N V\ t\ N\ d W_n t\ W_n V\ t\	W_v N V\ to\	/P W V \t\ N\ /P W V\ N\ to\ /P W P V\ t\ N\ /P W P V\ to\
whose	W t\ W V\ t\ W t\ N\ W V\ t\ N\ W t\ N\ N\ W N V\ t\ N\ N\ W N V\ t\ N\		/P W V\ to\ N\ /P W V\ t\ N\ N\ /P W P V\ t\ N\ N\ /P W P V\ to\ N\ /P W V\ t\ N\ /P W V\ to\ /P W P V\ t\ N\ /P W P V\ to\
when	W t\ N\ d		/P W V\ t\ N\
where	W V\ t\ N\ d W V\ to\ d		/P W V\ to\

	after $NW_n\backslash$:	*after* $VW_v\backslash$, *also:*	*after* $NW_n\backslash$ P; VW_v P:
how		same represen-	
		tations as for	
		when, where, but	
why		occurring only	
		after W_v (very	
		rarely after W)	
whether		W_v V\ t\ N\ d	
		W_v t\ N\ d	
		W_v V\ to\ d	

Column 2 gives the prepresentations, in addition to the W...sequences of column 1, that will cancel after W_v. In addition, the *wh*-words in this table are represented by the above sequences beginning W or W_v, with N replacing the W or W_v: *who*→N t\, N V\ t\; etc. This provides for the occurring of *wh*-words as string-heads of N-replacer (*What he said is true*). Further, *whether*, and *wh*-words plus *ever* (e.g. *whatever*),→the corresponding W or W_v representations (except those ending with *to*), but with the W removed: *whomever*→t/ N\ d; N V\ t\ N\ d. In addition, *who*→W_1, *which*→W_1, W_2; *what*→W_1, W_2; *whom*→W_2; *whose*→W_3 *when, where, how, why*→W_4; these representations are for the occurrence of *wh*- words in questions (see below).

C_s (*because, since, before, that*)→D V\ t\ N\; D V\ t\ N\ D\; D t\ N\; D t\ N\ D\.

C_g (*since, before, despite*: conjunctions which occur before Ving)→D Ving\; D Ving\ D\.

C_b (*while*: conjunctions which occur before Ω_b)→D Ω_b\.

C (*and, or, but,* and, with some additional details, *than, as*)→C.

Aside from T, every category with a representation X has also a representation X X\ C\; every one having a representation of the form X Y\ or /Z X Y\ has also a representation X X\ C\ Y or /Z X X\ C\ Y\ (i.e. each string-head can be followed by C and a similar string-head, after the string remainder has been cancelled). Furthermore, for all those sequences of categories X Y which can be repeated around C (e.g. especially t V C t V *will buy and will sell*), the last category of the sequence has a representation containing the inverse of the sequence, followed by C: Y Y\ X\ C\ (e.g. t V C t V→t. V V\ t\ C\.C.t.V, which cancels to t V).

In addition, *than*→A\; V\; V\ t\.

All these inverses cancel everything except the center (independently occurring) string of each sentence-form. To cancel the center string we could make one part of it the inverse of the other; but it is more convenient to represent the sentence punctuation by the inverse of the center string, and to put this punctuational representation at the head rather than the end of the sentence.

.→V\ t\ N\ d; t\ N\ d; rare N\ V\ t D\ (*Here sat he. There was a man*).

?→$\Omega_b^\backslash$ N\ Ω_b $V_b^\backslash$ $t_s^\backslash$ (*Was he here?:?* t_s V_b N E→$\Omega_b^\backslash$ N\ Ω_b $V_b^\backslash$ $t_s^\backslash.t_s$. V_b /Ω_b.N.E); $\Omega_z^\backslash$ N\ Ω_z $V_z^\backslash$ $t_s^\backslash$ (*Had he gone?*); aside from these cases[24], V\ N\ t\ (*Will he go?*);

V\ t\ $W_1^\backslash$ (*Who will go?:?* W_1 t V→V\ t\ $W_1^\backslash$.W_1.t.V); N V\ N\ t\ $W_2^\backslash$ V\ t\ N\ $W_3^\backslash$; N V\ N\ t\ N\ $W_3^\backslash$; V\ N\ t\ $W_4^\backslash$; rarely also the representa- tion for period (e.g. *You went?*)

!→V\; N\.

If more detailed subcategories are recognized, especially in *D, A, N*, some of the multiplicity of representations could be reduced, and there would be less danger of sentence-representations cancelling even when the sentence- form is not well-formed, due to a fortuitous combination of inverses. For example, the adjectives A_s and nouns N_s and verbs V_s which have a nominal- ized sentence as their subject (e.g. *Whether he went is doubtful. That he went is a fact*) could be represented, in addition to the regular representations for *A, N, V*:

$$V_s→^\backslash t \,^\backslash It\ N\ t\ V\ V\backslash\ t\backslash\ N\backslash\ that\backslash$$
$$^\backslash t \,^\backslash It\ N\ t\ V\ V\backslash\ to\backslash\ N\backslash\ for\backslash$$
$$^\backslash t \,^\backslash It\ N\ t\ V\ V\backslash\ to\backslash$$
$$^\backslash t \,^\backslash It\ N\ t\ V\ W_v^\backslash$$

A_s and N_s→N /V_b /t /It N t V followed by the same four left inverse portions above. Then *It surprised me that he went*→It.t. / t.\It N t V V\ t\ N\ that\.that. N.t.V. And *It is important for him to go*→It t. V_b N\.N /V_b /t /It N t V V\ to\ N\ for\. for.N.to.V.

Certain conjunctions require that certain words in the conjoined string not be the same individual words as corresponding one in the parallel string. Such requirements are not directly expressible in constituent or string analyses of language, nor in the present inverse representation, since all of these deal with word-classes and not with individual words. This applies to the requirement for *than* and *or* that the string they introduce contain at least one different word (and for *but*, generally at least two) than the parallel string preceding them: *He may write or he may phone, He wrote more than he phoned*, but not *He wrote more than he wrote*. And it applies to the requirement in the comparative that if the word A in the conjoined string, which corresponds to the carrier A of *-er* (or *more* or *less*) or to the word of

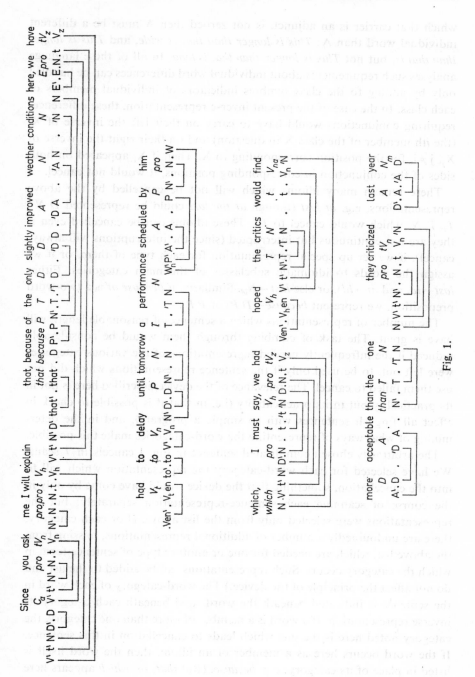

Fig. 1.

which that carrier is an adjunct, is not zeroed then A must be a different individual word than A: *This is longer than that is wide*, and *This is longer than that is*, but not *This is longer than that is long*. In all of these language analyses such requirements about individual word differences can be handled only by adding to the class symbols indicators of individual members of each class. In the case of the present inverse representation, these difference-requiring conjunctions would have to carry on their left the inverse of X_i (the ith member of the class X in question) and on their right the inverse of X_j, $j \neq i$, for the position corresponding to X. Then if X_i appeared on both sides of the conjunction in corresponding positions, it would not cancel.

There remain many idioms which will not be cancelled by the above representations, e.g. *at last* (though *at the last* could be represented $D \: N \backslash$. $T_t.'T_t \: N$, which would cancel to D). These idioms can be cancelled even if they are not continuous but interrupted (since the interruptions will always cancel), if we set up special representation for each type of them, or if we assign the words to idiomatic subclasses of the main categories. Either *last* → $Id \backslash$, and *at* → $Id \backslash$, or else *last* → N_{id}. Similarly, if *because of* is a two-word preposition, we represent *because* → $D \: P \backslash$ or $P \: P \backslash$.

The number of representations which a sentence of reasonable length will have is great. The task of combing through them would be considerably reduced if the infrequently needed representations of the various categories were left out, to be used only if the sentence representations which did not use them failed to cancel. The relevance of the device described here is not in its practicality but in its practicability (i.e. in that it is possible to check in effect all English sentences with so simple a program), and in the determining of what ways of representing the word-categories make this possible.

The arbitrarily chosen complicated sentence in Fig. 1 cancels in 7 scans. We have selected for each word-category the representation which will fit into the cancellation, something that the device would have come by only in the course of scanning each sentence-representation separately; but the representations were selected only from the list above. (For each category, there are undoubtedly a number of additional representations, missing from the above list, which are needed for one or another type of sentence-form in which the category occurs. Such representations can be added to the list and do not affect the principle of the device.) The word-category of each word in the sentence is indicated beneath the word; and beneath each category its inverse representation. If a word is a member of more than one category, the category noted here is the one which leads to cancellation in this sentence. If the word occurs here as a member of an idiom, then the word itself is listed in place of its category: e.g. *because*. (But *that, to, which* appears here as categories each with only one word as member.[25])

NOTES

[1] To this we have to add the rare cases of encircling (where the outer string is adjunct to the inner), and of a string $A_1 A_2$ which is intercalated into a string $B_1 B_2$, yielding $A_1 B_1 A_2 B_2$. In English, one type of intercalation, which has a marking word, is N_1 and $N_2 t_1 V_1$ and $t_2 V_2$ respectively (*He and she played and sang respectively*).

[2] An idiomatic word-complex is a word sequence whose insertability into strings is not identical with the insertability otherwise stated for its word-categories. E.g. *in general* is the category sequence *P A. P A* does not otherwise occur as a string, but *in general* is a string insertable at many points of other strings. That is, an idiom is, in string-analysis, a sequence of categories which differs from the sequences that are permitted or required at the sentence position in which it occurs.

[3] A cycling device of the types presented here was proposed in Z. S. Harris, *String Analysis of Sentence Structure* (Papers on Formal Linguistics, 1), The Hague 1962, p. 52. Its power has since been studied by John Myhill, but without the restriction to a memory of pre-fixed length such as the kinds of memory-restriction proposed in the two sections of this paper. Determining what is the simplest device for string-representation makes it possible to raise the question of comparing the various methods of sentence analysis and representation in respect to the simplicity of the devices that can check well-formedness in their terms.

[4] Correspondingly to (b) and (c), if Y is the end of a string which is inserted to the left of X, or if Y is the end of a string inserted to the left of a string ending in X, then $Y \to X\backslash$ and $X \to X$ or else $Y \to Y$ and $X \to /Y$. The arrow can be considered as sending the word-categories on the left into the new representation on the right; but it can also be considered as defining each different string-occurrence of each word-category in terms of the new representation. The alphabet of the new representation contains fewer different symbols than does the alphabet of word-categories.

[5] If a category is represented as $X\backslash$ then X is required. If a category is represented as $X\backslash$ or $Y\backslash$, then X is permitted, and so is Y. For these modalities in string theory, cf. p. 44 of *op. cit.*, note 3.

[6] If Y is the head of some string whose remainder is W, then the representation of Y will contain $W\backslash$ (e.g. it may be $Y W\backslash$), since Y has a string-relation to W. The actual sequence of categories is then not $X Y Z$ but $X Y W Z$, and one representation would be $Z\backslash Y\backslash$. $Y W\backslash.W.Z$ (see note 8), which cancels. Similarly, if X is followed by two string heads Y, Z, in that order, then $X \to Z\backslash Y\backslash$, the inverses appearing in the inverse order.

[7] Suggested by Aravind K. Joshi.

[8] The dots separate the representations of the successive categories.

[9] If it is thought desirable to specify that there is a string relation obtaining between *hear* and the particular preposition *of*, then it is possible to subclassify P so that each preposition becomes a unit category. Thus,

> *of* $\to$ of; ; of N\
> *to* $\to$ to; to N\
> *hear* $\to$ V of\; V /N of\; V /N /of
> *attribute* $\to$ V to\ N\; V /N to\; V /N to\N\, V /N /to N\

The other representations of *of*, *to*, etc. will parallel those of *P* (cf. p. 92).

Using this representation, *books of which I heard* becomes $N W_n\backslash.of.W N V\backslash t\backslash N\backslash.N.$ *t* $V /N /of$. Since all P must in any case have W-conjugate representations, in addition to their other representations (i.e., $P_i \to W P_i W\backslash$) in order to handle cases similar to these, we represent *of* here as W of $W\backslash$, which cancels.

Note that almost all categories in the verb object can be excised by means of *wh*-markers or question-words: *How easy did he make the test? How well did he behave? The man whom he attributed the painting to, the man to whom he attributed the painting, the painting which he attributed to Masaccio, books which I was looking for, books for which I was looking,* though not *the fool who I thought him* or *the bomb off which I touched.*

In these sentences A, D, N, and $P N$ have been excised from the objects of the various verbs which require them. The representations of the excision markers will thus contain A, D, and N; and the representations of the verbs will contain $/A$, $/D$, $/N$, and $/(P N)$, in addition to the $A\backslash$, $D\backslash$, $N\backslash$, and $(P N)\backslash$ which they contain for sentences without excisions. But now, since the markers occur to the left of the verb, the inverses of the excised categories $/A$, $/D$, $/N$, and $/(P N)$, must be placed at the leftmost end of the sequence of category inverses which sense the remainder (if any) of the object: Thus,

> $make \rightarrow$ V A$\backslash$N$\backslash$; V $/$AN$\backslash$; V $/$NA$\backslash$;
> $behave \rightarrow$ V D$\backslash$; V $/$D;
> $attribute \rightarrow$ V to$\backslash$ N$\backslash$; V $/$N to$\backslash$; V $/$(to N) N$\backslash$; V $/$N to$\backslash$ N$\backslash$;
> $hear \rightarrow$ V of$\backslash$; V $/$(of N); V $/$N of$\backslash$

A similar procedure is necessary in the case of objects of prepositions and adjectives (e.g. *aware of the problem*), for here too excision is possible. [John Robert Ross].

[10] We do not try to have the device select those representations of each category which would match (cancel) the other categories in the given sentence-form, for this would require the whole apparatus of string-analysis, which is not needed since all string relations have already been expressed in the representation, so that all that is now needed is a local check of each representation.

[11] $X X\backslash C\backslash$ permits the cancellation of $C X$ after X: *Can and may* $\rightarrow t\ t\backslash C\backslash.C.t$; *However and moreover* $\rightarrow$ & &$\backslash$ $C\backslash.C.$&$\ /$&, which cancels.

[12] Except in the case of W below, the convention for subscripts will be that $X\backslash$ cancels X and X_i; but $X_i\backslash$ does not cancel X nor does $X_i\backslash$ cancel $X_j.j \neq i$.

[13] In some cases, a word-category sequence $X Y$ occurs in the string positions of Z. In such cases, instead of directly representing these string relations of X and Y, we can assimilate $X Y$ to the representation already set up to Z, by $X \rightarrow Z Y\backslash$: i.e. in addition to expressing the string-relation within X Y (by writing $Y\backslash$) we express the fact that the string relations of $X Y$ are those of Z (by writing Z). Then $X Y \rightarrow Z Y\backslash.Y$, cancelling to Z.

[14] Hence for a given occurrence of N in a sentence, the representation that would cancel might be $N N\backslash$ or $/T N N\backslash$ or $/Q N N\backslash$, or $/A N P\backslash$, etc.

[15] The position of the x is empty or is occupied by any of the left inverse sequences on the right of N, perhaps all except $E\backslash$, $A_d\backslash$; and also by any of these followed by $C\backslash$ on its right.

[16] These are cases in which an N sequence is an adverbial subordinate clause.

[17] The position of z is empty or is occupied by any of the left inverse sequences which appear after N in the list above: $E P\backslash$, $E W_n\backslash$, etc. The z provides for cancelling the next string-head on N, which will follow the string in which the z is placed. If after an N-occurrence there are inserted two strings $A = A_h A_r$ (A_h: string-head of A:A_r remainder of A) and $B = B_h B_r$, we need $N \rightarrow N A_h\backslash$ and $A_h \rightarrow A_h B_h\ A_r\backslash$. Then the category sequence $N A_h A_r B_h B_r \rightarrow N A_h\backslash.A_h B_h\backslash A_r\backslash.A_r.B_h B_r\backslash.B_r$, which cancels to N. Hence to N we add the inverse of the heads of all strings insertable after N; and to each string-head A_h we add the inverse of the head of any next-inserted string, followed by the inverse of the remainder of the string A_r.

[18] The $/N$ provides for nouns which have been permuted to the left: *The book he tore the cover of* $\rightarrow$ T. $/T N N V\backslash t\backslash N\backslash.N.t.V N\backslash.T./T N P\backslash.P /N$, which cancels to N. The $D N\backslash$ is for $P N$ category-sequences which occur in roughly the same positions as adverbs: *At that time*, etc. The $D\backslash$ in $D D\backslash N\backslash$ provides for another $P N$ that may follow.

[19] The i ranges over the subscripts of V in the following list. Ω_i is the sequence of inverse-symbols following the symbol V_i in the representation of V_i.

[20] These above types of representation in respect to C apply also to V_iing, V_ien.

[21] The position of the d is occupied by $D\backslash$, or is empty. The symbol d should also be inserted immediately before the leftmost left-inverse in every representation of V, thus $V_i \rightarrow V_{np} d P\backslash d N\backslash$; $V_{np}/ N d P\backslash$, etc.

[22] Making *I think, I wonder* into an adverbial clause: *Everyone will, I think, try it; Will he go, I wonder?*

[23] In addition, *that* → that: after: V_h, $V_{h'}$; and *that* is also included in the pronouns.

[24] But including $V_z N$: *Did he have time?* as well as *Had he time?* Note that E is a case of Ω_b.

[25] The pre-print of this paper was issued in *Transformations and Discourse-Analysis Papers* 51 (1962), University of Pennsylvania. In November 1962, John Myhill gave a paper in the Moore School formalizing this automaton and relating it to the two-way erasing automata of Rabin and Scott. In 1965, Irwin D. J. Bross and co-workers, at the Roswell Park Memorial Institute, Buffalo, programmed this automaton with certain modifications and successfully analyzed the sentences of medical reports (some 200 sentences). See P. A. Shapiro, Acorn, *Methods of Information in Medicine* 6 (1967) 153–162.

DISCOURSE ANALYSIS*

* See the later *Discourse Analysis Reprints*, Papers on Formal Linguistics, 2, Mouton, The Hague 1963.

XIX

DISCOURSE ANALYSIS

This paper presents a method for the analysis of connected speech (or writing).[1] The method is formal, depending only on the occurrence of morphemes as distinguishable elements; it does not depend upon the analyst's knowledge of the particular meaning of each morpheme. By the same token, the method does not give us any new information about the individual morphemic meanings that are being communicated in the discourse under investigation. But the fact that such new information is not obtained does not mean that we can discover nothing about the discourse but how the grammar of the language is exemplified within it. For even though we use formal procedures akin to those of descriptive linguistics, we can obtain new information about the particular text we are studying, information that goes beyond descriptive linguistics.

This additional information results from one basic fact: the analysis of the occurrence of elements in the text is applied only in respect to that text alone – that is, in respect to the other elements in the same text, and not in respect to anything else in the language. As a result of this, we discover the particular interrelations of the morphemes of the text as they occur in that one text; and in so doing we discover something of the structure of the text, of what is being done in it. We may not know just WHAT a text is saying, but we can discover HOW it is saying – what are the patterns of recurrence of its chief morphemes.

Definite patterns may be discovered for particular texts, or for particular persons, styles, or subject-matters. In some cases, formal conclusions can be drawn from the particular pattern of morpheme distribution in a text. And often it is possible to show consistent differences of structure between the discourses of different persons, or in different styles, or about different subject-matters.

1. PRELIMINARIES

1.1. *The Problem*

One can approach discourse analysis from two types of problem, which turn

Language **28**, No. 1 (1952), 1–30.

out to be related. The first is the problem of continuing descriptive linguistics beyond the limits of a single sentence at a time. The other is the question of correlating 'culture' and language (i.e. non-linguistic and linguistic behavior).

The first problem arises because descriptive linguistics generally stops at sentence boundaries. This is not due to any prior decision. The techniques of linguistics were constructed to study any stretch of speech, of whatever length. But in every language it turns out that almost all the results lie within a relatively short stretch, which we may call a sentence. That is, when we can state a restriction on the occurrence of element *A* in respect to the occurrence of element *B,* it will almost always be the case that *A* and *B* are regarded as occurring within the same sentence. Of English adjectives, for instance, we can say that they occur before a noun or after certain verbs (in the same sentence): *the dark clouds, the future seems bright*; only rarely can we state restrictions across sentence boundaries, e.g. that if the main verb of one sentence has a given tense-suffix, the main verb of the next sentence will have a particular other tense-suffix. We cannot say that if one sentence has the form *N V*, the next sentence will have the form *N.* We can only say that most sentences are *N V*, some are *N*, and so on; and that these structures occur in various sequences.

In this way descriptive linguistics, which sets out to describe the occurrence of elements in any stretch of speech, ends up by describing it primarily in respect to other elements of the same sentence. This limitation has not seemed too serious, because it has not precluded the writing of adequate grammars: the grammar states the sentence structure; the speaker makes up a particular sentence in keeping with this structure, and supplies the particular sequence of sentences.

The other problem, that of the connection between behavior (or social situation) and language, has always been considered beyond the scope of linguistics proper. Descriptive linguistics has not dealt with the meanings of morphemes; and though one might try to get around that by speaking not of meanings, but of the social and interpersonal situation in which speech occurs, descriptive linguistics has had no equipment for taking the social situation into account: it has only been able to state the occurrence of one linguistic element in respect to the occurrence of others. Culture-and-language studies have therefore been carried on without benefit of the recent distributional investigations of linguistics. For example, they list the meanings expressed in the language by surveying the vocabulary stock; or they draw conclusions from the fact that in a particular language a particular set of meanings is expressed by the same morpheme; or they discuss the nuances of meaning and usage of one word in comparison with others (e.g. in stylistics).

Culture-and-language studies have also noted such points as that phrases are to be taken in their total meaning rather than as the sum of the meanings of their component morphemes, e.g. that *How are you* is a greeting rather than a question about health – an example that illustrates the correlation of speech with social situation. Similarly, personality characteristics in speech have been studied by correlating an individual's recurrent speech features with recurrent features of his behavior and feeling.[2]

1.2. *Distribution within Discourse*

Distributional or combinatorial analysis within one discourse at a time turns out to be relevant to both of these problems.

On the one hand, it carries us past the sentence limitation of descriptive linguistics. Although we cannot state the distribution of sentences (or, in general, any inter-sentence relation) when we are given an arbitrary conglomeration of sentences in a language, we can get quite definite results about certain relations across sentence boundaries when we consider just the sentences of particular connected discourse – that is, the sentences spoken or written in succession by one or more persons in a single situation. This restriction to connected discourse does not detract from the usefulness of the analysis, since all language occurrences are internally connected. Language does not occur in stray words or sentences, but in connected discourse – from a one-word utterance to a ten-volume work, from a monolog to a Union Square argument. Arbitrary conglomerations of sentences are indeed of no interest except as a check on grammatical description; and it is not surprising that we cannot find interdependence among the sentences of such an aggregate. The successive sentences of a connected discourse, however, offer fertile soil for the methods of descriptive linguistics, since these methods study the relative distribution of elements within a connected stretch of speech.

On the other hand, distributional analysis within one discourse at a time yields information about certain correlations of language with other behavior. The reason is that each connected discourse occurs within a particular situation – whether of a person speaking, or of a conversation, or of someone sitting down occasionally over a period of months to write a particular kind of book in a particular literary or scientific tradition. To be sure, this concurrence between situation and discourse does not mean that discourses occurring in similar situations must necessarily have certain formal characteristics in common, while discourses occurring in different situations must have certain formal differences. The concurrence between situation and discourse only makes it understandable, or possible, that such formal correlations should exist.

It remains to be shown as a matter of empirical fact that such formal correlations do indeed exist, that the discourses of a particular person, social group, style, or subject-matter exhibit not only particular meanings (in their selection of morphemes) but also characteristic formal features. The particular selection of morphemes cannot be considered here. But the formal features of the discourses can be studied by distributional methods within the text; and the fact of their correlation with a particular type of situation gives a meaning-status to the occurrence of these formal features.

1.3. *Conjunction with Grammar*

The method presented here is thus seen to grow out of an application of the distributional methods of linguistics to one discourse at a time. It can be applied directly to a text, without using any linguistic knowledge about the text except the morpheme boundaries. This is possible because distributional analysis is an elementary method, and involves merely the statement of the relative occurrence of elements, in this case morphemes. To establish the method for its own sake, or for possible application to non-linguistic material, no prior knowledge should be used except the boundaries of the elements.

However, when we are interested not in the method alone but in its results, when we want to use the method in order to find out all that we can about a particular text, then it is useful to combine this method with descriptive linguistics. To this end we would use only those statements of the grammar of the language which are true for any sentence of a given form. For example, given any English sentence of the form $N_1 \, V \, N_2$ (e.g. *The boss fired Jim*), we can get a sentence with the noun phrases in the reverse order $N_2 - N_1$ (*Jim – the boss*) by changing the suffixes around the verb[3]: *Jim was fired by the boss*. The justification for using such grammatical information in the analysis of a text is that since it is applicable to any $N_1 \, V \, N_2$ sentence in English it must also be applicable to any $N_1 \, V \, N_2$ sentence in the particular text before us, provided only that this is written in English. The desirability of using such information is that in many cases it makes possible further applications of the discourse-analysis method.

How this happens will appear in § 2.33; but it should be said here that such use of grammatical information does not replace work that could be done by the discourse-analysis method, nor does it alter the independence of that method. It merely transforms certain sentences of the text into grammatically equivalent sentences (as $N_1 \, V \, N_2$ above was transformed into $N_2 \, V^* N_1$), in such a way that the application of the discourse-analysis method becomes more convenient, or that it becomes possible in particular sections of the text where it was not possible to apply it before. And it will be seen that the decision where and how to apply these grammatical trans-formations need not be arbitrary but can be determined by the structure of the text itself.

The applicability of the discourse-analysis method in particular texts can be further increased if we not only use the ordinary results of grammar but also extend descriptive linguistics to deal with the special distributions of individual morphemes. There are cases, as will be seen in § 2.33 below, when we would like to use information not about all the morphemes of some class (like the transformability of V into $V*$) but about a particular member of the class, about a restriction of occurrence which is true for that one morpheme but not for the others of its class. Such information is not in general available today; but it can be obtained by methods which are basically those of descriptive linguistics.

Finally, the applicability of discourse analysis in particular texts can sometimes be increased if we draw our information not only from the grammar of the language but also from a descriptive analysis of the body of speech or writing of which our text is a part. This larger body of material may be looked upon as the dialect within which the text was spoken or written, and we can say as before that any distributional statement which is true for all sentences of a given form in that dialect will also hold for any sentence of that form in the text under consideration.

2. THE METHOD

2.0. *The Nature of the Method*

We have raised two problems: that of the distributional relations among sentences, and that of the correlation between language and social situation. We have proposed that information relevant to both of these problems can be obtained by a formal analysis of one stretch of discourse at a time. What KIND of analysis would be applicable here? To decide this, we consider what is permitted by the material.

Since the material is simply a string of linguistic forms arranged in successive sentences, any formal analysis is limited to locating linguistic elements within these sentences – that is, to stating the occurrence of elements. We cannot set up any method for investigating the nature or composition of these elements, or their correlations with non-linguistic features, unless we bring in new information from outside.

Furthermore, there are no particular elements, say *but* or *I* or *communism*, which have a prior importance, such as would cause us to be interested in the mere fact of their presence or absence in our text. Any analysis which aimed to find out whether certain particular words, selected by the investigator, occur in the text or not, would be an investigation of the CONTENT of the text and would be ultimately based on the MEANINGS of the words selected. If we do not depend upon meaning in our investigation, then the only morphemes or classes which we can deal with separately are those which have grammatically stated peculiarities of distribution.

Since, then, we are not in general interested in any particular element selected in advance, our interest in those elements that do occur cannot be merely in the tautologic statement THAT they occur, but in the empirical statement of HOW they occur: which ones occur next to which others, or in the same environment as which others, and so on – that is, in the relative occurrence of these elements with respect to each other. In this sense, our method is comparable to that which is used, in the case of a whole language, in compiling a grammar (which states the distributional relations among elements), rather than in compiling a dictionary (which lists all the elements that are found in the language, no matter where).

Finally, since our material is a closed string of sentences, our statement about the distribution of each element can only be valid within the limits of this succession of sentences, whether it be a paragraph or a book. We will see in § 2.33 that we can sometimes use information about the distribution of an element outside our material; but this can be only an external aid, brought in after the distribution of the element within the discourse has been completely stated.

2.1. *General Statement of the Method*

It follows from all this that our method will have to provide statements of the occurrence of elements, and in particular of the relative occurrence of all the elements of a discourse within the limits of that one discourse.

2.11. *Elements in Identical Environments*

We could satisfy this requirement by setting up detailed statements of the distribution of each element within the discourse, just as in descriptive linguistics we could set up individual statements summarizing all the environments (i.e. the distribution) of each element in various sentences of the language. However, such individual statements are unmanageably large for a whole language, and are unwieldy even for a single text. In both cases, moreover, the individual statements are an inconvenient basis for inspection and comparison, and for the deriving of general statements. Therefore, in discourse analysis as in descriptive linguistics, we collect those elements which have like distributions into one class, and thereafter speak of the distribution of the class as a whole rather than of each element individually.

When two elements have identical distributions, this operation of collecting presents no problem. In descriptive linguistics, however, the opportunity rarely occurs, since few words have identical distributions throughout a language.[4] It may occur more frequently in a repetitive text, where two words may be always used in identical parallel sentences – e.g. in stylistically balanced myths, in proverbs, in sloganeering speeches, and in 'dry' but meticulous scientific reports.

2.12. *Elements in Equivalent Environments*

In the much more frequent case where two elements occur in environments which are almost but not quite identical, we may be able to collect them into one distributional class by setting up a chain of equivalences connecting the two almost identical environments.[5] This is done in descriptive linguistics when we say that the class of adjectives A occurs before the class of nouns N, even though a particular A (say *voluntary*) may never occur before a particular N (say *subjugation*). It is done in discourse analysis when we say that two stretches which have the same environment in one place are equivalent even in some other place where their environment is not the same.

Suppose our text contains the following four sentences: *The trees turn here about the middle of autumn; The trees turn here about the end of October; The first frost comes after the middle of autumn; We start heating after the end of October.* Then we may say that *the middle of autumn* and *the end of October* are equivalent because they occur in the same environment (*The trees turn here about –*), and that this equivalence is carried over into the latter two sentences. On that basis, we may say further that *The first frost comes* and *We start heating* occur in equivalent environments. (The additional word *after* is identical in the two environments.) Such chains, which carry over the equivalence of two stretches from one pair of sentences where their environment is indeed identical to another pair of sentences where it is not, must of course be constructed with adequate safeguards, lest everything be made equivalent to everything else, and the analysis collapse. This problem appears also in setting up classes in descriptive linguistics; the kind of safeguards necessary in discourse analysis will be discussed in § 2.21.

More generally, if we find the sequences $A\,M$ and $A\,N$ in our text, we say that M is equivalent to N or that M and N occur in the identical environment A, or that M and N both appear as the environment of the identical element (or sequence of elements) A; and we write $M = N$. Then if we find the sequence $B\,M$ and $C\,N$ (or $M\,B$ and $N\,C$) in our text, we say that B is (secondarily) equivalent to C, since they occur in the two environments M and N which have been found to be equivalent; and we write $B = C$. If we further find $B\,K$ and $C\,L$, we would write $K = L$ by virtue of their having occurred in the secondarily equivalent environments B and C; and so on. As an example, let us continue our text fragment with the following sentence: *We always have a lot of trouble when we start heating but you've got to be prepared when the first frost comes*. Then we would say that *We always have a lot of trouble* is equivalent (for this text) to *but you've got to be prepared*.

Saying that $B = C$ does not mean that they are IN GENERAL equal to each other, or that they MEAN the same thing. The equal-sign is used only because the relation between B and C satisfies the technical requirements of the relation which is generally marked by that sign. All we mean when we write $B = C$ is that this relation is a step in a chain of equivalences: on the one hand, B and C are found in equivalent environments (M and N); and on the other, any two environments in which B and C are found will be considered equivalent (K and L).

It is not relevant to ask, 'Is it TRUE that $B = C$?' or 'Have we the RIGHT to say that $K = L$ merely because $B = C$ and because $B K$ and $C L$ occur?' All that is proposed here is a method of analysis; the only relevant questions are whether the method is usable, and whether it leads to valid and interesting results. Whether the method is usable can be judged on the basis of its operations, without regard to its results, as yet unseen. Whether these results are of interest will be considered in § 3 below, where we will see that the chains of equivalence reveal a structure for each text. There is no question whether we have the 'right' to put $K = L$, because all we indicate by $K = L$ is that $B K$ and $C L$ occur and that $B = C$. The justification will depend on the fact that when we put all the equivalences together we will obtain some information about the structure of the text.

2.13. *Equivalence Classes*

After discovering which sequences occur in equivalent environments, we can group all of them together into one equivalence class. In our formulaic statement we have $A = B$ (both occur before M), and $A = C$ (both before N), and $B = C$, so that we consider A, B, C all members of one equivalence class. Similarly, M, N, K, L are members of another single equivalence class. In our example, *The trees turn here in* (T_1) and *The first frost comes after* (T_2) and *We start heating after* (T_3) are all members of one equivalence class T, while *the middle of autumn* (E_1) and *the end of October* (E_2) are members of another equivalence class E. There is yet a third class E' consisting of *We always have a lot of trouble when* and *but you've got to be prepared when*. E' is obviously related to E, since both occur with the last two members of T. But E occurs AFTER T, whereas E' occurs BEFORE T.

In terms of these classes, the five sentences of our text fragment can be written as six formulas (since the last sentence was a double one): $T E, T E, T E, T E, E' T, E' T$. It is clear that we cannot make one class out of E and

E'; but we can say that when the order of E and T is reversed (when E is 'reflected' in T), we get E' instead of E. If we change the members of E' to the form they would have if they came after T instead of before, then those changed members of E' become regular members of E. For example, we might say *We start heating at the cost of a lot of trouble always, but the first frost comes in a way you've got to be prepared for.* This sentence has the form $T E, T E$. The new phrase *at the cost of a lot of trouble always* is a member of E by virtue of its occurrence after T; we can mark it E_3. Of course, we must show that it is equivalent to *We always have a lot of trouble*, except for the reversed position in repect to T; to show this, we need techniques which will be discussed in § 2.33. Similarly, we must show that the new E phrase *but ... in a way you've got to be prepared for* (E_4) is the T reflection of the E' phrase *but you've got to be prepared when.* If we can show these two reflection-equivalences, we can replace the two E' phrases by the changed phrases which we get when we put them in the E position. As a result we have two more members of E, and no peculiar E' class.

In such ways we can set up equivalence classes (like E) of all sequences which have equivalent environments, i.e. the same equivalence classes on the same side (before or after), within the text. The elements (or sequences of elements) which are included in the same equivalence class may be called equivalent to, or substituents of, each other. We will see later (§ 3.3) that in some respects (especially in extensions of the text) they may be considered substitutable or interchangeable for each other. In that case the equivalence class may also be called a substitution class.

Note especially that the operation of grouping non-identical forms into the same equivalence class does not depend upon disregarding small differences in meaning among them, but upon finding them in equivalent environments. This means either finding them in identical environments (*the middle of autumn* and *the end of October* both occur in the environment *The trees turn here in* –) or else finding them in environments which are at the ends of a safeguarded chain of equivalences (*The first frost comes* and *We start heating* occur in the equivalent environments *after the middle of autumn* and *after the end of October*). The method is thus fundamentally that of descriptive linguistics and not of semantics.

2.14. *Sentence Order*

At this point we come to an operation not used in descriptive linguistics: representing the order of successive occurrences of members of a class. In descriptive linguistics order comes into consideration only as the relative position of various sections of a sequence, as when the order of article and noun is described by saying that the first precedes the second along the line of a noun phrase. In discourse analysis we have this kind of order as among the sections of a sentence, e.g. the different orders of E and E' in respect to T.

The order of successive sentences, or of some particular word class in various sentences (say, the relation of successive subjects), is not generally relevant to descriptive linguistics, because its distributional statements are normally valid within only one sentence at a time. Here, however, where we are dealing with a whole discourse at once, this problem is a real one. If we were considering each sentence separately, and relating it to others only for purposes of structural comparison, we could say (as in descriptive linguistics) that each sentence in our text fragment consists of $T\,E$. But since we are speaking of the text as a whole, we cannot say that it consists merely of $T\,E$ six times over. The particular members of E and of T are different in the various sentences; and these differences may be (for all we know) peculiar to this text, or to a group of similar texts.

Our text fragment can be structurally represented by a double array, the horizontal axis indicating the material that occurs within a single sentence or subsentence, and the vertical axis (here broken into two parts) indicating the successive sentences:

$$T_1\,E_1 \qquad T_3\,E_2$$
$$T_1\,E_2 \qquad T_3\,E_3$$
$$T_2\,E_1 \qquad T_2\,E_4$$

In this double array, the various symbols in one horizontal row represent the various sections of a single sentence or subsentence of the text, in the order in which they occur in the sentence (except insofar as the order has been altered by explicit transformations in the course of reducing to symbols, as in the change from E' to E). The vertical columns indicate the various members of an equivalence class, in the order of the successive sentences in which they occur.

The reason why the order of symbols in a row may differ from the order of elements in a sentence, is that our linguistic knowledge of sentence structure enables us to deal with the elements separately from their order. We do this when we disregard in our symbols any order that is automatic and that would reappear as soon as our symbols are translated back into language, as when *but* ... is included in E_4 even though it is necessarily separated from E_4 in the actual sentence (since *but* generally occurs at the beginning of a sentence structure, no matter which section of the sentence it may be related to). We also perform this separation of elements from their order when we replace some non-automatic order which has morphemic value by the morphemes which are grammatically equivalent to it; for example, when we replace

$N_1 \, V \, N_2$ by $N_2 \, V^* N_1$ (replacing *The boss fired Jim* by *Jim was fired by the boss*); or when, in our text fragment, E' before T is replaced by E after T.

In contrast with this cavalier treatment of horizontal order, we cannot alter anything about the order within a vertical column. Here we have no prior linguistic knowledge to tell us which orderings of sentences (if any) are automatic and therefore not to be represented, or which orderings can be replaced by different but equivalent orderings. A closer study of sentence sequences in the language may some day give us such information in the future; for instance, to take a very simple case, it might show that sentence sequences of the form *P because Q* are equivalent to sequences of the form *Q so P*, or that *P and Q* is interchangeable with *Q and P* (whereas *P but Q* may not be similarly interchangeable with *Q but P*).[6] Furthermore, a closer study of a particular text, or of texts of a particular type, may show that certain whole sequences of sentences are equivalent or interchangeable; and with this information we may be able to simplify the vertical axis of the double array, for example by finding periodically repeated vertical patterns. Pending such specific information, however, the vertical axis is an exact reproduction of the order of the sentences or subsentences in the text.

2.15. *Summary*

We can now survey the whole method as follows. We call elements (sections of the text – morphemes or morpheme sequences) equivalent to each other if they occur in the environment of (other) identical or equivalent elements. Each set of mutually equivalent elements is called an equivalence class. Each successive sentence of the text is then represented as a sequence of equivalence classes, namely those to which its various sections belong. We thus obtain for the whole text a double array, the horizontal axis representing the equivalence classes contained in one sentence, and the vertical axis representing successive sentences. This is a tabular arrangement not of sentence structures (subjects, verbs, and the like), but of the patterned occurrence of the equivalence classes through the text.

If the different sentences contain completely different classes, the tabular arrangement is of no interest; but this is generally not the case. In almost every text there are passages in which particular equivalence classes recur, in successive sentences, in some characteristic pattern. The tabular arrangement makes it possible to inspect this pattern; and we can derive from it various kinds of information about the text, certain structural analyses of the text, and certain critiques of the text. For the equivalence classes, which are set up distributionally, the tabular arrangement shows the distribution. For the text as a whole, the tabular arrangement shows certain features of structure.

2.2. *Procedure*

We will now illustrate the procedure in detail by applying it to a specific text, of a type as common today as any other that reaches print[7]:

Millions Can't Be Wrong!

Millions of consumer bottles of X– have been sold since its introduction a few years ago. And four out of five people in a nationwide survey say they prefer X– to any hair tonic they've used. Four out of five people in a nation-wide survey can't be wrong. You too and your whole family will prefer X– to any hair tonic you've used! Every year we sell more bottles of X– to satisfied customers. You too will be satisfied!

2.21. *Determining the Equivalence Classes*

The first step in discourse analysis is to decide which elements are to be taken as equivalent to each other, i.e. placed in the same column of the tabular arrangement. This is not always automatic – simply a matter of finding which elements have identical environments; for (1) there may be several ways of breaking a sentence down into equivalent parts, and (2) we must decide which way to look for the less obvious equivalence chains.

The simplest starting point is to consider the more frequently repeated words of the text. Almost every text has particular words which occur a great many times[8]; and these will often be key words of that text. The various occurrences of such a word can certainly be put into one column, i.e. one equivalence class. And the neighboring words can be put into another single equivalence class because they occur in identical environments. In our text no key words are apparent; but we can start with the identical, and hence of course equivalent, repeated sequence *can't be wrong*. Then *Millions* is equivalent (for this text) to *Four out of five people in a nationwide survey*, since both occur before that sequence.

This first step might of course also be performed for such repeated words as *of*. But if we were to collect all the environments of the word *of*, we could not use the resulting equivalence class to build up a chain of further equivalences, because nothing else would be found in their environment. Whereas the class containing *Millions* and *Four out of five...*, which we obtain from repetitions of *can't be wrong*, will be found, in the paragraphs below, to tie up with other sections of our text.

From this utilization of repetitions we go on to construct chains of equivalence – that is, we ask what other environments occur for *Millions* and for *Four out of five....* For *Millions* we have one other environment, namely *of consumer bottles*, etc. It will turn out in our further work (§ 3.2) that this environment clashes with the environments of *Four out of five*.... Therefore we will tentatively set aside the sequence *of consumer bottles*, etc. As for *Four out of five people in a nationwide survey*, we find it in one other environment: before *say they prefer X– to any hair tonic they've used.*

We proceed along this equivalence chain by looking for some other environment in which *say they prefer X–* ... occurs. There is one such occurrence, but it differs by having *you* where the first occurrence has *they*. At first it seems that this difference makes it impossible for us to consider the two sequences equivalent, since our method provides for no approximation technique, no measurement of more and less difference, such as might permit us to say that these two sequences are similar enough to be considered equivalent. Indeed, since we do not operate with the meanings of the morphemes, the replacing of *they* by *you* might constitute a great difference (as it would if the whole text dealt with the distinction between 'you' and 'they'). As they stand, therefore, these two sequences would be left unrelated by our method; at most that method could separate out the identical and the different portions. It so happens, however, that a little consideration shows these two sequences to be contextually identical – that is, identical in respect to their relevant environment or context. This will be seen in § 2.31.

In constructing chains of equivalence the first safeguard is adherence to the formal requirements of the method. If we never make any approximations, never overlook some 'small' difference in environment, we will be certain that any two members of one equivalence class have at least one environment in common. If we wish to put two elements into one class even though no environment of one is identical with some environment of the other, it will have to be at the cost of some explicit assumption, added to the method, which equates the two environments or nullifies their difference.

The final factor in our decision to include or not to include two elements in one equivalence class is the way the resulting class will function in the analysis of the text, i.e. the kind of double array we get by using that class. This factor must play a part, since there are often various possible chains of equivalence that equally satisfy our method. The criterion is not some external consideration like getting the longest possible chain, but rather the intrinsic consideration of finding some patterned distribution of these classes, i.e. finding some structural fact about the text in terms of these classes. In other words, we try to set up such classes as will have an interesting distribution in our particular text. This may seem a rather circular safeguard for constructing equivalence chains. But it simply means that whenever we have to decide whether to carry an equivalence chain one step further, we exercise the foresight of considering how the new interval will fit into our analyzed text as it appears when represented in terms of the new class. This kind of consideration occurs in descriptive linguistics when we have to decide, for example, how far to subdivide a phonemic sequence into morphemes.[9]

One might ask what right we have to put two words into one equivalence class merely because they both occur in the same environment. The answer is that the equivalence class indicates no more than the distributional work which its members do in the text. If the two words occur only in identical or equivalent environments in this text, then in this text there is no difference in their distribution (aside from their order in the column, which is preserved). We are not denying any difference in meaning, or in distribution outside this text.

So far we have recognized two equivalence classes. One, which we will mark *P*, at present includes

> *Millions*
> *Four out of five people in a nationwide survey*

The other, which we will mark *W*, at present includes

> *can't be wrong*
> *say they prefer X– to any hair tonic they've used*

2.22. *Segmentation*

Once we have a rough idea of what equivalence classes we wish to try out in our text, we segment the text into successive intervals in such a way as to get, in each interval, like occurrences of the same equivalence classes. If our classes so far are *P* and *W*, and if we have a few *P W* successions, we try to segment into intervals each containing precisely one *P* and one *W*. For example, the title of the advertisement is represented by *P W*. The first sentence after the title seems to contain a *P* (the word *Millions*), but the rest of the sentence neither equals nor contains *W*; hence the sentence is as yet unanalyzed, and even its *P* is in doubt.

Assignment of an element to a particular class is always relative to the assignment of its environment. The elements are not defined except in relation to their environment. For all we know, *Millions* in this sentence might not even be the same word as *Millions* in the title. In descriptive linguistics two phonemically identical segments are the same morpheme only if they occur in the same morpheme class: *sun* and *son* would presumably have to be considered the 'same' morpheme, no less than *table* (of wood) and *table* (of statistical data). If they occur in different morpheme classes, e.g. *sea* and *see*, they certainly are not the same morpheme; and if we want to keep in view the connection between (*a*) *table* and (*to*) *table*, we have to speak of classed and unclassed morphemes, and say that the unclassed morpheme *table* appears both in the *N* class and in the *V* class. Similarly, if *Millions* occurs twice we try to consider it a repeated 'same' morpheme (hence in the same class), and so consider its two environments equivalent. But we may find later that a better text-analysis is obtained by not considering those two environments equivalent (because the first environment is equivalent to one sequence *A* in the text, while the second is equivalent to a different sequence *B* which is not equivalent to *A*). In that case we may have to consider the two occurrences of *Millions* as belonging to two different classes. In § 3.2, we will find this to be the case here.

To return to our segmentation. The second sentence in our text is *P W*, and the third is *P W*. Hence we try to segment our text into successive stretches each of which will contain just *P W* and no more. These stretches will then be the successive rows of our double array. They will often be whole sentences, but not necessarily: they may also be the separate sections of a compound sentence, each of which has its own sentence structure (as in the two *E' T* of § 2.13). But they may also be any other stretches taken out of the sentence. For example, if we found in our advertisement the sentence *Millions of people – four out of five – can't be wrong when they say they prefer X–*, which as it stands seems to consist of *P P W W*, we would try to reduce it to two *P W* intervals. Such less obvious segmentations require care, since we want not only the *P* and the *W* occurrences to be the same in each interval, but also the relation between *P* and *W* to be the same. When each whole sentence in a string is reduced to *P W*, the relation between *P* and *W* in each interval is the same; from descriptive linguistics we know it is the relation of subject to predicate. We do not need to use this specific information in tabulating our text as a succession of *P W*, but we do assume that whatever the relation between *P* and *W* in one interval, it is the same in all the other intervals. Otherwise we would be wrong in saying, when we see such a double array as the successive *T E* of § 2.14, that the successive intervals are identical in terms of *T* and *E*. Techniques for checking the sameness of the relation between the equivalence classes in each row will be discussed in §§ 2.32–3.

2.23. *Sets of Like Segments*

The attempt to divide a text into intervals containing the same equivalence classes (in the same relation to each other) will not generally succeed throughout a whole text. There may be individual sentences here and there which simply do not contain these classes. These may turn out to be introductory sentences, or offshoots of some other set of equivalence classes. And there may be successive sections of the text, each of which contains its own equivalence classes different from those of other sections. These may be paragraph-like or chapter-like sub-texts within the main text.

In the course of seeking intervals which contain the same classes, our procedures will discover the limits of this sameness, i.e. the points at which we get text-intervals containing different classes. In the general case, then, a text will be reduced not to a single set of identical rows (each row, like TE, representing an interval with the same equivalence classes), but to a succession of sets of identical rows, with occasional individually different rows occurring at one point or another.

Having obtained this result, we compare the various sets and individual rows to see what similarities and differences exist among them in the arrangement of their classes, whether the specific classes are different or not. We try to discover patterns in the occurrence of such similarities among the successive sets and individually different rows. For example, let a text come out to be $AB\ TE\ TE\ TE\ A'B'\ EP\ EP\ AB\ KD\ LM\ LM\ K'D'\ MS\ MS\ MS\ FBV\ MS$. Then, using $[TE]$ to indicate a set of TE intervals, and temporarily disregarding the FBV, we can represent the text by $AB\ [TE]\ A'B'\ [EP]\ AB\ KD\ [LM]$ $K'D'\ [MS]$. We note, further, that $AB\ [TE]\ A'B'\ [EP]$ and $KD\ [LM]\ K'D'$ $[MS]$ are structurally identical: both have the form $w\ [xy]\ w'\ [yz]$. This form is a particular relation of w, x, y, and z. Our text consists of two occurrences of this structure, with the w of the first occurrence (that is, the AB) appearing again between the two structures (or before the second structure), and with a unique FBV before the end of the last structure.

2.3. *Accessory Techniques*

The main procedure, as described in the foregoing section, must be refined and supplemented by a number of accessory techniques.

2.31. *Independent Occurrence*

The distribution of equivalence classes (their pattern of occurrence), and the segmentation of intervals containing them, depend on what we recognize as an occurrence of an element. At first sight, this would seem to be trivial: in the stretch *say they prefer X– to any hair tonic they've used* we obviously find *say* once, *they* twice, and so on. Closer consideration, however, will show that not all occurrences of elements are independent: there are some elements which occur, in a given environment, only when some other element is present. This situation is known from descriptive linguistics; for example, the *–s* of *he walks* is taken not as an independent element but as an automatic concomitant of *he*, by comparison with *I walk, you walk*[10]; and in forms like *both he and I* the *and* always occurs if *both* is present, so that *both ...and* can be taken as one element rather than two. In the same way, if in a particular text we find identical (repeated) or different elements, of which one occurs only if the other is present, we conclude that these occurrences are not independent of each other, and mark their joint occurrence as a single element in the representation of the text.

For *they prefer X– to any hair tonic they've used*, our only comparison is *You too and your whole family will prefer X– to any hair tonic you've used*. In each case, the stretch before *prefer* contains the same word that we find before *'ve*. We can therefore say that the word before *'ve* is not independent; rather, the choice of one or the other member of the set *they/you* depends on which word of that set occurs before *prefer*. Writing *Q* as a sign to repeat that member of the set *they/you* which occurs in the stretch before *prefer*, we obtain:

> they prefer X– to any hair tonic Q've used
> You...will prefer X– to any hair tonic Q've used

It now appears that by reducing these stretches to their independent elements, the latter sections have become identical. On this basis, the beginning sections of these two sentences are found to have identical environments, and hence to be equivalent. Since the first of these beginning sections was included in our class *P*, we can now include the section *You too...* in *P* as well.[11]

This is only one kind of dependent occurrence. There are many others which have to be investigated; and the resulting information is of use both to discourse analysis and to a more detailed descriptive linguistics.

One major example is that of the pronouns. If the advertisement had read *You...will prefer it* instead of *You...will prefer X–*, we would at first regard *it* as a new element, to be placed in a new equivalence class. However, the occurrence of *it* is dependent on the occurrence of *X–*: if the preceding *X–* had contained the plural morpheme (*X–s*), the pronoun in this sentence would have been *them*. Other words of the *it* group, say *he* or *you*, will not occur here as long as *X–* occurs in the preceding sentence; but they could occur if certain other words were used in place of *X–*. The same is true of words like *this/these, who/which*, which also depend on particular words occurring somewhere else in the passage. Without using any information about the meaning of these pronouns, or about their 'referring' to preceding nouns, we can conclude from their distribution in the text that they are not independent elements: they contain a (discontinuous) portion of the occurrence of the morpheme with which they correlate.

Another type of dependent occurrence is found in such expressions of cross reference as *each other* and *together*, which carry out in language some of the functions filled in mathematical expressions by variables – but in the vaguer and more complex way that is characteristic of language. The sentence

Foster and Lorch saw each other at the same moment is normal; but if we drop the words *and Lorch*, every native speaker of English will immediately replace *each other* by something else. To put it differently: we will not find any sentence that contains *each other* but does not contain either the expression *and Z* or a plural morpheme in the relevant noun. Furthermore, though we will find the sentence *Electrons and positrons attract each other*, we will not find – at least in a physics textbook – the same sentence with the words *and positrons* omitted, unless there are also other changes such as *repel* in place of *attract*.

It may be noted that dependent elements are especially prone to be assigned to different equivalence classes in their various occurrences, since each occurrence of them is assigned to the class of whatever element correlates with that particular occurrence. If the text contained *You will prefer X–, You will prefer it, The survey showed, It showed*, the first occurrence of *it* would be assigned to the class of *X–*, the second *it* to the class of *survey*.

In all such cases the special relations of dependent occurrence among particular elements can be eliminated by considering the dependent element to be simply a portion of that element with which it correlates (upon which its occurrence depends). It should be clear that when we speak of dependence, the term is only required to apply within a particular text. The dependence of pronouns or cross-reference words upon some neighboring noun may hold in every text in which these words occur; but the dependence between the two occurrences of *they* or of *you* in our text is peculiar to this text. Elsewhere we may find the sentence *they prefer X– to any hair tonic you've used*; but in this particular text such a sentence does not occur. It is for that reason that in this text we can tell what the second pronoun must be by looking at the first one.

2.32. *Subdivisions of Sentences*

The recognition of dependent elements affects our decision concerning the number of intervals into which a particular sentence is to be subdivided.

Where an element has dependent portions spread over a domain, we generally have to consider the whole domain as entering into one interval with that element. For example, in *they prefer X– to any hair tonic they've used* we have established that the two occurrences of *they* are interdependent in this text. Hence we can analyze this section into *they* (occurring over both positions) plus ...*prefer X– to any hair tonic* ... *'ve used*; and similarly for the sentence with *you* (also over both positions). This is a more general treatment than that of § 2.31, which gave favored status to the first occurrence of *they* and of *you* by considering the second occurrence to be dependent on the first, and which made the identity of the two sentences in their latter portions depend on their both containing the same kind of dependence (Q). The present treatment eliminates dependence by viewing the single *they* or *you* as occurring over two positions, and makes the second parts of the sentences identical without qualification. The effect of this new treatment is that since the two-position *they* stretches over almost the whole length of the second part, the whole of that second part has to be kept in the same interval as *they*. The consolidation of the two occurrences of *they* thus precludes our setting up two intervals here; otherwise we might have set up two intervals: *they prefer*..., and either *they've used* or *Q've used*.

On the other hand, there are cases where recognition of dependence leads us to distinguish more intervals than we might otherwise. Take the sentence *Casals, who is self-exiled from Spain, stopped performing after the fascist victory*. If we investigate the text in which this is imbedded we will find that the *who* is dependent upon *Casals*, much as the second *they* above is dependent upon the first: the text includes *And the same Casals who*..., but later *The records which*.... We may therefore say that the *who* 'contains' *Casals*, i.e. either continues it or repeats it. But which does it do? If *who* continues *Casals*, we have one interval, the first section (C) being *Casals who*, while the second section (S) is *is self-exiled...stopped*.... If *who* repeats *Casals* instead of continuing it, we have two intervals, one imbedded in the other: the first consists of *Casals* (again C) plus *stopped performing* (marked S_1), the second of *who* (taken as an equivalent of *Casals*) plus *is self-exiled* (S_2). We would be led to the second choice only if we could show in terms of the text that *is self-exiled*...and *stopped performing*...are two separate elements (not just two portions of one long element) – for example, if we found in the text two additional sentences: *The press failed to say why he stopped performing, etc. But he has stated publicly why he is self-exiled, etc.* In either case *who* contains *Casals*. But if the original sentence is *Casals who S*, we analyze it as $C\ S$, whereas if (on the basis of the later sentences) we view the original sentence as *Casals who $S_2 S_1$*, we analyze it as $C\ C\ S_2\ S_1$, and divide it into two intervals $C\ S_2$ and $C\ S_1$, with the result that S_2 and S_1 are equivalent since they both occur after C. The only difference between taking a dependent element as a continuation and taking it as a repetition is in the number of intervals – one or two – into which we then analyze the total.

We have seen here that when a sentence contains an element A which is dependent upon B, we have the choice of taking the whole sentence as one interval, with A simply a continuation of B, or as two intervals – one containing B and the other containing A in the same class as B. The latter choice will generally be taken if the rest of the sentence can be divided into two comparable sections, one to go with A and the other with B.

Choices of this type can arise even where there are no dependent forms. For example, in our second text we have the further sentence *The self-exiled Casals is waiting across the Pyrenees for the fall of Franco*. We wish to put *self-exiled* in the same class as *is self-exiled...*, since the same morphemes are involved (provided we can show from the text itself that *self-exiled* is equivalent to *self-exiled from Spain*). This gives us the peculiar sentence structure $S_2 \, C \, S_3$, as compared with the previous $C \, S$ sentences. Now if by good fortune the text also contained the sentence *Casals is waiting across the Pyrenees for the fall of Franco* (which is too much to ask in the way of repetition), we would be in position to make the following analysis. We have as sentences of the text $C \, S_1$, $C \, is \, S_2$, $S_2 \, C \, S_3$, $C \, S_3$. The sequences S_1 and S_2 and S_3 are all members of one equivalence class S, since they all occur after C. Our problem lies with the maverick $S_2 \, C \, S_3$. Let us now say that any sentence $X_1 \, A \, X_2$ can be 'transformed' into $A \, is \, X_1 : A \, X_2$.[12] This means that if $X_1 \, A \, X_2$ occurs in the text, then $A \, is \, X_1 : A \, X_2$ also occurs in the text. In that case we will consider $X_1 \, A \, X_2$ equivalent to $A \, is \, X_1 : A \, X_2$; as a new structure our maverick has disappeared. We replace $S_2 \, C \, S_3$ by the transformationally equivalent $C \, is \, S_2$ and $C \, S_3$, both of which occur elsewhere in the same text.

We may proceed on this basis even to transformations which are not already justified by the text, provided they do not conflict with the text. Thus, we find in the text the sentences *The memorable concerts were recorded in Prades... The concerts were recorded first on tape*. We can represent this as $M \, N \, R_1 : N \, R_2$ (the equivalence of R_1 and R_2 being shown, let us suppose, elsewhere in the text), and we would transform the first sentence into $N \, is \, M : N \, R_1$. This does not mean that we claim that our transformation $N \, is \, M$ (*The concerts were memorable*) actually occurs in the text, or that there is no stylistic or other difference between saying *The memorable concerts were recorded in Prades* and saying *The concerts were memorable: The concerts* (or *They*) *were recorded in Prades*. All that our transformation means is that $M \, N \, R_1$ is taken as equivalent to $N \, is \, M : N \, R_1$ because $S_2 \, C \, S_3$ is actually found as an equivalent of $C \, is \, S_2 : C \, S_3$, in the sense that both occur in the modified text.

On the one hand, we have eliminated from our tabular arrangement the peculiar interval structure $M \, N \, R_1$ or $S_2 \, C \, S_3$ – peculiar because the other intervals all have the form $N \, R$ or $C \, S$. On the other hand, we have discovered that M (or rather *is M*) is a member of the R class. But our most important result is that a sentence may be represented as two intervals even when it does not contain two sets of the requisite equivalence classes. This happens when we can show that a single class in the sentence relates independently to two other classes or elements elsewhere. That class is then repeated, once in each interval; and each interval will indicate separately its relation to one of the other classes.[13]

These difficulties in dividing a sentence into intervals arise from questions about the manner in which the equivalence classes relate to each other. In a sentence, the various morphemes or sequences do not merely occur together; they usually have a specific relation to each other which can be expressed by one or more morphemes of order: *You wrote Paul* and *Paul wrote you* differ only in their morphemic order. If we find several $C\ S$ intervals in our text, that means that C has a particular relation to S – that of occurring with it and before it. Since we are operating without meaning, we do not know what this relation is, but we are careful to represent the same morphemic order in the sentence by the same class order in the interval. Now when we find $S_2\ C\ S_3$, we do not know how this order relates to the order $C\ S$, and we can make no comparison of the two sentences. It is therefore desirable to rearrange the unknown $S_2\ C\ S_3$ so that it will contain the same classes in the same order as other intervals – and of course we must show that the re-arrangement is equivalent, for this text, to the original. In most cases this can be done only if we break the unknown sentence, by means of such trans-formations as have been discussed above, into two or more intervals, in such a way that the smaller intervals have a form which occurs in this text.

In this way we get a great number of structurally similar intervals even in a text whose sentences are very different from each other.

2.33. *Grammatical Transformations*

Up to this point we have seen how the structure of a text can be in-vestigated without using any information from outside the text itself. The straightforward procedure is to set up equivalence classes, and to discover patterned (i.e. similar or partly similar) combinations of these classes in successive intervals of the text. Often, however, we get many small classes and dissimilar intervals, because the sentences are so different from each other; when this happens, we find that by comparing the sentences of the text we can sometimes show that one section of one sentence is equivalent (for this text) to a different section of another sentence, and therefore contains the same classes. The extent to which we can do this depends upon the amount of repetition in the text.

We raise now the question of advancing further in the same direction by using information from outside the text. The information will be of the same kind as we have sought inside the text, namely whether one section of a sentence is equivalent to another (in the sense that $M\ N\ R$ is equivalent to N *is* $M: N\ R$). It will go back to the same basic operation, that of comparing different sentences. And it will serve the same end: to show that two otherwise different sentences contain the same combination of equivalence classes, even though they may contain different combinations of morphemes. What is new is only that we base our equivalence not on a comparison of two sentences in the text, but on a comparison of a sentence in the text with sentences outside the text.

This may seem to be a major departure. One may ask how we know that any equivalence discovered in this way is applicable to our text. The justification was given in § 1.3 above: if we can show that two sequences are equivalent in any English sentences in which they occur, then they are equivalent in any text written in English. If in any English sentence containing $X A Y$, the $X A Y$ is equivalent to A is $X: A Y$, then if we find $S_2 C S_3$ in our English text we can say that it is equivalent to C is $S_2: C S_3$.

But what is 'equivalence'? Two ELEMENTS are equivalent if they occur in the same environment within the sentence. Two SENTENCES in a text are equivalent simply if they both occur in the text (unless we discover structural details fine enough to show that two sentences are equivalent only if they occur in similar structural positions in the text). Similarly, two sentences in a language are equivalent if they both occur in the language. In particular, we will say that sentences of the form A are equivalent to sentences of the form B, if for each sentence A we can find a sentence B containing the same morphemes except for differences due to the difference in form between A and B. For example, $N_1 V N_2$ is equivalent to N_2 is V-en by N_1 because for any sentence like *Casals plays the cello* we can find a sentence *The cello is played by Casals*.

We do not claim that two equivalent sentences necessarily mean exactly the same thing, or that they are stylistically indifferent. But we do claim that not all sentences are equivalent in this sense: the relation of equivalence is not useless, as it would be if it were true for all sentences. For example, $N_1 V N_2$ is not equivalent to N_1 is V-en by N_2, because the latter form will be found only for certain N_1 and N_2 forms (*I saw you* and *I was seen by you*) but not for all forms (we will not find *Casals is played by the cello*).[14] We claim further that the application of this grammatical equivalence from outside the text will enable us to discover additional similar intervals in our text, beyond what we could get merely from comparing the text sentences with each other. Thus, we can show that in various environments *who, he*, etc. are grammatically equivalent to the preceding noun, and that N_1 who $V_1 V_2$ is equivalent to $N_1 V_2: N_1 V_1$. Then, in *Casals, who is self-exiled...stopped performing...*, we have two intervals $C S_1: C$ is S_2. We would have this result (without having to worry whether *Casals who* is one continued occurrence of C or two repeated occurrences) even if there were no other occurrences of *who* within the text, i.e. when no analysis could be made of *who* on internal textual grounds. The usefulness of grammatical equivalence is especially great if, for example, we have a number of intervals all containing *Casals*, besides many others interlarded among the first but containing *he*, and if we can find no common textual environments to show that *Casals* and *he* are equivalent. As soon as we accept this equivalence grammatically, we can show that all the environments of *Casals* are equivalent to those of *he*; and this in turn can make other equivalences discoverable textually.

Grammatical equivalence can be investigated more systematically if we introduce a technique of experimental variation. Given a sentence in form A and a desired form B, we try to alter A by only the formal difference that exists between it and B, and see what happens then to our A. Given *The memorable concerts were recorded...*, suppose that we want to make this $M N R$ sentence comparable in form to previous intervals beginning with N. To this end, we seek a variation of the sentence beginning *The concerts*. We may do this by putting an informant into a genuine social speech situation (not a linguistic discussion about speech) in which he would utter a sentence beginning *The concerts* and containing the words *memorable* and *recorded*.[15] Or we may do it by the tedious job of observation, hunting for a sentence that begins with *The concerts* and contains *memorable* and *recorded*. By either method, we might get *The concerts were memorable and were recorded*, or something of the sort[16], whence we learn that when M (or any adjective) is shifted to the other side of N (its following noun) one inserts *is*; $M N$ is equivalent to N *is* M. In this way we discover that when $M N R$ is shifted to a form beginning with N, an *is* appears between N and the following M.

This technique of varying the grammatical form of a sentence while keeping its morphemes constant cannot be used within a text; for there all we can do is to inspect the available material. But it can be used in the language outside the text, where we have the right, as speakers, to create any social situation which might favor another speaker's uttering one rather than another of the many sentences at his disposal. It is especially useful in a language like English, where so many morphemes occur in various grammatical classes.

The preceding paragraph indicates the basic safeguard in applying grammatical equivalence to extend our textual equivalence classes. We do not merely ask, What sentence-forms are equivalent to $M N R$? There may be many. We ask instead, Since $N...$ is a common form in this text, and since we find also $M N R$, can we replace this by an equivalent sentence of the form $N...$? The direction of change is not arbitrary, but comes entirely from the text. As before, it is a matter of dividing our sentences into the most similar intervals possible All we ask is whether there is a grammatical equivalence which would connect $M N R$ with the form $N...$; the answer is yes, provided an *is* appears in the form. This in turn yields *is M* as equivalent to *R*. As elsewhere in linguistics, the method does not collapse all sentences into any arbitrary form we choose; it simply enables us to describe the rarer forms of the text (*M N R*) in terms of the common ones (*N*...).

For analysis purely within the text, all we need to know are the morpheme boundaries. To utilize grammatical equivalences we need to know also the morpheme class to which each morpheme in our text belongs, since grammatical statements concern classes rather than individual morphemes. The grammatical statement in this instance is that adjective + noun is equivalent to noun + *is* + adjective; to apply it to our sequence *M N*, we must know that the *M* is an adjective and the *N* a noun.

It has been found empirically that a relatively small number of grammatical equivalences are called upon, time after time, in reducing the sentences of a text to similar intervals. Hence even a non-linguist can get considerable information about the text by using (in addition to the internal textual method) a prepared list of major grammatical equivalences for the language. Some frequently used equivalences are given here, without any evidence for their validity, and with only a very rough indication of the sentence-environments in which they hold[17]:

(1) If we find $X\,C\,Y$, then $X = Y$ (X is equivalent to Y). The C is a conjunction like *and, but, or*, or else, under special circumstances, a phrase like *as well as, rather than, A-er than*. The X and Y must be in the same grammatical class. Thus, in *I phoned him but he was out*, X and Y are each $N\,V$; in *I saw it but went on*, the Y is only the verb phrase *went on*, and hence the X can include only the verb phrase *saw it* (not the whole sequence *I saw it*). It follows that $N_1\,V_1\,C\,N_2\,V_2$ is equivalent to two intervals $N_1\,V_1 : N_2\,V_2$, and $N\,V_1\,C\,V_2 = N\,V_1 : N\,V_2$.

(2) The sequence N_1 *is* N_2 indicates that $N_1 = N_2$. The class of *is* includes *remains* and other verbs.

(3) $\acute{N}_1\,\acute{N}_2$, with a primary stress on each N, indicates that $N_1 = N_2$; e.g. *The pressure P increases* is equivalent to *The pressure increases* and *P increases*.

(4) $N\,V$ (*that*) $N\,V = N\,V : N\,V$; e.g. *I telegraphed that we'll arrive tomorrow* is equivalent to *I telegraphed: We'll arrive tomorrow*.

(5) $N_1\,V\,N_2 = N_2\,V^*N_1$, where V and V^* are respectively active and passive, or passive and active.

(6) $N_1\,P\,N_2 = N_2\,P^*N_1$; e.g. (*They seek*) *the goal of certainty* is equivalent to some such form as (*They seek*) *certainty as a goal*. The change in prepositions when two nouns are reversed is far greater than the corresponding change in verbs. In verbs the change is effected simply by adding or subtracting the passive morpheme and the word *by*; in prepositions it is effected by replacing one form by an entirely different form. The pairs of equivalent

prepositions are not fixed: between certain nouns, the substitute for *of* may be *as*; between others it may be *with*. Nevertheless, it is possible to find structures in which the nouns of the sequence $N_1 \, P \, N_2$ are reversed.

(7) $N_1 \, P \, N_2 = A_2 \, N_1$, i.e. the morpheme of the second noun occurs in an adjectival form before the prior noun, as in *medical training* for *training in medicine*.

(8) Pronouns like *he*, and certain words with initial *wh-* and *th-*, repeat a preceding noun. Which noun they repeat (when there are several nouns preceding) depends on the details of the grammatical environment; usually it is the immediately preceding noun, or the last noun that occurs in a comparable grammatical environment. Thus, *who = the man* in *The man who phoned left no name* ($N \, who \, V_1 \, V_2 = N \, V_2 : N \, V_1$); *who = my roommate* in *The man spoke to my room-mate, who told him to call again* ($N_1 \, V_1 \, N_2 \, who \, V_2 = N_1 \, V_1 \, N_2 : N_2 \, V_2$). There are many variant ways of determining which noun is repeated by a pronoun, and which verb belongs with each noun. In *the man who phoned*, no subject can be inserted before *phoned*, hence *who* must be taken as subject. In *The man I phoned was out*, we reduce first to *I phoned: The man was out*; then, since no object can be inserted after *phoned* in the original sentence, we set *the man* as the object [18] of *phoned* and obtain the equivalent *I phoned the man: The man was out* ($N_1 \, N_2 \, V_1 \, V_2 = N_2 \, V_1 \, N_1 : N_1 \, V_2$).

(9) $N \, V_1, \, V_2\text{-}ing = N \, V_1 : N \, V_2$; e.g. *They escaped, saving nothing* is equivalent to *They escaped: They saved nothing*.

(10) $N_1 \, C \, N_2 \, V \, X = N_1 \, V \, N_2 : N_2 \, V \, N_1$. Here X represents a class of cross-reference expressions like *each other*; e.g. *The Giants and the Dodgers each beat the other twice* is equivalent to *The D beat the G twice: The G beat the D twice*. The equivalence differs somewhat for different groups of X forms.

(11) $A \, N \, V = N \, is \, A : N \, V$, as in the example *The self-exiled Casals...* in § 2.32. So also $N \, V \, A \, N_1 = N \, V \, N_1 \, who \, is \, A = N \, V \, N_1 : N_1 \, is \, A$; e.g. *They read the interdicted books = They read the books which were interdicted = They read the books: The books were interdicted*.

(12) $N_1 \, V \, N_2 \, P \, N_3 = N_1 \, V \, N_2 : N_1 \, V \, P \, N_3$. That is, a double object can be replaced by two separate objects in two intervals which repeat the subject and verb; e.g. *I bought it: I bought for you* for *I bought it for you*.

These grammatical equivalences preserve the morphemes and the grammatical relations among them, though in a changed grammatical form. We cannot get $N_1 \, V \, N_2 = N_2 \, V \, N_1$, because that would change the subject-object relation to the verb; but $N_2 \, V \, ^{*} \, N_1$ is obtainable as an equivalent of $N_1 \, V \, N_2$ because the verb too is changed here, in a way that preserves its grammatical relation to the now reversed nouns. Preservation of the grammatical relations is essential, because such relations are always to be found among the morphemes in a sentence. That is to say, there are restrictions of substitutability and order and intonation among the various morphemes (or morpheme classes) in a sentence; and when we move from one sentence to an equivalent sentence, we want upon moving back to the original sentence to get back the same restrictions – since the original, like all sentences, is defined by the restrictions among its parts. Therefore, when we break up a sentence into various intervals for a tabular arrangement, we do not want two combinations of the same equivalence classes (say our first and second $T E$ combinations above) to represent different grammatical relations. Accordingly, when we transform a sentence containing certain equivalence classes, we are careful to preserve the original grammatical relations among them.

Sometimes, however, we find sections of a sentence which contain none of our equivalence classes; that is (in the simplest case), they contain no material which recurs elsewhere in the text. The grammatical relation of unique sections to the rest of the sentence must be preserved in our tabular arrangement no less than the relation of recurrent sections; but here we escape the problem of preserving their relation while changing their relative position, since we have no reason to change their position at all: it is only our equivalence classes that we wish to rearrange. All we want of this non-recurrent material is to know its relation to our equivalence classes, and to indicate this relation in our analysis. We may not be able to learn this from a study of our text alone; but we can learn it by bringing in grammatical information or experimental variation. For an example we return to the sequences *Casals, who is self-exiled from Spain* ... and *The self-exiled Casals* .... If the latter is $S_2\ C$, the former is $C,\ C$ is S_2 *from Spain*. Since *from Spain* does not recur, we want only to know where to keep it when we arrange our equivalence classes, i.e. what its relation is to these classes. From the grammar we know that in sentences in the form $N\ V\ A\ P\ N$ the smallest unit of which $P\ N$ is an immediate constituent is $A\ P\ N$, and that this $A\ P\ N$ is replaceable by A alone.[19] Therefore, if the A happens to be a member of one of our equivalence classes while the $P\ N$ is not, we associate the $P\ N$ with the A in its equivalence column by writing $A\ P\ N$ instead of A as the member of the class.

More generally, material that does not belong to any equivalence class, but is grammatically tied to a member of some class, is included with that member to form with it an expanded member of the class in question. Thus, *self-exiled from Spain* is now in the same class as *self-exiled*. The justification for this is that since the material does not occur again in this text (or occurs again only in the same grammatical relation to the same equivalence class), its only effect, when the text is represented in terms of particular equivalence classes, is precisely its relation to the particular member to which it is grammatically tied.

An interesting special case arises when two members of the same equivalence class constitute jointly the next larger grammatical unit of their sentence (i.e. are the immediate constituents of that unit), for example when the two are an adjective and a following noun, where $A \ N = N$. In such a case we may consider that the two together constitute just one member of their class, and fit together into a single interval. If we took them as two occurrences of their class, we would have to put each occurrence into a separate interval.

Grammatical information is especially useful in the recognition of sentence connectives. These morphemes are easily identified from formal grammar, quite independently of their meaning, but may not be identifiable as such on purely textual evidence. Their importance lies in the fact that many sentences of a text may contain the same classes except for some unassigned words, often at the beginning, which are grammatically connecters or introducers of sentences; they stand outside the specific classes which comprise the sentence or interval. In our tabular arrangement these elements can be assigned, by their grammatical position, to a special front column. We can go beyond this and assign to this front column any material which is not assignable to any of the equivalence columns. Sometimes such connecting material is not immediately obvious; note that many sentences of the form $N \ V \ that \ N_1 \ V_1$ can be analyzed as consisting of the equivalence classes $N_1 \ V_1$, with the $N \ V$ *that* relegated to the front column. Consider, for example, *We are proud that these concerts were recorded by our engineers.* Here the known members of equivalence classes are *concerts* and *recorded.* The preceding words do not recur in the text and are not grammatically tied to any particular class member. Quite the contrary, they can be grammatically replaced by introductory adverbs like *indeed*, even though in a purely grammatical sense they are the major subject and predicate of the sentence.

In addition to making use of the grammatical relations of whole grammatical classes, we can use information about the relation of particular morphemes or grammatical subclasses to grammatical classes. For instance, it is possible to establish that intransitive verbs (in some languages) form a subclass which never occurs with an object and which is equivalent to a transitive verb plus an object. In a given text, this may enable us to put a transitive verb with its object in the same column as a comparably placed intransitive verb.

Finally, there are a great many detailed equivalences which apply to particular morphemes. This information is not provided by descriptive linguistics, which deals generally with whole morpheme classes. But it can be obtained by linguistic methods, since it deals with matched occurrences and special restrictions, though in most cases it is necessary to study the restrictions over more than one sentence at a time. Suppose, for example, that we find the words *buy* and *sell* in a text. Their environments in that text may not be sufficiently similar to place them in the same equivalence class, even though it might promote the analysis of the text if we could do so. But if we investigate a good number of other short texts in which the two words occur, we will find that the two often appear in matched environments, and that in certain respects they are distributional inverses of each other; that is, we will find many sequences like N_1 *buys from* N_2: N_2 *sells to* N_1 *(I bought it from him at the best price I could get, but he still sold it to me at a profit).* If the environments of *buy* and *sell* in our text are similar to the matched environments of the other short texts, we may be able, by comparison with these wider results, to put the two into one equivalence class in our text after all, or even to analyze one as the inverse of the other.

In this way we can put more words into one textual class than would otherwise be possible, and we can make use of what would seem to be special semantic connections between words (as between *buy* and *sell*, or even between a transitive verb and the presence of an object) without departing from a purely formal study of occurrences. The reason is that differences in meaning correlate highly with differences in linguistic distribution; and if we have two related words whose distributional similarities cannot be shown within the confines of our text, we will often be able to show them in a larger selection of texts, even of very short ones.

The kind of outside information which has been indicated here has been only sketched in scattered examples, both because the field is vast and because a great deal remains to be done. Further work in this direction will not only be useful to discourse analysis but will also have interest as an extension of descriptive linguistics.

3. RESULTS

3.1. *The Double Array*

As a product of discourse analysis we obtain a succession of intervals, each containing certain equivalence classes. For a tabular arrangement we write each interval under the preceding one, with the successive members of each class forming a column, as in § 2.14 above. The very brief text of § 2.32 is arranged as follows.[20]

$$C \quad S_1$$
$$C \quad S_2 \quad (S_2 \text{ after } C \text{ is } is \text{ } S_2)$$

$$C \quad S_2 \quad (=S_2 \, C \text{ without the } is)$$
$$C \quad S_3$$
$$N \quad R_0 \quad (=M \, N; \; R_0 = is \, M)$$
$$N \quad R_1$$
$$N \quad R_2$$

The horizontal rows show the equivalence classes present in each interval, arranged according to their order (or other relation) within the interval. The vertical columns indicate the particular members of each class which appear in the successive intervals. Material which is a member of no equivalence class, but is grammatically tied to a particular member of some class, is included with that member in its column; thus *in Spain* is included in the first S_2. Material which is a member of no equivalence class, and is not grammatically tied to a particular member of some class, is placed in a front column (not illustrated here), which will be found to include morphemes that relate the sentences or intervals to each other, or mark some change in several classes of a single interval. The tabular arrangement thus represents the original one-dimensional text in a two-dimensional array, where each element has two coordinates: one horizontal, in respect to the other elements of its interval, and one vertical, in respect to the other members of its class.

This double array can be viewed as representing the whole text, since every morpheme of the text is assigned to one class or another in the array, and since the array preserves the relations among the morphemes. Even when a large number of textual and grammatical transformations have been carried out, the classes and their members are defined at each step in such a way that the text can always be reproduced from the array plus the full definition of the classes in it. The individual intervals in the array may not be 'idiomatic' – that is, they may not naturally occur in speech. But the preservation of idiom is not one of the requirements of our method. All we ask is that the succession of intervals should be textually and grammatically equivalent to the original text. Although the array may suggest a critique or a possible improvement of the text, it is not meant to be used instead of the original.

The double array can also be viewed as indicating the purely distributional relations among the equivalence classes which figure in it. From this viewpoint we can operate upon the tabular arrangement and investigate its properties. We can develop ways of simplifying the array, for example by drawing out common elements, or by grouping together larger sets of equivalent sequences than we used in the formation of the array. We can learn how to accommodate various special cases, such as a mobile class which appears in close relation now with one class now with another, or which appears a different number of times in various intervals. We can try to regularize or 'normalize' the array by matching all the intervals, so as to establish a single 'normal' interval with which all the actual intervals can be compared: for instance, given an interval from which one of the classes is absent, we can try to transform it into one that includes all the classes, preserving equivalence during the transformation. We can attempt to formulate a general statement covering the changes in successive members of a class as we go down a column, in a effort to 'explain' or 'predict' the particular form taken by the classes of each interval – that is, to derive the successive intervals from the normal form.

All such operations with the array have the effect of isolating the most general independent elements in terms of which we can describe the text (ultimately the horizontal and vertical axes), and of bringing out their relations to each other in the text. In this sense all such operations are but further refinements of our initial procedures.

3.2. *Findings*

Various conclusions can be drawn about a particular text or type of text by studying the properties of its double array, either directly or in its most simplified forms. Many of these conclusions may well have been obtainable intuitively without such formal analysis; but intuition does not yield results that are either explicit or rigorous. In some respects, moreover, the complexity and size of the material make it impossible for us to draw all the relevant conclusions without painstaking formal analysis. The sample texts used in the present paper have been necessarily too short and too simple to show what kind of conclusions the analysis yields about a particular text or style; that must be left for a future presentation of a longer sample text, though the details of method and the range of conclusions obtainable by means of it could be shown only through the analysis of a great many discourses. To give some slight idea of these conclusions, we will complete here the analysis of our first text (§ 2.2).

The analysis was left at the following point: *P* has as members *Millions, Four out of five people in a nationwide survey, You too will, (and) your whole family will. W* has as members *can't be wrong, prefer X– to any hair tonic... 've used.* Four of the sentences (including the title) are represented by five *P W* intervals.

At this point it is difficult to proceed without recourse to grammatical equivalence (see note 11). In *Four out of five...say they prefer...* we have *P* and *W* but with *say they* intervening. If our text happened to contain *they* and *four out of five...* in equivalent environments, we could analyze this sentence directly. In the absence of this, we appeal to the grammatical equivalence of *they* with the preceding comparably-situated noun: *four out of five*...as subject of *say*, parallel to *they* as subject of *prefer*. We therefore put *they* into the same class *P* as *four out of five*. Then the sentence becomes *P say P W*, which is analyzed as two intervals *P say: P W*, on the basis of the formula *N V (that) N V = N V: N V*; and on this basis *say* is a member of *W*, since it occurs after *P* to make a whole interval.

We now turn to the last sentence: *You too will be satisfied*. The first part is a known *P*; hence *be satisfied* is included in *W*. This gives us a start for working on the preceding sentence, *Every year we sell more bottles of X– to satisfied consumers*. Now *X– to satisfied consumers* is grammatically *X– to A N*, which is equivalent to *X– to N: N is A*. In this way we obtain an interval *consumers are satisfied*; and since the second part of this is *W*, we place *consumers* in *P*. The rest of the sentence contains new classes: Since *bottles* occurs elsewhere in the text, we regard it as representing a possible equivalence class and mark it *B*; with this occurrence of *B* we associate the word *more*, which does not occur elsewhere and which is grammatically tied to *bottles*. Since *sell* occurs elsewhere in *sold* (=*sell*+part of the passive morpheme), we mark it *S*; and we associate with it *every year*, which is grammatically tied to it. (*Every year* is similar in only one morpheme to *since...years ago* in the first sentence; rather than try to get these phrases into new equivalence classes, we note that each is tied to the member of *S* that occurs near it, and we associate each phrase with its member of *S*). There remains *we*, which is not grammatically part of either the *B* phrase or the *S* phrase; even though it seems not to occur again, we place it tentatively in a new class *I*. (We will see below that a zero form of *I* may be said to occur in the first sentence.) Thus we get *I S B to P*. This in turn can be somewhat simplified, since it is grammatically equivalent to *I S B: I S to P*.

Finally there is the first sentence, *Millions of consumer bottles of X– have been sold since its introduction a few years ago*. If we start with *Millions* as a known *P*, we obtain an unanalyzable remainder beginning with *of*. Instead, we match *bottles of X– have been sold* with *we sell bottles of X–*. The first has the form $N_1 V$; the second is $N_2 V N_1$. Grammatically, *have been sold* is *sell*+past+passive; hence if we take *sell* as *V*, then *been sold* is V^*. Grammatically also, *V*+passive+*by N* is equivalent to *V*+passive alone (*is sold by us = is sold*). Hence the lack of any *by us* after *sold* does not prevent our matching the two clauses. To *we sell bottles* as $N_2 V N_1$ we match *bottles have been sold* as $N_1 V^* = N_1 V^* N_2$; we can even say that the passive morpheme, with or without the following 'agent' (*by* + *N*) is equivalent to the subject of the active verb (i.e. the verb without the passive morpheme). If *we sell bottles of X–* is *I S B*, then *bottles of X– have been sold* is the equivalent $B S^* I$ with zero *I*. The section *since...years ago* we associate with the preceding S^*, as also the past-tense morpheme, since neither of these figures elsewhere in our equivalence classes. *Millions* and *consumer* are both members of P^{21}, but there is no way of making use of this fact. Grammatically, *consumer bottles* is $N_1 N_2 = N_2$, and *millions of N_2* is $N_3 P N_2 = N_2$, so that the whole sequence is grammatically tied to *bottles* (as *more* was tied to *bottles* above), leaving the sentence as $B S^* I$. This means that there are two occurrences of P words which are lost by being included in an occurrence of B. There is no other distributional relation that this *Millions* and this *consumer* have to any other class occurrence in the text (except their analogy to *more*); hence there is no way of including them in the double array. The same morphemes indeed occur elsewhere as P, but in different relations to other classes.

This points up the confusing relation of the title to the first sentence. If we start with the title, we come upon *Millions* in the first sentence and assign it to P, on the basis of the title, only to find that there is no class P in the final analysis of the sentence. (The millions who can't be wrong turn out to be bottles.[22]) If we begin with the body of the advertisement, we have a class P (*four out of five; you*) which relates to W, and a class B (*bottles, millions of ... bottles*) which relates to S; and if we then proceed to the title, we find there the W preceded not by any known P word or by a new word which we can assign to P, but by a word which has elsewhere been associated with a member of B. (The bottles show up as people.) This is the formal finding which parallels what one might have said as a semantic critique – namely, that the text of the advertisement (millions of bottles sold; many people cannot be wrong in preferring X–) fails to support the title (millions cannot be wrong).

The double array for the advertisement is not interesting in itself:

$P W$	*Millions of People Can't Be Wrong!*
$B S^* I$ (the B containing pseudo-P)	*Millions of consumer bottles ... have been sold ...*
$C P W$	*And four out of five people ... say*
$P W$	*they prefer X– ...*
$P W$	*Four out of five people ... can't be wrong.*
$P W$	*You too will prefer X– ...*
$P W$	*your whole family will prefer X– ...*
$B S^* I (= I S B)$	*Every year we sell more bottles of X–*
$S^* I$ to P	*we sell to consumers*
$P W$	*consumers are satisfied*
$P W$	*You too will be satisfied!*

3.3. *Interpretations*

The formal findings of this kind of analysis do more than state the distribution of classes, or the structure of intervals, or even the distribution of interval types. They can also reveal peculiarities within the structure, relative to the rest of the structure. They can show in what respects certain structures are similar or dissimilar to others. They can lead to a great many statements about the text.

All this, however, is still distinct from an INTERPRETATION of the findings, which must take the meanings of the morphemes into consideration, and ask what the author was about when he produced the text. Such interpretation is obviously quite separate from the formal findings, although it may follow closely in the directions which the formal findings indicate.

Even the formal findings can lead to results of broader interest than that of the text alone. The investigation of various types of textual structure can show correlations with the person or the situation of its origin, entirely without reference to the meanings of the morphemes. It can also show what are the inherent or the removable weaknesses (from some given point of view) of a particular type of structure. It can find the same kinds of structure present in different texts, and may even show how a particular type of structure can serve new texts or non-linguistic material.

Finally, such investigation performs the important task of indicating what additional intervals can be joined to the text without changing its structure. It is often possible to show that if, to the various combinations of classes that are found in the existing intervals of the text, we add intervals with certain new combinations of classes, the description of the textual structure becomes simpler, and exceptions are removed (provided we leave intact any intrinsic exceptions, such as boundary conditions). The adding of such intervals may regularize the text from the point of view of discourse analysis. If for example our text contains $A \, B: A \, C: Z \, B$, we may say that Z is secondarily equivalent to A, since both occur before B, but only A before C. If there are no textually intrinsic exceptions governing this restriction on Z, we can on this basis add the interval $Z \, C$ to the text. In this extended text the equivalence $A = Z$ is now a matter of complete substitutability in an identical range of environments, rather than just the secondary result of a chain of equivalences. The addition of such intervals has a very different standing from the addition of arbitrary intervals to the text. If we want to know what is implied but not explicitly stated in a given text, or if we want to see what more can be derived from a given text than the author has already included, this search for adjoinable intervals becomes important.

4. SUMMARY

Discourse analysis performs the following operations upon any single connected text. It collects those elements (or sequences of elements) which have identical or equivalent environments of other elements within a sentence, and considers these to be equivalent to each other (i.e. members of the same equivalence class). Material which does not belong to any equivalence class is associated with the class member to which it is grammatically most closely tied. The sentences of the text are divided into intervals, each a succession of equivalence classes, in such a way that each resulting interval is maximally similar in its class composition to other intervals of the text. The succession of intervals is then investigated for the distribution of classes which it exhibits, in particular for the patterning of class occurrence.

The operations make no use of any knowledge concerning the meaning of the morphemes or the intent or conditions of the author. They require only a knowledge of morpheme boundaries, including sentence junctures and other morphemic intonations (or punctuation). Application of these operations can be furthered by making use of grammatical equivalences (or individual morpheme occurrence relations) from the language as a whole, or from the linguistic body of which the given text is a part. In that case it is necessary to know the grammatical class of the various morphemes of the text.

Discourse analysis yields considerable information about the structure of a text or a type of text, and about the role that each element plays in such a structure. Descriptive linguistics, on the other hand, tells only the role that each element plays in the structure of its sentence. Discourse analysis tells, in addition, how a discourse can be constructed to meet various specifications, just as descriptive linguistics builds up sophistication about the ways in which linguistic systems can be constructed to meet various specifications. It also yields information about stretches of speech longer than one sentence; thus it turns out that while there are relations among successive sentences, these are not visible in sentence structure (in terms of what is subject and what is predicate, or the like), but in the pattern of occurrence of equivalence classes through successive sentences.

NOTES

[1] It is a pleasure to acknowledge here the cooperation of three men who have collaborated with me in developing the method and in analyzing various texts: Fred Lukoff, Noam Chomsky, and A. F. Brown. Earlier investigations in the direction of this method have been presented by Lukoff, Preliminary analysis of the linguistic structure of extended discourse, University of Pennsylvania Library (1948). A detailed analysis of a sample text will appear in a future number of *Lg.* (see Paper XX of this volume.)

[2] Correlations between personality and language are here taken to be not merely related to correlations between 'culture' and language, but actually a special case of these. The reason for this view is that most individual textual characteristics (as distinguished from phonetic characteristics) correlate with those personality features which arise out of the individual's experience with socially conditioned interpersonal situations.

[3] When the verb is transformed to suit such an inversion of subject (N_1 above) and object

(N_2), we may call the new verb form the conjugate of the original form, and write it V^*. Then an active verb has a passive verb as its conjugate, and a passive verb has an active verb as its conjugate.

[4] Two personal names may have identical distributions. Thus, for every sentence containing *Bill* we may find an otherwise identical sentence containing *Jim* instead.

[5] I owe a clarification of the use of such chains to the unpublished work of Noam Chomsky.

[6] Mathematics, and to a greater extent logic, have already set up particular sentence orders which are equivalent to each other. This equivalence can be rediscovered linguistically by finding that the distribution of each sequence is equivalent to that of the others. Our interest here, however, is to discover other equivalences than those which we already know to have been explicitly built into a system.

[7] This is the actual text of an advertisement, found on a card which had presumably been attached to a bottle of hair tonic. A considerable number of advertisements have been analyzed, because they offer repetitive and transparent material which is relatively easy to handle at this stage of our experience with discourse analysis. Many other kinds of texts have been analyzed as well – sections of textbooks, conversations, essays, and so on; and a collection of these will be published soon.

[8] This will be true, though to a lesser extent, even in the writing of those who obey the school admonition to use synonyms instead of repeating a word. In such cases the synonyms will often be found in the same environments as the original not-to-be-repeated word. In contrast, when a writer has used a different word because he intends the particular difference in meaning expressed by it, the synonym will often occur in correspondingly different environments from the original word.

[9] Cf. Harris, *Methods in Structural Linguistics*, Chicago 1951, 160. (The fourth impression appeared under the title *Structural Linguistics* in 1960.) It goes without saying that this vague use of foresight is a preliminary formulation. Detailed investigations will show what may be expected from different kinds of equivalence chains, and will thus make possible a more precise formulation of safeguards.

[10] The *-s* is also a part of all singular nouns (*The child walk-s*, etc.). Or else *walks, goes*, and the like can be taken as alternants of *walk, go*, etc. after *he* and singular nouns.

[11] Before this can be done, some further operations must be carried out to reduce *Four out of five ... say they prefer ...* to two *PW* sequences: *Four ... say ...* and *They prefer ...*, with the sentence *You ... will prefer ...* as a third *PW* sequence. Otherwise, the words *say they* would be left hanging, since the *P* section (equivalent to *Millions*) is only *Four out of five people in a nationwide survey*, and the corrected *W* section (identical with the *W* of *You ... will prefer ...*) is only *prefer X– to any hair tonic Q've used*. See § 3.2 below.

[12] In such formulas as *A is X_1: AX_2*, the italic colon indicates the end of a sentence or interval. (It is used instead of a period because that might be mistaken for the period at the end of a sentence in the author's exposition.)

[13] The case which we have been considering here is the important one of the sequence adjective + noun + verb, in which the noun relates independently to the adjective and to the verb. The adjective can be represented as a predicate of the noun in the same way as the verb. This will be discussed in § 2.33 below.

[14] True, one might claim that this last sentence is still 'grammatical'. But present-day grammar does not distinguish among the various members of a morpheme class. Hence to require that sentence *B* must contain the same morphemes as sentence *A* is to go beyond grammar in the ordinary sense.

[15] To give a crude example, one can read the text sentence *The memorable concerts were recorded* in company with an informant, and then stop and say to him, in an expectant and hesitant way, 'That is to say, the concerts——', waiting for him to supply the continuation.

[16] We may find a great many sentences beginning with *The concerts* and containing the other two words, e.g. *The concerts were not memorable but were nevertheless recorded*. These sentences will contain various words in addition to those of the original sentence; but the only new word which will occur in ALL sentences of the desired form *N M R* (or rather in

a subclass of the *N M R* sentences) will be a form of the verb *to be*. Hence this is the only new word that is essential when changing to that form.

[17] *A* for adjective, *N* for noun, *V* for verb, *P* for preposition. Subscripts indicate particular morphemes, regardless of their class.

[18] The only way to express the exclusion of an object here purely in terms of occurrence of elements is to say that the object already occurs. This cannot be *I*, since that is the subject of *phoned*; hence it must be the other *N*, *the man*.

[19] Semantically one would say that the *PN* 'modifies' the *A*.

[20] The array given here represents the following sentences, taken from a review of some recent phonograph records: *Casals, who is self-exiled from Spain, stopped performing after the fascist victory … The self-exiled Casals is waiting across the Pyrenees for the fall of Franco … The memorable concerts were recorded in Prades … The concerts were recorded first on tape.* (The other sentences analyzed in § 2.32 were composed by me for comparison with these.) The sentences do not represent a continuous portion of the text. This fact limits very materially the relevance of the double array; but that does not concern us here, since the array is intended only as an example of how such arrangements are set up.

[21] We have *consumers* in *P*; and since the singular-plural distinction does not figure in our classes, we can associate the dropping of the *-s* with the occurrence of *consumers* in the first sentence. By dropping the *-s* from the *P*-element *consumers* we get a *P*-form *consumer* for the sentence.

[22] Since *millions of consumers* would be a natural English phrase (P_1 of $P_2 = P_2$), the effect of using the almost identical sequence *millions of consumer* in front of *bottles* is to give a preliminary impression that the sentence is talking about *P*; but when one reaches the word *bottles* one sees that the subject of the sentence is *B*, with the *P* words only adjectival to *B*.

XX

DISCOURSE ANALYSIS: A SAMPLE TEXT

This paper offers an example of how connected discourse can be formally analyzed in such a way as to reveal something of its structure. The method used here was described in a previous paper, 'Discourse Analysis', *Lg.* **28** (1952), 1–30. It consists essentially of the following steps: given a particular text, we collect those linguistic elements (morphemes or sequences of morphemes) which have identical environments within a sentence, and we call these equivalent to each other; thus, if we find the sentences $A\ F$ and $B\ F$ in our text, we write $A = B$ and say that A is equivalent to B or that both are in the same equivalence class. We further collect those linguistic elements which have equivalent (rather than identical) environments, and we call these also equivalent to each other; if we find the sentences $A\ F$ and $B\ E$, and if $A = B$ (because $B\ F$ occurs too), then F is secondarily equivalent to E, and we write $F = E$. (Note that in the sentence $A\ F$, A is the environment of F, and F is the environment of A.) This operation enables us to collect many or all of the linguistic elements or sections of any particular text into a few equivalence classes. For example, if our text consists of the sentences[1] $A\ F$: $B\ E$: $C\ G$: $B\ F$: $M\ E$: $A\ G$: $N\ E$: $N\ G$: $M\ H$, we set up two classes: one class to include A, B (because of $A\ F$ and $B\ F$), C (because of $A\ G$ and $C\ G$), M, and N (because of $B\ E$ and $M\ E$ and $N\ E$); the other class to include F, E (because of $B\ F$ and $B\ E$), G (because of $A\ F$ and $A\ G$), and H (because of $M\ E$ and $M\ H$).[2]

In addition to recognizing that such classes are discoverable in our text, we go on to represent the text in terms of these classes. That is, we state in what way the members of these classes occur in our text, in what way the text can be said to consist of these classes. The difference between the first step and this one is like the difference between a word-class list or dictionary and a grammar: the dictionary tells us what words occur in the language, the word-class list tells us how they are collected into such classes as noun or adjective – i.e. which words occur in equivalent environments; but it is only the grammar that tells us how these words, as members of these classes, constitute the sentences of the language – i.e. how the sentences can be said to consist of these classes. In an analogous way we can ask what place the particular equivalence classes have in the construction of a text. In our small text above it is very simple: each sentence of the text contains one member of the first class followed by one member of the second class. The matter would be more complicated if the text also contained sentences built out of other classes than these two; for example, if it contained some entirely different sentence *P Q*, which could not be analyzed in terms of the other sentences of the same text. We would then have to add this information in describing the construction of the text.

To take a shorter example with actual words, let our text consist of three sentences: *His attitudes arose out of his social position: He was influenced by his social position: His attitudes arose out of a restricted world-view.* Here we put *his attitudes arose out of* and *he was influenced by* into one substitution class *A* because they both occur before *his social position.* And we put *his social position* and *a restricted world-view* into one class *B* because they both occur after *his attitudes arose out of.* We call the members of a class equivalent to each other even though they may not be equivalent in meaning or in morphemic content, simply because they are equivalent in respect to environments in a particular text. Even in this respect, they are not identical: *his social position* occurs after *he was influenced by,* whereas *a restricted world-view* does not. A text in which all members of a class had identical environments would perhaps be rather trivial; in any case, we do not generally find such texts.

Granted that it is useless to look for elements that have identical environments throughout, one may nevertheless ask: what point is there in grouping together elements which have at least one environment in common? The answer is not merely that it is possible to set up such classes, but rather, that when we set them up we often obtain some structural picture of the text. For the short text above, we can make the structural statement that all the sentences consist of *A B,* even though one possible *A B* sentence does not occur: *He was influenced by a restricted world-view.* The present treatment will make no attempt to justify this criterion of equivalence (*A = B* if they have at least one environment in common). Some of the relevant explanation has been given in the previous article. But ultimately the justification will rest upon the kind of results that are obtained with the aid of this equivalence. Our sample text will therefore be analyzed here in an empirical spirit, with the result – as will appear later – that at least some structural information about the text can be obtained by means of the analysis.

We consider the following text[3]:

[A large measure of nationalization (or socialization) of industry and of economic planning is inescapable. Recent history shows all nations, regardless of ideology, moving in that direction. But evidence grows that complete nationalization, overall planning, and the totalitarian state inevitably feed one into the other, at the cost of all individual values.]

Hence the basic principles of economic reconstruction must include:

1. The limitation of nationalization, or socialization, to large-scale industry. Socialization of monopoly enterprises, which dominate 70 per cent of American industrial activity, is enough to end the economic crisis and to build a new economic order with a policy of production for human welfare and freedom.

2. In addition to this limitation, socialized industry should be made to assume *functional organizational forms* that promote diversity, self-government, and decentralization within a state that, whatever new economic functions it may acquire, would still remain a limited-power state.

In a highly complex, organized world, organizational forms are important, since – depending on their character – they can support either totalitarianism or freedom. Public enterprises must be prevented from assuming forms that promote absolute centralization of economic power in the state. [They can and should be autonomous in organization, operation, and direction, independent of government except for over-all policy. The model is the public corporation of the TVA type, but with greater autonomy and with functional directorates representing management, workers, and consumers. These public corporations or authorities are neither direct state enterprises nor under civil service; they are operated as economic, not political, institutions. They provide the greatest amount of decentralization, with authority distributed on successive functional levels, encouraging employee and community participation and regional self-government, as well as greater efficiency. The public corporations in a particular industry are thus not formed into one "government trust", easily controlled by the state's top bureaucracy; they are independent and compete with one another within the relations of planning. A national government agency with final control can be set up to crack down on public corporations *if and when* they violate the mandates under which they operate.]

[Such organizational forms of public enterprise prevent an absolute centralization of economic power. At the same time they provide diversity and pluralism with their checks-and-balances.] Economic freedom is strengthened by retention of free private enterprise in small independent business and in agriculture, and by encouragement of cooperatives.

There is no economic need to socialize small independent business, in which ownership is combined with management; its existence is no bar to planning for economic balance and welfare. [This is also true of farmers, all of whom should become free independent farmers under use-ownership, with cooperatives for large-scale farming and for the purchase and sale of commodities and other purposes.] Cooperatives, because of their voluntaristic nature and self-government, can be major supports of economic freedom since they are forms of "social enterprise" independent of the state. Free private enterprise and cooperatives alike serve economic freedom by serving as a check-and-balance to public enterprise and the state. They can serve freedom especially in the opinion industries – film, the press, book publishing, radio – where a diversity of enterprise promotes group, minority and individual liberty of ideas, while absolute state control means their limitation or suppression.

How shall we set about analyzing this text? If we analyze each sentence down to some basic structure such as *N V I* (noun phrase + verb phrase + intonation), we reduce the text to a mere invariant succession of these structures. This is a much too powerful reduction – one that could be applied to any set of English sentences, whether they constitute a continuous discourse or not. And it is a reduction that tells us nothing about this text in particular.

If we try to find out, say, what all the subjects and all the predicates are in this text, we obtain a seemingly unorganizable hodgepodge. For example, the head noun of the subject in the first unbracketed sentence is *principles*, in another sentence it is *industry*, in a third it is *freedom*.

Instead of directly applying the grammatical categories of English, therefore, we look for the specific regularities of this one text. To this end, we ask first what morphemes or sequences can be substituted for each other – not in English as a whole, but again in this particular text. Different occurrences of the same element obviously can substitute for each other [4]: if we find *enterprise* in two sentences, we can interchange the two occurrences of this element without changing the text; if we find the morpheme sequence *socialize* in one of the last sentences, and then again before the morpheme *-ed* in *socialized*, and again before *-ation* in *socialization* (in the first two sentences), we can replace the first occurrence of *socialize* by the last (aside from morphophonemic and orthographic changes) without altering the text.

As in descriptive linguistics, we now go beyond occurrences of morphemically identical segments to occurrences of different segments with identical environments. In the present text, there is no direct case of two morphemes occurring in identical environments, such as can be found in some other texts. But there is indirect evidence for identity of environment. In one of the sentences we have *Public enterprise*; in another sentence we have *Socialization of monopoly enterprise*. The environments of these two phrases in their respective sentences are at first blush quite different; but the bracketed sentence which follows *Public enterprise* contains the passage *They can and should be...independent...*, and (as we will see below) this occurrence of *They* can be replaced by *Public enterprise*. Further down, in another bracketed sentence, we have *Public corporations of the T V A type...They are independent...*, where it can be shown that the occurrence of *They* is replaceable by *Public corporations of the T V A type*. We still have to show that the remainder of the two sentences, before and after *independent*, does not affect our results; to do this we demonstrate that these remainders are all equivalent to *independent*, and thus do not affect the relation of *independent* to *They* (and to the phrases which can replace *They*). Finally, we will show that *can and should be* is substitutable in this text for *are*.

All this may seem confusing and uncertain. It is nothing more, however, than a selected chain of substitutions, each substitution being justified on grounds of the kind given above. It is a chore to find a chain of substitutions which will carry us, say, from *Public enterprise* to *Socialization of monopoly enterprise* – if indeed any such chain happens to exist in the text. But once we have found the chain, it is easy to check whether each of the substitutions in it is valid. If we can establish the chain mentioned above (see note 15), we can say that *Public enterprise* and *Public corporations of the T V A type* are substitutable for each other in this text, since they both occur in the environment of *are independent* (or more exactly in environments which are equivalent to *are independent*). Similar chains of substitutions show that *Public corporations* is in turn substitutable for *Socialization of monopoly enterprise*.

Besides substitutions like this within the text, we use some of the results of the descriptive grammar of English to go beyond the criterion of identical environment. For example, at the beginning of the text we have *The limitation of nationalization, or socialization, to large-scale industry*. Now *socializ(e)* occurs elsewhere in our text; *nationalization* does not, though it occurs in some of the bracketed sentences. What is the status of this new phrase – *nationalization, or socialization* – which we have here? Is it substitutable for *socialization,* or is it something else? From English grammar, we know that a sequence consisting of a noun+a conjunction (a word like *and* or *or*)+ another noun is substitutable for a single noun by itself [5]: $N C N = N$. That is, in any sentence that contains *nationalization or socialization*, this can be replaced by *socialization* alone (or by any noun) and will still yield an English sentence. But will it yield a sentence of this text? In order to satisfy this last requirement, we restrict this general English rule of substitution to our text by saying that if our $N C N$ is replaced by one of the nouns of this same sentence, we obtain a sentence equivalent to the original one. That is, within any text $N_1 C N_2 = N_1$ and $N_1 C N_2 = N_2$, while in English grammar as a whole $N C N = N$ (any N, not necessarily one of the two in $N C N$).

More exactly, in place of any sentence containing $N_1 C N_2$ we can put two sentences, one containing just N_1 and the other just N_2, but both otherwise identical with the original sentence. Carrying out this replacement upon the sequence *The limitation of nationalization, or socialization, to large-scale industry*, we then get two sequences: *The limitation of nationalization to large-scale industry* and *The limitation of socialization to large-scale industry*. Either or both of these sequences can replace the original sentence of our text, with no change except in style. Of course, because of this difference in style, it would no longer be the same text; but we can create a modified text, identical with the original one except for this replacement, and say that the two texts are (on grounds of substitution) equivalent aside from style. It is in this sense that we can say that if we find $N_1 \, C \, N_2$ in our text, then N_1 is substitutable in our text for N_2.

In this way we can show that two morpheme sequences are substitutable for each other in a text even when they do not occur in the same environment. We do this, however, only by applying within the limits of our text those equivalences which have been found for the language in general, i.e. which can be applied to any utterance of the language.

We now take up the unbracketed sentences of our text one by one, numbered for reference from (1) to (9).

> (1)   *Hence the basic principles of economic reconstruction must include: 1. The limitation of nationalization, or socialization, to large-scale industry.*

We notice first that this constitutes a single English sentence in spite of the capitalization of *The*, except for the colon and the figure *1*. The intonation indicated by the colon would lead us to expect the two parallel sections (*1* and *2*) to follow the colon within the same sentence; but the section beginning with *2* is a separate later sentence, with a long sentence intervening. Since the colon intonation followed by *1* alone does not occur in English sentences, we will regard it as a written device, and will read the sentence without the colon and the *1*.

The subject noun-phrase is *the basic principles of economic reconstruction*; we will symbolize it by *R*. The verb is *must include*. The word *Hence*, which precedes the subject, will be found – quite apart from its meaning – to be a member of a class of words in this text (as elsewhere) which belong neither to the subject nor to the predicate, and which we can therefore treat as intersentence connectives. The proof will not be shown here, since only two other such words occur in the present excerpt.[6]

The object noun-phrase is *the limitation of socialization to large-scale industry*, with *socialization* as well as *nationalization* separately substitutable for *nationalization, or socialization* (by the discussion above). Since *socialization* occurs frequently in this text, we mark it *S*, so as to be able to consider separately its 'privileges of occurrence' (as Bloomfield called them), i.e. its substitutions.

The remainder of the phrase is then *the limitation of ... to large-scale industry*. The extraction of one noun (*socialization*) out of the original phrase may seem to do violence to the grammar. Grammatically, the first noun of a phrase is its head: $N_1 \, P \, N_2 = N_1$ (the numbers identify the individual nouns, and *P* is preposition) – if only because it is the first noun that agrees with the following verb as to number. In *A box of chocolates is fine,*

Boxes of chocolates are fine, Boxes of candy are fine, the plural morpheme extends over the verb (*is–are*) and over the first noun (*box*) of the subject phrase, but not over the second. In terms of meaning, too, we would ordinarily say that the second noun in a phrase modifies the first: *machines for calculation* are *calculating machines*, so that $N_1 P N_2 = A_2 N_1$ (*A* is adjective; and the number indicates that it is based on the same morpheme as N_2); *relatives of my mother* are *my maternal relatives* (again $N_1 P N_2 = A_2 N_1$).

However, on closer consideration we find that the head of a phrase may be its second noun instead of its first. *A great number of people* is *numerous people* in terms of meaning and of morpheme rearrangement: $N_1 P N_2 = A_1 N_2$. After some N_1, indeed, it is the N_2 that has (or lacks) the plural suffix in agreement with the verb: *A great number of people are coming, A lot of people are coming, Lots of milk is good for you*. Finally, the order of N_1 and N_2 is not as immutable as might be supposed. $N_1 P N_2$ can often be changed to $N_2 P N_1$ with a suitable change of the preposition; for example, sentences containing *the goal of greater production* can be replaced – in terms of meaning, but also by informant experiments – by sentences otherwise identical (aside from possible grammatical adjustments) containing *greater production as goal* instead. We can consider *as* to be the inverse or conjugate (*) of *of*, since *of* is replaced by *as* when the order of nouns is inverted: $N_1 P N_2 = N_2 P^* N_1$.

These examples do not contradict the fact that the head of an English noun phrase is usually the first noun. It is the first noun which is usually the ultimate subject: *the poet of Greece* is a man, not a country, and is followed by *he*, not *it*. But in some cases we will find in a text that a noun phrase is replaced by its second noun, as though that were the head: for *Boxes of candy* we find in equivalent environments *Amounts of candy*, and finally just *Candy*. We have also seen that in some cases the second noun of a phrase is grammatically the head. What is most important for our present purposes: given a phrase in which one noun is the head or subject, we can alter it grammatically, e.g. by inverting it, into a phrase in which the subject is the other noun. Returning to our text, we invert *the limitation of socialization*, and obtain something like *socialization as limited* (*to large-scale industry*), from which we extract the head noun, *socialization*, since we are interested in this particular noun as a repeated element of this text. We are then left with *limited to large-scale industry* as an additional element of the sentence, adjectival to the head noun; we will mark this additional element *L*.

All this discussion has been necessary to find out what to do with the peculiar segment *the limitation of ... to large-scale industry*. This segment was left on our hands when we extracted the key word *socialization*, and we wanted to know how it relates grammatically to that word. We have now found that this segment is grammatically equivalent to a phrase like *limited to large-scale industry*, appearing as a modifying adjective of *socialization*. The first sentence has been reduced to the form: *R must include S L.*

> (2) *Socialization of monopoly enterprises, which dominate 70 per cent of American industrial activity, is enough to end the economic crisis and to build a new economic order with a policy of production for human welfare and freedom.*

The first word is our *S*. The phrase *of monopoly enterprises* is grammatically on a par with *limited to large-scale industry*, since both are adjectival phrases following *socialization*. That these two phrases are substitutable for each other follows from various occurrences of *monopoly* elsewhere in the article (outside the quoted section that we are analyzing)[7], especially from the phrase *large-scale industry and monopoly*; for it was agreed above that if we find $N_1 \ C \ N_2$ in our text, then N_1 is substitutable for N_2. *Monopoly enterprises* is therefore our *L* again, since it is equivalent to *limited to large-scale industry*.

The phrase *which dominate 70 per cent of American industrial activity*, separated by comma intonation, is an adjectival phrase following *monopoly enterprises*. In English grammar, adjective + noun can be replaced by noun alone. This particular adjectival phrase contains no morphemes that figure in the analysis of this text (except for the element *industry*, which figures only with adjectives of the *L* group, but which appears here without these *L* morphemes). Hence it throws no new light on the substitution possibilities of those morphemes. For purposes of our present analysis, we can therefore apply here the rule $A \ N = N$ of English grammar, and say that *monopoly enterprises, which dominate 70 per cent of American industrial activity*, is equivalent (as far as substitutional relations in this text are concerned) to *monopoly enterprises* alone, i.e. to our *L*.[8]

The economic crisis occurs elsewhere in the article (outside the quoted section) as a substituent of *statism*, which in turn occurs elsewhere in the article as a substituent of *absolute state power*. Since *absolute state power* and its equivalents are thus equivalents of *the economic crisis*, we will indicate each of these by *T*.

Thus far we have: *S L is enough to end T.*

We now turn our attention to the remainder of the second sentence, beginning with *and to build*. By noting the effect of the conjunction *and*, we can show that this remainder is the equivalent of a whole new sentence. We do this by applying the conjunction formula $X \ C \ X = X$ (note 5); to make use of it, we must find a section having the form $X \ C \ X$. For this purpose, we complete our phrase *and (C) to build... (X_2)* by adding before the *and* as much of the preceding material (X_1) as is grammatically equivalent to X_2 (*to build*...) which follows the *and*. This X_1 is obviously *to end the economic crisis*, which is of the same grammatical structure as *to build*... On the basis of this $X_1 \, C \, X_2$ (*to end*...*and to build*...) we can now say that X_2 is substitutable for X_1: *to build a new economic order*...is substitutable for *to end the economic crisis*. Furthermore, since X_1 occurs after *S L is enough*, we derive that its substituent X_2 can also occur after *S L is enough*. This means that we can replace the second sentence by two sub-sentences: *S L is enough X_1* and *S L is enough X_2*. The first of these has already been tentatively analyzed. We now consider the second one: *S L is enough to build*...

In this latter sub-sentence the one significant morpheme which occurs frequently in our text, and which will be useful for substitutions, is *freedom*. Equivalent to this is *welfare*, by the rule $N \, C \, N = N$; and *human welfare* is a substituent of *welfare*, by the rule $A \, N = N$. However, *freedom* is the last of four noun phrases, each adjectival to the preceding one. In order to treat *freedom* here as a substituent of the other occurrences of *freedom* (where it is the object of the main verb), we would like to interpret the *freedom* in this sentence as the object of the verb *to build*, instead of a thrice-removed modifier of the object. To do this, we take the whole object phrase: N_1 (*a new economic order*) P_1 (*with*) N_2 (*a policy*) P_2 (*of*) N_3 (*production*) P_3 (*for*) N_4 (*human welfare and freedom*). By repeated application of the rule $N_1 \, P \, N_2 = N_2 \, P^* \, N_1$, we can invert this long noun phrase into its equivalent $N_4 \, P_3^* \text{-} N_3 \, P_2^* \, N_2 \, P_1^* \, N_1$ (something like *human welfare and freedom through production as the policy of a new economic order*).[9] In the inverted form, *freedom* (or its substituent, *human welfare and freedom*) is the object, and the other noun phrases are adjectival to it. The whole inverted phrase is equivalent to *freedom*, since $N_1 \, P \, N_2 = A_2 \, N_1 = N_1$. *Freedom*, in turn, is shown by other occurrences in this article (outside the quoted section) to be a substituent of *not totalitarian dictatorship*; and *totalitarian dictatorship* is shown by various occurrences in the article to be a substituent of *absolute state power*, which we have marked above by T. Hence *freedom* is equivalent to *not* plus *absolute state power*; we will indicate it by $-T$ (using the minus sign as a mark for *not*).

The second sub-sentence is therefore: *S L is enough to build $-T$.*

We have broken our original sentence into two sub-sentences on the basis of the *and* in the object; since it was only the object that was doubled, both sub-sentences have the same subject and verb. They are: *S L is enough to end T and S L is enough to build $-T$.*

We are now in a position to compare the second sub-sentence with sentence (1) of our text. The *economic reconstruction* of that sentence is shown by other occurrences in this article to be equivalent to *freedom*. To make use of this fact, we invert the whole R phrase, *the basic principles* (N_1) *of* (*P*) *economic reconstruction* (N_2) by applying the rule $N_1 \, P \, N_2 = N_2 \, P^* \, N_1$. Since the words *basic principles* do not occur elsewhere in the text, they will not affect our analysis; we can eliminate them from further consideration by using the fact that they occupy an adjectival position in the inverted phrase: $N_2 \, P^* \, N_1 = A_1 \, N_2 = N_2$. That is to say, our original R phrase *the basic principles of economic reconstruction* (which is $N_1 \, P \, N_2$) can be replaced by *economic reconstruction* (N_2) alone – that is, by an equivalent of *freedom*. Since *freedom* is $-T$, the whole R phrase is thus a substituent of $-T$.

Sentence (1) is thus reduced to $-T$ *must include* $S \, L$. Let us compare this with the second half of sentence (2), $S \, L$ *is enough to build* $-T$. We can bring out the similarity between these two by inverting the order of subject ($-T$) and object ($S \, L$) in sentence (1). This can be done in any English sentence by changing the verb from active to passive (or from passive to active). If we mark this change by an asterisk, we can write $N_1 \, V \, N_2 = N_2 \, V^* \, N_1$. Hence we can replace the sentence $-T$ *must include* $S \, L$ by $S \, L$ *must be included in* $-T$. If we now compare this with $S \, L$ *is enough to build* $-T$, it is clear that the two verb phrases have identical environments ($S \, L \dots -T$) and are therefore substitutable for each other. We will indicate each of them by the letter I.

Finally, we compare these two occurrences of $S \, L \, I \, -T$ with the $S \, L$ *is enough to end* T of the first half of sentence (2). It is at once apparent that *is enough to end* occurs in the same environment as $I-$, and is therefore a substituent of it. There is reason, however, for writing it $-I$ here rather than $I-$; for the minus sign (representing *not* and the like) in $S \, L \, I \, -T$ is part of the T phrase, before which it is written. But the minus sign included in *is enough to end* is part of the verb phrase; and this fact we indicate by writing it before the I.

The first two sentences of our text have now been analyzed as three sentence structures: $S \, L \, I \, -T$. $S \, L \, -I \, T$. $S \, L \, I \, -T$. We will see that all the other sentences of this text can be reduced to a similar structure, and that certain conclusions about the grammar of the text can be drawn from this fact.

> (3)   *2. In addition to this limitation, socialized industry should be made to assume functional organizational forms that promote diversity, self-government, and decentralization within a state that, whatever new economic functions it may acquire, would still remain a limited-power state.*

Since we disregarded the number *1* in sentence (1), we will disregard the *2* in this sentence.[10]

The subject phrase is *socialized industry*. In *socialized* we have our S. It is true that the grammatical form is different from the previous occurrences of S; but it can be shown that the difference is immaterial to this text. In the previous occurrences we had two noun phrases S and L, one of which was adjectival to the other. The fact that the S was previously the head of the phrase (as in *socialization of monopoly enterprise*), whereas here it is the adjectival part, is not important for our text analysis, since we could make the S of the preceding sentences adjectival to L by inverting $N_1 P N_2 = N_2 P^* N_1$ (e.g. *monopoly enterprise under socialization*). In sentence (3) we have S in adjectival form, equivalent to the S in an inverted form of the previous occurrences: *socialized N_1* is equivalent to *N_1 under socialization*, because $A_2 N_1 = N_1 P N_2$ (adjective before the noun is equivalent to pre-position-plus-noun after the noun).

It remains to ask whether *industry* is equivalent to our L, and where we should assign the phrase *In addition to this limitation*. By itself, *industry* is not our L, since it is not by itself substitutable in our text for *large-scale industry*. But we can show that *In addition to this limitation* is a $P N$ (more exactly $P N P N$) which is adjectival to *industry*, and that it replaces the adjective *large-scale*. We show this by first considering the word *this*. The morphemes *th* and *wh* (or the words *this, that, which*, etc.) constitute in English grammar a discontinuous extension of some previously (or later) occurring word or word sequence.[11] Since *this* is here an adjective of *limitation*, it marks the repetition of the previous adjective of *limitation*. The word *limitation* occurs in sentence (1) with *to large-scale industry* as its adjectival (or 'modifying') $P N$. Hence *this* repeats *to large-scale industry*. Our last problem concerns the grammatical relations within the broken phrase *in addition to this limitation, ... industry*. Grammatically, this phrase is equivalent to *industry, in addition to this limitation*. In view of what has been said of the word *this*, the latter phrase is equivalent to *industry with the limitation to large-scale industry*, which in turn is equivalent to our L.[12]

When we turn to the object phrase, we find that at several points in this article, outside the quoted passage, *diversity* occurs in the same environment as *freedom*. It is therefore $-T$. So are *self-government* and *decentralization*: they are substitutable for *diversity*, since $N, N, and N$ contains two con-junctions, and the sequence $N C N C N$ implies that each N can substitute for the other. The adjectival $P N$ phrase *within a state that would still remain a limited-power state* can be reduced to something like *within a limited-power state*[13], which occurs elsewhere in the article as a substituent of *freedom*, and hence as $-T$. This whole $P N$ phrase is then a $-T$ adjective for the three preceding $-T$ nouns. Since $A N = N$, the combination of a $-T$ adjectival phrase with a $-T$ noun is certainly equivalent to a $-T$ noun phrase; hence the whole combination is equivalent to $-T$.

The reader may ask why we are so careful with this adjectival phrase, when previously we dropped two adjectival phrases (*which dominate 70 per cent of American industry* and *basic principles of*) by using the rule $N P N = A N = N$. The answer is that the phrases previously disposed of do not contain words which are relevant in the analysis of this text, i.e. which belong to one of our substitution classes. They do not affect the substitution classes we set up; all that is necessary is to show, by such elimination rules as $A N = N$, that disregarding the adjectival phrase does not affect the grammatical position of the relevant word (e.g. T) with respect to the other relevant words (e.g. $S L$) of the sentence. In contrast, the words *limited-power state* recur elsewhere in the article, and we have to see if they connect our three $-T$ nouns with some other element of the analysis, of if they leave them equivalent to $-T$.

The phrase *whatever new economic functions it may acquire* is another adjectival element (or parenthetical sentence) of the noun *a state*, with *it* replacing *a state* (by the rule in note 11). The adjectival element contains no material relevant to our analysis; including it in the noun phrase of *state* (on the grammatical basis $A N = N$) does not affect the substitutional standing of that noun in this text.

The preceding three paragraphs give us a complete reduction of the object phrase in sentence (3). We find that each of the words *diversity, self-government*, and *decentralization* is $-T$. The whole remainder, *within a state...*, is also $-T$, due note being taken of the included phrase *whatever...acquire*, which has no effect on the analysis.

There remains the verb phrase. This connects the subject $S L$ with the object $-T$. If we compare our present sentence, $S L$ plus verb phrase plus $-T$, with the preceding sentence $S L I -T$, we see that the verb phrase here is substitutable for I. That means that our present sentence is also $S L I -T$. We can, however, make some reduction in this verb phrase, because two words in it, *functional organization*, occur elsewhere in the article as substituents of $-T$. To effect this reduction, we interpret the sequence of words *to assume functional organizational forms that promote diversity* as equivalent to something like the sequence *to assume forms that have functional organization* (X_1) *and that promote diversity* (X_2). The justification for this equivalence is that adjectives which precede a noun can be replaced equivalently, in English grammar, by adjectival phrases after the noun. The same morphemes can be rearranged into an equivalent grammatical form: *functional organizational forms* ($A_1 N_2$) can be replaced by *forms with functional organization* or *forms that have function organization* (both $N_2 P N_1$). The latter equivalent is important for us because it has the same grammatical form as the phrase *that promote diversity*. Hence if we use this particular equivalent, as we are grammatically permitted to do, we obtain the full phrase *that have functional organization* (X_1) *(and) that promote diversity* (X_2).[14]

Our sentence is now: *S L should be made to assume forms that have functional organization and that promote diversity* ... This is equivalent to a double sentence: *S L should be made to assume forms that have functional organization* and *S L should be made to assume forms that promote diversity* (by the rule in note 5, and the analysis of *to build and to end* above). Since *functional organization* and *diversity* are each $-T$, it follows from comparison with preceding sentences of the form $S L I - T$ that the two similar verb phrases in this double sentence, *should be made to assume forms that promote* and ... *that have*, are each equivalent to I.

The third sentence too has thus been reduced to a double occurrence of $S L I - T$.

(4) *Public enterprise must be prevented from assuming forms that promote abolute centralization of economic power in the state.*

The word *enterprise* does not by itself represent our L, and *public* is not a substituent of *socialized*. However, the sequence *public enterprise* occurs elsewhere in this article in the same environment as *public corporations*, which in turn occurs in the same environment as *socialized industry*. Hence the sequence *public enterprise* represents $S L$.[15]

The object phrase *absolute centralization* ... *in the state* is shown by various occurrences in this article to represent T: compare, among others, *absolute state power*, cited above, *absolute centralization* in note 15, and *absolute state control* in the last sentence of our text.

The verb phrase, connecting the subject $S L$ and the object T, is therefore equivalent to $-I$, as in the first part of sentence (2). If we compare *should be made to assume forms that promote* (as I) with *must be prevented from assuming forms that promote* (as $-I$), we see that the minus is represented by the difference between *made to* and *prevented from* (*must* being taken on other evidence as equivalent to *should*, and the *-ing* being grammatically automatic after *from*).

The sentence is then $S L - I T$.

(5) *Economic freedom is strengthened by retention of free private enterprise in small independent business and in agriculture, and by encouragement of cooperatives.*

Economic freedom is $-T$, like *freedom* alone. In this text, when a word is itself T (or $-T$, like *freedom*), the adjective *economic* does not affect its membership in that class. We can see this by comparing *absolute centralization of economic power in the state* (T) with *absolute centralization* and *absolute state power* (both T).

Free private enterprise is equivalent to *cooperatives* in sentence (8), where each is shown to be the minus (or opposite) of $S\,L$ as a unit; we can write this as $-(S\,L)$, or better as $-S\,-L$. *Small independent business* is shown to be $-L$ by several occurrences elsewhere in this article as the negative of *monopoly*. *Free private enterprise in small independent business* is thus $-S\,-L$ *in* $-L$. This reduces to $-S\,-L$, by the rule $N_1\,P\,N_2=N_1$. The addition of *and in agriculture* to this phrase does not affect its standing as $-S\,-L$, since *agriculture* does not occur otherwise in the text.

The words *retention of* and *encouragement of* before the two occurrences of $-S\,-L$ similarly have no effect on the analysis, since they do not occur in comparable environments elsewhere in this article, and are not substituents of anything that figures in our analysis. Hence we say that *encouragement of cooperatives=cooperatives*, by the rule $N_1\,P\,N_2=N_2\,P^*\,N_1=N_2$. If the author had used words like *retention* in sentences (7) and (8) as he did in (5) and (6) (e.g. if we found *retention of cooperatives serves economic freedom*), we would consider *cooperatives* to be only $-L$ (instead of $-S\,-L$), and *retention* would be $-S$ (the opposite of *nationalization*). This would have semantic support; but in view of the substitutibility of *encouragement of cooperatives* here with *cooperatives* alone in sentences (7) and (8), it is not possible.

So far we have $-T$ *is strengthened* $[by\,-S\,-L,\,and\,by\,-S\,-L]$. The brackets are inserted here to show the form $[X\,C\,X]$, which can be replaced by either X alone. This yields $-T$ *is strengthened by* $-S\,-L$ twice over. If we invert this sentence to the active (by $N_1\,V\,N_2=N_2\,V^*\,N_1$, as in the discussion at the end of sentence (2)), we obtain $-S\,-L$ *strengthens* $-T$. Elsewhere in this article, we find *strengthens* substitutable for *is*, which will turn out in sentence (6) to be I.

The sentence is thus $-S\,-L\,I\,-T$.

(6) *There is no economic need to socialize small independent business, in which ownership is combined with management; its existence is no bar to planning for economic balance and welfare.*

Economic need occurs elsewhere in this article as a substituent of *self-government*, hence is $-T$ (as in sentence (3)). *Small independent business* is $-L$ (as above). The phrase *in which … management* is adjectival to this $-L$ and does not affect its classification here, since the significant morphemes of this phrase do not occur elsewhere in the text. *There* is grammatically a precursor repetition of *to socialize small business…*, holding the subject position for that phrase; one could recast the sentence into something like *To socialize small independent business … is not an economic need*. The phrase *to socialize small independent business* is the subject, and on the basis of our previous work is classified as $S\,-L$.

The verb *is* is *I*, on the basis of several other occurrences (cf. the examples in note 15). The word *no*, like *not* (see under sentence (2)), is minus. For *is no* we put $-I$.

The first part of the sentence, then, is $S-L-I-T$.

The section after the colon is grammatically a separate sentence. The object is $-T$, because *welfare* occurs as such in the second part of sentence (2), and *balance* is here equivalent to it (by $N\ C\ N=N$). The adjective *economic* does not affect the standing of a $-T$ word[16]; and the word *planning*, which does not figure in our analysis, can be made adjectival to *welfare* by inverting *planning for ... welfare* on the basis of $N_1\ P\ N_2 = N_2\ P^*\ N_1$; this would give us something like *welfare and economic balance through planning*.

The predicate *is no bar* contains $-I$ (for *is no*) plus the word *bar*.[17] The subject *its existence* contains *it* as a repetition of *small business*, hence as $-L$. In order to determine the standing of the remaining words, *'s existence* and *bar*, we consider the sentence as it now stands: $-L$ *'s existence* $-I$ *bar* $-T$. We first note that *'s existence* is the head of the phrase containing $-L$, and is thus equivalent to *the existence of* (*it*). It is therefore in the same grammatical position as *to socialize* above, which is the head of the phrase *to socialize small independent business* (containing $-L$), and which is equivalent to *the socialization of* (*small independent business*). Comparison of our present sentence with the $S-L-I-T$ above suggests that *'s existence* contains S; but it is hard to see how this fits in with the presence of the word *bar*, which is lacking in the first sub-sentence. We will see that when *diversity* occurs as the head of the subject phrase of *I*, it is equivalent to $-S$ (in sentence (9)), and *continue to exist* is elsewhere in this article equivalent to *diversity*. Hence we class *'s existence* as $--S$. Putting this $-S$ before the $-L$ (because the grammatical relation between the two is the same as in the preceding S $-L$), we obtain $-S-L-I$ *bar* $-T$. When we compare this with the preceding $S-L-I-T$, we see that they are identical except for the extra minus (before S) and the word *bar*. To find what we must do with *bar*, we search for comparable pairs of sentences. The best we can find are such other pairs as the $S-L-I-T$ above and the $S\ L\ I\ -T$ of sentence (2). These are identical except that one has two minus signs more than the other; there are no pairs in which one sentence has just one minus sign more than the other. On this basis, we consider *bar* to be equivalent to a minus sign.[18]

If we assign *bar* to the predicate, we obtain $-S-L--I-T$.

> (7)   *Cooperatives, because of their voluntaristic nature and self-government, can be major supports of economic freedom since they are forms of "social enterprise" independent of the state.*

We first consider the main sentence *Cooperatives can be major supports of*

economic freedom. Economic freedom is $-T$ (from sentence (5)). The predicate *can be major supports of* is I: *support* occurs as I in one of the bracketed
sentences; *is a support* is grammatically equivalent to *supports* (*is* $N_1 = V_1$);
can be is a substituent of *is* in this text (see note 15); *support* is substitutable
for *major support* (by $AN=N$). Hence, *can be major supports of* is equivalent
to *support*, which is I. We thus obtain *Cooperatives* $I -T$. If we compare this
with previous sentences of the form $S L I -T$, it follows that *cooperatives* is
a substituent either of $S L$ or (by note 18) of $-S -L$. The partial substitutibility of *cooperatives* with *small independent business* in sentence (5)
suggests that we have $-S -L$ here, rather than $S L$.

The main sentence is thus $-S -L I -T$.

We now consider the phrase *because of their voluntaristic nature and self-
government*. This can be included in the subject, as an adjectival phrase which
contains no words except *self-government* relevant to our analysis. We have
seen under sentence (6) that when words which are substituents of *diversity*
(as *self-government* is) occur in $-L$ phrases they have $-S$ force; hence this
adjectival phrase does not affect the standing of the subject as $-S -L$.

The final section contains a new sentence; *They are forms of "social
enterprise" independent of the state.*[19] *They* repeats *cooperatives*, and is therefore $-S -L$. *Are* is I, since it is grammatically the same as *is*. *Independent*
occurs in note 15 as $-T$. *Of the state* is a $P N$ phrase included in the noun-
phrase modifier *independent*, and adjectival to this $-T$ word. *Forms of
"social enterprise"* is a noun phrase in grammatical apposition to *independent*
and hence equivalent to it (apposition being included among the conjunctions
C of $N C N=N$, as it was in note 14). We thus obtain a double sentence:
They are forms of "social enterprise" and *They are independent of the state.*[20]

This secondary sentence is thus a double occurrence of $-S -L I -T$.

> (8)   *Free private enterprise and cooperatives alike serve economic
> freedom by serving as a check-and-balance to public enterprise
> and the state.*

The first part is an independent sentence: *Free private enterprise and cooperatives alike serve economic freedom*. The word-pair *and ... alike* is a conjunction, by virtue of which *free private enterprise* is equivalent to *cooperatives*
and hence to $-S -L$. *Economic freedom* is $-T$. Comparison of the resulting
$-S -L$ *serve* $-T$ with the previous $-S -L I -T$ shows that *serve* is a
member of I.

The second part can be converted into an independent sentence for purposes of analysis by the following grammatical equivalence: $N_1 V_2 (P)V_3 ing$
$= N_1 V_2 : (C) N_1 V_3$. That is, a sentence containing two verbal phrases (with
or without a preposition between them), with *-ing* after the second verb, can

be matched by two sentences containing the same morphemes as the original sentence, but with the subject repeated before the second verb and the *-ing* omitted (together with the preposition, if any), with or without an inter-sentence connective *C*. For example, *Cooperatives succeed by economizing* can be matched by *Cooperatives economize: Thus they succeed.* (The order of sentences can be reversed, depending on the inter-sentence connective used.[21])

We thus obtain for the second part the equivalent sentence *They serve as a check-and-balance to public enterprise and the state. They* repeats the preceding $-S-L$. *Serve* is *I*. The remainder, the object, is $-T$ by comparison with the preceding $-S-L\ I\ -T$. This is supported by the occurrence of *checks-and-balances* elsewhere as $-T$.[22]

We thus have again two occurrences of $-S-L\ I\ -T$.

> (9) *They can serve freedom especially in the opinion industries – film, the press, book publishing, radio – where a diversity of enterprise promotes group, minority and individual liberty of ideas, while absolute state control means their limitation or suppression.*

Our first independent sentence ends just before the *where*. *They* repeats the subject of the preceding sentence, and is therefore $-S-L$. The object, *freedom*, is $-T$. The sentence thus become $-S-L\ can\ serve\ -T$. Comparison with $-S-L\ is\ -T$ shows that *can serve* is a substituent of *is*, hence a member of *I*. The analysis of the phrase *especially in the opinion industries* raises certain grammatical problems. It should probably be taken as adjectival to the subject, since its head-noun *industries* is a substituent of one of the two head-nouns of the subject, *enterprise*. In this text adjective + *industry* is either *L* or $-L$. Since the whole phrase is adjectival to a $-L$ subject, it is clear that *opinion industries* is $-L$ rather than *L*. As to the list enclosed by dashes, each of its four members is an equivalent of the preceding head-noun *industries*; the dashes and the commas function as the conjunction *C* of *N C N=N*. The sentence accordingly remains $-S-L\ I\ -T$.

The next sub-sentence that can be grammatically extracted is *where a diversity of enterprise promotes group, minority, and individual liberty of ideas*. By virtue of its *wh* morpheme (see above, at note 11 in the text), *where* is substitutable for the preceding noun phrase *in the opinion industries* (plus the dash-enclosed list). Hence the subject in this sub-sentence is (putting *diversity*, which is the head of the phrase, in front) *a diversity of enterprise in the opinion industries*. Since the subject in the preceding sub-sentence is *free private enterprise and cooperatives in the opinion industries*, and since *diversity* is a substituent of *freedom* in all positions in this article, we may expect that the two subject phrases are equivalent, both $-S-L$. This is supported by the fact that *promotes* is elsewhere substitutable for *serve* and is thus *I*, while *liberty* is elsewhere substitutable for *freedom* and is thus $-T$; the remaining words in the object phrase are all adjectives of *liberty*. We thus obtain $-S -L I -T$.

The final sub-sentence is *while absolute state control means their limitation or suppression*. The word *while* fills two grammatical functions: it repeats the *wh* of the preceding clause, and serves as an interconnection *C* between the two clauses.[23] Replacing the *wh* by that to which it is equivalent, we obtain as the subject of this sub-sentence *absolute state control in the opinion industries*. We know that *absolute state control* is the opposite or negative of *diversity*, since in object position the latter is $-T$ and the former is T.[24] When *diversity* occurs as the head of the subject phrase, preceding $-L$, we find it to be $-S$. Hence when *absolute state control* occurs as the head of the subject phrase, preceding $-L$, it must be S.[25]

The verb *means* occurs elsewhere as an *I*, though the evidence for this equivalence is not complete.

In the object phrase, *their limitation or suppression*, the plural *their* repeats the grammatically equivalent adjective phrase derived from a plural noun, *of ideas*, in the preceding sentence. This final sub-sentence can therefore be written, with the aid of the analysis so far, as $S -L I$ *the limitation or suppression of ideas*, which may be compared with the $S -L -I -T$ of sentence (6). The argument of note 18 means that if $S -L -I -T$ occurs in this text, then $S -L I T$ (with two minuses fewer) can also occur. If we compare this possible $S -L I T$ with our present $S -L I$ *the limitation or suppression of ideas*, we see that *the limitation or suppression of ideas* is equivalent to T.[26]

The final clause can then be taken as $S -L I T$.

We now rewrite the sentences of our text in terms of the equivalence classes that we have obtained:

(1)	S	L	$I -T.$
(2)	S	L	$-I \ T.$
	S	L	$I -T.$
(3)	S	L	$I -T.$
(4)	S	L	$-I \ T.$
(5)	$-S -L$		$I -T.$
(6)	$S -L$		$-I -T.$
	$-S -L -$		$-I -T.$
(7)	$-S -L$		$I -T.$
	$-S -L$		$I -T.$

$$
\begin{array}{lll}
(8) & -S\ -L & I\ -T. \\
& -S\ -L & I\ -T. \\
(9) & -S\ -L & I\ -T. \\
& -S\ -L & I\ -T. \\
& S\ -L & I\ \ \ T. \\
\end{array}
$$

Only five marks, aside from the period, occur in these sentences. In describing English grammar we say that all sentences consist of combinations of N, V, and the like, where N is defined as a class of certain mutually substitutable words, V as another class, and so on. Similarly, in describing the structure of this particular text, we can say that the sentences consist of combinations of S, L, and so on, where S is defined as a class of morpheme sequences substitutable for each other IN THIS TEXT, L as another class, and so on. Just as English $N\ V$ represents *The clock stopped* and also *His private phone was tapped* and countless other sentences, so $S\ L\ I\ -T$ represents several of the sentences (1), (2b) and (3) discussed above. The phrases represented by $S\ L$ are the grammatical subjects of I, but they need not occur at the beginning of the sentence, since the verb can be put in the passive (as I^*). The minus sign represents an even more diverse set of elements: *not, no, de-* (in *decentralization* as compared with *centralization*), or simply the difference FOR THIS TEXT between *prevent* and *provide* (somewhat as the plural morpheme is among other things the difference between *feet* and *foot*).

Just as sentences in English grammar consist of only certain combinations of N, V, etc. ($N\ V$ but not $N\ N$), so the sentences of this text consist of only certain combinations of our equivalence classes. Each sentence consists of one each of the elements S, L, I, T (in that order), with an odd number of minus signs variously placed among them.

This is, then, a structural analysis of our text. We have discovered what is common to all the sentences, or at any rate to all of a particular group of them. We see what morpheme sequences are represented by the same mark – that is, what sequences are equivalent. We see how the sentence structure, in terms of these marks, varies as the text goes on, and how the morpheme sequences represented by each mark vary in successive sentences.

Since we have a formal description of the sentences of the text, we can say what properties a sentence must possess to fit this description. That is, we can say what criteria (in terms of S, L and so on) a new sentence must satisfy to be formally identical (in terms of these elements) with the sentences of the text. We do this for English grammar when we say that any $N\ V$ is an English sentence, even if it is quite nonsensical or has never been spoken. Analogously, we may be able to find new sentences which are formally admissible within the structural analysis of this text. For example, a sentence of the form

$-SLIT$ would satisfy the structural analysis, even though no actual sentence of the text happens to show this form. Such a sentence might read something like this: *The existence* (6) *of monopoly enterprises* (2) *is enough to build* (2) *economic crisis* (2).

Almost the only way to avoid admitting this sentence as formally equivalent to the others would be to state the structural analysis of the text as follows: Sentences of the text contain one each of the elements *S, L, I, T*, with a single minus before any but the first mark; or with three minuses placed before the first two marks and the last, or before the last three; or with five minuses placed one before each mark with an extra one before the third. This amounts simply to listing the individual sentence types actually found. If we generalize the collection of types, and say that each sentence of the text contains $S\,L\,I\,T$ with a single minus sign before one or another of the marks (and frequently with additional minus signs, always odd in total number), we will be admitting the new form $-S\,L\,I\,T$ as formally equivalent to the actually occurring $S\,L\,I\,-T$, etc.

If we are interested in a deductive technique, we may claim that from the existing sentences we can 'derive' the new form $-S\,L\,I\,T$. In a semantic interpretation, we might claim that the new $-S\,L\,I\,T$ has for this text the same meaning or 'value' as the existing sentences; or else we might consider that there is a particular difference in meaning between $-S\,L\,I\,T$ and the other sentences which explains its omission. A purely formal description simply notes the extent to which the excluded sentence $-S\,L\,I\,T$ is similar in form to the included sentences.

In any case, we can say that there are certain structural features (structural in terms of the substitutive relations worked out here) which are common to all the sentences of this text; and that one sentence of this structure – perhaps the more 'extreme' sentence – is lacking from the collection. This does not mean that all the sentences are saying the same thing; that would depend on how different the various members are which we have included in each equivalence class. On the other hand, the equivalence in structure is not devoid of meaning. It is not something that could have been shown for any set of sentences, no matter how unrelated. The structural equivalence shows that IN RESPECT TO THESE CLASSES – *S, L, I, T*, and minus – the sentences are indeed all saying the same thing; otherwise they could not all have been brought to the same form in terms of these classes. Other texts may have other characteristics, not necessarily including equivalence of sentence types.

Before leaving our sample text we must observe that the results mentioned in the last four paragraphs are only a few of those that can be obtained from analyses of this type. Nor are the particular methods used here the only ones possible. In fact, the method of determining substitutability in this paper was inadequate at several points, because of the brevity of the text; in a full-scale analysis, the frequent references to other sections of the article would not be acceptable without further justification. Both the method and its results need more discussion; meanwhile, the analysis of a sample text may give some idea of what can be done.

NOTES

[1] Italic colons represent periods between sentences of the original text; cf. *Lg.* **28**, 17, note 10a. (Paper XIX of this volume.)

[2] If we take a member of a class, say *A*, we can always find at least one other member (*B*) which at least once has the same environment that *A* has once. (They both occur before *F*, though *B* also occurs before *E*, while *A* also occurs before *G*.) Not every member of the class does this: *M* occurs only before *E* and *H*, while *A* occurs only before *F* and *G*. But if *M* and *A* have nevertheless been put in the same class, then they must at least once occur in equivalent if not identical environments. The *E* environment of *M* and the *F* environment of *A* are equivalent because both appear among the environments of some one member (*B*). These formulaic statements may be hard to apprehend intuitively; but the examples which will come out of the sample text below should make the relations clear.

[3] This is a complete and separate section of an article by L. Corey, entitled 'Economic Democracy without Statism' (*Commentary*, August 1947, 145–6). The bracketed sentences will not be analyzed here. They are of the same general structure as the others, but are left out in order to keep the present paper within reasonable limits. In a forthcoming publication of a group of analyzed discourses, this text will be analyzed in toto, so that the reader can satisfy himself as to the application of the present results to the whole text.

This text has been selected, not because it is particularly easy to analyze, but – quite the contrary – because it exhibits the problems and techniques of discourse analysis in great variety. Many discourses, such as scientific writing and conversational speech, are simpler to analyze. The first three unbracketed sentences here are particularly complicated, but the reader will find that the rest of the text is quite readily analyzable after these have been worked through.

Reprinted by permission of Nathan Glazer, Associate Editor of *Commentary*.

[4] Since this analysis is presented as an empirical attempt, each step will be justified with a minimum of theoretical grounding; and at the same time only such operations will be developed as are required for this particular text. Therefore we will not raise at this point the question whether different occurrences of the same morpheme may turn out to be homonyms belonging to two different classes of the text, and so in some sense not substitutable for each other.

[5] More generally, a sequence consisting of any segment + conjunction + another segment of the same grammatical class is replaceable by a single segment of that class ($XCX = X$). This holds whether a comma intonation encloses the conjunction + second segment or not: i.e. both for *nationalization, or socialization*, and for *nationalization or socialization*.

[6] This treatment will have to be justified in the fuller analysis of the text which will be published elsewhere.

[7] Problems of validity are raised when we draw, here and at some points below, upon substitutions which occur elsewhere in the article, outside the quoted section analyzed here. For a complete analysis we would have to treat a text long enough to contain within itself all the required substitutions.

[8] A more careful analysis of phrases beginning with *which* would show that such adjectival phrases serve as repetitions of the phrases that precede them, so that our present phrase is equivalent to (or a repetition of) *monopoly enterprises*, and therefore substitutable for it. This, with other grammatical considerations useful in discourse analysis, is mentioned in the paper cited in the first paragraph.

⁹ The inverted form is not stylistically equivalent to the original. In some cases, the derived equivalent forms are not stylistically acceptable at all. This does not nullify the use of the equivalence as an intermediate step in our analysis.

¹⁰ The boldface numbers are of course not in the text. They are used here only to facilitate reference to the sentences.

¹¹ The same is true of most occurrences of *he, it*, etc. As a simple example, consider the equivalence of *I have a dollar watch: This is all I need*, and *I have a dollar watch: A dollar watch is all I need*. Note that the plural morpheme stretches over the noun and the *th* which is a discontinuous extension or repetition of it: *I have some dollar watches: They are all I need*.

¹² *In addition to* can for convenience be replaced by some single preposition like *with*, because $NPN = N$ and $PNPN = PN$, so that PNP (such as *in addition to*) can be replaced by a single P. Further use of the $NPN = N$ formula enables us to consolidate *industry* (N_1) *with* (P) *the limitation to large-scale industry* ($N_2 = L$) into N_2 alone, that is into our L. In all these changes we have not dropped any word which figures in the analysis of this text, but have merely performed certain grammatically equivalent substitutions in order that the words which follow *socialize* might be grammatically comparable to the words which follow *socialize* in sentences (1) and (2). The fact that these words turn out to be our old L is due not to our grammatical manipulations but to the recurrence here of the same morphemes: *this* (repeating *large-scale*) and *industry*.

¹³ The reduction is effected as follows. By the laws of English grammar, a relative pronoun (e.g. *that*) plus a verb (with or without a following object) constitutes an adjectival phrase to the preceding noun: *N that V = AN (the tower that leans = the leaning tower)*. Then *would still remain a limited power state* is adjectival to the noun *state*. And *within* plus this adjectival element plus the noun *state* is a PAN phrase which is itself adjectival to the preceding nouns *diversity*, etc. An alternative method of obtaining this reduction can be based on the fact that, for a certain group V_1 of English verbs (including *is* and *remains*), $N_1 V_1 N_2$ implies that N_1 and N_2 are substitutable for each other: e.g. in *He is a man.* In the parenthetical sentence *that* (N_1) *would still remain* (V_1) *a limited-power state* (N_2), we can therefore substitute *a limited-power state* (N_2) for *that* (N_1). But by note 11, *that* merely repeats the preceding *a state*, hence *limited power state* is substitutable for *state* in the phrase *within a* ...

¹⁴ Our original sentence had *functional organizational* (A_1) *forms that promote diversity* (A'_2). On grammatical grounds we have said that the first three words here are equivalent to *forms that have functional organization*. How does this equivalence connect grammatically with what follows? If we try to insert it in the sentence, we obtain *forms that have functional organization that promote diversity*. The subject of *promote diversity* is *forms* in the original sentence and therefore here too (since we are making no grammatical alteration); this is shown by the fact that the plural morpheme (which extends over subject and verb) extends both over *forms* (in the -*s*) and over *promote* (in the third-person lack of -*s*). Our only problem now is to discover why the phrase that we obtain does not read grammatically: where is the expected *and* after *organization*? We understand this as follows. The combination of a relative (*that*) plus a verb (*have* or *promote*) whose subject is *forms* has the grammatical standing of an adjectival phrase following *forms*, which in turn has the grammatical standing of an adjective preceding *forms*: thus *forms that promote diversity* is equivalent to *forms with promotion of diversity*, or to *diversity-promoting forms*. If we mark an adjectival phrase following a noun by A', we will find that we have here changed our original A_1 *forms* A'_2 into *forms* $A'_1 A'_2$. The result reads peculiarly because we expect something like *and* after *organization*, between the two A'. But this is no problem because the occurrence of conjunctions between adjectival segments is automatic. Conjunctions or commas (marking a special intonation) occur between adjoining adjectival segments of like syntactic structure: *a long, dull book* (A, AN), or *the fellow who called and who asked for you* (NA' *and* A'). Commas sometimes but not always occur between adjoining adjectival segments of unlike syntactic structure: *a fellow I know, who asked for you* (NA', A'), but also *a fellow I know who asked for you* ($NA'A'$). Conjunctions do not

occur between adjectives preceding a noun and an adjectival phrase following the noun. Therefore, when we change ANA' into $NA'A'$ we move from a form in which a conjunction does not appear to a form in which a conjunction appears automatically. If we supply this conjunction, we finally obtain *forms that have functional organization and that promote diversity (NA' and A')*.

[15] As an example of the chain of substitutions we note the following excerpts from the bracketed sentences of our text. The first step is to show that *public enterprise* is substitutable for *public corporations*. Compare *They can and should be independent* (where the *They* follows right after *Public enterprise* and hence repeats it): *They are independent* (where the *They* follows right after *public corporations*). To complete this substitution we must show the equivalence (for this text) of *can and should be* with *are*. First, *can and should be* is equivalent to *can be* (X_1 and X_2 can be replaced by either X alone); second, *be* is the same verb morpheme as *are*; third, *can* + verb is substitutable here for the verb alone, because we have *cooperatives serve economic freedom* in sentence (8) and in the next sentence *They can serve freedom*. The remaining step is to show that *public corporations* is substitutable for *socialized industry*. We have *Socialized industry ... made to promote ... decentralization* (sentence (3)) and *They provide ... decentralization* (where *They* follows immediately after *public corporations*). The required equivalence of *made to promote* and *provide* is given by the fact that the addition of minus to either of these is equivalent to *prevent*: compare *prevent from promoting* in sentence (4) with *made to promote* in sentence (3). And compare in the bracketed sentences: *public enterprises prevent absolute centralization* ($S L - I T$), and in the next sentence *they provide diversity* ($S L I - T$); these two sentences are parallel to our 3 and 4 except that *made to promote* is replaced by *provide*. By this circuitous route we show that *public enterprise* is substitutable for *socialized industry*, which is our $S L$.

[16] As in sentence (5). In other cases, however, the occurrence of *economic* may affect the status of a word which is not itself $- T$. In one of the bracketed sentences, for example, we have *economic, not political, institutions*. Here *economic* affects the standing of the phrase. Similarly, the word *need* in *economic need* does not occur by itself (hence has no standing by itself), and it is the whole AN phrase here which equals $- T$.

[17] One might prefer to consider the words *no bar* as part of the object. This is immaterial; it would merely shift the position of two minus signs from the I to the T.

[18] The argument can be stated as follows. Given $S L I - T$ of sentence (2), let us consider the first part of sentence (6) analyzed as $S - L I no - T$ (before we represent *no* by a minus). Here we have two sentences which are equivalent except that the second contains an extra minus and an extra word (in this case *no*); and the extra word turns out to be the same morpheme as one of the members (*not*) of the class marked minus. The two sentences therefore differ only in that the second has two minuses more than the first. We repeat this analysis when we compare $- S - L - I bar - T$ with $S - L - I - T$. In this pair, minus + *bar* is substitutable for minus + *no* in the other pair. Hence *bar* is equivalent to *no*, and is a member of the class marked minus.

[19] In breaking up this sentence into two, for convenience of analysis, we leave out *since*, which, like the *hence* of sentence (1), is outside the subject, verb, and object phrases, and serves to connect sentences.

[20] Our original sentence consisted of subject + verb + [object + conjunction + object] (where brackets indicate the domain of the conjunction, as at the end of sentence (5)). This is equivalent to a double sentence: subject + verb + object, twice over. A similar equivalence was seen at the end of sentence (3).

[21] Of course, this will not apply to all sentences of this form. In some cases *VPVing* is substitutable rather for a single V: *succeed in economizing* is replaceable by *economize* alone, or the like. The specific conditions for this equivalence cannot be discussed here.

[22] Note that when *public enterprise* occurs as the subject of I it is a substituent of $S L$. When it occurs as an adjectival phrase to a $- T$ object it is simply included in the object phrase. This is an example of homonyms (in respect to substitution classes), such as were mentioned in note 4.

23 In a somewhat different way the *where* also filled these two functions, as do many *wh* and *th* words.

24 Or if we had marked *diversity* in object position as *R* (as we marked its substituent in sentence (1)), *absolute state control* would be marked $-R$ when in object position.

25 In doing this, we assume that *absolute state control* has the same relation to *diversity* in the subject position as it has in the object position of the same sentence type (group of equivalent sentences). In object position *diversity* is $-T$ and *absolute state control* is *T*. When we see that in subject position of the same sentence type *diversity* is $-S$, we take *absolute state control* in that position as *S*.

26 More exactly: if we replace *the limitation or suppression of ideas* by *T* we obtain a possible sentence of this text. Let us call an analysis of a sentence 'successful' when each morpheme in it is assigned to a substitution class in such a way that the sequence of substitution classes represented by the sentence is a sequence which occurs elsewhere in the text. Then assigning *the limitation or suppression of ideas* to *T* yields a successful analysis of our sentence, though we have not shown that it is the ONLY successful analysis.

XXI

CULTURE AND STYLE IN EXTENDED DISCOURSE

This paper will propose a method for analyzing extended discourse, with sample analyses from Hidatsa, a Siouan language spoken in North Dakota.

There are several lines of investigation which might lead one to analyze extended discourse. One such line of investigation is a direct continuation of descriptive linguistics: Descriptive linguistics yields statements about the occurrence of morphemes, words, and the like within a sentence. That is to say, it states how the occurrence of one class of morphemes (or words) is restricted in terms of the occurrence of some other class of morphemes (or words) within the same sentence. Having obtained this result, one might readily ask how the occurrence of one sentence is restricted in terms of the occurrence of other sentences within the larger discourse. It is clear that there is some restriction of this kind; for if we stop short in the course of any text, for example at the end of the present sentence in this paper, the probability that certain particular English sentences will occur next is greater than the probability that certain others will occur. (It is more probable that the next sentence here would contain certain linguistic terms, or English learned words, or that it should have assertion-intonation and be of considerable length, than that it should contain names of automobiles, or specifically colloquial words, or that it should have exclamation-intonation and be short. This has indeed just been the case.) Nevertheless, it has not in general been possible to state how the occurrence of one sentence is restricted in terms of the occurrence of another within the larger discourse. Attempts to find regular sequences of particular sentence types within a text have generally been unsuccessful.

Another line of investigation which might lead one to analyze extended discourse is the distinction between what descriptive linguistics states to be 'possible' in the language (i.e., to constitute a sentence in the language) and what is actually said. As is well known, descriptive linguistics states, for example, that a particular sentence type is a sequence of particular morpheme or word classes. However, it is not the case that every member of one

S. Tax (ed.), *Indian Tribes of Aboriginal America*, Proceedings of the 29th International Congress of Americanists, The University of Chicago Press, 1952, 210–5.

of these classes occurs in the same sentence or phrase with every member of the other class. Certain combinations of particular members do not occur, but it would be difficult to use the regular techniques of descriptive linguistics in order to yield efficient statements as to what combinations do not occur. The analysis of extended discourse may provide techniques for such investigations, since, as will be seen below, it deals with the question of what particular members occur within the same discourse.

Yet another line of investigation which might lead one to analyze extended discourse is the correlation between linguistic behavior and other social or interpersonal behavior and relations. Here lies the question of what is the difference between the languages of two different cultures; what is the difference between the uses of language of two communities which have important cultural differences but descriptively or grammatically much the same language. Here also is the question of style – what differences in use of language are to be found in different social groups, different persons, different subject-matters, and so on. If we consider the speech of people who are using different styles, or come from different cultural backgrounds, we find that the individual sentences they use may be different, but in ways that cannot be efficiently stated within descriptive linguistics. Furthermore, many of their individual sentences may be identical, but they may occur in different orders, or intermingled with different other sentences. The problem is therefore not one that can be met by the present tools of descriptive linguistics. Nor can it be met by the tools of culture analysis, since these are much too unspecific and otherwise inadequate to yield precise differentiations in language use. It becomes, therefore, a question of comparing samples of the discourse of one group, person, or subject-matter with that of another. What is needed is a body of techniques that can show precisely what are the differences between one extended discourse and another.

We consider first what type of techniques are available for the analysis of extended discourse. Since an extended discourse differs from a single sentence only in being longer, the type of analysis that is possible is on the whole similar to the type of analysis that can be made of a single sentence. In both cases, the basic requirement is that the elementary parts, say the morphemes, be unambiguously identifiable, so that we should always be able to say whether a particular part is an occurrence of a given morpheme or of another morpheme. In both cases, too, the basic operation is substitution: we ask whether a particular part or sequence of parts is substitutable for another, as the word *political* or the phrase *relatively inconspicuous* are substitutable for the word *scientific* in the sentence *We held a scientific meeting*.

One might ask: If the basic analysis here is the same as that used in descriptive linguistics, how are we to expect further results from applying it to extended discourse? The answer is the difference in the domain of application. In descriptive linguistics this analysis is traditionally used only within the limits of one sentence at a time. Except for certain parts of syntax, the linguist does not seek the relation between some part of one sentence and some part of another. At the same time, however, he obtains his results from all the sentences in his sample of the language. If he sets up a class A which occurs before a class N, that means that this order is to be found throughout his material, except in stated circumstances. Instead of all this, we can take a single body of extended discourse, and analyze it as a separate domain. On the one hand, we would then consider the occurrence of any particular morpheme not only in respect to the other morphemes of the sentence but also in respect to the other morphemes throughout the discourse. On the other hand, we would not consider morphemes as substitutable for each other if they were found to be so in other sentences of the language, but only if they were found to be substitutable in sentences of this particular discourse. We would thus obtain a grammar of this discourse by itself.

When the basic operation of substitutability is applied in this way, much of the analysis will take on a somewhat different form than in descriptive linguistics. The criteria and types of classification will be different, as also the possibilities of interrelation among the members of a class. In somewhat the same way, if we view phonology and morphology as applying the same basic operations, but to short stretches of speech and to full sentences respectively, we will find that these same basic operations yield in phonology types of classes and inter-class relations which differ from those that these operations yield in morphology, as a result of the different domains used in the two cases.

The primary operation in analyzing a text of extended discourse, then, is to set up what may be called context classes, parallel to the phonemes of phonology or the morpheme classes of morphology. Members of a context class are substitutable for each other within the text. That is to say, if in a sentence of our text we replace one word by another word of its context class, we obtain another sentence of our text. For example, if our text contains the sentence *We held a scientific meeting*, and if the words *scientific* and *annual* are members of the same context class (for our text), then our text should also contain the sentence *We held an annual meeting*.

In most texts it is impossible to find many sentence pairs of this kind, which differ in only one word. However, we will frequently find pairs of sentences within a text that will differ only in having different members of two or more context classes. For example, if we set up for our text a context class containing *held* and *heard*, as well as other words, and another context class containing *meeting* and *lecture*, we may find in our text the sentence *We heard an annual lecture.* This method can, of course, be used in such a way as to make very many sentences of a text identical in their context-class composition. Similarly, the classification methods of descriptive linguistics can be used in such a way as to make very many sentences in a given language identical in their structure: for example, all sentences of the major English type can be said to consist merely of an N sequence plus a V sequence. However, just as morpheme classes can be used in a more refined way, to give a greater number of sub-types of English sentences, so context classes can be used in a more refined way, to yield a greater number of differentiated sentence types within the text.

Once we have stated the sentences of our text as particular sequences of context classes, we find that many statements about our text become possible. We may find that many sentences, either successive ones or not, are identical in terms of their context classes. Sentences which are not identical may be partially identical in their context classes. We may then investigate the pattern of occurrence of a particular context class through the various sentences, or through the sentences of a particular type; and we may consider how the occurrence of this context class is restricted in terms of the occurrence of some other context class. We may also consider the order of the members of a context class, in the successive sentences which contain that context class.

From all these investigations, we can obtain a description of this text in terms of its context classes. We may then compare this text with others, to see whether the occurrences of context class are similar (even if the context classes themselves are not). Or we can take various texts of one person, one social group, or one subject-matter, and compare them with texts of another, in order to see what the structures of the first have in common as against the structures of the other texts. Finally, we may wish to correlate that which is common in the structures of the first group of texts with the non-linguistic behavior or relations that are common to the people who spoke or wrote them.

We now consider two Hidatsa texts, the first a narration of a culturally important public event, and the second a casual narration of some private activities of the speaker. (Both were transcribed from recordings made by the same informant, Charlie Snow, in the course of work done by Carl Voegelin and me.)

The first text[1] reports the activities of the Water Buster clan in retrieving their sacred skulls from a museum, so that they might pray to them for rain. The word *wa.'a.htu.'as* (skulls) occurs very frequently, and was taken as the starting point for context-class formation. We denote it by S. We then consider the environments of S, and notice that every sentence which contains S also contains a word ending in -c, -k, or -wa (all clause-enders, meaning final-verb, non-final-verb, and *while it is*, respectively) immediately after (rarely one or two words after, and twice immediately before). These clause-ending words contain *wa* (we) twice, I once, and the various third-person plural overt and covert forms in all other cases. Furthermore, in a few cases the verb is composed of two stems, e.g., *watawa.'a.htu.'as wahku.ci-wa.wa.ha.'ac* (our-skulls we-to-get we-want). If we now compare these two-stem cases with the cases when one or more words intervene between S and the verb, we note a parallel: *wa.'a.htu.'as aru'i.ku.ci se'ehta u.waca'as ri.ha.'awa* (the-skulls to-get for-that money while-they-put). We can say that the last three words here are substitutable for the second stem in the two-stem verbs. In one pair, the two final verbs are the same: *watawa.'a.htu.'as o.kirure iska'ac* (our-skulls to-go-after they-planned); *wa.'a.htu.'as o.kure'e iska.k* (the-skulls an-owner [for them] they-planning).

On this basis, we may form two context classes: the final verb F, which is here removed from S by an intermediate stem or word; and the intermediate stem or word I (which never have the clause-enders above; the stem differs from the word only in having no main stress). The remaining verbs (i.e., words with clause-enders), which occur immediately after S, can be shown to be substitutable for F, and are thus put in the same context class. The sentences containing S thus have the composition S (I) F, the F including a WE, I, or THEY morpheme.

We now consider the sentences which do not contain S. Some of them contain *wiripa.ti* (Water Busters) plus a word ending in -c, -k, or -wa. We place these words into one context class; since some of the members are identical with members of F, this class is substitutable for F. Other sentences have the same clause-ending words (or others), but with *ruxpa.ka* (people), *e.c.iri* (everyone), *iha* (others), instead of Water Busters. We put all these in a class W, and all the clause-ending words that occur with them into F. Finally, much the same verbs occur in clauses by themselves, and these too are put in F. The prefix THEY which occurs with these F is substitutable for W+THEY in the clauses that contain W: *wiripa.ta'as e.ca kiruwac.ihka.'ac* (the-Water-Busters all they-gathered); *kiruwac.ihka.k* (they-gathering). Hence the prefixes THEY, WE, and I, which occur with F in the sentences containing S, can also be placed in the context class W. The sentences which contain S now have the composition S (I) W-F; and the sentences which do not contain S have the composition W F, the W being in some cases only a prefix. (A few additional substitutions have to be made in order to bring certain other sentences into the W F form; but these will not be carried out here.)

The only remaining sentences or clauses are *xare.c* (it rained), *wi.k.a.rus.a ki'ahuk* (even-grass becoming-plentiful). These are substitutable for each other in their environments, and may be denoted as R clauses.

Finally, a number of sentences of all types have initial clauses ending in -*ru*, -*k*, -*wa*, and containing words which do not appear in the rest of the sentence: *wa.ra i.piraka.ci e.raha.ru* (years twenty in-the-past); *a.tawa* (in the morning); *se'eruha.k* (then).

The text as a whole is a long series of S(I)W-F clauses and W F clauses, alternating in very short groups or singly, with a few R clauses interspersed toward the end. It may be noted that there are no sentences consisting of just S plus a verb whose subject the S would be (i.e., whose prefix would be part of the S).

We now consider the second text, reporting some personal experiences. Here the majority of words end in -*c*, -*k*, -*wa*; i.e., most clauses consist of just one word, with its prefix and its verbal clause-ending. In the first three clauses the prefix is I; we mark the clauses, with their prefix, stem, and clause-ender, by I. In some of these clauses, words with zero ending (often indicating what might be called a noun) or with -*hta* (to), -*kua* (in) precede the main word; since these words can be replaced by zero, the clauses containing them will also be denoted by I: *hawa se'ehta ware.c* (then there-to I-went); *ware.c* (I-went).

The last I clause in this initial group contains the word *sehi.wa* (Chippewa): *se'eruha.k sehi.wa wa.wasiwa* (then a Chippewa I-hired). The next clause is *wa.hiric* (he works), and for five more clauses the subject of the main word is HE. We denote these six clauses by H. There follow about ten I clauses, half of them having some word in addition to the main one. In the last of these the word is *watawa.karista* (my child). The next five clauses (C) have HE for the prefix, with MY CHILD specified in two of them as the HE in question. Then follow seven I clauses, followed by five clauses (B) with third-person prefix, in the first two of which *wa.hti* (boats) is specified as the subject. Then come fourteen I clauses, in the first few of which there is reference to traveling on the boats. The last of these is *a.tawa wa.ki-waka.'ac* (in-the-morning prayer we-reached; i.e., it was Sunday). The next clause is *wa.pixupa.wa ruxpa.ka akihtia wa.ki'ati ihtiawa wa'as.ak* (on-Sunday the-people many the-prayer-house the-big-one filling). This is followed by three third-person clauses (P) with PEOPLE or OTHERS as subject. Then follow four I clauses, and eight third-person clauses with MY CHILDREN as subject.

We thus have a simple sequence of groups of clauses: I, H, I, C, I, B, I, P, I, C. Every other group is I. The groups are fairly long. In about half the transitions from one group to the following one, a side word in the last clause of a group appears as the subject of the main word in the next group.

Various additional features might be pointed out about the order of stems within each of these groups, and so on, but space does not permit.

Even this cursory presentation of the analysis of the two texts shows that considerable difference can be found between them in the way their context classes occur in respect to each other. More detailed analysis brings further differences to light. One cannot, of course, make inferences about the difference between formal and conversational narration in Hidatsa merely on the basis of this material. But if such analysis is carried out independently on a sufficient number of formal narrations, and also on a sufficient number of conversational ones, and if the common features in the structures of the first group were compared with the common features of the second, we might expect to obtain results that could be correlated with the particular social and interpersonal relations involved in these two types of activity among the Hidatsa.

NOTE

[1] This text is published in Lowie, Harris, and Voegelin, *Hidatsa Texts*, 287.

TRANSFORMATIONS*

* See the earlier Section 2.33 in Discourse Analysis, *Lg*. **28** (1952), Paper XIX ofth is volume, and the later *Mathematical Structures of Language*, Interscience Tracts in Pure and Applied Mathematics 21, Interscience-Wiley, New York 1968.

XXII

INTRODUCTION TO TRANSFORMATIONS

1. WHAT TRANSFORMATIONS ARE

Linguistic transformations can be viewed as an equivalence relation among sentences or certain constituents of sentences.

We begin with a set of sentences in a language, each provided with an analysis into constituents; these constituents in turn may be provided with an analysis into sub-constituents, and so on. The constituents are collected into classes, and we can say that a given sentence is a case of a particular sequence of constituent classes. (The interest, of course, is in such classes in terms of which a convenient description of all sentences of the language is possible.) If A_k is a sentence or constituent which is analyzed into constituent parts which are members, successively, of classes $B, ..., C$, we call the form or set A of all A_k a construction of $B, ..., C$.

We now note that if we take the set A of all constructions $B_i \, C_j$ (all constructions whose first constituent is a member of B and second a member of C), we will often find that not all combinations of $B \, C$ occur in any corpus however large; not for all i, j does $B_i \, C_j$ occur. Certain of these non-occurrences can be eliminated by an appropriate constitution of the basic linguistic elements. For example, if *The dogs – are – funny* is $\bar{N}_1 \, B_1 \, A_1$ and *The dog – is – funny* is $\bar{N}_2 \, B_2 \, A_1$, we will fail to obtain as an English sentence $\bar{N}_2 \, B_1 \, A_1$: *The dog are funny*. Since *are* occurs only if its $\bar{N}^1$ contains the morpheme[2] *s* (or contains certain listed N), while *is* occurs only if its $\bar{N}$ does not contain this *s* morpheme, we say that *are* is simply the variant of *is* when its $\bar{N}$ contains this *s* morpheme; *are* then ceases to be a separate morpheme or a separate member of B. The two sentences then become $\bar{N}_1 \, B_2 \, A_1$ and $\bar{N}_2 \, B_2 \, A_1$, and the non-occurrence is eliminated.

Quite apart from such situations, we notice that the set A will contain certain $B_i \, C_j$ combinations, while other combinations do not occur, or occur only to the accompaniment of particular responses by the speakers of the language (indicating bizarreness, etc.). If A is a construction of n constituents $B, C, ...$, we will say that A is satisfied for certain n-tuples of members of

Transformations and Discourse Analysis Papers 2 (1956), Linguistics Department, University of Pennsylvania.

these constituents $(B_1 C_1 ..., B_2 C_2 ..., B_3 C_3 ...,$ and so on) when these specific member-combinations $(B, C, ...,$ etc.) actually occur as instances of the construction A. Thus the construction $\bar{N} tV \bar{N}$ may be satisfied in a given corpus for the triples *the bomb, killed, people* and *people, saw, the bomb*, and many others, but most likely not for the triple *music, heard, hydrogen*.

It is possible to find in a language two or more constructions which contain the same constituents (in different order, or with various added material), e.g. $\bar{N}_i tV \bar{N}_j$ and $\bar{N}_j$ *is Ven by* $\bar{N}_i$ (*People are killed by the bomb*). In such cases, if the two constructions are satisfied by the same n-tuples of members of their constituents, we say that the two constructions are transforms of each other. For example, the triples that satisfy $\bar{N}_i tV \bar{N}_j$ also satisfy (in reverse order as indicated) $\bar{N}_j$ *is Ven by* N_i (e.g. also *The bomb is seen by people*, etc.); and any triples that hardly occur in the first hardly occur in the second (*Music heard hydrogen, Hydrogen was heard by music*). Also $\bar{N}_i$'s V *ing* $\bar{N}_j$ is a transform of these, being satisfied for the same triples (*The bomb's killing people..., People's seeing the bomb...*). In contrast $N_i tV \bar{N}_j$ and $\bar{N}_j tV N_i$ are not transforms of each other (i.e. the construction $\bar{N} tV \bar{N}$ is not satisfied for the reverse of triples which satisfy it): we will hardly find *The bomb saw people*, and not very likely *People killed the bomb*. (The fact that some triples satisfy both forms – *The old man sought death* and *Death sought the old man* – does not make these transforms of each other.)

Various experimental methods may be set up to determine whether two constructions which contain the same constituents are indeed transforms of each other. For example, we can ask various speakers of the language to say many examples of each construction, to see whether much the same n-tuples appear for each. Or, given a list of n-tuples which satisfy one construction, we can ask if (or in what manner) people will accept the same n-tuples for the other construction.

2. TRANSFORMATIONS AND RESTRICTED TRANSFORMATIONS

A few major transformations for English are:
1. $S_i \leftrightarrow S_j$: transformations which send a sentence of one grammatical form S_i into another grammatical form S_j.[3]
1.1. $N_1 t V N_2 \leftrightarrow N_2 t$ *be Ven by* N_1 (active and passive) as above. The t indicates the tenses (or tenses and auxiliaries such as *will, can*): t *be = is, can be*, etc.; V *en = seen, taken, heard*, etc.
1.2. $N_1 t V J \leftrightarrow N t$ *be V J'*: *She danced, She was a dancer; He writes plays, He is a writer of plays*. (J' indicates that if the object begins with N, the word *of* is inserted before it.)
1.3. $N_1 t V J P N \leftrightarrow N_1$'s *Vn t be P N*: *He arrived with great fanfare; His*

arrival was with great fanfare. (Vn indicates a verb so affixed as to occur in noun position: *arrival, arriving.*)

1.4. $N_1 t V N_2 \leftrightarrow N_2$ *is* $wh\text{-}pro\text{-}N_2 N_1 t V$: *They sought fame; Fame is what they sought.* (*wh-pro-N_i* indicates words like *what, who,* the second morpheme of which is a pronoun of N_i.)

1.5. $N_1 t V N_2 \leftrightarrow It t be N_1 wh\text{-}pro\text{-}N_1 t V N_2;$ $It t be N_2 wh\text{-}pro\text{-}N_2 N_1 t V$: *He saw the supervisors; It was he who (that) saw the supervisors; It was the supervisors whom (that) he saw.* (Appropriately different transformations exist for verb-objects other than N; and the set of these can be summarized by saying that what follows the *wh-pro-N_i* is S^-, i.e. the original sentence minus N_i, whether N_i was in the subject or in the object.)

1.6. $N t V \leftrightarrow there t V N$: *A girl appeared; There appeared a girl.*

1.7. $N t V_g N_2 P N_3 \leftrightarrow N t V_g N_3 N_2$: *I gave the book to him; I gave him the book.* (V_g: verbs like *give, show.*)

1.8. $N_1 t V N_2 \leftrightarrow N_2 N_1 t V$: *He despised the public; The public he despised.*

2. Transformations which send a sentence containing some N_1 into a form which is not a sentence (but may be considered grammatically a noun-modifier) and which is inserted into some other sentence which contains the same N_1 (usually next to that N_1), in such a way that N_1 appears only once.

2.1. $N t be A \rightarrow A N$: *Books are interesting; interesting books.* (Combined with, say, *He got some books out* to form *He got some interesting books out.*)

2.2. $N t be P N \rightarrow N P N$: *The bulbs are from Holland; bulbs from Holland.*

2.3. $N_1 t be N_2 \rightarrow N_1, N_2$: *The striker is a union member; The striker, a union member,...* (Combined with *The striker refused to move* to obtain *The striker, a union member, refused to move.*)

2.4. $N t V J \rightarrow N_i wh\text{-}pro\text{-}N_i S^-$: *The bulbs are from Holland; the bulbs which are from Holland; American cars have fins, fins which American cars have.* (These would be combined with other sentences that share the N_i selected by the *wh*-word. E.g. with *The fins are ridiculous* we obtain *The fins which American cars have are ridiculous.*)

2.5. $N_1 t V N_2 \rightarrow N_2 for N_1 to V$: *A member may propose the plan; plan for a member to propose.* (E.g. combine with *I have got the plan* to obtain *I have got the plan for a member to propose.*)

2.6. $N_1 t V N_2 \rightarrow N_1 to V N_2$: *A member to propose the plan.* (Combine with *I have found a member* to obtain *I have found a member to propose the plan.*)

2.7. $N_1 has N_2 \rightarrow N_1\text{'s} N_2; N_2 of N_1$: *The book has value; the book's value, the value of the book.*

2.8. N_1 t V $N_2 \rightarrow N_2$-$Ving$ N_1 (Compound noun): *The fascists burned books; book-burning fascists.* (Combine with *They fought the fascists* to obtain *They fought the book-burning fascists.*)

2.9. Almost all compound nouns that end in N (not Vn) are transformed from sentences (in almost all of which the order of the words is the reverse of the order in the compound), which combine with other sentences containing the last N of the compound: For example, *tube-socket* (←*the socket of the tube*←*The tube has a socket*) combines with sentences containing *socket*, e.g. with *The socket wasn't soldered* to form *The tube-socket wasn't soldered.*)

3. Transformations which send a sentence into a form which is in general not a sentence and which enters as the subject or object (or as noun-like follower of P) in another (host) sentence.[4]

3.1. N_1 t V $J \rightarrow (N_1\text{'s})$ Vn (J'): *He read the note; His reading (of) the note, The reading (of the note).*

3.2. N_1 t V $J \leftrightarrow (N_1\text{'s})$ $Ving$ J: *He ran for help; (his) running for help.*

3.3. N t $V \leftrightarrow Ving$ N: *Dogs bark; barking dogs.*

3.4. N t $V \leftrightarrow Ving$ of N: *The barking of dogs.*

3.5. N_1 t V $J \leftrightarrow N_1$ $Ving$ J: *He wrote it; [They found] him writing it;* pronominal N_1 is then in the objective case, in 3.5–8, 4.2–3.

3.6. N_1 t V $J \leftrightarrow$ for N_1 to V J: *For him to take it [is useless].*

3.7. N_1 t V $J \leftrightarrow N_1$ V J: *He took it; [I let] him take it.* (This occurs when the preceding V, in the host sentence, S_1, is *let, make, see, hear,* etc.)

3.8. N_1 t be $N_2 \leftrightarrow N_1$ N_2: *He is a fool; [I consider] him a fool.* (The host V in S_1 is *consider, call, think,* etc.)

3.9. N_1 t V $J \leftrightarrow$ (that) N_1 t V J: *He came; [I believe] that he came; [I believe] he came.* (The preceding V, in S_1, is *believe, think, know,* etc.)

3.10. N_1 t V $J \leftrightarrow$ "N_1 t V J": *He came; [I said] "He came."* If the V in the host sentence is *say, think,* etc., any sentence may appear in quotes as its object.

In 3.1–3.5 the basic change consists in replacing the t by ing; in 3.6 t is replaced by *to*. In all of type 3, the whole transformed (nominalized) sentence occupies the position of an $\bar{N}$ in the host sentence, which is thus incomplete unless this $\bar{N}$ position is filled.

4. Transformations which send a sentence into a form which is in general not a sentence, and which is adjoined as modifier to another sentence:

4.1. N t V $J \rightarrow N$ $Ving$ J: *The hour is late; The hour being late [, we left].*

4.2. N t V $J \rightarrow$ with N $Ving$ J: *Everyone ran forever; With everyone running forever [we felt something was wrong].*

4.3. *N t be J→with N J: The war was over; With the war over [, things improved].*

4.4. Here can also be added the conjunction (*and, because*, etc.), comparative (*-er than, as...as*, etc.), and cross-reference words (*each other*, etc.) which show one sentence as adjoined to another.

In addition to these regular transformations there are very many transformations which are limited to particular lists of words or special conditions. Most of these restricted transformations are members of a few fixed transformation schemata.

3. KERNEL

We have seen that a sentence form (whether independent, or combined with another, or included as an $\bar{N}$ inside another sentence) can be considered the transform of some other sentence form. When homonymous sentences are suitably distinguished, this is an equivalence relation, and a sentence form may be a transform of several other forms (as is seen above). However, we can select a base set of sentence forms, in such a way that each sentence form of the language will be a transform of one or another of this base set. For the data covered in 2 above, it would be sufficient to select $N t V$, $N t V N$, $N t V P N$ (and so for other types of verb object), $N t V_g N$ to N, N is A, N is $P N$, N is N, N has N.

Each sentence covered by this analysis would then be factored into transforms of the base sentence forms. E.g. *The boy came* is a base form itself (i.e. the identity transform of $N t V$). *The comet was seen by everybody* is the 1.1 transform of $N t V N$ *(Everybody saw the comet)*. And *The book was shown him by the dealer* is the product of two transforms of a base sentence: 1.1 of *The dealer showed him the book* which in turn is 1.7 of *The dealer showed the book to him*. Furthermore, *He's taller than you* is the sum of one (host) sentence (*He's tall*)+a comparative conjunction *-er than*+a transform of another (host-related) sentence (*You are tall*). Finally, *The barking of dogs disturbed him* is the sum of *Dogs bark* (in transform 3.4)+ $\bar{N}$ *disturbed him*. And *The bulbs from Holland arrived* is the sum of *The bulbs are from Holland* (in transform 2.2)+*The bulbs arrived*.

In this way, every sentence can be analyzed as the sum (with particular connectives) of one or more base sentences, each undergoing one or more transformations (including the identity transformation, which leaves a base sentence unchanged). The transformations thus provide a factorization of all sentences; and if certain degeneracies (homonymities) can be properly marked, they provide a unique factorization of the set of sentences (thus marked). The set of transformations is thus a quotient set of the set of homonymity-marked sentences. If we map the set of sentence forms on the set of transformations, those sentence forms which go into the identity transformation are called the kernel of the set of sentence forms.

The language structure then consists of a set of kernel sentence forms (or sentences) and a set of transformations. All sentences of the language are obtained by applying one or more transformations to one or more kernel sentences, in accordance with stated rules of application. It is possible to select the kernel in such a way as to maximize the simplicity of the total description of all sentences in these terms.

4. APPLICATIONS

Transformations are of interest for structural linguistics – for the theory of language structure, for operational investigations in it, for a treatment of homonymities and other problems in language analysis, etc. Partly independently of this, they seem to have a range of applications in areas where language or linguistic structure are involved (either as an object or as a medium of investigation). For example, since languages are much simpler in their kernel sentences than in their full sentences, translation may be procedurally simplified if the material to be translated is first reduced to kernel sentences, and then the kernel sentences are translated. This is particularly relevant since languages seem to be more similar to each other in their kernel sentence forms than in their final resultant sentences (after transformations). More interesting is the possibility that transformations are less well remembered than kernel sentences. This is to say, if people hear a discourse (a string of sentences), there is reason to think that they are more likely to remember the kernel sentences which were involved than the actual form of the sentences as heard (i.e. the form which resulted from the operation of various transformations upon the kernel sentences).

NOTES

[1] All constituents are understood in respect to their construction. Hence $\bar{N}$ here is the $\bar{N}$ of the construction $\bar{N} B A$.

[2] A morpheme is the basic element of morphological structure of a language. (The whole linguistic discussion here is within morphology.) Morphemes can in turn be obtained by a particular relation among phonemes or sound-types (these being the basic elements of the phonological structure of language). However, for our present purposes it will suffice if we take them as the primitive elements in terms of which the constituent structure of our set of sentences can most simply be stated. At one stage of approximation, then, we have as morphemes *is, are, dog*, and *s* (the last having variant forms in certain environments, such as *en* after *ox* and change of *a* to *e* after *man*—to yield *men*). The decision as to what is a morpheme (and whether two parts like *en* after *ox*, and *s* elsewhere, are variants of the same

morpheme) is made not on the basis of meaning but on the basis of how simple is the description of all constructions in terms of these morphemes.

[3] In general, if *D* (adverbial phrases, e.g. *entirely*) or *P N* (preposition + noun phrases, e.g. *at this time*) occur with *V* in a sentence, they also occur in its transform. The symbol *J* is used below for the object of a verb.

[4] (*X*) means that *X* may occur or may be omitted (deletion). *J* indicates whatever may be the object of the preceding verb: zero, *N*, *P N*, etc. Square brackets contain the host sentence.

XXIII

CO-OCCURRENCE AND TRANSFORMATION
IN LINGUISTIC STRUCTURE

0. SUMMARY

This paper defines a formal relation among sentences, by virtue of which one sentence structure may be called a transform of another sentence structure (e.g. the active and the passive, or in a different way question and answer). The relation is based on comparing the individual co-occurrences of morphemes. By investigating the individual co-occurrences (§ 1.2; § 2) we can characterize the distribution of certain classes which may not be definable in ordinary linguistic terms (e.g. pronouns, § 2.6). More important, we can then proceed to define transformation (§ 1.3), based on two structures having the same set of individual co-occurrences. This relation yields unique analyses of certain structures and distinctions which could not be analyzed in ordinary linguistic terms (§ 3). It replaces a large part of the complexities of constituent analysis and sentence structure, at the cost of adding a level to grammatical analysis. It also has various analytic and practical applications (§ 5.7), and can enter into a more algebraic analysis of language structure (§ 5.2, 4, 6) than is natural for the usual classificatory linguistics. A list of English transformations is given in § 4. The main argument can be followed in § 1.11 (Co-Occurrence Defined), § 1.2 (Constructional Status), § 1.3 (Transformation Defined), § 2.9 (Summary of Constructions), § 3.9 (Summary of Sentence Sequences), § 5 (The Place of Transformations in Linguistic Structure).[1]

1. THE METHOD OF ANALYSIS

1.1. *Individual Co-Occurrence*

The range of individual co-occurrence of a morpheme (or word) i is defined first of all as the environment of morphemes (or words) which occur in the same sentences with i (in some body of linguistic material). This is indeed the initial information available for morphological structure. Given utterances or sentences and given the morphemes, we can say that each morpheme i has

Presidential address, Linguistic Society of America, 1955. *Language* 33, No. 3 (1957), 283–340.

the particular morphemes j, k, ... as co-occurrents in the sentences in which i appears. Each morpheme has a unique set of co-occurrents (except for special morphemes such as some paradigmatic affixes which all occur with the same set of words and in the same sentences).

The individuality of morphemes in this respect makes it difficult to set up any compact description of a language. However, some morphemes have very similar (though not identical) sets of co-occurrents: thus, the set of co-occurrents for *cloth* – e.g. *The ( ) tore, The ( ) was torn, Get me a ( ) quick* – may have many morphemes in common with the set for *paper*, certainly many more than with the set for *diminish*. This suggests that morphemes can be grouped into classes in such a way that members of a class have rather similar sets of co-occurrents, and each class in turn occurs with specific other classes to make a sentence structure. In structural linguistics this classification is not set up on the basis of relative similarity of co-occurrents, but rather on the basis of a particular choice of diagnostic co-occurrents: *cloth* and *paper* both occur, say, in the environment *the ( ) is* (i.e. after *the* and before *is*), where *diminish* does not appear; we call this class N. And *diminish* and *grow* both occur, say, in *It will ( )*, where *paper* and *cloth* do not; we call this class V. The diagnostic environments (stretches of co-occurrents) are chosen in such a way that the resulting classes permit compact statements about co-occurrence. For example, *cloth, paper, diminish, grow* all show some differences in their environments, so that no simple summary can be made. But in terms of the classes N and V we can say that every N occurs before some V in the environment *the ( ) V*, and every V occurs in the environment *the N ( )* for some N.

When we proceed to describe the structure of sentences (i.e. the choices of morphemes that occur in a sentence) in terms of these classes, we find that the work is of manageable proportions. In the sentences of any given language, only certain sequences of classes (set up as above for that language) will be found; and these sequences which constitute the sentences can be described as the products of a small number of elementary class sequences (constructions) which are combined in certain stateable ways; for instance, the class sequence T N P N V (*The fear of war grew*) results from the elementary class sequences T N V and N P N by the substitution operation N P N = N.[2] This compact description of sentence structure in terms of sequences of classes is obtained, however, at a cost: statements such as N P N = N or 'T N V is a sentence structure' do not mean that all members of N P N have been found in the same environments as all members of N, or that all sequences of members of T, N, and V in that order have been found as sentences.

On the other hand, to describe a language in terms of the co-occurrences of the individual morphemes is virtually impossible: almost each morpheme has a unique set of co-occurrents; the set varies with individual speakers and with time (whereas the class combinations are relatively permanent); it is in general impossible to obtain a complete list of co-occurrents for any morpheme; and in many cases a speaker is uncertain whether or not he would include some given morpheme as a co-occurrent of some other one. Individual co-occurrence is thus not just the limiting case of morpheme classes, where the number of members per class is one. Classes are essentially different because they are defined by a diagnostic environment, chosen to yield a class-sequence structure.[3]

1.11. It follows that individual co-occurrence cannot be used, as indeed it has not been used, as the basic element of morphological construction. Even for discussions of individual co-occurrence itself, it is convenient to use the framework of classes and constructions. This leads now to an adjusted definition: For classes K, L in a construction c, the K-co-occurrence of a particular member L_i of L is the set of members of K which occur with L_i in c: For example, in the A N construction found in English grammar, the A-co-occurrence of *hopes* (as N) includes *slight* (*slight hopes of peace*) but probably not *green*. The K-co-occurrence of L_i is not necessarily the same in two different K L constructions: the N-co-occurrents of *man* (as N_i) in N_i *is a* N may include *organism, beast, development, searcher*, while the N-co-occurrents of *man* in N_i's N may include *hopes, development, imagination*, etc.

1.2. *Constructional Status*

Although, as we have seen, individual co-occurrence cannot be used directly in discovering morphological relations, we do not have to disregard it (as we do in structural linguistics). In spite of the impossibility of obtaining complete or definite co-occurrence data, we can still consider various indirect questions (absolute or relative), such as whether a particular morpheme or class has some special property in its co-occurrence set, or how the co-occurrence sets of two classes or class sequences compare. Such questions can fit into the class structure because each co-occurrence check would be within stated classes and constructions (by the adjusted definition); and the results can be then phrased as new statements, again about classes and constructions, as will be seen below. From the point of view of structural linguistics, this amounts to asking one of the few types of outside questions that are still relevant to it, for these are questions which are couched in terms of the raw data of structural morphology (the occurrence of morphemes in sentences), and which lead to additional information about inter-class relations, yet which had not been asked in the original study of class environments.

Individual co-occurrences can be expressed in structural terms by saying that they are the values for which a structural formula is satisfied. That is, if we regard each statement about constructions (N P N=N, or T N V=S) as a formula which holds when particular morphemes (or sequences of them) occur in the positions indicated by their class marks, then we can say that the particular combinations of morphemes which co-occur in various instances of a construction are those which satisfy it (i.e. those for which the formula holds).[4]

We consider now the major applications of individual co-occurrence data within constructional morphology.

Given a construction (which is recognized by its place within larger constructions, up to a sentence), we can see some relations or different statuses among the participating classes by noting details of class occurrence for each class. For example, given the A N construction (*slight hopes*), we note that it is substitutable for N alone but not for A alone: both *slight hopes* and *hopes* occur in *Their ( ) faded*. We can express the constructional equivalence A N=N by defining in the place of these two a composite construction (A)N, with the parentheses indicating occasional omission; and in this new construction we can say that N is the 'head', meaning that it always is present when the construction occurs. Another kind of differential status for the classes in a construction is seen when one class has a correlation between its subclasses and some other element in or out of the construction (grammatical agreement); e.g. when nouns have each a particular gender suffix while the neighboring adjective takes whichever gender suffix the noun has. (Again we might say that the noun is the 'head'.)

To these considerations, the data about individual co-occurrence add a new factor. We note that in T A N V (*The slight hopes faded*) each N_i has a specific set of V-co-occurrents which is hardly affected by the preceding A, while A does not (the V-co-occurrents of each A_i depend on the following N). Thus N is that class in the A N construction which has fixed co-occurrence sets outside. Considerations of this type are available also in cases where the previously mentioned differentia of status are absent: in the construction N v V (noun plus tense or 'auxiliary' plus verb: *It faded, It grows, We may swim*) both V and v are always present, but each V_i has fixed N-co-occurrents (*hopes may grow*, but probably not *hopes may swim*), while each v_i occurs with any N that is in the co-occurrence set of its V, and with no other.

All these considerations together (the position, co-occurrence ranges, and other properties of classes or subconstruction with a construction) determine what we may call the constructional status or relation of each participating class or construction in a (larger) construction. We find various types of status in respect to individual co-occurrence: in Vv neither class has restricted co-occurrences (each v_i occurs with all V, and each V_i with all v), but in V P (*chalk up, tie up, tide over*) both have. In A N each class has fixed co-occurrences in the other, but only N has fixed co-occurrences in the neighboring V. The types of constructional status are useful in characterizing each construction, and in analyzing various less obvious constructions (§ 2).[5] Many of them serve to explicate intuitively-known grammatical relations: in the A N type one says that A modifies N. Finally, the types of constructional status themselves are partly determined by investigable conditions, such as the size of the participating classes.

Aside from the matter of constructional status there are certain subclasses of the major classes which are characterized only by peculiarities of their individual co-occurrence (§ 2.6).

1.3. *Transformations Defined*

In addition to investigating the types of co-occurrence for various classes in a construction, as in § 1.2, we can compare the co-occurrences in two different constructions which contain the same classes. In many such constructions, as in N's N and N *is a* N above, the co-occurrences are different. In some constructions the co-occurrences are about the same, and it is for these that transformations will be defined.

If two or more constructions (or sequences of constructions) which contain the same n classes (whatever else they may contain) occur with the same n-tuples of members of these classes in the same sentence environment (see below), we say that the constructions are transforms of each other, and that each may be derived from any other of them by a particular transformation. For example, the constructions N v V N (a sentence) and N's V*ing* N (a noun phrase) are satisfied by the same triples of N, V, and N (*he, meet, we; foreman, put up, list;* etc.); so that any choice of members which we find in the sentence we also find in the noun phrase and vice versa: *He met us, his meeting us...; The foreman put the list up, the foreman's putting the list up ...* Where the class members are identical in the two or more constructions we have a reversible transformation, and may write e.g. N_1 v V $N_2 \leftrightarrow N_1$'s V*ing* N_2 (and the set of triples for the first = the set for the second).[6]

In some cases all the n-tuples (the choices of one member each out of the n classes) which satisfy one construction (i.e. for which that construction actually occurs) also satisfy the other construction, but not vice versa. For example, every triple of N_1, V, and N_2 in the N_1 v V N_2 'active' sentence (with some exceptions discussed below) can also be found, in reverse order, in the N_2 v *be* V*en by* N_1 'passive' sentence: *The kids broke the window, The window was broken by the kids; The detective will watch the staff, The staff will be watched by the detective.* However, some triples satisfy only the second sequence and not the first: *The wreck was seen by the seashore*. Such cases may be called one-directional or nonreversible transformations: $N_1 v V N_2 \rightarrow N_2 v$ *be* V*en by* N_1 (and the set of triples for the second includes the reversed set for the first). In some cases a transformation appears nonreversible because of some particular circumstance (such as the homonymity in the two *by*-constructions here), or because one construction is much less frequent (so that some word choices are not found in it), or the like. It may then be possible to formulate it as a reversible transformation with restricted conditions.

There are also cases in which many or most but not all of the n-tuples that satisfy one construction also satisfy another; such constructions are then not transforms of each other, but may have some kindred relation (§ 4.5). Finally, at the other extreme, if two constructions of the same classes have no n-tuples in common, so that any word choice which satisfies one fails to satisfy the other, we have yet another relation of linguistic interest.

Since transformations are based not on the absolute contents of a set of co-occurring n-tuples, but on the similarity between the sets for different constructions, we do not even require a yes-or-no decision on whether any given n-tuple is in the set. We can accept graded decisions, and we do not even have to assert that any particular n-tuple never occurs. For example, the formulation might be that to the extent that any n-tuple satisfies $N_1 v V N_2$ it also satisfies N_1's V*ing* N_2: *he, meet, we* certainly in both forms; *moon, eat, cheese* doubtfully or for particular environments in both forms; *soup, drink, abstraction* hardly at all in either form.

There may be differences in some respects between the sets satisfying two constructions, without precluding a transformational relation. For example, all or certain ones of the n-tuples may be less frequent or natural in one construction than in another. Differences of this kind need not restrict the transformation, if they can be indicated in an adequate manner.

As to the differences between the same-class constructions – for there must of course be differences between them – these may consist of difference in order, or in individual morphemes (affixes or words), or in added small or large classes. If it is impossible to specify which members of the added classes occur in each instance of the constructions, the statement of the transformation remains incomplete (§ 4.5).

One condition (mentioned above) which requires some discussion concerns the sentence environment in which the constructions are being compared. If the rest of the sentence, outside the constructions under consideration, is not taken into account, then for example N V*ed* and N *will* V would be transforms of each other; for the same pairs of N, V occur before -*ed* as with *will* (*The cliff crumbled, The cliff will crumble*). If, however, it is required that the rest of the sentence be identical, these are not transforms, for -*ed* and *will* differ in some of their more distant co-occurrents: *The cliff crumbled yesterday* but *The cliff will crumble tomorrow*. There are various reasons for excluding such pairs as -*ed* and *will*. One is that this yields transformations that can be usefully distinguished from the direct constructional operations, such as the combination of classes Vv, or the combining of T and -*s* 'plural' with N (§ 5.6). Another reason is that the meaning difference in pairs like -*ed*/*will* seems much greater than that which is characteristic for transformations (see below).[7]

The general requirement can be stated as follows: no domain (section of the sentence or the like) to which the two constructions are grammatically connected may admit co-occurring morphemes for one of the constructions which are not admitted for the other. Thus the adverbial position at the end of the examples above is connectable both to N V*ed* and to N *will* V (both N V*ed* D and N *will* V D are grammatical sentence formulas); therefore it would have to admit the same members in both cases, if these two are to be transforms. The effect of this requirement is to make the identity of co-occurrence stretch over the maximal grammatical domain, i.e. to preclude any inequality (restrictions) of co-occurrence that would narrow down what the grammar permits. In this sense the requirement safeguards the characteristic of transformations, which is to have no co-occurrence restrictions that are correlated with the difference between the two constructions (i.e. with zero as against *be* ... -*en* ... *by* plus reverse order in the active/passive, or with -*ed* as against *will* in the present rejected case). Note that this formulation does not contravene the transformational standing of N v V N and N's V*ing* N, even though the sentence environment of the latter is lacking in the former. The latter, being a noun phrase, is always connected to the remaining constructions of its sentence (*We're uncertain about his meeting us; The foreman's putting the list up caused the wildcat*). But these additional sentence-parts cannot be connected to N v V N since that is a sentence in itself, hence their absence here is due to grammatical conditions and not to any inequality of co-occurrence.

The consideration of meaning mentioned above is relevant because some major element of meaning seems to be held constant under transformation. There may be differences in meaning between two constructions that are transforms of each other, due to their external grammatical status: e.g. the fact that N v V N is a sentence while N's V*ing* N is a noun phrase. There may be differences of emphasis or style, as between the active and the passive. And certain transforms have specific meaning differences associated with the specific morphemes they add, as between assertion and question. But aside from such differences, transforms seem to hold invariant what might be interpreted as the information content. This semantic relation is not merely because the same morphemes are involved. For example, *The man bit the dog* (N_2 v V N_1) contains the same morphemes as *The dog bit the man* (N_1 v V N_2), but it describes quite a different situation; and N_2 v V N_1 is not a transform of N_1 v V N_2, for many triples satisfy one but not the other (*The citizens destroyed the barracks* and *The bystander reported the accident* will hardly occur in reverse order). In contrast *The man was bitten by the dog* (N_2 v be V en by N_1) describes more or less the same situation as *The dog bit the man*, and is a transform of N_1 v V N_2, as seen above.

The determination and explication of this meaning relation is no simple matter, and will be only touched upon in § 5.7. But it points to one of the major utilities of transformational analysis.

1.4. *Determining the Evidence*

To establish the transformations in any given language we need methods, and if possible an organized procedure, for seeking (§ 1.41) what constructions may contain identical co-occurrences; these methods should if possible be general, but additional ones may be based on special features of the language. And we need methods of checking (§§ 1.42–3) the co-occurrences in each construction, so as to see if they are indeed identical.

1.41. *Domains of Transformation*

To find domains that may be transforms, we need to consider only constructions, since it appears that a given class has specifiable relations (restrictions) of individual co-occurrence only in respect to constructions, e.g. the relations appear between the head A class and nonhead class of a construction (N and A respectively in A N), or between the head of construction c and the head of construction k when c + k in turn constitute a larger construction (N head of the noun phrase and V head of the verb phrase in the sentence T A N + V v D, *The new girl laughed loudly*). There are no co-occurrence relations between the A and the D here, these being two nonheads in the two constructions; but there is such a relation within the adjective phrase D A, where the A is the head (*partly new*). These domains may, however, be sequences of constructions, as when we wish to compare the sentence sequence T N_1 V_2. T N_1 D V_3 T N with T N_1 *who* V_2 D V_3 T N_4 (*The king abdicated,* ⁂ *The king soon resumed the throne* vs. *The king who abdicated soon resumed the throne*).

The constructions must of course contain the same classes, the co-occurrences of whose members are to be checked; in the case of construction sequences some of the class members (indicated by class symbol with subscript) may occur twice, as the repeated N_1 in the last example above.

The search for same-class constructions may become complicated, especially in languages where different class sequences can substitute for each other in the same constructions; for example, the position of A in the A N construction can be occupied also by N na (making it N na N *childish laugh*), so that if we seek constructions containing two N we have not only N *is* N, N P N (*Pines of Rome*), and the like, but also the Nna N case of the A N construction.

The conditions of search may be different according as the morphemes which are added in one or both constructions (added to the classes that are same in both) are affixes or words, and according as they are uniquely specified morphemes, members of a small class, or members of a large class. For if the two constructions are expected to be transforms, the added material should not restrict which class members are going to occur; for example, in comparing $A_1 ly A_2$ (*exceptionally large, undesirably noisy*) with $A_1 A_2 ness$ (*exceptional largeness, undesirable noisiness*) we might as well ask at the start if *-ness* occurs with all A (or with all of a specifiable subclass of A); for if it does not, then various values of A_2 will be lacking before *-ness* while present in the other construction; i.e., the other construction will be satisfied by some values which will not satisfy the *-ness* construction. Affixes are more likely, in many languages, to occur with only a restricted number of particular members of their neighboring class, so that constructions containing them often have other co-occurrences than same-class constructions which do not contain them. Among the affixes that do not restrict the members of their neighboring class are what are called paradigmatic affixes, such as tenses; however, such affixes often restrict word choices elsewhere in the sentence, as in the case of *-ed* and *will* above.

Given these considerations, there are various ways of collecting sets of tentative transforms. One can simply select sequences of morphemes and seek the same combinations in other constructions. One can go through the types of class construction in the language – affixings, compound words, word constructions, sentence sequences; eliminate those in which the added material introduces unique restrictions on the main classes; note which constructions contain the same classes (with changes of order or additions), or have subtypes with the same classes (like the N na N subtype of A N); and chart each set of same-class constructions in some manner convenient for checking which of them have the same co-occurrences satisfying the same classes. One can make a preliminary test by choosing a wide semantic and morphological scatter of n-tuples satisfying one n-class construction and seeing if this arbitrary group also satisfies the other constructions of the same classes. Finally, one can go through some texts in the language, and for each construction or sequence of them ask what other combination of the same major morphemes would be substitutable (acceptable to author or reader) in the same place in the text.[8]

1.42. *Obtaining Co-Occurrence Ranges*

To check whether the co-occurrences are identical in two n-class constructions (suspected of being transforms), we obtain a list of n-tuples which satisfy the first construction and ask about each one whether it also satisfies the second; and vice versa. Or we hold constant $n-1$ members of an n-tuple, and ask for a list of members of the nth class satisfying the first construction and a list of members of that class satisfying the second. For example, to test N_1 v V N_2 and N_2 v *be* V*en by* N_1, we begin, say, with *The cat drank* ( ) and ask for a list of words that would fil out thel sentence, and then we offer ( ) *was drunk by the cat* and ask for a list of words that would fill out that sentence.

Such checking of individual co-occurrences is not practicable without an informant, i.e. a more or less native speaker of the language. It is impossible to survey everything that has been said or written in a language, even within a specified period. And if we wanted a sample that would serve for the language as a whole, we would need an impracticably large body of texts or other material. Work with an informant can be carried out under partly controlled conditions by various methods of eliciting, i.e. by presenting him with linguistic environments which favor the appearance of utterances relevant to our investigation, without influencing him in any way that might bring out utterances which would not sometimes occur naturally. Instead of wading through masses of speech and writing in search of the co-occurrents of *The cat drank*, we present this environment to a speaker and obtain a whole list. One has to guard, of course, against various factors which might bring out co-occurrents that would not occur outside the eliciting situation.

It is possible in various ways to control the validity of the elicited results for the language as a whole. Different informants may be asked for parallel lists, or one may be asked to fill one construction while a second fills the other. The validity of the lists as a sample of the co-occurrence range for the whole language may be checked by letting the sample grow: we may obtain a list of 50 items for *The child saw* ( ) and 50 for ( ) *was seen by the child*, and then an additional 50 each, and see if the two lists become more nearly identical as they grow, or – more relevantly – if the similarity increases faster with the growth of these lists than is the case when we build up two lists for *The child saw* ( ) and ( ) *saw the child*.

1.43. *Testing for Identity of Co-Occurrence Ranges*

In these applications, eliciting is like ordinary observation, i.e. hunting about for occurrences of our constructions, except that here the relevant data are concentrated. Questions of validation, statistical or other, are essentially the same as for ordinary observational data. However, eliciting can also be used to test whether a particular co-occurrent is acceptable, something which enables us to check whether the two sets of n-tuples satisfying two constructions are identical or only increasingly similar; observation and ordinary eliciting can only indicate similarity. In this test-eliciting we take the co-occurrents observed for one construction but not obtained for the other, and ask the informant whether he would say them or has heard them. This is a very different type of experimental condition. It involves new and great sources of error, due to the suggestiveness of the material presented to the informant, or due to his own response to the unusual linguistic situation. There are also uncertainties in the result: the informant may say that he is not sure, or his response may reveal unsureness. And the results involve a new measure: degree or type of acceptability (natural, uncomfortable, nonce-form); for example, if we are testing co-occurrents of ( )ish, an informant may be uncertain about *grandfatherish*, consider *deepish* uncomfortable, and *countryside-ish* a nonce-form, and reject *uncle-ish* or *wise-ish* outright.

Since we cannot test all the co-occurrents of each construction in the other, we try to test a wide variety, checking to see if any relevant subclass satisfies one but not the other. Thus we may test co-occurrents of widely different meanings, or of different morphological structures: in comparing A N and N *is* A, we may test not only A but also A aa like *largeish*, N na like *childish*, and V va like *speaking*. We may test any co-occurrents which seem to be peculiar, or metaphoric, or productive, to see if they also occur in the other construction. We may thus find the specific co-occurrents which are actually rejected (not merely have not been found) for one of the constructions; these co-occurrents become diagnostic for saying explicitly that the two constructions are not transforms.

1.44. *Summary*

We may say, then, that to determine transformations we need to find same-class constructions which seem relevant, collect and compare the co-occurrences in each, and test to see if differences between them are upheld. If one construction is less frequent (e.g. the passive as against the active), it is usually more convenient to begin with this, and test to see if all its co-occurrents also satisfy the more frequent construction. It is of interest to note whether the relative frequency and the relative acceptability (from natural to nonce) of the co-occurrents are similar in both constructions, and to see if we can list or characterize those co-occurrents which have not been found (or have been diagnostically rejected) in one construction as against the other.

The results can often be summarized in a chart of same co-occurrence, which organizes all the different constructions that exist for a given set of classes keeping constant the same co-occurrences, where the set is satisfied in all the constructions by the same set of members.

2. CO-OCCURRENCE AS A STRUCTURAL PROPERTY

2.0. Just how much grammatical knowledge is needed before transformations can be investigated depends in part on how much work is put into discovering the transformations. It may be enough merely to identify the morphemes and to have a constructional analysis of the simpler sentence types (as in § 5.4). For the present formulation, however, we will assume the whole of the usual structural grammar of the language, in order not to have to distinguish parts which are not needed.

2.1. *Dependent Elements in Constructions*

While some parts of grammar may not be needed, it is helpful if the parts which are used (e.g. the morpheme classes and the major constructions) have a very detailed analysis; for then the transformations are more apparent. This means a detailed investigation of how the occurrence of one morpheme or sequence (or stress or tone) in a sentence depends on the occurrence of some other in the same sentence or nearby, so that a change in one is accompanied by a change in the other. For example, if we offer an informant the utterance *The letter was returned* ⨯ *It must have been misaddressed* and ask him to substitute *The letters* for *The letter*, it is almost certain that he will also substitute *They* for *It*. If we get as many tense substitutions as we can in the sentence *The dog bit me as if he had been a man* we will probably find some tense combinations lacking, indicating some dependence between the two tense morphemes in this position. Some elements are completely dependent, as the *my* (or the *I*) in *I saw myself.*

In general, we can express certain dependent occurrences within a construction by a single discontinuous morpheme: Given *this book* but *these books*, and *The refugee became my friend* but *The refugees became my friends*, we can say that there is a discontinuous -*s* 'plural' which occurs after both A and N of the A N construction, and after both N of the N *is* N construction (and after just N when it occurs alone). This is preferable to saying that there are two occurrences of -*s,* but that each appears only if the other does. Similarly, given *I see* but *He sees*, and *You know* but *The child knows*, we can say that every N except *I* and *you* has another discontinuous -*s* (variant of 'present') which appears after the N V construction if there is no -s 'plural' after the N.

In contrast, when we find dependent occurrence between two neighboring constructions, it may be more useful to say that a given element has occurred twice (i.e. that the two constructions have an element in common), than to say that a single element extends discontinuously over both constructions. One such case appears when a morpheme in one construction varies with a corresponding morpheme in the other: *I saw the doctor whom you by-passed* but *I saw the book which you by-passed*; similarly *The letter ... It ...* and *The letters ... They ...* above.[9] Here we can describe the dependence by saying that *-om, -ich, it* are positional alternants of *doctor, book, letter* respectively, in the positions illustrated. That is, in *I saw the N_i wh( ) you by-passed*, the ( )*om* and ( )*ich* are variant forms of certain N_i, and in the experimentally varied sequence *The N_i was returned* ( ) *must have been misaddressed*, the *it* is a variant form of the N_i.

Another type of dependence between two constructions appears when construction c (in the neighborhood of construction k) never contains a particular morpheme or class which is present in k. In such cases, if c is a unique construction in the grammar, whereas c plus the absent morpheme or class would be an otherwise known construction, we may say that the morpheme or class in question indeed occurs in c but in the form of a zero; that is, when the morpheme or class in question occurs in both c and k, its variant form in c is zero. We thus avoid having a unique construction in c. For example, in *The shelf is wider than the closet* we may obtain an additional A (with intonational change), as in *The shelf is wider than the closet is deep*, but the A will not be the same as the preceding one (*wide*). We can then say that, if there is no second A, a zero variant of the morpheme *wide* occurs at the end of the original sentence; so that although *wide* is the one A that seems not to occur there, we so to speak explain this by saying that *wide* is already present but in a zero form. Since *more than* and ( )*er than* occur in general between two whole sentence structures (*He knows more than I know, The shelf is wide* + ( )*er than* + *the closet is deep*), having just an N after ( )*er than* would be a unique construction for that position: *The shelf is wide* + ( )*er than* + *the closet*. This unique construction is avoided by saying that the morphemes *is wide* of the first sentence structure are present also in the second construction, so that the second is also a sentence structure. Note that this satisfies the meaning of the sentence, which indeed refers to the width of the closet.

This explanation is useful even when there is no dependence to be analyzed as a double occurrence. For example, in constructions like *I know whom you by-passed* or *Whom did you by-pass?* the V *by-pass* is never followed by an object N, though elsewhere it is. We can then say that *whom* — or, for other reasons, just the ( )*om* — is itself the object N_2 of *by-pass*, so that ( )*om you by-passed* becomes the well-known construction N_1 v V N_2 with the N_2 moved up. We avoid having unique constructions like *you by-passed* without object N.

These few examples will illustrate without further discussion the kind of detailed analysis which is entirely in terms of classes and constructions.[10] It will be found useful for what follows, in several respects. First, it helps specify the domain of a construction, or of what one might call a grammatical relation: *The one who knows doesn't tell* and *The ones who know don't tell* show that both V (*know, do*) carry the discontinuous -*s* of *The one*. Second, it shows the type of many obscure constructions, by eliminating some morphemes (as being discontinuous parts of others), discovering the presence of some (as alternant forms of others), and assigning some to known classes (by comparing their constructional status, e.g. for the -*om* object). For example, the sentence last cited seems to be a new complex construction N_1 *who* V_2 V_3, with both V connected to the same N; but analyzing -*o* as an alternant of the preceding N reveals two N V constructions, $N_1 V_2$ and -*o* $(= N_1) V_3$, without denying the fact that both V are related to *The one*. Third, the present kind of analysis separates out various relevant subclasses. For example, the plural morpheme extends over both N in N *was* N, N *seemed* N, etc. but not in N *saw* N (*The refugees saw my friend, The refugees saw my friends*). This puts *is, seem, become*, etc. into a special V subclass.

2.2. Considerations from Co-Occurrence

We now proceed to take into consideration, as a correction upon the class-construction grammar, any data of interest concerning the individual co-occurrences of members of each class.

Individual co-occurrence can be used even to identify a morpheme (or word) in cases where the phonemic composition does not suffice (i.e. in homonymity). For example, *flight* can be identified as *fly* plus a vn suffix and also as *flee* plus a vn suffix. Which of these it is in a given appearance depends on whether its co-occurrences in the sentence (or even beyond) conform to those of *fly* or to those of *flee*: in *rocket flight* we have the same co-occurrence as in *the rocket flies*; in *flight from danger* we have it as in *flee from danger*; and in *flight of the Polish crew to Denmark* we can match both *flew* and *fled* in *the Polish crew* ( ) *to Denmark*. Here indeed both identifications – and both meanings – are simultaneously operative. Somewhat analogously, we can consider the morphemic division of, say, *joker* and *hammer*: these are both N, *joke* and *ham* both exist as V, and V + er = N, so that one might ask if *hammer* is ham + -*er*. However, the co-occurrences of *joker* generally conform to those of *joke* (*He is a joker* and *He jokes* both occur before *even on serious subjects*, or *in the old slapstick style*, etc.), which is not in general the case for *hammer* and *ham: It is a hammer* but *He hams*; ( ) *for heavy construction* as against ( ) *instead of answering seriously*.[11]

The use of individual co-occurrence in investigating constructional status has been mentioned in § 1.2. This can be used to check or carry further the constructional results of § 2.1. For example, it follows from the methods of § 2.1 that *-om* or *-ich* are alternant forms of their preceding N_i and are at the same time objects of the V_j following (i.e. have the same grammatical relation to the V_j as does N_k in the N V_j N_k construction). This is supported by the fact that the N_i preceding *-om* N V_j or *-ich* N V_j is indeed one of the N_k co-occurrents of V_j: we can find both *doctor* and *book* in *He by-passed the* ( ).

Some constructions which have the same classes are nevertheless distinguishable by co-occurrence. For example, in such constructions as *The strain made him speak* the second V will always be one of the co-occurrents of the second N (in an N V sentence) but not necessarily of the first: *speaks* occurs after *He* but hardly after *The strain*. We can therefore say that N_2 is the subject of V_2, and that N_1 V_1 N_2 V_2 contains an N_2 V_2 sentence-construction.

The methods touched upon in §§ 2.1–2 will now be applied to obtain certain grammatical analyses in English which will be particularly useful in the subsequent statement of English transformations.

2.3. *P N and D*

Only the most relevant distinctions about these two constructions will be mentioned here. There are many subclasses of P and of D which differ in position relative to other classes, and in type of co-occurrence with the members of these other classes. Among P, for example, *to* occurs before all V morphemes as well as before N; *of, at, from, into, for* have constructional relation only to their following N; *in, up, over,* etc. have constructional relation either to following N (*walk up the hill*) or to preceding V (*slice the meat up*). Among D, *very* occurs only before A or D, *quite* also before P N, *downward* etc. after V, A*ly* before A*ly*, A, or V, and after V, and often at the beginning of a sentence. Occasionally sequences P P occupy the position of one P (*over to the side*).

Of the members of P which occur after V, particular V P pairs co-occur (*think it over* but not *think it across*). The construction P N, in contrast, has very few restrictions on co-occurrence within it; but here the interest attaches rather to the co-occurrences of P N as a unit with other parts of the sentence. P N occurs directly after N with minor restrictions of co-occurrence: many but not all N P N triples occur (*time of day, store near the corner*).

Analogously after V: many but hardly all triples satisfy V P N (*leave at night, pass in a rush*). Certain P N occur in any of several sentence positions, initially or finally or between the N and the V, often separated by comma intonation; these seem to have no co-occurrence restriction to the N or to the V (*At this point he thought it over*). The P N after N are similar in constructional status to A before N, and there is a partial similarity in the co-occurrence restrictions (where we can get the same classes in both, e.g. N_1 na N_2 and N_2 P N_1 *wooden table* and *table of wood*; but not for *wooden smile, kind of wood*). The other P N, after V and in several sentence positions, are similar to D in constructional status and again partially in co-occurrence restrictions.

Some sequences require more detailed constructional analysis: V P N may be V P+N (*slice up the meat*, also *slice the meat up*) or V+P N (*crawl up the bank*, but not *crawl the bank up*); similarly for V P P N, etc. And in V N_1 P N_2 the N_1 P N_2 may be a unit as above, i.e. it may be one of the triples which satisfies N_1 P N_2 in any position; the usual case then is a V N_1 pair plus an N_1 P N_2 triple (*receive reports of unrest*). Or N_1 P N_2 may be a triple which hardly occurs except after this V (or certain V); then it may be a V N_1 pair plus a V P N_2 triple (*take the child to the laboratory*).[12]

Within N P N there are several different types which are relevant to transformations. Certain N pairs which occur in N_1 P N_2 also occur in N_1, N_2 (i.e. with only comma intonation between them) or in N_1 *is* N_2; in these cases the sentence environment which occurs around N_1 P N_2 can often also be found around N_1 or N_2 alone: *I like the job of sorting; I like the job; I like sorting; The job is sorting; This job, sorting, ...* Similarly *They moved toward the goal of greater production; The goal is greater production*, etc. We might call these parallel N P N.[13]

By contrast, the great majority of N_1 P N_2 triples do not satisfy the other formulas above; and the sentence environments of these N_1 P N_2 will be found around N_1 alone but not in general around N_2; cf. *This raised hopes for a settlement* and *This raised hopes*. N_1 has the same external co-occurrents as N_1 P N_2, but N_2 does not. In other respects too the N_1 is the head of the construction, e.g. only the N_1 participates in discontinuous morphemes that reach outside the construction: *A list of names is appended; Lists of names are appended; Hopes of peace are rising*. The P N_2 here has a constructional status (and co-occurrence pairing with N_1) somewhat similar to that of A; we may call it the P N=A type.

In some N_1 P N_2 triples the head is N_2. That is, it is N_2 and not N_1 that occurs in the same sentence environments as the whole N_1 P N_2; and in many of these it is the N_2 rather than the N_1 that gets the discontinuous morpheme which extends to the next construction: *A number of boys were arguing; Lots of color brightens it; A part of the Moguls were illiterate*. Here it is the N_1 P that is similar in status and co-occurrence to A, and the type may be called N P=A.

There are certain N_1 *of* N_2 (to be called reversible) which also occur in reverse order N_2 P N_1 (with P being *of* or some different P) in the same sentence environments. The N_1 here is usually one of a roughly stateable subclass including *set, type, group, class: This type of bacteria grows readily; Bacteria of this type grow readily* (it is not claimed that the meanings are identical); *A clump of some villagers was milling about; Some villagers in a clump were milling about.* Reverse order in same environment (usually with change of P) also is found for some of the preceding types: *A great number of boys were arguing; Boys in great number were arguing.*[14]

For the P N=A type of N_1 P N_2, and to a lesser extent for the other types, we can often find the same triples appearing in the construction N_1 *is* P N_2: *The hopes are for a settlement; This type is of bacteria, The bacteria are of this type.* However, certain triples cannot be obtained in the latter construction: *point of departure, time of day.* These are often the cases which seem more 'idiomatic'; they may be called compound N P N, akin to compound words. A related close-knit sequence is the P_1 N_2 P_3 N_4 in which the P_1 N_2 P_3 occurs throughout in the same individual sentence environments as a single P: *He phoned in regard to a job; They won by dint of a fluke.* The N_2 P_3 N_4 members of this construction do not occur in N_2 *is* P_3 N_4, and some do not even occur together except after P_1. The analysis here is not $P_1 + N_2$ P_3 N_4, but P_1 N_2 P_3 (=compound P, compare the P P compounds mentioned above)+N_4.

2.4. *C*

Members of the class C (*and, but, more than,* etc.) have in general the property that they occur between two instances of the same construction. Given an utterance containing C, it is in general possible to find a construction X immediately before C and a construction Y immediately after C, such that X and Y have the same status within the next larger construction; examples are *a pale but cheerful face*: two A within an N phrase; *the low wages and long hours in Detroit*: two A N sequences within an N phrase; *The low wages and the long hours were the chief causes*: two N phrases within a sentence; *Either I go or you go*: two sentence structures within a sentence. This means that both X alone and Y alone can occur in the same structural environment as X C Y: *a pale face, a cheerful face.*[15] In some cases it seems as though we do not have identical constructions on both sides of C: *I'll take the first and you the second; We got there on time but not he; He came, and fast; He's bigger than you.* In § 3.1, however, it will be seen that the shorter construction in each case contains zero forms of morphemes which are visible only in the longer construction, and precisely enough zeros to make it the same construction.

It has been pointed out[16] that the positions in which C occurs can be used to test the immediate constituents of a structure, that is the successive breakdown of a structure into the next largest constructions which are included within it. The two conjoined subconstructions have the same constituent status in the larger construction. For example, we have *He shingled and painted the roof.* The immediate constituents of *shingled the roof* are *shingled* and *the roof*; for *painted the roof* they are *painted* and *the roof*; and the two constituents *shingled* and *painted* are joined by C within their common next-larger construction ( ) *the roof.* But we do not have *He climbed to and painted the roof.* The immediate constituents of *climbed to the roof* are *climbed* and *to the roof*.

In addition to the equivalence in external status for both constructions, the two constructions around C are in general accepted more comfortably in English when their internal structure is similar: *bigger and better* rather than *big and better.* But this does not apply when junctures separate off C plus the second construction: *big, and better,...*

Not only the class environments, but also the individual co-occurrences of X and of Y alone are often the same as for X C Y. This holds for certain members of C: *and*, many occurrences of *or*, etc. Even for *and* there are certain pairs of X Y which do not occur singly in the same individual environments in which they occur together: *She and I don't see eye to eye; Sugar and water make syrup; It rocked to and fro.* These pairs, or certain properties of them as a subclass, can be investigated, in order to distinguish them from all the others. There are great differences, both in this and other respects, among the various C.

2.5 *v (Auxiliaries)*

If we compare *He paints, He painted* with *He doesn't paint, He dóes paint, Did he paint?, Only then did he paint, I painted and so did he,* we see that in the presence of certain conditions (*not*, emphatic stress, question intonation, etc.) V + its suffix is replaced by *do* + that suffix + V; and that in a subset of these conditions (question, or after certain words) *do* + the suffix further changes places with the preceding N. If we consider that the main V here remains *paint*, it will not be easy to explain the occurrence of *do* here. If we consider that the main V in the altered sentences is *do*, with *paint* as some secondary element (as it is e.g. in *He learned to paint*) the grammar will be simpler. But it will turn out that the individual sentence environments in these altered sentences will be identical with those where *paint* is the V, even though in the altered sentences the V is now *do*. This is not the case in other sentences where *paint* is a secondary element: the individual sentence environments around *doesn't paint* are closely related to those around *paint*; but for, say, *learned to paint* we can find environments where *paint* might not occur, such as *He learned to paint from the impressionists*.

If now we compare *He will paint* with *He will not paint, He will paint, Will he paint?, Only then will he paint, I'll paint and so will he*, we see that under the same conditions the V + auxiliaries (*will, can*, etc.) do not change, except that in the subset of conditions mentioned above the auxiliary changes place with the preceding N. This and other considerations which will appear in §§ 2.5, 6 suggest that the *-s, -ed* be considered affixes of *paint* even after they move in front of it, and that the *do* which precedes them be considered not a morpheme at all but only a phonemic carrier for the suffixes when they do not have their V before them. (The suffixes occur only after a phonemic word, and interchange in position with V leaves them without a phonemic word.)

On this basis we can now analyze the forms which have neither suffix nor auxiliary: *They paint, They do not paint, They dó paint, Do they paint?, Only then do they paint, We paint and so do they*. We say that there is a zero suffix (variant of the *-s*) after the V *paint*, which moves in front of the V under the conditions indicated. Like the other suffixes, this zero is always attached to a preceding phonemic word, and here receives the carrier *do*.[17]

There are now two different interchanges of position ('inversions'). One is that the suffixes *-ed* and zero (with variant *-s*) of V appear in front of V under all the conditions of the type illustrated above; they then have the carrier *do*. The other is that both of these suffixes and also the auxiliaries *will, can*, etc. appear in front of the preceding (subject) N in the subset of conditions exemplified above. The first inversion simply brings the suffixes over to the auxiliary position, when certain elements (including the emphatic) come before the V.[18]

The class v has the following properties: (1) each occurs with each V; (2) V never occurs without some v or other, nor v without some V (apparent exceptions will be discussed in § 2.63, § 2.7); (3) each v may have some restrictions as to the separable D, P N in its sentence (e.g. *-ed* will hardly occur directly with *tomorrow*); (4) but aside from such restrictions, which apply to a given v equally for all V, the individual sentence environments of each V remain the same no matter what the v. Note that this is not the case for, say, *learned to paint, learned to talk*, where the sentence environments differ in various ways from those of *painted, talked*.

The first and third of these three properties also apply to the constructions in *He is painting, He has painted, He has been painting*. All constructions of this type can be described by saying that between the v and the V there occur, sometimes but not always, *have ( )en, be ( )ing*, or the first of these followed by the second; the empty parentheses mark the location of the following V word (including *have* and *be*). Then *He paints, He can paint* have v V; *is painting, may be painting* are v + *be* ( )*ing* + V; *has painted, had painted, will have painted* are v + *have* ( )*en* + V; *has been painting, could have been painting* are v + *have -en* + *be -ing* + V. These constructions may be viewed as expansions of v, constituting v-phrases of which the v proper is the head.[19]

2.6. *Pro-Morphemes*

In class-structural terms the traditionally recognized category of pronoun cannot be defined. *I, he, this*, etc. are members of N by their class environments (e.g. all occur before V to make a sentence), but no adequate further distinction can be found for them. However, in terms of individual co-occurrence they are a distinct group. If we ask for the V-co-occurrents following *which* in *The bird which* ( ) or *I spotted the bird which* ( ), we will find, in both cases, a list including *sang, flew, fluttered, was shot*, etc. If we ask for the V-co-occurrents following *The bird* ( ) we will obtain a similar list (and can elicit an identical list). If we ask for the V-co-occurrents of *which* in *The wall which* ( ) or *I was watching the wall which* ( ), we will get *cracked, collapsed, was repainted*, etc., and this is also the list for *The wall* ( ). In general, the V-co-occurrents following *which* (those V whose subject is *which* by the methods of § 2.1), in each sentence in which *which* appears, equal the V-co-occurrents of the N immediately preceding the *which* in that sentence.[20] Now consider the fact that *which* may occur after any member of a particular (nonhuman) subclass of N. If we ask what is the total list of V-co-occurrents that follow *which* in all of its appearances (i.e. in any sentence whatever), we will see that it equals the total V-co-occurrents of all the members of its subclass. In one or another appearance of *which* we may find any V-co-occurrent of *bird*, or of *wall*, or of *book*, etc. Analogous properties will hold for other words traditionally called pronouns.

We can now generalize. There exist morphemes whose X-co-occurrents (for each class X in constructional relation to them), in each sentence, equal the X-co-occurrents of a morpheme (of class Y) occupying a stated position (or one of several stated positions), relative to them, in the same sentence (or sequence of sentences), and whose total X-co-occurrents in all the appearances of these morphemes equal the sum of the X-co-occurrents of all the members of the class Y (which occupies the stated position relative to them). Such morphemes will be called pro-morphemes of the class Y, or pro-Y. If the Y position with the same X-co-occurrents (roughly what is called the antecedent position) is uniquely determined, the pro-Y will be called bound. If it is not completely determined, the pro-Y may be called indeterminately bound; in this case we cannot tell definitely to which antecedent the pro-Y 'refers'. The pro-Y can be viewed in each sentence as a positional (variant) form of its antecedent in that sentence, as was done for *-om* and *-ich* in § 2.1.[21]

2.61. *Pronouns*

The morphemes *he*, *I*, etc. which appear as pro-morphemes of the class N usually occur indeterminately bound, so that one cannot specify without investigation which preceding or following N has the same range of co-occurrents: *Mark came too late; Carl had taken his painting and gone off.* In many cases this pronoun is not bound at all, that is, it does not have the co-occurrence range of (and does not refer to) any N in its neighborhood, as in a story in which a character is never referred to except as *he*. Such pro-morphemes may be called free; they lack the pro-morpheme property of having antecedents, but possess the other property of having a co-occurrence range equal to the sum of co-occurrence ranges of a stateable class (N). This is equivalent to saying that in each appearance of a pronoun, including a free pronoun, one can always find some noun of its subclass that could substitute for it, i.e. could be found in its position in that sentence.[22]

One can study, for each structure that contains pro-morphemes, the degree and type of uncertainty in their boundedness (in the location of their antecedents), by such structural methods as their participation in discontinuous morphemes (*the man* will not be an antecedent for *they*), by the restriction of some pro-morphemes to particular subclasses (*the man* is not an antecedent for *she*), and by testing the co-occurrence ranges of the pro-morpheme and its putative antecedents.

Some pro-morphemes have stateable antecedents only in very few structures. For example, *I* and *you* have N, *he*, or *she* as their antecedents, but only when in particular quote positions: N *said 'I...', ...said to* N *'You...'*; and they are replaced by *he* or *she* when the quote intonation is replaced by *that*: N *said that he...* In addition, *I* and *you* replace each other in the question-answer sequence.

In some cases, a small set of pronouns covers (between them) the whole N class, each member of the set having only some subclass of N as its antecedent: *he* and *she* and *it*. Other pronouns range over the whole N or some subclass of it: *this, that, some, another, everyone*, etc.[23]

All these are (with some individual differences) pro-morphemes of the full N-phrase (including N-phrase P N-phrase=N-phrase: *The book of old songs... It...*). This is a way of stating the fact that we do not find, for example, *the* or *old* before *it*, or *of songs* after *it*. These are therefore pro-N-phrases, and are members of the class N-phrase rather than of the class N. Hence *he, this*, etc. include T within them (i.e. they constitute a recurrence, or a variant form, of some neighboring N-phrase with its *the, a, some*, etc.), and this gives them an individuating semantic effect. That is, in *The man ... he...*, the pro-morpheme *he* indicates a recurrence not merely of the morpheme *man* but of the particular *man* individuated by its article *the*.

In addition, *one* occurs as a pro-N (except for mass nouns), not a pro-N-phrase: *He bought a large painting, but I'd prefer a small one; As to exams, the hardest ones are still to come.* There are also zero pro-N, whose antecedent is always in another sentence structure: *Her hair is lighter than her brother's* (where *hair* may be repeated in full, or by zero pro-N); *The people tried but soon gave up* (where *the people* recurs after *but* in the pro-N-phrase *they* or zero).[24]

2.62. *The wh-Pro-Morphemes*

If we consider *who*[25], *which, what, where, when, why*, etc., we find that they can all be described as occurring in a specific position, namely before a sentence structure S_2 which lacks some particular constituent. The methods of § 2.1 show that the *wh-* word has precisely the status of this constituent.[26] Furthermore, since *wh-* is common to all these we extract it as a morpheme which indicates this construction as a whole, while the residues of each *wh* word are morphemes each with the specific constructional status of the section that is lacking in S_2. The *wh-* itself then precedes a complete S_2 (made complete by inclusion of the post-*wh-* element). In the thus completed S_2, *-o* is subject N-phrase, *-om* object N, *-ose* is N's (which is a member of A), *-ich* and *-at* are N or A (A if an N follows, as in *which books, what books*), *-ere, -en, -ither*, etc. are P N, and *-y* (of *why*) can be taken as P N or C S (subordinating conjunction plus sentence).

There are three main positions in which the whole *wh-* + S_2 occurs: with question intonation, as adjective-phrase after nouns, and as object or subject of another sentence. The list of post-*wh-* morphemes is slightly different after each of these.

wh- S*?: Who took the book?, Where did it go?, Where did it come from?, From where did it come?.* Here the post-*wh-* pro-morpheme is free, except that it will be shown in § 3.3 to parallel (and to be pro-morphemically bound to) the corresponding N, P N, etc. in the accompanying assertion (*It went to the right*). The *wh-* here may be viewed as a member of the class of sentence introducers or connectors.

In the other two positions, *wh-* + S_2 is imbedded within another sentence S_1.

N *wh-* S_2 (excluding *what, why*) occurring in any N-phrase position within S_1; the post-*wh-* morpheme filling any N (or, in the case of *-ere* etc., any P N) position within S_2; *The villagers who escaped reached home; He picked a* *flower which had dropped; I met the fellow whose papers I found; In the place which I mentioned.* P preceding *wh-* goes with the post-*wh-* morpheme in S$_2$: *From the place in which I stood* (*-ich* pro-N of *the place*); it parallels *wh-* + P N: *From the place where I stood* (*-ere* is P plus pro-N of *the place*). In each case the post-*wh-* pro-morpheme is bound to the immediately preceding N word as antecedent (or if N P N precedes, then to one of these N). Within its following S$_2$ the post-*wh-* morpheme can fill any N or P N position. Like other bound pro-N-phrases, the post-*wh-* pro-morpheme refers to the same individual as its antecedent. The *wh-* S$_2$ can be viewed as an A-phrase of the preceding N (like *The villagers escaping from the camp reached home*); and when it is separated off by comma intonation it has the co-occurrence characteristics of a descriptive A (*The villagers, who had escaped,...*; see § 3.8). The *wh-* in this construction can therefore be considered an sa morpheme (i.e. a morpheme which is added to a sentence and yields an adjective), or as a conjunction C between the two sentence structures (*The villagers reached home* and *The villagers escaped, I met the man* and *I had found the man's papers*).[27]

wh- S$_2$ as subject or object: Here the post-*wh-* pro-morpheme is free, with no antecedent, and fills a place in its S$_2$. In *wh-* S$_2$ V, the *wh-* S$_2$ is subject of V: *What happened is history; Where I went is irrelevant.* In N + object-requiring V + *wh-* S$_2$, the whole *wh-* S$_2$ may seem (by co-occurrence comparisons) to be the object of the preceding V: *I saw who was there.* The *wh-* here may be viewed as an sn morpheme, making an S into a subject or object N-phrase. For other cases, however, it is simpler to say (as perhaps can also be said for the cases above) that S$_2$ is not the object or subject of S$_1$, but an independent sentence which shares a free pro-morpheme with S$_1$: *I found what you lost* being *I found* N$_i$ (*-at*) + *You lost* N$_i$ (*-at*); the *wh-* is then a conjunction.[28] In P *wh-* N and *wh-* P N, the N is shared, but the P belongs to either or both of S$_1$ and S$_2$ depending on whether their V require P. P only in S$_2$: *I know with whom he sat; I know whom he sat with* (*I know -om* + *he sat with -om*); *I know where he sat* (*I know* + the pro-N part of *-ere*; + *He sat* + the P part of *-ere* + the pro-N part of *-ere*). P only in S$_1$: *I cooked with what* (*ever*) *we had* (*I cooked with -at* + *We had -at*); *I kept looking for what he had come with* (*I kept looking for -at* + *He had come with -at*); but in *wh-* P N (*-ere* etc.) the P is hardly ever excluded from S$_2$. P in both: *I cooked with what he had cooked* (*I cooked with -at* + *He had cooked with -at*); *I stayed where we had lived previously* (*I stayed* + *-ere* as P plus pro-N + *We had lived previously* + *-ere* as P plus pro-N).[29]

2.63. *Pro-V*

If we compare *I'll go if you will* with *I'll go if you will go*, we see that *go* can have a zero variant in its second occurrence; this zero is analogous to, say, *-o* as second-occurrence variant of *the man* in *the man who*, and satisfies the conditions for being called a pro-verb. In all cases like the short form above, the one V (*go*) is in the V-co-occurrence for both N (*I, you*), and is the antecedent of the bound zero pro-morpheme at the end. The auxiliary v may be different (*I'll go if you can't*) or the same, but in any case it occurs in full in the second part, so that the pro-morpheme covers only the V and not v+V (there is no *I'll go if you*). When we consider *I left when he did*, we understand (on the basis of § 2.5) that this is the same construction: after the second N there is no V (*did*) but only the *-ed* tense (member of v) with a carrier *do*. The pro-V here is not *do* but zero, as in the other members of v. We find the tenses and other auxiliaries intermingled in *I left so that he would, I can go if they did*. We therefore analyze *I can* not as N+V but as N+v+zero pro-V, the antecedent V being usually present in the neighborhood. This accords with the absence after *can* and the like of the third-person *-s* which is found after all V.

The zero is actually a pro-morpheme of the V-phrase, including V P constructions, the object N and V+P N 'indirect object': *I'll go up if you will, He likes the 19th-century but I don't*. It is possible to have a pro-V with an object different from the antecedent; but in that case the auxiliary is included and we have a pro-vV: *I got the first copy and he the second*.[30]

In some constructions we can find, beside a full recurrence of the antecedent or a zero pro-V, also *do it, do that*, and *do so* as pro-V: *I'll buy some pictures* (or: *I'll go over*) *if you will ( ) too*. But after *so* as a separate morpheme, the pro-V is zero: *I went over and so did he* or *and so will he*. All these too are pro-V-phrase, and have the internal structure of a V+object. The original object can then recur as P N of the pro-V-phrase: *They repaid Tom; They did it to him but not to me*.

After *wh-* the pro-V is *-at ... do: I don't know what he will do* or *What will* (or *did*) *he do?* (the 'antecedent' in the following answer may be *He disappeared, He sold the books*, etc.).

These pro-V are usually bound, the antecedent appearing in another sentence structure within the same sentence, or sometimes farther away in the neighborhood. Some of them also occur free: *Wait, I'll do it; He does it with a flourish*. All these contrast with *do* as a direct member of V: *This will do; When did you do the carvings?; I did them last summer*. (Note that the pro-V *do it* has no plural *do them*.)

Specific constructions have specific pro-V. For example, in *He'll manage better than I* we have full recurrence (*than I'll manage*), zero pro-V (*than I will*) and zero pro-vV (*than I*). In *Some spoke French and some German* we have full recurrence (*spoke German*) or zero pro-vV. In *I'll go rather than have you go* we find full recurrence and any pro-V except zero (*than have you do it*).

2.64. *Pro-A, pro-S, pro-N-Pair*

A few morphemes satisfy the conditions for being pro-morphemes of A: *this, that*, and a number of words like *aforementioned, other*; also the second morphemes in *which, what*.

Of greater interest are the pro-S. In certain constructions and sentence sequences, *this, that, it, so*, zero, etc. operate as pro-S (or rather as pro-morphemes of S made into an N-phrase). The antecedent S (or nominalized S) is often immediately preceding. The pro-S can always be substituted by the antecedent, in nominalized form: *I'll go down there myself – that should do it (My going down there myself should do it)*; *I don't like him – Why so?* (or *So I see*); *He said he didn't do it, and I believe it* (or *I believe he didn't do it*). And the-*y* of *why* may be considered a pro-C S: *Why would you choose it? – I would choose it because it's easy.*[31]

Among other pro-morphemes, we might note the crossreference words. These occur as object of two N and a V, when otherwise the two N occur as subject and object of that V: *Men and women marry each other*, but *Men marry women* and *Women marry men*. The *each other* may then be viewed as a promorpheme of the N pair, distributing them in respect to the V.

2.7. *Two-V Constructions*

Constructions including two V (*let go, want to have met, stop going*, etc.) are complicated in their details, and cannot be completely structured without the aid of transformations. For our present purposes we will only note the main types and characteristics, omitting many details. Constructions with *to* V, V*ing* occurring alone (*The first problem is learning; To learn is not enough*) will be considered not here but in § 4. In many of the constructions considered here and in § 2.8 only certain members of V occur, so that complicated overlapping subclasses of V are determined by these forms, i.e. by whether they may be followed by V, *to* V, V*ing*, V N N, N, etc. In all cases the second V lacks the v (tenses or auxiliaries) though in some cases it may have the expansion of v, such as *be* ( )*ing, have* ( )*en*.

In all these cases both V are in the co-occurrence range of the preceding N. If we find, for example, *The dog came running, The clock stopped ticking, The boy tried to cough*, and *The clock began again, ticking loudly*, we can also find not only *The dog came, The clock stopped*, etc. but also *The dog ran, The clock ticked, The boy coughed*, etc. Both V are in the co-occurrence range of the first N in N V N, V*ing* (sometimes even without the comma): *The clock tolled the hour, ticking loudly*; but not for a sequence N V N V*ing* that never admits of a comma (*The stranger heard the clock ticking*), where the second V is not necessarily in the co-occurrence range of the first N. It follows from this that in constructions of the first types indicated above, there is a particular constructional relation between the first N and each of the V. This relation could be expressed by saying that N is the subject of each V, or perhaps by saying that the two V form a composite V phrase whose subject is that N.

We consider first the constructional relations in the simplest case, where this problem does not come up: *The phone-call reminded me to be rushing off, He saw the car stalling on the tracks, He saw the car stall on the tracks.* Here the first N is (in general) in the subject range only of the first V, and the second N is so for the second V. At the same time the second N is in the object range of the first N V. The first V is always a V that can be (or always is) followed by object N. Furthermore, when the second N happens to be the same person as the first, it is replaced by a pronoun + *self*, as is general for a same-person object: *I reminded myself to go.* When the second V happens to be the same as the first, it recurs in full, not in pro-V: *I remind you to remind him.* This is the only two-V form that has a regular passive: *The car was seen by him stalling* (or: *to stall*) *on the tracks.* We may call this the $N_1 V_1 N_2 + N_2 V_2$ type; the V_2 is of course a complete V-phrase, with or without an object N.

We next consider *I remember the dog barking there, His mates admired his speaking out, We let the water flow, I like children to behave.* Here the first N is subject of the first V but not of the second (the second V is not necessarily in the co-occurrence range of the subject N); the second N, however, is the subject of the second V. Furthermore, the first V is always one that can occur with object N; many of these first V (e.g. *like*) occur always with object N. So far, the relations are the same as in the preceding type. The difference, however, is that the second N is not necessarily one which is in the object range of the first N V; note *The scare made the girl scream.* Even where the second N is in the object range of the first N V, discourse analysis methods may show that it is not so in the given sentence, and this will in general fit our intuitive sense of the meaning: the person with opinions about behaving, above, probably does not like children. Since something in the sentence has to have the status of object to the first N V, we can say that if it is not the second N, then it is the whole second N V, writing the whole as $N_1 V_1 (N_2 V_2)$. While we cannot compare the co-occurrences of this whole class of $N_2 V_2$ pairs with objects elsewhere, we find many of them, when their structure is an N-phrase, occurring as object of the very same $N_1 V_1$: *I like children's behavior, I remember the dog's bark* (or *barking*); the sequence *his speaking out* above can be analyzed as it stands as an N-phrase.[32]

A related construction is seen in *He avoided working, The longshoremen wanted to strike.* Here both V are in the range of the N as subject, and we might think of a two-V phrase. Since in the previous construction, however, we generally fail to find cases where the second N is identical with the first, we can say that the examples before us are simply those cases of the previous construction where the second N is the same as the first. That is to say, when the second N is identical with the first, even as to specific individual, it is (in general) represented by zero: *I wanted to write* is $N_1 V_1 (N_1 V_2)$ while *I wanted you to write* is $N_1 V_1 (N_2 V_2)$.[33]

We now consider the constructions where we find in the position of *to* also *in order to, so that,* and other sequences: *I need a ladder for you to paint the wall* (also: *in order for you to paint the wall*). Here not only the second V (as in the previous construction), but both V, are complete V phrases, each with its object if it is a V that in general occurs with objects. Hence there is no problem of seeking some part of the second N V which may be object to the first. Each N is, by co-occurrence ranges, subject of the V after it. We can see this type therefore as two conjoined N V structures, even though they are connected by words like *for* (which we might not expect as conjunctions), and even though the second verb has *to* instead of v. We may write it $N_1 V_1 C N_2 V_2$.

We further find *in order to* and the like substitutable for *to* even without a subject N for the second V: either because there is no second N at all (*I rose to speak*), or because the second N is object of the first V and is perhaps not in the subject range for the second V: *I need a ladder to fix that spot, I want a book to read*). Here too we note that the preceding construction in general lacked cases in which the second N is the same as the first, and we can say that in general when the second N denotes the same individual as the first it takes a zero form. The second V then has as subject a zero recurrence of the first N, and is indeed always in the co-occurrence range of the first N. This is $N_1 V_1 C N_1 V_2$.

There remain some sequences V *to* V, and V V*ing* which are not easily regarded as such $N_1 V_1 + N_1 V_2$ combinations. This is because we have these with a single N_1 but cannot obtain them naturally with N_2; hence we cannot say that the zero is an N which happens to be the same as the first: *I'll go to sleep* (we can hardly match this with *I'll go for him to sleep* or the like), *We begin to observe* (no *We begin for someone to observe*), *He tried to stop, He tried stopping, I'll go on doing it.* These constructions contain a small subclass of V in their first position, and this subclass may be considered an auxiliary V which is added to many (though not necessarily all) V to make a larger V-phrase. The second V is the head of this V-phrase, since the rest of the sentence fits characteristically into the co-occurrence range of the second V rather than of the first. These auxiliary V + *to* or + *ing* are indeed somewhat similar to the *is+ing*, except that the latter occurs with all V, and also that it precedes these auxiliary V.

2.8. *V N N Constructions*

Two chief types of constructions seem to have two object N after the V. In one of these, e.g. *give the fellow a book, ask him a question*, the first N is always one which also appears in the P N range of that V (*give to the fellow, ask of him*); the second N may be one which is not in that range (*give tone to a book*, but hardly *ask P a question*).[34] Only a small number of V, the subclass V^a, occur with such two object N.

A very different group is seen in *The oil magnates made Harding president, The committee named him an honorary member, We found the barn a shambles*, etc. The V here, in general different from V^a, comprise a subclass V^b. Neither N is necessarily in the P N range of the V. The distinguishing property is that the two N are always in each other's co-occurrence range (in the same order) for the construction $N_1 V^n N_2$ (where V^n is a V subclass including *be, become, seem, remain*, etc.). That is, we can find sentences *Harding is president, He became an honorary member, The barn remained a shambles*. Furthermore the two N participate jointly in discontinuous morphemes which extend beyond a structure, such as *-s* 'plural': *He named them honorary members*.[35]

There are various constructions related to this one. Many members of V^b occur also with A or P N in the position of the second object N: *They made him enthusiastic, We consider him too unserious, The staff found him in poor health*. Other V, outside V^b, occur with A (and not N) in this second 'object' position: *throw the door open*. Some members of V^b and some other V occur with *as, to be*, etc. between the two N, and the second N position may be occupied by V*ing* as well as by A or P N: *I see this as their only hope, We regard them as progressing satisfactorily, We consider him to be too unserious*.[36]

In the passive, there are two forms, both with the first N as passive subject: *He was named an honorary member by the committee* and *He was named by the committee an honorary member; He was found (to be) in poor health by the staff* and *He was found by the staff (to be) in poor health*. The first form is similar to the passive of V P constructions (N+V P+N): *He took the project over, The project was taken over by him*. In both cases the second member after the V (*an honorary member* and *over*) comes right after the V in the passive, when the first member, *he* and *the project*, appears as subject. However, in the V N N case there is the alternative form with the second member separated from the passive verb (*named by the committee an honorary member*), which does not exist for the V P+N case (there is no *was taken by him over*). The same two passive forms occur for V N D: *He shut the door quietly* has *The door was shut quietly by him* and *The door was shut by him quietly*. The passive placing of second post-V members seems therefore to be a general property, and does not imply that all similarly placed second members have the same constructional status. That is, we do not have to judge that *an honorary member* has a relation to *named* similar to that of *over* to *took*.[37]

2.9. *Summary of Constructions*

A detailed analysis of the class constructions within each sentence type may make it possible to say that, of two sentence types A and B, A has the same construction as B except for the addition of some x: A = B + x. For example, *He didn't go = He went + not* (§ 2.5). When we add to this a consideration of the actual word choices (individual co-occurrences) we may be able to show that a single n-class construction is satisfied by several different sets of n-tuples, sets which occur elsewhere in different constructions. For example, N P N is satisfied by one set of triples which also occur in reverse order (N_2 P N_1), and by another set in which the two N may each occur alone in the position of the N P N, and so on (§ 2.3). When we compare various partially similar constructions we may find that one of them can be considered a special case of another. For example, *who went* can be considered a special case of an N V sentence (like *Carl went*) on the basis of considerations which make *-o* a special member of N (§ 2.1, § 2.6). And when we compare the word choices in partially similar sentences (§ 2.2) or in neighboring sections of a sentence (§ 2.1), we may find that undecidable or unique constructions can be reinterpreted (by environmental considerations) as special cases of known constructions, as when *He knows more than I* is shown to be *He knows + more than + I know*. By so comparing sentences with similar or neighboring sentences, we prepare the ground for showing that all sentence structures are combinations or transformations of just a few simple sentence structures.

In particular, we note (§ 2.3) various subtypes of D and of P (including P P), to distinguish V P + N from V + P N, and V N + P N from V + N P N. Within N_1 P N_2 we distinguish the parallel type (where both N_1 and N_2 are substitutable for N_1 P N_2), the majority type P N = A (where only N_1 is substitutable for N_1 P N_2), the type N P = A (where N_2 is the head and substitutable for N_1 P N_2), the reversible type (where by the side of N_1 P_i N_2 there is also a substitutable N_2 P_j N_1), the compound type, and the P N P = P type (which do not occur in N_1 *is* P N_2).

Concerning C (§ 2.4) we note that they occur between two instances of the same construction; i.e. given a construction Z containing C, it is possible to find a subconstruction X immediately before C and another subconstruction

Y immediately after C, such that X and Y separately, and also X C Y, have the same status within the next larger construction Z.

In § 2.5, a class v was set up, including the tenses -*ed* and zero (without variant -*s*) and the auxiliaries *will, can*, etc. In the presence of *not*, emphatic stress, question intonation, etc., the suffix members of v (the tenses proper) move in front of their V to the position of the other v; they then appear with *do* as phonemic carrier. In the presence of question intonation and certain prefixed words, all v move in front of their subject N. There is also a v-phrase expansion: *have -en* and *be -ing* between the v and the following V.

§ 2.6 defined a set of subclasses called pro-morphemes. A small subclass of Y is called pro-Y if its X-co-occurrence range (for each constructionally related class X) equals the sum of X-co-occurrence ranges of all members of Y: e.g. the sum of V-co-occurrences of *he, she*, and *it* equals the sum of the V-co-occurrences of all N. A pro-Y is bound if, in each sentence in which it occurs, its X-co-occurrents when in that environment equal the X-co-occurrents of the particular Y which occupies a specified neighboring ('antecedent') position in respect to the pro-Y. Free (not bound) pro-N-phrases: *he, she, it, this*, etc. Pro-N: *one*, zero (§ 2.61). Pro-N (and -A) after *wh-* (§ 2.62) in the *wh-* question, in N *wh-* S_2 (bound to preceding N), and in *wh-* S_2 as subject or object of S_1 (free). Pro-V-phrase: zero (bound), and free pro-V: *do it*, etc. (§ 2.63). Pro-A and pro-S (*this*, etc.) and bound pro-N-pair (*each other*) (§ 2.64).

With the aid of the above, it is possible to analyze two-V constructions into several types (§ 2.7): $N_1 V_1 N_2 + N_2 V_2$ *The call reminded me to rush*; $N_1 V_1 (N_2 V_2)$, the second sentence being object of the first, as in *The scare made the girl scream*; $N_1 V_1 (N_1 V_2)$ as in *He avoided working* (the subject of V_2 being a zero recurrence of the subject of V_1); $N_1 V_1 C N_2 V_2$ as in *I want a ladder (in order) for you to paint the wall*; $N_1 V_1 C N_1 V_2$ as in *I want a book (in order) to read*; and V_1 *to* V_2 or $V_1 V_2ing$ extended V-phrases (where no second subject could appear before *to* V_2 or V_2ing) as in *He tried to stop*.

In § 2.8, V N N constructions are analyzed into $V N_1 N_2$ as variant of $V N_2 P N_1$, for certain V, as in *give him a book, give a book to him*; and $N V (N_1 N_2)$ for other V, the $N_1 N_2$ being object of the V (and also occurring in N_1 *is* N_2 sentences), as in *The oil magnates made Harding president*.

From all this we can go on (§ 3.1) to show that in complicated sentences in general the two or more sections are separate simple sentence structures which have been combined in one of these relations or another.

3. TRANSFORMATIONS IN SENTENCE SEQUENCES

3.0. Certain sequences of two or more sentences have a special form for one of the sentences (usually the second): e.g. *Some groups have rebelled frequently* ※ *Some only rarely*, or *I've just been over there* ※ *Oh, you were there?* In addition, many sentences which have what might be called complex structures can be analyzed as containing a sequence of two or more sentences or sentence structures, some or all of which have special forms: *I met him coming back*. In all these cases the sections with special forms (*Oh, you were there?* or *him coming back*) can be shown to be transforms of ordinary independent sentences, in the sense of the definition of § 1.3. These transforms can thus be viewed as variant forms of sentences. Some of these variant forms are positionally bound, occurring only in particular sentence sequences, e.g. *Some only rarely* or *him coming back*. Others also occur outside of the sentence sequences, e.g. *Oh, you were there?*

To obtain this result we first have to show that the sections in question occur in specifiable positions with respect to other sentences or sentence sections. Then we have to show that the sections in question are complete sentence structures, in the sense that they contain the same constructions as a sentence, with the same relations among these constructions. Finally, we have to show that they are transforms of independently occurring sentences, that is, that every n-tuple of morphemes that satisfies one of these special variant forms also satisfies an independent sentence.

The first task has been partly covered in § 2, where special sections were singled out from many sentence structures. These sections have various grammatical relations, of course, to the rest of the sentence in which they occur: in *I hear he returned* the *he returned* is the object of *I hear*; and in *The ticket which was lost is replaceable* the *which was lost* is an adjectival phrase of *ticket*. But that does not prevent these sections from having internal sentence structures on their own. In addition to these special sections within larger sentences, there is a host of particular sentence sequences, of which many will be listed below. In all of these, the special sentence form is often characterized by particular features: question intonation, contrastive stress, reduced main stress, special introductory words before the special ('secondary') sentence (*and, though*, etc.) or before both sentences (*some ... some ...*, *some ... others ...*, etc.).

The second task, to show that the special sentence forms or sentence sections are complete sentence structures internally is accomplished by methods of structural linguistics as in § 2.1 and of individual co-occurrence as in § 2.2. It is primarily a matter of filling out the special form by showing that it contains pro-morphemes or zero variants of elements which are present in the neighboring ('primary') sentence or sentence section, and that these can be filled out precisely up to the point of giving the secondary section the internal structure of a sentence. This will be sketched in § 3.1.

Finally, the fact that these are indeed transforms will be discussed in Part 4, where both these and the other transformations of English will be listed.

The result of Part 3, then, will be to show that various types of sentence sequence and of complicated sentences are the product of one sentence with the transform of another sentence. There are certain transformations which so to speak change a sentence into a noun-phrase or an adjectival phrase or a subordinate or coordinate clause. That is, given sentence S_2, such a transform of it $T S_2$ occurs next to another sentence S_1, with $T S_2$ filling one of these positions (N-phrase, etc.) within S_1. There is no correlation in English between the transformations and the positions they fill: several different transformations – $T_1 S_2$, $T_2 S_2$, etc. – may fill the same position within S_1 (e.g. there are several ways in which S_2 may be nominalized and appear as object of S_1); and the same transformation $T_1 S_2$ may fill different positions in S_1. Quite apart from its transformational form, there are restrictions of individual co-occurrence dictating which S_2 will fill which positions in S_1: not all $S_1 S_2$ combinations occur.

3.1. *Pro-Morphemes and Zero-Recurrence in Sentence Sequences*

If we consider sentence sequences (or complicated sentence structures) in which one section contains pro-morphemes, we can often show that the pro-morpheme has the same co-occurrence relations as some particular 'antecedent' morpheme or word or phrase present in the neighboring section (§§ 2.1, 6). If we consider sections that are added to sentence structures (*but not I* after *He spoke there*) or imbedded within them (*committing myself* in *I avoided* [ ]), and if we compare certain of these sections with whole sentences, we find that there exist sentences which contain precisely the words of these sections plus words that are absent in these sections but are present in the neighboring one, e.g. *I did not speak* as compared with *not I*. Instead of merely noting the absence of such words from these sections, we can say that the whole sentences have certain positions filled which are empty in these sections. We put it this way because we can then proceed to say that these positions are actually not empty but are occupied by zero morphemes. We discover these zero morphemes by finding that the exigencies of grammatical description (in particular the methods of §§ 2.1, 2) point to the effect, in these sections, of certain elements which are not visible in them but are present in neighboring sections; and instead of saying that the morphemes of the neighboring section reach over to affect the choice of morphemes in the other, we say that zero variants of those morphemes occur in this other section and operate within it – or, equivalently, that when this other section contains morphemes, identical with those of the neighboring section, these morphemes may have zero as a variant form in that position.

This effect (on our section) which is correlatable with morphemes of the neighboring section, and which we thus attribute to the presence in our section of zero variants of those morphemes, is the restriction of co-occurrence range for the various elements of our section. For example, in *He spoke there but not* ( ), we may find various other N, not only *I*, but always such N as are in the subject range of *spoke*. Hence we say that *spoke* recurs in *not I*, though in a zero variant form.

The result of this analysis, as we have seen, is to find in each such sentence sequence, or complicated sentence structure, a sequence or a combination of two sentences, such that some morphemes recur in both sentences. These sequences then become merely a special case of all sentence sequences and combinations – the case when some morphemes happen to be identical in the two sentences.

We now look upon these structures as sentence combinations in which recurring morphemes have been replaced by pro-morphemes or zero variants. Whether the morpheme recurs in full or in pro-morpheme or zero form, depends upon the particular type of sentence combination, on the class of the morpheme, and on the position of the class in the sentence. Only sketchy indications can be given here of the mass of detail.

In some sentence combinations there are certain positions in which a recurring morpheme is always zero, for instance the A in *That one is wider than this one is* (though a different A is given in full: *That one is wider than this one is deep*). Similarly the second subject N in *I avoided going*, the sentences being *I avoided* ( ) and *I went*; a different second subject appears in full (*I avoided Tom's haranguing*). In some sentence combinations there are positions in which a recurring morpheme appears either in full or as zero. In *He would buy books rather than records* (where *he would buy* is zeroed after *than*), we can also find *He would buy books rather than buy records* (where only N and v are zeroed). Similarly we have *Some people do ⁕ Some people don't*, as well as *Some people do ⁕ Some don't*. In some positions we find either full recurrence or pro-morphemes, but not zero, as for the second subject N in *The ideas kept changing as the ideas spread*, more comfortably ... *as they spread*. In some positions the recurring morphemes may appear either in full, in pro-morpheme, or in zero forms, as is the case for most classes after *and*: *The man bought the books and the man sold the books, The man bought the books and he sold the books, The man bought the books and sold the books*. In some positions a recurring morpheme always appears as pro-morpheme, e.g. after *wh-*.

As to the effect on each class, some classes have no pro-morpheme, e.g. the auxiliary and tense class v. Some classes are hardly ever zeroed by themselves, e.g. v (perhaps in such forms as *Well, I might go and he stay*).

The zeroing operates on constituents; thus the v V + N (object) construction may recur in full (*I'll take a copy and he'll take a copy too*), or in pro-mor-pheme of the V N (*I'll take a copy and he'll do so too*), or in zero of V N but full recurrence of v (*I'll take a copy and he will too*), or in zero of the whole v V N (*I'll take a copy and he too*), or in pro-morpheme only of the N (*I'll take a copy and he'll take one too*); other possibilities do not appear. In two sentences connected by *and*, the recurring material around any constituent can be replaced by zero, provided the *and*, together with the remaining constituent, is joined to the corresponding constituent in the first sentence: *The cheap and dishonest electioneering continued* can be derived by such zeroings from *The cheap electioneering continued and the dishonest election-eering continued.*[38]

The position in which the recurring morpheme takes a variant form is specifiable, completely or partly, with respect to the particular sentence combination. In the case of bound pro-morphemes and zeros the antecedent is usually completely specified. In the case of free pro-morphemes, the full morpheme will be replaced by a pro-morpheme in the second sentence or after a subordinating conjunction, but hardly otherwise: *Bill will do it if he can; If Bill can, he'll do it; If he can, Bill will do it*; but hardly *He will do it, if Bill can* (in the last case *He* is presumably the pronoun of some other antecedent).

3.2. *Types of Sentence Combination*

Establishing the antecedents of pro-morphemes, and placing zero morphemes within sentence combinations, can show that these sequences or complicated structures contain two or more sections, each of which has a sentence-like internal structure. It remains to investigate the different types of combination.

In some of these combinations what we may call the secondary section be-comes a full sentence as soon as the pro-morphemes and zeros are replaced by the corresponding morphemes from the primary section. Examples are the sentence sequences question–answer and assertion–question (*The book disappeared* ✕ *What disappeared?*). Many irregular sentence structures appear only in a context: *I can't decide where to go* ✕ *Maybe to New York*. Here the second sentence is filled out to consist of the introducer *maybe* + zero variant of subject *I* + zero variant of verb *go* + P N *to New York* 'answering' the pro-P N *where*. There are also matched introducers: *Some people will come* ✕ *Some won't* or *Others won't*, where the second sentence has zero for *people* and for *come*. Most conjunctions (*and, or, either ... or, more than*, etc.) occur between two sentence structures that usually have a single sentence intonation, and are in many cases not recognizable as two sentences until the zeros are established. Yet another example is the *wh-* set

(*The fellow whose pen you lost is back = The fellow is back + You lost the fellow's pen*).

In other combinations the second section can be shown indeed to have the constructional relations of a sentence among its parts, but the whole may not have the external form of a sentence. Zeros and pro-morphemes may not even be involved in it. Such are the V without v (but usually with -*ing* or *to*): *Being alone, he didn't go*, where zero subject *he* can be shown before *being*; *For John to win, he would have to try harder* or *To win, John would* ... with zero *John* before *to win*; *him coming* in *I met him coming*. Such also are the nominalized sentences imbedded in others: *I resent his coming*. And such are the A N and N P N and other constructions that will be seen below to be extractable. In all these cases the sentence-like structures will be shown to be transforms of ordinary sentences; thus, *being alone* and *he being alone* are transforms of *He is alone*.

Aside from this question whether the filled-out section is a sentence or only a transform of a sentence, we may consider another distinction: whether the primary section is an independent sentence by itself or whether it requires the presence of the secondary. For example, the primary is self-sufficient before C S (conjunction + secondary S): *The car rounded the corner and stopped* is filled out to *The car rounded the corner + and the car stopped; I like him better than her* is filled out to *I like him + better than I like her*. It is also self-sufficient when the secondary is a *wh-* phrase separated by comma intonation, or a descriptive A or P N: *Snakes, which have no teeth, can't bite*. And in the N V $N_2 + N_2$ V type of combination (§ 2.7): *I met him returning home = I met him + him* (or zero *he*) *returning home*. Various members of sentence sequences are also self-sufficient, e.g. an assertion or answer occurs independently of the question.

In contrast with this there are structures in which the primary section does not occur as a sentence by itself, without the secondary section either as a constituent of the primary or as a neighbor, sometimes specifically before it or after it. This may be because the structure of the primary is incomplete or because the individual co-occurrences would not appear without the secondary. Examples are certain matched introducers (e.g. *On the one hand*...), or the N V $N_2 + N_2$ V type of combination when the shared N_2 is a pronoun (§ 2.62: *I saw who came = I saw who + who came* or *I saw $N_i + N_i$ came*). In these cases the primary is not independent of the secondary (though for different reasons). Another example is in nominalized sentences which are subjects or objects of the primary: *I think (that) he can, He said 'It won't do', I announced your coming, Bees buzzing around annoyed him* (where the primary is N *annoyed him*). Finally the primary is not independent when the secondary is a *wh-* phrase without comma intonation, or a partitive

A or P N (such as A_i, A_j in *Some* N_k *are* A_i. ※ *Some are* A_j), because the co-occurrences may then be different: one may find *Dogs which bark don't bite* or *A barking dog doesn't bite* even if one does not find *Dogs don't bite.*

Several additional distinctions characterize the various types of sentence combination; some of these will become apparent as they are surveyed. In the following pages the sentence combinations will be grouped by their major structural features rather than by the transformations that appear in them, since the latter will be summarized in Part 4. These structural classifications are the question sequence, matched sentences, conjunctions, word-sharing, nominalized sentences, and the *wh-* forms.

3.3. *The Question Sequence*

We consider sequences of sentences in which the second has zero recurrences based on the first. A special case of this is the sequence of assertion and question (*John came here* ※ *He did?* or *Did he?* or *Who came, did you say?*), or question and answer (*Who came?* ※ *John* or *Did John come?* ※ *Yes, he did*). In each pair, the composition of one sentence can be described in terms of its predecessor, and is indeed seen to be a transform of it.

When the question is of the yes-no type, it contains a particular question element, the intonation, together with an optional interchange of v with subject N. The answer may contain the words *yes* or *no*. Aside from this, in the assertion-question and the question-answer pairs the second sentence repeats the first. The repetition may have zero recurrence for everything after the subject N+v (*He'll come to you* ※ *He will?* and *Will he come to you?* ※ *He will.*), or for everything after N v V N (*Did he take it yesterday?* ※ *Yes, he took it.*); or it may have zeros for the whole N v V N before any added material (*Will he get some today?* ※ *Yes, today.*), or just for the N v V while repeating the object N (*I'll take these two* ※ *Just these two?*). Note that we cannot repeat the N v V and zero the object N (we cannot very well answer *Yes, he'll get* or ask *Will you take?*). If the first sentence of the sequence is of the N_1 V_1 (N_1 V_2) type (§ 2.7), the second V may be zeroed by itself: *I'd like to go* ※ *You'd like to?* The second sentence may thus repeat or zero the sections of its predecessor in any of the above ways: *Will he take these two today?* ※ *Yes, he will*, or *Yes, he will take these two* or *Yes, these two* or *Yes, today*. In addition, the second sentence may have bound pro-morphemes in the manner that we have noticed for any secondary sentence: *Yes, he will take them* or *Yes, he will do so*. But in all cases the zeros and pro-morphemes are variants of their antecedent in the first sentence, so that the second sentence is a variant form of a full sentence. Sometimes some of the zeros are in the first sentence rather than the second. A notable characteristic of this sequence is that the altered forms occur equally in the question or in the assertion, depending only on which is the second.

When the question is of the *wh-* type, it contains *wh-* and its intonation, with a pro-morpheme following the *wh-*. This may be a pro-subject N (*-o, -at, -ich*), pro-object N (*-om, -at, -ich*), pro-A (*-ose; -at, -ich* before N), P + pro-N (*-en, -ere,* etc.), pro-V-phrase (*-at do*), etc. The part which is pro-morphemed in the question appears in full in the assertion, whatever the order of the two may be. Aside from this, the special forms are as above. The first sentence of the sequence, whether assertion or question, is generally complete. The second sentence contains the post-*wh-* pro-morpheme (if it is the question) or specific morphemes of the same constructional status (if it is the answer), and the remaining sections of the first sentence may be repeated, pro-morphemed, or zeroed just as in the yes-no question.[39]

Since each question contains the same words as its neighboring assertion (aside from interchanging *you* and *I*), we can say that it is obtained by a transformation (from that assertion) which takes place in the presence of the question elements. In the case of the *wh-* questions, there is the additional transformation of substituting the post-*wh-* pro-morpheme as a positional variant of the constructionally corresponding section of the assertion.

3.4. *Matched Sentences*

There are in English, in addition to the question-assertion pairs, other sequences of matched sentences, namely sequences in which both sentences contain the same words in all but one or two positions. Those sequences are characterized by having contrastive stress or reduced stress on the second sentence (the last, if there are more than two); and by having the possibility of zero variants for the recurrent words in all but one of the sentences (usually in all but the first). Since all these characteristics may be found in other successions of sentences, one could say that the ones described above are merely those successive sentences which have various words in common. However, for transformational purposes it is convenient to consider these sentence sequences separately, because they are marked by certain introducers or adverbial phrases which thus become transformation indicators.

The more obvious type is the case of matched introducers, in which all sentences of the sequence have either the same or related introducing words: *Some people are cynical* ※ *Some are not* (also *Some people are not* or *Some are not cynical* or *Some are innocent,* etc.). Another pair of introducers is seen in *Some people are cynical* ※ *Others are not* etc. Since *some ... some ...* seems to occur with the same sentences as *some ... others...,* it may itself be considered a transform of *some ... others...,* quite apart from the relation between the two successive sentences in each case. There are many other matched introducers: *A few ... a few...*, *A few ... others...*, and in general pairs of partitive adjectives (e.g. *Reasoned decisions are sure to do some good here* ⸽ *Arbitrary ones are less so*). In all these cases the subject N or the whole subject N-phrase, and the object N-phrase or the whole V-phrase, including the object, may have zero form in the second sentence (if the words are the same as in the first); after partitive A there is usually a pro-N (*ones*) for the subject, rather than a zero.

In another type of matched sentences we find all but one of the sentences (usually all but the first) containing special D or P N (or even appositional elements to the N and V sections), but otherwise repeating all or most of the words of the primary sentence: *The boys got home early* ⸽ *They really did* ⸽ *And so did we*, or *Tim gets up early* ⸽ *We all do*. Here the V may be zeroed, but not the subject N (except in particular circumstances).

The various sentences of a matched sequence are not transforms of each other, since there is generally some difference even between their expanded forms (aside from differences in the introducers), e.g. *The boys got home early, The boys really got home early, We got home early*. However, each reduced sentence is a transform of the complete sentences which we obtain by filling in its pro-morphemes and zeros: *They really did* is a transform of *The boys really got home early*. Each set of matched introducers constitutes a discontinuous morphemic element (*some ... some...*, *a few ... others ...*) which provides the distinctive environment for the transformation.[40]

3.5. *Conjunctions*

A somewhat different type of sequence is that marked by conjunctions (*and, since*, etc.). Here we have two sentence structures joined by a morpheme of the conjunction class C. In the case of some members of C the two sentence structures always have a single sentence intonation extending over them: *He's taller than I am*. For many other members of C the two sentence structures sometimes have a single sentence intonation, sometimes separate intonations (often with comma intonation on the first, reduced or contrastive stress on the second): *I'll go there if I can* and *I'll go there, if I can*. Many members of C appear sometimes with matched introducers: *Some ... But others ....*

Another difference between conjunctions and matched introducers is that the two or more sentences joined by conjunctions may have no words in common, and yet the conjunctions or intonations may be the same as when they have. However, in those cases where the two sentences have the same words in corresponding positions, the occurrence of zeros and pro-morphemes is much the same as in matched sentences. The details as to which positions may be zeroed (or in some cases must be zeroed) differ for different members of C, and also differ when the C occurs with comma intonation. For many C the subject N is never zeroed (but the V often is): so for *because, since, if, as if, as, unless, though, while* (*The sailors got the raise because they had organized for it; The children can see the trees next fall if they don't this fall*).[41] For some C a large part of the primary sentence may be zeroed (or given in pro-morpheme or in full) in the secondary sentence; and for some C certain positions of the primary sentence are always zeroed in the secondary: *He is quick rather than careful.* For some C, if only one constituent in the second-ary sentence contains different words from the primary, all the repeated words may be zeroed, and the remaining constituent may be conjoined directly to its corresponding constituent in the primary. Thus we have *He and I will come*, which we can derive from *He will come and I will come*, or *I can and will go* from *I can go and I will go*. In varying degrees this is the case for *and, or, either ... or ..., but, as well as, that is*, etc. The sections of the lead sentence that are zeroed after *and* and a few other C have been indicated near the end of § 3.1. A complete statement for all C involves a considerable body of detail.[42]

Most C occur before the second sentence; in the case of a few C the sentence with C may precede the other: *Since you won't, I'll go* or *Since you won't go, I will.* A few C are discontinuous, with one part occurring before each sentence: *Either you go or I will, If you go then I may too.* It is possible to distinguish certain subclasses of C, such as coordinating and subordinating, on the basis of the co-occurrence ranges within each sentence, or of the relative positions of the sentences; e.g. whether each pair of sentences also occurs in reverse order for the same C.[43]

As in matched sentences, each reduced sentence is a transform of the com-plete sentence which we can reconstruct on the basis of the primary sentence, even though the reconstructed sentence has various sections which differ from the primary. Each different rule for zeroing is a different though related transformation, which takes place in the presence of the particular members of C for which that rule holds. The transformation of note 41 is yet another, for particular C. The original long sentence is not merely the sum of the reconstructed sentences, but the sum of these with their conjunctions.[44]

3.6. *Word Sharing*

In § 3.5 we saw cases of two sections joined by a conjunction; in most cases one of these was clearly a sentence structure, while the other could be ex-panded into a sentence structure with the aid of the zero variants. Below we will see cases which are often quite similar, except that they are not so conveniently marked by a conjunction; they are complicated sentences which can be shown to contain transforms of two or more sentences. In § 3.5 the two sentences are simply joined by a conjunction, and then often words are zeroed if they are the same as in the corresponding constructional position in the conjoined sentence. In the new type below, the sentences always have a word in common (otherwise they are not joinable), and they are joined by sharing their common word; that is, the word occurs only once, so that the two constructions which contain it overlap, or one is included in the other. The secondary sentence does not in general contain zero variants, except in that it does not repeat the word which it has in common with the primary sentence; but it contains various transformational changes.

A case rather similar to that of conjunctions (of the type in note 41) is N V V*ing* (*I was there working*), also N V, V*ing* (*I was there, working*), and N V *to* V (*I came to learn*), and N V A or N V, A (*We waited, breathless*; also with N-phrase or P N in place of A). Here the co-occurrence ranges show that the subject of the second V (or of *is* A) is the same as the subject of the first V. This can be analyzed as $N_1 V_1$ + zero conjunction + $N_1 V_2$ (with the N_1 recurrence zeroed, and with the further transformation of replacing the second v by *to* or *ing*, or *be* + v). Or it can be analyzed as two sentences $N_1 V_1 + N_1 V_2$ (overlapping around the common N_1, and with the same further transformation as above).[45] A special case of this is the appositional sentence, e.g. *The stranger, a Frenchman, could not understand* from *The stranger could not understand* and *The stranger was a Frenchman*.

In the cases above the shared word is in the same constructional status in both sentences. When we have two sentences in which the shared word is not in the same constructional status, we can no longer apply the zeroings that occur with conjunctions; here the nonrepetition of the shared word can no longer be considered such a zero, but must be due to a new method of combining S.

We first consider cases like *I asked him to deny it, We finally found it lying in a corner, We saw it high above us*. In all these cases the second N is both the object of the first V and the subject of the second V. These are then transforms of $N_1 V_1 N_2 + N_2 V_2$ (*We finally found it* + *It lay in a corner*, etc.). The transformations consist in the second sentence overlapping the first around the common word (i.e. not repeating the common word), as above; and in replacing the second v by *to* or *ing*, or dropping *be* + v (e.g. from *It was high above us*). We can usually find the same underlying sentences joined in a conjunction sequence, in the manner of § 3.5; but then the transformations and the resultant are different (e.g. *We finally found it as it lay in a corner, I asked him if he would deny it;* note that the meaning is affected by the particular member of C).

When the common word is the object of both sentences, they overlap by having the second sentence in the passive transformation: *I bought a house built by him* from *I bought a house* + *He built a house*. Transforming the second sentence into the passive makes this object into a special case of the shared object-subject above, since *a house* is the subject of the passive.[46]

A different case arises in sentences like *The leaning tower collapsed, The plane-grounding order was issued at ten, They designed a circuit with a servo*, and in general wherever an N has subsidiary A or P N phrases constructionally attached to it. In all the cases where the A N pairs also satisfy N *is* A (*leaning tower*, and *the tower leans*) and where the N P N triples also satisfy N *is* P N (*the circuit is with a servo*), we can extract two sentences, e.g. *The tower collapsed* + *The tower leaned* or *The order was issued at ten* + *The order grounded planes*. Any sentence, then, which contains N_i in any position can combine by word-sharing (i.e. by sentence-overlapping) with the transform of any sentence which begins N_i *is* ( ); that is, it can so combine with any construction whose head is this N_i (e.g. A N_i, or N_i P N).[47]

3.7. *Constructionally Included Sentences*

Another type of sentence combination occurs when a transform of one sentence occupies a constructional position within another sentence: *They let the newcomer speak*, where *the newcomer speak* is object of *They let*, but neither *the newcomer* nor *speak* alone would occur as object. In the word-sharing combination the shared word fills a position in both sentences: in *I bought a house built by him*, we find *a house* both in the object range for *I bought* and also in the subject range for *built by him*. In such combinations it is not even necessary to find any grammatical relation between the two sentences, since each has its own complete structure; they simply overlap in sharing a word. In the present case, however, only the subsidiary sentence has a complete structure: *the newcomer speaks*, transformed by dropping the v into *the newcomer speak*. The primary sentence does not have a complete structure unless the subsidiary is taken as filling some status within it: *They let* does not otherwise occur without an object, and neither *the newcomer* nor *speak* but only their sum is in its object range.

In many cases of N_1 V_1 N_2 V_2, there is confusion or even homonymity between the analysis above as N_1 V_1 (N_2 V_2), with N_2 V_2 as object, and the word-sharing analysis N_1 V_1 N_2 + N_2 V_2 (§ 3.6). This is so because N_2 may happen to be in the object range of V_1, yet in a particular sentence the object of V_1 may be the whole N_2 V_2 sentence. Whether a given N_1 V_1 N_2 V_2 belongs to one type or the other can be discovered by noting what other combining transformations are possible for the particular N_1 V_1 and N_2 V_2. For example, in *Everyone heard my brother denying the story* (in word-sharing analysis: N_1 V_1 N_2 + N_2 V_2 N_3), we find the same words also satisfying the transformation N_1 V_1 N_2 C N_2 V_2 N_3 (*Everyone heard my brother as he denied the story*), but in *Everyone awaited the reports announcing victory* ($N_1 V_1 [N_2 V_2 N_3]$, in included-construction analysis) we find the same words also satisfying the transformation $N_1 V_1 N_2$ *that* $V_2 N_3$ (§ 3.8: *Everyone awaited the reports that announced victory*) and not the conjunction transformation. The distinction is also seen in the passive: *My brother was heard denying the story by everyone* or ... *was heard by everyone denying the story*, but *The reports announcing victory were awaited by everyone*. In such cases, then, we can say that *brother* is separately the object of S_1 and the subject of S_2, while *reports announcing victory* as a whole is the object of S_1. Both analyses apply in the case of homonymity: for *The new pilot saw the paper lying there in the corner*, we have *The paper was seen by the new pilot, lying there in the corner* and *The paper was seen lying there in the corner by the new pilot* (both passives of $N_1 V_1 N_2 + N_2 V_2$, and both having the same meaning); but also *The paper lying there in the corner was seen by the new pilot* (passive of $N_1 V_1 (N_2 V_2)$, and with an appropriately different meaning).

When one sentence occupies a constructional position within another (without word-sharing), the position which it occupies is that of an N. There are many transformations that nominalize a sentence for such insertion, among them N V*ing* (as above), N V without the v (*the newcomer speak*), *if* or *whether* or *that* or zero plus N v V (*I wonder if he went, I insist that he went, I heard he went*), *that* or zero plus N V without the v (*I prefer that he go, I insist he leave*), *for* N *to* V (*For him to go is foolish*), N's V*ing* (*His leaving disturbs me*), etc. (§ 4.3).

The N position which is occupied by the transformed sentence may be the subject or object of the primary sentence, or virtually any other N, as in P N after V in *I count on his leaving*, P N after N in *The danger of his leaving is past*.

3.8. *Sentences combined by wh-*

The two types of sentences containing *wh-* (aside from questions, § 2.62) can be analyzed as sentence sequences connected by *wh-*, with some N, P N, or A of the secondary sentence S_2 replaced by a pro-morpheme which stands immediately after the *wh-* at the beginning of S_2.

In the first type, the *wh-* (plus the subsidiary sentence S_2) occurs after any N of the primary sentence S_1; the following pro-morpheme has this N (or the first N of N P N) as its antecedent, though it may have any N or P N status in its own subsidiary sentence: *The fellow who passed, The fellow for whom I got it* or *The fellow who(m) I got it for, The place in which it was* and *The place where it was*. The whole *wh-* + S_2 thus occupies a constructional position within S_1, being an A phrase of one of its N. It is comparable to the word-sharing combinations (in particular to the last paragraph of § 3.6) in that S_2 always has an N in common with S_1. But the transformational machinery is different, since the common word is not overlapped but repeated in pro-morpheme (something which permits the use here of more complex S_2). Other words in S_2 which are identical with words of the same status in S_1 may be zeros as in parallel sentences. When the *wh-* $+ S_2$ is intonationally separated it has the properties of a descriptive A: *The report, for which I'd been waiting all day, finally arrived.* Otherwise it can occur in matched sentences like a partitive adjective.

In this post-N type, a *wh-* word which is subject of its S_2 may have a variant *that* (*The fellow that passed*), and a *wh-* word which is object of S_2 (or part of P N with the P at the end of S_2) has variants *that* and zero (*The fellow I saw, The fellow that I got it for, The fellow I got it for*). These are subsidiary transformations of the *wh-* group.

The other main type has *wh-* $+ S_2$ after the V or V-phrase of S_1. The *wh-* $+ S_2$ occupies the position of subject, object, or P N of S_1, depending on the structure of S_1.[48] The pro-morpheme after *wh-* has its own status within S_2: *-o* is subject N, *-om* is object N, *-at* is N, *-ere* is P N; hence we find *who saw, whom I saw, in what I found it, what I found it in, where I found it,* but not *where happened* (where *-ere* would have to be subject). In this type the pro-morpheme is free, and has no antecedent in S_1. There is thus no parallelism or word sharing here between S_1 and S_2, and the relation between them is the same as in the nominalized sentences of § 3.7. It is also possible, however, to regard these as a special type of word-sharing combination if the pro-morpheme, rather than the whole *wh-* $+ S_2$, is considered to be the object, subject, or P N of S_1 (according to the conditions of note 48), and at the same time to occupy whatever status it occupies within S_2. The transformational machinery in S_2 is of course the same by either analysis.

In the *wh-* positions of this post-V type we also find *wh-* words $+$ *ever*: *Whatever I do seems to be wrong.* However, *wh-* words $+$ *ever*, and *wh-* words $+$ certain special environments, occur in secondary sentences of the zero-C type mentioned in note 41: *Whatever you think, I'm going; I'm going no matter what you say.* We have here a *wh-* transform of S_2 with a zero-C combination of S_1 and S_2.

3.9. *Summary of Sentence Sequences*

We review all the cases where successive sentences are combined. In almost all such sequences one sentence (often the first) is not transformed and may be called the primary sentence. This can be determined for each type of combination.

There are several different co-occurrence relations between the S. Two or more sentences may each be completely independent of each other (except for transformational effects, to be mentioned below), as in some S C S. All but the primary sentence may be dependent in that some of their word co-occurrences do not appear in primaries, or in that S_1 and S_2 (with their particular word co-occurrences) do not occur in reverse order with the same connective (§ 3.2, some from § 3.4, some S C S, first type in § 3.8). Or all the sentences may be dependent in that each contains elements that occur only in the neighborhood of the other, as in contrasting partitive adjectives. The question sentence may be considered completely dependent, since it is identical with the assertion, except for transformations and the introductory (or connective) question element.

There are also different constructional relations between the sentences in a sequence. Two or more sentences may be grammatically independent. Or one sentence may occupy an unessential position in the other, e.g. constituting an A-phrase, or a P N, or an appositional N-phrase within the other (end of § 3.6, first type in § 3.8, and note 41). Or one sentence may fill an essential position within the other, as its subject or object phrase (§ 3.7, end of § 3.8).

There are various types of connective between the sentences. In respect to intonation there may be mere succession of two sentence intonations (§ 3.2), or contrastive stress, or reduced stress or comma intonation on the secondary sentences; or the secondary sentence (in its transform) may simply be included in the intonation of the primary (e.g. *wh-* forms without comma). In respect to connecting morphemes there may be matched introducers, question markers, conjunctions between the sentences or before each one (and these 'coordinating' if the two S are reversible within the same text, 'subordinating' if not), P before a nominalized secondary sentence (note 41), *wh-* of both types. Finally, the overlapping of § 3.6 may be considered a type of connection, as also the positioning of S_2 in the subject or object or other position of S_1 (§ 3.7).

The types of transformation, mainly in secondary sentences, are as follows: pro-morphemes in all parallel sentences (§§ 3.2–5), and in a special way in § 3.8; zeroing of parallel recurrent elements in parallel sentences (with different details for different connectives); inversion after the question element; and bringing the pro-morpheme constituent to the beginning of S_2 after *wh-*; dropping of v or *be* + v and in some cases adding *to* or *ing* to V; and many nominalizations of the secondary sentence. In § 3.6 one can say that the shared word is zeroed in the secondary sentence.

In many cases the same S_1 S_2 sequence may occur with various connectives between them, or with various transformations on S_2, with the resultant meaning either virtually the same or different according to the connectives and the transformations in question.

4. THE TRANSFORMATIONS OF ENGLISH

4.0. The following list presents the major English transformations in bare outline. Each of these accords with the definition that the same n-tuples of class members satisfy the two or more constructions which are transforms of each other. A detailed discussion of each transformation cannot be given here; the reader can test them himself, although in some cases more complicated methods may be needed in order to characterize and isolate exceptions or special cases. This is not a complete list. Perhaps it is impossible to determine a complete list for any language; but this, if it is true, will not affect either the practical or the theoretical use of transformations. The transformations will be noted in three main groupings: those that occur in independent sentences (S↔S); those that occur in sequential sentences (S₁↔S₂); and those that occur in sentences that occupy the position of an N-phrase (S↔N). Minor groupings will be noted below.

4.1. *S↔S*

The main types here are passive, introducers, alternative order, and various transformations of individual words.

4.11. N_1 v V $N_2 \rightarrow N_2$ v *be* V*en by* N_1 (passive): *The children were drinking milk, Milk was being drunk by the children.* Morphemically, *be -en* looks like one of the expanded members of v. But whereas every subject-verb pair that satisfies one member of v satisfies every other (*The children drink, The children were drinking*, etc.), they do not necessarily satisfy *be -en* (we would hardly find *Milk drank*). This *be -en* occurs after any member of v, including the expansions *be -ing, have -en*; the suffix part of all three occurs after the next verb morpheme in the sequence: *The children + ed + be -ing + drink + milk, Milk + ed + be -ing + be -en + drink + by + the children.* The N above represents any N-phrase. The V represents every V word, V P compounds (those in which the P may occur at sentence end: *They tore the paper up*), and certain other V+P: *The paper was torn up by them, His attempts were laughed at by everybody.*[49]

When N_2 is itself a transform of a sentence, we have two cases. If the transform has the internal structure of an N-phrase, it is treated as such: *The liberal weeklies opposed his sending the troops, His sending the troops was opposed by the liberal weeklies.* If the transformed secondary does not itself have an N-phrase structure (even though it occupies the position of an N-phrase in the primary sentence), or if it is a word-sharing combination rather than the object of the primary, then the passive of the primary sentence has either or both of the following two forms (§ 2.7, § 3.7): N_1 v V N_2 X↔N_2 v *be* V*en* X *by* N_1 or N_2 v *be* V*en by* N_1 X (X represents whatever follows N_2 in the transformed secondary active sentence). Thus *The crowd trapped the secret police in their barracks, The secret police were trapped in their barracks by the crowd*, or *The secret police were trapped by the crowd in their barracks*.[50] Any additional material in the original sentence (introducers, D, P N) appears without change in the passive. The *by* of this transformation is homonymous with *by* as member of P[51]; and in some cases the whole transform of N_1 v V_2 N_3 is homonymous with the transform of N_4 v V_2 N_3 to which has been added *by* N_1 (as a P N): *They were seen by the front office* is a transform of *The front office saw them* but also a transform of N_4 *saw them by the front office*. The homonymy is made possible by the dropping of N_4 (§ 4.4). Because of this homonymy we cannot say that all N_2 v *be* V*en by* $N_1 \leftrightarrow N_1$ v V N_2, so that the transformation appears one-directional.[52]

4.12. *Introducers.* There are a number of individual words or word sequences which occur before any sentence, so that we have a transformation S $\leftrightarrow$ Introducer + S. Some of these sequences are members of the classes P N or D; others are N V or N V *that*. Examples: for V which do not occur with objects, N v V $\leftrightarrow$ *There* v V N (*A boy came, There came a boy*); and with certain exclusions, N_1 v V N_2 $\leftrightarrow$ *There* v V N_2 N_1 (*At this point there hit the embankment a shell from our own lines*). Another such transformation is S $\leftrightarrow$ *There* v *be* + certain nominalizations of S (§ 4.3): *There was a barking of dogs, There was much chasing of cats by the dogs, There are the dogs chasing the cats, There will be people waiting there*.[53]

4.13. Certain similar introducers transform into an S any N (or A or P N) word or phrase (not merely one which is itself transformed from an S): *It* or *There* + v *be* (*It's a report, There will be a report*); this can be viewed as a grammatical element making N into S (an ns element by note 2). Combining this with other transformations (by *wh-* or word-sharing combinations) yields various types of transformed sentences: N v V $\leftrightarrow$ *It's* N *that* V (*It's my brother that came*, also with *who* or *which* or zero in position of *that*); N v V $\leftrightarrow$ *There's* N *that* v V; N v V + ( ) *is* A $\leftrightarrow$ *It's* A *for* N *to* V (*It's good for him to try*, via the nominalized first sentence occurring as subject of the second: *For him to try is good*); etc.

4.14. Alternative orders occur occasionally in several constructions, chiefly the following: N_1 v V $N_2 \leftrightarrow N_2$ N_1 v V (*The public he always despised*); N_1 v V N_2 X $\leftrightarrow N_1$ v V X N_2 (X being the rest of the nominalized sentence whose subject is N_2, or being the P of V P compounds, or certain D), as in *He threw the door open, He threw open the door*. When of two sentences with the same subject one is made secondary by dropping the v or v + *be* (§ 4.3), the common subject may come before or after the remainder of the secondary: N, X, V $\leftrightarrow$ X, N V (*He, an inveterate libertarian, opposed the measure*). The two sentences here are N *is* X and N V.[54]

4.15. A few transformations can be set up in the environment of particular subclass or individual words. For a subclass V^g which includes *give* and *tell*, $V^g \, N_1 \, N_2 \leftrightarrow V^g \, N_2 \, to \, N_1$ (*give him this, give this to him*). As an individual example: $N_1 \, v \, be \, more \, A$ (or A*er*) *than* $N_2 \leftrightarrow N_2 \, v \, be \, less \, A \, than \, N_1$ (*The sun is larger than the earth, The earth is less large than the sun*). But by no means can all logical or semantic opposites be transformationally paired in such a way. And even where this seems possible (for example between $N_1 \, v \, buy \, N_2$ *from* N_3 and $N_3 \, v \, sell \, N_2 \, to \, N_1$), there are usually so many special cases as to make these at best quasi-transformations (§ 4.5).

4.2. $S \leftrightarrow S_2$

There are quite a few transformations which change an independent sentence into a sequential one, these being the sentence combiners (or sequence markers) of §§ 3.2–5 and § 3.8 with their attendant changes in the secondary sentence (including the order changes of note 54). This includes bound pro-morphemes in general (including *other*, many occurrences of *both*, etc.); the various distributions of zero recurrence for the various matched introducers, conjunctions, and other types of parallel sentences, including question; the specific matched introducers, question markers (with their *you/I* interchange), members of C, and *wh-*. All of these sentence-combiners have specific meanings, something which is not clearly the case for other transformations. We may consider these sentence combiners to be morphemic elements (which they generally are), and the attendant changes to be transformations. Many transformations are common to a variety of sentence-combiners, e.g. the zero recurrence. We may say then that the main transformations which are limited to S_2 position after various sentence combiners are these: bound pro-morphemes, zero recurrence, and certain order changes.

4.3. $S \leftrightarrow N$

The final large group contains transformations which nominalize a sentence, i.e. change to a form that can appear in one of the N-phrase positions of another sentence. Note that the transformations of § 4.2 do not themselves carry any structural function, for example to combine sentences or to make them into questions; this is done by the morphemic elements that appear in each case. Here we can say similarly that the various transformations do not themselves nominalize their sentences, but that this effect is due to the appearance of the sentences in particular constructional positions within other sentences. The sentences then are N-phrases by virtue of their position; but the transformations apply only when they are in these positions.

Almost all these transformations involve dropping the v (and often the associated *be*, before A and N phrases); in most, the v is replaced by *to* or *-ing*. Particulars are given in the next thirteen subsections.

4.301. N_1 v V $(N_2) \leftrightarrow N_1$'s V*ing* $((of)$ $N_2)$, and V*ing* $((of)$ $N_2)$ *by* N_1 (parentheses indicate occasional occurrence): *your reading (of) these things, reading (of) these things by you.*[55] The result has an N-phrase structure, with V*ing* as head, (of) N_2 and N_1's or *by* N_1 as modifiers (N_1 and N_2 being themselves whole N-phrases with their own T, A, etc.); hence V*ing* may have *-s* 'plural', and if it is subject of the primary sentence this *-s* will extend to the V of the primary: *Your reading of these things is incisive, Your readings of the play are incisive.*[56] N *is* N sentences (see note 49) occur only in the first of these transformations, and without the *of*: *your being a writer, the door's being open.*

4.302. N v V $\leftrightarrow$ V*ing* N, the N being the head of the resulting N-phrase. Here the whole v, including its expansion, is dropped, so that the V is a single word. The N usually is also a single word; the T and most A that preceded N now precede the whole sequence V*ing* N: *barking dogs; the dangerous barking dogs.* Although this transformation differs from the preceding in various respects, homonymy between them is possible in a particular case: when nothing precedes the V*ing*, and no T precedes the N_2 above, and the N_1 above is dropped (§ 4.4), and of course when the N happens to be in both the subject range and the object range of the V. Thus *The lobbyist visited some journalists* $\rightarrow$ *Visiting journalists* (*, he thought, might help his plans*); *Journalists visited the new premier* $\rightarrow$ *Visiting journalists* (*, he thought, might help his plans*). In those constructional situations in which homonymy is possible the transformation is one-directional; for, given V*ing* N, we do not know whether a pair V, N that satisfies it also satisfies N v V or also satisfies v V N. The homonymy disappears if a long morpheme appears, because of the difference in headship: *Visiting journalists was indeed helpful, Visiting journalists were indeed helpful.* The present transformation holds for V without object N. For V with object N it occurs often (as above), the object being then either dropped or prefixed to the V: $\hat{N}_2$-V*ing* N_1 (often only a nonce form: *a journalist-visiting lobbyist*).

4.303. N v V $\leftrightarrow$ V*ing of* N, with V*ing* as head: *the barking of dogs.* Here V is as above, and homonymy is again possible with the transformation of § 4.301, when its subject N_1 is dropped: in *reading of plays, plays* is transformed from the object (§ 4.301); in *barking of dogs, dogs* is transformed from the subject.

4.304. N_1 v V $(N_2) \leftrightarrow N_1$ V*ing* (N_2). This does not have the internal structure of an N-phrase; it occurs as object (after V or P), but not as subject of another sentence, the N_1 having an object affix when it is a pronoun (cf. § 4.308): *They found the lobbyist* (or *him*) *visiting journalists.* It also occurs after C, in which case the N_1 is subject (and often zero, if the parallel primary sentence has the same subject): *They turned off, he going first; Taking the hint, he went away.* From sentences of the form N *is* N we have, for example, *They turned off, he being first.*

The next group replaces v by *to* rather than *-ing.*

4.305. N_1 v V (N_2) $\leftrightarrow$ *for* N_1 *to* V (N_2). This transformation occurs when its sentence is subject of another, or secondary to another; despite the *for*, it is an N-phrase, not a P N-phrase: *For him to visit journalists* (*is useless*); when the transformation is from the passive, for example, we have: *He praises paintings* → *Paintings are praised by him* → *For paintings to be praised by him* (*is most unusual*).

4.306. N_1 v V (N_2) $\leftrightarrow$ N_1 *to* V (N_2), with N_1 as head. This occurs when its sentence is subject or object of another sentence: *Actors to play the part* (*are plentiful*); (*We want*) *him to visit journalists.*

4.307. N_1 v V N_2 → N_2 *to* V: *paintings to praise.* This transform of its sentence may be found in any N position of another sentence. The N_1 is often present nearby, often with some P preceding: (*Good*) *parts to play are rare for him.*

The remaining transformations contain neither *to* nor *-ing.*

4.308. N_1 v V (N_2) $\leftrightarrow$ N_1 V (N_2). This occurs when the sentence is object of certain V (*make, let, have, feel, see, hear*, etc.) in another sentence: *He took it* → (*I let*) *him take it.* The whole v, including expansions, is dropped. Some of these V of the primary sentence also occur with other transformations of the secondary: *I saw him take it, I saw him taking it.* This transformation also occurs, with other V of the primary sentence, after *that* or its zero variant: *I insist* (*that*) *he be there* (from the sentence *He is there*), *We demand* (*that*) *he stop it.* Here the N_1 does not have the object affix when it is a pronoun. As elsewhere, the object affix is determined not by the transformation but by the relation of the secondary sentence to the primary, i.e. by the combining element, which in one case is *that* and in the other is object position; *that* + S_2 can occur as subject of S_1 as well as object of S_1.

4.309. N_1 v V (N_2) $\leftrightarrow$ *that* N_1 v V (N_2), or with zero variant of *that*. This occurs as subject or object of other sentences, after particular V of the other sentence: *I believe* (*that*) *he went; I insist* (*that*) *he is there; That he took it is certain.* Although the same V of the primary sentence (*insist*) may appear with this transformation and with the preceding one, it appears in the two cases as member of different V subclasses, and the meaning is different.

4.310. N_1 v V (N_2) $\leftrightarrow$ 'N_1 v V (N_2)'. Any sentence may appear unchanged except for the intonation of quotation, after certain V (*said*, etc.) of the primary sentence, its status being object of that V.[57]

Aside from participating in many of the v-dropping transformations above, sentences of the form N *is* N (in the sense of note 49) have the following transformations.

4.311. N_1 v *be* $N_2 \leftrightarrow N_1$ N_2 as object of another sentence (after certain V): *They considered him a police agent*; also after some members of C (*as*, zero C), in which case N_1 does not have an object affix when it is a pronoun, and often is zeroed: (*As*) *a police agent, he was hunted down by the rebels*. The transform occurs in any N position of the primary sentence when N_2 is P N, or when N_2 is marked off by comma intonation; the relation of the secondary sentence to the primary is then of the word-sharing type. We see both cases in *The fellow from Paris, a small hamlet nearby, spoke up*.

4.312. N *is* A $\leftrightarrow$ A N in the word-sharing combination: *The storm is distant* $\rightarrow$ *The distant storm (rumbled)*.

4.313. N_1 *has* $N_2 \leftrightarrow N_1$'s N_2; the result may appear (as a word-sharing combination) whenever N_2 appears.

4.4. *Many-One Transformations*

Most of the preceding transformations are one-one in the sense that for each individual sentence there is one transform and conversely (except for cases of homonymity). The N_1 v V $N_2 \rightarrow N_2$ *to* V (§ 4.307) is many-one, in that various sentences (with different subjects) have the same transform. All the v-dropping transformations may be considered many-one in this sense. Other many-one transformations follow.

4.41. Free pro-morphemes, e.g. N_1 v V $\rightarrow$ *He* (or *She* or *It*) v V. These transformations are S$\rightarrow$S and I(S)$\rightarrow$I(S), where I(S) indicates transformed S. For example, *The Hungarians rebelled* $\rightarrow$ *They rebelled; The rebels' setting up councils* (*led to a shadow government*) $\rightarrow$ *Their setting up councils* ... If I(S) is a nominalization, its pro-morpheme is a pro-S (really pro-nominalized-S), e.g. *This led to a shadow government*.

4.42. Dropping of *by* N, both in S$\leftrightarrow$S and in S$\leftrightarrow$N transformations; and the dropping of N's and *for* N in the S$\leftrightarrow$N group. In all these cases the sections that are subject to dropping have the structural position of P N and A, positions which are sometimes filled and sometimes not filled (i.e. which may structurally be considered droppable). As a result we have by the side of *Milk was being drunk by the children* also *Milk was being drunk*; by the side of *Your reading these things* also *Reading these things*; etc.

4.5 *Quasi-Transformations*

There are many cases in which two constructions fall short, in one respect or another, of satisfying the conditions for a transformation. These cases may nevertheless be of interest for various purposes, and may even be usable as transformations in restricted applications. Here only a brief indication will be given of the main types of quasi-transformations.[58]

One type of failure to meet the conditions is that in which the domain of transformation is smaller than a sentence. This is particularly of interest when the domain covers everything except separable D and P N phrases (those that can be separated by comma intonation), for example N_1 v V (N_2) $\leftrightarrow N_1$ v *not* V (N_2). In the transformations of §§ 4.1–4 it is understood, for the formulas given, that anything additional which occurs in the original sentence occurs also in the transform. Here this is no longer true. All central sentence constructions (subject phrase + verb phrase + N and P N object phrases), with most of the separable D and P N phrases, occur also with *not*. But some separable D and P N phrases and other constructions do not occur so, or else are altered when *not* is added: *not* would hardly occur without further change in *How silent it all seemed!* or *She looked up at last*. This is the case with some separable D and P N and some introducers, which occur with every central construction but not with every (other) separable D or P N. Even v can be considered a quasi-transformation of this type: N_1 + present tense + V $(N_2)\leftrightarrow N_1$ v V (N_2), or N V $(N_2)\leftrightarrow$N v V (N_2); in the second formulation the starting point N V is not a full sentence. We can go on from here to consider additions which have no restrictions of co-occurrence on the classes near them, but do have restrictions on the members of classes elsewhere in the sentence.

We have another failure to meet the conditions when the set of n-tuples that satisfies one construction is only partly similar to the set that satisfies the other construction, or almost but not quite identical with it. This is the case, for example, when the transformation holds for some not readily stateable subclasses. Thus, for certain subclasses of N_1 and N_2 we have the relation N_1 *is* $N_2\leftrightarrow N_2$ *is* N_1. It is also the case when the transformation holds for many but not all the members of a class, as in such individual quasi-transformations as N v V$\leftrightarrow$N v *succeed in* V*ing*, or N v V$\leftrightarrow$N v *be able to* V, or for the examples of § 4.15 and notes 52 and 56. We have such incompleteness, for example, in the quasi-transformation V A*ly* $\rightarrow$ A V*er* (*walk slowly, slow walker*), or in the various transformations that apply to various triples in the N P N construction (for example, there are some subclasses for which N_1 P_2 $N_3 \rightarrow N_3$ P_4 N_1 holds: *groups of people, people in groups*). Other construction pairs which are partially satisfied are N_1 P N_2 and N_2 na N_1, or V_1 P N_2 and V_1 N_2 na *ly* (*a push with energy, an energetic push, he pushed with energy, he pushed energetically*).

Quasi-transformations of this incomplete type show certain relations between the constructions concerned. Furthermore, many of them are productive; that is, co-occurrences which are present in one of the two constructions but lacking in the other frequently appear in the second as new formations, thus making the co-occurrences in the two constructions more nearly similar. Constructions related by quasi-transformations may be a major avenue for productivity, as the extension of morphemes to co-occurrents or constructions in which they had not previously appeared.

A third failure to meet the conditions for a full transformation appears when a quasi-transformation specifies for one of its components a class rather than an individual morpheme. This may happen if we can say that for certain N subclasses, N_1 of $N_2 \rightarrow N_2$ P N_1; but the choice of P depends on the individual members of N. Or if for given subclasses, N_1 P $N_2 \rightarrow N_2$ na N_1; but the choice of na depends on the particular co-occurrence of na with N (*wooden* but *national* etc.). Such relations are more useable if the class whose member remains to be specified is a small class. Even when the class is a large one, however, such a relation may be of interest, if some particular situation is afoot. For example, for many V we have $V_1 \rightarrow V_i$ V_1 vn. That is, the V_1 appears in nominalized form preceded by a new V_i; the new V_i (and its choice depends on the V_1) does not have here any of its usual meanings, but contributes some aspectual meaning while verbalizing the V_1 vn: *give a push, take a look, take a step, do a dance, make an analysis*, etc. Here too the quasi-transformational relation seems to be productive.

Cases of this type can be formulated by saying, for example, that for each N-pair (out of a subclass of N-pairs) there exists a particular (choice of) na, such that N_1 P $N_2 \rightarrow N_2$ na N_1.

A fourth type of quasi-transformation appears when part of an addition to a construction has transformational or quasi-transformational status, while another part has not. Thus, N v *make* or N v *let* can be added as primary sentence to almost any other sentence (the secondary having the transformation of § 4.308), but the choice of N depends in part on the individual words of the secondary.

Finally, some transformations may hold only if particular words are present in neighboring sentences. These are textually dependent transformations (§ 5.7).

5. THE PLACE OF TRANSFORMATIONS IN LINGUISTIC STRUCTURE

5.1. *Elementary Transformations*

The difference between any two constructions which are satisfied by the same n-tuples of their word classes comprises a transformation. When we compare the constructional differences that are contributed by various transformations we may see that one such difference is the sum of two others; that is, the effect of one transformation can be obtained by successive application of the other two, perhaps in a particular order. For example, N_1 v V $N_2 \rightarrow N_2$ v *be* Ven (*I saw him, He was seen*) is obtainable by the ordered succession of N_1 v V $N_2 \rightarrow N_2$ v *be* Ven by N_1 (§ 4.11) and S by $N_1 \rightarrow$ S (dropping by N_1, or more generally dropping a separable P N, § 4.42). Furthermore, comparison of various transformations may show that these can be combined out of certain elementary changes, even if these do not occur by themselves. Any transformation which is not obtainable by combining the effect of two or more other simpler transformations will be called an elementary transformation.

5.2. *The Algebra of Transformations*

The existence of elementary transformations makes it possible to regard all transformations as compoundings of one or more elementary ones. There are a great many transformational relations among constructions, e.g. N_1 v V $N_2 \rightarrow$ *by* wh + pro-morpheme v *be* N_1 V*en ?* is a transformation (*The workers rejected the ultimatum, By whom was the ultimatum rejected?*). The list in Part 4 is relatively short because it is in approximately elementary terms; the transformation just cited is not listed, but can be obtained from § 4.11 plus the question transform of § 4.2.

If we now consider a transform to be the effect of perhaps several elementary transformations, rather than always of just a single transformation, we have to see in what way the various elementary transformations can occur together. Here we have to bring into consideration the fact that transformations are restricted to particular structural environments. This is most obvious for the transformations of § 4.2 and § 4.3, since, for example, zero recurrence appears only in secondary parallel sentences, and dropping of v without replacement by *to* or *-ing* occurs only after certain V (*make, let*, etc.). But it is also true for the other transformations, since, for example, the passive occurs only for sentences with N v V N structure, hence not for N *is* N.[59] In view of this, we have to recognize that a given transformation does not apply to all sentences. And a given transformation T_1 operating on an appropriate sentence S_1 may leave the structure of S_1 altered in such a way that another transformation T_2, or for that matter T_1 again, cannot be applied to the altered T_1 S_1 even if it could have been applied to S_1 itself. For example, the passive T_p carries S_1 *The Hungarian workers staged a sit-down strike* into T_p S_1 *A sit-down strike was staged by the Hungarian workers*; but to the resultant T_p S_1 we can no longer apply T_p (to yield T_p T_p S_1), because the resultant has the structure N v V P N, which is not in general subject to T_p (see note 49).

It is sometimes possible to analyze the observed transformations into elementary ones in more than one way; and for each different analysis, the detailed algebra of how these elementary ones are compounded to yield the observed resultants will be correspondingly different.

The successive application of elementary transformations can be called their product. For example, the sentence *May there be mentioned now a certain secret?* can be derived from N *may mention now a certain secret* by the product of transformations T_p T_d T_t T_q described in §§ 4.11, 42, 13, and 2 (question) respectively; along the way we have T_p S (*A certain secret may be mentioned now by* N), T_p T_d S (*A certain secret may be mentioned now*), T_p T_d T_t S (*There may be mentioned now a certain secret*). Some products may not occur; or they may occur in one order but not in the other (e.g. T_d, dropping of *by* N, obviously occurs after but not before T_p). But this situation may be partly remedied by regarding certain transformations as positional variants of others.[60] Furthermore, all products may be said to occur, vacuously in some cases, if we say that wherever T_i S does not observably occur (where S itself may be the resultant of various transformations), T_i will be said to occur with the identity value. That is, identity is treated as a positional variant of T_i for all positions where T_i does not otherwise occur. Under this view, T_p T_p S for example occurs, but equals T_p S. This rather Herculean solution is of course of no interest except in cases where particular useful results can be obtained from it. Where products of particular transforms do occur in both orders, the result may or may not be the same; it usually is, e.g. T_p T_q $S_i = T_q$ T_p S_i.

It is clear that we have here a set of transformations with a base set (the elementary transformations), with products of the base members yielding the various other members of the set. Multiplication in the product may be associative (in the mathematical sense), and it may be commutative, depending on the properties of the transformations in the particular language and in part on how the various elementary transformations are defined. We can now define an identity transformation as one which leaves an S unchanged. An inverse can then be defined for each transformation, as that which will undo the effect of the transformation in question: the inverse T_p^{-1} of T_p is N_2 v *be* V*en by* $N_1 \rightarrow N_1$ v V N_2. The inverse T_i^{-1}, however, is of limited algebraic interest, because it usually occurs only after T_i, and will not combine with other T.

5.3. *Addition (Concatenation) of Transformed Sentences*

Many of the transformations appear only when their sentence occurs with another, in some secondary status to that other. Which particular sentences occur together is a matter of co-occurrence, like which members of two classes co-occur in a sentence. But how the sentences with their sequential transformations combine is of interest as showing an operation among transformed sentences, different from that of § 5.2.

We have seen three general types of sentence-combining, each with its characteristic transformations: parallel sentences, overlapping sentences (by word-sharing), and sentences nominalized as subjects or objects of others. These can be combined and recombined, so long as the conditions for applying them are satisfied; but each combination requires a new sentence to co-occur with the others. As an example we take the rather involved sentence *For the refugees from Budapest to have made so much of my arranging their border-crossing seemed to me sadder than anything else they did*. Here *The refugees cross borders* (with pronoun *they*) is nominalized as object of *I arranged* ( ). This in turn is nominalized as object of *The refugees have made so much of* ( ). This overlaps *The refugees were from Budapest*; and it also is nominalized as subject of ( ) *seemed sad to me*. The latter is conjoined by *-er than* with the zeroed parallel sentence ( ) *seemed sad to me* whose subject (the only part of the parallel sentence not zeroed) is *anything else*, to which is added by sentence overlap the *wh-* transform of *they did anything else* (with zero variant of the *which* pronoun of *anything else*, and *they* pronoun of the correspondingly placed *the refugees*). Various sentences or combinations here, including the whole, could carry various non-sequential transformations of the type of § 5.2, within the limits of their application. For example, the complete sentence could take the question transformation, aside from considerations of style (which could be lightened by using a different nominalization at the beginning).

5.4. *The Kernel*

It follows from §§ 5.2 and 5.3 that each sentence in the language can be expressed in terms of sequential and nonsequential transformations. Given any sentence, we can check it for all transformations; we will then find the sentence to consist of a sequence of one or more underlying sentences – those which have been transformed into the shapes that we see in our sentence – with various introductory or combining elements (as in § 3). We have thus a factorization of each sentence into transformations and elementary underlying sentences and combiners; the elementary sentences will be called sentences of the kernel of the grammar. Any two different sentences will have different factorizations, either the kernel sentences or the transformations being different; but one sentence may have two different factorizations, since two one-directional transformations (applied to partly different kernel sentences) may yield the same resultant sentence (homonymy).[61]

The kernel is the set of elementary sentences and combiners, such that all sentences of the language are obtained from one or more kernel sentences (with combiners) by means of one or more transformations. Each kernel sentence is of course a particular construction of classes, with particular members of the classes co-occurring. If many different types of construction were exemplified by the various kernel sentences, the kernel would be of no great interest, especially not of any practical interest. But kernels generally contain very few constructions; and applying transformations to these few constructions suffices to yield all the many sentence constructions of the language. The kernel constructions of English seem to be only these:

N v V (for V that occur without objects)
N v V P N (for P N that have restricted co-occurrence with particular V)
N v V N
N *is* N
N *is* A
N *is* P N
N *is* D

In addition there are a few minor constructions, such as

N *is between* N *and* N.

There are also some inert constructions which hardly enter into transformations (except quotation):

e.g. N!, *Yes*.[62]

Finally, there are the combiners and introducers of § 3, and the intonationally separable introducers and D and P N phrases, all of which occur with any kernel sentence. The V in these formulas includes V P compounds and V D; the A includes D A; the N includes compound N and special forms like unitary (compound) N P N, and carries various T and post-T words (quantifiers etc.) as well as *-s* 'plural'.[63]

Different decisions at various points in the analysis of transformations will yield a somewhat different set of kernel structures. The result, however, will not make a great deal of difference for the picture of the structure of the language, and even less for the structure of language in general.

Kernel sentences contain in general no parts that repeat elements elsewhere in the sentence or in other sentences near-by; such repetition has been eliminated by the setting up of independent elements (independent within a sentence) in structural linguistics, and by the removal of dependences on other sentences in the course of transformational analysis.[64] The importance of this independence among kernel sentences is that the further grammar, the grammar of how kernel sentences are built up into the actual sentences of the language, does not have to specify very closely which kernel sentences are to be combined with which, except for the relatively loose restrictions of co-occurrence that hold among sentences. If two kernel sentences nevertheless have a special co-occurrence relation to each other, this must be stated in the grammar of constructions beyond the kernel – the grammar which contains the transformations and any other information that may be required to build all sentences.

In addition to exhibiting the minimal sentence constructions, the kernel sentences are thus also the domain of the major restrictions of co-occurrence in the language. The restrictions that determine which member of a class occurs with which member of its neighbor class are contained in the list of actual sentences that satisfy each of the kernel constructions. By the nature of transformations, they do not affect these co-occurrences. The word-co-occurrences in all sentences of the language are in general those of the kernel sentences, so that the only restrictions that remain outside the kernel are the much looser ones determining which sentences combine with which. In view of this, one may raise the question whether the kernel sentences may not be subdivided further into minimal domains of co-occurrence restriction, out of which the kernel sentences would then be built according to the grammar of kernel constructions (chiefly by means of a word-sharing combination of those minimal domains). In effect, this means extracting N V, V N (object), V P N, V D, and D A out of the structures which contain these (and the various compound words), and combining, say, $N_i V_j + V_j N_k$ to yield a sentence $N_i V_j N_k$.

5.5. *Effect of Transformations in the Language Structure*

Transformations have some particular effects in the over-all structure of the language. They make possible an unbounded variety and length of sentences out of the stock of kernel sentences, thanks to the unbounded repeatability of various sequential transformations. They give an organized view of complex sentences (cf. Parts 2 and 3). As a result, they provide solutions for the structure of some constructions which are hardly solvable in the usual linguistic terms, for instance the structure of *flying planes* in *Flying planes is my hobby*; and can explain what are the differences in the two structures of a homonymous sentence (e.g. *They appointed a fascist chief of police*: both *A fascist is chief of police* transformed as object of *They appointed ( )*, and *(The) chief of police is a fascist* transformed as word-sharing overlap in *They appointed a chief of police*).[65]

Transformations can specify in general the differences and the similarities among sentences. Consider for example these four very similar sentences:

S_1 *Mary has a sad fate.*
S_2 *Mary's fate is sad.*
S_3 *Mary's fate is a sad one.*
S_4 *Mary's is a sad fate.*

These are transformed from some or all of three kernel sentences:

K_1 *Mary has a fate.*
K_2 *Fate is a fate.*
K_3 *Fate is sad.*

The following transformations are involved:

For S_1: K_3, overlap with K_1.
For S_2: K_1, N *has* N→N'*s* N, overlap with K_3.
For S_3: K_1, N *has* N→N'*s* N, overlap with K_2 (first N);
K_2, pro-N of second N;
K_3, overlap with K_2 (second N).
For S_4: K_1, N *has* N→N'*s* N, overlap with K_2 (first N);
K_2, zero recurrence of first N;
K_3, overlap with K_2 (second N).

It is of interest to see that these sentences, which we would intuitively describe as semantically equivalent or almost equivalent, have the same kernel sentences – except that some of them lack K_2, which we would hardly expect to contribute a semantic change – and differ only in transformations.

Transformations often overcome structural restrictions of the kernel grammar. For example, the subject of a sentence is always present in English; but it can be dropped by transforming into the passive and then carrying out the drop transformation of § 4.42.[66] Or a sentence N v V, without object or even P N, can be given the passive transformation by first applying a pro-V-phrase transformation (§ 4.41): *He stumbled unexpectedly, He did it unexpectedly, It was done by him unexpectedly.*

In many cases, transformations add flexibility in a direct way. They may change the grammatical status of a sentence into that of an N-phrase, thus making it possible to relate the sentence to an outside N V or V N, etc. They may bring out one part of the sentence for primary attention. And of course they yield stylistic variations.

5.6. *Co-Occurrence and Transformation in Structural Theory*

Important properties of linguistic structure are definable with respect to co-occurrence and transformations. Those constructional features of grammar which are well known from descriptive linguistics are in general limited to the kernel. In the kernel, the constructions are built up as concatenations of various included constructions, down to morpheme classes; various classes or sequences of classes (and their members) are substitutable for each other in particular positions of these constructions. Transformations cannot be viewed as a continuation of this constructional process. They are

based on a new relation, which satisfies the conditions for being an equivalence relation, and which does not occur in descriptive linguistics. All
sentences which are described in constructional terms must have a specific
constituent analysis, since the constructional analysis proceeds in terms of
immediate constituents (component subconstructions). This is not necessary,
however, for all sentences in transformational analysis. Some of the cruces
in descriptive linguistics have been due to the search for a constituent
analysis in sentence types where this does not exist because the sentences are
transformationally derived from others. For this and other reasons a
language cannot be fully described in purely constructional terms, without
the transform relation.[67]

Some of the special operations on constructions which are set up in
descriptive linguistics can be described in terms of transformations instead.
For example, much of the expansion of constructions (e.g. A N = N, i.e. A N
is substitutable for N) is obtainable as a result of the sentence-overlapping
transformations; this will be more general if the kernel constructions are
subdivided into co-occurrence domains (§ 5.4, end). Transformations have
partial similarity to certain elements and relations of descriptive linguistics.
Most important of these is the similarity of transformations to variants, both
free and positional. However, if A is to be a variant of B, A must be substitutable for B, or must have environments complementary to those of B,
and the environments of A and B must be otherwise identical. These conditions cannot be explicitly met in the case of sentences because in descriptive
linguistics environments are defined only up to sentence boundaries.

A major difference between the kernel and the rest of the language structure
is that the individual co-occurrences among members of classes are in
general contained within the kernel. The kinds of problems that are associated
with this – for example the statistical determination of co-occurrents, the
scaling of acceptance of co-occurrents, the differences among samples – all
refer to the kernel. Between the kernel and the transformational structure it
may be convenient to recognize a border area containing some of the types of
quasi-transformations and productivity.

Finally, as has been mentioned, the kernel (including the list of combiners)
is finite; all the unbounded possibilities of language are properties of the
transformational operations. This is of interest because it is in general
impossible to set up a reasonable grammar or description of a language that
provides for its being finite. Though the sample of the language out of which
the grammar is derived is of course finite, the grammar which is made to
generate all the sentences of that sample will be found to generate also many
other sentences, and unboundedly many sentences of unbounded length. If
we were to insist on a finite language, we would have to include in our gram-

mar several highly arbitrary and numerical conditions – saying, for example, that in a given position there are not more than three occurrences of *and* between N. Since a grammar therefore cannot help generating an unbounded language, it is desirable to have the features which yield this unboundedness separate from the rest of the grammar.

Our picture of a language, then, includes a finite number of actual kernel sentences, all cast in a small number of sentence structures built out of a few morpheme classes by means of a few constructional rules; a set of combining and introducing elements; and a set of elementary transformations, such that one or more transformations may be applied to any kernel sentence or any sequence of kernel sentences, and such that any properly transformed sentences may be added sequentially by means of the combiners.

The network of individual co-occurrence in language can provide more analysis of linguistic structure than is involved in transformations alone. The co-occurrences can provide us with a relation in language with respect to which we can discover a system of algebraic structures and algebraic relations in language. The central method here is to set up for each construction of two or more classes C_1, C_2, ... a correspondence which associates with each member of C_1 those members of C_2 that occur with it in that construction, and so on. The mappings differ for different constructions; several of them are many-valued, and the individual associations vary for different samples. It turns out, however, that permanent structures can be permanently characterized by particular types of mappings. The different structures so distinguished turn out to be significantly different in the economy of the language.

5.7. *Applications*

Transformations are applicable in various studies or utilizations of systems of a generally linguistic type. There are specific applications, for example, in linguistic typology – comparison of different types of language structure.[68]

The chief outside uses of transformations, however, depend upon their special meaning status. Meaning is a matter of evaluation, and cannot be fitted directly into the type of science that is developed in structural linguistics or in transformation theory. Still, for various purposes it may be possible to set up some practical evaluation of meaning; and with respect to most of these evaluations, transformations will have a special status. That many sentences which are transforms of each other have more or less the same meaning, except for different external grammatical status (different grammatical relations to surrounding sentence elements), is an immediate impression. This is not surprising, since meaning correlates closely with range of occurrence, and transformations maintain the same occurrence range.

When we have transformations which are associated with a meaning change, it is usually possible to attribute the meaning change to the special morphemes (combiners, introducers, subclasses of the primary V) in whose environment the transformation occurs. To what extent, and in what sense, transformations hold meaning constant is a matter for investigation; but enough is known to make transformations a possible tool for reducing the complexity of sentences under semantically controlled conditions.

It is possible to normalize any sequence of sentences by reducing each one to its kernels and their transformations. The text then becomes longer, but its component sentences are simpler, as is the kernel grammar according to which they are written. The kernel sentences are then available for comparison or arrangement, both within the discourse and as among discourses, in a way that the original sentences were not. Transformations can be checked by comparing the textual environments of a sentence and its transform, to see whether, say, a given N V N triple which occurs in a given environment of other sentences will also occur in the same environment when it is transformed to the passive. Methods of this kind can be used to make various quasi-transformations acceptable as transformations in a given discourse, or to make one-directional transformations useable in both directions.

Transformations are much needed in discourse analysis; for though the method of discourse analysis is independent of them, the complexity of many sentences makes discourse analysis hardly applicable unless the text has first been normalized by transformations. For discourse analysis it is often not necessary to reduce sentences to their kernels, but only to transform those sentences and sections which contain the same words in such a way that they have the same structure, if this is possible.

NOTES

[1] The study of transformations arose out of the attempt to construct a method for analyzing language samples longer than a sentence; a preliminary list of English transformations is given in Z. Harris, 'Discourse Analysis', *Lg.* **28** (1952), 18–23 (Paper XIX of this volume). Although the present paper was presented at the 1955 meeting of the Linguistic Society in Chicago, some of the details on English transformations have been added since that time, in connection with a project of the National Science Foundation.

From a time when this work was still at an early stage, Noam Chomsky has been carrying out partly related studies of transformations and their position in linguistic analysis: see his dissertation, *Transformational Analysis* (University of Pennsylvania, 1955); and his paper 'Three Models for the Description of Language', *IRE Transactions on Information Theory*, IT-2, No. 3 (1956),113–24; now also his book *Syntactic Structures*, The Hague 1957. My many conversations with Chomsky have sharpened the work presented here, in addition to being a great pleasure in themselves.

[2] Notation: Morpheme and word classes: N (noun) and V (verb) as above; A (adjective) includes *large, old, extreme,* etc.; *T* (article) includes *the, a*; P (preposition) includes *of,*

from, to, etc.; C (conjunction) includes *and, or, but*, etc.; D (adverb) includes *very, well, quickly*, etc. Classes of affixes (mostly suffixes, some prefixes): na indicates an affix such that N + na (i.e. the sequence N na) yields an A word (a word substitutable for A morphemes): *papery, cloth-like*. Similarly vn after V yields an N word: *growth*; nn after N yields an N word: *growths, childhood*; and so on. And v (tense and verb 'auxiliary' class, § 2.5) includes *-ed will, can*, etc. S stands for sentence. The equivalence A = B indicates that if sequence A occurs in a sentence, the substitution of B for A also yields a sentence. All these classes apply specifically to English; the analyses and transformations below have been set up for English data, although the principles are general and not limited to any particular language.

[3] It might be argued that individual co-occurrence is essentially different from morphological classification simply because it is a direct reflection of the speaker's combinations of meanings, and is therefore not subject at all to investigation for distributional regularities. No doubt the speakers' meanings, or the knowledge and perceptions of the body of speakers, is a major factor in building up the co-occurrence set of each morpheme. But linguistic productivity, and other factors which are determined at least partly by structural and historical factors, also affect co-occurrence: different noun-making suffixes occur in *avoidance* and *evasion* for no semantic reason; *killing* occurs in *a ( ) sense of humor* but perhaps not in *a ( ) laugh*. Furthermore, it frequently happens that morphemes in one of their co-occurrences have idiomatic meanings which cannot reasonably be drawn from the meanings of the component morphemes in any other occurrences, so that one can hardly claim that the occurrence in question was based on the meaning of the morphemes. Nor can one easily predict what combinations will appear: *I saw them off* but not *I noticed them off; There's trouble ahead* and *There's trouble afoot; dressed chicken* but not *undressed chicken*. A seed catalog describes a marigold as *exceedingly double*, though one might not have expected a quantifier before a number word. The observed co-occurrences thus have to be taken as raw data for classification and comparison; they cannot be adequately derived from some nonlinguistic source such as 'the desired combinations of meanings'.

[4] It can be readily seen that the statement 'there is a stateable set of B-co-occurrents for each A_1 in the construction A B' is equivalent to 'the construction A B is satisfied (i.e. instances of it actually occur) for a stateable set of $A_i B_j$ pairs'. For our present purposes, it will be sufficient to describe a construction thus: a construction is a sentence, or a class sequence such that some construction is defined as a combination of that class sequence plus other class sequences. Thus T A N V is a sentence construction; T A N (a member of the set of N-phrase constructions) and V (a member of the set of V-phrase constructions) are each constructions, since N-phrase plus V-phrase defines a sentence. For all except certain transformational sentences we can replace the words above by these: A construction is a sentence, or an immediate constituent of a construction.

[5] An example of indirect use of these considerations. Since the classes A and N in English contain in general different morphemes and words, the A-co-occurrence of N_i in A N_i and the N-co-occurrence of N_i in N_i *of* N will be different sets. But many A words contain N morphemes (having been formed by N + na: *wooden, glassy*); and for these N na N_i constructions (a subset of A N_i) we find that the N-co-occurrents are partially similar to the N-co-occurrents of N_i in N_i *of* N (*wooden table, table of wood, glassy surface, surface of glass*, but only *glassy stare*). This suggests that the status of N_i relative to ( ) *of N* is similar to the status of N_i relative to N na ( ), and hence relative to A ( ), since N na is just a subset of A. (Note that the difference of meaning between *glassy surface* and *surface of glass* is not relevant here.)

[6] Same subscript means same member of the class: the second appearance of N_1 indicates the same morpheme as the first N_1.

[7] This requirement excludes, among others, the cases of small classes whose members have the same immediate neighbors but different co-occurrents elsewhere in the sentence, e.g. *and, or*.

[8] Examples of all these will be given in a later paper, describing how transformations are actually set up for a language.

⁹ These are examples of two major types of environmental effect. In the first, the absent combinations (e.g. *book whom*) do not occur in ordinary use of the language. In the second, the absent combinations (e.g. *The letter was returned ≠ They must have been misaddressed*) can be found, but usually with different textual environment, often with different intonation, and in any case not as the statistically checked experimental result of asking the informant to substitute *The letter* for *The letters*.

¹⁰ Further analyses will become possible in § 2.2 when we add the consideration of individual co-occurrence; while the further step of setting up transformations (§§ 3.0ff.) is based on the added consideration of identical co-occurrences (§ 1.3).

¹¹ Two constructions of the same n classes may also be distinguished by their n-tuples, as two morphemes of the same phonemes are distinguished here. For example, if P N (*at this time* etc.) occurs in various sentence positions, we merely consider it the same construction but in different positions. If, however, the particular pairs of P and N are partly different in different positions (say at sentence beginning and medially), we define two separate P N constructions.

¹² There are many special cases, homonymities, etc. which must be left for a later discussion.

¹³ There is a minor special case of N₁ P N₂ in which the two N have both parallel and P N = A characteristics, e.g. in *crushed against the wall of the building* or *heard the paddle of the canoe*. Internally the N P N is of the P N = A type. But in relation to the preceding V, each N occurs in similar sentence environments as object N of that V. That is, N₁ and N₂ occur in same sentence environments after this V, even though they do not otherwise, and in respect to this they are parallel.

¹⁴ The P N = A type of N₁ P₃ N₂ also often occurs in reverse order, N₂ P₄ N₁, but with different sentence environment, usually different P, and with a change of headship: *The name of the lists is 'Soldiers killed in battle'*. Since the environment is not held constant, there is little interest in this unless some particular relations can be stated, e.g. between the P₃ and P₄ choices.

¹⁵ Where X (or Y) in the given environment participates in a discontinuous morpheme extending to another construction, we find this participation on both X and Y of X C Y: *He reads, He reads and writes*. Certain C may be defined as participating in such an extending morpheme even where their X or Y alone would not: in N₁ *and* Nⱼ V, the V generally shows the plural morpheme even when N₁ V or Nⱼ V alone does not (*A man and woman are here* but *A man is here*).

¹⁶ By Noam Chomsky.

¹⁷ This zero morpheme meets the requirements for a zero – of being determined by observable conditions (namely *I*, *you*, and plurals as subject); and it satisfies the meaning of V + zero, which is not just V in general but V in the present tense. The *-s* 'third person singular' can now be considered an alternant of this zero, occurring with the remaining subjects.

¹⁸ For convenience, we will henceforth consider the *-ed* and zero (and *-s*) suffixes to be members of the auxiliary class v; this requires us to view *could, should*, etc. as independent members of v rather than as *can, shall*, etc. + *-ed*. Alternatively we can regard the suffixes as a separate class, and *could* as *can* + *-ed*, etc. But *should, would* often occur in environments where *-ed* does not otherwise occur (e.g. *I would, if he will too*). Furthermore, we would have to note that *can* etc. occur with *-ed* (to make *could*) but not with *-s* (*He can*, but *He sees*). Note in the whole analysis the departure of structural considerations from historical antecedents.

¹⁹ These are only combinations that constitute verb structures. To each of these can be added *be -en* just before the V, forming the passive of that construction; but this involves also a certain rearrangement of the sentence environment (§ 4.11). A few other combinations occur, as in *He has had stolen from him two invaluable manuscripts*, which seems to contain v + *have -en* + *have -en* + V. But the constituent analysis here is not *he* (subject N) + *has had stolen* (V) + P N + object N-phrase, for these cannot be rearranged like other N, V, P N, or replaced here by other N, V, P N. This sentence has to be analyzed

as a transformation; even without that the *stolen* would be taken with *from him*, not with *has had*. Note the alternative form *He has had two invaluable manuscripts stolen from him.*
[20] The N being subject of the V. If *which* follows N P N, either of the N may be the one with similar co-occurrents: *I was watching the wall of books which* ( ).
[21] In English the antecedent is almost always in a different sentence structure from the pro-morpheme, though both sentence structures may be within the same sentence. (Sentence structure is used here to mean any sequence which is a transform of a sentence, such as *which had cracked* in *The wall which had cracked finally collapsed*.) An exception is pronoun + *self*, whose antecedent is almost always the subject: *Carl saw himself, Carl went by himself, Carl himself saw it*. This can perhaps be analyzed as not a pronoun but just a morpheme *self* (different from *the self*), with the subject having a discontinuous repetition (in pronoun form) before this *self*. However, pronoun + *'s* (which is a member of A) occurs freely in the same clause as its antecedent N: *He took his books.*
[22] The total co-occurrence range of a free *he* equals the total co-occurrence ranges of all bound *he*. A marginal case is such pronoun occurrences as unstressed *you're, we're, one's* in ( ) *only young once*, which can perhaps be replaced by all members of N, or perhaps only by a new subclass of N (*people, Jim*, etc.; whereas *one* can otherwise be substituted by any N). In contrast, the *it* of *It's raining* is not a pro-morpheme at all: almost no other morpheme can substitute for it here, so that this *it* is just a member of N.
[23] We also find *some* as a member of T (article class) in *some person*. Many words are members of more than one class.
[24] The *s* of *ours, yours*, etc. and the *n* of *mine* are also pro-N: *I'll take my book and you take yours*.
[25] The following analysis will show *who* to contain the morpheme *wh-* even though it lacks the phonemic /hw/.
[26] Various additional considerations show that these morphemes belong to the classes missing in the sentence structure that follows them. For example, P occurs in general only before N, but it also occurs before *whom, which, what* (*to whom, from which*, etc.). Throughout § 2.62 N indicates N-phrase: the *wh-* words replace a full N-phrase and do not have T or A before them; and V will be used for V-phrase. Whenever S is written here directly after *wh-* it is understood that some part of this S is occupied by the post-*wh-* morpheme, e.g. *...who went* is *wh-* S, the *-o* being the subject N; *whom I saw* is *wh-* S, the *-om* being the object N.
[27] We find *that* in place of *who, whom, which*, and a zero morpheme in place of *whom, which*, when no P precedes these: *a flower that had dropped, the place I mentioned*. We regard *that* or zero as variants of *wh-*, with the *-o, -om, -ich* appearing after it in a zero variant. In the first S$_1$ *wh-* S$_2$ type below, *that* or a zero morpheme replaces the *wh-*, with the post-*wh-* morpheme appearing in full in S$_2$: *I know who came, I know that he came*. Justification for these analyses becomes apparent when all the constructions are compared.
[28] It is impossible to give here all the co-occurrence characteristics which justify these analyses, but as an example note that in sentences like *I found what you lost* the two verbs are always such as have some nouns (not merely pronouns) which are common to both their object ranges. We would hardly find, for example, *I bit what you extrapolated*.
[29] Among minor occurrences of *wh-* note these: *wh-* S constituting an independent subject N-phrase, primarily in N *is* N sentences and passives (*Who did it is a question, Who did it can no longer be discovered*); *wh-ever* S as independent N-phrase (*Whoever did it was a fool*); the construction *What a clean job !*; *while* as a C. Sentences like *I know where* may be analyzed as *I know where S* with the S present in a zero pro-morpheme; the antecedent S is usually present in the neighborhood.
[30] After constructions like *I am going, I have gone*, the second part is *but he isn't, but he hasn't*, not *but he doesn't*. The *is* and *has* operate like members of v. After *I will be going* the second part is *and so will you be* or *and so will you*, with the *be* repeated like a member of v or zeroed like a V. A similar situation occurs in N *is* N sentences: *He's a fool but she isn't, He'll be late but she won't be* or *but she won't*. And the case is similar for V *to* V and V V*ing* sequences: *I'll try to catch it if you will* or *if you try*.

[31] In *He came, and fast*, we satisfy the property of C of always occurring between identical constructions, by saying that a zero pro-S of *he came* occurs before *fast*. This is supported by the fact that the D word in the position of *fast* will always be in the D-co-occurrence of the verb of the preceding section (*came*).

[32] There are many subtypes. For example, there is no *The scare made the girl's scream*. Note the general similarities to the constructions of § 2.8.

[33] Some first V have a P before the second V: *insist on going, insist on you going, succeed in taking, stop noticing, stop him from noticing, stop him noticing*.

[34] It will be noted later that for each such construction V N_1 N_2 the same morphemes also occur in the construction V N_2 P N_1: *give a book to the fellow, ask a question of him*. But this is a transformational criterion, such as we are skirting here: the constructional status here is to be determined only by grammar and co-occurrence ranges. Some additional transformational properties characterize only this structure: the transformation of replacing the second N by its pro-N generally involves interchange of the two N (*give it to the fellow*) but not so for the first N (*give him a book*); there are two passive transformations, one of which shows the P N character of the first N (*A book was given to the fellow, The fellow was given a book*).

[35] Similarly in N V^n N: *They are honorary members*. The *shambles* above does not conflict since it is preceded by the singular *a* and is hence singular like its first N *barn*.

[36] This construction is thus seen to have some similarities to the N_1 V_1 (N_2 V_2) of § 2.7 (*We heard it flow* etc.), although the V_1 there is not in the V^b subclass. When transformations are considered, these two will be found to be special cases of the same transformation.

[37] Furthermore, V has restricted co-occurrence relations to P (i.e. there are specific V P pairs) in such forms as *He took the project over*, but V does not seem to have specific pairs with the second N of V N N. A different analysis of this and of forms like *threw the door open* is proposed by Noam Chomsky.

[38] There may be small differences in meaning, and large differences in style; this does not affect the fact (but only the interpretation) of the co-occurrence equivalences discussed above or the transformational equivalences discussed below.

[39] There is also a minor type of question-assertion sequence, as in *Did you go to Rome, or to Paris?, Did you, or she, do it?*. These have two like constituents joined by *or*, with a rising intonation on the first and a falling intonation at sentence-end. (It is distinct from the yes-no question *Did you or she do it?* with one rising intonation.) The assertion here is *I went to Rome* or *To Rome* (and *She* or *She did* or *She did it*). The two or more constituents joined by *or* function like the post-*wh-* morpheme of that status (*to Rome, or to Paris* functions like *where*; the pro-morpheme equals a disjunction of members of its class). That is, the assertion always contains a constituent of that constructional status (e.g. *To Rome*, or perhaps *Neither, just to Marseilles*) and repetitions, pro-morphemes, or zeros of the rest of the question as above.

[40] From this it follows, incidentally, that two matched sentences do not occur in identical environments even if their introducers seem to be identical: they really appear in two different positions in respect to their one discontinuous matching introducer: *people are cynical* occurs in position ( )$_1$ and *people are not cynical* occurs in position ( )$_2$ of the environment *Some* ( )$_1$ *Some* ( )$_2$.

[41] Some of these C occur also with a different transformation, in which the subject N is zeroed and the V has *-ing* instead of a tense or auxiliary v: *The sailors got the raise while (still) organizing for it*. When the reconstructed secondary would be N *is* N, N *is* A, or N *is* P N, this transformation may treat *is* as a V or may drop the *is*, when the subject N is zeroed: *The sailors got the raise while being on duty* or *while on duty*. In this transformation the secondary sentence (C + S_2) often appears first: *While walking home, we found this stone*. In *Walking home, we found this stone* we can say there is a zero member of C. With zero and certain other C, the zeroed subject N is followed by *to* V in the place of v V: *To get there we must rush; They rushed so as to get there on time*.

[42] Certain occurrences of *and* and *or* cannot be regarded as deriving in this way from two

sentences; e.g. *Sugar and water make syrup* (compare *Sugar with water makes syrup*), *They argued back and forth, a black and white drawing, She and I disagreed.* It is generally possible to characterize these cases. Certain specific combinations of specific morphemes + *and* fall in this category, e.g. *between* N *and* N (*I lost it somewhere between Fifth and Sixth*). In the case of N *and* N V *each other* (*Electrons and positrons repel each other*) we do not directly expand the N *and* N because of the pro-N-pair *each other*.

[43] The distinctions have to be drawn carefully. Coordinating conjunctions do not necessarily have reversible order: *The goldfish ate too much and died.*

[44] *He is richer than you* is not *He is rich* + *you are rich* but *He is rich* + *-er than* + *you are rich.* Cf. Edward Sapir, 'Grading: A Study in Semantics', *Philosophy of Science* **11** (1944), 93–116.

[45] The first sentence may have an object, as in *I phoned him to learn what was going on,* transformed from $N_1 V_1 N_2$ and $N_1 V_2$. Superficially this can be confused with the next case below ($N_1 V_1 N_2$ and $N_2 V_2$) until the various co-occurrence ranges are checked, as also the substitutability of C (*I phoned him in order to ...*). When both N_1 and N_2 are in the subject range for V_2, the sentence is ambiguous, and both analyses (and both meanings) are possible. (Such homonymities appear wherever a single resultant structure is obtained from different transformations and underlying sentences.) Example: *We saw him up there* from *We saw him* + *We were up there* or from *We saw him* + *He was up there.*

[46] Another transformation for two sentences with the same object will be seen in § 3.8. The shared words, like the zeros of the parallel sentences (§§ 3.3–5) and bound pro-morphemes in general, are not merely two independent occurrences of the same morpheme. Rather, the morpheme in question extends into the shared, zero, or pro-morphemed position in the next sentence. Hence the meaning of the underlying sentences is not merely that I bought a house and that he built a house, but that the house that I bought and the one that he built are the same.

[47] This formulation overlooks the fact that certain sentences containing N_1 may not co-occur with some particular N_1 *is* ( ) sentences. The more exact statement therefore is: Any sentence S_1 which contains an N_1-phrase (provided the N_1-phrase is a transform of an N_1 *is* [ ] sentence) can be analyzed as a shared-word combination of S_1 with N_1 in place of the N_1-phrase + the corresponding N_1 *is* ( ) sentence.

[48] Cf. the end of § 2.62.

[49] But other V + P N do not have this transformation: there is no passive of *The flowers grew near the wall.* Nor does the passive occur with N *is* N sentences: *They became refugees, We are at peace.* In N *is* N sentences the long morphemes -*s* 'plural' etc. extend over both N; the position of the second N can be occupied by any N-phrase, P N-phrase, or A-phrase (including V*ing*, or V*en* from the passive); and a certain subclass of V including *become, remain*, etc. occurs in the position of *is*.

[50] The V P mentioned above operates like the first X position. All these examples have shown the passive of a primary S_1 which includes a secondary S_2 in one of its N positions. The secondary S_2 could be transformed into a passive without affecting the primary: *Many thousands watched the daredevils race the cars, Many thousands watched the cars being raced by the daredevils.* Or both primary and secondary can be transformed: *The cars being raced by the daredevils were watched by many thousands.* In the shared-word sequence (§ 3.6), the primary sentence can be transformed, but the secondary only if the result fits with the restrictions on word-sharing. In contrast, there is no passive of V *to* V constructions because these do not constitute a single sentence structure composed out of S_1 and S_2 but two parallel structures (§ 3.5): *I phoned to meet him.*

[51] The *by* which is a member of P has restrictions of co-occurrence; that is, it occurs between certain V_i and N_j and not between others. The *by* of the passive occurs between any V_i and N_j which satisfy $N_j V_i$.

[52] Among the many details omitted here are the characterizations of such exceptions which do not transform as *It caught fire.* There is a partial transformation with -*able* in the position of -*en*: *The milk is drinkable by the children.* But there are various restrictions on the occurrence of this -*able*, so that it can only be considered a quasi-transformation (§ 4.5).

Note that there is a semantic addition in -*able* such as we do not have in the -*en* passive.

[53] There are many other introducers, with the constructional status of D, P N, or N V *that*, which occur with almost any sentence: *perhaps, certainly, in general, It is probable that*, etc. We could propose transformations, for example: $S \leftrightarrow It$ *is probable that* S; or $N v V D \leftrightarrow How$ D N v V! (*How quickly he came!*). Since there may be some S with which these do not occur, we have to consider them quasi-transformations (§ 4.5); note that they contribute more specific semantic additions than do the transformations.

[54] Certain dependent order changes may be mentioned here, though they can be regarded as part of the sentence-elements with which they occur. Most of these are limited to S_2 position (after particular combining elements). The order change $N v \rightarrow v N$ is usual with the question intonation, and always with the element *wh-?*; the inversion of tenses with *not* can be expressed by assuming *not* to occur before v and adding $not v \rightarrow v not$; and the bringing of the pro-morphemed section to the beginning of the sentence occurs always after *wh-*.

[55] Here and in the other transformations it is only the v proper (auxiliary or tense) that is dropped. The expansions of v (*be -ing, have -en*) remain, and the -*ing* is added to the first of them (except that the sequence *being* V*ing* is avoided): *He has read* → *His having read, He has been reading* → *His having been reading.*

[56] After -*s* the parenthesized *of* always occurs. More restrictedly, as a quasi-transformation, we have $Ń_2$-V̇*ing* in the position of V*ing* (*of*) N_2: *your play-readings.* Another quasi-transformation is N_1 *is a* V*er of* N_2, $Ń_1$ *is a* N_2-V̇*er*, and (dropping the N_1) $Ń_2$-V̇*er*: *He is a play-reader*, etc.

[57] In a quoted-sentence object of N_1 *said to* N_2, *I* is a pronoun of N_1, *you* is a pronoun of N_2. The position of the quote marker can be occupied by *that* (or zero), in which case the special pronoun relations above do not hold, and certain changes occur in the v.

[58] The case where the set of n-tuples that satisfy one construction is included in the set of n-tuples that satisfy another construction (rather than being identical with that other set) is a one-directional transformation (e.g. § 4.11), but does not have to be regarded as a quasi-transformation.

[59] In general, a given structure may be subject to several transformations, e.g. N v V N, or the object N (or any N) position in a primary sentence. And a given transformation may occur in more than one structure, e.g. zero recurrence, or N v inversion. It may be possible to characterize for a given language what types of transformations occur in what types of structures.

[60] If two transformations occur in complementary products, so that they do not both occur in the same position, we can call them positional variants of each other, and say that they are the same transformation (but with the observed different values in the different positions).

[61] The set of all sentences is closed with respect to transformations. If homonymous sentences can be suitably distinguished or marked, the set of all transformations (all the occurring products of the elementary transformations) yields a partition of the set of sentences. The set of transformations is thus a quotient set of the set of sentences. If we now map the set of sentences into the set of transformations (so that each sentence is associated with the particular product of transformations that is present in it), then those sentences which are carried into the identity transformation are the kernel of the set of sentences with respect to this mapping. These kernel sentences are precisely the underlying elementary sentences mentioned above.

[62] But V! is an N v V kernel sentence with zero variant of *you*, plus exclamatory intonation. Note that only sequential sentences, or sentences with internal evidence of zeros (as in the case of V!), are built up to full sentence structure. The traditional *Fire!* is left as it stands; we cannot know with what words to fill it out.

[63] Most cases of V*ing* will occur under V (either from *is -ing*, as an expansion of v, in V, or else from various transforms of V). But some cases are members of A; these appear in co-occurrences which are not the same as those of the corresponding V. Example: *unyielding*, and *understanding* in *He has a very understanding manner.*

[64] The sentences of a kernel are therefore maximally independent of each other; one can say that they give the least possible information about each other. (In contrast, transforms obviously contain information about each other, as do sequential sentences.) Nevertheless, some kinds of dependences between sentences cannot be removed by the methods mentioned here, and remain in the kernel. Such are for example dependences among loose and unspecifiable subclasses, e.g. the partitive adjectives of a particular noun: the occurrence of one of them in a kernel sentence tells us that a partly similar sentence with another partitive adjective of that noun also exists in the kernel.

[65] Both types of problems are discussed in detail and provided with a theoretical framework in Noam Chomsky's dissertation, *Transformational Analysis*.

[66] Such added flexibilities are often attained when a transformation gives the sentence the form of a different structure which has that flexibility, in this case the similarity between the passive and an N V P N sentence with omittable P N.

[67] This has been shown by Noam Chomsky, in the reference given in note 1.

[68] There are also possible applications in translation, for many languages are more similar in their kernel sentences than in their total structure (the transformations, and especially the details of the transformations, being more different). Translational equivalences can be established for the kernel combinations of words, and if necessary even for the elementary transformations as such. There is also some reason to think that the kernels may function differently in memory and thought from the transformations.

XXIV

LINGUISTIC TRANSFORMATIONS FOR
INFORMATION RETRIEVAL

ABSTRACT. This paper discusses the application to information retrieval of a particular relation in linguistic structure, called transformations.[1] The method makes possible the reduction of a text, in particular scientific texts, to a sequence of kernel sentences and transformations, which is roughly equivalent in information to the original text. It seems possible to determine the division into kernels in such a way that each adjusted kernel will carry about as much information as is likely to be called for independently of the neighboring information in the article. A text may therefore be stored in this form (perhaps omitting, by means of formal criteria, any sections which are unnecessary for retrieval), and its individual kernels may be retrieved separately. Since the carrying out of transformations depends only on the positions of words in a sentence, and not on knowledge of meanings, it seems possible that at least part of this operation can be performed by machine; the more so since the method does not require any judgment about the subject matter, or any coding of the concepts of a particular science.

1. LANGUAGE STRUCTURE

Methods such as are presented here are possible because language can be objectively studied as a part of nature, and it is then found to have an explicitly stateable formal structure. It can be objectively studied if one considers speech and writing not as an expression of the speaker which has particular, introspectively recognized, meanings to the hearer; but rather as a set of events – sound waves or ink marks – which may be said, if we wish, to serve as tool or vehicle for communication and expression. This set of events, the many occurrences of speaking and of writing, can be described in terms of a structural model. We can say that each such occurrence is composed of parts (mostly successive in time), and that these parts (words, or word parts, or sounds) are collected into various classes, e.g., the class of words N (noun). These classes are defined not by meaning but by the position of the words relative to each other. Any property of language which is stated only in terms of the relative occurrence of physically describable parts is called 'formal'.

Each language is found to have a formal structure, and the structures of various languages are similar to each other in various respects. In each language we find that we can set up and classify elements called 'morphemes'

Proceedings of the International Conference on Scientific Information (1958), 2, NAS-NRC, Washington D.C. 1959.

(word parts, such as prefixes, or indecomposable words) in such a way that the various classes of these morphemes occur (in speech and writing) in a regular way relative to each other. The domain of this regularity is called a sentence. We can identify a few sequences of morpheme classes (and sequences of sequences), and show that every sentence is one or another of these sequences, but this only with the aid of recursive formulations.

In this way, the structure of language can be shown to have algebraic properties. This may seem strange to those who expect language to be irregular or full of exceptions. It is true that there are a great many special details if we try to approach anything like a complete description of a language. And it is true that each word has its own particular range of other words with which it occurs in a sentence; for example, a given noun occurs before certain verbs and not others. Nevertheless, the sequence of word classes that constitutes a sentence is definite for a given language, and even the fact that every word has a unique range of other words with which it occurs turns out to provide a basis for regularities in the language structure, as will be seen in 1.1.[2]

1.1. *Transformations*

For our present purposes, the only structural feature we have to consider is transformations, and as much of language structure as is required in order to operate with these. We begin by defining a construction as a sequence of n word or morpheme classes in terms of which a sentence or another construction is structurally described. For example, $A N$ (as in *charged atom*) is a two-class sequence, and $T N Ving N$ (as in *the atoms emitting electrons*) is a three-class sequence (neglecting the T), both of which constitute a construction 'noun phrase' which we may write N'.[3] $N is A$ (as in *Power is evil.*) and $N V$ (as in *Justice sleeps.*) are two-class sequences, and $N V N$ (as in *Denaturation affects rotations.*) or $N is V en by N$ (as in *Results were recorded by observers.*) are three-class sequences, all of which constitute sentences.[4]

A construction is satisfied for certain particular members of its n classes if the sequence of those n words (those members of its n classes) actually occur as a case of that construction. For example, $A N$ is satisfied for the pairs (*charged, atom*), (*clean, room*), (*large, room*) and a great many others. $T N Ving N$ is satisfied for the triples (*atom, emit, electron*), (*atom, contain, electron*), (*molecule, emit, electron*), (*worker, work, overtime*) and a great many others. It might seem that not much can be done with this: the satisfaction list for each construction is very large; and it is impossible to say that one or another n-tuple does not satisfy the construction. Thus we cannot say that the noun phrases *charged room* or *atoms evicting overtime* would not occur somewhere. We can only say that in some sample of the language the pair (*charged, room*) did not occur in the construction $A N$, or that even in a very large sample the triple (*atom, evict, overtime*) did not occur as a sentence construction. Nevertheless, we can obtain a useful result by considering (for a given sample of the language) not the absolute lists of n-tuples that satisfy a given construction, but the similarities among the lists that satisfy different constructions.

If two constructions R, S which contain the same n word classes (with possibly additional individual morphemes, e.g., $A N$ and N *is* A) are each satisfied for the same list of n-tuples of members of these classes, we call the two constructions transforms of each other[5]: $R \leftrightarrow S$. If the satisfaction list for R is a proper subset of the satisfaction list for S, we say that R transforms one-directionally into S: $R \rightarrow S$. For example $A N \rightarrow N$ *is* A: every pair satisfying $A N$ can also be obtained in N *is* A (*The atom is charged*, etc.), but there are certain subtypes of A which occur in the latter but not the former. Similarly $T N_1$ *Ving* $N_2 \leftrightarrow N_1 V N_2$ (the subscripts distinguish the different occurrences or members of classes): every triple found in one construction can also be found in the other (compare the examples above with *The atoms emit electrons; Denaturation affecting rotations...*). And $N_1 V N_2 \leftrightarrow N_2$ *is Ven by* N_1: as in *Electrons are emitted by the atoms; Rotations are affected by denaturation*. But $N_1 V N_2 \leftrightarrow N_2 V N_1$: both may be satisfied for the ordered triple (*nature, imitate, art*), if we have *Nature imitates art* and *Art imitates nature*; but we are likely to find the ordered triple (*atom, emit, electron*) only in the first (not finding the sentence *Electrons emit atoms*). Another example: The sentence construction N_1, N_2, V (e.g., *The tapestry, a masterpiece, faded.*) is not a transform of $N_1 V N_2$ (we don't find *The tapestry faded a masterpiece*), but it is a transform of the sentence sequence $N_1 V. N_1$ *is* N_2 (as in *The tapestry faded. The tapestry is a masterpiece*).

1.2. *Kernels*

We thus see that many sentence constructions are transforms of other sentence constructions, or of sequences of these, or include subconstructions (such as noun phrases) which are transforms of some sentence construction. Transformation is an equivalence relation among constructions (in particular, homonymity-marked sentences) in respect to their satisfaction lists.[6] The transformations thus provide a partition of the set of such sentences. Furthermore, it is possible to find a simple algebra of transformations by showing that some transformations are products of others (base transformations): for example, $T N_2$ *being Ven by* N_1 and $N_1 V N_2$ meet the conditions for being transforms of each other (*The electrons being omitted by atoms* and *Atoms emit electrons*); but we can say that this is the product of two transformations which have been mentioned above; $N_1 V N_2 \leftrightarrow N_2$ *is Ven by* N_1 (yielding *Electrons are emitted by atoms*) and $N_1 V N_2 \leftrightarrow T N_1$ *Ving* N_2 (where the new *V* is *is*, and the original *Ven by* is carried after *is* as a constant of the transformation; i.e., *is emitted by↔being emitted by*).

Every sentence structure is the product of one or more (base) transformations of some other sentence structure, or the sum of products of transformations (if its parts are themselves transforms of sentences) of some sentence structure; if it is not, we say it is the identity transform of itself. If we can suitably mark homonymities, we obtain that every sentence structure is a unique sum of products of transformations of certain elementary sentence structures. The set of transformations is then a quotient set of the set of such sentences, and under the natural mapping of the set of sentences onto the set of transformations, those sentences which are carried into the identity transformation are the kernel of the set of sentences; these sentences of the kernel are the elementary sentences.

In English, these kernel sentences have a few simple structures, chiefly *N V* and *N V P N*, *N V N* and *N V N P N*, *N is N*, *N is A*, *N is P N*. Every sentence, therefore, can be reduced by transformation to one or more of these; and combinations of transformations of these generate every sentence. The complex variety of the unbounded number of English sentences can therefore be described in terms of a small number of kernel structures, a small number of base transformations with their algebra [7], and a small number of recursive rules for sentence combination and a dictionary.

2. APPLICATION TO INFORMATION RETRIEVAL

The possibility of applying transformations to information retrieval rests on the fact that, by standards of information or meaning which are of interest to science, a sentence carries the same information as do the kernels and transformations of which it is composed (after allowing for the differences inherent in the particular transformation, such as being a sentence or being a noun phrase). In particular, paraphrastic transformations can be disregarded. This is not the case, for instance, for belles-lettres or poetry in particular, or for material where association or the use made of the language vehicle is itself a relevant part of the expression or communication. For scientific, factual, and logical material, however, it seems that the relevant information is held constant under transformation, or is varied in a way that depends explicitly on the transformation used. This means that a sentence, or a text, transformed into a sequence of kernels and transformations carries approximately the same information as did the original.[8] It is for this reason that a problem like information retrieval, which deals with content, can be treated with formal methods – precisely because these methods simplify linguistic form while leaving content approximately constant.

The usefulness of transformation to information retrieval is due in part to the fact that scientific report and discussion does not utilize all the structure which is made available by language, such as the differences between paraphrastic transforms of the same kernel, the various verbs and affixes which are roughly synonymous with respect to science, and so on. There is an extra redundancy in language when used in science, and the removal of some of this redundancy, by establishing what distinctions are not utilized, would make possible a more compact and more lucidly organized storage of the content of scientific writing. This is not the same as a reduction of English sentences to their logical equivalents. The tools of logic are not sufficient for a representation of the statements and problems of science.

Transformational analysis makes it possible to store a text as a sequence of kernels and transformations on them. One might ask what advantage there is in this as against merely storing the text in original form. If a searcher asks for anything which interrelates two words a, b, the fact that a, b both occur in the same sentence does not guarantee that there is a relation between them; and a, b may be related while occurring in two neighboring sentences (e.g., if there are certain connectives between the sentences). Hence, either he must be given the whole article, or he will miss some relevant sentences and get some irrelevant ones. In contrast, kernels and their connectors specify the relation among words. Hence it is possible to extract, from a storage containing many articles, precisely those kernels or kernel sequences in which a, b are related (or related in a particular way). It thus seems possible both to store a whole article (transformed), to be called out as such, and also to draw upon it, if desired, for individual kernels separately. Problems attendant upon this are discussed in Section 3.

Once a text has been organized grammatically into a sequence of kernels and transformations, a further operation of reduction becomes possible. It is possible to compare corresponding sections of various kernels, and on this basis first to eliminate repetition, and secondly to separate out to some extent the sentences that have different status in respect to retrieval; e.g., sentences which are not worth storing, or sentences which should be stored but not indexed, and perhaps even those which should be used as an abstract of the article. The basis for this is discussed in Section 4.

The methods discussed here do not require the exercise of any knowledge of the subject matter of the article, nor do they require any coding of the relevant concepts of each science.

3. INFORMATIONAL KERNELS

The kernels that are obtained from transformational analysis are determined by the set of transformations that can be found in the given language. It was found that reduction of texts to kernels yielded stretches too small for efficient retrieval. Consider, for example, the sentence:

> The optical rotatory power of proteins is very sensitive to the experimental conditions under which it is measured, particularly the wavelength of light which is used.

Transformed down to kernels, this becomes:

connector[9]	kernel
	the power is rotatory
	rotation is optical
,,	,, ,, of proteins
,,	,, ,, very sensitive to the conditions
	,, ,, are experimental
wh ,,	,, ,, measured under ,, ,,
particularly ,,	,, ,, very sensitive to the wavelength
	,, is of light
wh	,, is used

We would like to obtain larger kernels, preferably of the size and structure that would provide separate kernels for the separate requests of information search. Larger kernels can be obtained simply by omitting some of the transformations, for each omission of a transformation would leave some section or distinction intact. If we can find that certain transformations are responsible for separating out (into different kernels) items that we would like to keep together, we would omit these transformations, and the regular application of the remaining transformations would give us kernels closer to the size and type we want.

This result can be to a large extent obtained by omitting the transformations that separate adjuncts from their centers.[10] As we apply one transformation after another to reduce a sentence (all those which are applicable to that sentence), we reach a stage in which the reduced component sentences have the structure of kernels indicated above (end of Section 1.2) except that the N and V have various adjunct phrases ($A, P N$, etc.) associated with them; e.g., *The rotatory properties of proteins depend on wavelength* (reduced from the example in Section 5). The next applicable transformations here would break this up into:

> the properties depend on wavelength
> ,,   ,,   are of proteins
> ,,   ,,   ,, rotatory

Here *the rotatory properties of proteins* is a noun phrase, with *properties* as center and *of proteins* and *rotatory* as two adjuncts. If for information retrieval purposes we omit these adjunct-extracting transformations, we obtain larger kernels that are closer to retrieval needs.

However, this overshoots the mark, because some phrases which are grammatically adjuncts may be of independent informational interest. It turns out that many of these are phrases which contain the same words as appear in center positions in neighboring kernels. It is therefore useful to introduce a second type of operation, over and above the transformations. This is to compare the words in every long adjunct with the neighboring center words. The result provides a criterion for further transformation. If the adjunct contains (perhaps two or more) words which are centers in other kernels, that adjunct is transformed into a separate kernel; otherwise it is not.

4. RETRIEVAL STATUS OF KERNELS

The operation of comparison introduced in the preceding paragraph is not hard to carry out once we have kernels, each with its two or three centers and their adjuncts. This same operation, once it is introduced, can be put to wider use in deciding how to treat various kernels.

The various sentences of an article differ in informational status, and even certain sentences which may be of interest to readers of the article may not be requested or useful in retrievals. The distinction is sharper in the case of kernels, because transformations usually separate out what we might consider side remarks, comments about methodology or prior science of the article, and so on, from the kernels that carry the central material of the article. This happens because in many cases the different types of material necessarily occupy different grammatical subsections of the original sentence.

If we now compare the centers of the various kernels, we find that the sections which carry the main material of the article are generally characterized by having certain words occur over and over in various relations to each other. These are the kernels from which the abstract should be selected. The kernels of this type are usually also the ones which are likely to be separately useful in answer to search, so that these kernels should be indexed.

Adjoining these kernels are sections which are adjuncts of them or separate kernels connected to them, and which in many cases contain at most one of the words which are centers of the main kernels. These sections often report conditions, detailed operations, and the like, which apply to the main kernel. This material is not needed in the abstract, and in most cases only its most repeated centers would be wanted in an index for retrieval.

There are also metadiscourse kernels which talk about the main material (e.g., discussing the problems of the investigators). These contain words entirely different from those of the main kernels, except that they often contain one word from a main kernel or a pronoun referring to a main kernel. Such kernels may be omitted from storage except in cases where they are retained as modifiers of a main kernel. In any case they need not be indexed.

Finally, there are in many cases kernels which have a vocabulary of their own, not as repetitively interrelated as the vocabulary of the main kernels. These are often comments about the underlying science of the article, including general methodology; in most cases they need not be stored for retrieval purposes.

This characterization of informational statuses is tentative and rough, but the relevant fact is that properties of the type mentioned in each case can be recognized by means of the comparison operation introduced above. To the extent that there is a correlation between the types of word recurrence and the informational status of kernels, it will be possible to set up the comparison operation in such a way as to make the desired distinctions and thus to determine which kernels are to be stored, which of these are to be indexed, and which abstracted. A great deal of investigation is still required here.

5. STORED TEXTS

The operations indicated above transform a text into a sequence of kernels with standard structure. A convenient way of providing for further operations on the kernels (whether retrieval or further analysis) is to mark off the main internal structures of each kernel, since these will have already been established in the course of applying transformations. Each kernel can be divided into at most five sections:

> 0. Connectors (binary operators) to other kernels (e.g., *or, because, however, if...then*); unary operators on the kernel (e.g., *not, perhaps, surprisingly enough*).
> 1. Subject noun phrase: center N and its adjuncts.
> 2. Verb phrase, including its adjunct D and $P N$ (preposition plus noun phrase).
> 3. Post-verb ('object') N or A or $P N$ phrase: center and its adjuncts.
> 4. Adjuncts of the kernel as a whole (usually $P N$ or connected sentence).

There are various problems in determining this analysis of each kernel as it is produced by transformations from the original sentence, though in most cases the original sentence structure determines the analysis readily. Nor is this the only way in which kernel structure can be arranged. Of the above sections, 0 and 4 (and perhaps 3) may be empty in a given kernel.

The various kernels in an article, or in a neighborhood within the article, can be compared in order to discover repetitions. If the words of section n of kernel m (written m.n) are identical with the words of section p of kernel q, or if m.n contains a grammatical pronoun of q.p, then in position m.n we merely record the address of q.p instead of repeating the words. If only part of a section is repeated this can be indicated by marking this part (as a subdivisional address) and recording the specific address at the point of repetition. If the repetition is of the corresponding sections 1, 2, or 3 in the preceding kernel (the most frequent situation), we may simply leave the repeating position empty. For example,

$$
\begin{array}{llllll}
\textit{kernel} \\
\textit{address} \\
m & 0 & {}^1\text{E F} & {}^2\text{G} & {}^3\text{H} & {}^4\text{J} \\
m+1 & {}^0\text{K} & {}^1\text{L} & {}^2\text{G} & {}^3\text{M F} & {}^4
\end{array}
$$

would be recorded:

$$
\begin{array}{llllll}
m & 0 & {}^1\text{E }{}^5\text{F} & {}^2\text{G} & {}^3\text{H} & {}^4\text{J} \\
m+1 & {}^0\text{K} & {}^1\text{L} & {}^2 & {}^3\text{Mm5} & {}^4
\end{array}
$$

Articles contain so many repetitions as to make this useful. Similarly, if one kernel contains a whole kernel (or a pronoun of it) within it, we record the address of the repeated kernel in the position which includes it. However, if as often happens the containing kernel is of a metadiscourse type (e.g., *We have found that* ...) it would be recorded (in full or in summary form) in the 0 section of the kernel which it contained, or else omitted altogether. As an example, we take a sentence drawn from the same text as the previous examples:

One phase of this research, the dependence of the rotatory
$$N_1 \qquad\qquad\qquad\qquad\qquad N_2$$
properties of proteins on wavelength, is recorded here because
$$V_3 \qquad\qquad C$$
it is of special importance to the problem at hand.
$$N_1\ V_4$$

The centers of the noun and verb phrases are marked by N_i, V_j.

The structure of the sentence in terms of these phrases is:

$$N_1,\ N_2,\ V_3\ C\ N_1\ V_4$$

Three transformations are applicable here, first separating out the sentence structures, then transforming the constructions within a sentence structure:

1. S_{123} C $S_{14} \leftrightarrow S_{123}$. C S_{14}.
2. N_1, N_2, $V_3 \leftrightarrow N_1$ is N_2. N_1 V_3.
   (S_{123} indicates the sentence containing the words marked
   1, 2, 3.)

Comparison shows that the words of N_2 recur as centers of other kernels; therefore N_2 is transformed into a sentence in order to be recorded as a separate kernel:

The dependence of the rotatory properties of proteins on wavelength

V_5n   of N_6 P_7 N_8
3. V_5n of N_6 P_7 $N_8 \leftrightarrow N_6$ V_5 P_7 N_8.

If these three transformations are applied and the section markers are indicated, we obtain:

1. [0] [1] One phase of this research [2] is [3] 2
2. [0] [1] The rotatory properties [2] of proteins depend on [3] wavelength
3. [0] [1] 1.1 [2] is recorded here
4. [0] because [1] [2] is of special importance to the problem at hand

Comparison shows that the words of kernels 1, 3, 4 do not recur in the article; these kernels would not be marked for indexing, and it is most likely that further investigation of their word subclasses would lead to their rejection from storage. On this basis also kernel 1 would be replaced by having the words *one phase of this research is* placed in section 0 of kernel 2.

Various modifications and empirically tested criteria can be added to these operations. For example, if the title consists of N_1 plus adjunct X (or if the first sentence of a paragraph contains such N_1 X) then all occurrences of *the N_1* in the article (or paragraph) can be credited with a repetition of X, i.e., *the $N_1 = N_1$ X*. If further investigation specifies the situation in which words like *condition, property* have the status of pronouns, i.e., in which they constitute repetitions of something previously stated, then these words could, like pronouns, be replaced by the words they repeat (or rather, by the addresses of those words). If a list of synonyms can be established for various relational verbs, classificatory nouns, and the like, it would be possible to consider each of those words a repetition of any of its synonyms. On this basis, for example, kernel 2 above turns out to be entirely a repetition of other kernels in the same article, and can therefore be omitted. Such a synonym list goes part way toward indicating logical equivalence between sentences, but only in the direction and to the extent that scientific writing actually permits.

When there is a connector between two kernels, each time one of the kernels is retrieved, the connected one will be picked up also (except that a kernel may not have to pick up those which are subordinate to it). If the connector at p refers to a kernel m which is not contiguous, the address of m would be added to the connector at p. The instructions for this arrangement, as for the others mentioned above (such as the section division of kernels), could be obtained as a by-product in the course of carrying out transformations.

In the kernels which are marked for indexing, a suitable criterion can be set up; for example, all words may be indexed except those in a stated list (*the, some*, etc.), or we might index only the center words and the words which are centers of the adjuncts. If someone searches for kernels that connect two words (or their synonyms), the index will yield two long lists of addresses; addresses occurring in both lists give the desired kernels. There are certain strong connectors such that a word occurring in one of the connected kernels may have an important relation to a word in the other (though this is not the case for other connectors or for unconnected kernels). Kernel sequences with such connectors will receive only a single address, so that if a person asks for two words, the index will find the same address under each of them, even if they are in different but strongly connected kernels.

6. MACHINE APPLICATION

The nature of the operations which have been described above is such that they may in principle be performable by machine; in particular, they have been based on the position which words occupy, not on meanings. This is, of course, quite different from discovering the structure of a language, which is also based only on the relative occurrence of physical entities, but is not reducible to such simple formulation. The general question about machine performance of these operations hinges on whether a decision procedure can always be found for the requisite work, and on whether it would be sufficiently short in all cases.

Much of the analysis of language structure is based upon comparison of the positions of a great many words in a great many sentences. This would take too long on a machine. However, the results of this analysis can be built into the machine. For example, there can be a dictionary which gives the class membership of each word, or, where a word is a member of more than one class, determines the class membership on the basis of the class membership of neighboring words. And there can be a list of transformations, each stated in terms of a particular class sequence; if a transformation depends upon particular members of a class this would be indicated under those members in the dictionary. Nevertheless, there may remain various distinctions which are necessary in order to determine the applicable transformation but which cannot be recognized by the machine in terms of the material immediately available to it. The most obvious case is that of homonymities, where no formal division is possible because two different transformational products have the same physical shape.[11]

In other cases, an analysis (or a choice between two analyses) is decidable, but on the basis of such a network of subclass relations as a human being can keep in mind but is beyond the storage and time capacities of machine use. In such cases it may be necessary to pre-edit the text, that is to insert at certain points in the text marks which the machine would use in deciding what transformation to use. This editing would require only a practical knowledge of the language, not any special knowledge of the subject matter.

The possibilities then are about as follows. The original text is first read into the machine (perhaps by a print reader, if one can be developed at least for selected fonts in which the major journals are printed). If any pre-editing marks are needed, they would be included in the text; word space, punctuation marks, and paragraph space will of course be noted. The machine then works on a sentence at a time, getting from its dictionary the class and special transformations of each word in the sentence. The representation of the sentence as a sequence of classes (with occasional markers for special transformations) constitutes, with the aid of a stored program for separating out the main phrases, the instructions for carrying out the transformations. (This is not done by a simple left-to-right reading of the marks.) These transformations produce from the original sentence a sequence of tentative kernels, each with its connectors and main grammatical sections marked.

At each paragraph division the machine would institute the comparison operation over the kernels of that paragraph (and perhaps with a check of the main kernels of the preceding paragraph). First, the main words of each long adjunct would be compared with the centers of the various kernels, to see if the adjunct should be transformed into a kernel. The words of each section of each kernel would then be compared in order to replace repetition by kernel-and-section addresses. This would have to be done over stretches longer than one paragraph. Here as elsewhere various simplifications are possible. For example, it might be sufficient to compare the various sections 1 with each other and with the sections 3. There would be few repetitions between these sections and section 0 or 2. Also, the machine might stop this comparison operation if it has gone through say a paragraph plus two sentences (i.e., into the second paragraph) without finding a repetition to the section it is checking. A table of synonyms could be used to extend what is considered a repetition.

Next, the centers of each kernel would be compared to see which kernels have the same centers in different relations (e.g., with different adjuncts), and other characterizing conditions. The results of this comparison would indicate whether a kernel is to be rejected or transformed into a section (chiefly 0) of an adjoining kernel, or stored, and whether it is to be indexed, and perhaps whether it is to be included in the abstract. The kernels would then be stored, and their centers or other indicated words would be marked with their address and sent to the index storage.

The whole of this work – linguistic analysis, formulation of the transformations, characterization of informational status, and machine application – is far from done. The remarks presented above indicate only the results at the time of writing.

7. FURTHER POSSIBILITIES

One advantage in the operations proposed here is that they pave the way for further reduction and organization of scientific texts. Discourse analysis would be a step in this direction; transformations are a preliminary to it, while the comparison operation may be considered the first operation of discourse analysis. If further steps become mechanizable in a reasonable way, it would then be possible to carry out further comparisons and reductions on the stored standardized kernels of the text.

More important, as a by-product of analyzing and storing a great many texts it may be possible to collect experience toward a critique of scientific writing and an indication of useful modifications in language and in discourse structure for scientific writing. Science uses more than logic or mathematics but less than language; and in some respects it uses formulations for which language is not very adequate. However, since scientific communication operates via language (except for mathematical expressions, graphs, and illustrations), detailed investigation of how the language is used gives us some picture of what would be a more useful quasi-linguistic system for science.

NOTES

[1] Z. S. Harris, 'Co-occurrence and Transformations in Linguistic Structure', *Lg.* **33** (1957), 283–340, (Paper XXIII of this volume.) A discussion of the place of transformations in linguistic theory is included in Noam Chomsky, *Syntactic Structures* (1957). The further method of discourse analysis mentioned below is preliminarily presented in Z. S. Harris, 'Discourse Analysis', *Lg.* **28** (1952), 1–30, (Paper XIX of this volume.) The application to information retrieval has been investigated with the support of the National Science Foundation.

[2] Aside from this there are homonymities in language, i.e., structurally different words or sequences that have the same sounds and may therefore be physically indistinguishable; these are degeneracies of the language structure. And there are ambiguities, i.e., cases

where the hearer cannot tell which of several meanings of a sentence was intended; structural analysis cannot help in this case, except perhaps by such methods as discourse analysis.

[3] Marks for positionally defined word classes in English: N noun (*bridge, idea*, etc.), V verb (*see, erupt*, etc.), A adjective (*new, fortuitous*, etc.), T article or quantifier (*the, some*, etc.), D adverb (*very, $A + ly$*, etc.), P preposition (*of, without*, etc.), C conjunction (*and, but*, etc.). S indicates a sequence having sentence structure. For x, y ranging over these values, y is defined by $Xy = Y$, i.e., y is something added to a member of class X such that the sequence Xy is a member of class Y (occurs in the positions of Y). E.g., $An = N$, and *-ness, -ism* are members of this n, as in *largeness; $Vn = N$*, and *-ment, -ion* are members of this n, as in *treatment, construction*.

[4] Sentences may also be described in terms of noun-phrases and comparable constructions, with N' occupying the position of N, as in N' *is* A (e.g., *The atoms emitting electrons are charged.*).

[5] Since the satisfaction lists for each construction are not closed, and vary somewhat with the sample, 'same' here can only mean 'approximately same'. However, it is possible to establish, by means of linguistic eliciting methods or otherwise, whether this sameness holds between two constructions or does not.

[6] But in addition to these, we may define certain one-directional transformations as a partial ordering relation.

[7] There are also various restricted transformations which apply only under particular conditions.

[8] Further work may be desired on the question of information constancy under transformation. For example, one can test experimentally whether kernels are remembered (and forgotten), whereas paraphrastic transformations are largely unnoticed. Or one can consider each transformation and see what changes are involved (what morphemes and orderings are changed) and what meaning attaches to each change.

[9] In addition, the sharing of words between kernels (indicated by ditto marks) is also a connector between them.

[10] If for every occurrence of construction X Y in sentence environment Z, we can find also the construction Y (but not X) alone in environment Z, we call Y the center of X Y and X the adjunct. Thus in a construction A N V D (e.g., *The blue liquid boiled rapidly.*) N and V are the centers, constituting an N V kernel (*The liquid boiled*), and A is adjunct of N, D adjunct of V.

[11] Where this yields an ambiguity, such that the reader might indeed interpret the form in two ways, we would presumably want to leave the ambiguity unresolved, i.e., not carry out the transformation.

XXV

TRANSFORMATIONS IN LINGUISTIC STRUCTURE

Empirically, a language is a set of discourses – things said or written. Each discourse can be shown to be a sequence of (one or more) sentences (or certain fragments of sentences), a sentence being the largest stretch of language whose composition can be described in certain compact ways. (It is possible to state additional properties of a discourse, but not – at least at present – direct rules of how it is composed.) There are several ways of analyzing the structure of sentences, and the applicability of one does not falsify the others. The most common method, both in traditional grammar and in modern linguistics, is to describe sentences as composed of certain constituents, e.g., subject and predicate, and these in turn of certain smaller constituents (say, subject as composed of noun and its modifiers; predicate as composed of verb plus object), and so on until we arrive at morphemes (morphologically indivisible words, stems, affixes). This can be stated in a compact hierarchy of rules or mappings, the rules and their hierarchy all showing some regular character. All sentences, or all of a distinguished subset of sentences, are composed in this way. The various constructions, like 'noun-modifier', 'subject', are only intermediate constructs of the hierarchical operation of the rules.

In contrast, transformational analysis describes sentences as being composed of sentences, rather than of parts which are themselves not sentences. Rather than ask how one can analyze a sentence into parts and those parts further into parts, and so on, we now ask whether there is an interesting way, not *ad hoc*, for decomposing a sentence into sentences, and those into yet other sentences, until one reaches certain elementary sentences which are not further decomposable.

In the case of English, and of the other languages investigated up to now, these elementary sentences turn out to be from two to five words long. To have some picture of this decomposition, consider the sentence: *The book was picked by the man*. It is decomposable, via a particular operation, into a single sentence: *The man picked the book*, plus passive operator. Similarly,

Proceedings of the American Philosophical Society **108**, No. 5 (1964), 418–22. (Read April 25, 1964.)

The man who spoke just left, would be decomposable into two sentences: *The man just left, The man spoke*, with a *wh*-connective between them. (This is the *wh* of *who, which, when*, etc.)

Now, it is necessary to indicate by what criteria one would determine whether a sentence is or is not composed of another sentence.

Let us take a sentence form, which is to say a sequence of word classes, with possibly certain small grammatical words or affixes such as *is*, which we will call the constants of that form. We take first the grammatical form $N_1 \ V \ N_2 \ P \ N_3$. (*N*: noun, *V*: verb, *P*: preposition; the subscript numbers are only to identify the various N). There are very many sentences of this form. Some of them are more acceptable, some are less acceptable. Let us consider a number of them—for convenience, all containing the same verb, *mail*.

> *The man mailed a letter to the office.*
> *The man mailed a letter to the child.*
> *The man mailed a letter to the moon.*

The last is questionable, even though it may become a reasonable sentence. However, in this listing we shall not exclude sentences on the basis of meaning. We are seeking here a structural relation among sentences (that is, a relation between sentence structures); and in order to establish this we seek first some usable difference among the sentences of each form. The difference may be in acceptability, in type of meaning, etc. In the sequel we shall see that we do not use the actual fact of whether a sentence is acceptable or not, or what its meaning is, but some relation formulated on this property, a relation which will be preserved in the structural equivalence we are about to define.

We continue, then, with:

> *The man mailed the moon to the sun*
> *The office mailed the house to the letter.*

and finally:

> *The idea mailed the moon to cheese*

which some people would say is ungrammatical, while others would say it is nonsensical (whatever the precise meaning of 'nonsensical' may be).

Among these and any sentences in a form, there are differences in meaning. Meaning, however, is not the best criterion not only because it is difficult to determine, but also because it is too individual: Every sentence has a meaning which perhaps differs in some sense from that of any other sentence.

Each sentence also has some property of acceptability, as being fully natural, nonsensical, barely grammatical, etc. Many sentences are roughly equivalent in this respect, and it is this criterion which we shall consider here. But for our present purposes it does not matter what criterion one uses. Other non-trivial properties, in respect to which the sentences in a form can be scaled, can suffice.

Now, let us consider some other sentence forms containing the same word-classes: for example, $N_1 \ V \ N_3 \ N_2$. We have *The man mailed the office a letter*. This may be a bit less acceptable than *The man mailed a letter to the office*, but this is not relevant, as we shall see.

> *The man mailed the child a letter.*
> *The man mailed the moon a letter.*
> *The man mailed the sun the moon.*
> *The office mailed the letter the house.*
> *The idea mailed cheese the moon.*

All except the most natural sentences of the $N_1 \ V \ N_2 \ P \ N_3$ form may be a bit less comfortable when rearranged into this form. But what is relevant is that the differences in acceptability among the various sentences in the $N_1 \ V \ N_2$ $P \ N_3$ form are preserved in the $N_1 \ V \ N_3 \ N_2$ form.

As I said, it does not matter for our purposes whether one uses acceptability or normalcy of meaning, or any scalable property that one wishes, or whether one uses measures of response, e.g., measuring how long it takes a hearer to recognize the sentence.

We can consider another form, e.g., $N_2 \ was \ Ven \ (by \ N_1) \ P \ N_3$, where parentheses indicate omittability.

> *The letter was mailed (by the man) to the office.*
> *The letter was mailed (by the man) to the child.*
> *The letter was mailed (by the man) to the moon.*
> *The moon was mailed (by the man) to the sun.*
> *The house was mailed (by the office) to the letter.*
> *The moon was mailed (by the idea) to cheese.*

Here, too, any differences among the sentences, as to which are more and less acceptable in this form, are preserved in respect to the $N_1 \ V \ N_2 \ P \ N_3$ form and the $N_1 \ V \ N_3 \ N_2$ form. Recasting a sentence from one of these forms to the others does not affect its difference in acceptability relative to the identically recast sentences in the same forms.

In setting up this relation I have called it 'transformation', since it is a transformation of members of a set into other members of the set, preserving some important properties: It is the rearranging of the words of a sentence from one form into another in which the difference among the sentences of a form, as to acceptability, or as to like properties, is preserved.

Now, let us take another case. Let us take the form $N_1 \, V \, N_3 \, P \, N_2$. Here we have:

> The man mailed the office to a letter.

Note that a sentence which was perfectly acceptable in the first form becomes not acceptable, or nonsensical, in this new form. Then we have:

> The man mailed a child to the letter.
> The man mailed the moon to a letter.
> The man mailed the sun to the moon.
> The office mailed the letter to the house.
> The idea mailed cheese to the moon.

Sentences which differed greatly in their acceptability in the other forms are equally unacceptable in this form; and some sentences which were non-sensical in the other forms are acceptable when rearranged here. That difference between sentences which was found in the first form and pre-served in the other two no longer obtains here. Some sentences in this form may be sensible, some may not be sensible; but the differences between them, when their words are rearranged in this way, are not the same as the differences among them in the other forms. This form, then, is not a trans-form of the others, even though it is the simplest permutation of the first form. It may, of course, be a transform of something else.

Another form which is not a transform of $N_1 \, V \, N_2 \, P \, N_3$ is, for example, $N_1, N_2, \, V P \, N_3$:

> The man, the office, mailed to a letter; The man, a child, mailed to a letter; etc.

The definition of transformation can be refined to be a relation, not between forms, but among sets of sentences such that each set has a unique range of forms into which its sentences can be rearranged transformationally. The decision as to whether two forms are transformations of one another becomes far more complicated if we want to consider cases in which some of the sentences (word-choices) in a form are transformed into another form, while others are not. Here there is the difficulty of distinguishing the rea-sonable transformations from chance sets of sentences whose acceptability-difference is preserved when their words are rearranged into another form. However, internal checks can be made to support the distinction. And the fact that the transformations of a language form a tightly knit structure, as we shall see, shows that they have not been defined in an *ad hoc* manner.

The decision as to whether one sentence is a transform of another is based not upon the individual sentences, but upon the forms which the sentences have and upon the differences in acceptability among the sentences within a form. The decision is not based in a direct way upon the meaning of the words.

Since many people have questioned the attitude of formal linguistics to meaning, I should remark that the avoidance of defining linguistic relations on the basis of meaning is not because meaning is considered to be pointless. It is because we are trying, among other things, to discover a formal basis or correlate to meaning rather than to assume meaning as an undefined linguistic primitive.

It is not always the case, though it often happens, that the sentences in one form mean the same as their transforms in another form. Some people may say that there is a difference in meaning between the passive and the active, hence between *The man mailed the letter to the office* and its transform *The letter was mailed by the man to the office*. But it is very different from the difference in meaning between *The man mailed the letter to the office* and its nontransform *The man mailed the office to the letter*. There are, it is true, transformations which bring in a large difference in meaning. For instance, the question and the negative are transformations, since they simply permute some words of the sentence, add constants, in the same way for all of the sentences of a given form; and this without changing the difference in acceptability. But the difference in meaning which is due to the transformation is the same for all sentences, and does not affect the relative acceptability of the sentences. (Differences of truth result from negation, differently for different sentences, while the question eliminates any property of truth; but truth is not directly involved in defining transformations.)

So though there may be a change in meaning due to a transformation, the change is either stylistic or subjective, in contrast to the objective difference in information between sentences which are not transforms of each other (as in the example above); or else there is a change of a logical or operational type, which is constant for all the sentences of the form. The difference between (a) transformational and (b) other changes in meaning, which result when the words of a sentence are rearranged (a) transformationally, or (b) otherwise, may help in distinguishing two senses of meaning – stylistic and quasi-logical as against substantive – which may be useful for the retrieval and analysis of the information contained in scientific discourse.

Sentential transformations, as we have seen them here, are a relation among sentences. Indeed, they are an equivalence relation, though not exactly on sentences but rather on readings of sentences. (A sentence may have two or more grammatically distinct readings, each of which has transformations different from those of the others. Such a sentence is called grammatically ambiguous.) However, we can define the difference in form between two transforms of each other as a directed operation producing one out of the other. This is useful when we speak in terms of decomposing and composing sentences.

In English, and in the few languages which have been partially studied transformationally, it turns out that all transformations are either unary, i.e., operate on one sentence to produce a sentence, or else binary, i.e., operate on two sentences to produce a single sentence. Every sentence of the language is thus decomposed by (the inverse of) a binary transformation into two sentences (with a binary operator on them), or else by (the inverse of) a unary transformation into one sentence with a unary operator on it. Each sentence of these decomposition products is in turn decomposable either into two sentences with a binary on them or one sentence with a unary on it. And so on till we reach the elementary sentences. Each sentence of the language can therefore be represented in a unique way (except, in some cases, for order) by a sequence of elementary sentences with unary and binary operators on them and on the operators. Thus we represent (avoiding compact symbolisms): *The book was taken by a man whom he and I know.*

1. *A man took the book.*
2. Passive (1)
3. *He knows a man.*
4. *I know a man.*
5. *and* (3, 4), with repeated corresponding words zeroed.
6. *wh* (2, 5) with respect to *man* (more exactly: with respect to the first *N* of 1 and the last *N* of 3, 4).

This representation supplies a normal form for every sentence, that is, a fixed form in which every sentence can be written; and I should explain that since transformational methods are entirely formal, i.e., based on the combinations of words as members of classes, and not based upon meanings, the obtaining of the normal form can be done mechanically. In fact, it can be done in principle by a computer, and in principle for all sentences of the language (although there are problems of idiomatic expressions and the like). The transformational rules decompose one form into another. The computer can be programmed to recognize forms as sequences of classes (possibly with the omission of something that is expected as part of the sentence), plus stated constants such as *is* and *-en* and *by* of the passive. On this basis the computer can rearrange the words of the sentence into the form of the decomposition-product sentence, and so down to the elementary sentences (which, because of an algebraic property which they have, I have called the kernel sentences) and the unary or binary operations on them.

The normal form opens the way to a large number of applications. For instance, suppose that in a scientific article every sentence in the article is decomposed in this way. (This is something which we have actually carried out). Then we shall find that certain kinds of information (e.g., about the events that are being studied) are contained in the kernel sentences, certain kinds of information (e.g., about the analyses and activities of the scientists) are contained in a certain set of meaning-carrying unary operators on the kernel sentences, and certain kinds of information (e.g., quasi-logical relations) are contained in a different set of unary operators and in the binary operators.

Furthermore, if two words are informationally related to each other, that is, if the article speaks about some connection between their concepts, the two words are necessarily to be found inside of one kernel sentence (plus certain adjuncts) or in two kernel sentences which are connected to each other by certain chains of binary operations. A statement of this kind cannot be made about unanalyzed sentences, for two words can occur in one sentence, even next to each other, without having any contentual relation; and two concepts may be related in a sentence without one of them being expressed by any word in the sentence (e.g., if the word has been dropped owing to a zeroing transformation).

I should say that, in addition to this, there is a mathematical character to this theory, because what we have here is a set of objects, sentences, and an operation on the set itself, an operation which decomposes or composes the objects in this set into other objects of this set, either one or else two at a time. What is of special interest here is that the objects on which this and other mathematically defined operations act are objects of the real world, the set of sentences of a language.

There is one fact which has to be stated, in addition to the existence of the transformational relation. This is that the transformations of a language form a tightly knit structure. It is not the case that each language simply has some arbitrary permutations and constant-addings which create a new form out of an old form, in such a way that the sentences of the old form are to be found also (as transforms) in the new form. Rather, it turns out that in each language there is a very small set of operations on sentences, which satisfy the definition of a transformation and which have an understandable, often informationally or grammatically functional, character. The hundred or so major transformations that a language has are each a particular application or succession of some of these elementary transformations.

I shall now give a sketch of the elementary sentence structures and transformations for English. The kernel structures are primarily (each with tense before the verb; I disregard here certain problems of *the*, etc.):

N V	A tree fell.
N V N	A rock struck a tree.
N V P N	A child relies on luck.
N V N P N	The man attributed the picture to Vasari.
N be A	The man is glad.
N be P N	The box is near a corner.
N be $D_{loc.}$	The man is here.
N be N	Man is a mammal.

The elementary transformations are:

(1) Adjuncts (in effect, modifiers) to the parts of a kernel sentence or to the whole sentence. E.g.:

to *N:*	*a, only,* etc.	*(a man, men only)*
to *A:*	*very, quite,* etc.	*(very large)*
to *V:*	*quite, just,* etc.	*(I just forgot)*
to *K* (kernel sentence):		*however,* etc.

(2) Sentence operators. These are special verbs (with their subjects or their objects), or adjectives or nouns, which operate on a sentence by making it their object or their subject. E.g.:

> *I know that he came.*
> *I wonder whether he came.*
> *I know of his coming.*
> *That he came surprised me.*
> *That he came is clear.*
> *That he came is a fact.*
> *His coming is clear.*

Each of these can operate on any sentence of the language, including their own resultants:

> *He suspects that I know that he came.*

There are restricted forms of these operators in which the subject of the operator and the subject of the included sentence are necessarily identical (the second usually zeroed):

> *He does (his) studying at night.*
> *He tried to come.*
> *He began to come.*

There are also several major groups of adverbs which appear as adjuncts of the verb, but also as operators on the sentence:

He speaks slowly.
His speaking is slow.

(3) Connectives between two sentences:

coordinate (*and, or, but*) between any two sentences,
comparative (*than, as*) between two sentences the first of which
contains a comparative marker (*more, less,* etc.);
subordinate (*because, while, after,* etc.) between any two sentences;
wh-words between two sentences which contain an identical
noun; the common *N* is omitted from the second sentence,
and the *wh* plus second sentence becomes an adjunct of the
common *N* in the first:
[The book was poor] wh- *[He read the book]* →*The book
which he read was poor.*

(4) Under specific conditions, zeroing of words which can be determined
from other words (or from other occurrences of the same word) in the
sentence: Compare *I want you to go* with *I want to go,* where obviously the
subject of the second verb is zeroed when it is the same as the subject of the
first.

(5) There are certain analogic extensions of these elementary transformations, which produce forms like those produced above but on slightly
different subclasses of words.

(6) There are inverses of all these transformations, which take a sentence
that looks like (but is not) the resultant of one of these transformations and
creates a pseudo-original for it. This is a frequent event, and is similar to
what has been called back-formation in linguistics. It is an unexpected
result that many transformations, such as *The writing of letters was by him,
His writing was of letters,* from *He wrote letters,* are simply inverses of the
elementary transformations listed above. Others, such as *A letter is what
he wrote, It is letters that he wrote, What did he write?* are successions of the
above.

(7) Finally there are certain permutations which create peculiar sentences
in which the syntactic character of the parts are unchanged even though
their position is changed. Thus in *This I like,* the word *this* is still the object
of the verb even though it is in first position. So also for *this* in *This say the
scientists.*

All the elementary transformations (and therefore all the complex transformations which are built out of them), aside from this last group, form
sentences whose structure is similar to the kernel structures except for a

limited number of additions and changes which are specified when we list the transformations. Each transformation acts on particular structures (of the kernel, and resultants of particular transformations) and produces out of them a particular structure. Thus one transformation can act on the resultant of another, if the earlier one has produced a structure which matches the operand of the later one as to constants, arrangement of word-classes, and the subclasses involved. The complicated transformations, such as the question, are simply successive applications of these elementary transformations, matching resultant and operand. It is the detail of matching subclasses, of limitations as to which words take which affixes, and the like, that makes language so complicated. The essential structure is simply that which has been sketched here.

XXVI

THE ELEMENTARY TRANSFORMATIONS

INTRODUCTION

In transformational theory, the first result is that there is an equivalence relation among certain subsets of sentences in respect to their word choices. The second result is that the transformations, in each language, are not just an otherwise uncharacterized set of changes from one sentence structure to another. A small number of constants appear in many transformations, and only a few types of structures are seen in the resultants. If, therefore, we consider a transformation as possibly an operation on word-selections, or on the elementary sentence structures that are satisfied by these characteristic word-selections, we may seek to divide such operations into a small set of elementary operations.

The search for elementary operations is supported by the fact that there are many cases of apparently unrelated transformations containing in part the same constants: e.g. -*ing* in

> He is reading it.
> He began reading it.
> His reading of it was denied.
> I saw him reading it.
> The reading of it was by him.
> Every student reading it will get credit.

In a morphological analysis of language this would constitute no problem, since we would merely say that -*ing* is added to *V* in various circumstances. However, it is clear that -*ing* and other affixes are not merely morphological operations, since they appear only in conjunction with particular other changes in other words of the sentence. Each appearance of -*ing* on *V* is therefore part of a coordinated occurrence of a number of changes in specifiable parts of the sentence; i.e. it is only part of a larger (transformational) change over the whole sentence.[1] But if we have a fair number of transformations each of which contains -*ing* as part of it, we would then

Excerpts from *Transformations and Discourse Analysis Papers* 54 (1964).

have a number of unrelated whole-sentence changes each of which includes the adding of -*ing* to *V*. This is not reasonable. We would like to show that all addings of -*ing* have one source. But we have seen that each transformation is made up not of separately existing changes in various parts of the sentence, but of a single transformational change over a whole sentence; and if a transformation φ_1 is decomposable at all into components, then each component is itself a transformation over the whole sentence, and φ_1 is simply a succession (product) of the component transformations. Therefore, if we want one source for the addings of -*ing*, we have to find one elementary transformation, which adds -*ing* to *V* as part of a change over the whole sentence; this elementary transformation is then included as a stage, i.e. a component transformation, in obtaining every transform that contains -*ing*.

We now present a set of elementary transformations φ which operate on the elementary sentence structures *K*, yielding $\varphi\, K$, and which also operate on $\varphi\, K$, in such a way that every $\varphi\, \varphi \ldots \varphi\, K$ is a possible sentence structure (given that the constants required by the φ find the environment which permit their occurrence), and that every actual sentence is a satisfaction of one of the $\varphi\, \varphi \ldots \varphi\, K$. It should be remarked at the outset that a list of elementary transformations, adequate for the above purpose, can be stated in several different but of course closely related ways. The main result is not that there exist these particular operations rather than others, but that it is possible to find one or another set of a few elementary operations such that between any two sentence-sets which are transforms of each other there exists a succession of sentence-sets, each obtainable from (i.e. different from) the preceding one by one of these elementary transformations, with each intermediate set containing sentences of the language (or forms which are constructed like sentences except that the particular *n*-tuple involved refuses to admit the constants required by that elementary transformation).

It will be further seen that the elementary transformations are not merely such as suffice for the above purpose, but also have a very reasonable character. They consist of: (1) three types of increments, i.e. structures added to *K*: insertions among the *K*-positions, operators on *K*, and connectives between two *K*; (2) a morphophonemic zeroing of recoverable redundant words[2]; (3) extensions of the above operations to new subclasses of their operands; (4) certain elementary permutations. This simple character of the elementary transformations makes it preferable to provide for aberrant sentence-sets as special *K*-types rather than as special transformational types.

0. SENTENCES OF THE KERNEL (K)

We begin with certain categories of words which can be defined morphologically by what affixes they take, or alternatively in a circular manner by the major transformations which can operate on all the words of a particular category:

N: noun (*man, book*)
V: verb (*exist, take, rely*)
P: preposition (*in, of*)
A: adjective (*large, clear*)
D: primitive adverb (*here, now, very, almost*)
t: two tense morphemes: *-s* (and zero, $\emptyset$) 'present', *-ed* 'past'.

Each elementary sentence K is a particular ordered n-tuple of words (with the assertion intonation or punctuation) satisfying one of the following structures, i.e. sequences of categories.

Σ	t	V	Ω_1	Ω_2	
N	t	V_0			A man came.
N	t	V_n	N		The man found gold.
N	t	V_p	P N		The man relied on gold.
N	t	V_{np}	N	P N	The man attributed the letter to Shaw.
N	t	V_{nn}	N	N	The man gave Shaw a letter.
N	t	be	N		A whale is a mammal.
N	t	be	P N		The book is on the desk.
N	t	be	A		The box is small.
N	t	be	D_e		The box is here.
It	t	V_{it}			It rained. It's May 8.
There	t	V_{th}	N		There's hope.

The symbols Σ (subject), t, V, Ω (object), will be used to indicate the K-segments which are listed beneath them.[3] The subscripted V indicate particular subcategories of V which occur with the particular values of Ω. Some members of these subcategories are two-word sequences $V D_p$ (D_p: certain prepositional adverbs): *look up* (as in *look the number up* vs. *look up the street*); these could also be analyzed as ordinary V with a restricted D_p adverb following, but some of the positions of D_p are different from those of D. Where the particular t is irrelevant, the t will be omitted from formulas, and t *be* will be written *is*.

The V_{nn} is a small subcategory of dative verbs. Its sentences could be obtained from the V_{np} structure, at the cost of a special transformation. The D_e is a small subcategory of locational adverbs. The V_{it} is a small subcategory of V, including *be*, followed by certain time-subcategories of N and A. The structure differs from those above it in that Σ contains only the one word *it*, which does not take inserts or plural (as N does) though it accepts other operations that N accepts. The last K structure differs from the others in that *there* is not a member of N, and takes almost no transformations of N; and the morphophonemic plural of *be* (which is a member of the small V_{th} subclass) depends on the N in the Ω column, whereas it otherwise depends on the Σ column.

One or two additional K-structures may be needed for small subcategories of V, e.g. $N\,t\,V_c\,N_c$, where the $\Omega = N_c$ contains collective or plural N_c (including N and N, etc.): *They collected a crowd.*

The words in the K consist for the most part of single morphemes (e.g. *house*, not *establishment*). A word in K which contains more than one morpheme is not divisible transformationally; that is, the sentence containing the complex word cannot be transformationally related to a sentence containing that word minus some of its morphemes: e.g. *nation*.

It is clear from the above that a slightly different set of K structures could be proposed instead of the list given here. Each difference would have to be compensated for by some corresponding alteration in the transformations which operate on the K. The over-all differences would be small, and the character of the theory would not be affected.

It is also clear that all the K structures fit into a single family of partially similar category-sequences. They are all cases of a single sequence $\Sigma\,t\,V\,\Omega$, where each of these symbols is a disjunction of a few interrelated categories with restrictions as to which value of one symbol can occur with which value of another: Σ is N, or rarely *it* or *there*; V is a disjunction of the subcategories of V; Ω is Ω, or the sequence $\Omega_1\,\Omega_2$; Ω_1 is $N, P\,N, A, D_e$; Ω_2 is $P\,N$ or N.

1. INSERTION

Each category, whether in the K structures or in the increment structures below, may have certain morphemes before or after it in the K or increment, without affecting its position in the structure, i.e. its occurrence as a value of $\Sigma, t, V, \Omega_1, \Omega_2$, or of a particular segment of an increment. E.g. there may be appended:

next to N: *a, some* and other quantifiers on the left (q_l); certain D and $P\,N$ (and some $P\,A$), like *only, in particular*, on the right (q_r): *He in particular should go.*

next to V: morphologically elementary adverbs *quite, just* and D_b *(merely, simply)* which are morphologically derived but not syntactically derived, i.e. are not transforms of their morphological source: *He merely slept, $\nexists$ His sleeping was mere.* Here also *not* and emphatic stress, placed between t and V.

next to A: morphologically elementary adverbs *quite, very*: and certain suffixes, e.g. *-ish* (*The box is small, The box is smallish*). To the comparative adjectives A_c, chiefly, *less, more*, there may be appended certain adverbs of comparative degree: *far, little: His seriousness is little less than yours.*

left of t: The almost closed set *can, may, will*, etc. can be viewed as inserted before t, or else as included in the category t.

right of X: To the right of various categories or segments X of K or increment, certain primitive $C\,X$ may be inserted: *back and forth, more or less.*

within K: placed before or after any word of K (less comfortably before N in Ω): adverbial asides such as *however, moreover, in general, in particular*. These are called sentence adjuncts.

As insertions we also count the large sets of locally inserted adverbs D, $P\,N$ which can appear also as predicates *is A, is P N* on the whole K:

D_m: adverbs and $P\,N_m$ of manner, appended to V (except *be*, in general) and to A: *He sang the songs slowly*; also in the form A_m in *His singing of the songs was slow*. Particular members of D_m occur naturally with particular members of V, A, much like the word-selection differences within K. No other increments, neither the other D nor any other increments, have restrictions of an intra-K character on co-occurrence. This would make it desirable to consider the D_m as part of the K, or as part of a second K with connective, e.g. *He sang the songs* and *The singing was slow*. However, any convenient formulation of this type can be shown to be transformationally equivalent to setting up *He sang the songs* and *His singing of the songs was slow*, so that we end up with D_m being appended to the K as a whole.

D_g: adverbs and $P\,N_g$ of degree, appended to A: *He is only moderately successful*; also (though less naturally) in the form A_g in *His success is only moderate*.

D_c: adverbs of comparison appended to A when the comparative conjunction follows: *They are less clear than I expected*; also in the form A_c in *Their clarity is less than I expected* (see 3.2). The most characteristic D_c are: before *than*: *-er* (A_c form: *more*), *less*; before *as*: *as* (A_c form: *as much*); before *for--to*: *enough, too* (A_c: *too much*); before *that*: *so* (A_c: *such*).

D_t: adverbs and $P\,N_t$ of time, appended to K: *He sings these songs frequently*; also *His singing these songs is frequent* (*occurs frequently*).

These categories of D and $P\,N$ can be considered as being primitively inserts, which are transformable into sentence-operators (2.3) *is A, is P N* (and *occurs D_t, occurs P N_t*). Alternatively, they can be considered as being primitively sentence-operators, which are transformable into *D, P N*. The considerations for this will be discussed below. In any case, a number of alternative formulations are possible for *D* (and *P N*) in general and for *D_m* in particular.

Some of the individual inserts proposed here are similar to larger classes of increments, e.g. to *D* or *C K* in general. However, they are unique in form or position and would require special transformations to derive them from the larger classes of increment. We therefore take them as primitive inserts, and indeed may use these as models for some transformational extensions of occurrence of the larger classes. This is much the same as the choice in the case of the special *K*-structures which can more easily be taken as primitive than be derived from the major *K*-structures.

2. OPERATORS ON VERB AND SENTENCE

There are certain increments on *K* which occupy some of the *Σ, V, Ω* positions of the sentence that results from their operation, hence are not merely inserts: e g. *I deny* operates on *He came*, yielding *I deny that he came*, where *Σ = I, V = deny, Ω = that he came*. Each of these increments consists of a new word which is morphologically a member of *V* (*know, expect, is*, etc.), plus certain words or morphemes affixed to the *K* which is receiving the increment or to the *V* of that *K: know that K, expect N's Ving of Ω* (where *N V Ω* is the *K*), *is Ving* (where *V* is the *V* of the *K*). In addition, the new *V* of type 2.3 have their own *Σ* or *Ω* (but not both, so that they do not constitute a whole *K*). It will be seen that these increments can be considered as operators on *K*. The subtypes are:

Operators *Y* on verb (2.1), e.g.
    He studies eclipses→He is studying eclipses.
Operators *U* on *V Ω* (2.2), e.g.
    He studies eclipses→He is a student of eclipses.
    He studies eclipses→He makes studies of eclipses.
Operators *W* on whole *K* (2.3), e.g.
    He studies eclipses→We know that he studies eclipses.
    He studies eclipses→His studying eclipses surprised us.
    He studies eclipses→That he studies eclipses is clear.

2.1. *Operators Y on Verbs*

There are two operators *be--ing, have--en*, on *V* which send

N t V Ω → N t be Ving Ω,
N t V Ω → N t have Ven Ω.

The V on which these Y operate includes all other V, including the V in the U and W operators noted below; Y do not operate on Y, except that *have--en* operates on *be--ing*: *He has been studying eclipses*, but ∄ *He has had studied eclipses*, ∄ *He is being studying eclipses*, ∄ *He is having studied eclipses*. Also *be--ing* does not normally operate on *be* and on certain V such as *know*: ∄ *I am knowing this.*[4]

2.2. *Operators U on V Ω*

A far more complex set of operators U contains subtypes graduated from similarity to Y over to similarity to W. They all have the form:

N t V Ω → N t U Vm P Ω,

where $P Ω$ stands for P (usually, *of*) plus $Ω$ if $Ω$ begins with N, and for $Ω$ alone otherwise (i.e. P = zero if $Ω$ does not begin with N). The *Vm* here stands for *Vn, Ving, to V*; and when $U = be$ or certain related verbs, also *Va*. In some subtypes of U there is a transformation (4.24) which repeats the $Σ$, yielding a W-like form as though both the U and also the K on which it operates each had a $Σ$:

N_i t U Vn P Ω → N_i t U N_i's Vn P Ω

He takes a walk daily → He takes his walk daily.
This repetition of N_i does not occur for certain U, e.g. *be*, but occurs with the other U.

The various subtypes of U operate on V, U and W within the restrictions specified for that subtype; but they do not operate on Y: ∄ *He began having studied eclipses.*

The main subtypes are given in 'Transformational Theory', § 3.2.

2.3. *Operators W on K*

This set of operators consists of two main types: $W_{.s}$ in which the K is after the operator, and appears as $Ω$ of the operator; and $W_{s.}$ in which the K is before the operator and appears as its $Σ$. $W_{.s}$ consists of $N V_s$ before the K; and $W_{s.}$ consists of $V_s, Ω$, *is* A_s, *is* N_s after the K. Depending on the subtype of V_s, A_s, N_s the K itself is deformed ('nominalized'):

by inserting *that, whether*, before K: *that he bought books;*
or by $N (t) V Ω → for N to V Ω$: *for him to buy books;*
or by changing *(t) V → Ving* or *Vn*; and subject $N → N's$, *by N*, or *of N*;
and (1) $Ω → P Ω$ (usually *of* $Ω$), or (2) leaving $Ω$ unchanged even if it begins

with N: (1) *His purchase of books*, (2) *his buying books, the buying of books by him, the singing of birds.*[6]

The various subtypes yield the following, operating on *He wrote the letter:*

$W_{.h}$:   → I know that he wrote the letter.[7]

$W_{.w}$:   → I wonder whether he wrote the letter, I wonder what he wrote.

$W_{.f}$:   → I prefer (for) him to write the letter.

$W_{.f}$ operates only on K ($t=should$). Some of its members are also in a subset of $W_{.h}$ which requires that the K on which it operates have $t=should$:

> *I prefer that he (should) write the letter.*

The deformation of K (including K with increment) by adding *that, whether, for* will be marked Kn^0.

$W_{.g}$:   → I awaited his writing of the letter.

W_{pg}:   → She responded to his writing the letter.

The deformation of K (with possible increment, except *be--ing*), into N's *Ving* Ω will be marked Kn'; the W_{pg} have $P\ Kn'$ as Ω.

$W_{.n}$:   → They imitated his signing of the letter. This inhibits the formation of colonies by the bacteria.

W_{pn}:   → This differs from his signing of the letter.

The deformation of K (including of K with increment, except Y) into N's *Vn* of Ω (n including *-ing*) will be marked Kn; the W_{pn} have $P\ Kn$ as Ω. Kn may have, instead of N's, also *by N* or, if $V=V_o$, also *of N: They imitated the signing of the letter by the clerk, They imitated the singing of birds.*

The Kn deformation of *N is A, N is N* is:

N is A→*N's An*, and as above *An of N: He stressed its clarity.*
N is N→*N's Nn: They sought his friendship.*

Kn (and in respect to the Σ, also Kn') is similar to N with inserts on it, in respect to many further operations.

W_h. (comprising V_h, is A_h, is N_h) with deformation of K into *that K:*
→ That he wrote the letter surprised me.
→ That he wrote the letter is clear.
→ That he wrote the letter is a fact.

W_w. (comprising V_w, is A_w, is N_w) with deformation of K into *whether K:*
→ Whether he wrote the letter worried them, What he wrote worried them.
→ Whether he wrote the letter is unclear, What he wrote is unclear.

→ Whether he wrote the letter is a question, What he wrote is a question.

W_f. (comprising V_f, is N_f; and is A_f with possibly *of N, for N* after it), with deformation of K into *for N to V Ω*, and also into *that N should V Ω*:

→ For him to write letters angered them, That he should write letters angered them.

→ For him to write letters is queer, That he should write letters is queer.

→ For him to write letters is the plan, That he should write letters is the plan.

→ For him to write letters is nice (of him), That he should write letters is nice.

→ For him to write letters is important (for him), That he should write letters is important.

W_g. (V_g, is A_g, is N_g), where the deformation of K is Kn':

→ His writing the letter angered them.

→ His writing the letter is surprising.

→ His writing the letter is a fact.

W_n. (V_n, is A_n, is N_n), with deformation of K into Kn:

→ His writing of the letter simulates earlier styles.

→ His writing of the letter is intelligent.

→ His writing of the letter is a piece of high style.

We can look upon these W as operators on K, or as verbs which make a K into their subject or object. In addition, there are verbs which make their object an ordered pair (N, K), or else $(N_i, K$ with N_i as Σ and with $t = should$):

W_{nt}:   I told him (that) it was late, I said to him that she had come.
W_{nw}:   I asked (of) him whether she had come.
W_{nv}:   He commanded them to lead←(*) He commanded them that they should lead.

These can be considered operators on the N, K pairs indicated.[8] The K on which the W operate can take all increments, except that one of the Y cannot occur on a K which is deformed into Kn', and no Y on a K which is deformed into Kn. The K on which the W operate can also take almost all other transformations. Therefore the operand of W may be written Sn instead of Kn (i.e. nominalized arbitrary sentence).

In addition to the W, there are secondary (derived) sentence-operators, namely the adjuncts $D, P N$, and the subordinate conjunctions C_s, which appear not only in their original forms as inserts at the V, or as conjunctions, but also in a sentence-operator form: D_m, etc., in the list of Section 1: *He* *sang quietly, His singing was quiet; C*ₛ *in He sang the anthem because they insisted, His singing the anthem was because they insisted.* The deformation of the *K* (with whatever increments), when it becomes the subject, is *Kn'* and *Kn* for some of these secondary operators, *Kn* alone for the others:

$$\text{N t V }\Omega\text{ D}_t \rightarrow \text{N's Ving }\Omega\text{ t be A}_t$$
He wrote this letter recently→His writing this letter was recent.

Similarly $K\,PN_t \rightarrow Kn'$ is PN_t *(He wrote the letter on Monday, His writing the letter was on Monday)*, and $K\,C_s\,K \rightarrow Kn'$ is $C_s\,K$ *(He wrote the letter before he knew, His writing the letter was before he knew)*. In all of these cases a certain subcategory of *V* *(occur, take place*, etc.) can appear in the place of *be*. Note that the *t* which is lost from *Kn'* appears in the sentence-operator verb: *He wrote...*; *His writing was...*. For the adverbs of manner, we have similarly:

$$\text{N t V }\Omega\text{ D}_m \rightarrow \text{N's Ving of }\Omega\text{ t be A}_m$$
He sang quietly→His singing was quiet.

and similarly for PN_m, and for the adverbs of degree:

$$\text{N t be D}_g\text{ A} \rightarrow \text{N's An t be A}_g$$
He was moderately angry→His anger was moderate.

and similarly for D_c, the comparative adverbs.

The operator form of these *D, PN,* and C_s is less comfortable than their adverb and conjunction form, and is morphologically more complex, (requiring *be* and the deformations of the *K*; though the *D* is complex in that it adds *-ly* to the *A*). However, the combination of these operations with other operations on the same *K* is more easily stated on the basis of the sentence-operator form of these operations than on the basis of the adverb and conjunction forms.

It will be seen later that the forms here called secondary sentence operators can be derived from the insertion (*D, PN*) and conjunction (*C*ₛ*K*) forms, and that secondary insertion-forms can be derived from the *W* (*That he wrote it is clear→Clearly, he wrote it; For him to write the letter was important for him→ He wrote the letter, importantly for him*). Also most *W* which take Kn^0 deformations on their *K* can secondarily take *Kn'* (or *P Sn'*) deformations:

I know that he bought the books→I know of his buying the books;

and *W* which take *Kn'* can also take *Kn*:

His buying the books occurred Tuesday→His buying of the books occurred Tuesday.

3. CONNECTIVES

There is also an operation on two sentences, which inserts a connective C before the second sentence (which begins after the primary sentence). It can be looked upon as a binary transformation: $C(S_1, S_2) = S_1 C S_2$; for some connectives, the $C S_2$ is inserted at an appropriate interior point of S_1. Or it can be seen as a succession of two unary operations: C operating as a string-head on S_2 to yield $C S_2$ (which is not in general a sentence and can be considered a non-nominal deformation of S_2), followed by $C S_2$ operating as a right or interior insert to S_1.[9]

3.1. C_s: The large set of subordinate conjunctions *if, because, while, when, after, -ing, so that, rather than,* etc. occur in $S_1 C_s S_2$, and take the transformation $\rightarrow S_1 n'$ is $C_s S_2$: *He waited because he hoped they would come; He waited, hoping they would come.*

3.2. C_{co}. The comparative conjunctions *than, as* (and *for--to, that*) have some of the properties of C_s, but are restricted to occur after a primary Σ is $D_c A_i$ sentence (with appropriate D_c which in some cases follows the A_i); in the sentence-operator form this becomes

$A_i n$ of Σ_1 is A_c than (or: as) $A_i n$ of Σ_2
$A_i n$ of Σ_1 is A_c for--to (or: that) S:
The play is less clear than the novel $\leftrightarrow$ The clarity of the play is less than the clarity of the novel.
The play is sufficiently innocuous for the censors to pass it. $\leftrightarrow$ The innocuousness of the play is sufficient for the censors to pass it.

The C_{co} are like C_c in the zeroings they permit (4.2). For D_c, see 1 above.

3.3. C_c. The coordinate conjunctions *and* (including comma intonation), *or, but*; these occur in $S_1 C_c S_2$ but do not take the sentence-operator transformation which we saw in $C_s K \rightarrow$ is $C_s K$ (i.e. $\nexists$ *His coming is or her going,* etc.). The three C_c are distinguished in that *and* requires no difference between S_1 and S_2, *or* requires at least one difference, *but* requires at least two differences (or one, in the case of paired predicates):

He went and he went.
He will come or she will come.
He will go but she will not go.

($\nexists$ *He will go but she will go,* but $\exists$ *He will go; but he will return*).

3.4. *wh.* The morpheme *wh* connects, to a primary S_1 which contains some N_i, a second sentence S_2 which contains (or, after permutations, begins with) the same N_i. (In the case of adverbial PN of time, and place, manner, etc. S_2 begins with PN_i.)

> I know the man. wh The man came. $=$ I know the man who came.
> I know this place. wh In this place he lived. $=$ I know the place where he lived.

The N_i (or PN_i) of S_2 is then pronouned into the second part of the wh-word; and wh S_2 is then inserted directly after the N_i in S_1. If $S_1 = X N_i Y$, and if we write $\check{X}$ for the pronoun of X, and S-X for S with the X part of it omitted, then we have:

> S_1 wh $S_2 = X N_i$ (,) wh $\check{N}_i$ S_2-N_i (,) Y.
> The man left. wh The man was here.
> $=$ The man (,) who was here (,) left.

The (,) indicates that wh S_2 may be separated off by commas from S_1, or not. When wh S_2 is not separated off by commas, the meaning of the wh is somewhat different and N_i is not (in general) a proper noun; and under certain conditions (depending on the t and the differences between the S) this wh S_2 takes a transformation related to the subordinating conjunctions (in particular, if, provided that, and the like):

> S_1 wh $S_2 \rightarrow S_1$ C_s S_2

where C_s is any of several C_s related to if, according to the word choices in S_1, S_2:

> People who are jobless are bitter.
> People are bitter if they are jobless.

Like C_c, so also wh does not have a sentence-operator form.

4. ANALOGIC EXTENSIONS

In addition to the incremental and redundancy-removing operations (note 2), each defined on some class or subcategory of operands, there are certain analogic extensions which apply one or another operation to some further subclass of operands related to but outside that for which the operation had been defined. These extensions work in only a small number of specifiable ways. In the main, given two transformationally related sentence sets, $S_a(X')$ and $\varphi S_a(X')$, which contain subclass (usually a word-subcategory) X' of X, and given a case $S_a(X'')$, of the same sentence structure containing a different subclass X'' of X, the analogic extension yields $\varphi S_a(X'')$.

In 4.1–6, we give examples of the specific kinds of extensions. Many transforms, such as the passive, can be reached as end-points of not one such extension but a succession of them. It will be seen that these extensions do not open the way to arbitrary forming of sentences. They all lead to only a certain range of sentence structures: only structures which are identical with the resultants of the incremental and redundancy operations above, except for permitting additional subclasses in stated positions within the resultants. And even of these structures, most of the analogic operations (all except that of 4.6) produce only such sentences as can be obtained from the previously existing sentences by extending to a new subclass a previously existing difference (in most cases transformational) among sentences of some other subclass. Thus, where previously we had the difference between S_a and $\varphi\, S_a = S_b$ just for X' (with X'' occurring only in S_a), now we have that difference also for X'' (since X'' now occurs in both sentence forms). The extensions thus bring in neither new sentence forms (if the forms are defined in terms of classes X rather than of subclasses X') nor, except for the 4.6 case, new transformational pairs of sentence-forms.

It must be stressed, however, that the choice of which subclasses become the subject of analogic extension, and which do not, seems quite arbitrary, within present knowledge. There are no clear criteria which determine, within the limits stated above, where analogy will act. Some of the factors at work here may be the same as those involved in historical change; but this would require considerable investigation.

4.1. *Extending an Elementary Operation*

The simplest kind of analogic extension is the case in which a transformation from S_a to $S_b = \varphi\, S_a$ has been defined over a subcategory X' and the starting form, S_a, exists for another subcategory X'' of the same category X:

From $S_a(X') \rightarrow S_b(X')$
and $S_a(X'')$
_____
we obtain $S_b(X')$

A simple example of this is the moving of many $A\ ly$ and PN members of post-V inserts into the other insert positions in a K on the analogy of the sentence-adjunct category (whose members are primarily of the form $A\ ly$ and PN) which are defined as occurring both in the post-V and in the other insert positions in K. Thus, given *He prefers Bach generally, He generally prefers Bach, Generally he prefers Bach*, we obtain from *He solved the problem slowly, He solved the problem with difficulty*, also *He slowly solved the problem, Slowly he solved the problem*, and *He with difficulty solved the problem, With difficulty he solved the problem.*[10] Note that pre-*V* inserts such as *quite,* and post-*V* adverbial *A* (not *A ly*) such as in *He ran fast,* do not share this extension.[11]

This permutation of adverbs into all insert positions extends also to A_s *ly, P* $V_s n$ (adverbial forms of sentence-operators, 4.25) and to the many forms of $C_s S$ (subordinate connectives). All of these sequences share with $A_m ly$ a certain range of positions.[12] They all occur as inserts (in effect, adverbially) at *K* end, and they all can take the *K* as their subject (K_n *is* A_m, *Kn is* A_s, *Kn is* C_s *S*). The fact that they can all move into the various insert-positions of *K* can be taken as an analogic extension, to this whole set of inserts, of the mobility of the $A_m ly$ subset of this set. Thus we obtain:

> He, clearly, is the one. Clearly, he is the one.
> He at our suggestion went there. At our suggestion he went there.
> The student's missing of the solution was because he didn't ask the right question.
> The student missed the solution because he didn't....
> The student, because he didn't..., missed the solution.
> Because he didn't..., the student missed the solution.

4.2. *Inverses*

The possibility of extending a transformational operation to a new subclass does not depend upon the direction of the operation.

From $\qquad$ $S_a(X') \rightarrow S_b(X')$
and $\qquad\qquad\qquad$ $S_b(X'')$
$\qquad\qquad\qquad$ ―――――――――
we obtain $\quad S_a(X'')$

Given a transformation from structure S_a to structure S_b, for sentences containing a subcategory X' of X, and given a structure S_b which contains in the corresponding position a subcategory X'' of the same X, we often find a back-formed S_a of X''. The set of sentences $S_a(X'')$ not only extends the transformational relation between S_a and S_b to the subcategory X'', but also shows that a transformational relation between S_a and S_b can be obtained (in terms of our basic operations) in the sense $a \rightarrow b$ in the case of X' and in the sense $b \rightarrow a$ in the case of X''.

We thus have inverses of the basic operations. This does not mean simply the undoing of an operation which has occurred; that would not be apparent unless the operation had left some morphophonemic or other effect which was not removed when the operation was undone. Rather, it means the carrying out of the inverse operation on a sentence in which the operation has not occurred (but which has a form similar to the resultant of the operation, for otherwise the inverse would not find the conditions necessary for its being carried out).

The possibility of carrying out such inverses (as contrasted with simple undoing) rests on our being able to find material which looks like the forms produced by the $a \rightarrow b$ transformation but which in fact did not result from $a \rightarrow b$. 'Looks like' means, as before, consisting of a (different) subcategory (X'') of the same category X to which the X' subcategory belongs, and carrying an outside (last) affix of the same kind as X' receives in the course of $a \rightarrow b$ (if indeed X' receives any affix in the course of $a \rightarrow b$). A major source of inverses is in the resultants of the sentence-operators, for when the Σ or Ω of the operator has such forms as N's $Ving$ of N, Vn of N by N deformed from N V N, the N's and PN here have the form and position of inserts which we would expect if just the $Ving$, and Vn, as N-equivalents, were the Σ or Ω of the operator, and if the N's and PN had been brought in as inserts from *The Vn is PN* or the like (by 3.4).

4.21. *Inverse of Insertion*

Since insertion is the placing of certain word-category sequences into a K (as sentence adjunct), or next to a part of K (as local insert), its inverse would be the excision, from an S, of insert-like material, i.e. of material that is similar to inserts in its word-class and affix composition, and is similarly placed, but which was not in fact brought in as insert. These latter may be called pseudo-inserts. Such pseudo-inserts are the subjects and objects of S under operators, which take such forms as Σ's, *of* Ω. As was seen above, certain ones of these drop, whereas Σ (and in most cases Ω) not in adjunct form do not. However, such PN and N's drop only when the N is redundant ('Transformational Theory', 5.2). Inverses of insertion do not seem to occur except under these conditions.

4.22. *Inverse of Sentence-Operators*

Since the sentence-operators, though verbs, are in general different from the verbs of a K, there is little opportunity to remove a K verb as though it were a sentence-operator-verb V_s. However, this possibility arises in the case of the U_b operators, especially *have, do, make*, and U_{ap}, which are morphemically identical with certain K-verbs. Thus, we have N t $V_2 \rightarrow N$ t U_{ap} $V_2 n$ (or with $V_2 n$ otherwise in the Ω of U_{ap}): *He dreamt* $\rightarrow$ *He dreamt a dream; He fought* $\rightarrow$ *He put up a fight*. When we now have N_2 which occur in N_1 t $V_{ap} N_2$ (or with N_2 otherwise in the Ω of V_{ap}), we obtain N_1 t N_2 (v), where the (v) indicates that the N_2 is operated on as a V even though it carries no verbalizing suffix v (i.e. it has v=zero): *He ate (had) breakfast* $\rightarrow$ *He break-*

fasted; He put up a wall around it→He walled it. Thus, just as V_2 above was replaced by $U_{ap} V_2n$, so here we replace $V_{ap} N_2$ by $N_2(v)$.

In most cases, given $S_a(X')→S_b(X')$, any additions of an affix to X' would occur in the derived S_b as part of the $a→b$ effect. If we find a derived form that contains a zero affix (on some subclass X''), the likelihood is that the derivation is obtained by an inverse operation, and that the resultant is affixless because it parallels the source form on a related subclass X''.

4.23. *Inverses of Connectives; Denominalization*

Situations arise in which a connective which was not originally in the sentence is removed, so that $S_1 C S_2→S_1 . S_2$. This can happen only if the connective had been brought in secondarily by the inverse of a connective-dropping operation. Such a situation occurs widely and with many different resultants, out of a K under sentence operator. Some of the examples below could indeed be routed differently as the inverse of the nominalizing deformation which sends $K→Kn$ under W.

From 2.3 we have $N_0 V_{.s}$ acting on $N V N_2$ (or $N V PN_2$) to yield $N_0 V_{.s}$ N's $Vn PN_2$ (where Vn includes *Ving*): *We reported their purchase of gouaches*, from *They purchased gouaches.* If we apply here the inverse of the *wh, is* constant-excision ('Transformational Theory', 5. 212) we bring in a secondary *wh, is* obtaining

$$N_0 V_{.s} Vn \text{ wh } N\text{'s } Vn \text{ is } PN_2$$

or

$$\text{wh } Vn PN_2 \text{ is } N\text{'s.}$$

> We reported a purchase. wh Their purchase is of gouaches.

If we now apply the inverse of the *wh*-operation (the operation 3.4 that takes two sentences, S_1, S_2 with common N_i, and produces S_1 wh $\check{N}_i S_2$-N_i, we obtain two sentences

$$N_0 V_{.s} Vn. N\text{'s } Vn \text{ is } PN_2.$$

or

$$Vn PN_2 \text{ is } N\text{'s.}$$

> We reported the purchase. Their purchase was of gouaches.

or

> The purchase of gouaches was theirs.

The same process takes place for *by N* in the position of N's.
From

> We reported the purchase of gouaches by them.

or

> We reported the purchase by them of gouaches.

we obtain

> We reported the purchase. The purchase by them was of gouaches.

or

> The purchase of gouaches was by them.

or also

> The purchase was of gouaches.

and

> The purchase was by them.

This variety of forms arises from the fact that each *is*-excision ('Transformational Theory', 5.212) changes one Ω into a pseudo-insert, i.e. into something which has the form and transformability of an insert:

> The picture which was on the wall fell → The picture on the wall fell.
> The picture which was new fell → The new picture fell.
> The new picture which was on the wall fell → The new picture on the wall fell.

When we find in a sentence an N (or an N-equivalent such as *Vn*, 4.2 above) with two inserts or pseudo-inserts, we can apply the inverse of *is*-excision to one insert in such a way as to carry the other insert with the N into the newly constructed sentence, or to leave it in the sentence from which we started:

> The new picture on the wall fell →
> The new picture which was on the wall fell →
> The picture fell. The new picture was on the wall.

or

> The new picture on the wall fell →
> The new picture which was on the wall fell →
> The new picture fell. The picture was on the wall.

The constructing of a new sentence by such bringing in of *is* before pseudo-inserts will be called denominalization.

The denominalization described here produces the *is PN* forms of adverbial *PN* which were discussed in Section 1. Thus the form *his writing of the letter with trepidation*, which has the form of N (i.e. *Ving*) with pseudo-inserts (N's, *PN*), becomes *His writing of the letter was with trepidation*, which has the form of a sentence. We have:

KPN_m:	He wrote the letter with trepidation.
→ $KnPN_m$ (under W)	We doubt his writing of the letter with trepidation.
→ Kn is PN_m:	His writing of the letter was with trepidation.

Similarly for C_sK:

KC_sK:	He wrote the letter because he was angry.
→ Kn' C_sK:	We doubt his writing the letter because he was angry.
→ Kn' is C_sK:	His writing the letter was because he was angry.

The situation is more complicated for A_mly, because here there is a change to A_m:

He wrote the letter hesitantly.
We doubt his writing the letter hesitantly.

To obtain the A_m, without -*ly*, in *His writing of the letter was hesitant* we have to appeal to the analogy of A_s (*His writing of the letter is certain*) in 4.6.

In denominalization, the necessary *is* can be brought in only before such sentence-segments as are of the kind before which *is* would have been dropped in nominalization (2.3) or in constant-excision. Hence this does not occur for C_cK: *He wrote the letter and she mailed it.* Under W, we have Kn C_c Kn: *We doubt his mailing the letter and her sending it.* No *is* can be brought in before C_cK.

A possible example of the inverse of an inverse is the case of PN (and P Sn) inserts to a K which become the subjects of that K. These are forms like the instrumental:

(1)   He broke the plank by (or: with) a blow of the fist.
(2)   A blow of the fist broke the plank;

or verbs like *cause, indicate, demonstrate* which have both:

He caused their return by (his) publishing the news.

and

His publishing the news caused their return.

The second member of each pair can be obtained from the first by the following extension:

If we begin with N_1 V N_2, we can obtain under certain W operators the deformation *the Ving of N_2 by N_1*, from which we can reconstruct, as above, *The Ving of N_2 is by N_1*, which is thus a transform of N_1 V N_2.

Now if we begin with

N_1 V N_2 by N_3: He broke the plank by a blow of the fist

we can obtain under the W the deformation

N_1's Ving of N_2 by N_3: his breaking of the plank by a blow of the fist,

from which we can reconstruct not only

His breaking of the plank was by a blow of the fist

but also (since not all the pseudo-inserts have to be included)

(3)   The breaking of the plank was by a blow of the fist.
The Ving of N_2 is by N_3.

If we extend to this form the transformational relations of the similar *The Ving of N_2 is by N_1* above, we have that (3) is a transform of

(2) N_3 V N_2: A blow of the fist broke the plank.

In this double inverse we have two successive extensions to new subcategories. First, whereas *is*-excision was defined on the K_2 after a *wh*-connective, its inverse here acts on the Σ and the adverbial *by*-inserts of the main K itself under an operator. Second, we extended to the adverbial *by*-inserts the inverse of the operation which had given us *is by N_1* from an N_1 subject.

The inverse of an inverse also appears in the following succession: Given, e.g.

(1) N is A P N, N V Ω P N
He is silent about his past,

we get, under operators:

(2) N's An P N, N's Ving Ω P N
His silence about his past.

and by inverse of *is*-excision:

(3) N's An is P N, N's Ving Ω is P N
His silence is about his past.

as well as other forms (e.g. *An P N is N's*).

When the inverse of this whole succession (or of the first change above) is applied, by extension, to forms (2, 3) in which the *N's* is not derived from the Σ of the V or the A, we obtain new sentences of the form (1) *N is A P N, N V Ω P N* in which the subject N is not the kernel Σ of this *is A, V Ω*:

His smoothness in speaking →
He is smooth in speaking.
(*) The book's surprise to us is in (its) selling well →
The book surprised us in selling well.

(*) The book's oddness in selling well →
The book is odd in selling well.[13]

4.24. *Inverse of Redundancy Removers; Extraction*

In 4.23 we saw various cases of the inverse of the *is*-excision and the *wh*-excision operating on nominalized S (under W). A somewhat different case operates on an original *wh* (3.4) but then produces a secondary *wh* (by inverse of *wh, is*-excision) yielding the very important 'extraction' structures. We start with K_1 *wh* K_2, say $K_1 = N\ V\ N_i$, $K_2 = N_2\ V_2\ N_i$, or $N_i\ V_2$, obtaining

(1) $N\ V\ N_i$ wh $\check{N}_i\ N_2\ V_2$
I know the mayor whom he meant.
(2) $N\ V\ N_i$ wh $\check{N}_i\ V_2$
I saw the book which fell.

Now in *I bought the book which was on the shelf* → *I bought the book on the shelf*, we have excision of the constants *wh, is*. If the inverse of this excision is applied by extension to (1, 2), where the *wh* had never been excised, we obtain

$N\ V\ N_i$ wh $\check{N}_i$ is wh $\check{N}_i\ N_2\ V_2$
I know the mayor who is whom he meant.
$N\ V\ N_i$ wh $\check{N}_i$ is wh $\check{N}_i\ V_2$
I saw the book which is what fell.[14]

If we separate the two sentences in each case (inverse of connective, 4.23), we obtain

I know the mayor. The mayor is whom he meant.
I saw the book. The book is what fell.

We thus have *The book is what fell* as transform of *The book fell*, *The book is what he took* as transform of *He took the book*, etc.

In various situations there take place inverses of the operations which zero words after an antecedent (4.2). Here belongs the pleonastic repetition of the subject after certain U operators, which makes them similar to W operators (*He began his studying* ← *He began studying*). Here too we may mention the repeating of the Σ which takes N is A in *Ving* Ω (← $N\ V\ \Omega\ A\ ly$, below) into N is A in N's *Ving* $P\ \Omega$: *He is lengthy in presenting these reports, He is lengthy in his presenting of these reports.*

The inserting of classifier N_{cl} in some forms may also be taken as the inverse of the dropping of N_{cl} before *wh*-inserts and after A inserts:

N_2 is A_s for N_1 to V → N_2 is an $A_s\ N_{cl}$ for N_1 to V
A novel is easy (for anyone) to read →
A novel is an easy book (for anyone) to read.

4.25. *Inverses of Analogic Extensions*

Once an analogic extension is established, there may be an inverse of it on yet some other subclass. Thus if $A_m ly \rightarrow is\ A_m$ and $PN_m \rightarrow is\ PN_m$ (on an analogy between $A_m ly$ and $is\ A_s$, 4.6 below), we then have further the inverse is $A_s \rightarrow A_s ly$:

> His being the right one is clear, →
> He is the right one, clearly;

and from $is\ P\ V_s n$ we have adverbial $P\ V_s n$:

> His resigning was at our suggestion.
> (from We suggested his resigning, 4.23, 52) →
> He resigned at our suggestion.

In this way the sentence-operators are transformable into adverbs of the K on which they had operated.

Another example is a possible inverse of insert-moving. The rare moving of $wh\text{-}\tilde{N}_i\ S\text{-}N_i$ from its position after N_i to the end of the K (if no N is passed on the way) can be taken as the inverse of the moving of $C_c\ N_i$ from the end of the K to the position after N_i. *My friend came, whom I had mentioned to you← My friend whom I had mentioned to you came.* Compare: *My friend came, and I too→ My friend and I came.*

Here also belong the inverses of inverses seen in 4.23.

4.3. *Missing Sources*

There are cases in which a form, S_b, appears for one subcategory X' (or for all subcategories except X'') only as a result of a transformation ($\leftarrow S_a$), whereas for another subcategory, X'', only S_b occurs and not S_a.

$$S_a(X') \rightarrow \quad S_b(X')$$
$$S_b(X'')$$

but $\nexists\ S_a(X'')$. If S_b is understandable only as a transformational resultant, how is the source S_a absent for X''? This situation appears most obviously when $a \rightarrow b$ involves affixes, and the absence of a sentence form S_a is due to the absence of its morphological form in the case of words of the X'' subclass. Thus, from *He believes this* we have *He finds this believable, This is believable to him*; we have also *He finds this credible, This is credible to him*, but $\nexists$ *He cred- this.* Here we either have to set up a source outside the set of actual S, namely * $S_a(X'')$, or else $S_b(X'')$ has to be taken as an elementary form even though S_b is a derived form on another subclass X'.

An only distantly similar case is that in which the $S_a(X')$ is not missing but rare, or has a particular twist of meaning. Thus, from $N\ t\ V\ \Omega$ we have

$N\,t$ be $Ving\,\Omega$, $K\,C_s\,N\,t\,V\,\Omega$, etc. for non-zero Ω, e.g. *He studies physics, He is studying physics, He tires when he studies physics*, whereas for many V with zero Ω the first form occurs by itself only very limitedly: *He is coming, They flee when he comes*, etc., but only in special circumstances *He comes*. From the point of view of construction, the $N\,t\,V\,\Omega$ form is the source for these V as it is for the others.

4.4. *Intermediate Resultants; Products of Operations*

A related but less difficult situation arises in:

$$S_a(X') \rightarrow S_b(X') \rightarrow S_c(X')$$
$$S_a(X'') \qquad\qquad S_c(X'')$$

but $\nexists\,S_b(X'')$. Here $S_c(X')$ is such that it is best obtained from S_b (and not directly from S_a), but the form S_b either does not exist or is very restricted for the subcategory X''.

4.41. *Rare Intermediates*

We first consider intermediates which are missing or at least marginal for some members of a category, but are acceptable for other members.
Consider:

> Who came? (He came.)
> What will he take? (He will take the book.)
> When will he come? (He will come later.)

We see that the question can be related to its set of answers by substituting a *wh*-word for the Σ, Ω, or adverbial inserts (D, PN, *because S*) of the answer (and then permuting t with Σ). This, however, seems not to explain the form

> What will he do? (He will write an answer.)

The *what* here clearly substitutes for the $V\,\Omega$ (*write an answer*), but the *do* is inexplicable: It cannot be a pro-verb since the other *wh*-questions (above) do not contain a pronoun of the questioned word (other than in the *wh*-word itself). The *do* cannot be an auxiliary because an auxiliary (*will*, etc.) is present. The only way to explain this form in the same terms as the other *wh*-questions is to relate it to (*) *He will do the writing of an answer* in which the *Ving* Ω is the Ω of *do*. This form is obtained by U_b operator *do* on *He will write an answer* (2.25)[15], and occurs for many verbs, at least in special circumstances[16], but not for all. We thus have a known operator-transformation $N\,t\,V\,\Omega \rightarrow N\,t\,do\,Ving\,\Omega$, for a large subclass of V, and a known *wh*-transformation operating not on V but on Σ, and on adverbial inserts, and hence on *Ving* Ω when it is the Ω of an operator, e.g. $N\,t\,V\,\Omega \rightarrow what$

t N V? (He wrote an answer. What did he write?, He tried writing an answer. What did he try?).

The only unusual feature here is that many V undergo the *do* operator-transformation only when the resultant receives the *wh*-transformation immediately thereafter. The *do* resultant does not exist by itself. This is tantamount to saying that whereas for some V we have *do* operating on V, and then *wh* operating on the resultant, for other V only the product (succession) of *wh* on *do* acts as a single operation.

4.42. *Missing Intermediate*

An analysis of the above kind is needed also for the cases of intermediate resultants of an operation succession φ_1, φ_2 which are missing when φ_1, φ_2 act on one morphological category but which are present when φ_1, φ_2 act in the same way on other morphological categories.

Consider:

	The book and also the pencil fell.
from:	The book fell and also the pencil.
from:	The book fell and also the pencil fell;

or:	I can and will finish it.
from:	I can finish it, and will.
from:	I can finish it, and I will finish it;

or:	He may, but you must, attend that session.
from:	He may attend that session, but you must.
from:	He may attend that session, but you must attend that session.

It is clear that on $N\ t\ V\ \Omega\ C_c\ N\ t\ V\ \Omega$ there are two transformations here: one zeroes those parts of the second K_2 which are identical with corresponding parts of the first K_1; and then in the resultant, if the residue after C_c is an unbroken segment of K_2, there is a permuting transformation which sends C_c plus the residue to the position right after the corresponding segment of K.

If now we take *He bought the rings and he wore the rings*, we find *He bought and wore the rings*, but no **He bought the rings and wore*; similarly *He bought and she wore those rings* but no **He bought those rings and she wore*. If we account for this by saying that $V\ \Omega$ is a single element, we find that it is not so in the case of C_{co} (*He bought more rings than he wore, He bought more rings than she wore*), and in various other forms. In the present terms we can simply say that on Ω in $C_c K$, only the product of the permuting and zeroing transformations acts, whereas on the other K parts each of these acts separately; i.e. on these others the resultants of the first transformation exists independently of its being acted on by the second.

Another example is in zeroed Σ after C_s. We have for certain C_s:

$K_1 \ C_s \ K_2$ He said it after he drove here.
$K_1 \ P_s \ K_2 n$ He said it after his driving here.
zeroed Σ's   He said it after driving here.

but for *while*:

He said it while he drove here.
∄ He said it while his driving here.
He said it while driving here.

We have to say that for a subset of C_s the two transformations, $K_2 n$ and zeroing, occur only as parts of a product of elementary transformations, and not separately.

4.43. *Required Transformations and Morphophonemics*

The methods which have here been seen to be necessary in order to account for certain forms can also be used to describe required changes in syntax or morphology. A required change is always a change which takes place in the position or phonemic content of some word in a sentence when the word or sentence enters a particular situation. The change is always conditioned upon some other change. Thus when, compared with *walk-walked*, we have *go→ went*, the change *go→wen-* occurs if the past-tense morpheme is added (this morpheme in turn having the forms -*d*, -*t*, etc. depending on what it is added to). In our present terms we can say that whereas other V accept the past tense independently, *go* accepts only the product of *go→wen-* and past tense, but not either of them independently.

There is little advantage in such a formulation, since a *go→wen-* operation is not otherwise known. The case was different in examples of 4.41–42 where both of the operations which are involved were known for a certain class of operands, and the peculiar situation could be explained by saying that for a subclass of these operands the operations indeed occurred but not separately. Nevertheless the use of such a formulation even when one of the operations is unique may be of interest in that it separates out the common operation which is then to be acting on the unique member of a class no differently than it acts on the rest of the class.

There is here a further consideration of policy. Since transformations are a relation on (non-ordered) sentence pairs, both sides of the relation naturally exist as sentences. When we evoke a system of directional operations sufficient to characterize the transformations, the source and resultant of each operation are directly relatable to existing sentences, since these operations are simply a base set, with direction, selected out of the set of transformations. Since both sides of an operation exist, the operation is not required; i.e. we have a sentence whether or not we carry out the operation. The cases of transformational changes which are required are few and have a limited character, as in the zeroing of repeated A in the comparative (*He is taller than she*), or in the $t\ \Sigma$ permutation in the question. It would be of some interest to be able to formulate these exceptional changes in a way more similar to the main body of transformations. Now in 4.41-42 we saw certain aberrant situations which could be produced out of the known transformations, without denying the lack of intermediate forms, by saying that in certain cases only a product of operations acts, and not each operation separately. It is not that these particular operations are required for the subclass of operands in question, since the subclass can avoid both together. What is required for the given subclass is the succession, i.e. that the application of one operation implies the application of the other. Once we have to do with such required products we can extend the succession-requirements to do the work that is otherwise done by required transformations, if we can show that at least one part of each required operation (which, as noted above, always contains two parts) consists of an operation which is known on other operands, and is there independent and not required. This is indeed always the case. Both for the conditional variants of phonemics and morphology and for the few required operations in syntax, it is possible to separate out (1) a non-required event acting on a class of operands, and (2) for a particular subclass a change in composition or position, perhaps unique, such that that subclass will not undergo (1) without (2), i.e. it will undergo only the product of the two.

As an example we note the transformational relation between *The man has white hair* and *The man with white hair*: $\not\exists$ *The man is with white hair*. But we have N *has* $N \rightarrow N$ *is P N* (4.51) for other P (for certain N pairs). We can say that N *has* $N \rightarrow N$ *is with* N (and in many cases $\rightarrow N$ *is of N*) takes place only when followed by the *is*-excision operation: *the man who has white hair* $\rightarrow$ **the man who is with white hair* $\rightarrow$ *the man with white hair*. That is, only the product of the two occurs.

4.5. *Extending a Transformational Relation*

There are cases of a normally obtainable $S_a(X'')$ and an inexplicable $S_b(X'')$ where $a \rightarrow b$ does not exist as an elementary transformation, but where for another subcategory X', $S_a(X')$ and $S_b(X')$ are transforms of each other by reason of some complicated chain of elementary operations, or by reason of both being derived from the same source. These intermediate steps do not exist for X''. In such cases, we can say that

from $\quad\quad S_a(X') \leftrightarrow S_b(X')$
and $\quad\quad S_a(X'')$
$\overline{}$
we obtain $\quad\quad\quad\quad S_b(X'')$

These situations can be considered merely special cases of X'' missing the intermediate steps through which X' goes, except that the succession of elementary operations that make $S_b(X')$ a transform of $S_a(X')$ is clearly irrelevant to X'', whereas in 4.3, 4 the missing forms would make syntactic sense for X'' as for X', and are missing for morphological or similar reasons.

4.51. *Secondary U*

One type is that in which $S_a(X')$ and $S_b(X')$ are both obtained from the same source via two members of the same set of operations. For example, the category of operations U contain subcategories of operators which are closely related to each other in form (all utilizing the *be, have* which are also members of Y) and in meaning:

N t V Ω → N t be Va P Ω   He is responsive to it, He is suspicious of it.
N t V Ω → N t be P Vn P Ω   He is in receipt of it.
N t V Ω → N t have Vn P Ω   He has love for it, He has suspicions about it.

Somewhat less closely related are the further subcategories of U:

$\quad\quad\quad\quad$ N t V Ω → N t U_n P Ω $\quad\quad$ He takes a look at it.
$\quad\quad\quad\quad$ N t V Ω → N t U_{ap} Vn P Ω $\quad\quad$ He feels love for it.

These all have a transformational relation to each other, with small differences in meaning of a modal rather than substantive kind. The relation can be stated as a succession of operations (including inverses) from one U to another: e.g. *N has Vn* ↔ *N U_{ap} Vn* is decomposable into *N has Vn → N V N U_{ap} Vn*. The existence of this relation on *Vn, Va* is the basis for an occasional and not always comfortable operation on *N, A* which is in effect a transformation among secondary U, operating on *N, A* instead of on *Vn*:

$\quad\quad\quad\quad$ is $\quad$ A ↔ is P An ↔ has An ↔ U_{ap} An[17]:
$\quad\quad\quad\quad\quad\quad$ It is adequate, He is young.
$\quad\quad\quad\quad\quad\quad$ It is of adequate quality.
$\quad\quad\quad\quad\quad\quad$ It has adequacy, He has youth.
$\quad\quad\quad\quad\quad\quad$ It exhibits adequacy.

V_{ap} N↔has N↔is P N↔is Na:
> He has money, He has wit.
> He is in the money.
> He is moneyed, He is witty.

As an indication of the U_{ap} character of certain V_{ap} before N, note that in *He had a party↔He gave a party, He threw a party*, the pronouning of *party* (e.g. in **He threw it*) is limited, like the pronouning of *Vn* in *N U Vn* (**He took it ← He took a look*), and not like the pronouning of *N* after ordinary *V*).

Such transformations among sentences containing U and V_{ap}, together with adverbs and nominalization ($K \rightarrow Kn$) and denominalization ($Kn \rightarrow K$), account for a variety of unusual sentence-types, such as *He plays a fast game, His game is fast*.

4.52. *Mirroring*

There is an operation of mirroring *X is Y → Y is X* (occasionally *X is P_i Y → Y is (P_j) X*), which occurs only for *is* which is brought in by analogic operations (e.g. inverse of constant-excision, and *is P←has*).[18]

This operation can be accounted for in a number of ways. One way is to start with the fact that in the *N is N_{cl}* type of *K* the order is reversed when the N_{cl} has a specific insert: (1) *A trout is a fish*, (2) *This fish is a trout*. The latter is thus derived from the former in the course of inserting *this*. With addition of *wh K_2* we obtain *The fish which you saw is a trout*, etc. Now if the N_{cl} is of a very general kind a particular analogy arises. This happens if we take, e.g. *The thing is a book, That is a book*, together with *The thing fell, That fell*. We obtain:

> The thing which fell is a book.
> That which fell is a book.

Similarly

> The one whom he meant is the mayor.

This form differs from (4.24)

> The book is what fell.
> The mayor is whom he meant.

in about the way that (2) differs from (1). The forms are in part analogically extended toward each other, producing:

> What fell is a book. What fell is the book.
> A book is that which fell. The book is that which fell.

This *Y is X↔X is Y*, where *X=N, P N, Vn of Ω* and *Ving*, and *Y=*the

remainder of the K (X) plus constants, is then the basis for an operation
Y is $X \rightarrow X$ is Y (or Y is P_i $X \rightarrow X$ is P_j Y where the *is* has come in as noted
above.[19] Examples of this mirroring are:

> N's Vn is of $N_2 \rightarrow N_2$ is N's Vn
> His purchase is of these books, These books are his purchase.
> Vn of N_2 is N's $\rightarrow$ N's is Vn of N_2
> The purchases of books were his, His were the purchases of books.
> N's Ving of Ω U_{ap} $A_m n$[20] $\rightarrow A_m n$ is P N's Ving of Ω
> His speaking has (or: shows, etc.) elegance, Elegance is in his speaking.

4.53. Σ of K into Σ of Operator

Equivalent sources can give rise to a transformational relation, as in the
two ways of dropping redundant Σ in insert form: For certain W operators
(and for U operators after they have received a pleonastic subject for their
operand), we have redundancy-removal of the following type:

> N_i's $V_s$ing of N_i's Ving $\Omega \rightarrow N_i$'s $V_s$ing of Ving Ω

and

> N_i's $V_s$ing of N_i's Ving $\Omega \rightarrow$ The $V_s$ing of N_i's Ving Ω
> His beginning of his painting of landscapes
> His beginning of the painting of landscapes
> The beginning of his painting of landscapes.

For these $V_s ing$ and *Ving*, we thus have relations of the following type:

> N's $V_s$ing of Ving $\Omega \leftrightarrow$ The $V_s$ing of N's Ving Ω.

This type of relation is extended, as an operation, to those V_s which did not
have their own Σ, and to certain A_s in W, and more weakly to A_m:

> The surprise to us in the book's selling well $\rightarrow$
> (*) The book's surprise to us in selling well;
> The oddness of the book's selling well $\rightarrow$
> (*) The book's oddness in selling well;
> The smoothness of his speaking $\rightarrow$
> His smoothness in speaking.

In this way the insert-form Σ of the operand appears as the insert-form Σ of
the operator.[21]

4.54. Derived V

There are also more complicated cases of transformational equivalences.

For example: We have seen transformations which send V into V_a, V_n; and A into An; and N into Na. These have been described here as the 'nominalization' of K under operators and as analogic extensions of this operation. The few cases of Nv, Av, Vv, in which a V is morphologically created, present a different problem. They cannot be merely inverses of the above, for they involve unique affixes which must be primitive:

> It is red, It reddens.
> It is large, He enlarges it.
> They sat, He seated them.
> They were in a house, He housed them.

The first is like an inverse of a U-operator *be* (2.2):

> It shakes → It is shaky, It is shaken.

The others bring in a new causative Σ and thus parallel the W operators:

> It is large, He made it large.
> They sat, He had them sit.
> They were in a house, He put them in a house.

The parallel between $N_0\ t\ Xv\ N$ and $N_0\ t\ V_s\ N\ X$ (e.g. *He enlarged it* and *He made it large*) as two equivalent transforms of $N\ t\ X$ (X: small subcategories of N, A, V; with *be* added to t before $X = N$, A) is extended: in the case of N, into a productive $N_0\ t\ Vn\ N$, where the X is a N with zero v suffix:

> They booked a reservation.
> (They put a reservation into a book)[22];

and in the case of V, into a productive 'zero causative' $N_0\ t\ V\ N$, where we can consider the V to be, also, V with zero v suffix:

> They walked the patient.
> (They helped him walk).

4.55. *Passive*

As a difficult and doubtful example, we take the passive: The inverse of *wh*, *is*-excision (4.23) followed by mirroring (4.52) and a transformation among secondary U (4.51, with intermediates absent, as in the last paragraph of 4.43) provides a complex path to the passive. That (1) the passive is related to (2) the constructing of a sentence out of the operand of a W (4.23) is clear from the similar forms and restrictions in (1) and (2). Under W, one of the Kn forms is

> Ving of Ω by Σ

and the *by* Σ, which is a characteristic of the passive, occurs in *Sn* primarily if the *V* has an Ω beginning with *N* (2.3), which is again a characteristic of the passive. Interestingly enough, the range of Ω and pseudo-Ω which are difficult or impossible for the passive are also difficult or impossible for this *Kn*. From *The Champion ran a mile, The candidate spoke two hours:*

> (They reported) the running of a mile by the champion.
> A mile was run by the champion.
> ∄ (They reported) the speaking of two hours by the candidate.
> ∄ Two hours were spoken by the candidate.

Furthermore, this *Sn* form, like the passive, does not apply if $V = be$ or verbs of the *be*-set (*seem, become*). From the *Kn* form above, we obtain:

> by 4.23:   (The) Ving by Σ is of Ω
> by mirroring: Ω is P Ving by Σ
> by *U*-transformations: Ω is Ven by Σ,

the *-en* being a particular adjectivizing suffix after *V* (as in 2.21). The intermediate forms exist hardly or not at all, and we would have to say, as in 4.43, that it is only the product of these elementary operations (and not each of them separately) which takes us from:

> He saw the book.
> through: N V$_s$ the seeing of the book by him.
> to: The book was seen by him.

4.6. *New Relations*

In a few cases an operation is formed where no relation had existed. In these cases,

given $S_b(X')$
and $S_a(X'')$
we obtain   ⎯⎯⎯⎯⎯⎯
                          $S_b(X'')$

Here, not only are X', X'' closely related subcategories of *X*, but also the differences between S_a and S_b must be within some specifiable limit, of the kind that can be traversed by a single new operation. However, a general statement about the limits for these differences between S_a and S_b is not available at present.

The operation

> S A$_m$ly → Sn is A$_m$

> He wrote the letter hesitantly→His writing of the letter was hesitant,

has to be accounted for by some route such as the following: We have by denominalization (4.23)

$$S \; P \; N_m \to Sn \; is \; P \; N_m$$
He spoke with trepidation→His speaking was with trepidation.

We also have nominalization of sentences containing PN_s members of W (when the whole sentence is nominalized under further W):

$$Sn \; is \; PN_s \to Sn \; PN_s$$
His speaking is at my suggestion →
(I deny) his speaking at my suggestion.

In the same class as PN_m there is $A_m ly$; and in the same class as $is \; PN_s$ there is $is \; A_s$ (*is certain*, etc.). We can say that, on this analogy, $A_m ly$ is denominalized into the new $is \; A_m$, yielding

His writing of the letter is hesitant,
like: His writing of the letter is certain.

There is an inverse of this operation, which takes $Sn \; is \; A_s \to S, \; A_s ly$, and more rarely makes the other W operators into adverbial inserts in the S which was the operand of the W:

He wrote the letter, certainly.
He wrote the letter, to my knowledge.

A similar situation may explain the permuting of the residue of $C_c S$ after zeroing. There is a small number of primitive $C_c X$ (i.e.$\leftrightarrow C_c S$) adjoined to the right of a word of class X: *good and ready, by and large*. In $K_1 \; C_c \; K_2$, if $K_1 = Y_i \; X_i \; Z_i$ and $K_2 = Y_i \; X_j \; Z_i$ (X, Y, Z: successive portions of their identically structured K), then K_2 is zeroed down to X_j, and

$$Y_i \; X_i \; Z_i \; C_c \; X_j \to Y_i \; X_i \; C_c \; X_j \; Z_i.$$

The permuting of $C_c X_j$, which makes it similar to, though in certain respects not identical with, an insert to the right of X_i, is a case of 4.6, if we take

$$S_b(X') = C_c X'$$

as primitive insert on the right of X_i, and

$$S_a (X'') = C_c X'' \leftarrow C_c S$$

when it is after K_1, producing

$$S_b(X'') = C_c X''$$

when it is to the right of X_i.

The forming of a new relation also seems to account for

$$Sn^0 \ V \ \Omega \rightarrow It \ V \ \Omega \ Sn^0.$$

We have a primitive

It seems that S, It is merely that S,

e.g. *It's merely that I couldn't wait*, etc., as a W (of $N \ V_s$ type) on S which gives a resultant like the *It* type of K. Here the position of *it* cannot be taken by any other word: and no source with Sn^0 as Σ is possible: $\nexists$ *That S seems*, $\nexists$ *That S is merely*. These therefore cannot be taken as transforms of some other form. In *That S V_s. Ω* and the other $Sn^0 \ V_{s.} \ \Omega$, we can see an extension of *It V that S* from the small subcategory $V_{.s} =$ *seems, is merely*, etc. to $V =$ those $V_{s.}$, *is A_s, is N_s* which have $\Sigma =$ *that S, whether S, for S*.

Other cases of new relations may be

$$Sn^0 \rightarrow Sn', \quad Sn' \rightarrow Sn$$

as operands of W, so that a W whose operand was Sn^0 can also take Sn' etc.: this presumably because some W had both.

I know that he went, I know of his going.

Also $C_s S \rightarrow P_s \ Sn$: *He left since I came, He left since my coming*; presumably because some words were in both C_s and in P; and because P, which in K occurs only before N, comes to occur before Vn and Kn under U and W (2.2, 23). Similarly, the fact that most, but not all, U_g are in U_t and vice-versa (2.23) may be obtained from separate U_g and U_t memberships (with perhaps some overlap), with words then spreading from one to the other. Also $N \ V_{nn} \ N_2 \ N_1 \rightarrow N \ V \ N_1 \ to \ N_2 \ (V_{nn} =$ *give, write*, etc.) on the analogy of $N \ V_{np} \ N_1 \ to \ N_2 \ (V =$ *attribute, affix*):

He gave me the book.
He gave the book to me.
He attributed the book to me.

5. ASYNTACTIC PERMUTATIONS

There are a few permutations (mostly either literary or else required as morphophonemics) which differ from all the above operations in that they produce a sentence-structure which differs from the K structures, and in that the permuted parts retain their pre-permutation relation to the other parts of the K (i.e. the apportionment of transformational effects on the various K-parts).[23] Thus in *This say all the scientists, $\Omega \ V \ \Sigma \leftarrow \Sigma \ V \ \Omega$*, the number-agreement with the V is retained by the original Σ. The effect is thus that the grammatical relations are not changed; no syntactic realignment has taken place. There is no extension here of an operation to new subclasses, and also no apparent increment. But there is reason to argue that these permutations are morphophonemic changes which follow upon the entry of an increment. The carrying out of the permutation may then permit the zeroing of the increment, since it shows that the increment had been present.

5.1. *Inversion*

A rare transformation, with rather literary flavor, is

$$\Sigma \, t \, V \, X \rightarrow X \, t \, V \, \Sigma$$

where $X = \Omega$ (including either Ω_1 or Ω_2 but not both together) or adverbial D or PN:

> A man sat nearby $\rightarrow$ Nearby sat a man.
> The Don rolls quietly $\rightarrow$ Quietly rolls the Don.
> The scientists say this $\rightarrow$ This say the scientists.
> He is a fool $\rightarrow$ A fool is he.

This differs from mirroring in that the X in the new position is still the Ω, and the V does not change its number to agree with the X. Also the V remains unchanged and is the V of the K, not one produced by an operation. This permutation is comfortable when the Σ is very long.

> The following units, A, B, and C, are returning home $\rightarrow$ Returning home are the following units: A, B, and C.

It is the more uncomfortable, the more possibility there is of X being mistaken as the Σ: *The girls saw five Martians $\rightarrow$ Five Martians* (as Ω) *saw the girls.*

5.2. *Concessive Permutation*

After certain C_s chiefly of concessive meaning:

> $C_s \, N \, t \, V \, \Omega \, D \rightarrow D \, C_s \, N \, (t) \, V \, \Omega$,
> $C_s \, N \, t \, V \, \Omega \rightarrow V \, \Omega \, C_s \, N \, t$ (U not including *be*)
> $C_s \, N \, t \, V \, \Omega \rightarrow \Omega \, C_s \, N \, (t) \, V$
> Though he plays the flute softly $\rightarrow$ Softly though he plays the flute.
> Though he would play the flute $\rightarrow$ Play the flute though he would
> Though he would play the flute $\rightarrow$ The flute though he would play
> Though he is young $\rightarrow$ Young though he is.

The (t) indicates that in certain cases, even in current English, the *t* is missing in the resultant (*Young though he be*).

5.3. *t Σ Permutation*

For certain *K*-initial *D* it is required or permitted to have *D t Σ V Ω* instead of the usual *Σ t* order:

> Little did I think that he would come.

This order also occurs when the *if* variant of *whether* is dropped after V_s whose *Ω* begins with *whether:*

> I wonder if (whether) he will come or not →
> I wonder, will he come or not.

The *D* in question have in most cases a concessive or restrictive meaning, but not in all cases:

> They will never know it, They never will know it, Never will they know it.
> They will hardly guess it, They hardly will guess it, Hardly will they guess it.
> They will only slowly return, They only slowly will return, Only slowly will they return.

We also have

> (*) Little I would have guessed it, Little would I have guessed it.
> Much I would have liked it, Much would I have liked it.

This permutation also appears with the dropping of the C_s member *if*: *Had I known I would have gone; Should he come, I will call you.* Also in S_1 of the *D S_1 than S_2* construction: *Hardly had he left than she returned.* Also with a few non-concessive introducers of secondary *S*: (*He went and so will I (go)*).[24]

When *t* is a suffix or zero, then if *V=be* (whether as *Y* or otherwise), or if *V=have* as member of *Y* (or optionally otherwise), what permutes is *t be, t have*. Before other *V*, a suffix or zero *t* which remains separated from its *V* receives the non-morphemic morphophonemes of *do*, whereupon it becomes pronounceable as a word. To understand this, we start with the form *Σ t V Ω*, and say that in those cases where the tense is not a word (but a suffix, or zero: ∅) it is then morphophonemically moved to be appended after the *V*:

> The man will arrive
> *The man -ed arrive → The man arrived.
> *The man -s arrive → The man arrives
> *The men ∅ arrive → The men arrive.

When the *t* is separated from the *V* by its permutation with Σ (or, as will be seen below, by certain *D*), this morphophonemic moving does not take place. The suffix or zero *t* is not pronounceable by itself as a word. The morphophonemes of *do* which are then placed before it give it word structure.[25] Thus *did, does, do* are not verbs or pro-verbs (there is room for neither since a *V* follows), nor operators on *V* (as is *have*), but morphophonemic carriers for *-ed, s,* and ∅ tense affixes.

Certain *D*, chiefly *not* and emphatic stress, are inserted between *t* and *V*, yielding, e.g.

$$\Sigma \text{ t not } V \ \Omega.$$

The resulting forms are not due to a permutation of the *t*, but rather to the prevention of the normal moving of suffix *t* to after the *V*:

> The man will not arrive.
> The man did not arrive.
> The man does not arrive.
> The men do not arrive.
> The man did arrive.

5.4. *Length Permutation*

Permuting of a shorter portion of a form to occur before another (usually longer) portion takes place in certain specified situations: It takes place within the material following a $V \Sigma V X Y \to \Sigma V Y X$ if *X* is longer: *X Y* are chiefly $\Omega_1 \ \Omega_2$ or ΩD. This is required in some cases, optional in most: **They broke up it→They broke it up*[26], *They broke up the game → They broke the game up; He attributed the painting to her→He attributed to her the painting* (but *He attributed it to her* does not change); *He read a very long letter which was on the desk slowly→He read slowly a very long letter which was on the desk* (but *He read the letter slowly* does not change).

It takes place also between *N* and the material that is inserted to the right of it. The problem arises particularly with the *wh-K₂* insert, whose length can be reduced by excision of the *wh-* and *is*. If after the dropping of the *wh-* word and *is*, the residue of K_2 is only an *A* (including *Ving, Ven* without explicit or zeroed *Ω* or *D* following) or a compound word, or in certain cases just another *N*, then the residue permutes to the left of the *N: long book, China doll, broken promises, sleeping beauty, wood-burning stove*; but *the promises broken (by them), a person sleeping (at the time)*; and *the man here, the man present*. This permutation is required. The position of the insert to the right or left of *N* always depends on the length of the insert (before and after any excisions).

In all these cases length is understood not purely in terms of number of phonemes or morphemes. It is a grammatical quantity, roughly correlating with number of morphemes (and, to a slight extent, of phonemes), but in detail formulated so as to describe accurately which parts appear to the left of which other parts.[27] Note that comma is itself a contributor to length, so that comma-containing inserts on N (e.g. *wh* K_2 with comma) never permute to the left.

6. KERNEL-LIKE RESULTANTS

If we now consider the resultant of an elementary transformation on a sentence structure, we find that this resultant is itself identical with some of the previously recognized sentence structures, or different from it in only a manner to be specified here. The well-formedness conditions for an elementary sentence structure are that it be a sequence $\Sigma\ t\ V\ \Omega$, where the symbols indicate precisely the categories or subcategories of words listed in Section 0.[28] The well-formedness conditions for the resultants of an elementary transformation are the same, except that the insertions given in Section 1 are permitted before or after the indicated parts of the elementary sentence, and the definitions of Σ, V, Ω are extended to include certain new subcategories or sequences. In this sense, the resultant of an operation on K (or on a K-like structure) is K-like, where 'K-like' means that the structure is identical with K except for the additions and definition-extensions noted in 6.1–5. In addition, the asyntactic operations add the permutations listed in 6.6.

We now consider the resultants of each of the elementary transformations.

6.1. The resultant of an insertion which adds J_r to the right or J_l to the left of X in K satisfies the well-formedness conditions for K if we accept $X J_r$ or $J_l X$ whenever we would accept X in K.

6.2. The resultants of the sentence-operators and verb-operators satisfy the well-formedness conditions for K if *that K, whether K, for N to V* Ω and *N Ving* Ω are permitted to satisfy Σ or Ω_1 (the N case) or Ω_2 (the PN case) in K, and if *Ving* Ω, and *Ving*, and *Vn* and *An* are permitted to occupy the position of Σ and of N in Ω, with *N's* or *of N* or *by N* (with various restrictions) being right and left inserts to these, and $P\ \Omega$ being a right insert to *Ving* or *Vn*, and finally if *Ving* Ω, *Va* and *PVn* are permitted to occupy the position of A in Ω. In addition we note that the operators themselves satisfy the well-formedness conditions for parts of an elementary sentence, consisting as they do of either V (for the Y and U operators) or $V\ \Omega$, or $N\ V$, including *be* with A, N, PN objects; to the latter we have to add C_sK and P_sKn as Ω of *be*. The various subcategories of V brought in by these operators are in many cases morphemes which were not members of V in K.

6.3. The resultants of the connective operation satisfy the well-formedness conditions for an elementary sentence only if we add to these conditions the permission for K to be followed by $C_s K$ or $C_c K$ or $C_{co} K$ (in which latter case there must be a D_c in the first K), and for N to be followed by wh K as right insert.[29]

6.4. The redundancy operation does not disturb the well-formedness schema because it is so restricted as not to affect the Σ or V or K[30], but only the Ω of K, and secondary K or inserts into K. The zeroing of Ω in 'Transformational Theory', 5.23 produces a sentence of N V_0 type. In this case the well-formedness conditions have to be extended so that a verb which was in the category requiring $\Omega = N$, PN object must now be included also in the category which is followed by $\Omega =$ zero. The zeroing of constants and appropriate words occurs only in a K_2 which has been adjoined to a K_1, and the zeroing of non-insert-form words on the basis of an antecedent occurs only in a K_2 on the basis of an antecedent in K_1.[31] Thus the verb be, even though it is a constant of a transformation, cannot be zeroed in $This$ is $what$ I $took$; but the be of K_2 after wh is dropped with the wh as in The $cable$ $from$ $home$ $arrived$. Note that if a noun has an antecedent within the same K it is not zeroed, but may be replaced by pronoun plus $self$, as in He saw $himself$. As to the zeroing of words which are in insert-form, this obviously does not affect well-formedness since inserts are merely permitted (6.1). These remarks referred to the zeroing of elements. In contrast, the pronouning of elements can occur in any positions of secondary or paired structures (with the antecedent in the other structure); or the pronoun replaces a disjunction of N from a disjunction of sentences. To include pro-morphemes in the well-formedness conditions, we need only include the pro-morpheme of a category as a member of that category. In this way the redundancy operation permits zeros to occur in certain positions of an adjoined K_2, thus affecting the well-formedness for such insertions; but it does not otherwise affect the well-formedness conditions for K.

6.5. The analogic extensions operate on given well-formed sentences and produce only a sentence set identical to one of the given forms except for a stated different subcategory or sequence occurring in place of one of the categories of the given form. The mirror operation produces a novel form in that all the Ω of be, and not only N, may appear in Σ position if they are missing in a certain way from the new Ω, e.g. $Here$ is $where$ he was, $Here$ is $where$ he $stood$, $Nice$ is $hardly$ $what$ he is.

6.6. The asyntactic permutations produce in general sentence structures which are not K-like, but are describable in terms of K-structure, as permutations of its parts.

6.7. We can summarize the operands and resultants of the elementary transformations in the following table, omitting all details:

TRANSFORMATION	OPERAND	RESULTANT
Insertion J	X of K	$J_l\, X$ or $X\, J_r$ substituting for X
Verb-operators Y	$N\, V\, \Omega$	$N\ Y\ Ving/en\ \Omega$
$V\, \Omega$-operators U	$N\, V\, \Omega$	$N\ U\ (N's)\ Vm\ (of)\ \Omega$[32]
Sentence-operators W	S (incl. K)	$N\ V\ S\bar{n},\ S\bar{n}\ V\ \Omega$[33]
Connectives C	$S_1,\, S_2$	$S_1\ C\ S_2$
(exc. wh)		
Connective wh	$K_1\ (N_i),$	$K_1\ (N_i\ wh\ \breve{N}_i\ S_2\text{-}N_i)$
	$S_2\ (N_i+)$[34]	
Redundancy removal	$Sn,\ CS,$ and a few other increments	reduced forms of $Sn,\ CS,$ and, in a few cases, of K.

7. SUCCESSIVE APPLICATION OF THE OPERATION

Each transformation φ_i has been defined here as operating on an operand of a certain form; a K or K-pair structure, which the φ_i may require to have certain limitations as to subcategories of words in stated K-parts, or as to identity of certain words in the two K. Now each transformation φ_j produces specified changes in the form; and for certain transformations, φ_i operates on the resultant of φ_j in the same way that φ_i operates on a K. This can be expressed by broadening the definition of the operand of φ_i to include the additions, subcategory-changes, etc. that φ_j has introduced.

7.1. *The Trace of a Transformation*

For this purpose, it is useful to specify the changes introduced by each φ.

We define the trace of φ_i as the difference (in V, pre-tV, and post-tV parts) in the resultant of φ_i as against the operand of φ_i.

φ	TRACE
J:	J before or after stated parts of K.
W:	V_s for V, with mostly human N for Σ (i.e. the pre-tV part), $S\bar{n}$ for Ω (i.e. the post-tV part); or else Sn for Σ, and $V_{s.}\Omega$ (incl. *is* A_s, *is* N_s) for $V\,\Omega$.
U:	U for V, Vm *(of)* Ω (with possibly $N's$ repeating the N of Σ).
Y:	Y for V, $Ving/en\ \Omega$ for Ω.
$C_c,\ C_{co}$:	C_cS as J_r after K; $C_{co}S$ as J_r after Σ *is* A_c.
with zeroing:	C_cX as J_r after X; $C_{co}S$ as J_r after X containing D_c.
C_s:	C_sS as J on K.
wh:	$wh\ \breve{N}_i\ S\text{-}N_i$ as J_r on N_i.
zeroing:	$Vn\ \Omega,\ Vn$ instead of $Sn',\ Sn$ as Ω of W; zero instead of N as Ω of certain V; etc.

The traces of the various analogic extensions and inverses consist in that a particular subcategory (or category or sequence) in a stated part of K is different from the subcategory for that part in the definition of K, or of the φ on that K.

It can be shown that the trace of a transformation is never entirely zeroed (or, rather that this is a safe assumption to make), even though parts of the trace may be zeroed.

We can now say that if φ_i operates on a resultant $\varphi_j K$, then φ_i operates on $\varphi_j K$ precisely as φ_i operates on the parts of K, except that if any part X_i of the K has been replaced by a trace of φ_j, the φ_i operates on that trace of φ_j in X_i as it would operate on the X_i. It is then possible to say for each φ_i whether it will or will not operate on a given φ_j: for particular i, j, either $\varphi_i (\varphi_j K)$ occurs or it does not occur.

To sum up: Because the resultant of an operation φ_j on K is K-like, it is possible for an operation φ_i defined on K to operate on the resultant of φ_j on K. In general, φ_i can operate on K if the K has the particular conditions required in the definition of φ_i. And φ_i can operate on φ_j if φ_j introduces the conditions for φ_i, or if K had the conditions for φ_i, and φ_j did not destroy them, or, finally, if the definition of φ_i is extended so as to accept in a stated K position the new material brought into it by φ_j. It is therefore possible to draw up a table showing which operations can be carried out on the resultants of which operations. Each operation φ_j produces a particular kind of K-like structure, so that if an operation is able to act on the resultant of φ_j it can do so no matter whether φ_j in turn had been applied to a K or to the resultant of some φ acting on a K, and so on.

7.2. *Independent Transformations on K*

In principle we do not need the additional concept of two transformations operating separately on a K. However, for many classes of φ, $\varphi_j \varphi_i K = \varphi_i \varphi_j K$; and furthermore both these resultants are identical with what we would get if we could combine separately the effect of φ_i on K and the effect of φ_j on the same K. This happens when the traces of φ_i and φ_j do not alter the operand of the other, as when one J is added to one part of a K and another J to another part of the same K, or when a J is added to a part of a K while a sentence-operator $N V_s$ *that* is added to the whole K. Even when two J are added to the same part X of the same K, their action is independent if each operates only in respect to the X:

$$J_1: X \to J_1 X; J_r: X \to XJ_r$$
$$J_1 (J_r X) = J_r (J_1 X): X \to J_1 X J_r.$$

If the two J on the same X are added to the same side of X, they are independent if the second J to be added operates without reference to the earlier J, i.e. operates only in respect to the X. In this case the latter-added J would be closer to the X than the earlier-added J:

Hence, if

$$J_r: A \text{ X } B \to A \text{ X } J_r \text{ B},$$

then
$$J_{r1}: A \text{ X } B \to A \text{ X } J_{r1} \text{ B}$$

and
$$J_{r2}: A \text{ X } J_{r1} \text{ B} \to A \text{ X } J_{r2} \text{ } J_{r1} \text{ B}$$

Thus
$$J_{r2} (J_{r1}x) = X J_{r2} J_{r1},$$

while
$$J_{r1} (J_{r2}X) = X J_{r1} J_{r2}.$$

It should be noted that while J_{r1} follows J_{r2} to yield $X J_{r1} J_{r2}$, and J_{r2} follows J_{r1} to yield $X J_{r2} J_{r1}$, both orderings of J_{r1}, J_{r2} are possible in this example, to yield one sentence or another.

Although we have defined no separate primitive activity of summing the separate operation of two φ on the same K, we can say that in the above conditions the effect of φ_i on $\varphi_j K$ is the same as a summing of the independent effects of φ_j on K and φ_i on K. The need to specify that φ_i occurs on $\varphi_j K$ remains only for transformation pairs in which the operand K-parts of one are altered by the trace of the other.

7.3. *Transformations operating on Resultants*

J, which are defined to operate on the K-parts, can also operate on the new $N V_{.s}$ or $V_{s.}$ Ω (including *is A_s, is N_s*), U, and Y, since these are simply new subcategories of the categories occupying K positions. But J does not operate in general on the new Σ and Ω which are deformed from the underlying S or $V \Omega$ on which W, U operate. Nor does J operate in general on J, or on C.[35]

W, U, Y operate on any resultant of these, since each of these produces an $N t V \Omega$, which is the form of the operand. Where the Σ or Ω of W is Sn^0, the S (in Sn^0) can carry any transformations, since Sn^0 is merely any S preceded by *that, whether, for--to*. Where the Σ or Ω is Sn' or Sn, the S can carry only such transformations as can be operated on by these nominalizations.[36]

The C operate on two sentences S_1, S_2 to produce a single sentence $S_3 = S_1 C S_2$ (with $C S$ as J on K), or $S_3 = S_1$ plus a local J as residue of the $C S_2$. Therefore they can operate on their own resultant: $C (S C S, S)$ and $C (S, S C S)$, as well as on resultants of almost all other φ. In the case of C_{co}, each of the two S has to be of the form *An is A_c* (or a form derived therefrom), with the result that C_{co} can only repeat on a pair $S C_{co}S$, $SC_{co}S$.

In the repetition of *wh*, two different results are obtained, according as whether the N_i common to S_2 and S_3 is the same as the N_j common to S_1 and S_2, or not. If $i=j$, then we have from S_1 *wh* S_2:

$$X_1 \; N_i \; Y_1 \; wh \; N_i \; S_2\text{-}N_i = X_1 \; N_i \; wh \; \breve{N}_i \; S_2\text{-}N_i \; Y_1$$

and repeating the operation for $(S_1 \; wh \; S_2) \; wh \; S_3$:

$$(X_1 \; N_i \; wh \; \breve{N}_i \; S_2\text{-}N_i \; Y_1) \; wh \; N_i \; S_3\text{-}N_i =$$
$$X_1 \; N_i \; wh \; \breve{N}_i \; S_3\text{-}N_i \; wh \; \breve{N}_i \; S_2\text{-}N_i \; Y_1$$

Thus, $S_1 \; wh \; S_2$:

The book which he wrote is rather poor;

with $wh \; S_3$:

The book which sold so well which he wrote is rather poor.

If $i \neq j$, i.e. if different N in S_2 are involved in the two applications of wh, then, taking as an example $S_2 = N_j \; V_2 \; N_i$: we have from $S_2 \; wh \; S_3$:

$$N_j \; V_2 \; N_i \; wh \; N_j \; S_3\text{-}N_j = N_j \; wh \; \breve{N}_j \; S_3\text{-}N_j \; V_2 \; N_i$$

and from $S_1 \; wh \; (S_2 \; wh \; S_3)$:

$$X_1 \; N_i \; Y_1 \; wh \; (N_i \; N_j \; wh \; \breve{N}_j \; S_3\text{-}N_j \; V_2) = X_1 \; N_i \; wh \; \breve{N}_i \; N_j \; wh$$
$$S_3\text{-}N_j \; V_2 \; Y_1.$$

Thus, $S_2 \; wh \; S_3$:

The quartet which the prince commissioned was to make him famous.

with $wh \; S_1$:

The quartet which the prince who favored Beethoven commissioned was to make him famous.

We see here that the repetition of wh takes two different forms, not because of a different mode of operation, but because of the extra degree of freedom in wh as to which N is common to the participating sentences.

The zeroing operations have only limited possibilities of repetition, because of the way they operate originally. Thus given $S_1 \; C_c \; S_2 \rightarrow S_1 \; C_c \; X_2$, there are only limited possibilities for zeroing in S_3 in the resultants $(S_1 \; C_c \; X_2) \; C_c \; S_3$ or $S_3 \; C_c \; (S_1 \; C_c \; X_2)$.
Thus from $S_1 \; C_c \; S_2 \; C_c \; S_3$:

John likes Bach and I like Bach and I like Stravinsky.

we obtain $(S_1 \; C_c \; X_2) \; C_c \; S_3$:

John and I like Bach and I (like) Stravinsky.

where the second I cannot be zeroed because its would-be antecedent I is only in an insert $(C_c \; X_2)$ within S_1. Or we obtain $S_1 \; C_c \; (S_2 \; C_c \; X_3)$:

John likes Bach and I (like) Bach and Stravinsky.

where the second *Bach* cannot be zeroed because it carries an insert $(C_c X_3)$ in S_2 which its antecedent in S_1 does not. Similarly, in $S_1 C_c S_2 C_c S_3$:

> John likes Bach and I prefer Mozart and John likes Stravinsky.

nothing can be zeroed because S_2 contains no words with antecedents in S_1, and S_3 none with antecedents in S_2.[37]

We thus have different repetition effects: In a sequence of conjoined S, the zeroing (and difference-counting) in each S depends on the preceding S. In any sequence S_1 *wh* S_2 *wh* S_3, the form of *wh* S_3 depends on S_2 or on S_1 (depending on the N which S_3 shares with its antecedent). In a repetition of J on a K, each J acts independently on the K. And C_{co} repeats only on a C_{co} pair. All these effects, however, differ only because of the conditions met in each case by the single mode of operation of φ on φ defined above.

7.4. *Same Increment in Different Transforms*

If a particular increment can be transformed from one φ-type into another, e.g. from J or C to W, it will have a different relation to other φ-applications, according to the φ-type in which it is appearing. For example, since the C increment in $S_1 C_s S_2$ can be transformed into the W increment in $S_1 n$ *is* $C_s S_2$, we can have this W from repeat, yielding $(S_1 n$ *is* $C_s S_2)n$ *is* $C_s C_3$:

> His going there was because he thought she was still in.
> His going there being because he thought she was still in was because he wanted to see her.

This can be transformed back into $S C_s S$ form:

> He went there because he thought she was still in, because he wanted to see her.

But we also have *wh* on this Sn *is* $C_s S$, yielding

> $(S_1 n$ *is* $C_s S_3)$ *wh* $(S_1 n$ *is* $C_s S_2) \rightarrow$
> $S_1 n C_s S_2$ *is* $C_s S_3$ [38]:
> His going there was because he wanted to see her.
> His going there was even though he was still tired.
> His going there even though he was still tired was because he wanted to see her.

Transforming back into $S C_s S$ form, we obtain

> He went there, even though he was still tired, because he wanted to see her.

In a similar way, one can obtain

$(S_1$n is P_s S_2n) wh $(S_2$n is C_s $S_3)$

His going there was because of his wanting to see them.

His wanting to see them was because they were famous.

His going there was because of his wanting to see them because they were famous.

He went there, because he wanted to see them because they were famous.

Other combinations of repeated C_s-transforms are possible, all ultimately reducible to a sequence of subordinate conjunctions $S \, C_s S \ldots C_s S$, in which the various transformational equivalents are discernible as different readings, partially distinguished by commas, of the long sentence.

In a similar way we have:

His quiet announcing of the defeat affected everyone.

from:

wh $\begin{cases} \text{His announcing of the defeat affected everyone. } (W) \\ \text{The announcing of the defeat was quiet. } (W \text{ form of } D_m). \end{cases}$

Without zeroing of *wh-* and the constant *was*, this is identical with:

His announcing of the defeat, which was quiet, affected everyone.

In contrast, there is:

His announcing the defeat quietly affected everyone.

from *affected everyone* operating as $V_{s.}$ Ω on:

He announced the defeat quietly.

But the latter has the transform (as above)

His announcing the defeat was quiet.

and if the $W \Omega$ operates on this transform we obtain the equivalent

His announcing of the defeat being quiet affected everyone.

In the first case, we have W on K and D_m on K (the latter necessarily in W form) connected by comma-*wh*. In the second case, we have W operating on D_m which has operated on K.

8. THE NETWORK OF SENTENCE DIFFERENCES

We can now consider what is the effect of the elementary operations above, and hence all transformations (which are only successions of these), on the set of sentences in the language. The fact that the resultants of these operations (except for the asyntactic) are K-like means that given an initial set of K sentences which have different K structures for different subcategories, the operations yield additional sets of sentences showing the same structural differences, except that for the new sentences, these structural differences now obtain between sentence sets which have the same sets of word-selections. Furthermore, the fact that the analogic operations do their part of this only by paralleling existing transformational relations (except in the case of 4.6) means that the kinds of structural difference for same word-selection are only those brought in by the increment and redundancy operations (and by the 4.6 analogy). Each of the elementary operations increases the variety of material (subcategories, sequences) occupying K-positions (Σ, V, Ω or next to these), without adding to the stock of word-selection-acceptances of sentences of the kernel.[39]

The main effect, then, of elementary transformations is to bring the word-selections of one K_i structure into the form of another K_j structure; i.e. a transformation φ_i takes the sets of simultaneous occupants of the K_i positions, together with some constants of φ_i, into particular positions of K_j. It is for this reason that we can look upon a transformation as an operation, which derives the presence of a particular set of word-selections occupying the positions of K_j from their occupancy of positions of K_i.

The problem of transformations as directional operations can only be touched upon here. There are many considerations which support a view of the elementary transformations as being directed operations, and not merely equivalences. In the case of the increments (including affixation) and redundancy-removing, it is clearly natural to think of an operation from a structure A to a structure consisting of A plus increment or excision, rather than merely to say that a set of word-selections occurs with and without these increments or excisions. There is also the fact of linguistic productivity, in which we can see the novel appearance of the word-selection of some structure A appearing in a structure B in which it had not occurred before. There are also situations in which the word selections of form S_a and those of S_b appear both in S_c and in S_d. This can be conveniently described by saying that while two operations took the word-selections of S_a into S_c, and of S_b into S_c, one further operation took those of S_c into S_d. Thus forms with $\Sigma = Sn^0$ come from various sources, but all participate on $Sn^0 \ V \ \Omega \rightarrow It \ V \ \Omega \ Sn^0$.

The existence of operations along a directed path may be seen in the residue left by some of the intermediate operations. An example of this is in the transformations which require or prefer the presence of a D, even though the D seems not to be involved in the transformationally related forms. For example, there is for certain V a transformational relation between $N_1 \ V \ N_2$ and $N_2 \ V \ D$, a relation which is supported by the fact that it is productive, though uncomfortable:

> People sell this book, This book sells easily.
> They pasted the wallpaper, The wallpaper didn't paste nicely.

The $N_2 V$ cannot be directly related to the $N_1 \ V \ N_2$ by any known operation; and in any case we have to explain why the form is much more acceptable with D than without it. The D, however, can serve to indicate a possible succession of elementary operations which would account for $N_2 \ V \ D$:

(1)	$N_1 \ V \ N_2$	He sells this book.
(2)	$N_1 \ V \ N_2 \ A \ ly$	He sells this book easily.
(3)	One $V \ N_2 \ A \ ly$ (indefinite pronoun)	One sells this book easily.
(4)	One's $Ving$ of N_2 is A	One's selling of this book is easy.
(5)	The $Ving$ of N_2 is A (drop indef. Σ)	The selling of this book is easy.
(6)	$N_2 \ V \ A \ ly$	This book sells easily.

We obtain (6) from (5) by the inverse of the $K \ A \ ly \rightarrow Kn \ is \ A$ operation (Section 4.6) which had given (4) out of (3). The form $Ving \ of \ N \ is \ A$ has two sources, one in which the N is the Σ (*The singing of birds was soft*), and one in which the N is the Ω (*The singing of the chorales was loud.*); these are in general discriminable only by co-occurrence. If a sentence of this form receives an inverse of $K \ A \ ly \rightarrow Kn \ is \ A$ toward the 'wrong' source, we obtain such a result as (6) from (1) above. In this way there arises a limited relation $N_1 \ V \ N_2 \ A \ ly \rightarrow N_2 \ V \ A \ ly$. The D is present, therefore, because it was a step in the succession of operations; since it was the nominalization of K under *is A* that made it possible to reconstruct N_2, instead of the lost N_1, as the Σ.

There can thus be little doubt as to the descriptive value of a succession of operations to take us from one form to another. Nevertheless, there are many difficulties in the way of taking a directed operation as the only relation between different S-forms of the same word-selections set. One is the existence of inverse operations (4.2), which, even though they act on a different set of word-selections than the operation they are paralleling, show that the direction of the original operation was not a determining characteristic of it. In fact, nothing in the analogic extensions, which is to say nothing in the way the first operations (1–4) are used for further extension, depends upon the direction of the initial set of operations. $A \rightarrow B$ and $B \rightarrow A$, and sequences of such, serve equally well as a model for producing a new B' out of A'.

The fact that some forms B' can be described as related to A' on the analogy of a relation between B and A, even though an A' source does not exist (4.3), or at the cost of saying that only the product of the operations involved in $A \rightarrow B$ acts on B' (4.4, 5), suggests that it is not the (directed) path to B that is paralleled in producing B', but rather the pairing A, B.

Finally, if S_b can be related to S_a by a long succession of elementary operations, it will often be found that it can also be related to S_a by other successions of elementary operations. The long paths are often not unique.

There are thus many problems about a system of directed operations which takes us from the K to all the resultant sentences of the language. But even if one does not wish to accept a particular path of elementary transformations between S_a and S_b as a 'derivation' of S_b from S_a, it remains that if the difference between S_a and S_b is more than an elementary transformation, then sentences having partial (intermediate) differences between S_a and S_b exist, in most cases. And even if the particular K and elementary operations proposed here are rejected in favor of some other set of K and transformations, the fact would remain that for every sentence in the language we would be able to find other sentences containing the same word-selection and differing from it in structure by only the differences exhibited in the elementary operations above (or in some equivalent set of elementary differences) or in some succession of them. The elementary transformations constitute, for the sentences of the language, a system of connectives more than of derivations.

It is this network of elementary differences among sentences, in particular sentences of the same word-selection, that is the most definite result. Indeed, small differences reaching over a range of sentence structures can be seen even outside of transformations. The similarity of all K structures, as expressed in $\Sigma \, t \, V \, \Omega$, is not transformational. In the U operators, we saw several sets of operators which ranged in many properties from ones similar to Y to ones similar to W; but the various subcategories of U contained different words, so that in general one U form is not a transform of another.

In the case of sentences which are transformationally equivalent, the differences are of a much more definite kind: They are not simply a matter of similarity, but are the precise differences which are sufficient to house the increments and excisions in kernel-like forms (i.e. in a stated and minor extension) of the K structures. The differences thus form a system, namely that of 2.1–4. It is natural to view the moving of a word-selection set over one of these differences as a derivation.[40] But in some cases a descriptively possible derivation is historically unnatural. For example, it is possible to derive the plural affix from sequences N *and* $N \ldots$ *and* N; whereas *and* cannot be derived from the plural affix. Similarly, by using otherwise existing operations, it is possible to derive all question forms and imperative forms from assertion forms with performative W operators; but one might hesitate to claim that indeed questions exist in the language only by virtue of this derivation. The descriptive derivations are nevertheless of interest both for a systematic analysis and a normalization of the structure of language, and also for the transformational equivalence which they show between, e.g. singular and plural sentences, or assertions and questions.

9. SUMMARY

We have seen here that the sentences of English can be characterized by a small family of elementary sentence structures and a few small families of elementary transformations on these. Specifically:

(1) a small family of elementary sentence forms $K = \Sigma\, V\, \Omega$ ($\Sigma = N$; $\Omega =$ zero, N, PN, and a few more), each K-form having particular word-selections for its categories.

(2) three types of increment to K: inserts to K or to parts of K, mostly short, and all in very small classes except for the adverbs; operators on V and on K which themselves become the V of the resultant K-like structure; connectives which adjoin a second K to a first.

(3) the removal of material which becomes redundant when two entities (K, insert, or operator) are juxtaposed in accordance with (2) above. The zeroing is carried out in such a way that the resultant maintains a K-like structure (6). Since only material that can be determined is dropped, we can say that the material is still morphemically present, that only its phonemes become zero, and that the language therefore has no dropping of morphemes.

(4) analogic extensions of these operations and their inverses, to sub-categories on which they had not been defined, but in such a way as to produce new sentences of structure similar to extant sentences. Only rarely does this involve the setting up of new transformational relations.

(5) a very few asyntactic operations which permute the parts of a K so that it is no longer K-like.

These structural components are also semantically characterizable. Strong co-occurrence restrictions on words appear only within a K, and between V and the D_m (PN_m) insert. The insertions are in general modifiers of that next to which they are inserted. The V of the K, and the Y, U and W operators are all verbs or predicates with distinct semantic differences between one set and the other. The semantic differences among the various types of C can be readily related to differences in the requirements which they make as to the similarity between the two K which they connect. And so down to more delicate distinctions in subcategories. Idioms and metaphors are distin-

guishable as word-co-occurrences which do not accept all of the transformations that the others in their set do. Linguistic jokes and nonce forms
are distinguishable as extensions, usually of type 4.6, made on one member of
a word-selection set and not on the rest.

And above all: all substantive information is contained in the K and the
incremental operations. Redundancy removal, analogic extension, and the
asyntactic permutations vary the style or subjective character of a sentence
but not its information. And every S can be mapped by these transformations
onto the K and increments it contains (in their particular interrelation).

The elementary operations are not so loose as to permit all word combinations to appear as an English sentence. One can study the total range of
structures (say, within any given length) that can be produced by any combination of these operations, and it will be seen that they produce a particular
set of category-sequences and, within these, only particular rearrangements
of the occupants of K positions. As a result, the structure of English sentences,
without taking into account the K-occupant rearrangements, remains the
$\Sigma\ t\ V\ \Omega$ of the K, except that the values of these variables is now given not
only by the list for K, but also by the additions and changes due to the
elementary operations.

Every K structure is a model for some transformation, and every word-
selection set is present in more than one structure, i.e. enters into transformations. Every transformation is an elementary operation (an elementary
difference) or a succession of these. Every sentence is a K, or can be said to be
obtained from a K by a succession of elementary operations. No new concepts are needed to explain the form of this or that sentence, except for
restrictions on the application of elementary operations, or for the arbitrariness of which subclass extensions are made by the analogic operation.
More generally, aside from specifiable petrified forms, only such sentences
exist in the language as differ from other sentences of the same word-
selections by various ones of the elementary differences only or by products
of these. If we think in terms of the obvious gross transformations, such as
passive and question, then we see that each sentence makes its large transformations out of material that is also used in different combinations in
other transformations; each use of such material being necessarily itself a
component transformation over the whole sentence. Thus for a sentence
to fit into the grammar is for it to participate in this network of transformational differences.

NOTES

[1] 'Change' here refers to: the adding of a morpheme which does not occur in elementary
sentences (called sentences of the kernel), e.g. affixes, such as *-ing*; the appearance, as a

constant of transformations, of certain morphemes which occur also in kernel S (e.g. informationally weak V like *be, do*; metaphorical uses of certain V like *take*, and of P like *by*); the permutation of certain kernel-S parts (e.g. of Σ and Ω in *So says he*). S indicates sentence.

2 The operation of zeroing is not presented here because it is discussed in 'Transformational Theory', § 5.2, *Lg.* **41** (1965). (Paper XXVII of this volume.)

3 In addition to these symbols, X_j (where $j =$ one of the defined subcategories of X) indicates the j subcategory of X, and Xy indicates a word of category X which upon receiving affix y occurs in the position of category Y. X_i, where i is a number or an undefined subscript of X, indicates an individual member i of X. $K(X)$ indicates K containing X; aside from this, (X) indicates that X is omittable from the form in which it appears. $\breve{X}$ indicates a pronoun of X. Occasionally, X/Y will be used to indicate 'X or Y'. * or $\not\exists$ before an example indicates that it does not occur as a sentence of the language; (*) indicates that it is uncomfortable except in suitable context. The position which a word X occupies in a structure A will be called the position of X; or a position in A, or an A-position.

4 There is a third, very restricted member of this set, the *be--en* of *He is gone*.

5 V_s indicates either $V_{.s}$ or $V_{s.}$.

6 The forms $N's, of N, by N$ which the Σ receives, and the form (1) $P \Omega$ which the Ω may receive, are similar structurally (and in their acceptance of many further operations) to certain primitive inserts on N (sec. 1). They will be called insert-forms of Σ, Ω. The forms *Ving, Vn* are similar to N in their acceptance of many operations (including plural).

7 A special subset of $W_{.h}$ is seen in *It seemed that he wrote the letter, It is merely that he wrote the letter*, etc., where *be* plus *not* or D_g, and a few V of the *be*-set, occur only with *It* as Σ (as in the K-structure with *It*).

8 Although the Kn^0 are most conveniently analyzed as Σ and Ω of W, like Kn' and Kn, an alternative analysis could take them as separate K connected by *that, whether, for* to another K built out of the W. Such an alternative is particularly suggestive for the W which have N as well as K in their object. There is indeed a similar form in certain marginal C_s: *that* in *He fled to the woods, (in order, so) that he might live; for* in *He shouted loudly, (in order) for them to notice him; They called a strike, (in order, so as) to protect their working conditions; whether* in *I'll go, whether they come or not*. Whereas the C_s connect a K_2 to a preceding K_1, these three (with *if* also) connect K to an operator W which may be looked upon as an 'incomplete' K: $N V$ or $V \Omega$.

9 The insert-character differs for the various C: C_sS is like an insert on K (sentence-adjunct); *wh S* is like an insert to the right of N; C_cX (as residue of C_cS, inserted to the right of X) is somewhat like an adjunct on X, but an N subject in singular with *and N* inserted after it takes plural verb.

10 Various $A, P N$ are variously comfortable in these positions, and there is some confusion with those $A ly, P N$ (usually separated by commas) that come from $N is A, N is P N$; *Slowly, he rose* (in the sense of 'being slow', not 'in a slow manner').

11 A rather special case of this moving of sentence-adjunct-like material may be involved in *For N to V N_2 is A_s* $\rightarrow$ *N_2 is A_s for N to V: For him to say this is easy, This is easy for him to say*. The *for N* has indeed the form of a mobile insert, but the *to V* is only distantly similar to the *to V* Ω which is a C_sS insert, for here the *to V* is moved while Ω remains. The separation of *to V* from its Ω might be understood if the permutation of the *to V* went through an intermediate $\Omega \Sigma V$ operation (5.1) yielding *N_2 for N to V is A_s: This for him to say is easy*.

12 I.e., they can all, together with A_m, be looked upon as subclasses of a super-class of sentence-predicates, defined by occurrences in this range of positions.

13 For the source forms, see 4.53. Those with (*) are uncomfortable, but can be found in context.

14 The change from *which* to *what* here presents a problem.

15 The same intermediate $N t do Ving \Omega \leftarrow N t V \Omega$ is needed for *Writing letters is what he*

does all day ← (*) *He does writing letters all day* ← *He writes letters all day*, and for *All that he does is feel bad* ← * *He does only feeling bad* ← *He only feels bad*.

[16] One might not think, for example, that *do dying* occurs, but cf: *What does one learn from Berenson's last years except that dying is better done in Italy?* Or: *Most generals do their dying in bed*.

[17] For *An* we may find *A* with classifier N_{cl} of that *A*.

[18] After mirroring, the *Y* is the new Σ: thus if the new Σ is an *N* in the plural the *is* becomes plural.

[19] This mirroring does not occur for the *is-ing* of *He is buying books*, where the *is* is part of a discontinuous constant of the verb-operator.

[20] From *N's Ving of Ω is A_m*, by transformation among the *U* (4.51); and this latter from *N V Ω $A_m$ly*, by 4.6.

[21] A further operation on these is seen at the end of 4.23.

[22] In 4.51 we had *N* with zero v suffix in N_0 t N_1 v N_2 ← N_0 t V_{ap} N_1 P N_2 as inverses of N_0 t V_{ap} V_m P N_2: *He watered the plants, He gave water to the plants; He kicked the door, He gave a kick to the door*.

[23] A few other transformations lead to more limitedly novel structures, as in the Σ-loss in the imperative V Ω ! ('Transformational Theory', 5.213) marked by the imperative intonation. The non-*K*-like structure of the question derives in part from the performative-dropping ('Transformational Theory' 5.213) which again is marked by intonation, and in part from 5.3.

[24] Properties of both the *D* and C_s cases are seen in the t Σ permutations in *Neither will he go* (or: *Neither he will go*) *nor will you*.

[25] Morphophonemes, not phonemes, of *do*; because this non-morphemic carrier of the tense goes through the same morphophonemic changes as would *do* in the same environment.

[26] Instead of this, we can merely say that the pronoun *it* can replace *the game* in *They broke the game up*, but not (for reasons of length) in *They broke up the game*.

[27] Thus the D_e adverbs, e.g. *here*, do not permute (as in *the man here*) while *A* permute (as in *the long book*).

[28] There are also certain exclamations and petrified expressions.

[29] The connectives carry additional well-formedness restrictions, within the general restrictions on *K*, as to similarities among the *K* on which they operate.

[30] Redundant Σ is dropped in the imperative and in such special forms as *Coming*!

[31] With the exception of zeroed V Ω in primary K_1 from antecedent in $C_s K_2$: *If you won't go, I will*.

[32] For *Vm*, see 2.2.

[33] *S$\bar{n}$* stands for Sn^0, Sn', and Sn.

[34] *K* may contain *J* and a few *J*-like reductions of *wh*, but not other connectives. $S(N_i +)$ means that the N_i is the first word of *S*, at least after a permuting operation.

[35] The occurrence of D_g on C_s originates in the sentence-operator form: *He came primarily because she was sick* ← *His coming was primarily because she was sick*. Thus, *primarily* is D_g on *was* rather than on C_s.

[36] Some details were given in 2.1–3.

[37] This chain property characterizes the zeroing procedure of C_c but not all zeroing procedures. The chain appears in C_c even when zeroing is not involved: the difference which *or, but* require in connected *S* do not apply between S_3 and S_1 in S_1 C_c S_2 C_c S_3. *C* is an operation on pairs.

[38] The form *Sn is C_s* is often uncomfortable. However, it is a possible form, and is subject to *wh* because *Sn* is operated on here in the same way that *N* is. If we did not want to go through this form we would need another formulation for this kind of C_s repetition.

[39] A partial exception: The D_m (adverbs of manner, Section 1), alone of all the increments, have a selection restriction, to the *V*, of the kind that obtains within a *K*. While the D_m appears in an insert position, various transformations bring it and its *V* into positions of a

K structure, thus producing a new selectional relation within a *K* structure. As to the asyntactic operations, they neither increase the variety of material nor do they add to the stock of selections.

[40] The historical and the psychological reality of these derivations is another matter. Some undoubtedly reflect the path of development of a form. Others may be only a way of exhibiting the parallel to various component transformations. Still others may show an analogic trend which is growing in the language. What does not show the past may be showing the future.

XXVII

TRANSFORMATIONAL THEORY*

1. STYLES OF GRAMMAR AND PROPERTIES OF SENTENCES

It may be helpful to understand transformational analysis in the light of other styles of grammatical analysis. The establishment of descriptive linguistics as a successful research method, and the piling up of grammatical descriptions, have made possible the investigation of various types of grammatical relation. Different ways of analyzing sentence-structures have been found or proposed; these are characterized by different kinds of aspects in terms of which the sentences of a language are described. Traditional grammar established various distinguished segments of sentences which were hierarchically subdivided into smaller segments (in a manner made explicit by Leonard Bloomfield, as the method of immediate constituents), or were altered by a grammatical process (in a manner developed, for example, in the work of Edward Sapir). Another decomposition is given by string analysis, in which each sentence is segmented into one center string and a number of adjunct strings which are adjoined to the center or adjunct strings.

In describing sentence structure, string analysis differs from constituent analysis primarily in that it isolates a distinguished elementary sentence and elementary adjuncts within each sentence, whereas constituent analysis does not directly express the fact that the heads of the various constituents of a sentence or constituent X, at a given level of constituency, make up a sentence or adjunct string which can by itself appear in the linguistic environments in which X appears. That is, if a sentence or adjunct string X consists of constituents A (composed, in constituent terms, of head-of-A plus remainder-of-A) and B (composed of head-of-B plus remainder-of-B), then the environments in which the sequence head-of-A plus head-of-B can occur are closely related to the environments in which X can occur: they are the same (as in *I walked home briskly. The air was clear* and *I walked home. The air was clear*) or the same except for parallel remainders within connected sentences (as in *I walked slowly. But John walked briskly*), or the like.[1] Thus in the sentence

> *However, a sample which a young naturalist can obtain directly is often of value*

we have

(1) center string: *a sample is of value;*
(2) adjunct on 1: *however;*
(3) right-adjunct on subject of 1: *which a naturalist can obtain;*
(4) left-adjunct on subject of 3: *young;*
(5) (right)-adjunct on verb of 3: *directly;*
(6) adjunct on 1: *often.*[2]

If we compare the statements in string analysis with those in constituent analysis, we see that constituent analysis gives a hierarchical subdivision (in principle unbounded) of a sentence and its parts into parts, whereas string analysis gives a center and adjuncts, the adjoining of some adjuncts being in principle unboundedly repeatable. The fact that an adjunct may adjoin another adjunct is equivalent to part of the hierarchy in constituent description, but certain pseudo-hierarchical features of constituent description are replaced by the sequential composition of elementary strings and by the repeatability of certain adjunctions.[3]

Transformational analysis yields yet another decomposition of sentences: into sentences and operations on them, ultimately into elementary sentences K and elementary operations φ which operate on K and φ. The operations (transformations) thus decompose a sentence into sentences. In the above example we have (using here a rough formulation of transformations):

(1) elementary sentence: *a sample has value;*
(2) elementary sentence: *a naturalist obtains a sample;*
(3) elementary sentence: *a naturalist is young;*
(4) *however* (sentence-insert) operating on sentence 1, yielding a sentence;
(5) *often* (sentence-insert) operating on sentence 1, yielding a sentence;
(6) *has* $N \rightarrow is$ *of N* (for a certain subcategory of N);
(7) *wh-* connective on sentences 1, 2, yielding a sentence;
(8) *can* (verb-operator) on sentence 2;
(9) *directly* (adverbial insert) on sentence 2;
(10) *wh-* connective on sentences 2, 3, yielding a sentence;
(11) zeroing of *who is* in 10, with permutation of remainder of sentence 3.

Transformational analysis is relevant to linguistics because (1) it is possible to give formal and reasonable criteria for decomposing a sentence into sentences, and this by means of a reasonably small set of transformations; (2) the set of sentences of the language has an interesting structure, and one which has a semantic interpretation, under the transformational operations; (3) the set of transformations also has an interesting structure, and is not merely an arbitrary list of operations sufficient to decompose sentences into sentences. Transformational analysis is of particular interest, first, because it can be described and investigated with algebraic tools, and second, because it provides exceptionally subtle analyses and distinctions for sentences.[4]

To interrelate these analyses, it is necessary to understand that these are not competing theories, but rather complement each other in the description of sentences.[5] It is not that grammar is one or another of these analyses, but that sentences exhibit simultaneously all of these properties. Indeed one can devise modifications of languages, say of English, which lack one property while retaining the others; but the result is not structurally the same as the original language. Thus English sentences, taken transformationally as they now are, would have no simple string structure if the words due to separate elementary sentences were intermixed irregularly in the transformational resultant; and the sentences would have no string structure at all if transformations combined morphemes from separate elementary sentences into novel product-morphemes (portmanteau blends).

Each of these properties can be used as the basis for a description of the whole language because the effects of the other properties can be brought in as restrictions on the chosen property. For example, the string restriction on transformations can be expressed as follows: Consider a string of 21 positions, which can be expanded by repeatable insertion of s, l, r on s, l, r:

$$s \, l \, N \, r \, s \, l \, V \, r \, s \, l \, \Omega_1 \, r \, s \, l \, P \, r \, s \, l \, N_2 \, r \, s$$

where the tense (and auxiliaries) is left out to be added after any transformations, and where

s: adjunct on sentence

l, r: left and right adjuncts of their neighboring category

N, V, P: noun, verb, preposition word-categories

Ω_1: first section of object; may be empty

$P \, N_2$: second section of object; empty except for some cases of $\Omega_1 = N, A$

(If Ω_1 or P or $P \, N_2$ is empty, their l, r, and following s positions are also empty.) We can say that each transformation takes the words which are in specified positions of one or of two such strings and sends them, with possibly some added constants (including primitive adjuncts and operators) and zeroings, into specified positions of such a string. This conforms with two facts: that sentences have a quite limited string structure, and that transformations operate on a sentence, or on two, to produce a sentence.[6] The string property of the resultant sentence can thus be stated as a restriction on the transformation which yields that resultant.

Conversely the effect of each transformation on a sentence can be stated as a restriction on the string structure of that sentence. This is seen as follows:

Consider the string structure of a subset of sentences which we will call elementary. Here all the s, l, r positions are empty, and the N, V, Ω_1, P, N_2 positions are filled by particular subcategories (largely of unimorphemic words). It can be shown that each transformation which operates on an elementary sentence brings into one or another of the positions a subcategory which had not occurred there in the string structure of the sentence on which the transformation had operated. By asking what subcategories occur in each string position of a sentence – which is a question in purely string terms – we obtain the same information about the sentence as we would by asking what transformations had operated to produce the sentence.

Comparable statements can be made for constituent analysis, and in this sense each of these major sentential properties can be formulated so as to include the relevant effects of the other properties and so as to describe in its own terms the whole set of sentences.[7] In organizing a language description around one or another of these properties, the main difference lies not in the sentences which can be described, but in the way in which the description relates each sentence to certain others, i.e. in the various subsets of sentences that the description creates. Constituent analysis groups all sentences having similar hierarchical complexities; string analysis groups sentences which have the same center, or the same types of adjunction; transformational analysis groups sentences which have the same kernel (elementary) sentences, or the same transformations – i.e. each transformation is a set of sentence pairs, and transformational theory creates or characterizes these pairs.

However, the greatest interest in each of these properties lies not in its utilization as an organizing scheme for grammatical analysis, but in the statements which can be made, uniquely in terms of the given property, about the structure of language. For example, in terms of the string property we can make the fundamental statement that if we define in a given language a small set of center strings and a few sets of adjunct strings – each set being characterized by its adjoining a particular type of string at a particular point in it – then (aside from grammatical ambiguity) each sentence can be decomposed in a mechanical way into one center sentence and certain adjunct strings.[8] There are, besides, additional interesting statements which can be made in terms of each property. For example, in terms of string analysis, we can say that the discontinuous elements of constituent analysis present no problem of noncontiguity (relation at a distance). Every relation (co-occurrence or selection, agreement, structural composition, etc.) holds within a string (among the symbols of a string) or else between a string (or its first member) and the string to which it is adjoined. Thus the 'movable' adjective in Latin, and the 'detached' relative clause of *My friend came, whom I had mentioned to you*, are indeed distant from their nouns, but they are contiguous to the string containing that noun; they cannot be non-contiguous to that string or its adjuncts.

It should be mentioned that the investigation of the several basic properties of sentences, and the possibility of using each as the central method of sentence analysis, are different from the question of the logical forms of grammar as a theory of language. The properties, e.g. the transformational relation, can be studied empirically; and a particular form of grammar can use various of these properties.[9]

2. CRITERIA FOR TRANSFORMATION

Before considering the transformational structure of a language, it might be well to state under what conditions two sentences (or sets of sentences) are transforms of each other; here we offer this, rather than a definition of transformation. Take an n-place form, i.e. a sequence of n symbols for word-categories such as N, V, with possibly some individual morphemes which will be called constants of the form e.g. (1) $N_1 \ t \ V \ N_2 \ P \ N_3$ (t: tense morpheme; the subscripts are only for distinguishing the various occurrences of N).

We now take ordered n-tuples of words, each containing one member for each word-category in the sentence-form, e.g. (2):

> *man, give, book, to, boy.*
> *man, give, book, to, girl.*
> *man, give, boy, to, table.*

The result of substituting the words of an n-tuple for the category-symbols of the sentence-form (allowing for morphophonemic and other requirements, such as the article) will be called a satisfier of the form, e.g. (3):

> *The man gave a book to the boy.*
> *The man gave a book to the girl.*
> *The man gave a boy to the table.*

Among these satisfiers there are some differences in their acceptability as sentences, differences which make them partially ordered on a scale of naturalness, likelihood of occurrence in particular language use (e.g. scientific articles, fairy tales), type (including, presumably, timing) of response by particular hearers, or the like. Or the satisfiers are differentiated, not linearly, on several such scales.

Consider now another sentence form of the same n word-categories, say (4) $N_2 \ t \ be \ Ven \ by \ N_1 \ P \ N_3$. If we find a set of n-tuples whose satisfiers X of the first form have the same order on this scale as their satisfiers Y of the second form, we say that the two forms can be taken as transforms of each other for that set of n-tuples (or: the two sets of sentences can be transforms of each other).[10] Whether they are indeed so taken will depend on whether the set of n-tuples is not ad hoc, i.e. whether it can be characterized in some useful way in respect to other sets of n-tuples: for example, whether the set appears again in transformations to yet other sentence-forms, whether the set is characterizable by some morphological or syntactic property (e.g. if it contains all V which can have – or lack – certain affixes, or certain types of object), whether the complement set of n-tuples participates in other transformations, and so on. This is much the same kind of consideration as is used in determining what categories of words are worth setting up in linguistic structure. As with all linguistic classifications, the chosen criteria suffice for the great bulk of the material; however, scattered residues will be found which do not satisfy all the requirements of the chosen criteria, but can be analyzed in such a way as to fit with the analysis of the bulk of the language. Thus after the main transformations have been set up, it will be convenient to define certain transformations for small sets of words which are not otherwise recognized as sets. Such treatments are unavoidable throughout linguistic analysis, because of the existence of aberrant detail in language.[11]

It should be clear that the interest here is not in the actual acceptances that a given n-tuple has in a given form (something which is often difficult to evaluate), but in the fact that the ordering of acceptability for a set of n-tuples is the same in several sentence forms (even if the actual acceptabilities, or the amount of difference in acceptability, may differ in the several forms). This suffices to relate the several forms in respect to the given set of n-tuples.

By this criterion, we can take forms (1) and (4) as transforms of each other (written (1)↔(4)) for a set of n-tuples including (2), since the acceptability-ordering of (2) in (3) is the same as in (5):

> *A book was given by the man to the boy.*
> *A book was given by the man to the girl.*
> *A boy was given by the man to the table.*

Both in (3) and in (5) the first two n-tuples yield normal acceptance, while the third gives one pause. But when the same n-tuples are used as satisfiers of (6) $N_1\ t\ V\ N_3\ P\ N_2$, we get a different acceptability-ordering:

> *The man gave the boy to a book.*
> *The man gave the girl to a book.*
> *The man gave the table to a boy.*

Hence (1)↔(6).

Furthermore, the transformation (1)↔(4) does not hold for such n-tuples as (7):

> *man, practise, hour, on, Tuesday*
> *man, walk, mile, on, Tuesday*

which are acceptable in (1), but have no or only special acceptance in (4); as in

> ∼∃ *An hour was practised by the man on Tuesday.*
> ∼∃ *A mile was walked by the man on Tuesday.*

Note, however, that (7) is acceptable in (8) N_1 *V for* N_2 *P* N_3 as in

> *The man practised for an hour on Tuesday.*
> *The man walked for a mile on Tuesday.*

so that for (7) we have (1)↔(8).

In the light of this criterion we can see, for example, that (9) N_1 *t V* N_2 is not a transform of (10) N_2 *t V* N_1. True, there are n-tuples whose acceptability-ordering is presented in the two forms, e.g. in *John saw Bill* and *Bill saw John*. But for each *V* there can be found nouns whose acceptability-ordering as objects of that *V* is not the same as their acceptability-ordering as subjects of it, as can be seen from *Can the deaf see the blind?* Even if the *N* are restricted to personal names we can find such cases, as in *Did John see Helen Keller?*[12] There is thus no independent property which would characterize the n-tuples whose acceptability-ordering is the same in (9) and (10) from those for which it is not.[13]

Similarly, (11) *A* N_1 *t V* N_2 is not a transform of (12) N_1 *t V A* N_2. For (11) is a transform of the pair of forms (13) N_1 *t V* N_2, N_1 *is A* (by the connective *wh* on N_1), while (12) is a transform of (14) N_1 *t V* N_2, N_2 *is A* (by the connective *wh* on N_2); and even if N_1 and N_2 are the same word, we can always find, for each *V*, some set of *A* such that the acceptability-ordering of n-tuples containing these *A* in (11) and in (13) is not preserved (in the manner of note 12) in (12) and in (14).

It is possible to define transformations, as a relation among sentences, in various ways.[14] All adequate formulations ultimately yield virtually the same transformations for a language.[15] The formulation sketched here in terms of acceptability-differences fits into the fact that there is no well-defined set of sentences in a language. Rather, some word sequences are clearly sentences, others are odd or even undecidable as to sentencehood in one or another way, and some are entirely impossible. In terms of transformational theory, we can say that all these differences and types of acceptability are to be found in the elementary sentence-forms, in respect to the satisfaction of these forms by various word n-tuples. The transformations preserve the acceptability-ordering (and so the normalcy, jocularity, marginality, etc.) of these n-tuple satisfactions, from the elementary sentence-forms into all the other sentence-forms of the language. It is thus possible to find a precise set of transformations in a language without having to state a precise set of sentences for the language. Transformations simply tell us that the sense in which an n-tuple satisfies a particular complex sentence-form is the same as that in which it satisfies some other (and ultimately, some elementary) sentence-form. As happens so often in science, in order to describe a particular set of phenomena we have to start with a class of objects which is different from our initial interest but which is precisely definable and in respect to which we can describe our particular phenomena. In the present case, we set out to describe a relation among sentences, but we have to define a relation among sentence-forms in respect to certain n-tuples which satisfy them.[16]

3. THE TRANSFORMATIONS

The transformations of English fall into certain types which in gross character seem to be the case for many other languages too.[17]

3.1. *Unaries*

There are unary transformations between two sentence-forms. These include some in which word-categories are permuted (or, rarely, repeated or dropped), usually with the addition of some constant words or morphemes. In most or all of these there is no substantive change of meaning, e.g. between the active and the passive. In addition to the well-established transformations, there are transformations which are barely acceptable or are used only in particular linguistic environments: e.g. *He works at night→His work is at night, He prepared the experiment→The preparation of the experiment was by him.* Many of these latter transformations come in families, in which the individual transformations apply a particular change to various parts of the sentence-form; e.g. the important set of extraction transformations: *His story describes Sicily→His story is what describes Sicily, It is his story that describes Sicily, Sicily is what his story describes, It is Sicily that his story describes.* We could also find *He left it on the table→The table is what he left it on.* In several such families we find parts of the sentence for which the transformation is more complicated or difficult, e.g. the extraction of the verb in *Describing Sicily* (or: *To describe Sicily) is what his story does.* There may even be parts of the sentence such that we cannot say whether the family of transformations extends to them or not: *He wrote the story within one week→ (?) One week is what he wrote the story within, *Within one week is when he wrote the story.*

Many such cases of difficult or uncertain transformations would not even be noticed if it were not for having a family of transformations, which operate in comparable ways on various parts of a sentence, and which we then discover to be neither definitely acceptable or definitely unacceptable on certain other parts of the sentence, but rather partially acceptable in various ways.

As will be seen, the great majority of transformations listed below operate on all words of the major word-categories on which they act, or on all words which do or don't come from particular other transformations (e.g. the passive does not act on N_2 which have come from the P-zeroing transformation of § 3.4). A few, like the instrumental, act on a particular subcategory of V, N, etc. And a few, like the middle, act on small subcategories but are productive with weakened acceptability outside the subcategory.

The transformations of a language can be grouped in various ways. Here we will group the main unary transformations of English in a way that will be useful for the further decomposition of transformations in § 5 below.

One type of transformation is that which permutes parts of an elementary sentence (and, in some cases, an insert to it), without adding any constants, in such a way as to yield a form that differs from any elementary sentence-form of the language. Such are:

$N_1 \ t \ V \ N_2 \rightarrow N_2 \ N_1 \ t \ V$: *I like this, This I like.*
$N_1 \ t \ V \ N_2 \rightarrow N_2 \ t \ V \ N_1$: *All the scientists say this,*
This say all the scientists.

There is no change in the syntactic character of the parts (i.e. the subjection to major transformations and morphophonemics, as in plural agreement): e.g. *This* does not become the subject and does not agree in number with *say*. Hence we may call these the ASYNTACTIC transformations. They are uncomfortable except in cases where the permuted object is stressed and where ambiguity is not likely (e.g. *This say*... is not ambiguous because the number differs). All other transformations yield sentences which have elementary sentence-forms (though with new items satisfying some of the symbols) plus, possibly, adjuncts.

Another small type of transformation is the addition of PLEONASTIC material in a way that does not destroy elementary sentence-form (e.g. the addition being in the form of an insert):

$N_1 \ t \ V \ N_2 \rightarrow N_1 \ t \ V \ N_1\text{'s} \ N_2$: *He learned a lesson,*
He learned his lesson.

(*his* is not independent here; $\sim\exists$ *He learned her lesson*, except in a different sense, with a different transformational analysis).

An important transformation is the replacement of words (chiefly nouns) by PROWORDS (pronouns): *The man came, He came.*

Another transformation is the substitution one for another of semantically weak verbs or VERBALIZING suffixes, which give various forms to sentences whose information is carried by two nouns, or by noun and adjective:

> *He lived in a room there, He stayed in a room there, He roomed there.*
> *It has value, It is of value.*
> *He was sick, He became sick, He sickened.*

Yet another is the replacement of subject by object in what we may call the MIDDLE (between active and passive):

> *I attach this interpretation to your words, This interpretation attaches to your words.*

Another is the transformation which MIRRORS a sentence in its verb *be*:

> *Mathematics is his forte, His forte is mathematics.*

Then there is the large set of MODULATIONS noted above:

> *His work is at night; The preparation of the experiment was by him.*

In these the nominalized verb appears as subject; but related to these are transformations in which the subject is replaced by the object or by an added indirect object peculiar to certain verbs:
e.g. the PASSIVE:

> $N_1 \ t \ V \ N_2 \rightarrow N_2 \ t \ be \ Ven \ by \ N_1$: *He saw the man,*
> *The man was seen by him.*

and passive-like transformations:

> $N_1 \ t \ V \ N_2 \rightarrow N_2 \ t \ be \ Ven \ P \ N_1$: *The plan involves him, He is involved in the plan.*

and the INSTRUMENTAL (on a subcategory of V):

> $N_1 \ t \ V \ N_2 \ with \ N_3 \rightarrow N_3 \ t \ V \ N_2$: *He cut the meat with a knife, The knife cut the meat.*

There is a set of quotation-forms and intonationally-marked moods:
Quotation: *Social means not individual* → '*Social' means not individual.*
Question: *He took the book* → *Did he take the book?, Who took the book?, What did he take?, What did he do?*
Imperative: *Take the book!*
Optative: *Would that he took the book!*

Finally, there is the family of EXTRACTIONS mentioned above (*Sicily is what his story describes*, etc.), and the ZEROING OF INDEFINITE PRONOUNS which is seen in deletion of the object:

He read all day ← He read things all day,

in adjective used as noun:

I prefer the larger ← I prefer the larger one,

and in such limited constructions as indefinite pronoun (or classifier-noun) plus preposition before noun of receptacle:

The whole room laughed ← All those in the room laughed.

3.2. *Nonsentential Increments*

The pure unaries listed above rearrange the words of a sentence, with some zeroings or the addition of constants or repetitions. There are other operations, which add to a sentence-form a whole category of words. These naturally alter the meaning of the sentence, but the added meanings are not like the concrete meanings of the words in the elementary sentence; rather, they are metasentential (in the sense of talking about the meanings in the sentence), or relational, or aspectual, or they refer to conditions of time, place, and manner, and so on. The addition of any of these increments to a sentence yields again a sentence, and the resultant (as also in all the pure unaries except the asyntactic) has an elementary sentence-form (with new items satisfying some of the symbols) plus, possibly, adjuncts. It is therefore possible to consider the addition of these increments to be unary transformations.

The main incremental unaries are the inserts, verb-operators, and sentence-operators.

All inserts are adjuncts (modifiers) on a sentence or on one of its parts. A sentence of the form $X_1 X_2 X_3$, with an insert J adjoined to X_i, is a sentence with center $X_1 X_2 X_3$ and adjunct J on X_i.

LOCAL INSERTS adjoin certain small subcategories, of vaguely quantitative meanings, e.g. *a* to the left of N, *very* to the left of A, *quite* to the left (or right) of V (or A), *almost* to the left of V or P.

TENSE INSERTS, which can perhaps be best considered as operating on t (tense), have particular transformations on them, e.g. *not* (to the right of t in the sentence-form), the auxiliaries (*can, may*, etc.) to the left of t.

SENTENCE-INSERTS occur in all positions, before or after any symbol of an elementary sentence-form, e.g. *however, in general*. Some of these have conjunctional force, others can be viewed as irregular residues of conjoined sentences; but as they appear at present, they form a set of primitive inserts (not regularly derivable from second sentences).

ADVERBIAL INSERTS, D (mostly Aly) and $P N$, have some subcategories only to the right of V (e.g. *down, out*), others in all or most of the positions that sentence-inserts occupy.

All VERB-OPERATORS bring in a new V of certain special subcategories, change the original V into what might be called the object of the new V (Vn, Va, etc.); some also add or change a preposition before the N_2 object of the old V.[18] Thus:

$$N_1 \, t \, V \, \Omega \rightarrow N_1 \, t \, V_{new} \, Vx \, (P) \, \Omega.$$

A special set of verb-operators (symbolized by Y) includes *be-ing* and *have-en*: *He is writing a story, He has written a story.*

The other verb-operators (marked U) fall into several subcategories, of which the main ones are the following:

be Va (P): A complicated set of changes, acting on special subcategories of V e.g.

>*This destroys our trust → This is destructive of our trust.*
>*He loves Italy → He is in love with Italy.*
>*It irritated them → It was (very) irritating to them.*
>*He is clever → He is being clever.*
>*The door sticks → The door is stuck.*

be Vn P: acting on most V, mostly with *-er*:

>*He studies eclipses → He is a student of eclipses.*
>*He builds bridges → He is a builder of bridges.*

U_g *Ving*, U_t *to V*: on every V:

>*He began building bridges, He began to build bridges.*
>*He stopped building bridges.* (But $\sim \exists$ *He stopped to build bridges*).

U_{hg} *Ving*, U_{ht} *to V*: only on sentences whose subject is taken in a human-like sense.

>*He tried building bridges, He tried to build bridges.*
>*The electron tries to escape.*

U_d *(the) Ving P*: on most or all V, but with varying acceptability.

>*He does the building of bridges,*
>*He began the building of bridges.*

U_m *Vn P*: on many V which have Vn (with zero or real affix):

He does studies of eclipses.
He makes studies of eclipses.
He began the study of eclipses, He began a study of eclipses.
He thinks of a repeat → He has thoughts of a repeat.

U_n *a Vn P*: for each *U* just a few particular *V*, unextendable, with *n* usually zero.

He kicked the door → He gave a kick to the door.
He looked at it → He took a look at it, He gave a look at it.

U_{ap} *Vn P*: particular *U* 'appropriate' to particular *V*; the U_{ap} is often the same morpheme as the *V* or a classifier of it:

He slept quietly → He slept a quiet sleep.
He fears it → He feels fear of it.

Finally, there are the SENTENCE-OPERATORS (marked *W*), formed out of particular subcategories of *V, A, N*. These are *N V* whose object is a slightly deformed sentence, or they are *V* Ω (including *is A, is N, is P N*) whose subject is a similarly deformed sentence.[19] The deformations are[20]:

$N t V \Omega$: *(that)* $N t V \Omega$
    (that) $N V \Omega$ } marked Sn^0
    if $N t V \Omega$
    N's Ving Ω, marked *Sn'*
    N's Vn of Ω, marked *Sn*

Examples:

I know (that) he came.
I prefer (that) he come, I prefer for him to come.
I wonder if he came or not, I wonder whether he came or not.
She appreciated his having signed the letter.
They imitated his signing of the letter.
That he came surprised me, ...is a fact, ...is the trouble.
That he came is important, For him to come is important.
Whether he will come or not is the question.
His leaving school occurred two years ago.
His leaving of school was secretive.

There are additional forms which occur only as objects of particular *N V* and *N is A*. These include:[21]

(P) N_i *that* N_j *t V* Ω
(P) N_i *if* N_j *t V* Ω
(P) N_i *that* N_i *V* Ω, variant N_i *to V* Ω

> (P) N_i P N_i's *Ving* Ω, with (P) N_i's zeroed (for some W, necessarily)
> P *Sn'*
> P *Sn*
> N V Ω, with N accusative if pronoun.

Examples:

> *I told him that she came.*
> *I reported to him that she came.*
> *I asked (of) him if she came or not.*
> *I ordered them that they be present, I ordered them to be present.*
> *I required of them that they be present, I required of them to be present.*
> *I restrained him from going, I got him to thinking.*
> *I refrained from buying paper-backs.*[22]
> *I am aware of his having come.*
> *I made him come.*[23]

There is also a zero (and affix) causative in which the W contains no new verb, but the N and V of the operand sentence are permuted:

> *The children sat → He seated the children.*
> *The patient walked → The nurse walked the patient.*

Just as in the pure unaries we had a pairing of sets of sentences with and without certain structural changes, so in the incremental unaries we have a pairing of sets of sentences with and without certain increments; the increments either are adjuncts or contain new verbs, and the new verb has either the old V Ω as its object or else the whole old sentence as its subject or object. In each case the paired sentence-forms are satisfied by the same n-tuples with acceptability-ordering preserved, so that they are transforms of each other for the given n-tuple sets. The structural difference in each pair can be considered an operation which operates on the simpler member of the pair, as operand, to yield the other member as resultant.

3.3. *Binaries*

There are also binary transformations operating on two sentences to yield a resultant sentence. No conjunctional transformations operate on three sentences at a time; but this may not apply to the connective verbs mentioned below. All the conjunctional transformations except the connective verbs leave the first sentence unchanged (at least initially, before any further transformation operates) and add a connective C or a deformation or both to the second sentence, the modified second sentence having then (precisely or partially) the position of an adjunct in respect to the first. Thus, the connective *and* on the pair *The man talked, The man drove* yields

> *The man talked and the man drove; The man talked and drove.*

The connective *after* yields:

> *The man talked after he drove; After he drove the man talked;*
> *The man talked after driving;* etc.

The *wh*-connective yields:

> *The man who drove talked.*

Furthermore, most of the connectives require particular similarities and particular minimal differences between the two sentences on which they act. Thus, in the coordinate conjunctions, *and* requires no differences, *or* requires at least one difference, *but* requires at least one difference in the predicate[24]:

> *Years passed and years passed.*
> *He will go or she will go.*
> *He bought books but she bought flowers.*

In the pure comparative conjunctions, the two participant sentences can always be transformed into (or from) a canonical N *is* A form (below). In the *wh* (relative clause) connective, the two sentences must have a noun in common (i.e. the same member of the N category, as enlarged by any transformations, must appear in both), and in the second sentence the common noun must be in a position from which it can be permuted to the head of its sentence by an existing transformation. Thus:

> *wh* [*The man talked about it, The man drove*]
> = *The man who drove talked about it.*
> *wh* [*His friend talked about it, His friend I saw* ← *I saw his friend*]
> = *His friend whom I saw talked about it.*

In the subordinate conjunctions and the secondary comparatives (e.g. *enough for*), the specification of differences is more involved and requires investigation.

The connectives of English fall into a few subcategories which are differentiated by the transformations that can operate upon them (§ 3.4):

Coordinate conjunctions: *and, or, but* (and secondarily comma, semicolon, period). These permit particular zeroings and permutations; e.g. $\sim \exists$ *and he came, I went.*

Subordinate conjunctions, C_s, in various subcategories:

because, etc. before S: *I came because he arrived.*

while before S, *Ving* Ω: *I came while he arrived, I talked while driving.*

after before S, Sn':   *I came after he left, I came after his having left.*

during before Sn: *I came during his signing of the letter.*

These permit different zeroings and permutations; e.g. ∃ *Because he came, I went.*

Comparative conjunctions: *-er* (or: *less*) *than, as much as* between two sentences (not necessarily elementary) of *N is A* form. Existing transformations relate this form to other sentence-forms, in the course of which the first ('adverbial') part of the connective (*-er, less, as*) is moved into various positions of the first sentence as a marker of what is being compared. As an example of a comparative sentence: *A larger frame arrived than we had ordered.* Its canonical transform: *The frame which arrived is large | er than | the frame which we had ordered (is large).* Weakened conditions on this yield the properties of secondary comparatives, e.g. *The frame is too large to order.*

The *wh*-connective takes a sentence containing a particular N_i and a second sentence beginning (after suitable transformations) with the same N_i, replaces N_i by a pronoun of it attached to *wh*; and inserts the thus deformed second sentence as a right adjunct on the N_i in the first sentence: as above. *wh* also operates on the ordered pair $(S_i, S_i n\ V\ \Omega)$: *He left, which surprised me*←*wh (He left, His leaving surprised me)*.

To the binaries must be added the subcategories of *V* which have two deformed *S*, one as subject and one as object:

> *That he felt responsible indicates that he knew everything.*
> *That he knew everything follows from his having felt responsible.*
> *The change of temperature caused a change of plans.*
> *The size of the frame which arrived exceeded the size which we had ordered.*

Although these have the combined features of *W* with object *S* and *W* with subject *S*, they are not operators on a single sentence, as are the *W*, but on two. Some of them can be related to subordinate and comparative conjunctions. In any case, they are connectives which do not leave the first sentence unchanged, so that some of the string properties of conjunctions do not apply to these connective *V*.[25]

3.4. *Unaries on Increments and Binaries*

To complete the transformational analysis of English sentences, we recognize transformations which operate on the resultants of increments and binaries somewhat as the pure unaries (§ 3.1) operate on elementary sentences: they permute, repeat, and zero various parts (symbols) of the resultant sentence form, and add constants.

In the first place, various of the pure unaries are extended to operate on some of these resultants. This requires the extension of the argument of the unary; so that if for example the passive has been defined on certain N_1 t V N_2, the domain of V and N_2 is now extended to include U and $Ving$ Ω respectively (but not U and to $V\Omega$):

> *Europeans soon began printing → Printing was soon begun by Europeans*

(but no passive of *Europeans soon began to print*), and also to include verbs of W and $Sn°$ or Sn' or Sn:

> *They recognize that he came → That he came is recognized by them.*

Of greater interest are the new, nonelementary, unaries which appear specifically on incremental and connected sentences. A simple example of these is the permutation of t and N in the presence of certain D (adverbs)[26]:

> *He would little care to see her → Little would he care to see her.*

Another permutation related to increments is the preference, in a sequence of syntactically parallel items, to have the longer ones come later; this is especially strong after the V, among the objects and verb-adjuncts. Thus:

> Ω_1 Ω_2 in the elementary S: *He referred a man to the office.*
> short D[27], and Ω: *He broke up the game.*
> Ω shortened by pronouning: *He broke it up.*
> Ω_1 lengthened by adjunction: *He referred to the office a man who had been making persistent inquiries.*

The adverbial increments D, primarily P N and those containing *-ly*, are transformable into the position of A and V members of W with sentential subject:

> $SD_t → Sn'$ occurs D_t, Sn' is A_t
> $SD_m → Sn$ is A_m

Here D_t indicates P N or *Aly* of time and place, and A_t the corresponding P N or A; *occur* stands for a set of synonymous verbs (*take place*, etc.); and the tense of *occur* or *be* is the tense of the S (lost in Sn'). Similarly for D_m of manner.

> *He spoke there on Tuesday. His speaking there occurred on Tuesday. His speaking there was on Tuesday.*
> *He may break the toys frequently. His breaking the toys may occur frequently.*
> *His breaking the toys may be frequent.*
> *He broke the toys vindictively. His breaking of the toys was vindictive.*

In addition, the A_m of manner take a transformation like certain A members of W: *N's Ving Ω is $A \rightarrow N$ is A in Ving Ω.*

> *He was vindictive in breaking the toys.*
> *He was vindictive in his* (or: *the*) *breaking of the toys.*

Similarly, in W:

> *For him to do this is helpful; He is helpful to do this.*

Among the transformations which involve only small subcategories of words are these:

The zeroing of P in $P N$ of measure: *He ran for two hours $\rightarrow$ He ran two hours.*

The repeating of the subject after certain U: *He took a walk $\rightarrow$ He took his walk.*

On W, there are the variants within the deformation of S as noted above. Furthermore, every subcategory of W that occurs with Sn° has a transformation $\rightarrow Sn'$, and every W that occurs with Sn' has a transformation $\rightarrow Sn$:

> *I know that he signed the letter $\rightarrow$ I know of his having signed the letter $\rightarrow$ I know of his signing of the letter.*

Also, every sentence of the form $Sn^{\circ} V \Omega \rightarrow It V \Omega Sn^{\circ}$:

> *That he came is odd $\rightarrow$ It is odd that he came.*

The various W on S are also transformable into the positions of D as adjuncts on that S; e.g.

> *I know that he came $\rightarrow$ He came, to my knowledge.*
> *He came, as I know.*
> *He came, I know.*
> *That he came is clear $\rightarrow$ He came, clearly.*

Given an S which is the object of a W, if the subject of the S is the same (in referent) as the subject of the W (or as the Ω_1 of the W if the given W has such an Ω_1), the subject of the operand S is zeroed (with various special conditions):

I asked that I might come   → *I asked to come.*
I asked him that he should come → *I asked him to come.*

The transformations on connectives are of three main kinds: interchanges among the connectives; zeroing of repeated or otherwise redundant material; permuting of the second sentence.

The main interchange among connectives is that certain subordinate conjunctions C_s become conjunctional preposition P_s and in some cases finally adverbs:

$$C_s \; N \; t \; V \, \Omega \rightarrow \begin{Bmatrix} C_s \; Ving \; \Omega \\ P_s \; (N's) \; Ving \; \Omega \end{Bmatrix} \rightarrow Vingly$$

while he smiled, while smiling, smilingly

There are also transformations between conjunctions and the binary verbs.

The zeroing occurs under different conditions for different conjunctions. In C_s, $V\,\Omega$ is zeroed if identical with the $V\,\Omega$ of the first sentence; but it may be zeroed in the first sentence if the second S with C_s precedes:

I will go if you will.
If you will go, I will.

In C_s and P_s forms with *-ing* in the second sentence, the subject must or may be zeroed (depending on the conjunction) if identical in referent with subject or object of the first sentence:

I returned, after driving all night.

In coordinate conjunctions, words in the second sentence (under the conjunction) are zeroed if they are identical with the words in the corresponding string position in the first sentence; but there are certain restrictions, and even certain references to the position of the words in the underlying elementary sentences.

He bought books and she bought flowers   → *He bought books and*
                                               she flowers.
He bought books and she too bought books → *He bought books and*
                                               she too.

In comparative conjunctions, the zeroing is much like that of the coordinate conjunctions, with some interesting differences.

In addition, there is zeroing of words in the second sentence which can be determined (up to synonymity) from other words in it. This appears in the zeroing of *is* (with zeroing of referent repeating subject) in

If he is free, he will go → *If free, he will go.*

It appears in the zeroing of *wh*-word plus *is* in

The mountain which is very angular is the Matterhorn → The very angular mountain is the Matterhorn.

It appears in more complicated ways in the zeroing of 'appropriate' V in certain compound nouns, and in the zeroing of *each other* after reciprocal verbs.

$C_s S$, in any of its transformations, can be permuted into any sentence-insert position in the first sentence. Second sentences headed by coordinate or comparative conjunctions can be permuted to a particular point in the first sentence: the coordinate to immediately after the word which corresponds to the last non-zeroed word under the conjunction (*He and she too bought books*); the comparative to immediately after the word in the first sentence which carried the comparative marker (*A larger frame than we ordered has arrived*).

3.5. *How the Transformations Operate*

The pure unaries, the increments, and the binaries have been defined as operations from elementary sentences to a resultant sentence. The non-elementary unaries (§ 3.4) were defined on specific resultants, yielding a new resultant. All of these can also operate on particular other sentence-structures which have resulted from the prior operation of other transformations. To see why this is possible, we note certain restrictions on the set of elementary sentences and on the set of transformations, restrictions which will become more apparent in the discussion of elementary transformations below. (1) All elementary sentence-forms are similar to each other in certain features: all consist of a subcategory of N plus t plus a subcategory of V plus an Ω structure determined by the V subcategory. (2) All transformations are defined initially on one or some of the elementary sentence forms, or else on the resultants of transformations which have been defined on elementary sentence forms. (3) The resultant of a transformation differs from its operand (and therefore from some elementary sentence form) by only certain limited differences: either there has only been an insertion to the right or left of one of the symbols of the form, or the subcategories which are the domains of the symbols have been changed[28], or the order of symbols is no longer the same as in one of the elementary sentence forms.

For an operation φ_j, defined on elementary sentence forms, to operate also on the resultant of an operation φ_i, it is necessary only to extend the domain of the argument of φ_j so as to include the effects due to φ_i. Thus, since the passive operates on *He began the smoking of cigars*, i.e. on the resultant of U_{gr}, we extend the definition of the passive to apply not only to the domains of V and N_2 in the elementary sentence forms, but also to the new V subcategory which includes *begin* and to *the Vn* (for all the elementary sub-categories of V) as satisfying the N_2 symbol. But since the passive does not operate on *He began to smoke cigars*, i.e. on the resultant of U_t, we do not extend the domain of N_2, as argument of the passive, to include *to V*; we need not then specify here whether *to V* is or is not the Ω of *begin*, since we are not defining the symbols absolutely, but only in respect to the various transformations for which their domain has to be specified. And, since the passive defined on N_1 *t V* N_2 fails to operate on the resultant of *P*-zeroing before *N* of measure (see note 28), we say: *N* of measure is not included in the elementary domain of N_2 for *V* other than measure-verbs, so that the passive does not operate on sentences containing such *N* of measure as elementary sentences; and when we extend the definition of the passive, we do not extend it to *N* of measure after nonmeasure *V*.

Transformations can therefore be defined as operations on elementary sentences and on the resultants of transformations. This in turn is equivalent to defining transformations as operations on elementary sentences and on transformations. When we extend the argument of a transformation to include the effects of particular transformations, we are specifying which transformations can follow upon which transformations, and so giving their partial ordering. With their arguments defined in this way, the transformations need not be further ordered in respect to each other; although when we give a transformational characterization of a particular sentence we may have to specify a partial ordering among the transformations for that particular resultant. Thus *Smoking of cigars was begun by them* is Passive of U_g of *They smoked cigars*, while *Cigars began to be smoked by them* is U_g of Passive of *They smoked cigars*. The question of which transformations can repeat is also included in this specification of arguments.

When so specified, the transformations can be said to be able to occur whenever the conditions of their argument (including the availability of any necessary affixes for the particular words selected) are met. That is, every sentence that can be formed by the defined transformations should be a possible sentence, with an acceptability determined by the n-tuples and the transformations.[29]

The brief sketch above of the transformations of English and of their mode of operation is thus a sketch of a transformational grammar of English. Many problems remain concerning the precise domain of certain transformations, and whether certain relations among sentences satisfy the criteria of being a transformation; and there are problems in the boundaries between transformational structure and other features of language. However, a transformation once established is not normally falsifiable by further research; and the existence of the transformational relation and the general properties discussed below of the set of sentences under this relation, and of the set of transformations, are not shaken by individual problems concerning transformations.

4. THE SET OF SENTENCES UNDER TRANSFORMATIONS

When we describe the set of sentences in terms of the transformational relation, we have the following.

There is a family of elementary (axiomatic) sentence forms, the kernel of the set of sentence forms under mapping onto the set of transformations. The sequence of symbols $N\ t\ V\ \Omega$ (Ω=zero, N, $N\ P\ N$, etc. according to the subtype of V) is the well-formedness requirement for the sentences of the kernel. The well-formedness requirement for the other sentences, transformationally related to the kernel sentences, is the same, except that:

(1) Stated local inserts may appear to the left or right of stated symbols; transformed sentences headed by *wh*, and by coordinate and comparative conjunctions, may appear to the right of stated symbols (with zeroed *wh- is*; also to the left); and sentence inserts, including sentences headed by subordinate conjunctions, may appear before or after any symbol of the kernel sentence.

(2) The domain of V is extended to include the verbs of (a) Y, U and (b) W[30], with the domain (a) of Ω being correspondingly extended to include V with various affixes (including *to*), and (b) of the subject N or the Ω (or, for the binary verbs, both) being extended to include $Sn°$ or Sn' or Sn.

(3) A sentence headed by a conjunction (or, more rarely, subject or object of W) may have to have certain similarities or differences with respect to the sentence to which it is being conjoined (or to the W under which it is), and may (or in some cases must) have certain of its symbols satisfied by zero. In a very few situations symbols of a sentence are satisfiable by zero when a second sentence is conjoined to it in a particular way.

(4) Almost any word X of the elementary sentence, or else an adverbial insert X on it, can appear as the value of the subject N (or object of the verb *be*) when *wh* plus pronoun of X plus the rest of the elementary sentence appears as the object of *be* (or the subject N): *Nice is what he is, How he speaks is quietly.*

(5) A few permutations occur: of $N\ t$ after certain D and under question intonation; of Ω to the head of the sentence under question and contrastive intonations.

(6) Satisfiers of N positions can be replaced by pronouns (including *wh*-pronouns under question intonation).

We thus have, for nonkernel sentences, a secondary well-formedness requirement derived from kernel well-formedness, and one which could as well be expressed in string or other terms as in transformational terms. A stronger composition rule specifies the nonkernel sentences transformationally in respect to the kernel sentences: Given a number of sentences in a kernel form, which have among them a particular acceptability-ordering or differentiation (not necessarily linear), all successions of transformations which are permitted, by the definition of their argument, will produce sentences preserving the same acceptability-ordering or differentiation. These transformations therefore specify a decomposition of each derived sentence into a kernel sentence, or if some of the transformations were binary, into more than one kernel sentence. This decomposition can be used to give each sentence of the language a normal form, which represents that sentence as a set of kernel sentences with partially-ordered transformations operating upon them (each transformation operating on one or on two kernel sentences, or else on a transformation). Sentences which are grammatically ambiguous (i.e. homonymous) will have more than one normal representation.[31]

If a sequence of words (or of refined word subcategories) is not decomposable by transformations into one or more kernel sentences (or refined kernel sentence forms), then that sequence is ungrammatical. If it is so decomposable, then it has a certain kind and degree of acceptability as a sentence, which is some kind of reasonable sum of the acceptabilities of the component kernel sentences and the acceptability effects of the transformations which figure in the decomposition.

This decomposition, or normal form, is of special interest because of various correlations with vocabulary, information-content, etc. The kernel sentences are not only short and of simple form, but are also composed of a restricted and simple vocabulary: mostly concrete nouns and verbs and adjectives, and mostly unimorphemic words. Most morphologically derived words are not in the kernel, because in almost all cases it is not that a word takes on an affix of its own accord, in order to modify its meaning or change its category; but rather a sentence changes its form by a transformation and as part of the constants of this transformation some of the words take on affixes. Thus *boy→boyhood* appears in transformationally related sentences like *He was yet a boy, He was yet in his boyhood;* *theory→theorize* in such transformationally related sentences as *He made a theory about this, He theorized about this.* The kernel words are mostly concrete, because action nouns, nouns of result, and many abstract nouns are in general nominalizations of sentences under *W* and *U* operators (*This item covered him adequately, This item gave him adequate coverage*), because many intellectual and relational words are themselves *W* operators on a sentence (*–is a fact,*

–is obvious, believe that–), because various words of aspect or mode of action are *U* operators (*try to–, begin to–*), and so on. It can even be shown that pronouns, numbers, most plurals, most occurrences of *the*[32], etc. can be brought into the sentences by existing types of transformations, and need not be taken as occurring in the kernel sentences.

In addition, there is a correlation of different parts of the normal form with different kinds of selection (co-occurrence restrictions). The usual kind of word-selection occurs in kernel n-tuples and between *V* and *D* (adverbial inserts on verb). Between *U* operators and the operand kernel *V* there is in some cases a weak selection; there is a dependence between certain *W* or C_s and the *t* of the kernel under them; and there is a restriction on the amount and kind of difference between the two sentences joined by a connective.

In view of all this, it is clear that transformations provide not only a possible grammatical analysis, but also one that is particularly subtle and has various semantic correlations.

5. THE SET OF TRANSFORMATIONS

The interest of transformations for a theory of language structure would be greater if the transformations of a language are not just a set of differences or operations between sentences, but a set that has some coherent structure of its own. The possibility of finding such a structure is heightened by the fact that certain constants appear in various transformations (something which itself would have to be explained): e.g. *-ing* in *Y, U (He is buying books, He began buying books, He began the buying of books)* and *W (His buying of the books surprised me)* and C_s (*He left without buying the books*). What is more, in their various occurrences the constants are placed in similar ways in respect to the kernel symbols and the other constants: e.g. *by* precedes the original subject *N* and follows a nominalization or adjectivization of the original *V* both in the Passive, *The books were bought by him*, and also under *W, The buying of the books by him surprised me*. This suggests that these constants are not merely local morphological affixes, but parts of a syntactic (i.e. sentence-wide) activity with interrelated affixes over specified parts of the kernel, which gives the kernel sentence a particular deformation as operand of some operator or connective: e.g. the forms under *Y, U, W, C_s*.

Furthermore, when we see that the same constants appear in different kinds of syntactic situation, e.g. *by* in the deformation under *W* and in the unary Passive, we can ask if one of these forms is the result of a transformation on the other, so that the constant appears in the later form simply because it was carried over from the earlier. Such an analysis would require that many transformations which seem to be single, e.g. the Passive, are really the resultants of some smaller transformation B operating on the resultant of another, A – smaller, in the sense that only part of the passive form would be due to B, the rest being due to the A on which B had operated. Since we have thus entered upon the situation of successions of transformations, discussed in § 3.5, it becomes relevant that the resultants of many transformations are of only a few string forms (e.g. the resultant of some transformations is like a kernel form; the resultant of the Sn deformations N's Ving of N, Ving of N by N, under W and P_s is like N with right and left adjuncts); this makes it easier for other transformations to operate on the resultants of the first.

We have thus reached the possibility of decomposing transformations into component (divisor) transformations which we may call ELEMENTARY OPERA-TIONS. We try to carry this out in such a way that (if possible) every constant is introduced by only one transformation (which must then be a divisor of every resultant containing that constant), and in a way that yields a reasonable set of elementary operations and a derivation rule to obtain all transformations out of them. This turns out to be not entirely attainable for English. The situation for English is as follows. Transformations have two properties. One, they distribute certain changes over specified parts of a sentence form A. Two, the result is a sentence form B, and the acceptability-ordering for the n-tuples of A is preserved in B. The optimal divisors into which we can break up the transformations of English fall just short of these properties in the following way.

There are a few divisors whose resultant or operand is not quite acceptable as a sentence, or is a deformation of a sentence (type 3 below), but such that the next divisor operating on it yields an acceptable sentence. Thus the question-answer pair *What does he do? He draws cartoons* can be analyzed in the same way as *What does he draw? He draws cartoons* and *Who draws cartoons? He draws cartoons* only by relating *What does he do?* to *He does drawing of cartoons* and then the latter to *He draws cartoons*. In this way we can reach a set of elementary transformational divisors which have the following property: every transformation of the language is either one of these divisors or else a particular succession of them. Except for divisors of type 3 below, those resultants of a divisor which, for many n-tuples, are not acceptable as sentences are nevertheless acceptable for certain n-tuples or in the presence of certain kinds of adjuncts. Thus *He does drawing of cartoons* may be barely acceptable; *He did smoking of cigars* (between *What did he do?* and *He smoked cigars*) is rather unacceptable; but *He does teaching* is acceptable.

5.1. *The Elementary Transformations*

The elementary (axiomatic) operations (in a few cases, nonindependent divisors) into which the transformations of English can be decomposed turn out to be a rather reasonable set:

(1) Local and sentential inserts and adverbial inserts, which do not affect the syntactic status (i.e. the subjectability to transformations) of the sentence parts to which they are adjoined.

(2) Operators Y, U, W on verb and on sentence, which introduce a new verb, with the original V or sentence being deformed as object or subject of it.

(3) Connectives, which head a sentence and may require a deformation of it, after which the connective-headed sentence is inserted into another sentence by the first operation above.[33]

(4) The zeroing of redundant material. Whereas the three transformational divisors listed above were all increments, this fourth one drops words from a sentence, but only words whose presence can be reconstructed from the environment. Hence we can say that the material is still morphemically present, that only its phonemes become zero, and that the language therefore has no dropping of morphemes. Nevertheless, this zeroing is real enough to be a transformational divisor in the derivation rule for transformations (§ 5.3).

5.2. *Zeroing of Redundant Material*

Since this operation is not easy to observe, a more detailed study of it will be given here.

Zeroing eliminates, from (usually) secondary members of a sequence of K and W, such words Z as can be determined (up to local synonymity[34]) from the particular words which occupy certain positions in the sequence distinguished relative to Z. Z therefore carries no information in the given sentence.

In all cases, what is removed is a redundancy that has arisen out of the juxtaposing of a kernel sentence K with an operator or insert, or with another K (or a disjunction or conjunction of K). Removal of redundancy is carried out in a way that leaves the resultant similar to some K form. The sentences which lack a word, because of a redundancy removal, have structures of the same kind as sentences without redundancy removal: e.g. *He denied his having slept, He denied having slept* (where the Ω loses a word, but remains Ω). This is so because most redundancy removal is in those parts of a sentence which have the form of an insert (e.g. the *his* above, which is like an insert in the Ω), or in a limited way in the Ω of the sentence.

The material that is zeroed in English is mainly 'appropriate' words (§ 5.21), repetitive words (§ 5.22), and indefinite pronouns (resulting from disjunctions or conjunctions of sentences, § 5.23).

5.21. *Appropriate Words*

The first type of redundancy removal operates in an insert or a secondary K, i.e. a $C K$, or a K that is under an operator. To consider the actual forms, it will be helpful first to define 'appropriate X', X_{ap}; X here ranges over the relation-expressing categories V, P, the operator W, and perhaps classifier-nouns N_{c1}. The X_{ap} of a particular word in a structure is the member (or members) of X which is the main co-occurrent of that word in that structure, for the given subject matter. That is, X_{ap}, in a K or insert or operator, is a particular member of category X which in the given culture or subject matter (e.g. conversation or science) is accepted (understood) as the main word to occur with the particular other words of that K or insert or operator, or with the particular word to which the K or insert is adjoined. In a form $A_i X_{ap} B_i$, the X_{ap} means not its full dictionary meaning but that which primarily carries out the X-relation (e.g. verb-relation) of A_i to B_i (in the present discourse).[35] Several words of category X may equally satisfy $A_i X_{ap} B_i$; they are then locally synonymous in respect to $A_i \dots B_i$.

In many circumstances, specified below, the X_{ap} can be eliminated; other members of X cannot. There is no loss of information, for the absence of the X which is required in the $A X B$ structure (whose presence is evidenced by the remaining $A B$), points to the X_{ap} which is determined (up to local synonymity) by the individual words of the $A_i B_i$. Thus from *violin-prodigy* we generally reconstruct *violin-playing prodigy*, and from *violin-merchant* we generally reconstruct *violin-selling merchant*. In any case, the grammatical reality of X_{ap} lies in the fact that it and not other X can be zeroed in this way (or that X_{ap} is the only X that occurs in the given position). This treatment enables us to relate in a simple and reasonable way such aberrant forms $A B$ (e.g. compound nouns N-N) with grammatically regular form $A X B$.[36]

5.211. *Conditions for dropping V_{ap}.* The chief environmentally determined redundancy is in V_{ap} and the related *is* P_{ap}, which may be dropped when it occurs in an insert, or in the subject or Ω of the operator. Thus many compound nouns of the form N_2-N_1 are derived as follows:

$$N_2\text{-}N_1 \leftarrow N_2\text{-}V_{ap}ing\ N_1 \leftarrow N_1\ V_{ap}\ N_2$$

e.g.

> *the milkman*
> $\leftarrow$ **the milk-delivering man*
> $\leftarrow$ *The man delivers milk* connected by *wh* to *man* in some other S.

Similarly, when N_1 *is* P_{ap} N_2 is connected by *wh* to N_1, we obtain N_2-N_1: *He painted the clothes-closet*$\leftarrow$*wh* [*He painted the closet. The closet is for clothes*] (or *The closet contains clothes*, or the like).

Under an operator, when the K or its V is deformed, with $N V \rightarrow Ving\ of\ N$

(*Brecht wrote*→*writings of Brecht*) and *V N*→*to V N* (*to study French*), the *Ving* and *to V* can be dropped if *V* is V_{ap}.[37]

> *The writings of Brecht make good reading* → *Brecht makes good reading.*
> *I began to study French*   → *I began French.*

To hear would not drop in *I began to hear French.*

> *I began to read the book* → *I began the book.*
> *I began to write the book* → *I began the book.*

But *to buy* does not drop in *I began to buy the book.* The appropriateness may also be determined by the operator, as in *The storm* (*crash, noise,* etc.) *caused the damage* (←*the occurrence of the storm*... etc.). In contrast, in *The ending of the storm caused the damage, The brevity of the storm caused the damage,* the words *the ending of, the brevity of* would not drop.[38]

Similarly, *When do you expect him to come?* (or *to arrive* etc.)→ *When do you expect him?*; but in *When do you expect him to speak?* (or *to leave*), the *to V*, not being *to* V_{ap} for the operator *expect,* does not drop.[39]

Much investigation is still needed in the question of X_{ap}, since careful justification is necessary before absent words are reconstructed. Evidence of a dropped V_{ap} is particularly clear when a plural subject has a singular verb: *Too many cooks spoils the broth*←*Having* (or *The action of*) *too many cooks spoils the broth* (the common form *Too many cooks spoil the broth* is not understandable literally); *Two apparently opposed parties is the answer*← *Having*... As another example, consider a word which must be followed (when in category *P*) by a N_t of time, or (when in category P_s) by *Sn*, but which appears followed by *N* not of time: *It's the best bargain since Manhattan*←...*since the purchase of Manhattan*.[40]

A case of Ω_{ap} is *each other* as Ω of reciprocal *V*. The reciprocal *V* (for which $N_1 V N_2$↔$N_2 V N_1$: *She met him, He met her*) do not occur without Ω except as a result of a dropped Ω=*each other*: *He and she met*←*He and she met each other*; while *Tom and Jim argued*←*Tom and Jim argued with each other*, or←*Tom argued and Jim argued.* But in nonreciprocal *V*, the *each other* does not drop: *He and she dislike each other.*

5.212. *Dropping of constants.* The dropping of words which are constants of certain forms can be taken as a grammatical parallel to the dropping of X_{ap}: the constants are X_{ap} of the forms. In certain insert and object forms of those *K* whose *V* is *be* (or has been reduced to *be*), the *be* is dropped. In *the people here*←*the people who are here* we have the *wh* word plus tense plus *be* dropped from the insert *who are here,* whereas another *V* in this position would not be dropped: *the people who ate here*↔*the people here.* When a *K* whose *V* is *be* becomes the object of certain *W* operators or of certain P_s, the *be, to be,* or *being* may be dropped: *They left him angry* but *They left him feeling ill*[41]; *While ill, he thought of it,* but *While delivering milk, he thought of it.*

The dropping of a constant in a particular form gives rise to one of the most common transformations, namely the sharing transformation which takes two *K* that contain identical N_i and makes the residue of the second *K* into an adjective or other insert to the N_i in the first *K*. We start with K_1 *wh* K_2, in which K_2 necessarily contains an N_i which also occurs in K_1. K_2 is permuted so that N_i is its first part. The N_i at the head of the K_2 is replaced by a pronoun which becomes the second part of the *wh*-word: *I picked up the book which fell.* The *wh*-word (i.e. *wh* plus pronoun) may be replaced by *that,* which carries less information than *who* or *which,* since it does not specify the subcategory of N_i (something which however can be discovered from the N_i itself immediately preceding). Furthermore, in all cases where the constant, whether *wh*-word or *that,* is not followed by the verb K_2, the *wh*-word or *that* may be dropped: *I picked up the book which you dropped, I picked up the book you dropped.*

Here an additional use of the redundancy-removal operation comes into play: If the verb following the *wh*-word is the constant *be* (or certain U_d operators like *do* in *He does writing*), or V_{ap}, then both the *wh*-word and the *V*-constant or V_{ap} of K_2 may be dropped:

> *I described the tree which was nearby* →
> *I described the tree nearby.*

We thus obtain the very frequent and important situation of *wh*-less K_2 inserts on *N*, including the one-word left (and right) adjuncts of *N: I saw the people present* from *I saw the people who (that) were present, I saw the new book* from *I saw the book which (that) was new, I saw the milkman* from *I saw the man who (that) delivers milk (*or *brings* or *sells milk).*[42]

5.213. *Dropping of performative operators.* Related to the dropping of predictable material is the dropping of certain sentence-operators which have performative force (so that no information loss results from dropping them) and whose existence is indicated by characteristic intonations in the *K* on which they had operated. This is the case in English for the question and the imperative. As can be shown, all questions (both yes-no and *wh*-) are obtainable in a simple way, and without appeal to special transformations, from a particular *W* operator on a disjunction of *S*:

> *I ask if S_1 or S_2 ... or S_n*

where the *or S_2 ... or S_n* can be promorphemed into a droppable *or not,* with *if* → *whether:*

> *I ask whether S₁ (or not)*

e.g. *I ask whether he will go (or not) → I ask: Will he go (or not)? → Will he go?* If in the disjunction only one word, say the object, varies, we have:

> *I ask if he will take the pen or he will take the pencil … or he will take the brush.*
> *→ I ask whether he will take the pen or the pencil … or the brush.*
> *→ I ask what he will take.*
> *→ I ask: What will he take?*[43] *→ What will he take?*

Similarly, we obtain the imperative from:

> *I request (order, etc.) you that you (please) take it.*
> *→ I request (order, etc.) you: (Please) take it.*
> *→ (Please) take it!*

In each case, the deformed operand with its intonation is unique to the particular *W*; therefore the *W* is zeroable.

Similar considerations apply to quoted material. Thus we can derive:

> *'Long' contains four letters.*
> *← The word 'long' contains four letters.*
> *← wh [The word contains four letters, The word is 'long']*

with

> *The word is 'long'.*
> *← 'Long' is a word.*
> *← Long is a word.*

where the quotes are a unique transformation for the subjects of the kernel sentences *X is a word, X is a term,* etc.

In such ways we can eliminate the moods, quotes, etc. from the kernel, and show that they are not independent meaning-carrying operations but simply variants occurring under unique operators or kernel-words (such as *word*). Furthermore, *Will he go?* is then directly transformed not from *He will go* but from *I ask whether he will go*; and *'Long' contains four letters* is not transformed from *Long contains four letters* but from *The word 'long' contains four letters* (with source noted above).

It is possible also to say that any sentence *S* may be derived from its occurrence under droppable operators which leave it unchanged. Thus in

> *Someone says that S. → Someone says: S.*

the conditions of § 5.213 would permit the dropping of the operator, leaving *S*. Similarly, since an informationless operator which can occur on all *S* would be droppable by § 5.213, we could say that any S occurrence may be derived from its occurrence under such an operator. In particular, we could think of cycles consisting of the adding of such an operator and its zeroing:

He returned.

plus operator: → *His returning occurred.*
zeroing: → *He returned.*

As was noted near the beginning of § 3.4, in these forms the tense (and auxiliaries) moves to the operator when the tenseless *Sn'* is formed. This situation enables us to explain the difference between *He may return* in the sense of his volition and *He may return* in the sense of likelihood. The first is:

He returns.

plus *may*: → *He may return.*

The second is:

He   returns.

plus operator: → *His returning occurs.*
plus *may*: → *His returning may occur.*
zeroing of operator: → *He may return.*

The difference between the two meanings is then due not to the meaning range of *may* but to a difference in transformations.

5.22. *Repetitive Material*

The second type of redundancy removal also operates only in secondary K, and permits or requires the dropping of a word (with certain appended constants, if they are present) if the same word precedes (rarely, follows) it, as antecedent, in a distinguished position of its primary K_1 or of the operator on the K.

The simplest case is in K_1 *wh* K_2, where the common N immediately following the *wh* is pronouned and becomes the second part of the *wh*-word.

A repetitive subject (if it has been transformed into the form of an insert) or adverbial $P\ N$ (but not normally Ω) is zeroed under W, P_s. Thus when certain W with N_i subject (or Ω_1) operate on a K whose subject is N_i, the second N_i drops if it is in insert-form: in *I prefer that I should go first* there is no zeroing, but in the transform of this *I prefer for me to go first→I prefer to go first*. Similarly *I insist that I should go, I insist on my going→I insist on going*. Similarly, *I told him to go←I told him that he should go*; but there is no zeroing in *I told him that she should go, I told him that he was wrong*. There are other operators (e.g. *oppose*) after which the zero before *Ving* (e.g. *I oppose smoking*) is of type § 5.23 below.

Several conditions for zeroing a referent-repeating subject are found in S_2n after certain P_s. Thus: *He stopped after entering*←*He stopped after his entering* (or: *entry*); since *after* is also C_s, we also have *He stopped after he entered.* After *while*, we have (as C_s) *He stopped while he spoke* and (as P_s) *He stopped while speaking,* but the intermediate is lacking: $\sim\exists$ *He stopped while his speaking.* Zeroing of the subject of S_2n is the same whether the antecedent is the subject of S_1, as above, or the Ω of S_1, as in *He stopped her after (her) entering.* In many situations, therefore, the zeroed subject is ambiguous as to antecedent: *He caught them while leaving the hall.*

A different kind of zeroing of repeated words is found after the coordinate and comparative connectives and C_s, as was seen in § 3.4.

The answer after a question, and the question after an assertion, may zero the $V \Omega$, or the whole sentence except for the answering or questioning word: *I will go. You will?, What will he get? A book.*[44]

5.23. *Zeroing of Indefinite Pronouns*

The third type of redundancy operation permits the pronouning (or, in certain cases, dropping) of disjunctions (more rarely, conjunctions) of all the words in a category or subcategory. These disjunctions of words come from disjunctions of elementary sentences. If *n* is the number of words in subcategory *N*, we have:

N_1 *or* N_2 ... *or* N_n V_i Ω_i
←N_1 V_i Ω_i *or* N_2 ... *or* N_n
← N_1 V_i Ω_i *or* N_2 V_i Ω_i ... *or* N_n V_i Ω_i.
I or you ... or she will go.
I will go, or you, ... or she.
I will go or you will go ... or she will go.

In a variety of positions, such disjunctions of *N* are pronouned. They are zeroed only in insert-forms, and in Ω and before *wh*-insert. When this zeroing occurs, we may say that the disjunction is first replaced by an indefinite pronoun, and that this pronoun is then zeroed.[45] No loss of information results from such zeroing, since the disjunction could carry no information (beyond the grammatical presence of the category, which remains evident from the environing residual structure).

Dropping of insert-form indefinite pronouns (e.g. *someone's, by someone*) is seen when secondary *K* receive the form of adjectives or *P N*, and may be dropped, with a meaning equivalent to the indefinite pronoun of subject and Ω. Thus

The place has been taken.
← *The place has been taken by someone.*

← *The place has been taken by* N_1, *or by* N_2 ... *or by* N_n.
← *The place has been taken by* N_1 ... *or the place has been taken by* N_n.
← N_1 *took the place* ... *or* N_n *took the place.*[46]

Under certain sentence-operators, the insert-form subject of the operand K is zeroed when it is an indefinite pronoun, rather than when it is identical with the subject or Ω_1 of the operator.

> *He opposes drinking.* ← *He opposes anyone's drinking.*
> *He says to wait.* ← *He says for people to wait.*
> *The job requires having patience.* ← *The job requires one's having patience.*

The same is the case for

> *To find the book is important.*
> ← *For someone to find the book is important.*

When this subject of the K is not in insert form, the disjunction is pronouned but not zeroed:

> *The job requires that one have patience.*

Other types of disjunction-zeroing take place in certain particular non-insert positions.

The most widespread of these is the zeroing of indefinite object, which occurs with many but not all V: *He reads* ← *He reads something* ← *He reads* N_1 *or* N_2 ... *or* N_n.[47] That this Ω-zeroing is indeed of the disjunction of objects for the given V, and not of a single Ω, is supported by the fact that metaphorical and idiomatic objects are not pronounable or zeroable: the idiomatic sense of *If I know how to read the signs correctly* is not preserved in *If I know how to read correctly.*

There is also a situation in which, given an indefinite pronoun[48] which carries a *wh*-insert, the pronoun is dropped, leaving the insert to carry the grammatical relations of the N (or, we might say, leaving a zero N whose presence is recognized from the insert).[49] This is the case of forms like

> *I read what he wrote.*
> ← *I read that* (or: *the things*) *which he wrote.*
> ← *I read* N_1 *which he wrote and* N_2 *which he wrote* ... *and* N_n *which he wrote.*

That we indeed have here a zero N, invisible as to phonemes but tangible morphemically, is supported by the fact that certain transformations which operate on *wh*-forms do not operate on those *wh*-forms which are merely inserts to a zeroed *N*. Thus, the transformation *W*, as in:

$$Sn° \; V \; \Omega \rightarrow It \; V \; \Omega \; Sn°$$

operates not only on *Sn°* under *W*, as in:

> *What he will say is not known. → It is not known what he will say.*
> *Who will come doesn't interest me. → It doesn't interest me who will come.*

but also on the extraction form of *K* (with *that* in place of *what*)[50]:

> wh $\check{N}_i$ S-N_i is N_i → It is N_i that S-N_i
> *What he needs is money. → It is money that he needs.*
> (*) *Who said so was John himself. → It was John himself who said so.*

However, the transformation does not operate on

> *What he wrote was (widely) read.*
> $\sim \exists$ *It was (widely) read what he wrote.*[51]

even though the subject is of the same form as in the extraction. This is so because the subject here has zero *N*:

> *What he wrote was (widely) read. ← That which he wrote was (widely) read.*

with *that* zeroed, but morphemically present. Indeed, when the pronoun is human, it is usually not zeroed:

> *The one whom they opposed was voted down.*

5.3. *The Derivation Rule on the Elementary Operations*

We can now return to the four axiomatic transformational divisors, i.e. the elementary operations of § 5.1, and attempt a rule of derivation which specifies almost all transformations[52] on the basis of them.

Consider two sentence forms *A*, *B*, each containing some subcategory *X* and therefore written *A(X)*, *B(X)*. If between *A(X)* and *B(X)* there holds some succession of the elementary operations, then given the corresponding form *A(X′)* containing a subcategory *X′* similar to *X*, there is a possibility of finding *B* of *X′*:

$$\frac{\begin{array}{l} A(X) \leftrightarrow B(X) \\ A(X') \end{array}}{B(X').}$$

It should be understood that while B(X') is a transform of A(X'), it is not derived from A(X') by a transformation, but is derived from the above rule. Derivation is therefore to be taken in the sense of this rule, and is not identical with transformation in its definition.

The above is an analogic rule of a form relevant to linguistic change.[53] It is of a tenuous character, because we cannot specify what similarities are sufficient for this rule to operate, and what is the likelihood that the extension of the A(X)–B(X) relation to A(X') will indeed have much acceptability. These matters require investigation, although a complete specification of these two conditions is not be be expected, if the development of language is not internally determinate. Nevertheless, a reasonable interpretation of the similarity conditions for X, X' suffices to characterize the transformations of English from the four (or, with note 52, five) types of elementary operation by means of this rule.

If the relation in the major premise is $A \to B$ defined on X, in the sense that B(X) is derivable from A(X) by one or more of the operations, then B(X') looks like an extension of the argument of these operations to include X' as well as X. E.g. the transformation on W operators

$$Sn° \ V \ \Omega \to It \ V \ \Omega \ Sn°$$

is extended to operate on sentences of the extraction form (2) *wh- S is X* as well as on (1) *Sn° V Ω*. The *Sn° V Ω* itself includes *wh- S is A, wh- S is N: Whether he took it is unclear, Whether he took it is the question, What he took is the question, Who took it is the question,* etc. The sentences of the form (2) *wh- S is X* constitute an important set of sentences, pronouning at the head of *S* an *X* whose range is *N, P N, Ving Ω, D,* and certain *Ω* including *A: What he took is a book, Who said so is John, Where he stayed was with me, How he argued was quietly, What he is is clever.* Although these are very different from (1) *Sn° V Ω* in range and in grammatical character, there are a number of structures in (1) and (2) which are similar, as sequences of symbols, i.e. of constants and categories. We thus find the *It* form (with *that* replacing the *wh*-words except for *who* and rarely *when, where*), yielding *It is X that S-X: It is a book that he took, It is John who said so, It was clearly that he argued,* etc.[54] We could have said from the start that the *It* transformation operates on both structures. However, since the extraction (2) has a complicated derivation we can describe the application to it of the *It* transformation as a separate step, derived from *It* on *W* operators.

If the relation is $A \leftarrow B$ defined on X, the deriving of B(X') looks like an inverse transformation from A(X'). Thus, we can zero a repetitive subject under *W*:

(1)   *We prefer our studying French.* → *We prefer studying French.*

while in the parallel *We prefer her studying French* there is no zeroing. Now given sentences under *U*:

(2)   *We began studying French (last year).*
        We had thoughts about it.

we derive

(3)   *We began our studying French (last year).*
        We had our thoughts about it.

The two-subject form (3) cannot be the source of the one-subject form (2), since there are no two independent subjects in (3): $\sim\exists$ *We had their thoughts about it*, and *U* is defined as not introducing a second subject. Hence we can only understand (3) as obtained from (2) as an extension of (1).

If the transformational relation between *A* and *B* on *X* is not a single divisor, the formation of $B(X')$ makes the *A-B* difference look like a single operation from $A(X')$, even if such a transformation does not exist. Thus, if we start first with certain *U*, as in

He laughed → He gave a laugh; He had a laugh

we have a transformational relation between *He gave a laugh* and *He had a laugh* even though no elementary operation takes us from one to the other (and indeed the only succession of elementary operations that would take us from one to the other would be the inverse of a member of *U: He gave a laugh→He laughed* followed by another member of *U: He laughed→He had a laugh*). Given now

He had a party

we extend the transformational relation above, which had been defined on *Vn*, to such *N* (like *party*) as are the Ω of sets of *U*-like members of *V*; in this way we can obtain

He gave a party

(or vice versa), even though no verb *partied* exists to connect these two by elementary operations. This yields derived transformation directly from one *U*-like *V* to another, before certain *N*.

A surprising result is that many transformational shapes of a sentence are best obtainable from the elementary operations by going through the *W* operators. This is so because many of these transforms are virtually identical with the *Sn* under *W*, except that the sentential form has *is*. Thus the *Sn* forms of *They purchased the gouaches* under a *W* include:

(1)   *We reported their purchase of gouaches* (or: *their purchasing*)
      We reported the purchase of the gouaches by them
      We reported the purchase by them of the gouaches
      We reported their gouache-purchase.

Consider now a sentence beginning with *N is* under the *wh*-connective, with excision of *wh- is* (§ 5.212):

(2)   *He tore a picture; The picture was on the wall* →
      He tore the picture which was on the wall →
(3)   *He tore the picture on the wall.*

Since all *Sn* have the morphological form of *N* with adjuncts, the set (1) is similar to (3) except for subcategory: both consist of N_1 plus *t V* plus N_2 with adjuncts. We therefore form from the set (1), on the analogy of the difference between (3) and (2), i.e. by the inverse of *wh- is* excision and of *wh* connective:

> *We reported the purchase. Their purchase was of the gouaches.*
>   (or: *The purchase of the gouaches was theirs.*)
> *We reported the purchase. The purchase of the gouaches was by them* (or: *The purchasing…*)
> *We reported the purchase. The purchase by them was of the gouaches.*
> *We reported the purchase. The gouache-purchase was theirs.*

And so for all *Sn*-forms, although some of these new sentence forms have low acceptability. Such derivations can yield the sentence modulations, as in *The purchase of gouaches was theirs*.

In addition to these directly derivable forms, there are transformational forms which show further operations upon these derivations. Thus, starting from

> *The purchasing by them was of gouaches*

we may be able to obtain, by transformational steps similar to mirroring (§ 3.1) and a *be Va P* type of *U* (§ 3.2), the passive:

> *Gouaches were purchased by them*

This derivation is particularly uncertain because the intermediate steps are similar but not identical to the known forms of mirroring and *U*. Nevertheless, the relation of the passive to the *Sn* noted above is supported by the following similarities. In both, the original subject takes *by* and becomes appended after the deverbalized *V*. Both reject the same pseudo-objects: From *The champion ran a mile, The candidate spoke two hours*:

> *(They reported) the running of a mile by the champion.*
> *A mile was run by the champion.*
> $\sim \exists$ *(They reported) the speaking of two hours by the candidate.*
> $\sim \exists$ *Two hours were spoken by the candidate.*

And neither applies if $V = be$ or verbs of the *be*-set (*seem, become*). There is no Passive of *He was sick, He seemed sick*, and

> $\sim \exists$ *They reported the being sick by him.*
> $\sim \exists$ *They reported the seeming sick by him.*

As a somewhat different case, consider a peculiar English sentence form, whose character can be explained only by some kind of derivation from W. This is the form containing *is to: The bomb is to go off at three.* On the one hand, such sentences are peculiar in that no auxiliaries can be added: $\sim \exists$ *The bomb will be to go off at three.* On the other hand, each *is to* sentence carries the meaning of intention or of arranging for an outcome, even though the intender does not appear in the sentence. Now if we consider the W operators which take the form

(1) $N \, t \, V \, (P) \, N_i$ *that* N_i *should* $V \, \Omega \rightarrow$
(2) $N \, t \, V \, N_i$ *to* $V \, \Omega$,

we find that they have a characteristic meaning of arranging the $V \, \Omega$ for the N_i: *They set the bomb that it should go off at three* $\rightarrow$ *They set the bomb to go off at three, He fixed the show to open abroad*, etc. If on (2) we carry out successively the inverse of *wh- is* excision and the inverse of the *wh* connective, we obtain:

> $N \, t \, V \, N_i$ *to* $V \, \Omega \rightarrow$
> $N \, t \, V \, N_i$ *wh* $\check{N}_i$ *is to* $V \, \Omega \rightarrow$
> $N \, t \, V \, N_i \cdot N_i$ *is to* $V \, \Omega.$
> *He set the bomb to go off at three* $\rightarrow$
> *He set the bomb, which is to go off at three* $\rightarrow$
> *He set the bomb. The bomb is to go off at three.*

The form (2) is formed only out of (1) containing in its operand K the auxiliary *should* to which of course no further auxiliary can be added. The *to* (2) is a morphophonemic shape of this auxiliary *should* (in particular, *should* in the sense which it has in the operand of *set, arrange*) under certain operators, i.e. in certain new (insert-like) environments. The K-like form which the inverses produce out of (2) merely adds the V-constant *be* to this *to*. Hence no auxiliaries can be added to *is to*, and the meaning of the source *arrange that N should* is retained in *N is to*.

A remark on the direction of derivation: The great similarity between these sentence forms and *Sn* under *W* makes it clear that one should be derived from the other. One might think of deriving the *Sn* from the independent *S* forms, by saying that we could go in the opposite direction, and obtain the *Sn* by *wh*-connective between such sentences as *We reported the purchase, They set the bomb* (instead of the *W* operators) and these new *S* forms. However, since the same verbs *report, set*, etc. appear also as undoubted *W* operators on *that they purchased, that the bomb should go off* (and each with different *Sn°* deformations of the operand *S*, at that), we would have to have the *W* operators in *S* anyhow, and it is far simpler to have a single transformation *Sn°→Sn*, and then the new *S* forms from the *Sn*.

If we now make a quick check of the unaries in § 3.1, we find that they are all either successions of the elementary operations or else derivable from them by the rule of § 5.3, and so for the unaries of § 3.5. Thus the asyntactic require the fifth operation (note 52). The pleonastic *N's* is the inverse of the repetition zeroing under *W*. Pronouning can be considered a process like zeroing, but not simply a stage toward it, since the conditions for the two differ in important respects (see note 44). The derivation of the modulations and the passive have been discussed above. The middle can be obtained via *S→Sn is* A_m followed by an inverse:

> *He fitted the door snugly*
> → *His fitting of the door was snug*
> → *The fitting of the door was snug*
> → *The door fitted snugly*

the last being the inverse of the same *S→Sn is* A_m transformation on intransitive *V*, as in *The chirping of the birds was cheery←The birds chirped cheerily*.

6. THE SET OF SENTENCES UNDER THE ELEMENTARY OPERATIONS

When we consider the set of sentences under the elementary operations we find a new situation. In the case of the set of sentences under transformations (§ 4), we saw that if two sentences were related, it was always possible to state a transformation or succession of these from one to the other. Because of the nature of the derivation rule on the elementary operations, we now have sentences which are related to each other in the theory of elementary operations, without one being derived from the other by any succession of elementary operations (as in the interchange of *U*, § 5.3). What does hold between any two related sentences, however, is that the difference between them is always a sum of elementary differences, where an elementary difference is the difference between the operand and resultant of an elementary operation. We might therefore reach an analysis of sentences as a sum of elementary sentences and elementary differences; in some cases the order of accumulating the differences is nonunique, though the problem of alternative ways of deriving a form may become complicated only where certain inverses are involved.

NOTES

* The details of transformational analysis which the present paper summarizes have appeared or are to appear in various issues of *Transformations and Discourse Analysis Papers*, Department of Linguistics, University of Pennsylvania, and of *Papers on Formal Linguistics*, Mouton & Co., The Hague. I wish to thank Henry Hiż for valuable criticisms of the present manuscript.

[1] This is a simplified statement, omitting various restrictive conditions.

[2] The immediate-constituent analysis would give:

> Subject: *a sample which a young naturalist can obtain directly*
> Predicate: *is often of value,*

with *a sample* and *is* and *of value* eventually appearing as heads. The existence of a sentence *A sample is of value*, and its relation to the analyzed sentence, are not expressed by the constituent analysis.

[3] A distinction should also be made here between hierarchical operations and simple classification. The fact that some strings are partially similar, or that some strings occur in the same positions, may be expressed by collecting these strings into a class or schema. This serves only for an abbreviation of a linguistic description that could be made without such classification, so that there is no hierarchical linguistic operation here.

[4] This is not to say that there are no further subtleties of sentence structure which have yet to be treated. There remain problems concerning morphological and other restrictions on the application of transformations, concerning quasi-idiomatic constructions, concerning classifier-relations between words, etc.

[5] The pitting of one linguistic tool against another has in it something of the absolutist postwar temper of social institutions, but is not required by the character and range of these tools of analysis.

[6] The complete statement is a bit more complicated, because certain sentences have a string structure different from the one shown here (though closely related to it); e.g. *This I like*. Correspondingly, certain transformations produce or act upon these other string structures. The actual transformations of a language are of course a small subset of the ones admitted by the above statement, a subset distinguished by certain additional string restrictions and by the essential transformational properties described below in this paper.

[7] Because of the mass of idiomatic and quasi-idiomatic expressions in language, each type of description has to treat of various special small categories of words, and in some cases even of unique words. But in the case of string and transformational analyses, and less adequately in the case of constituent analysis, the statements for aberrant and idiomatic material can be made in the terms of the given description (constituent, string, or transformation) or in limited extension or weakenings of the rules of that description. In these analyses, the treatment of difficult material does not require us to go completely outside the terms of the given description into the terms of another or into the metalanguage.

[8] A program for string analysis by computer exists, and a transformational program has been designed. A transformational program can utilize in part the results of a string analysis. The less detailed program which analyzed sentences on the Univac in 1959 used a combination of string analysis and constituent analysis.

[9] This applies, for example, to the formulation of grammar in terms of partially ordered homomorphisms which was sketched in Z. S. Harris, 'From Morpheme to Utterance', *Lg.* 22 (1946), 161–83 (Paper VI of this volume) and which has been given an explicit form in Noam Chomsky's rewriting rules; also to the precise theory of generative grammar proposed and formulated by Chomsky in a series of major papers, especially in his *Syntactic Structures*, The Hague 1957. Cf. also his interesting 'Three Models for the Description of Language', *IRE Transactions on Information Theory*, IT-2 (1956).

[10] This formulation has to be extended, as it readily can be, to two further cases: where the second sentence form lacks one of the word categories (due to zeroing); and where we start with two sentence forms, A_1 and A_2, each with its own scale of satisfiers, plus a connective, and compare with a sentence form B containing the word categories of both (or at least, allowing for zeroing, the word categories of one form) where the acceptability-order of the n-tuples of B is summed in some regular way (related to the connective) from the acceptability-order of the corresponding n-tuples of A_1 and A_2. This criterion of a preserved acceptability-ordering is not easy to investigate and use. However, it clearly holds for all the pairs of satisfier-sets X, Y, where we would clearly want a transformational relation between X and Y. And if we find n-tuples which satisfy one form (with satisfiers X) with different acceptability-ordering than when they satisfy another form (with satisfiers Y), we indeed do not wish to call Y a transform of X, e.g. we may hesitate to consider the use of the passive form in scientific writing as a passive transform of the active.

[11] Such extension of a type of analysis into parts of the language where the analysis could not have been independently established does not make the analysis arbitrary. The existence of the relation in question has already been established over a large part of the language. Once we have seen, in this large part of the language, what are the effects of this relation, we may be able to show that similar effects exist in the rest of the language and may be attributed to the same relation.

[12] One might say *Can Helen Keller see a person with her fingers?*, but the acceptability would be rather special, and even more so for a simple *Did Helen Keller see John?* There is also *Can Helen Keller 'see' a person with her fingers?*; but this can be derived, by a transformation that produces quotation, from something like *Can Helen Keller do something which is called seeing a person with her fingers?*

[13] One might propose, as such a property: personal names used purely as examples for this discussion, and not identified with any real or fictional person. But such n-tuples have no acceptability difference among them in any sentence-form, so that they do not provide a basis for saying that (9)↔(10).

[14] Note in particular the formulations proposed by Henry Hiż in 'Congrammaticality, Batteries of Transformations, and Grammatical Categories', in *Proceedings of Symposia in Applied Mathematics*, vol. 12, American Mathematical Society 1961; also in his 'The Role of Paraphrase in Grammar', *Monograph Series on Languages and Linguistics*, vol. 17 (1964). The definition of transformation can also be adjusted for various purposes. Starting with transformations defined as an equivalence relation between satisfier-sets (the X and Y above), we can speak of transformations between sentences (corresponding members of these sets) or between sentence forms (for certain n-tuples satisfying them). In a different way, we can speak of transformations operating on sentences, or operating on elementary sentences and on transformations (§ 3.5 below).

[15] This holds also for the transformations as they appear in the theory of Noam Chomsky and in the applications by his students, even though in this case they are set up formally not as a relation between sentences but as instructions in the course of generating sentences (from already-generated simpler sentences). See Noam Chomsky, 'A Transformational Approach to Syntax', in A. A. Hill (ed.), *Proceedings of the Third Texas Conference on Problems of Linguistic Analysis in English, 1958* 1962, 124–58, reprinted in J. A. Fodor and J. J. Katz (eds.), *The Structure of Language*, 1964.

[16] Acceptability-difference is a refinement of the criterion of co-occurrence, which had been used in the original presentation of transformations in Z. S. Harris, 'Distributional Structure', *Word* 10 (1954), 146–62 (Paper XXXVI of this volume); 'Co-occurrence

and Transformation in Linguistic Structure', *Lg.* **33** (1957), 283–340 (Paper XXIII of this volume). The criterion of co-occurrence presented difficulties, because it is doubtful if we can say that a certain n-tuple does not occur at all in a given sentence form. A more important reason for seeking a refinement on co-occurrence is that transformation preserves not only the occurrability of n-tuples but also the degree to which they can occur and the sense and nuance with which they occur. See end of note 10.

[17] The specific lists for English, on which the present commentary draws, are given in various papers, from Z. S. Harris, 'Discourse Analysis', *Lg.* **28** (1952), 1–30, § 7.3 (Paper XIX of this volume), and through various issues of the *Transformations and Discourse Analysis Papers.* In the following discussion, the terminology of operations and the symbol → will often be used instead of the terminology of (equivalence) relations and the symbol ↔. This is only because once we have a transformational relation between forms *A* and *B*, it is convenient (in order to define a useful set of base transformations, § 5) to develop a formulation in which *B* is obtained from *A* by an operation, with *A* being the simpler or descriptively prior form. In terms of the elementary operations (§ 5), the primitive is no longer the equivalence relation but a set of incremental and zeroing operations (§ 5.1), which produce one form out of another, $A \rightarrow B$. However, this direct operational formulation does not suffice for the extensions of § 5.3.

[18] *Vn* for nominalized verb, i.e. *V* with zero or other affix occurring in the positions of *N*; and so for *Va*, etc. (*P*) in the formulas below indicates that some cases covered by the formula have *P* and others do not. *S* for sentence. The words 'subject' and 'object' (or Ω) represent not constituents but the pre-*t* and post-*V* material in the elementary sentence forms, and material brought into these positions by specified operations on these forms.

[19] One could also analyze this structure not as *N V* or *V* Ω operating on *S*, but as *N V X* and *X V* Ω (as sentences) with an *S* replacing the *X*. E.g. *I know that he came* = *I know something* plus *He came. That he came is a fact* = *Something is a fact* plus *He came.* Among the various difficulties with such an analysis is the fact that for some of these *W* verbs there is no natural *X*: e.g. *I hope that he will come* would require at best *I hope for something.* The difference in analysis is one of convenience of description. It does not affect the essential existence or properties of transformations.

[20] More precisely, the *if* entry is *if S_1 or S_2 ... or S_n.* There is a *whether* variant of *if*, and in certain situations a *whether* variant of *that*. Also, *that N V* Ω has the variant *that N should V* Ω and in certain positions necessarily *for N to V* Ω. *Sn'* is distinct from *Sn*, because it can contain *Y*: *His having been present was denied. Sn* includes *Ving* as well as *Vn*, with *of* before objects beginning with *N*: *His purchasing of the books was deliberate, His retention of the report was deliberate. Sn* can be taken to include also the deformation *N's An* (*His quickness*) from *N is A*, and *N's Nn* (*His manhood*) from *N is N.*

[21] Other limited or variant objects of *W* can be seen in, for example, *I prefer it that he should come.* Also *P N_1 that $N_1(t)$ V* Ω has a variant *N_1 to V* Ω: *I believe about him that he is wrong, I believe him to be wrong, I know him to have come late*; this variant is comfortable primarily if *V = be* or if *Y* has operated on *V*. For a particular subcategory of *W*, *to be* in this object is zeroed, yielding: *I believe him wrong, I consider him an authority, I find him at fault.* Note that *I ordered them present* is obtained here from *I ordered* (*about them*) *that they be present*, while *I ordered them to be present* is obtained from *I ordered them that they be present* (in the object list below); the latter means that the order was addressed to them, but the former does not.

[22] For the necessary zeroing of N_i's when the subject of *W* is N_i, see below.

[23] Among limited objects of particular *W* there is *I let go of it* (in addition to *I let it go*).

[24] This is a crude statement of the differences required by *but*.

[25] There is also a possibility of operating on three sentences at once, e.g. *S_1 related S_2 to S_3.*

[26] A similar permutation in the question *Would he see her?* etc. will be seen below to be occasioned by the dropping of *if*. Permutations like *This I like* in the elementary sentence could also be considered to depend upon the addition of a stress morpheme, and so based upon an increment. The position of *not* in respect to tense in *He did not go*, etc., can be ana-

lyzed as the original position and not a permutation; but there are other special transformations on *not*.

[27] Or rather than D: second morpheme of V.

[28] This can happen as the result of permutation, as when the passive $N_1 t V N_2 \to N_2 t$ Ven by N_1 puts as the domain of the first N of the resultant the word category which had been the domain of the second N in the operand. It happens as the result of zeroing, as when the zeroing of P in $P N$ of measure, $N V P N \to N V N$, brings into the apparent Ω position to V a noun of measure which had not been in the domain of the Ω of that V (e.g. *minute* is in the domain of the Ω of *tick off*, as in *The clock ticked off a minute* $\to$ *A minute was ticked off by the clock*, but it is not in the Ω of *pause*, as in *He paused for a minute* $\to$ *He paused a minute* where $\sim \exists$ *A minute was paused by him*). It also happens as the result of adding constants, as in *He smoked cigars* $\to$ *He began the smoking of cigars*, where *began* becomes the value of V and we can say that *the smoking* becomes the value of Ω in respect to any transformation which is defined on Ω and accepts *the smoking* as Ω of *began*.

[29] Since every transformation leaves its effect, if only in the choice of subcategory for a given category symbol, the precise statement of arguments and of operands and resultants for each transformation opens the way to computation of transformational decomposition. There exist cases of φ_i followed by a zeroing which has the effect of an inverse of φ_i, but these have to be recognized only when a trace has been left, i.e. when some φ_j has intervened (for an example, see end of § 5.213).

[30] Under W we have to include *is* A_m of manner, and also the binary verbs.

[31] A sentence can be ambiguous because of the range of meanings of a word in it (e.g. *I like the sound; I like the Sound*) or because of a degeneracy (homonymity) resulting from transformations (e.g. *They have shined shoes.* $\leftarrow$ *They have shoes which are shined*, by zeroing of *which are* $\leftarrow$ *wh* (*They have shoes. The shoes are shined.*); and also *They have shined shoes* $\leftarrow$ *They shined shoes* by the Y operator *have Ven*). In the former type, dictionary ambiguity, the ambiguity disappears when some of the other words in the *n*-tuple are varied (e.g. *The boat sank in the Sound*). In the latter, grammatical ambiguity, the ambiguity remains no matter how the n-tuple is varied, so long as the altered n-tuples can occur at all in the two grammatical sources.

[32] For this analysis of *the*, see the papers of Beverly Robbins in the *Transformations and Discourse Analysis Papers*, and in her *The Definite Article in English Transformations*, Papers on Formal Linguistics, No. 4, Mouton & Co., The Hague, 1968.

[33] In this form we no longer have binary transformations. Each binary is the result of a divisor of type 3 (whose resultant is not a sentence) followed by a divisor of type 1 (operating on a sentence, with a deformed sentence as increment).

[34] 'Local synonymity' is used for synonymity in respect to the particular environing words in a structure.

[35] This is an extreme example of the fact that when a word occurs in a sentence, it does not carry its full dictionary meaning, but only such meaning as can constitute a normally accepted (or, depending on the discourse, a jocular, shocking, etc.) meaning in relation to the other words with which it is grammatically juxtaposed.

[36] Though the determiners of X_{ap} may be the other words of the K, the zeroing does not occur in a K by itself, but only when one form is juxtaposed to another (as happens also in morphophonemics). Within a K or an insert or operator by itself there is no redundancy which is removable. In those K in which a particular subcategory of Ω, or a particular subject-object pair, determine that a particular V (or set of locally synonymous V) is the main one, the V may be replaced by a constant of low semantic specificity (e.g. *have* or *be* or *is P*); but the V will not be zeroed (something which would produce a new kind of V-less sentence): *He wrote a poem* $\to$ *He did a poem*; $\sim \exists$ *He poem*.

[37] Here the $V_{ap}ing$ and *to* V_{ap} do not have the form of inserts. However, dropping them only changes the form of the subject or object to N, which is a respectable grammatical form. Note that the plural agreement is a late morphophonemic operation, after the zeroing.

[38] Although the evidence that one form has been derived from another by the dropping of some material is of the same kind here as throughout, it is less obvious in the cases discussed here. The evidence that (1) N_1 *caused* $N_2 \leftarrow$ (2) *The* $V_{ap}ing$ *of* N_1 *caused* N_2 is that for every sentence of form (1) there exists a sentence of form (2), the difference in acceptability between various N_1, N_2 choices in (1) being the same as in (2). Furthermore, this holds only for $V = occur, happen, act$, etc. and not for $V = end, is brief$, etc. In contrast, for N_1 *ate* N_2 we don't find *The* *Ving of* N_1 *ate* N_2. Hence *cause* here is not a V which simply occurs in a K, but is a sentence operator. I.e. its subject (and Ω) is a deformed K. When we find N (other than 'human' N) as its subject, this N is obtained from the deformed K by dropping the *Ving*; and the *Ving* drops only if it is the appropriate one for *cause*.

[39] Dropping *to* V_{ap} is different from zeroing repetitive V_1 or *to* V_1 after an antecedent *to* V_1 (§ 5.22): *I spoke and I expect him to.*

[40] Going beyond language to specialized subject-matter languages which contain greater restrictions, methods of this kind could be used to achieve more simply characterizable subjects, objects, etc. Thus *to measure a room* could be taken as reduced from *to measure the length* (etc.) *of a room; to rig the convention* from *to rig the voting* (or *the activity* etc.) *of the convention, to load the gun* from *to load the cylinder of the gun.* In this way the Ω of the V would also become more explicit.

[41] Under certain sentence operators, the K is only (or primarily) of the *be* type; and after certain of these the *be* is then always dropped: *I call him a fool; I consider him a fool, I consider him to be a fool.*

[42] But if the V of K_2 is not *be* or the appropriate verb, the *wh*-word remains: *I saw the man who buys milk* (unless this man has been familiarly regarded as being the person with a characteristic relation to milk, in this case an inveterate buyer of it: he might then be referred to as *the milkman*).

[43] The collecting of the disjunctional N, the formation of the *wh*-words, the N t permutation (when N is available, hence no permutation in *Who will go?*), are all transformations which appear elsewhere too. The W needed for the question are those that take *if*. The W needed for the imperative are those that permit *please* in the operand. That the lost subject of the operand is uniquely *you* is seen from *Wash yourself!* etc.; it is therefore zeroable as N_{ap}.

[44] We can define a set of proword substitutions which are similar to various types of zeroing, but operate under somewhat different conditions. Thus the disjunctions and conjunctions of § 5.23 may be replaced by indefinite pronouns and by certain words operating as classifiers (e.g. *people* in the sense of *someone*; *act* in the sense of *do something*) in all syntactic situations, and by zero in only certain syntactic ones. Words of almost all categories (chiefly N) can be replaced by prowords of that category and by words that are semantically inclusive in respect to them; this is more likely to occur if the word is referent-repeating. The zeroing of repetitive material (§ 5.22) is similar only to this last, but occurs also in some syntactic situations in which pronouning does not occur (e.g. *while Ving*) and also in various categories which have no proword. The zeroing of 'appropriate' words (§ 5.21) is related to a much more general system of locally appropriate sub-categories, which includes synonyms and certain kinds of antonyms as well as sets of words based on looser local semantic similarity.

[45] This relation of zero to pronoun does not hold in § 5.22, where a word is zeroed only if it is the same word as the antecedent; nor in § 5.21.

[46] The ambiguity of *Every place has been taken by someone* arises from the two possible orderings of the disjunctional operation (which yielded *someone*) and the conjunctional operation (which yielded *every*). We begin with

$$A_i \text{ place has been taken by } N_j$$

If we first make a conjunction on the A (i.e. A_1 *place has been taken by* N_1 *and* A_2 *place has been taken by* N_1 ... *and* A_n *place has been taken by* N_1) we obtain

$$\text{Every place has been taken by } N_1.$$

If here we make a disjunction on the N (i.e. *Every place has been taken by N_1 or every place has been taken by N_2 ... or every place has been taken by N_m*) we obtain

Every place has been taken by someone

in the sense of

($\exists N$) ($\forall A$) *A place has been taken by N.*

However, if in the original sentence we first make a disjunction on the N, yielding

A_1 place has been taken by someone

and on this a conjunction on the A, we obtain

Every place has been taken by someone

in the sense of

($\forall A$) ($\exists N$) *A place has been taken by N.*

[47] There is a possibility that this Ω-zeroing can be derived through the Sn form, where Ω has insert form.

[48] In the example given here, *what* can be replaced by *whatever*; and what has been dropped is *anything, the things*, etc., which are pronouns for disjunctions of N. However, there are also cases in which *what* can be replaced by *the single thing that*, or the like; in such cases, what has been dropped is a pronoun or a classifier N_{c1} for a single N: *I heard what he said and you heard it too; What he planted has grown to be quite a tree.*

[49] A partly similar case is the rare dropping of pronoun or N_{c1} which may occur after certain *the A*, where the *the* indicates a lost *wh*-insert connected to that N: *the true $\leftarrow$ the things which are true. This is mine $\leftarrow$ This is my N_1 or N_2...or N_n; This is his $\leftarrow$ This is his N_1 or N_2...or N_n.*

[50] $\hat{X}$ for pronoun of X. S-N_1 indicates S with N_1 omitted.

[51] The apposition with comma is different: *It was (widely) read, what he wrote.*

[52] Almost all, because there remain a few pure permutational (asyntactic) transformations. To derive these, we would have to add a fifth type of elementary transformation which carries out restricted permutations.

[53] See in particular Henry M. Hoenigswald, *Language Change and Linguistic Reconstruction*, Chicago 1960.

[54] As an example of a limitation on similarity, note that the *It* transformation does not extend to zero N plus *wh-S*: see the end of § 5.23.

XXVIII

DECOMPOSITION LATTICES

This paper presents the transformational decomposition of paragraphs from scientific texts. The decomposition is displayed in a form that shows the order relation among the transformations. In the decomposition of a sentence, a transformation-occurrence φ_1 is an upper bound of another one, φ_2, if the operand of φ_1 contains φ_2; and φ_1 is the least upper bound of φ_2 if there is no φ_3 such that φ_1 is an upper bound of φ_3 and φ_3 is an upper bound of φ_2. It will be seen that each decomposition is a lattice if the sentence contains only one kernel-sentence ('kernels'), and like a semi-lattice otherwise. We say 'like' because in this case right and left are distinguished: $X \, C \, Y \neq Y \, C \, X$; $C = $ conjunction. To distinguish these we draw a main branch through C for X in X C Y and for Y in Y C X:

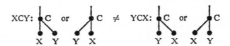

Only the 'correct' reading is presented for each sentence; we assume that, given a set of all possible decompositions of a sentence (each differing in meaning from the others), it will be possible, by comparisons among neighboring sentences, to select the 'correct' (intended) reading.

Though many detailed problems remain, it seems that the decompositional path to a given set of kernel sentences (K) is unique. However, in the present state of transformational theory, it may be that for certain sentences, a particular reading can be decomposed into different kernels and transformations, depending on whether we use certain conjectured transformations; examples of this are given (e.g. parts 2, 3 of S1 of text I).

The procedure for obtaining the decomposition is as follows: Starting with the given sentence (S), we ask what unary or binary transformation can be undone at this point; the residual sentence must be transformationally related to the given sentence. We present a unary as a node on a line going to the right, and a binary as a node joining a downward or upward line to the line going right. If more than one transformation can be undone in this

Transformations and Discourse Analysis Papers 70 (1967).

sentence, we treat them as an unordered set of transformations at this point. The resultant of undoing a transformation or an unordered set of transformations is again a sentence, and we repeat the procedure on the resultant sentence. (We may find unordered sets of sequences of transformations, as in *more and more – appears as* in part 1 of S1 of text I). The procedure can be checked by recomposing the sentence from the kernels obtained by the decomposition. In the resulting lattice, the universal points are sentences, the residual kernel sentences being the null points at the right. (This orientation is used here, instead of having the universal point at the top, in order to facilitate writing the language material along the lattice lines.) Nodes along a line are unary transformations; nodes at a junction of two lines which do not meet again are binary transformations. Each transformation operates on the combined resultant of all transformations not to its left to which it is connected by lines. As a pictorial convention, transformations operating independently on subject, verb, object, are written in that order from top downwards (e.g. *it, probably, the* in S3 of text I). (Right angles in the drawing are made so that the unary transformations on a K should appear along a

horizontal line: ⌐__   is equivalent to ——< .)

The set of all component sentences of the given S is obtained from the lattice of transformations as follows: Going in either direction: For each node (including S and K, at the ends), with n lines entering the node, each choice of m of these lines ($1 \leq m \leq n$) identifies a sentence which is the joint resultant of the nearest nodes on these m lines, operating on the resultants of the next nodes further out. Each such sentence is transformationally intermediate between the sentences, connected to it by lines, to its left and those not to its left. Both directions have to be used if all component sentences are to be obtained.

For an example of component sentences, for $m = 1$, taken in each direction, see under S1 of text I. For an example of the cross-product component sentences (for each choice of m, $1 \leq m \leq n$), see under S8 of text I.

One type of component sentence may not be obtained from the above, as follows: In

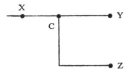

X may be an operator on C, or it may operate on Y or on Z in the form which they receive under C, or on the Y C Z entity. In all these cases, X could not be applied to the right of C. But in some cases, the X could have operated on

Y and on Z separately, with the resultant of X Y C X Z being the same as X operating on Y C Z. In such cases, X Y and X Z are component sentences too, although the figure shows only X (Y C Z). Examples of such X: D, plural, zeroings in both Y and Z. E.g. in S4 of text I.

Remarks about the transformations:

V_{ap} indicates any appropriate verb for the given kernel or transformation.

U indicates any appropriate verb-operator: $N V \Omega \rightarrow N U VnP \Omega$ (e.g. *effects removal of gland, has function, suffers death, has importance*). Ω indicates the object of a V; P: preposition; V: verb; N: noun.

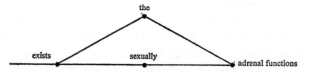 S, including specified U such as $\overset{is \ Va}{\bullet\!\!-\!\!-\!\!-\!\!\bullet}$ S, means that the $V \Omega$ of S are operated on by the U: *N is important → N has importance. A tumor masculinizes → A tumor is masculinizing.*

S, where W represents any verb having a sentence (nominalized) as its subject or object (but not both), means that the S receives an appropriate nominalized form:

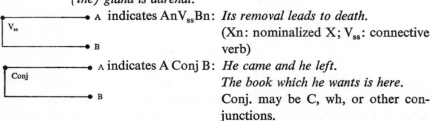

A sexual function of the adrenal exists.

$\overset{0}{wh}$ indicates connective wh-word (*which*, etc.) which is zeroed together with following *is: adrenal gland ← gland which is adrenal*. Although derivation via *wh* is uncomfortable in many cases, such as the above, it fits the rest of the grammar: *prime gland ← gland which is prime*.

In all cases of [A ——wh——→ B; ——→ C], B and C have a noun in common, and it is understood that C is transformed so that this common noun comes first, if it is not already first in C: *adrenal is a gland → (the) gland is adrenal.*

[V_{ss} ——→ A; ——→ B] indicates $AnV_{ss}Bn$: *Its removal leads to death.* (Xn: nominalized X; V_{ss}: connective verb)

[Conj ——→ A; ——→ B] indicates A Conj B: *He came and he left. The book which he wants is here.* Conj. may be C, wh, or other conjunctions.

$\overset{o}{X}$ indicates the zeroing of X.

the, this, and other pro-adjectives are traces of lost C K: e.g. *the adrenal←adrenal (pair) is unique.*

it and other pronouns are traces of lost CK too.

all, plural, and other quantifiers and indefinite pronouns are traces of conjunctions and disjunctions of K, hence of CK...CK.

In some cases, imperfectly established limited transformations would yield more reasonable K; this may be the only source of non-unique decomposition (above). Informationally unreasonable and repetitive K are in any case unavoidable. Thus in S5 of text I *gland is gland* is inescapable if we are to have an occurrence of *gland* to which we can attach *whose different functions....* The source without *gland is gland* would be:

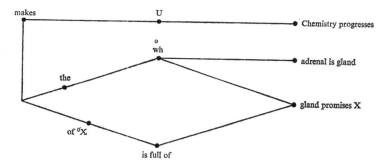

which yields *Progress of chemistry makes the adrenal gland full of promise*; then *whose functions...* would have to be attached to the first *gland*, which would differ in meaning from the given S5. We could also have:

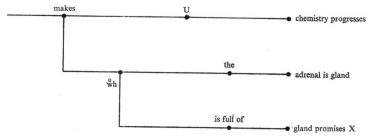

yielding: *The progress of chemistry makes the adrenal (into) a gland full of promise.*

However, this contains: *The progress of chemistry makes the adrenal (into) a gland*, and this may not be a desired component sentence of S5.

TEXT I: P. Delost, *La fonction sexuelle de la cortico-surrénale*, sentences 1–9, translated:

S1: *The adrenal appears more and more as a prime endocrine gland; its importance grows in the animal scale; among the mammals, it has become indispensable for life, its removal leads rapidly to death; its functions are multiple.*

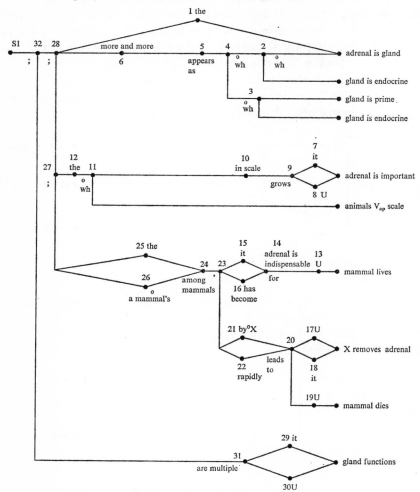

Alternatives:

Part 2: In the following, the transformation X would have to rearrange the words of D_1, D_2:

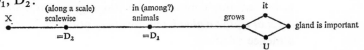

Part 3: PASAP is the appropriate passive-like transformation, e.g. *X requires Y→Y is indispensable for X*. It could be avoided by having as K: *Adrenal is indispensable for mammal*. But it is not clear that this yields *among mammals* (or only *for mammals*).

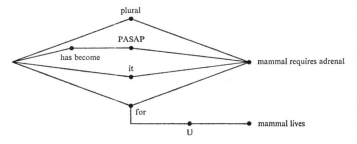

We assume that part 3 (nodes 14–27) is especially related to part 2 (i.e. adjoined to it), while parts 2–3 and part 4 are independently adjoined to part 1.

Examples of component sentences, excluding the cross-product ones (with automatic features such as *a* added):

Resultant of node
1: The adrenal is a gland.
2: An adrenal is a gland which is endocrine.
   An adrenal is an endocrine gland.
3: A gland which is endocrine is prime (of prime importance).
   An endocrine gland is prime.
4: An adrenal is an endocrine gland which is prime.
   An adrenal is a prime endocrine gland.
5: An adrenal appears as a prime endocrine gland.
6: An adrenal appears more and more as a prime endocrine gland.
7: It is important.
8: An adrenal has importance.
9: Its importance grows. Note that *grows* operates on the combined resultant of *it* and of U. When a sentence-operator, W, or a conjunctional verb, V_{ss}, operates on the resultant of a verb-operator, U, on K, the effect is as though W operated on a complete nominalization of K: thus

yields: A gland has function; then: A function of a gland is important. whereas

yields: Functioning of a gland is important; or: That a gland function is important.

The V_{ss} case appears below in *leads to*

10: Its importance grows in (along) a scale.

11: Its importance grows in an animal scale (or: a scale of animals).

12: Its importance grows in the animal scale.

13: A mammal has life.

14: An adrenal is indispensable for a mammal's life.

15: It is indispensable for a mammal's life.

16: An adrenal has become indispensable for a mammal's life.

17: X effects an adrenal's removal.

18: X removes it.

19: A mammal suffers death.

20: Its removal by X leads to a mammal's death.

21: Its removal leads to a mammal's death.

22: Its removal by X leads rapidly to a mammal's death.

23: It has become indispensable for a mammal's life; its removal leads rapidly to a mammal's death.

24: Among mammals, 23.

25: Among the mammals, 23.

26: Among mammals, it has become indispensable for life, its removal leads rapidly to death.

27: 13; resultant of 25 and 26.

28: The adrenal gland appears more and more as a prime endocrine gland; 27. (The resultants of 1 and 6 are not combined until the operation of 28. If part 1 (nodes 1–6 and their K) had been a separate sentence, the resultants of 1 and 6 would have been combined immediately.)

29: It functions.

30: An adrenal has a function.

31: Its functions are multiple. (Under W, the resultant of U is completely nominalised into *A function of an adrenal*, or, with the resultant of *it*, into *Its function*. Certain W, such as *are multiple*, automatically introduce a plural on the subject of this nominalised operand.)

32: 28; 31. This ≡ S1.

Examples of the component sentences of part 1, going in the decompositional direction in which each node indicates the removal of the transformation named at that point:

−1: An adrenal appears more and more as a prime endocrine gland.

−6: The adrenal appears as a prime endocrine gland.

−5: The adrenal is a prime endocrine gland.

−4: The adrenal is an endocrine gland. The endocrine gland is prime.

−3: A gland is prime. The gland is endocrine.
−2: The adrenal is a gland.

Note that most of these component sentences are not quite identical with those obtained in the other direction, above.

S2: *Though the functions of the medulla and of the adrenal cortex daily show themselves more numerous, one must confess that their mechanisms of action are as yet quite imperfectly established.*

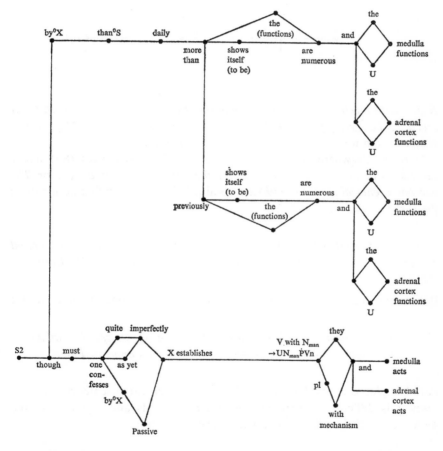

Part 1: What is conjoined by *more than* is lost, but in the presence of the adverb *daily* on U (*shows itself*), the *than S* which would be most readily zeroable here would be: *than the functions...had previously shown themselves to be numerous.*

The U is assumed to be in the operand of *numerous* because *of* is repeated. In contrast, *The functions of the medulla and the adrenal cortex* might perhaps be better obtained from:

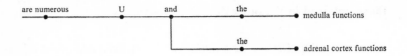

Part 2: A slightly different reading (and meaning) would give:

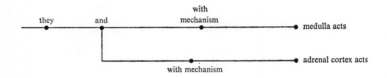

N acts with mechanism→*N has mechanism of action*; like *N talks with great speed*→*N has great speed of talking*. In symbols: V with N_{man}→UN_{man} of Vn. N_{man}: certain nouns of manner, such as *mechanism*.

Here as elsewhere we assume that nominalized sentences (Sn) under sentence operators (e.g. *X establishes their mechanism of action*, or *The adrenal's removal leads to death*) are obtained via a U which first nominalizes the verb:

$$X \text{ removes adrenal} \rightarrow X \text{ effects removal of adrenal} \Bigg\} \rightarrow X\text{'s removal of adrenal}$$
$$Y \text{ dies} \qquad\qquad \rightarrow Y \text{ suffers death} \qquad\qquad \text{leads to } Y\text{'s death.}$$

But in many cases the Sn is more natural than the presumed intervening U:

$$N \text{ talked with speed } \xrightarrow{?} N \text{ shows speed of talking} \rightarrow \Big\} \ N\text{'s speed of talking}$$
$$\underline{\qquad\qquad\qquad\qquad\qquad\qquad} \rightarrow \Big\{ \ \textit{impressed me.}$$

Part 1 is placed above Part 2 to indicate the order in the sentence. In some cases it is difficult to represent the order of words and segments in the sentence (as distinct from the order of transformations).

> S3: *The adrenal cortex certainly regulates the electrolyte balance and acts on the metabolism of the glucides; it probably intervenes in the metabolism of the proteins and the lipids; it presumably participates in the balance of the blood and the connective tissue.*

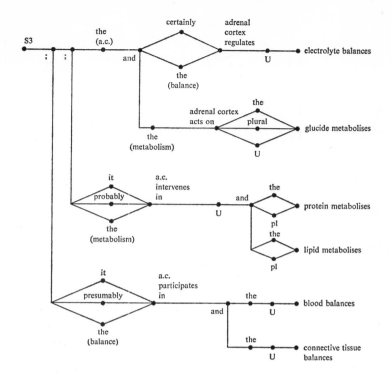

Part 1: The sentential residue should perhaps be *Electrolyte is in balance,* in the form of U operating on a dubious *Electrolyte balances.*

In sequences of *and* or *;* or *,* it is not clear whether the third part should be added to the first part (as is done above) or to the second; and so on. It should be clear that in all cases of a conjunction, we assume that there appear to the left of the conjunction a zeroing of identical portions of the secondary sentence sufficient to yield the resultant sentence as it appears here.

> S4: *This gland reveals itself as the pivot of the defense of the organism against all attacks, and as regulator, perhaps more than the hypophysis, of numerous physiological functions.*

Parts 2ff.: Perhaps X's should come immediately to left of *regulates, are numerous.* No *plural* is given to the right of *numerous,* because *plural* is automatic with *numerous.* (Diagram is on next page.)

> S5: *The progress of chemistry, which has made it possible to extract from the adrenal cortex a considerable quantity of*

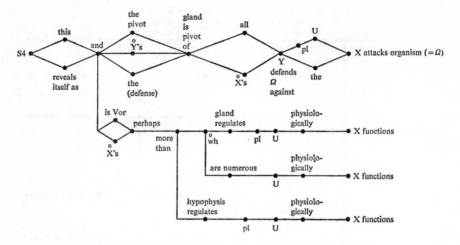

*hormones, has made the adrenal gland into one full of promise,
whose different functions have not ceased to surprise us.*

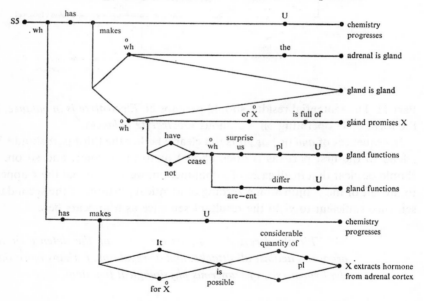

considerable quantities of is a quantifier with its classifier (*quantity*):=
in considerable quantity, considerable as to quantity, etc.

Here, *wh* inserts a conjunctional sentence S_2CS_3, into S_1, with the first word
of S_2 and of S_3 being the noun which each of these has in common with
S_1: *gland.*

S_1: *The adrenal gland is a gland.*

S_2CS_3: *A gland is full of promise; the gland's functions have not ceased to surprise us.*

When we insert the S_2CS_3 into S_1, by *wh*, we obtain: *The adrenal gland is a gland which is full of promise, whose functions have not ceased to surprise us.*

The second *wh*-word is not subject to the zeroing of *wh*-word plus *is*, while the first one is. Hence when we perform this zeroing, only the first is affected, yielding: *The adrenal gland is a gland full of promise, whose functions have not ceased to surprise us.*

In contrast, note $\overset{o}{wh}$ on S_1 *and* S_2, in S7, where the parallelism in S_1 *and* S_2 permits a zeroing in S_2.

S6: *Among these, the new idea of a sexual function merits all our attention.*

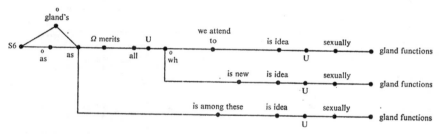

$\Sigma \text{ V } \Omega \rightarrow \Omega$ merits Σ's Vn.

The analysis of *Among these* is not certain.

S7: *It is the observations of human pathology, furnished by the masculinizing and feminizing tumors of the adrenal cortex, then the observations, in certain animal species, of a genital stimulation coming from the adrenals, and finally the recent findings of chemistry, showing the similarity between the hormones secreted by the adrenal and the sexual glands, which have directed us in this path.*

Xa indicates adjectivized X.

In $\boxed{\quad\overset{ing}{}}$ the *ing* is a subordinate conjunction.

Instrumental: *Y finds that K, in chemistry* → *Chemistry finds that K.*

$\Sigma \text{ V } \Omega \rightarrow \Omega$ is a V ing of Σ: *that K is a finding of chemistry.*

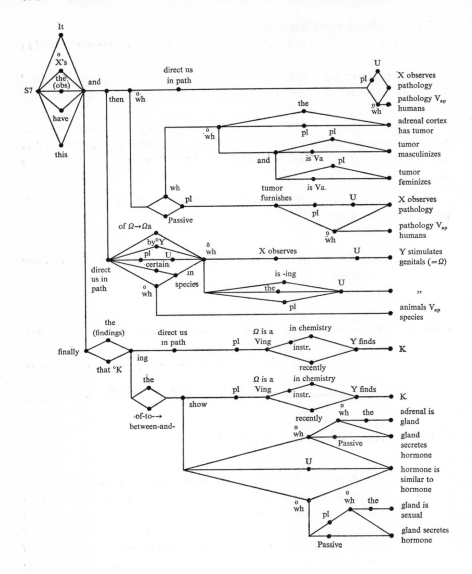

Then: *Findings of chemistry that K direct us in this path....*

Such K as *gland is sexual* are of course dubious; *gland V$_{ap}$ sex* would be better.

If the meaning was that the three contributions together, not severally, 'directed us in this path', we would take S7 as zeroed from *It is the combination of A then B and finally C which has directed us.* For *It,* see S9.

S8: *Does a sexual function of the adrenal exist?*

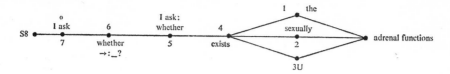

The complete list of component sentences, in the direction of composition, is:

     K: An adrenal functions.
     1:   The adrenal functions.
     2:   An adrenal functions sexually.
     3:   An adrenal has a function.
  1, 2:   The adrenal functions sexually.
  1, 3:   The adrenal has a function.
  2, 3:   An adrenal has a sexual function.
1, 2, 3:   The adrenal has a sexual function.
     4:   A sexual function of the adrenal exists.
     5:   I ask whether a sexual function of the adrenal exists.
     6:   I ask: Does a sexual function of the adrenal exist?
     7:   Does a sexual function of the adrenal exist?

The same components appear in the direction of decomposition:

     S: Does a sexual function of the adrenal exist?
   −7:   I ask: Does a sexual function of the adrenal exist?
   −6:   I ask whether a sexual function of the adrenal exists.
   −5:   A sexual function of the adrenal exists.
   −4:   The adrenal has a sexual function.
   −3:   The adrenal functions sexually.
   −2:   The adrenal has a function.
   −1:   An adrenal has a sexual function.
 −3, 2:   The adrenal functions.
 −3, 1:   An adrenal functions sexually.
 −2, 1:   An adrenal has a function.
−3, 2, 1:   An adrenal functions.

> S9: *It is this that we are going to try to establish, leaving the hypotheses aside, but analyzing in a precise manner the principal observations, and appealing to all latest investigations, which are indispensable for affirming the existence of such a function.*

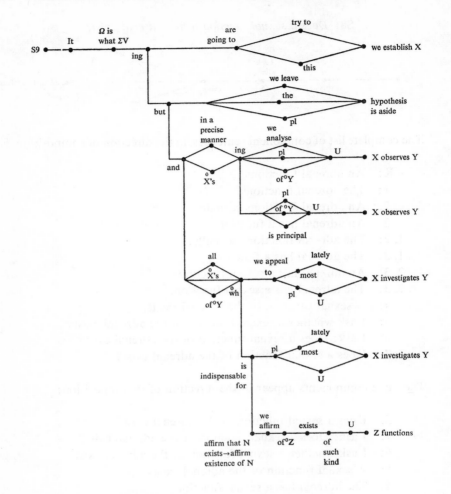

Ω is what V: We establish this→This is what we establish.

$$\left.\begin{array}{l} \text{That} \\ \text{wh} \\ \text{for} \end{array}\right\} KV\Omega \rightarrow It\ V\Omega \left\{\begin{array}{l} \text{that} \\ \text{wh} \\ \text{for} \end{array}\right\} K.$$

If the sentence on which *It* operates is *N is what ΣV* we assume an intervening→*what ΣV is N*, and then the *It* operation. Similarly, $\Sigma V\Omega \rightarrow \Sigma$ is what $V\Omega \rightarrow$ what $V\Omega$ is $\Sigma \rightarrow It$ is Σ that $V\Omega$, as in S7: *Observations direct us→It is observations that direct us.*

Clearly, the objects of the K here, and *hypotheses* (and *pathology* in S7) come from K, so that *establish, is aside, observe, investigate* (and V_{ap} *humans* in S7) are operations.

TEXT II: N. Tinbergen, *Social Behaviour in Animals*, p. 1, sentences 3–6:

> *Not all aggregations of animals however are social. When, on a summer night, hundreds of insects gather round our lamp, these insects need not be social. They may have arrived one by one, and their gathering just here may be clearly accidental; they aggregate because each of them is attracted by the lamp. But Starlings on winter evenings, executing their fascinating aerial manoeuvres before settling down for the night, do really react to one another; they even follow each other in such perfect order that we may be led to believe that they have superhuman powers of communication.*

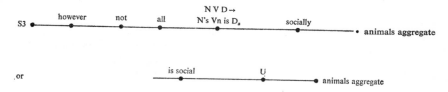

depending on how such adverbs are treated.

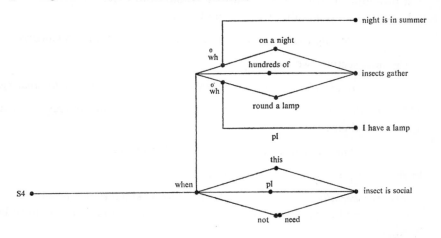

If two transformations operate as a product but not singly, they are written together (in the order fitting their other occurrences) so that no sentence is formed between them: *need not*.

In S5: Since the N is one which can be pronouned in this environment, it must be *insects*.

Each of, and differently *one another, each other*, decompose into disjunctions of the K to which they are attached; but for simplicity this is not

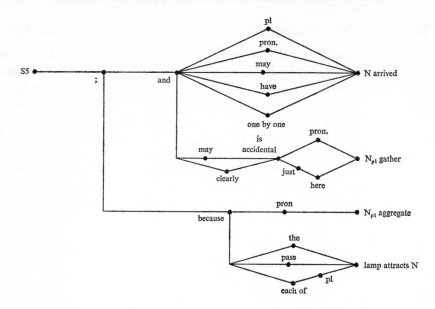

shown here. Even plural could be treated in this way. Pronouns (*they, this*) and pro-adjuncts (*the, this*) also are derivable from C K.

In S6: Σ's: repeat subject under the U:

> *starling executes manoeuvre→starling executes its manoeuvre*

In the next section, we have

> *It (starling) makes a manoeuvre→Its manoeuvre is fascinating.*

Although the two cases of *its manoeuvre* have different sources, *wh* can operate on them:

> *Starling executes its fascinating manoeuvre.*

In *for the night, the* is part of an idiom?

manoeuvre aerially→executes aerial manoeuvres, since *aerial* is adjunct of place or type; but *fascinating* is from W on *manoeuvre* and therefore must be brought in by *wh*.

Superhumanly, with superhuman power, etc. is D of means.

D/V: *N V D$_{means}$→N is Da in Ving; N V P N$_{means}$→N has N$_{means}$ of Ving.*

Note: Because S4 seemed stilted, two paraphrases of it were attempted, in order to see how their analyses would compare with that of S4:

S4(1) *Insects need not be acting socially when they gather in hundreds round our lamp on a summer night:*

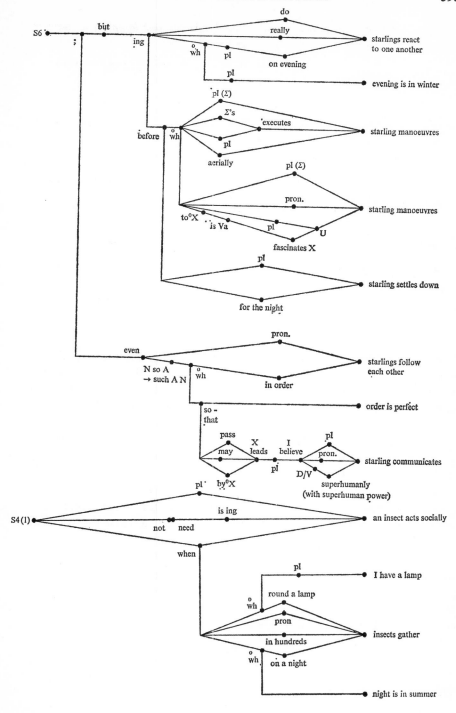

S4(2) *The hundreds of insects which gather round our lamp on a summer night need not be acting socially in doing so:*

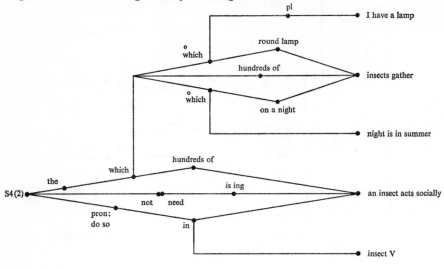

APPENDIX

The lattices, together with the left–right orientation, are nothing more than a presentation of the partially ordered transformational decomposition of a sentence. When a sentence S is fully decomposed into its elementary (kernel-) sentences K and transformations φ (especially into its base transformations), the result is an excessively repetitive structure. This constitutes no short-coming, because such a derivation of the given S is somewhat comparable to writing out a proof with the full regalia of logical symbolism and with every step fully presented. It is necessary to see that this can be done. For practical purposes the lattices can be simplified by recognizing certain common trans-formational products as single named steps in a transformational deri-vation. This is especially desirable for the analogic φ (e.g. Passive) but is also desirable for other paraphrastic products (e.g. Extraction: *This fell→This is what fell, What fell is this*; It-extraction: *→It is this that fell*; Question; Imperative; plural and numbers instead of conjunctions of S; indefinite pronouns instead of disjunctions of S). This applies also to recognizing *wh* as a separate conjunction, though it is derivable from *and* or *if*. Other common paraphrastic products are:

φ_s→D: His arrival is on Tuesday→He arrives on Tuesday.

V/D interchange: He speaks hurriedly→He is hurried in speaking

This is limited in complicated ways.

Nominalization-strengthening:

I know that he buys books→I know of his buying books

I wonder whether he buys books→I wonder about his buying books.

I prefer that he (should) come→I prefer his coming

His writing letters is frequent→His writing of letters is frequent.

Differences in detail in how we define the transformations (and their ability to repeat) lead to somewhat different lattices for the same (unambiguous) S. One can choose definitions which lead to a simpler algebra of transformations. Or one can choose definitions which lead to simpler lattices. There are also different ways of analyzing certain subclasses (including words like *system, kind,* etc.) which can support transformations that other words cannot.

When at a φ_c one S is secondary, it enters the φ_c node on a horizontal line. When the φ_c is a verb (e.g. *states*) neither S is secondary; the first (leftmost) S is then the subject of the connective verb.

If the trace (physical effect in the sentence) of φ_1 appears earlier in the sentence than the trace of φ_2, φ_1 will be shown to the left of φ_2 in the lattice, as far as is possible. Also where possible, *wh* on the left (or above) connect to the subject of their primary S, and *wh* on the right (or below) to its object.

Ň indicates an indefinite pronoun, which will be zeroed as soon as it enters an adjunct form (e.g. of Ň); this zeroing is not shown in the lattice.

Plural (pl) is a non-paraphrastic φ which can be considered a member of φ_a (local adjuncts); or it can be derived from a conjunction of the kernel-sentence or operator on which it operates.

Paraphrastic non-base operators are named (e.g. Passive), or their effect is shown (e.g.→the,→of like kind).

In these decompositions, we use a definition of *wh* which permits more than one *wh* to operate, unordered, on a single N.

wh requires that the secondary S should begin with a N (or P N) which appears in the primary S. If this shared N is not at the head of the secondary S a permutation brings it there; in some cases we do not show this permutation, for simplicity.

The usual lattice form is illustrated only for $S_{1,2}$. It is easier to read but harder to write.

Condon and Shortley, *Theory of Atomic Spectra,* Appendix: Universal Constants and Natural Atomic Units.

> *Measurements in physics are statements of relation of the quantity measured to quantities of like kind which are called units. It is*

customary to build up the system in such a way that the unit of any kind of physical quantity is defined in terms of three convention-al units of mass, length and time. The choice of the basic units for these quantities is wholly arbitrary, the general order of mag-nitude in the centimetre-gram-second system being such that the numerical measure of quantities occurring in ordinary laboratory experiments is of the general order of unity. Thus the velocity of light in the cgs system is 3×10^{10} cm sec^{-1}. The centimetre and second being so chosen that 1 cm sec^{-1} is of the order of velocities of common experience, the bigness of the number measuring velocity of light on this system is simply a statement that velocities of common experience are very small compared with that of light.

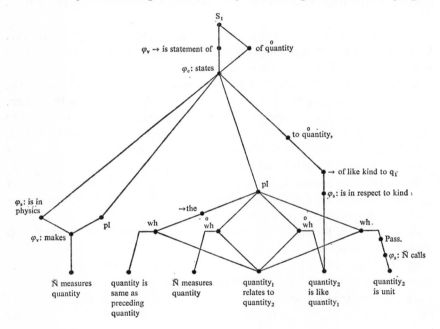

Remarks to S_1:

Depending on how φ_s is defined, we could say that φ_s here operates on φ_v. φ_s alone would yield: *N's measuring of quantity is in physics.* φ_v alone would yield: *N makes measurement of quantity.* φ_s on φ_v would yield: *N's measure-ment of quantity is in physics.* One could also attempt a definition in which these φ_v and φ_s were independent of each other.

The explanation of *the* as due to repetition of *quantity* required us to assume that the object of the first K was *quantity*, which is zeroed after the first K is connected to *q relates to q*. This means that the first occurrence of *quantity* in the connected sentence is zeroed on the basis of a later occurrence. Such direction of zeroing is so limited that the present case may not fit the rest of the language. Since it is by no means a certain derivation, and other derivations for *the* could be proposed here, the peculiarity of the zeroing may make this analysis unjustified. The alternative is *Ň measures Ň* as first K, and something like *quantity is under consideration here* (or: *is unique*) instead of *q is same* as source for *the*.

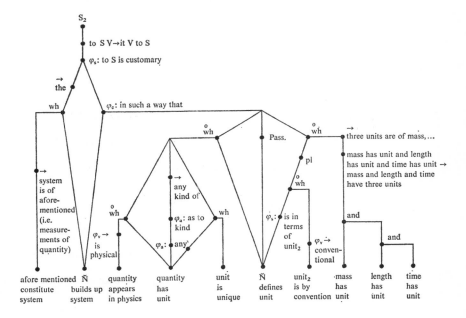

Remarks to S_2:

the system←system is (constituted) of things mentioned above.

as to kind is a φ_a on *any*, which is φ_a on *quantity*. We go through this route because the alternative would be *unit is of a kind* (← *a kind has a unit*) and *kind is of quantity* (←*quantity exists* or *appears in kinds*), which is very unsatisfactory. The φ: *any as to kind→any kind of* occurs for certain property-classifiers (e.g. *sort, size, manner, form*).

In a science-sublanguage we would probably have a single K: *unit₁ is defined in terms of unit₂*, which is semantically better.

Note that the other sense of *conventional* (human subject) would be derived from *N follows convention.*

The number n before *X* is a pronoun for n−1 occurrences of *and X* after the *X* in question. When *3 units are of*... is joined by *wh* to *in terms of units* we get *in terms of 3 units of*. Somewhat similarly if *ideas are acceptable in*

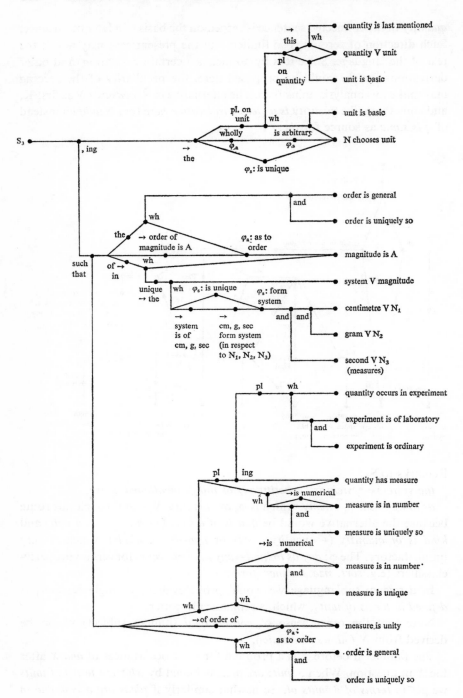

science is joined by *wh* to *express ideas* we get either *express ideas (which are) acceptable in science* or *express acceptable ideas in science.*

Instead of φ_c: *in such a way that* we could have *in a way* or *in way X* both to *N builds up system* and to *N defines unit* (as a φ_s), and then the φ_c is just *that* (or *so that*). There are various problems with the dropping of the second *in a way* and the entering of pro-adjective *such.*

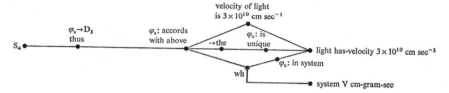

Remarks to S_{3-5}:

V is for V_{ap}, the appropriate verb, in this case *has* or the like. Further down it is *measures, consists of, has to do with,* etc. We take as K: *N has-velocity X,* though if no regard were given to the special subclass properties of *velocity,* the preceding K could be derived from two K: *N has velocity, velocity is X.* Words of the subclass of *velocity, size, cost,* etc. are classifiers of certain values on a scale. Certain paraphrastic transformations are possible with these words, as in:

> N cost $5.
> The cost of N is $5.
> $5. is the cost of N.
> The cost of $5...
> The $5. cost...

Some of these transforms appear here for *velocity,* and for *kind, order.*

$\varphi_s \rightarrow D$: virtually all sentence operators can be transformed into adverbs: *I know that he came → He came to my knowledge, He came, as known to me. That he came surprised us → He came, surprisingly for us. His writing is slow. → He writes slowly.*

$\overset{\text{o o}}{wh}$ indicates a *wh* which is followed by the zeroing of the preceding N, i.e. the N which had been common to the two sentences connected by the *wh.*

> $\big\{$ X is small compared with Y
> $\big($ wh: X is a velocity of common experience
> → X which is a velocity of common experience
>   is small compared with Y
> → velocity of common experience is small
>   compared with Y.

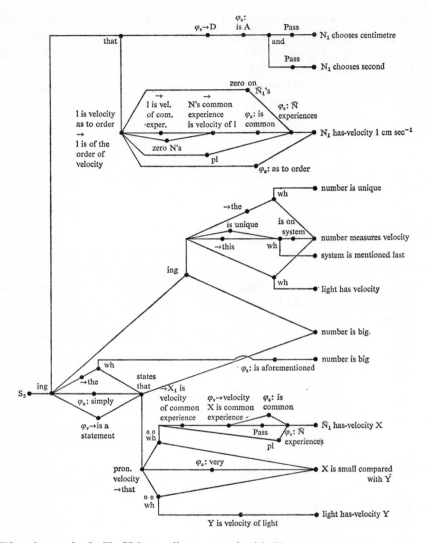

We take as single K: X is small-compared-with Y

and: X is large-compared-with Y

like the comparative K: X exceeds Y, X is larger than Y

and: X equals Y, X is as large as Y.

S_5 shows some of the zeroings of adjunct Ň, not shown elsewhere.

XXIX

ALGEBRAIC OPERATIONS IN LINGUISTIC STRUCTURE

Mathematical linguistics includes on one hand the applications of mathematical calculation to investigations of the systemic phenomena of natural language. On the other, it includes the study of the objects of linguistics as mathematical objects. The latter is possible because natural language, which is a set of discourses (utterances), can be described as a distinguished subset of sequences in a set of arbitrary symbols. The interest here is not in constructing a mathematically definable system which has some limited relation to language (as a simplification or a generalization or a small subset of it), but in formulating in a mathematical system precisely those properties sufficient and necessary to characterize the whole of natural language and its unique power.

The fact that grammatical elements are arbitrary is seen as follows: In every known language, the elements (sounds, words) which enter into grammatical relations (i.e. into interrelated combinations in various discourses) are pre-set in each user of the language. That is, they have to be learned, and are not just understood directly through any inherent relation to their meanings. The elements are also discrete: Speech-sounds, it is true, are continuous, but the elements of the grammar are only certain distinctions among the speech-sounds, particular to each language. Both the sound-distinctions, and also the words (each identified by a sequence of sound-distinctions) differ in different languages, in a manner unrelated to any differences among the meanings expressed in the different languages. The discrete and socially fixed pre-set words are necessarily arbitrary sound-sequences: they cannot be determined by the continuous and changing world of meanings and by individually differing experience.

A further necessary property is the redundancy of language. In every discourse, the elements are linearly ordered. The set of grammatical elements and relations is finite: their number is limited by the fact that they are individually learned. The set of discourses (and sentences) is denumerable. Because natural languages are apprehendable without reference to any prior language (as in a person's first language), it must be the case that not

Read to the International Congress of Mathematicians, Moscow 1966.

604 STRUCTURAL AND TRANSFORMATIONAL LINGUISTICS

all the combinations of elements appear in discourses; for the location of word-boundaries among the successive sounds, and the identification of the words, depends upon the high redundancy of the elements in discourses, i.e. the non-occurrence of many sound and word sequences. Discovering which sequences occur, and which do not, is an empirical problem for each language. Finding general ways of characterizing the ones that occur is the central problem of structural linguistics. In mathematical linguistics, one seeks to formulate this characterization as mappings among subsets of a set of arbitrary objects.

Various mathematical applications are used in determining the grammatical elements for a particular language, and in characterizing the combinations of them which occur in discourses.

In determining the elements, the particular sound-distinctions, which are represented by the phonemes (roughly, letters of the alphabet) for a given language, are determined from the agreement of hearer and speaker in distinguishing utterances which are not repetitions of each other; an utterance is thus identified by its sequential distinctions from all utterances which are not repetitions of it. A discourse can then be segmented into its successive words by introducing, among the successive phonemes or letters, the boundaries of words and of morphemes (which are the affixes and stems in words). This can be done by taking a large number of discourses which have the same first n letters and counting how any different $(n+1)$th letters appear in them. Each value of n for which the count at $n+1$ (after various adjustments) is a maximum is a word or morpheme boundary. Word boundaries are thus points of greater freedom for phoneme combination in a set of discourses. This result is due to the fact that the redundancy in language is unevenly distributed through the length of discourses, in a way which permits the defining of segments of a discourse which are sequences of classes of smaller segments.

In characterizing the combinations of words which occur in a discourse: we first collect words or morphemes into a few classes on the basis of gross properties of occurrence, and within each of these into a large number of subclasses. If this were not possible, the set of grammatical relations could be as large as the set of all subsequences of sentences. The constraints on the combinations of word classes, i.e. on the occurrence of one class due to the occurrence of other classes in the neighborhood, can be stated within the bounds of a certain segmentation of discourses; these segments are called sentences. Beyond this, there are constraints on what combinations of sentences occur in a discourse (more exactly, how the word-choices in one sentence are determined by the word-choices in neighboring sentences).

One constraint, the string property, provides that every sentence of a language can be analyzed as containing an elementary sentence (a center string) to which have been adjoined certain other strings. Each elementary string is a stated sequence of word-classes, and is a member of a particular class of strings; each language has a reasonably small number of string-classes (about 20). Each class of strings is defined by the property that its members adjoin strings of particular other classes at particular points in those strings. The rule for deriving all sentences from the center strings states that the class of center strings is the elementary subclass of the class of sentences, and that the result of adjoining a string of some class A to a string of some class B is a string of class B. In this way, a sentence has the word-class sequence of an elementary sentence, with certain other word-class sequences inserted. The interpretation is that each inserted sequence is subsidiary to its host.

A further constraint, the constituent property, provides that if the inserted string is defined in respect to a particular part of the host string, it is inserted immediately (aside from repetition of such insertion) to the right or left of that part. This makes a modifier contiguous to the particular word it modifies, within the host string, so that a sentence appears constructed from whole constituents (a subject with its modifiers, a verb with its modifiers, etc.). However, there are some insertions which do not obey this constraint, and more so in some languages than in others.

A third constraint, the transformational property, provides that every sentence of a language can be decomposed into elementary sentences of the language with transformations on these, a transformation being a relation between a sentence, or a pair of sentences, and a sentence. In this way, each sentence contains the word-sequences (in their word-class assignments) of one or more elementary sentences, each component word-sequence or pair of these being recast by particular transformations. The traces which these transformations leave in the sentence are permutations, additions of fixed morphemes, and word-omissions. Each language has a number of transformations (about 100), in only a few (about 5) types of traces. The string and constituent properties appear as constraints on the traces produced by the transformations, the most important such constraint being that for all except a small number of transformations, the resultant of a transformation is similar to an elementary sentence: i.e. transformations defined on elementary sentences can operate also on resultants of transformations.

We turn now to the other activity in mathematical linguistics, formulating linguistic objects as mathematical objects. The richest material for this lies in the set of sentences under transformations. For this reason, we now consider this relation, which can be defined in several ways. We begin by noting that word-sequences are not simply in or out of the set of sentences. Rather, a word-sequence may be a completely acceptable sentence (e.g. *This book fell upon the cup*), or one which is accepted as a metaphor, joke, etc. (*His words fell upon deaf ears*), or nonsensical (*This book climbed the cup*), or as occurring in particular technical subject-matter (*These values approach infinity*), etc.; one can also readily find a word-sequence for which speakers of the language disagree or are uncertain as to whether it is a sentence (e.g. *The rabbit took a run. The cup was fallen upon by this book*). In any given sentence form, i.e. any sequence of word-classes (as variables) with possibly some fixed words (constants), the sentences of that form (having particular word-choices as values of the variables) can thus be partially ordered in respect to types of acceptability, or classified in respect to type of discourse.[1] We then find that there exist other sentence-forms of the same word-classes in which the word-choices have the same acceptability-ordering or discourse-classification. E.g. under the passage from $N_1 V N_2$ to *It is N_1 that $V N_2$*, we have, corresponding with the above examples: *It was this book that fell upon the cup. It was his words that fell upon deaf ears. It was this book that climbed the cup. It is these values that approach infinity. It was the rabbit that took a run. It was the cup that was fallen upon by this book.*[2] Given two sentence-forms, defined over the same domain of the variables, in which the acceptability-ordering or discourse-classification of the choices of values is preserved under the passage from one form to the other, we say that for each of these choices of values, the sentence A_i obtained in one form A is a transform of the sentence B_i obtained in the other form B: $A_i = \varphi B_i$. We say that A_i contains (the trace of) φ. The difference φ between A_i and B_i is a transformation.

These transformations constitute an equivalence relation among sentences, and provide a partition of the set of sentences. Because products of certain transformations are degenerate (produce the same trace), one can find a word-sequence appearing in more than one partition, in which case it is ambiguous and can be considered to be more than one homonymous sentence.[3] If each transformation over a given domain of the variables is taken in one direction, we can obtain a mapping of the set of sentences onto the set of transformations, where each sentence is sent to the transformation (or transformational product) whose trace it contains. The kernel of this mapping is then the finite set of elementary sentences which go into the identity transformation. These 'kernel sentences' are the ones into which every sentence can be decomposed via transformations. It is possible, instead of defining the transformations as operating on sentences, to define them as operating on elementary sentences and on transformations. This yields a finitary system of arguments for the transformations, and establishes in the set of transformations a structure of how transformations operate on each other. When the set of transformations is investigated, it further turns out that (in the few languages so far checked) all transformations are products in a set of base transformations which has only some five types of structure. Among these, the conjunctions have a special property, of requiring each value of a variable in the conjoined sentences to occur in more than one sentence. As a result, the conjunctions can be treated (like the other transformations) as unary operations on a sentence, since to a given sentence S_i a given conjunction C_j appends not any arbitrary sentence but only one out of a set of sentences which is determined by S_i, C_j. They can also be treated as binary operations in the set of sentences, if we say that C_j on an arbitrary pair S_i, S_k produces not $S_i C_j S_k$ but $S_i CS \ldots CSC_j S_k$, the intervening CS being from a set determined by C_j, S_i, S_k.

Several structures of interest can be defined in the set of sentences on the basis of the transformations. For example, we can decompose a sentence into its elementary sentences, by first carrying out all the transformations which are defined, in the direction of decomposition (from the given sentence to the elementary sentences), on the sentence-form of that sentence. This yields a sentence, on which we then repeat the process, until we reach the elementary sentences. We thus obtain a partially ordered set of transformations taking us from the given sentence to the set of its residual elementary sentences. If a word-sequence is ambiguous, it will decompose into more than one set of elementary sentences (or, in certain situations, elementary sentences with particular transformations). For each word-sequence and set of its residual sentences, the lattice of the intervening decompositional transformations is unique. We can thus pair each sentence S_i with a set of elementary (or otherwise residual) sentences $\{S_{Ri}\}$, in such a way that each word-sequence which is n-fold ambiguous has n different pairings. There is a homomorphism from the set of these pairings onto the set of sentences, such that each pairing identifies one grammatical meaning (or analysis) of its first member. Each of these pairings, $(S_i, \{S_{Ri}\}_j)$ for each i, j, is unambiguous, and the set of them is indeed the minimal set of subsets of sentences which maps homomorphically onto the whole set of sentences but which contains no ambiguity. One can also ask how to construct a maximal such set.

From each S_i-pairing lattice of transformations we can form a graph whose vertices are all the partial sentences of S_i under that pairing, i.e. all the sentences which can be formed from any residual sentences of that lattice by any of its ordered transformations. If S_i (in a certain pairing) is itself a partial sentence of some S_j (in a corresponding pairing) the graph for S_i will be a subgraph of the graph for S_j. Since for every sentence there is some sentence of which it is a partial, and for any two sentences there is some sentence of which both are partials, the graphs of all sentences are subgraphs of one graph. The properties of this graph (which would present a single sentence which includes all sentences of the language) are of course of some interest; and the question arises whether a different graph could be constructed from it in which each sentence of the language occurs only once.

We now introduce another property of language in respect to which interesting subsets of the set of sentences can be defined. This is the fact that every natural language, like the formal languages, can be characterized by an axiomatic system: a vocabulary of symbols (word-subclasses), an elementary set of well-formed sequences of these (sentence-forms or strings), and a derivation rule which from well-formed sequences produces well-formed sequences. The string and transformational analyses mentioned above are examples of such axiomatizations. We consider, in the set of sentences, a subset whose axiomatization intersects with, and is not a proper part of, the axiomatization of the whole set. This situation occurs in natural language: an example is a body of scientific writing. The technical terms of a science constitute special word-classes which occur only in particular well-formed sequences. Many of the same words exist in the language as a whole, but not in special classes and without these special sentence-forms. There are thus some axioms for the sentences in science which do not occur for the sentences of the language as a whole. On the other hand, there are certain types of sentences which occur in natural language but not in its science subset, e.g. poetic forms. Thus there are axioms for the whole language which do not occur for the sentences of its science subset. We can now make a conjecture that, for S_s in the science subset and S_l in the language but not in the science subset, the resultant of a binary operation C_i on (S_s, S_l) is again a sentence of the science subset. This is suggested by the fact that the C_i would require the addition of further CS until the words of S_s are repeated in the resultant, with the presumed effect that the subject-matter of S_s is preserved in the resultant.

A more important property of language involving a special subset of its sentences is that the metalanguage of a language is itself a set of sentences and a subset of the whole language. This includes the axiomatization, every grammatical description of the language, and all such individual sentences of the metalanguage as 'S_i' *is a sentence of English*. Various results ensue, such as the fact that certain impredicative sentences, the syntactic core of the paradoxes, which name a sentence within itself (*This sentence is...*), can be separated off from other sentences. An important result is the fact that metadiscourse sentences can be inserted into the discourse about which they speak: if some discourse occurs only in particular circumstances, we can conjoin this statement about the discourse to the discourse itself. This not only makes the definition of all linguistic objects independent of any outside universe, but also makes possible the regularization of the word-repeating requirement of conjunctions. As an example of the metalanguage subset of sentences, we note that each transformational lattice of S_i can be read as a metalinguistic sentence (*Transformation A operates on residual sentence B*) which in turn has a lattice which can be read as a sentence, and so on. Similarly, the simpler process of going from S_i to 'S_i' *is a sentence* can be repeated without end. The set of non-metalinguistic sentences can be mapped isomorphically, in several different ways, onto a set of metalinguistic sentences, which are carried by the same isomorphism onto a further set of metalinguistic sentences, and so on without end. For each sentence (in particular, each non-metalinguistic one) there are several denumerable sets of metalinguistic ones.

There are also other sets, not referrable to transformations, which can be defined and their structure studied. For example, since there are only a few string-relations that a word can have to its next neighbor in a sentence, we can define symbols (which include right and left inverses) representing all the string-relations that each word-class can have to each class which neighbors it in any sentence. When a sentence is represented by sequences of these symbols, a cycling automaton, which cancels every pair consisting of a symbol and its inverse, suffices to check whether an arbitrary word sequence is a sentence, and of what string structure. The structure of this set of symbols, and the structure of a sentence as represented by these, differs from the other sets defined in linguistics.

Since the structures mentioned above related mostly to the central linguistic problem of characterizing what occurs in discourse, we can now consider what is the mathematical form of the whole theory of language. Pure constituent and string theories deal with regular word-sequences, but their entities (sentences) are one-many with respect to grammatical meaning (being ambiguous), and with respect to regularity of neighborhood within discourses. Transformational theory deals with discourses.[4] A discourse (in contrast with an arbitrary assemblage of sentences) has a certain type of structure of its own. A sentence S_i within a discourse has a word-choice relation to neighboring sentences, and can be paired with transforms of S_i which have the same word-choice relation to their neighboring sentences. Discourses are unambiguous (or can be extended to be so), as are sentences paired to neighboring word-choices, or sentences paired to appropriate transforms (in particular, to their residual sentences). Transformational theory is thus a theory of sentence pairs; its adequacy is supported by the claim that no word-sequence is a sentence without being a member of a transformational sentence-pair.[5]

Mathematical linguistics is still undeveloped. Many more structures, involving various fields of mathematics, may still be found in it. So far, the structures have been from abstract algebra: mappings and relations between them. Semi-groups, and in particular free semi-groups, easily describe language; but groups are not found, because inverses occur very limitedly in the structures so far defined. There are partially ordered sets, and systems of partial transformations, with various restrictions that suggest structures of interest. There are certain kinds of graphs. There are interesting problems of recursion and automata, with various methods for enumerating the set of sentences or other sets. Stochastic processes appear, but in limited ways. The structure of formal languages and of programming languages is closely related to part of natural language structure. Mathematical logic serves as a tool in investigating and formulating the material, rather than as an equivalent system (because of the absence in natural language of an equivalent to truth tables).

The results of structural and mathematical linguistics have various applications. They provide explications or solutions to many problems involving language, sentence, meaning, and the like: e.g. that ambiguity and paraphrase arise from particular types of transformation-succession in a lattice; that one can determine the presumably intended meaning of a sentence by relating its decompositions to those of neighboring sentences. They provide necessary material for theories of discourse and of semantic information: e.g. that information involves the repeating of words, and discourse involves the repeating of elementary sentences. They define a normal form for each sentence of the language, in such a way that the similarities and differences among sentences can be stated in a unique way which correlates with their informational relations. They provide methods for computer analysis of each sentence into elementary sentences plus transformations, or into strings. This has been done in various ways, including by an automaton, or by a single scan which gives a picture of what can be understood serially at each successive word of the sentence. Finally, because of the close correspondence between the (computer) normalization of a sentence and the information in the sentence, it should be possible to devise computer processing and comparing of the information contained in scientific articles, and it may be possible to see something of the structure of the language of science.

NOTES

[1] This may have to be generalized to say that in each sentence-form, the sentences have $n \geqslant 1$ acceptances each, and the sentences are ordered or classified for each of the n values.

[2] In contrast, the passage from $N_1\ V N_2$ to $N_2\ V N_1$ would yield *The cup fell upon the book* (acceptable), *Deaf ears fell upon his words* (nonsensical and not a metaphor), *Infinity approaches this value* (not in the same technical subject-matter as the example above), *A run took the rabbit* (nonsensical rather than uncertain), etc. N: noun, V: verb.

[3] But in this paper it is considered one sentence, with ambiguity.

[4] In principle, discourse neighborhood can replace the acceptability criterion.

[5] This statement is made possible by the fact that even idioms and other grammatical exceptions can be formulated as extensions of existing grammatical rules.

XXX

THE TWO SYSTEMS OF GRAMMAR:
REPORT AND PARAPHRASE

Transformation and Discourse Analysis Papers 79 (1969).

1. INTRODUCTION

1.0. *Summary*

From an attempt to isolate the independent elements of sentence construction, we arrive at two different and separately acting grammatical systems, which contribute to this construction: a system of predicates (with *and, or*) and a system which can be considered an extension of morphophonemics (which is change purely of phonemic sequences). The predicate system carries all the objective information in the sentence, and the most natural interpretation of its structure is that of giving a report. The morphophonemic system is interpretable as being paraphrastic, and changes at most the speaker's or hearer's relation to the report. The grammar of the language as a whole is simply the resultant of these two systems.

The method used to obtain this result arises from the characteristic problem of structural linguistics: that not all combinations of elements, but only certain ones, occur as acceptable sentences. This limitation is clearly related to the information-bearing power of language. We see this relation in the fact that elements whose environments are complementary to each other (e.g. *am* and *are* in *I am going, You are going*) cannot be the bearers of informational differences (unless their different neighbors are then zeroed); and elements whose environments differ in particular ways have corresponding differences in meaning.

If element A requires element B in its environment, or if all of the environments of A have certain similarities and differences with respect to all of the environments of B, then we say that A is (syntactically) dependent on B.

The question now arises whether we can isolate all these dependences (i.e. restrictions on element-combination) into particular paraphrastic transforms of the restricted sentences, leaving other transforms of the same sentences without the restrictions. This is achieved by showing that one can obtain, within transformational methods, unrestricted free or automatic source-sentences for all sentences which contain restricted word-combinations (§§ 2, 3), and by showing that forms which are restricted to particular subsets of words (having particular properties) can be derived without resort to this dependence (§ 4).

The set of restrictionless transforms that is obtained contains paraphrases of all sentences of the language. It is a sublanguage, closed under the non-paraphrastic transformations (6.2, 3), and in it the choices and the relative positions of words are not affected by any dependences aside from a few very general formation-rules (7.2, 7.5). Within these basic structures of sentences, and within the limits of the vocabulary, the word-combinations are determined solely by the combinations of information (more precisely, the report) that is being expressed. This sublanguage can be put into an operator form far simpler than is possible for the language as a whole (§ 5). The operators in the construction of a sentence are apparently linearly ordered. They consist of predicates (verb; or *be* plus adjective or noun or preposition) or *and*, *or*; each resultant of an operator is formed by placing the operator word after its first argument, thus forming the word sequence that is the sentence.

The sublanguage carries all the objective information, or report, which is carried in the language, and can be used without the rest of the language. Indeed, every sentence of the language can be decomposed (by an algorithm) into a sentence of the report-sublanguage (containing all that is reported in the original sentence) plus various paraphrastic transformations. But if the sentence contains pronouns or other referentials (including covert ones) whose antecedent can be in some other sentence of the discourse, this antecedent cannot in general be determined by a sentence-decomposing algorithm. A discourse in the language can be reduced to one in the sublanguage by reducing each sentence to its source in this sublanguage. Many sentences, more precisely word-sequences that can be read as a sentence, are grammatically ambiguous, i.e. have more than one source from which they could be transformationally derived. This is due to transformational degeneracies: different transformations which yield the same word-sequence, or zeroings and pronounings of different material. In many cases, a comparison of the alternative sources of a sentence with those of neighboring sentences in the discourse shows which of its sources best fits which source of the neighbors. The report which is carried in the original discourse is preserved in the reduced discourse, aside from ambiguities; but now various processings of the information in the reduced discourse can be performed in orderly ways that were unavailable for the original discourse.

In the sublanguage the connection between the simple syntactic relations in it and the meaning of words and classes becomes much sharper than in the language as a whole. Investigation of what kind of information can be borne in language, and how language can be modified to carry other kinds of information, is made possible by analysis of the structure of this report-sublanguage, in which every item of structure is relevant to the informational burden that language carries. The few types of predicates (7.2) which impose and preserve partial orderings in their operands,[1] together with *and*, *or*, are found to be sufficient and necessary for the information that language can carry. And the simple method of placing the fixed-argument operator-word (the predicate or *and* or *or*) between the argument words (7.5) is found sufficient to enable a parentheses-less string of words (i.e. a sentence) to indicate the operator-structured information that language carries.

The whole of the rest of the language can be derived out of this sublanguage, as source, by a system of paraphrastic transformations (morphophonemics of syntactic sequences), which themselves have a particular grammatical structure, and a subjective (or purely paraphrastic) semantic character. They bring in no new independent words (or new report) into the sentence, but are especially useful for abbreviation. It is these paraphrastic transformations that bring in grammatical ambiguity and complex (and simultaneously differing) string relations (affixes and positionings) among the words of the sentence.

One can, of course, make a description of the whole language, but it is now possible to see that there is no coherent structure in the grammar of a whole language. The whole grammar is a resultant of two quite different structures, the second operating on the prior one. Each system is coherent, as being derivable from a tightly interrelated set of primitives, in a way that the whole grammar is not; and each has a natural interpretation. Together they account for the forms and the interpretation (meaning) of the whole language.

1.1. *An Extension of Transformational Analysis*

In transformational analysis, we define over the set of sentences of a language some of them wholly acceptable and some less so, an equivalence relation 'transformation' (written ↔) between two subsets of sentences, each being of a particular sentence-form.[2] This relation preserves the acceptability-ordering of the corresponding sentences of the two forms. It has been found that there are two types of transformations: One, the paraphrastic (T), holds between two sentence-forms, A, B, each having the independent variables $x_1, x_2, ..., x_n$, when each ordered set of n-tuples of values of these variables determines the same acceptability-ordering for the sentences it produces out of A as for those it produces out of B.

The other, the incremental, holds between two sentence-sets, B of m variables, and C containing these m variables and at least one additional variable called C's increment, when, given an ordered set of m-tuples of values of the common m variables, the acceptability-ordering which this set of m-tuples determines for the sentences of B is related in certain readily summarizable ways to the acceptability-ordering it determines for the sentences of C. The chief relation is the following: Let A be a sentence-set of the variables $x_1, ..., x_{m-1}$ with an acceptability-ordering for the $m-1$-tuples of values, B a sentence-set of the same variables with an incremental x_m, and C a sentence-set of the same m variables with an incremental x_{m+1}. Then for each value of x_{m+1} in C, the acceptability-ordering for the $m-1$-tuples of values of $x_1, ..., x_{m-1}$ in respect to each value of x_m is the same as it is in B.[2a] Thus the ordering of the sentences of C consists, in this case, of an ordering of x_m for each value of x_{m+1} and an ordering of the $m-1$-tuples of values for each value of x_m, the latter ordering being carried over from B and there from A.

Thus we have a paraphrastic transformation between *N V Aly* and *N's Ving is A*, as in:

The ball rolls slowly,   and: The ball's rolling is slow
(both normal word-choices, even though the second is less comfortable),

The rock rolls slowly,   and: The rock's rolling is slow
(both normal word-choices),

The photon rolls slowly,   and: The photon's rolling is slow
(both peculiar or nonsensical).

In contrast, there is no transformation between $N_1 V N_2$ and $N_2 V N_1$:

A truck carried a boat,   and: A boat carried a truck
(both normal), but

Man invented ether, and: Ether invented man
(the first normal, the second nonsensical).

And we have an incremental transformation in the increment *slowly* (or *is slow*), as is seen in the fact that, with *roll* as value of x_m we have the same acceptability-ordering for *The ball rolls slowly, The rock rolls slowly, The photon rolls slowly* as for *The ball rolls, The rock rolls* (both normal) and *The photon rolls* (peculiar or nonsensical). In contrast, *The man slept* is normal, and *The microbe slept* is peculiar, but both *The man slept slowly*, and *The microbe slept slowly* are peculiar. Thus *slowly* (as x_{m+1}) preserves the acceptability of sentences with *roll* (as x_m) but reduces it for sentences with *sleep* (as x_m). Increments impose an ordering upon their immediate argument (which is the x_m in this case), and the acceptability-ordering of their resultant sentences (C, here) is a product of the ordering of x_m under the increment, and the ordering of the $m-1$-tuples for each x_m.

The increment in C may therefore be considered an operator (note 1) operating on the $x_1, ..., x_m$ sentence-form and altering in a particular way the acceptability produced there by the m-tuples of values.

In some cases of A↔B, one or more of the variables in B has a domain e which is only a proper subset of its domain d in A: we write A(d) for A over domain d, and B $(e \subset d)$. In such cases, the transformation holds only for the smaller domain e (of B); or else we can define a directed transformational operator A→B, more precisely A(d)→B$(e \subset d)$, which derives B$(e \subset d)$ out of A(d) as a transform of A over the smaller domain e.

This is not the only situation in which a directed transformation, →, is defined. In some transformational work there is a different, though not conflicting, interest in defining an operator →. Because there are degenerate transformations, so that there can be T_i: A→B and T_j: C→B, we may find that the domain of some variable x_i in the A-form is a proper subset of the domain of x_i in B. In these degenerate cases, the domain of x_i in B is completely covered by the domains of x_i in A, C, and in any other proposed sources for the form B. The situation is different for the analysis proposed in this paper. Here if the domain of x_i in B is only a proper subset of the domain of x_i in A, then there are no transforms, different from B, which cover the residue of the domain of x_i in A. In such a case we must take A as the source, from which B is derived. For if we did not, then indeed A could be derived from B (instead of B from A) for that part of the domain of x_i which is common to both A and B; but the A form for the residue of the domain of x_i would still have to be formed in A, since by assumption it could not be derived from any other form over that residual domain.

The methods proposed in the present paper examine the domains of the transformations, in particular the incremental ones, and thereby determine a particular organization of the transformations. The chief method used here will show that, given an incremental A(d)→B$(e \subset d)$, we can find some sentence-form B*(d) (of the same independent variables as B$(e \subset d)$, but without the reduction of domain in any variable), such that A(d)↔B*(d) is an unrestricted incremental transformation and B*(d)→B$(e \subset d)$ is a restricted paraphrastic transformation.[3] Finding B*(d) makes it possible to separate increments from domain-restriction, i.e. to remove domain-restriction from the increments.

1.2. *An Extension of Free Variation in Structural Linguistics*

From the point of view of linguistic structure the methods proposed here investigate free variation among morphemic elements. Structural linguistics deals with the distribution of elements, i.e. the environmental restrictions on their combinability in making sentences of the language. The fundamental relations are: two elements A, B, may be complementary variants of each other (if all sentence-making environments of A differ in part from all those of B); or they may be free variants of each other (if B occurs in the same environments as A, and if sentences which differ only in having B instead of A are considered structurally equivalent); or else they are distinct ('contrastive'). In phonology, complementary variants are well known (e.g. English unaspirated *t* after *s* but aspirated *t* after word-initial), as are free variants (e.g. English released and unreleased *t* before word-end). In morphology, only complementary variants are well known. They occur with small phonemic difference (e.g. *knive-* before plural, but *knife* otherwise) and with large (e.g. *be* after *to* and the auxiliaries or before *-ing*, *am* after *I*, *are* after *you* and plural, *is* otherwise). Complementary variation is known not only for A, B at identical positions of their respective environments, but also in more complicated cases; e.g. the discontiguous morphemic entity, which consists of a plural suffix after the noun and a (perhaps different) plural suffix after the adjective is complementary to the non-discontiguous plural suffix after an adjective-less noun: the former occurs only when the environment contains noun plus adjective (*-s ... -s* in *Il y a deux erreurs graves*), and the latter only when the environment contains only a noun and no adjective (*-s* in *Il y a deux erreurs*).

Free variants are hardly considered in morphology. There are a few cases with small phonemic difference; e.g. *ekənamiks* and *iykənamiks* for *economics* pronounced with initial *e* or *i y*; or *I'll* and *I will*. And there may be a few with large phonemic difference: e.g. *etcetera* and *and so on*. But there is no recognition of any large system of free variation, or of free variation which involves various positions distributed thoughout the sentence, and so on. One reason for this non-recognition was the lack of instances where such free variation was of use in the formulation of morphological structure. Another was the question of what criterion would determine that a given A and B were in free variation to each other, i.e. what would determine that sentences with A were to be considered equivalent to those having B instead of A.

The syntactic relevance of recognizing morphological free variants may be seen for example in the fact that this relation is necessary in order to obtain the analyses proposed in this paper; and the morpheme sequences which are found to be free variants of each other are not similar in phonemic composition, and are in some cases not similar in the sentential position they occupy, or even in their immediate syntactic statuses. As to the criterion for determing that sentences containing A are equivalent to those containing B (as free variant) instead of A: it is that replacing A by B does not change the acceptability-ordering of the sentences. In other words, sentences with A are paraphrastic transforms of sentences having B instead of A.

In particular, there is one type of paraphrastic transformation which assures the possibility of the type of analysis proposed in this paper. This is due to the fact that not only does every language contain meta-linguistic sentences (including definitions and grammatical statements), but also every sentence S_i can have conjoined to it or operating upon it all the grammatical and definitional statements about it. S_i with these added meta-statements can then be considered as the source for S_i, which is derived from the source by zeroing the known metastatements.[3a] If a restricted or non-predicate apparent increment I has no free variant which is unrestricted and of predicate form, we can always operate on the I-bearing sentences with a metastatement M defining the I. M need not contain the I restriction, and can be in the form of a predicate on the I-bearing sentence. Under the M operator, the I would be a morphophonemic entity due to the M which defines it and states its presence in the operand of M. The I-bearing sentence is then a morphophonemic variant of the sentence having the M operator.

The inclusion of free variation as a relation utilized within morphology completes the utilization of the fundamental relations of structural linguistics. In the present paper this relation is used for the existing vocabulary of language. It can later be used (§ 9) in conditions that go beyond the vocabulary, somewhat as phonemic long components used complementary variants beyond the conditions of sequential phonemes.

2. UNRESTRICTED FREE VARIANTS FOR RESTRICTED OPERATORS

The whole work of distributional linguistics has been to replace restricted elements by less restricted ones. In transformational analysis, a restricted transformational operator is one whose domain is only a proper subset of the domain of its operand: e.g. the apparent transformation $NV \rightarrow N$ be $Ving$ does not apply to certain V ($\nexists$ I am $knowing$). The major method of the present paper involves a reformulation of each restricted incremental operator, in such a way that the restriction to a subdomain applies only to a paraphrastic transformation which follows after the increment has operated. This is achieved mainly by finding an unrestricted free variant for the restricted increment (§ 2), secondarily by adding to the grammar unrestricted morphophonemic sources for the restricted forms (§ 3), and finally by finding for the grammatically restricted lists (sub-classes) of words certain environing words whose presence can determine the subclass properties (§ 4).

2.1. *Be-ing*

The *be-ing* operator which yields, e.g. *I am writing poetry* from *I write poetry* has a restricted domain in that it does not operate on certain verbs: $\not\exists$ *I am knowing English*, $\not\exists$ *I am owning a car*. If we seek free variants for this operator on the verb, we find them in a few perhaps stilted operators on the sentence such as *be in process, be on: My writing poetry is in process*. Although these are in themselves far less comfortable than *be-ing*, the acceptability-ordering (and nuance) of sentences with *be in process* (or its equivalents) and of those with *be-ing* is approximately the same for the same sets of word-values.[4] The passage between these sentence-forms is accomplished by well-established transformations over these domains. First the argument-skipping transformation (8.1 (9)):

> My writing poetry is in process → I am in process of writing
>   poetry.

as in:

> My driving is slow → I am slow in driving.

And then:

> I am in process of writing poetry → I am writing poetry.

by zeroing of *in process of* as a constant of this form, i.e. as the only segment which is zeroable to produce *N is Ving* with unchanged object of *Ving*. The derivational connection between *be in process* and *be-ing* is supported by the fact that *be in process* has the same domain restriction[5]: One would not say *My knowing English is in process, My owning a car is in process*. However, what makes this derivation of interest to our present purposes is the fact that whereas the domain restriction of *be-ing* is more or less an unbreakable grammatical rule, in the case of *be in process* it appears rather as a matter of selection (co-occurrence), which can be changed by adding operators that would affect the reasonableness of the selection, or by cultural changes in what it is acceptable to say. Thus we can extend the selectional domain by adding something which really treats the owning of a car as a process, e.g. *My owning a car is finally in process*; this may then extend with some difficulty to *I am finally owning a car*, although in the latter both the acceptability and the meaning are more uncertain. Also if one can some day trace the course of neurophysiological processing of knowing, which so far has not been seen as a process, we may be able to say *My knowing English is in process*. We thus have an increment *be in process*, which makes no restriction on its operand sentences, except for selection; and a paraphrase (zeroing to *be-ing*) which freezes this selection as a grammatical restriction. Extensions of the selection, as in *My owning a car is finally in process*, are not readily zeroed to *be-ing*.

A major respect in which the source proposed here is unrestricted is in the possibilities of further increments on this increment. *Be-ing* cannot be nominalized: From *I write* we have *My writing is regrettable*, but for (1) *I am writing*, ∄ *My being writing is regrettable*. In other forms, *be* is nominalizable by *-ing*: *My being here is regrettable*. This restriction does not apply to the source form, which can be nominalized under operators: From (2) *My writing is in process* we have (3) *My writing being in process is regrettable*. Here as in many other examples below the source form is uncomfortable, but becomes more comfortable when something is added, as in (4) *My writing being still only in process is regrettable*. The only source from which the expanded form (4) can be directly derived, by certain incremental operators, is (3); hence (3) must exist. The reason for (4) being more comfortable than (3) is that (3) is derived from (2) which is overshadowed by its short transform (1), whereas (4) is derived from (5) *My writing is still only in process*, which is not as fully overshadowed by its short transform (6) *I am still only writing*. And the reason for (5) being less overshadowed than (2) is presumably that the increments *still only* which operate on the 'continuative' operator of (1), (2) as their argument, are more explicitly related to their argument in its source form (*is in process*, in (5), where they appear as adjuncts on it) than in its short transform (*is ... ing*, in (6)).

2.2. *Very*

While most adverbs of degree (e.g. *considerably*) occur with (modify) all predicate forms, both verb and adjective, the adverb *very* does not occur with verbs. This makes it seem that there is here an intrinsically different modifier for adjectives. We can find, however, free variants of *very*, such as *to a great extent*, which occur freely with all predicate forms: *He favors is to a great extent*, *He is favorable to it to a great extent*, *He is cold to a great extent*. We can then say that there is an unrestricted operator on sentence (in effect, on predicates) *to a great extent*; and that over the adjective subset of predicates (e.g. *cold*, *favorable*) this has a free variant *very*, which provides the same acceptability-ordering as does *to a great extent*. This analysis simplifies the transformational connection in such sentence pairs as

> The room darkened to a great extent

and

> The room became very dark (←The room became dark to a great extent).

If *very* were not a transform of an adverb which operates also on verbs, we would not be able to derive the sentences with deverbal adjectives (e.g. *He is very fussy*) from their verb sources (e.g. *He fusses to a great extent*).

2.3. *Adverbs of Manner*

About adverbs of manner two restrictions are known: In their predicate form they require the *of*-nominalization of their operand: *His driving of the car is quite slow,* ∄ *His driving the car is quite slow* (whereas for time-adverbs both nominalizations occur: *His driving of the car is quite frequent, His driving the car is quite frequent*). And only a particular subclass of morphemes occurs as manner-adverbs (as others are time-adverbs, etc.), in some cases depending on the verb. Thus *unexpectedly* is an adverb of fact: *He pronounced my name unexpectedly* ← *That he pronounced my name was unexpected*. *Continuously* is an adverb of time-distribution: *He rubbed it continuously* ← *His rubbing it continued*. *Unfairly* is of fact or of manner, depending on the verb: *He tipped them off unfairly* ← *That he tipped them off was unfair*; *He divided the gifts unfairly* ← *His dividing of the gifts was unfair* (*in manner*). However, we can find for these adverbs certain free variants of them which are not restricted:

> He pronounced my name in an unexpected manner.
> He rubbed it in a continuous manner.
> He tipped them off in an unfair manner.

In all these cases *in A manner* ↔ *Aly* (writing *A* for adjective). The restriction of particular *A*, to being manner-adverbs or other adverbs, is therefore not in the increment *in A manner*, which is available for all adjectives within selectional dependence upon the verb, but in the paraphrastic change *in ... manner* → *-ly* which is used only for adjectives that are characteristically manner, or are such for the given verb.

Furthermore, although *of* is required as above when *manner* is absent, we find nominalization without *of* when *manner* is present: *His driving of the car is slow in manner, His driving the car is slow in manner, The manner of his driving of the car is slow, The manner of his driving the car is slow*; ∄ *His driving the car is slow*. Here we have a free variant of *A* of manner which is not restricted to *of*; the restriction to *of* occurs for the paraphrastic reduction of *in ... manner* → *-ly*.

2.4. *Subjunctive*

In English the subjunctive occurs under certain operators: under operators on sentence, e.g. *I request that he go there* (as contrasted with *I deny that he goes there* (or *will go*)); and in the second operand of conjunctions on sentence-pairs, e.g. *I won't go for fear* (or: *lest*) *he go there* as contrasted with *I won't go because he goes there* (or *will go*). It thus appears as a grammatical property restricted to these and perhaps other situations. However, we can find free variants in which these operators appear without the subjunctive: *I request his going there*, no different from *I deny his going there*; and *My not going is for fear of his going there*, no different from *My not going is because of his going there*. Hence the increments of the class of the sentence-operator *request* and of the conjunction *for fear* are not restricted to occurring on the subjunctive form of their operand sentence. The domain restriction comes in later, in the paraphrastic free variant of the type

I request his going → I request that he go.

This transformation operates not on all *N's Ving* under sentence operators and conjunctions, but only for the ones under a subdomain of sentence-operators and conjunctions: specifically in English those sentence-operators and conjunctions in which the time-location adverb of the operand sentence is dependent upon the time-location adverb of the sentence-operator or the primary sentence preceding the conjunction.

For *deny*, the time-location adverb of the operand sentence is independent:

I denied yesterday that he went the day before yesterday.
I denied yesterday that he will go tomorrow.
I will deny tomorrow that he went yesterday.
I will deny tomorrow that he will go the day after tomorrow.

But for *request*, the time-location adverb of the operand sentence always indicates a later time than that of *request*; or, less specifically, the operand sentence can be viewed as always containing a (zeroable) time-order adverb *afterwards* or *subsequently*:

I requested the day before yesterday that he go yesterday (or: that he go afterwards).
I requested yesterday that he go tomorrow (or: that he go afterwards).
I will request tomorrow that he go the day after tomorrow (or: that he go afterwards).
∄ I requested yesterday that he go the day before yesterday.
∄ I will request tomorrow that he go yesterday.

Similarly, for *because* we have independent time-adverbs:

I went yesterday because he went the day before yesterday.
I went yesterday because he will go tomorrow.
I will go tomorrow because he went yesterday.
I will go tomorrow because he will go the day after tomorrow.

But for *for fear* or *lest* the second is dependent upon the first:

I went the day before yesterday lest he go yesterday (or: afterwards).

I went yesterday lest he go tomorrow (or: afterwards).

I will go tomorrow lest he go the day after tomorrow (or: afterwards).

∄ I went yesterday lest he go the day before yesterday.

∄ I will go tomorrow lest he go yesterday.

We see then that the paraphrastic free variant transformation from *N's Ving*
to *that NV* (the subjunctive) occurs in operand sentences under those operators which impose a time-location dependence upon the operand (or which,
equivalently, always permit the word *subsequently* (or: *afterwards*) in their
operand). There are, of course, various details which are omitted here. There
are some verbs, e.g. *request*, whose operand always contains *afterwards* and
which never have a tense on their argument. There are some which take
afterwards usually but perhaps not always, and which may therefore sometimes appear with a tensed argument: *I suggest that he go, I suggest that he
possibly went by himself* (or: *I suggest that he might have gone by himself*).
There are some verbs which have both the *afterwards* and the tensed arguments: *I insist that he go, I insist that he went.* In some cases the tensed argument may be of a variant of the untensed: *I prefer that he go, I prefer that he
went now.* In other languages, the subjunctive is determined by morphemes
expressing possibility, not only by morphemes (such as *afterwards*) expressing
time-order.

2.5. *Time-Conjunctions*

If we consider the time-ordering conjunctions *before, after, until, since, while,*
etc., we find complex restrictions as to the tenses of the verbs which they
connect. It has been shown[6] that if certain compound tenses and verbs are
characterized as being either perfective or else imperfective, these restrictions
can be organized into a few readily stateable requirements, e.g. that the verb
following *before* or *after* be perfective (while the verb preceding the conjunction can be either perfective or imperfective), and that either both verbs be
past or else both verbs be future. (The present tense which is replaceable by a
synonymous future tense is considered here as future.) Thus we have:

(1)   He returned (yesterday) before she arrived (yesterday).

(2)   He will return (tomorrow) before she arrives (tomorrow) (or:
         will arrive).

But

(3)   ∄ He will return (tomorrow) before she arrived (yesterday).

(4)   ∄ He returned (yesterday) before she will arrive (tomorrow).

It should be noted that while (3) could be said to be excluded as having an impossible meaning, (4) is perfectly reasonable but grammatically excluded.

As in the preceding cases, it turns out that the language contains free variants which are not restricted, and which are related to (1)–(4) by known paraphrastic transformations:

His return yesterday was before her arrival yesterday.

His return tomorrow will be before her arrival tomorrow.

(5)! His return tomorrow will be before her arrival yesterday.

(6) His return yesterday was (or: will have been) before her arrival tomorrow.

The tenses in (1)–(4) correlate with the time-location adverbs of their verbs. But whereas *before* is restricted to certain tense-pairs, ⌊*be before* ⌋is not restricted by the time-location pairs whose tenses would have restricted *before*. The time-relation which was reasonable but grammatically excluded in (4) is acceptable for *be before* (6). And the time-relation which was unreasonable and grammatically excluded in (3) is not grammatically excluded though still unreasonable here (5). In (5), as in the case of *be-ing*, we have found for a form which is grammatically restricted a free variant which is only selectionally restricted; and, as for *be-ing*, the selectional restriction is changeable due to new sentence-environments or cultural contexts: (5) can indeed be contained in such a sentence as *Gödel's backward-running time could make one's return tomorrow be before one's arrival yesterday*. Thus *before* plus tense is a free variant of *be before* over part of the domain of *be before*: The subdomain is characterized by both of the time-location adverbs under *be before* being such as determine the past tense, or both determining the future tense, and by the second verb being perfective.

It further turns out that all the other ('time-ordering') conjunctions which have such tense and perfectivity restrictions are free variants (preserving acceptability-ordering) of other subdomains of *be before* plus certain additions. First, *be after* plus reflection of operands in the operator (the operand interchange, 8.1 (8)) is a free variant of *be before* over its whole domain:

Her arrival yesterday was after his return yesterday.

Her arrival tomorrow will be after his return yesterday.

Then, *after* plus tense plus reflecting the two operands in the operator is a free variant of *be before* over the following subdomain: the time-location adverbs are as for *before*, and the first verb (under *be before*) must be perfective. When both verbs are perfective we can form out of

His return was before her arrival

both
>He returned before she arrived

and
>She arrived after he returned.

When only the second is perfective, then from

>His continuing to work was before her arrival

we can form

>He continued to work before she arrived

but not

>⌐ She arrived after he continued to work.

And when only the first is perfective, then from

>Her arrival was before his continuing to work

we can form

>He continued to work after she arrived

but not

>⌐ She arrived before he continued to work.

The other time-ordering conjunctions can also be shown to be free variants, over other subdomains, of *be before* plus more complex additions.

The sentences containing *be before* have many other free variants. One of these makes a desirable source. It is the form in which *be before* is simply a verb between two time-nouns:

>His return at 3 P.M. was before her arrival at 3:15 P.M.
>His return at the hour of 3 P.M. was before her arrival at the hour of 3:15 P.M.

(7)   3 P.M., which was the hour of his return, is before 3:15 P.M., which was the hour of her arrival.

Each of the first two sentences is derivable from the one below it by known paraphrastic transformations. In (7) we see finally that one of the free variants is different in an important respect: instead of *be before* as a connective verb (transformable into a conjunction) between two nominalized sentences containing time-location adverbs, we now have *be before* as a verb between time-nouns, and two *wh*-conjunctions connecting two sentences with time adverbs to these time-nouns.

The source of (7) is:

(8)   (The hour of) 3 P.M. is before (the hour of) 3:15 P.M.
(9)   His return was at (the hour of) 3 P.M.

(10)   Her arrival was at (the hour of) 3:15 P.M.

with (9) and (10) being each joined to (8) by *wh-*.
   In the case of time-connectives without time-location adverbs, e.g. in

His return was before her arrival

we have to assume that the source contained unspecified time-predicates:

(8')   A time is before a time.
(9')   His return in the past was at a time.
(10')   Her arrival in the past was at a time.

If we operate on the ordered (9'), (10') with two *wh-* operators (themselves derived from *and*) on the successive *time* of (8'), we obtain (with automatic *the*):

(11)   The time of his return in the past was before the time of her arrival in the past.

Zeroing *the time of* as a constant in respect to *be before*, we obtain:

(12)   His return in the past was before her arrival in the past,

whence by tense-transplacing and second-operand tensing (which make a conjunction out of the verb *be before* 5.5, 8.1 (10), (12)):

(13)   He returned before she arrived.

If the time and perfectivity conditions for the tense-transplacing are not satisfied, the conjunction form as in (13) is not reached. Furthermore, if the two source sentences under the *wh-* (i.e. (9') and (10') here) do not have past or future (from *is in past, is in future* predicates) the derivation cannot reach (13) and we are left with

His return is before her arrival.

In (8)–(10) and (8')–(10') we see how the whole system of inter-sentence time-connectives can turn out to be a free variant of one verb, *be before* (or *precede*) on time-nouns, plus the *wh-*connective.

2.6. *Comparatives*

A somewhat similar situation arises in the case of the comparative. The comparative has certain grammatical restrictions. It involves not only a conjunction between two sentences but also a comparative morpheme placed next to a particular word (the one in respect to which the comparison is being made) in the first sentence[7]:

(1)   More men read books than women (read) magazines.

(2)   Men read more books than women (read) magazines.

In the second operand sentence of each pair, there are unique zeroings (discussed below), which are seen in, e.g.:

(3)   More men read books than read magazines.
(4)   Men read more books than (they read) magazines.
(5)   Men read more books than are worthwhile.

but no zeroing in:

(6)   More men read books than there are books which are worth-
           while.

After zeroing, the *than*... can be permuted, but not to before the compari-son-bearing word in the first sentence:

(7a)   More men read books than women (do).
(7b)   More men than women read books.
(7c)   Men read more books than women (read).
           ∄ Men than women read more books.

Finally, the comparative is restricted in repetition. In the case of other con-junctions (except *wh-*), if a conjunction C has operated on a pair of sentences S_1, S_2, yielding a new sentence S_1CS_2, it can then operate on a further pair consisting of this resultant and a third sentence: $(S_1CS_2)CS_3$ or $S_3C(S_1CS_2)$:

           (He left because it was late) because he had to be back in time.

In contrast, the comparative repeats only on pairs of pairs, yielding (S_1CS_2) $C(S_3CS_4)$:

(8)   He is richer than she more than you are richer than me.

but ∄ $(S_1CS_2)CS_3$:

(9)   ∄ He is richer than she more than you are (rich).

There are many free variants to the comparative form. One in particular turns out to be free of the various restrictions of the comparative conjunction. We consider, for

(10)   He is richer than she (is).

the free variant (via (10″) below):

(10′)   The amount of his riches is more than the amount of her riches.

or with morphophonemic *exceed* for *be more than*:

           The amount of his riches exceeds the amount of her riches.

On the basis of (10′) we can form a free variant to (8):

(11)   The excess of (the amount of) his riches over hers exceeds the excess of (the amount of) your riches over mine.

And here we can also form $(S_1CS_2)CS_3$, which was impossible in (9):

(12)   The excess of (the amount of) his riches over hers exceeds (the amount of) your riches.

In the new form we have no comparative conjunction: As in (8)–(10) of 2.5, (10′) is formed out of a certain elementary sentence form (13) plus two sentences connected to (13) by the *wh*-connective:

(13) N_i is more than N_j (by N_k),

where N_i, N_j, N_k are any numbers; or they may be pronouns and classifiers of the numbers, such as the words *number, amount, degree*. To (13) are joined (by *wh*-):

(14) N_i is the amount of his riches ← His riches amount to N_i.
(15) N_j is the amount of her riches ← Her riches amount to N_j.

The result of connecting (14) and (15) by *wh*- to (13) is:

N_i, which is the amount of his riches is more than N_j, which is the amount of her riches.

As in (8′)–(10′) of 2.5, we can form this set also when the nouns of (13) are unspecified quantities, if we allow these further nouns to be subject and object of *is more than*:

(13′)   An amount is more than an amount (by an amount).
(14′)   His riches have an amount.
(15′)   Her riches have an amount.

When (14′), (15′) are each connected by *wh*- to (13′), and addressed respectively to the first two occurrences of *amount*, we obtain (comparably to (11)–(13) of 2.5):

(10′)   The amount of his riches is more than the amount of her riches.

and, by zeroing of *the amount of* as a constant of *is more than*:

(10″)   His riches are more than her riches (or: than hers).

and by tense-transplacing, second-operand tensing, and zeroing we obtain the comparative conjunction:

(10)   He is richer than she.

The source set of type (13)–(15), (13')–(15') explains the special zeroing of the comparative conjunction. In this source there is under the second *wh-* (i.e. in the (15)-type sentence) an established zeroing of repeated material in positions corresponding to their antecedents in the (14)-type sentence. Thus from

> N_i, which is the (number of) men who read books, in more than
> N_j, which is the (number of) men who read magazines

we obtain by zeroing of the indefinite N_i, N_j and of parallel repetitions:

> The (number of) men who read books, is more than read magazines.

Here operand interchange under *wh-* yields the somewhat dubious:

> Men read books who are more than read magazines.

With zeroing of *who are* and permuting of *more* to the left of its host (8.4(6)):

> (3)   More men read books than read magazines.

The permutation of 8.4 (6) can operate not on *more* alone but also on *more than read magazines* (i.e. on *more* together with its adjunct), yielding:

> More men than read magazines read books.

The fact that *than*… is never permuted to before *more* (see (7) above) is due to the fact that the permutation operates on *than*… only as right adjunct of *more*. It is *more* that is permutable, and *than*… only with it.

Similarly, from a source

> N_i, which is the (number of) books which men read, is more than
> N_j, which is the (number of) magazines which men read

we obtain (4) via

> The books which men read are more than the magazines (which they read).

And from a source

> N_i, which is the (number of) books which are read, is more than
> N_j which is the (number of) books that are worthwhile

we obtain (5) via

> The books which men read are more than are worthwhile.

And from a source

> N_i, which is the (number of) men who read books, is more than
> N_j, which is the (number of) books that are worthwhile

we obtain (6) via

> The men who read books are more than the books that are worthwhile.

The *wh-* on two operand sentences with a common N always brings the common N in its second operand to the start of the second operand, where it is pronounced onto the *wh-*. The common N in (13)–(15) is always a quantity (as the common N in (8)–(10) of 2.5 is always a time-noun), and the noun which bears the quantity is automatically brought up after it (by the string effect of *wh-*, 2.8, 8.4 (6)). It is this that puts the compared (quantified) word at the start and that determines what are the corresponding positions for zeroing. When the tense-transplacing and second-operand tensing make the verb *is more than* into a conjunction *than*, the operand sentences undergo a string change and the compared word may no longer be at the start.

Note that for (6) the second *books* is not zeroable under the source *wh-* because it is not in a position corresponding to that of the first *books*, whereas for (5) the second *books* was in a corresponding position and zeroable. The (13)–(15)-type of source shows that the comparative has not merely one compared word, the bearer of *more* in the first compared sentence (i.e. the word quantified by N_i), but also a second compared word, in the second sentence (i.e. the word quantified by N_j). The zeroing rules under the comparative conjunction, which seem complex and unique, turn out to be almost entirely the normal zeroings under *wh-* in the source form shown here.

Like all paraphrases in this paper, these transformations are not semantically determined equivalences but established transformations, preserving acceptability-ordering. And the intermediate sentences in the derivation, and the source sentences in (13)–(15), exist in the language, even if they are felt to be cumbersome. It should also be noted that the precise form of the elementary sentences, and precisely which paraphrastic transformations are to be used in the derivation, need not concern us in the present problem, though they would concern a detailed grammar of English. All that is important here is that the comparative conjunction, like the time-order conjunctions, can be paraphrastically derived from an elementary sentence form and the *wh-* connective, and that the source forms do not have the restrictions in domain or in further operability which the derived forms have. The special properties of the comparative are thus merely the result of a few established transformations operating on this unrestricted source.

The discussion above shows that the comparative conjunction has a free variant, in the (13)–(15) source form, which does not have the grammatical peculiarities of the comparative: it does not have a comparative marker which has to be placed in the first operand sentence; its zeroings and permutations are mostly the normal ones for the source form; and it is not restricted as to repetition or other further transformability. Also, the source form is semantically more explicit, in that it naturally distinguishes a quantified (and compared) word in the second operand sentence as well as in the first.

As in other cases, we find that many sentences can be said in the source form which cannot be said (or can be said only by some special adjustment) in the more common derived form. These are the sentences which are excluded by the restrictions that are required for the paraphrastic derived form.

Thus, we have seen in (12) that we could form the source for the (SCS)CS comparison, where the short form (9) was excluded: (12) resulted from joining three sentences to the N_i, N_j, N_k of (13). If only one sentence, say (14), is adjoined by *wh-* to (13) we obtain (if N_j is, say, $5.):

(16)   The amount of his riches is more than $5.

or:
His riches exceed $5.

where, as in (9) the comparative-conjunction form does not exist:

(17)   ∄ He is richer than $5.

We find additional source sentences which lack a comparative-conjunction paraphrase if we note the zeroings involved in (1)–(7). In all these cases, the source proposed here has zeroable material: identical words in parallel positions. Thus the source of (1) would be:

(18)   The number of men who read books is more than the number of women who read magazines.

And the source of (2) is:

(19)   The number of books which men read is more than the number of magazines which women read.

In these and the other cases the quantified words have the same position in the source sentences, so that the two *wh-* clauses in (18), or in (19), have identical structures.[8] If, however, we take a sentence of this type in which the two *wh-* clauses have different structures, we find that in certain cases the direct comparative-conjunction form does not exist:

The number of men who read books is more than the number of magazines which women read.
∄ More men read books than magazines women read.[9]

Similarly, for

> The number of books which men read is more than the number
> of women who read books.
> ⌐ Men read more books than women who read books.

To summarize the situation for the comparative: We have found that there is
an incremental system, not restricted to any subdomain, which consists of
any sentence of the elementary form (13) to which are joined by *wh-* any
sentences with quantity-predicates as in (14), (15). Under certain conditions,
when there are certain parallelisms (which may be due to zeroings) in the
sentences joined to (13), the section preceding *than* is transformed into a
sentence, and *than* becomes a conjunction. It is this last transformation, a
paraphrastic one, which is restricted; and certain source-sets of the (13)–(15)-
type cannot receive this transformation.

The comparative with *less than* is readily obtained from *more than*. And
the *as … as* comparative can also be obtained from *more than*; or *is as*
(*equals*) can be considered another member of the class of *is more than*
(*exceeds*), except that it involves no *by* N_k. Hence by the side of (13) there is
also

(20) N_i is as N_j; N_i equals N_j.

2.7. *Special Comparatives*

Related to the comparative, there are several highly restricted and seemingly
arbitrary sentence-forms. These too are found to be free variants of the comparative source (13) or (20) plus (14), (15) of 2.6, with simple additions.

One set is seen in:

(1)   He is too ill for you to leave now.
           He is so ill that you should not leave now.

These are derivable by morphophonemic replacements (*too* and *so … that …*
should not for *more … than is appropriate*) from

> He is more ill than is appropriate for your leaving now (or: for
> you to leave now)

which is derivable by tense-transplacing and zeroing, as in 2.6, from

(2)   The degree of his illness is more than the degree of his illness
           which is appropriate for your leaving now

which is derived from (13) of 2.6:

(3) N_i is more than N_j (by N_k); or: A degree is more than a degree
           (by a degree).

joined by *wh-* with

(4)   He is ill to a degree (N_i).

(5)   His being ill to a degree (N_j) is appropriate for your leaving now.

Another set is seen in:

(1')   It's solid enough to break the wall.
It is so solid that it can break the wall.

These are morphophonemically derivable (with *enough* and *so...that... should* for *as...as is appropriate*) from

> It is as solid as necessary (or: appropriate) for its breaking the wall (or: for it to break the wall).

from (as above)

> The amount of its solidity is as the amount of solidity of it necessary (or: appropriate) for (its) breaking the wall.

which is derived from (20) of 2.6:

> N_i is as N_j (or: N_i equals N_j); or: An amount equals an amount.

joined by *wh-* with

> N_i is the amount of its solidity; It is solid to an amount (N_i).
> N_j is the amount of its solidity necessary (or: appropriate) for it to break the wall; Its being solid to an amount (N_j) is necessary for its breaking the wall.

Thus the forms with *too* and *enough* are a special case of the (13)–(15) system of 2.6. They are derived from it by regular zeroings and special morphophonemics from the two forms (13) and (20) respectively, when the two *wh*-sentences are:

> N_i is the amount of $S_1 n$; or: $S_1 n$ is an amount N_i.
> N_j is the amount of $S_1 n$ appropriate for $S_2 n$[10]; or: $S_1 n$ being in an amount N_j is appropriate for $S_2 n$.

This derivation explains why there are precisely two sets, (1) and (1'), of these sufficiency-comparisons: they arise from the two sources (13) and (20) of 2.6.

Another special comparative is found in the proverb form

(6)   The bigger they are the harder they fall.

This is derivable by somewhat unusual applications of zeroing from three occurrences (a, b, c) of the whole (13)–(15) system of 2.6:

(a): N_i exceeds N_j by N_k.
         N_i is how big they are (or: N_i is the amount of their bigness).
         N_j is ... (here: some zeroable S containing a quantity).

which transforms into

(7) N_k is the excess of how (much) bigger they are (than ...).
(b): M_i exceeds M_j by M_k.
         M_i is how hard they fall.
         M_j is ... (here: some zeroable S containing a quantity).

whence the transform:

(8) M_k is the excess of how (much) harder they fall (than ...).
(c): (9) N_k is as M_k.

The remaining sentences of the (c) set are (7) and (8), the resultants of (a) and (b); then (c) transforms to

    N_k which is the excess of how (much) bigger they are is as M_k
        which is the excess of how (much) harder they fall.

Standard zeroings take this into:

    The excess of how (much) bigger they are is the excess of how
        (much) harder they fall.

whence the unusual constant-zeroing of *excess of how* (*much*) and *is* produces the irregular form (6).

If instead of (9) we had had its paraphrastic transform

    As N_k is so is M_k

we would have obtained

    As they are bigger so they fall harder.

This derivation shows why (6) is available only for *more* and *less* (note: *The less he knows the better*) but not for *as* ($\nexists$ *The as much he knows the as good*): for the derivation uses essentially, in (7)–(9), the *by* N_k, *by* M_k which is available only with *is more than*, *is less than*. And it explains the permutation in *the bigger they are* as being due to the *how* in (a), (b).

2.8. *Wh-*

The main use of *wh-*, namely that in which the morpheme following the *wh-* is a pronoun of a preceding (but possibly zeroed) N or PN, has been analyzed as a free variant which morphophonemically replaces *and*, plus a sentence identifying the pronoun with its located antecedent, by *wh-*. Thus:

> He found the book which had disappeared.

can be derived by zeroing and the above morphophonemics from such sources as:

> He found a book and a book had disappeared and 'book' of preceding sentence indicates the same individual as 'book' of sentence preceding that.

Thus, *wh-* occurs only between two sentences in which the same noun appears with certain restrictions.

The main interest of such derivations for our present purpose is that, differently from *wh-*, *and* is not restricted as to the two sentences which it joins together, and even the added sentence about individual sameness is not grammatically restricted. E.g. the sequence which does not satisfy this restriction: *He found a card and he wrote a letter*: *and 'house' of preceding sentence is the same individual as 'book' of sentence preceding that* is nonsensical rather than ungrammatical. Thus the increment *and* is unrestricted; and the increment which consists in adding the sentence about sameness is restricted only in meaningfulness of selection. In contrast, *wh-*, which is a free variant of these together, is grammatically restricted: it cannot be said in a grammatical sentence which does not derive from occurrences of a common noun in two operand sentences.

2.9. *Vocabulary*

A more complicated problem is that of the restricted vocabulary. There are many words whose environment is limited in ways that are characteristic of grammatical restriction rather than of meaningful selection. It can be shown that unrestricted free variants are available for these words or their sequences.

A simple example is the case of restricted single words which have unrestricted synonyms. Thus the noun *flock* occurs primarily in *of birds* (not all birds, at that), *of sheep*, *of parishioners*, or in transforms of these. In all its occurrences there are various free variants available, such as *congregation* or *assemblage*, which are not themselves restricted except selectionally. If we take the unrestricted word as the transformational source, we can then say that for a particular subset of the environments of this word there is a free-variant morphophonemic transformation to the restricted form.

More generally, all idioms have unrestricted free variants. The words of an idiomatic sequence (e.g. *he threw in the towel*) have a special restriction to each other, and sometimes to the environment, in the environments in which they constitute an idiom, as in *In the competition to see who could throw more towels in through the window he threw in the towel by refusing to throw in any towel*. Similarly, in the environments where this is an idiom, ∄ *He threw in two towels*. And in many idioms and metaphors various further transformations do not operate. Such restrictions do not apply to various free variants of the idioms, e.g. in this case *give up*, which preserve acceptability-ordering of their environments, even though these may not be felt subjectively as perfect synonyms of the idiom.

The claim made here for idioms has to do with the availability of specific free variants, and is not based on any general principle that everything can be said in a language. There are indeed things that cannot be precisely said: e.g. it is difficult to state a precise paraphrase of that which is intended in *They came in one after the other* (where the first person came in after no one).

3. UNRESTRICTED MORPHOPHONEMIC SOURCE FOR RESTRICTED OPERATORS

In § 2 we saw that many incremental operators with restricted domain had, over their own domain, free variants whose domain in turn was not restricted. There remain certain operators which do not have unrestricted free variants, but which nevertheless permit the formulation of an unrestricted source. This is possible first of all in the case of two or more forms which are complementary in their environments: in that case it has become customary to define a morphophonemic source, which does not exist in at least certain of the environments (where it is marked *), and to say that the morphophonemic source occurs in all environments, except that where it is marked * it is automatically (necessarily) changed in shape into the form that is indeed found there. This is done not only in individual cases such as *knife-knives* and in more prominent situations such as irregular verbs (*be*, etc.), but also in many paradigmatic situations such as number and gender agreement, and conjugations.

The morphophonemic source can still be formulated secondly, in a more complicated situation: when two forms contrast in some environments but are complementary in others. This situation, which in phonemics was called neutralization, is uncomfortable if we seek to state what are the independent elements in all sentences. The situation arises, for example, in gender if some nouns are only feminine, e.g. *la rivière*, while other nouns have both masculine and feminine forms, e.g. *le lion, la lionne*. In this case the feminine endings on *rivière* and the words in the scope of its agreement have to be considered to be simply phonemic portions of *rivière*, while the feminine ending in *lionne* is a morpheme (in effect an adjective) independently adjoinable to *lion*.

3.1. *Plural*

A clear case of this neutralization is the plural affix. In *The books fell* as against *The book fell*, the *-s* is an independent morpheme, in effect an adjective. In *Three books fell* the *-s* is not independent: ⫫ *Three book fell*, and *books* is a complementary variant of *book* in this environment. We can avoid this situation by noting that for every *N pl.* (noun plus plural suffix), in every environment where it has no quantifier, there is a free variant containing an indefinite plural pronoun, e.g. *two-or-more N pl.*:

> I need books.
> I need two-or-more books.

We consider a subset of English which has all English sentences except that instead of each sentence containing unquantified *N pl.*, it has the corresponding sentence with *two-or-more N pl.* In this subset, the plural suffix is never independent: it is always determined by such quantifiers as *two, three, many, two-or-more*. We now replace all the cases of *two books, many books, two-or-more books*, etc., by a newly created morphophonemic source **two book, *many book, *two-or-more book*, etc. In English, the plural suffix is a restricted increment, not occurring after *one N*. But in the above subset of English with its morphophonemic source there is no independent plural morpheme: There are only various quantifiers *one, two, many, two-or-more*, and each of these is unrestricted; and there is a pronunciation *two books* for the source **two book*, etc. The restricted plural is now no longer due to adding a restricted increment; rather, it is due to restricted morphophonemics, which pronounces the phonemes of *pl.* after certain quantifiers but not after *one, half*, etc., and it is due to the zeroing of a particular quantifier once this morphophonemic *pl.* was present, thus producing out of *two-or-more N pl.* a free variant *N pl.*

It is not necessary to suppose that every noun without *pl.* is singular, either in meaning or grammatically. In the grammar, the category 'singular' is no longer relevant (nor is 'plural' except as the domain of a particular morphophonemic change). In meaning, there is no reason to consider un-pluralized mass-nouns as either singular or plural: e.g. in *water*, or even *much water, more water*; while *the waters* has to be considered as ← **the two-or-more water*.

3.2. *Tense*

A similar but more complex case is that of tense. The tense of a verb is dependent on the time-location adverb of that verb: *I went yesterday.* ∄ *I went tomorrow.* But tense occurs also as an independent element on verbs lacking a time-location adverb: *I went. I will go.* Again we have neutralization. As above, we can find a free variant with general time-location adverb for every tensed verb which lacks a time-location adverb, and we consider the latter to be zeroed from the former:

> He went. ← He went in the past (or: before now).
> He will go. ← He will go in the future (or: after now).
> He goes. ← He goes at present (or: now).

In the longer forms above the tense is always dependent, so that these can be derived from untensed morphophonemic sources, or nominalization:

> *He go in the past; or: His going is in the past.
> *He go in the future; or: His going is in the future.
> *He go at present; or: His going is at present.

In these source sentences the morphophonemically automatic *be* does not have to be *was* or *will be*; and its form *is* is clearly no indication of present time (which would be meaningless here) but is a morphophonemic requirement.

In sentences without time-location adverb (this can occur only when the sentences are operands), and in particular in the sentences as they are about to be nominalized under time-location predicates as immediately above, we cannot have had a tensed source. Here the tenseless morphophonemic form must have been the source: *He go. Semantically, the time of such forms is indefinite or indeterminate, rather than being some kind of generalized present.

Timeless source sentences actually exist as operands. In *My going may turn out to be a great mistake* there is no indication of the time of *my going*, and there is no reason to say that this sentence is a degenerate grammatical ambiguity from precisely three sources: *My going in the past may...*, *My going in the future may...*, *My going at present may....* The same timeless operand sentence is seen in *I returned because of his departure.* It would go against the conditions necessary for zeroing to derive ... *because of his departure* from ...*because he departed* or from ...*because he will depart*, since such a derivation would lose time-information, whereas morphemes are zeroed only if they can be reconstructed from the remaining environment (although two different zeroings may yield degenerately the same residual sentence). Hence *I returned because he will depart* is a transform of *I returned because of his future departure* and not of *I returned because of his departure*; the latter has no tensed transform for the second operand.

Tenseless operand forms exist for every operator: no operator in English requires a tensed V as argument. Those for which the operand can be tensed, also have a tenseless form of the operand as in *I regret his departure, They made him leave.* This explains why every tensed operand has a tenseless apparent transform but not conversely: (1) *That he went is a fact,* (2) *His going is a fact*; *His driving is slow, ∄ That he drives is slow.* For we now see that (1) is a transform not of (2) but of *His going (being) in the past is a fact.* But *is slow* does not operate on time predicates: *His driving in the past was slow* is derived not from *is slow* on *is in the past,* but from *and* on the two increments *is in the past, is slow,* producing *His driving which was in the past was slow, His past driving was slow.* Hence *is slow* has only tenseless operands, while *is a fact* has both tensed and tenseless.

The occurrence of tensed forms can be described as a free variant or automatic change (required variant) of time-location adverbs; but doing so requires a rather complicated statement of, first, when this variant occurs and, second, which tense goes with which particular adverbs.

First, when does tensing occur?

Under certain sentence-operators (e.g. *demand*) the argument verb is never tensed, and under certain operators on sentence-pairs (e.g. *in order that*) the second argument is never independently tensed. As for the subjunctive in 2.4, the time-location adverb A of the argument in question is partially though not entirely dependent upon the time-location adverb B of the sentence-operator in the first case or of the primary sentence in the second case: A is never in the past in respect to B. In these cases, an operand sentence which occurs in the nominalized form *N's Ving* can be transformed into the 'subjunctive' form *that NV, that N should V, for N to V,* but not into the tensed (indicative) form *that N tense V.*[11]

A few other operators, whose arguments are also never past relative to them, have their operands neither nominalized (*N's Ving*) nor subjunctive but only a tenseless *NV*:

> They made him go.
> They let him go.

Other sentence-operators never have tensed operands for other reasons. Because predicates of manner do not operate on time-predicates (as in *is slow* above) they have only nominalized operators:

> His driving has (or: is in) a hesitant manner.
> The manner of his driving is hesitant.
> His driving is hesitant (in manner).

The operand is tensed only via the tense-transplacing T (8.1 (10)), in which the predicate becomes an adjunct (adverb; 8.4 (8)):

> He drives in a hesitant manner.
> He drives hesitantly.

In all other situations, there are free variants in which the untensed operands occur tensed.

The tense-transplacing transformations (8.1 (10)) move the tensing from the last operator (the one which is not itself an operand) to its first argument. E.g.:

(3)   Her return tomorrow is because of his departure yesterday.

(4)   → She will return tomorrow because of his departure yesterday.
         Her driving will always be slow (in manner).
         → She will always drive in a slow manner (or: slowly).

A tensed free variant (8.1 (12)) also occurs in the second argument-verb under certain V_{vv} (7.2, in particular those consisting of *be P*, e.g. *be because of*) and under *be before*:

(3)   → Her return tomorrow is because he departed yesterday.

(4)   → She will return tomorrow because he departed yesterday.
         His return was before her arrival→
            His return was before she arrived.
         He returned before her arrival→
            He returned before she arrived.

Under the comparative, this happens only if the first argument-verb is tensed:

(5)   His riches are more than her riches ↔≠ His riches are more than
         she is rich.

(5)   → He is rich more than she is.

Finally, the predicate analysis of §§ 4, 5 makes possible a simple formulation of the occurrence of tensing: In every sentence the predicate operator which is not itself an operand (except of *and, or*) is tensed. That is to say that when, in constructing a sentence, we stop the construction after applying a particular predicate operator (with possibly *and, or* operators on it), this operator is then tensed: the tensing can be considered an automatic variant (a required morphophonemic form) of placing a period or sentence-intonation upon the word-sequence. It is better to take period as an independent entity, with tense as automatic in respect to it, than to take tense as independent, because tense also occurs in other positions (above) where it is not independent but a free variant. The tensing should also not be considered to be simply the morphemic realization of the act of asserting, because in its free variant occurrences it is neither more nor less assertion than is its un-tensed variant: Both forms of the operand are equally asserted in *I announced his having come on time, I announced that he came on time*; the tensed *he came* is not asserted in *I wonder if he came*; and the untensed operand is implicitly asserted in *I made him bring it*.

Second, given that tensing is a free or automatic variant, it remains to state how the particular tense is determined. A verb is tensed with *-ed* if it has on it any past-time adverb or predicate (including the general *in the past* or the like, which is then zeroable). A verb is tensed with (the auxiliary) *will* if it has on it any future-time adverb or predicate (including the general *in the future* or the like which is then zeroable). A verb is tensed with zero (with variant *-s* after third person singular subject) if it has any present-time adverb or predi-cate (including the zeroable *at present*, etc.) or if it has no time-location operator (in which case it has not been restricted to being in the past or in the future, so that it often means unspecified or distributed as to time). An example of the latter is seen in *His going is in the past*.

There are a number of amendments to the above. If the verb is a sen-tence-pair operator its tense is partially restricted by the time-location of its two operands:

> His having arrived will spoil their leaving on time soon.
> His having arrived spoiled their leaving on time soon.
> ∄ His having arrived will spoil their having left on time.
> ? ∄ His arriving an hour from now spoiled their leaving on time
>   soon.

Under certain forms of certain operators, the tense of the operand is deter-mined not only by the time-location of the operand but also by that of the operator. Thus

> He announced her being ill in the past.→ He announced that she
>   was ill, He announced that she had been ill.
> He announced her being ill in the present.→ He announced that
>   she was ill.

The same operands have different tenses in the 'direct discourse' transforms of the above sentences:

> He announced: 'She was ill'.
> He announced: 'She is ill'.

4. RESTRICTION DETERMINED BY ENVIRONMENT

In § 2 it was seen that certain increments which appeared to be restricted to particular subsets of the domain of a variable could be derived from unrestricted increments. In § 3 it was seen that certain other restricted operators were variants determined by the presence of other operators, i.e. of particular morphemes in the environment (e.g. quantifiers or time adverbs). Here we consider how yet other grammatical forms, which appear to be restricted to words of some particular subset, are derivable as variants of particular morphemes which are present in the environment of words of that subset.

What is eliminated in § 4 is mostly restrictions on certain paraphrastic transformations, rather than on increments. However, the elimination of these restrictions requires certain added complexities in the source form of the increments upon which the transformations operate (e.g. 4.1, 4.3), and it is therefore being considered here.

4.1. *Subjunctive*

This type of situation has already been met in the subjunctive (2.4), where the non-tensing of the operand was due to a particular dependence between the time-adverb of the operand and that of the operator.

It was seen there that all sentences containing this time dependence had as one of their free variant transforms a sentence which contained the statement of that time-dependence: *subsequently*, or *afterwards*, or the like. In the formulation of grammar there is a great difference between saying that the subjunctive occurs in the operands of verbs that necessarily (or normally) have this time-dependence to them, and saying that the subjunctive occurs in the operands of those verbs that necessarily (or normally) impose the word *afterwards* on them. For in the latter case, we can simply say that the subjunctive is a free variant of the required *afterwards*; and the required *afterwards* can be considered as simply a part of those verbs which always impose it on their arguments. It is true that the requirement of *afterwards* can be considered a classifier of a subset of words, but it can also be considered a morphemic segment of those verbs and thus simply a part of the sentences in which those verbs occur, a part that can be replaced by free variants of it. Then the source form of *request* would be *request-for-afterwards*.

The analysis of *afterwards* will be clearer if we use here the operator notation of §§ 6–7 (see note 1), in which X(Y, Z) indicates that X is operating on the pair Y, Z as its arguments; in elementary sentences the verb is taken as operating on its subject and object (7.1). Then *I request that he go* is in operator notation:

request-for-afterwards (I, go (he)),

and in the actual string of words (7.5):

> *I request-for-afterwards his going

which becomes by length-permutation (8.1 (6)):

> I request his going afterwards,

where the presence of the required *afterwards* prevents the morphophonemic operation of tensing and leaves a tenseless transform

> I request that he go (afterwards).

4.2. *Adverbs of Manner*

The appeal to environment has also been met in the predicates of manner (2.3), which were seen to be derived from adjectives (in principle, arbitrary ones) plus the word *manner*: (1) *His driving of trucks was hesitant* ← (2) *His driving (of) trucks was in a hesitant manner* ↔ *The manner of his driving (of) trucks was hesitant*. What makes them adverbs of manner is that the words *in ... manner* had occurred with them, but were zeroable and zeroed. Furthermore, since the nominalization with *of* before the object (1) is required only when *manner* is absent, we see that the requirement is a variant of *manner*: (1) and (2) are free variants of each other. And indeed the verbs which have *manner* as object (not as part of a predicate) also have this *of*-nominalization when *manner* is zeroed: *They imitated the manner of his driving (of) trucks, They imitated his driving of trucks*. Of course, in order to determine the special transformation (in this case, *of*), the determining environment (in this case, *manner*), if it is zeroed, must be present at the moment of application of the special transformation.

4.3. *Reciprocals*

Free variation to environing morphemes is seen in the case of the reciprocal verbs. For all verbs, a sentence of the form:

> A saw B and B saw A

can be transformed into:

> A and B saw B and A respectively.

which transforms into:

> (1)   A and B saw each other.

There is a particular subset of verbs in English, called reciprocal, after which *each other* can be paraphrastically zeroed:

> A met B and B met A.
> A and B met B and A respectively.
> (2) A and B met each other.
> (3) A and B met.

In such a derivation, the zeroing of *each other* in (2) but not in (1) is determined by the presence of *met* in (2) as against *saw* in (1): that is, the determining environment is a particular subset of words, the reciprocal verbs, V_{rec}, which have to be listed.

However, there is another way of arriving at (3) which has the same grammatical character as in 4.1. We note that the reciprocal verbs, for which (3) occurs in the sense only of *each other*, are precisely the verbs V_{rec} for which

> (4) A V_{rec} B and A's V_{rec}ing B implies B's V_{rec}ing A.
> (4') A V_{rec} B and that A and B V_{rec} B and A respectively is implicit.

are transforms of

> A V_{rec} B

as in:

> A met B and that A and B met B and A respectively is implicit.

Therefore the sentence:

> A met B and B met A
> → A and B met B and A respectively

has various transforms of the type (pronouned from (4')):

> (5) A and B met B and A respectively, and this is implicit.

Of course, this is not to say that (4) may not occur for verbs not in V_{rec}, when they have particular A, B or particular conditions (which could be appended to the sentence): e.g. in a given situation we might have (6) *He saw her and his seeing her implied her seeing him.* But (6) would not be a transform of *He saw her*, preserving acceptability-ordering for all choices of subject and object.

We can now say that what is zeroable is the transformational case (as in (4') but not (6)) of *B and A respectively and this is implicit*, which indeed meets the informationlessness criterion for zeroing. To zero this segment requires no appeal to a determining environment. (3) is then derived not from (2) but from (5).

At this point one might think that all that has been gained is a shifting of the definition of the V_{rec} subset, from a subset defined by a list to one defined by having the transforms (4). However, the difference is that now the reduced form (3) is derived by zeroing the zeroable material in (5) and not from any checking of the environment; but the cost is that the source form of *met* is now as in (5). The V_{rec} can occur without the adjoined implication of (4) and (5), and in that case the zeroing does not take place; in that case the V_{rec} can only reach the form with *each other*, in which it does not differ from any other verb. Furthermore, as in 2.4, the availability of (4), (5) is not as sharp a grammatical restriction as would be thought from the listed V_{rec}. There are verbs, e.g. *equal*, which are fully acceptable in forms (4) and (5), and can with hesitation be used in form (3). As before, the source forms have some freedom in selection of co-occurrents, while the paraphrastically shortened forms (3) are frozen into grammatical subjects. Here as elsewhere (e.g. 2.1), what is sharply grammatical in the transformational paraphrase system is derived from what is flexibly selectional (co-occurrence) in the source sentences.

4.4. *Sentence nominalization. Sn*

A more important problem replacing subset lists by source environments is the choice of forms (deformations) taken by operand sentences under various sentence-operators.

Just as some operators get the subjunctive (i.e. do not get tense) on their operand, so other operators have other special deformations of their operand. Most of these are variants of the basic *N's Ving* deformation of 7.5. Thus for a certain subset of V_{nv} operators (7.2) such as *prevent*, the operand N_1 *'s Ving* N_2 is transformable to N_1 *from Ving* N_2 (*They prevented his taking it, They prevented him from taking it*); which is not the case for, say, *regret* (*They regretted his taking it, ∄ They regretted him from taking it*).

A particularly difficult case is the subset of V_v operators (7.2), such as *undergo*, whose most common sentence form has for the subject of the operator the same individual as the object of the argument: (1) *He underwent (elaborate) testing*. Since the subject of *undergo* is not an independent variable, we cannot say that *undergo* is V_{nv}, i.e. an operator on a noun (as its subject) and verb (which in turn carries its own subject and object). We have to say that *undergo* is V_v, i.e. an operator on a verb (which carries its own subject and object), and that by some transformation the object of the operand verb comes to be the subject of the V_v. The source form would have to be something like, for (1):

> N's (elaborate) testing of him was an undergoing (or: an experience).

Then we would have to say that there is a transformation, for these operators but not for others, in which the object of the argument becomes the subject of the operator:

He underwent N's (elaborate) testing of him

and, with zeroing of indefinite *N's* and of the now repetitive *of him*:

He underwent (elaborate) testing.

In contrast, many (but not all) V_v operators have the argument-skipping transformation (8.1 (9)), in which the subject (not the object) of the argument becomes the subject of the operator:

Their (elaborate) testing of him was hard work.

→ They worked hard at (an elaborate) testing (of) him.

The number of different operand deformations under different subsets of operators is not large. The detailed derivation of free variants of these deformations leads to uncomfortable and even marginal forms. However, the hope is that one can find free variants which will contain specific morphemes peculiar to the various subsets, such as would make it possible to set up a source in which these morphemes were present as a (classifier) part of the operator and were then replaced by the deformation common to that operator. This is what was done in deriving the subjunctive (on the operand) from *for afterward* affixed to the operator. In this method, the source of *prevent* might be something like *prevent-in-respect-to-the-subject* (of the argument verb), and the source of *undergo* might be something like *an-under-going-for-the-object* (of the argument verb).

We could obtain the various deformations of the operand sentence quite simply if we were willing to have an operator act on a pair consisting of an argument B and an argument C which must itself be an operator on B. In that case, *prevent*, for example, would be

prevent (N, N_i, $V(N_i, N)$)

and *undergo* would be

undergo (N_i, $V(N, N_i)$).

However, this is a less economical description than the one above, since it sacrifices the principle that each variable must be independent, and therefore it does not show the limitation in the range of combinations, or the semantic relations, as directly as does the first description.

5. PREDICATIONAL SOURCE FOR INCREMENTS

5.0. *Introduction*

The attempt in § 2 to reformulate restrictions and subsets by finding free or automatic variants to the various increments has in many cases turned up variants which had the form, in respect to the rest of the sentence, of a predicate operating on sentences. The term 'predicate' is used here to indicate verb or its linguistic equivalent: e.g. in the order of appearance above *be in process, be to great extent, be of slow manner (have slow manner), be easy, demand, be before (precede), be more than (exceed), be in past, imply.* In all these cases the predicational form could be considered the source, from which the other forms are paraphrastically derived, so that the grammatical restrictions are on the paraphrase, not on the source. This raises the question whether every increment has a variant form that is a predicate, which could then be taken as source even if no restrictional advantages are gained thereby. If there was a single relative position in the sentence, such that all increments could be derived paraphrastically from operators having that position relative to their operand, it would be convenient for the simplicity of a theory of language, and it would show that all other syntactic relations are merely paraphrases of the single relation in the source. This is all the more important when the source is largely restrictionless and yet carries all the objective information carried in language. For then we can see that a single relation of certain argument-specific operators to their arguments suffices to carry the objective information. We therefore consider for each increment the set of free (or automatic) variants which it has,[12] and we survey all the sets to see if there is some one form which is to be found in every set – preferably the form in which the operator is a predicate in the above sense. If in a given set of variants (transforms) we do not find such a form, we will try to see at what morphophonemic or other cost a variant of this form can be added to the set.

In what follows, many of the attempts to derive increments from a predicate source will seem forced. Some derivations from predicate form have grammatical justification, even if they are not entirely obvious: the moods (5.6) and most of the noun-adjuncts (5.1), verb-adjuncts (5.2), and auxiliaries (5.3). The remaining noun-adjuncts (chiefly quantifiers, *the*) and verb-adjuncts are few and special. It can be argued that there is good reason to try to regularize them (to predicate form), and that relevant classifications are brought to light in the process (e.g. about *all, the*). However, one might claim that even if this is the case there is no point in forcing the verb-operators (e.g. *begin, take a*) and subordinate conjunctions into the framework of predicates. These are major distinct constructions of grammar, and it seems quite unreal to derive them from uncomfortable or non-existent predicates. Even the fact that many verb-operators occur also as predicates, and that many subordinate conjunctions have associated verb forms, does not alter the grammatical specialness of these non-predicate forms.

However, the intention in this chapter is not to claim that the predicates are sources in any sense except the very special one used here, namely that the established transformations plus a heavy use of morphophonemics suffice to produce all the increments out of predicate forms, and that often these forms are clear syntactic sources in that they are less restricted as to domain or further operability. Thus aside from the standard paraphrastic transformations, the only difference between the normal sentences and the predicate system is morphophonemic, i.e. is in phonemic shape and position. The implications for information, and for the relation of information to syntactic structure, are obvious.

When we can show that no more than one type of operator-operand relation is needed for language, we can deduce one of the major properties of language computability. When grammar is presented with several kinds of operators – adverbs, conjunctions, etc. – it is clear that there are restrictions on the operator combinations, and that these restrictions preserve a certain connectedness among the sentence-parts. For example, *I clearly remember its being put in service with great to-do* is transformable to *I remember its being put in service with great to-do with clarity*, but not to *I remember its being put in service with clarity with great to-do*. The lines connecting *remember* to its adjunct *with clarity* and connecting *put in service* with its adjunct *with great to-do* cannot cross. This does not have to be presented as a special condition on sentence-construction. For when all the segments in a sentence are seen to be brought in by a single type of incremental operator, we see that this connectedness is due to the fact that in each sentence-construction the single operator-type can bring in the segments in only one order.

The predicate source is possible because the different morphological and apparently syntactic classes of words – adjectives, subordinate conjunctions, etc. – do not have different combinability in the language than do particular classes of predicates that can be considered to correspond to them. There is no noun-adjunct that cannot be paraphrased by a conjoined sentence containing that noun, nor any subordinate-conjunction-sentence which cannot be paraphrased by a sentence-pair with an inter-sentence verb. So many grammatical constructions turn out to be derivable from predicates, and so many difficult constructions are conveniently explainable in this derivation, that the syntactic relation here is clearly not external to the language. The predicate sources are not morphologically simple. Since the syntax of a language describes the combinings and relative positionings of elements in sentences, we see that the predicate sources are syntactic primitives and not morphological ones, and they represent (by paraphrastic transformation and morphophonemics) all the morphemes of no matter what morphological class which have identical combinability relative to other morphemes. Just as phonemes are not necessarily phonetically simple, so the syntactic elements determined here are not necessarily morphologically simple, though many of them are.

5.1. *Noun Adjuncts*

We first note briefly the primitive adjuncts of nouns: *the, all, many, only,* etc. The adjuncts, other than these, of a noun N_i are all derived from predicates of another sentence whose subject is also N_i, the second sentence having been adjoined by *wh-* (2.8) to the given occurrence of N_i: *The heavy book fell* ← *The book which is heavy fell* ← *wh-* (*The book fell, The book is heavy*). The numbers and some of the quantifiers can also be derived in this way: *Five books fell* ← *Books which numbered five fell* ← *wh-* (*Books numbered five, Books fell*); although at a later stage the numbers could be derived from repetitions (under *and*) of the singular sentences.

Indefinite and universal quantifiers such as *all* cannot be derived from some number of repetitions under *and*, nor do they appear by themselves as predicates of the nouns to which they are adjoined: ⫫ *The men are all*. However, these quantifiers carry explicit or implicit (i.e. zeroed) references to a domain over which they are taken; and indeed these quantifiers can be derived from appropriate predicates connecting their noun to this domain. E.g. for *all*: *All the men in the room left* ← *Men comprising the set in the room left*: *All books must be returned* ← *All books which have been taken must be returned* (or the like) ← *Books covering the set of those which have been taken must be returned*; *All men die* ← *Men exhausting the set of* (*what is called*) *men die*. The permutability of *all* (*Men all die*; *Men die, all of them*) supports such a derivation.

As to *the*, there may be several sources, from one or another of which we can derive each occurrence of *the*, according to its environment.[13] Certain cases of *the* are automatic in the presence of certain adjuncts of the noun. Others are free variant replacements for such adjuncts as *which has just been mentioned*.

5.2. *Verb Adjuncts*

There are a few adverbs of degree which do not have predicate transforms: *I quite forgot; I simply forgot* (≠ *My forgetting was simple*). As in the case of *very* (2.2), these can be derived from synonymous predicate-transformable adverbs of degree or conjoined clauses which satisfy the conditions for being free variants of them: e.g. *quite* from *completely*, *simply* from *without qualification*.

Almost all adverbs have predicate transforms. That the predicate forms are the source has been shown from 2.3 and from the fact that adverbs generally operate semantically on all adverbs which are between them and the verb: Each adverb arose as a predicate operating on the previous adverbial predicate: *He has been writing clearly recently.* ← *His writing clearly has been recent.* ← *His writing being clear has been recent.*

A special problem exists in the case of *not*. *S→ not S* is an incremental transformation: Not only does it derive one sentence from another, but it preserves subject-matter context (*The values approach infinity* and *The values do not approach infinity* occur in the same subject-matter sublanguage); and like all incremental transformations it preserves acceptability-ordering over a large subdomain (*The flower fell* and *The flower did not fall*, as against *The flower thundered* and *The flower did not thunder*).

First, we note that all negatives are derivable from *not* on the verb (i.e. in the sentence). Thus *We lost no time* ← *We did not lose (even a little) time*; and *non* occurs more acceptably on predicate nouns (e.g. *non-student*, derived from a verb) than on primitive operand nouns (such as *chair*). Secondly, not too much morphophonemics is involved in deriving *not* as adjunct on verb from **is not* as predicate on sentence. Such a derivation is indeed needed for *It is not that S₁ (but that S₂)*, which has to be derived ← **That S₁ is not*, by the well-established transformation seen in *It is false that he came* ← *That he came is false.*

If **is not* is taken as a predicate which operates on sentence we find that its further transformations are similar to those of other sentence-operators, except for morphophonemic details. E.g. when we operate with an additional increment, say *may help*, on these sentence-operators we obtain:

> *My driving is not. → My not driving may help.
> My driving is (in the) future. → My future driving may help.
> My driving is slow. → My slow driving may help.

Another peculiarity of *not* appears in the argument-skipping transformation (8.1 (9)) which is seen in

> My driving continued. → I continued driving.
> My driving was slow. → I was slow in driving.

Here *not* is peculiar in that the verb receives no affix (as it receives none under the auxiliaries), and the tense and auxiliaries are placed before the *not*:

> *My driving was not. → I did not drive.

This leads to certain degeneracies: In *not* operating on *may* operating on *I drive*, we have *not* on *I may drive*, which yields the word-string *I may not drive*, meaning: it is not the case that I may drive, my driving is not possible or allowable. Here we have *not* placed after *may* by the argument-skipping transformation, though this transformation otherwise puts the last operator before its argument (8.1 (9)). Now, in *may* operating on *not* on *I drive*, we have *may* on *I do not drive* (or: *my not driving*) where the same transformation produces, ambiguously, the same word sequence *I may not drive*, meaning: it is possible that I will (or: do) not drive, my not driving is a possibility.

Aside from this, the different placings of *not* in the sentence, which mean negation of different parts of the sentence, are appropriately derivable from different orderings of the **is not* predicate in the ordering of predicates that constructs the sentence. This is the same as we have seen for the different placings of adverbs (also derived from predicates).

A special situation that may be treated here is that of preposition P following verbs. The P may be considered an adverbial operator on the verb in most cases (e.g. *He looked up*), even though the source with the adverb as predicate is asterisked (**His looking was up(ward)*): the tense-transplacing transformation is required here. In the forms with an object, two main types are distinguishable: (1) having no permutation of P, e.g. *They looked out the window* (or: *up the street*) (∄ *They looked the window out*); (2) having permutation of P, e.g. *They threw out the food*, *They threw the food out*. Here there is in many cases a (not very comfortable) transform (2′) *They threw the food so that it was out*. We might distinguish a type (3) which differs from (2) only in not having this transform, e.g. *They looked up the number* (or, ambiguously to the above, *up the street*), *They looked the number up*.

Type (1) can be derived from a prepositional predicate on a pair: (V, N):

out (look (they), window).

producing the uncomfortable source form

Their looking is out the window

and by tense-transplacing

They look out the window.

This is the operator form that would represent case-endings in languages which have such.

Type (2) can be derived from a prepositional predicate on a verb with object:

out (throw (they, food))

producing the source form:

Their throwing of the food is outward

and by tense-transplacing:

> They throw the food out

and by length-permutation on short objects (8.1(6))

> They throw out the food.

The conjunctional transform (2′) results from the fact that the operator *out* is more precisely *out-in-respect-to-the object* in the manner of 4.4 (end).

Type (3) could be derived from a two-morpheme verb:

> look up (they, number)

producing

> They look up the number

and with length-permutation on short objects:

> They look the number up.

5.3. *Compound Tense; Auxiliaries*

There are two other problems of finding a predicate source for verb-operators, which are special to English and related languages: the auxiliaries and the compound tense in *has gone, is gone.*

In the matter of *have-en* we note that there are certain environments in which it is not independent. We will consider here the tensed and tenseless positions of *have-en.*

For the tensed position: By itself, *have-en* seems independent: *He has gone, He went.* But under certain operators it is not: (1) *He has gone by now,* $\not\exists$ *He went by now; At the time of his arrival I had already gone,* $\not\exists$ *At the time of his arrival I already went.* In (1) we can say that *by now* has automatically (morphophonemically) produced the *have-en.* In environments in which *have-en* and the past contrast ((2) *He has gone twice today. He went twice today.*) we can then say that some increment like *by now* had been present and had morphophonemically produced the *have-en* form, and had thereafter been zeroed. The source of (1), (2) would then be something like (3) **His going is by now, *His going is twice by now today.* The required morphophonemics in (3) would produce *His going has been by now,* whence tense-transplacing yields (1).

For the tenseless position: Not only do we find *have-en* on verbs with *-ing,* where tense does not occur, but we find that in some environments the tenseless *have-en* is related to the past-tense rather than to the tensed *have-en.* Thus (4) *I regret his having gone at just that moment* is not the resultant of *regret* operating on (5) $\not\exists$ *He has gone at just that moment,* since (5) does not exist. If we compare (4) and also *I regret his going right now* with *He went at just that moment* and *He goes right now*, it is clear that (4) is the result of *regret* operating the source-form of *He went at just that moment*. That is, *have-en* is a complementary variant here of the ordinary past tense.

In (4), the increment which produced *have-en* could not be *by now*, since *just at that moment* would not co-occur with *by now* (hence (5) is unacceptable). Since *his having gone* in (4) can occur with *yesterday* and other past-time morphemes, but not with future-time morphemes, it follows from the method of 3.2 that there had been present here the ordinary time-location *in the past*. Since *in the past* cannot be transformed into the tense *-ed* when, as in (4), it is in a nominalized sentence, it is here transformed into *have-en*. Thus *have-en* is here a variant of *-ed*.

The fact that *have-en* can appear as a morphophonemic variant of two time-operators – *by now* and *in the past*, in two different environments – makes its derivation more delicate. But it shows that *have-en* is not itself an operator (of a physical type which is unusual in the language and hence inconvenient for a compact structuring) but is a morphophonemic change brought in by an operator (or, in different environments by different operators); and we can now choose the source form of these operators to be the predicate form.

The conditions which determine the producing of *have-en* also involve the perfectivity or imperfectivity of the operand verb: e.g. not all environments which require *have-en* on *go* will also require it on *like* (*At the time of his arrival I already liked it*).

As to the auxiliaries. These are words having many of the properties of the operators on verb which, as will be seen (5.4), can be derived with large or small cost from predicates (operators on sentence). The auxiliaries differ (in English) in that their operand verb is affixless (*began going, began to go* but *can go*); and they do not occur in deformed operands (e.g. nominalized sentences), hence cannot operate on each other (∄ *can may go*); also *not* operating on them is placed after and not before them. These properties are also characteristic of tense. But we have seen that the tense can be derived as a transform of time-operators, and that it is only the tense-transform of the time-operators that cannot occur in the deformed-operand forms of sentence: the source form of the time-operators, or other transforms of them such as the *have-en* in (4), do occur there. We will attempt a similar source for the auxiliaries.

For one auxiliary, the case is almost as good as for the past tense, for we have the same dependence upon a set of time-operators. This is *will*, and we can say, as in 3.2, e.g.:

His coming is tomorrow → He will come tomorrow.

and with zeroing:

> His coming is in the future → He will come in the future →
> He will come.

For the other auxiliaries we do not have such a convenient classifier relation to a set of predicates which can be said to produce the auxiliary morphophonemically. All we can do is to seek a synonymous predicate whose acceptability-ordering the auxiliary preserves. Then we can propose something like:

(6)   For him to go is an ability (or: a capability, possibility) →(7)
He is able to go. → (8) He can go.

(6)→(7) is the argument-skipping transformation. (7)→(8) is a unique morphophonemic one: Support for it can be found in the use of *is able to* instead of *can* wherever *can* cannot occur or is disappearing from use. This is seen in nominalizations: (9) *He can clear 7 ft., but his ability to do it is less than it was*; or under the past-operator: *He can not clear 7 ft. now but in his college years he could still do so*, which today is more likely to be (10) *He can not clear 7 ft. now but in his college years he was still able to do so*.

Additional support for the predicate source of the auxiliaries is seen in the way many of them have two meanings of the following type: (11) *A boy can jump all day (and not get tired) ← A boy's jumping all day (and not getting tired) is a capability* (or: *possibility*); *A boy is able to jump all day*. In contrast: (12) *A boy can speak five languages, (but it is rare) ← A boy's speaking five languages occurring is a possibility, (but it is rare)*; *The occurrence of a boy's speaking five languages is a possibility*; *A boy's speaking five languages is capable of occurring*. In (11) the action is a capability; in (12) the occurrence of the action is. The source (11) has *is a capability* operating on *jump*; the source of (12) has *is a capability* (or: *possibility*) operating on *occur* operating on *speak*. The same structure as in (12) appears in (13) *A boy can jump all day (without getting caught)*. The sentence common to (11) and (13) is ambiguous, and the ambiguity is due to the zeroing of *occur* in (13) as in (12).

The analysis of *can* is paralleled for *may, must* if we take (with *that* as a morphophonemic constant due to the operator):

> He may go. ← That he go is potential.
> He must go. ← That he go is obligatory.

In addition, there are, though somewhat in disuse, *shall* (now synonymous to *will*), and the resultants of past on *will* (*would*), *shall* (*should*), *can* (*could*) and very rarely *may* (*might*). A different kind of source appears in *should* (or *would, might*), which is produced as a variant of zero (non-tensing) under the 'subjunctive' sentence-operators and sentence-pair-operators:

(14)   I request that he go; I request that he should go.
        He left early lest he miss her; ⋯ lest he should miss her.

This analysis treats the auxiliaries as merely a subset of predicates (expressing types of readiness) which transform like the verb-operators (5.4) but have morphophonemic properties somewhat like those of the time-predicates. Then when auxiliaries are under an operator requiring a deformation, the operator simply operates on their source and not on the auxiliary form. More precisely, the morphophonemic transformation from the source to the auxiliary form does not occur in the same situations where tensing cannot occur (except for the variant of non-tensing as in (14)). It is the transformation to auxiliary form that is restricted. And, as elsewhere, the source does not have the restrictions that the transform has: it occurs in the predicate position as in (6), and under nominalization as in (9), and under time-operators as in (10).

In view of the secondary status of the auxiliaries, it is not surprising that the subset is not sharply closed. Most of the relevant morphophonemics apply optionally also to *need* (*He need go but once* ← *His going is a need but once*, and the like), *dare* (usually under *not*), and *ought* only under *not* (*He ought not go* ← *That he go is not a duty*, or *an owing*, or the like). Less close are certain specially restricted verb-operators with *to* which are losing the phonemic and morphemic recognizability of their *to*: *used to, has to, is going to, is supposed to*. These too could be derived from synonymous predicates.

In respect to the affixless form which the arguments of the auxiliaries receive, it may be noted that a similar affixless verb-argument appears under the predicates *make, let* (*I made him go, I let him go*). Compare the *to V* operands under V_v such as *important* (*For him to go is important*) and V_{nv} such as *prefer* (*I prefer for him to go*); and *that*-operands under V_v such as *is a fact* (*That he went is a fact*) and V_{nv} such as *know* (*I know that he went*).

5.4. *Verb-Operators*

A major type of increment in many languages is the verb-operator, which is seen in e.g. *He ceased writing*, and *He delayed writing*, as against *He wrote*. Verb-operators can be derived from sentence-operators (predicates on a sentence) by several paraphrastic transformations, chiefly by argument-skipping (8.1 (9)), as in

(1)   He ceased writing. ← His writing ceased.

like

       He is hesitant in driving. ← His driving is hesitant;

and, differently, by zeroing of a repeated subject, as in

(2)   He delayed writing. ← He delayed his writing.

If the subject of the operand is different from the subject of the operator, zeroing of course does not occur, and we do not obtain the effect of a verb-operator: *He delayed her writing.*

The great bulk of English verb-operators can be derived from sentence-operators in one or the other of these two ways. For derivations as in (1): Appropiately to their untensed operand (verb plus *to* or *-ing* or nominalization) these verb operators come from sentence-predicates whose argument is not tensed: Thus we have:

> He is irresponsible to see her. ← For him to see her is irresponsible.

and also for predicates whose arguments can be tensed or not:

> He is likely to see her. ← For him to see her is likely, That he will see her is likely.
> He is certain to see her. ← For him to see her is certain, That he will see her is certain.

but not for predicates whose argument must be tensed unless it is nominalized:

> $\not\exists$ He is probable to see her; $\exists$ That he will see her is probable.

In many cases the verb-deformation after the argument-skipping remains what it was under the predicate increment, e.g.:

> He began writing. ← His writing began.

However, there are cases of *to V* after the verb-operator transform, where the operand was *Ving* (and not *to V*) under the predicate source:

> He began to write, $\not\exists$ For him to write began.

Similarly:

> He (just) happened to come on time. ← His coming on time (just) happened.

In some cases there is an added morpheme:

> He persisted in talking. ← His talking persisted.

And the predicate may be a noun instead of a verb:

> He took the trouble to see her. ← For him to see her took trouble.

The question may be raised whether these are indeed paraphrastic transforms of each other, since there seems to be a noticeable difference in meaning.

However, the acceptability-orderings seem to be preserved throughout. And the difference in meaning is the subjective one of attributing the new predicate to the subject of the operand sentence: but this is precisely what the form change does explicitly, and it is felt, though more weakly, in other cases of the argument-skipping transformation, as in *He is hesitant in driving* ← *He has a hesitant manner in driving* ← *He drives in a hesitant manner*.

The other derivation, of (2), is seen in clear cases such as

He regretted writing it. ← He regretted his writing it.

(cf. *He regretted her writing it*), and also in less clear cases such as

He missed meeting her. ← He missed his meeting her.

where we may be uncertain about *He missed our meeting her*. For several verb-operators it is not clear whether their source predicates are of one kind or the other: If *He stopped their writing us* exists and is derived from *stop* operating on the pair (*he, they write us*), then

He stopped writing us. ← He stopped his writing us.
= stop (he, write (he, us)).

However, if *He stopped their writing us* is not really acceptable, or if it is derived from *He made them stop writing us* (which is *make* operating on *They stop writing us*), then

He stopped writing us. ← His writing us stopped.
= stop (write (he, us)).

This is a detailed problem of English transformations; and the language may be changing in this respect so that both solutions may be possible and no solution 'right'. In either case, a predicate source is available.

In some cases a predicate variant can indeed be found (e.g. *is an attempt* as variant of *attempts to*) but with unwontedly and unwantedly complex restrictions. Consider verb-operators like *try, attempt*, perhaps restricted to subjects denoting living organisms: *The dog tried to move?* ∄ *The book tried to move*; but without restriction: *The dog tends to move, The book tends to move*. If this were derived from an operator on sentence, e.g. *The dog's moving is a try*, we would have an operator restricted to particular subjects of its operand:[14]

try (move (dog))

where *try* restricts the argument (*dog*) of its argument: ∄ *try* (*move* (*back*)) as above. However, to an uncertain extent *try* may be derived from operators on the pair (N,S) if we accept such sentences as *He tried that the scaffold should remain*: then the restriction to living subject becomes a restriction of *try* in the domain of its own first argument: in

try (he, remain (scaffold))

the restriction of *try* is to its own first argument (*he*), which is the normal situation for operators. Even if such sentences are (or have become) unacceptable in English, their place is taken by a circumlocution: *He tried to have the scaffold remain.* If *have* here is taken as the argument of *try*, then the restriction holds for the subject (argument) of the argument. But if *try to have* is taken as a variant of *try* in all cases where the subject of *try* is not the same as the subject of the argument (*remain* as against *move, go*) of *try*, then we obtain *I try to go* as *try* operating on (*I, go* (*I*)), producing *I try* (*for me*) *to go*, and *I try to have it remain* as *try* operating on (*I, remain* (*it*)).

When the verb-operators involve a morphologically limited adjectivizing or nominalizing of the verb they may be hard to match with a predicate (on that verb) which might be considered their source. In such cases, a search for a predicate form involves us in what seems to be primarily semantic considerations of synonymy. One can propose various predicate variants for certain increments on verbs, but it is hard to know whether the predicates show the same acceptability-ordering on their verbs as the increments do:

> The government is repressive ← The government's repression is characteristic (or: is a disposition).

Intermediate transforms are: via argument-skipping to

> The government has a character of repression

and, by morphophonemic change between the adjectivizers *of* and *-ive*, to

> The government has a repressive character.

By the same transformations plus zeroing, we derive

> He is (very) frightening to them ← His frightening them has a (great) effect (or: impression).

And:

> He is an actor ← His acting is occupational

The most difficult search for a predicate source is in the case of verb operators on nominalized verbs: *have a look, give a look, make a trip*, etc. They almost all have the meaning of some bounded segment of activity, as is also seen in their time-duration adverbs: *He walked all day,* ∄ *He had a walk all day.* We would expect to derive these nominalizations from a predicate (or a choice of predicates) that state the bounding, but words that would preserve acceptability-ordering are hard to come by in this case:

> I had a walk. ← My walking was an event (or: was in an amount).

The problem is one of the availability of words. That an action-bounding operator is involved may be seen not only from the duration-adverbs and the like, but also from the fact that those adjectives of *have a walk* which are not in the adverb-selection for *walk* are explicable as adjectives of the action-bounding operator which had been the source of *have a*:

> I had a short walk. ← My walking had an extent and the extent was short.

A special case of verb-operators are those on *be* which permit *be* to be then zeroed: *He appears ill.* ← *He is ill.* These can be derived by argument-skipping and morphophonemics from a predicate: *His illness is apparent.* Many of the predicate forms do not occur except as presumable sources for the argument-skipping transformation: e.g. we have to derive *He seems to be ill.* ← **His being ill seems*; *He became ill.* ← **His illness became* (though marginally ∃ *His illness came to be*).

5.5. *Subordinate Conjunctions*

The subordinate conjunctions can be readily put into predicate form. Almost all of them appear in the following transforms:

(1)   He left because she arrived: $S_1 C S_2$.
(2)   He left because of her arrival: $S_1 P_v S_2 n$.
(3)   His leaving was because she arrived.
(4)   His leaving was because of her arrival: $S_1 n \ V_{vv} \ S_2 n$.

In (1) we have a conjunction C; in (2) what would be called a preposition P_v. In (3) we have a form (due to the transformation of 8.1 (11), cf. (3), (4) of 3.2) which does not really fit any classical grammatical classification since, *His leaving was* does not occur as a sentence in English, so that the following *because* is not a conjunction and indeed has no category; this is an example of how transformational analysis treats structures that cannot be analyzed except ad hoc in non-transformational grammar (8.4 (9)). In (4) we have a verb V_{vv} on two nominalized sentences, i.e. a predicate whose argument is a verb-pair. We can take (4) as the source and derive the other forms by paraphrastic transformations from it. It will then be found that these transformations operate on only a subset of the verb-pair predicates: some V_{vv} are not transformed into C, e.g. *spoil, be due to.* Thus:

> His leaving spoiled her arrival
> His leaving was due to her arrival.

These V_{vv} can be transformed almost up to (2) by a simulator of tense-transplacing. We add S_1C before (4), and then zero:

(5)   He left, (with) his leaving spoiling her arrival →
       He left, spoiling her arrival.

When the V_{vv} contains *be*, tense-transplacing can operate, producing the structure of (2):

His leaving was due to her arrival.
→ He left due to her arrival.

When the second operand is changed to *the fact that S* or the like, instead of nominalized S, we obtain such forms as

He left due to the fact that she arrived,

in which *due to the fact that* may be considered a member of the set of conjunctions, existing in the form (1).

These considerations not only show how members of V_{vv} can transform toward that subset of V_{vv} which has a transform called subordinate conjunction; they also help to organize the transformations operating on various subdomains of V_{vv} (like the zeroing of *his leaving* in (5)), as a step toward showing that some conjunctions are variants of other conjunctions, under suitable transformations.

The deriving of one conjunction from another, or rather from other V_{vv}, may also be supported by restriction-removal of the kind seen in § 2. Thus *whereas* is restricted to sentence-pairs which differ at two points: *I play violin whereas she plays piano* (the specific contrasting is not essential, as in *I play violin whereas she goes to museums*); ∄ *He went whereas I went*. Somewhat differently, *but* is restricted to sentence-pairs which differ at least in their verb-plus-object segment, and preferably at two points: *I play violin but she plays piano*, but also *I went but (I) missed him* (∄ *I went whereas I missed him*), *I came late but I left early, I smoke a lot but I smoke mild cigarettes*; ∄ *He went but I went*. One might think that this double contrast is a need of the concessive meaning. However, *whereas* and *but* can be shown to be free variants of *despite* (in the case of *but*: with an added sentence about what is the expectation of S_2, given S_1). *Despite* does not have this restriction: *He went despite my going*; and even (with special meaning) *He is educated despite his being educated*. Thus the restriction is made only in the paraphrastic transformations which, for slightly different subdomains yield *whereas, but* out of *despite*. It is not a property of the source increment, the predicate *despite*.

5.6. *Moods*

The above survey of increments has shown that at one cost or another, every

type of increment (except *and, or*) can be derived from a predicate on sentences. In addition, certain apparent increments have been shown in transformational analysis to be obtained by paraphrastic transformations from
other incremental forms. In particular, this is the case for the various grammatical 'moods'. All question forms, both the yes-no form (*Are you going?*) and
the *wh-* form (*When are you going? What will you take?* are paraphrastic
transformations of *I ask you whether you are going or not. I ask you when you
are going* (or: *whether you are going at time A or ... or you are going at time
Z*). *I ask you what you will take* (or: *whether you will take A or ... or Z*). The
imperative, e.g. *(Please) go!*, is derived from *I command* (or: *request*) *you that
you (please) go.* The optative *Would that he returned!* is derivable from *I
would that he returned, I wish that he would return.* And so on. That is to say,
these forms are obtained not by an increment of an intonation (plus some
changes) to an existing sentence, but by paraphrastic transformation from
known types of predicate operators.

The sources reached in many of these derivations have the additional advantage of being less restricted, in the manner of § 2. For example, the question form does not appear under sentence-operators except those which
produce that form. We have (1) *I ask you: Is she reading it?* ← (2) *I ask you
whether she is reading it* (*or not*), (2) being indeed the source of (1). But $\nexists$
He told them: Is she reading it? and $\nexists$ *He is waiting with the book while: Is she
reading it?* However, the source form of the question occurs freely under all
sentence-operators: $\exists$ *He told them* (*that*) *I ask you whether she is reading it*
(*or not*), $\exists$ *He is waiting with the book while I ask you whether she is reading it*
(*or not*). The paraphrastic transformation to the question form occurs in certain of the operator-environments in which the source form occurs (e.g.
under *and: I'm reading it and is she reading it?*) but not in all, as above.

5.7. *And, Or*

Two incremental operators have been left without any indication of how they
could be derived from predicates: *and, or.* One might think of replacing *and*
operating on S_1, S_2 by a predicate *conjoins* on S_1, S_2; and so for *or*. But this
may not fit as simply into the grammar as the previous predicate sources.

In any case, one can show that *and* is an operator only on sentences. It is
always possible to derive *and* in predicates from *and* or other operators on
sentence. And even *and* on nouns can be so derived. This has already been
seen, for example, in the reciprocal verbs (4.3); many other cases of N_1 *and*
N_2 can be derived from N_1 *with* N_2 or from *the set consisting of* N_1 *and* N_2 ←
the set contains N_1 *and the set contains* N_2. A particular problem here is that
of the collective verbs V_{coll}, e.g. *gather*, which are restricted to subjects or
objects consisting of *N and N*, or *N and N and ... and N* (at least 3), or instead

to certain collective nouns N_{coll} such as *set, crowd, group*. Here one can say that, in the source, V_{coll} selects only (in effect, is restricted to) N_{coll} as subject or object. The cases with *N and N* would be derived as follows:

> N and N and N gathered at the corner.[15]
>
> ←N_{coll} which consisted of N and N and N gathered at the corner.
>
> ←wh- (N_{coll} gathered at the corner: N_{coll} consisted of N and N and N).

The second operand here can be built up as follows:

> N_1 is a member of N_{coll} and N_2 is a member of N_{coll} and N_3 is a member of N_{coll}. → N_1 and N_2 and N_3 are members of N_{coll}.

On this there operates *is complete* or *is exhaustive*, yielding:

> N_1 and N_2 and N_3's membership of N_{coll} is exhaustive.
>
> →N_1 and N_2 and N_3 exhaust (the membership of) N_{coll}.
>
> →N_{coll} consists of N_1 and N_2 and N_3.

We now ask whether *and* between sentences is not simply a morphophonemic form of period between successive sentences in a discourse. Such an analysis does not seem adequate, first because it leaves the parallel problem of *or*, and secondly because *and* (and *or*) also operates on untensed (and period-less) sentences under all operators. In particular, *or* is essential under *ask, wonder* and similar operators, and *and* is essential in the derivation of the numbers, reciprocal verb, collectives, etc., and in specifying the operand-domain (the scope of operation) of certain zeroings (and of *wh-* plus pronouns). There are other operations which depend not upon *and* but upon the successive (and addressable) periods among sentences of a discourse: These are, above all, pronouns and the more subtle methods of reference[16], and also discourse structure.

6. RESULT

6.1. *Summary of Reductions*

We begin with the set of sentences {S}, as given in transformational linguistics, and with the sets of incremental transformations (or operators) and of paraphrastic transformations T defined on it. On the set of increments, the following grammatical reductions have been proposed in §§ 2–5:

For each individual incremental operator A, if it is restricted to a subdomain of values of the variables in its argument or in the operators upon it, we seek a free variant for A which is not restricted in this way. The unrestricted variant is taken as source; the restrictions are on the T (§ 2).

For each incremental operator A which is restricted in operator or argument domain, but does not have an unrestricted free variant, we seek one or more increments (one of which may be zero) each of which occurs with a subdomain of operator or argument which is complementary to that of the others and to that of A, such that the sum of the subdomains is the unrestricted domain of the variables in question. If we find increments which are only partly complementary, we try to make them completely complementary by assuming a zeroable element to occur in certain environments of one of the increments. An unrestricted morphophonemic source sentence (*S) is formed for the complementary variants (§ 3).

If a paraphrastic transformation T is restricted to a particular subdomain A′ of its operand A, we try to assume a zeroable operator Z (possibly a metalinguistic one) which A′ can accept on selectional (co-occurrence) grounds, such that T can operate on Z and thereby operate on those occurrences of A′ which are under Z. E.g., T may be a free variant of Z (§ 4). This is discussed here because it affects the form of the source increment.

We choose a particular sentence-position in respect to arguments, such that, for each incremental operator which does not occur in that position in respect to its argument (when it forms a sentence with its argument) we seek a free variant – if necessary, a metasentence one – that has this position; and if none is available we construct a morphophonemic source (*S) which does. For English and many other languages, this sentence position is the 'predicate' position, namely that of V, be $N(P)$, be $A(P)$, be P (§ 5).

6.2. *An Unrestricted Subset of Sentences*

Each of these steps can be carried out over all the transformations of the language. The first three steps produce free or complementary (automatic) variants which are unrestricted, and which can be taken as sources of the restricted ones. The last step gives to all increments a single source sentence-position. The recognizing or forming of these source-sentences is of special interest because of the following construction:

First, we form the set $\{S\}^+$ by adding to $\{S\}$ all the morphophonemic source-sentences *S introduced by the steps of §§ 2–5 or the conventional methods of structural and transformational linguistics. Then $\{S\}^+$ contains, for example, the tenseless *He go, as well as He goes. Second, we form a set $\{I\}$ consisting of all the source-sentences (asterisked or not) established in the above steps, plus all those other sentences of $\{S\}^+$ (again, whether asterisked morphophonemic sources or actual sentences) which contain only increments, and are not paraphrastic transforms. These will be unrestricted increments, since the restricted ones will have been treated in §§ 2–5. Then $\{I\}$ is a restrictionless subset of $\{S\}^+$, and is obtained by removing from the sentences of $\{S\}^+$ all effects (traces) of T, leaving each residual sentence to consist only of the arguments and incremental operators specified in 7.2.

We now consider the relation of {I} to {S-I}, its complement in {S}$^+$. The sentences in {S-I} are products of increments and paraphrastic transformations T, while those of {I} contain no T-traces. If for each sequence of increments and primitive arguments which constitutes the non-paraphrastic material of some sentence in {S-I} there exists in {I} a sentence composed of precisely that sequence, then it follows that for each sentence A of {S-I} there is some sentence A' of {I} such that A is a paraphrastic transform of A', and is derivable from A' or from the same increment-sequence as in A', by certain T.

To show this, it is sufficient that, for all pairs of an increment and a T, if there exists a sentence

$$S_i = \text{increment}_i \text{ on } T_j \text{ on } S_k.$$

then there must exist a sentence differing only in the T_j-trace[17]

$$S_h = \text{increment}_i \text{ on } S_k.$$

That is, there should be no case of a T enabling an increment to operate on a sentence (or more precisely on an increment-sequence) on which it would not operate otherwise. This demand seems to be satisfied in English and in other languages, as has been sketched in §§ 2–5. In contrast, there are many cases in which a T prevents an increment from operating on an increment-sequence on which it otherwise can operate. E.g. if

(1)   He is writing

is derived by zeroing from

(2)   He is in process of writing,

then we have nominalizing sentence-operators on (2), as in (2') *His being in the process of writing is (quite) frequent*, but not on the resultant of zeroing, i.e. not on (1): Hence (1') ∄ *His being writing is (quite) frequent.* Also: The question does not occur under sentence-operators, as in ∄ *They suspect is he going* (5.6), but the source of the question does: *They suspect that I ask you whether he is going or not*, or even (though less certainly) *They suspect that I ask you: is he going* or: *They suspect that I ask you: Is he going?* The increment *They suspect* does not operate on the zeroing of *I ask you*, or equivalently the zeroing of *I ask you* does not operate (is not addressable) under the increment *They suspect*.

For every S_i, S_h pair as above, the question arises whether the T_j component of S_i must be ordered in among the incremental components, or whether we can formulate the T components in such a way that they would operate after all the incremental components. In other words, can we always obtain S_i by T_j (possibly reformulated) operating on the corresponding {I}-sentence S_h?

Thus, in investigating the relation between {I} and {S-I}, we now consider the placing of the T in respect to the increments. One arrangement would have each T in a sentence operate as soon as its operand has been formed. That is to say, if a T which is defined on arguments X, Y has operated in the construction of a sentence, then it must have operated before any further increments on X, Y. In such an analysis, the operator representation of the sentence requires no special addressing in the argument of the T. Thus, the two (ambiguous) analyses of

> I dislike his speaking because she can't.

would be

(3)   dislike (I, T_z(because (speak (he), not (can speak (she))))))

in the sense of *His speaking because she can't is disliked by me* and

(3') T_z(because (dislike (I, speak (he)), not (can (speak (she)))))

in the sense of *His speaking is disliked by me because she can't speak*. In each case the T_z zeroes the word which is repeated (in a position corresponding to its antecedent) under the immediate operand of T_z. Of course, the increment *I dislike* could also have operated without the T_z. In both analyses we would have

> I dislike his speaking because she cannot speak.

which in the sense of (3) is:

(4)   dislike (I, because (speak (he), not (can (speak (she)))))

and in the sense of (3') is:

(4')   because (dislike (I, speak (he)), not (can (speak (she)))).

In (3) *dislike* has operated on T_z, whereas in (4) it did not. In some cases, an increment does not operate on a particular T. Such an increment is found only on the T-less operand, as in (1), (2) above:

for (2'): be frequent (be in process (write (he))).

for (1'): $\not\exists$ be frequent (T_z (be in process (write (he)))).

An alternative arrangement to the above is that all T in a sentence operate after all increments have operated. This is a more complex description, for it requires the arguments of each T to be provided with addresses in the sentence, indicating on what segments or operators in the sentence the given T is operating. Thus, in this decomposition, (3) above would appear as:

$$T_{z(because)} (\text{dislike (I, because (speak (he), not (can (speak (she)))))})$$

In both of these types of T-placing some addressing may in some cases be needed to indicate what word in the argument is zeroed. In the second type, however, the restrictions would be due not to an increment refusing to operate on a T (as for (1′) above) but rather to the T refusing to operate on (i.e. be addressable to) the operands of certain increments. Thus we would have, for (1′):

$$\not\exists\ T_{z(in\ process)} (\text{be frequent (be in process (write (he))))}$$

6.3. *A Sublanguage for Objective Information*

The result indicated above, that {S-I} contains only paraphrases of sentences of {I}, gives a new importance to the traditional linguistic search for removing restrictions. Modern linguistic analysis, whether descriptive, structural or transformational, has always sought to remove restrictions. Of course, the restrictions could not really be removed, but only moved: For example, in phonology, the great number of sounds that are heard in a language are organized into just a few phonemes; but this is at a cost, for whereas there was previously no such distinction as one between an element and its pronunciation (or its gross acoustic shape in the world of physical events), we now have to say that each phoneme may have more than one pronunciation, according to its environment. The total number of sounds remains naturally the same, but the number of statements necessary to describe them all may be greatly reduced, and the writing far simplified.

In the present case, the fact that {I} contains all the increment-combinations, which in interpretation means roughly all the objective information, that can be carried in {S}$^+$ gives a particular importance to shifting all subdomain restrictions out of {I}: it means that the subdomain restrictions are not necessary for expressing the objective information carried by language. That is to say, one can carry all the objective information of language in a system containing no such restrictions. Moving the restrictions is therefore in this case not merely a matter of structural compactness or elegance, but a gain for the interpretation and for the utilization of language-information, because the restrictions have here been moved out of a distinguished part of {S}$^+$, leaving that distinguished part as a far simpler system which is nevertheless capable of doing all the objective informational work.

This completes the restriction-removal activity of sentence (but not discourse) grammar, in so far as applies to the existing vocabulary of the language. (A step beyond this will be indicated in § 9.) This bringing to completion creates an effect which the various partial restriction-removals could not produce: Metalinguistically, it brings out the semantic interpretation of syntax: one can now see that each syntactic element (variable, operator-type, etc.) enters into combinations in a way that is directly interpretable by the meanings they carry. Linguistically, {I} is a system in which (within the limitations of how information is represented by morphemes) syntactic form and objective information correlate well: every two different pieces of such information are expressed by different sentences; but it is not at all excluded that, even when paraphrastic transformations are eliminated, the complex semantic overlappings in the vocabulary would permit two different sentences to carry the same information.

In studying the relation of {I} to {S}$^+$, the major question that remains at this point is to what extent the sentences in {I}, which are the source-sentences from which the sentences of {S-I} are derived, are themselves sentences of the original set {S} (and hence free variants of the sentences of {S-I}), and to what extent, and in what way, they are asterisked morphophonemic source-sentences, formed for {S}$^+$ but not extant in {S}: From the sentences in {I} which are not asterisked, those sentences of {S-I} whose source they are are derived by T. These T also derive some sentences of {S-I} from other ones. If the sentences in {S-I} for which asterisked sources have been formed in {I} differ from these asterisked sources (i.e. are derivable from them) by no more than these same T, it would mean that all sentences of {S-I} (i.e. all the remaining sentences of the language) are derived from all sources in {I} only by T. This would hold whether the source sentences in {I} are real or asterisked. In English, all sentences in {I} are of the form *S because they lack the required tensing (and in some cases also plural) morphophonemics. Nevertheless, in the case of English and many other languages, such asterisked *S sources as have to be formed in {I} satisfy the condition of differing from S only by established T.

When this condition is satisfied, then {S}$^+$ is only a slight extension of the set of real sentences {S}, for it involves no extension of the set T which derive all sentences from others, except for adding new morphophonemic changes to the list of morphophonemic T. In fact it is only a regularization of the domain of T, i.e. of the T-relation among sentences. It is then worth calling {S}$^+$ an extended natural language, and {I} (for all its asterisked members) a subset of that language. It may, however, happen in some languages that some of the asterisked sources differ from the sentences in {S-I} (that are to be derived from them) by T*, where T* are paraphrastic operations which differ from T or which include T as only a proper part. Then {I}, which contains these asterisked sources, can no longer be reasonably viewed as a subset of what we would consider a (slightly extended) natural language. Rather,

{I} would have to be considered a projection of {S-I}. This situation might be the case in some languages for the fourth step above (§ 5), when we seek a single positional relation that all increments have to the sentences onto which they are added. If such a relation is not attainable with any morphophonemics that would fit into the given language, it may still be attainable in principle, as a purely syntactic rather than also morphemic relation. In that case, the purely syntactic form could be simply the operator notation, which identifies each increment as an operator on a particular argument.

We now begin with $\{S\}^+$ as an empirically given set of sentences with the addition of asterisked source-sentences. Transformational theory shows that it contains a base set K of elementary sentences ('sentences of the kernel') from which all other sentences are derived, and two sets of transformations, the incremental and the paraphrastic, by which the sentences of $\{S\}^+$ are derived from other members of $\{S\}^+$. The empirical set $\{S\}^+$ is closed under these transformations, and it is as such that we call $\{S\}^+$ a language. $\{S\}^+$ is also closed under T above, taking {I} as the base set. When {I} is a subset of $\{S\}^+$, it is a sublanguage of the language $\{S\}^+$. This is so because the operators in {I} are the increments, which derive members of {I} from other members of {I} and ultimately from the base set of elementary sentences (K or *K, i.e. morphophonemic sources of K), which is contained in {I}. {I} is closed under the incremental operators.

Although both {I} and its complement {S-I} are subsets of $\{S\}^+$, the structures (grammars) of each of these are not subgrammars of that of $\{S\}^+$. The subsets have been separated on the basis of grammatical properties: presence or absence of T, and hence of all the environmental ('distributional') and string properties (§ 8) that T bring in. Therefore the grammars of {I} and of {S-I} each contain relations which are lacking in the grammar of $\{S\}^+$ (or in the grammar of the set of real sentences {S}). As will be seen below, they are each simpler and more transparent systems than is the grammar of the whole language, and have interpretations which do not naturally arise from the grammar of the whole language.

7. THE PREDICATE SYSTEM

7.0. *The Metalanguage*

In considering the structure of {I}, we note first that the removal of restrictions and the environment-filling method of § 4 eliminate most of the metagrammar needed for stating the grammar of {I}. Each increment can be provided with an indication (a subscript) of its argument variables, and every sequence consisting of increments operating on variables that match their arguments is well formed, i.e. is in {I}.

7.1. *The Base*

When the increments are viewed, like the T, as transformations from one subset of sentences (those satisfying the argument requirements) to another (those containing the increment as their latest – i.e. not operated on – operator), then we have to take the elementary ('kernel') sentences or their morphophonemic sources as a base set K or *K within {I}; from K or *K, the sentences of {I} are generated by the increments. However, we have seen that all increments except *and, or* form their resultant sentences by serving as the verbal segment in respect to their argument. It therefore becomes convenient to look upon the elementary sentences as being themselves the resultants of an operator (their verbal segment) acting upon their primitive arguments (their subject and object nouns). Then the operators of {1} are not only the increments but also the verbal segments of the elementary sentences. The primitive operands are the subjects and objects of the elementary sentences. The operators are now no longer transformations from sentences to sentences, but operations which produce a sentence when carried out on a sentence or non-sentence operand. Indeed, if we can show that the increments affect only the most recently operating (i.e. not already operated on) verbal segment of their operand, we can define the argument of each increment to be certain operators rather than a whole sentence. This analysis presents, of course, a purely syntactic relation; the physical contents – what morphemes in what positions – will be considered in 7.4, 5.

7.2. *The Operators*

For English the primitive arguments are primarily the concrete N, and the main operator sets are:

V_n: e.g. *exist, be tall, be a mammal, be up.*

V_{nn}: e.g. *eat, be father of, be near (to).*

V_{nnn}: e.g. *be between ... and*; possibly *give ... to.*

V_v: e.g. *be a fact, continue.* Thus *His smoking continues* would be: *continue (smoke (he)).*

V_{nv}: e.g. *think,* In almost all arguments which contain both v and n, the n indicates the subset of nouns which denote living beings: it is only these that can be related to the v by the given operator. Thus *I think he drinks tea* would be: *think (I, drink (he, tea)).*

V_{nnv}: e.g. *tell.*

V_{vv}: e.g. *be because of, correlate with.*

V_{nvv}: e.g. *relate ... to.*

C_{vv}: *and, or.*

Special subtypes of *V* with *v*-arguments carry particular classificatory morphemes, as in *request-for-afterwards* (4.2), *an-undergoing-for-the-object* (4.4). We may also wish to recognize a *V* whose argument is a constant, e.g. *rain, late* (Whence morphophonemically *It's raining, It's late*).

Each operator operates on its arguments to produce a sentence. Those whose arguments include operators (V) are increments. The others form elementary sentences.

The products (sequences) of operators are associative, even though the conjunctional transforms of many V_{vv} are not. The C_{vv} and certain of the V_{vv} are interpretationally commutative in the sense that while S_1 *and* S_2 is a different sentence than S_2 *and* S_1 it carries the same objective information. It is not certain that C_{vv} must be taken as binary rather than n-ary (for $n > 1$) in argument. In constructing a sentence, the operators are apparently linearly ordered. Each can then occur whenever its arguments are present (and not already operated on). The ordering and repeatability possibilities of an operator are determined by its arguments.

To these must be added one operation quite different from these operators. In this operation we pair each occurrence (in a discourse) of an element or sequence of elements A with an address which indicates the position of A in the discourse or in any stated segment of the discourse (e.g. sentence or structurally identified section of a sentence). In the actual form of the sentence and discourse or a sequence of phonemes, morphemes, words, etc., the address of A states that A is the *n*th occurrence, in a given segment of the discourse, of a member of the class of A. In the operator form, if an operator B contains within its argument the address of A, then the address states what position A occupies in the operand of B. This addressing is implicit in the linear ordering of phonemes and words which comprise a discourse, and in the ordering of operators and their arguments, as morphemes, by which we represent the actual sentences and discourses. This addressing is necessary for the metadiscourse operators which are included within the grammar of the language, and for certain paraphrastic T (e.g. zeroing of repeated words in particular relative positions). It is also needed if we try to place all T after all increments (end of 6.2).

Finally: what is produced by the operator is a sentential string, but not quite a sentence because it lacks the sentence-intonation (period) and its attendant morphophonemics (primarily tensing). The placing of the period takes a sentential string out of {I} for then it can no longer be operated on by the operators of {I}, or by the T-operators of {S-I}. Similarly for sentential strings produced in {S-I}.

7.3. *The Values*

The arguments and operators in formulas are class-marks, i.e. variables over certain domains. Each value A_i of an operator A imposes a partial ordering of acceptability (or subject-matter classification) on the values of its argument B; but A apparently leaves unaltered the partial orderings in which B otherwise participates. That is, the partial ordering of acceptability which B had imposed upon the arguments of B, and any partial ordering of acceptability which B has in respect to any other operator on B (if B can be an argument of more than one operator – see immediately below), are invariant under A's operating on B.

In what variable (or variables) of its operand does each value of an operator impose a partial ordering of acceptability on the values of the variable? This variable in the operand would be the effective argument of the operator. The question is important for the fundamental problem of operator-syntax, namely: what is the relevant argument of each operator? And the main, and still partly open, question in whether the increments are linearly or partially ordered is a matter of how increments relate to each other in respect to the arguments on which they impose an acceptability-ordering.

7.4. *Morphemic Shape*

For the most part, each operator introduces into the sentence one morpheme, and of only the predicate morpheme classes: *V, be A (P), be N (P), be P*; aside from *and, or.* The *be* is clearly morphophonemic and not an independent morpheme. The operator N are e.g., classifiers (*mammal, fact*) and relations (*father*), and are not the same morphemes as in the concrete N class. There are, however, many cases in which the demands of simple and consistent syntactic relations make us assume a morphologically complex form as the syntactic source, as when we take, say, *His acting is an occupation*, or the like, as source (via argument-skipping) for *He is an actor*. Where there is a conflict between syntactic regularity and morphological regularity, we see that the operator system is a syntactic one.

The operator system is morphologically convenient in another way too. To a large extent, each morpheme is a value of only one operator: thus the *-ing* of *be-ing* (*He is running*), as also the *-ing* of verb-operators (*He continued running*), are derived from the *-ing* of sentence nominalization (*His running continued.*).

7.5. *String Shape*

Although every sentence and discourse is a sequence of morphemes, the only way in which grammatical descriptions have succeeded in characterizing which sequences are those that constitute sentences has been by finding among the morphemes of the sentence certain relations which are not immediately apparent from their positions. In transformational theory, and especially in the further reduction of §§ 2–5, this relation is that of operator to argument. A sentence can be fully represented by a linear or partial ordering of operators, each operating on a prior one, with the innermost operating on primitive arguments. The argument of each operator can be written in parentheses. The sentences of a natural language, however, do not use parentheses and do not directly indicate the operator-argument relation. The possibility of representing in a string of words the same thing that the operator notation represents, is achieved in language by means of an apparatus which can best be described in two stages: In {I} it is done by means of a classification of morphemes in respect to their known arguments, and by means of a relative positioning of operator and arguments (see below); these together give the morphemes of {I}-sentences a 'string' relation to each other: what is subject, predicate, object, etc. In {S-I} it is achieved as follows: when T produces B out of A, it makes particular changes in the relative positions of the morphemes of A, and may give them the appearance of different operator-argument relations. Thus these morphemes appear in changed string relations to each other in B; the relative positioning is important because on it are defined certain prominent morphophonemics such as the location of tensing or the agreement of verb with subject in respect to plural. In many of these changes, the participating morphemes receive particular constants (usually affixes) marking the change. We can say that the string relation of {I} are produced by the operators of {I}, and the string changes (to new string relations) in {S-I} are produced by T.

Given the transformational representation of a sentence, i.e. the operator relations among the morphemes in it, and the T if any, we can determine the positions and string-relation constants of the morphemes, i.e. we can determine the actual word-sequence that is the sentence. And conversely: Given the word sequence and a grammatical lexicon, i.e. a list of which morphemes belong to which operator (or argument) classification, we can determine (in some cases, ambiguously) the string relations in this sequence and thence the operator relations and the T.

Here we consider the string shape of the {I} operators in English; the string changes in {S-I} are noted in 8.4. A major advantage in having found (§ 5) a single positional relation in respect to the argument, which the sources of almost all increments would have, is that this gives a single string structure to all source sentences, i.e. to {I}. It shows that a single positional (syntactic) relation suffices for all the operators of {I}. As among these, *and* and *or* differ from all the other operators (the predicates) only in morphophonemic respects, below. Such string complexity as there is in {I} is due to the nested superposing of the syntactic relations of those elements which are in the given sentence both operators and arguments. In {I}, the ordered morphemes of an operator A concatenate with its sequence of arguments B, in such a way that the operator morphemes occupy even-numbered positions, and the ordered arguments the odd-numbered positions, in the resultant sequence:

$$A_1 A_2 \ldots A_n (B_1, B_2, \ldots, B_n B_{n+1}) = B_1 \overgroup{A_1 \; B_2} \; A_2 \ldots B_n \overgroup{A_n \; B_{n+1}}.$$

The interpretation, both in the operator notation and in the word-concatenation, is that the B_1 is the subject of A_1 (as predicate) and B_2 the direct object, and the remaining B what may be called indirect objects. Under a predicate operator (but not *and, or*), when one of the arguments B_p is itself a predicate, there is attached to B_p a constant which depends upon the first morpheme of the operator. This constant indicates that the predicate is also an argument; the main constant is *-ing* or other nominalizing affix (zero under the operator *make*, etc.). If an argument B itself has arguments C, these stay concatenated to B as a single entity in respect to A; and if B receives a nominalizing constant then C receives an adjectivizing constant, primarily: *'s* (mostly for first operand under B), *by* (only for first operand under B), *of* (rarely on the first operand if it occurs on the second operand under B). The choice of constants is free, or depends on C. Thus when B becomes an operand of A, then C receives constants which mark the relation it had to B before B had become an operand. The constants (and positions) indicate the operator-argument relations that had existed in the sentence before A operated on it.

The string structures in {I} are therefore such as the following:

$V(N)$:   exist (gas) = *gas exist → Gas exists.

$V(N, N)$:   between and (N, L, M) = *N between L and M → N is between L and M.

$V_0(N, V_1, V_2)$: relate to (I, grow, increase) = I relate ... growth to ... increase.

Here the arguments of the two operand-verbs V_1, V_2, were not shown, in order to bring out the positional relation of the new operator V_0 to its immediate arguments. If we take the resultant of the above with

$V_1(N)$: grow (tree) = *Tree grow,

$V_2(N)$: increase (rain) = *Rain increase,

we obtain

relate to (I, grow (tree), increase (rain)) = I relate the tree's growth to the rain's increase.

The *-th* and *'s* are parts neither of the operator nor of the argument. They are constants indicating the superposition of syntactic statuses: *-th* nomina zation of V_1 under V_0; *'s* adjectivization of subjects when their verb becomes an argument. Similarly, the -s and is above are neither in the operator nor in the argument, but are morphophonemic effects. See also 8.5 (1), (2).

In the case of all operators but *and, or* the words entering the second position in the resultant string are of the predicate morpheme-classes (7.4) and can undergo certain T (argument-skipping, certain zeroings, placing of the morphophonemic tense). In the case of *and, or* the morphological class is different and the T which can operate on them are fewer and different (different zeroings and permutations).

The fact that there is one position, relative to all arguments, which is taken by all operators, and the further fact that the operators belong to morphologically recognizable classes of known arguments, makes the word strings which are sentences of {I} readily computable. That is to say, it makes their operator-argument (i.e. syntactic) relations recognizable to the hearer word by word, without waiting for parenthesis-closings. (It will be seen in § 8 that the T bring considerable complexity, and even degeneracies, into the recognizability of the operator-argument relations of the words, but without destroying computability.) To the extent that different morphemes occur as values of the different variables, the operator-argument relations are more immediately recognizable. To the extent that certain morphemes (or merely phoneme-sequences) occur as values of more than one class-variable (e.g. of both V_{nn} and V_{nv}) the operator-argument relations are less transparent in {I}, and in {S-I} ambiguities may result.

7.6. *Relation to Linguistic Analysis*

In the {I} sublanguage more can be said than had been thought sayable in {S}, because regular sources are discovered whose existence had been put into shadow by the more compact but more restricted variants. Such restrictions as exist in {I} are more like the semantically reasonable and changeable restrictions of selection (co-occurrence) than like the grammatical restrictions of unbreakable 'rules'.

The meanings of words and of constructions are seen more sharply than in the language as a whole. For example, when we see the source of the comparative, which is e.g. for *He is richer than she*:

> n is more than m.
> His riches amount to n.
> Her riches amount to m,

we see that indeed the comparative does not include *He is rich* as an immediate syntactic source (but only *N is the amount of his riches*), just as it does not include the meaning of that sentence in its direct meaning[18].

The approach in descriptive linguistics had been to sweep everything under the carpet, i.e. to obtain regular grammar at the cost of irregular source. Thus the subjunctive could be presented as what occurs after verbs that require the subjunctive; and then the non-subjunctive form *I request his going* is obtained from the subjunctive by a transformation. In the present work, however, we want the source to be as regular as possible, since we want its structure to contain no complexity other than what is required by its informational burden. The only cost that we can admit is in the morphophonemic complexity of the source; for this is unrelated to the objective information, though it complicates the subjective task of coding and decoding. Thus in the case of the subjunctive we would first note that this can be viewed in English as a morphophonemic change from a tenseless (and non-subjunctive) form; then in considering the verbs which require or permit this morphophonemic change, we would try to characterize them not by a list but by the fact that they selectionally always have *subsequently* or the like in their environment (or, indeed, as part of them) in such a way that (as in § 4) the subjunctive form would be a free variant replacement or a free or required accompanying variant of that accompanying word.

As the operators become unrestricted, and as subset listings are replaced by the presence of classifier morphemes in the environment, we begin to have elements whose properties are no longer inherent but due only to their positional relations and whose combinations (i.e. positional relations) are sufficiently regular and simple to permit of something approaching a mathematical characterization. It also becomes possible to find relations of relations, such as elements whose positional relations are the inverse of each other's: e.g. *before* and *after* are inverses of each other when they are taken as V_{vv} (or as V_{nn} on two time-nouns) but not when they are taken as conjunctions.

8. THE MORPHOPHONEMIC SYSTEM

8.0. *Introduction*

The paraphrastic transformations T, which operate on the sentences of {I} and of {S-I} to produce the sentences of {S-I}, can be considered an extension of morphophonemics. Morphophonemics is the change of the phonemic shape of a morpheme; if automatic, the change appears when the morpheme occurs in the environment of particular other morphemes. The T include such changes (from the source morphemic shape, 7.4); but they also include changes in the positional relations of the morphemes (from those of 7.5). As in morphophonemics, the original syntactic relations of the source sentence are not lost, although secondary syntactic relations are superposed (8.5); and there are various other changes: e.g. at what point of the sentence the hearer is apprised of particular syntactic elements (8.2). All this applies also to morphophonemics, though in a much simpler way. Hence all T can be considered to be morphophonemic, or perhaps to constitute a corresponding relation of syntaxomorphemics: the change of the morphemic (and ultimately phonemic) shape of a syntactic element or sequence. The change occurs freely in all or in certain syntactic (i.e., now, operator) environments, or requiredly (automatically) in certain syntactic environments.

The difference between the increment system and the paraphrastic T system is roughly that between the directly useable activities of life and the institutional apparatus which channelizes these activities. Like social institutions, the T system structures, facilitates, slants, and petrifies the activities-for-use of the {I} system, and is inflexible, conventional, and in part historically accidental; and in some cases it stands in the way of further development of the use-activities, i.e. of the directly meaningful expressions of {I}. Indeed, the relations between {I} and {S-I} can be studied as a very special case of the relations between activities-for-use and their institutionalization.

8.1. *The Morphemic and String Changes*

In the case of English, the changes which are introduced by each T can be seen from the list of established paraphrastic transformations plus the further cases of T required by the sources proposed above (§§ 2–5).

The (1) zeroing and (2) pronouning T replace certain morphemes or sequences by zero or pronominal variant of them, usually at the same site in the sentence (though some pronominal variants occur at a stated other site: e.g. the ones after *wh-*). Zeroing can affect the string relations of the remaining words. Thus, certain expected operands are zeroable, e.g. *arrive, come* under *expect*, yielding *I expect him to come* → *I expect him.* In the resultant, *him* is the object of *expect*, so that *expect* now occurs with a noun as object as well as with a sentence as object. Note that in *I expect him to come, him* is not the object of *expect*, but the subject of the object (*him to come*) of *expect*.

(3) The T which are purely morphophonemic in the ordinary sense of the word replace certain morphemes (not simply phonemes, although this is a matter of definition) by others, and not always at the same site.

(4) An extreme case is the one which produces a single morpheme out of a specially structured sequence: e.g. *the* from *wh-* plus certain second operands (5.1); *wh-* from *and...and...same...* (2.8, 8.2).

The permutational T change the sites of words in the sentence, i.e. their relative positions.

(5) Some permutations do not change the receptivity of the words to other morphophonemics (e.g. tensing and adjunction), and what is subject and object: *So he says* ← *He says so.* Such is the moving of verb-adjuncts and

sentence-adjuncts (8.4) to before the verb or the subject: *He hesitantly drove the truck, Hesitantly he drove the truck.*

(6) A major set of these are the length-permutations, which act on post-verb syntactic entities to put short ones before long ones: *They looked up the number,* but *They looked it up.*

(7) There are some restricted permutational changes which affect in unique ways the subject-object relations of their operand sentence: the *It*-form (*That he came is certain → It is certain that he came*), and the *There*-form (*There is a man coming*).

(8) Other T change the words' string relations to each other, as in the interchange of two operands (e.g. Passive), or

(9) in the argument-skipping T which shifts the operator to a lower argument: A(B(C)) → A(C), as in *His driving is hesitant → He is hesitant in driving.* Here the *hesitant* which had been the predicate of the sentence **He drives* appears as the predicate of the noun *He.*

(10) There is a widespread tense-transplacing T which shifts the predicate status (the location of tensing) from the latest operator to its argument, as in *His death was in March → He died in March.* There are reasons for taking the former as the source; but in any case two sentences would have to be related by a transformation, whose effect is to move the predicate status from one to the other.

(11) And there is a free variant in which the morphophonemic operation of tensing (or non-tensing in the subjunctive 2.4) together with a constant such as *that* occurs on the V-arguments of many operators: *I deny his going in the past → I deny that he went.*

(12) On the second argument-verb under certain operators (see 3.2, (3)–(5)) tensing occurs as free variant (with no constant).

8.2. *The Interpretation of T*

In structural linguistics, morphophonemic changes do not change the meaning of a morpheme, since the meaning of morphemes does not depend on its phonemes, which is all that morphophonemics changes. But there can result a change as to where in the sentence the hearer is apprised of the presence of a particular morpheme. Thus in a question beginning *Will . . .* the hearer knows nothing of the subject until he hears it, but in a question beginning *Am . . .* the hearer knows beforehand that the subject is *I.*

The morphemic and string changes of the type of 8.1 produce various (or no) modifications of the information in their operand sentences, but always without altering the objective information carried by their base sentences in {I}. Pronouning and zeroing neither destroy nor add information; they are carried out in such a way that the dropped morphemes (or their equivalents) can be reconstructed from the residue. However, they can give an indication, earlier than in the source, of the identity of individual reference of certain words: *I saw a boy and spoke with him* ← *I saw a boy and spoke with a boy and the two boys were the same*. And they can lead to degeneracies (ambiguities): *I met John, and Mary too*. ← *I met John and I met Mary too*, or ← *I met John, and Mary too met John*. In many cases they do little more than abbreviate the sentence: *He explained this and left* ← *He explained this and he left*.

Many zeroings, and certain other T, occur when a particular argument is the expected one for the given operator (or vice versa) – expected in the culture as a whole, or in a particular subject matter, or in a particular conversation, etc. Thus from the source operator *be in A manner*, the *manner* is zeroable if the particular A is one which is more expectably an adjective of manner than some other adjective, e.g. of occurrence (in 2.3). Hence it is zeroable in *He spoke in a hesitant manner* → *He spoke hesitantly*, but not in *He arrived in an unexpected manner* ↮ *He arrived unexpectedly*. This and some other changes, such as the zeroing of *to arrive* under *expect*, and the conditions for *but*, make expectability a property in {S-I}, though not in {I}.

In transformations which are restricted to a subset of the domain, the resultant receives a more restricted meaning, expressing the effect of the increment upon this more limited environment. Thus, whereas the source *be before* simply means 'prior', the time-conjunction *before* has rather the meaning of 'prior within the same subjective time-segmentation', since it only relates two past events to each other, or two future events.

In some T, especially such as bring a word out to the beginning of a sentence, there is an attention-directing effect upon the meaning of a sentence: e.g. *This in particular I like* ← *I like this in particular*, and the passive, etc. In some T, this device is less a matter of directing attention to a particular word in the sentence as of directing to that word the argument status in some further operator: e.g. *I have a book which you want* is most directly derivable from *wh-* on the pair *I have a book, a book you want*, which is derivable from something like $n-2$, *I have a book and*, $n-1$, *you want a book and*, *n*, *book of $n-1$ is same individual as book of $n-2$*. (The n are addresses in the discourse.)

If we consider carefully the meaning effect of all T, we see that they do not alter the objective report that is carried in their operand, and ultimately in the {I} sentence to which they relate; this is hardly surprising since by definition they do not alter the acceptability-ordering of the word n-tuples. However, while some of the T are indeed simple paraphrases with no appreciable change in nuance, others add discernible nuances which can perhaps be best summarized as subjective, for the hearer or for the speaker. Some of these simply affect when in the course of hearing the sentence the hearer is apprised of a given content in the sentence. Some affect what the hearer learns from a sentence by bringing in local ambiguity (which is resolved later on in the sentence) or unresolved ambiguity. Some T involve the criterion of what is considered an expectable operator or arguments at a given point in the sentence construction. Others give special syntactic status to the subjective tense, i.e. the relation between when the sentence is said and when what it says occurs. Others call attention to a particular segment of the sentence. There are various kinds of such effects which are due to the T, and the matter requires investigation. It is in any case clear that we can distinguish, on syntactic grounds, three interpretationally-different properties: objective report, subjective discrimination, and pure paraphrase (including paraphrase for convenience of discourse, i.e. of relation to neighboring sentences). Such a distinction in the interpretation of language might not have been thought of without the evidence from transformations. But this fact need not surprise us, since the history of structural linguistics has shown that precise grammatical analysis throws light on the meanings borne in language. And indeed a test of a syntactic method is whether it makes predictable the meanings of sentences, or the modifiability of their meanings – in short, whether it contributes to the elimination of meaning as an independent primitive of linguistics.

8.3. *Creation of Subsets*

The effect of the T upon the sentences of {I} yields certain new features in the grammar of the whole language. One of these is the creation of grammatical subsets of the major word or morpheme classes. In {I} there are virtually no restrictions in the domain of operations, and virtually no subclasses. Such subclasses as there are, are a matter of changeable selection rather than fixed grammatical subclasses: e.g. the living-being or human-like subjects of many increments whose arguments contain both N and V (*know*, etc.). The nonexistence of closed subclasses remains unchanged for those T which do not apply to a restricted subdomain. However, those T which are restricted are defined in respect to a particular subdomain. The defining institutionalizes the subdomain and therefore freezes it, creating an unchanging grammatical fact. This holds even for the T-restrictions which are based on {I}-selections. Thus in {I} certain adjectival increments more naturally select *occurrence* than *manner* (2.3); but in T, the zeroing of *in manner* (as against zeroing *in occurrence*) fixes certain *Aly* as being adverbs of manner: *hesitantly*, but not *unexpectedly*.

In some cases, the net effect of several morphophonemic T is to create a subset of operators which are distinct in terms of the overt grammar: e.g. the auxiliaries *can, may*, etc.

8.4. *String Change*

It was seen in 8.1 that the T change the morphemic shapes or relative positions of syntactic entities (or both). The result is that new kinds of string relations are created, which were not found in {I}.

(1) Some T (8.1 (5), (6)) produce resultants in which the relative positions of the entities of their operand sentence are changed, without altering the interpretation of the concatenation in 7.5, or the status of the entities as arguments of further T. Thus in *This I say.* ← *I say this.*, the *I* remains the subject, and the *say* remains the location for tensing.

(2) Some T produce unique string relations not found in any other sentence-form: the not quite appositional status of *that S* under *It*, and the status of *It, There* (8.1 (7)).

(3) Some T only change the form of a syntactic entity without changing the string relations among the entities. Thus in the zeroing *I play piano and he violin* ← *I play piano and he plays violin*, the second argument under *and* has zero form while its arguments in turn remain, producing the new word-concatenation *he violin* whose operator structure is *0 (he, violin)*; 0 here is for zero.

(4) Some T produce word sequences that are new for a particular environment (i.e. under particular operators) but do not constitute new types of word sequence for the language. Thus the zeroing *to arrive* under *expect* produces, e.g., *I expect him*, where *him* is a new type of object for *expect*, but not for other V of the language; hence the change has merely shifted *expect* from being only in V_{nv} to being also in V_{nn}.

(5) Many T produce a new string relation, which may be called the host-adjunct relation. When we zero *He left and he returned* → *He left and returned* we obtain, as above, a new form for second arguments under *and*: in this case an operand whose operand in turn in zero. But when we zero and permute *He left and she left* → *He and she left* we obtain a new syntactic entity *and she*, different from the ones found in {I}. For whereas *He left and she left* is the concatenation of words corresponding (by 7.5) to

$$\text{and (left (he), left (she))}$$

the word sequence *He and she left* has an interrupting operator (*and*) with an incomplete operand. Interruptions of this kind, headed by *and* or *or*, are found to contain a sub-sequence of the second operand of the *and*, a sub-sequence whose internal string relations (or status) are the same as those of the material immediately preceding the interruption. Hence we call the interruption an adjunct of the immediately preceding syntactic entity. Here fits *wh-* on sentence: *He left, which surprised me* ← *wh- (He left, His leaving surprised me)* ← *He left and his leaving surprised me*.

(6) Adjuncts, of noun, also result from the T which produces *wh-* out of *and* (8.2) and permutes it, as in *The book which you want is lost*, where *which you want*, transformed from *and you want the book*, has the new string relation of adjunct to *book* (in *The book is lost*).

(7) Many of these *wh-* adjuncts may have their constants zeroed and are then permuted to before their host; where they become a left-adjunct to the host: *The picture which is small is nicer* → *The small picture is nicer*.

(8) Adjuncts, of verb and sentence, also result from other types of T. The tense-transplacing T (8.1 (10)) which shifts the predicate status (both as interpretation of 7.5 and as location for tensing) from the latest operator to its argument leaves the latest operator without any defined string status in terms of 7.5: Hence in *He died in March*, or *He died quietly* (← *His death was quiet*) the *in March* and *quietly* are called adjuncts of the new predicate *died* (which had also been the previous predicate before *was in March* or *was quiet* had operated). Similarly for this T on V_{vv}: *His leaving was because of her arrival* → *He left because of her arrival*, where *because of her arrival* is now an adjunct. When both this T and the second-operand tensing (8.1 (12)) operate on V_{vv}, we have an adjunct consisting of a subordinate conjunction plus its second operand: *He left because she arrived*.

(9) When the second-operand tensing operates on V_{vv} without the tense-transplacing, we obtain a unique string-relation for the subordinate conjunction plus its second operand: *His leaving was because she arrived*.

(10) Finally, the adjuncts (8) above can be permuted to various points of the remaining sentence, their host: *His leaving was because of her return* → *He left because of her return*; *He left because she returned* → *Because of her return, he left*; *Because she returned, he left*. Similarly: *In March he died*. Again, the permuted segment no longer fits into the string relations introduced in 7.5; it has to be called an adjunct on the residual sentence *He left*.

(11) There is one string relation which results from certain T which can with difficulty be fitted into the relations of 7.5. This is found in the resultant of the argument-skipping T that changes A(B(C)) into A(C); the B which is left over can be considered in some cases as an adjunct of A and in other cases the second argument of A: In *He is hesitant in driving* we can take *in driving* as adjunct of *is hesitant* (whereas in *His driving is hesitant*, we had *is hesitant* as operator on *driving*); In *The franc began deteriorating* we can take *deteriorating* as second argument (object) of *began* (whereas in *The franc's deterioration began* we had *began* as operator on *deterioration*).

(12) A change in the status of certain adjuncts occurs as a result of T which zero the host, in particular situations. This appears in *I like the bigger* ← *I like the bigger one*; *His reading is mostly politics* ← *That which constitutes his reading is mostly politics*; *What he found was valuable* ← *That which he*

found was valuable. In such cases the string status of subject or object is taken by an adjective or a segment of certain complex operands.

8.5. *String Properties under T*

In all this we see that in certain cases a T creates in its resultant a relation among the concatenated words (or word sub-sequences) of a sentence that differs from anything present in {I}. In addition to the subject, predicate, and objects of 7.5, we have now adjuncts, which can be attached to one of these or to the string as a whole. These adjuncts are formed by various T out of the latest operator in a sentence, or out of a (permuted) V_{vv} plus its second operand, or out of (permuted) *and*, *or* plus its second operand (after zeroing). The result of this adjunct-making is to leave the first operand sentence (under a one-sentence or two-sentence operator) as a center string with the structure of 7.5, while the operator (together with its second operand, if it has one) becomes an adjunct of the center or of some part of the center. Many of these adjunct forms are marked by certain constants, in addition to being usually permuted next to their host. In their constants, and in their positions next to their host, they bear some resemblance to the operand of an operand in 7.5. There is also some interpretational similarity: In the string form of A(B(C)) in 7.5., the relation of A to B is unaffected by the presence or nature of C (except perhaps for certain problematic cases). And in the case of adjuncts, the string relations among the non-adjunct entities are unaffected (except for certain problematic cases) by whether any of them are hosts to adjuncts, and of what kind.

Many T also bring in certain innovations in the relations among the string analyses of sentences. One such is the ambiguity exemplified in *I met John, and Mary too* (8.2). Different zeroings and permutations, operating on different sentences, may degenerately produce identical strings of words, although in each case the string of words has string relations (and grammatical meanings) appropriate to the particular operator sequence and T which produced it.

Another such innovation is the fact that the resultants of many T exhibit two or more simultaneous syntactic relations in the meaning of the sentence. This is so because the string relations of the sentence on which the T operated have not been effaced in the resultant. The constant of the T are indicators of a change, rather than simply markers of the string relations in the resultant; hence they indicate the string relations in the operand sentence as well as those in the resultant.

Constants which indicate change have already been seen in the operands of an operand (7.5): given $V_1(N_1, N_2) = N_1 V_1 N_2$, we find that when V_1 becomes an operand as in $V_0(V_1)$ we obtain $V_0(V_1(N_1, N_2)) = N_1$'s V_1ing of

N_2V_0. Thus:

(1)   Students composed jazz.
(2)   Students' composing of jazz continued.

where *Students' composing of jazz* is positionally the subject of *continued*, but within it the constants (and positions) show that *students* is the subject of *compose*, and *jazz* its object. In this case, and throughout the sentences of {I}, no two words show two different string relations to each other.

In the resultants of many T, however, the constants and the meaning of the sentence exhibit both the new and the former string relations among the same words (since no new words except for constants are brought in by T). Thus in the passive of (1),

(3)   Jazz is composed by students,

jazz is the subject of *is composed* (by position and by the morphophonemics of the plural subject-verb agreement that is associated with the string form of 7.5); but the constants *be-en* on the verb indicate that this string relation is a mutation from the verb-object relation in the sentence on which the passive had operated. And indeed, at the same time that it is subject of *be composed*, *jazz* has the selectional properties and the meaning of an object of *compose*. Similarly the *by* shows that *students*, which is in the adjunct of *be composed*, is the subject of *compose*. Further, in the argument-skipping transform of (2),

(4)   Students continued composing jazz,

students has subject relation to *continue*; but the *-ing* on the following verb *compose* (together with the V_v membership of *continue*) indicates that *students* had the subject relation to *compose* in the sentence from which (3) was derived. If we take the passive of (4) we obtain

(5)   The composing of jazz was continued by students,

where *the composing of jazz* is the subject, and *by students* the adjunct, of *be continued*; but as in (3) the constants *be-en*, *by* show that *composing jazz* (or *the composing of jazz*) is the object, and *students* the subject, of *continue*; and as in (4) the *-ing* shows that *students* is the subject of *compose* in the sentence form prior to the action of the argument-skipping T. And if we take the passive under the increment of (2) we obtain

(6)   Jazz' being composed by students continued,

where *jazz* is marked both as the subject of the operand *be composed* and as the object of *compose*. And the argument-skipping transform of (6) is

(7)   Jazz continued being composed by students,

where *jazz* is the subject and *be composed* the object of *continue*; but as in (4) *be composed* is also the prior subject of *continue*, in which case *jazz* is the subject and *by students* the adjunct of the operand *be composed* (under *continue*), where the *be-en* shows that *jazz* is the object and *students* the subject of *compose*.

The comments above list only a few of the string-relations among the words in these transforms, but they suffice to show that many different (but not conflicting) string relations appear in the various transforms. The string relations in the {I} sentence from which the transforms are derived is always indicated, as well as all the string relations in each transform along the line of derivation from {I}. If we compare (7) above with (5), we find that the same two T produced them, but in different order of application. The simultaneous systems of string relations in (7) and (5) are however quite different, except that both contain the string relations of their common {I} source. It is reasonable to say that the meanings of all these string relations are present in the sentence (e.g. *jazz* in (7) being the subject of both *continue* and *be composed* and the object of *compose*), but they do not seem to be ordered as meanings, although to arrive at them requires an ordered undoing of the transformations that had produced the final resultant sentence.

If we go from the ordered operator notation (i.e. of transformations) to the natural string of words, the various constants and positionings are the trace, in the word-string, of each ordered transformation upon its operand sentence; they are changes in the sense that each transformation makes a change upon its operand. If we go from the actual word sequence to its transformational representation, then the constants and the positions have to be taken not as objects in a static description of the sentence, but as the result of ordered changes: certain ones of them have to be reorganized as the latest change (due to the latest transformation); when they are undone we arrive at the operand sentence on which that change had been made, and then have to recognize what is now the latest change, which had produced that (operand) sentence in turn; and so on to the base.

It must be stressed that there are certain properties common to almost all string changes, such that they preserve the general properties of the string structure of {I}, or change them in only a few generally stateable ways. Hence the whole language has an almost coherent string structure which applies to all sentences (though in part vacuously to the sentences of {I}). Nevertheless even here there are some exceptions to coherence, as in the string structure of the moods (5.6).

8.6. *Invariants*

From the foregoing survey of the T, and of how they change the string structure of a sentence, we can see what it is that is preserved under T: It is the operator order of the {I} source, or equivalently the {I}-string relations (7.5) among words of the sentence. This gives the objective grammatical meaning of the syntactic relation among the words, and is reachable from any T resultant by a computation (which may contain ambiguous degeneracies). The T add no new morphemes other than constants marking string-change, and the only added meanings that these string changes bring in are subjective without affecting the objective grammatical meaning carried over from the {I} source.

In addition, the T preserve, by definition, the independent variables and the acceptability-ordering of the sentences (or, equivalently, the selection-ordering for the words in the sentences), and so the meanings of the sentences.

The {I}-operator ordering and objective meaning of a sentence are therefore invariants of sentences under T.

8.7. *Structure of* {S-I}

Just as we can state the sub-language grammar of {I} (7.2), so we can state one for {S-I}. In {S}⁺ we take {I} as base, and T as the operators. Each T is defined on particular transformations (increments or T) as arguments. Each resultant sentence can be operated on by a partially ordered subset of T, or equivalently by a string relation of its words which includes a particular change from the string relation of the same words in the operand sentence.

The set of T can be organized in more than one convenient way since there are only a few different types of T (partly indicated in 8.1) and there are various similarities among the types. What is important in the kind of analysis proposed here, is that all T be recognized, and distinguished from the increments. How the T are formulated, and whether a given T is to be decomposed into two or more successive elementary T, is not essential to decomposing the grammar of the language into the two systems {I} and {S-I}. As long as there was no evidence concerning what was the core of language, the main goal of structural linguistics was to eliminate restrictions and increase regularity in the relative occurrence (the combinations) of language elements. There was no other criterion for finding what was linguistically essential, out of languages which obviously contained many inessential restrictions and irregularities. For this reason, every reduction of the data to more regular and basic elements had to be considered, even if it seemed to be based on chance similarities in the data. However, given a base whose reality is supported by absence of restriction, simplicity of structure and reasonableness of interpretation, we are no longer in the position of simply extracting every irregularity possible toward a residue that is defined only by its irreducibility. We now are given, for analysis, both an initial language and a final base to which to reduce it. The bases – the primitive arguments N, or the elementary sentences K, or the paraphraseless sublanguage {I} – are indeed irreducible, but they are so in respect to explicit operations. In organizing the data as a set constructed from a base (or reducible to it) by certain operators, we no longer go merely by what eliminates an irregularity, but rather by what is the best way of arranging operations that will reach from one structure to the other. Differences of opinion as to what are the base operations (e.g. whether the numbers should be derived from a count on occurrences of *and*), or inefficiencies in their action, are no longer crucial; one can leave room for historical chance, for unused productivity, etc.

8.8. *Derivation*

In {S}$^+$ we speak of deriving the sentences of {I} from its elementary sentences K or *K, because each derivation adds an increment while preserving the properties (operator order, string relations though in modified form, selection and meaning) of the operand sentence. We speak of deriving the sentences of {S-I} from those of {I} because (a) in those T-derivations which apply to only a subdomain of their operand sentences (in {I} or in {S-I}) the sense of the derivation can only be from the form which applies over a larger domain to that which holds for a smaller domain (even if the former is morphemically complex or uncomfortable); and (b) the other T-derivations, where there is no reduction of domain, are of the same kind as (a).

The course of derivation also has good interpretation, in that the interword grammatical relations which are passed through in the various stages of a derivation are preserved in the simultaneous string-relations of the resultant sentence (8.4), and in that the traces of intermediate derivational stages are left in the lexical shift of words. Thus the meaning of something like 'bounded event' which adheres to *talk* in *His talks are inspirational* comes from the predicate in *His talking was in a piece* (or: *was an event*) which is the source of *He had a talk*, *He gave a talk* (5.4), which is a stage in the derivation. As far as we can see, no relation and no meaning is present in a sentence except those that are due to the primitive arguments, the ordered {I}-operators and the T which appear in its derivation.

The existence of one apparent derivation for a sentence does not always mean that there is no other derivation for the same sentence, which may avoid some difficulties present in the first. Thus the reciprocal verbs could be derived from a zeroing of *each other* determined by an environing V_{rec}, but

more satisfactorily (from the point of view of metatheory) from a zeroing of
and this is implicit as in 4.3.

The sources for these derivations are set up here only in a structural sense.
However, some of them reflect the course of history by reconstructing a form
which had diverged into separate forms. Other sources, quite the contrary,
reflect the detailed limitations upon the combinability of words: There are
some words which have no linguistic utilization (combinability) beyond certain operator or operand environments, and it is this limitation that makes
them useable as particular sources or as derivable from particular sources.

9. BEYOND THE PRESENT ANALYSIS

The distinguishing of the {I} and {S-I} systems of language requires much
further work. Aside from questions of individual transformations and
derivations, there is the general problem of the detailed structure of each of
these systems: Do they depend on (or affect) only their immediate argument or
also the argument of their argument, and if so how far down? What operations are linearly ordered and what partially ordered? What types of domain
restriction appear in T, and what kind of subjective information do the T
carry? The distinction between objective and subjective information, which
arises out of the {I}-{S-I}-distinction, would also bear consideration. Within
{I}, where more is sayable than might at first have been thought for language,
the question arises what remains unsayable due to its structural limitation.

There is also the possibility of utilizing and even modifying the structural
characteristics of {I}. The removal of transformational paraphrase leaves {I}
as an information-processing system of a particular kind – and of a widespread kind, since this is human language. Sharper versions of an information
processing structure may be found, if an {I} system is constructed for the
sublanguages of particular sciences, where much dictionary paraphrase (which
is due to semantic overlapping in the vocabulary) can be isolated and eliminated, so that the correlation of structure and report becomes sharper, and
the particular relations of the science would be brought out sharply.

The structure of {I} applies to the morphemes that exist in language, and
to the particular meaning-ranges which they have, i.e. to the way information is represented by morphemes. The fact that part of its structure is achieved
by utilizing the limitations upon use of morphemes (8.7) suggests that if
we could find further limitations upon morpheme use we might obtain a still
more compact {I}. Such further limitations undoubtedly exist in language,
but they are limitations not upon morphemes but upon (synonymous) morpheme sets. This happens because in many cases we can find morphemes A,
B such that B is a free variant (and synonym) of A over only certain but not

all of the operator or operand environments of A: that is, a word may have synonyms in all its occurrences i.e. in all its environments, but not always the same synonym. Such free variation will have been missed in the methods of §§ 2–5, which, for each morpheme, dealt with the whole set of its occurrences, i.e. with the whole set of its environments in all its occurrences.

In establishing useful primitives of morphology, morphemes were freed from the need to be phonemically simple. In the methods of the present paper, useful primitives of syntax are sought by freeing them from the need to be morphemically simple. That is, we did not take each morpheme and classify it with those having similar combinability. Instead we sought morphemes and sequences of morphemes that had free or complementary variation to each other and called them all a single syntactic element. Now we can consider the further possibility of freeing the syntactic primitive from vocabulary simplicity, i.e. from having to represent morphemes each in the full range of its occurrence. We can consider how a given morpheme may be a member of one syntactic element in some of its occurrences, and of another element in others. Of course, methods have to be developed to decide how to partition the range of occurrences of a morpheme without being arbitrary or trivial. The partition would have to be similar for a whole class of morphemes, and each morpheme would have corresponding different synonyms in each subset of its range. But it is not clear that effective tests can be made for this.

If a useable method could be developed for discovering all of these sectional free variations (synonym sets), we would eliminate all sectional synonymity (and homonymity, which does not hold between synonym sets). Such a further reduction may be practicable for particular small word classes (e.g. the V_{vv} and the subordinate conjunctions which are transforms of them), or within sublanguages of science.

The method envisioned here may be applicable in a special situation. In general, we cannot expect to be able to go beyond morphemes toward freer syntactic primitives. The reason is that morphemes have too much selectional flexibility to be replaceable by some more fundamental relation that would express the restrictions on their selection. Language is everywhere expandable and changeable; hence there is no value of a variable (say, a particular morpheme in the V class) about which we can say that it cannot have a particular other value of a variable in its syntactic environment (say, a particular N morpheme as its subject). However, there may be characterizable subsets of language, such as the sublanguages for particular sciences, in which a part of the vocabulary is restricted as to its syntactically environing vocabulary. In a sublanguage in which we can delimit the acceptability of syntactically environing morphemes of a morpheme A in class X, we can discover whether there are other morphemes B, C in the same class X such that a subset p of the environments of B and a subset q of the environments of C together equal the environment-set of A. If this is found to be the case, we can redefine A as being two homonymous morphemes, A_p and A_q in class X, A_p being a free variant and synonym of B_p, and A_q a free variant and synonym of C_q. If this can be done to an important part of the sub-language vocabulary, then instead of the relevant values of the morpheme-class variables being the morphemes A, B, C, they would be now certain environmental subsets of morpheme occurrences, namely p, q, etc. Here the p value of the variable X would have A and B as its freely-varying phonemic representation, and the q value of X would have A and C as its freely-varying phonemic representation.

When p and q are taken as the values of X, there are no homonymities: for whereas A_p and A_q could have been considered homonymous morphemes, now they are simply variant forms belonging to different values. And synonymities have been eliminated: for whereas some of the occurrences of morpheme B had been synonymous to some of the occurrences of morpheme A, now the phoneme-sequence of B_p and the phoneme-sequence of A_p are merely variant phonemic forms of a value p. In this part of the vocabulary, we can then characterize the values of the variable (morpheme-class) X not phonemically but syntactically, i.e. by their occurring with particular values of environing variables (as for the subsets p of A and B above). In this situation, the phonemic representation of the values, e.g. the free-variant A and B forms of p, becomes part of morphophonemics, in {S–I}, and is no longer part of the informational {I}. For morphophonemics is the change of the phonemic shape of a morpheme (as value of a class-variable) in the environment of certain other morphemes, and the phoneme sequences of A and of B are the change (from zero) of the phonemic shape of p, which is a (morphemic) value of X, in the environment of certain values of other variables.

Syntax is initially bound to phonemes because it starts out to state the independent restrictions on the combinability of phonemes, the sentences being given as phoneme sequences. But in the special conditions considered here, we would be able to define the elements not as phoneme sequences (morphemes) but as values of variables which are characterized, purely syntactically, as occurring with certain other values of other variables. The co-occurrence of these values would be in {I}; the phonemic shapes of these values would now be in {S-I}.

NOTES

[1] An operator X_{yz} (Y, Z) is defined as acting on certain arguments Y, Z (written as subscripts), i.e. on certain variables on which it imposes a partial ordering of values. A sen-

tence is produced by the words of an operator A being concatenated with the words of its argument B; and the words of argument B being in turn concatenated with the words of its argument C, if B have any C; and so on. In the sentence, the word-string produced by the arguments B of A together with the arguments C of B, and so on, are the operand of A.

[2] A sentence-form is a sequence of variables and constants, the constants being particular morphemes and the variables being symbols for word- (or morpheme-) classes. The words in the class constitute the domain of the variable. Replacing the n independent variables of a sentence-form by an n-tuple of values from the stated domains produces a sentence S of that sentence-form.

[2a] In the initial condition, A is not a sentence-set but a set of N-arguments, and in B the x_m is not an increment but the predicate of an elementary sentence (7.2).

[3] Here A is the source of B*, written A→B*, on the general grounds of transformational analysis (Z. Harris, *Mathematical Structures of Language*, Interscience Tracts in Mathematics, Vol. 21, Wiley, New York, 1968, p. 62–3).

[3a] Op. cit. note 3, §§ 5.4, 5.6. 3–4.

[4] Also, the sense of an ongoing act in the special use of *be-ing* before adjectives and nouns (*He is being clever, He is being a man*) is seen in the other form: *His being clever is in process, His being a man in in process* (is something going on).

[5] Also by the fact that this finally makes it possible to derive all occurrences of *-ing* from a single source.

[6] Richard I. Kittredge, *Transformations and Discourse Analysis Papers*, University of Pennsylvania 1969. The classifications 'perfective' and 'imperfective', introduced in this connection by Kittredge, are used here tentatively, pending further investigation.

[7] In the sentence after *than* (or *as*) parentheses indicate optional zeroing; but if a word of that sentence is omitted then this is due to required zeroing.

[8] The comparative-conjunction form is also obtained when the quantified words in the two source sentences have different positions, provided that they are the same word so that the second occurrence has been zeroed: *The number of men who read books is more than (the number of men whom) you can count. More men read books than you can count.*

[9] The nearest we come to this is the makeshift and semantically unclear *More men read books than there are magazines which women read.* A more acceptable situation of this type is seen in (6).

[10] *Sn* indicates nominalized sentences. The subscripts identify the sentences.

[11] That the subjunctive does not bring in independent morphemes but only a form that is automatic in respect to its operator is seen in the fact that a subjunctive occurrence of a sentence can be zeroed as a repetition of a non-subjunctive occurrence of that sentence: *He opposed it more than I expected (that he would oppose it)*. For the parenthesized segment to be zeroed, it must consist only of its antecedent (the segment, aside from tense, in *He opposed it*) plus entities that are determined by (and reconstructed from) the residual *I expected*.

[12] I.e. its battery of transformations in the sense of H. Hiż, 'Congrammaticality, Batteries of Transformations, and Grammatical Categories', in *Proceedings, Symposium in Applied Mathematics* 12, American Mathematical Society, 1961, 43–50. The view presented in this section is close to that reached on other grounds by A. K. Joshi in his *Properties of Formal Grammars with mixed types of rules and their linguistic relevance* (University of Pennsylvania 1969), and in A. K. Joshi, S. R. Kosaraju, H. Yamada, String Adjunct Grammars, *Transformations and Discourse Analysis Papers* 75 (University of Pennsylvania 1968). Both Mr. Hiż and Mr. Joshi have also contributed valuable criticisms to the present paper.

[13] Beverly Levin Robbins, *The Definite Article in English Transformations*, Papers on Formal Linguistics, Mouton, The Hague, 1968.

[14] Since it will be seen that *move* is the argument of *try*, and *dog* is the argument of *move* (7.1), this means that *try* would have a domain restriction on the argument of its argument.

[15] This cannot be derived from *N gathered and N gathered and N gathered* because of the restriction of *gather* to N_{coll}.

[16] H. Hiż, Referentials, *Semiotica*, Vol. I, 2 (1969), 136–166.

[17] S_h should be obtainable from S_i by recognizing the trace of T_j, removing increment$_i$ and T_j, and reapplying increment$_i$. It has to be shown that the increment can always be applied even without the intermediate T, and that its meaning effect is then unchanged.

[18] As was noted by Edward Sapir in his paper 'Grading' in D. G. Mandelbaum (ed.), *Selected Writings of Edward Sapir*, University of California 1958, p. 122ff.

ABOUT LINGUISTICS

XXXI

GRAY'S *FOUNDATIONS OF LANGUAGE*

Louis H. Gray: *Foundations of Language*, Macmillan, New York, 1939.

In the interpretation of his data, neglect of the structural method cuts the linguist off from the organization of all non-historical facts. The author sees only the historical interpretation: "It becomes necessary to be thoroughly versed in the history of each language before one can render a scientific judgement upon any of the phenomena which it presents" (2); the "method of procedure [of linguistics] is essentially the same as in investigation of any problem of history" (4). To get the real meaning of words, therefore, we must know not only how they are used, but also their history: "If the student of literature ... is ignorant of the historical development of words and their arrangements, ... he sunders himself from that which will give him a keener appreciation of literature" (142). And of the syntax of a language at various periods: "The later period is seldom fully intelligible without knowledge of the earlier" (226). Such appeals to history are beside the point, since the meaning of forms and of their arrangements is necessarily given by a complete description of how they are used, i.e. of what they mean to the people who use them.

The practical results of this position appear throughout the book. Some interpretations are historical: the proof that in nominal sentences we do not have an omission of a copula is that "originally there was no such thing as a copula" (230). Others are comparative: "Phonology, morphology, and etymology may be studied with fair adequacy with the help of tables of sound correspondences" (226; there is no hint that these may be studied by themselves as systems in a single language). Still others are semantic: "The sentence consists essentially of two parts. ... Sentences containing only a noun, such as *fire, murder,* are really elliptical and require a verb to make their meaning complete, *there is, is being committed*" (228–30). Such explanations are necessarily irrelevant, and may lead to incorrect analysis, as in the last example cited. The structural relations are clouded. Elements are accounted similar or different according to their original state: "Grammatically, nouns

Language 16, No. 3 (1940), 216–30. Excerpts. This material is reprinted here only because it contains an early expression of the modern linguistic viewpoint.

and adjectives are identical; their functional differentiation ... was a later development" (169); "In Indo-European ... the pronoun for the third person is, in reality, a demonstrative" (173); "Outward identity of form does not necessarily imply essential and historical unity" (2), so that homonyms of different origin are considered descriptively separate, even if they would now be the 'same word' in the speaker's judgment. "The Latin ablative has three general connotations: 'from', 'with', and 'in'; they are irreconcilable so far as Latin alone is concerned. If, however, we compare Latin declension with Sanskrit, we find that the Latin ablative is a combination" (19–20). But for Latin this is a single morphological relation, not three irreconcilable ones. The division into three is merely what a Sanskrit or English speaker would find in Latin (though an English speaker might well find some other division, since the one above is not based on any category of his language); it reflects nothing in the Latin language. Insofar as any parts of utterances in a given language have the same form, and are used in the same way in respect to the other parts, they are necessarily identical in any sense which we can investigate.

Failure to organize data by their place in the structure often leads to unsatisfactory classifications. Thus we find the verbal prefixes of Semitic (*hi-*, *ta-*, etc.) mentioned together with root determinatives (Arabic *na-* in *našara*, also IE *-ent-*, *-tor-*, etc.; 156–8); but the former can be used with almost any verb, are members of a closed contrastive set (category), and exist not by themselves but only in conjunction with certain vowel patterns, while the latter are ordinary and non-contrastive suffixes, each limited to a few particular roots. Translated words are called foreign (132) even if they have been formed in accordance with the structural processes of the language; no indication is given that a word like Ger. *übersetzen*, though it would be regarded as a translation in a study of inter-language contacts, is structurally indistinguishable from other German words. Lack of structural analysis thus enables the author to call some scientific terms "linguistically correct, both elements being drawn from the same language", while others are "linguistically unjustifiable, whose components are taken from different languages" (148). One need hardly point out that for the speaker it makes no difference if the elements come from one language or two, but only if the phonological and morphological structure of the form is the same as that of other words in his language. The difficulties of classification come out clearer when, after describing genders, Gray mentions the Bantu classes, saying: "It is not quite certain whether these classes can properly be termed genders" (190), though the Bantu classes differ in important respects from IE genders, and can only be described in terms of their structural position in Bantu. Similarly, Gray looks upon case as being not a grouping of morphological relations in a language, but something existing of itself: "We may reckon the number [of case-forms] as at least thirty-six, of which IE has eight" (191). But the only number of case distinctions which can be listed is the largest one observable in any particular language (much below 36). To list a series of case significations is arbitrary and useless, for every language covers all the noun relations that exist in its utterances. The inessive of Finnish is partly or wholly equalled in the locative of Latin or the genitive of Arabic, so that these three cannot be added to each other in this list; on the other hand, the accusative or genitive of Latin and of Arabic cover different functions, and cannot be equated and counted as one in the list. The author ascribes "one [case] each to Modern French, Italian, Spanish" (191). But one case is no case; if the formal relation of nouns to other words is the same for all nouns in that language, then it is pointless to set up a class of nouns having that relation (case).

In view of all this, it is not surprising that no adequate statement of phonemic analysis appears in this book. The nearest we come to it is this: the speaker "normally hears (i.e. specifically recognizes) only those individual words or sounds which he feels necessary for understanding the force of the sentence collectively" (225). Disputed interpretations of the phoneme are mentioned (61), but there is no indication that, whatever the interpretation, all linguists use it in much the same way. Phonemes are used because every language can be most conveniently described in terms of a number of such units; but this is a result of structural analysis, and does not emerge here. The further result, that certain linguistic events can be described as determined by phonemic structure, is also omitted. Thus, in describing the difficulty of pronouncing foreign sounds (5), there is no mention of the interference of the speaker's native phonemic habits. In speaking of the "effect midway between voiced and voiceless" which voiceless lenes make on "the unaccustomed ear" (51), what is meant is an ear accustomed to voiced lenes and voiceless fortes. The author arranges sounds according to length, sonority, etc., and gives such rules as that short vowels become shorter yet before voiceless consonants (57–60), without indicating that in the phonemic structure of any given language only certain of these phonetic differentiae and habits (rules) are significant, while others don't exist or are non-distinctive. There is also no discussion of phonemic distribution, i.e. of the various positions in which each phoneme may occur, the absence of phonemic contrasts in certain positions (neutralization), etc. Morphophonemes are omitted, presumably so as not to complicate the account, although they or their equivalent are necessary in any discussion of linguistic regularity. These omissions were possible only because the author did not consider the existence of a phonologic structure in each language.

Neglect of structural analysis of each language leads to disregard of the differences between language structures. This is true even of the different structures of successive periods of the same language, as when Gray says "Hebrew usually has the Arabic word-order" (239), which was true at one period of Hebrew, but not at another. Gray is quite aware of the principle that each language should be "judged on its own merits" (166), but fails to apply it structurally. Hence, he offers a "formula for a word in any inflected language" (159), whereas the structure of words in various languages is quite different; it is meaningless to combine the structural analyses of words in languages of different structure, as may be seen from H. J. Uldall's letter which Gray courteously prints on pp. 146–7. The verb is defined as "a word characterised by inflexion, if inflected at all, for person" (178); but this does not define the verb e.g. in Southern Paiute or Zuni, nor will it serve for Hidatsa, where any stem may take on any personal element, and may then take on any of a class of final (syntactic) elements, some of which would make the form verbal (for us) while others would not. Further on we read that "the accusative has a terminative or illative signification ... as in Latin" (193); but in Arabic most of these significations would appear in the genitive.

How much distortion may result, is seen from the statement "prepositions serve as substitutes for inflexion in analytic languages" (157). Descriptively, we would not make such a statement, for as far as these languages are concerned, the prepositions have their own place in the economy, and substitute for nothing. But, what is more important, this statement conceals a possible great difference in the economy of languages between the in-flexions and the prepositions (which often, indeed, have replaced inflexions historically). For if the inflexions are grouped into a closed contrastive set (category: e.g. cases, aspects), then every form of the class concerned (here nouns, verbs), as it occurs in speech, necessarily belongs to one of the in-flexions as against the others; and forms without inflexional element (if there are such: e.g. vocative in some languages, jussive in Semitic) contrast formally with the other inflexions of that category as having a zero inflexional element. On the other hand, in languages where the analogous utterance has merely a preposition or the like, the contrast within a closed group of possibilities does not exist; the preposition contrasts now with all the other words of the same form-class which could stand in that position, and the utterance has no formal description in that language beyond the syntactic pattern which is realized in that particular combination of words.

Since one cannot do entirely without structural interpretations, the linguist who does not explicitly work out the structure of other languages is in danger of interpreting them in terms of his own. Most of the slips listed above have been in the direction of regarding English or IE categories as general distinctions which must exist, if with different details, in all languages. The grammatical statements are mostly based on IE: e.g. in the discussion of persons (203) there is no mention of the Algonquian obviative (fourth person). Gray is justified, in that he announces that he will stress IE (vii), but readers will assume that these descriptions cover all or most languages. This home influence becomes more apparent in the examples which follow. In listing non-IE distinctions, the author writes: "Many languages carefully distinguish in the pronoun between inclusive and exclusive forms" (182). But, of course, they distinguish this no more carefully than anything else; it is merely that English speakers are not accustomed to making such a distinction. A Hidatsa speaker might say that English carefully distinguishes between singular and plural. Again: "So meagre is the language (Aranta) that it is frequently impossible to determine the meaning of its words without knowledge of the circumstances under which they are spoken" (155). But the meaning of linguistic forms in any language is known primarily from the circumstances in which they are spoken, and one can use the short-cut of translating them into a second language only to the extent that the second language has roughly similar distinctions between the meanings of its own linguistic forms. The same slip appears when the author says, concerning the usefulness in Asia and elsewhere of an international language based upon Latin: "Knowledge of the phonology and morphology would be fairly easy to gain; but the vocabulary would remain hopelessly alien" (36). He can say this only because Latin phonology and morphology are sufficiently similar to those of the languages he knows. To a Chinese or Navaho, they would be as alien as the vocabulary, and far harder to acquire. (His suggestion of reviving Latin for this purpose likewise misses the point that the desideratum in an international language is a simple structure.)

The structural method is basically the placing together of any formal features of a language which in respect to any criterion are similar. Sounds in each language may be grouped according to certain phonetic features and certain complementary distributions in respect to the other sounds in the flow of speech; we find this classification into phonemes particularly convenient because in terms of it we can briefly identify the sounds of any utterance in that language. The phonemes may be grouped according to the positions they can occupy in respect to other phonemes, and insofar as this yields distinct classes, such as consonants and vowels, we may describe in terms of them the shapes of linguistic forms in that language, and the relations between certain partially similar forms. In the same way, we arrange various features of the occurrence of morphemes: the positions each one occupies in respect to other morphemes, the types of combinations into which it can enter, the particular morphemes with which it actually combines.

Such arrangements give us various classifications which supplement each other. If we find two or more morphemes which enter into complementary (contrastive) combinations, but whose meanings are the same, and the sum of whose positions in these combinations is the same as those of single morphemes, we group them as suppletive variants (e.g. *is, am, are*). Where we find many morphemes whose positions and range of combinations is the same, we group them into a major form-class; and where we find that some of these will combine only with particular members of the other classes, we group them into sub-classes.

We call this 'structure', because all these statements and classifications for any given language can be organized in terms of particular units (phonemes, morphemes, etc.) and relations existing among them. We call it 'pattern', because many of the relations crisscross each other, often in parallel lines. Some linguistic facts will escape the investigator who does not try to arrange the initial classifications into possible networks, who does not look for relations between the relations. If the relations between certain sub-classes may be arranged into a category, their place in the structure will be quite different from that of relations which cannot be so arranged. Thus the difference between a category of tenses, and a number of semantically similar morphemes (words or affixes) referring to time, is that the absence in an utterance of any such morpheme means that it is indifferent as to time, whereas the absence (if that is possible) of any tense-morpheme from an utterance in which the tense-category is used indicates a particular kind of time-reference (expressed by zero-affix) contrasted to the time-reference of all the other tense-morphemes. That this patterning of linguistic facts is not a forced laboratory arrangement, follows from the fact that it determines an important type of linguistic event: analogic change. Analogic new formations, whether or not they become accepted (or yield forms already existing in the language), can be simply described on the basis of the existing pattern. Therefore, whereas phonetic change may yield new classifications in the language, analogic change never can, but only adds a new member to an existing class, frequently transferring a form from a rare (small) class to a common (large) one in the same category.

It is important to recognize that language is a system of units and their relations, because that often serves as our criterion of what material is language and what is not. Only on this basis do we exclude at present the vast and as yet unorganized fields of expressive modifications (e.g. anger-modulations, intonations of sarcasm, etc.), and of the linguistic differentiae used by particular sections of the community (e.g. characteristic intonations of girls, etc.). All these have conventional phonetic forms and meanings, no less than language proper, and are marked off from language only because

we cannot analyze them structurally in the same way. It is therefore un-
fortunate that Gray uses 'language' (for French *langage*) to include the
babblings of infants (15), which do not involve any linguistic system, or that
he should put in one category American Indian 'winter counts', which were
not based on the system of language, and our own writing, which shows a
one-to-one correspondence with our language structure (18–9). The same
considerations suffice to disallow his separation of morphology from syntax,
as belonging to two different orders of linguistics, the 'mechanical' and the
'psychological' (145); for the type of predications is the same in both:
relations of order, combination, and the like among linguistic forms, the
difference between the two lying usually in the individuals (linguistic forms)
of which they treat.

Some of the difficulties encountered in this book suffice to show why the
structure of a language can be described only in terms of the formal, not the
semantic, differences of its units and their relations. Though Gray says that
classification must be by form (which, however, he defines as "morphology
viewed in the light of historical development", 165), the criteria which are
actually used in the book are semantic almost throughout. Thus, "the
ultimate identity of the noun and the adjective are clearly shown in such
abstracts as *the beautiful*, which are practically synonymous with *beauty*"
(169); but the semantic identity does not alter the structural fact that their
phonetic forms and their relations to other words (e.g. to *the*) are different.
Again: "A verb is the sole part of speech which can form a complete sentence"
(230); but whether in any given language a verb can or can not do this is a
question of the formal structure of that language, and can not be stated
on the basis of the semantic value of verbs. Again: "The ultimate distinction
between a compound and a non-compound is purely semantic: has, or has
not, the word-combination acquired a special and distinct connotation"
(160). In each language, however, we would find regular formal differences,
as in *res'publica: 'res'publica* and all the other examples Gray gives; were it
not so, how could we distinguish between compounds and 'idioms' (since
Gray uses that term, 9), which also have special connotation, but are
formally phrases of separate words? The statement "The singular denotes
either a single thing, or a group of things regarded collectively; the plural
more than one thing regarded as individuals" (179) is wrong even for English
(e.g. *the masses* is a 'collective' in Gray's sense above, but is plural in form);
it is irrelevant for languages of different structure, e.g. those which have no
plural but only a distributive; and it is useless in any case, being circular. For
how do we know if a number of things is regarded collectively or individually?
– for the most part, by whether the word is in the singular or in the plural.

The treatment of aspects here is a good example of the irrelevance of semantic classification. The IE ingressive, terminative, etc., are given together with the Semitic reciprocal (207), without any indication that these meanings are expressed in IE by determinatives (*n*, *sk*, etc.) which are added to a few particular bases, but in Semitic by a prefix + vowel-pattern which may be used with almost any root and which is a member of a closed category of contrastive aspects without which no Semitic verb exists. And on p. 204 we find: "The meaning of many verbs in itself denotes their aspects; e.g., English *strike* is instantaneous while *beat* is durative", a distinction which has no formal basis and which is entirely inconsequential to linguistic structure, for if we desire we can make an endless number of similar non-formal distinctions in any material. True, after the formal mechanism of a language has been worked out, it may be interesting to ask how it compares with other languages in meeting the same situations, i.e. in the rough classification of meanings, but that cannot be done before the structure is described.

Explanations of the causes of linguistic events are unwise at the present stage of our knowledge. The logical analysis of ideas, which is used by several European linguists today, is irrelevant to linguistic structure. When Gray says "From the point of view of strict logic, there should be no neuter nominative. An inactive thing cannot, theoretically, have the active function implied by possession of an active (i.e., nominative) case" (192–3), he merely shows that these logical categories have nothing to do with it, because, in various languages, nouns in the neuter class do have the affix and sentence position called nominative. Nor is anything gained through teleological explanations, such as that a particular lengthening occurs "to compensate for the loss of a phoneme" (66); the same facts are stated if we say that the loss is a condition for the lengthening.

Particularly undesirable are psychological explanations. They add nothing, as when we read concerning the use of the second person familiar pronoun: "words tabued as too exalted or too debased for ordinary use may be employed as terms of familiarity.... In all these cases the true second person is employed only in addressing the Deity or, at the other extreme, children, servants", etc. (265). It is pointless to explain a single linguistic relation by two different psychological relations, as is necessary here. Even if we could find a single psychological relation in terms of which these two situations would be similar, it would give us, indeed, a single range of meaning for 'tutoyer', but would not 'explain' it. These explanations are ad hoc: "The cow has practically only one designation throughout IE, since her one special function is to give milk. The horse, on the other hand, is used for many purposes" and therefore various names have developed in various languages (268). When it comes to etymologies, Gray recognizes the exegetical character of such methods (279). They cannot be tested, and arise from no evidence beyond the linguistic fact itself: e.g. "Progressive assimilation is mechanical.... In regressive assimilation and metathesis the process is psychological" (73), whereas all we can say about both is that they are the result of bad timing in a set of habitual motions.

Psychological explanations are often circular: "The earliest stages of IE had no future, but as need arose to express future time and, consequently, to denote such a tense, a number of devices were adopted" (20); the tense is there because they had need of it, and the proof that they had need of it is that the tense is there. Even on their own level they may not be sufficient causes: words suffer pejoration because of the "natural desire to veil unpleasant facts by pleasant words" (266); but why does this occur only for certain such facts and words, and not for others? In some cases they break down, as when Gray writes: "names for parts of the body ... show curious transfers of meaning" (270); facts are 'curious' only if the explanation offered for their class fails to cover them, and it is the explanation that is at fault, not the fact that is curious. Investigators who use such explanations often miss possibilities of further formal analysis. On p. 239 the author writes: "practically only the psychological element remains to explain the arrangement of the words of the sentence"; but if he had not been satisfied with such a statement, he would, on closer analysis, have found the class and sub-class selections that make up most of syntax.

Any psychological or sociological interpretation of language is permissible (and by the same token every one is irrelevant) so long as it does not conflict with the results of linguistic investigation; which of them is desirable can only be decided in terms of the other sciences. It is more efficient, therefore, to formulate the units and relations and events of language directly in linguistic terms. The statements of a science should be given in a form available to all those who are interested in it; they must refer to such features as the scientist, with his apparatus and method, can distinguish or measure.

Thus, however we may individually look upon 'meaning', the meaning of linguistic forms must be made identifiable by some linguistic definition. It avails nothing to say that it is a mental concept, or that it "becomes clear only when the word's history is studied" (251). The meaning of a linguistic form may best be defined as the range of situations in which that form occurs, or more exactly, it is the features common to all the situations in which the form occurs and excluded from all those in which it does not. This furnishes a test which, though impossible in practice, is at least conceivable. In practice, we use approximations to this: the meaning of a form class is the contrast between its positions and combinations and those of the other form classes; the meaning of individual morphemes is approximated by contrasting the situations in which they occur in an utterance with the situations in which the same utterances occur without them, and so on. With such a definition, a statement like the following would be an obvious corollary: "when a word is borrowed by another language, it may come to diverge widely in meaning from its earlier sense" (273). It is a corollary because borrowing is the use of a foreign word in a native utterance, in a situation in which that word would be used in the foreign language. The only uses of the word which are directly equivalent in both languages are those occurring in the situations in which the borrowing takes place (in which the native speaker is constructing an analogy to the foreign utterance). All further occurrences of the word in native utterances are determined by native conditions; the range of situations (i.e. the full meaning) of the word in the foreign language is not borrowed.

With an apparatus of linguistic definitions, the work of linguistics is reducible, in the last analysis, to establishing correlations. Correlations between the occurrence of linguistic forms and the occurrence of situations (features of situations) suffice to identify meanings; the term 'to signify' can be defined as the name of this relation. There is therefore no need to regard 'sign' or 'symbol' as primitive terms of linguistics. To say that linguistics is a 'science sémiologique' is to push its foundations back to a 'science' which cannot be studied objectively, to a relation of 'signifying' (16–7) which requires something like teleology for its understanding. And correlations between the occurrence of one form and that of other forms yield the whole of linguistic structure. The fact that these correlations may be grouped into certain patterned regularities is of great interest for psychology; but to the pattern itself need not be attributed a metaphysical reality in linguistics. Gray speaks of three aspects of language (15–8), basing himself on the langue–parole dichotomy of de Saussure and many Continental linguists. This division, however, is misleading, in setting up two parallel levels of linguistics. 'Parole' is merely the physical events which we count as language, while 'langue' is the scientist's analysis and arrangements of them. The relation between the two is the same as between the world of physical events and the science of physics. The danger of using such undefined and intuitive criteria as pattern, symbol, and logical a prioris, is that linguistics is precisely the one empirical field which may enable us to derive definitions of these intuitive fundamental relationships out of correlations of observable phenomena.

Gray's interest in the history of forms is such that he frequently offers speculations about their origin. E.g. "the pronoun is, in all probability, the source of the categories of number and gender, and of case" (175; in all languages?); "the personal pronoun is the most primitive of all parts of speech; the one for the first person was the earliest" (177). Such guesses conjure up a false picture of language stages which had only pronouns, and the like. Early stages can be pictured, if at all, not by arguing the respective merits of various parts of our present structures, but by tracing the development of our structures as a whole. There is also the danger of giving psychological explanations of the origins of our structure, on the assumption that the categories of language are determined by preconceived ideas (though that still would not explain the structural form). Thus: "The chief source of grammatical gender seems to lie in animism.... The masculine was the animate, concrete", etc. If a word, e.g. 'tree', had different genders, it was because "the tree was sometimes regarded as a mere lifeless, sexless, inanimate thing (neuter), sometimes as a female (feminine, passive) living producer, and sometimes as a male (masculine, active) living producer.... It is interesting to note that the conclusions here reached on strictly linguistic evidence had already been attained in principle by the author of the fourteenth century *Grammatica speculativa*" (184–7).

Here and there appear value judgments which might well have been omitted: "the more developed languages" (179); "It does not seem pedantic to regard such losses [of the *I shall: you will* distinction] as retrogressions" (98); "true education, as contrasted with the mere acquisition of facts and 'practicality' which now passes for it, is impossible without knowledge of the Greek language and love of its literature" (429); "Only when a minority-language becomes a means for violent subversive political activities does governmental action appear to be justifiable" (119; but it is always the government that decides what is subversive).

XXXII

TRUBETZKOY'S *GRUNDZÜGE DER PHONOLOGIE*

N. S. Trubetzkoy: *Grundzüge der Phonologie* (Travaux du Cercle Linguistique de Prague, 7), Prague 1939.

In this unfinished study, his last work, Trubetzkoy presents a final version of his phonological theories and applies them to the phonemic systems of a large number of languages. The book discusses the relation of phonology to other studies (5–30), the nature of phonemes (30–41), how to determine the phonemes of a language (41–59), relations between phonemes in general analysis (59–80) and in particular languages (80–206), neutralization (206–18), phonemic combinations (clusters, 218–30), phonological statistics (230–41), and boundary-markers (junctures, 241–61).

This volume shows, even more than did his shorter works, the breadth of Trubetzkoy's knowledge and the intricacy and incisiveness and cerebral character of his scientific analysis. However, precisely because this is the last statement of his theoretical work, it is desirable to criticize here some features of the Prague Circle's terminology. The point at issue is the Prague Circle's occasionally mystical use of philosophical terms. Now, it is not necessary for us to agree on our idea of the nature of a phoneme: whether we are to understand it as a class of sounds (each sound being itself a slice out of a continuum of sound), or regard it as some new entity containing a 'characteristic' sound plus an on-glide and an off-glide. For linguistic work it suffices to know how to recognize the phonemes of a language. But Trubetzkoy offers a specific picture of the phoneme as a 'functional' sound: "The phonologist considers in the sound only that which fills a specific function in the language system" (14). And having established such units of function, he speaks of language structure, in contrast to speech, as "something general and constant" (5). Such talk may be considered a matter of taste. It makes no difference what picture each linguistic worker has of a phoneme, so long as each performs the same operations upon it.

The Prague Circle terminology, however, has two dangers: First, it gives the impression that there are two objects of possible investigation, the

Sprechakt (speech) and the *Sprachgebilde* (language structure), whereas the latter is merely the scientific arrangement of the former. Second, talking about function, system, and the like, without defining them in terms of operations and relations, fools even the linguistic worker. For by satisfying him with undefined psychological terms it prevents him from continuing his analysis. Thus Trubetzkoy says that each word is, in the language structure, a *Gestalt*, and that it therefore "always contains something more than the sum of its parts (i.e. of the phonemes), namely a unity (*Ganzheitsgrundsatz*) which holds the sequence of phonemes together and gives the word its individuality" (35). Had he not been satisfied with such words, he would have been forced to seek for the physical events which enable us to consider the word as a unity and not merely a sequence of phonemes. And he would undoubtedly have realized that this physical event is usually the 'zero juncture' (see below) defined as the juncture between phonemes of one morpheme (or the like) in contrast to other junctures. Had he recognized this he could not have written his next sentence: "In contrast to the individual phonemes, this word-unity cannot be localized in the body of the word."

In his introductory material Trubetzkoy gives a general approach to phonology. On pp. 17–8 he follows Bühler's division of the act of speech into three 'aspects': features of sound characteristic of the speaker, features constituting the appeal to the hearer, features referring to the content of discourse. He indicates that phonology can build only upon the third of these divisions. On p. 29 he distinguishes three phonological functions: 'distinctive or meaning-distinguishing' (phonemes proper), 'culminative or crest-making' (stress, etc.); 'boundary-marking' (junctures).

The definition of the phoneme given here is typical for the Prague Circle. The instructions on how to recognize the phonemes of a language closely follow, with some improvements, Trubetzkoy's important pamphlet *Anleitung zu phonologischen Beschreibungen* (1935).

This review will discuss the three chief contributions of the present volume: (1) Trubetzkoy's method of phonemic patterning; (2) neutralization; (3) junctures.

(1) The main point at issue is Trubetzkoy's method of phonemic patterning. Looking at his whole theoretical work, we can find in it three steps: first, the recognition that phonemes are not absolute but relative, that what is relevant in phonemics is only the contrast between one group of sounds and another; second, the selection of a particular contrast-criterion in terms of which to compare the phonemes; third, studying the relations between the contrasts and working out a pattern which describes these relations.

The first step is basic to phonemics, and Trubetzkoy and the Prague Circle performed a great service in clarifying and stressing it. Trubetzkoy was always keenly aware that phonology, like any science, dealt only with what was relevant to it. And he stressed, perhaps more than anyone else, that no feature or group of sounds was relevant in itself, but only if it contrasted with another to distinguish morphemes. For example, lengthening of vowels is phonologically irrelevant in English, where it is positionally conditioned, but phonologically relevant in several European languages, where its presence or absence yields different morphemes.

The second step will be discussed later.

The third step, charting the relations between the contrasts, is complexly and competently handled, although few of us would accept Trubetzkoy's particular system of charting. Trubetzkoy studies the relations between phonemic contrasts in terms of a rather old-fashioned logic of limited scope. Modern logic and especially modern mathematical methods have developed much more powerful procedures of analysis, although the question whether and in what way they can be applied to linguistic relations cannot be discussed here.

Since many linguistic workers in America may want to have some idea of Trubetzkoy's method, a few of its lines will be indicated here. Phonemes are points in a network of contrasts. Two phonemes which have no features in common (in respect to the criterion chosen; see the second step below) cannot be contrasted. Two phonemes which have in common some feature which no other phoneme has are in UNIDIMENSIONAL contrast. Two phonemes whose common feature is also common to some other phoneme are in PLURIDIMENSIONAL contrast. The unidimensional contrasts are fewer but more interesting than the other. Pluridimensional contrasts are HOMOGENEOUS if they obtain between phonemes which are endpoints of a chain of unidimensional contrasts; otherwise they are HETEROGENEOUS. Homogeneous pluridimensional contrasts are LINEAR if only one chain can be constructed; otherwise they are NON-LINEAR. Pairs of phonemes having similar contrasts between them may be equated in a PROPORTIONAL formula. Various proportional chains may criss-cross, thus presenting a network pattern. Two phonemes in particularly close and limited contrast form a RELATION-PAIR. The difference between them is a RELATION-MARKER. The two phonemes are considered identical except that one has the marker of their private relation while the other does not; they would be represented not as A:B but as A:(A+a). A closed network of relations among a group of phonemes constitutes a RELATION-BUNDLE.

This is but the skeleton of Trubetzkoy's system. It is vaguer and more difficult to keep in mind than would appear necessary. But complexity alone does not suffice to condemn it; any logical or mathematical analysis would seem complicated as long as it is strange. The test of its value should primarily be: What results does it give? In answer we must note that its only results are a patterning of the phonemes (which cannot be checked against anything else) and a correlation with the incidence of neutralization (70–6). Other procedures of studying the relations among phonemic contrasts may produce more important results.

It is in the second step, selection of the contrast-criterion, that one may differ with Trubetzkoy's work. For in order to study the relations between phonemic contrasts one must first have selected what kind of contrast to investigate. Those which Trubetzkoy studies are the phonetic contrasts. He does not say that he is intentionally selecting these rather than any other. He merely uses them as though they were the natural and necessary ones to consider. He sets up certain phonetic criteria: localization and degree of the obstacles to passage of air; 'co-articulation' features such as palatalization; resonance chamber; etc. It is in these terms that he lists phonemic contrasts. E.g. English [t] and [d] contrast unidimensionally in respect to voicing, the other phonologically relevant phonetic features being common to both of them.

But there are other criteria in terms of which one may study the contrasts between phonemes. Chief among these is the positional distribution ('privileges of occurrence' in Bloomfield's *Language*). It is possible to contrast the positions in which each phoneme of a language may and may not occur, to see which phonemes differ much or little in this respect. Trubetzkoy was quite aware of this. On p. 206 he discusses the importance of considering these distributional contrasts, and in the following section he modifies the patterning of the phonetic contrasts by some results from distributional contrasts.

However, it is pointless to mix phonetic and distributional contrasts. If phonemes which are phonetically similar are also similar in their distribution, that is a result which must be independently proved. For the crux of the matter is that phonetic and distributional contrasts are methodologically different, and that only distributional contrasts are relevant while phonetic contrasts are irrelevant.

This becomes clear as soon as we consider what is the scientific operation of working out the phonemic pattern. For phonemes are in the first instance determined on the basis of distribution. Two positional variants may be considered one phoneme if they are in complementary distribution; never otherwise. In identical environment (distribution) two sounds are assigned to two phonemes if their difference distinguishes one morpheme from another; in complementary distribution this test cannot be applied. We see therefore that although the range of phonetic similarity of various occurrences of a phoneme is important, it is the criterion of distribution that determines whether a given sound is to be classified in one phoneme or another. And when, having fixed the phonemes, we come to compare them, we can do so only on the basis of the distributional criterion in terms of which they had been defined. As in any classificatory scheme, the distributional analysis is simply the unfolding of the criterion used for the original classification. If it yields a patterned arrangement of the phonemes, that is an interesting result for linguistic structure.

On the other hand, the types and degrees of phonetic contrast (e.g. whether all the consonants come in voiced and unvoiced pairs) have nothing to do with the classification of the phonemes; hence they do not constitute a necessary patterning. This is not to say that phonetic comparisons of the phonemes may not be interesting. It may indeed be desirable to work out patterns of the phonetic relations between phonemes and see how they compare with the distributional pattern. But that would be a new correlation, interesting for diachronic linguistics and for linguistic psychology, e.g. for the question: How do the physical (phonetic) differences within the ranges of phonemes (events to which people conventionally react uniformly) compare with the differences between different phonemes (events to which they react differently)? In synchronic linguistics, it is only the distributional pattern that would show what work each phoneme can do, what operations can be performed upon each, i.e. what its place is in the structure.

(2) The two most important contributions of Trubetzkoy's last volume are his detailed (though not complete) discussions of neutralization and junctures. Both of these are fairly new terms in linguistics, representing procedures of analysis which have only recently become explicit.

Two phonemes may be contrasted in some positions but not in others, if in these other positions only one of them can occur. For example, English [b] and [p] are not contrasted after [s], because only one of them can occur after [s]. Neutralization (*Aufhebung*) is the term for such lack of contrast in specific positions. It is a relation analogous to positional variants and is central in the description of phonemic distribution. This is the only distributional problem analyzed by Trubetzkoy. Like other European linguists, he discusses whether the phoneme in neutralized position should be regarded as representing one of the neutralized phonemes or both together, and so on. For example, is the second phoneme in English *spin* [p] or [b], or [P] representing both? Trubetzkoy also notes (217–8) that for each language there are certain phonemic environments with maximum phonemic contrasts and others with maximum neutralization.

The value of Trubetzkoy's discussion is limited by the fact that he groups together all neutralizations, both those which would be eliminated in morphophonemic formulae (in cases where the neutralized and contrasted positions of a phoneme occur in two forms of the same morpheme) as well as those which constitute the purely phonemic positional limitations of the phoneme in question (where no morpheme could have it in both neutralized and contrasted positions).

(3) In the final section Trubetzkoy discusses boundary-markers (*Grenz-signale*). He lists various negative markers, phonetic and phonemic forms that can occur only medially in a morpheme or word: e.g. certain clusters in some languages, and positional variants which foreshadow the following phoneme only if it is in the same morpheme or word. He also lists positive markers which, in various languages, betray the presence of a morpheme or word boundary: e.g. positional variants or clusters which occur only at morpheme or word initial or final, clusters which occur only across such boundaries, bound accent, and change of vowel-harmony.

Much of this is included in the analysis of what we call junctures, namely the type of contact between phonemes. In such analysis of a given language the contact between phonemes within a morpheme might be called zero juncture, while contacts across morpheme, word, and other boundaries, if they differ from zero, are given successive names. This method not only organizes all the boundary-markers which Trubetzkoy recognizes, but also reveals certain relations which Trubetzkoy's method would probably miss. For example, morphemes of a given class may combine with certain morphemes without any boundary indication (zero juncture), whereas they undergo morphophonemic alternations when combined with certain other morphemes (e.g. Nootka junctures of stems with suffixes; see Sapir and Swadesh, *Nootka Texts*, grammatical survey). In Trubetzkoy's system morphophonemic alternations which do not yield non-medial clusters may be overlooked; in a juncture analysis a special juncture must be recognized to account for the alternation.

These remarks suggest that a different approach may yield results beyond those of Trubetzkoy. However, this can in no way detract from the value of Trubetzkoy's vanguard work, since discussion of neutralization and junctures is so recent that no writer can give a complete presentation. Even where his method was unsatisfactory, Trubetzkoy's knowledge and interest and intuition in phonology were so great as to bring out most of the important points.

XXXIII

SAPIR'S *SELECTED WRITINGS*

Selected Writings of Edward Sapir in Language, Culture, and Personality (Edited by DAVID G. MANDELBAUM), University of California Press, Berkeley and Los Angeles, 1949.

This volume brings together some of the most important material in linguistics and in the social studies which touch upon linguistics. The writings of Edward Sapir are invaluable for their complete grasp of linguistics, for their approach to language and culture and personality, for the wonderful working of data which they exhibit. We all know what a never-ending source of learning and delight this was to Sapir's students and friends. Now it becomes available to those who would learn today, to whoever can appreciate both subtlety and independence of thought.

In going through the articles reprinted here, I was impressed with how well they read after all these years: how much was still new or freshly put in the articles I had never read before; how much more I could see now in the articles which I had already read in the original publication. The work is in no way dated. Aside from further organization of morphological analysis, Sapir's linguistic analysis is equal to the best that has yet been done, and his understanding of language as a system is better than anything in the field. In personality studies there has been more recent work along the lines that Sapir foreshadowed, but no superior formulation has superseded his. Quite the contrary: the deepest understandings of the interrelation of culture and personality are still to be found in his writings. And as for culture, Sapir's comments are a breath of fresh air not only because of their intrinsic worth, but also because they bear the imprint of an era when social criticism and understanding went farther than today: in the debunking carried out by the intellectuals during the gilded twenties, and in the left liberalism with which many Americans responded during the thirties to the undisguised inadequacy of their own social structure.

The articles selected for this volume give an excellent coverage of Sapir's three specialties, and every reader will appreciate not only the trouble that

Language 27, No. 3 (1951), 288–333.

Mandelbaum went to in putting the book together, but also the wisdom of Mandelbaum's selection. The items are arranged under three headings: Language (The nature of language; Studies of American Indian languages; Studies of Indo-European and Semitic languages), Culture (The general view; American Indians; Literature and music), and The interplay of culture and personality; with a complete bibliography of Sapir's writings appended. Perhaps the most interesting articles are these: 'Language' (from the *Encyclopedia of the Social Sciences*); 'Sound Patterns in Language'; 'Communication' (also from the *ESS*); 'The Function of an International Auxiliary Language'; 'Central and North-American Languages' (from the *Encyclopaedia Britannica*); 'Internal Linguistic Evidence Suggestive of the Northern Origin of the Navaho'; 'Culture, Genuine and Spurious'; 'Fashion' (from the *ESS*); 'Time Perspective in Aboriginal American Culture'; 'Cultural Anthropology and Psychiatry'; 'The Unconscious Patterning of Behavior in Society'; 'Why Cultural Anthropology needs the Psychiatrist'; 'Psychiatric and Cultural Pitfalls in the Business of Getting a Living'; 'The Emergence of the Concept of Personality in a Study of Cultures'.

The importance of all these reprinted articles makes it even clearer than before that Sapir's unpublished material should be made available. There are many unpublished notes and lists of comparisons in American Indian languages. These have first claim, but everything else should also be collected and arranged. As examples of the most important, we might mention Sapir's Yana dictionary materials and his Comparative Wakashan note books, both of which are in Morris Swadesh's hands; the latter he is now editing for the Library of the American Philosophical Society. We need have no concern about whether it would be fair to Sapir's memory to publish his unfinished work. The material contains contributions which should not be lost; and Sapir himself prepared an early paper, 'Grading', for publication in a relatively unfinished state.

We will consider here the material in all three sections of the present volume, both because the treatment and approach in the culture and the personality sections is similar to that in the linguistics section, and because linguists should know the whole Sapir and should understand how he combined his interests in language, in culture, and in personality.

1. LANGUAGE

1.1. *Descriptive Linguistics: Process; Analysis in Depth*

Sapir puts the essential statements of modern linguistics in postulational or definitional form: "Not only are all languages phonetic in character; they are also phonemic"; and morphemes are "conventional groupings of such phonemes" (8–9).[1] But by the side of this, we find his characteristic approach in depth. Phonemes are presented not as a classification of phonetic events or types, but as the result of a process of selection: "Between the articulation of the voice into the phonetic sequence ... and the complicated patterning of phonetic sequences into ... words, phrases, and sentences there is a very interesting process of phonetic selection and generalization." And concerning the phonemic constituency of morphemes we find: "the limiting conditions [of morphemes] may be said to constitute the phonemic mechanics, or phonology, of a particular language". The term 'limiting conditions' aptly relates the range of morpheme construction to the range of phoneme combination.

Sapir thus sees the elements of linguistics and the relations among them as being the results of processes in language. The descriptive structure of a language can, of course, be regarded as the result of many processes of change, as de Saussure pointed out in his example of the cross section of a tree-trunk in relation to the growth and vertical axis of the tree.[2] This kind of interest appears in Sapir's 'Glottalized Continuants', and will be discussed below.

Process or Distribution. Sapir, however, also used this model of an "entity as a result of process" within descriptive linguistics proper. Consider, for example, those environmental ranges by virtue of which two sound types never contrast: say the fact that in a certain language no morpheme contains two vowels in succession; and that in any word which contains one morpheme ending in a vowel, followed by a second morpheme beginning with a vowel, a glottal stop is pronounced between these two vowels. When we speak in terms of distribution and classification, we would say that no morpheme contains the VV sequence, and that all morphemes which end in V before consonant or juncture have alternants ending in V? before vowel (before any following morpheme which begins with a vowel). Hence the VV sequence never occurs across morpheme junction, just as it does not occur within a morpheme. In contrast with this, Sapir would say that no two vowels could come together (within a morpheme), and that when a particular morpheme conjunction would have the effect of bringing two vowels together a glottal stop comes in as a protective mechanism to keep them apart. This kind of model appears in much of Sapir's grammatical work and in the work of some of his students, as for example in Newman's handsome analysis of Yokuts.[3]

We can consider this simply as a method of description, an alternative to our present formulations, which we make in terms of the classifying of occurrences. The process model has the advantage of being more dramatic, and often of reflecting the actual historical changes (the inter-morphemic glottal stop may well have been a later development).[4] It has the greater

advantage of opening the way to a more subtle descriptive analysis –
something always dear to Sapir's heart – by giving a special secondary
status to some parts of the descriptive structure. For example, we may be
missing something when we say innocently that VV does not occur across
morpheme boundary (while VʔV and VCV do): the VʔV which we find
there may not be fully equivalent to the VCV which result from morphemes
ending in -VC plus morphemes beginning in V- (or from -V plus CV-); for
one thing, these VCV alternate with -VC and V- when their morphemes
occur separately, whereas the VʔV alternate with -V and V-; for another, the
frequency of VʔV (differently from VCV) may be much greater in those
positions where morpheme boundaries can occur than in other positions.[5]
On the other hand, the process model has the disadvantage of bringing into
descriptive analysis a new dimension – the relations of one distribution to
another distribution – which does not fit well into the algebraic character of
the present bald statements of distribution. There is need for further elaboration of descriptive techniques, in order to make room for such refinements
among our direct distributional statements.

The Process and its Result. We can also consider the use of the process
model as an activity of the linguists who use it; and we can then say that
aside from such personality reasons as may have dictated Sapir's use of it, it
also occupies a determinate position from the point of view of the history of
science. It seems to constitute a stage in the separation of descriptive method
both from historical analysis and from the older psychologizing of grammatical forms. The older grammars did not distinguish descriptive from
historical statements, so that the history of the glottal stop at word boundary
would have been combined with the statement of the absence of vowel
sequences there. The older grammars assigned reasons for speech forms:
people said VʔV (with 'intrusive glottal stop') in order to avoid VV which
they did not otherwise pronounce.[6] Finally, the older grammars frequently
failed to distinguish morphological from phonological considerations, so
that the morphophonemic fact about VʔV appearing for -V+V- would be
given together with the phonemic fact about the absence of VV. The formulations in terms of process give expression to all this while at the same
time separating descriptive linguistics from the rest. This is achieved by the
dual character of these formulations: the 'process' of protecting the cross-
boundary -V+V- yields the 'result' that VʔV occurs.

The process section of this formulation takes cognizance of such factors as
were brought out by the older linguistics (or by Sapir's interest in descriptive
detail); the result section gives the distributional statement as an item in a
separate science of distributions.[7]

Process in Language Structure. The process model led to a characterization of linguistic structures in terms of the types of process involved in them. A grammar was viewed as consisting of so much prefixation and suffixation, so much internal change or reduplication, used at such and such points.[8] Much of what was called process concerned the changes in or near a given form as its environment varied. For example, there is an internal change in *knife* (to *knive-*) when -*s* 'plural' appears in its environment. There is another internal change in *sing* (to *sang*) which can occur without any change in environment: *You sing well* ~ *You sang well*. (But if we vary the environment to *I like to* ( ), we exclude *sang* and find only *I like to sing*.) There is a process of suffixation that adds -*ed* to many English words without any accompanying change in environment, or when the environment is changed to include *yesterday*, but never directly after *will* or *to: I walk, I walked, I walked yesterday, I will walk, I want to walk.* Today we would say that *knife* and *knive* are alternants of one morpheme, and that the internal change there is a morphophonemic alternant of zero (other morphemes, like *spoon*, have no change before -*s*). We would say that *sang* consists of *sing* plus some other perfectly respectable morpheme, and that this other morpheme (change of /i/ to /æ/) is an alternant of the morpheme -*ed*.

To speak only of the presence of internal change, suffixation, reduplication in a language is to tell merely what is the phonemic history of a morpheme and its neighborhood, as the morpheme is tracked through its various environments. To speak only of the fact that some nouns have alternant forms before -*s* (or that some nouns before -*s* are complementary to other nouns not before -*s*), and that -*ed* has various alternant forms, is to give bare distributional statements with the merest nod to the phonemic composition of the morphemes.

To speak of internal change and suffixation and the like as occurring under particular environmental conditions is to give a detailed distributional statement of morphemes as phonemic groupings. This last can be described as a combining of today's distributional interests with the interest in process of Sapir (and, in morphology, Bloomfield) and various European linguists; it is a direction of development which would be fruitful in the present stage of linguistics. It would be fruitful because linguistics has at present one technique for stating the relation of phoneme to morpheme (morphemes are arbitrary combinations of phonemes) and another for stating the general relation of morpheme to utterance (utterances are composed of stated distributions of morphemes). To take greater cognizance of the phonemic composition of morphemes is to come nearer to the direct relation of phoneme to utterance (utterances are composed of stated distributions of phonemes). This goal will presumably never be reached, because there will always be arbitrary elements in the phonemic composition of morphemes.

But if we can make general statements about part of this field, as by noting when the morphemes or alternants consist of added new phonemes or of repeated phonemes or of exchanged phonemes, we leave less that is arbitrary and outside our generalized statements.

1.2. *Linguistic Structure: Pattern*

Sapir's greatest contribution to linguistics, and the feature most characteristic of his linguistic work, was not the process model but the patterning of data. Both of these analytic approaches were of course used by many linguists beside Sapir, but Sapir made major contributions to both lines of development. For patterning we have, first of all, his famous 'Sound Patterns in Language' (1925), which is reprinted here on pages 33–45. Here he pointed out that what is linguistically significant is not what sounds are observed in a given language but under what linguistic circumstances (i.e. in what distribution) those sounds occur. The phraseology of course is prephonemic, but (or since) the article is one of the cornerstones of phonemic analysis.

Sapir's search for patterns pervaded not only his phonemic but also his morphological work, as anyone would know who saw him working over his large charts of Navaho verb forms. His morphological patterning may be seen in his analysis of paradigms in his book *Language* (Ch. 5), and in his Navaho work, and in his published and unpublished American Indian material. His phonemic patterning is amply evident in the articles reprinted in this volume.

Since the original appearance of his articles, patterning has become an everyday matter for linguistics. Phonemic analysis seems quite obvious today. Morphological analysis is more procedural now than in Sapir's book *Language* (1921). Some of the earliest organized work in morphophonemic patterning was carried out by Sapir[9] or under his influence.[10]

Today the distinction between phonemic and morphophonemic patterns is quite prominent. In 'La réalité psychologique des phonèmes' (1933; English version printed here on pp. 46–60), Sapir includes both kinds without explicit distinction. Phonemic examples (from native responses) are: writing /ḥi/ in Nootka for phonetic ḥɛ, ɛ being the allophone of *i* after *ḥ* (54); reconstructing the Southern Paiute allophone *p* when post-vocalic -βaʻ 'at' was experimentally pronounced after pause (49; initial *p* and post-vocalic β are positional variants of each other); writing [p'] with prior release of oral closure and ['m] with prior release of glottal closure equivalently as /ṗ/ and /ṁ/, because the distributional features of [p'] and ['m] are equivalent (56–7; both occur at syllable beginning where clusters do not occur, neither occurs at syllable end where other types of consonants occur, plus a morphophonemic equivalence). Morphophonemic examples (from native responses) are: recognition of the difference between the phonemically identical Sarcee /dìní/ 'this one' and /dìní/ 'it makes a sound' based on the form of the stem before suffixes, e.g. /-í/ 'the one who', where we find /dìná·ª/, /dìnít'í/, morphophonemic stem *nít'* (52–3); writing Nootka morphemic *s-s* (with morpheme boundary between them) as morphophonemic *ss*, and phonetic [V̆s·V] as containing phonemic /s/ – [s·] being the allophone of /s/ after short vowel and before vowel – even though this *ss* is phonemically /s/: in the morphophonemic writing *tsi· qšit'lassatłni* 'we went there only to speak' (containing *'as* 'to go in order to' and *sa* 'only') the *ss* is phonemically identical (and phonetically equivalent) with the /s/ of /tłasatł/ 'the stick that takes an upright position on the beach' – phonetically [tłas·atł] and with morphemic boundary *tła-satł* (54–5).

Language Classification. The variegated kinds of patterning, once recognized, invited attempts at some kind of organization. To organize the patterns of each language into a total structure of that language, and to investigate and compare the kinds of structuralization, was not possible until much more work had been done around these patterns. What was done instead by Sapir and others was to classify patterns (case system etc.) and to classify language types on this basis. To a large extent this was what Sapir did in his famous classification of (North) American Indian languages into six major groups (169–78). It is clear from the considerations explicitly presented by Sapir in this article (and also from the difficulty of conceiving any discoverable genetic relation among some of the families, for example in the 'Hokan-Siouan' group) that this classification is structural rather than genetic, though in many cases it suggests possible genetic connections that can be supported by further research.

Sapir also proposed a general method of classifying languages on the basis of types of grammatical patterning (in his book *Language*), but neither he nor others followed it up. For since there was no organizing principle for all patternings, such as would arise out of an analysis of the full possibilities of linguistic patterning and of their structural interrelations, the classification work was a useful but temporary way of noting what formal features occur in languages, and which of them occur together. The classification results could not in themselves be used for any further work, except to suggest distant genetic relationships as in the American Indian classification. (In contrast, if a fully organized – though not necessarily one-dimensional – classification of complete language structures is ever achieved, the results would be useful for understanding the development of linguistic systems, for discovering the limitations and further possibilities of language-like systems, etc.) The piling up of research in distribution and its patterns has made it possible by now to talk about the place of one pattern relative to others, and about the way these fit into a whole structure. With more work of this type we may be able to say wherein and to what extent two languages differ from each other, and thus approach a structural classificatory principle.

Descriptive Function. This structural limitation did not affect the general linguistic approach that was made possible by recognition of patterning. Sapir's patterning is an observable (distributional) fact which he can discover in his data and from which he can draw those methodological and psychological considerations which he cannot observe directly, such as function and relevance, or perception and individual participation. He can the more readily do this because his patterning is established not directly on distributional classification but on an analysis in depth of the way in which the various elements are used in the language. The 'way the elements are used' is equivalent to their distribution; but talking about such use gives a depth which is lacking in direct classification of environments.

Thus Sapir uses the patterning of elements in order to express their function (their functional position within the language): "to say that a given phoneme is not sufficiently defined in articulatory acoustic terms but needs to be fitted into the total system of sound relations peculiar to the language is, at bottom, no more mysterious than to say that a club is not defined for us when it is said to be made of wood and to have such and such a shape and such and such dimensions. We must understand why a roughly similar object, not so different to the eye, is no club at all. ... To the naive speaker and hearer, sounds (i.e. phonemes)[11] do not differ as five-inch or six-inch entities differ, but as clubs and poles differ. If the phonetician discovers in the flow of actual speech something that is neither 'club' nor 'pole', he, as phonetician, has the right to set up a 'halfway between club and pole' entity. Functionally, however, such an entity is a fiction, and the naive speaker or hearer is not only driven by its relational behavior to classify it as a 'club' or a 'pole', but actually hears and feels it as such" (46–7).[12]

Perception. In a related way, patterning is used as a basis for the structuring of perception. Sapir reports that English-speaking students often mistakenly hear *p*, *t*, or *k* instead of a final glottal stop; and after learning to recognize a glottal stop, they often mistakenly hear a glottal stop at the end of words ending in an accented short vowel (they write *smɛ'* for *smɛ*). He then points out (59–60) that the second type of error is simply a more sophisticated form of the first. Since words ending in accented short vowel do not occur in English, the students who fail to recognize the glottal stop in *smɛ'* cannot perceive the words as *smɛ* (since such words are out of their pattern) and therefore (selecting a consonant nearest ') hear it as *smɛk* or the like. Later, when they know about glottal stops and hear *smɛ*, they can still perceive only a word ending in a consonant and (selecting a consonant nearest zero) hear it as *smɛ*'.

This effect upon perception is claimed not only for such phonemic hearing, but also for the structuring of experience in terms of the morphological and vocabulary patterns of the language: "Even comparatively simple acts of perception are very much more at the mercy of the social [more exactly: linguistic] patterns called words than we might suppose. If one draws some dozen lines, for instance, of different shapes, one perceives them as divisible into such categories as 'straight', 'crooked', 'curved', 'zigzag' because of the classificatory suggestiveness of the linguistic terms themselves" (162).

System. Sapir goes on to recognize patterning as one of the basic characteristics of language: "Of all forms of culture, it seems that language is that one which develops fundamental patterns with relatively the most complete detachment from other types of cultural patterning" (164). Had he used the descriptive word 'consists of' instead of the process word 'develops', he might have gone beyond this to add that we can even use this linguistic patterning to determine what is to be included in 'language'. There are scattered bits of speech-like noises – coughing, crying, shrieking, laughing, clucking – which may or may not be considered part of 'language' on one basis or another, but which we count out of language because they do not fit into its detached patterning.

Out of all this Sapir was able to make important generalizations about language as a system. Recognition of the detachment of linguistic patterning leads to the statement that "the patterning of language is to a very appreciable extent self-contained and not significantly at the mercy of intercrossing patterns of a non-linguistic type" (165). This explicit talk about the fact of patterning makes possible the distinction between the grammar (specific pattern) and grammaticalness (degree of patterning) of language: "In spite of endless differences of detail, it may justly be said that all grammars have the same degree of fixity. One language may be more complex or difficult grammatically than another, but there is no meaning whatever in the statement which is sometimes made that one language is more grammatical, or form bound, than another" (9–10).

From this, Sapir could go on to an interesting formulation of the adequacy of language. We all know the statement that any language can be used as the vehicle for expressing anything. Sapir removes the air of triviality from this by saying, "New cultural experiences frequently make it necessary to enlarge the resources of a language, but such enlargement is never an arbitrary addition to the materials and forms already present; it is merely a further application of principles already in use and in many cases little more than a metaphorical extension of old terms and meanings" (10). In other words, the adequacy of language is not simply definitional, but derives from the possibilities of extension and transference within the language structure, without either disregarding or destroying the structure. "The outstanding fact about any language is its formal completeness. ... No matter what any speaker of it may desire to communicate, the language is prepared to do his work. ... Formal completeness has nothing to do with the richness or the poverty of the vocabulary. ... The unsophisticated natives, having no occasion to speculate on the nature of causation, have probably no word that adequately translates our philosophic term 'causation', but this shortcoming is purely and simply a matter of vocabulary and of no interest whatever from the standpoint of linguistic form. ... As a matter of fact, the causative relation ... is expressed only fragmentarily in our modern European languages ... [but] in Nootka ... there is no verb or verb form which has not its precise causative counterpart" (153–5). Sapir might have continued here to point out that the work of language in communication and expression can be carried out both by grammatical form and by vocabulary (though with different effect), since one can insert *to cause to* before any English verb somewhat as one can add a causative element to every Nootka verb.[13] Hence what is important is not so much the distinction between grammatical form and vocabulary, as the fact that the distribution of grammatical elements, and so the grammatical structure, can change in a continuous deformation (the structure at any one moment being virtually identical with the immediately preceding structure), and that vocabulary can be added without limit (and changed in meaning). What we have, therefore, as the basic adequacy of language is not so much the static completeness of its formal structure, but rather its completability, or more exactly its constructivity without limit.

1.3. *Language as Social Activity*

The Fact of Patterning. A person who is interested in the various kinds and relations of patterns, for their own sake, can establish pattern and structure as bland distributional arrangements, and thence move toward the mathematical investigation of the combinatorial possibilities. Sapir, however, was interested in the fact of patterning, and what could be derived from the discovery that language was so patterned a bit of human behavior. This was not only because Sapir was above all an anthropologist, but also because of the particular development in linguistic science at the time.

From de Saussure to the Prague Circle and Sapir and Bloomfield, the fact of patterning was the overshadowing interest. In the later work of this period in linguistics we find attempts to analyze and classify these patterns, but the big result was still the very existence of structure. This was the big advance in several sciences at the time. In the late depression years, when neither admiration of Russia nor war preparations in America had as yet obscured the scientific and social results of Karl Marx, Leonard Bloomfield remarked to me that in studying *Das Kapital* he was impressed above all with the similarity between Marx's treatment of social behavior and that of linguistics. In both cases, he said, the activities which people were carrying out in terms of their own life situations (but in those ways which were socially available) turned out to constitute tight patterns that could be described independently of what people were about. In language, they communicate, or pronounce words they have heard, but with the descriptive result of maintaining a patterned contrast between various subclasses of verbs or the like. In economic behavior, they may do various things just in order to make profit, but with the descriptive result that the producing population becomes increasingly removed from control over its production. Sapir saw this fact of patterning even more clearly – in language, in culture, and later in personality. Throughout his writings one sees how impressed he was with this fact, one which was also being stressed at the time (but with less happy success) in other social sciences. In his comments about language as patterned behavior he reached the heights of his subtlety, and pioneered a form of research which few have as yet taken up.

Talking as Part of Behavior. About the very act of talking he says: "While it may be looked upon as a symbolic system which reports or refers to or otherwise substitutes for direct experience, it does not as a matter of actual behavior stand apart from or run parallel to direct experience but completely interpenetrates with it. ... It is this constant interplay between language and experience which removes language from the cold status of such purely and simply symbolic systems as mathematical symbolism or flag signaling. ... It is because it is learned early and piecemeal, in constant association with the color and the requirements of actual contexts, that language, in spite of its quasi-mathematical form, is rarely a purely referential organization" (11–2). This understanding of the relation of language to other experience is involved also in the view that psychological suggestion (and, in extreme form, hypnotism) is in essence the same as talking. In *The Psychology of Human Conflict* (174), E. T. Guthrie says: "Suggestibility is the result of learning a language. When we acquire any language, such acquisition lies in associating the sounds of the language with action. The use of suggestion is merely the use of these acquired cues. ... There is no essential difference between causing a man to perform some act by suggestion and causing him to perform that act by request." Arthur Jenness amplifies[14]: "In the past, the subject has been drowsy when the word 'drowsy' has been spoken, and the state of drowsiness has thereby become conditioned to the word 'drowsy'. The word 'drowsy' repeated later *under the proper circumstances* tends to elicit drowsiness."

Sapir's point has the merit that instead of referring language back to an undefined and dangerously over-used 'symbolism', he presents it as a direct item of behavior, associated with other behavior: "If language is in its analyzed form a symbolic system of reference, it is far from being merely that if we consider the psychologic part that it plays in continuous behavior" (12).[15] In order to treat of the 'symbolic' character of language, he says that symbols "begin with situations in which a sign[16] is disassociated from its context" (566); and he adds, "Even comparatively simple forms of behavior are far less directly functional than they seem to be, but include in their motivation unconscious and even unacknowledged impulses, for which the behavior must be looked upon as a symbol" (566–7). Language, then, is just an extreme type (and a physiologically and structurally separable portion) of the associations and dissociations that occur in all behavior.

Sapir goes on to distinguish two characteristics (and origins, and types) of symbols: the "substitute for some more closely intermediating type of behavior", and the "condensation of energy" (565–6). His first or 'referential' symbolism, like telegraphic ticking, is the one we all know in science and technology[17]; his second, like the washing ritual of an obsessive, is that which occurs in psychoanalysis. In ordinary behavior, and even in language, both are blended.[18]

Forms and Meanings. Sapir's interest in language as patterned behavior, in some respects continuous (associated) with other behavior and in some respects dissociated from it (symbolic), enabled him to use readily the morphological approach current at the time. Grammars were usually organized not only on the basis of the formal (distributional) relations of elements[19], but also on the basis of the major relations between form and meaning – such as whether there are gender or tense paradigms. Sapir accepted this as a basis for grammatical description, and used it in distinguishing language types.

This kind of consideration is quite different from the purely formal one. The formal typology would note to what extent linguistic elements have positional variants (i.e. environmentally determined alternants), what kinds of combinations of classes there are to be found, at what points in the structure we find domains of varying lengths (as against unit length of operand), and the like. The form–meaning typology notes the importance of noun classification on the basis of gender, or the like; to this Sapir added the criterion of "the expression of fundamental syntactic relations as such versus their expression in necessary combination with notions of a concrete order. In Latin, for example, the notion of the subject of a predicate is never purely expressed in a formal sense, because there is no distinctive symbol for this relation. It is impossible to render it without at the same time defining the number and gender of the subject of the sentence" (21).

The correlation of form and meaning is, however, only one side of linguistic typology. It can tell us whether certain meanings are always either explicitly included or explicitly excluded (like the plural in *book ~ books*), or are undefined when absent (as in Kwakiutl, where nothing is indicated about number if no explicit plural morpheme is given). It can tell whether some meanings are very frequently indicated, as any paradigmatic morpheme like the English plural would be. It can tell what meanings are expressed together, as in the Latin example cited above. But the differences are largely in degree. As Sapir recognized, even a meaning which is not paradigmatically expressed can be expressed in any given language, even though absence of the morpheme would not then mean presence of its paradigmatically contrasted meaning (as absence of *-s* indicates singular, or absence of *-ed* and the *will*-class indicates present). The fact that a particular meaning is expressed as a grammatical category (rather than, say, in a separate noun) is of interest to cultural history (443), but is not essentially different from having the meaning expressed by any morpheme, of any class (100).

Which meanings or kinds of meaning are expressed by which kinds of structural elements (paradigmatic sets, large open classes like nouns, etc.) is nevertheless of considerable interest in discussing a language as social behavior. It may affect perception, and may in part determine what can be efficiently said in that language. Sapir pointed out, for example, that the Nootka translation for *The stone falls* would be grammatically equivalent to *It stones down* (something like the difference between *Rain is falling* and *It's raining*), and commented that such differences show a "relativity of the form of thought" (159).

Meanings. This line of interest led to research of a purely semantic character. Around 1930, Sapir wrote three long semantic papers as preliminary researches toward an international auxiliary language: 'Totality' (Language Monograph No. 6); 'The Expression of the Ending-Point Relation in English, French, and German' (in collaboration with Morris Swadesh; Language Monograph No. 10); and 'Grading' (reprinted here on pp. 122–49). We can distinguish several problems in these investigations. First, there was some analysis of the purely semantic relations among the meanings themselves. For example, Sapir says: "Grading as a psychological process precedes measurement and counting. ... The term four means something only when it is known to refer to a number which is 'less than' certain others" (122). And farther on: "Judgments of 'more than' and 'less than' may be said to be based on perceptions of 'envelopment'" (i.e. of successively inclusive bounds). Such analysis could be aided by the abstract study of relations in mathematics and logic (as in the relation between order and quantity which is involved on p. 124), and perhaps also by investigations along the lines of experimental psychology into basic (not culturally determined) perception and behavior.

Second, we find analysis of the precise meanings of the relevant words of a given language. Sapir was always an artist at bringing out the complexities of meanings hidden in a particular word, or in someone's use of the word in a given situation. Here he does this in a more formal way. He shows, for example, that there are two different uses of *good, near,* and other grading terms (126–8): referred to an absolute norm (e.g. *brilliant,* or *better* in *Thanks. This one is better*); and referred to comparison (e.g. *better* in *My pen is better than yours, but I confess that both are bad*); note that one wouldn't say *A is more brilliant than B, but both are stupid.* In this second category we have *good* in the sense of *of what quality* (*How good is it? Oh, very bad*), and *near* in the sense of *at what distance* (*How near was he? Still quite far*). Similarly, he points out that many grading terms "color the judgment with their latent affect of approval or disapproval (e.g. 'as much as' smuggles in a note of satisfaction; 'only' and 'hardly' tend to voice disappointment)" (139).[20]

Third, from his analysis of the total meanings which are expressed in each word, Sapir isolates various factors of meaning, chiefly the following: the distinction between grading with reference to a norm and grading with reference to terms of comparison (125–6), noted above; open and closed gamuts of grading with one central or two end norms (127–30); reversible and irreversible sets (132–3); direction of increase or decrease (and also goal) implied in the grading word, as in *good: better* versus *good: less good* (134–5, exemplified in note 20); the intrusion of affect in regard to the grade (and the goal) (139–44, and cf. note 20). Such isolating of 'elements of meaning' is not subject to the usual criticisms directed against semantic work, because it is an empirical linguistic investigation. It does not derive elements of meaning from some deductive system of presumed basic meanings, but discovers what elements can be separated out from the total meaning of each word; and it discovers this by comparing the various words of a semantic set, by seeing the linguistic environment in which these occur, and the social situation or meaning of each use.

All these investigations involving meaning, when carried out with the kind of approach that Sapir used, have validity and utility. The formal analysis of language is an empirical discovery of the same kinds of relations and combinations which are devised in logic and mathematics; and their empirical discovery in language is of value because languages contain (or suggest) more complicated types of combination than people have invented for logic. In much the same way, we have here an empirical discovery of elements of meaning in natural languages, instead of the seemingly hopeless task of inventing basic elements of meaning in speculative abstract semantics.[21] True, the particular elements we obtain depend on the languages considered and upon the degree and type of analysis. But it serves as a beginning, to suggest what kind of elements can be isolated and arranged in varied patterns, which ones can be combined within a single morpheme (with what effect), what would result from expressing some of them in grammatical forms and others in ordinary words, and so on. We thus obtain both a picture of how meanings are expressed in languages, and a suggestion of how other ways can be constructed.

Communication and Expression. Having surveyed the relation of talking to other behavior, and the meaning of talk, we turn now to the place that talking occupies in the life of a person – what might be called the function of speech.

Sapir points out that talking fills various functions beside communication. There is first the direct expressive effect to oneself of talking and of the way one talks. To this Sapir adds the symbol of social solidarity that is expressed by having speech forms in common – in the nicknames of a family, in professional cant, in all sorts of small and large common-interest groups: "No one is entitled to say 'trig' or 'math' who has not gone through such familiar and painful experiences as a high school or undergraduate student. ... A self-made mathematician has hardly the right to use the word 'math' in referring to his own interests because the student overtones of the word do not properly apply to him" (16). Finally, because of the dissociated character of language, there is "the important role which language plays as a substitute means of expression for those individuals who have a greater than normal difficulty in adjusting to the environment in terms of primary action patterns" (18). Such functions of language, though episodically mentioned by linguists, merit further study, even though these functions are often filled more adequately by other behavior – gesture, symbol, art, and the like. As a method of communicating, however, no other behavior compares with language. Writing originated as an independent method of communicating, but Sapir points out that "true progress in the art of writing lay in the virtual abandonment of the principle with which it originally started" (13): the pictorial and direct symbolization of experience was replaced by symbolization of words; and we may add that in most systems the direct symbolization of words was replaced by signs for the sounds of speech.

Of non-verbal communication, such as railroad lights or wigwagging, he adds that "while they are late in developing in the history of society, they are very much less complex in structure than language itself" (107). This statement holds only in certain senses. It is true that each field of mathematics, and all of them together, can deal with but a small range of subjects. And the symbols and statements (equations) and sequences of statements of mathematics may each, taken individually, be less complex than those of language. But the possibility of including the results (output) of one relational statement into the terms of another, by means of successive definitions, makes it possible for mathematical statements to carry a far greater communication load than linguistic statements on the same subjects: compare any mathematical formula but the most trivial with its translation into English. Furthermore, developments in electrical circuit systems, in electronic control instruments, and in electronic computers open the possibility of highly complicated activities equivalent to communication. The ultimate communicational operation in these instruments is simpler than in mathematics (and much simpler than the countless experiential associations of language), since it is generally reducible to *yes–no* (closing or opening a circuit) or to a distribution of a given current as among several branches in the circuit (depending on the resistance of each branch). Nevertheless, the innumerable possible lay-outs of paths, and the rapid and numerous occurrences of the basic operation, may enable these instruments to carry more complex communication than language can, within a limited range of subject-matter.

Sapir notes, indeed, that non-verbal communication may be more useful even when it is not more complex (or because it can be more simple); namely "where it is desired to encourage the automatic nature of the response. Because language is extraordinarily rich in meaning, it sometimes becomes a little annoying or even dangerous to rely upon it where only a simple this or that, or yes or no, is expected to be the response" (107).

Behind the discussion of language as a method of communication lies the less important but still relevant question of just how much of language-like communication is language proper. This is largely the question of the intonations and gestures which occur with speech. Sapir says: "The consistent message delivered by language symbolism in the narrow sense may flatly contradict the message communicated by the synchronous system of gestures, consisting of movements of the hands and head, intonations of the voice, and breathing symbolisms. The former system may be entirely conscious, the latter entirely unconscious. Linguistic, as opposed to gesture, communication tends to be the official and socially accredited one" (105).

While all this is quite true, a few cautions may be in place. Some of the intonations may be reducible to patterned sequences of a few contrasting tones (tone phonemes), and may thus be considered morphemes no less than the ordinary morphemes with which they occur: in English this may be true of the assertion or command intonations, but not of the ones for excitement or for irony.

This means that the question of which intonations are part of language and which are gestural sounds is simply the question of which of them can be described like the other elements of language – as combinations and sequences of phonemic elements (in this case phonemic tones). In turn, this means that at least some of the distinction between gesture and language is a matter of the linguist's methods of analysis. This is not to say that the distinction is not important. The fact that ordinary morphemes and some intonations can be described as fixed combinations of fixed phonemic elements, while other intonations and all gestures cannot be so described, reflects a difference in the explicitness and type of use of these two groups of communicational (and expressive) activities.

For the linguist, one group is language, the other is not. For the hearer and the speaker the difference may be one of degree, with decreasing awareness and explicitness as we go from morpheme to morpheme-like intonations to other intonations and gestures. But there is still considerable awareness of gesture and intonation, which most people can understand with nicety. And there is often great unawareness of the 'accredited' linguistic communication and expression, as when a person reveals his attitudes or wishes by what we call his 'natural choice of words' (with or without the hearer's understanding of what lies behind this choice).

The decision of what to include in the linguistic structure rests with the linguist, who has to work out that structure, and is simply a matter of what can be fitted into a structure of the linguistic type. The question of what activities constitute what kind of communication is largely an independent one, and is answered by observing the kind of use people make of the various communicational and expressive activities.

Constructed Language. So far the description and analysis. It is fine to do this for its own sake. It is fine to obtain from this work generalizations and predictions about language, or interconnections with more general problems about the patterning of behavior. However, the linguist who has all these results in his hands is also able to construct something with it, to synthesize something by means of his knowledge. He can carry out critiques of people's language and communication activities, showing what is being effected by them, or how they fall short by one standard or another. He can use his particular analytic experience in devising combinatorial techniques, not only of linguistic material. He can try to construct a communication system (and perhaps a representation system) more efficient and free than existing languages.

This last is always an attractive task to any linguist who is interested in the productive potentialities of his work. It is little wonder that Jespersen and Sapir, two linguists who were avidly interested in life and in their work, were each concerned with the construction of a superior language.

The most obvious source of interest lay in the need for international communication. Because Sapir's anthropological horizons were naturally wider than Jespersen's, the problem was more complicated for him because 'international' meant for him more than just the western world: "As the Oriental peoples become of more and more importance in the modern world, the air of sanctity that attaches to English or German or French is likely to seem less and less a thing to be taken for granted, and it is not at all unlikely that the triumph of the international language movement will owe much to the Chinaman's and the Indian's indifference to the vested interests of Europe" (119). Furthermore, an international language meant more than a pidgin auxiliary: "It is perfectly true that for untold generations to come an international language must be auxiliary, must not attempt to set itself up against the many languages of the folk, but it must for all that be a free powerful expression of its own, capable of all work that may reasonably be expected of language" (113). Special audiences for it already exist, as in the 'social unity' of the scattered scientific world (108); but Sapir recognized the social blocks: "Any consciously constructed international language has to deal with the great difficulty of not being felt to represent a distinctive people or culture. Hence the learning of it is of very little symbolic significance for the average person" (31). Under possible future political circumstances, however, such a language might conversely be "protected by the powerful negative fact that it cannot be interpreted as the symbol of any localism or nationality" (113). And Sapir's comment quoted above about the possible effect of the Asiatics on the establishment of an international language is an example of the kind of social need which alone would bring such a language into currency.

The need for a language of international communication arises not only from the fact that communication without it may be impossible (where people do not know each other's language), but also from the fact that it may be inefficient (where one depends on translation, interpreters, or one's limited knowledge of a foreign tongue). We are here dealing with the question of information loss in translation. On this subject Sapir says: "To pass from one language to another is psychologically parallel to passing from one geometrical system of reference to another. The environing world which is referred to is the same for either language; the world of points is the same in either frame of reference. But the formal method of approach to the expressed item of experience, as to the given point of space, is so different that the resulting feeling of orientation can be the same neither in the two languages nor in the two frames of reference" (153).

There is however a difference between the two cases. One might claim that what is said in one geometric frame (or language) is different from what is said in another, or that the relation of the given information to its universe (or to other bits of information) is different in one from its translation in the other. Still, any identification of a point or relation in, say, Cartesian coordinates can be given completely in, say, polar coordinates, and conversely (though the 'translation' may be more complicated than the original statement). This does not in general hold for language translation. Except for relatively simple parts of the physical world (like the smaller numbers), or very explicitly described parts of it (like the set-up of a scientific experiment), we cannot get a description of the physical world except as variously perceived by the speakers of one language or another.[22] It is therefore not in general possible to see how two language systems depart from their common physical world, but only how they depart from each other. The question of translation is the question of correcting for the difference between the two systems. But neither system can be referred to an absolute physical system (as is possible in the case of scientific terminology), nor is there at present any general method for establishing equivalence relations among them (as can be done among geometric frames of reference). Therefore it does not seem possible to establish a general method for determining the information loss in translating from one language to another, as Wiener would do on the basis of his measure of 'amount of information'.[23]

These two types of difficulty in international communication may have been the major stimulus to the many attempts at forming auxiliary languages. To Sapir, however, as to some linguists and logicians, there was also the incentive of fashioning a superior language system. He was well aware of the limitations of our language, which both narrows our perception and prevents us from expressing adequately some of the things we have perceived: "As our scientific experience grows we must learn to fight the implications of language. ... No matter how sophisticated our modes of interpretation become, we never really get beyond the projection and continuous transfer of relations suggested by the forms of our speech. After all, to say 'Friction causes such and such a result' is not very different from saying 'The grass waves in the wind'" (10–1). He was also able to show that linguistic systems are much less satisfactory than might appear: "The fact that a beginner in English has not many paradigms to learn gives him a feeling of absence of difficulty ... [but] behind a superficial appearance of simplicity there is concealed a perfect hornets' nest of bizarre and arbitrary usages ... We can 'give a person a shove' or 'a push', but we cannot 'give him a move'.

... We can 'give one help', but we 'give obedience', not 'obey'. ... 'To put out of danger' is formally analogous to 'to put out of school', but here too the analogy is utterly misleading, unless, indeed, one defines school as a form of danger" (114–5).

Because of his sensitivity to these limitations, Sapir had in mind "an engine of expression which is logically defensible at every point and which tends to correspond to the rigorous spirit of modern science" (112). He pointed out that the inadequacies of language systems have led to the development of separate systems of symbolism in mathematics and symbolic logic (118). The problem was therefore one of constructing a language system which by its structure would avoid ambiguities and inefficiencies, would be a conformable vehicle for our present scientific understandings, and would be able to change with growth of our understanding. However, there may well be a distinction between the construction of an international language for flexible use in ordinary life, and that of a scientific language which would not only express in its structure the various types of relations, of operations and operands, known to science, but would also have the truth-value retention of a logical system.[24]

The program called for a language that would be easy to learn for people coming with the background of the existing languages, and that would be as simple as possible in its structure, while selecting the kind of structure that would fit the scientific understanding of the world. Because these were his interests, Sapir did not try to construct a language, like Jespersen's Novial, but tried rather to find out what should go into the construction of such a language. Even his investigation of phonetic symbolism is relevant here, as showing what meanings might be less arbitrarily expressed by particular sounds. The investigations which he made specifically for the International Auxiliary Language Association were the semantic papers mentioned above, which would show how useful or harmful it was to have certain meanings expressed together within a morpheme, and what component factors of meaning could be extracted from given words by seeing how they are used. The questions of what meanings could be conveniently expressed by what kinds of structural elements, and of what patternings and formal structures were possible, were not touched by Sapir.

1.4. *Change in Language*

Sapir's tendency toward analysis in depth, which he could express within descriptive linguistics by means of the process type of formulation, led also to the historical investigation of patterned features. In the process formulation, time was not involved, and depth was a matter of various analytic layers of the system. We now consider investigations in which depth was a matter of historical time, of various successive forms of the system through time.

A descriptive pattern can of course be viewed as being just an interesting arrangement of the data. However, since Sapir saw it as the result of various distributional processes (such as protective mechanisms) among the elements, he could readily see it also as the result of various historical processes affecting the elements. An instance is the historical addition of a glottal stop between morpheme-final vowel and morpheme-initial vowel in the example cited earlier: in terms of descriptive process, the ʔ in -V+V- was based on a descriptively prior absence of -VV-; in terms of history the ʔ in -V+V- may actually have been a late development, due analogically to the absence of -VV-.

A detailed example of this is the discussion of glottalized continuants in certain west-coast languages. After making it clear that all or most of the types ẏ, ẇ, ṁ, and ṅ are distinct phonemes in the languages under consideration, Sapir points out that they are "so singular that it is tempting to seek evidence accounting for their origin" (226–7). Their singularity is partly distributional (in Navaho, these alone of all consonants do not occur as word-initial), partly morphophonemic (in Navaho, these occur in morphemic environments which can be otherwise shown to have once contained a *d* morpheme, 228–9). For Wakashan (Nootka and Kwakiutl), he shows that these consonants go back to coalescences of ʔ or *h* with neighboring continuants (244); the argument is far too involved and detailed to be summarized here (230–44). In the course of his analysis, Sapir shows that additional glottalized continuants probably existed once in Wakashan (231), and that Boas' 'hardening' process is not the opposite of his 'softening' but is simply a glottalized softening (233). The whole reconstruction, based on comparative evidence, is then used to suggest that when phonetically 'weak' consonants drop they may leave influences in neighboring phonemes, i.e. that they are absorbed rather than dropped (244). With this background, Sapir then reconstructs Indo-European laryngeal bases out of various sets of irregular cognates (245–50), by explaining the various consonantal irregularities as regular reflexes of the effect of lost laryngeals (i.e. of their absorption).

The same methods of investigation are apparent in the famous series of articles on word cognates and word borrowings in Indo-European, Semitic, and other Mediterranean languages, which began to appear in 1934. Two of these are reprinted here (285–8, 294–302); all are of course listed in the bibliography. Studies of loanwords were prominent in this series, because they made it possible to consider the effect of each language system on the form of the word, and to explain otherwise unexplained forms. These papers, together with that on glottalized continuants, are masterpieces of brilliant association, bringing together all sorts of apparently unrelated data, and of meticulous responsibility to every possibly relevant consideration or counter-argument. To discuss what Sapir does in them would take as much space as the original articles; only a careful reading can reveal their remarkable craftsmanship. Some aspects of the method of work used in them, however, will be discussed in Part 4 below.

Much of this brilliance and craftsmanship went into Sapir's painstaking work on Tocharian, which was one of his main projects during those years, and most of which is as yet unpublished.

In addition to all this work, which was of a unique character and bore the stamp of his personality, Sapir also carried out standard work in comparative linguistics, as for example in the *Encyclopaedia Britannica* article on 'Philology', or in 'The Concept of Phonetic Law as Tested in Primitive Languages by Leonard Bloomfield' (73–82), in which he presented Bloomfield's Algonkian reconstructions and his own Athabascan ones.

Sapir being what he was, he not only carried out historical linguistic investigations but also made historical linguistic interpretations. In his book *Language* (Chapter 7), he suggested that similarities among genetically related languages which were too late for their common ancestry, but which could not easily be explained as diffusion, might be explained by a 'drift' which occurs in each of these languages independently of the other but along parallel lines of development. This view has been generally questioned and disregarded by linguists, although data that may support it are not lacking.[25] Sapir granted that such drift could be explained only on the basis of what he sometimes called 'configurational pressure' in the structure with which each of the sister languages started. That is to say, the parent structure may have contained certain imbalances or irregularities, or may otherwise have favored the occurrence of certain changes rather than others; and as this structure developed in various separate places (in what became the various daughter languages) it underwent some of these structurally favored changes in several places independently of each other. Elsewhere, Sapir uses the concept of drift, i.e. of structural favoring as a source of change, to explain the bulk of changes – differentiating ones as well as parallel ones (23). Little, however, can be done with this concept until we can say what kind of structure favors what kind of change in it, i.e. until we can specify 'configurational pressure' and then test to see if it operates.

In addition to this tentative suggestion about the direction of linguistic change, Sapir commented on the even more general problem of the rate of change. There have been various conditional suggestions, as for example that languages with tightly knit structures (e.g. Semitic) change more slowly than those with looser structures (e.g., in comparison, Indo-European). To this Sapir added the general statement that all languages change much more slowly than culture (26–7) and at a more even rate (433)[26], although he thought that changes in both rates might be interconnected: "The rapid development of culture in western Europe during the last 2000 years has been synchronous with what seems to be unusually rapid changes in language" (102). He then used this statement for a possible explanation of why there is no structural correlation between the patterning of language and the patterning of culture: even if there was once a "more definite association between cultural and linguistic form, the different character and rate of change in linguistic cultural phenomena ... would in the long run very materially disturb and ultimately entirely eliminate such an association" (101, also 26 and 102).

2. CULTURE

Sapir's primary standing was as an anthropologist; but since the bulk of his technical work was in linguistics, his understanding of culture was affected by the experience gained from analyzing language. It was quite natural to transfer this experience, because he dealt with language as an item of culture (166). There are other though less central ways of treating linguistic material: as a separate set of physiological actions (in experimental or articulatory phonetics), as a problem in hearing and in acoustic engineering (in acoustic linguistics), as an example of combinatorial relations (and other problems of mathematical logic). Sapir did not deal with these. He did not even deal with the technical analogs between the structure of language and the structure of music, though he was deeply interested and proficient in music, and though it is very natural to think of analyzing thematic patterning, phrasing, and the like in music with the techniques developed for language.[27]

The central aspects of language with which he dealt involved basically the same problems as culture: the behavior of individuals along lines that are patterned for the whole social group (see his 'psychology' in Part 3 below); the patterned relations that can be seen among items of language, and among items of culture (e.g. phonemics); the way linguistic forms are used (linguistic usage as an example of custom, 366; the modification of words as a mocking technique in the article 'Abnormal Types of Speech in Nootka', 179–96); diffusion (as in the loanword articles); historical change, where not only is the process of change closely related for language and for culture, but also specific changes in one may be related to changes in the other and may throw light upon them (as in the monograph on time perspective, cf. 432–3).

In addition, cultural and speech behavior simply occur together, and are distinguished from each other by the linguist and the ethnologist more than by the people whose actions are being studied. "Some day the attempt to master a primitive culture without the help of the language of its society will seem as amateurish as the labors of a historian who cannot handle the original documents of the civilization which he is describing" (162).

2.1. *Cultural Patterning*

This argument – that conditions and actions are to be treated in culture only in terms of their relation to other items of the culture – runs closely parallel to the argument made in the article 'Sound Patterns in Language.' This applies even to the question of what environmental items are included in the culture: "The mere existence of a certain type of animal in the physical environment of a people does not suffice to give rise to a linguistic symbol referring to it. It is necessary that the animal be known by the members of the group in common and that they have some interest, however slight, in it" (90). And it applies to the question of what actions are cultural: "Ordinarily the characteristic rhythm of breathing of a given individual is looked upon as a matter for strictly individual definition. But if the emphasis shifts to the consideration of a certain manner of breathing as due to good form or social tradition or some other principle that is usually given a social context, then the whole subject of breathing at once ceases to be a merely individual concern and takes on the appearance of a social pattern" (546). Compare the argument in the article on sound patterns, that the sound of blowing out a candle is not speech whereas the rather similar *wh* sound is speech (33–4).

Similarly, a distinction is drawn between innovation (non-cultural) and fashion (cultural): "If there is a shortage of silk and it becomes customary to substitute cotton for silk ... such an enforced change of material, however important economically or æsthetically, does not constitute a true change of fashion. ... If people persist in using the cotton material even after silk has once more become available, a new fashion has arisen" (374). Just as a sound in one language may have quite a different phonemic place from a similar sound in another language, so "Gothic type is a nationalistic token in Germany, while in Anglo-Saxon culture the practically identical type known as Old English has entirely different connotations" (376).

The actual patterns within culture are far less easily describable in terms of intricate combinatorial relations than is the case for linguistic patterns. Sapir described cultural patterns, as for example in 'The Social Organization of the West Coast Tribes' (468–87), where, in discussing their groupings according to rank, he shows that various privileges are as characteristic of rank as is authority (473–4), and that these perquisites of rank are handed down from holder to heir (475–6), and finally connects it all into a social pattern: "The idea of a definite patrimony of standing and associated rights which, if possible, should be kept intact or nearly so. Despite the emphasis placed on rank ... the individual as such is of very much less importance than the tradition that for the time being he happens to represent" (476). This is the kind of patterning that Sapir worked out for culture – specific, and achieved by interrelating variegated data into a single whole. He had too much experience with the intricate and demonstrable patterns of linguistics, and with the great difference between a pattern within a language and the structure of a whole language, to speak of a whole culture as constituting a unified pattern. He did not call one society 'Dionysian', or another 'oral-sadistic' – even though (or rather because) he had an early and deep understanding of psychoanalytic theories, as is evidenced by his reviews of Freud and Freudian writers (522–32).

Function of Patterns. His picture of cultural patterns was quite different from the views of the functionalists. He argued specifically that cultural patterns do not correlate readily with social function (339–40) and that "it is more than doubtful if the gradual unfolding of social patterns tends indefinitely to be controlled by function" (341). He was sensitive to the relevance of each behavioral item, and noted when the pattern of an activity revealed that something beyond its social function was involved. Concerning fashion, for example, he shows that the same role is played by all fashions, no matter what their cultural content – namely giving people an opportunity to express themselves without exceeding the bounds of custom, i.e. "to legitimize their personal deviation". Therefore fashions are not relevant to function, where function is understood as the avowed social content of a behavior: "Functional irrelevance as contrasted with symbolic significance for the expressionism of the ego is implicit in all fashion" (381).

Because of his interest in bringing such points home, Sapir failed to mention the more indirect and subtle functions which these patterns could still be shown to have. He did this, indeed, in showing the personality function of the fashion pattern; but in the example of Gothic and Old English type he could have pointed out that while the pattern point of this type face is quite different in Germany and in England, still there is some functional similarity: in both areas the type face represented a symbolism with some national (or national-historical) aura, as contrasted with an efficient search for clear printing. Similarly, in a very early paper (1919) we find: "A magic ritual which, when considered psychologically, seems to liberate and give form to powerful emotional æsthetic elements of our nature, is nearly always put in harness to some humdrum utilitarian end – the catching of rabbits or the curing of disease" (319; the next sentence has it "functionally or pseudo-functionally interwoven with the immediate ends").

But the magic ritual often has another function, the maintenance of certain social rankings, or of the privileges of a particular occupational group; and the ritual is useful for this function precisely because it can serve it indirectly. Hence we see that while the ritual has undoubted expressive value, it also has some intrinsic social function aside from its pseudo-function – which last is merely the function (or social correlate) of its outcome rather than the function of the specific behavior peculiar to it.

A similar question of remoter social effect may be raised at another point in the same paper: "[A genuine culture is one] in which no important part of the general functioning brings with it a sense of frustration, of misdirected or unsympathetic effort. ... If the culture necessitates slavery, it frankly admits it. ... It does not make a great show in its ethical ideals of an uncompromising opposition to slavery, only to introduce what amounts to a slave system into certain portions of its industrial mechanism" (315). But one cannot have an arrangement like slavery in a society without having certain effects that are excluded from the 'genuine culture'. Where there is any exercise of power by one group over another, the ruled will have cause enough for 'a sense of frustration'. If the power is overt, the ruling group presumably has to justify its actions to itself (and will often insist that the ruled accept that justification), with all sorts of resultant effects upon the ideology, the rationalizations, and the social forms at least of the rulers. If the power is covert, the ruling group has to conceal the actual social relations from the ruled (and often also from itself), with the result that there are many social forms whose indirect social function is not recognized, that the ideal culture differs widely from the real, and that there are many other features which are precisely excluded from the picture of the 'genuine' culture.

From all these examples, it follows that a greater (though indirect and remote) functional character can be shown for social patterns. Sapir did not miss all this, as would be obvious to anyone who knew him. But he did not use this material in his generalizations, whether because of his desire to correct for the superficial functionalism that was often espoused, or because his linguistic interests made him favor intra-cultural explanations as against those involving social organization or economics. In a few places he refers to culture instead of social and economic organization (although, of course, the former could be understood to include the latter): "As a result of cultural reasons of one kind or another a local dialect gets accepted as the favored or desirable form of speech within a linguistic community that is cut up into a large number of dialects" (85). Or consider: "In custom bound cultures, such as are characteristic of the primitive world, there are slow non-reversible changes of style rather than the often reversible forms of fashion found in modern cultures. ... It is not until modern Europe is reached that the familiar merry-go-round of fashion with its rapid alternations of season occurs" (377). Sapir did not work into his generalization here the factor which he mentions on the next page, and without which this modern change appears strange: "The extraordinarily high initial profits to be derived from fashion and the relatively rapid tapering off of profits make it inevitable that the natural tendency to change in fashion is helped along by commercial suggestion" (378). Similarly, Sapir speaks of "the nuclei of consciousness from which all science, all art, all history, all culture, have flowed as symbolic by-products in the humble but intensely urgent business of establishing meaningful relationships between actual human beings" (581) – failing to add "and the business of obtaining food and making a living". Yet further on in the same article he points out brilliantly that "personalities live in tangible environments and that the business of making a living is one of the bed-rock factors in their environmental adjustment. ... For all practical purposes a too low income is at least as significant a datum in the causation of mental ill-health as a buried Oedipus complex or sex trauma" (588).

In all these cases we seem to see an understanding come clear in the specific analysis, but not used in the generalization. This was not like Sapir, who used to create powerful new generalizations by extracting every bit of implication out of his subtle analyses of specific points. We can only assume that he failed to follow up his own analyses here because they were too far from the main directions of his cultural interests, which were in linguistics and in personality.

Inertia of Patterns. Certainly his linguistic experience may have influenced him to give more weight to cultural inertia (or lag) than is its due. In language, of course, this seems an unquestionable fact. Not only is there the barely changing persistence of grammatical structure, but there is also the "adaptive persistence" of vocabulary, "which tends to remain fairly true to set form but which is constantly undergoing reinterpretation. ... For example, the word robin refers in the United States to a very different bird from the English bird that was originally meant. The word could linger on with a modified meaning because it is a symbol and therefore capable of indefinite reinterpretation" (368). In one or two places comparable statements are made for culture and social organization: "the universal tendency for groups which have a well defined function to lose their original function but to linger on as symbolically reinterpreted groups. Thus a political club may lose its significance in the realistic world of politics but may nevertheless survive significantly as a social club in which membership is eagerly sought by those who wish to acquire a valuable symbol of status" (362). And more generally: "Old culture forms, habitual types of reaction, tend to persist through the force of inertia" (317). Now it is of course true that forms often persist; but instead of saying merely that they may persist, we can specify some of the conditions which make them persist: for example, if the political club is an organ of a ruling group which no longer operates through politics but still maintains a social ruling position. Such formulations make it unnecessary to appeal to a principle of inertia, since persistence like anything else will then appear to have causes (or, at least, particular antecedents). One can then see that the word *robin* was used for the new bird if the settlers had no name for it and at the same time had little occasion to use the old word *robin* in their new homes (and if the birds had some sufficient similarities). And the political club became a prestige club because status was still a functioning part of the social organization, and this club was available for a status-symbol since it was losing its political function and was associated with a socially powerful class.

2.2. *Cultural Change*

Just as Sapir dealt not only with the patterns of language but also with their historical depth, so he dealt both with culture patterns and with their sources in culture history. In 'The Social Organization of the West Coast Tribes' (468–87) he analyzes their clan and crest organization, and from a distributional description of the crests – where they occur, which occur together, which represents a subdivision of the other – he works out a time perspective for them, showing which can be presumed to be earlier, reconstructing the earlier relations of the crests, and buttressing all this by the kind of names the clans have, and the like (480–7). All this is very similar to the kind of work he did in historical linguistics based on distributional descriptive analysis. In addition, Sapir did the standard type of investigation, making historical linguistic analyses in order to derive historical interpretations of social and cultural contact – for example in his Tocharian work (e.g. 'Tibetan Influences on Tocharian', 273–84).

The whole of such historical analysis, both for culture and for language, was organized by Sapir in his famous 1916 monograph *Time Perspective in Aboriginal American Culture: A Study in Method* (reprinted 389–462). This monumental work shows how one can judge the age of cultural elements from their relation to various other cultural and linguistic items, and thus place the present cultural elements into a chronological perspective in respect to each other. Not only is half the material here linguistic, but the method used in reconstructing the purely cultural chronology is closely related to the methods of historical linguistics. Thus, "inferential evidence for time perspective" is divided into two main parts, one dealing with the evidence from ethnology (400–32), the other with the evidence from linguistics (432–60). The ethnologic evidence is divided into evidence from cultural seriation (400–2), cultural associations (402–10), geographical distribution (subdivided into diffusion, 410–25, and cultural areas and strata, 425–32). The linguistic evidence is listed under language and culture (432–4), inferences from analysis of words and grammatical elements (434–44), and geographical distribution of culture words (444–51), of linguistic stocks (452–8), and of grammatical features (458–60).

Suspicion of greater age attaches to the simpler forms of a cultural element (e.g. the single-figure Nootka totem pole as against the more elaborate poles to the north, 401)[28]; the logically prior forms (e.g. realistic designs as against the geometric ones derived from them, 401)[29]; the elements which are presupposed by others (the art of dressing skins must be older than the tipi, 402–3)[30]; the more stereotyped forms and those frequently referred to in ceremonies and the like (404); forms with widely ramified associations in the culture (407) and with elaboration of detail (408); isolated elements which seem out of context (409, though these may be borrowings rather than survivals); elements which are distributed over a larger area (412–3) and occur in those tribes which are nearer the center of the area of distribution (412)[31]; and elements whose area of distribution is a broken one (their diffusion having preceded the break, 423–4). Various cautions have to be observed throughout, such as the possibility of parallel or convergent developments in various tribes, which may account (instead of diffusion) for the distribution of an element (420). Also, the age of a cultural element need not be the age of the complex in which it is set in one or more tribes (413–4). One can then reconstruct the culture of an area by eliminating all the latecoming elements, and may find that it then forms a continuous culture area with its neighbors, or that it reveals an earlier areal cleavage, or the like (426). Sapir goes on to argue against the notion of a culture stratum, i.e. a group of elements which go back to a common period and which move together though not technically related to each other (427–30).

Linguistic evidence suggestive of antiquity of culture elements is of several kinds: non-descriptive terms for the element, as against terms which analysis (whether obvious or not) shows to be descriptive (e.g. English *king* from OE *cyning*, derivative of *cynn* 'kin', 435)[32]; meaningless place names (435); the meanings of the component elements in descriptive (i.e. morphologically derivative) words whose later meaning is not the sum of its parts (e.g. *spinster* is composed of elements meaning 'one who spins', whence certain cultural inferences may be drawn, 439); culture complexes having more ramified vocabulary (440–1); words of cultural interest having survival features in their grammar (e.g. *oxen*, 441; but words with regular grammar may be equally old, 442)[33]; cultural elements expressed by affixes (which are of more certain antiquity than stems, 443); elements whose names are diffused widely (444–5)[34]; any words shown to be from the parent stage of a language family by the fact that the daughter languages contain cognates of it (449); borrowed words shown to be subject to (hence older than) the operation of some phonetic change in the borrowing language (450); widely spread, and in particular heavily diversified, language families (452; "A tribe may overrun a large territory at a very much more rapid rate than a language splits up into two divergent dialects").[35]

In somewhat later work, Sapir dealt more generally and interpretatively with cultural change. Thus, he shows how technical innovations which are not in themselves changes of custom can become changes of custom because of their relation to other culture items: "The introduction of the automobile, for instance, was not at first felt as necessarily disturbing custom, but in the long run all those customs appertaining to visiting and other modes of disposing of one's leisure time have come to be seriously modified by the automobile as a power contrivance" (367). This is quite similar to phonologization in linguistics, the process whereby a non-phonemic sound change comes to alter the phonemic pattern of the language. Elsewhere, Sapir also suggested a cultural drift, somewhat like the drift he proposed in linguistics: "Wherever the human mind has worked collectively and unconsciously, it has striven for and often attained unique form. The important point is that the evolution of form has a drift in one direction, that is seeks poise, and that it rests, relatively speaking, when it has found this poise" (382).

By far his most interesting and valuable remarks about culture change came out of his interrelating of cultural form and individual activity. He saw culture change as stemming from the reactions of individuals, and culture itself as the deposit and growing framework of interpersonal behavior. A full discussion of this, however, is possible only after his treatment of the individual is surveyed, and the subject will therefore be taken up in the next section.

3. PERSONALITY

From the early thirties on, Sapir's great new interest was the interrelation of personality and culture. To the study of personality he brought two special backgrounds. His linguistic experience gave him rigor in the treatment of behavior. His ethnologic background contributed relativism and emphasized the place of social forms in the growth of a personality. Although he is considered by many to be the chief figure in this field, his formulations have hardly been understood or used by any professionals, because they are so incisive and lead so readily to social criticism.

Before we consider the personality-and-culture formulations, we will survey Sapir's statements on psychology and personality in general.

3.1. *Personality as a System*

Sapir saw personality as he saw language and also culture—as a systemic result of interrelated processes. He defined the psychiatric view of personality as "an essentially invariant reactive system" (560). Because of this there is little wonder that he was so impressed with the depth analysis and the coherent systematization of personality that marked the Freudian schools as against the older trait psychology (513).

After arguing that psychiatry cannot deal with the individual except in terms of his social (interpersonal) relations (512), and that cultural anthropology cannot deal with culture except in terms of individual behavior (512, 515, 569), Sapir asks what he calls the social-psychological question: "What is the meaning of culture in terms of individual behavior?" (513). His answer is that individual behavior is the individual's selection and personal systemization of what we can observe in the gross as social behavior (when we disregard the personality selection but use social correlates instead). "We have thus defined the difference between individual and social behavior, not in terms of kind or essence, but in terms of organization. To say that the human being behaves individually at one moment and socially at another is as absurd as to declare that matter follows the laws of chemistry at a certain time and succumbs to the supposedly different laws of atomic physics at another" (545).

Whatever is the character of particular social forms, then, is also the character of the individual behavior which carries out those social forms. The individual who carries out the forms cannot say, 'This is not me; it is a social form'. It is his behavior, and Sapir speaks of "the world of meanings which each one of these individuals may unconsciously abstract for himself from his participation in these interactions" (515).

From this it follows that what the anthropologist and linguist describe as social and linguistic patterns are at the same time patterns of individual behavior.[36] With the prime example of language patterning at his hand, Sapir shows how the speaker of a particular language uses the particular pattern of that language no matter what he is saying (550–3). He then proceeds to the important point that this patterning is 'unconscious' for the individual (549). When these patterns are described impersonally, for the language or the culture as an abstraction or an aggregate, the question of whether they are 'conscious' is meaningless. But once we take into consideration that the individual's behavior is patterned along much the same lines, we have to recognize that it is not a 'conscious' arrangement of behavior for him. "Not all forms of cultural behavior so well illustrate the mechanics of unconscious patterning as does linguistic behavior, but there are few, if any, types of

cultural behavior which do not illustrate it. ... There is not only an unconscious patterning of types of endeavor that are classed as economic, there
is even such a thing as a characteristic patterning of economic motive. Thus,
the acquirement of wealth is not to be lightly taken for granted as one of the
basic drives of human beings. One accumulates property, one defers the
immediate enjoyment of wealth, only in so far as society sets the pace for
these activities and inhibitions" (556–7).

One might ask what is the importance of recognizing the unconscious
status of these patterns in the individual who carries them out. The answer:
it is of interest to our understanding of the personality because it points out a
major set of activities which never rises up into awareness. And it gives a
clear parallel to the better-known cases, of the more personally clouded
behavior which has not entered into awareness. Writing before his close
association with Harry Stack Sullivan, Sapir discussed unconscious behavior
in a way which fits in closely with Sullivan's picture of awareness: the
unconscious is not always something suppressed, but includes the individual's patterning of his behavior along the lines of the cultural patterns
(549).

3.2. *Sapir's 'Psychology': Individual Participation in Social Patterns*

At this point it becomes possible to explain Sapir's use of the word 'psychology' in his linguistic and ethnographic discussions, something which has
disturbed many of his readers. He did not use it to explain linguistic forms, as
many linguists had done in the past; he would never say, for example, that a
language contained three genders because people 'needed' to distinguish
male, female, and neuter objects. Quite the contrary, he was a master at the
craft of stating one linguistic occurrence in terms of other, partially similar,
linguistic occurrences[37]; and his work and explicit statements were major
factors in raising linguistics above the level of the circular and ad-hoc
psychological explanations which had been the order of the day. In culture
and in personality, as in language, he argued for formal explanations as
against 'psychology'. In his article on Group, he says: "In the discussion of
the fundamental psychology of the group such terms as gregariousness,
consciousness of kind and group mind do little more than give names to
problems to which they are in no sense a solution. The psychology of the
group cannot be fruitfully discussed except on the basis of a profounder
understanding of the ways in which different sorts of personalities enter into
significant relations with each other" (363).[38] And in the article 'Fashion':
"A specific fashion is utterly unintelligible if lifted out of its sequence of
forms. It is exceedingly dangerous to rationalize or in any other way psycholo-
gize a particular fashion on the basis of general principles which might be

considered applicable to the class of forms of which it seems to be an example" (375–6).

A detailed examination of Sapir's use of *psychology* and kindred words shows they refer not to some new forces within the individual which can affect his language, culture, or personality, but simply to the fact that the individual participates in linguistic, cultural, and personality patterns. This is the meaning – i.e. the use – of the word; and it is quite different from what many thought it meant. Characteristically, the sentences containing *psychology* or its equivalents have two parts, the first in terms of formal pattern and the second in terms of the 'psychological' participation in the pattern. An example: "In other languages, with different phonologic and morphologic understandings ... '*m* and '*p* would have a significantly different psychologic weighting" (57–8).

The meaning "individual participation in a pattern" comes out clearly: "the formal procedures which are intuitively employed by the speakers of a language" (9); "the psychological difference between a sound and a phoneme" (54); "In Sarcee ... there is a true middle tone and a pseudo-middle [i.e. morphophonemic] tone which results from the lowering of a high tone to the middle position because of certain mechanical rules of tone sandhi. I doubt very much if the intuitive psychology of these two middle tones is the same" (40). This is also the use of the word *feel*: "Since no word can begin with a cluster of consonants, both '*p* and '*m* [which occur initially] are felt by Nootka speakers to be unanalyzable phonologic units [i.e. not clusters]" (57); "the English theory of syllabification feels the point of syllabic division to lie in the following consonant" (59); "*se battre* gives the Frenchman the same formal feeling as *se tuer*" (116).[39]

This individual participation in patterns is then said to be unconscious: "unconscious linguistic forms which in their totality give us regular phonetic change" (161; elsewhere, in discussing drift, linguistic change is attributed to the patterning of the language); "unconscious phonologic pattern" (58); "the subconscious character of grammatical classification" (101). It was easier for a linguist than for anyone else to recognize that the "patterns of social behavior are very incompletely, if at all, known by the normal naïve individual" (549), and Sapir used language as his main example of this (552–5). He says that the development of an individual's participation in a pattern is unconscious: "in each case an unconscious control of very complicated configurations or formal sets is individually acquired" (555); "the language-learning process, particularly the acquisition of a feeling for the formal set of a language, is very largely unconscious and involves mechanisms that are quite distinct in character from either sensation or reflection" (156). "The unconscious nature of this patterning consists not in some mysterious function of a racial or social mind ... but merely in a typical unawareness on the part of the individual of outlines and demarcations and significances of conduct which he is all the time implicitly following" (548). Since the socially patterned behavior figures in the life of each participating individual, the effect of the pattern is observable not only in the linguist's or anthropologist's analysis but also in the individuals themselves. This is the meaning of Sapir's phrase 'configurational pressure': "Owing to ... the lack of obvious paradigmatic relationship of *ʔi·ṅiʔ* and *diṅí* to *di-...-ní*, it is safe to assume that the [historical] analyses that we have given, however clear to the dissecting linguist, have not the 'configurative pressure' that would justify our considering the phoneme *ṅ* as merely a resultant of *d+n*. If such an interpretation was at one time possible, it is probably no longer the case from a purely descriptive point of view" (227).[40]

Then configurational pressure would be what makes the speakers change their speech in such pattern-favored directions as analogic levelling. The static equivalent of it is simply the individual's patterned perception. His participation in patterned behavior determines his perception of that behavior. His perception of one utterance, for example, is structured by his knowledge of partially similar other utterances. A case in point is phonemic hearing: "it was this underlying phonologic configuration that made Alex [Sapir's Nootka informant] hear *'m* as sufficiently similar to *p̓* to justify its being written in an analogous fashion" (57). Or mishearing: "Owing to the compelling, but mainly unconscious, nature of the forms of social behavior, it becomes almost impossible for the normal individual to observe or to conceive of functionally similar types of behavior in other societies than his own, or in other cultural contexts than those he has experienced, without projecting into them the forms that he is familiar with" (549). "Thus, the naïve Frenchman confounds the two sounds 's' of 'sick' and 'th' of 'thick' in a single pattern point – not because he is really unable to hear the difference, but because the setting up of such a difference disturbs his feeling for the necessary configuration of linguistic sounds" (555–6).

We can now understand why Sapir had to stress the fact that the individual's participation in these patterns is unconscious. It is precisely because the individual is not aware of the way his behavior is patterned that he cannot explicitly compare his patterning with that of others, and so has his perception of others' behavior determined in advance. His awareness is restricted to certain aspects of his behavior, to the particular use he is making of his patterned actions, but does not extend to the resulting pattern. Thus Sapir points out that an unending cycle of fashion is the pattern for a society organized as ours is; but it results from the interplay of people bridging the gap to the next class above them, while the class above expresses its status by creating fashions that distinguish it from the one below; the result is an unending cycle (375).

It is important to understand how Sapir used these terms, both because it removes any hint of psychologizing, and also because it nets us two results: the reminder, first, that each person's behavior is patterned by his participation in these social forms (§ 3.1 above); second, that the structuring of perception is related to the individual's lack of awareness of how his behavior is patterned. Nevertheless, the vocabulary available to Sapir leaves certain unclarities which will have to be eliminated in future work. For the generation of linguists which has learned, from Sapir and Bloomfield, to avoid psychological explanations, the use of such words as *feel* and *intuitive* is uncomfortable. In contexts dealing with culture and personality the words may slip by unnoticed. For example, Sapir analyzes the West Coast Indians' system of ranking to be not an individual ranking (as it appears in the immediately observable behavior) but a method of preserving sets of privileges down through the generations. He then summarizes this analysis and attributes some of this to the individual participating Indian: "'For men may come and men may go', says the line of descent with its distinctive privileges, 'but I go on forever'. This is the Indian theory as implied in their general attitude" (477). At the same time Sapir recognizes that this is an 'unconscious patterning' descriptive of the society, rather than an explicit attitude of the individual: "One accumulates property ... only insofar as society sets the pace" (557).

It would be more rigorous if in all these fields we only recognized, first, the analytically discovered social pattern which results from the behavior of the individuals, and second (following Sapir), the unaware participation of the individuals in this pattern – i.e. the fact that the individual's behavior follows along the patterned lines. Whether, and in what sense or to what degree, the individual feels his participation, is a matter for separate investigation, though there are many reasons to think (as Sapir did) that the individual may somehow do so.

Another reason for being careful about this formulation is that it seems to make the individual merely a creature of the social pattern, someone who 'actualizes' it by participating in it. Sapir himself was quite sensitive to this danger, and used the pattern to detect variation as well as conformity: "To one who is not accustomed to the pattern, [the individual] variations would appear so slight as to be all but unobserved. Yet they are of maximum importance to us as individuals; so much so that we are liable to forget that there is a general social pattern to vary from" (534). Perhaps the relation of the individual behavior to the social pattern could be more generally expressed by saying that the social pattern (i.e. the behavior of the other individuals in society) provides experience and a model which is available to each individual when he acts.[41] Just how he will use this available material depends on his history and situation: often enough he will simply imitate it, but not always. This formulation does not say that the individual participates in the social pattern (and sometimes varies from it), or that he feels it; it says that he uses it as available material when he acts. It will appear below that this formulation fits Sapir's own view of the position of the individual in society.

3.3. *The Relation of the Individual to the Culture*

The crux of Sapir's happy and fruitful understanding of the relation between individual and culture is that it is a reactive relation. The culture is seen not as a matrix in which the individual is stamped, but in the best tradition of the Enlightenment as part of the environing situation (together with the physical conditions) within which the individual operates: "The social forces which thus transform the purely environmental influences may themselves be looked upon as environmental in character insofar as a given individual is placed in, and therefore reacts to, a set of social factors" (89).[42]

Sapir makes the implications explicit: "Culture is not something given but something to be gradually and gropingly discovered" (596). "[Society] is only apparently a static sum of social institutions; actually it is being reanimated or creatively reaffirmed from day to day by particular acts of a communicative nature which obtain among individuals participating in it" (104).[43] This recognition of the difference between the social patterns or channels and people's behavior or interrelations gave Sapir insight into the relation of social form to individual life. He was thus able to distinguish the efficiency of technology from the efficiency of the human use of it: "The telephone girl who lends her capacities, during the greater part of the living day, to the manipulation of a technical routine that has an eventually high efficiency value but that answers to no spiritual needs of her own is an appalling sacrifice to civilization. As a solution to the problem of culture she is a failure – the more dismal the greater her natural endowment. ... The American Indian who solves the economic problem with salmon-spear and rabbit-snare operates on a relatively low level of civilization, but he represents an incomparably higher solution than our telephone girl of the questions that culture has to ask of economics" (316).[44]

Sapir was further able to distinguish between social function and personal function: "The increasing ease of communication is purchased at a price, for it is becoming increasingly difficult to keep an intended communication within the desired bounds. A humble example of this new problem is the inadvisability of making certain kinds of statements on the telephone" (108).

Sapir could hardly have had wire-tapping in mind as an example in this remark (which was published in 1931), but the intrusion upon privacy which has developed since he wrote these lines shows how much perspicacity can result from the understanding with which one approached a problem. Sapir was interested in how such social techniques as communication relate to the individual's life, and was therefore able to recognize the general fact that privacy can be lost and controls can be exercised.

Sapir's final conclusion was: the observables are people and patternable behavior. Society is just the "state in which people find themselves", and culture is the abstracted pattern of their behavior (576). "The true locus of culture is in the interactions of specific individuals" (515). The continuity and permanence of culture is provided for in a way that explains both its permanence and its changeability: "We shall have to operate as though we knew nothing about culture but were interested in analyzing as well as we could what a given number of human beings accustomed to live with each other actually think and do in their day to day relationships. We shall then find that we are driven, willy-nilly, to the recognition of certain permanencies, in a relative sense, in these interrelationships, permanencies which can reasonably be counted on to perdure but which must also be recognized to be eternally subject to serious modification of form and meaning with the lapse of time and with those changes of personnel which are unavoidable in the history of any group of human beings" (574).

This formulation is strongly supported by the fact that the culture of the individual is not the same as the whole culture of a society but is rather a selection and subsection within it. Sapir pointed this out, and used it productively: "It is impossible to think of any cultural pattern or set of cultural patterns which can, in the literal sense of the word, be referred to society as such. There are no facts of political organization or family life or religious belief or magical procedure or technology or æsthetic endeavor which are coterminous with society or with any mechanically or sociologically defined segment of society. The fact that John Doe is registered in some municipal office as a member of such and such a ward only vaguely defines him with reference to ... 'municipal administration' ... If John Doe is paying taxes on a house ... and if he also happens to be in personal contact with a number of municipal offices, ward classification may easily become a symbol of his orientation ... But there is sure to be another John Doe ... who does not even know that the town is divided into wards and that he is, by definition, enrolled in one of them" (515-6).[45]

Viewed in terms of the society, the fact that no cultural item extends over the whole population means that the 'whole' culture is a composite of varying and overlapping subcultures. Viewed in terms of the individual, it means that persons within a society may differ from each other in various cultural respects: "If we make the test of imputing the contents of an ethnological monograph to a known individual in the community which it describes, we would inevitably be led to discover that, while every single statement in it may, in the favorable case, be recognized as holding true in some sense, the complex of patterns as described cannot, without considerable absurdity, be interpreted as a significant configuration of experience, both actual and potential, in the life of the person appealed to" (593). More than that, all this means that only particular items of culture (i.e. of patterned interpersonal experience) and not others are interrelated within particular personalities: "[Personality is not] a mysterious entity resisting the historically given culture but rather a distinctive configuration of experience which tends always to form a psychologically significant unit and which ... creates finally that cultural microcosm of which official 'culture' is little more than a metaphorically and mechanically expanded copy" (595).

The implication is that society and culture do not determine and control people as fully as the social scientists suppose or would like to suppose. The social scientists may be led to their beliefs by the supra-individual composite arrangement of their data, or by their occupational position in schools and administrative offices. But their statements represent an occupational ideology rather than a relativistic understanding. It is true, of course, that each person is considerably affected by the patterned behavior, demands and expectations, of those around him. "Some modes of behavior and attitude are pervasive and compelling beyond the power of even the most isolated individual to withstand or reject. Such patterns would be, for example, the symbolisms of affection or hostility ... and many details of the economic order" (517). However, even here it may be possible to view the acquiescent response of the individual not as submission to control, or as being stamped by a matrix, but as participation in ways (ways of recognizing affection, ways of functioning economically) which are available to him – the compelling character being due precisely to their pervasiveness, i.e. to the fact that the person has at the time no alternative way for recognizing people's affection or for interrelating with them in production.

For Sapir, then, the individual's relation to the culture is that he acts and in particular interrelates with others, and that in developing his ways of acting he makes use of his particular experience as to the behavior of others. This differs from the naive formulations of perception, which would make the individual merely a reflection of the culture, perceiving everything in terms set by the culture.[46] Sapir supports his position by pointing to cultural individuality: "Vast reaches of culture, far from being in any real sense 'carried' by a community or a group as such, are discoverable only as the peculiar property of certain individuals, who cannot but give these cultural goods the impress of their own personality" (594–5).

3.4. *The Relation of the Individual to Society*

The discussion hitherto has dealt with the behavior of others which an individual observes and with which he interacts. The anthropologist, as also the linguist, organizes his description of this behavior into a culture pattern. The individual observes the behavior, imitating it or varying upon it or whatever, but without explicitly recognizing the various behaviors as inter-related points in some pattern. Nor does the individual recognize the effect (the 'function') of the pattern if the pattern has some other effect than its component behaviors. This is the meaning of Sapir's statement that the patterning is unconscious (549). One can say that the individual pronounces *met* with a certain tongue position and *mat* with another, simply because he has learned to pronounce each word so, and not because the difference in tongue position is needed in order to preserve the phonemic patterning of /e/ and /æ/. And when the child's mispronunciation is corrected, he is told simply to say it more like the person who is doing the correcting; he is not told to speak in such a way as to keep *met* and *mat* (and certainly not /e/ and /æ/) apart. Similarly, when Sapir analyzes West Coast rankings, he obtains a pattern which could hardly be present in the Indians' awareness (474–5).

The importance of recognizing the purely analytic status of the pattern lies in this: it means that the individual's participation in culture patterns is something quite different from the conformity that keeps a person from "deviating from the norm". When a 'deviant' is corrected, it is not in the name of the pattern or of its function – since these are not generally explicit – but in the name of the individual behaviors and their functions.[47] The relation of the individual to culture patterns is therefore something quite different from the relation of the individual to social demands for conformity. Culturally patterned behaviors vary in the degree of social demands associated with them. Some are sought out by the individual, e.g. the ways of scientific investigation which the student learns – though even here there are sub-patterns that are imposed rather than sought out: Russian students must not accept Morgan's genetics; American students find (far less violently, to be sure) that they had better not accept Lamarck. Other culturally patterned behaviors are not so much imitated (learned) for their own sake as imposed upon individuals by demands for conformity.

Sapir's great preoccupation with the relation of the individual to culture patterns and to conformity (the 'givenness' of culture and so on) is due to a growing awareness of the distinction between these two. The cultural environment which "the individual is placed in, and therefore reacts to" is the culture pattern itself (as 'exemplified' in the patterned behaviors); the only pressure that these patterns may exert upon the individual is their own "configurational pressure". In contrast, the pressure to imitate the culturally patterned behaviors, i.e. to conform, is not a matter of the patterns at all but simply of social control.

Where Sapir had argued for the validity of patterns as describing or 'explaining' behavior, he argued against the idea that these patterns involve conformity. "Cultural anthropology, if properly understood, has the healthiest of all scepticisms about the validity of the concept 'normal behavior' ... Personalities are not conditioned by a generalized process of adjusting to 'the normal' but by the necessity of adjusting to the greatest possible variety of idea patterns and action patterns according to the accidents of birth and biography" (514–5). From this, and from the statement that almost no cultural item covers the whole population, it follows that individuals conform much less than is supposed. The administrative social scientist expects the conformity of the 'coordinated man'. He considers any person who does not conform to a particular cultural item to be a 'deviant' – an invidious word which came to be used after the term 'abnormal' could no longer be defended. (More recently, the term has been 'maladjusted', to indicate that the experts should adjust the person.) But that person is merely trying to do what everyone else does: to use his experience in meeting the problems of living. If he does the identical things that others in his society do, it is because he meets similar problems and has had similar experiences upon which to draw – not primarily because he is the creature of the culture pattern. If he does different things, it is because he has had somewhat different experiences or has integrated them into different values (or into a different level of understanding within the basic common values).

The many indisputable cases of conformity are therefore seen not as 'human nature' but as the result of specific pressures by specific people to make people conform. It was because of this whole chain of understandings, no less than because of his personal humanistic values, that Sapir was so alert to all cases of control and so subtle in analyzing them. He recognized submission to cultural control even when the submission was clouded in apparent independence: "[Followers of fashion] are not fundamentally in revolt from custom but they wish somehow to legitimize their personal deviation without laying themselves open to the charge of insensitiveness to good taste or good manners. Fashion is the discreet solution of the subtle conflict" (374). He recognized the effect of control even in social requirements which the controllers claim to be innocent, as in the following remark about the acquiescence involved in communication: "Imitation, while not communicative in intent, has always the retroactive value of a communication, for in the process of falling in with the ways of society one in effect acquiesces in the meanings that inhere in these ways. When one learns to go to church, for instance, because other members of the community set the pace for this kind of activity, it is as though a communication had been received and acted upon" (105–6).[48] And to take an example of joint cultural and social control: when Sapir says, "Human beings do not wish to be modest; they want to be as expressive – that is, as immodest – as fear allows" (380), he is defining the cultural expectation called 'modest' as a contradiction of human expressiveness, and points to the social situation (fear) which gives the victory to the cultural demand.

Looking at all this from the point of view of the individual, Sapir not only saw fearful submission where social scientists often see natural conformity, and independent expression where they see deviation, but also resistance of the individual where they see failure of cultural conditioning: "In spite of all these standardizing influences, local dialects have persisted with a vitality that is little short of amazing. Obviously the question of the conservation of dialect is not altogether a negative matter of the inertia of speech and of the failure of overriding cultural influences to permeate into all corners of a given territory. It is, to a very significant degree, a positive matter of the resistance of the local dialects to something which is vaguely felt as hostile" (86).

The resistance of individuals or subgroups consists in their use of particular ways in spite of the demands of others that they change to other ways. Sapir sees the ways of the individual or the subgroup as constituting a subculture in themselves (515, 519), so that the individual is never 'wrong' while the majority culture is 'right'. Speaking of an Indian who denies a cultural form which others accept, he says: "If we think long enough about Two Crows and his persistent denials, we shall have to admit that in some sense Two Crows is never wrong. ... The fact that this rebel, Two Crows, can in turn bend others to his own view of fact or theory or to his own preference in action shows that his divergence from custom had, from the very beginning, the essential possibility of culturalized behavior" (572).[49]

Sapir's question of the relation of individual to society is, then, not the administrator's problem of "the extreme limits within which human behavior is culturally modifiable", but the human being's problem of making his way through life. Hence, Sapir does not assume that the individual should adjust to society, but asks how valid or adequate the cultural ways are for the individual who has to make do with them (513). His deep criticisms of our own culture (especially in 'Psychiatric and Cultural Pitfalls in the Business of Getting a Living', 578–89, and 'Culture, Genuine and Spurious', 308–31) shows how important these inadequacies were to him.

3.5. *The Individual and Cultural Change*

Control and the adequacy of cultural forms are important not only in themselves, but also for their relation to cultural change. Since Sapir saw culture in general as being the continuing interrelation of people, he naturally saw cultural change as stemming from changes made by individuals (425). The problem then becomes one of investigating under what circumstances changes appear in the individual behavior. This would include, among others, the fact that the act of change can itself be a personality expression, the differences in what each person learns from his experiences with others, the possible operation of a tendency for formal configuration (Sapir's 'drift' in language and in culture), and the reaction to controls and cultural inadequacies. Cultural inadequacies lead to attempts at change, as Sapir implies in saying that mathematics had to develop its own language and that people have to fight the trammels of their own language (cf. note 45). "It is sometimes necessary to become conscious of the forms of social behavior in order to bring about a more serviceable adaptation to changed conditions" (558). The direction is toward liberation: "The attitude of independence toward a constructed language which all national speakers must adopt is really a great advantage, because it tends to make man see himself as the master of language instead of its obedient servant" (119). To this extent an observer who is unaware of the cost to the individuals of their participation in particular social forms – costs due to the inadequacy of the forms, or due to their control effect – would not be able to understand the changes that arise from people's attempts to escape these costs, from the tendency to take up or develop other forms that do not involve such costs whenever these become available to the people.

The changes which the individual attempts in his own life, whether for any of the reasons mentioned above or for other reasons, can become the changes of culture. Sapir illustrates this by having his maverick Indian, Two Crows, interchange A and Z in the alphabet order. "No matter how many Two Crows deny that two and two make four, the actual history of mathematics, however retarded by such perversity, cannot be seriously modified by it. But if we get enough Two Crows to agree on the interchange of A and Z, we have what we call a new tradition" (571). The change may be made by making new use of existing social patterns which are available to the individuals in question, but that does not make it any less a change: "Thus, the particular method of revolting against the habit of church-going in a given society, while contradictory, on the surface, of the conventional meanings of that society, may nevertheless receive all its social significance from hundreds of existing prior communications that belong to the culture of the group as a whole" (106).

The importance, then, of seeing the origins of these changes in the individual lives is that the changes make sense in terms of the individual lives in which they originated. "We cannot thoroughly understand the dynamics of culture, of society, of history, without sooner or later taking account of the actual interrelationships of human beings" (575). "That culture is a super-organic, impersonal whole is a useful enough methodological principle to begin with but becomes a serious deterrent in the long run to the more dynamic study of the genesis and development of cultural patterns because these cannot be realistically disconnected from those organizations of ideas and feelings which constitute the individual" (512). In his famous rationalistic criticism of supra-human social 'forces' as accounting for history (or as manifesting themselves in history), 'Do we need a "Superorganic"?', Sapir wrote: "The social is but a name for those reactions or types of reaction that depend for their perpetuation on a cumulative technique of transference, that known as social inheritance. This technique, however, does not depend for its operation on any significantly new 'force'. ... Social science is not psychology, not because it studies the resultants of a superpsychic or super-organic force, but because its terms are differently demarcated".[50]

It is possible of course to find long-range correlations and regularities in the time-sequence of cultural patterns and social conditions. These can be described as social or cultural causes of historical change. Sapir's formulation does not deny this. The particular material and social conditions in which people find themselves at any particular time and place determine to a large extent the kind of problems they encounter, problems which are dealt with in biologically favored directions. The cultural patterns that are available to people at any particular time and place favor particular kinds of patterned behavior: the obedient conformists will all be doing much the same thing; those who tend more toward personal variation and expression will be using essentially the same underlying patterns as a base upon which to vary or express; those who react more actively against the costs of controls and of cultural inadequacies all find much the same controls and inadequacies to overcome; and those changes which are elicited by response to the formalism of the patterning (the drift) are in a direction suggested by the existing configuration.[51] Changes which are attempted at any one time will therefore be intimately connected with the cultural patterns existing at that time, and will lead to patterns which differ in certain directions rather than in others, and which are not entirely different and unrelated to the previous patterns. A more or less continuous and directional shift, with observable regularities, is therefore often discernible in the history of cultural patterns taken by themselves, even though the agency of change is the reaction of the individual.

3.6. *Culture in the Structure of the Personality*

Sapir approached the problems of personality from his analysis of culture, and his contributions lay in showing relationships between culture and the development of the personality. Like Sullivan, he found that "the locus of psychiatry turns out not to be the human organism at all in any fruitful sense of the word but the more intangible, yet more intelligible, world of human relationships and ideas that such relationships bring forth" (512).[52] Since he also said much the same of culture (515), he denies "the conventional contrast of the individual and his society" (519). His statement that each individual or group constitutes a subculture (519), which he connects with the fact that each culture pattern reaches only some part of the population, enabled him to see structural parallels between personality and culture. An individual's mental breakdown "invites a study of his system of ideas as a more or less distinct cultural entity which has been vainly struggling to maintain itself in a discouraging environment" (520).

This formulation, which at first may seem to be just a manner of speaking, leads to interesting results when taken seriously. For it means that the individual's ways of relating to people constitute a complete system which can do for him all the work done by a national culture. The psychiatric problem is then one of clearing up sources of difficulty within the individual's existing system of understandings and behaviors, rather than of getting the person to become a part (or participant) of the supra-individual culture. "Psychiatrists who are tolerant only in the sense that they refrain from criticizing anybody who is subjected to their care and who do their best to guide him back to the renewed performance of society's rituals may be good practical surgeons of the psyche. They are not necessarily the profoundly sympathetic students of the mind who respect the fundamental intent and direction of every personality organization" (521).

This structural similarity between personality and culture led Sapir to see cultural items as factors in the development of the personality. He speaks of the confusion between the personal and cultural implications of experience in childhood, "when the significant personality is interpreted as an institution and every cultural pattern is merely a memory of what this or that person has actually done" (590). "The more obvious conflicts of cultures with which we are familiar in the modern world create an uneasiness which forms a fruitful soil for the eventual development, in particular cases, of neurotic symptoms and mental breakdowns but they can hardly be considered sufficient to account for serious psychological derangements. These arise not on the basis of a generalized cultural conflict but out of specific conflicts of a more intimate sort, in which systems of ideas get attached to particular persons, or images of such persons, who play a decisive role in the life of the individual as representative of cultural values" (510–1). Hence "it is a dangerous thing for the individual to give up his identification with such cultural patterns as have come to symbolize for him his own personality integration" (519–20).

The difficulties which are intrinsic to the culture patterns thus have a direct relation to difficulties in persons who participate in these patterns: "Mechanisms which are unconsciously evolved by the neurotic or psychotic are by no means closed systems imprisoned within the biological walls of isolated individuals. They are tacit commentaries on the validity or invalidity of some of the more intimate implications of culture" (513). The same relation appears in more chronic but milder forms that no one would think of treating because almost everybody in the society is affected in one way or another. A 'social' example: "The endless rediscovery of the self in a series of petty truancies from the official socialized self becomes a mild obsession of the normal individual in any society in which the individual has ceased to be a measure of the society itself" (375). An 'economic' example: "For all practical purposes a too low income is at least as significant a datum in the causation of mental ill-health as a buried Oedipus complex or sex trauma" (588). A 'cultural' example (speaking of an impoverished overworked farmer): "It is only when the sober, inevitable, corroding impoverishment of the farmer's personality is lit up by some spectacular morbidity of sex or religion that the psychiatrist or novelist or poet is attracted to him. The far more important dullness of daily routine, of futile striving, of ceaseless mental thwarting, does not seem to clamor for the psychiatrist's analysis" (588).

In view of all this, it is not surprising that Sapir opposes all ideas of 'adjusting' individuals to society. His critique of our society and of its effects upon personality comes as groundwork for considering how a society and culture could be more satisfactorily structured, just as his critique of the form-meaning relation in existing languages was offered as groundwork for considering how a more satisfactory language could be constructed. The question can be one of adjusting cultural patterns to the individual (which is one of the types of cultural change, as has been seen), rather than adjusting individual to culture. In his article 'The Unconscious Patterning of Behavior in Society', Sapir ends by saying: "Complete analysis and the conscious control that comes with a complete analysis are at best but the medicine of society, not its food" (559). Which means: Do not take it as food; but also: Do take it as medicine.

4. CONCLUSION

Sapir's methods of work were essentially the same in language, in culture, and in personality. He was outstanding not only for his contributions but also for his methods and his presentation. His writing was often an artistic expression, as in the article 'Psychiatric and Cultural Pitfalls in the Business of Getting a Living'; or a masterpiece of getting the point across, as in 'Why Cultural Anthropology needs the Psychiatrist'. He could make very subtle definitions of words, as in some of his encyclopedia articles (365, 373), and very perceptive formulations, as in his summary of Jung (530–1).

Three major work methods of his were so impressive that everyone sensed them, even if only vaguely: his ability to extract results out of elusive data; the dramatic way in which his conclusions came out of his data; the sensitivity and critical independence with which he approached his problems.

His handling of elusive data was related to a very clear sense of the structure of the line of scientific argument. Data that were too uncertain in the light of a loosely constructed argument become relevant when the argument is built up more carefully. For example, when Sapir argued that Wakashan glottalized continuants developed out of glottal stop plus continuant, he showed that there were reasons to analyze initial $\dot{y}$ as reduced from earlier $\text{?}+\text{vowel}+y$ – something which would not have been thought of if he had not needed it in his chain of argument. Of course, this is what happens in all use of data for scientific conclusions, except that Sapir carried it out with greater detail and finesse. Many of his tours de force came simply out of scientific and artistic integrity: he would not be satisfied with a minimally sufficient chain of argument, but would cast about to see if there were any possible counter-arguments to discuss, any data that could be elucidated in the light of the new conclusions (and elucidation which would in turn lend further support to the conclusion). Thus, after showing the development of $\text{?}+\text{continuant}$, he remarked that there are a number of words in *ha-* which look like irregular reduplications, and that this reduplicated *ha-* occurs more frequently before glottalized continuants than one would expect; from this he proceeded to show that another source of glottalized continuants is $h+\text{continuant}$ (240; and note the more complicated point about IE *y-*, 247). He never dismissed weak data, but analyzed it for what it was worth. In the monograph on time perspective he showed that though density of population in an area would normally not be considered in any discussion of the antiquity of settlement in that area, since it could be due to geographic conditions, nevertheless consideration of the density can be useful in conjunction with other data (399–400; cf. also 381, 214).

The dramatic structure of his argument resulted both from the many interweaving details and the disposing of counter-arguments, and also from his habit of using his straightforward data to build up a working hypothesis, then bringing in large-scale considerations to show it as a reasonable and expectable conclusion, and finally explaining complicated data in the light of all this, in a way that both proves the hypothesis and shows how much work it can do. He did this at many points, characteristically in explaining Navaho forms (e.g. 216–7, 218–9), Indo-European laryngeals (e.g. 248–9, 296–7), and the way in which Yana expresses in a single word what English gives in a fairly complicated sentence (552). These things have to be read to appreciate their construction.

Sapir's sensitivity and something of his critical approach may be seen in many of the quotations cited above. His critical independence is perhaps best seen in his treatment of his own society. He did not at all mind making searching and incisive comments about modern society, both in his anthropological papers and in various popular articles; and if these comments often had the effect of exclaiming 'But the emperor has no clothes on', this was due to the situation he was describing rather than to a prior intention on his part. A few examples will suffice.

About the ideal of the 'cultured person' current in this society he says: "It is an attitude of perhaps even more radical aloofness than snobbishness outright. ... Another of its indispensable requisites is intimate contact with the past. ... But perhaps the most extraordinary thing about the cultured ideal is its selection of the particular treasures of the past which it deems worthiest of worship ... [This] selection of treasures has proceeded chiefly according to the accidents of history" (309–10). About the actual 'ethnologist's' culture he says: "in the case of America ... a chronic state of cultural maladjustment has for so long a period reduced much of our higher life to sterile externality ... the present world wide labor unrest has as one of its deepest roots some sort of perception of the cultural fallacy of the present form of industrialism" (318).

In a discussion of "economic factors in personal adjustment", Sapir gives a poignant novelistic sketch, written with sad irony, of the interlace of economic and social and personal problems in the tragedy of a typical low-paid professional (586–7). With this he contrasts the position of Banker C, asking what are the services for which he receives his income: "Should any impertinent, thoroughly unscientific, snooper whisper to the economist that, so far as he can see, C's $500,000.00 income (in virtue of his vice-presidency of the X bank plus shareholdership in the Y company plus investment in the Z oilfields of Mexico plus a long list of other services rendered his fellowmen) seems to be strangely unaffected by the tissue of physical and psychological performances of the psycho-physical entity or organism called C, it making apparently little difference whether C is on hand to instruct one of his secretaries to cut his coupons or is resting up in the Riviera, the economist loses patience" (583). Sapir sums up the economic factor in personal adjustment by asking, in regard to the underpaid professional's breakdown,

"Why should not the psychiatrist be frank enough to call attention to the great evils of unemployment or lack of economic security?" (588). And he adds: "As to C, the interest of the psychiatrist in his moods, conflicts, and aspirations is perennial. ... Perhaps C too inclines to suffer from an economic ill – that obscure, perverse, guilt feeling which, the psychiatrist tells us, so often festers in one's heart of hearts when one tries to balance one's usefulness to society with the size of one's income. ... Is it conceivable that good mental hygiene, even expert psychiatry, may find it proper to recommend some share of income reduction...?" (589).

Although most of Sapir's comments refer to the position of the individual, he also touched on more typically sociological matters, often with an ironic note. Speaking of how a Frenchman fails to see the difference between our *s* and *th*, since the difference lies primarily in our structuring of these sounds, he adds: "It is as though an observer from Mars, knowing nothing of the custom we call war, were intuitively led to confound a punishable murder with a thoroughly legal and noble act of killing in the course of battle" (556). Speaking of the dependence of fashion on social factors, he says: "In a democratic society, for instance, if there is an unacknowledged drift toward class distinctions fashion will discover endless ways of giving it visible form. Criticism can always be met by the insincere defense that fashion is merely fashion and need not be taken seriously" (376). And in respect to acculturation from above, a matter in which anthropologists today are unavoidably interested, he remarks: "A culture may well be quickened from without, but its supersession by another, whether superior or not, is no cultural gain. Whether or not it is attended by a political gain does not concern us here. That is why the deliberate attempt to impose a culture directly and speedily, no matter how backed by good will, is an affront to the human spirit. When such an attempt is backed, not by good will, but by military ruthlessness, it is the greatest conceivable crime against the human spirit, it is the very denial of culture" (328).

So refreshing is this freeness and criticalness, that we are brought to a sharp realization of how such writing has disappeared from the scene. In part, this was the writing of pre-administrative anthropology. We have seen that Sapir was against the very idea that culture is 'given': "This metaphor is always persuading us that culture is a neatly packed up assemblage of forms of behavior handed over piecemeal, but without serious breakage, to the passively inquiring child. I have come to feel that it is precisely the supposed 'givenness' of culture that is the most serious obstacle to our real understanding of the nature of culture and cultural change and of their relationship to individual personality" (596). It is to be expected that the present situation, in which anthropology finds itself helping to make it 'given' [53], would affect the current picture of culture and the way of writing about it: "Canned culture is so much easier to administer" (330). However, important as this development in anthropology may be in explaining why Sapir's writing is so different, it is not the only source of Sapir's way of writing. In part, too, this source was the difference between the atmosphere of a depression period and the atmosphere of the continuous war period which replaced it. And in part it was Sapir.

NOTES

1 Page numbers refer directly to the volume under review, without specifying the particular article involved. I would like to call attention to Stanley S. Newman's very interesting review of this book *IJAL* **17** (1951), 180–5, in which there is some explanation of Sapir's unusual style of writing.

2 Ferdinand de Saussure, *Cours de linguistique générale*, 125.

3 Stanley S. Newman, *Yokuts Language of California*, New York 1944. (See Paper XII of this volume.)

4 Cf. Sapir's article on glottalized continuants (225–50), and Henry M. Hoenigswald, 'Sound Change and Linguistic Structure', *Lg.* **22** (1946), 138–43.

5 To make this more explicit: Suppose all word-initial morphemes have two or more syllables (vowels). Then the probability of finding ʔ rather than some other consonant after the FIRST vowel of a word is related simply to the frequency of the medial glottal stop. The probability of finding ʔ after the SECOND vowel is related to the frequency of the glottal stop (medial and at the end of morphemes) plus the frequency of morphemes which end with a vowel (and of morphemes which begin with a vowel). However, the probability of finding other consonants (not ʔ) after the second vowel is related merely to the frequency of those consonants medially and at morpheme-end.

6 How different Sapir's psychologism is from this will be discussed in Part 3 below. For the moment, it is worth noting that Sapir's grammatical formulations stayed within linguistic categories. In descriptive linguistics he would not say that people inserted a glottal stop so as to avoid the sequence VV, but that the glottal stop constituted, in respect of medial VV, a 'protection' (in cross-boundary position) of that non-occurrence of VV. The primacy of medial VV over the cross-boundary case is maintained, but in terms of the structure rather than in terms of people's intervention in their own speech behavior.

7 We can say that the use of base forms in morphophonemics – as in Leonard Bloomfield's 'Menomini morphophonemics', *TCLP*, 8 (1939), 105–15 – is a further step from history or process toward purely distributional statements.

8 It is interesting that Bloomfield's work, which (as suggested above) represents a later stage in this particular development, presents phonemes no longer as the result of process but as direct classification, whereas the morphology is still largely described in terms of process. Cf. the chapters on phonology and on morphology in his book *Language*.

9 In Sapir and Swadesh, *Nootka Texts* Philadelphia 1939, 236–9.

10 As in Morris Swadesh and C. F. Voegelin, 'A Problem in Phonological Alternation', *Lg.* **15** (1939; written some years earlier), 7.

11 Sapir means: sounds as phonemically heard (perceived, structured) by the naive speaker and hearer.

12 Note 'relational behavior' for our 'distribution'. The hearer might also classify it as a 'bad pole', so that even if the difference between the halfway sound and the regular sounds is noticed and not lost, it is nevertheless referred to (i.e. structured in terms of) the functionally (distributionally) determined points of the pattern.

13 We omit here the important difference that an English verb by itself contrasts most

immediately with the small class of affix combinations (e.g. verb plus -*ed*), and only secondarily with a vast class of phrasal sequences in which that verb could be set (of which *to cause to do so-and-so* is one), while a Nootka verb by itself contrasts with a few specific combinations of verb plus affix (of which the causative affix is one), and only secondarily with the large class of phrasal sequences.

[14] *Hypnotism*, 496 (where the Guthrie quotation is given in full) = Chap. 15 of J. McV. Hunt (ed.), *Personality and the Behavior Disorders*, Vol. I.

[15] This was published in 1933. The novelty of this view may be seen from the fact that in 1929 Sapir had given it a more traditional formulation: "If I shove open a door in order to enter a house, the significance of the act lies precisely in its allowing me to make an easy entry. But if I 'knock at the door', a little reflection shows that the knock itself does not open the door for me. It serves merely as a sign that somebody is to come to open it for me" (163–4). His later understanding would suggest that the knock can be viewed instead as a tool, an indirect step in the course of getting the door opened (like the stick with which Köhler's ape knocks down the banana, or the lever with which we pry up a rock). It is part of the continuous behavior which makes the person inside unlock the door for us, or which makes him ready for our intrusion. It is not a 'substitute for shoving' but rather the equivalent for shoving in a society where people are customarily apprised of a visitor's arrival. In social situations where this is not customary (as among intimates), one indeed opens the door without knocking.

[16] For 'sign' we should say: any associated behavior, such as a noise.

[17] Note Martin Joos's statement of it in the last paragraph of his paper 'Description of Language Design', *Jour. Acoustic Soc. America* **22** (1950), 707.

[18] It is conceivable that there might have been yet another element of symbolism in language, if the noise behavior that became dissociated had had such a relation to the situation with which it was associated as would be independently arrived at by every speaker (or by every speaker in the given culture). Such associations occur in onomatopoetic elements (14), and they would have made words more a matter of individual expression than of arbitrary social learning. Sapir found some traces of such phonetic symbolism by a neat use of the methods of experimental psychology; part of this work appears in the present volume (61–72), part is as yet unpublished.

[19] E.g. what large open classes there were (such as stems, or distinct verb and noun classes) which occurred with small closed classes (such as affixes, or distinct verb and noun affixes in various environmental subclasses).

[20] It is always possible, of course, to overlook various environmental factors in analyzing the meanings of words. Sapir says (140): "If a quantitative goal is to be reached by increase, say 'ten pages of reading', *more than* necessarily has an approving ring (e.g., 'I have *already* read *more than three pages*', though it may actually be less than four), *less than* a disapproving ring (e.g., 'I have *only* read *less than eight pages*', though it may actually be more than seven). On the other hand, if the quantitative goal is to be reached by decrease, say 'no more reading to do', *more than* has a disapproving ring (e.g., 'I have *still more than three pages* to do', though actually less than four remain to be done), *less than* an approving ring (e.g., 'I have *less than eight pages* to do', though more than seven pages remain to be done out of a total of ten)." – If the form of the verb were taken into consideration here, it might be possible to show that the approving ring comes from the conjunction of *more* with the past tense and *less* with *to do*, the disapproving ring from *more* plus *to do* and *less* plus the past tense. To isolate the 'affect in grading', which Sapir seeks here, we extract an element 'approval' out of *more* plus past and *less* plus future, and an element 'disapproval' out of the opposite combinations.

[21] As is well known, logic and especially semantics are also based in part upon the language of their practitioners, and are limited by their linguistic experience. However, this linguistic basis is not explicit because usually unacknowledged; narrow because usually limited to European languages; and arbitrary because not subject to explicit empirical and analytic techniques or to controls.

[22] See E. Sapir and M. Swadesh, 'American Indian Grammatical Categories', *Word* **2**,

(1946), 103–12 – an item not included in the bibliography. On p. 111 Swadesh quotes a perfectly valid note of Sapir's: "Naiveté of imagining that any analysis of experience is dependent on pattern expressed in language. Lack of case or other category no indication of lack functionally. ... In any given context involving use of language, lang. response is not to be split up into its elements grammatically nor sensorimotorly but kept as unit in contextual pattern." Elsewhere, however, Sapir says: "The 'real world' is to a large extent unconsciously built up on the language habits of the group ... The worlds in which different societies live are distinct worlds, not merely the same world with different labels attached" (162). There is no contradiction here, since the 'environing world' is the physical world, whereas the 'real world', in quotes, is also called 'social reality' (162) and constitutes the physical world as socially perceived: "Even the simplest environmental influence is either supported or transformed by social forces" (89); "The physical environment is reflected in language only insofar as it has been influenced by social forces" (90).

[23] Norbert Wiener, *Cybernetics*, Chap. 3, esp. 75–9.

[24] For an example of how particular logical relations can be built into a constructed language, consider the 'newspeak' of George Orwell's novel *Nineteen eighty-four*. One of the distributional features which is only lightly suggested in his system is the technique (not unknown in our real languages) of letting opposites equal or replace each other in certain environments, with the result that no distinction between opposites (say between *war* and *peace*) can be made in the language.

[25] Cf. Zellig S. Harris, *Development of the Canaanite Dialects*, New Haven 1939, 99–100.

[26] An echo of this appears in the work of Sapir's student Morris Swadesh on rate of vocabulary change. Cf. in particular his Salish investigations, carried out under the auspices of the Boas Collection in the American Philosophical Society Library, and published in 'Salish Internal Relationships', *IJAL* 16 (1950), 157–67.

[27] His writings on music dealt with its relation to poetry rather than to linguistic structure. See for example his article 'The Musical Foundations of Verse', *JEGP* 20 (1921), 213–28.

[28] Comparison of the page references in this paragraph with those in the preceding one will indicate which point is included in which category. Thus, simplicity of form is discussed under the seriation of culture elements from the simple or primary to the derived.

[29] But one must guard against such other factors as simplification of a form in the course of borrowing (402).

[30] But a cultural element (e.g. ritual use of tobacco) may be borrowed without its chronological antecedent (cultivation of the tobacco plant; 403).

[31] Larger areas will often not mean greater age, since some elements diffuse faster than others (e.g. elements which are not secret, or are detachable from their context, 414–5), and some environments favor quicker diffusion (e.g. areas covered by related languages, or lines of easy communication, 416–9).

[32] But some languages favor descriptive word formations (437); and old non-descriptive words may have been changed in meaning to apply to a later culture element (438).

[33] And languages differ in their hospitality to analogic regularization of grammar (442).

[34] In language, unlike culture, borrowed material can often be readily recognized by its phonetic structure, morphological unanalyzability, length, or the like, and can be traced to its language of origin (445–9).

[35] In discussing what can be learned historically from the way a language family is spread and diversified (453–8), Sapir says that the fact that both Aleut and Eskimo are spoken in Alaska, while only Eskimo is spoken in Canada, supports Alaska as the center of dispersion of Eskimo. But such considerations will not hold if there are successive waves of emigration from a center, which pile up at coast-lines or other boundaries, thus making the periphery more differentiated in language than the center (cf. the diversified Semitic periphery as against the Arabian center).

[36] In some cases, as in social organization or linguistic usage and vocabulary, the individual carries out only a part of the socially observed pattern (516), and we cannot say that his selection of behavior is the same as the social pattern. In other cases, as in grammatical

structure, the individual's behavior is virtually the same as that which is described for the society as a whole.

[37] E.g. of 'explaining' an unusual suffix by analyzing it as a combination of two suffixes which are members of classes whose sequence would indeed occur precisely in the position occupied by the strange suffix.

[38] In linguistics, the analog to "the way personalities enter into relations with each other" is the distributional interrelation of elements.

[39] Note also the 'feeling' due to the range of occurrences of the morpheme -ké·h in Navaho (220–2).

[40] A descriptive pattern would have been the same as a configurational pressure on the individual speakers; a historical reconstruction would not.

[41] Sapir seems to say that the native 'grasps' the social pattern, while the outside observer just sees the resultant behavior (547). But by observing enough of the behavior, the observer can see as much as the native has grasped. The native himself has grasped it only by observing a great deal of behavior; he is a 'participant observer' of his own society. Hence the social patterns are really not 'felt' by him, but observed; the observations are experiences upon which he can draw when he acts.

[42] Gordon Childe, *What Happened in History*, 8: "In practice ideas form as effective an element in the environment of any human society as do mountains, trees, animals, the weather and the rest of external nature. Societies, that is, behave as if they were reacting to a spiritual environment as well as to a material environment."

[43] The siren of literary effect, which is not always identical with meticulous statement, sometimes led Sapir into such sentences as this (106): "It is largely the function of the artist to make articulate these more subtle intentions of society." Some writers really mean it when they refer to the 'subtle intentions of society'; Sapir obviously did not.

[44] The 'higher solution' lies in the fact that the Indian makes fuller use of available technical knowledge, and has more opportunity to participate in the arranging of his own work, and to make any changes in it. If he fails to carry out any developments in his own work, it is because he lacks the immediate need or the means to make such changes, not so much because he is restricted as to his own activities (as he would be in our society) by orders from others and by a tight organizational structure into which he fits as a cog. One might argue that not only our society has such restrictions, and that the problem is not so much whether primitive societies are freer of them but rather how in our society the people who work can become more free of such limitations. But Sapir's comment is more important as a critique of his own culture than as a commendation of the Indian's – which is natural, since Sapir knew the detailed difficulties of his own culture better, and since these touched him more closely.

[45] In two somewhat earlier articles, Sapir talked in a more standard anthropological manner without recognizing the limitations of cultural uniformity that were stressed in the excerpt quoted above: "[A Haida Indian] cannot be born, become of age, be married, give feasts, be invited to a feast, take or give a name, decorate his belongings, or die as a mere individual, but always as one who shares in the traditions and usages that go with the Killer-whale or associated crests" (345). "If we leave the more sophisticated peoples and study the social habits of primitive and barbaric folk, we shall find that it is very difficult to discover religious institutions that are as highly formalized as those that go under the name of the Roman Catholic Church or of Judaism. Yet religion in some sense is everywhere present. It seems to be as universal as speech itself and the use of material tools" (346). Sapir's own argument above leaves little room for doubt that we could find many actions by Haida individuals which would manage to keep clear of any crest identification, just as the second John Doe avoided involvement in the ward system; and that many primitive individuals are free of any religious identification, just as are many moderns. It is quite understandable that Sapir should have noticed the individual differences in his own society and missed them – or simply not had the data – in other societies which he necessarily knew in far less detail. When anthropologists have turned to write about their own society, they have customarily found conformity and acceptable conditions, in

contrast with the class controls and major cultural inadequacies which they found in enemy or primitive societies. It is to Sapir's credit that he used his critical powers where they might do most good: in remarks about his own society. He might omit some individual variation or some cultural critique of a primitive society, but he would be sure to fight it out at home. (See § 3.3, end, and Part 4 below.)

[46] Sapir sometimes spoke of language as determining people's perception: "The 'real world' is to a large extent unconsciously built up on the language habits of the group" (162). In later work he says rather that a particular language can "help and retard us in our exploration of experience" (11) – i.e. retard us but not stamp us irrevocably; that mathematics has gone on to develop its own alternative system (118), rather than remaining blocked by perceptions based on language; and that "as our scientific experience grows we must learn to fight the implications of language" (10), rather than accept it as inevitable that we can do no more than reflect the existing linguistic structure.

[47] What the anthropologist constructs are cultural patterns. What members of the society observe, or impose upon others, are culturally patterned behaviors.

[48] Princeton University official register 1941 § 33.3 (257): "Freshmen and sophomores are required to attend at least one-half of the Sunday services in the University Chapel in each quarter of the academic year. ... To be appreciated, the service of public worship must be experienced and this is the basis of the requirement for chapel." One can imagine what communication Sapir would have recognized when the regents of the university whose press published this volume of his selected writings demanded oaths of its faculty and fired the non-submissive.

[49] Sapir adds: "We have said nothing so far that is not utterly commonplace. What is strange is that the ultimate importance of these commonplaces seems not to be thoroughly grasped by social scientists at the present time". The strangeness disappears, of course, when one remembers that the social scientists are not catering to the rebels. As John F. Embree says (*American Anthropologist* NS 52 [1950], 431), "The applied anthropologist ... advises managers how to manage their workers; he has been little concerned to advise the managed how to maintain their own social interests vis-a-vis the managers".

[50] Sapir, 'Do we need a "Superorganic"?', *American Anthropologist* NS **19** (1917), 444. This article is not included in the present volume.

[51] This effect of the formal configuration may be seen most readily in limited well-structured fields, such as music or some particular science. Aside from the more generally social factors that lead to particular developments and tendencies in each field, it seems probable that the existing pattern at any one time (the kind of scales used, the type of composition potentialities which have been well investigated) favor certain directions of change, rather than others, by those who try out changes.

[52] The effect of culturally patterned interpersonal relations is treated by Harry Stack Sullivan, *Conceptions of Modern Psychiatry*.

[53] Cf. John F. Embree, 'A Note on Ethnocentrism in Anthropology', *American Anthropologist* NS **52** (1950), 430–2.

XXXIV

EDWARD SAPIR

Edward Sapir was one of the founders of formal descriptive linguistics and modern cultural anthropology, and a pioneer in personality studies, who brought to these fields a subtle and rigorous search for pattern and a strong psychological and humanistic approach. He was born in Pomerania (Germany) on Jan. 26, 1884 and was four years old when his family moved to the United States. He came to American Indian languages and ethnology as a student of Franz Boas. From 1910 he was chief of the Division of Anthropology in the Geological Survey of Canada. In 1925 he was appointed to a professorship in anthropology and general linguistics at the University of Chicago; in Chicago, after the death of his first wife, he found happiness in his marriage to Jean McClenaghan. In 1931 he became Sterling Professor at Yale University (where, in a cause célèbre, an attempt to exclude him from the Faculty Club because he was Jewish was countered by certain resignations from the Club); he died in New Haven on Feb. 4, 1939.

Although his bent was toward problems of style, perception, and delicate shades of meaning, Sapir's work methods and criteria were objective and rigorous. It was this that gave him his exceptional importance, taking him beyond both the massing of irrelevant data and the speculation on concepts that could not be defined or investigated in the real world. His explicit methodological interest was the search for patterns and for interactions among the entities within a pattern. This constant property, together with his remarkable capacity for involved chains of reasoning, gave Sapir's work a personal stamp and a breath-taking beauty which can be seen in his writings even by those who did not experience the fascination of the rich and committed personality from which it all came.

In linguistics, Sapir was an originator of phonemic theory, which analyzes the sounds of a language in reference to a particular system of sound-differences that are recognized (in each sound-environment) in that language. His approach to phonemes was based not only on distribution (as it was in the contemporary work of Leonard Bloomfield and N. Trubetzkoy) but also on the perception and the patterning of sounds ('Sound Patterns in

Prepared for the *International Encyclopaedia of the Social Sciences*.

Language'). Sapir was also an originator of the concept of the morphophoneme, which classifies together such occurrences of different phonemes as replace each other in the different phonemic shapes which a word (or morpheme) may have when it occurs in different morphemic environments. Here too his grounds were in part the speaker's perception of phonemic replacement ('La réalité psychologique des phonèmes'; *Nootka Texts*).

Objectively, Sapir was, with Bloomfield, a founder of the distributional method which characterizes descriptive linguistics (especially of the 'American' school). This method classifies each part of a sentence (sound, morpheme, etc.) on the basis of their different neighboring parts in the various sentences in which that part occurs, rather than on the basis of meaning, phonetic properties, etc. The importance of this method is not only in its being self-contained, but also in that its universe and its terms of reference are so explicit that one can discover all sorts of hidden relations which are observable only by second-order disturbances in the overt distributional system: masked and combined phonemes, neutralized phonemic differences, zeroed morphemes, and the like. Sapir's formulation of the aberrant phenomena was nevertheless at times not in distributional terms but in terms drawn from biological processes. While this reduced the incisiveness and generality of the developing distributional theory, it gave an indication that further systemic factors might be involved – factors of equilibrium, of dynamics, etc. – in understanding the sources of the aberrant phenomena or the place they occupy in the descriptive system (and ultimately in understanding the source of the system itself). Thus Sapir might say that if, in a given language, a two-vowel sequence never occurs inside a morpheme and does not usually arise when two morphemes adjoin each other in a word, the rare cases where such adjoining would result in a two-vowel sequence is (in some languages) avoided by a 'protective mechanism' of a glottal stop or the like pronounced between them (as in French liaison *t*).

In morphology, to which the distributional methods were coming more slowly, the formulation in terms of process was used more widely. Here some purely descriptive phenomena were viewed as processes (such as 'suppletion' for the replacement of stems in certain word-groups, e.g. in *am, is, be*); these do not bear the systemic biological connotation of the mechanism cited above.

He published less in ethnography, but his critical and theoretical papers on cultural anthropology were as important in their day as were his linguistic papers later. In one, the epoch-making 1916 monograph *Time Perspective in Aboriginal American Culture*, he showed how one can judge the age of cultural elements from their relation to other cultural and linguistic items; this brought the first sophisticated historical treatment to anthropology. In another, 'Do we need a "Superorganic"?' (1917), he argued against positing supra-human or superpsychic social 'forces' as accounting for social institutions and history.

These and other papers show Sapir's two main views of culture. One is that culture is a pattern of items, the various cultural items being interrelated to each other in various ways, rather than each directly and separately satisfying a function (this as against functionalist anthropology). The other is that the culture exists via the participation in it of the various individuals in the community. It is not a mold which completely and uniformly stamps each individual, and it cannot claim the individual at the points where he does not participate (515–6).[1] The individual has a reactive relation to the culture. Individuals thus differ from each other in their cultural participation, and the difference between individual and social behavior is in the individual's selection and personal systematization of what we can observe in the aggregate as social behavior (513, 545). For cultural change, the implication of this is that cultural items, including social institutions, continue only by virtue of the acceptance (even if forced) of the population; different views and actions on the part of the population bring a change in the culture (571) – though the problem of the circumstances in which such different reactions arise and spread was only hinted at in Sapir's work and is even less in evidence in other anthropological writing.

Writing in the brave days of early anthropology, and in the heady critical atmosphere of depression years, when the inadequacies of economic and social institutions were visible to the naked eye, Sapir saw society not as something over and above people but as a body of institutions which exists by virtue of people's actions (104) and which can be judged by how it satisfies the needs and capacities of people (316). Sapir was utterly opposed to conformity and to the imposition of social norms (really, the interests of powerful institutions) upon the individual: "Cultural anthropology, if properly understood, has the healthiest of all scepticisms about the validity of the concept 'normal behavior'. ... Personalities are not conditioned by a generalized process of adjusting to 'the normal' but by the necessity of adjusting to the greatest possible variety of idea patterns and action patterns" (514–5).

Given his individual-oriented view of cultural patterns it is not surprising that Sapir became very interested in Freudian psychology and later found himself in accord with Harry Stack Sullivan, with whom he developed a close association. For him, as for Sullivan, "the locus of psychiatry turns out not to be the human organism at all in any fruitful sense of the word but the more intangible, yet more intelligible, world of human relationships and ideas that such relationships bring forth" (512). His view was that the individual makes, in original unawareness, a personal organization of his participation in the culture, just as he accepted Sullivan's view that the individual develops his character structure in original unawareness. Awareness comes with need for change: "It is sometimes necessary to become conscious of the forms of social behavior in order to bring about a more serviceable adaptation to changed conditions" (558). In his last years, Sapir wrote a few articles on personality and culture with a depth of sympathy and understanding which constitute a monument to him and to his period.

NOTE

[1] These and the following page references are to D. G. Mandelbaum, (ed.), *Selected Writings of Edward Sapir*, Univ. of California Press 1949. (See Paper XXXIII of this volume.)

XXXV

ELICITING IN LINGUISTICS
(with C. F. Voegelin)

IMITATION AND REPETITION

In any eliciting we are trying to get the informant to say utterances which will be partly or wholly similar to other utterances which we found in our previously obtained text, or which we or someone else have said in the informant's hearing. That is, we want the elicited utterance to repeat some part of the earlier utterance. It is therefore desirable to understand the linguistic status of elicited repetitions.

One of the considerations upon which the validation of eliciting rests is therefore the distinction between repetition and imitation. In his *Language and Language Disturbance*[1], Kurt Goldstein points out that when people normally reproduce the speech of another they do not imitate the actual sounds which they have heard, but 'repeat' the utterance in their own pronunciation. The reproduction which they offer is not an attempt to get as close as possible to the original which they heard. Such an attempt at approximation is what we get when we imitate a bird-call, or an unknown language, or the peculiar intonation of some individual. In contrast with this, when we 'repeat' someone's utterance, the sounds which we make may be quite different from the sounds which he had made (and which we had heard), because our voice and our pronunciation are different. Indeed, we make no attempt to modify our pronunciation so as to make it temporarily more similar to his, nor are we even aware of how his pronunciation differed from ours.

What, then, is the connection between what the other person said and what we said? If the sounds are different, in varying degrees and directions, what makes our bit of talking a reproduction or 'repetition' of his? Before the days of phonemic theory, before the idea of phonemic distinction had become explicit, we would have said that our bit of talking was accepted as a repetition of his because it was very similar to his, or more similar than any other bit of talking would be, or because it meant the same thing.

There are various reasons why explanations of this type are less than satisfactory. Suppose we repeat the other person's original statement twice, one of our repetitions being physically (acoustically) more similar to his than the other was. Would our less similar reproduction be any less a 'repetition' of his original statement than our other one? Suppose we misunderstood the meaning of his original statement (as we could if it contained a homonym), or suppose some words in his statement had a different or private meaning to us, so that when we repeated his original statement we meant by it something different from what he meant (and suppose the difference could be demonstrated), would our reproduction be any less a repetition for that reason? (It is true that a third person would understand the same thing by his statement and by our repetition, so that the meaning difference should not apply here; but that goes back to the matter of phonemic distinctions. Furthermore, even a third person might see different meanings in the original and the repetition if some accompanying gestures or gestural intonations were different, or if the words meant different things when coming from the original speaker and from the repeater.)

Today we can indicate quite simply what is involved in a repetition: a repetition contains the same phonemes as that which it repeats. If one person says 'yes', and we repeat 'yes', our sounds may differ greatly from his, but both his speech and ours contained the same phonemes /yes/ (and often the same phonemic intonation). In the case of dialects which have small phonemic differences between them, but which are mutually intelligible (and often not even distinguished by the speakers), a repetition is marked by containing the same morphemes rather than the same phonemes. For example, consider a conversation between speakers of two Philadelphia dialects. Speaker A has the same phoneme /æ/ in 'I can' and in 'a can'; speaker B has a different phoneme in 'I can' from his 'a can'. Now when B hears A say 'I can' he will repeat 'I can' not with the phoneme /æ/ even though that is what A used and even though B has /æ/ in his dialect. Instead B will say 'I can' with his second phoneme, and both A and B will accept this phonemically different utterance as B's repetition of A's utterance.

An utterance therefore either is or is not a repetition of another utterance depending on whether it does or does not contain the same phonemes or morphemes. There is no question of approaching the other utterance by closer or less close 'repetitions', as there is a question of an imitation approaching closer to the original bird-call, or to the foreign language, or to some one's pronunciational peculiarity, and approximating the original as closely as we can make it.

This difference between repetition and imitation is one of the indications of the usefulness of a phonemic theory and analysis. One might say that it is one of the indications that people do indeed operate with phonemic distinctions and with the allophone (the positional variant of a phoneme) as a class of free variants (the actual pronunciations). From the point of view of eliciting, it is also one of the indications that we are dealing with authentic linguistic material. As long as our informant repeats what he said, or even what we have said, or as long as he repeats the morpheme we seek in a repetition of the environment in which we are interested, we have an utterance of the language, that is, a combination of phonemes or morphemes of the language. As soon as the informant imitates a pronunciation or a (phonemic or morphemic) combination which we have offered him, we cannot assume that the result is an utterance of the language in question.

TEXTLET ELICITING

The bulk of eliciting carried out by linguists in the past has been what may be narrowly called 'morphological'. It investigated the possibilities of combination within word length. When dealing with words of syntactic importance, however, such as sentence connectives or phrase introducers, eliciting consists of obtaining full sentences which include one or another of the words under investigation. Neither morphological eliciting nor the eliciting of syntactic elements exhaust information which has grammatical relevance. For example, the structure of one sentence may depend on the structure of a preceding sentence, without this dependence being expressed in a specific syntactic element – as when there are restrictions in the sequence of tenses in successive sentences (*consecutio temporum* in some Semitic and other ancient languages). More important than this, even, is the situation when a given verb in one sentence is likely to be followed by a particular other verb in the next sentence; such special relations between two verbs can be readily illustrated in two English sentences. Thus, take as our first sentence: *He bought the car from the Ford garage at an unusually low price.* If one of the following sentences in the text contains (a) *the [Ford] garage* (as subject), (b) *the car* or *it* or the like (as 'direct object'), (c) *him* (as 'indirect object'), there is an expectancy that the verb between (a) and (b) will be *sold to*. A possible second sentence might be: *But the garage still sold it to him at a profit.*

The relationship between the two sentences cited can be discussed on two levels. First there is the question as to whether the second sentence would be inevitable, given the first sentence, or even whether the second would be at all likely to follow the first. The answer to this question depends upon whether or not certain restrictions are included, namely whether *garage* is to occur as the subject, and *him* as the indirect object of the sentence. Without this restriction, the occurrence of *sold* in the second sentence is not discussable; with the restriction mentioned, however, the occurrence of *sold* is likely or probable or expectable, though of course not inevitable.

Whatever statistical interest may attach to the preceding question, it has nothing to do with the next question, which is: What is the relation between *bought* and *sold*? This is the grammatical level of the discussion. We call this relation between *bought* and *sold* grammatical rather than semantic, because it can be stated in terms of limitation of distribution.

For the case above, this limitation is as follows. Given a sentence with subject and indirect object, followed by a second sentence in which these two are inverted or interchanged (subject becoming indirect object; indirect object becoming subject), then *buy* (*from*) in one sentence will have a high probability of being accompanied by *sell* (*to*) in the other sentence. Just as the term *tribelet* may be applied to a tribe so small that each individual in the population may enjoy face-to-face relationship with every other individual, so we may use here the term *textlet* for a sequence of sentences just long enough to contain a limitation of distribution of the kind discussed above. Such a textlet will in general contain more than one sentence.

It is clear that we find the type of limitation discussed above among sentences of a large text; from all such sentences we select the particular sentences which constitute a textlet. The question remains whether one can elicit textlets.

The chances are about equal that we will succeed or that we will fail in eliciting textlets. In general one succeeds in eliciting when the environment or the linguistic materials with which the informant approaches the utterances are large – large in respect to the linguistic materials with which the informant completes the utterance. Thus, if the informant approaches the utterance with *many book*..., he will complete the utterance with -*s* (altogether, *many books*); or more generally, it is easy to elicit a suffix, given an appropriate stem. In the case of textlet eliciting, the informant approaches the problem with a first sentence (*he bought a car from a garage*...) plus the grammatical conditions for the second (interchange of subject and indirect object); he completes the utterance when (or if) he replaces *bought* by *sold*.

THE VALIDITY OF ELICITING

Eliciting is a method of adding data to the corpus of material on which the linguist bases his analysis. For example, if the corpus is one short text in Shawnee, there may occur in it some nouns whose gender cannot be judged from this text alone; by asking for the plural of the nouns in question one can determine from the suffix for plural whether the nouns are animate or inanimate. Having done this we know more about the gender of the morphemes in question than we would have known from the text alone.

When the linguist works with texts or overheard conversations, he has language data as they occur in the language; he builds his analysis on environmental (distributional) comparisons of the elements which he has found in this corpus. Frequently the linguist finds that he would like to have more information about the distribution of a particular element, more environments in which it occurs, so as to compare its distribution more fully with that of other elements. He would therefore like to have additional data which contains this particular element. And usually, since he will be comparing the distribution of this element with that of specific other elements, he would like to know whether his element occurs in certain environments in which the other elements do. If these combinations occur in utterances of the language, they would presumably show up in his texts or conversational material sooner or later. Eliciting is merely a method of making available to the linguist those particular utterances which would show up in his material sooner or later, but which he would like to obtain now (if they occur at all).

Eliciting is therefore a method of selecting utterances out of the great body of utterances which an informant may say in the course of speaking his language. This fact of selection does not prejudice the validity of his now enlarged corpus (to which this selected material has been added) as long as the linguist is not studying the frequency of occurrence of elements or combinations, but only the fact that they occur. One may still consider whether the process of eliciting affects this last – whether it brings up utterances that would not otherwise occur in the language.

Obviously, in any form of eliciting, the linguist is affecting the occurrence of utterances. In order to bring up a particular utterance, the linguist has to say something or show something to the informant, or play back some recording. He creates for the informant (or for the linguist-informant set-up) a situation in which the informant is more likely than before to produce the utterance in question if that is an utterance of the language. Four such situations follow.

It may be an ordinary situation for the speakers of that language. If so, the informant will say something which is ordinarily said in the language, the only selection due to the linguist being in the occurrence of that utterance at this particular moment.

Or the situation may be culturally unusual for the informant, in which case he may produce an utterance which may not have occurred previously, or which would not otherwise occur. This does not mean that the utterance is not linguistically acceptable, because it is an essential characteristic of languages that they produce for new cultural situations utterances which may be new but which are structurally – grammatically – similar to other utterances of the language. (This is what we mean when we say that a language can be used to talk about anything.) The combinations of elements which occur in new situations may indeed be new, but these are minor novelties, e.g. of which particular noun occurs before which particular verb. When larger innovations do come in a language, and new combinations of whole classes develop, they come out of linguistic causes – apparently – rather than out of novel cultural situations in which speaking may be done.

The new situation which the linguist has created with the informant, in trying to elicit a particular combination of elements, may be a partially linguistic situation. That is to say, the informant may react to the linguistic element or combination which the linguist is interested in. The danger is not that the informant may wish to please the linguist. (Amenable people exist all over the world, but they speak their language naturally.) The danger is that the informant may react to the linguistic objective of the eliciting, or to what he thinks is the linguistic objective of the eliciting, and produce an utterance affected by this linguistic consideration.

Finally, the linguist can create a purely linguistic situation by speaking the informant's language not like a native, but like a non-native. He may offer a form which no native would say; as soon as he does so, he has added that form to the corpus of non-native utterances of that language, and he has added a linguistic experience to the informant. The informant may be affected by this; for example, the new combination may seem to him to be a perfectly reasonable one and he may not know that it is new. This is the danger known as 'spoiling the informant'. An utterance by him based on what he heard from the linguist may be one which would not have occurred in the language were it not for his experience in hearing non-native speech.

The first two situations described above had no special linguistic characteristics, and do not invalidate the material obtained by eliciting. The latter two have special non-native linguistic characteristics, and make it uncertain whether the linguistic form of the informant's response would have occurred natively.

NOTE

[1] New York 1948, pp. 71, 103.

XXXVI

DISTRIBUTIONAL STRUCTURE

1. DOES LANGUAGE HAVE A DISTRIBUTIONAL STRUCTURE?

For the purposes of the present discussion, the term structure will be used in the following non-rigorous sense: A set of phonemes or a set of data is structured in respect to some feature, to the extent that we can form in terms of that feature some organized system of statements which describes the members of the set and their interrelations (at least up to some limit of complexity). In this sense, language can be structured in respect to various independent features. And whether it is structured (to more than a trivial extent) in respect to, say, regular historical change, social intercourse, meaning, or distribution – or to what extent it is structured in any of these respects – is a matter decidable by investigation. Here we will discuss how each language can be described in terms of a distributional structure, i.e. in terms of the occurrence of parts (ultimately sounds) relative to other parts, and how this description is complete without intrusion of other features such as history or meaning. It goes without saying that other studies of language – historical, psychological, etc. – are also possible, both in relation to distributional structure and independently of it.

The distribution of an element will be understood as the sum of all its environments. An environment of an element A is an existing array of its co-occurrents, i.e. the other elements, each in a particular position, with which A occurs to yield an utterance. A's co-occurrents in a particular position are called its selection for that position.

1.1. *Possibilities of Structure for the Distributional Facts*

To see that there can be a distributional structure we note the following: First, the parts of a language do not occur arbitrarily relative to each other: each element occurs in certain positions relative to certain other elements. The perennial man in the street believes that when he speaks he freely puts together whatever elements have the meanings he intends; but he does so only by choosing members of those classes that regularly occur together, and in the order in which these classes occur.

Second, the restricted distribution of classes persists for all their occurrences; the restrictions are not disregarded arbitrarily, e.g. for semantic needs. Some logicians, for example, have considered that an exact distributional description of natural languages is impossible because of their inherent vagueness. This is not quite the case. All elements in a language can be grouped into classes whose relative occurrence can be stated exactly. However, for the occurrence of a particular member of one class relative to a particular member of another class it would be necessary to speak in terms of probability, based on the frequency of that occurrence in a sample.

Third, it is possible to state the occurrence of any element relative to any other element, to the degree of exactness indicated above, so that distributional statements can cover all the material of a language, without requiring support from other types of information. At various times it has been thought that one could only state the normative rules of grammar (e.g. because colloquial departures from these were irregular), or the rules for a standard dialect but not for 'substandard' speech or slang; or that distributional statements had to be amplified by historical derivation (e.g. because the earlier form of the language was somehow more regular). However, in all dialects studied it has been possible to find elements having regularities of occurrence; and while historical derivation can be studied both independently and in relation to the distribution of elements[1], it is always also possible to state the relative occurrence of elements without reference to their history (i.e. 'descriptively').

Fourth, the restrictions on relative occurrence of each element are described most simply by a network of interrelated statements, certain of them being put in terms of the results of certain others, rather than by a simple measurement of the total restriction on each element separately. Some engineers and mathematicians (as also phoneticians and experimental psychologists) who have become interested in language have sought a direct formulation of the total restrictions on occurrence for each element, say for each sound.[2] This would yield an expression for how the occurrences of each element depart from equiprobability, and so would give a complete description of the occurrences of elements in the language. Now it is of course possible to enumerate the relative occurrences of a finite set of elements in finitely long utterances; but direct enumeration is of little interest because it yields no simple description of the over-all occurrences of elements, and because it does not order the restrictions in such a way that the larger restrictions get stated before the smaller ones. In contrast with this, it is possible to describe the occurrence of each element indirectly, by successive groupings into sets, in such a way that the total statements about the groupings of elements into sets and the relative occurrence of the sets are fewer and simpler than the total statements about the relative occurrence of each element directly.

We obtain then an ordered set of statements in terms of certain constructs – the sets at successive levels. Since the ordering of statements can be arranged so that the earlier ones will deal with the more inclusive sets, we can stop the process of setting up these statements at any convenient point, and accept the unfinished list of statements as an approximation to the distributional facts – knowing that the subsequent statements will only make subsidiary corrections to the earlier statements. (This is not the case for the direct enumeration of restrictions, where the restrictions to be enumerated after a given point may be greater than those enumerated before.)

In view of this we may say that there is not only a body of facts about the relative occurrence of elements in a language, but also a structure of relative occurrence (i.e. of distribution). Hence the investigation of a language entails not only the empirical discovery of what are its irreducible elements and their relative occurrence, but also the mathematical search for a simple set of ordered statements that will express the empirical facts.[3] It may turn out that several systems of statements are equally adequate, for example several phonemic solutions for a particular language (or only, say, for the long vowels of a language). It may also be that different systems are simpler under different conditions. For example, one system may be adequate in terms of successive segments of sound (with at most stress and tone abstracted), while another system may be simpler if we admit the analysis of the sounds into simultaneous components of varying lengths. Or one system of stating distribution in respect to near neighbors (the usual environment for pho-nemic solutions) may be simple by itself, but if we are to imbed it in other statements about farther neighbors we may find that when we choose a modified system the statements covering the imbedding are simpler (i.e. a different phonemic solution may be more convenient for use in statements about morphemes). If the distributional structure is to be used as part of a description of speech, of linguistic behavior, then we will of course accept only such structures as retain a passably simple relation to the phonetic features. But for some other purpose, such as transmission or systemic analysis, phonetic complexity may be no serious objection. In any case, there is no harm in all this non-uniqueness[4], since each system can be mapped onto the others, so long as any special conditions are explicit and measurable.

Various questions are raised by the fact that there can be more than one (non-trivial) structural statement for a given language. Can we say whether a particular item of structural analysis contributes to the simplicity of the system? It may be possible to do this: For example, if a given analysis involves a particular classification of elements (say, verbs), we may try some variation on this classification (say, by subdivision into transitive and intransitive – distributionally defined) and see whether the resulting analysis is simpler or not. Can we say what is invariant under all the possible distributional structures for a given body of data? For example, for all the phonemic solutions in a given language, there remains constant the minimal network of phonemically distinct utterance-pairs in terms of which we can distinguish every phonemically distinct utterance.

The various structural systems considered here all have this in common, that they list items and their occurrences. There is at least one other type of structural statement which is essentially distributional but couched in different terms. This is the style which describes one linguistic form as being derived by some process (operation) from another. The item style says: Form A includes elements $e+f$ while form B includes elements $e+g$; and thus it describes all forms as combinations of elements. The process style says: Form A is derived from B by changing f into g; and thus it describes most forms as derived from certain base forms. The combinatorial or item style, which has a more algebraic form, is more parsimonious and representative for much of linguistic data. The process style, which is more similar to historical statements, is useful in certain situations, especially in compact morphophonemics.[5] Both styles are based solely on the relative occurrence of parts, and are therefore distributional.

1.2. *Reality of the Structure*

Some question has been raised as to the reality of this structure. Does it really exist, or is it just a mathematical creation of the investigator's? Skirting the philosophical difficulties of this problem, we should in any case realize that there are two quite different questions here.

One: Does the structure really exist in the language? The answer is yes, as much as any scientific structure really obtains in the data which it describes: the scientific structure states a network of relations, and these relations really hold in the data investigated.[6]

Two: Does the structure really exist in the speakers? Here we are faced with a question of fact, which is not directly or fully investigated in the process of determining the distributional structure. Clearly, certain behaviors of the speakers indicate perception along the lines of the distributional structure: for example, the fact that while people imitate non-linguistic or foreign-language sounds, they 'repeat' utterances of their own language[7] (i.e. they reproduce the utterance by substituting, for the sounds they heard, the particular corresponding variants which they habitually pronounce; hence the heard sounds are perceived as members of correspondence sets). There are also evidences of perception of sounds in terms of their morphophonemic memberships.[8]

A reasonable expectation is that the distributional structure should exist in the speakers in the sense of reflecting their speaking habits.[9] Indeed, responses along the lines of distributional structure can be found in experimental psychology work.[10] However, different speakers differ in the details of distributional perception. One speaker may associate the stem of *nation* with that of *native*, while another may not: should the morpheme analysis be different for the two idiolects (individual dialects)? Even if we take the speaking habits to be some kind of social summation over the behaviors (and habits) of all the individuals, we may not find it possible to discover all these habits except by investigating the very speech events which we had hoped to correlate with the (independently discovered) habits.

If, as Hockett proposes, we measure the habits by the new utterances which had not been used in the structural description, we have indeed a possible and sensible measure; and this applies both to real productivity (the use of elements in environments in which they had not occurred before), and also to arbitrarily unused data (utterances which may have occurred before but which had not been used in deriving the distributional structure). However, even when our structure can predict new utterances, we do not know that it always reflects a previously existing neural association in the speakers (different from the associations which do not, at a given time, produce new utterances). For example, before the word *analyticity* came to be used (in modern logic) our data on English may have contained *analytic*, *synthetic*, *periodic*, *periodicity*, *simplicity*, etc. On this basis we would have made some statement about the distributional relation of *-ic* to *-ity*, and the new formation of *analyticity* may have conformed to this statement. But this means only that the pattern or the habit existed in the speakers at the time of the new formation, not necessarily before: the 'habit' – the readiness to combine these elements productively – may have developed only when the need arose, by association of words that were partially similar as to composition and environment.

For the position of the speakers is after all similar to that of the linguist. They have heard (and used) a great many utterances among which they perceive partial similarities: parts which occur in various combinations with each other. They produce new combinations of these along the lines of the ones they have heard. The formation of new utterances in the language is therefore based on the distributional relations – as changeably perceived by the speakers – among the parts of the previously heard utterances.[11]

Concerning any habit, i.e. any predisposition to form new combinations along particular distributional lines rather than others, we know about its existence in the speakers only if we have some outside evidence (such as association tests), or if new formations of the type in question have been formed by these speakers. The frequency of slips, new formations, etc., is enough to make us feel that the bulk of the major structural features are indeed reflected in speaking habits – habits which are presumably based, like the linguist's analysis, on the distributional facts. Aside from this, all we know about any particular language habit is the probability that new formations will be along certain distributional lines rather than others, and this is no more than testing the success of our distributional structure in predicting new data or formations. The particular distributional structure which best predicts new formations will be of greatest interest from many (not all) points of view; but this is not the same as saying that all of that structure exists in the speakers at any particular time prior to the new formations.[12]

2. DISTRIBUTION AND MEANING

2.1. *Is there a Parallel 'Meaning Structure'?*

While the distinction between descriptive (synchronic) structure and historical change is by now well known, the distinction between distributional structure and meaning is not yet always clear. Meaning is not a unique property of language, but a general characteristic of human activity. It is true that language has a special relation to meaning, both in the sense of the classification of aspects of experience, and in the sense of communication. But the relation is not simple. For example, we can compare the structures of languages with the structure of the physical world (e.g. the kind of phenomena that are expressed by differentiation and integration in calculus), or with what we know about the structure of human response (e.g. association, transference). In either case, it would be clear that the structure of one language or another does not conform in many respects to the structure of physical nature or of human response – i.e. to the structure of objective experience from which we presumably draw our meanings. And if we consider the individual aspects of experience, the way a person's store of meanings grows and changes through the years while his language remains fairly constant, or the way a person can have an idea or a feeling which he cannot readily express in the language available to him, we see that the structure of language does not necessarily conform to the structure of subjective experience, of the subjective world of meanings.[13]

All this is not to say that there is not a great interconnection between language and meaning, in whatever sense it may be possible to use this word. But it is not a one-to-one relation between morphological structure and anything else. There is not even a one-to-one relation between the vocabulary and any independent classification of meaning: We cannot say that each morpheme or word has a single or central meaning; or even that it has a continuous or coherent range of meanings. Accidents of sound change, homonymity, borrowing, forgotten metaphors, and the like can give diverse meanings to a number of phonemic occurrences which we have to consider as occurrences of the same morpheme. Aside from this, if we consider the suggestion of Kurt Goldstein[14] that there are two separate uses and meanings of language – the concrete (e.g. by certain brain-injured patients) and the abstract – it would follow that the same grammatical structure and much the same vocabulary can carry quite different types of speaking activity.

The correlation between language and meaning is much greater when we consider connected discourse. To the extent that formal (distributional) structure can be discovered in discourse, it correlates in some way with the substance of what is being said; this is especially evident in stylized scientific discourse (e.g. reports on experimental work) and above all in the formal discourses (proofs) of mathematics and logic. However, this is not the same thing as saying that the distributional structure of language (phonology, morphology, and at most a small amount of discourse structure) conforms in some one-to-one way with some independently discoverable structure of meaning. If one wishes to speak of language as existing in some sense on two planes – of form and of meaning – we can at least say that the structures of the two are not identical, though they will be found similar in various respects.

2.2. *Are Morphemes determined by Meaning?*

Since there is no independently known structure of meanings which exactly parallels linguistic structure, we cannot mix distributional investigations with occasional assists from meaning whenever the going is hard. For example, if the morphemic composition of a word is not easily determined, we cannot decide the matter by seeing what are the component meanings of the word and assigning one morpheme to each: Do *persist, person* contain one morpheme each or two? In terms of meaning it would be difficult to decide, and the decision would not necessarily fit into any resulting structure. In terms of distribution we have *consist, resist, pertain, contain, retain*, etc. (related in phonemic composition and in sentence environment), but no such set for *person*; hence we take *persist* as two morphemes, *person* as one.

Although rough indications of meaning are often used heuristically to guess at the morphemes of a word or utterance, the decision as to morphemic composition is always based on a check of what sections of that word or utterance are substitutable in a structured (patterned) way in that environment; as roughly indicated in the example above.

Where the meanings (in most cases, the translations) are not immediately suggestive, the analysis is laboriously distributional without any heuristic aids to test. For example in the Cherokee verb prefixes, we find scores of forms[15], e.g. /agwalənɔ́ʔəgi/ 'I started', /sdəgadhénoha/ 'I and another are searching for you', /sdəgadhénohəgi/ 'I searched for you two'. These have obviously personal reference, but it is impossible to separate out a small set of phonemic segments which will mean 'I' or 'I as subject', 'I as object', etc. It is nevertheless possible to discover the morphemes distributionally. First we identify the words by their distributional relation to the rest of the sentence. We find that certain words with many different stems and a few different prefixes have certain types of environment in common. For example /zinəgali'a/ 'I am cleaning' and /agiyoseha/ 'I am hungry' occur in certain environments in which /uniyoseha/ 'they are hungry' does not occur. We take a set of words each with different stems but which have the same environment in the sense referred to above. We will assume that the sameness in this feature of the environment correlates with some morphemic part that is the same in all these words (and is obviously not the stem).[16] This means that the different prefixes of these words contain alternants of the same morpheme; and we try to state a morphophonemic relation between /z/, /(a)g/, etc., giving the environing conditions (in phonemic rather than morphemic terms if possible) in which each alternant occurs: we write the morpheme {z} and translate it 'I'. Another set, containing e.g. /ozinəgaliʔa/ 'I and others are cleaning', /ogiyoseha/ 'I and others are hungry', would thus be analyzed (in the same manner, but with the aid of {z}) as containing two morphemes, {o} 'others' and {z} 'I'. If we now turn to the set containing /osdinəgaliʔa/ 'I and another are cleaning', /oginiyoseha/ 'I and another are hungry', etc., our morphophonemic knowledge about {z} enables us to separate out /d,/ /n/ etc. as alternants of some third morpheme {n}, with undetermined meaning. In /iginiyoseha/ 'you and I are hungry' our known morphophonemics enables us to analyze the prefix as an alternant of {z} plus an alternant of this same {n}, where it seems to have the meaning 'you'. However, in /hinəgaliʔa/ 'you (sg.) are cleaning' we are unable to fit the /h/ into the morphophonemic regularities of {n}, and thus set up a new morpheme {h} 'you'; and in /sdinəgaliʔa/ 'you two are cleaning' we can satisfy the morphophonemic regularities by saying that there are two morphemes: the /s/ alternant of {h} plus the /d/ alternant of {n}.

In this way we can divide each prefix into a unique combination of morphophonemic alternants of the following morphemes: {z} 'I', {h} 'you (sg.)', {a} 'third person sg.', {i} 'plural' (always including 'you', at least due to absence of {o}), {o} roughly 'person(s) excluding you', {n} roughly 'another person, you as first choice'. These morphemes were obtained as solutions to the environmental regularities of the prefixed phonemes. The translations offered above are an attempt to assign a single meaning to each on the basis of the meanings of all those words in which it occurs. If we write the prefixes morphophonemically, then the meanings of some of the occurring combinations are: {ozn} (phonemically /osd/ etc.) 'I and he', {oz} 'I and they', {zn} 'I and you (sg.)' {iz} 'I, you, and they', {h} 'you (sg.)', {hn} 'you two', {in} 'you (pl.)'. From this we can try to extract (as above) a single meaning contribution which {n} or {o} or {i} bring to each combination in which they are included. But it was not the isolation of these complicated central meanings (if that is always non-trivially possible) that led us to recognize {n} etc. as morphemes. We do not even know that these central meanings exist for the speakers: the speakers may be subjectively using two homonymous {n} morphemes, or they may be using these prefix combinations as fixed whole entities with only a vague impression of the phonemic and morphophonemic regularities.[17]

So far, we have not touched the great majority of verb forms, those which have objects together with the subjects. By using the morphophonemic relations established previously, we are able to extract the morphemes above from some of these new combinations, and small extensions of the morphophonemics reveal these morphemes in yet other combinations. Then we analyze the prefix in /gəiha/ 'I am killing you' as {z} + {n}, and in /sgwúsədohda/ 'you covered me' as {h} + {z}; and certain order statements about the two prefix components indicate the subject-object relation. The remaining phonemes of some of these prefixes can be grouped by rather simple morphophonemics into a few additional morphemes like {g} 'animate object'; and so we finally obtain a morphemic analysis of all the prefixes. This analysis does not necessarily correlate with any meaning units we may have in mind about person and number. For example, it gives the same morphemes {znn} for the prefix in /sdəgadhénoha/ 'I and another are searching for you (whether sg. or dual but not plural)' and in /sdəgadhénohəgi/ 'I searched for you two'. Even if we find different phonemes with different meanings, e.g. /izə-gow'diha/ 'I and he see you (pl.)' and /izəy-olighi/ 'I and they know you (sg.)' the analysis may say that these are alternants of the same morphemic composition {izn}; in that case both meanings can be obtained for each form.

The methods indicated so sketchily above suggest how the morphemic composition of a word or utterance can be determined by the occurrence of each phoneme sequence relative to others: e.g. *per, con* relative to *sist, tain;* or /z/ /gi/, /o/, etc. relative to various features of environment which are common to /z/ and /gi/ as against /o/. The final decision as to morphemic analysis always depends on this relative occurrence of phoneme sequences, since the grammar then proceeds to state compactly the relative occurrence of the morphemes. That is, we set up as morphemes those phonemic sequences (or features) such that all utterances are compactly statable relative occurrences of them.

The chief difficulty with this is that it provides us only with a criterion that tells us whether a given phoneme sequence is a morpheme or not; more exactly, whether a particular segmentation of an utterance (once we propose it) divides it into morphemic segments. It does not provide us with a procedure which will directly yield a morphemic segmentation of an utterance. There is available, however, a procedure which yields most if not all of the morphemic segmentations of an utterance. In outline it is as follows: Given any test utterance, associate many utterances whose first phoneme is the same as that of the test utterance; and note how many different phonemes follow the first in these utterances. Then consider utterances whose first two phonemes are the same as the first two of the test utterance, and note how many different phonemes follow the first two in these. And so on. If after the first n phonemes the number of different phonemes which follow the nth (in the associated utterances) is greater than the number after the first $n-1$ phonemes or the first $n+1$, then we place a tentative morpheme boundary after the nth. Various operations are needed to correct and check the correctness of each result; but together with the final test of patterned relative occurrence, this yields the morphemes of a language without any reference to meaning or informant response.

2.3. *Meaning as a Function of Distribution*

Distribution suffices to determine the phonemes and morphemes, and to state a grammar in terms of them. However, both (a) in determining the elements and (b) in stating the relations between them, it turns out that the distributional structure does not give ideal coverage. It must either leave many details unsaid, or else become extremely complicated. For example: (a) Morphemes are determined on the basis of a patterned independence (replaceability in utterances) in respect to other morphemes (or phoneme sequences); but not all morphemes have the same degree of independence: compare *hood* (*boyhood*) with *ness* (*bigness*). (b) The grammatical statements group morphemes into classes, and then say that certain sequences of these classes occur; but not every member of the one class occurs (in any actual body of data) with every member of the other: not every adjective occurs with every noun. Finally we may mention one other respect in which distribution fails to cover all the facts about speech occurrence: (c) We can state distributional regularities only within narrow domains – for phonology usually the immediately neighboring phonemes, for morphology usually the sentence or some part of the sentence.

At all these points where simple distributional regularities are no longer discoverable, people often revert to the position of our man in the street (§1.1) and say that here the only determinant is meaning: (a) *hood* has a meaning which ties it to certain few nouns; (b) with a given noun, e.g. *doctor*, there will be used those adjectives that make sense with it; (c) beyond the sentence there are no significant formal restrictions on what one says, and sentences are strung along purely according to meaning. Now meaning is of course a determinant in these and in other choices that we make when we speak. But as we make these choices we build a stock of utterances each of which is a particular combination of particular elements. And this stock of combinations of elements becomes a factor in the way later choices are made (in the sense indicated in the last two paragraphs of §1.2); for language is not merely a bag of words but a tool with particular properties which have been fashioned in the course of its use. The linguist's work is precisely to discover these properties, whether for descriptive analysis or for the synthesis of quasi-linguistic systems. As Leonard Bloomfield pointed out, it frequently happens that when we do not rest with the explanation that something is due to meaning, we discover that it has a formal regularity or 'explanation'. It may still be 'due to meaning' in one sense, but it accords with a distributional regularity.

If we investigate in this light the areas where there are no simple distributional regularities, we will often find interesting distributional relations, relations which tell us something about the occurrence of elements and which correlate with some aspect of meaning. In certain important cases it will even prove possible to state certain aspects of meaning as functions of measurable distributional relations.

(a) There are different degrees of independence (§3.3). We find complete dependence in the various phonemes of one morpheme, or in the various parts of a discontinuous morpheme (including grammatical agreement). In *hood* we have sufficient independence to make it a separate morpheme, but it is limited to very few predecessors. In *ness* there is more independence. The degree of independence of a morpheme is a distributional measure of the number of different morphemes with which it occurs, and of the degree to which they are spread out over various classes or subclasses. The various members of a distributional class or subclass have some element of meaning in common, which is stronger the more distributional characteristics the class has. The major classes have the kind of common meanings that are associated, say, with the words 'noun' or 'adjective'.

(b) The fact that, for example, not every adjective occurs with every noun can be used as a measure of meaning difference. For it is not merely that different members of the one class have different selections of members of the other class with which they are actually found. More than that: if we consider words or morphemes A and B to be more different in meaning than A and C, then we will often find that the distributions of A and B are more different than the distributions of A and C. In other words, difference of meaning correlates with difference of distribution.

If we consider *oculist* and *eye-doctor*[18] we find that, as our corpus of actually occurring utterances grows, these two occur in almost the same environments, except for such sentences as *An oculist is just an eye-doctor under a fancier name*, or *I told him Burns was an oculist, but since he didn't know the professional titles, he didn't realize that he could go to him to have his eyes examined*. If we ask informants for any words that may occupy the same place as *oculist* in sentences like the above (i.e. have these same environments), we will not in general obtain *eye-doctor*; but in almost any other sentence we would. In contrast, there are many sentence environments in which *oculist* occurs but *lawyer* does not: e.g. *I've had my eyes examined by the same oculist for twenty years*, or *Oculists often have their prescription blanks printed for them by opticians*. It is not a question of whether the above sentence with *lawyer* substituted is true or not; it might be true in some situation. It is rather a question of the relative frequency of such environments with *oculist* and with *lawyer*, or of whether we will obtain *lawyer* here if we ask an informant to substitute any words he wishes for *oculist* (not asking what words have the same meaning). These and similar tests all measure the probability of particular environments occurring with particular elements, i.e. they measure the selections of each element.

It is impossible to obtain more than a rough approximation of the relatively common selection of a given word (with almost no indication of its rarer selection). But it is possible to measure how similar are the selection approximations of any two words (within various sets of data). If for two elements A and B we obtain almost the same list of particular environments (selection), except that the environment of A always contains some X which never occurs in the environment of B, we say that A and B are (complementary) alternants of each other: e.g. *knife* and *knive-*. If A and B have identical environments throughout (in terms of our data tests) we say that they are free variants: e.g. perhaps for /ekənamiks/ and /iykənamiks/ *economics*. If the environments of A are always different in some regular way from the environments of B, we state some relation between A and B depending on this regular type of difference: e.g. *ain't* and *am not* have frequent differences of a certain type in their environments (*ain't goin'* but *am not going*) which we would call dialectal. If A and B have almost identical environments except chiefly for sentences which contain both, we say they are synonyms: *oculist* and *eye-doctor*. If A and B have some environments in common and some not (e.g. *oculist* and *lawyer*) we say that they have different meanings, the amount of meaning difference corresponding roughly to the amount of difference in their environments. (This latter amount would depend on the numerical relation of different to same environments, with more weighting being given to differences of selectional subclasses.) If A and B never have the same environment, we say that they are members of two different grammatical classes (this aside from homonymity and from any stated position where both these classes can occur).

While much more has to be said in order to establish constructional methods for such a classification as above, these remarks may suffice to show how it is possible to use the detailed distributional facts about each morpheme. Though we cannot list all the co-occurrents (selection) of a particular morpheme, or define its meaning fully on the basis of these, we can measure roughly the difference in selection between elements, say something about their difference in meaning, and also (above and §4.1) derive certain structural information.

(c) If we investigate the relative occurrence of any part of one sentence in respect to any part of the neighboring sentences in the same discourse, we will find that there are certain regularities (§3.5 end). The sequence of sentences is not entirely arbitrary; there are even certain elements (e.g. pronouns) whose occurrence (and meaning) is specifically related to the grammatically restricted occurrence of certain other morphemes in the neighboring sentences (§4.1, first paragraph). Such regularities (and meanings) will not extend from one discourse to another (except to another related in some relevant way to the first, e.g. successive lectures of a series). A consecutive (or seriate) discourse of one or more persons is thus the fullest environmental unit for distributional investigation.[19]

3. DISTRIBUTIONAL ANALYSIS

We now review briefly the basic analysis applicable to distributional facts.

3.1. *Element*

The first distributional fact is that it is possible to divide (to segment) any flow of speech into parts, in such a way that we can find some regularities in the occurrence of one part relative to others in the flow of speech. These parts are the discrete elements which have a certain distribution (set of relative locations) in the flow of speech; and each bit of speech is a particular combination of elements. The first operation is purely segmenting, arbitrary if need be. The first step of segmenting has to be independent of any particular distributional criterion, since we cannot speak of distributional relations until we have not only segments but also a similarity grouping of them (§3.2). After the first segmenting of utterances, each segment is unique and has a unique environment (completely different from every other one); after the segments have been compared, and 'similar' ones grouped together, we find that various of these similarity groupings have partially similar and partially different environments. Hence we can speak about the distributional relations of these similarity groupings.

If we wish to be able, in the later operations (§3.3–4), to obtain elements (or classes of elements) whose distributions will have maximum regularity, we have to divide not only the time flow into successive portions, but also any single time segment (or succession of time segments) into simultaneous components (of one segment length, e.g. a tone, or longer, e.g. a pitch-stress contour). After we have set up the phonetically more obvious segmentations and simultaneities, and have studied their distribution, we may find that more regular distributions can be obtained if we change our original segmentation of elements, even to ones that are phonetically less obvious, and even if some of our adjusted elements become components which extend over various numbers of other elements.

3.2. *Similarity*

Another essential distributional fact is that some elements are similar to others in terms of certain tests; or are similar in the sense that if we group these similar elements into sets ('similarity groupings'), the distribution of all members of a set (in respect to other sets) will be the same as far as we can discover. This reduces ultimately to the similarity of sound segments under repetition, or in the pair test: x_1 is similar to x_2 but not to y_1 if, when one native speaker repeats x_1z, x_2z, y_1z, ..., a second speaker can guess correctly whether x_1z as against y_1z is being said, but not whether x_1z as against x_2z is being said. We call x_1 and x_2 free variants of each other (or members of a similarity grouping). Note that the pair test involves discrimination of sound but not of meaning.

3.3. *Dependence (Serial)*

To obtain a least set of elements sufficient for description we join any elements which are completely dependent: if A is a set of similar elements (a similarity grouping) and so is B, and (in a particular type of environment) only AB occurs (not necessarily contiguously), never A or B alone, then we set up AB as a single element (a single set of similar elements).

Thereafter we don't have any two elements which are completely dependent upon each other in occurrence. But our elements have various degrees of dependence: for each element we can say that any utterance (or shorter domain) which contains it will also contain such and such other classes. For example, morpheme A may occur always close to (i.e. within a statable distance from) any one of a few or many B_1, B_2, ... If the sequence B_1A

occurs in environments X, it may be that B_1 by itself also occurs in X (e.g. *kingdom* and *king*), or that B_1 does not (e.g. *kingly* and *king*). The B_1 with which A occurs may all have the same types of environment when they occur without A (e.g. all predecessors of *dom* are nouns), or some may have one type and some another (e.g. *ish* occurs with both nouns and adjectives). These are a few of the various degrees and types of occurrence-dependence which an element can have to the elements that occur in the same utterances as it does.

3.4. *Substitutability (Parallel)*

It will in general appear that various elements have identical types of occurrence-dependence. We group A and B into a substitution set whenever A and B each have the same (or partially same) environments X (X being at first elements, later substitution sets of elements) within a statable domain of the flow of speech. This enables us to speak of the occurrence-dependence of a whole set of elements in respect to other such sets of elements. Some of the types of partial sameness of environment were listed in §2.3(b).

The elements of distributional structure are usually obtained by the operations of §3.1, §3.2 and the first paragraph of §3.3. The distributional relations are usually combinations of §3.3 and §3.4. For example, *hood* occurs after few morphemes N_1, N_2, ... of a certain substitution set ('nouns'), *ish* after many of them, *s* and its alternants after all or almost all of them. $N_i + hood$ or $N_i + s$ occur in the same large environments in which N_i occur alone. But $N_i + ish$ occur in different environments than N_i alone; however *ish* also occurs after many members of another substitution set, A_1, A_2, ... ('adjectives'), and both $N_i + ish$ and $A_i + ish$ occur in the larger environments of A_i alone.

3.5. *Domains*

All the statements about dependence and substitutability apply within some specified domain, the domain being determined either by nature (e.g. silence before and after an utterance) or by the types of environment within which there is regularity (e.g. the narrow restriction of *hood* is only to what precedes it, and only to the first morpheme in that direction). It is often possible to state the co-occurrences of elements within a domain in such a way that that domain then becomes the element whose co-occurrences are regular within a larger domain: e.g. the occurrences of stems and suffixes within word-length, and of words within phrases. Common types of domain are the word, phrase, clause. In many cases the stretches of speech covered by certain long pitch and stress components (or fixed sequences of short pitch and stress components) are identical with the domains of distributional relations: word, sentence.

Although grammar has generally stopped with the sentence, it is possible to find distributional regularities in larger domains. There are certain sentence sequences in which the second can be described as a fixed modification of the first (e.g., with certain restrictions, in the case of questions and answers in English). There are certain types of distributional relation (e.g. between English active and passive, between *buy* and *sell*) which have particular kinds of regularity in (not necessarily immediately) neighboring sentences. For example, if one sentence contains noun A+active (transitive) verb B+noun C, and a neighboring sentence contains C+verb+A, there is a certain likelihood that the verb will be the passive of B; or if the neighboring sentence contains C+the passive of B+some noun, there is a certain likelihood that the second noun will be A or some noun which elsewhere in that discourse has similar individual environments (selection) to those of A. And if one sentence contains A *buys* B *from* C, and a neighboring sentence contains C *sells* B *to*+some noun, there is a good likelihood that the noun will be A or an environmentally similar noun (and given C+some verb+B *to* A, we may expect the verb to be *sell* or some environmentally similar one).[20]

Finally, if we take a whole connected discourse as environment, we find that there are certain substitution sets of morphemes which occur regularly (relative to the other sets) throughout the discourse or some portion of it[21]; these are not the major substitution sets of the language (e.g. nouns) or its grammatical subclasses, but new groupings which are often relevant only to that one discourse. And there are certain sequences of these sets which constitute the subdomains of the discourse, i.e. such that the sets are regular within these intervals and the intervals are regular within the discourse; these intervals are not necessarily sentences or clauses in the sense of grammatical structure. The regularities in a discourse are far weaker and less interrelated than those within a sentence; but they show that occurrence-dependence (and the environment relevant for distribution) can extend throughout a whole discourse.

3.6. *Data*

The distributional investigations sketched above are carried out by recording utterances (as stretches of changing sound) and comparing them for partial similarities. We do not ask a speaker whether his language contains certain elements or whether they have certain dependences or substitutabilities. Even though his 'speaking habits' (§1.2) yield regular utterances, they are not sufficiently close to all the distributional details, nor is the speaker sufficiently aware of them. Hence we cannot directly investigate the rules of 'the language' via some system of habits or some neurological machine that generates all the utterances of the language. We have to investigate some actual corpus of utterances, and derive therefrom such regularities as would have generated these utterances – and would presumably generate other utterances of the language than the ones in our corpus. Statements about distribution are always made on the basis of a corpus of occurring utterances; one hopes that these statements will also apply to other utterances which may occur naturally. Thus when we say that the selectional difference in *oculist/lawyer* is greater than in *oculist/eye-doctor* (§2.3), or that the selection of nouns around the passive verb is the same as the selection around the active verb but with inverted order (§4.1), we mean that these relations will be approximated in any sufficiently large corpus (especially one built with the aid of eliciting), and that they will presumably apply to any sufficiently large additions to the corpus.

In much linguistic work we require for comparison various utterances which occur so infrequently that searching for them in an arbitrary corpus is prohibitively laborious. To get around this, we can use various techniques of eliciting, i.e. techniques which favor the appearance of utterances relevant to the feature we are investigating (without influencing the speaker in any manner that might bring out utterances which would not have sometimes occurred naturally). In particular, investigations of the selections of particular morphemes (§2.3, 4.1) can hardly be carried out without the aid of eliciting. Eliciting is a method of testing whether a certain utterance (which is relevant to our investigation) would occur naturally: in effect, we try to provide a speaker with an environment in which he could say that utterance – if he ever would naturally say it – without extracting it from him if he wouldn't. For example, if we are testing the active/passive relation we might offer a speaker noun A_1 + transitive verb B_1 and ask him to complete the sentence in many ways, obtaining a particular selection C_1, C_2, ... after the verb. Then we can offer a speaker the passive verb $B_1 + A_1$ and ask him to begin the sentence in many ways, checking whether we get about the same selection C_1, C_2, ... before the verb. We can repeat this for various A_i, and then for various B_i.

4. DISTRIBUTIONAL RELATIONS

The methods of §3 yield first of all a representation of each utterance as a combination of elements. They also yield a set of statements about the utterances: what elements and regularities of combination suffice to represent the utterances. One can go beyond this and study the kinds of regularities, and the kinds of relations among elements. As was pointed out at the end of §2.3(b), certain correlations may be discovered even in those distributional facts which are too individual to be directly useful.

4.1. As an example of the latter we may consider selectional similarity. For instance, it is impossible to list all the verbs that follow each particular noun, or all the verbs that follow *who*. But it is possible to state the following relation between the verb selection of nouns and the verb selection of *who*: Under an eliciting test as in §3.6, we will get after *The pianist* – much the same verbs as we will get after *The pianist who* –, and so for every noun. This means that the verb selection of *who* is the same as the verb selection of the noun preceding *who*. We have here a distributional characteristic that distinguishes such pronominal elements from ordinary nouns.

Or we may consider the active/passive relation mentioned in §3.6. If we take a large number of sentences containing a transitive verb in English, e.g. *The kids broke that window last week*, we can elicit sentences consisting of the same verb but with the passive morpheme, the same nouns before and after it but in reverse order, and the same remainder of the sentence, e.g. *That window was broken by the kids last week*. Some of these sentences may be stylistically clumsy, so that they would not occur unless some special circumlocution were involved; but they are obtainable by otherwise valid eliciting techniques.[22] In contrast, if we seek such inversion without the passive, we will fail to elicit many sentences: we can get *The kids saw Mary last week* and *Mary saw the kids last week*; but to *The kids saw the movie* we will never – or hardly ever – get *The movie saw the kids* (even though this sentence is grammatical). Or if we seek such selectional similarity (with or without inversion) for *broke/will break* or the like, we will find the same selection as to preceding and following nouns, but not always as to the rest of the sentence: *The kids broke that window* and *The kids will break that window*, but not *The kids will break that window last week* or *The kids broke that window if they don't watch out*. It thus appears that, using only distributional information about an ordinarily elicited corpus, we can find a relation between the active verb and the passive verb which is different from the relation between *-ed* and *will*.

4.2. The distributional regularities can themselves be a subject of study. One can consider recurrent types of dependence and substitutabilities that are found in a language (or in many languages), and find on one level such relations as "subject" and "object" (semantic names for distributional positions), and on a higher level of generality such relations as 'constituent' and 'head of a construction' (if A occurs in environment X, and AB does too, but B does not, then A is the head of AB). One can consider the parts of a grammar which permit alternative distributional analyses, and check their relation to language change and dialect or idiolect interrelations (since probably every linguistic structure has some points which are structurally in flux). One can investigate what are the structural characteristics of those parts of a language which are productive. Furthermore, one can survey what is similar and what is different in a great many language structures, and how linguistic systems in general differ from such partially similar systems as mathematics and logistic 'languages', sign languages, gestures, codes, music.

NOTES

[1] The investigation of historical regularity without direct regard to descriptive (synchronic) structure was the major achievement of the linguists of the late eighteen hundreds. There are incipient studies of historical-descriptive interrelations, as in H. M. Hoenigswald, 'Sound Change and Linguistic Structure', *Lg.* 22 (1946), 138–43; cf. A. G. Juilland, 'A Bibliography of Diachronic Phonemics', *Word* 9 (1953), 198–208. The independent study of descriptive structure was clarified largely by Ferdinand de Saussure's *Cours de linguistique générale*, the Prague Circle in its *Travaux du Cercle linguistique de Prague*, Edward Sapir in various writings, and Leonard Bloomfield's *Language*.

[2] These approaches are discussed by Martin Joos, 'Description of Language Design', *Journal of the Acoustical Society of America* 22 (1950), 702–8, and W. F. Twaddell, *ibid.* 24 (1952), 607–11.

[3] For a discussion of simplicity in this connection, see a forthcoming article by Noam Chomsky, 'Some Comments on Simplicity and the Form of Grammars'.

[4] Y. R. Chao, 'The Non-Uniqueness of Phonemic Solutions of Phonetic Systems', *Bulletin of the Institute of History and Philology, Academia Sinica* 4 (1934), 363–98. Cf. the two solutions of Annamese phonemes in M. B. Emeneau, *Studies in Vietnamese (Annamese) Grammar*, 9–22.

[5] This kind of formulation is best expressed in the work of Sapir and Newman; cf. reviews of *Selected Writings of Edward Sapir* (ed. by D. Mandelbaum) in *Language* 27 (1951), 289–92 (Paper XXXIII of this volume); and of Stanley Newman, *Yokuts Language of California* in *International Journal of American Linguistics* 10 (1944), 196–211 (Paper XII of this volume).

[6] An opposition has sometimes been claimed between real facts and mathematical manipulation of structure. This claim ignores the fact that science is (among other things) a process of indicating much data by few general statements, and that mathematical methods are often useful in achieving this. Mathematical and other methods of arranging data are not a game but essential parts of the activity of science.

[7] As pointed out by Kurt Goldstein, *Language and Language Disturbances*, 71, 103.

[8] E.g. in Edward Sapir, 'La réalité psychologique des phonèmes', *Journal de Psychologie Normale et Pathologique* 30 (1933), 247–65 (translated in David Mandelbaum, ed., *Selected Writings of Edward Sapir*, 46–60). (See Paper XXXIII of this volume.)

[9] C. F. Hockett, review of *Recherches structurales* in *International Journal of American Linguistics* 18 (1952), 98.

[10] As pointed out to the writer by A. W. Holt.

[11] This applies to the grammatical innovation involved in new formations; the selection of morphemes within a class is determined, not only by these "grammatical" associations but also semantically. Cf. the first paragraph of §1.1 above.

[12] Here we have discussed whether the distributional structure exists in the speakers as a parallel system of habits of speaking and of productivity. This is quite different from the dubious suggestion made at various times that the categories of language determine the speakers' categories of perception, a suggestion which may be a bit of occupational imperialism for linguistics, and which is not seriously testable as long as we have so little knowledge about people's categories of perception. Cf. for the suggestion, Benjamin L. Whorf, 'The Relation of Habitual Thought and Behavior to Language', *Language, Culture and Personality (Sapir Memorial Volume)* (ed. by A. I. Hallowell, L. Spier, and S. Newman),

75–93; 'Languages and Logic', *The Technology Review*, 1941, 43–6; and against it, Eric H. Lenneberg, 'Cognition in Ethnolinguistics', *Lg.* **29** (1953), 463–71; Lewis S. Feuer, 'Sociological Aspects of the Relation Between Language and Philosophy', *Philosophy of Science* **20** (1953), 85–100.

[13] In E. G. Schachtel's 'On Memory and Childhood Amnesia', *Psychiatry* **10** (1947), 1–26 it is suggested that the experiences of infancy are not recallable in later life because the selection of aspects of experience and the classification of experience embodied in language, which fixes experience for recall, differs from the way events and observations are experienced (and categorized) by the infant.

[14] *Human Nature in the Light of Psychopathology: The William James Lectures for 1938–39*, ch. 3.

[15] The following analysis can be fully understood only if one checks through the actual lists of Cherokee forms. The few forms cited here are taken from William D. Reyburn, 'Cherokee Verb Morphology II', *International Journal of American Linguistics* **19** (1953), 259–73. For the analysis, see the charts and comments in Reyburn's work and in Z. S. Harris, 'Cherokee Skeletal Grammar', and 'Cherokee Grammatical Word Lists and Utterances', in the Franz Boas Collection of the American Philosophical Society Library.

[16] This assumption is based on the fact that each morpheme has a different distribution (§2.36), so that same feature of environment points to the same morpheme.

[17] Since new formations of these combinations do not appear, we cannot apply the productivity tests of §2.1 to discover the speakers' morphemic recognition.

[18] This particular pair was suggested to me by Y. Bar-Hillel, who however considers that distributional correlates of meaning differences cannot be established.

[19] It should be clear that only after we discover what kinds of distributional regularities there are among successive elements or sections in discourses can we attempt any organized semantic interpretation of the successions discovered. Various types of discourses have various types of succession (of sentences, clauses, or other intervals). In mathematics and the constructed 'languages' of logic, certain conditions are imposed on what sentences can appear in succession in their connected discourses (proofs): each sentence (line in a proof) has to be a theorem or else derived from a preceding sentence in a particular way. This situation does not hold for natural languages, where the truth-value of logic is not kept constant through successive sentences, and where the types of succession are more varied.

[20] Such relations as that of active to passive, or *buy* to *sell*, are essentially substitutability relations (§3.4), i.e. they show that certain elements have similar environments (e.g. partially inverted ones). The fact that they may appear in neighboring sentences is a serial relation (§3.3) which is a secondary characteristic of certain substitutabilities. Relations like that of active to passive are different from the essentially serial relations of successive intervals of a discourse, discussed at the end of §3.5.

[21] The fact that a discourse contains several or many occurrences of a given substitution class, often in parallel positions, brings out a rare relation in linguistics: the order of occurrence of various members of the same class. Something like this comes up in compound nouns, or in successions of two or more adjectives (sometimes with preferred order). Usually, if two members of a class occur in one domain, their order is not regular (e.g. in most cases of N *and* N); but in compound nouns, for instance, certain members are frequent in the first N position, and others in the second.

[22] There will be a few exceptions where the passive is not obtainable. And if we try to elicit the active on the basis of the passive, we run into the difficulty of distinguishing between *by* of the passive (*The letter was finished by Carl*) and *by* as preposition (*The letter was finished by noon*).

XXXVII

A LANGUAGE FOR INTERNATIONAL COOPERATION

Proposals for an international auxiliary language were relatively widespread in the decades around the turn of the century, when hopes for a more decent and reasonable world society were common and perhaps a bit innocent. The proposals, too, were too simple to be viable. The languages were constructed with some arbitrariness; and there was not enough knowledge of how a language could be constructed so as to be more adequate for carrying particular kinds of information and discussion, or so as to be more easily used by the speakers of the existing major languages. And little thought was given to the question of what conditions, and what chains of social events, might lead to the actual use of such an auxiliary language. It is possible now to consider these questions somewhat more carefully.

POTENTIAL USES OF A WORLD-WIDE AUXILIARY LANGUAGE

The failure of past proposals does not mean that languages for communication across linguistic boundaries are impossible. Occurrences of an auxiliary lingua franca are known in various places in the world: pidgin English in the South Sea Islands, Swahili in eastern Africa. Such auxiliary tongues enable speakers of different languages to converse with each other. And the mere learning of a second language is not a difficult matter. In border areas (e.g., at the German-French border) and in countries in which different languages are spoken (e.g., Morocco, with Arabic and Berber) large parts of the population can speak a second language. The failure of the proposed international languages has been due not to the impossibility of maintaining a second or auxiliary language but to lack of a social basis, of real occasion for its use. There is also no need to fear that an international language would soon break up into local dialects. Modern communication operates against dialect formation. And an auxiliary language would have little regional life, and is not likely to be increasingly swallowed up by the local language.

Preventing World War III: Some Proposals (ed. by Q. Wright *et al.*), Simon & Schuster, New York, 1962.

It is not easy to see what pressing and continuing uses such a language could have in the world of today, and for what groups of people. One use might be a lingua franca for scientists, and for other occupational groups which deal with their colleagues in other countries. But the language could hardly be kept up if its only use was in occasional conversations. If a Japanese learns English in order to read scientific articles, he will hardly use an international language in speaking to an English scientist. A lingua franca for science could perhaps be maintained if scientific works for international use (excluding those textbooks or research and discussions which are used only locally) were all translated into a common auxiliary language, so that scientists would not have to learn foreign languages (aside from the auxiliary) in order to read the works of foreign scientists or in order to talk with them.

At present, few scientific articles are translated (except, for war reasons, between Russian and English), and only the major scientific books get translated into a few other languages, usually only after several years. Many scientists acquire some knowledge of the major languages of science (and of politics); in effect, Russian-satellite scientists can read Russian, and scientists in the rest of the world often learn English. In the smaller or less technological countries, scientists often write their major articles in English. However, for most people, reading the foreign language is harder and slower, with the result that in the major countries working scientists, after their school days are over, read little except what is written in their own language. In some fields, like physics, the problem is reduced because the great bulk of major articles is published in English or Russian; in mathematics, chemistry, and biology, the concentration is far less. This whole situation fosters certain insularities and delays in the scientific work of various countries – though this is not to say that different schools of work in a science are not desirable, and inevitable, even within a single country, on the basis of close personal communication.

Translating scientific, technical, and practical writing in a routine manner, perhaps even mechanically, into a specially constructed common language would be easier than translation of all writing between arbitrary languages, because of the greater explicitness and simplicity of the grammar of scientific writing, and because these grammatical features can be reflected in the constructed language. We here distinguish science writing from the language arts, and from writing in the fields of values, opinion, and persuasion (criticism and comment, philosophy, politics, propaganda), where translation is more a matter of judgment, and where a constructed language, necessarily poor in connotations, ranges of meaning, grammatical allusion, and the like, may prove an inadequate vehicle. The translation problem is less important here, because it is precisely in the language arts and value fields (which are less technical and have wider audiences) that books are widely translated at present.

It thus appears that a real social use exists for something which is technically possible: a common language for translation, and for talking with foreigners, in scientific and practical matters. This may be too limited a use, involving too restricted an audience, to constitute by itself the occasion for the rise of such a language. Other realistic uses are possible, for example in the growing international travel, and in technological activities requiring direct, even if brief, communication among people of different parts of the world. There are also uses related to linguistic theory and application. For example, we will see, when we discuss some technical problems of constructing the language, that a well-constructed detailed auxiliary would be of great value to linguistic research, and would have some of the properties useful for an intermediate translation language (for translating from one language to the auxiliary and from it to the second language).

It is of course possible that if a sensible, promising, and not too difficult language is devised, those who wish to establish contact with people in other countries might learn and use this language. Although such plans have failed in the past, this kind of use might possibly develop in the shadow of the bomb. The fact that man has never had an auxiliary language in the sense considered here is not in itself an argument against the possibilities of the future, just as the absence of a complex decent social structure in the past is no argument against the possibility of one in the future. Under the new conditions and dangers that are developing, men may be led to do what they have not needed or been able to do in the past.

The presence of possible social uses, however, and even of social needs, is no guarantee that a particular solution, or any solution, will arise. Every social institution and behavior has been adjusted to by the people involved, and the process of changing is usually more difficult and costly to them than going on with the existing ways, no matter how inefficient or harmful these may be. Gradual changes go on all the time, but these rarely make a major difference, and in any case can hardly bring about such a specific thing as an international language. Sharp changes and overturns also pepper human history; but these appear in special and extreme circumstances, of a kind not foreseeable for such an incidental as an auxiliary language. When extreme circumstances do come, they can in general make use only of already developed alternatives, rather than suddenly create new social forms (though the new use of existing social alternatives may look like a new social form). In this sense, social preparation in a direction which seems to us possible and desirable may not be wasted, even if we cannot foresee the need or opportunity which may bring it into real life. The creation of an auxiliary language may therefore be worth attempting, even if we can only guess at the pressures and chains of circumstances that might bring it into use or at its possible consequences for the development of actions and attitudes transcending national lines.

However, our present interest in an auxiliary language is not as a tool for such specific needs, but as a social instrument which might facilitate the cooperation of individuals in spite of national conflicts, and which might have some effect toward counteracting the divisive national languages and cultures. Naturally, one cannot expect too much. The opinion-molding institutions and the instruments of social control enable the ruling social elements in each nation to affect the opinions and actions of their population in the direction of international hatreds and conflicts, far more than such supranational considerations as the common human destiny and emotions, the increasingly world-wide sciences and arts, and the direct communication made possible by a general human language, could affect people toward world peace and cooperation. Nevertheless, we cannot doubt that people could feel themselves more a part of an interrelated world population if they had a common language which they could use with other human beings of whatever land. And aside from how people feel and see themselves, there is also the matter of practical possibilities of behavior.

If people were able to talk to each other across national boundaries, it would be easier for people (as distinct from translator-equipped governments) to exchange opinions on their common problems, and to act jointly. Such communication is more possible today, with the increased international travel and with the possibility of world-wide immediate conversation through communication satellites. Finally, if we are to face reality, rather than just hope that the interests of ruling groups and the inability to act of ruled populations will somehow run their course without nuclear war, we may have to think of a situation in which the governments have destroyed themselves together with much of their populations, and in which the remaining people will have to find direct ways of dealing with each other.

It might be mentioned in passing that the possibility of a single world language, presumably with local dialects, would not represent a great loss for human culture. In former years it was felt that the diversity of languages was a desirable fact, offering various shapes that variously inform human perception, thought, and literary invention. More recent research, especially into the transformational basis of language, suggests that all languages are very similar in basic structure. The greatest differences among languages is in their culturally least important aspect: the different choice of words for particular meanings. There are also important differences among the languages in respect to which general properties (time, number, etc.) are expressed by elements whose choice must be specified (e.g. singular and plural in English) and which ever are expressed by elements which need not be specified (e.g. the plural number – two, three, etc.; in contrast there are languages in which one must specify singular, dual, or plural). It is possible that the choice of properties which must be specified in a given language affects the perception of speakers of that language. There are also differences in details of sentence structure. The basic structure of sentences is nevertheless apparently much the same for all languages.

STRUCTURE OF A WORLD-WIDE LANGUAGE

We have seen that an auxiliary language may be more likely to come into use if it is technically superior for various purposes, and much easier to learn, than the existing major languages of the world. While it might seem impossible to construct a language easily learnable for the people of many different countries, modern linguistics gives considerable information on how this can be attempted. And we must realize that whereas Esperanto was merely based on Latin, with elements from current European languages, today's language would have to suit not only the Germanic-Romance-Slavic languages, but also Chinese and Japanese, some of the major languages of Southeast Asia, Indic and Dravidian, Arabic, and perhaps the main Finno-Ugric and African languages.

Before we consider the structure of an auxiliary language and how it should relate to the existing ones, it should be mentioned that no language can be constructed directly on the basis of general laws of thought, or any fixed system of concepts and relations. No laws of thought adequate to language, and no sets of terms and operations sufficient or necessary for science, are yet known. What is known today about the processes of thought, or about the universe of discourse and the methods of statement for science as a whole, is uncertain, vague, episodic, and lacking in definitive frame of reference. The systems of logic and mathematics are explicit and powerful, but apply only to truth-value and to a few kinds of relations, most of them ultimately set-theoretic. They are not sufficient for science, for practical affairs, or for the value-judgmental fields. Natural language, however, has been sufficient for man; or rather, man has only been able to express explicitly that which he could put into language, with the addition of such special tools as mathematics, representational methods like graphs, and the apparatus of gesture. For the part handled by language, the only method available now is not to find out semantically what the speaker really means and express this in some new system natural to all people, but to follow whatever way natural language has developed for expressing things in an open, inadequate but adjustable, system – in effect, simply to translate what the speaker says into an intermediate common language which the hearer or reader can understand. An auxiliary language would therefore be based not on some theory of thought and knowledge but on the existing languages.

The learnability and intertranslatability of the auxiliary can be best considered under three heads: sounds (and writing), vocabulary, grammar.

Sounds

The sounds of a language are arbitrary. The only thing that can be asked is that the auxiliary should not contain any sounds or sound-combinations which speakers of any major language cannot discern or pronounce, and above all should not contain any sound-distinctions which are automatic sound-replacements in any major language (whose speakers have learned to disregard these particular sound-differences). Furthermore, since the sounds of the auxiliary will be pronounced by each person in a manner related to his own language, the auxiliary should avoid such sounds or letters as would be pronounced in unrecognizably different ways by different people. Beyond this, the only consideration is that the sounds be simple and clearly distinguishable. Finally, the auxiliary would have to contain some approximation to the sounds used in the present scientific terms and international words, since they would be incorporated into the language. All these requirements restrict the advisable complement of sounds, and some compromises will have to be made; but the cautions indicated here can be followed in practice to a considerable extent.

There is also the matter of the writing system – undoubtedly alphabetic, and most likely based on the very widespread Latin letters. But problems would arise in assigning letters to the sounds in such a way as to minimize confusions and difficulties.

Vocabulary

Vocabulary presents more complicated problems. The many international words – scientific, cultural, political – would undoubtedly be retained, and in a form which most speakers can recognize on the basis of their own pronunciation or spelling of the word. For the mass of remaining vocabulary, the burden of learning should presumably be spread among the major languages in some way. That is, some words would be taken from each major language, so that the speakers of that language would at least not have to learn those particular words. Various considerations can be used in deciding which words should be taken from which language – depending, for example, on the semantic adequacy of the word, on the amount of help that this word is likely to give to those who know it in remembering or guessing the meaning of other words which occur with it in a sentence of the auxiliary language.

In addition to this question about the stock of words – what sound-sequences shall be taken for the various meanings – there are two more complicated problems with respect to vocabulary.

One is the ranges of meaning for each word. The way in which range of meaning is cut up for assignment to words differs in different languages: in English, *floor* means flooring and house-level, while *plane* means flat surface; but in Italian, *pavimento* means flooring, while *piano* means house-level and flat surface. As a result, the translation of *floor* is sometimes *pavimento* and sometimes *piano*, while the translation of *piano* is sometimes *floor* and sometimes *plane*. Since people who use the auxiliary language will be translating from their own (more, even, than people who just learn a foreign language), they will tend to use the words of the auxiliary with the meaning-ranges of their own language. In making the dictionary of the auxiliary, in stating what meaning-ranges each word has and what its translation is in each language (for each of its meanings), it will be necessary to seek such an assignment of meaning-ranges to words as will be easiest to translate for each major language, and at the same time will offer least misunderstanding between speakers of different languages. And this without greatly increasing the number of words in the vocabulary; for one costly direction of solution is simply to reduce the range of meaning of each word by introducing separate words for each discernible meaning. All this is a very cumbersome problem. However, investigations in this area may be useful for current activity about translation; and it is therefore possible that they may be carried out.

Grammar

The other problem leads from vocabulary to grammar. It is the question of how the vocabulary shall be divided as between independent and derived words. In German, *Grundlage* contains the word *Grund*, 'ground'; its translation in English, *foundation*, is just a noun-form of the independent verb *found*, 'establish'. Thus a word W in one language may contain ('be derived from') certain other words, Y, Z of that language; whereas its translation W' in another language may not contain the corresponding words (translations) Y', Z' of the other language; W' may be an independent word, or it may contain words other than Y', Z'. Since the stock of words in a language is one of the hardest things to learn, being arbitrary and large, it is desirable to have a relatively small stock of independent words and prefixes and suffixes, and to have the great bulk of the words of the language built up out of these independent words and affixes. However, it is necessary that the way in which words are built up (the 'rules' by which words are 'derived' from other words) should be as simple as possible, as consistent as possible with the way people think and speak, and describable in a general way, so that if anyone forms a word – new or just unknown to him – out of parts, people anywhere can understand its meaning fairly accurately from the component elements and the rules of combination – plus the environment in which the word is used. And it is desirable that the methods and meanings of these combining operations be translatable into, or understandable on the basis of, those of the major languages.

Finally, we have to consider the way in which words are arranged so as to form a sentence. Here certain linguistic results are particularly useful. In all languages, speaking and writing consists of a series of word-strings, each string being what we may call a sentence. It appears that in all languages there are certain simple sentence structures, with all of the more complicated or longer sentences being built up out of these (either by combining two sentences – themselves simple or combined – or by altering the shape of a simple or combined or already altered sentence). To a large extent, and perhaps to as complete an extent as the language is analyzed, these operations of combining and altering sentences depend not on the meaning or individuality of the sentences, but only on their structure and word-classes. This means that, for each language separately, a method can be found for breaking down each sentence into its component sentences and the operations used on them, or for applying the operations to simple sentences so as to obtain complex ones. Furthermore, the substantive meaning (though not the stylistic effect) of each sentence is not changed by this reduction; it is equivalent to the meaning of the component sentences and operations (especially the combining operations). Finally, while the operations of one language may differ appreciably from those of another, the simple sentence structures are rather similar, much more similar than the complex sentences of the two languages.

As a result of all this, if for each major language we find the method of decomposing its complex sentences into its simple ones, we would have a simpler ('basic') version of that language: namely, its simple sentence structures plus its operations (chiefly the combining ones). If the auxiliary is constructed so as to be as similar as possible, or rather as translatable as possible, to the simple versions of each major language, we would have a very effective auxiliary. In order to learn the auxiliary, each person would have to learn how to reduce the sentences of his own language, and then how to translate between his reduced sentences and the auxiliary. Learning how to decompose the sentences of one's own language is tantamount to learning the grammar of one's language in this form. And translation from the reduced sentences is related to the general method of a proceduralized translation, for translation between the reduced versions of two languages, directly or through an intermediate like the auxiliary, is much easier and more orderly than translation from the complex sentences of one language to those of another.

SEMANTIC CONFUSIONS VS. CONFLICTING INTERESTS

Any discussion about the possibilities of a world-wide language for cooperation among people must first clear away the common misconception that semantics is a key to mutual understanding. Neither in social nor in international conflicts can peace or understanding be reached by overcoming semantic confusions. For the conflicts are due not to semantic differences, but to real clashes of interest – between employer and employed, between ruler and ruled, between competing economic and governmental groups.

Not only are semantic confusions not causes of class and national conflicts; they do not even deepen these conflicts to any appreciable degree. The chief effect they have on the conflicting sides is to diffuse the conscious scope of conflict, so that each group does not even understand the opponents' arguments, and pays them little heed, where if it did understand them it would merely oppose them more explicitly. If workers talk about their customary practices and pace in carrying out the work they do, while the boss talks about management prerogatives in allocating or in timing their work, no conflict will be reduced by bringing these terms to a common denominator. If the American government speaks about freedom (or about the occupation of Eastern Europe), and the Russian government about bread (or about colonialism), no lessening of the cold war can be expected from clarifying the arguments. As always, the attack on the opponent will contain much truth, the defense of oneself will be mealy-mouthed and dishonest. If one makes a critique of the meaning of 'free' for the victims of all the employers, institutions, and courts that cooperated with McCarthyism, if one asks what is the meaning of 'workers' state' for the Russian regime, one may find hoary techniques of propaganda, but no key to peace. And with the social and international differences inherent in the structure of the human world today, it is certain that crucial conflicts will occur which no semantics can mitigate.

Even the more powerful critique by the sociology of knowledge can only show what economic and political conditions motivate each opponent, partly expressed and partly camouflaged by what he says; it cannot in general lead to a resolution of the conflict. The function that the semantic camouflages have, indeed, is to square the actions of governments and economic or political groups with the values which they, or those whose support they need, maintain at least overtly. A semantic clarification therefore will often have the effect not of removing error or of bringing people's understandings together, but of unmasking this camouflage. The unmasking, however, does not free the actor to act differently, nor the supporter to remove his support, because the direction of action and support is limited by the possibilities and needs of each group: the interests of the Russian government in controlling Eastern Europe remain even after the meaning of 'people's democracy' for Hungary or wherever is unmasked; the interests of American business and government in Guatemala and Cuba remain, independently of the way the question is treated in public statements; the employer has to get as much as he can from his workers, even if the 'agitators' whom he blames are semantically clarified as being the dissatisfactions and needs of the employees; and the workers have to find employment under some employer even if they understand that employment means not just work but the control of others over their work.

The chief case where something like verbal camouflage has a deep effect, making people accept and support situations which they might otherwise oppose, is in systems of outlook and belief, for example religious or national, which the members of a population find around them from childhood on. By the same token, however, no semantic analysis can by itself free the people from the concepts and attitudes which are inculcated by these long-term formulations and which are integrated with the existing institutions of control, social intercourse, and production.

All this is not to say that clarification of meanings, in the popular sense of 'semantics', and unmasking of social sources in the sense of the sociology of knowledge, are not valuable. But these critiques can affect the world which they describe only in certain social constellations, those same ones in which positive ideals (such as freedom of belief, rationalism, civil liberty and equality, socialism) can be moving forces – that is when ideas, critical or positive, can be weapons: when the social groups to whom the ideas are addressed have alternatives actually available to them – in terms of the organization of work, of different international alliances and military possibilities, etc. – which the ideas can help them use.

We have stressed here the limitations of popular semantics, in order to remove any expectation that an international language would lead to common understanding (most social conflicts and not a few wars are fought within a common language), or that it can be so constructed as to have explicit and fixed meanings which would deter intentional or unintentional falsification. Every language (excluding formal systems, such as mathematics) has to be open to new meanings and extensions of meaning and to new understandings; no language can be structurally protected from containing false or confusing statements. Methods of checking and criticizing may be developed, based both on logic and on the structure of scientific writing, which would be useful in recognizing or correcting falsehoods, ignorance, or points of view. But such methods would be *ex post facto* tests of what has been said; they cannot (except in restricted conditions) be built in as *a priori* structure of the language in order to limit what can be said.

INDEX OF SUBJECTS

- restriction 618
environmentally determined redundancy 559
equal 320
- -sign 320
equated 108
equation 105, 109ff, 214, 230, 231, 247, 258
equilibrium 766
equiprobability 776
equivalence 347, 525; *see also* grammatical equivalence
- class 320, 321, 323, 324, 326, 332, 333, 349
- classes recur 323
- of morpheme sequences 224, 230
- relation 383, 387, 448, 460, 482, 573, 574, 615
- relation among sentences 606
equivalent 320, 618, 619
- environment 319, 320, 321, 349, 350ff
- sentence-form 334
erase 291
Eskimo 217, 249
every 576
evidence 397
exception 434, 455, 459
exceptional change 506
excised 307
excision 289, 496, 516, 527; *see also wh-* excision
  marker 308
  of *wh-is* 569, 570
exclamatory intonation 456
excluded 632
exclusion 348
exist 621, 654, 665, 688
- for the speaker 783
existence 675
existing vocabulary 667
exocentric 119, 215, 286, 287
expanded form 621
expanded member 338
expansion 414, 438, 456
- of construction 448
expectability 679
expectable 680
expectancy 771
expectation of sentence 661
expected argument 679
explaining 763
explanation 785
explicit 6, 100, 120, 123, 131, 190, 238, 243, 287, 766
ex post facto test 805
express 803

expressible in language 780
extend domain 553
- of argument 552
extended category 517, 520
extended natural language 668
extended text 345
extended well-formedness conditions 518
extending operation 494
extending substitution 100
extending transformational relation 506, 540, 568
extension 29, 483, 499, 500, 501, 513, 514, 526, 527, 529, 567, 572, 573, 574, 611, 720
- of analysis 7, 8
- of argument 549, 567
- of meaning 804
- of morphophonemics 613, 676, 783
- of selection 620
- of set of sentences 668
- of substitution classes 104
- of transformational analysis 615
external grammatical status 449
extract morphemes 783
extraction 501, 502, 540, 543, 566, 567, 596

facilitate 677
fact 461
factorization 387, 444; *see also* unique factorization
failure of well-formedness 270, 271
falsehood 805
falsification 804
families 540
- of structures 278
family of transformations 541
Fanti 30
farther neighbor 777
feminine 94, 101
few constructional rules 449; *see also* simple description
few elementary operations 483
few members 143
few morpheme classes 449
few morphemes 243
few types of structure 482
final 69, 70, 71
- base 687
- set 265
finitary system of arguments 606
finite 263, 448, 603
- memory 255
- number 280
- set of elements 776
- set of kernel structures 273

replaced 183, 201, 561, 647
replacement 91, 211, 542
replacing 184, 574, 619
report 613, 614, 615; *see also* speaker's
   relation to report, structure and report
  – -sublanguage 614, 615
represent 140, 161
representation of utterance 791
representational method 799
reproduce utterance 778
require 261, 263, 266, 269, 284, 295, 296,
   307, 308, 412, 525, 563, 626
required *afterwards* 643, 644
required article 133
required change 505, 677
required morph 60
required morphophonemic form 641
required neighbor 268
required operation 506
required permutation 513, 516
required product 506
required transformation 505, 506
required variant 640
required zeroing 691
requirement 287, 292, 751
re-run of computation 255
residual sentence 607, 609
residual structure 564
residue 275, 280, 281, 286, 296, 298, 411,
   504, 512, 516, 525, 538, 543, 617, 687
resistance of individual 752
respectively 287, 288, 307, 644, 645
restatement 217, 235
restrict 398
restricted alternant 83
restricted comparative 628
restricted co-occurrence 393, 394, 454
restricted distribution 115, 775
restricted domain 620, 637
restricted environment 61
restricted form 503
restricted increment 619, 623
restricted meaning 679
restricted member 530
restricted morpheme 250
restricted morphophonemics 638
restricted occurrence 373
restricted operator 619, 643
restricted paraphrastic transformation 617,
   664
restricted permission 288
restricted permutation 577
restricted position 54
restricted selection 112
restricted sentence 614

restricted sequence 67
restricted source 662
restricted subdomain 680
restricted tense 642
restricted transformation 387, 471, 633, 656,
   679
restricted variant 625, 675
restricted verb-operator 656
restricted vocabulary 636
restricted word-combination 614
restriction 27, 58, 61, 63, 65, 129, 408, 410,
   485, 510, 551, 552, 556, 576, 622, 624,
   627, 628, 632, 636, 637, 643, 649, 658,
   659, 661, 663, 667, 675, 678, 686, 790;
   see also grammatical restriction, special
   restrictions, structural restriction, well-
   formedness restrictions
– across sentence boundary 314
– domain 680
– in domain 631
– of co-occurrence 440, 445
– of co-occurrence range 422
– of individual co-occurrence 421
– of occurrence 65, 238, 314, 317, 456
– of substitutability 228
– on combinability 690
– on element-combination 613
– on randomness 238
– on relative occurrence 776
– on selection 689
– on string structure 535
– -removal 661; *see also* removal of
   restrictions
restrictionless source 648
restrictionless transform 614
restrictive meaning 515
restrictive statement 92
resultant 258, 275, 276, 482, 496, 497, 517,
   519, 520, 521, 522, 525, 528, 546, 552,
   553, 557, 558, 575, 614, 665, 674, 677,
   679, 683, 685, 686; *see also* intermediate
   resultant
– sentence 527, 535, 546, 579, 587, 617, 686
– sequence 674
– string 675
– two systems 613
reverse 140, 143, 156
– order 384, 394, 396, 428, 433, 452, 792
reversible 149, 151, 406, 433
– order 455
– transformation 394, 395
reversing 156
revised grammar 156, 157
revised structure 157
right 253, 279, 485, 516, 543, 552, 554, 561,

INDEX OF SYMBOLS AND TERMS